# Adult Psychopathology
# and Diagnosis

# Adult Psychopathology and Diagnosis

Sixth Edition

Edited by

Michel Hersen and Deborah C. Beidel

WILEY

John Wiley & Sons, Inc.

*Library of Congress Cataloging-in-Publication Data:*

Adult psychopathology and diagnosis/edited by Michel Hersen and Deborah Beidel.—6th ed.
    p.; cm.
  Includes bibliographical references and indexes.
  ISBN 978-0-470-64194-1 (cloth: alk. paper); 978-1-118-13883-0 (eMobi); 978-1-118-13884-7 (ePub); 978-1-118-13882-3 (ePDF)
    1. Psychology, Pathological.   2. Mental illness—Diagnosis.   I. Hersen, Michel.   II. Beidel, Deborah C.
  [DNLM: 1. Mental Disorders—diagnosis.   2. Adult.   3. Mental Disorders—psychology. WM 141]
  RC454.A324 2012
  616.89—dc23                                                                                  2011019561

Printed in the United States of America

10 9 8 7 6 5 4 3 2

# Contents

# Preface

This is the sixth edition of *Adult Psychopathology and Diagnosis* and the first that does not bear Samuel M. Turner's name due to his untimely passing. But his spirit is here, and Deborah Beidel and I dedicate this volume to him.

Since publication of the previous edition, new data continue to emerge that force us to continuously reconsider how we approach and conceptualize psychological disorders. Psychopathology is a vibrant field and continuing discoveries regarding the roles of genetics, neurobiology, and behavior require that we continue to update this volume for students and professionals alike. We believe that our eminent authors have captured both major changes and more nuanced findings in their respective chapters.

The sixth edition contains 19 chapters divided into two parts (Part I: Overview; Part II: Specific Disorders). Part I has four chapters by experts in the field: Chapter 1: Mental Disorders as Discrete Clinical Conditions: Dimensional Versus Categorical Classification; Chapter 2: The Problem of Dual Diagnosis; Chapter 3: Structured and Semistructured Interviews for Differential Diagnosis: Fundamentals, Applications, and Essential Features; and Chapter 4: Impact of Race and Ethnicity on the Expression, Assessment, and Diagnosis of Psychopathology.

Part II on Specific Disorders includes 15 chapters that cover many of the diagnostic entities and problems seen in daily clinical work by our colleagues in hospitals, clinics, and private practice. Approximately 30% of the chapters have new authors for this edition. Additionally, as a testament to the vibrancy of the field of psychopathology, the former anxiety disorders chapter has now been split into two chapters: (Chapter 11: Panic Disorder, Agoraphobia, Social Anxiety Disorder, and Specific Phobias; and Chapter 12: Generalized Anxiety Disorder, Posttraumatic Stress Disorder, and Obsessive-Compulsive Disorder) in order to adequately address the extensive work in these areas. Furthermore, Gender Identity Disorders has been removed from the Sexual Disorders and Paraphilias chapter and now stands as Chapter 16.

To the extent possible, we have asked our gracious contributors to follow a standard format. Exceptions, of course, were granted as dictated by the data inherent in each chapter. Generally, however, each chapter has a Description of the Disorder, a Case Study, and material documenting Epidemiology, Clinical Picture, Course and Prognosis, Diagnostic Considerations, Psychological and Biological Assessment, and Etiological Considerations. Each chapter also contains a Summary.

Many individuals have contributed to the sixth edition of this book. First, we thank our experts, who agreed to share their vast knowledge about their areas of study. Second, we thank Carole Londeree for her very fine editorial assistance. And finally, we thank Patricia Rossi and her exceptionally professional staff at John Wiley & Sons, for understanding the importance of this area in clinical psychology.

Michel Hersen, Hillsboro, Oregon
Deborah C. Beidel, Orlando, Florida

# Contributors

**Michelle Accardi**
Department of Psychology
Binghamton University (SUNY)
Binghamton, NY

**Patricia A. Areán, PhD**
Department of Psychiatry
University of California,
    San Francisco
San Francisco, CA

**Gordon J. G. Asmundson, PhD**
Department of Psychology
University of Regina
Regina, Saskatchewan, Canada

**Evelyn Behar, PhD**
Department of Psychology
University of Illinois at Chicago
Chicago, IL

**Melanie E. Bennett, PhD**
Department of Psychiatry
University of Maryland
    School of Medicine
Baltimore, MD

**Joanna Berg**
Department of Psychology
Emory University
Atlanta, GA

**Lori A. Brotto, PhD**
Department of Obstetrics
    and Gynecology
University of British Columbia
Vancouver, BC, Canada

**Cynthia M. Bulik, PhD**
Department of Psychiatry and
    Department of Nutrition
University of North Carolina at
    Chapel Hill
Chapel Hill, NC

**Colleen Cleere**
Department of Psychology
Binghamton University (SUNY)
Binghamton, NY

**Dennis R. Combs, PhD**
Department of Psychology
University of Texas at Tyler
Tyler, TX

**Daniel Conybeare**
Department of Psychology
University of Illinois at Chicago
Chicago, IL

**Frederick L. Coolidge, PhD**
Department of Psychology
University of Colorado at Colorado
    Springs
Colorado Springs, CO

**Bernadette M. Cortese, PhD**
Department of Psychiatry and
    Behavioral Sciences
Medical University of South Carolina
Charleston, SC

**Stacey B. Daughters, PhD**
Department of Behavioral and
    Community Health
University of Maryland
College Park, MD

**Leilani Feliciano, PhD**
Department of Psychology
University of Colorado at Colorado
    Springs
Colorado Springs, CO

**Thomas A. Fergus**
Department of Psychology
Northern Illinois University
Dekalb, IL

**Timo Giesbrecht, PhD**
Department of Experimental
    Psychology
University of Maastricht
Maastricht, The Netherlands

**Selvija Gjonbalaj-Marovic, PhD**
Department of Psychiatry
University of Maryland School of
    Medicine
College Park, MD

**Gerald Goldstein, PhD**
Psychological Service
Veterans Affairs Medical Center
Pittsburgh, PA

**Whitney L. Gore**
Department of Psychology
University of Kentucky
Lexington, KY

**Sophia Grewal**
Psychological Service Center
Pacific University
Portland, OR

**Marisela M. Gutierrez, MS**
Department of Psychology
University of Texas at Tyler
Tyler, TX

**Jordana L. Hemberg**
Department of Behavioral and
    Community Health
University of Maryland
College Park, MD

**Christopher J. Hopwood, PhD**
Department of Psychology
Michigan State University
East Lansing, MI

**Michelle M. Hospital, PhD**
Department of Psychology
Florida International University
Miami, FL

**Sandra Jenkins, PhD**
Psychological Service Center
Pacific University
Portland, OR

**Sheri L. Johnson, PhD**
Department of Psychology
University of California
Berkeley, CA

**Carolin Klein, PhD**
Department of Obstetrics
    and Gynecology
University of British Columbia
Vancouver, BC, Canada

**Anne A. Lawrence, MD, PhD**
Department of Psychology
University of Lethbridge
Lethbridge, Alberta, Canada

**Susan Tinsley Li, PhD**
Psychological Service Center
Pacific University
Portland, OR

**Scott Lilienfeld, PhD**
Department of Psychology
Emory University
Atlanta, GA

**Steven Jay Lynn, PhD**
Department of Psychology
Binghamton University (SUNY)
Binghamton, NY

**Suzanne E. Mazzeo, PhD**
Department of Psychology
Virginia Commonwealth University
Richmond, VA

**Harald Merckelbach, PhD**
Department of Experimental Clinical
    Psychology
University of Maastricht
Maastricht, The Netherlands

**David J. Miklowitz, PhD**
Department of Psychiatry –
    Semel Institute
University of California
Los Angeles, CA

**Anne E. Mueller, MA**
Department of Psychology
University of Colorado at
    Colorado Springs
Colorado Springs, CO

**Kim T. Mueser, PhD**
Department of Psychiatry and
    Community and Family
    Medicine
Dartmouth College Medical School
Hanover, NH

**Jason Peer, PhD**
Department of Psychiatry
University of Maryland
    School of Medicine
Baltimore, MD

**Daniel L. Peluso**
Department of Psychology
University of Regina
Regina, Saskatchewan, Canada

**Brenna N. Renn**
Department of Psychology
University of Colorado
Colorado Springs, CO

**Jessica M. Richards**
Department of Behavioral and
    Community Health
University of Maryland,
    College Park
College Park, MD

**Daniel L. Segal, PhD**
Department of Psychology
University of Colorado at Colorado
    Springs
Colorado Springs, CO

**Linda C. Sobell, PhD**
Center for Psychological Studies
Nova Southeastern University
Fort Lauderdale, FL

**Mark B. Sobell, PhD**
Center for Psychological Studies
Nova Southeastern University
Fort Lauderdale, FL

**Michel A. Thibodeau**
Department of Psychology
University of Regina
Regina, Saskatchewan, Canada

**Katherine M. Thomas**
Department of Psychology
Michigan State University
East Lansing, MI

**Sara E. Trace, PhD**
Department of Psychiatry
University of North Carolina at
    Chapel Hill
Chapel Hill, NC

**Thomas W. Uhde, MD**
Department of Psychiatry &
  Behavioral Sciences
Medical University of South
  Carolina
Charleston, SC

**David P. Valentiner, PhD**
Department of Psychology
Northern Illinois University
Dekalb, IL

**Andrei Vedeniapin, MD**
Department of Psychiatry & Behavioral
  Sciences
Medical University of South Carolina
Charleston, SC

**Eric F. Wagner, PhD**
College of Public Health and Social
  Work
Florida International University
Miami, FL

**Thomas A. Widiger, PhD**
Department of Psychology
University of Kentucky
Lexington, KY

**Kenneth J. Zucker, PhD**
Department of Psychiatry
  and Psychology
University of Toronto
Toronto, Ontario, Canada

# PART I

## OVERVIEW

# CHAPTER 1

# Mental Disorders as Discrete Clinical Conditions: Dimensional Versus Categorical Classification

THOMAS A. WIDIGER and WHITNEY L. GORE

"IN *DSM-IV*, THERE is no assumption that each category of mental disorder is a completely discrete entity with absolute boundaries dividing it from other mental disorders or from no mental disorder" (American Psychiatric Association [APA], 2000, p. xxxi). This carefully worded disclaimer, however, is somewhat hollow, as it is the case that "*DSM-IV* is a categorical classification that divides mental disorders into types based on criterion sets with defining features" (APA, 2000, p. xxxi). The categorical model of classification is consistent with a medical tradition in which it is believed (and often confirmed in other areas of medicine) that disorders have specific etiologies, pathologies, and treatments (Guze, 1978; Guze & Helzer, 1987; Zachar & Kendler, 2007).

Clinicians, following this lead, diagnose and conceptualize conditions presented in *DSM-IV-TR* as disorders that are qualitatively distinct from normal functioning and from one another. *DSM-IV-TR* provides diagnostic criterion sets to help guide clinicians toward a purportedly correct diagnosis and an additional supplementary section devoted to differential diagnosis that indicates "how to differentiate [the] disorder from other disorders that have similar presenting characteristics" (APA, 2000, p. 10). The intention of the manual is to help clinicians determine which particular mental disorder provides the best explanation for the symptoms and problems facing the patient. Clinicians devote initial time with a new patient to identify, through differential diagnosis, which specific disorder best explains a patient's presenting complaints. The assumption is that the person is suffering from a single, distinct clinical condition, caused by a specific pathology for which there will be a specific treatment (Frances, First, & Pincus, 1995).

Authors of the diagnostic manual devote a considerable amount of time writing, revising, and researching diagnostic criteria to improve differential diagnosis. They buttress each disorder's criterion set, trying to shore up discriminant validity and distinctiveness, following the rubric of Robins and Guze (1970) that validity of a diagnosis rests in large part on its "delimitation from other disorders" (p. 108). "These criteria should . . . permit exclusion of borderline cases and doubtful cases (an undiagnosed group) so that the index group may be as homogeneous as possible" (Robins & Guze, 1970, p. 108).

Scientists may devote their careers to attempting to identify the specific etiology, pathology, or treatment for a respective diagnostic category. Under the assumption that the diagnoses do in fact refer to qualitatively distinct conditions, it follows that there should be a specific etiology, pathology, and perhaps even a specific treatment for each respective disorder. The theories, hypotheses, findings, and disputes as to specific etiology, pathology, and/or treatment of a respective mental disorder largely inform the respective chapters of professional, graduate, and undergraduate texts on psychopathology, such as this current edition of *Adult Psychopathology and Diagnosis*.

However, the question of whether mental disorders are in fact discrete clinical conditions or arbitrary distinctions along continuous dimensions of functioning has been a longstanding issue (Kendell, 1975), and its significance is escalating with the growing recognition of the limitations of the categorical model (Hyman, 2010; Widiger & Clark, 2000; Widiger & Samuel, 2005). The principal model for validation of mental disorder diagnostic categories was provided by Robins and Guze (1970), who articulated five fundamental phases: clinical description, laboratory study, delimitation from other disorders, follow-up, and family studies. However, the research that has accumulated to date has not supported validity of the delimitation of the disorders from one another:

> Indeed, in the last 20 years, the categorical approach has been increasingly questioned as evidence has accumulated that the so-called categorical disorders like major depressive disorder and anxiety disorders, and schizophrenia and bipolar disorder seem to merge imperceptibly both into one another and into normality . . . with no demonstrable natural boundaries. (First, 2003, p. 661)

As expressed by the Vice Chair of *DSM-5*,

> the failure of *DSM-III* criteria to specifically define individuals with only one disorder served as an alert that the strict neo-Kraepelinian categorical approach to mental disorder diagnoses advocated by Robins and Guze (1970), Spitzer, Endicott and Robins (1978), and others could have some serious problems. (Regier, 2008, p. xxi)

As acknowledged by Kendell and Jablensky (2003), "it is likely that, sooner or later, our existing typology will be abandoned and replaced by a dimensional classification" (p. 8).

In 1999, a *DSM-5* Research Planning Conference was held under joint sponsorship of the APA and the National Institute of Mental Health (NIMH), the purpose of which was to set research priorities that would optimally inform future classifications. One impetus for this effort was the frustration with the existing nomenclature.

> In the more than 30 years since introduction of the Feighner criteria by Robins and Guze, which eventually led to *DSM-III*, the goal of validating these syndromes and discovering common etiologies has remained elusive. Despite many proposed candidates, not one

laboratory marker has been found to be specific in identifying any of the *DSM*-defined syndromes. Epidemiologic and clinical studies have shown extremely high rates of comorbidities among the disorders, undermining the hypothesis that the syndromes represent distinct etiologies. Furthermore, epidemiologic studies have shown a high degree of short-term diagnostic instability for many disorders. With regard to treatment, lack of treatment specificity is the rule rather than the exception. (Kupfer, First, & Regier, 2002, p. xviii)

*DSM-5* Research Planning Work Groups were formed to develop white papers that would set an effective research agenda for the next edition of the diagnostic manual. The Nomenclature Work Group, charged with addressing the fundamental assumptions of the diagnostic system, concluded that it will be "important that consideration be given to advantages and disadvantages of basing part or all of *DSM-V* on dimensions rather than categories" (Rounsaville et al., 2002, p. 12).

The white papers developed by the *DSM-5* Research Planning Work Groups were followed by a series of international conferences whose purpose was to further enrich the empirical database in preparation for the eventual development of *DSM-5* (a description of this conference series can be found at www.dsm5.org). The first conference was devoted to shifting personality disorders to a dimensional model of classification (Widiger, Simonsen, Krueger, Livesley, & Verheul, 2005). The final conference was devoted to dimensional approaches across the diagnostic manual, including substance use disorders, major depressive disorder, psychoses, anxiety disorders, and developmental psychopathology, as well as the personality disorders (Helzer, Kraemer, et al., 2008).

The purpose of this chapter is to review the *DSM-IV-TR* categorical diagnostic approach. The chapter begins with a discussion of the problematic boundaries among the *DSM-IV-TR* categorical diagnoses. We then focus in particular on depression, alcohol abuse and dependence, personality disorders, and intellectual disability. We conclude with a discussion of the shift within *DSM-5* toward a dimensional classification.

## DIAGNOSTIC BOUNDARIES

In an effort to force differential diagnosis, a majority of diagnoses in *DSM-III* (APA, 1980) contained exclusionary criteria specifying that a respective disorder could not be diagnosed if it occurred in the presence of another disorder. These exclusions by fiat did not prove to be effective (Boyd et al., 1984) and many were deleted in *DSM-III-R* (APA, 1987). As expressed at the time by Maser and Cloninger (1990), "it is clear that the classic Kraepelinian model in which all psychopathology is comprised of discrete and mutually exclusive diseases must be modified or rejected" (p. 12).

Many *DSM-IV-TR* diagnostic criterion sets, though, continue to include exclusionary criteria that attempt to force clinicians to make largely arbitrary choices among alternative diagnoses (APA, 2000), and it is also evident that there continues to be a highly problematic rate of diagnostic co-occurrence (Kessler, Chiu, Dember, & Walters, 2005; Krueger & Markon, 2006; Maser & Patterson, 2002; Widiger & Clark, 2000). The term *comorbidity* refers to the co-occurrence of distinct disorders, apparently interacting with one another, each presumably with its own etiology, pathology, and treatment implications (Feinstein, 1970). If one considers the entire diagnostic manual (which has not yet been done by any epidemiological study), it would likely be exceedingly rare for any patient to meet the criteria for just one disorder, and the comorbidity rises even further if one considers lifetime co-occurrence. Brown, Campbell, Lehman, Grisham, and Mancill (2001) reported that 95% of individuals in a clinical setting who meet criteria for lifetime major depression or dysthymia also meet criteria for a current or past anxiety disorder. In the case of psychopathology, comorbidity may be saying more about the invalidity of existing diagnostic distinctions than about the presence of multiple coexisting conditions (Krueger, 2002; Widiger & Edmundson, 2011).

Diagnostic comorbidity has become so prevalent that some researchers have argued for an abandonment of the term *comorbidity* in favor of a term (e.g., *co-occurrence*) that is more simply descriptive and does not imply the presence of distinct clinical entities (Lilienfeld, Waldman, & Israel, 1994). There are instances in which the presence of multiple diagnoses suggests the presence of distinct yet comorbid psychopathologies, but in most instances the presence of co-occurring diagnoses does appear to suggest the presence of a common, shared pathology and, therefore, a possible failing of the current diagnostic system (Krueger & Markon, 2006; Widiger & Clark, 2000).

> Comorbidity may be trying to show us that many current treatments are not so much treatments for transient "state" mental disorders of affect and anxiety as they are treatments for core processes, such as negative affectivity, that span normal and abnormal variation as well as undergird multiple mental disorders. (Krueger, 2002, p. 44)

Diagnostic criteria are developed and modified in order to construct a disorder that is as homogeneous as possible, thereby facilitating the likelihood of identifying a specific etiology, pathology, and treatment (Robins & Guze, 1970). However, the typical result of this effort is to leave many cases unaccounted for. In addition, despite the best effort to construct homogeneous and distinct syndromes, *DSM-IV-TR* is still replete with heterogeneous conditions with overlapping boundaries (Smith & Combs, 2010). New diagnostic categories are added to the nomenclature in large part to decrease clinicians' reliance on the nonspecific, wastebasket label of "not otherwise specified" (NOS). NOS is among the most frequently diagnosed disorders within clinical populations (Widiger & Edmundson, 2011). The function of most of the new disorders that are added to the manual does not appear to involve the identification of uniquely new forms of psychopathology. Their purpose is generally instead to fill problematic gaps. Notable examples for *DSM-IV* included bipolar II (filling a gap between *DSM-III-R* bipolar and cyclothymic mood disorders), mixed anxiety-depressive disorder (a gap between anxiety and mood disorders), depressive personality disorder (personality and mood disorders), and postpsychotic depressive disorder of schizophrenia (schizophrenia and major depression) (Frances et al., 1995).

When new diagnoses are added to fill gaps, they have the ironic effect of creating additional boundary problems, thereby making differential diagnosis even more problematic (Phillips, Price, Greenburg, & Rasmussen, 2003; Pincus, Frances, Davis,

First, & Widiger, 1992; Pincus, McQueen, & Elinson, 2003). One must ask, for instance, whether it is really meaningful or useful to determine whether mixed anxiety-depressive disorder is a mood or an anxiety disorder, whether schizo-affective disorder is a mood disorder or a form of schizophrenia (Craddock & Owen, 2005), whether postpsychotic depressive disorder is a form of depression or schizophrenia, whether early-onset dysthymia is a mood or a personality disorder (Widiger, 2003), whether acute stress disorder is an anxiety or a dissociative disorder (Cardena, Butler, & Spiegel, 2003), whether hypochondriasis is an anxiety disorder or a somatoform disorder, whether body dysmorphic disorder is an anxiety, eating, or somatoform disorder, and whether generalized social phobia is an anxiety or a personality disorder (Widiger, 2001a). In all of these cases, the most accurate answer is likely to be that each respective disorder includes features of different sections of the diagnostic manual. Yet the arbitrary and Procrustean decision of which single section of the manual in which to place each diagnosis must be made by the authors of a categorical diagnostic manual, and a considerable amount of effort and research is conducted to guide this decision, followed by further discussion and research to refute and debate whatever particular categorical decision was made.

## DEPRESSION

Mood disorders is a section of the APA diagnostic manual for which presence of qualitatively distinct conditions is particularly difficult to defend, especially for the primary diagnoses of dysthymia and major depressive disorder. Discussed here will be early-onset dysthymia, the continuum of depression, and subthreshold major depression, along with more general points concerning the boundary between mood and personality disorder.

*Early-Onset Dysthymia*   There is no meaningful distinction between early-onset dysthymia, an officially recognized mood disorder diagnosis, and depressive personality disorder, a proposed diagnosis within an appendix to *DSM-IV-TR* (APA, 2000). In fact, much of the empirical and conceptual basis for adding dysthymia to the *DSM-III* (APA, 1980) came from research and clinical literature concerning depressive personality (i.e., Keller, 1989). As acknowledged by the principal architects of *DSM-III*, dysthymia is "roughly equivalent to the concept of depressive personality" (Spitzer, Williams, & Skodol, 1980, p. 159). Depressive personality disorder was included within the mood disorders section of *DSM-III* despite the recommendations to recognize its existence as a disorder of personality (Klerman, Endicott, Spitzer, & Hirschfeld, 1979), because it resembled the symptomatology of other mood disorders (i.e., depressed mood) more than it resembled the symptoms of other personality disorders (e.g., schizoid). However, whereas mood disorders are defined largely by similarity in content (i.e., mood being the predominant feature; APA, 2000), the personality disorders are defined largely by form (i.e., early onset, pervasive, and chronic), often with quite different content (e.g., schizoid also shares little resemblance to histrionic personality disorder).

After *DSM-III* was published it became evident that many of the persons who were consistently and characteristically pessimistic, gloomy, cheerless, glum, and sullen (i.e., dysthymic) had been that way since childhood and that in many cases no apparent or distinct age of onset could be established. In other words, its conceptualization as a personality disorder became apparent. *DSM-III-R*, therefore, added an early-onset subtype (APA, 1987) and acknowledged that "this disorder usually begins in childhood, adolescence, or early adult life, and for this reason has often been referred to as a Depressive Personality" (APA, 1987, p. 231).

Personality disorder researchers proposed again for *DSM-IV* to include a depressive personality disorder diagnosis. They were told that in order for it to be included, it needed to be distinguished from the already established diagnosis of early-onset dysthymia, a task that might be considered rather difficult, if not unfair, given that the latter construct was based in large part on the former construct. Nevertheless, the *DSM-IV* Personality Disorders Work Group developed a proposed diagnostic criterion set that placed relatively more emphasis on cognitive features not currently included within the criterion set for dysthymia (including early-onset), as well as excluding somatic features (Task Force on DSM-IV, 1991). This criterion set was provided to the *DSM-IV* Mood Disorders Work Group to include within their *DSM-IV* field trial to determine empirically whether it was indeed possible to demarcate an area of functioning not yet covered by early-onset dysthymia, or at least identify persons not yet meeting diagnostic criteria for early-onset dysthymia.

The proposed criterion set was successful in reaching this goal (Phillips et al., 1998), which perhaps should not be surprising as no criterion set for a categorical diagnosis appears to be entirely successful in covering all cases. However, the Mood Disorders Work Group was equally impressed with the potential utility of the depressive personality diagnostic criteria for further describing and expanding the coverage of dysthymia (Keller et al., 1995) and therefore incorporated much of the proposed criteria for depressive personality into their proposed revisions for dysthymia, including early-onset (Task Force on DSM-IV, 1993). The *DSM-IV* Task Force recognized that it might be problematic to now require the personality disorder researchers to further redefine depressive personality to distinguish it from this further revision of dysthymia. Therefore, the *DSM-IV* Task Force decided instead to include both criterion sets in the appendix to *DSM-IV* (along with the original criterion set for dysthymia within the mood disorders section), with the acknowledgment that there may not be any meaningful distinction between them (APA, 1994; Frances et al., 1995). It is likely that in *DSM-5* depressive personality disorder will be deleted from the appendix, and the depressive personality traits will be incorporated into the criterion set for dysthymia.

*The Continuum of Depression*   The common view is that many instances of sadness (or even depression) do not constitute a mental disorder. Persons can be very sad without having a mental disorder. However, a simple inspection of the diagnostic criteria for major depressive disorder would not lend confidence to a conceptualization of this condition as being qualitatively distinct from "normal" depression or sadness (Andrews et al., 2008). Persons who are just very sad will have most of the same attributes (if not all of them) but just at a lesser degree of severity. The diagnostic criteria for major depressive disorder include depressed mood, loss of interest or pleasure, weight loss (or gain), insomnia (or hypersomnia), psychomotor retardation (or agitation), loss of energy, feelings of worthlessness, and/or diminished capacity to make decisions (APA, 2000). Each of these diagnostic criteria is readily placed along a continuum of severity that would shade imperceptibly into what would be considered a "normal" sadness or depression. *DSM-IV-TR*, therefore, includes specific thresholds for each of them, but they are clearly arbitrary thresholds that simply demarcate a relatively higher level of severity from a lower level of severity (e.g., "nearly every day" or "markedly diminished," and at least a "two week" period; APA, 2000). The diagnosis requires five of these nine criteria, with no apparent rationale for this threshold other than it would appear to be severe enough to be defensible to be titled as a "major" depressive episode, as distinguished from a "minor" depressive episode, which is then distinguished from "normal" sadness (APA, 2000).

Depression does appear to shade imperceptibly into "normal" sadness (Andrews et al., 2008). Ustun and Sartorius (1995) conducted a study of 5,000 primary care patients in 14 countries and reported a linear relationship between disability and number of depressive symptoms. Kessler, Zhao, Blazer, and Swartz (1997) examined the distribution of minor and major symptoms of depression using data from the National Comorbidity Survey. They considered the relationship of these symptoms with parental history of mental disorder, number and duration of depressive episodes, and comorbidity with other forms of psychopathology. Respective relationships increased with increasing number of symptoms, with no clear, distinct break. Sakashita, Slade, and Andrews (2007) examined the relationship between number of symptoms of depression and four measures of impairment using data from the Australian National Survey of Mental Health and Well-Being, and found that the relationship was again simply linear, with no clear or natural discontinuity to support the selection of any particular cutoff point.

Taxometrics refers to a series of related statistical techniques to detect whether a set of items is optimally understood as describing (assessing) a dimensional or a categorical construct (Beauchaine, 2007; Ruscio & Ruscio, 2004). Other statistical techniques, such as cluster or factor analyses, presume that the construct is either categorical or dimensional (respectively) and then determines how best to characterize the variables or items in either a categorical or dimensional format (respectively). Taxometric analyses are uniquely intriguing in providing a direct test of which structural model is most valid in characterizing the set of items or variables.

Several taxometric studies have been conducted on various symptoms and measures of depression. The first was provided by Ruscio and Ruscio (2000) in their taxometric analyses of items from the Beck Depression Inventory and, independently, items from the Zung Self-Rating Depression Scale in a sample of 996 male veterans who had received a diagnosis of posttraumatic stress disorder but also had a high prevalence rate of major depressive disorder, as well as a sample of 8,045 individuals from the general population (60% female) who completed the items from the Depression scale of the Minnesota Multiphasic Personality Inventory (MMPI). They indicated that "results of both studies, drawing on three widely used measures of depression, corroborated the dimensionality of depression" (Ruscio & Ruscio, 2000, p. 473).

The taxometric findings of Ruscio and Ruscio (2000) have been subsequently replicated, including taxometric analyses of (1) structured interview assessments of *DSM-IV-TR* major depressive disorder symptoms and, independently, items from the Beck Depression Inventory in a sample of 960 psychiatric outpatients (Slade, 2007); (2) major depressive disorder diagnostic criteria assessed in the 1,933 persons who endorsed at least one criterion in the Australian National Survey of Mental Health and Well-Being (Slade & Andrews, 2005); (3) self- and parent-reported depressive symptoms in 845 children and adolescents drawn from the population-based Georgia Health and Behavior Study (Hankin, Fraley, Lahey, & Waldman, 2005); (4) responses to MMPI-2 depression scales completed by 2,000 psychiatric inpatients and outpatients (Franklin, Strong, & Greene, 2002); (5) an epidemiologic survey of depressive symptoms within 392 college students (Baldwin & Shean, 2006); (6) Beck Depression Inventory items reported by 2,260 college students (Ruscio & Ruscio, 2002); and (7) depression items in the Composite International Diagnostic Interview as administered in the National Comorbidity Survey to 4,577 participants who endorsed the item concerning a lifetime occurrence of sad mood or loss of interest (Prisciandoro & Roberts, 2005). However, in contrast to the findings from these eight taxometric studies, three taxometric studies have supported a latent class taxon, including semistructured interview assessments of *DSM-IV-TR* major depressive disorder symptoms in 1,800 psychiatric outpatients (Ruscio, Zimmerman, McGlinchey, Chelminski, & Young, 2007), interview and self-report assessments of depression in 1,400 high school students (Solomon, Ruscio, Seeley, & Lewinsohn, 2006), and self-report and interview data on depression in 378 adolescents receiving treatment for depression (Ambrosini, Bennett, Cleland, & Haslam, 2002). In sum, the bulk of the evidence does appear to support a dimensional understanding of depression, but there is some ambiguity and inconsistency in the taxometric findings (Beach & Amir, 2003; Beauchaine, 2007; Widiger, 2001b).

*Subthreshold Major Depression*   Depression is a section of the diagnostic manual that does have considerable difficulty identifying or defining a clear boundary with "normal" sadness. Subthreshold cases of depression (i.e., persons with depressive symptoms below the threshold for a *DSM-IV-TR* mental disorder diagnosis) are clearly responsive to pharmacologic interventions, do seek treatment for their sadness, and are often being treated within primary care settings (Judd, Schettler, & Akiskal, 2002; Magruder & Calderone, 2000; Pincus, McQueen, & Elinson, 2003). These facts contributed to the proposal to include within an appendix to *DSM-IV* a diagnosis of "minor depressive disorder," for which it is acknowledged "can be difficult to distinguish from periods of sadness that are an inherent part of everyday life" (APA, 2000, p. 776).

Wakefield (2007) has been critical of the *DSM-IV-TR* criteria for major depressive disorder for including an inconsistently applied exclusion criterion. The diagnosis excludes most instances of depressive reactions to the loss of a loved one (i.e., uncomplicated bereavement). Depression after the loss of a loved one can be considered a mental disorder if "the symptoms persist for longer than two months" (APA, 2000, p. 356). Allowing persons just 2 months to grieve before one is diagnosed with a mental disorder does appear to be rather arbitrary. Perhaps more importantly, it is also unclear if depression in response to other losses should not also then be comparably excluded, such as depression secondary to the loss of a job or physical health (Wakefield, Schimtz, First, & Horwitz, 2007). Why the loss of a person is treated so differently from the loss of health or a job is not clear.

On the other hand, one could argue alternatively that all exclusion criteria should be removed. Perhaps the problem is not that depression in response to a loss of a job or physical disorder should not be a disorder, analogous to bereavement (Wakefield, 2007); perhaps the problem is that bereavement should be a mental disorder (Bonanno et al., 2007; Forstmeier & Maercker, 2007; Widiger & Miller, 2008). What is currently considered to be a normal depression in response to the loss of a loved one does often, if not always, include pain and suffering, meaningful impairment to functioning, and is outside of the ability of the bereaved person to fully control—the essential hallmarks of a mental disorder (Widiger & Sankis, 2000). Depression is a reasonable response to the loss of a loved one, a psychological trauma, but many physical disorders and injuries are reasonable and understandable responses to a physical trauma. Loss is perhaps best understood as part of the etiology for the disorder, not a reason for which the disorder is not present (Widiger, in press). One of the proposals for *DSM-5* is in fact to remove the bereavement exclusion criterion (see www.dsm5.org).

## ALCOHOL ABUSE AND DEPENDENCE

One of the sections of the *DSM-IV-TR* for which a categorical model of classification and conceptualization has had a firmly entrenched tradition is the substance use disorders. Alcoholism in particular has long been conceptualized as a qualitatively distinct disease (Garbutt, 2008; Goodwin & Guze, 1996). A significant change to its diagnosis and conceptualization occurred with *DSM-III-R* (APA, 1987), when it shifted from being understood as a purely physiological dependence to a broader and less specific behavioral dependence (Carroll, Rounsaville, & Bryant, 1994; Edwards & Gross, 1976). "Dependence is seen as a complex process that reflects the central importance of substances in an individual's life, along with a feeling of compulsion to continue taking the substance and subsequent problems controlling use" (Schuckit et al., 1999, p. 41). To many, the diagnosis does still refer to a disease, but one that is developed through a normal social learning history (Kandel, 1998).

However, the diagnosis is likely to be broadened further in *DSM-5*, wherein it would be referred to as a behavioral addiction that would also include pathological gambling (Martin, 2005; Petry, 2006; Potenza, 2006). Pathological gambling has been considered by many substance use and pathological gambling researchers and clinicians to be an addiction, but it could not be included within the substance-related disorders section because it does not involve the ingestion of a substance (Bradford, Geller, Lesieur, Rosenthal, & Wise, 1996). Proposed for *DSM-5* will be an abandonment of this requirement, replacing the section of substance-related disorders with a new section concerning "addiction and related disorders" (see www.dsm5.org).

This new class of disorders could now contain a wide variety of possible behavioral addictions, including an excessive participation in shopping, sex, or the Internet. As stated on the *DSM-5* website, along with pathological gambling, "other addiction-like behavioral disorders such as 'Internet addiction' . . . will be considered as potential additions to this category as research data accumulate" (APA, 2010, "Substance Related Disorders," para. 1). "This 'slippery slope' makes it difficult to know where to draw the line demarcating any excessive behavior as an addiction" (Petry, 2005a, p. 7). In fact, proposed for inclusion in the sex disorders section of *DSM-5* is hypersexual disorder, which can indeed be identified as a sex addiction (Kafka, 2010; Ragan & Martin, 2000; Winters, 2010).

The boundary between a behavioral addiction and substantial interest in an activity that a person finds highly pleasurable will be difficult to demarcate. For example, on the basis of the proposed criteria for an Internet hypersexual disorder, a person who partakes in Internet pornography would meet diagnostic criteria if he or she enjoyed it for longer than 6 months, engaged in the activity for a period of time that a clinician considered to be excessive (i.e., the amount of time considered to be excessive is not objectively specified), did so at times in response to feeling bored, did so at times to help relieve stress, reduced the activity due to transient feelings of guilt or doubt but then resumed the activity later when these feelings subsided, and/or continued to enjoy Internet pornography despite a clinician's belief that it causes emotional harm to the person or to someone else. Beyond a concern that any disapproved and/or harmful activity will be classified as mental disorders in *DSM-5* (Petry, 2005b), it would seem evident that the boundary between the presence versus absence of a behavioral addiction will be rather fuzzy.

The distinction between harmful substance use and a substance abuse (or dependence) is also unclear and indistinct. Presumably, persons can choose to consume alcohol without being compelled to do so by the presence of a mental disorder. The *DSM-IV-TR* diagnostic criteria for substance abuse (and dependence) are fallible indicators for harmful and dyscontrolled usage (e.g., use more than originally intended, continue to use despite social consequences, and reduction of other activities in preference for the substance; APA, 2000). The greater number of these indicators of dyscontrol that are present, the more likely that there is in fact dyscontrol, but none can be considered infallible in the identification of dyscontrol, and no particular number of them clearly demarcates a boundary between presence versus absence of dyscontrolled usage. It is not even clear how much purportedly volitional or regulatory control a normal, healthy person has over adaptive, healthy behaviors (Bargh & Ferguson, 2000; Howard & Conway, 1986; Kirsch & Lynn, 2000; Wegner & Wheatley, 2000), let alone the boundary between controlled and dyscontrolled harmful usage. Both normal and abnormal human functioning is, at best, the result of a complex interaction of apparent volitional choice with an array of biogenetic and environmental determinants.

The distinction between alcohol abuse and dependence is equally fuzzy. Abuse has generally been considered to be simply a residual category and/or a less severe form of dependence (Saunders, 2006). Some of the diagnostic criteria for abuse are contained within the criterion set for dependence (e.g., interference with social, occupational, or recreational activities), which is always a problem for disorders that would be considered to be qualitatively distinct. It is largely for this reason that the *DSM-IV-TR* diagnoses of abuse and dependence will likely be subsumed into one diagnosis of substance use disorder in *DSM-5*.

Diagnostic criteria for alcohol dependence were written largely in an effort to describe a prototypic case of the disorder, a practice that is followed for all but a few of the disorders throughout *DSM-IV-TR* (Frances et al., 1995). However, prototypic cases are typically understood to be the most severe cases and/or the cases that involve all possible features or symptoms of the disorder (First & Westen, 2007). The construction of diagnostic criterion sets in terms of prototypic cases does work to an extent, but it also fails to adequately describe many of the actual cases, including the subthreshold cases, and perhaps even the typical cases, depending upon the distribution of features and symptomatology within the population. Constructing criterion sets in terms of prototypic cases can be comparable to confining the description and diagnosis of (for instance) mental retardation to the most severe variant of intellectual disability, and then attempting to apply this description to all of the less severe variants—a method of diagnosis that would obviously be sorely limited. The limitations of this approach are now becoming more closely appreciated in the diagnosis of dyscontrolled substance use and, more specifically, alcohol use disorders, where the existing criterion sets are failing to adequately describe (for instance) dyscontrolled and impairing alcohol usage in adolescents (Crowley, 2006) and other "diagnostic orphans" (Saunders, 2006).

The limitation is perhaps most clearly demonstrated in studies using item response theory (IRT) methodology. IRT allows the researcher to investigate the fidelity with which items are measuring a latent trait along the length of its continuum, contrasting, for instance, the amount of information that different diagnostic criteria provide at different levels of the latent trait (Muthen, 2006). Some diagnostic criteria, for instance, might be most useful in distinguishing among mild cases of the disorder, whereas other diagnostic criteria are most useful in distinguishing among the more severe cases of the disorder. Several IRT analyses have now been conducted for the diagnosis of substance dependence (and other disorders), and the findings are remarkably consistent (Reise & Waller, 2009). Existing diagnostic criterion sets (and/or symptoms currently assessed in existing instruments) cluster around the high end of the disorder as opposed to being spread out across the entire range of the continuum (e.g., Kahler & Strong, 2006; Langenbucher et al., 2004; Muthen, 2006; Proudfoot, Baillie, & Teesson, 2006; Saha, Chou, & Grant, 2006). This consistent pattern of results is in stark contrast to what is traditionally found in cognitive ability testing, where IRT analyses have been largely developed and previously applied (Reise & Waller, 2009).

It is evident from the IRT analyses that the existing diagnostic criterion sets are sorely inadequate in characterizing the lower and even middle range of substance use dysfunction, consistent with the *DSM-IV-TR* description being confined to a prototypic case (of the presumably qualitatively distinct disorder). If alcohol usage was conceptualized along a continuum, the job of the authors of the diagnostic manual would be to construct a description and measurement of the disorder that adequately represents each of the levels or degrees to which the disorder appears along this continuum rather than attempt to describe the prototypic case. The *DSM-IV-TR* (and *DSM-5*) criterion sets are confined to only the most severe cases and are not describing well a large proportion of persons with clinically significant alcohol use dysfunction. As a result, clinicians must continue to rely on the nondescriptive, wastebasket diagnosis of NOS to describe the lower range of the continuum (Saunders, 2006).

PERSONALITY DISORDERS

There are three major problematic boundaries for the personality disorders: (1) the boundaries between personality disorders and other mental disorders, (2) the boundaries between personality disorders and normal personality, and (3) the boundaries among the personality disorders. Discussed first will be the boundaries with other mental disorders, followed by the other two boundaries.

*Boundaries With Other Mental Disorders*   Among the proposals considered for the personality disorders at the *DSM-5* Research Planning Conference (Kupfer et al., 2002) was the suggestion to replace the diagnosis of personality disorder with early-onset and chronic variants of existing Axis I mental disorders (First et al., 2002). This might appear at first blush to be a radical proposal, and perhaps it is. However, it does have support from a variety of sources.

There is no clear or consistent boundary between the personality disorders and many other mental disorders, particularly certain mood, anxiety, impulse dyscontrol, and psychotic disorders (Krueger, 2002). In fact, *DSM-IV-TR* schizotypal personality disorder has long been classified as a form of schizophrenia rather than as a personality disorder in the World Health Organization's *International Classification of Diseases* (*ICD-10*; WHO, 1992), the parent classification for the APA's *DSM-IV-TR*. Schizotypal personality disorder is genetically related to schizophrenia, most of its neurobiological risk factors and psychophysiological correlates are shared with schizophrenia (e.g., eye tracking, orienting, startle blink, and neurodevelopmental abnormalities), and the treatments that are effective in ameliorating schizotypal symptoms overlap with treatments used for persons with Axis I schizophrenia (Parnas, Licht, & Bovet, 2005; Raine, 2006).

On the other hand, there are also compelling reasons for continuing to consider schizotypal as a personality disorder (Raine, 2006). Simply because a personality disorder shares a genetic foundation with another disorder does not then indicate that it is a form of that other disorder. Contrary to viewing schizotypal personality disorder as a variant of schizophrenia is that the disorder is far more comorbid with other personality disorders than it is with any other schizophrenia-related disorder; persons with schizotypal personality disorder rarely go on to develop schizophrenia; and schizotypal symptomatology is seen in many persons within the general population who lack any genetic association with schizophrenia and who would not be appropriately described as having some form of schizophrenia (Raine, 2006).

However, a fate similar to that of schizotypal personality disorder in *ICD-10* (WHO, 1992) and depressive personality disorder in *DSM-IV* (APA, 1994) could await the other personality disorder diagnostic categories in a future edition of the diagnostic manual (First et al., 2002). For example, social phobia was a new addition to *DSM-III* (Spitzer et al., 1980; Turner & Beidel, 1989). It was considered then to be a distinct, circumscribed condition, consistent with the definition of a phobia as a "persistent, irrational fear of a *specific* object, activity, or situation" (APA, 1994, p. 336, our emphasis). However, it became apparent to anxiety disorder researchers and clinicians that the fears of many of their patients were rarely so discrete and circumscribed (Spitzer & Williams, 1985). Therefore, the authors of *DSM-III-R* developed a generalized subtype for when "the phobic situation includes most social situations" (APA, 1987, p. 243).

*DSM-III-R* generalized social phobia, however, merged into the *DSM-III* diagnosis of avoidant personality disorder. Both were concerned with a pervasive, generalized social insecurity, discomfort, and timidity. Efforts to distinguish them have indicated only that avoidant personality disorder tends to be, on average, relatively more dysfunctional than generalized social phobia (Turner, Beidel, & Townsley, 1992; Widiger, 2001a).

*DSM-IV* provided no solution. In fact, it was acknowledged that generalized social phobia emerges "out of a childhood history of social inhibition or shyness" (APA, 1994, p. 414), consistent with the concept of a maladaptive personality trait. An argument raised for classifying this condition as an anxiety rather than as a personality disorder was that many persons with the disorder benefit from pharmacologic interventions (Liebowitz, 1992). "One may have to rethink what the personality disorder concept means in an instance where 6 weeks of phenelzine therapy begins to reverse long-standing interpersonal hypersensitivity as well as discomfort in socializing" (Liebowitz, 1992, p. 251). Of course, one might also have to rethink what the anxiety disorder concept means when an antidepressant is an effective form of treating an anxiety disorder. In addition, it is unclear why a maladaptive personality trait should not be responsive to a pharmacologic intervention (Knorr & Kessing, 2010; Knutson et al., 1998; Tang et al., 2009). In any case, the authors of *DSM-IV-TR* concluded that these two conditions "may be alternative conceptualizations of the same or similar conditions" (APA, 2000, p. 720).

There does not currently appear to be a meaningful distinction between avoidant personality disorder and generalized social phobia (APA, 2000; Tyrer, 2005; Widiger, 2003). Some suggest that the best solution is to simply abandon the personality disorder diagnosis in favor of the generalized anxiety disorder (First et al., 2002; Schneider, Blanco, Anita, & Liebowitz, 2002). "We believe that the more extensive evidence for syndromal validity of social phobia, including pharmacological and cognitive-behavioral treatment efficacy, make it the more useful designation in cases of overlap with avoidant personality" (Liebowitz et al., 1998, p. 1060). The reference to treatment efficacy by Liebowitz et al. (1998) falls on receptive ears for many clinicians who struggle to obtain insurance coverage for the treatment of maladaptive personality functioning. It is often reported that a personality disorder diagnosis is stigmatizing, due in large part to its placement on a distinct axis that carries the implication of being an untreatable, lifetime disorder (Frances et al., 1991; Kendell, 1983). For reasons such as these, the Assembly of the American Psychiatric Association (which has authoritative governance over the approval of revisions to the diagnostic manual) has repeatedly passed resolutions to explore proposals to move one or more personality disorders to Axis I in large part to address the stigma and lack of reimbursement for their treatment.

Just as the depressive, schizotypal, and avoidant personality disorders could be readily subsumed within an existing section of Axis I, borderline personality disorder could be reclassified as a mood dysregulation and/or impulse dyscontrol disorder; obsessive-compulsive personality disorder could be reclassified as a generalized and chronic variant of obsessive-compulsive anxiety disorder (although there is in fact only weak evidence to support a close relationship between the obsessive-compulsive anxiety and personality disorders; Costa, Samuels, Bagby, Daffin, & Norton, 2005); and antisocial personality disorder could be an adult variant of conduct (disruptive behavior) disorder. The five other *DSM-IV-TR* personality disorders (i.e., narcissistic, histrionic, dependent, paranoid, and schizoid) are relatively more difficult to reclassify in this manner.

However, any difficulty with shifting the narcissistic, histrionic, dependent, paranoid, and schizoid personality disorders into an existing Axis I disorder could become moot in *DSM-5*, as they are proposed for deletion (see www.dsm5.org). Narcissism (Miller, Widiger, & Campbell, 2010; Pincus & Lukowitsky, 2010; Rhodewalt & Vohs, 2005; Ronningstam, 2011) and dependency (Bornstein, 2011; Hammen, 2005) are well-validated constructs within the general personality literature, but these two diagnoses, along with the histrionic, have a strong psychodynamic heritage (Millon et al., 1996). The trend in psychiatry is toward a neurobiological perspective (Hyman, 2010; Insel, 2009; Widiger, in press). Personality disorder constructs with a strong psychodynamic connotation are unlikely to be missed in the effort to shift psychiatry toward a particular theoretical perspective (Widiger, 2011).

In sum, the future of all the personality disorder diagnostic categories might be reformulation as early-onset chronic variants of existing Axis I disorders, as explicitly proposed at the initial *DSM-5* Research Planning Conference (First et al., 2002). A difficulty with respect to this proposal—beyond the fundamental concern that the diagnostic manual would no longer recognize the existence of maladaptive personality functioning—is that it might just create more problems than it solves (Widiger, 2003). It is well established that persons have constellations of maladaptive personality traits that have significant consequential life outcomes (Ozer & Benet-Martinez, 2006; Roberts & DelVecchio, 2000). These personality traits are not currently well described by just one or even multiple personality disorder diagnoses (Clark, 2007; Trull & Durrett, 2005; Widiger & Trull, 2007), and they will be described even less well by multiple diagnoses across the broad classes of mood, anxiety, impulse dyscontrol, psychotic, and disruptive behavior disorders.

*Boundaries With Other Personality Disorders and Normal Personality*   Rounsaville et al. (2002) suggested that the first section of the diagnostic manual to shift to a dimensional classification should be the personality disorders. The personality disorders have been among the most problematic of disorders to be diagnosed categorically (First et al., 2002; Kendell, 1989). It is the norm for patients to meet diagnostic criteria for more than one personality disorder (Clark, 2007; Lilienfeld et al., 1994; Livesley, 2003; Trull & Durrett, 2005). Excessive diagnostic co-occurrence is in fact the primary reason that 5 of the 10 personality disorder diagnoses are proposed for deletion in *DSM-5* (Skodol et al., 2011). It is perhaps self-evident that persons are not well described by just one trait term. Each person has instead a constellation of personality traits, many of which are adaptive and some of which may also be maladaptive. There is little reason to think that it would be different when a person is said to have a personality disorder (Widiger & Trull, 2007).

There also appears to be no clear or distinct boundary between normal and abnormal personality functioning. The *DSM-IV-TR* diagnostic thresholds were not set at a point that has any theoretical or clinical significance. They are arbitrarily set at half or one more than half of the diagnostic criteria (APA, 2000). In fact, all of the personality disorders are readily understood as extreme and/or maladaptive variants of normal personality traits distributed within the general population; more specifically, they are the domains and facets of the five-factor dimensional model (FFM) of general personality structure (Widiger & Trull, 2007).

The FFM consists of five broad domains of general personality functioning: (1) neuroticism (or emotional instability), (2) extraversion versus introversion, (3) openness versus closedness, (4) agreeableness versus antagonism, and (5) conscientiousness versus undependability. The FFM was derived originally through empirical studies of the trait terms within the English language (L. Goldberg, 1993). Language can be understood as a sedimentary deposit of the observations of persons over the thousands of years of the language's development and transformation. The most important domains of personality functioning are those with the most number of trait terms to describe and differentiate the various manifestations and nuances of a respective domain, and the structure of personality is suggested by the empirical relationships among these trait terms. The initial lexical studies with the English language converged well onto a five-factor structure (Goldberg, 1993). Subsequent lexical studies have been conducted on many additional languages (e.g., German, Dutch, Czech, Polish, Russian, Italian, Spanish, Hebrew, Hungarian, Turkish, Korean, and Filipino), and these have confirmed well the existence of the five broad domains (Ashton & Lee, 2001; Church, 2001). The five broad domains have been differentiated into more specific facets by Costa and McCrae (1992) on the basis of their development of and research with the NEO Personality Inventory-Revised (NEO PI-R), by far the most commonly used and heavily researched measure of the FFM.

Studies have now well documented that all of the *DSM-IV-TR* personality disorder symptomatology is readily understood as maladaptive variants of the domains and facets of the FFM (O'Connor, 2002, 2005; Samuel & Widiger, 2008; Saulsman & Page, 2004; Widiger & Costa, 2002). Saulsman and Page (2004) concluded that "each of the personality disorders shows associations with the five-factor model that are meaningful and predictable given their diagnostic criteria" (p. 1075). As acknowledged by Livesley (2001b), "all categorical diagnoses of *DSM* can be accommodated within the five-factor framework" (p. 24). As expressed by Clark (2007), "the five-factor model of personality is widely accepted as representing the higher-order structure of both normal and abnormal personality traits" (p. 246). The problematic diagnostic co-occurrence among the *DSM-IV-TR* personality disorders is well explained by the extent to which each of the personality disorders shares traits of the FFM (Lynam & Widiger, 2001; O'Connor, 2005).

Widiger, Costa, and McCrae (2002) have proposed a four-step procedure for the diagnosis of a personality disorder from the perspective of the FFM, as an alternative to the existing diagnostic categories. The first step is to obtain a hierarchical and multifactorial description of an individual's general personality structure in terms of the five domains and 30 facets of the FFM. Widiger and Lowe (2007) provide a discussion of optimal instruments for this assessment. The second step is to identify problems in living associated with elevated scores. Problems in living associated with each of the 60 poles of the 30 facets of the FFM are provided in Widiger et al. (2002) and McCrae, Löckenhoff, and Costa (2005). Each of these problems is considered within the sociocultural context in which the person must function, as some personality traits can be quite adaptive within some contexts but maladaptive within others (Wakefield, 2008; Widiger & Costa, 1994). The third step is to determine whether the impairments reach a clinically significant level that would warrant a diagnosis of personality disorder. This can be done through simply a sum of the impairments associated with each facet or through a more inferential consideration of the configuration or interaction of traits (Wakefield, 2008). The latter is more consistent with traditional personality disorder theory, but the former would be simpler and more reliable. The fourth step is optional: a quantitative matching of the individual's FFM personality profile to prototypic profiles of diagnostic constructs (e.g., Miller & Lynam, 2003; Trull et al., 2003). An illustration of this four-step procedure was provided by Widiger and Lowe (2007).

The FFM of personality disorder has several advantages over the existing categorical approach. It would help with the stigmatization of a personality disorder diagnosis, because no longer would a personality disorder be conceptualized as something that is qualitatively distinct from general personality traits. All persons vary in the extent of their neuroticism, in the extent to which they are agreeable versus antagonistic, and in the extent to which they are conscientious, impulsive, and/or undependable (McCrae & Costa, 2003). The FFM of personality disorder will provide not only a more precise description of each person's individual personality structure but also a more complete picture through the inclusion of normal, adaptive traits, recognizing thereby that a person is more than just the personality disorder and that aspects to the self can be adaptive, even commendable, despite the presence of the maladaptive personality traits. Some of the personality strengths may also be quite relevant to treatment, such as openness to experience indicating an interest in exploratory psychotherapy, agreeableness indicating an engagement in group therapy, and conscientiousness indicating a willingness and ability to adhere to the demands and rigor of dialectical behavior therapy (Sanderson & Clarkin, 2002). The FFM of personality disorder would also bring to the psychiatric nomenclature a wealth of knowledge concerning the origins, childhood antecedents, stability, and universality of the dispositions that underlie personality disorder (Widiger & Trull, 2007). Further discussions of this proposal are provided by Widiger and Mullins-Sweatt (2009).

## INTELLECTUAL DISABILITY

Rounsaville et al. (2002) and others have suggested that the personality disorders section should be the first to shift to a dimensional classification, apparently not fully appreciating that one section has long been dimensional: mental retardation. Many persons write as if a shift to a dimensional classification represents a new, fundamental change in the diagnostic manual (e.g., Regier, 2008). For much of the manual, such a shift would certainly represent a fundamental change in how mental disorders are conceptualized and classified (Guze, 1978; Guze & Helzer, 1987; Robins & Guze, 1970). Nevertheless, there is a clear precedent for a dimensional classification of psychopathology already included within *DSM-IV-TR*: the diagnosis of mental retardation (APA, 2000).

Mental retardation in *DSM-IV-TR* is diagnosed along a continuum of intellectual and social functioning; more precisely, "significantly subaverage intellectual functioning: an IQ [intelligence quotient] of approximately 70 or below" (APA, 2000, p. 49), along with related deficits or impairments in adaptive functioning. This is consistent with steps one and two of the FFM of personality disorder (Widiger & Trull, 2007). An IQ of 70 does not carve nature at a discrete joint or identify the presence of a qualitatively distinct condition, disease, or disorder. On the contrary, it is a quantitative cutoff point along the dimension of intelligence. An IQ of 70 is simply two standard deviations below the mean (American Association on Mental Retardation [AAMR], 2002).

Intelligence involves the ability to reason, plan, solve problems, think abstractly, comprehend complex ideas, learn quickly, and learn from experience (AAMR, 2002). Intelligence, like personality, is distributed as a hierarchical, multifactorial continuous variable. Most persons' level of intelligence, including most of those with mental retardation, is the result of a complex interaction of multiple genetic, fetal and infant development, and environmental influences (Deary, Spinath, & Bates, 2006). There are no discrete breaks in its distribution that would provide an absolute distinction between normal and abnormal intelligence. The point of demarcation for the diagnosis of an intellectual disability (the current term for the disorder and the term to be used in *DSM-5*) is an arbitrary, quantitative distinction along the normally distributed levels of hierarchically and multi-factorially defined intelligence. This point of demarcation is arbitrary in the sense that it does not carve nature at a discrete joint, but it was not, of course, randomly or mindlessly chosen. It is a defensible selection that was informed by the impairments in functioning commonly associated with an IQ of 70 or below (AAMR, 2002). For example, a previous cutoff point of an IQ of 79 identified too many persons who were in fact able to function independently.

In addition, the disorder of mental retardation is not diagnosed simply by the presence of an IQ of 70 or below. It must be accompanied by a documented impairment to functioning. "Mental retardation is a disability characterized by significant limitation in both intellectual functioning and in adaptive behavior as expressed in conceptual, social, and practical adaptive skills" (AAMR, 2002, p. 23). Persons with IQ scores lower than 70 who can function effectively would not be diagnosed. The diagnosis is understood in the context of the social, practical requirements of everyday functioning that must be met by the person (Luckasson & Reeve, 2001). The purpose of the diagnosis is not to suggest that a specific pathology is present, but to identify persons who, on the basis of their intellectual disability, would be eligible for public health care services and benefits to help them overcome or compensate for their relatively lower level of intelligence.

Many instances of intellectual disability are due in large part to specific etiologies, such as tuberous sclerosis, microcephaly, von Recklinghausen's disease, trisomy 21, mosaicism, Prader-Willi syndrome, and many, many more (Kendell & Jablensky, 2003). Nevertheless, disorders that result from these specific etiologies are generally understood as medical conditions, an associated feature of which is also an intellectual disability that would be diagnosed concurrently and independently as mental retardation. The intellectual disability that is diagnosed as a mental disorder within *DSM-IV-TR* is itself a multifactorially determined and heterogeneous dimensional construct falling along the broad continuum of intellectual functioning. "The causes of intellectual disabilities are typically complex interactions of biological, behavioral/

psychological, and sociocultural factors" (Naglieri, Salter, & Rojahn, 2008, p. 409). An important postnatal cause for intellectual disability is "simply" psychosocial deprivation, resulting from poverty, chaotic living environment, and/or child abuse or neglect. As expressed in *DSM-IV-TR*, "in approximately 30%–40% of individuals seen in clinical settings, no clear etiology for the mental retardation can be determined despite extensive evaluation efforts" (APA, 2000, p. 45). In sum, intellectual disability may serve as an effective model for the classification of the rest of the diagnostic manual, including mood, psychotic, personality, anxiety, and other mental disorders.

## *DSM-5* AND DIMENSIONAL CLASSIFICATION

The modern effort to demarcate a taxonomy of distinct clinical conditions is often traced to Kraepelin (1917). Kraepelin (1917), however, had acknowledged that "wherever we try to mark out the frontier between mental health and disease, we find a neutral territory, in which the imperceptible change from the realm of normal life to that of obvious derangement takes place" (p. 295). The Robins and Guze (1970) paradigm for the validation of categorical diagnosis has also been widely influential within psychiatry (Klerman, 1983; Kupfer et al., 2002). In 1989, L. Robins and Barrett (1989) edited a text in honor of this classic paper. Kendell (1989) provided the final word in his closing chapter. His conclusions, however, were curiously negative: "Ninety years have now elapsed since Kraepelin first provided the framework of a plausible classification of mental disorders. Why then, with so many potential validators available, have we made so little progress since that time?" (Kendell, 1989, p. 313). He answered his rhetorical question in the next paragraph: "One important possibility is that the discrete clusters of psychiatric symptoms we are trying to delineate do not actually exist but are as much a mirage as discrete personality types" (Kendell, 1989, p. 313).

It is stated in the first paragraph of the introduction to *DSM-IV-TR* that "our highest priority has been to provide a helpful guide to clinical practice" (APA, 2000, p. xxiii). First (2005) argued in his rejoinder to proposals for shifting the diagnostic manual into a dimension model that "the most important obstacle standing in the way of its implementation in *DSM-V* (and beyond) is questions about clinical utility" (p. 561). However, one should question whether the existing diagnostic manual in fact has appreciable clinical utility (Mullins-Sweatt & Widiger, 2009; Widiger & Mullins-Sweatt, 2010). "Apologists for categorical diagnoses argue that the system has clinical utility being easy to use and valuable in formulating cases and planning treatment [but] there is little evidence for these assertions" (Livesley, 2001a, p. 278). First (2005) suggested that "the current categorical system of *DSM* has clinical utility with regard to the treatment of individuals" (p. 562), yet elsewhere has stated that "with regard to treatment, lack of treatment specificity is the rule rather than the exception" (Kupfer et al., 2002, p. xviii). The heterogeneity of diagnostic membership, the lack of precision in description, the excessive diagnostic co-occurrence, the failure to lead to a specific diagnosis, the reliance on the NOS wastebasket diagnosis, and the unstable and arbitrary diagnostic boundaries of the *DSM-IV-TR* diagnostic categories are matters of clinical utility that is a source of considerable frustration for clinicians and public health care agencies (Mullins-Sweatt & Widiger, 2009).

Work on *DSM-5* is now well underway, and it is evident that a primary goal is to shift the manual toward a dimensional classification (Helzer, Wittchen, Krueger, & Kraemer, 2008; Regier, Narrow, Kuhl, & Kupfer, 2010). This effort is a clear recognition of the failure of the categorical system (D. Goldberg, 2010). Nevertheless, it also appears that the shifts likely to take place in *DSM-5* will be neither fundamental nor significant. The effort will fall considerably short of a true paradigm shift. Current proposals appear, for the most part, to be quite tentative, if not timid. "What is being proposed for *DSM-V* is not to substitute dimensional scales for categorical diagnoses, but to add a dimensional option to the usual categorical diagnoses for *DSM-V*" (Kraemer, 2008, p. 9). None of the mental disorders, including even the personality disorders, will convert to a dimensional classification in *DSM-5* (see www.dsm5.org).

As acknowledged by Helzer, Kraemer, and Krueger (2006), "our proposal not only preserves categorical definitions but also does not alter the process by which these definitions would be developed. Those charged with developing criteria for specific mental disorders would operate just as their predecessors have" (p. 1675). In other words, work groups will continue to develop diagnostic criteria to describe prototypic cases in a manner that will maximize homogeneity and differential diagnosis (Robins & Guze, 1970; Spitzer, Williams, & Skodol, 1980), thereby continuing to fail to adequately describe typical cases and again leaving many patients to receive the diagnosis of NOS.

Dimensional proposals for *DSM-5* have been posted on the official APA website (see www.dsm5.org), but all of the proposals are only to develop "supplementary dimensional approaches to the categorical definitions that would also relate back to the categorical definitions" (Helzer, Wittchen, et al., 2008, p. 116). These dimensions will serve only as ancillary descriptions that will lack any official representation within a patient's medical record. They will have no alphanumerical code and may then not even be communicated to any public health care agency.

Even the proposal for a dimensional model of personality disorder falls well short of providing a truly integrated dimensional model of normal and abnormal personality functioning. The dimensional model proposed for *DSM-5* does not include any normal, adaptive personality traits. The description is confined to abnormal, dysfunctional traits. Rather than indicate how the model is well integrated with general personality research, emphasis is given instead for how it is inconsistent with the FFM (i.e., Clark & Krueger, 2010). Two of the dimensions (i.e., compulsivity and schizotypy) are even said to be qualitatively distinct from normal personality functioning, with no counterpart whatsoever in general personality structure (Krueger et al., 2011).

Kraemer, Noda, and O'Hara (2004) argue that in psychiatry "a categorical diagnosis is necessary" (p. 21). "Clinicians who must decide whether to treat or not treat a patient, to hospitalize or not, to treat a patient with a drug or with psychotherapy, or what type, must inevitably use a categorical approach to diagnosis" (Kraemer et al., 2004, p. 12). This is a not uncommon perception, but it is not an accurate characterization of actual clinical practice (Widiger & Mullins-Sweatt, 2010). In many common clinical situations, the decision is not in fact black and white. Clinicians and social agencies make decisions with respect to a frequency of therapy sessions, an extent of insurance coverage, a degree of medication dosage, and even degrees of hospitalization (e.g., day hospital, partial hospitalization, residential program, or traditional hospitalization).

It is evident that these different clinical decisions are not well informed by a single, uniform diagnostic threshold. The current diagnostic thresholds are not set at a point that is optimal for any one particular social or clinical decision, and the single diagnostic threshold is used to inform a wide variety of different decisions. A dimensional system has the flexibility to provide different thresholds for different social and clinical decisions and would then be considerably more useful for clinicians and more credible for social agencies than is the current system. A flexible (dimensional) classification would be preferable to governmental, social, and professional agencies, because it would provide a more reliable, valid, explicitly defined, and tailored means for making each respective social and clinical concern. It is for this reason that the authors of *DSM-5* will include supplementary dimensional scales to facilitate particular clinical decisions (e.g., Shear, Bjelland, Beesdo, Gloster, & Wittchen, 2008).

*DSM-III* is often said to have provided a significant paradigm shift in how psychopathology is diagnosed (Kendell & Jablensky, 2003; Klerman, 1983; Regier, 2008). Much of the credit for the innovative nature and success of *DSM-III* is due to the foresight, resolve, and perhaps even courage of its Chair, Dr. Robert Spitzer. The primary authors of *DSM-5* fully recognize the failure of the categorical model of classification (Kupfer et al., 2002; Regier, 2008; Regier et al., 2010). They have the empirical support and the opportunity to lead the field of psychiatry to a comparably bold new future in diagnosis and classification, but it does not appear that this shift will in fact occur.

Most (if not all) mental disorders appear to be the result of a complex interaction of an array of biological vulnerabilities and dispositions with many significant environmental, psychosocial events that often exert their effects over a progressively developing period of time (Rutter, 2003). The symptoms and pathologies of mental disorders appear to be highly responsive to a wide variety of neurobiological, interpersonal, cognitive, and other mediating and moderating variables that help develop, shape, and form a particular individual's psychopathology profile. This complex etiological history and individual psychopathology profile are unlikely to be well described by single diagnostic categories that attempt to make distinctions at nonexistent discrete joints along the continuous distributions (Widiger & Samuel, 2005). Publication of *DSM-III* provided a significant, major advance in the diagnosis and classification of psychopathology (Klerman, 1983). It is perhaps time, now, to move on.

## REFERENCES

Ambrosini, P. J., Bennett, D. S., Cleland, C. M., & Haslam, N. (2002). Taxonicity of adolescent melancholia: A categorical or dimensional construct? *Journal of Psychiatric Research, 36,* 247–256.

American Association on Mental Retardation. (2002). *Mental retardation: Definition, classification, and systems of support* (10th ed.). Washington, DC: Author.

American Psychiatric Association. (1980). *Diagnostic and statistical manual of mental disorders* (3rd ed.). Washington, DC: Author.

American Psychiatric Association. (1987). *Diagnostic and statistical manual of mental disorders* (3rd ed., rev. ed.). Washington, DC: Author.

American Psychiatric Association. (1994). *Diagnostic and statistical manual of mental disorders* (4th ed.). Washington, DC: Author.

American Psychiatric Association. (2000). *Diagnostic and statistical manual of mental disorders, text revision* (4th ed., rev. ed.). Washington, DC: Author.

American Psychiatric Association. (February 2010). Include pathological (disordered) gambling within addiction and related disorders. Retrieved from: www.dsm5.org/Proposed-Revisions/Pages/proposedrevision.aspx?rid=210

Andrews, G., Brugha, T., Thase, M., Duffy, F. F., Rucci, P., & Slade, T. (2008). Dimensionality and the category of major depressive episode. In J. E. Helzer, H. C. Kraemer, R. F. Krueger, H. U. Wittchen, P. J. Sirovatka, & D. A. Regier (Eds.), *Dimensional approaches to diagnostic classification: Refining the research agenda for DSM-V* (pp. 35–51). Washington, DC: American Psychiatric Association.

Ashton, M. C., & Lee K. (2001). A theoretical basis for the major dimensions of personality. *European Journal of Personality, 15*, 327–353.

Baldwin, G., & Shean, G. D. (2006). A taxometric study of the Center for Epidemiological Studies depression scale. *Genetic, Social, and General Psychology Monographs, 132*, 101–128.

Bargh, J. A., & Ferguson, M. J. (2000). Beyond behaviorism: On the automaticity of higher mental processes. *Psychological Bulletin, 126*, 925–945.

Beach, S. R. H., & Amir, N. (2003). Is depression taxonic, dimensional, or both? *Journal of Abnormal Psychology, 112*, 228–236.

Beauchaine, T. P. (2007). A brief taxometrics primer. *Journal of Clinical Child and Adolescent Psychology, 36*, 654–676.

Bonanno, G. A., Neria, Y., Mancini, A., Coifman, K. G., Litz, B., & Insel, B. (2007). Is there more to complicated grief than depression and posttraumatic stress disorder? A test of incremental validity. *Journal of Abnormal Psychology, 116*, 342–351.

Bornstein, R. F. (2011). Reconceptualizing personality pathology in *DSM-5*: Limitations in evidence for eliminating dependent personality disorder and other *DSM-IV* syndromes. *Journal of Personality Disorders, 25*(2), 235–247.

Boyd, J. H., Burke, J. D., Jr., Gruenberg, E., Holzer, C. E., III, Rae, D. S., George, L. K., . . . Nestadt, G. (1984). Exclusion criteria of *DSM-III*: A study of co-occurrence of hierarchy-free syndromes. *Archives of General Psychiatry, 41*, 983–989.

Bradford, J., Geller, J., Lesieur, H. R., Rosenthal, R., & Wise, M. (1996). Impulse control disorders. In T. A. Widiger, A. J. Frances, H. A. Pincus, R. Ross, M. B. First, & W. W. Davis (Eds.), *DSM-IV sourcebook* (Vol. 2, pp. 1007–1031). Washington, DC: American Psychiatric Association.

Brown, T. A., Campbell, L. A., Lehman, C. L., Grisham, J. R., & Mancill, R. B. (2001). Current and lifetime comorbidity of the *DSM-IV* anxiety and mood disorders in a large clinical sample. *Journal of Abnormal Psychology, 110*, 585–599.

Cardeña, E., Butler, L. D., & Spiegel, D. (2003). Stress disorders. In I. Weiner, G. Stricker, & T. A. Widiger (Eds.), *Handbook of psychology, Vol. 8: Clinical psychology* (pp. 229–249). Hoboken, NJ: John Wiley & Sons.

Carroll, K. M., Rounsaville, B. J., & Bryant, K. J. (1994). Should tolerance and withdrawal be required for substance dependence disorder? *Drug and Alcohol Dependence, 36*, 15–20.

Church, A. T. (2001). Personality measurement in cross-cultural perspective. *Journal of Personality, 69*, 979–1006.

Clark, L. A. (2007). Assessment and diagnosis of personality disorder: Perennial issues and an emerging reconceptualization. *Annual Review of Psychology, 58*, 227–257.

Clark, L. A., & Krueger, R. F. (2010, February 10). Rationale for a six-domain trait dimensional diagnostic system for personality disorder. Retrieved from www.dsm5.org/Proposed Revisions/Pages/RationaleforaSix-DomainTraitDimensionalDiagnosticSystemforPersonality Disorder.aspx

Costa, P. T., & McCrae, R. R. (1992). *Revised NEO Personality Inventory (NEO PI-R) and NEO Five-Factor Inventory (NEO-FFI) professional manual.* Odessa, FL: Psychological Assessment Resources.

Costa, P. T., Samuels, J., Bagby, M., Daffin, L., & Norton, H. (2005). Obsessive-compulsive personality disorder: A review. In M. Maj, H. S. Akiskal, J. E. Mezzich, & A. Okasha (Eds.), *Personality disorders* (pp. 405–439). Hoboken, NJ: John Wiley & Sons.

Craddock, N., & Owen, M. J. (2005). The beginning of the end for the Kraepelinian dichotomy. *British Journal of Psychiatry, 186*, 364–366.

Crowley, T. J. (2006). Adolescents and substance-related disorders: Research agenda to guide decisions on *Diagnostic and Statistical Manual of Mental Disorders, fifth edition* (DSM-V). *Addiction, 101*(1), 115–124.

Deary, I. J., Spinath, F. M., & Bates, T. C. (2006). Genetics of intelligence. *European Journal of Human Genetics, 14*, 690–700.

Edwards, G., & Gross, M. (1976). Alcohol dependence: Provisional description of a clinical syndrome. *British Medical Journal, 1*, 1058–1061.

Feinstein, A. R. (1970). The pre-therapeutic classification of co-morbidity in chronic disease. *Chronic Disease, 23*, 455–468.

First, M. B. (2003). Psychiatric classification. In A. Tasman, J. Kay, & J. Lieberman (Eds.), *Psychiatry* (2nd ed., Vol. 1, pp. 659–676). Hoboken, NJ: John Wiley & Sons.

First, M. B. (2005). Clinical utility: A prerequisite for the adoption of a dimensional approach in *DSM. Journal of Abnormal Psychology, 114*, 560–564.

First, M. B., Bell, C. B., Cuthbert, B., Krystal, J. H., Malison, R., Offord, D. R., . . . Wisner, K. L. (2002). Personality disorders and relational disorders: A research agenda for addressing crucial gaps in *DSM.* In D. J. Kupfer, M. B. First, & D. A. Regier (Eds.), *A research agenda for DSM-V* (pp. 123–199). Washington, DC: American Psychiatric Association.

First, M. B., & Westen, D. (2007). Classification for clinical practice: How to make ICD and *DSM* better able to serve clinicians. *International Review of Psychiatry, 19*, 473–481.

Forstmeier, S., & Maercker, A. (2007). Comparison of two diagnostic systems for complicated grief. *Journal of Affective Disorders, 99*, 203–211.

Frances, A. J., First, M. B., & Pincus, H. A. (1995). *DSM-IV guidebook.* Washington, DC: American Psychiatric Press.

Frances, A. J., First, M. B., Widiger, T. A., Miele, G., Tilly, S. M., Davis, W. W., & Pincus, H. A. (1991). An A to Z guide to *DSM-IV* conundrums. *Journal of Abnormal Psychology, 100*, 407–412.

Franklin, C. L., Strong, D. R., & Greene, R. L. (2002). A taxometric analysis of the MMPI-2 depression scales. *Journal of Personality Assessment, 79*, 110–121.

Garbutt, J. C. (2008). Alcoholism. In S. H. Fatemi & P. J. Clayton (Eds.), *The medical basis of psychiatry* (3rd ed., pp. 227–249). Totowa, NY: Humana Press.

Goldberg, D. (2010). Should our major classifications of mental disorders be revised? *British Journal of Psychiatry, 196*, 255–256.

Goldberg, L. R. (1993). The structure of phenotypic personality traits. *American Psychologist, 48*, 26–34.

Goodwin, D. W., & Guze, S. B. (1996). *Psychiatric diagnosis* (5th ed.). New York, NY: Oxford University Press.

Guze, S. B. (1978). Nature of psychiatric illness: Why psychiatry is a branch of medicine. *Comprehensive Psychiatry, 19,* 295–307.

Guze, S. B., & Helzer, J. E. (1987). The medical model and psychiatric disorders. In R. Michels & J. Cavenar (Eds.), *Psychiatry* (Vol. 1, pp. 1–8). Philadelphia, PA: Lippincott.

Hammen, C. (2005). Stress and depression. *Annual Review of Clinical Psychology, 1,* 293–319.

Hankin, B. L., Fraley, R. C., Lahey, B. B., & Waldman, I. D. (2005). Is depression best viewed as a continuum or discrete category? A taxometric analysis of childhood and adolescent depression in a population-based sample. *Journal of Abnormal Psychology, 114,* 96–110.

Helzer, J. E., Kraemer, H. C., & Krueger, R. F. (2006). The feasibility and need for dimensional psychiatric diagnoses. *Psychological Medicine, 36,* 1671–1680.

Helzer, J. E., Kraemer, H. C., Krueger, R. F., Wittchen, H.-U., Sirovatka, P. J., & Regier, D. A. (Eds.). (2008). *Dimensional approaches in diagnostic classification.* Washington, DC: American Psychiatric Association.

Helzer, J. E., Wittchen, H.-U., Krueger, R. F., & Kraemer, H. C. (2008). Dimensional options for *DSM-V*: The way forward. In J. E. Helzer, H. C. Kraemer, R. F. Krueger, H.-U. Wittchen, P. J. Sirovatka, & D. A. Regier (Eds.), *Dimensional approaches to diagnostic classification. Refining the research agenda for DSM-V* (pp. 115–127). Washington, DC: American Psychiatric Association.

Howard, G. S., & Conway, C. G. (1986). Can there be an empirical science of volitional action? *American Psychologist, 41,* 1241–1251.

Hyman, S. (2010). The diagnosis of mental disorders: The problem of reification. *Annual Review of Clinical Psychology, 6,* 155–179.

Insel, T. R. (2009). Translating scientific opportunity into public health impact. A strategic plan for research on mental illness. *Archives of General Psychiatry, 66,* 128–133.

Judd, L. L., Schettler, P. J., & Akiskal, H. S. (2002). The prevalence, clinical relevance, and public health significance of subthreshold depressions. *Psychiatric Clinics of North America, 25,* 685–698.

Kafka, M. P. (2010). Hypersexual disorder. A proposed diagnosis for *DSM-V*. *Archives of Sexual Behavior, 39,* 377–400.

Kahler, C. W., & Strong, D. R. (2006). A Rasch model analysis of *DSM-IV* alcohol abuse and dependence items in the National Epidemiological Survey on Alcohol and Related Conditions. *Alcoholism: Clinical and Experimental Research, 30,* 1165–1175.

Kandel, E. R. (1998). A new intellectual framework for psychiatry. *American Journal of Psychiatry, 155,* 457–469.

Keller, M. B. (1989). Current concepts in affective disorders. *Journal of Clinical Psychiatry, 50,* 157–162.

Keller, M. B., Klein, D. N., Hirschfeld, R. M. A., Kocsis, J. H., McCullough, J. P., Miller, I., . . . Shea, M. T. (1995). Results of the *DSM-IV* mood disorders field trial. *American Journal of Psychiatry, 152,* 843–849.

Kendell, R. E. (1975). *The role of diagnosis in psychiatry.* Oxford, England: Blackwell Scientific.

Kendell, R. E. (1983). *DSM-III*: A major advance in psychiatric nosology. In R. L. Spitzer, J. B. W. Williams, & A. E. Skodol (Eds.), *International perspectives on DSM-III* (pp. 55–68). Washington, DC: American Psychiatric Press.

Kendell, R. E. (1989). Clinical validity. In L. N. Robins & J. E. Barrett (Eds.), *The validity of psychiatric diagnosis* (pp. 305–321). New York, NY: Raven Press.

Kendell, R. E., & Jablensky, A. (2003). Distinguishing between the validity and utility of psychiatric diagnosis. *American Journal of Psychiatry, 160,* 4–12.

Kessler, R. C., Chiu, W. T., Dember, O., & Walters, E. E. (2005). Prevalence, severity, and comorbidity of 12-month *DSM-IV* disorders in the National Comorbidity Survey replication. *Archives of General Psychiatry, 62*, 617–627.

Kessler, R. C., Zhao, S., Blazer, D. G., & Swartz, M. (1997). Prevalence, correlates, and course of minor depression and major depression in the National Comorbidity Survey. *Journal of Affective Disorders, 45*, 19–30.

Kirsch, I., & Lynn, S. J. (2000). Automaticity in clinical psychology. *American Psychologist, 54*, 504–515.

Klerman, G. L. (1983). The significance of *DSM-III* in American psychiatry. In R. L. Spitzer, J. B. W. Williams, & A. E. Skodol (Eds.), *International perspectives on DSM-III* (pp. 3–26). Washington, DC: American Psychiatric Press.

Klerman, G. L., Endicott, J., Spitzer, R. L., & Hirschfeld, R. M. (1979). Neurotic depressions: A systematic analysis of multiple criteria and meanings. *American Journal of Psychiatry, 136*, 57–61.

Knorr, U., & Kessing, L. V. (2010). The effect of selective serotonin reuptake in healthy subjects. A systematic review. *Nordic Journal of Psychiatry, 64*, 153–163.

Knutson, B., Wolkowitz, O. M., Cole, S. W., Chan, T., Moore, E. A., Johnson, R. C., . . . Reus, V. H. (1998). Selective alteration of personality and social behavior by serotonergic intervention. *American Journal of Psychiatry, 155*, 373–379.

Kraemer, H. C. (2008). *DSM* categories and dimensions in clinical and research contexts. In J. E. Helzer, H. C. Kraemer, R. F. Krueger, H.-U. Wittchen, P. J. Sirovatka, & D. A. Regier (Eds.), *Dimensional approaches to diagnostic classification: Refining the research agenda for DSM-V* (pp. 5–17). Washington, DC: American Psychiatric Association.

Kraemer, H. C., Noda, A., & O'Hara, R. (2004). Categorical versus dimensional approaches to diagnosis: Methodological challenges. *Journal of Psychiatric Research, 38*, 17–25.

Kraepelin, E. (1917). *Lectures on clinical psychiatry* (3rd ed.). New York, NY: William Wood.

Krueger, R. F. (2002). Psychometric perspectives on comorbidity. In J. E. Helzer & J. J. Hudziak (Eds.), *Defining psychopathology in the 21st century: DSM-V and beyond* (pp. 41–54). Washington, DC: American Psychiatric Publishing.

Krueger, R. F., Clark, L. A., Watson, D., Markon, K. E., Derringer, J., Skodol, A., & Livesley, W. J. (2011). Deriving an empirical structure of personality pathology for *DSM-5*. *Journal of Personality Disorders, 25*(2), 170–191.

Krueger, R. F., & Markon, K. E. (2006). Reinterpreting comorbidity: A model-based approach to understanding and classifying psychopathology. *Annual Review of Clinical Psychology, 2*, 111–133.

Kupfer, D. J., First, M. B., & Regier, D. A. (Eds.). (2002). Introduction. In D. J. Kupfer, M. B. First, & D. A. Regier (Eds.), *A research agenda for DSM-V* (pp. xv-xxiii) Washington, DC: American Psychiatric Association.

Langenbucher, J. W., Labouvie, E., Martin, C. S., Sanjuan, P. M., Bavly, L., Kirisci, L., & Chung, T. (2004). Application of item response theory analysis to alcohol, cannabis, and cocaine criteria in *DSM-IV*. *Journal of Abnormal Psychology, 113*, 72–80.

Liebowitz, M. R. (1992). Diagnostic issues in anxiety disorders. In A. Tasman & M. B. Riba (Eds.), *Review of psychiatry* (Vol. 11, pp. 247–259). Washington, DC: American Psychiatric Press.

Liebowitz, M. R., Barlow, D. H., Ballenger, J. C., Davidson, J., Foa, E. B., Fyer, A. J., . . . Spiegel, D. (1998). *DSM-IV* anxiety disorders: Final overview. In T. A. Widiger, A. J. Frances, H. A. Pincus, R. Ross, M. B. First, W. Davis, & M. Kline (Eds.), *DSM-IV sourcebook* (Vol. 4, pp. 1047–1076). Washington, DC: American Psychiatric Association.

Lilienfeld, S. O., Waldman, I. D., & Israel, A. C. (1994). A critical examination of the use of the term "comorbidity" in psychopathology research. *Clinical Psychology: Science and Practice, 1*, 71–83.

Livesley, W. J. (2001a). Commentary on reconceptualizing personality disorder categories using trait dimensions. *Journal of Personality, 69*, 277–286.

Livesley, W. J. (2001b). Conceptual and taxonomic issues. In W. J. Livesley (Ed.), *Handbook of personality disorders: Theory, research, and treatment* (pp. 3–38). New York, NY: Guilford Press.

Livesley, W. J. (2003). Diagnostic dilemmas in classifying personality disorder. In K. A. Phillips, M. B. First, & H. A. Pincus (Eds.), *Advancing DSM: Dilemmas in psychiatric diagnosis* (pp. 153–190). Washington, DC: American Psychiatric Association.

Luckasson, R., & Reeve, A. (2001). Naming, defining, and classifying in mental retardation. *Mental Retardation, 39*, 47–52.

Lynam, D. R., & Widiger, T. A. (2001). Using the five factor model to represent the *DSM-IV* personality disorders: An expert consensus approach. *Journal of Abnormal Psychology, 110*, 401–412.

Magruder, K. M., & Calderone, G. E. (2000). Public health consequences of different thresholds for the diagnosis of mental disorders. *Comprehensive Psychiatry, 41*, 14–18.

Martin, P. R. (2005). Affirmative viewpoint. *The American Journal on Addictions, 14*, 1–3.

Maser, J. D., & Cloninger, C. R. (1990). Comorbidity of anxiety and mood disorders: Introduction and overview. In J. D. Maser & C. R. Cloninger (Eds.), *Comorbidity of mood and anxiety disorders* (pp. 3–12). Washington, DC: American Psychiatric Press.

Maser, J. D., & Patterson, T. (2002). Spectrum and nosology: Implications for *DSM-V*. *Psychiatric Clinics of North America, 25*, 855–885.

McCrae, R. R., & Costa, P. T. (2003). *Personality in adulthood: A five-factor theory perspective* (2nd ed.). New York, NY: Guilford Press.

McCrae, R. R., Löckenhoff, C. E., & Costa, P. T. (2005). A step toward *DSM-V*: Cataloguing personality-related problems in living. *European Journal of Personality, 19*, 269–286.

Miller, J. D., & Lynam, D. R. (2003). Psychopathy and the five-factor model of personality: A replication and extension. *Journal of Personality Assessment, 81*, 168–178.

Miller, J. D., Widiger, T. A, & Campbell, W. K. (2010). Narcissistic personality disorder and the *DSM-V*. *Journal of Abnormal Psychology, 119*, 640–649.

Millon, T., Davis, R., Millon, C. M., Wenger, C. M., Van Zuilen, M. H., Fuchs, M., & Millon, R. B. (1996). *Disorders of personality: DSM-IV and beyond* (2nd ed.). New York, NY: John Wiley & Sons.

Mullins-Sweatt, S. N., & Widiger, T. A. (2009). Clinical utility and *DSM-V*. *Psychological Assessment, 21*, 302–312.

Muthen, B. (2006). Should substance use disorders be considered as categorical or dimensional? *Addiction, 101*(1), 6–16.

Naglieri, J., Salter, C., & Rojahn, J. (2008). Cognitive disorders of childhood. Specific learning and intellectual disabilities. In J. E. Maddux & B. A. Winstead (Eds.), *Psychopathology: Foundations for a contemporary understanding* (2nd ed., pp. 401–416). Mahwah, NJ: Erlbaum.

O'Connor, B. P. (2002). A quantitative review of the comprehensiveness of the five-factor model in relation to popular personality inventories. *Assessment, 9*, 188–203.

O'Connor, B. P. (2005). A search for consensus on the dimensional structure of personality disorders. *Journal of Clinical Psychology, 61*, 323–345.

Ozer, D. J., & Benet-Martinez, V. (2006). Personality and the prediction of consequential outcomes. *Annual Review of Psychology, 57*, 401–421.

Parnas, J., Licht, D., & Bovet, P. (2005). Cluster A personality disorders: A review. In M. Maj, H. S. Akiskal, J. E. Mezzich, & A. Okasha (Eds.), *Personality disorders* (pp. 1–74). Hoboken, NJ: John Wiley & Sons.

Petry, N. M. (2005a). Negative rebuttal. *The American Journal on Addictions, 14*, 6–7.

Petry, N. M. (2005b). Negative viewpoint. *The American Journal on Addictions, 14*, 4–5.

Petry, N. M. (2006). Should the scope of addictive behaviors be broadened to include pathological gambling? *Addiction, 101*(1), 152–160.

Phillips, K. A., Gunderson, J. G., Triebwasser, J., Kimble, C. R., Faedda, G., Lyoo, I. K., & Renn, J. (1998). Reliability and validity of depressive personality disorder. *American Journal of Psychiatry, 155*, 1044–1048.

Phillips, K. A., Price, L. H., Greenburg, B. D., & Rasmussen, S. A. (2003). Should the *DSM* diagnostic groupings be changed? In K. A. Phillips, M. B. First, & H. A. Pincus (Eds.), *Advancing DSM: Dilemmas in psychiatric diagnosis* (pp. 57–84). Washington, DC: American Psychiatric Association.

Pincus, A. L., & Lukowitsky, M. R. (2010). Pathological narcissism and narcissistic personality disorder. *Annual Review of Clinical Psychology, 6*, 421–446.

Pincus, H. A., Frances, A., Davis, W., First, M., & Widiger, T. (1992). *DSM-IV* and new diagnostic categories: Holding the line on proliferation. *American Journal of Psychiatry, 149*, 112–117.

Pincus, H. A., McQueen, L. E., & Elinson, L. (2003). Subthreshold mental disorders: Nosological and research recommendations. In K. A. Phillips, M. B. First, & H. A. Pincus (Eds.), *Advancing DSM: Dilemmas in psychiatric diagnosis* (pp. 129–144). Washington, DC: American Psychiatric Association.

Potenza, M. N. (2006). Should addictive disorders include non-substance-related conditions? *Addiction, 101*(1), 142–151.

Prisciandaro, J. J., & Roberts, J. E. (2005). A taxometric investigation of unipolar depression in the National Comorbidity Survey. *Journal of Abnormal Psychology, 114*, 718–728.

Proudfoot, H., Baillie, A. J., & Teesson, M. (2006). The structure of alcohol dependence in the community. *Drug and Alcohol Dependence, 81*, 21–26.

Ragan, P. W., & Martin, P. R. (2000). The psychobiology of sexual addiction. *Sexual Addiction & Compulsivity, 7*, 161–175.

Raine, A. (2006). Schizotypal personality: Neurodevelopmental and psychosocial trajectories. *Annual Review of Clinical Psychology, 2*, 291–326.

Regier, D. A. (2008). Forward: Dimensional approaches to psychiatric classification. In J. E. Helzer, H. C. Kraemer, R. F. Krueger, H.-U. Wittchen, P. J. Sirovatka, & D. A. Regier (Eds.), *Dimensional approaches to diagnostic classification: Refining the research agenda for DSM-V* (pp. xvii–xxiii). Washington, DC: American Psychiatric Association.

Regier, D. A., Narrow, W. E., Kuhl, E. A., & Kupfer, D. J. (2010). The conceptual development of *DSM-V*. *American Journal of Psychiatry, 166*, 645–655.

Reise, S. P., & Waller, N. G. (2009). Item response theory and clinical measurement. *Annual Review of Clinical Psychology, 5*, 27–48.

Rhodewalt, F., & Vohs, K. D. (2005). Defensive strategies, motivation, and the self: A self-regulatory process view. In J. Andrew & C. S. Dweck (Eds.), *Handbook of competence and motivation* (pp. 548–565). New York, NY: Guilford Press.

Roberts, B. W., & DelVecchio, W. F. (2000). The rank-order consistency of personality traits from childhood to old age: A quantitative review of longitudinal studies. *Psychological Bulletin, 126*, 3–25.

Robins, E., & Guze, S. B. (1970). Establishment of diagnostic validity in psychiatric illness: Its application to schizophrenia. *American Journal of Psychiatry, 126*, 107–111.

Robins, L. N., & Barrett, J. E. (Eds.). (1989). *The validity of psychiatric diagnosis*. New York, NY: Raven Press.

Ronningstam, E. (2011). Narcissistic personality disorder in *DSM-V*: In support of retaining a significant diagnosis. *Journal of Personality Disorders, 17*(2), 89–99.

Rounsaville, B. J., Alarcon, R. D., Andrews, G., Jackson, J. S., Kendell, R. E., & Kendler, K. (2002). Basic nomenclature issues for *DSM-V*. In D. J. Kupfer, M. B. First, & D. E. Regier (Eds.), *A research agenda for DSM-V* (pp. 1–29). Washington, DC: American Psychiatric Association.

Ruscio, A. M., & Ruscio, J. (2002). The latent structure of analogue depression: Should the Beck Depression Inventory be used to classify groups? *Psychological Assessment, 14*, 135–145.

Ruscio, J., & Ruscio, A. M. (2000). Informing the continuity controversy: A taxometric analysis of depression. *Journal of Abnormal Psychology, 109*, 473–487.

Ruscio, J., & Ruscio, A. M. (2004). Clarifying boundary issues in psychopathology: The role of taxometrics in a comprehensive program of structural research. *Journal of Abnormal Psychology, 113*, 24–38.

Ruscio, J., Zimmerman, M., McGlinchey, J. B., Chelminski, I., & Young, D. (2007). Diagnosing major depressive disorder XI: A taxometric investigation of the structure underlying *DSM-IV* symptoms. *Journal of Nervous and Mental Disease, 195*, 10–19.

Rutter, M. (2003, October). *Pathways of genetic influences on psychopathology*. Zubin Award Address at the 18th Annual Meeting of the Society for Research in Psychopathology, Toronto, Ontario.

Saha, T. D., Chou, S. P., & Grant, B. F. (2006). Toward an alcohol use disorder continuum using item response theory: Results from the National Epidemiologic Survey on Alcohol and Related Conditions. *Psychological Medicine, 36*, 931–941.

Sakashita, C., Slade, T., & Andrews, G. (2007). An empirical analysis of two assumptions in the diagnosis of *DSM-IV* major depressive episode. *Australian and New Zealand Journal of Psychiatry, 41*, 17–23.

Samuel, D. B., & Widiger, T. A. (2008). A meta analytic review of the relationships between the five-factor model and *DSM-IV-TR* personality disorders: A facet level analysis. *Clinical Psychology Review, 28*, 1326–1342.

Sanderson, C. J., & Clarkin, J. F. (2002). Further use of the NEO PI-R personality dimensions in differential treatment planning. In P. T. Costa & T. A. Widiger (Eds.), *Personality disorders and the five factor model of personality* (2nd ed., pp. 351–75). Washington, DC: American Psychological Association.

Saulsman, L. M., & Page, A. C. (2004). The five-factor model and personality disorder empirical literature: A meta-analytic review. *Clinical Psychology Review, 23*, 1055–1085.

Saunders, J. B. (2006). Substance dependence and non-dependence in the *Diagnostic and Statistical Manual of Mental Disorders (DSM)* and the *International Classification of Diseases (ICD)*: Can an identical conceptualization be achieved? *Addiction, 101*(1), 48–58.

Schneider, F. R., Blanco, C., Anita, S., & Liebowitz, M. R. (2002). The social anxiety spectrum. *Psychiatric Clinics of North America, 25*, 757–774.

Schuckit, M. A., Daeppen, J.-B., Danko, G. P., Tripp, M. L., Smith, T. L., Li, T.-K., . . . Bucholz, K. K. (1999). Clinical implications for four drugs of the *DSM-IV* distinction between substance dependence with and without a physiological component. *American Journal of Psychiatry, 156*, 41–49.

Shear, M. K., Bjelland, I., Beesdo, K., Gloster, A. T., & Wittchen, H.-U. (2008). Supplementary dimensional assessment in anxiety disorders. In J. E. Helzer, H. C. Kraemer, R. F. Krueger, H.-U. Wittchen, P. J. Sirovatka, & D. A. Regier (Eds.), *Dimensional approaches to diagnostic classification: Refining the research agenda for DSM-V* (pp. 65–84). Washington, DC: American Psychiatric Association.

Skodol, A. E., Bender, D. S., Morey, L. C., Clark, L. A., Oldham, J. M., Alarcon, R. D., . . . Siever, L., J. (2011). Personality disorder types proposed for *DSM-5*. *Journal of Personality Disorders, 25*(2), 139–169.

Slade, T. (2007). Taxometric investigation of depression: Evidence of consistent latent structure across clinical and community samples. *Australian and New Zealand Journal of Psychiatry, 41*, 403–410.

Slade, T., & Andrews, G. (2005). Latent structure of depression in a community sample: A taxometric analysis. *Psychological Medicine, 35*, 489–497.

Smith, G. T., & Combs, J. (2010). Issues of construct validity in psychological diagnoses. In T. Millon, R. F. Krueger, and E. Simonsen (Eds.), *Contemporary directions in psychopathology: Toward the DSM-V and ICD-11* (pp. 205–222). New York, NY: Guilford Press.

Solomon, A., Ruscio, J., Seeley, J. R., & Lewinsohn, P. M. (2006). A taxometric investigation of unipolar depression in a large community sample. *Psychological Medicine, 36*, 973–985.

Spitzer, R. L., Endicott, J., & Robins, E. (1978). Research diagnostic criteria: Rationale and reliability. *Archives of General Psychiatry, 35*, 773–782.

Spitzer, R. L., & Williams, J. B. W. (1985). Proposed revisions in the *DSM-III* classification of anxiety disorders based on research and clinical experience. In A. H. Tuma & J. Maser (Eds.), *Anxiety and the anxiety disorders* (pp. 759–773). Hillsdale, NJ: Erlbaum.

Spitzer, R. L., Williams, J. B. W., & Skodol, A. E. (1980). *DSM-III*: The major achievements and an overview. *American Journal of Psychiatry, 137*, 151–164.

Tang, T. Z., DeRubeis, R. J., Hollon, S. D., Amsterdam, J., Shelton, R., & Schalet, B. (2009). Personality change during depression treatment. A placebo-controlled trial. *Archives of General Psychiatry, 66*, 1322–1330.

Task Force on DSM-IV. (1991, September). *DSM-IV options book: Work in progress*. Washington, DC: American Psychiatric Association.

Task Force on DSM-IV. (1993, March). *DSM-IV draft criteria*. Washington, DC: American Psychiatric Association.

Trull, T. J., & Durrett, C. A. (2005). Categorical and dimensional models of personality disorder. *Annual Review of Clinical Psychology, 1*, 355–380.

Trull, T. J., Widiger, T. A., Lynam, D. R. & Costa, P. T. (2003). Borderline personality disorder from the perspective of general personality functioning. *Journal of Abnormal Psychology, 112*, 193–202.

Turner, S. M., & Beidel, D. C. (1989). Social phobia: Clinical syndrome, diagnosis, and comorbidity. *Clinical Psychology Review, 9*, 3–18.

Turner, S. M., Beidel, D. C., & Townsley, R. M. (1992). Social phobia: A comparison of specific and generalized subtypes and avoidant personality disorder. *Journal of Abnormal Psychology, 101*, 326–331.

Tyrer, P. (2005). The anxious cluster of personality disorders: A review. In M. Maj, H. S. Akiskal, J. E. Mezzich, & A. Okasha (Eds.), *Personality disorders* (pp. 349–375). Hoboken, NJ: John Wiley & Sons.

Ustun, T. B., & Sartorius, N. (Eds.). (1995). *Mental illness in general health care: An international study*. London, England: John Wiley & Sons.

Wakefield, J. C. (2007). The concept of mental disorder: Diagnostic implications of the harmful dysfunction analysis. *World Psychiatry, 6*, 149–156.

Wakefield, J. C. (2008). The perils of dimensionalization: Challenges in distinguishing negative traits from personality disorders. *Psychiatric Clinics of North America, 31*, 379–393.

Wakefield, J. C., Schmitz, M. F., First, M. B., & Horwitz, A. V. (2007). Extending the bereavement exclusion for major depression to other losses: Evidence from the National Comorbidity Survey. *Archives of General Psychiatry, 64*, 433–440.

Wegner, D. M., & Wheatley, T. (2000). Apparent mental causation: Sources of the experience of will. *American Psychologist, 54*, 480–492.

Widiger, T. A. (2001a). Social anxiety, social phobia, and avoidant personality disorder. In W. R. Corzier & L. Alden (Eds.), *International handbook of social anxiety* (pp. 335–356). New York, NY: John Wiley & Sons.

Widiger, T. A. (2001b). What can we learn from taxometric analyses? *Clinical Psychology: Science and Practice, 8*, 528–533.

Widiger, T. A. (2003). Personality disorder and Axis I psychopathology: The problematic boundary of Axis I and Axis II. *Journal of Personality Disorders, 17*, 90–108.

Widiger, T. A. (2011). A shaky future for personality disorders. *Personality Disorders: Theory, Research, and Treatment* 2(1), 54–67.

Widiger, T. A. (in press). Classification and diagnosis: Historical development and contemporary issues. In J. Maddux and B. Winstead (Eds.), *Psychopathology: Foundations for a contemporary understanding* (3rd ed.). Mahwah, NJ: Erlbaum.

Widiger, T. A., & Clark, L. A. (2000). Toward *DSM-V* and the classification of psychopathology. *Psychological Bulletin, 126*, 946–963.

Widiger, T. A., & Costa, P. T. (1994). Personality and personality disorders. *Journal of Abnormal Psychology, 103*, 78–91.

Widiger, T. A., & Costa, P. T. (2002). Five-factor model personality disorder research. In T. A. Widiger & P. T. Costa (Eds.), *Personality disorders and the five-factor model of personality* (2nd ed., pp. 59–87). Washington, DC: American Psychological Association.

Widiger, T. A., Costa, P. T., & McCrae, R. R. (2002). A proposal for Axis II: Diagnosing personality disorders using the five-factor model. In T. A. Widiger & P. T. Costa (Eds.), *Personality disorders and the five-factor model of personality* (2nd ed., pp. 431–456). Washington, DC: American Psychological Association.

Widiger, T. A., & Edmundson, M. (2011). Diagnoses, dimensions, and *DSM-V*. In D. Barlow (Ed.), *Oxford handbook of clinical psychology* (pp. 254–278). New York, NY: Oxford University Press.

Widiger, T. A., & Lowe, J. (2007). Five factor model assessment of personality disorder. *Journal of Personality Assessment, 89*, 16–29.

Widiger, T. A., & Miller, J. D. (2008). Psychological diagnosis. In D. Richard & S. Huprich (Eds.), *Clinical psychology, assessment, treatment, and research* (pp. 69–88). Oxford, England: Elsevier.

Widiger, T. A., & Mullins-Sweatt, S. N. (2009). Five-factor model of personality disorder: A proposal for *DSM-V*. *Annual Review of Clinical Psychology, 5*, 115–138.

Widiger, T. A., & Mullins-Sweatt, S. (2010). Clinical utility of a dimensional model of personality disorder. *Professional Psychology: Research and Practice, 41*(6), 488–494.

Widiger, T. A., & Samuel, D. B. (2005). Diagnostic categories or dimensions: A question for *DSM-V*. *Journal of Abnormal Psychology, 114*, 494–504.

Widiger, T. A., & Sankis, L. (2000). Adult psychopathology: Issues and controversies. *Annual Review of Psychology, 51*, 377–404.

Widiger, T. A., Simonsen, E., Krueger, R. F., Livesley, W. J., & Verheul, R. (2005). Personality disorder research agenda for the *DSM-V*. *Journal of Personality Disorders, 19*, 317–340.

Widiger, T. A., & Trull, T. J. (2007). Plate tectonics in the classification of personality disorder: Shifting to a dimensional model. *American Psychologist, 62*, 71–83.

Winters, J. (2010). Hypersexual disorder: A more cautious approach. *Archives of Sexual Behavior*, *39*, 594–596.

World Health Organization. (1992). *The ICD-10 classification of mental and behavioural disorders: Clinical descriptions and diagnostic guidelines.* Geneva, Switzerland: Author.

Zachar, P., & Kendler, K. S. (2007). Psychiatric disorders: A conceptual taxonomy. *American Journal of Psychiatry, 164*, 557–565.

# CHAPTER 2

# The Problem of Dual Diagnosis

MELANIE E. BENNETT, JASON PEER, and SELVIJA GJONBALAJ-MAROVIC

R ESEARCH INDICATES THAT a substantial percentage of the general population with a lifetime psychiatric disorder has a history of some other disorder (Kessler, 1997; Kessler et al., 1994), and more than half of patients in psychiatric treatment meet criteria for more than one diagnosis (Wolf, Schubert, Patterson, Marion, & Grande, 1988). The issue of comorbidity broadly refers to combinations of any types of psychiatric disorders that co-occur in the same individual. A diagnostic pair that has received significant attention over the last two decades is that of mental illness and substance abuse. The term *dual diagnosis* describes individuals who meet diagnostic criteria for an Axis I or Axis II mental disorder (or disorders) along with one or more substance use disorders. Since the 1980s, rates of co-occurring mental illness and substance use disorders have been found to have increased sharply. This increase is likely owing to a range of factors including more specific diagnostic criteria for substance use disorders, as well as the development of standardized diagnostic interviews that allow for reliable and valid assessments of Axis I disorders in a range of patient populations (Wittchen, Perkonigg, & Reed, 1996). It is likely that these recently documented increases in rates of dual diagnosis reflect what was truly there all along—a frequent association between mental and substance use disorders that we have only now begun to measure accurately. It is now clear that dual diagnosis impacts all aspects of psychopathology research and clinical practice, from service utilization, treatment entry, and treatment retention to assessment and diagnosis of psychological problems to research on psychopathology and treatment outcome. In this chapter, we will review current data on rates of dual diagnosis, both generally and for specific domains of disorders, as well as discuss some of the ways in which dual diagnosis impacts the course, prognosis, assessment, and treatment of adult psychopathology. Finally, we will review current research on the etiology of dual diagnosis and highlight clinical and research directions.

## METHODOLOGICAL ISSUES IN DETERMINING
## PREVALENCE RATES OF DUAL DIAGNOSIS

There are several methodological issues to consider when evaluating the literature on the epidemiology of dual diagnosis. First, data come from both epidemiological and clinical studies, each of which has benefits and drawbacks. Several large-scale epidemiological studies examining rates of dual diagnosis in general population samples have been carried out since the mid-1980s. These studies provide representative information on rates of mental illness and substance use disorders, use structured diagnostic interviews, and generate results that are reliable and relevant to the population as a whole. Most of the information on rates of dual diagnosis comes from studies of clinical populations. Although such studies are not representative of the general population, they provide valuable information on the types of problems that are faced by individuals in treatment, as well as on the links between dual diagnosis, service utilization, impact on illness, and treatment outcome. Importantly, individuals with multiple disorders are more likely to seek treatment, a condition known as Berkson's fallacy (Berkson, 1949), so that estimates of the prevalence of comorbid disorders will be higher in clinical samples. Relatedly, factors such as inpatient or outpatient status and chronicity of illness may affect rates of dual diagnosis found in clinical samples. For example, research on patients with schizophrenia has found that more severely impaired inpatients are less likely to abuse substances than patients who are less ill (Mueser et al., 1990). Dual diagnosis rates have also been found to differ by setting, with hospital emergency rooms reflecting higher estimates than other settings (Barbee, Clark, Crapanzano, Heintz, & Kehoe, 1989; Galanter, Castaneda, & Ferman, 1988). In addition, several demographic variables correlate with substance abuse, and differences in these variables in clinical samples can influence prevalence rates. For example, gender and age both correlate with substance abuse: Males and those of younger age are more likely to abuse substances. Because studies of comorbidity in schizophrenia often use samples of inpatients who are more likely to be male, the comorbidity rate in schizophrenia found in research with clinical samples may be inflated, because males are both more likely to have substance use disorders and more likely to be inpatients in psychiatric hospitals.

Second, definitions of what constitutes dual diagnosis are far from uniform. Studies often use differing definitions and measures of substance use disorders, making prevalence rates diverse and difficult to compare. For example, definitions used to determine rates of dual diagnosis vary, ranging from problem use of a substance based on the frequency of use or the number of negative consequences experienced as a result of use, to abuse or dependence based on formal diagnostic criteria. This is a particularly important issue when formal diagnostic criteria for substance use disorders are used to assess dual diagnosis. Currently the two most widely used systems for psychiatric diagnosis and classification are the *Diagnostic and Statistical Manual, fourth edition*, text revision (*DSM-IV-TR*) (American Psychiatric Association, 2000), used primarily in the United States, and the *International Classification of Diseases, tenth edition* (*ICD-10*) (World Health Organization, 1993), used primarily in other countries. There are important features of these systems that influence how substance use disorders are diagnosed that can, in turn, influence rates of dual disorders. The diagnostic criteria for alcohol use disorders provide a good example (see Hasin, 2003, for a complete review). Both systems include a diagnosis of alcohol dependence that requires at least three symptoms be present from a list of six (*ICD-10*) or seven (*DSM-IV*) that include both physiological symptoms such as tolerance and withdrawal as well as nonphysiological symptoms such as impaired control, giving up other important activities, and continued use in the face of physical or psychological consequences.

Research has shown good reliability between *DSM* and *ICD* for dependence diagnoses (Hasin, 2003). In contrast, these systems differ with respect to diagnoses of alcohol abuse (as it is called in *DSM-IV*) or harmful use (as found in *ICD-10*). *DSM-IV* requires "recurrent use" that leads to at least one of four possible consequences (failure to fulfill obligations, use in situations in which it is physically hazardous, use-related legal problems, use despite recurrent social/interpersonal problems) in order to meet a diagnosis of alcohol abuse. *ICD-10* is more specific in its definition of "recurrent" ("The pattern of use has persisted for at least 1 month or has occurred repeatedly within a 12-month period") but less specific in describing those consequences that are "harmful," requiring only "clear evidence that alcohol use contributed to physical or psychological harm" and that a "pattern of use has persisted" (WHO, 1993). Such differences in criteria have no doubt contributed to findings of lower reliability between these categories (Hasin, 2003). Moreover, these sorts of differences are especially important when considering how rates of dual disorders compare across nations and cultures (see Room, 2006, for a review).

In addition, the methods used to determine psychiatric and substance use diagnoses can influence findings. The types of diagnostic measures used include structured research interviews, nonstructured clinical interviews, self-report ratings, and reviews of medical records. Although structured interviews are the most reliable method of diagnosis (Mueser, Bellack, & Blanchard, 1992), research with clinical samples will often employ less well-standardized assessments. Relatedly, studies measure different substances in their assessments of dual diagnosis, typically including alcohol, cocaine, heroin, hallucinogens, stimulants, and marijuana. Importantly, some substances are not typically considered in assessments of dual diagnosis. For example, nicotine is usually not considered a substance of abuse in dual diagnosis research, despite the high rates of use among individuals with both mental illness (Lasser et al., 2000) and substance abuse (Bien & Burge, 1990), as well as a growing literature that suggests that nicotine dependence has links, perhaps biological in nature, to both major depression (Quattrocki, Baird, & Yurgelun-Todd, 2000) and schizophrenia (Dalack & Meador-Woodruff, 1996; Ziedonis & George, 1997). Others have found elevated rates of psychiatric and substance use disorders in smokers (Keuthen et al., 2000). Taken together, factors such as the type of problematic substance use assessed, the measures that are used, and the specific substances that are included in an assessment all contribute to varying meanings of the term *dual diagnosis*.

A final methodological issue involves the split between the mental health treatment system and the substance abuse treatment system, and the impact that this separation has on dual diagnosis research. The literature on dual diagnosis really includes two largely separate areas of investigation: research on substance abuse in individuals with mental illness, as well as research on mental illness in primary substance abusers. In order to get an accurate picture of dual diagnosis and its full impact on clinical functioning and research in psychopathology, both aspects of this literature must be examined.

## FINDINGS FROM MAJOR EPIDEMIOLOGICAL STUDIES

Over the past 25 years, several large-scale epidemiological studies of mental illness have examined rates of dual diagnosis, including the Epidemiologic Catchment Area Study (ECA; Regier et al., 1990), the National Comorbidity Survey (NCS; Kessler et al., 1994), the National Comorbidity Survey Replication (NCS-R; Kessler & Merikangas, 2004), and the National Longitudinal Alcohol Epidemiology Study (NLAES; Grant et al., 1994). Although each study differs somewhat from the others in methodology, inclusion/exclusion criteria, and diagnostic categories assessed (see Table 2.1 for a brief description of methods for these studies), we can take several points from this literature that can contribute to our thinking about and understanding of dual diagnosis.

**Table 2.1**

Methods of Several Major Epidemiological Studies on Dual Diagnosis

| Study | Years | Methods |
| --- | --- | --- |
| ECA (Reiger et al., 1990) | 1980–1984 | Surveyed more than 20,000 adults in five cities across the United States both in the community and in institutions. Trained interviewers used the Diagnostic Interview Schedule to determine *DSM-III* diagnoses. Included affective, anxiety, and schizophrenia-spectrum disorders. |
| NCS (Kessler et al., 1994) | 1990–1992 | Assessed 12-month and lifetime prevalence rates for a range of psychiatric disorders in more than 8,000 noninstitutionalized individuals ages 15–54 across 48 states using the Composite International Diagnostic Interview (CIDI) and based on *DSM-III-R* criteria. |
| NLAES (Grant et al., 1994) | 1991–1992 | Examined rates of co-occurrence of alcohol and drug use disorders and affective disorders in a general population sample. The NLAES is a household survey of over 42,000 adults in the United States that utilized diagnostic interviews to assess *DSM-IV* diagnostic criteria for alcohol use disorders. |
| NCSR (Kessler et al., 2004) | 2001–2002 | Nationally representative face-to-face household survey of over 9,000 noninstitutionalized people ages 18 years or older. Diagnoses based on *DSM-IV* criteria assessed via CIDI interviews. |
| NESARC (Grant et al., 2004) | 2001–2002 | Nationally representative face-to-face survey of 43,093 noninstitutionalized respondents, 18 years of age or older, conducted by NIAAA. *DSM-IV* criteria for substance use disorders and nine independent mood and anxiety disorders were assessed with the Alcohol Use Disorders and Associated Disabilities Interview Schedule-DSM-IV Version (AUDADIS-IV), a structured diagnostic interview administered by lay interviewers. |

## Dual Diagnosis Is Highly Prevalent in Community Samples

First, epidemiological studies consistently show that dual diagnosis is highly prevalent in community samples. Each of these studies finds that people with mental illness are at greatly increased risk of having a co-occurring substance use disorder, and people with a substance use disorder are likewise much more likely to meet criteria for an Axis I mental disorder. For example, the Epidemiologic Catchment Area Study (ECA; Regier et al., 1990) was the first large-scale study of comorbidity of psychiatric and substance use disorders in the general population, and documented high rates of dual diagnosis among both individuals with primary mental disorders and those with primary substance use disorders. Overall, individuals with a lifetime history of a mental illness had an odds ratio of 2.3 for a lifetime history of alcohol use disorder and 4.5 for drug use disorder, a clear illustration of how those with mental illness are at substantially increased risk of having a comorbid substance use diagnosis. When examined by type of disorder, antisocial personality disorder (ASP) showed the highest comorbidity rate (83.6%), followed by bipolar disorder (60.7%), schizophrenia (47.0%), panic disorder (35.8%), obsessive-compulsive disorder (32.8%), and major depression (27.2%). Further analysis of ECA data (Helzer, Robbins, & McEvoy, 1987) found that men and women with posttraumatic stress disorder (PTSD) were 5 times and 1.4 times more likely, respectively, to have a drug use disorder as were men and women without PTSD. Substantial rates of dual diagnosis were also found in primary substance abusers (Regier et al., 1990). Overall, 37% of individuals with an alcohol disorder and 53% of those with a drug use disorder had comorbid mental illness.

Further analyses (Helzer & Pryzbeck, 1988) found that among those with alcohol use disorders, the strongest association was with ASP (odds ratio = 21.0), followed by mania (OR = 6.2) and schizophrenia (OR = 4.0). Like the ECA study, the NCS and that NLAES found markedly high rates of dual diagnosis. NCS (Kessler et al., 1994) findings showed that respondents with mental illness had at least twice the risk of lifetime alcohol or drug use disorder, with even greater risk for individuals with certain types of mental illnesses. Findings were similar for primary substance abusers: The majority of respondents with an alcohol or drug use disorder had a history of some nonsubstance use psychiatric disorder (Kendler, Davis, & Kessler, 1997; Kessler, 1997). Overall, 56.8% of men and 72.4% of women with alcohol abuse met diagnostic criteria for at least one psychiatric disorder, as did 78.3% of men and 86.0% of women with alcohol dependence (Kendler et al., 1997). Moreover, 59% of those with a lifetime drug use disorder also met criteria for a lifetime psychiatric disorder (Kessler, 1997). Likewise the NLAES (Grant et al., 1994; Grant & Harford, 1995) found that among respondents with major depression, 32.5% met criteria for alcohol dependence during their lifetime, as compared to 11.2% of those without major depression. Those with primary alcohol use disorders were almost 4 times more likely to be diagnosed with lifetime depression, and the associations were even stronger for drug use disorders: Individuals with drug dependence were nearly 7 times more likely than those without drug dependence to report lifetime major depression (see Bucholz, 1999, for a review). Such findings clearly illustrate that rates of dual diagnosis are significant among individuals with mental illness and primary substance abusers, and that many types of psychiatric disorders confer an increased risk of substance use disorder. Overall these studies find that a psychiatric diagnosis yields at least double the risk of a lifetime alcohol or drug use disorder.

## High Prevalence Rates of Dual Diagnosis Persist Over Time

A second important feature of rates of dual diagnosis is that they appear to be persistent. Examining how rates persist or change over time is important for several reasons. When the ECA and NCS findings were first published, the findings of high rates of both single and dual disorders were significant because they illustrated the many ways in which the understanding, assessment, and treatment of mental illness and substance use disorders were incomplete. The NCS in particular came under increased scrutiny, given that the rates it found for mental illness were even higher than those found by the ECA. Replications of these studies can demonstrate whether the high rates found in the first studies persist over time. In addition, since the first epidemiologic studies were conducted, *DSM* criteria have changed, leading to questions of how these diagnostic changes might impact illness rates. Finally, seeking treatment for mental distress, as well as use of medications for symptoms of depression and anxiety, are now more widely discussed and accepted than they were 10 to 20 years ago, and it is unclear how changing attitudes might impact rates of dual disorders. Findings from several replications of large epidemiologic studies indicate that even with changes in diagnostic criteria and attitudes about psychological distress, rates of dual disorders remain high. For example, the NCS was recently replicated in the NCS-R. The NCS-R (Kessler & Merikangas, 2004) shared much of the same methodology as the original NCS, repeated many questions from the original survey, and included additional questions to tap *DSM-IV* diagnostic criteria. Conducting these studies 10 years apart allows for an examination of the stability in rates of dual diagnosis, as well as how changes in assessment and diagnostic criteria impact the prevalence of dual diagnosis and other comorbid conditions.

Comparisons of data from both studies illustrate the persistent nature of dual diagnosis. That is, while specific values have changed from one interview to another, the overall picture of dual diagnosis remains the same: Prevalence rates are high, and people with mental illness remain at greatly increased risk for developing substance use disorders. For example, for major depressive disorder (MDD; Kessler et al., 1996) 38.6% of respondents who met criteria for lifetime MDD also had a diagnosis of substance use disorder based on NCS data, while 18.5% of respondents who met criteria for 12-month MDD also had a diagnosis of substance use disorder. Results from the NCS-R confirmed the high prevalence rates of dual diagnosis in people with MDD: 24.0% of those with lifetime MDD also met criteria for a substance use disorder, and 27.1% of those who met criteria for 12-month MDD also met criteria for a substance use disorder (Kessler, Berglund, et al., 2005). Although the exact percentages change over time, the rates for dual MDD and substance use diagnoses remain strikingly high over the 10 years between studies.

Similar comparisons can be made between the NLAES and a more recent NIAAA survey called the National Epidemiologic Survey on Alcohol and Related Conditions (NESARC; Grant et al., 2004). The NESARC stressed the need to ensure that diagnoses of mood and anxiety disorders were independent from substance use disorders. A comparison of the two studies shows that dual mood/anxiety and substance use disorders continue to be highly prevalent in community samples. For example, in the NLAES (Grant & Harford, 1995), respondents with a past-year diagnosis of major depression had a 21.36% rate of a co-occurring alcohol use disorder, compared with 6.92% of those without 12-month major depression (OR = 3.65). Similarly, high odds ratios were found for 12-month major depression and drug use disorders (Grant, 1995). Importantly, results of the NESARC confirm the persistent association of substance use disorders and affective disorders. People who met criteria for any 12-month mood disorder were 4.5 times more likely to meet criteria for substance dependence (range of 3.4 to 6.4 for the four mood disorders assessed). People who met criteria for any 12-month anxiety disorder were 2.8 times more likely to meet substance dependence criteria (range of 2.2 to 4.2 for the five anxiety disorders assessed). Examining the results in terms of prevalence rates is similar: 19.97% of those with any 12-month mood disorder had at least one substance use disorder (SUD), and 14.96% of those with any 12-month anxiety disorder had at least one SUD. Similarly, 19.67% of those with a 12-month SUD had at least one mood disorder, and 17.71% had at least one anxiety disorder. Overall, comparisons from replications of large epidemiologic studies illustrate the persistence of dual diagnosis over time.

## DUAL DIAGNOSIS IS ONLY ONE PART OF THE COMORBIDITY PUZZLE

A third issue that is highlighted in some epidemiological studies is the fact that the term and typical understanding of dual diagnosis may not accurately reflect the nature and complexity of the problem of co-occurring mental and substance use disorders. That is, co-occurring disorders can take many forms, and limiting attention to a particular number or combination of problems may restrict what we can learn about the links and interactions between mental illness and substance use disorders. As discussed previously, the term *dual diagnosis* has most often been used to refer to a combination of one mental illness and one substance use disorder. However, epidemiologic studies find high prevalence rates of three or more co-occurring disorders that include but are not limited to dual mental-SUD combinations. For example, Kessler and colleagues (1994) found that 14% of the NCS sample met criteria for three or more comorbid *DSM* disorders, and that these respondents accounted for well over half of the lifetime and 12-month diagnoses found in the sample. Moreover, these respondents accounted for 89.5% of the severe 12-month disorders, which included active mania, nonaffective psychosis, or other disorders requiring hospitalization or associated with severe role impairment. Other data from the NCS (Kessler et al., 1996) showed that 31.9% of respondents with lifetime MDD and 18.5% of those with 12-month MDD met criteria for three or more comorbid conditions. In the NCS-R, Kessler, Berglund, et al. (2005) found that 17.3% of respondents met criteria for three or more lifetime disorders. In addition, in examining projected lifetime risk of developing different *DSM* disorders, these authors reported that 80% of projected new onsets were estimated to occur in people who already had disorders. In examining 12-month disorders in the NCS-R sample, Kessler, Chiu, et al. (2005) found similar results: 23% of the sample met criteria for three or more diagnoses. As these authors state, "Although mental disorders are widespread, serious cases are concentrated among a relatively small proportion of cases with high comorbidity" (Kessler, Chiu, et al., 2005, p. 617). Taken together, these findings illustrate the importance of thinking about dual diagnosis in the context of the broader picture of comorbid conditions. People with dual mental and substance use disorders may in fact meet criteria for a combination of multiple mental and substance use disorders.

Such aggregation of mental and substance use disorders in a small proportion of people should influence conceptualizations regarding the processes underlying dual and comorbid conditions. In addition, comorbidity appears to be influenced by severity of mental illness. Using data from the NCS-R, Kessler and colleagues (2003) examined differences in rates of comorbid disorders (including but not limited to SUDs) in respondents with MDD of differing levels of severity. Specifically, respondents who met criteria for 12-month MDD were classified as showing mild, moderate, severe, or very severe symptoms, based on scores on the Quick Inventory of Depressive Symptomatology Self Report (QIDS-SR) for the worst month in the past year. As severity level increased, so did rates of comorbidity, defined as the percentage of respondents with two or more comorbid 12-month disorders, including substance use disorders. Specifically, 34.9% of mild, 58.0% of moderate, 77.3% of severe, and 82.1% of very severe MDD cases met criteria for two or more comorbid disorders. This finding of increased severity as number of disorders increases was also found for 12-month diagnoses (Kessler, Chiu, et al., 2005). This trend is another reminder that dual diagnosis and comorbidity labels represent heterogeneous groups of people who differ in meaningful ways that likely have significance in terms of assessment, treatment, and etiology of mental and substance use disorders. In sum, epidemiological studies are now able to tell us not only that dual diagnosis is highly prevalent but also that rates of dual disorders persist over time. In addition, we now have ample evidence to suggest that talking about dual disorders is actually a simplification of a complex problem in that patients often have more than two psychiatric disorders as well as use, abuse, or dependence on multiple substances. Such findings suggest that thinking about the causes of dual disorders may need to be broadened in order to be able to explain this range of diversity among dual-disordered patients.

## FINDINGS FROM STUDIES OF CLINICAL SAMPLES

The fact that dual diagnosis is fairly common in the general population serves to highlight the even higher rates found in treatment settings. Clinical studies of dual diagnosis have assessed general psychiatric patients, patients with specific psychiatric disorders, and primary substance abusing patients.

### DUAL DIAGNOSIS IN GENERAL PSYCHIATRIC PATIENTS

Clinical studies of dual diagnosis over the past 20 years indicate that one-third to three-quarters of general psychiatric patients may meet criteria for comorbid psychiatric and substance use disorders, depending on the diagnostic makeup of the sample and the level of chronicity represented (Ananth et al., 1989; Galanter, Castaneda, & Ferman, 1988; McLellan, Druley, & Carson, 1978; Mezzich, Ahn, Fabrega, & Pilkonis, 1990; Safer, 1987). Rates seem to fall in the higher end of this range for samples comprising more impaired patient populations. For example, Ananth and colleagues (1989) found that 72.0% of a sample of patients with schizophrenia, bipolar disorder, and atypical psychosis received a comorbid substance use diagnosis. Mezzich, Ahn, Fabrega, & Pilkonis (1990) conducted a large-scale assessment of dual diagnosis in more than 4,000 patients presenting for evaluation and referral for mental health problems over an 18-month period and found substantial rates of dual diagnosis among several diagnostic subsamples. The highest rates were seen among patients with severe mental illnesses such as bipolar disorder (45% diagnosed with an alcohol use disorder and 39% diagnosed with a drug use disorder) and schizophrenia or paranoid disorders (42% and 38% were diagnosed with alcohol and other substance use disorders, respectively). However, dual diagnosis was also pronounced in other patient groups. Specifically, 33% of patients with major depression were diagnosed with an alcohol use disorder, and 18% were diagnosed with a drug use disorder. Among patients with anxiety disorders, 19% and 11% were diagnosed with alcohol and other substance use disorders, respectively.

## DUAL DIAGNOSIS IN SAMPLES OF PATIENTS WITH SPECIFIC DISORDERS

Rates of dual diagnosis have been extensively studied among patients with severe mental illness, including schizophrenia (Dixon, Haas, Weiden, Sweeney, & Frances, 1991; Mueser et al., 1990), bipolar disorder (Bauer et al., 2005; McElroy et al., 2001; Salloum & Thase, 2000; Vieta et al., 2000), and major depression (Goodwin & Jamison, 1990; Lynskey, 1998; Merikangas, Leckman, Prusoff, Pauls, & Weissman, 1985; Swendsen & Merikangas, 2000). Findings show that dual diagnosis is common in such samples. Mueser et al. (1990) evaluated 149 patients with schizophrenia spectrum disorders and found that 47% had a lifetime history of alcohol abuse, while many had abused stimulants (25%), cannabis (42%), and hallucinogens (18%). Dixon and colleagues (1991) found that 48% of a sample of schizophrenia patients met criteria for an alcohol or drug use disorder. Chengappa, Levine, Gershon, and Kupfer (2000) evaluated the prevalence of substance abuse and dependence in patients with bipolar disorder. Among patients with bipolar I, 58% met abuse or dependence criteria for at least one substance, and 11% abused or were dependent on three or more substances. In the bipolar II group, the rate of dual diagnosis was approximately 39%. Baethge and colleagues (2005) followed a group of first-episode bipolar I patients and found that about one-third of the sample had a substance use disorder at the baseline assessment, and that patients using two or more substances showed poorer outcomes over the 2 years of the study. Bauer and colleagues (Bauer et al., 2005) conducted structured interviews with a large sample of inpatient veterans with bipolar disorder across 11 sites ($n = 328$) to examine rates of comorbid anxiety and substance use disorders. Results showed high rates of current (33.8%) and lifetime (72.3%) substance use disorders in the sample, along with a rate of 29.8% meeting criteria for multiple current disorders. Hasin, Endicott, and Lewis (1985) examined rates of comorbidity in a sample of patients with affective disorder presenting for treatment as part of the National Institute of Mental Health Collaborative Study of Depression and found that 24% of these patients reported serious problems with alcohol and 18% met diagnostic criteria for an alcohol use disorder.

In an examination of patients with major depression, bipolar disorder, and controls participating in the National Institute of Mental Health Collaborative Program on the Psychobiology of Depression, Winokur and colleagues (1998) found that affective disorder patients had substantially higher rates of dual substance use disorders than did controls.

Dual diagnosis is also common among patients with anxiety disorders. In their review of studies of dual anxiety and substance use disorders, Kushner, Sher, and Beitman (1990) found that rates differ by type of anxiety disorder, with social phobia (ranging from 20% to 36% rate of dual diagnosis) and agoraphobia (ranging from 7.0% to 27.0% rate of dual diagnosis) showing the highest rates of substance abuse comorbidity. Others have found a 22% rate of lifetime alcohol use disorder among patients with social phobia (Himle & Hill, 1991), a 10% to 20% rate for patients with agoraphobia (Bibb & Chambless, 1986), and up to a 12% rate of lifetime alcohol dependence among patients with obsessive-compulsive disorder (Eisen & Rasmussen, 1989). In addition, more attention is being given recently to dual substance abuse and PTSD in clinical samples. A growing literature examining this diagnostic combination finds high rates of dual diagnosis among patients with PTSD, with some findings as high as 80% (Keane, Gerardi, Lyons, & Wolfe, 1988). Research both with samples of veterans with PTSD and samples of women with assault- or trauma-related PTSD show strikingly high rates of comorbid substance abuse and dependence (see Stewart, Pihl, Conrod, & Dongier, 1998, for a review). Moreover, Breslau, Davis, Peterson, and Schultz (1997) interviewed a sample of 801 women and found that PTSD significantly increased the likelihood for later alcohol use disorder.

Recent work documents high rates of dual diagnosis among those with eating disorders. Higher rates of drug use have been found in samples of individuals with eating disorders than in controls (Krug et al., 2008), and studies of clinical samples show high overall rates of alcohol and drug use disorders. For example, Grillo, White, and Masheb (2009) assessed *DSM-IV* lifetime and current psychiatric disorder comorbidity in patients with binge-eating disorder and found that more than 73% of respondents had at least one lifetime diagnosis and 43% had at least one current psychiatric diagnosis, with almost 25% of the sample meeting criteria for a lifetime substance use disorder. Several studies have shown variation in rates of substance use disorders across the different types of eating disorders—anorexia nervosa, bulimia nervosa, binge-eating disorder—and subsets of disorders within these (Root et al., 2010). In addition, rates of comorbidity, including that with SUDs, may be associated with eating disorder severity, with those with more severe symptoms of eating disorder showing the highest rates of comorbid SUDs (Spindler & Milos, 2007).

Some of the highest rates of comorbidity are found for patients with personality disorders, especially antisocial personality disorder (ASP). Studies show that comorbid ASP accelerates the development of alcoholism (Hesselbrock, Hesselbrock, & Workman-Daniels, 1986), and that 80% of patients with ASP have a history of problem use of alcohol (Schuckit, 1983). In a recent review of studies on dual substance use disorders and borderline personality disorder (BPD), Trull and colleagues (2000) found that, across studies, more than 48% of patients with BPD met criteria for alcohol use disorders, and 38% of those with BPD met criteria for a drug use disorder. In a recent reanalysis of the NESARC data, Trull and colleagues

(2010) found high rates of dual personality disorders and SUDs. More than one-quarter of those with ASP (26.65%) met criteria for drug dependence, while even higher rates of drug dependence were found for those with histrionic (29.72%) and dependent (27.34%) personality disorders.

Important work is now illustrating the need to think more broadly about dual and multiple comorbidities and how these span Axis I and Axis II disorders. For example, a recent examination of data on generalized anxiety disorder from the NESARC study (Alegría et al., 2010) found a lifetime prevalence rate of generalized anxiety disorder with comorbid SUD of 2.04%. However, those with generalized anxiety disorder and comorbid SUD showed significantly higher rates of comorbidity of other psychiatric disorders than did those with generalized anxiety disorder alone, including higher lifetime rates of bipolar disorder, panic disorder, and ASP. A similar pattern was found for social anxiety in the NESARC data (Schneier et al., 2010): Respondents with both social anxiety disorder and comorbid alcohol use disorder were significantly more likely to earn diagnoses of mood, other anxiety, psychotic, and personality disorders, as well as additional substance use disorders and pathological gambling. Goldstein, Compton, and Grant (2010) examined rates of ASP in individuals with PTSD and how this combination of disorders affected risk of further comorbid psychiatric disorders. Compared to those with PTSD only, those with PTSD+ASP showed much higher rates of additional comorbid diagnoses. Specifically, those with PTSD+ASP met criteria for, on average, 5.7 additional lifetime Axis I diagnoses, while those with PTSD only met criteria for only 2.3 additional lifetime Axis I diagnoses. Rates of additional Axis II diagnosis were similar (2.5 additional Axis II diagnoses for those with PTSD+ASP versus 0.7 for those with PTSD only). Wildes, Marcus, and Fagiolini (2008) examined rates of eating disorders in individuals with bipolar disorder and found that a subset of individuals with bipolar disorder and loss of control over eating showed elevated rates of substance use disorders. In another study of individuals with bipolar disorder, Bauer and colleagues (2005) interviewed inpatients using the Structured Clinical Interview for *DSM-IV* and found that rates of comorbidity with SUDs were high (33.8% current, 72.3% lifetime), but that almost 30% of respondents had comorbid bipolar, SUD, and anxiety disorders. Such findings illustrate the importance of expanding our thinking regarding dual diagnosis into multiple comorbidities.

## DUAL DIAGNOSIS IN PATIENTS WITH PRIMARY SUBSTANCE USE DISORDERS

Substance-abusing patients in treatment are a heterogeneous group, encompassing a range of substances and levels of severity. Nonetheless, researchers have found high rates of dual disorders across diverse samples of patients seeking substance abuse treatment (Arendt & Munk-Jorgensen, 2004; Falck, Wang, Siegal, & Carlson, 2004; Herz, Volicer, D'Angelo, & Gadish, 1990; Mirin, Weiss, Griffin, & Michael, 1991; Mirin, Weiss, & Michael, 1988; Penick et al., 1984; Powell, Penick, Othmer, Bingham, & Rice, 1982; Ross, Glaser, & Stiasny, 1988; Rounsaville, Weissman, Kleber, & Wilber, 1982; Watkins et al., 2004; Weissman & Meyers, 1980). Findings of lifetime rates of psychiatric disorder range from 73.5% of a sample of cocaine abusers (Rounsaville et al., 1991) to 77% of a sample of hospitalized alcoholics (Hesselbrock, Meyer, &

Keener, 1985) to 78% of a sample of patients in an alcohol and drug treatment facility (Ross, Glaser, & Germanson, 1988). Findings of current psychiatric disorder are similarly high, ranging from 55.7% of a group of cocaine abusers (Rounsaville et al., 1991) to 65% in a general substance-abusing sample (Ross et al., 1988).

Further reflecting their diagnostic heterogeneity, substance abusers in treatment experience a range of comorbid psychiatric disorders. Among the most widely studied have been affective disorders, and treatment-seeking substance abusers show high rates of both major depression (Hasin, Grant, & Endicott, 1988; Hesselbrock et al., 1985; Merikangas & Gelernter, 1990; Mezzich et al., 1990; Miller, Klamen, Hoffmann, & Flaherty, 1996; Rounsaville, Weissman, Wilber, Crits-Christoph, & Kleber, 1982; Weissman & Meyers, 1980) and bipolar disorder (Strakowski & DelBello, 2000). Miller and colleagues (1996) surveyed a sample of more than 6,000 substance abuse treatment patients from 41 sites and found that 44% had a lifetime history of major depression. In a review of comorbidity of affective and substance use disorders, Lynskey (1998) found that the prevalence of unipolar depression among patients receiving treatment for substance use disorders ranged from a low of 25.8% for lifetime depression in a sample of 93 alcohol-dependent men (Sellman & Joyce, 1996) to a high of 67% meeting a lifetime diagnosis of major depression among a sample of 120 inpatients (Grant, Hasin, & Harford, 1989). Busto, Romach, and Sellers (1996) evaluated rates of dual diagnosis in a sample of 30 patients admitted to a medical facility for benzodiazepine detoxification and found that 33% met *DSM-III-R* criteria for lifetime major depression. Results from large studies of treatment-seeking substance abusers find that these patients show 5 to 8 times the risk of having a comorbid bipolar diagnosis (see Strakowski & DelBello, 2000, for a review). The importance of dual mental illness in substance-abusing samples lies in its link to functioning and treatment outcome. Burns, Teesson, and O'Neill (2005) studied the impact of dual anxiety disorders and/or depression on outcome of 71 patients seeking outpatient alcohol treatment. Comorbid patients showed greater problems at baseline (more disabled, drank more heavily) than did substance-abuse-only patients, a difference that persisted at a follow-up assessment 3 months later.

An extensive literature documents high rates of comorbid personality disorders in primary substance abusers (Khantzian & Treece, 1985; Nace, 1990; Nace, Davis, & Gaspari, 1991), especially ASP (Herz et al., 1990; Hesselbrock et al., 1985; Liskow, Powell, Nickel, & Penick, 1991; Morgenstern, Langenbucher, Labouvie, & Miller, 1997; Penick et al., 1984; Powell et al., 1982). In their evaluation of a large sample of treatment-seeking substance abusers, Mezzich and colleagues (1990) found that 18% of those with alcohol use disorders and almost 25% of those with drug use disorders met criteria for an Axis II disorder. Busto and colleagues (1996) found that 42% of their sample of patients undergoing benzodiazepine detoxification met *DSM-III-R* criteria for ASP. Morgenstern and colleagues (1997) assessed prevalence rates of personality disorders in a multisite sample of 366 substance abusers in treatment. Results showed that more than 57% of the sample met criteria for at least one personality disorder. ASP was the most prevalent (22.7% of the sample), followed by borderline (22.4%), paranoid (20.7%), and avoidant (18%) personality disorders. Moreover, the presence of a personality disorder doubled the likelihood of meeting criteria for a comorbid Axis I disorder. Brooner and colleagues (1997) assessed psychiatric disorders in 716 opioid abusers on methadone maintenance therapy and found that 47% of the sample met criteria for at least one disorder, with ASP and major depression being the most common co-occurring diagnoses. In addition, psychiatric comorbidity was associated with more severe substance use disorder. Kokkevi, Stephanis, Anastasopoulou, and Kostogianni (1998) surveyed 226 treatment-seeking individuals with drug dependence in Greece and found a 59.5% prevalence rate of personality disorder, with more than 60% of these patients meeting criteria for more than one personality disorder. Moreover, those with personality disorders were at twice the risk for meeting an additional Axis I diagnosis.

Findings are similar with anxiety disorders, with high rates of comorbid phobias (Bowen, Cipywnyk, D'Arcy, & Keegan, 1984; Hasin et al., 1988; Ross et al., 1988), panic disorder (Hasin et al., 1988; Penick et al., 1984), and obsessive-compulsive disorder (Eisen & Rasmussen, 1989) documented in substance-abusing populations. Thomas, Thevos, and Randall (1999) reported a 23% prevalence rate of social phobias in a large study of both inpatients and outpatients with alcohol dependence. Substance abusers also appear to be especially affected by PTSD (Cottler, Compton, Mager, Spitznagel, & Janca, 1992; Davis & Wood, 1999; Triffleman, Marmar, Delucchi, & Ronfeldt, 1995). In an analysis of cocaine-dependent patients in the National Institute on Drug Abuse Collaborative Cocaine Treatment Study, Najavitis and colleagues (1998) found that 30.2% of women and 15.2% of men met *DSM-III-R* criteria for PTSD. Recently, Back and colleagues (2000) found that 42.9% of a sample of cocaine-dependent individuals met criteria for PTSD, and Bonin and colleagues (2000) found a 37.4% rate of PTSD in a sample of patients attending a community substance abuse treatment program. In sum, the literature clearly documents high rates of dual substance abuse and psychiatric disorders for a variety of psychopathological conditions and in a range of patient populations. Findings from epidemiological studies show that dual diagnosis is relatively common in the general population, and results of clinical studies illustrate the frequency of dual diagnosis among individuals in treatment. That rates of dual diagnosis are similarly high in both mentally ill and in primary substance-abusing populations serves to highlight the serious difficulties in having two separate and independent systems of care for mental illness and substance abuse (Grella, 1996; Ridgely, Lambert, Goodman, Chichester, & Ralph, 1998), because both populations of patients are quite likely to be suffering from both types of disorders.

## CLINICAL IMPACT OF DUAL DISORDERS

The importance of dual diagnosis lies in its negative impact on the course and prognosis of both psychiatric and substance use disorders, as well as its influence on assessment, diagnosis, and treatment outcome. Individuals with dual disorders show more adverse social, health, economic, and psychiatric consequences than do those with only one disorder, and they show more severe difficulties, often a more chronic course of psychiatric disorder, and a poorer response to both mental health and substance abuse treatment. In the next section we review the ways that dual diagnosis impacts three general areas: patient functioning, clinical care, and research.

Impact of Dual Diagnosis on Patient Functioning

*Symptoms, Course of Illness, and Life Functioning*   Dual diagnosis severely impacts the severity and course of many disorders, especially among patients with serious mental illnesses such as schizophrenia, bipolar disorder, and recurrent major depression. Often these dually diagnosed individuals show a poorer and more chaotic course of disorder, with more severe symptoms (Alterman, Erdlen, Laporte, & Erdlen, 1982; Barbee et al., 1989; Hays & Aidroos, 1986; Negrete and Knapp, 1986), more frequent hospitalizations (Carpenter, Heinrichs, & Alphs, 1985; Drake & Wallach, 1989; Sonne, Brady, & Morton, 1994), and more frequent relapses than patients without co-occurring substance abuse (Linszen, Dingemans, & Lenior, 1994; O'Connell, Mayo, Flatow, Cuthbertson, & O'Brien, 1991; Sokolski et al., 1994). Haywood et al. (1995) found that substance abuse, along with medication noncompliance, was the most important predictor of more frequent rehospitalization among schizophrenia patients. Recently, Margolese and colleagues (2004) compared three groups of schizophrenia patients: those with current SUD, those with lifetime but not current SUD, and those with no current or history of SUD. Patients with current SUD showed more positive symptoms than both other patient groups, had higher scores on measures of depression as compared to the single diagnosis group, and were more likely than the single diagnosis group to be noncompliant with their medications. Winokur and colleagues (1998) found that patients with drug abuse and bipolar disorder had an earlier age of onset of bipolar disorder than those with bipolar disorder alone, as well as a stronger family history of mania.

Nolan and colleagues (2004) rated patients with bipolar or schizoaffective disorder on severity of manic symptoms, severity of depressive symptoms, and number of illness episodes over a 1-year period ($n = 258$). Results showed that ratings for mania severity were associated with comorbid substance abuse. Lehman, Myers, Thompson, and Corty (1993) compared individuals with dual mental illness and substance use diagnoses to those with just a primary mental illness and found that the dual diagnosis group had a higher rate of personality disorder and more legal problems. Hasin, Endicott, and Keller (1991) followed 135 individuals with dual mood and alcohol use disorders who were originally studied as part of the National Institute of Mental Health Collaborative Study on the Psychobiology of Depression. Although most had experienced at least one 6-month period of remission of the alcohol disorder at some point during the follow-up period, most had relapsed after 5 years. Mueller and colleagues (1994) examined the impact of alcohol dependence on the course of major depression over 10 years among individuals with depression who participated in the National Institute of Mental Health Collaborative Depression Study. Those who were alcohol dependent at baseline had a much lower rate of recovery from major depression than those with major depression alone, illustrating the negative impact of alcohol use disorders on the course of major depressive disorder.

Dual diagnosis is also a serious issue for patients with anxiety disorders such as PTSD (Najavitis, Weiss, & Shaw, 1997; Ouimette, Brown, & Najavitis, 1998). Overall, the combination of substance abuse and PTSD appears to be linked to higher rates of victimization, more severe PTSD symptoms in general, more severe subgroups of PTSD symptoms, and higher rates of Axis II comorbidity (Ouimette,

Wolfe, & Chrestman, 1996). Saladin, Brady, Dansky, and Kilpatrick (1995) compared 28 women with both substance abuse and PTSD to 28 women with PTSD only and found that the dual diagnosis group reported more symptoms of avoidance and arousal, more sleep disturbance, and greater traumatic event exposure than the PTSD-only group. Back and colleagues (2000) similarly found higher rates of exposure to traumatic events, more severe symptomatology, and higher rates of Axis I and Axis II disorders among cocaine-dependent individuals with PTSD as compared to those without lifetime PTSD. Moreover, evidence suggests that the combination of PTSD and cocaine dependence remains harmful over several years, with patients showing a greater likelihood of continued PTSD as well as revictimization several years after an initial substance abuse treatment episode (Dansky, Brady, & Saladin, 1998).

Dual diagnosis also exerts a profound impact on overall life functioning. Patients with severe mental illnesses such as schizophrenia who abuse substances appear to be particularly hard hit in this regard (see Bradizza & Stasiewicz, 1997, for a review; Kozaric-Kovacic, Folnegovic-Smalc, Folnegovic, & Marusic, 1995). Drake and colleagues consistently have found that individuals with schizophrenia and comorbid substance abuse show substantially poorer life adjustment than than do individuals with schizophrenia without substance abuse, and eat fewer regular meals (Drake, Osher, & Wallach, 1989; Drake & Wallach, 1989). Havassy and Arns (1998) surveyed 160 frequently hospitalized adult psychiatric patients and found not only high rates of dual disorders (48% of patients had at least one current substance use disorder; of these, 55.1% met criteria for polysubstance dependence) but also that dual diagnosis was related to increased depressive symptoms, poor life functioning, lower life satisfaction, and a greater likelihood of being arrested or in jail. Research similarly shows that patients with dual affective and alcohol use disorders show greater difficulties in overall functioning and social functioning than do patients with depression (Hirschfeld, Hasin, Keller, Endicott, & Wunder, 1990) or bipolar disorder (Singh, Mattoo, Sharan, & Basu, 2005).

Newman, Moffitt, Caspi, and Silva (1998) examined the impact of different types of comorbidity (including but not limited to substance abuse–psychiatric disorder combinations) on life functioning in a large sample of young adults. Multiple-disordered cases showed poorer functioning than single-disordered cases in almost every area measured, including health status, suicide attempts, disruption in performance of daily activities, the number of months disabled because of psychiatric illness, greater life dissatisfaction, less social stability (more residence changes, greater use of welfare for support, greater rates of adult criminal conviction records), greater employment problems, lower levels of educational attainment, and greater reports of physical health problems. Weiss and colleagues (2005) examined the interplay between bipolar disorder and recovery from substance use disorders on a range of quality-of-life factors in a sample of 1,000 patients with current or lifetime bipolar disorder. Specifically, three groups were compared: those with no history of SUDs, those with past SUDs, and those with current SUDs. Results showed that the current-SUD group had the poorest functioning, and both SUD groups reported lower quality of life and higher lifetime rates of suicide attempts than did the non-SUD group. Moreover, the toxic effects of psychoactive substances in individuals with schizophrenia and bipolar disorder may be present even at use levels that may not be problematic in the general population (Lehman, Myers, Dixon, & Johnson, 1994; Mueser et al., 1990).

*Cognitive Functioning* Increasingly, clinicians and researchers are focusing on cognitive functioning in persons with dual disorders. There is a range of cognitive impairments associated with psychiatric disorders, particularly serious mental illness (e.g., schizophrenia, bipolar disorder). Individuals with schizophrenia spectrum disorders demonstrate cognitive impairments across a range of cognitive domains when compared to normative comparison samples (Heinrichs and Zakzanis, 1998). While not as severe, individuals with affective disorders demonstrate similar impairments across a range of cognitive domains (Depp et al., 2007; Goldberg et al., 1993; Schretlen et al., 2007). These impairments are linked by modest to strong correlations to functional outcomes in schizophrenia (Green 1996) and bipolar disorder (Dickerson et al., 2004; Dickerson, Sommerville, Origoni, Ringel, & Parente, 2001). There is also evidence that in samples of individuals with primary substance use disorders, chronic or sustained substance use can contribute to cognitive impairment and resulting brain dysfunction (Bowden, Crews, Bates, Fals-Stewart, & Ambrose, 2001; Rogers & Robbins, 2001). Moreover, cognitive impairment has been implicated in substance abuse treatment outcomes in this population (Aharonovich, Nunes, & Hasin, 2003; Fals-Stewart and Schafer, 1992). Such findings suggest that substance use may exacerbate existing cognitive impairment, which may in part contribute to the poorer outcomes, experienced by persons with co-occurring serious mental illness (SMI) and SUD.

While this recognition has prompted clinical research efforts to adapt and develop new substance abuse interventions designed to accommodate some of the cognitive and motivational impairments associated with SMI (e.g., Addington et al., 1998; Bellack, Bennett, Gearon, Brown, & Yang, 2006; Ziedonis & George, 1997), other research efforts have been directed toward further description and explication of the role of cognitive impairment in individuals with dual diagnosis. The majority of this work has focused on SMI samples. On the one hand, there is concern about the possible exacerbation of existing cognitive impairment resulting from substance use among individuals with dual disorders, suggesting that these individuals would demonstrate poorer cognitive functioning when compared to those without SUD. On the other hand, some data suggest that engaging in behaviors necessary to obtain access to substances requires a higher level of functioning (Dixon, 1999; Mueser et al., 1990), and thus these individuals with dual disorders would have better cognitive functioning than individuals without SUD. With regard to cognitive functioning, the data are in fact mixed and overall suggest that there are few differences between those with SMI who have a current or history of SUD and those who do not. In a meta-analysis of 22 studies investigating neurocognitive functioning among individuals with schizophrenia, Potvin, Joyal, Pelletier, and Stip (2008) found that there was no difference on a composite score of cognitive functioning between those with SUD and those without. Furthermore, they found few differences between groups on specific cognitive domains or specific cognitive measures. Depp et al. (2007) also found no differences in cognitive functioning among a sample of individuals with bipolar disorder with and without SUDs. In contrast, Carey, Carey, and Simons (2003), in a sample of individuals with schizophrenia spectrum and bipolar disorders, found that those with a current SUD or former SUD both demonstrated better cognitive functioning than those who had never used substances.

The interpretation of these data is complicated by several substantive and methodological issues. First, there is some indication that impairment may vary depending on primary substance of abuse. Across the meta-analytic data, alcohol use was associated with poorer working memory performance, whereas cannabis use was associated with better problem solving and visual memory performance (Potvin et al., 2008). This finding is consistent with neuropsychological data from SUD samples without psychiatric diagnoses, where alcohol is associated with greater impairments than other drugs such as cocaine (Goldstein et al., 2004). However, types of substances are not always considered in dual disorder studies (e.g., Carey et al., 2003). Second, consistent with methodological limitations across the dual diagnosis research literature, the rigor with which samples have been characterized has been quite variable. Some studies have relied on chart diagnoses as opposed to diagnostic interview to identify SUD, few have verified drug status with urinalysis, and others have failed to characterize the severity, recency, or chronicity of substance use. With regard to the latter, analyses included in the Potvin et al. (2008) study indicated that as age increased, so did the cognitive impairment among those with SUD, suggesting that chronicity of use may be a moderating factor in cognitive functioning among dual disorders. Similarly, Carpenter and Hittner (1997) found that lifetime use of alcohol or cocaine (i.e., number of years of regular use) were the strongest predictors of cognitive impairment among a sample of individuals with mixed psychiatric diagnoses (affective and anxiety disorders) and SUDs.

These latter findings raise the related question of how cognitive impairment changes over time as a result of substance use in individuals with dual disorders. Few investigations have addressed this question. Using a group comparison design with carefully characterized samples, Carey et al. (2003) found no difference in cognitive functioning between individuals with SMI and current SUD versus those with past history of SUD (defined as not meeting full criteria for the past 6 months). Peer, Bennett, and Bellack (2009) compared individuals with schizophrenia who met *DSM-IV* criteria for current cocaine dependence and those who met criteria for remission on a brief neuropsychological battery and found few differences. This study also included a parallel analysis of samples of individuals with affective disorders and cocaine dependence versus remission, which yielded similar results. Although these studies used rigorous diagnostic criteria to characterize the samples, they are limited by their cross-sectional nature. That is, they did not evaluate within subjects change in cognitive functioning as a result of discontinuation of substance use. At least two longitudinal studies have been conducted that address this question. A brief longitudinal study of inpatients with schizophrenia with or without current cocaine dependence at admission found few changes in cognition as a result of abstinence from cocaine over an 18-day study period (Cooper et al., 1999). Furthermore, there were few differences in cognition between groups at baseline or at follow-up. McCleery, Addington, and Addington (2006) followed 183 individuals with a first episode of psychosis over a 2-year study period and assessed cognition and substance use. Results indicated that cognition largely remained stable over time, while substance use declined over the study period. Together these findings suggest that cognitive functioning may be relatively static among individuals with dual disorders. Indeed, in the general SUD literature, longitudinal data suggest there are only slight and/or inconsistent improvements in neurocognitive functioning after a period of abstinence from substances (Bates,Voelbel, Buckman, Labouvie, & Barry, 2005; Di Sclafani, Tolou-Shams, Price, & Fein, 2002; Horner, 1999).

There are at least two possible interpretations of these data: (1) given the significant cognitive impairment associated with SMI, substance use causes only minimal additional impairment; and (2) the toxic effects of substance use on cognition are not easily resolved following abstinence. In part, this research may be limited by the lack of sensitivity of the neuropsychological measures used for these particular research questions. With further advances in cognitive neuroscience, more refined measures that are more tightly linked to brain structures and functions impacted by chronic substance use will likely be developed (Rogers & Robbins, 2001). While candidate brain structures and neurotransmitter pathways are increasingly being identified in the general SUD literature (e.g., Goldstein et al., 2010; Goldstein & Volkow, 2002), significantly more work is needed to understand the specifics of cognitive functioning in dual disorders, both with regard to preexisting impairment as well as a sequelae of chronic substance use.

*Treatment Noncompliance and Violence*   Substance abuse often interferes with compliance with both behavioral and psychopharmacological treatments. Lambert, Griffith, and Hendrickse (1996) surveyed patients on a general psychiatry unit in a Veterans Administration medical center and found that discharges against medical advice (AMA) were more likely to occur among patients with alcohol and/or substance use disorders. Pages and colleagues (1998) similarly assessed predictors of AMA discharge in psychiatric patients. The presence of SUD and a greater quantity and frequency of substance use were among the most important predictors. Owen and colleagues (1996) followed a sample of 135 inpatients after discharge and found that medication noncompliance was related to substance abuse, and that this combination was significantly associated with lack of outpatient contact in the follow-up period. Specifically, those with dual diagnoses were more than 8 times more likely to be noncompliant with their medication. In a large-scale study of factors related to medication adherence in schizophrenia patients, Gilmer and colleagues (2004) found that substance abusers were less likely to be adherent to antipsychotic medication regimens than were schizophrenia patients who did not abuse substances.

Similar results were found in a review of factors that impede use of medication in individuals with bipolar disorder (Velligan et al., 2009): Many studies have found that substance use is a critical barrier to medication adherence. Such findings are especially important when linked to functioning and service use. For example, schizophrenia patients who were nonadherent with their medications were more than 2.5 times more likely to be hospitalized than those who were adherent (Gilmer et al., 2004). Verduin, Carter, Brady, Myrick, and Timmerman (2005) compared bipolar only, alcohol-dependent only, and comorbid bipolar and alcohol-dependent patients on several treatment variables, including number of outpatient psychiatric visits and length of psychiatric hospitalizations, in the year leading up to and including an index hospitalization at a veterans hospital from 1999 through 2003.

The comorbid group had fewer outpatient psychiatric visits and shorter inpatient hospitalizations than did either of the single disorder groups.

For many disorders, substance abuse and its associated noncompliance with treatment is linked not only to poorer outcomes but also to greater risk for violence (Marzuk, 1996; Poldrugo, 1998; Sandberg, McNiel, & Binder, 1998; Scott et al., 1998; Soyka, 2000; Steadman et al., 1998; Swanson, Borum, Swartz, & Hiday, 1999; Swartz et al., 1998) and suicide (Cohen, Test, & Brown, 1990; Goodwin & Jamison, 1990; Karmali et al., 2000; Landmark, Cernovsky, & Merskey, 1987; Pages et al., 1997; Verduin et al., 2005). In terms of violence, Fulwiler, Grossman, Forbes, and Ruthazer (1997) compared differences between two groups of outpatients with chronic mental illness: those with and without a history of violence. The only significant differences between the two groups involved alcohol or drug use. McFall and colleagues (1999) examined 228 male Vietnam veterans seeking inpatient treatment for PTSD and found that levels of substance abuse were positively correlated with violence and aggression. The combination of schizophrenia and ASP appears to put people at high risk for violence, especially when they are drinking (Joyal, Putkonen, Paavola, & Tiihonen, 2004).

In their recent examination of population-based registers of hospital discharge diagnoses and violent crime in a Swedish sample over 30 years, Fazel, Lichtenstein, Grann, Goodwin, and Langstrom (2010) found that risk for violent crime among individuals with bipolar disorders was almost entirely due to substance abuse comorbidity, with those with bipolar-only diagnoses showing extremely low risk for violent crime. Such findings illustrate the problematic impact of substance use on violence in individuals with psychiatric disorders.

Research also shows links between dual disorders and rate of suicide. In an analysis of epidemiological data from the NESARC, Oquendo and colleagues found that lifetime rates of suicide attempts were higher for those with dual bipolar disorder and alcohol use disorders (25.29%) than for respondents with bipolar disorder alone (14.78%) (Oquendo et al., 2010). Pages and colleagues (1997) surveyed 891 psychiatric inpatients with major depressive disorder and found that both substance use and substance dependence were associated with higher levels of suicidal ideation. Potash and colleagues (2000) examined the relationship between alcohol use disorders and suicidality in bipolar patients and found that 38% of subjects with dual bipolar and alcohol use disorders had attempted suicide, as compared to 22% of those with bipolar disorder only. Recently, McCloud, Barnaby, Omu, Drummond, and Aboud (2004) examined alcohol disorders and suicidality (defined as any record of self-harm or thoughts or plans of self-harm or suicide written in the medical record) in consecutive admissions to a psychiatric hospital. Problem drinking (as measured by the Alcohol Use Disorders Identification Test [AUDIT]) was strongly related to suicidality, with higher AUDIT scores (representing greater severity of problems with alcohol) showing higher rates of suicidality. Importantly, those with multiple comorbidities—patients who have more than two comorbid diagnoses—are at even higher risk for suicide. In such cases, the added impact on suicidality of trauma in general or comorbid PTSD in particular is great. Tarrier and Picken (2010) examined rates of suicide in individuals with dual schizophrenia and substance use disorders and found that rates of suicidality (based on scores on the Beck Suicidality Scale) were higher among those with comorbid PTSD. Cacciola and colleagues (2009) identified four groups among a sample of 466 male veterans: (1) substance use disorder only; (2) substance use disorder + PTSD; (3) substance use disorder + PTSD + another Axis I disorder; and (4) substance use disorder + another Axis I disorder. Lifetime rates of both suicidal ideation and suicide attempts were highest in the substance use disorder + PTSD + another Axis I disorder group. Such findings illustrate the ways that multiple comorbidities can further increase risk for suicidality.

Impact of Dual Diagnosis on Clinical Care and Related Factors

*Service Utilization and Health Care Costs*  The fact that clinical settings routinely demonstrate higher rates of dual diagnosis patients points to the fact that having both psychiatric and substance use disorders increases rates of treatment seeking. Increased service utilization among the dually diagnosed has been borne out in both large-scale household surveys and clinical studies. For example, Helzer and Pryzbeck (1988) examined data from the ECA study and found that, for respondents of both sexes with alcohol use disorders, the number of additional nonsubstance-use disorder diagnoses had a significant impact on treatment seeking: Those with more diagnoses reported greater utilization of treatment services. Grant (1997) examined the influence of comorbid major depression and substance abuse on rates of seeking alcohol and drug treatment in data collected from the National Longitudinal Alcohol Epidemiological Survey (NLAES; Grant et al., 1994). The percentage of individuals with alcohol use disorders seeking treatment practically doubled, from 7.8% to 16.9%, when a comorbid major depressive disorder was also present. Interestingly, the greatest rate of treatment seeking (35.3%) was found among respondents who met criteria for all three disorders—alcohol, drug, and depression—illustrating how the term *dual diagnosis* is somewhat misleading, because some individuals have two or more substance use and psychiatric disorders, and each might have an additive effect on negative outcomes.

Similarly, Wu, Kouzis, and Leaf (1999), analyzing data from the NCS, found that although 14.5% of patients with a pure alcohol disorder reported using mental health and substance abuse intervention services, more than 32% of patients with comorbid alcohol and mental disorders used such services. Menezes and colleagues (1996) studied the impact of substance use problems on service utilization over 1 year in a sample of 171 individuals with serious mental illness. Although the number of inpatient admissions was equivalent for those with dual disorders and those with mental illness only, the dual diagnosis group used psychiatric emergency services 1.3 times more frequently and spent 1.8 times as many days in the hospital than did the single disorder group.

Given their increased rates of service utilization, it is not surprising that dual diagnosis patients generally accrue greater health care costs than do patients with a single diagnosis (Maynard & Cox, 1998; McCrone et al., 2000). Dickey and Azeni (1996) examined the costs of psychiatric treatment for more than 16,000 seriously mentally ill individuals with and without comorbid substance use disorders. Patients with dual diagnoses had psychiatric treatment costs that were nearly 60% higher than the costs of psychiatrically impaired individuals without substance abuse. Interestingly, most of the increased cost was owing to greater rates of inpatient psychiatric treatment, suggesting that the impact of substance abuse on psychiatric symptoms and illness relapse is realized when patients require costly psychiatric hospitalization. Garnick, Hendricks, Comstock, and Horgan (1997) examined health insurance data files over 3 years from almost 40,000 employees and found that those with dual diagnoses routinely accrued substantially higher health care costs than those with substance abuse only. Such findings suggest that individuals with dual disorders access the most expensive treatment options (inpatient hospitalization, visits to emergency rooms) that are short-term in order to manage acute distress and fail to get the comprehensive and ongoing care they require.

These findings on rates of services use can be perplexing. For example, if dual diagnosis patients are accessing more and more expensive services, why do they consistently have more severe psychiatric symptoms, more substance-related problems, and poorer outcomes than do those with single disorders? As noted earlier, dual diagnosis patients appear to access expensive but short-term or acute treatment options more often while being noncompliant or not adhering to longer-term medication and outpatient treatment regiments. Other factors include lack of integrated care, as well as increased numbers of problems to treat associated with treating more than one disorder (Watkins, Burnam, Kung, & Paddock, 2001). In addition, researchers recently have begun to more closely examine the quality of services accessed by dual diagnosis patients. For example, in their study of patients with bipolar disorder with and without comorbid substance use disorders, Verduin and colleagues (2005) found that patients with bipolar disorder and comorbid substance abuse were less likely than patients with substance abuse alone to be referred to intensive substance abuse treatment.

Watkins and colleagues (2001) looked at the delivery of appropriate care to probable dual diagnosis patients assessed as part of the Healthcare for Communities Survey (a study of a subset of respondents from the Community Tracking Study, a nationally representative study of the civilian, noninstitutionalized people in the United States [see Kemper et al., 1996, for details]). Appropriate care included medications for severe mental illness (a mood stabilizer for bipolar disorder, antipsychotic medication for a psychiatric disorder), medications and/or psychosocial interventions for anxiety disorders or major depression, and at least four sessions of any sort of treatment in the past year. In addition, variables addressed included whether patients are receiving integrated care for dual disorders (receiving both mental health and substance abuse treatment from one provider) or comprehensive substance abuse treatment (defined as including inpatient or outpatient substance use treatment that included a physical examination, a mental health evaluation, or job or relationship counseling). Results showed that 72% of dual diagnosis patients did not receive any specialty mental health or substance abuse services (i.e., services provided by a mental health or substance abuse professional rather than a primary care physician), 8% received both mental health and substance abuse treatment (either integrated or by different providers), 23% received appropriate mental health care, and 9% received comprehensive substance abuse treatment. Other studies have found a disconnect between services accessed and services needed in dual diagnosis samples (Najavitis, Sullivan, Schmitz, Weiss, & Lee, 2004). Such findings suggest that the complicated clinical picture presented by dual diagnosis patients makes it difficult for patients and providers to determine and administer appropriate care.

*Physical Illness*   Dual diagnosis puts people at risk for different forms of illness and disease. One of the most significant health problems in this population is risk for HIV and AIDS. Individuals with dual diagnosis show greatly increased risk for HIV and AIDS. People with schizophrenia and other severe mental illness are now one of the highest-risk groups for HIV (Gottesman & Groome, 1997; Krakow, Galanter, Dermatis, & Westreich, 1998), and data indicate that substance use substantially increases the likelihood of unsafe sex practices (Carey, Carey, & Kalichman, 1997) and other high-risk behaviors in those with mental illness. For example, McKinnon and colleagues (1996) found that 17.5% of a sample of psychiatric patients had a history of injection drug use, 35% reported using drugs during sex, and 30% traded sex for drugs—all substance use behaviors that are highly risky in terms of the transmission of HIV and AIDS. In their sample of 145 psychiatric inpatients and outpatients in Australia, Thompson and colleagues (1997) found that 15.9% of dual diagnosis patients reported injection drug use, a figure that is 10 times higher than that found in the general population. Hoff, Beam-Goulet, and Rosenheck (1997) examined data from the 1992 National Survey of Veterans and found that the combination of PTSD and substance abuse increased the risk of HIV infection by almost 12 times over individuals with either disorder alone.

There is increasing evidence that other physical illnesses and high-risk health habits are also found more often in people with dual disorders. Stuyt (2004) found that 29.7% of a dual diagnosis sample had hepatitis C, a rate that is 16 times higher than that found in the general population. Salloum, Douaihy, Ndimbie, and Kirisci (2004) examined physical health and disorders in three groups of psychiatric patients hospitalized on a dual diagnosis treatment unit: a group with both alcohol and cocaine dependence, a group with alcohol dependence only, and a group with cocaine dependence only. Results showed that the group with both alcohol and cocaine dependence showed higher rates of a range of medical problems, including multiple hepatitis infections, than both single diagnosis groups. Jones and colleagues (2004) examined physical health problems among people with severe mental illness and found that 74% of the sample was treated for one chronic health condition, and 50% was treated for two or more. The two most highly prevalent chronic health conditions—pulmonary disease and infectious disease—were both associated with substance use disorders in this sample. Moreover, results of regression analysis showed that substance abuse, along with age and obesity, was a significant predictor of health problem severity. Ouimette, Goodwin, and Brown (2007) identified medical problems in SUD patients with and without PTSD. Those with dual SUD + PTSD had more cardiovascular, neurological, and total physical symptoms than those with SUDs alone. Others have found high rates of mortality and other dangerous health conditions among those with dual diagnosis (Batki et al., 2009; Dickey, Dembling, Azeni & Normand, 2004; Lambert, LePage, & Schmitt, 2003). Importantly, these higher rates of physical health problems can serve as additional barriers to achieving important recovery goals (Conover, Arno, Weaver, Ang, & Ettner, 2006).

*Legal Problems*   There is also evidence that individuals with dual diagnoses have more frequent contacts with the legal system. Clark, Ricketts, and McHugo (1999) followed a sample of individuals with mental illness and substance use disorders over 3 years to longitudinally examine legal involvement and its correlates in this population. The sample consisted of 203 patients receiving treatment in a dual diagnosis treatment program. Cost and use data were collected from a range of sources, including police, defenders, prosecutors, and jails. Interestingly, while rates of arrest were certainly high, patients were 4 times more likely to have encounters with the legal system that did not result in arrest. This suggests that frequency of arrest, while significant, is an underrepresentation of the frequency of contact that dual diagnosis patients have with the legal system. In addition, continued substance abuse over the follow-up period was significantly associated with a greater likelihood of arrest.

*Homelessness*   The combination of mental illness and substance abuse also increases risk for homelessness. In a study of patients with schizophrenia, Dixon (1999) found that those who used substances experienced not only greater psychotic symptoms and relapses, a higher incidence of violent behavior and suicide, elevated rates of HIV infection, increased mortality, and higher rates of treatment and medication noncompliance, but they were also more likely to live in an unstable housing situation or be homeless. Caton and colleagues (1994) compared a sample of mentally ill homeless men to a sample of mentally ill men who were not homeless and found higher rates of drug use disorders among the homeless group. Leal, Galanter, Dermatis, and Westreich (1999) assessed homelessness in a sample of 147 patients with dual diagnosis and found that those in the group with so-called protracted homelessness (no residence for 1 year or more) were significantly more likely than those patients without protracted homelessness to report a history of injection drug use. Recently, Folsom et al. (2005) examined risk factors for homelessness and patterns of service use among those who are homeless in a large sample ($n = 10,340$) of patients with severe mental illness from a large public mental health system in southern California. Homelessness was associated with a range of variables, including substance abuse—60.5% of the homeless mentally ill group showed a substance use disorder as compared to 20.9% of the non-homeless mentally ill group. Moreover, results of multivariate logistic regression showed that those with mental illness and substance abuse were more than 4 times as likely to be homeless than were patients who did not abuse substances.

*Issues for Women With Severe Mental Illness and Substance Abuse*   Importantly, dual diagnosis is often particularly problematic for individuals who are also otherwise underserved. As noted, individuals with schizophrenia appear to be particularly hard hit by the additional difficulties of SUD. Another such population is women with severe mental illness and substance abuse. Research on women with dual diagnoses has shown that those with comorbid severe mental illness and substance abuse show poorer retention in treatment (Brown, Melchior, & Huba, 1999) and elevated levels of anxiety, depression, and medical illness (Brunette & Drake, 1998), as well as being more difficult to engage in treatment and more underrepresented in treatment overall (Comtois & Ries, 1995). In addition, women with dual diagnoses appear to have alarmingly higher rates of sexual and physical victimization that are substantially higher than those observed among women in the general population (Gearon & Bellack, 1999; Goodman, Rosenburg, Mueser, & Drake, 1997). Prevalence rates for physical victimization for women with serious mental illness range between 42% and 64% (Jacobson, 1989), and other research finds that 21% to 38% of women with serious mental illness report adult sexual abuse (Goodman, Dutton & Harris, 1995). Among women receiving treatment in a residential therapeutic community, 49% reported physical abuse and 40% reported sexual abuse (Palacios, Urmann, Newel, & Hamilton, 1999). Data from 28 women and 24 men with serious mental illness and SUDs indicated that, when compared with men, women were more likely to report being physically (60% of women vs. 29% of men) and sexually (47% of women vs. 17% of men) victimized (Gearon, Bellack, Nidecker, & Bennett, 2003).

In addition, women with dual diagnosis are often affected by issues related to pregnancy and parenting. Grella (1997) summarized some of the many difficulties in terms of providing services for pregnant women with dual disorders, including receiving adequate prenatal care, use of substances and psychiatric medications while pregnant, and lack of coordinated treatment planning and provision among medical, psychiatric, and addictions professionals. Kelly and colleagues (1999) examined the medical records of all women delivering babies in California hospitals in 1994 and 1995 and found that women with both psychiatric and substance use diagnoses were at greatly elevated risk of receiving inadequate prenatal care. There are also substantial barriers to treatment and medical care for these women, including fears of losing custody of the unborn child or their other children, lack of medical insurance, and the often disjointed nature of available services for the medical and psychiatric care of these patients (Grella, 1997). Finally, when compared to men, women with dual diagnosis may have different treatment needs. Grella (2003) compared differences in substance use and treatment histories and perceptions of service needs between men and women diagnosed with severe mental illness (mood or psychotic disorders) on admission to inpatient drug treatment. Women reported greater needs for family and trauma-related services, and women with psychotic disorders had the greatest level of need of all the groups for basic services.

## PROVISION OF TREATMENT AND TREATMENT OUTCOME

Co-occurring SUDs raise problems for interventions that have been designed to impact specific psychiatric symptoms, or ones that have been validated on samples that have excluded dual diagnosis patients. In addition, clinicians often experience difficulties in making referrals for dual diagnosis patients in the current system of single disorder treatment that effectively separates the treatment systems for mental illness and substance abuse. The fact that patients must often be forced into single diagnostic categories no doubt results in SUDs being overlooked or ignored by treatment professionals who have expertise in treating only single conditions or in dual diagnosis patients not receiving both the psychiatric and the substance abuse treatment they require (Blanchard, 2000). Patients with dual diagnosis are more difficult to treat and show poorer retention in treatment as well as poorer treatment outcomes as compared to single disorder patients. Such findings tend to be true both for patients with primary mental illness and co-occurring substance abuse (see Drake et al., 1998, and Polcin, 1992 for reviews; Goldberg, Garno, Leon, Kocsis, & Portera, 1999), as well as for patients identified through substance abuse treatment programs with comorbid mental illness (Glenn & Parsons, 1991; Ouimette, Ahrens, Moos, & Finney, 1998; Rounsaville, Kosten, Weissman, & Kleber, 1986). An early study by McLellan et al. (1983) found that higher psychiatric severity was associated with poorer treatment outcome among alcohol and drug abuse treatment patients. Tomasson and Vaglum (1997) examined the impact of psychiatric comorbidity on 351 treatment-seeking substance abusers over a 28-month period and found that patients with comorbid psychiatric disorders at admission showed worse outcome in terms of mental health functioning at follow-up.

Ouimette, Gima, Moos, and Finney (1999) reported findings of a 1-year follow-up of three groups of patients with dual substance use and psychiatric disorders (psychotic disorders, affective/anxiety disorders, and personality disorders) as compared to a group of substance abuse–only patients. Although all the groups showed comparable decreases in substance use at follow-up, patients with dual diagnoses showed greater levels of psychological distress and psychiatric symptoms and lower rates of employment than did patients with only SUDs. In a 3-year follow-up of a sample of patients with alcohol use disorders, Kranzler, Del Boca, and Rounsaville (1996) found that the presence of comorbid psychiatric disorders, including depression and ASP, is generally associated with worse 3-year outcomes. Thomas, Melchert, and Banken (1999) examined treatment outcome in 252 patients in substance abuse treatment and found the likelihood of relapse within the year following treatment was significantly increased in patients with dual personality disorders. Specifically, 6% of patients with personality disorders were abstinent 1-year posttreatment, as compared with 44% of those with no diagnosed personality disorders. A study by Havassy, Shopshire, and Quigley (2000) examined the effects of substance dependence on treatment outcome in 268 psychiatric patients following two different case management programs. Regardless of program, dual diagnosis patients showed more negative outcomes than patients with only a psychiatric disorder. Such results illustrate that the dually diagnosed fare worse than patients with either SUDs or psychiatric disorders alone following treatment. Importantly, the fact that dual diagnosis patients are often found to still be adversely affected by psychiatric symptomatology following substance abuse treatment is a stark reminder that treatment strategies have yet to evolve that effectively address symptoms of both types of disorders.

## IMPACT OF DUAL DISORDERS ON ASSESSMENT AND DIAGNOSIS

There are numerous ways that dual diagnosis affects assessment and diagnosis, including symptom overlap, multiple impairments owing to different disorders, and substance-induced disorders resembling psychiatric disorders.

### Symptom Overlap

Symptom overlap is a significant complication in terms of assessment and diagnosis. The symptoms of many psychiatric disorders overlap with those of substance use disorders, making diagnosis of either class of disorders difficult. For example, *DSM* lists problems in social functioning as symptoms of both schizophrenia and substance use disorders. That some criteria can count toward multiple diagnoses can potentially increase comorbidity rates and can make diagnosis of substance abuse difficult. This overlap can work against identification of the psychiatric disorder in some cases. For example, high rates of dual substance use and bipolar disorders lead to an underdiagnosis of bipolar disorder, because of the often incorrect assumption that the behavioral manifestations of bipolar disorder are secondary to substance use (Evans, 2000). Others (Brady, Killeen, Brewerton, & Lucerini, 2000; Brunello et al., 2001) suggest that underdiagnosis can also be an issue with dual PTSD and substance use disorders.

### MULTIPLE IMPAIRMENTS OWING TO DIFFERENT DISORDERS

Substance use disorders are often overlooked in mental health settings in which patients present with a range of acute impairments that exert a negative impact on overall functioning. There is often diagnostic confusion in terms of whether a given impairment results from substance abuse, psychiatric disorder, both, or neither. For example, it is exceedingly difficult to determine the impact of substance abuse when serious mental illness profoundly affects all areas of functioning. Patients with severe mental illness in particular have a range of impairments in social, cognitive, occupational, and psychological functioning, and evaluating the negative impact of substance abuse is difficult when the functioning of individuals in this patient population is so poor to begin with. Moreover, *DSM-IV* diagnoses of substance abuse and dependence are based for the most part on diagnostic criteria that reflect substance use becoming more pervasive in a person's life and interfering with normal functioning. For example, criteria involve substance use impairing one's ability to work, engage in relationships, complete responsibilities, and participate in activities. However, such factors often do not apply to many patients with mental illness whose substantial level of impairment associated with the psychiatric disorder often precludes them from having a job, being in relationships, or engaging in other activities. It becomes unclear how to measure the negative impact of substance use when there are few competing demands, activities, or responsibilities to be disrupted.

### SUBSTANCE-INDUCED DISORDERS RESEMBLE PSYCHIATRIC DISORDERS

Diagnosis of psychopathology in the presence of substance abuse and dependence is especially difficult because symptoms of substance use and withdrawal can resemble psychiatric disorders (Schuckit, 1983; Schuckit & Monteiro, 1988). For example, long-term alcohol use and withdrawal can lead to psychotic symptoms, and abuse of amphetamines often results in psychotic symptoms that are identical to schizophrenia. Alcohol abuse and withdrawal also resemble symptoms of anxiety disorders (Kushner, Sher, & Beitman, 1990). Panic and obsessive behavior are often found with stimulant use and withdrawal from depressant drugs (Schuckit, 1983). Because symptoms of substance use and withdrawal can resemble psychiatric symptoms, differential diagnosis may be confounded. The lack of clear rules for differential diagnosis has important implications. Rates of dual diagnosis might be inflated, with individuals experiencing psychiatric disorders concurrent with alcohol or drug dependence being counted among those with dual disorder, although many of these symptoms will likely fade following a period of abstinence.

Incorrect treatment decisions may be made if interventions are aimed at what appear to be acute symptoms of psychiatric disorder but are in fact substance-induced symptoms. For example, Rosenthal and Miner (1997) review the issue of differential diagnosis of substance-induced psychosis and schizophrenia and stress that medicating what appears to be acute psychosis due to schizophrenia but is actually substance-induced psychosis is not only incorrect but also ineffective treatment. Schuckit and colleagues (1997) suggest that too little attention has been paid to the "independent versus concurrent distinction" as it applies to dual diagnosis. Some alcoholics suffer from long-term psychiatric disorders that are present before, during, and after alcohol dependence and require treatment independent of that for their alcohol abuse or dependence. However, many individuals present with substance-induced disorders, including depression, anxiety, and psychosis, that will remit after several weeks of abstinence. This suggests that much dual diagnosis, while distressing and clinically relevant in the short term, is temporary, likely to improve after several weeks, and thus holds different clinical and treatment implications from a true, independent psychiatric disorder. The data, taken from the Collaborative Study on the Genetics of Alcoholism, show that the majority of alcohol-dependent men and women did not meet diagnostic criteria for an "independent" mood or anxiety disorder that occurred outside of the context of the alcohol dependence. Specifically, there was no increased risk of a range of disorders in the alcohol-dependent sample, including major depression, obsessive-compulsive disorder, or agoraphobia. In contrast, there was an increased risk of independent bipolar, panic disorder, and social phobia.

Others have also found that a majority of dual diagnosis patients have concurrent psychiatric diagnoses that are likely owing to the effects of heavy substance use. Rosenblum and colleagues (1999) used an algorithm to determine whether individuals with co-occurring mood and cocaine use disorders have either an "autonomous" mood disorder—that is, one that either existed prior to the cocaine use disorder or persists during times of abstinence (similar to Schuckit's independent distinction)—or a "nonautonomous" mood disorder that followed from the cocaine use disorder and would remit during cocaine abstinence. Results showed that 27% of subjects were rated as having an autonomous mood disorder, while 73% were rated as having a nonautonomous mood disorder. At this point, differentiating independent from concurrent dual disorders requires significant investment in training interviewers and in interviewing patients. Such requirements often cannot be met in the day-to-day operations of mental health treatment programs. Moreover, multiple assessments may be necessary. For example, Ramsey and colleagues (2004) examined changes in classifying depressive episodes in alcohol-dependent patients as either substance-induced depression or independent major depressive disorder. Patients in a partial hospital program for alcohol treatment were assessed five times over a year for symptoms of MDD. Results showed that many (more than 25%) of the cases first categorized as substance-induced MDD were reclassified as independent MDD at some point during the year, owing to depressive symptoms that persisted once the patients had achieved a long period of abstinence.

IMPLICATIONS FOR NOSOLOGY

The fact that two disorders co-occur with great regularity raises the question of whether both categories actually represent two distinct disorders at all (Sher & Trull, 1996). For example, the literature regarding SUDS and ASP finds a high rate of comorbidity between the two disorders, one that is likely enhanced by the symptom overlap inherent in the ASP diagnosis. However, some suggest (Widiger & Shea, 1991) that such a high degree of co-occurrence between these two disorders may mean that these are not, in fact, unique diagnoses, but rather that such a pattern of comorbidity indicates the presence of a single disorder.

## IMPACT OF DUAL DIAGNOSIS ON PSYCHOPATHOLOGY RESEARCH

Dual diagnosis affects several areas that are critical to psychopathology research, including diagnosis, sample selection, and interpretation of research findings.

DIAGNOSTIC AND SAMPLE SELECTION ISSUES IN PSYCHOPATHOLOGY RESEARCH

An accurate diagnosis is a necessary starting point for any psychopathology study, and dual diagnosis presents an abundance of diagnostic challenges. Individuals with dual diagnoses may provide unreliable diagnostic information, or their data may be inaccurate because of greater severity of impairments. Alternatively, they may minimize their substance use and associated consequences, especially if they have much to lose by admitting to or honestly discussing their substance use, such as services, benefits (Ridgely, Goldman, & Willenbring, 1990), or child custody. The timing of a research diagnostic interview can also impact results, as answers and resulting diagnostic decisions may vary depending on type of use, stage of treatment, and psychiatric stabilization. The method of assessment also can impact diagnostic findings (Regier et al., 1998), and diagnoses given in a clinical setting may vary with those obtained through more structured methods (Fennig, Craig, Tanenberg-Karant, & Bromet, 1994). As presented previously, establishing an accurate diagnosis in individuals with active substance use or withdrawal can be problematic, as the effects of substance use can imitate the symptoms of various psychiatric disorders. Most diagnostic systems used in psychopathology research address this difficulty by asking if psychiatric symptoms have been experienced solely during the course of substance use, and may recommend assessment only after a sustained period of abstinence. However, patient reports may be inaccurate, and histories may be too extensive and complicated to allow for this level of precise understanding.

Finally, the issue of overlapping diagnostic criteria can pose a significant difficulty for psychopathology research, as common diagnostic criteria may contribute to the diagnosis of multiple disorders when in fact the psychopathology is better understood as a single pathological process rather than two distinct disorders (Blashfield, 1990; Sher & Trull, 1996). The overlap of SUDs with ASP is notably problematic, and this frequent comorbidity has long been recognized (Widiger & Shea, 1991). Krueger (1999) examined 10 common mental disorders using structural equation modeling and found that ASP loads onto a common "externalizing" factor along with alcohol and drug dependence, suggesting that substance dependence and ASP may share certain underlying features. Whether this overlap is indeed because of common conceptual characteristics or is an artifact of similar diagnostic criteria is unknown. All of these diagnostic issues impact research findings, in that poor diagnoses will necessarily lead to poor-quality data. Researchers can improve diagnostic reliability by conducting structured interviews, using collateral information and behavioral observation to inform diagnostic decisions, and assessing the patient at multiple time points (Carey & Correia, 1998).

In terms of sample selection, psychopathology and treatment outcome research tends to focus on single or pure disorders and routinely excludes dual diagnosis cases, a practice that has several implications for research. First, screening out dual diagnosis patients yields samples that are atypical. Most patients with one psychiatric disorder meet criteria for some other disorder. Eliminating patients with dual disorders means that the resulting sample is less impaired and less representative of patients who present for treatment, resulting in limited generalizability of research findings (Krueger, 1999). In addition, dual diagnosis patients often have other characteristics that are not adequately represented in the resultant study sample. For example, Partonen, Sihvo, and Lonnqvist (1996) report descriptive data on patients excluded from an antidepressant efficacy that screened out individuals with "chronic alcohol or drug misuse." As a result, younger male patients were likely to be excluded, with current substance abuse as the strongest excluding influence. Second, dual diagnosis impacts required sample sizes. In their examination of the impact of comorbid disorders on sample selection, Newman and colleagues (1998) discuss findings related to effect sizes of examining only single disorder cases versus the inclusion of dual disorder cases when analyzing group differences. Results showed that when dual disorder cases are excluded, larger sample sizes are required in order to detect small effect sizes. In contrast, retaining dual disorder cases yielded greater variance on study measures, resulting in larger effect sizes requiring smaller sample sizes. Third, psychopathology and treatment outcome research most often combines those with dual diagnoses together without classification by the specific type of drug use disorder. Whereas some might limit the scope of the study to alcohol only, most cast a wide net and include patients with alcohol, drug, and poly-substance-use disorders. For example, research on substance abuse among patients with severe mental illness typically includes disorders of any number or combination of substances, including alcohol, marijuana, cocaine, and heroin. The impact of grouping all substance use disorders together is unclear, but it certainly raises the possibility that research may miss important issues potentially particular to one substance. For example, it would not be surprising if interventions for patients with a greater number of drug use disorders or with both alcohol and drug use disorders required adaptations that are not necessary for patients with single-drug or alcohol-use disorders. Similarly, there are likely meaningful differences between patients who inject drugs and those who do not, patients who have long histories of substance dependence and those who do not, or patients who are dependent on cocaine or heroin versus those who are abusing marijuana.

The overall result of screening out those with substance use disorders from psychopathology and treatment outcome research is that there are very few data to inform treatment. For example, following completion of an antidepressant efficacy trial, Partonen and colleagues (1996) point out that they were left without information regarding the efficacy of antidepressants among patients with dual disorders. Given the significant rates of dual disorders found in clinical samples, such an omission is clearly problematic. In their discussion of the many complex issues surrounding comorbidity and psychopathology research, Sher and Trull (1996) question the advantage of studying pure cases when certain disorders occur together with such great frequency that there really may be no ultimate benefit of studying either one alone. It also is unclear how well findings from psychopathology and treatment outcome research will generalize to the larger population of individuals with a particular disorder if patients with dual diagnoses are not included. The epidemiological studies reviewed earlier clearly illustrate that a significant number of those with mental illness or substance abuse experience dual disorders. The relevance of single disorder research to this substantial population of dually impaired individuals is highly suspect, and excluding dual diagnosis cases yields samples that are not representative of those presenting for treatment.

However, routinely including dual diagnosis cases in psychopathology and treatment outcome research has its drawbacks. Sher and Trull (1996) and Krueger (1999) discuss the fact that if dual diagnosis cases are included in psychopathology research, understanding of both mental and substance use disorders is compromised, in that samples would be less well-defined. As a result, it would be unclear whether results could be attributed to the disorder under study or to comorbid disorders represented in the sample. In addition, comorbidity complicates longitudinal data because different patterns of comorbidity may emerge over time within individuals (Sher and Trull, 1996). One possible strategy for dealing with dual disorders in psychopathology and treatment outcome research is the use of samples that include comorbid cases in percentages found in the general population in order to increase the generalizability of findings (Newman et al., 1998; Sher and Trull, 1996). Widiger and Shea (1991) offer additional options, including having one diagnosis take precedence over another, adding criteria in order to make a differential diagnosis, or removing criteria shared by disorders. Sher and Trull (1996) additionally suggest statistically controlling for comorbidity via regression techniques but acknowledge that this practice can mask important common features of disorders.

## THEORIES OF DUAL DIAGNOSIS

This review makes two points clear: Dual diagnosis is highly prevalent, and it has a pervasive impact on both clinical and research domains. There now is general agreement that the time has come to define more precisely the mechanisms underlying dual diagnosis, which is a complex task for several reasons. Most important, there is a great degree of heterogeneity found in dual diagnosis populations. The numerous types of psychopathological disorders and substances of abuse ensure many dual diagnosis combinations. In addition, although the term *dual* is meant to describe cases with both mental illness and substance use problems, it can in actuality reflect more than two disorders (for example, an individual might meet criteria for an affective disorder, an anxiety disorder, and a substance use disorder). Thus it is unlikely that one explanation or causal model for dual diagnosis can explain the diversity of cases and experiences that are found. Models to explain dual diagnoses tend to fall into one of four general categories (see Mueser, Drake, & Wallach, 1998, for a review). Third variable or common factors models suggest that some shared influence is responsible for the development of both psychiatric and substance use disorders. The two types of causal models—secondary substance use disorder models and secondary psychiatric disorder models—posit that either type of disorder causes the other. Bidirectional models suggest that either psychiatric or substance use disorders can increase risk for and exacerbate the impact of the other. These models have been more or less described depending on the particular area of psychopathology. Examination of this literature finds that models of dual diagnosis are typically organized by disorder, with research focused on specific combinations of dual disorders rather than on the issue of dual diagnosis across disorders. Extensive reviews of models in each of these categories can be found (Blanchard, 2000; Mueser et al., 1998). The following section provides a review of some models of dual diagnosis in their respective domains of psychopathology.

## COMMON FACTORS MODELS

Common factors models suggest a shared etiological basis for psychiatric and substance use disorders. Most research has focused on genetics as the likely common factor. Results of numerous twin, adoption, and family studies clearly show that both mental illness and substance abuse run in families, and that familial aggregation of single disorders is substantial (Kendler, Davis, & Kessler, 1997; Kushner, Sher, & Beitman, 1990; Merikangas et al., 1985; Merikangas & Gelernter, 1990). Such findings have led to the hypothesis that commonly co-occurring disorders might be linked via common genetic factors. However, for genetics to serve as a viable common factor, family studies must show high rates of transmission of pure forms of both substance use and psychiatric disorders. For example, a proband with depression only should have an increased rate of alcoholism only in the individual's relatives in order to provide evidence of shared genetic etiology. Studies of familial transmission of a range of comorbid psychiatric and substance use disorders find that the evidence for a common genetic factor is lacking. Merikangas and Gelernter (1990) reviewed family, twin, and adoption studies of alcoholism and depression and concluded that familial transmission of pure forms of the disorders was not supported: "Depressed only" probands did not have increased rates of "alcoholism only" in their relatives, and "alcoholism only" probands did not have increased rates of "depression only" in their relatives. These authors stress that although familial aggregation of disorders is evident, the notion of a common genetic factor underlying the two is not supported, and the disorders appear to be transmitted separately. In subsequent analyses of familial transmission of comorbid depression and substance use disorders using data from the Yale Family Study of Comorbidity of Substance Disorders, Swendsen and Merikangas (2000) similarly found that there was no support for a common factors model: Mood disorders in the proband were not associated with an increased risk of alcohol dependence in relatives. Similar results have been reported with schizophrenia (Kendler, 1985), ASP (Hesselbrock, 1986), and patients with schizoaffective and bipolar disorders (Gershon et al., 1982).

Importantly, common factors other than genetics may exist. Several possible common factors might link substance use disorders and severe mental illness, including comorbid ASP, low socioeconomic status, and poor cognitive functioning (Mueser, Drake, & Wallach, 1998). For example, ASP is associated with both substance use disorders and severe mental illness. Mueser and colleagues (1999) examined the links between conduct disorder, ASP, and substance use disorders in patients with severe mental illness and found that both childhood conduct disorder and adult ASP were significant risk factors for SUDs. However, the status of ASP as a risk factor is unclear, given that problem substance use is part of the diagnosis of ASP, raising the possibility that ASP may be a byproduct of substance use disorder. Also, ASP is based in large part on criminality and socioeconomic status, both of which are difficulties that often go along with both substance use disorder and severe mental illness (Mueser et al., 1998).

Other researchers are proposing multivariate approaches to identifying common factors of dual disorders. One such model is described by Trull and colleagues (2000) to explain the high prevalence of dual substance use disorders and borderline personality disorder. These authors suggest that a family history of psychopathology inspires both dysfunctional family interactions and the inheritance of deviant personality traits that are associated with the development of both borderline personality disorder and substance use disorders. Specifically, the personality traits of affective instability and impulsivity are central to both disorders and are conceptualized as stemming from a combination of "constitutional and environmental factors" (Trull et al., 2000) that include inherited deficiencies in serotonergic functioning, in combination with a deviant family environment that may include associated childhood trauma. These factors in turn impact the development of borderline personality disorder and substance use disorder, both alone and in combination. These authors stress that while this model is currently speculative, more prospective, longitudinal studies with a developmental and multivariate focus will enable the pieces of the models to be evaluated simultaneously. This model provides an example of combining strategies from family studies and psychopathology research into a multivariate framework that provides rich details as to how two disorders could be developmentally related.

In fact, the description and measurement of multivariate influences in the development and maintenance of dual disorders are becoming increasingly sophisticated, spanning from neurophysiology to postnatal development factors such as family stress (Fishbein & Tarter, 2009). Several studies have focused on the identification of neurocognitive and neurophysiological vulnerability indicators for substance use and psychiatric disorders. The P3 event-related potential (ERP) is a neurophysiological measure of brain activity that occurs between 300 and 600 milliseconds after stimulus presentation and is implicated in cognitive information processing, response inhibition, and self-regulation (Begleiter & Porjesz, 1995; Fishbein & Tarter, 2009). Reduced P3 amplitude has been fairly consistently identified among individuals with an alcohol SUD who are abstinent, as well as in populations at high risk for SUD (e.g., sons of fathers with alcohol dependence) suggesting that it is a heritable preexisting vulnerability marker, or endophenotype, for alcohol use disorders (Begleiter & Porjesz, 1995).

As discussed previously, conduct disorder or, more generally, externalizing disorders often co-occur with SUDs. Reduced P3 has also been associated with externalizing disorders (e.g., ADD; Klorman, 1991), which suggests it may represent a common factor to both of these disorders (Iacono, Carlson, Malone, & McGue, 2002). In a large longitudinal community-based sample, Iacono and colleagues (2002) measured P3 amplitude and assessed for a series of disorders including attention deficit hyperactivity disorder, conduct disorder, ASP, and SUD in a sample of 502 male adolescents and their parents. Participants were assessed at age 17 and then reassessed 3 years later. Results indicated that reduced P3 amplitude was associated with not only a paternal history of SUD but also paternal history of ASP. It was also associated with childhood disorders of disinhibition including SUDs, and P3 amplitude at age 17 predicted the development of several disorders of disinhibition including SUD. The authors conclude that reduced P3 amplitude may be a common, genetically transmitted risk factor for a broad range of psychiatric disorders including SUD that share the common feature of behavioral disinhibition. It is anticipated that with continued advancements in cognitive neuroscience, similar endophenotypes will be identified that will facilitate the identification of common genetic risk factors for dual disorders.

## SECONDARY SUBSTANCE ABUSE MODELS

Secondary substance abuse models contend that mental illness increases vulnerability to substance use disorders. Probably the most widely discussed model of this type is the self-medication model, which asserts that individuals with psychiatric disorders use substances as a way to self-medicate psychopathological symptoms and relieve discomfort associated with the primary psychiatric disorder.

There are several types of studies used to examine applicability of a self-medication model to different forms of psychopathology. Some determine the ages of onset of dual disorders, with the idea being that SUDs developing after other Axis I psychopathology support the self-medication hypothesis. Some examine subjective reasons for use among patients with different disorders, while others correlate levels of symptoms with levels of substance abuse (from a self-medication perspective, greater symptoms should correlate with greater substance abuse). Another line of self-medication research involves investigating the types of substances used by different patient groups. According to a self-medication hypothesis, patients with certain psychopathological conditions should preferentially seek out and use substances that will directly impact symptoms associated with their specific psychopathology.

Support for a self-medication model varies depending on the type of mental illness under investigation. For example, although the model is popular among treatment providers working with patients with severe mental illness, empirical support for a self-medication model has not been compelling (see Mueser, Drake, & Wallach, 1998, for a review). Although it has been suggested that schizophrenia patients preferentially abuse stimulants to self-medicate negative symptoms (Schneier & Siris, 1987), this finding has not been replicated in other studies (Mueser, Yarnold, & Bellack, 1992).

Most important, studies fail to find evidence that specific substances are used in response to specific symptoms. Rather, patterns of drug use appear to be strongly associated with demographic factors and drug availability (Mueser, Yarnold, & Bellack, 1992). In addition, a self-medication model of SUDs in severe mental illness would predict that the more symptomatic patients would be at higher risk for substance use disorders (Mueser, Bellack, & Blanchard, 1992). Several studies, however, have found the opposite to be true: More severely ill patients are less likely to abuse substances (Chen et al., 1992; Cohen & Klein, 1970; Mueser, Yarnold, & Bellack, 1992), and patients with SUDs have better premorbid social functioning (Dixon et al., 1991). Although individuals with schizophrenia and other severe mental illnesses report a range of reasons for substance use—to alleviate social problems, insomnia, or depression; to get high; to relieve boredom; and to increase energy—few endorse using specific substances to combat particular psychiatric symptoms (see Brunette, Mueser, Xie, & Drake, 1997, for a review). Moreover, many studies have found that patients with schizophrenia report worsening of symptoms with substance abuse, including increased hallucinations, delusions, and paranoia (Barbee et al., 1989; Cleghorn et al., 1991; Dixon et al., 1991; Drake et al., 1989), and others have found that more severe symptoms of schizophrenia are not linked to more severe substance abuse (Brunette et al., 1997). Similarly, findings of increased rates of cocaine use among patients with bipolar disorder, interpreted by some to indicate self-medication of depressive symptoms, have been found upon review to more likely reflect attempts to prolong euphoric feelings associated with mania (Goodwin & Jamison, 1990).

Other secondary substance abuse models may be more relevant to patients with severe mental illness. A social facilitation model suggests that patients with severe mental illness may have fewer available opportunities for social interaction, and that substance abuse helps smooth the process of social engagement in patients who lack appropriate social and interpersonal skills. Finding that a large portion of substance use/abuse by individuals with schizophrenia occurs in a public setting, Dixon, Haas, Weiden, Sweeney, & Frances (1990) suggest that drug use may provide "isolated, socially handicapped individuals with an identity and a social group" (p. 74) or to fulfill needs for contact and acceptance (Mueser, Bellack, & Blanchard, 1992). Others offer an alleviation of dysphoria model; substance abuse represents an attempt to alleviate these negative mood states. Evidence for self-medication may be more relevant to dual diagnosis within other psychopathological disorders. For example, several reviews have found that self-medication may apply to dual PTSD and SUDs, especially among women with trauma-related PTSD. Three main theories (Chilcoat & Breslau, 1998) are (1) the self-medication hypothesis, which suggests that drugs are used to medicate PTSD symptoms; (2) the high-risk hypothesis, which suggests that drug use puts individuals at heightened risk for trauma that can lead to PTSD; and (3) the susceptibility hypothesis, which suggests that drug users are more likely to develop PTSD following exposure to a traumatic event. They then use data from a sample of more than 1,000 young adults who were randomly selected from enrollees in a large health maintenance organization and were followed longitudinally over 5 years in order to examine the timing of the development of both PTSD and substance use disorders. Those with a history of PTSD at baseline were 4 times more likely than those without PTSD to develop drug abuse or dependence at some point during the 5 years of the study. In contrast, baseline drug abuse/dependence did not confer any increased risk of subsequent exposure to trauma or to developing PTSD in those who did experience some traumatic event during the follow-up period.

Other data on dual SUD and PTSD (Stewart et al., 1998) that also lend support to a self-medication model include (1) development of substance abuse most often follows development of PTSD; (2) patients often report that they perceive substance use to be effective in controlling PTSD symptoms; (3) patients with both PTSD and substance use disorder report more severe trauma and a greater severity of PTSD symptoms, suggesting that substances are used in an effort to control greater psychiatric symptomatology; and (4) drugs of abuse may be related to different clusters of PTSD symptoms, suggesting that substance abuse may be linked to attempts to control intrusion or arousal symptoms of PTSD. These authors stress that although a self-medication model is likely too simplistic to explain all forms of PTSD–SUD comorbidity, at this point it provides a good fit for the current literature.

Recently there has been increased interest in neurobiological mechanisms that underlie dual diagnosis, particularly with respect to the ways in which mental illness and addiction share common neurological pathways. The foundation for this research is that neurobiological deficits and abnormalities that provide the basis for different forms of mental illness may predispose those with mental illness to substance abuse. This literature includes animal studies of dual diagnosis, where brain lesions are produced to simulate different forms of psychopathology. Factors such as the ability to experience reinforcement from drug use and differential patterns of use and/or cravings are examined. A good summary of this approach to dual diagnosis in schizophrenia is presented by Chambers, Krystal, and Self (2001). Briefly, increased vulnerability to substance use disorders in schizophrenia results from impairment in brain systems that are central to schizophrenia—the most important of which may be the mesolimbic dopamine system (MDS). According to this model, the MDS is implicated in the reinforcing effects of drug use (drug use increases dopamine levels), as well as in the development of schizophrenia (high dopamine levels are implicated as a major factor in the development of schizophrenia). In other words, these authors suggest that

> the neuropathology of schizophrenia may contribute to the vulnerability to addiction by facilitating neural substrates that mediate positive reinforcement. The putative neuro-pathology underlying schizophrenia involves alterations in neuro-anatomic circuitry that regulate positive reinforcement, incentive motivation, behavioral inhibition, and addictive behavior. (Chambers et al., 2001, p. 71)

Thus the neurobiological problems that give rise to schizophrenia also put the individual at heightened risk for developing SUDs. Several studies have found support for this sort of neurological linkage in schizophrenia. Chambers and Self (2002) studied rats with neonatal ventral hippocampal lesions (NVHL rats), a procedure that produces behavioral disturbances in rats that resemble the psychopathological behaviors seen in schizophrenia, including positive and negative symptoms and abnormal cognitive functioning (see Chambers & Self, 2002, and Chambers & Taylor, 2004, for details of the procedure and its effects). In comparison to controls (rats with sham lesions), NVHL rats showed faster rates of cocaine self-administration, higher degree of binge cocaine use, and faster relapse to cocaine use following a period of nonuse. Other studies using this and similar methodologies have generated similar findings (Chambers & Taylor, 2004).

Similar animal models are available for depression and substance use. In one model for depression, rats undergo bilateral olfactory bulbectomy (OBX), creating behavior that is biologically and behaviorally similar to depression in humans, including decreased pleasure seeking, disruptions in sleep, agitation, and other cognitive problems that respond only to chronic (and not acute) antidepressant treatment (see Holmes et al., 2002, for a thorough review). Importantly, this procedure also causes dopamine dysregulation in areas of the brain implicated in the reinforcing effects of drugs of abuse, again similar to those found in humans. In comparison to rats with sham lesions (Holmes et al., 2002), those with OBX lesions were more sensitive to the reinforcing effects of amphetamine. Specifically, they learned to self-administer amphetamine more quickly and had higher levels of stable amphetamine administration.

Other studies have used rats genetically bred for signs of learned helplessness as an operational definition of depression in rats. For example, Vengeliene and colleagues (2005) examined differences in alcohol intake between congenital learned helplessness rats (cLH) and congenital nonlearned helplessness rats (cNLH)—two lines of rats selectively bred for different escape reactions following inescapable shock (cLH rats do not try to escape the shock, even though they have not been exposed to it before, whereas cNLH rats will try to escape the shock). In this study, these two groups of rats were given access to alcohol and tap water for self-administration for 6 weeks and then underwent 2 weeks of no alcohol access followed by renewed access to alcohol for 4 days. Although results showed no differences in males, female cLH rats consumed greater amounts of alcohol than cNLH rats during the self-administration portion of the study and showed a more pronounced alcohol deprivation effect (greater consumption of alcohol following a period with no alcohol consumption). The authors suggest that inborn "depressive-like" behavior in female rats is associated with increase alcohol intake. These and other animal models of depression (Fagergren, Overstreet, Goiny, & Hurd, 2005) appear to be a useful avenue for the study of dual diagnosis involving depression and substance abuse. Such studies are finding that "depressed" animals respond differently than other animals to drugs and alcohol, providing interesting new leads in the search for biological mechanisms that lead to dual diagnosis.

The high rate of smoking among individuals with schizophrenia is another possible instance where a neurophysiological deficit predisposes individuals to engage in substance use. Rates of smoking among individuals with schizophrenia are exceedingly high when compared to the general population (de Leon et al., 1995; Hughes, Hatsukami, Mitchell, & Dahlgren, 1986). Individuals with schizophrenia tend to smoke more cigarettes (de Leon et al., 1995), smoke higher nicotine content cigarettes, and smoke harder in an attempt to extract higher doses of nicotine from cigarettes (Olincy, Young, & Freedman, 1997). Somewhat different than the self-medication of symptoms of schizophrenia discussed previously, intriguing data suggest that, for some individuals with schizophrenia, smoking may be an attempt to adapt to a neurophysiological deficit related to sensory gating. Specifically, Adler, Hoffer, Wiser, and Freedman (1993) investigated the impact of cigarette smoking on the P50 ERP. This ERP is involved in habituation to stimuli and functions to screen out irrelevant information. It is typically elicited with a sensory gating paradigm where two auditory clicks are presented in close temporal sequence. In intact sensory gating there is a diminished neurophysiological response to the second click. Functionally, this represents a screening out of less relevant information, thus allowing for the availability of more cognitive resources for the processing of new salient stimuli. Consistent with other research, Adler et al. (1993) found that in the case of individuals with schizophrenia, there is a failure to inhibit the response to the second click. However, when allowed to smoke freely, there was a normalization (i.e., greater inhibition in response to the second click), albeit lasting only briefly. In a second experiment, Adler, Hoffer, Griffith, Waldo, and Freedman (1992) investigated the impact of nicotine gum in first-degree relatives of individuals with schizophrenia who were nonsmokers and had a demonstrated sensory gating deficit (as measured by P50). Results were similar to the patient sample: Relatives demonstrated a transient improvement in P50 ERP. Interestingly, these effects were only found with a higher dose of nicotine gum (6 mg); pilot testing with lower doses failed to yield an effect (Adler et al., 1992).

Another well-documented psychophysiological deficit in individuals with schizophrenia that has also been identified in first-degree relatives is that of eye tracking dysfunction, namely smooth pursuit eye movement (SPEM; e.g., Holzman, 1987). Briefly, when required to visually track a moving object, impaired individuals demonstrate an increase in "catch-up" (due to tracking too slowly) and "leading" eye saccades (due to tracking too quickly or visually "jumping" ahead of the stimuli; Olincy, Ross, Young, Roath, & Freedman, 1998). Essentially, these saccades decrease the accuracy and efficiency with which individuals visually track a moving object. Olincy et al. (1998) found that in individuals with schizophrenia, performance on a SPEM task significantly improved when patients were allowed to smoke freely (compared to task performance after a 10-hour period of abstinence from smoking). Notably, after smoking there was a significant decrease in leading saccades, which the authors postulated was an indication of enhanced inhibition and similar to nicotine's normalizing effect in the P50 ERP. These neurophysiological findings have been linked to the alpha-7 nicotinic receptor, a low-affinity receptor that requires high doses of nicotine for activation, which may partially explain heavy smoking (i.e., extracting higher doses of nicotine) among individuals with schizophrenia (Adler et al., 1998). In addition to furthering our understanding of the impact of nicotine on the pathophysiology of schizophrenia, these findings have also helped contribute to the development of new cognitive-enhancing medications for individuals with the disorder (e.g., Olincy et al., 2006).

SECONDARY PSYCHIATRIC DISORDER MODELS

With some specific differences, these models suggest that substance abuse causes psychopathology. Schuckit and Monteiro (1988; Schuckit, 1983) stress that the use of or withdrawal from many psychoactive substances causes reactions that appear indistinguishable from psychiatric disorder. As reviewed earlier, these authors contend that substance use disorders are often mistakenly diagnosed as psychiatric disorders because of similar symptomatology, and that while serious psycho-pathology can be expected in the course of substance use disorder, substance-induced disorders are likely to remit following several weeks of abstinence. The case for substance-induced psychiatric disorder appears to be particularly relevant to dual substance use disorders and major depression. Raimo and Schuckit (1998) review the evidence in support of the idea that most cases of comorbid depression and alcohol dependence are substance-induced, including findings that (a) drinking can cause severe depressive symptoms; (b) treatment-seeking substance abusers show increased rates of depression that often remit following abstinence and in the absence of specific treatments for depression; (c) individuals with substance-induced depression do not show elevated rates of depression in family members; and (d) children of alcoholics show higher rates of alcohol use disorders but do not show elevated rates of major depression. These authors stress that while having indepen-dent depression in addition to alcohol abuse or dependence is certainly possible, most of the depression that is comorbid with alcohol use disorders is substance-induced and not independent in nature.

Following this example, Swendsen and Merikangas (2000) reviewed findings that are relevant to an etiological model of dual substance abuse and depression: (a) The onset of alcohol dependence typically precedes the onset of unipolar depression; (b) symptoms of depression often remit following several weeks of abstinence from alcohol; and (c) genetic studies do not support a shared genetic basis for comorbidity of depression and alcohol dependence. They suggest that the association between unipolar depression and alcohol dependence may best be described via a secondary psychiatric disorder model, in which chronic alcohol use causes unipolar depression, through either the considerable life stress that alcohol dependence promotes for the drinker in many important domains of functioning, or through the pharmacological properties of alcohol as a depressant substance.

## BIDIRECTIONAL MODELS

Bidirectional models propose that ongoing, interactional effects account for increased rates of comorbidity. Support for a bidirectional model for anxiety and alcohol dependence (Kushner, Abrams, & Borchardt, 2000) includes the following: (a) most patients with anxiety and alcohol use disorders report drinking to control fears and reduce tension; (b) drinking can cause anxiety (i.e., anxiety can result from long-term alcohol use, patients report increased anxiety after drinking, and withdrawal from alcohol can cause physiological symptoms of anxiety); (c) alcohol dependence can lead to anxiety disorders (i.e., alcohol dependence puts one at increased risk for later development of an anxiety disorder, and chronic drinking can cause neurochemical changes that cause anxiety and panic); and (d) anxiety disorders can lead to alcohol dependence (i.e., having an anxiety disorder puts one at increased risk for later development of alcohol dependence, alcohol provides stress-response dampening and reduces the clinical symptoms of anxiety, and many people use alcohol to self-medicate anxiety symptoms). The authors conclude that alcohol and anxiety interact to produce an exacerbation of both anxiety symptoms and drinking. Whereas initial use of alcohol provides short-term relief of anxiety symptoms, it negatively reinforces further drinking, leading to increased physiological symptoms of anxiety. They then propose a so-called feed-forward cycle wherein drinking is promoted by its short-term anxiety-reducing effects of alcohol, while anxiety symptoms are worsened by heavy drinking, leading to continued drinking in response to these worsened anxiety symptoms.

Although several caveats and issues remain to be clarified (i.e., the model seems to best fit with comorbid alcohol dependence and its relevance to drug use disorders is unknown; those for whom the anxiety disorder begins first would not necessarily experience the anxiety-reducing properties of alcohol in a way that would initiate the feed-forward cycle), the authors suggest that a bidirectional model can best explain existing findings and can focus future research on comorbidity of anxiety and substance use disorders. Moreover, this sort of bidirectional model highlights the possibility that unidirectional causal models are likely too simplistic an approach in explaining comorbidity. Rather, the relationship between psychiatric and substance use disorders is more likely characterized by complex interactions between the two disorders.

## SUMMARY AND FUTURE DIRECTIONS

We are at a critical juncture in the field of dual diagnosis and its impact both clinically and in research. Over the last three decades, efforts have focused primarily on identifying the problem of dual diagnosis—including its rates and consequences—and getting clinicians and researchers to think about dual disorders when pursuing their clinical or research work. We have learned much about the prevalence and impact of dual disorders from general population and clinical studies over the last several decades. Currently we can say with certainty that dual diagnosis is common, both in the general population and among clients in mental health and substance abuse treatment. Comorbid psychiatric and substance use disorders impact a large percentage of people, and dual disorders persist over time. Importantly, we are now beginning to see that patients who present with multiple diagnoses are the most difficult and complex patients to treat and understand. The notion of dual disorders may require reconceptualization as the frequency of individuals with two, three, or more comorbid psychiatric and substance use disorders continues to climb.

Looking ahead, probably the most critical issue facing assessment and diagnosis of dual disorders is that of multiple comorbidities—multiple substance use, psychiatric, and even medical disorders within individuals. This issue will be manifest in different ways across diagnosis, assessment, and research. First, the upcoming revision of *DSM* and scheduled publication of *DSM-5* in 2013 is sure to impact dual diagnosis in important ways. Currently there are several proposed changes to *DSM* criteria for psychotic, mood, and substance use disorders that will change the way we diagnose dual psychiatric and substance use disorders. For example, proposed revisions to the diagnosis of substance use disorders include merging abuse and dependence into a single Substance-Related Disorder that will require an individual to meet two diagnostic criteria for classification. Along with such a change, use of a measure of severity will allow for finer distinctions within this diagnostic category, such that less or more severe manifestations of disorder can be identified. Clearly, any change in the way that substance use disorders are identified will have an impact on rates of dual diagnosis. Combining abuse and dependence into one disorder could lead to higher rates of dual diagnosis in that individuals with less severe problems (abuse) who may have been overlooked or not included previously would now be counted. Moreover, it is being proposed that other non-substance-related addictive disorders, such as gambling addiction, be included in an expanded section that includes both substance-related and other addictive behaviors. The nature of dual disorders as a combination of substance use and psychiatric disorders may change if other addictive behaviors are included in a more prominent way in *DSM-5*.

Similarly, experts reviewing possible changes to *DSM-5* in the diagnosis of psychotic disorders are examining the proposal of including an Attenuated Psychotic Symptoms Syndrome as either a distinct disorder or as an Appendix for Future Research. Inclusion of this as a disorder will allow dual diagnosis to extend to individuals who are earlier in the developmental trajectory of a psychiatric disorder than others with more longstanding psychotic illnesses. This could impact the ways that age and dual diagnosis are related and has additional implications for the impact of dual disorders, especially if earlier identification leads to improved intervention and treatment. Proposed revisions to the diagnosis of mood disorders include a diagnosis of Mixed Anxiety Depression, given the high rates of comorbidity between major depressive disorder and anxiety disorders, especially generalized anxiety disorder. Such a change is relevant to our thinking about *dual* diagnosis and whether the term should updated from *dual* to *multiple* as a way to more accurately capture the reality that many cases of dual diagnosis really reflect multiple comorbid conditions.

Second, it is clear that research on psychopathology and its treatments is complicated by questions of dual diagnosis. Dual diagnosis impacts basic questions of research methodology: Who is included and excluded in dual diagnosis research? How are dual disorders handled in data collection and analysis? and How are research findings to be understood when individuals have multiple disorders? While acknowledging and adapting to the reality of multiple comorbidites within individuals will further complicate treatment research, it is essential that research explore ways to include and be applicable to individuals with multiple conditions. That is, it is increasingly less useful to explore the relationships between only two disorders, or to limit the development of treatments to individuals with two disorders, when many of those with comorbid conditions have more than two problems. Practically speaking, issues of mood, anxiety, and substance use are intertwined for many people, and research will need to address the understanding and treatment of these syndromes together rather than separately.

Finally, several models that explain dual diagnosis take into account the different types of psychopathology and substances of abuse, as well as the differences in disorder severity. Research linking neurobiological development of psychiatric disorders to substance abuse vulnerability highlights the need to incorporate biological and psychological constructs as we proceed in trying to understand dual diagnosis. The next step is to further examine causal mechanisms and determine how these models work given the significant heterogeneity seen in the dual diagnosis population. Although a range of theories has been proposed, more specific work is required to fully examine the links between mental illness and substance use disorders. Here again, research will have to adapt to the current reality of multiple comorbidities. At present it is unclear how prevailing models of dual disorders that are organized around a pair of problems are going to be relevant to individuals with three or more diagnoses. Overall, moving forward in our understanding of dual disorders will require that we focus on comorbidity and the connections among multiple problems as a way to best learn about and treat individuals.

## REFERENCES

Addington, J., el-Guebaly, N., Campbell, W., Hodgins, D. C., & Addington, D. (1998). Smoking cessation treatment for patients with schizophrenia. *American Journal of Psychiatry, 155,* 974–976.

Adler, L. E., Hoffer, L. J., Griffith, J., Waldo, M. C., & Freedman, R. (1992). Normalization by nicotine of deficient auditory sensory gating in the relatives of schizophrenics. *Biological Psychiatry, 32,* 607–616.

Adler, L. E., Hoffer, L. D., Wiser, A., & Freedman, R. (1993). Normalization of auditory physiology by cigarette smoking in schizophrenic patients. *American Journal of Psychiatry, 150,* 1865–1861.

Adler, L. E., Olincy, A., Waldo, M., Harris, J. G., Griffith, J., Stevens, K., . . . Freedman, R. (1998). Schizophrenia, sensory gating, and nicotinic receptors. *Schizophrenia Bulletin, 24,* 189–202.

Aharonovich, E., Nunes, E., & Hasin, D. (2003). Cognitive impairment, retention, and abstinence among cocaine abusers in cognitive-behavioral treatment. *Drug and Alcohol Dependence, 71,* 207–211.

Alegría, A. A., Hasin, D. S., Nunes, E. V., Liu, S. M., Davies, C., Grant, B. F., & Blanco, C. (2010). Comorbidity of generalized anxiety disorder and substance use disorders. Results from the National Epidemiologic Survey on Alcohol and Related Conditions. *Journal of Clinical Psychiatry, 71,* 1187–1195.

Alterman, A. I., Erdlen, D. L., Laporte, D. L., & Erdlen, F. R. (1982). Effects of illicit drug use in an inpatient psychiatric setting. *Addictive Behaviors, 7*(3), 231–242.

American Psychiatric Association. (1994). *Diagnostic and statistical manual of mental disorders* (4th ed.). Washington, DC: Author.

Ananth, J., Vandewater, S., Kamal, M., Brodsky, A., Gamal, R., & Miller, M. (1989). Mixed diagnosis of substance abuse in psychiatric patients. *Hospital and Community Psychiatry, 40,* 297–299.

Arendt, M., & Munk-Jorgensen, P. (2004). Heavy cannabis users seeking treatment: Prevalence of psychiatric disorders. *Social Psychiatry and Psychiatric Epidemiology, 39*(2), 97–105.

Back, S., Dansky, B. S., Coffey, S. F., Saladin, M. E., Sonne, S., & Brady, K. T. (2000). Cocaine dependence with and without post-traumatic stress disorder: A comparison of substance use, trauma history, and psychiatric comorbidity. *American Journal on Addictions, 9*(1), 51–62.

Baethge, C., Baldessarini, R. J., Khalsa, H. M., Hennen, J., Salvatore, P., & Tohen, M. (2005). Substance abuse in first-episode bipolar I disorder: Indications for early intervention. *American Journal of Psychiatry, 162*(5), 1008–1010.

Barbee, J. G., Clark, P. D., Crapanzano, M. S., Heintz, G. C., & Kehoe, C. E. (1989). Alcohol and substance abuse among schizophrenic patients presenting to an emergency psychiatric service. *Journal of Nervous and Mental Disease, 177,* 400–407.

Bates, M. E., Voelbel, G. T., Buckman, J. F., Labouvie, E. W., & Barry, D. (2005). Short-term neuropsychological recovery in clients with substance use disorders. *Alcoholism: Clinical and Experimental Research, 29*(3), 367–377.

Batki, S. L., Meszaros, Z. S., Strutynski, K., Dimmock, J. A., Leontieva, L., Ploutz-Snyder, R., . . . Drayer, R. A. (2009). Medical comorbidity in patients with schizophrenia and alcohol dependence. *Schizophrenia Research, 107*(2-3), 139–146.

Bauer, M. S., Altshuler, L., Evans, D. R., Beresford, T., Williford, W. O., & Hauger, R. (2005). Prevalence and distinct correlates of anxiety, substance, and combined comorbidity in a multi-site public sector sample with bipolar disorder. *Journal of Affective Disorders, 85*, 301–315.

Begleiter, H., & Porjesz, B. (1995). Neurophysiological phenotypic factors in the development of alcoholism. In H. Begleiter & B. Kissin (Eds.), *The genetics of alcoholism* (pp. 269–293). New York, NY: Oxford University Press.

Bellack, A. S., Bennett, M. E., Gearon, J. S., Brown, C. H., & Yang, Y. (2006). A randomized clinical trail of a new behavioral treatment for drug abuse in people with severe and persistent mental illness. *Archives of General Psychiatry, 63*, 426–432.

Berkson, J. (1949). Limitations of the application of four-fold tables to hospital data. *Biometric Bulletin, 2*, 47–53.

Bibb, J. L., & Chambless, D. L. (1986). Alcohol use and abuse among diagnosed agoraphobics. *Behavior Research and Therapy, 24*(1), 49–58.

Bien, T. H., & Burge, J. (1990). Smoking and drinking: A review of the literature. *International Journal of the Addictions, 25*, 1429–1454.

Blanchard, J. J. (2000). The co-occurrence of substance use in other mental disorders: Editor's introduction. *Clinical Psychology Review, 20*(2), 145–148.

Blashfield, R. K. (1990). Comorbidity and classification. In J. D. Master & C. R. Cloninger (Eds.), *Comorbidity of mood and anxiety disorders* (pp. 61–82). Washington, DC: American Psychiatric Association Press.

Bonin, M. F., Norton, G. R., Asmundson, G. J., Dicurzio, S., & Pidlubney, S. (2000). Drinking away the hurt: The nature and prevalence of posttraumatic stress disorder in substance abuse patient attending a community-based treatment program. *Journal of Behavior Therapy and Experimental Psychiatry, 31*(1), 55–66.

Bowden, S. C., Crews, F. T., Bates, M. E., Fals-Stewart, W., & Ambrose, M. L. (2001). Neurotoxicity and neurocognitive impairments with alcohol and drug-use disorders: Potential roles in addiction and recovery. *Alcoholism: Clinical and Experimental Research, 25*, 317–321.

Bowen, R. C., Cipywnyk, D., D'Arcy, C., & Keegan, D. (1984). Alcoholism, anxiety disorders, and agoraphobia. *Alcoholism Clinical and Experimental Research, 8*(1), 48–50.

Bradizza, C. M., & Stasiewicz, P. R. (1997). Integrating substance abuse treatment for the seriously mentally ill into inpatient psychiatric treatment. *Journal of Substance Abuse Treatment, 14*(2), 103–111.

Brady, K. T., Killeen, T. K., Brewerton, T., & Lucerini, S. (2000). Comorbidity of psychiatric disorders and posttraumatic stress disorder. *Journal of Clinical Psychiatry, 61*(Suppl. 7), 22–32.

Breslau, N., Davis, G. C., Peterson, E. L., & Schultz, L. (1997). Psychiatric sequelae of posttraumatic stress disorder in women. *Archives of General Psychiatry, 54*(1), 81–87.

Brooner, R. K., King, V. L., Kidorf, M., Schmidt, C. W., & Bigelow, G. E. (1997). Psychiatric and substance use comorbidity among treatment-seeking opioid abusers. *Archives of General Psychiatry, 54*(1), 71–80.

Brown, V. B., Melchior, L. A., & Huba, G. J. (1999). Level of burden among women diagnosed with severe mental illness and substance abuse. *Journal of Psychoactive Drugs, 31*(1), 31–40.

Brunello, N., Davidson, J. R., Deahl, M., Kessler, R. C., Mendlewicz, J., Racagni, G., . . . Zohar, J. (2001). Posttraumatic stress disorder: Diagnosis and epidemiology, comorbidity and social consequences, biology and treatment. *Neuropsychobiology*, 43(3), 150–162.

Brunette, M. F., & Drake, R. E. (1998). Gender differences in homeless persons with schizophrenia and substance abuse. *Community Mental Health Journal*, 34, 627–642.

Brunette, M. F., Mueser, K. T., Xie, H., & Drake, R. E. (1997). Relationships between symptoms of schizophrenia and substance abuse. *Journal of Nervous and Mental Disease*, 185, 13–20.

Bucholz, K. K. (1999). Nosology and epidemiology of addictive disorders and their comorbidity. *Psychiatric Clinics of North America*, 22(2), 221–239.

Burns, L., Teesson, M., & O'Neill, K. (2005). The impact of comorbid anxiety and depression on alcohol treatment outcomes. *Addiction*, 100(6), 787–796.

Busto, U. E., Romach, M. K., & Sellers, E. M. (1996). Multiple drug use and psychiatric comorbidity in patients admitted to the hospital with severe benzodiazepine dependence. *Journal of Clinical Psychopharmacology*, 16(1), 51–57.

Cacciola, J. S., Koppenhaver, J. M., Alterman, A. I., & McKay, J. R. (2009). Posttraumatic stress disorder and other psychopathology in substance abusing patients. *Drug and Alcohol Dependence*, 101(1-2), 27–33.

Carey K. B., Carey M. P., & Simons J. S. (2003). Correlates of substance use disorder among psychiatric outpatients: Focus on cognition, social role functioning, and psychiatric status. *Journal of Nervous and Mental Disease*, 191, 300–308.

Carey, K. B., & Correia, C. J. (1998). Severe mental illness and addictions: Assessment considerations. *Addictive Behaviors*, 23(6), 735–748.

Carey, M. P., Carey, K. B., & Kalichman, S. C. (1997). Risk for human immunodeficiency virus (HIV) infection among persons with severe mental illnesses. *Clinical Psychology Review*, 17, 271–291.

Carpenter, K. M., & Hittner, J. B. (1997). Cognitive impairment among the dually diagnosed: Substance use history and depressive symptom correlates. *Addiction*, 92, 747–759.

Carpenter, W. T. J., Heinrichs, D. W., & Alphs, L. D. (1985). Treatment of negative symptoms. *Schizophrenia Bulletin*, 11, 440–452.

Caton, C. L., Shrout, P. E., Eagle, P. F., Opler, L. A., Felix, A., & Dominguez, B. (1994). Risk factors for homelessness among schizophrenic men: A case-control study. *American Journal of Public Health*, 84, 265–270.

Chambers, R. A., Krystal, J. H., & Self, D. W. (2001). A neurobiological basis for substance abuse comorbidity in schizophrenia. *Biological Psychiatry*, 50, 71–83.

Chambers, R. A., & Self, D. W. (2002). Motivational responses to natural and drug rewards in rats with neonatal ventral hippocampal lesions: An animal model of dual diagnosis schizophrenia. *Neuropsychopharmacology*, 27, 889–905.

Chambers, R. A., & Taylor, J. R. (2004). Animal modeling dual diagnosis schizophrenia: Sensitization to cocaine in rats with neonatal ventral hippocampal lesions. *Biological Psychiatry*, 56, 308–316.

Chen, C., Balogh, R., Bathija, J., Howanitz, E., Plutchik, R., & Conte, H. R. (1992). Substance abuse among psychiatric inpatients. *Comprehensive Psychiatry*, 33, 60–64.

Chengappa, K. N., Levine, J., Gershon, S., & Kupfer, D. J. (2000). Lifetime prevalence of substance or alcohol abuse and dependence among subjects with bipolar I and II disorders in a voluntary registry. *Bipolar Disorder*, 2 (3, Pt. 1), 191–195.

Chilcoat, H. D., & Breslau, N. (1998). Investigations of causal pathways between posttraumatic stress disorder and drug use disorders. *Addictive Behaviors*, 23(6), 827–840.

Clark, R. E., Ricketts, S. K., & McHugo, G. J. (1999). Legal system involvement and costs for persons in treatment for severe mental illness and substance use disorders. *Psychiatric Services, 50*(5), 641–647.

Cleghorn, J. M., Kaplan, R. D., Szechtman, B., Szechtman, H., Brown, G. M., & Franco, S. (1991). Substance abuse and schizophrenia: Effect on symptoms but not on neurocognitive function. *Journal of Clinical Psychiatry, 52*, 26–30.

Cohen, L. J., Test, M. A., & Brown, R. J. (1990). Suicide and schizophrenia: Data from a prospective community treatment study. *American Journal of Psychiatry, 147*, 602–607.

Cohen, M., & Klein, D. F. (1970). Drug abuse in a young psychiatric population. *American Journal of Orthopsychiatry, 40*, 448–455.

Comtois, K. A., & Ries, R. (1995). Sex differences in dually diagnosed severely mentally ill clients in dual diagnosis outpatient treatment. *American Journal on Addictions, 4*, 245–253.

Conover, C. J., Arno, P., Weaver, M., Ang, A., & Ettner, S. L. (2006). Income and employment of people living with combined HIV/AIDS, chronic mental illness, and substance abuse disorders. *Journal of Mental Health Policy and Economics, 9*(2), 71–86.

Cooper, L., Liberman, D., Tucker, D., Nuechterlein, K. H., Tsuang, J., & Barnett, H. L. (1999). Neurocognitive deficits in the dually diagnosed with schizophrenia and cocaine abuse. *Psychiatric Rehabilitation Skills, 3*, 231–245.

Cottler, L. B., Compton, W. M., III, Mager, D., Spitznagel, E. L., & Janca, A. (1992). Post-traumatic stress disorder among substance users from the general population. *American Journal of Psychiatry, 149*(5), 664–670.

Dalack, G. W., & Meador-Woodruff, J. H. (1996). Smoking, smoking withdrawal and schizophrenia: Case reports and a review of the literature. *Schizophrenia Research, 22*, 133–141.

Dansky, B. S., Brady, K. T., & Saladin, M. E. (1998). Untreated symptoms of posttraumatic stress disorder among cocaine-dependent individuals: Changes over time. *Journal of Substance Abuse Treatment, 15*(6), 499–504.

Davis, T. M., & Wood, P. S. (1999). Substance abuse and sexual trauma in a female veteran population. *Journal of Substance Abuse Treatment, 16*(2), 123–127.

de Leon, J., Dadvand, M., Canuso, C., White, A. O., Stanilla, J. K., & Simpson, G. M. (1995). Schizophrenia and smoking: An epidemiological survey in a state hospital. *American Journal of Psychiatry, 152*(3), 453–455.

Depp, C. A., Moore, D. J., Sitzer, D., Palmer, B. W., Eyler, L. T., Roesch, S., . . . Jeste, D. V. (2007). Neurocognitive impairment in middle-aged and older adults with bipolar disorder: Comparison to schizophrenia and normal comparison subjects. *Journal of Affective Disorders, 101*, 201–209.

Dickerson, F. B., Boronow, J. J., Stallings, C. R., Origoni, A. E., Cole, S., & Yolken, R. H. (2004). Association between cognitive functioning and employment status of persons with bipolar disorder. *Psychiatric Services, 55*(1), 54–58.

Dickerson, F. B., Sommerville, J., Origoni, A. E., Ringel, N. B., & Parente, F. (2001). Outpatients with schizophrenia and bipolar I disorder: Do they differ in their cognitive and social functioning? *Psychiatry Research, 102*(1), 21–27.

Dickey, B., & Azeni, H. (1996). Persons with dual diagnoses of substance abuse and major mental illness: Their excess costs of psychiatric care. *American Journal of Public Health, 86*(7), 973–977.

Dickey, B., Dembling, B., Azeni, H., & Normand, S. T. (2004). Externally caused deaths for adults with substance use and mental disorders. *Journal of Behavioral Health Services & Research, 31*(1), 75–85.

Di Sclafani, V., Tolou-Shams, M., Price, L. J., & Fein, G. (2002). Neuropsychological perform-ance of individuals dependent on crack-cocaine, or crack-cocaine and alcohol, at 6 weeks and 6 months of abstinence. *Drug and Alcohol Dependence, 66,* 161–171.

Dixon, L. (1999). Dual diagnosis of substance abuse in schizophrenia: Prevalence and impact on outcomes. *Schizophrenia Research, 35,* S93–S100.

Dixon, L., Haas, G., Weiden, P., Sweeney, J., & Frances, A. J. (1990). Acute effects of drug abuse in schizophrenic patients: Clinical observations and patients' self-reports. *Schizophrenia Bulletin, 16*(1), 69–79.

Dixon, L., Haas, G., Weiden, P., Sweeney, J., & Frances, A. J. (1991). Drug abuse in schizo-phrenic patients: Clinical correlates and reasons for use. *American Journal of Psychiatry, 149,* 231–234.

Drake, R. E., Mercer-McFadden, C., Mueser, K. T., McHugo, G. J., & Bond, G. R. (1998). Review of integrated mental health and substance abuse treatment for patients with dual disorders. *Schizophrenia Bulletin, 24*(4), 589–608.

Drake, R. E., Osher, F. C., & Wallach, M. A. (1989). Alcohol use and abuse in schizophrenia: A prospective community study. *Journal of Nervous and Mental Disease, 177,* 408–414.

Drake, R. E., & Wallach, M. A. (1989). Substance abuse among the chronically mentally ill. *Hospital and Community Psychiatry, 40,* 1041–1046.

Eisen, J. L., & Rasmussen, S. A. (1989). Coexisting obsessive compulsive disorder and alcoholism. *Journal of Clinical Psychiatry, 50*(3), 96–98.

Evans, D. L. (2000). Bipolar disorder: Diagnostic challenges and treatment consideration. *Journal of Clinical Psychiatry, 61*(Suppl. 13), 26–31.

Fagergren, P., Overstreet, D. H., Goiny, M., & Hurd, Y. L. (2005). Blunted response to cocaine in the Flinders hypercholinergic animal model of depression. *Neuroscience, 132,* 1159–1171.

Falck, R. S., Wang, J., Siegal, H. A., & Carlson, R. G. (2004). The prevalence of psychiatric disorder among a community sample of crack cocaine users: An exploratory study with practical implications. *Journal of Nervous and Mental Disease, 192*(7), 503–507.

Fals-Stewart, W., & Schafer, J. (1992). The relationship between length of stay in drug-free therapeutic communities and neurocognitive functioning. *Journal of Clinical Psychology, 48*(4), 539–543.

Fazel, S., Lichtenstein, P., Grann, M., Goodwin, G. M., & Langstrom, N. (2010). Bipolar disorder and violent crime: New evidence from population-based longitudinal studies and system-atic review. *Archives of General Psychiatry, 67*(9), 931–938.

Fennig, S., Craig, T. J., Tanenberg-Karant, M., & Bromet, E. J. (1994). Comparison of facility and research diagnoses in first-admission psychotic patients. *American Journal of Psychiatry, 151*(10), 1423–1429.

Fishbein, D., & Tarter, R. (2009). Infusing neuroscience into the study and prevention of drug misuse and co-occurring aggressive behavior. *Substance Use and Misuse, 44,* 1204–1235.

Folsom, D. P., Hawthorne, W., Lindamer, L., Gilmer, T., Bailey, A., Golshan, S., . . . Jeste, D. V. (2005). Prevalence and risk factors for homelessness and utilization of mental health services among 10,340 patients with serious mental illness in a large public mental health system. *American Journal of Psychiatry, 162*(2), 370–376.

Fulwiler, C., Grossman, H., Forbes, C., & Ruthazer, R. (1997). Early-onset substance abuse and community violence by outpatient with chronic mental illness. *Psychiatric Services, 48*(9), 1181–1185.

Galanter, M., Castaneda, R., & Ferman, J. (1988). Substance abuse among general psychiatric patients: Place of presentation, diagnosis, and treatment. *American Journal of Drug and Alcohol Abuse, 14*(2), 211–235.

Garnick, D. W., Hendricks, A. M., Comstock, C., & Horgan, C. (1997). Do individuals with substance abuse diagnoses incur higher charges than individuals with other chronic conditions? *Journal of Substance Abuse Treatment, 14*(5), 457–465.

Gearon, J. S., & Bellack, A. S. (1999). Women with schizophrenia and co-occurring substance use disorders: An increased risk for violent victimization and HIV. *Journal of Community Mental Health, 35*, 401–419.

Gearon, J. S., Bellack, A. S., Nidecker, M., & Bennett, M. E. (2003). Gender differences in drug use behavior in people with serious mental illness. *American Journal on Addictions, 12*(3), 229–241.

Gershon, E. S., Hamovit, J., Guroff, J. J., Dibble, E., Leckman, J. F., Sceery, W., . . . Bunney, W. E. (1982). A family study of schizoaffective, bipolar I, bipolar II, and normal probands. *Archives of General Psychiatry, 39*(10), 1157–1167.

Gilmer, T. P., Dolder, C. R., Lacro, J. P., Folsom, D. P., Lindamer, L., Garcia, P., & Jeste, D. V. (2004). Adherence to treatment with antipsychotic medication and health care costs among Medicaid beneficiaries with schizophrenia. *American Journal of Psychiatry, 161*, 692–699.

Glenn, S. W., & Parsons, O. A. (1991). Prediction of resumption of drinking in posttreatment alcoholics. *International Journal of the Addictions, 26*(2), 237–254.

Goldberg, J. F., Garno, J. L., Leon, A. C., Kocsis, J. H., & Portera, L. (1999). A history of substance abuse complicates remission from acute mania in bipolar disorder. *Journal of Clinical Psychiatry, 60*(11), 733–740.

Goldberg, T. E., Gold, J. M., Greenberg, M. D., Griffin, S., Schulz, C., Pickar, D., . . . Weinberger, D. R. (1993). Contrasts between patients with affective disorders and patients with schizophrenia on a neuropsychological test battery. *American Journal of Psychiatry, 150*, 1355–1362.

Goldstein, R. B., Compton, W. M., & Grant, B. F. (2010). Antisocial behavioral syndromes and additional psychiatric comorbidity in posttraumatic stress disorder among U.S. adults: Results from Wave 2 of the National Epidemiologic Survey on Alcohol and Related Conditions. *Journal of the American Psychiatric Nurses Association, 16*, 145–165.

Goldstein, R. Z., & Volkow, N. D. (2002). Drug addiction and its underlying neurobiological basis: Neuroimaging evidence for the involvement of the frontal cortex. *American Journal of Psychiatry, 159*, 1642–1652.

Goodman, L. A., Dutton, M. A., & Harris, M. (1995). The relationship between violence dimensions and symptom severity among homeless, mentally ill women. *Journal of Traumatic Stress, 10*(1), 51–70.

Goodman, L., Rosenburg, S., Mueser, K. T., & Drake, R. (1997). Physical and sexual assault history in women with SMI: Prevalence, correlates, treatment, and future research directions. *Schizophrenia Bulletin, 23*, 685–696.

Goodwin, F. K., & Jamison, K. R. (1990). *Manic-depressive illness.* New York, NY: Oxford University Press.

Gottesman, I. I., & Groome, C. S. (1997). HIV/AIDS risks as a consequence of schizophrenia. *Schizophrenia Bulletin, 23*, 675–684.

Grant, B. F. (1995). Comorbidity between *DSM-IV* drug use disorders and major depression: Results of a national survey of adults. *Journal of Substance Abuse, 7*(4), 481–497.

Grant, B. F. (1997). The influence of comorbid major depression and substance use disorders on alcohol and drug treatment: Results of a national survey. *National Institute on Drug Abuse Research Monograph, 172*, 4–15.

Grant, B. F., & Harford, T. C. (1995). Comorbidity between *DSM-IV* alcohol use disorders and major depression: Results of a national survey. *Drug and Alcohol Dependence, 39*, 197–206.

Grant, B. F., Harford, T. C., Dawson, D. A., Chou, P., Dufour, M., & Pickering, R. (1994). Prevalence of *DSM-IV* alcohol abuse and dependence: United States,1992. *Alcohol Health and Research World, 18*(3), 243–248.

Grant, B. F., Hasin, D. S., & Harford, T. C. (1989). Screening for major depression among alcoholics: An application of receiver operating characteristic analysis. *Drug and Alcohol Dependence, 23*, 123–131.

Grant, B. F., Stinson, F. S., Dawson, D. A., Chou, S. P., Dufour, M. C., Compton, W., . . . Kaplan, K. (2004). Prevalence and co-occurrence of substance use disorders and independent mood and anxiety disorders: Results from the National Epidemiologic Survey on Alcohol and Related Conditions. *General Psychiatry, 61*(8), 807–816.

Green, M. F. (1996). What are the functional consequences of neurocognitive deficits in schizophrenia? *American Journal of Psychiatry, 153*, 321–330.

Grella, C. E. (1996). Background and overview of mental health and substance abuse treatment systems: Meeting the needs of women who are pregnant or parenting. *Journal of Psychoactive Drugs, 28*(4), 319–343.

Grella, C. E. (1997). Services for perinatal women with substance abuse and mental health disorders: The unmet need. *Journal of Psychoactive Drugs, 29*(1), 67–78.

Grella, C. E. (2003). Effects of gender and diagnosis on addiction history, treatment utilization, and psychosocial functioning among a dually-diagnosed sample in drug treatment. *Journal of Psychoactive Drugs, 35*(1), 169–179.

Grillo, C. M., White, M. A., & Masheb, R. M. (2009). *DSM-IV* psychiatric disorder comorbidity and its correlates in binge eating disorder. *International Journal of Eating Disorders, 42*(3), 228–234.

Hasin, D. (2003). Classification of alcohol use disorders. *Alcohol Research and Health, 27*(1), 5–17.

Hasin, D. S., Endicott, J., & Keller, M. B. (1991). Alcohol problems in psychiatric patients: 5-year course. *Comprehensive Psychiatry, 32*(4), 303–316.

Hasin, D. S., Endicott, J., & Lewis, C. (1985). Alcohol and drug abuse in patients with affective syndromes. *Comprehensive Psychiatry, 26*(3), 283–295.

Hasin, D. S., Grant, B. F., & Endicott, J. (1988). Lifetime psychiatric comorbidity in hospitalized alcoholics: Subject and familial correlates. *International Journal of the Addictions, 23*(8), 827–850.

Havassy, B. E., & Arns, P. G. (1998). Relationship of cocaine and other substance dependence to well-being of high-risk psychiatric patients. *Psychiatric Services, 49*(7), 935–940.

Havassy, B. E., Shopshire, M. S., & Quigley, L. A. (2000). Effects of substance dependence on outcomes of patients in a randomized trial of two case management models. *Psychiatric Services, 51*(5), 639–644.

Hays, P., & Aidroos, N. (1986). Alcoholism followed by schizophrenia. *Acta Psychiatrica Scandinavica, 74*(2), 187–189.

Haywood, T. W., Kravitz, H. M., Grossman, L. S., Cavanaugh, J. L., Jr., Davis, J. M., & Lewis, D. A. (1995). Predicting the "revolving door" phenomenon among patients with schizophrenic, schizoaffective, and affective disorders. *American Journal of Psychiatry, 152*, 856–861.

Heinrichs, R. W., & Zakzanis, K. K. (1998). Neurocognitive deficit in schizophrenia: A quantitative review of the evidence. *Neuropsychology, 12*, 426–445.

Helzer, J. E., & Pryzbeck, T. R. (1988). The co-occurrence of alcoholism with other psychiatric disorders in the general population and its impact on treatment. *Journal of Studies on Alcohol, 49*(3), 219–224.

Helzer, J. E., Robbins, L. H., & McEvoy, L. (1987). Post-traumatic stress disorder in the general population. *New England Journal of Medicine, 317*, 1630–1634.

Herz, L. R., Volicer, L., D'Angelo, N., & Gadish, D. (1990). Additional psychiatric illness by Diagnostic Interview Schedule in male alcoholics. *Comprehensive Psychiatry, 30*(1), 72–79.

Hesselbrock, M. N., Meyer, R. E., & Keener, J. J. (1985). Psychopathology in hospitalized alcoholics. *Archives of General Psychiatry, 42,* 1050–1055.

Hesselbrock, V. M. (1986). Family history of psychopathology in alcoholics: A review and issues. In R. E. Meyer (Ed.), *Psychopathology and addictive disorders* (pp. 41–56). New York, NY: Guilford Press.

Hesselbrock, V. M., Hesselbrock, M. N., & Workman-Daniels, K. L. (1986). Effect of major depression and antisocial personality on alcoholism: Course and motivational patterns. *Journal of Studies on Alcohol, 47*(3), 207–212.

Himle, J. A., & Hill, E. M. (1991). Alcohol abuse and anxiety disorders: Evidence from the Epidemiologic Catchment Area Survey. *Journal of Anxiety Disorders, 5,* 237–245.

Hirschfeld, R. M. A., Hasin, D., Keller, M. D., Endicott, J., & Wunder, J. (1990). Depression and alcoholism: Comorbidity in a longitudinal study. In J. D. Maser and C. R. Cloninger (Eds.), *Comorbidity of mood and anxiety disorders* (pp. 293–304). Washington, DC: American Psychiatric Association Press.

Hoff, R. A., Beam-Goulet, J., & Rosenheck, R. A. (1997). Mental disorder as a risk factor for human immunodeficiency virus infection in a sample of veterans. *Journal of Nervous and Mental Disease, 185*(9), 556–560.

Holmes, P. V., Masini, C. V., Primuaux, S. D., Garrett, J. L., Zellner, A., Stogner, K. S., . . . Crystal, J. D. (2002). Intravenous self-administration of amphetamine is increased in a rat model of depression. *Synapse, 46*(4), 4–10.

Holzman, P. S. (1987). Recent studies of psychophysiology in schizophrenia. *Schizophrenia Bulletin, 13,* 49–75.

Horner, D. (1999). Attentional functioning in abstinent cocaine abusers. *Drug and Alcohol Dependence, 54,* 19–33.

Hughes, J. R., Hatsukami, D. K., Mitchell, J. E., & Dahlgren, L. A. (1986). Prevalence of smoking among psychiatric outpatients. *American Journal of Psychiatry, 143*(8), 993–997.

Iacono, W. G., Carlson, S. R., Malone, S. M., & McGue, M. (2002). P3 event-related potential amplitude and the risk for disinhibitory disorders in adolescent boys. *Archives of General Psychiatry, 59,* 750–757.

Jacobson, A. (1989). Physical and sexual assault histories among psychiatric outpatients. *American Journal of Psychiatry, 146*(6), 755–758.

Jones, D. R., Macias, C., Barreira, P. J., Fisher, W. H., Hargreaves, W. A., & Harding, C. M. (2004). Prevalence, severity, and co-occurrence of chronic physical health problems of persons with severe mental illness. *Psychiatric Services, 55*(11), 1250–1257.

Joyal, C. C., Putkonen, A., Paavola, P., & Tiihonen, J. (2004). Characteristics and circumstances of homicidal acts committed by offenders with schizophrenia. *Psychological Medicine, 34*(3), 433–442.

Karmali, M., Kelly, L., Gervin, M., Browne, S., Larkin, C., & O'Callaghan, E. (2000). The prevalence of comorbid substance misuse and its influence on suicidal ideation among inpatients with schizophrenia. *Acta Psychiatrica Scandinavica, 101*(6), 452–456.

Keane, T. M., Gerardi, R. J., Lyons, J. A., & Wolfe, J. (1988). The interrelationship of substance abuse and posttraumatic stress disorder: Epidemiological and clinical considerations. In M. Galanter (Ed.), *Recent developments in alcoholism.* New York, NY: Plenum Press.

Kelly, R. H., Danielsen, B. H., Golding, J. M., Anders, T. F., Gilbert, W. M., & Zatzick, D. F. (1999). Adequacy of prenatal care among women with psychiatric diagnoses giving birth in California in 1994 and 1995. *Psychiatric Services, 50*(12), 1584–1590.

Kemper, P., Blumenthal, D., Corrigan, J. M., Cunningham, P. J., Felt, S. M., Grossman, J. M., . . . Ginsburg, P. B. (1996). The design of the community tracking study: A longitudinal study of health system change and its effects on people. *Inquiry, 33*(2), 195–206.

Kendler, K. S. (1985). A twin study of individuals with both schizophrenia and alcoholism. *British Journal of Psychiatry, 147*, 48–53.

Kendler, K. S., Davis, C. G., & Kessler, R. C. (1997). The familial aggregation of common psychiatric and substance use disorders in the National Comorbidity Survey: A family history study. *British Journal of Psychiatry, 170*, 541–548.

Kessler, R. C. (1997). The prevalence of psychiatric comorbidity. In S. Wetzler & W. C. Sanderson (Eds.), *Treatment strategies for patients with psychiatric comorbidity* (pp. 23–48). New York, NY: John Wiley & Sons.

Kessler, R. C., Berglund, P., Demler, O., Jin, R., Koretz, D., Merikangas, K. R., . . . Wang, P. S. (2003). The epidemiology of major depressive disorder: Results from the National Comorbidity Survey Replication (NCS-R). *Journal of the American Medical Association, 289*(23), 3095–3105.

Kessler, R. C., Berglund, P., Demler, O., Jin, R., Merikangas, K. R., & Walters, E. E. (2005). Lifetime prevalence and age-of-onset distributions of *DSM-IV* disorders in the National Comorbidity Survey Replication. *Archives of General Psychiatry, 62*, 593–602.

Kessler, R. C., Chiu, W. T., Demler, O., Merikangas, A. R., & Walters, E. E. (2005). Prevalence, severity, and comorbidity of 12-month *DSM-IV* disorders in the National Comorbidity Survey Replication. *Archives of General Psychiatry, 62*, 617–627.

Kessler, R. C., McGonagle, K. A., Zhao, S., Nelson, C. B., Hughes, M., Eshleman, S., . . . Kendler, K. S. (1994). Lifetime and 12-month prevalence of *DSM-II-R* psychiatric disorders in the United States. *Archives of General Psychiatry, 51*, 8–19.

Kessler, R. C., & Merikangas, K. R. (2004). The National Comorbidity Survey Replication (NCS-R): Background and aims. *International Journal of Methods in Psychiatric Research, 13*(2), 60–68.

Kessler, R. C., Nelson, C. B., McGonagle, K. A., Liu, J., Swartz, M., & Blazer, D. G. (1996). Comorbidity of *DSM-III-R* major depressive disorder in the general population: Results from the US National Comorbidity Survey. *British Journal of Psychiatry, 168*(30), 17–30.

Keuthen, N. J., Niaura, R. S., Borrelli, B., Goldstein, M., DePue, J., Murphy, C., . . . Abrams, D. (2000). Comorbidity, smoking behavior, and treatment outcome. *Psychotherapy and Psychosomatics, 69*, 244–250.

Khantzian, E. J., & Treece, C. (1985). *DSM-III* psychiatric diagnoses of narcotic addicts. *Archives of General Psychiatry, 42*, 1067–1071.

Klorman, R. (1991). Cognitive event-related potentials and attention deficit disorder. *Journal of Learning Disability, 64*, 179–192.

Kokkevi, A., Stephanis, N., Anastasopoulou, E., & Kostogianni, C. (1998). Personality disorders in drug abusers: Prevalence and their association with Axis I disorders as predictors of treatment retention. *Addictive Behaviors, 23*(6), 841–853.

Kozaric-Kovacic, D., Folnegovic-Smalc, V., Folnegovic, Z., & Marusic, A. (1995). Influence of alcoholism on the prognosis of schizophrenia patients. *Journal of Studies on Alcohol, 56*, 622–627.

Krakow, D. S., Galanter, M., Dermatis, H., & Westreich, L. M. (1998). HIV risk factors in dually diagnosed patients. *American Journal of Addictions, 7*(1), 74–80.

Kranzler, H. R., Del Boca, F. K., & Rounsaville, B. J. (1996). Comorbid psychiatric diagnosis predicts three-year outcomes in alcoholics: A posttreatment natural history study. *Journal of Studies on Alcohol, 57*, 619–626.

Krueger, R. F. (1999). The structure of common mental disorders. *Archives of General Psychiatry*, *56*, 921–926.

Krug, I., Treasure, J., Anderluh, M., Bellodi, L., Cellini, E., di Bernardo, M. . . . Fernández-Aranda, F. (2008). Present and lifetime comorbidity of tobacco, alcohol and drug use in eating disorders: A European multicenter study. *Drug and Alcohol Dependence*, *97*(1-2), 169–179.

Kushner, M. G., Abrams, K., & Borchardt, C. (2000). The relationship between anxiety disorders and alcohol use disorders: A review of major perspectives and findings. *Clinical Psychology Review*, *20*(2), 149–171.

Kushner, M. G., Sher, K. J., & Beitman, B. D. (1990). The relation between alcohol problems and the anxiety disorders. *American Journal of Psychiatry*, *147*(6), 685–695.

Lambert, M. T., Griffith, J. M., & Hendrickse, W. (1996). Characteristics of patients with substance abuse diagnoses on a general psychiatry unit in a VA medical center. *Psychiatric Services*, *47*(10), 1104–1107.

Lambert, M. T., LePage, J. P., & Schmitt, A. L. (2003). Five-year outcomes following psychiatric consultation to a tertiary care emergency room. *American Journal of Psychiatry*, *160*(7), 1350–1353.

Landmark, J., Cernovsky, Z. Z., & Merskey, H. (1987). Correlates of suicide attempts and ideation in schizophrenia. *British Journal of Psychiatry*, *151*, 18–20.

Lasser, K., Boyd, J. W., Woolhandler, S., Himmelstein, D. U., McCormick, D., & Bor, D. H. (2000). Smoking and mental illness: A population-based study. *Journal of the American Medical Association*, *284*(2), 2606–2610.

Leal, D., Galanter, M., Dermatis, H., & Westreich, L. (1999). Correlates of protracted homelessness in a sample of dually diagnosed psychiatric inpatients. *Journal of Substance Abuse Treatment*, *16*(2), 143–147.

Lehman, A. F., Myers, C. P., Dixon, L. B., & Johnson, J. L. (1994). Defining subgroups of dual diagnosis patients for service planning. *Hospital and Community Psychiatry*, *45*(6), 556–561.

Lehman, A. F., Myers, C. P., Thompson, J. W., & Corty, E. (1993). Implications of mental and substance use disorders: A comparison of single and dual diagnosis patients. *Journal of Nervous and Mental Disease*, *181*(6), 365–370.

Linszen, D. H., Dingemans, P. M., & Lenior, M. E. (1994). Cannabis abuse and the course of recent-onset schizophrenic disorders. *Archives of General Psychiatry*, *51*, 273–279.

Liskow, B., Powell, B. J., Nickel, E. J., & Penick, E. (1991). Antisocial alcoholics: Are there clinically significant diagnostic subtypes? *Journal of Studies on Alcohol*, *52*(1), 62–69.

Lynskey, M. T. (1998). The comorbidity of alcohol dependence and affective disorders: Treatment implications. *Drug and Alcohol Dependence*, *52*, 201–209.

Margolese, H. C., Malchy, L., Negrete, J. C., Tempier, R., & Gill, K. (2004). Drug and alcohol use among patients with schizophrenia and related psychosis: Levels and consequences. *Schizophrenia Research*, *67*(2-3), 157–166.

Marzuk, P. M. (1996). Violence, crime, and mental illness: How strong a link? *Archives of General Psychiatry*, *53*, 481–486.

Maynard, C., & Cox, G. B. (1988). Psychiatric hospitalization of persons with dual diagnoses: estimates from two national surveys. *Psychiatric Services*, *49*(12), 1615–1617.

McCleery, A., Addington, J., & Addington, D. (2006). Substance misuse and cognitive functioning in early psychosis: A 2-year follow-up. *Schizophrenia Research*, *88*, 187–191.

McCloud, A., Barnaby, B., Omu, N., Drummond, C., & Aboud, A. (2004). Relationship between alcohol use disorders and suicidality in a psychiatric population: In-patient prevalence study. *British Journal of Psychiatry*, *184*, 439–445.

McCrone, P., Menezes, P. R., Johnson, S., Scott, H., Thornicroft, G., Marshall, J., Bebbington, P., & Kuipers, E. (2000). Service use and costs of people with dual diagnosis in South London. *Acta Psychiatrica Scandinavica*, *101*(6), 464–472.

McElroy, S. L., Altshuler, L. L., Suppes, T., Keck, P. E., Jr., Frye, M. A., Denicoff, K. D., . . . Post, R. M. (2001). Axis I psychiatric comorbidity and its relationship to historical illness variables in 288 patients with bipolar disorder. *American Journal of Psychiatry*, *158*(3), 420–426.

McFall, M., Fontana, A., Raskind, M., & Rosenheck, R. (1999). Analysis of violent behavior in Vietnam combat veteran psychiatric inpatients with posttraumatic stress disorder. *Journal of Traumatic Stress*, *12*(3), 501–517.

McKinnon, K., Cournos, F., Sugden, R., Guido, J. R., & Herman, R. (1996). The relative contributions of psychiatric symptoms and AIDS knowledge to HIV risk behaviors among people with severe mental illness. *Journal of Clinical Psychiatry*, *57*(11), 506–513.

McLellan, A. T., Druley, K. A., & Carson, J. E. (1978). Evaluation of substance abuse in a psychiatric hospital. *Journal of Clinical Psychiatry*, *39*(5), 425–430.

McLellan, A. T., Luborsky, L., Woody, G. E., O'Brien, C. P., & Cruley, K. A. (1983). Predicting response to alcohol and drug abuse treatments: Role of psychiatric severity. *Archives of General Psychiatry*, *40*, 620–625.

Menezes, P. R., Johnson, S., Thornicroft, G., Marshall, J., Prosser, D., Bebbington, P., & Kuipers, E. (1996). Drug and alcohol problems among individuals with severe mental illnesses in South London. *British Journal of Psychiatry*, *168*, 612–619.

Merikangas, K. R., & Gelernter, C. S. (1990). Comorbidity for alcoholism and depression. *Psychiatric Clinics of North America*, *13*(4), 613–633.

Merikangas, K. R., Leckman, J. F., Prusoff, B. A., Pauls, D. L., & Weissman, M. M. (1985). Familial transmission of depression and alcoholism. *Archives of General Psychiatry*, *42*, 367–372.

Mezzich, J. E., Ahn, C. W., Fabrega, H., & Pilkonis, P. (1990). Patterns of psychiatric comorbidity in a large population presenting for care. In J. D. Maser & C. R. Cloninger (Eds.), Comorbidity of mood and anxiety disorders (pp. 189–204). Washington, DC: American Psychiatric Association Press.

Miller, N. S., Klamen, D., Hoffmann, N. G., & Flaherty, J. A. (1996). Prevalence of depression and alcohol and other drug dependence in addictions treatment populations. *Journal of Psychoactive Drugs*, *28*, 111–124.

Mirin, S. M., Weiss, R. D., Griffin, M. L., & Michael, J. L. (1991). Psychopathology in drug abusers and their families. *Comprehensive Psychiatry*, *32*(1), 36–51.

Mirin, S. M., Weiss, R. D., & Michael, J. L. (1988). Psychopathology in substance abusers: Diagnosis and treatment. *American Journal of Drug and Alcohol Abuse*, *14*, 139–157.

Morgenstern, J., Langenbucher, J., Labouvie, E., & Miller, K. J. (1997). The comorbidity of alcoholism and personality disorders in a clinical population: Prevalence rates and relation to alcohol typology variables. *Journal of Abnormal Psychology*, *106*(1), 74–84.

Mueller, T. I., Lavori, P. W., Keller, M. B., Swartz, A., Warshaw, M., Hasin, D., . . . Akiskal, H. (1994). Prognostic effect of the variable course of alcoholism on the 10-year course of depression. *American Journal of Psychiatry*, *151*(5), 701–706.

Mueser, K. T., Bellack, A. S., & Blanchard, J. J. (1992). Comorbidity of schizophrenia and substance abuse: Implications for treatment. *Journal of Consulting and Clinical Psychology*, *60*(6), 845–856.

Mueser, K. T., Drake, R. E., & Wallach, M. A. (1998). Dual diagnosis: A review of etiological theories. *Addictive Behaviors*, *23*(6), 717–734.

Mueser, K. T., Rosenberg, S. D., Drake, R. E., Miles, K. M., Wolford, G., Vidaver, R., & Carrieri, K. (1999). Conduct disorder, antisocial personality disorder, and substance use disorders in schizophrenia and major affective disorders. *Journal of Studies on Alcohol*, *60*(2), 278–284.

Mueser, K. T., Yarnold, P. R., & Bellack, A. S. (1992). Diagnostic and demographic correlates of substance abuse in schizophrenia and major affective disorder. *Acta Psychiatrica Scandinavica, 85*, 48–55.

Mueser, K. T., Yarnold, P. R., Levinson, D. F., Singh, H., Bellack, A. S., Kee, K., . . . Yadalam, K. G. (1990). Prevalence of substance abuse in schizophrenia: Demographic and clinical correlates. *Schizophrenia Bulletin, 16*(1), 31–56.

Nace, E. P. (1990). Personality disorder in the alcoholic patient. *Psychiatric Annals, 19*, 256–260.

Nace, E. P., Davis, C. W., & Gaspari, J. P. (1991). Axis II comorbidity in substance abusers. *American Journal of Psychiatry, 148*(1), 118–120.

Najavitis, L. M., Gastfriend, D. R., Barber, J. P., Reif, S., Muenz, L. R., Blaine, J., . . . Weiss, R. D. (1998). Cocaine dependence with and without posttraumatic stress disorder among subjects in the National Institute on Drug Abuse Collaborative Cocaine Treatment Study. *American Journal of Psychiatry, 155*(2), 214–219.

Najavitis, L. M., Sullivan, T. P., Schmitz, M., Weiss, R. D., & Lee, C. S. (2004). Treatment utilization by women with PTSD and substance dependence. *American Journal of Addictions, 13*(3), 215–224.

Najavitis, L. M., Weiss, R. D., & Shaw, S. R. (1997). The link between substance abuse and posttraumatic stress disorder in women: A review. *American Journal of Addiction, 6*(4), 273–283.

Negrete, J. C., & Knapp, W. P. (1986). The effects of cannabis use on the clinical condition of schizophrenics. *National Institute on Drug Abuse Research Monograph, 67*, 321–327.

Newman, D. L., Moffitt, T. E., Caspi, A., & Silva, P. (1998). Comorbid mental disorders: Implications for treatment and sample selection. *Journal of Abnormal Psychology, 107*(2), 305–311.

Nolan, W. A., Luckenbaugh, D. A., Altshuler, L. L., Suppes, T., McElroy, S. L., Frye, M. A., . . . Post, R. M. (2004). Correlates to 1-year prospective outcome in bipolar disorder: Results from the Stanley Foundation Bipolar Network. *American Journal of Psychiatry, 161*(8), 1447–1454.

O'Connell, R. A., Mayo, J. A., Flatow, L., Cuthbertson, B., & O'Brien, B. E. (1991). Outcome of bipolar disorder on long-term treatment with lithium. *British Journal of Psychiatry, 159*, 123–129.

Olincy, A., Harris, J. G., Johnson, L. L., Pender, V., Kongs, S., Allensworth, D., . . . Freedman, R. (2006). Proof-of-concept trial of an alpha7 nicotinic agonist in schizophrenia. *Archives of General Psychiatry, 63*(6), 630–638.

Olincy, A., Ross, R. G., Young, D. A., Roath, M., & Freedman, R. (1998). Improvement in smooth pursuit eye movements after cigarette smoking in schizophrenic patients. *Neuropsychopharmacology, 18*(3), 175–185.

Olincy, A., Young, D. A., & Freedman, R. (1997). Increased levels of the nicotine metabolite cotinine in schizophrenic smokers compared to other smokers. *Biological Psychiatry, 42*, 1–5.

Oquendo, M. A., Currier, D., Liu, S. M., Hasin, D. S., Grant, B. F., & Blanco, C. (2010). Increased risk for suicidal behavior in comorbid bipolar disorder and alcohol use disorders: Results from the National Epidemiologic Survey on Alcohol and Related Conditions. *Journal of Clinical Psychiatry, 71*(7), 902–909.

Ouimette, P. C., Ahrens, C., Moos, R. H., & Finney, J. W. (1998). During treatment changes in substance abuse patients with posttraumatic stress disorder: The influence of specific interventions and program environments. *Journal of Substance Abuse Treatment, 15*(6), 555–564.

Ouimette, P. C., Brown, P. J., & Najavitis, L. M. (1998). Course and treatment of patients with both substance use and posttraumatic stress disorders. *Addictive Behaviors, 23*(6), 785–795.

Ouimette, P. C., Gima, K., Moos, R. H., & Finney, J. W. (1999). A comparative evaluation of substance abuse treatment IV: The effect of comorbid psychiatric diagnoses on amount of treatment, continuing care, and 1-year outcomes. *Alcoholism: Clinical and Experimental Research, 23*(3), 552–557.

Ouimette, P., Goodwin, E., & Brown, P.J. (2007). Health and well being of substance use disorder patients with and without posttraumatic stress disorder. *Addictive Behaviors, 31*(8), 1415–1423.

Ouimette, P. C., Wolfe, J., & Chrestman, K. R. (1996). Characteristics of posttraumatic stress disorder-alcohol abuse comorbidity in women. *Journal of Substance Abuse, 8*(3), 335–346.

Owen, R. R., Fischer, E. P., Booth, B. M., & Cuffel, B. J. (1996). Medication noncompliance and substance abuse among persons with schizophrenia. *Psychiatric Services, 47*(8), 853–858.

Pages, K. P., Russo, J. E., Roy-Byrne, P. P., Ries, R. K., & Cowley, D. S. (1997). Determinants of suicidal ideation: The role of substance use disorders. *Journal of Clinical Psychiatry, 58*(11), 510–515.

Pages, K. P., Russo, J. E., Wingerson, D. K., Ries, R. K., Roy-Byrne, P. P., & Cowley, D. S. (1998). Predictors and outcome of discharge against medical advice from the psychiatric units of a general hospital. *Psychiatric Services, 49*(9), 1187–1192.

Palacios, S., Urmann, C. F., Newel, R., & Hamilton, N. (1999). Developing a sociological framework for dually diagnosed women. *Journal of Substance Abuse Treatment, 17*(1-2), 91–102.

Partonen, T., Sihvo, S., & Lonnqvist, J. K. (1996). Patients excluded from an antidepressant efficacy trial. *Journal of Clinical Psychiatry, 57*(12), 572–575.

Peer, J., Bennett, M. E., & Bellack, A. S. (2009). Neurocognitive characteristics of individuals with schizophrenia and cocaine dependence: Comparison of currently dependent and remitted groups. *Journal of Nervous and Mental Disease, 197,* 631–634.

Penick, E. C., Powell, B. J., Othmer, E., Bingham, S. F., Rice, A. S., & Liese, B. S. (1984). Subtyping alcoholics by coexisting psychiatric syndromes: Course, family history, outcome. In D. W. Goodwin, K. T. Van Dusen, & S. A. Mednick (Eds.), *Longitudinal research in alcoholism* (pp. 167–196). Boston, MA: Kluwer-Nijhoff.

Polcin, D. L. (1992). Issues in the treatment of dual diagnosis clients who have chronic mental illness. *Professional Psychology: Research and Practice, 23*(1), 30–37.

Poldrugo, F. (1998). Alcohol and criminal behavior. *Alcohol and Alcoholism, 33*(1), 12–15.

Potash, J. B., Kane, H. S., Chiu, Y. F., Simpson, S. G., MacKinnon, D. F., McInnis, M. G., . . . DePaulo, J. R., Jr. (2000). Attempted suicide and alcoholism in bipolar disorder: Clinical and familial relationships. *American Journal of Psychiatry, 157*(12), 2048–2050.

Potvin, S., Joyal, C. C., Pelletier, J., & Stip, E. (2008). Contradictory cognitive capacities among substance-abusing patients with schizophrenia: A meta-analysis. *Schizophrenia Research, 100,* 242–251.

Powell, B. J., Penick, E. C., Othmer, E., Bingham, S. F., & Rice, A. S. (1982). Prevalence of additional psychiatric syndromes among male alcoholics. *Journal of Clinical Psychiatry, 43* (10), 404–407.

Quattrocki, E., Baird, A., & Yurgelun-Todd, D. (2000). Biological aspects of the link between smoking and depression. *Harvard Review of Psychiatry, 8*(3), 99–110.

Raimo, E. B., & Schuckit, M. A. (1998). Alcohol dependence and mood disorders. *Addictive Behaviors, 23*(6), 933–946.

Ramsey, S. E., Kahler, C. W., Read, J. P., Stuart, G. L., & Brown, R. A. (2004). Discriminating between substance-induced and independent depressive episodes in alcohol dependent patients. *Journal of Studies on Alcohol, 65*(5), 672–676.

Regier, D. A., Farmer, M. E., Rae, D. S., Locke, B. Z., Keither, S. J., Judd, L. L., & Goodwin, F. K. (1990). Comorbidity of mental disorders with alcohol and other drug abuse. *Journal of the American Medical Association, 264,* 2511–2518.

Regier, D. A., Kaelber, C. T., Rae, D. S., Farmer, M. E., Knauper, B., Kessler, R. C., & Norquist, G. S. (1998). Limitations of diagnostic criteria and assessment instruments for mental disorders: Implications for research and policy. *Archives of General Psychiatry, 55,* 109–115.

Ridgely, M. S., Goldman, H. H., & Willenbring, M. (1990). Barriers to the case of persons with dual diagnoses: Organizational and financing issues. *Schizophrenia Bulletin, 16*(1), 123–132.

Ridgely, M. S., Lambert, D., Goodman, A., Chichester, C. S., & Ralph, R. (1998). Interagency collaboration in services for people with co-occurring mental illness and substance use disorder. *Psychiatric Services, 49,* 236–238.

Rogers, R. D., & Robbins, T. W. (2001). Investigating the neurocognitive deficits associated with chronic drug misuse. *Current Opinion in Neurobiology, 11,* 250–257.

Room, R. (2006). Taking account of cultural and societal influences on substance use diagnoses and criteria. *Addiction, 101*(1), 31–39.

Root, T. L., Pinheiro, A. P., Thornton, L., Strober, M., Fernandez-Aranda, F., Brandt, H., . . . Bulik, C. M. (2010). Substance use disorders in women with anorexia nervosa. *International Journal of Eating Disorders, 43*(1), 14–21.

Rosenblum, A., Fallon, B., Magura, S., Handelsman, L., Foote, J., & Bernstein, D. (1999). The autonomy of mood disorders among cocaine-using methadone patients. *American Journal of Drug and Alcohol Abuse, 25*(1), 67–80.

Rosenthal, R. N., & Miner, C. H. (1997). Differential diagnosis of substance-induced psychosis and schizophrenia in patients with substance use disorders. *Schizophrenia Bulletin, 23*(2), 187–193.

Ross, H. E., Glaser, F. B., & Germanson, T. (1988). The prevalence of psychiatric disorders in patients with alcohol and other drug problems. *Archives of General Psychiatry, 45,* 1023–1031.

Ross, H. E., Glaser, F. B., & Stiasny, S. (1988). Differences in the prevalence of psychiatric disorders in patients with alcohol and drug problems. *British Journal of Addiction, 83,* 1179–1192.

Rounsaville, B. J., Anton, S. F., Carroll, K., Budde, D., Prusoff, B. A., & Gawin, F. (1991). Psychiatric diagnoses of treatment seeking cocaine abusers. *Archives of General Psychiatry, 48,* 43–51.

Rounsaville, B. J., Kosten, T. R., Weissman, M. M., & Kleber, H. D. (1986). Prognostic significance of psychopathology in treated opiate addicts. *Archives of General Psychiatry, 43,* 739–745.

Rounsaville, B. J., Weissman, M. M., Kleber, H., & Wilber, C. (1982). Heterogeneity of psychiatric diagnosis in treated opiate addicts. *Archives of General Psychiatry, 39,* 161–166.

Rounsaville, B. J., Weissman, M. M., Wilber, C. H., Crits-Christoph, K., & Kleber, H. D. (1982). Diagnosis and symptoms of depression in opiate addicts: Course and relationship to treatment outcome. *Archives of General Psychiatry, 39,* 151–156.

Safer, D. J. (1987). Substance abuse by young adult chronic patients. *Hospital and Community Psychiatry, 38*(5), 511–514.

Saladin, M. E., Brady, K. T., Dansky, B. S., & Kilpatrick, D. G. (1995). Understanding comorbidity between posttraumatic stress disorder and substance use disorders: Two preliminary investigations. *Addictive Behaviors, 20*(5), 643–655.

Salloum, I. M., Douaihy, A., Ndimbie, O. K., & Kirisci, L. (2004). Concurrent alcohol and cocaine dependence impact on physical health among psychiatric patients. *Journal of Addictive Disorders, 23*(2) 71–81.

Salloum, I. M., & Thase, M. E. (2000). Impact of substance abuse on the course and treatment of bipolar disorder. *Bipolar Disorder, 2* (3, Pt. 2), 269–280.

Sandberg, D. A., McNiel, D. E., & Binder, R. L. (1998). Characteristics of psychiatric inpatients who stalk, threaten, or harass hospital staff after discharge. *American Journal of Psychiatry, 155*(8), 1102–1105.

Schneier, F. R., Foose, T. E., Hasin, D. S., Heimberg, R. G., Liu, S. M., Grant, B. F., & Blanco, C. (2010). Social anxiety disorder and alcohol use disorder co-morbidity in the National Epidemiologic Survey on Alcohol and Related Conditions. *Psychological Medicine, 40*(6), 977–988.

Schneier, F. R., & Siris, S. G. (1987). A review of psychoactive substance use and abuse in schizophrenia: Patterns of drug choice. *Journal of Nervous and Mental Disease, 175*, 641–650.

Schretlen, D. J., Cascella, N. G., Meyer, S. M., Kingery, L. R., Testa, S. M., Munro, C. A., . . . Pearlson, G. D. (2007). Neuropsychological functioning in bipolar disorder and schizophrenia. *Biological Psychiatry, 62*, 179–186.

Schuckit, M. A. (1983). Alcoholism and other psychiatric disorders. *Hospital and Community Psychiatry, 34*(11), 1022–1027.

Schuckit, M. A., & Monteiro, M. G. (1988). Alcoholism, anxiety, and depression. *British Journal of Addiction, 83*, 1373–1380.

Schuckit, M. A., Tipp, J. E., Bucholz, K. K., Nurnberger, J. I., Hesselbrock, V. M., Crowe, R. R., & Kramer, J. (1997). The life-time rates of three major mood disorder and four major anxiety disorders in alcoholics and controls. *Addiction, 92*(10), 1289–1304.

Scott, H., Johnson, S., Menezes, P., Thornicroft, G., Marshall, J., Bindman, J., . . . Kuipers, E. (1998). Substance misuse and risk of aggression and offending among the severely mentally ill. *British Journal of Psychiatry, 172*, 345–350.

Sellman, J. D., & Joyce, P. R. (1996). Does depression predict relapse in the 6 months following treatment for men with alcohol dependence? *Australian New Zealand Journal of Psychiatry, 30*, 573–578.

Sher, K. J., & Trull, T. J. (1996). Methodological issues in psychopathology research. *Annual Review of Psychology, 47*, 371–400.

Singh, J., Mattoo, S. K., Sharan, P., & Basu, D. (2005). Quality of life and its correlates in patients with dual diagnosis of bipolar affective disorder and substance dependence. *Bipolar Disorder, 7*(2), 187–191.

Sokolski, K. N., Cummings, J. L., Abrams, B. I., DeMet, E. M., Katz, L. S., & Costa, J. F. (1994). Effects of substance abuse on hallucination rates and treatment responses in chronic psychiatric patients. *Journal of Clinical Psychiatry, 55*, 380–387.

Sonne, S. C., Brady, K. T., & Morton, W. A. (1994). Substance abuse and bipolar affective disorder. *Journal of Nervous and Mental Disease, 182*(6), 349–352.

Soyka, M. (2000). Substance misuse, psychiatric disorder and violent and disturbed behaviour. *British Journal of Psychiatry, 176*, 345–350.

Spindler, A., & Milos, G. (2007). Links between eating disorder symptom severity and psychiatric comorbidity. *Eating Behavior, 8*(3), 364–367.

Steadman, H. J., Mulvey, E. P., Monahan, J., Robbins, P. C., Appelbaum, P. S., Grisson, T., . . . Silver, E. (1998). Violence by people discharged from acute psychiatric inpatient facilities and by others in the same neighborhoods. *Archives of General Psychiatry, 55*(5), 393–401.

Stewart, S. H., Pihl, R. O., Conrod, P. J., & Dongier, M. (1998). Functional associations among trauma, posttraumatic stress disorder and substance-related disorders. *Addictive Behaviors, 23*(6), 797–812.

Strakowski, S. M., & DelBello, M. P. (2000). The co-occurrence of bipolar and substance use disorders. *Clinical Psychology Review, 20*(2), 191–206.

Stuyt, E. B. (2004). Hepatitis C in patients with co-occurring mental disorders and substance use disorders: Is tobacco use a possible risk factor? *American Journal of Addictions, 13*(1), 46–52.

Swanson, J., Borum, R., Swartz, M., & Hiday, V. (1999). Violent behavior preceding hospitalization among persons with severe mental illness. *Law and Human Behavior, 23*(2), 185–204.

Swartz, M. S., Swanson, J. W., Hiday, V. A., Borum, R., Wagner, H. R., & Burns, B. J. (1998). Violence and severe mental illness: The effects of substance abuse and nonadherence to medication. *American Journal of Psychiatry, 155*(2), 226–231.

Swendsen, J. D., & Merikangas, K. R. (2000). The comorbidity of depression and substance use disorders. *Clinical Psychology Review, 20*(2), 173–189.

Tarrier, N., & Picken, A. (2010). Co-morbid PTSD and suicidality in individuals with schizophrenia and substance and alcohol abuse. *Social Psychiatry and Psychiatric Epidemiology*, online publication, August 15, 2010.

Thomas, S. E., Thevos, A. K., & Randall, C. L. (1999). Alcoholics with and without social phobia: A comparison of substance use and psychiatric variables. *Journal of Studies on Alcohol, 60*, 472–479.

Thomas, V. H., Melchert, T. P., & Banken, J. A. (1999). Substance dependence and personality disorders: Comorbidity and treatment outcome in an inpatient treatment population. *Journal of Studies on Alcohol, 60*(2), 271–277.

Thompson, S. C., Checkley, G. E., Hocking, J. S., Crofts, N., Mijch, A. M., & Judd, F. K. (1997). HIV risk behavior and HIV testing of psychiatric patients in Melbourne. *Australia and New Zealand Journal of Psychiatry, 31*(4), 566–576.

Tomasson, K., & Vaglum, P. (1997). The 2-year course following detoxification treatment of substance abuse: The possible influence of psychiatric comorbidity. *European Archives of Psychiatry and Clinical Neuroscience, 247*(6), 320–327.

Triffleman, E. G., Marmar, C. R., Delucchi, K. L., & Ronfeldt, H. (1995). Childhood trauma and posttraumatic stress disorder in substance abuse inpatients. *Journal of Nervous and Mental Disease, 183*(3), 172–176.

Trull, T. J., Jahng, S., Tomko, R. L., Wood, P. K., & Sher, K. J. (2010). Revised NESARC personality disorder diagnoses: Gender, prevalence, and comorbidity with substance dependence disorders. *Journal of Personality Disorders, 24*(4), 412–426.

Trull, T. J., Sher, K. J., Minks-Brown, C., Durbin, J., & Burr, R. (2000). Borderline personality disorder and substance use disorders: A review and integration. *Clinical Psychology Review, 20*(2), 235–253.

Velligan, D. I., Weiden, P. J., Sajatovic, M., Scott, J., Carpenter, D., Ross, R., & Docherty, J. P. Expert Consensus Panel on Adherence Problems in Serious and Persistent Mental Illness. (2009). The Expert Consensus Guideline Series: Adherence problems in patients with serious and persistent mental illness. *Journal of Clinical Psychiatry, 70*(Suppl 4), 1–46.

Vengeliene, V., Vollmayr, B., Henn, F. A., & Spanagel, R. (2005). Voluntary alcohol intake in two rat lines selectively bred for learned helpless and non-helpless behavior. *Psychopharmacology, 178*, 125–132.

Verduin, M. L., Carter, R. E., Brady, K. T., Myrick, H., & Timmerman, M. A. (2005). Health service use among persons with comorbid bipolar and substance use disorders. *Psychiatric Services, 56*(4), 475–480.

Vieta, E., Colom, F., Martinez-Aran, A., Benabarre, A., Reinares, M., & Gasto, C. (2000). Bipolar II disorder and comorbidity. *Comprehensive Psychiatry, 41*(5), 339–343.

Watkins, K. E., Burnam, A., Kung, F. Y., & Paddock, S. (2001). A national survey of care for persons with co-occurring mental and substance use disorders. *Psychiatric Services, 52*(8), 1062–1068.

Watkins, K. E., Hunter, S. B., Wenzel, S. L., Tu, W., Paddock, S. M., Griffin, A., & Ebener, P. (2004). Prevalence and characteristics of clients with co-occurring disorders in outpatient substance abuse treatment. *American Journal of Drug and Alcohol Abuse, 30*(4), 749–764.

Weiss, R. D., Ostacher, M. J., Otto, M. W., Calabrese, J. R., Fossey, M., Wisniewski, S. R., . . . STEP-BD Investigators. (2005). Does recovery from substance use disorder matter in patients with bipolar disorder? *Journal of Clinical Psychiatry, 66*(6), 730–750.

Weissman, M. M., & Myers, J. K. (1980). Clinical depression in alcoholism. *American Journal of Psychiatry, 137,* 372–373.

Widiger, T. A., & Shea, T. (1991). Differentiation of Axis I and Axis II disorders. *Journal of Abnormal Psychology, 100*(3), 399–406.

Wildes, J. E., Marcus, M. D., & Fagiolini, A. (2008). Prevalence and correlates of eating disorder co-morbidity in patients with bipolar disorder. *Psychiatry Research, 161*(1), 51–58.

Winokur, G., Turvey, C., Akiskal, H., Coryell, W., Solomon, D., Leon, A., . . . Keller, M. (1998). Alcoholism and drug abuse in three groups—bipolar I, unipolars, and their acquaintances. *Journal of Affective Disorders, 50*(2-3), 81–89.

Wittchen, H., Perkonigg, A., & Reed, V. (1996). Comorbidity of mental disorders and substance use disorders. *European Addiction Research, 2,* 36–47.

Wolf, A. W., Schubert, D. S. P., Patterson, M. B., Marion, B., & Grande, T. P. (1988). Associations among major psychiatric disorders. *Journal of Consulting and Clinical Psychology, 56,* 292–294.

World Health Organization (WHO). (1993). *International statistical classification of diseases and related health problems, tenth revision.* Geneva, Switzerland: Author.

Wu, L., Kouzis, A. C., & Leaf, P. J. (1999). Influence of comorbid alcohol and psychiatric disorders on utilization of mental health services in the National Comorbidity Survey. *American Journal of Psychiatry, 156,* 1230–1236.

Ziedonis, D. M., & George, T. P. (1997). Schizophrenia and nicotine use: Report of a pilot smoking cessation program and review of neurobiological and clinical issues. *Schizophrenia Bulletin, 23,* 247–254.

# CHAPTER 3

# Structured and Semistructured Interviews for Differential Diagnosis: Fundamentals, Applications, and Essential Features

DANIEL L. SEGAL, ANNE E. MUELLER, and FREDERICK L. COOLIDGE

STRUCTURED AND SEMISTRUCTURED interviews were developed in the 1970s to address an important problem in the mental health field: Clinicians and researchers alike had tremendous difficulty in making consistent and accurate diagnoses of mental disorders with unstructured clinical interviews. A major contributing factor to these diagnostic problems was the lack of uniformity or standardization of questions asked of respondents to evaluate the nature and extent of their psychiatric symptoms and to arrive at a formal diagnosis. Structured and semistructured interviews solve this problem by their very nature. As such, they have become increasingly popular and effective in the mental health field, leading to vastly improved diagnostic clarity and precision. The purpose of this chapter is to provide a basic introduction to structured and semistructured interviews used to assess and diagnose psychopathology among adults. We begin with a discussion of the basic types of applications of structured and semistructured interviews followed by an exploration of the major features, advantages, and drawbacks of structured and semistructured interviews. We conclude this chapter with a discussion of the most popular multidisorder structured and semistructured interviews used to diagnose clinical disorders and personality disorders as conceptualized by the current classification system, the *Diagnostic and Statistical Manual of Mental Disorders* (*DSM-IV-TR*; American Psychiatric Association [APA], 2000).

## BASIC ISSUES REGARDING STRUCTURED AND SEMISTRUCTURED INTERVIEWS

The most common method among mental health professionals to evaluate and diagnose their clients is the direct clinical interview (Segal & Hersen, 2010). Such interviews, however, can vary tremendously, especially regarding the amount of structure that is imposed. Indeed, some important differences exist between less structured interviews and more structured ones. Unstructured clinical interviews are dependent on the clinician's unique background, knowledge base, theoretical model, and interpersonal style, and thus are highly flexible. Within this unstructured approach, clinicians are entirely responsible for asking whatever questions they decide are necessary to reach a diagnostic conclusion. In fact, any type of question or topic (relevant or not) can be pursued in any way that fits the mood, preferences, training, specific interests, or philosophy of the clinician. As a consequence, one can imagine the variability across interviews from one clinician to another. On the other hand, structured interviews conform to a standardized list of questions (including follow-up questions), a uniform sequence of questioning, and systematized ratings of the client's responses. These questions are designed to measure the specific criteria for many mental disorders as presented in the *DSM-IV-TR*. These essential elements of structured interviews serve several important purposes, most notably that their use:

- Increases coverage of many mental disorders that otherwise might be overlooked.
- Enhances the diagnostician's ability to accurately determine whether particular symptoms are present or absent.
- Reduces variability among interviewers, which improves reliability.

These features of structured interviews add much in developing clinical psychology into a true science. For example, structured interviews are subject to evaluation and statistical analysis, and they can be modified and improved based on the published literature as to their psychometric properties.

But not all structured interviews are the same. In fact, the term *structured interview* is broad, and the actual amount of structure provided by an interview varies considerably. Structured interviews can be divided into one of two types: *fully structured* or *semistructured*. In a fully structured interview, questions are asked verbatim to the respondent, the wording of probes used to follow up on initial questions is specified, and interviewers are trained to not deviate from this rigid format. In a semistructured interview, although initial questions for each symptom are specified and are typically asked verbatim, the interviewer has substantial latitude to follow up on responses. The interviewer can modify or augment the standard inquiries with individualized and contextualized probes to more accurately rate specific symptoms. The amount of structure provided in an interview clearly impacts the extent of clinical experience and judgment needed to administer the interview appropriately: Semistructured interviews require clinically experienced examiners to administer the interview and to make diagnoses, whereas fully structured interviews can be administered by nonclinicians who receive training on the specific instrument. This latter difference makes fully structured interviews popular and economical, especially in large-scale research studies in which an accurate diagnosis is essential.

Structured and semistructured interviews have been created to assist with the differential diagnosis of all major Axis I clinical disorders and all standard Axis II personality disorders. Interviews used for psychiatric diagnosis are typically aligned with the *DSM* system and, therefore, assess the formal diagnostic criteria specified in the manual. However, structured interviews exist beyond those designed for *DSM* differential diagnosis. Other structured interviews are narrower in focus: for example, to assess a specific problem or form of psychopathology (e.g., eating disorders, substance abuse, borderline personality disorder features) in great depth. An excellent resource for information about a host of specialized interviews is provided by Rogers (2001). Our focus now turns to a discussion of some common functions of structured and semistructured interviews.

## APPLICATIONS OF STRUCTURED AND SEMISTRUCTURED INTERVIEWS

Whereas structured and semistructured interviews are used in many different venues and for many different purposes, their application falls into three broad areas: research, clinical practice, and clinical training.

### RESEARCH

The research domain is the most common application, in which structured or semistructured interviews are used to formally diagnose participants for inclusion into a study so that etiology, comorbidity, and treatment approaches (among other topics) can be explored for a particular diagnosis or group of diagnoses. Sound empirical research on mental disorders certainly requires that individuals assigned a diagnosis truly meet full criteria for that diagnosis. Another research application for structured interviews is to provide a standardized method for assessing change in one's clinical status over time. As noted by Rogers (2003), these types of longitudinal comparisons are essential for establishing outcome criteria, which is vital to diagnostic validity.

### CLINICAL PRACTICE

In clinical settings, administration of a structured or semistructured interview may be used as part of a comprehensive and standardized intake evaluation. Routine and complete administration of a structured interview is increasingly common in psychology training clinics, but doing so requires considerable training for clinicians and time for full administration. A variation on this theme is that sections of a structured interview may be administered subsequent to a traditional unstructured interview to clarify and confirm the diagnostic impressions. Widiger and Samuel (2005) provide another thoughtful alternative, especially regarding the assessment of personality disorders in clinical practice. They recommend the strategy of administering an objective self-report inventory, which is followed by a semistructured interview that focuses on the personality disorders that received elevated scores from the testing. This strategy is responsive to time constraints in clinical practice but also allows for collection of standardized, systematic, and objective data from the structured interview. Finally, we wish to emphasize that in clinical settings, structured interviews should not take the place of traditional interviews. Both can be performed, although at different times and for different purposes. The combination of the two approaches, integrated flexibly to meet the needs of the individual clinician and his or her clients, reflects the best of the scientist-practitioner model in which the science and art of assessment are both valued and valuable (Rogers, 2003).

Clinical Training

Use of structured or semistructured interviews for training mental health professionals is an increasingly popular and ideal application, because interviewers have the opportunity to learn (through repeated administrations) specific questions and follow-up probes used to elicit information and evaluate specific diagnostic criteria provided by the *DSM-IV-TR*. Modeling the questions, sequence, and flow from a structured interview can be an invaluable source of training for beginning clinicians.

## ADVANTAGES AND DISADVANTAGES OF STRUCTURED AND SEMISTRUCTURED INTERVIEWS

No assessment device in the mental health field is perfect, and structured and semistructured interviews are no exception to this truism. In this section, the strengths and weaknesses of structured interviews are discussed. Our intention is to give readers an appreciation of the major issues to be considered when deciding whether to use the structured interview approach to assessment. A brief summary of the advantages and disadvantages is presented in Table 3.1.

**Table 3.1**
Advantages and Disadvantages of Structured and Semistructured Interviews

| Advantages | Disadvantages |
| --- | --- |
| **Increased Reliability:** Because questions are standardized, structured interviews decrease variability among interviewers which enhances interrater reliability. Structured interviews also increase the reliability of assessment for a client's symptoms across time, as well as the reliability between client report and collateral information. | **May Hinder Rapport:** Use of structured interviews may damage rapport because they are problem-centered, not person-centered, and poorly trained interviewers may neglect to use their basic clinical skills during the assessment. |
| **Increased Validity:** Structured interviews assure that diagnostic criteria are covered systematically and completely. This is important because it serves to increase the validity of diagnosis. | **Limited by the Validity of the Classification System Itself:** Structured interviews used for diagnosis are inherently tied to diagnostic systems. Thus, they are only as valid as the systems upon which they are based. Furthermore, it is difficult to establish the validity of particular structured interviews because there is no gold standard in psychiatric diagnosis. |
| **Utility as Training Tools:** Structured interviews are excellent training tools for clinicians-in-training because structured interviews promote the learning of specific diagnostic questions and probes used by experienced clinical interviewers. In addition, nonclinicians can easily be trained to administer fully structured interviews, which can be cost effective in both research and clinical settings. | **The Tradeoff of Breadth versus Depth:** Structured interviews are limited because they cannot cover all disorders or topic areas. When choosing a structured interview, one must evaluate carefully the tradeoffs of breadth versus depth of assessment. |

## ADVANTAGE: INCREASED RELIABILITY

Perhaps the most important advantage of structured interviews is their ability to increase diagnostic reliability (*reliability* defined in this context refers to consistency or agreement about diagnoses assigned by different raters; Coolidge & Segal, 2010a). By systemizing and standardizing the questions interviewers ask and the way answers to those questions are recorded and interpreted, structured interviews decrease the amount of information variance in diagnostic evaluations (e.g., Rogers, 2001). That is, structured interviews decrease the chances that two different interviewers will elicit different information from the same client, which may result in different diagnoses. Thus, interrater reliability, or the likelihood that two different interviewers examining the same individual will arrive at the same diagnosis, is greatly increased.

Increased interrater reliability has broad implications in clinical and research settings. Because many psychological and psychopharmacological treatments are intimately tied to specific diagnoses, it is imperative that those diagnoses are accurate (Segal & Coolidge, 2001). Thus, if different clinicians interviewing the same client arrive at different diagnostic conclusions, it would be challenging to make a definitive decision about treatment. Similarly, accurate diagnosis is also essential for many types of clinical research, for example, studies that address causes and treatments of specific forms of psychopathology (Segal & Coolidge, 2001). Imagine a study examining different treatments for bipolar disorder. In such a study, it would be imperative to be certain that those patients in the treatment groups actually have accurate diagnoses of bipolar disorder. Researchers must be able to accurately and definitively diagnose participants with the disorder being studied before researchers can even begin to examine theories of etiology or effectiveness of treatment for that particular mental disorder.

In addition to increasing interrater reliability, structured interviews increase the likelihood that the diagnosis is reliable across time and across different sources of information (Rogers, 2001). In many clinical and research settings, individuals are in fact assessed on different occasions. Making multiple assessments could be dangerous if an interviewer evaluates a client in a different manner with different questions on different occasions. The client's presentation may be substantially altered, because the way the client is asked about those symptoms has changed instead of the client's symptoms or diagnosis being different. Using a standardized interview for multiple assessments helps ensure that if a client's presentation has changed, it is because his or her symptoms are actually different, not because of variance in interviews (Rogers, 2001). Likewise, in many settings, clinicians conduct collateral interviews with significant people in the client's life to glean a broader picture of the client's symptoms, problems, and experiences. Using a structured interview for both a client and a collateral source will likely increase the chances that discrepancies between the client and collateral informant are real, rather than a consequence of different interviewing styles (Rogers, 2001).

## ADVANTAGE: INCREASED VALIDITY

*Validity* of psychiatric diagnosis refers to the meaningfulness or usefulness of the diagnosis (Coolidge & Segal, 2010b). A required prerequisite for validity is reliability. Thus, by virtue of the fact that structured interviews greatly increase reliability of diagnosis, they also increase the likelihood that the diagnosis is valid. Structured interviews also improve the validity of diagnoses in other ways. The systematic construction of structured interviews lends a methodological validity to these types of assessments compared to unstructured approaches. Because structured interviews are designed to thoroughly and accurately assess well-defined diagnostic criteria, they are often better assessments of those criteria than unstructured interviews (Rogers, 2001). According to Rogers, clinicians who use unstructured interviews sometimes diagnose too quickly, narrow their diagnostic options too early, and miss comorbid diagnoses. Because structured interviews force clinicians to assess all of the specified criteria for a broad range of diagnoses, they offer a more thorough and valid assessment of many disorders compared to unstructured interviews.

In our experience, it is common for beginning clinicians who are performing an unstructured clinical interview to gather information about the presence or absence of only a few common mental disorders. Coverage of other disorders may be neglected during an unstructured interview if the interviewer is unfamiliar with the specific criteria of some disorders. Some unstructured interviews may also provide limited information about whether comorbid psychopathology exists or about the severity of the psychopathology. Because they incorporate systematic ratings, structured and semistructured interviews easily provide information that allows for the determination of the level of severity and the level of impairment associated with a particular diagnosis. Structured interviews provide the same information about comorbid conditions as well.

### ADVANTAGE: UTILITY AS TRAINING TOOLS

Structured interviews can be invaluable training tools for beginning mental health professionals as well as experienced clinicians who desire to enhance their diagnostic skills. Use of structured interviews in the training context may help clinicians develop or enhance their understanding of the flow, format, and questions inherent in a comprehensive diagnostic interview. With repeated administrations, much of a structured interview can be internalized by the clinician. In addition, use of structured interviews for training may reduce anxiety, especially among neophyte clinicians, because the format and flow of the interview is laid out clearly outlined for the interviewer. This type of structure can be helpful and calming for beginning clinicians, who may be initially overwhelmed by the diagnostic process and its inherent complexity.

Structured interviews can also be a useful means of training those who make preliminary mental health assessments: for example, intake staff at hospitals, so that clients are thoroughly and accurately evaluated in preparation for treatment planning. In the case of nonclinician interviewers, fully structured interviews are advisable because they minimize the amount of clinical judgment needed for accurate administration. Use of these trained paraprofessionals can make large-scale research studies cost effective.

### DISADVANTAGE: MAY HINDER RAPPORT

Despite advantages of structured interviews, their application is not without controversy. The most common criticism of structured interviews is that their use may damage rapport or the therapeutic alliance (Segal, Maxfield, & Coolidge, 2008), which is widely viewed as an essential component of effective psychotherapy. Attaining a reliable and accurate diagnosis of a client achieves a hollow victory if the process prevents the therapeutic alliance from forming, or in a more dramatic example of clinical failure, the client does not return for continued treatment. The well-known joke poking fun at medicine, "the operation was a success but the patient died," might be recast in terms of structured interviews as "the diagnosis was impeccable but the client fled treatment."

How exactly might structured interviews damage rapport? Perhaps most importantly, structured interviews may impede the connection between client and clinician because interviews are problem-centered rather than person-centered. There is a danger that interviewers may get so concerned with the protocol of their interview that they fail to demonstrate the warmth, empathy, and genuine regard necessary to form a therapeutic alliance. Indeed, the standardization of the interview may play out as "routinization" (Rogers, 2003). In addition, interviewers who are overly focused on the questions that they must "get through" in an interview may, as a consequence, miss important behavioral cues or other information that could prove essential to the case.

Proponents of structured interviews note that the problem of rapport-building during a structured interview can be overcome with training, experience, and flexibility (Rogers, 2003). We concur and emphasize the observation that "rapid inquiries or monotonous questioning represents clear misuses of structured interviews" (Rogers, 2003, p. 22). If interviewers make an effort to use their basic clinical skills, structured interviews can and should be conducted in such a way that establishes rapport and enhances understanding of the client. To ensure that this is the case, however, interviewers must be aware of the potential negative effects of structured interviews on rapport-building and make the nurturance of the therapeutic alliance a prominent goal during an interview, even when they are also focused on following the protocol. It behooves those who use structured interviews to engage their respondents in a meaningful way during the interview and to avoid a rote-like interviewing style that may alienate. On the other hand, not all clients have a negative perception of a structured interview that must be intentionally overcome. Some clients actually like the structured approach to assessment because it is perceived as thorough and detailed, and in these cases, rapport is easily attained.

## DISADVANTAGE: LIMITED BY THE VALIDITY OF THE CLASSIFICATION SYSTEM ITSELF

Earlier, we noted that proponents of structured interviews claim structured interviews may be more valid in general. The assumption inherent in this argument is that the *DSM* diagnostic criteria are inherently valid, which is a debatable point. One should recognize that *DSM* diagnostic criteria were developed to *reify* theoretical constructs (e.g., depression, schizophrenia), so there is no absolute basis on which criteria were created. Furthermore, mental disorders are social constructions, and they evolve over time as societies evolve. Although successive editions of the *DSM* have been better grounded in empirical research, and the criteria for some disorders (e.g., major depression) have solid research support, other disorders (e.g., most of the personality disorders) and their criteria have not been examined as consistently or as completely, therefore leaving questions about their attendant validity (Widiger & Trull, 2007). This point is also bolstered by the fact that criteria for some disorders have changed significantly from one edition to another in the evolution of the *DSM* (Coolidge & Segal, 1998; Segal, 2010). Furthermore, criteria for many disorders in the *DSM* are impacted by cultural and subcultural variations in the respondent (see Chapter 4 in this book), as well as by the age of the respondent. Indeed, criteria for many mental disorders do not fit the context of later life and, therefore, some criteria do not adequately capture the presentation of the disorders among many older adults (e.g., Segal, Coolidge, & Rosowsky, 2006; Segal, Qualls, & Smyer, 2011). Thus, certain criteria may be valid only for a particular group of individuals, at a particular point in time, at a particular age. The primary method clinicians currently use to conceptualize diagnoses (the *DSM*), while improving, is far from perfect. Because the *DSM* generally does poorly in attending to issues of age and diversity, interviews based on poor-fitting diagnostic criteria are similarly limited.

In addition to potential problems with *DSM* diagnostic criteria, another issue regarding structured interviews is that it is challenging to establish firmly validity of any particular structured interview. The quandary is that our best means of establishing the validity of a structured interview is to compare diagnoses obtained from such interviews to diagnoses obtained by expert clinicians or by other structured interviews. This is inherently problematic because we cannot be certain that diagnoses by experts or other structured interviews are in fact valid in the first place (Segal et al., 2008).

## Disadvantage: The Tradeoff of Breadth Versus Depth

A final criticism of structured interviews centers on the fact that no one structured interview can be all things in all situations, covering all disorders and eventualities. For example, if a structured interview has been designed to cover an entire diagnostic system (like the *DSM* that identifies several hundred specific disorders), then inquiries about each disorder must be limited to a few inclusion criteria. In this case, the fidelity of the official diagnostic criteria has been compromised for the sake of a comprehensive interview. If fidelity of the criteria is not compromised, then the structured interview becomes unwieldy in terms of time and effort required for its full administration. Most structured interviews attempt some kind of compromise between these two points of tension.

Thus, as to breadth versus depth of approach, users of structured interviews are forced to make a choice about what is most useful in a given situation. Both choices have their limitations. If clinicians or researchers decide to use an interview that provides great breadth of information, they ensure that a wide range of disorders and a great many different areas of a respondent's life are assessed. However, one may not have the depth of information needed to fully conceptualize a case. On the other hand, deciding to use an interview focused on a few specific areas will provide clinicians and researchers with a wealth of information about those specific areas, but it may result in missing information that could lead to additional diagnoses or a different case conceptualization. Thus, it is essential to understand that when choosing a particular structured or semistructured interview, there are often tradeoffs regarding breadth and depth of information.

## Weighing Both Advantages and Disadvantages

Our examination of the strengths and limitations of structured interviews highlights the importance of carefully contemplating what is needed in a particular clinical or research situation before choosing a structured interview. Structured interviews can be invaluable tools in both clinical and research work; however, it is essential that one does not use such tools without accounting for some of the problems inherent in their use. Rogers (2001) voiced the helpful perspective that it would be unwise to view the interviewing process as an either/or proposition (i.e., unstructured vs. structured interview). In certain situations, unstructured interviews may meet the objectives of a particular clinical inquiry more efficiently than a structured interview. For example, in a crisis situation, flexibility on the part of the clinician is required to meet the pressing demands of this fluid and potentially volatile interaction. However, in other cases, greater assurances that the diagnostic conclusions are valid and meaningful would take priority, for example, in clinical research or in the delivery of clearly defined psychotherapeutic intervention protocols. As noted earlier, integration of a nonstandardized or clinical interview with a structured or semistructured interview may also be an excellent option for clinicians and researchers.

Finally, despite some potential limitations to the use of structured and semistructured interviews, their use has clearly revolutionized the diagnostic process, vastly improving diagnostic reliability and validity. Such interviews have greatly improved clinical and research endeavors by providing a more standardized, scientific, and quantitative approach to the evaluation of specific symptoms and mental disorders.

## STRUCTURED AND SEMISTRUCTURED INTERVIEWS FOR DIFFERENTIAL DIAGNOSIS

In this section, we examine several popular structured and semistructured interviews. These interviews can be divided into those that focus on either Axis I clinical disorders or Axis II personality disorders. Axis I instruments include the Anxiety Disorders Interview Schedule for *DSM-IV*, Diagnostic Interview Schedule for *DSM-IV*, the Schedule for Affective Disorders and Schizophrenia, and the Structured Clinical Interview for *DSM-IV* Axis I Disorders. Axis II instruments include the Diagnostic Interview for *DSM* Personality Disorders, the International Personality Disorder Examination, the Structured Clinical Interview for *DSM-IV* Axis II Personality Disorders, and the Structured Interview for *DSM-IV* Personality. A general overview of each instrument is provided in Table 3.2. Each instrument assesses a variety of mental disorders and, therefore, can assist in the important task of differential diagnosis (i.e., a systematic way of discriminating among numerous possible disorders to identify specific ones for which the client meets the diagnostic threshold). Each interview also allows for an assessment of comorbid mental disorders on the diagnostic axis on which it focuses. Instruments presented in this chapter do not represent an exhaustive list of structured and semistructured interviews, but they are among the most common and well-validated ones. Interested readers are referred to Rogers (2001) and Summerfeldt, Kloosterman, and Antony (2010) for coverage of instruments not reviewed in this chapter.

**Table 3.2**

Comparison of Diagnostic Interviews for Both Axis I and II

| Name | Time Required | Format | Comment |
|---|---|---|---|
| Anxiety Disorders Interview Schedule for *DSM-IV* (Brown et al., 1994a) | 45 to 60 minutes | Semistructured, interviewer administered | Provides in-depth assessment of anxiety disorders and other frequently comorbid conditions (e.g., mood, substance use). Designed to be administered by trained mental health professionals with training in administration. Available in separate current and lifetime versions. |
| Diagnostic Interview Schedule for *DSM-IV* (Robins et al., 2000) | 90 to 150 minutes | Fully structured, computerized, closed-ended questions | Designed for epidemiological research. Includes all possible diagnoses in *DSM-IV*. Can be administered by nonclinicians, though interviewers must receive specialized training. |
| Schedule for Affective Disorders and Schizophrenia (Endicott & Spitzer, 1978) | 90 to 150 minutes | Semistructured, interviewer administered | Provides in-depth coverage on Axis I disorders, namely mood and psychotic disorders. Designed for administration by trained mental health professionals, and additional training in administration is required. |
| Structured Clinical Interview for *DSM-IV* Axis I Disorders (First et al., 1997a) | 45 to 90 minutes | Semistructured, interviewer administered | Covers Axis I *DSM-IV* disorders most commonly seen in clinical settings. Designed for use by professionals with knowledge of psychopathology, *DSM-IV* diagnostic criteria, and basic interviewing skills. Research Version and Clinical Version available. |
| Diagnostic Interview for *DSM-IV* Personality Disorders (Zanarini et al., 1996) | 90 minutes | Semistructured, interviewer administered | Designed to assess the 10 standard *DSM-IV* personality disorders. Requirements for administration include at minimum a bachelor's degree, at least 1 year of clinical experience with personality-disordered clients, and several training interviews. |

| International Personality Disorder Examination (Loranger, 1999) | 15 minutes (self-administered screen), 90 minutes (interview) | Contains self-administered pencil-and-paper questionnaire and semistructured interview | Evaluates personality disorders for both the *DSM-IV* and the *International Classification of Diseases, 10th edition (ICD-10)*. Intended for use by experienced clinicians with specialized training in administration. |
|---|---|---|---|
| Structured Clinical Interview for *DSM-IV* Axis II Personality Disorders (First et al., 1997) | 20 minutes (self-administered screen), 60 minutes (interview) | Contains self-report screening questionnaire and semistructured interview | Assesses the 10 standard *DSM-IV* Axis II personality disorders. Designed for administration by professionals with knowledge of psychopathology, *DSM-IV* diagnostic criteria, and basic interviewing skills. |
| Structured Interview for *DSM-IV* Personality (Pfohl et al., 1997) | 60 to 90 minutes | Semistructured interview | Comprehensive interview for *DSM-IV* personality disorders. Collateral sources encouraged. Requirements for administration include an undergraduate degree in the social sciences and 6 months' experience with diagnostic interviewing in addition to specialized training. |

## STRUCTURED AND SEMISTRUCTURED INTERVIEWS FOR AXIS I

*Anxiety Disorders Interview Schedule for* DSM-IV   The Anxiety Disorders Interview Schedule for *DSM-IV* (ADIS-IV; Brown, DiNardo, & Barlow, 1994a) is a semistructured clinician-administered interview designed to measure current episodes of anxiety disorders as defined by the *DSM-IV*. It provides differential diagnosis among anxiety disorders and includes sections on mood, somatoform, and substance use disorders, as anxiety disorders are frequently comorbid with such conditions. There are two versions of the adult ADIS-IV: the Standard Version, which provides only current diagnostic information, and the Lifetime Version (ADIS-IV-L; DiNardo, Brown, & Barlow, 1994), which offers both past and current diagnostic information. The ADIS-IV-L is similar in structure to the ADIS-IV, but contains separate sections that assess the occurrence of disorders in the past. The ADIS-IV can be used in both clinical and research settings.

At the beginning of the ADIS-IV, basic demographic information is collected as well as a short description of the presenting problem. This information gives the examiner an idea of which topics should be pursued in more detail throughout the interview. Following the presenting problem, the examiner asks the respondent "What would you say is the main reason that brought you here today?" and the response is recorded verbatim. Next, the respondent is asked to describe any recent struggles in functioning within the past year (e.g., school, work, relationships). The interview then continues with the assessment of anxiety disorders. This section begins with the more prevalent anxiety disorders (e.g., panic disorder, agoraphobia, social phobia) and is organized logically to reflect the shared symptoms among many anxiety disorders. Subsequent to this segment are sections assessing mood disorders, somatoform disorders, mixed anxiety/depression disorders, alcohol and substance use/dependence, and psychotic and conversion symptoms. A segment assessing the individual's family history of psychological disorders is also included. At the end of the ADIS-IV, the examiner administers the Hamilton Rating Scale for Depression and the Hamilton Anxiety Rating Scale. The clinician manual (Brown, DiNardo, & Barlow, 1994b) notes that these scales are useful as they provide a general assessment of current depressive and anxious symptoms.

Each section on the ADIS-IV includes items assessing diagnostic criteria for the given disorder. The examiner begins with several dichotomous yes/no initial inquiry questions, and answers of "yes" warrant asking more extensive questions to gauge the presence or absence of the particular disorder. In some sections, these dichotomous items are considered skip-out points in which, pending negative ratings, continuation is not necessary. Dimensional ratings are also obtained regarding both current and past experiences of major symptoms of the given disorder. As noted previously, the ADIS-IV-L contains separate sections for current and past occurrences of disorders, whereas the ADIS-IV assesses only current disorders. However, the ADIS-IV contains screening questions for past episodes in the initial inquiry items. If the respondent denotes a positive response to these particular screening questions, the clinician's manual recommends that the interviewer adapt other items in that section to obtain information about previous disorders. The manual notes that this information may be useful in differential diagnosis.

After the initial inquiry section, the clinician continues with the current episode segment of the interview, which provides items that collectively assess all diagnostic criteria for a particular disorder. The questions in the current episode section are arranged so that they begin as open-ended and are followed by more specific inquiries. The need for the more specific inquiries is contingent upon the response to the initial open-ended question. For instance, if the respondent provides a specific response to a question regarding the timeline of a given symptom (e.g., "The symptom began around one month ago"), then follow-up questions may not be needed. The current episode section also contains questions that assess the onset of the disorder and etiological factors. At the conclusion of the current episode section, the administrator again inquiries about past episodes of the disorder. The purpose of this repeated item is that the interviewer can reassess the previous occurrence of the disorder given the wealth of diagnostic information collected in that section. In the ADIS-IV-L, the current episode portion of the interview is followed by the past episode section, which is similar in structure to the current episode segment.

The ADIS-IV contains a score sheet in which the interviewer records diagnoses (including dates of onset) in addition to a diagnostic confidence rating (0–100, 100 indicating complete certainty). If the diagnostic confidence rating is less than 100, the interviewer must indicate why. Each disorder listed is given a rating of clinical severity ranging from 0–8, with higher numbers indicating more distress. Ratings of 0 indicate that there are no features of a given disorder present. These ratings are used to identify clinical versus subclinical disorders, such that ratings of 3 or below indicate subsyndromal symptomatology, and ratings of 4 and above indicate the presence of a disorder (as per the *DSM-IV* criteria). The ADIS-IV-L also contains a diagnostic timeline page, which synthesizes information regarding the temporal sequence of disorders as well as etiology.

The ADIS-IV is designed for use by experienced clinicians who are familiar with the *DSM-IV* as well as the ADIS-IV. Examiners are encouraged to use clinical judgment to determine whether an item should be read verbatim or reworded as needed (e.g., shortening length and complexity of questions for those with lower levels of education). Examiners are also encouraged to use their clinical judgment to gather further clarifying information from respondents and to decide when to skip certain sections of the interview.

Overall, both the ADIS-IV and ADIS-IV-L are popular and valuable tools in diagnosing anxiety disorders as well as frequently comorbid conditions. Studies have indicated empirical support regarding the reliability and validity of the ADIS-IV and ADIS-IV-L, and interested readers are referred to Grisham, Brown, and Campbell (2004) for a summary of the psychometric properties of both tests. The ADIS-IV and ADIS-IV-L have been translated into at least five other languages, and they also have been adapted into a version for use with children. The ADIS-IV interview and manual are available from Oxford University Press (www.us.oup.com).

*Diagnostic Interview Schedule for* DSM-IV   The Diagnostic Interview Schedule for *DSM-IV* (DIS-IV; Robins et al., 2000) is designed to ascertain the presence or absence of major mental disorders of the *DSM-IV* (APA, 1994). It is unique among the multidisorder diagnostic interviews in that it is a *fully structured* interview specifically designed for use by nonclinician interviewers, whereas the other interviews are semistructured. By definition, a fully structured interview clearly specifies all questions and probes and does not permit deviations.

The original DIS was developed in 1978 at the request of the National Institute of Mental Health Division of Biometry and Epidemiology, which was commencing a series of large-scale, multicenter epidemiological investigations of mental disorders in the general adult population in the United States. Development of a structured interview that could be administered by nonclinicians was imperative because of the prohibitive cost of using professional clinicians as interviewers. As a result, the DIS was designed as a fully structured diagnostic interview explicitly crafted so that it could be administered and scored by nonclinician interviewers.

To ensure standardized administration of the DIS-IV, computerized administration is required, which may be interviewer-administered or self-administered. In both formats, the exact wording of all questions and probes is presented to the respondent in a fixed order on a computer screen. Rephrasing of questions is discouraged, although DIS-IV interviewers can repeat questions as necessary to ensure that they are understood by the respondent. All questions are closed-ended, and replies are coded with a forced-choice "yes" or "no" response format. The DIS-IV gathers all necessary information about the person from his or her self-report. Collateral sources of information are not used. The DIS-IV is self-contained and covers all necessary symptoms to make many *DSM-IV* diagnoses. To this end, the *DSM-IV* diagnostic criteria for the disorders have been faithfully turned into specific questions on the DIS-IV. The coded responses are directly entered into a database during the interview, and the diagnosis is made according to the explicit rules of the *DSM-IV* diagnostic system.

Because the DIS-IV was designed for epidemiological research with normative samples, interviewers do not elicit a presenting problem from the respondent, as would be typical in unstructured clinical interviews. Rather, interviewers begin by asking questions about symptoms in a standardized order. Like most of the other structured interviews examined here, the DIS-IV has sections that cover different disorders. Each diagnostic section is independent, except where one diagnosis preempts another. Once a symptom is reported to be present, further closed-ended questions are asked about diagnostically relevant information, such as severity, frequency, time frame, and possibility of organic etiology of the symptom. The DIS-IV includes a set of core questions that are asked of each respondent. Core questions are followed by contingent questions that are administered only if the preceding core question is endorsed. Interviewers use a probe flowchart that indicates which probes to select in which circumstances.

For each symptom, the respondent is asked to state whether it has ever been present and how recently. All data about presence or absence of symptoms and time frames of occurrence are coded and entered into the computer. Consistent with its use of nonclinician interviewers who may not be overly familiar with the *DSM-IV* or psychiatric diagnosis, the diagnostic output of the DIS-IV is generated by a computer program that analyzes data from the completed interview. The output provides estimates of prevalence for two time periods: current and lifetime.

Due to its highly structured format, full administration of the DIS-IV typically requires between 90 and 150 minutes. To shorten administration time, the modular format makes it possible to drop evaluation of disorders that are not of interest in a particular study. Another option is to drop further questioning for a particular disorder once it is clear that the threshold number of symptoms needed for diagnosis will not be met. Although designed for use by nonclinician administrators, training for competent administration of the DIS-IV is necessary. Trainees typically attend a one-week training program at Washington University (St. Louis, Missouri), during which they review the DIS-IV manual, listen to didactic presentations about the structure and conventions of the DIS-IV, view recorded vignettes, complete workbook exercises, and conduct several practice interviews followed by feedback and review. Additional supervised practice is also recommended.

The psychometric properties of the original DIS and its revisions are excellent, and such data has been documented in an impressive array of studies. Interested readers are referred to Compton and Cottler (2004) for an excellent summary of the psychometric characteristics of the DIS-IV. Overall, the DIS-IV has proven to be a popular and useful diagnostic assessment tool, especially for large-scale epidemiological research. The DIS-IV has been translated into more than a dozen languages, is used in countries across the globe for epidemiological research, and served as the basis for the Composite International Diagnostic Interview used by the World Health Organization. For further information on DIS-IV materials, training, and developments, refer to the DIS-IV website (http://epi.wustl.edu).

*Schedule for Affective Disorders and Schizophrenia*  The Schedule for Affective Disorders and Schizophrenia (SADS; Endicott & Spitzer, 1978) is a semistructured diagnostic interview designed to evaluate a range of Axis I clinical disorders, with a focus on mood and psychotic disorders. Ancillary coverage is provided for anxiety symptoms, substance abuse, psychosocial treatment history, and antisocial personality features. The SADS provides in-depth but focused coverage of the mood and psychotic disorders and also supplies meaningful distinctions of impairment in the clinical range for these disorders. The SADS can be used to make many *DSM-IV* diagnoses, but it is not completely aligned with the *DSM* system representing a significant point of concern.

The SADS is intended to be administered to adult respondents by trained mental health professionals. It focuses heavily on the differential diagnosis of mood and psychotic disorders, with great depth of assessment in these areas. In the beginning of the interview, a brief overview of the respondent's background and psychiatric problems is elicited in an open-ended inquiry. The SADS is then divided into two parts, each focusing on a different time period. Part I provides for a thorough evaluation of current psychiatric problems and concomitant functional impairment. A unique feature of the SADS is that for the current episode, symptoms are rated when they were at their worst levels to increase diagnostic sensitivity and validity. In contrast, Part II provides a broad overview of past episodes of psychopathology and treatment. Overall, the SADS covers more than 20 diagnoses in a systematic and comprehensive fashion and provides for diagnosis of both current and lifetime psychiatric disorders. Some examples include schizophrenia (with six subtypes), schizoaffective disorder, manic disorder, hypomanic disorder, major depressive disorder (with 11 subtypes), minor depressive disorder, panic disorder, obsessive compulsive disorder, phobic disorder, alcoholism, and antisocial personality disorder (Endicott & Spitzer, 1978).

In the SADS, questions are clustered according to specific diagnoses. For each disorder, standard questions are specified to evaluate specific symptoms of that disorder. Questions are either dichotomous or rated on a Likert scale, which allows for uniform documentation of levels of severity, persistence, and functional impairment associated with each symptom. To supplement client self-report and obtain the most accurate symptom picture, the SADS allows for consideration of all available sources of information (i.e., chart records, input from relatives). In addition to the standard questions asked of each respondent, optional probes may be selectively used to clarify responses, and unstructured questions may be generated by the interviewer to augment answers to the optional probes. Thus, considerable clinical experience and judgment are needed to administer the SADS. To reduce length of administration and evaluation of symptoms that are not diagnostically significant, many diagnostic sections begin with screening questions that provide for skip-outs to the next section if the respondent shows no evidence of having the disorder. Administration of the SADS typically takes between 90 and 150 minutes. Formal diagnostic appraisals are made by the interviewer after the interview is completed. No computer scoring applications have been designed for the SADS because of the complex nature of the diagnostic process and the strong reliance on clinical judgment.

As noted earlier, the SADS was designed for use by trained clinicians. Considerable clinical judgment, interviewing skills, and familiarity with diagnostic criteria and psychiatric symptoms are requisite for competent administration. As such, it is recommended that the SADS only be administered by professionals with graduate degrees and clinical experience, such as clinical psychologists, psychiatrists, and psychiatric social workers (Endicott & Spitzer, 1978). Training in the SADS is intensive and can encompass several weeks. The process includes reviewing the most recent SADS manual and practice in rating written case vignettes and videotaped SADS interviews. Additionally, trainees typically watch and score live interviews as if participating in a reliability study with a simultaneous-rating design. Throughout, discussion and clarification with expert interviewers regarding diagnostic disagreements or difficulties add to the experience. Finally, trainees conduct their own SADS interviews that are observed and critiqued by the expert trainers.

Numerous additional versions of the SADS have been devised, each with a distinct focus and purpose. Perhaps the most common is the SADS-L (Lifetime version), which can be used to make both current and lifetime diagnoses but has significantly fewer details about current psychopathology than the full SADS and results in a quicker administration time. The SADS-L generally is used with nonpsychiatric samples in which there is no assumption of a significant current psychiatric problem. The SADS-Change Version is also popular and consists of 45 key symptoms from the SADS Part 1. Extensive study of the SADS suggests that it possesses excellent psychometric characteristics. See Rogers, Jackson, and Cashel (2004) for a comprehensive review of these data.

The SADS has been translated into several languages, but its primary use has been in North America. The SADS has been widely used in clinical research over the past three decades, and consequently has a large body of empirical data associated with it. As such, it is often the instrument of choice for clinical researchers desiring in-depth assessment of depression and schizophrenia. The extensive subtyping of disorders provided by the SADS is also highly valued by clinical researchers. However, owing to its length and complexity, the SADS is infrequently chosen for use in many traditional, pure clinical settings (e.g., community mental health centers).

*Structured Clinical Interview for* DSM-IV *Axis I Disorders*   The Structured Clinical Interview for *DSM-IV* Axis I Disorders (SCID-I) is a flexible, semistructured diagnostic interview designed for use by trained clinicians to diagnose many adult *DSM-IV* Axis I clinical disorders. The SCID-I has widespread popularity as an instrument to obtain reliable and valid psychiatric diagnoses for clinical, research, and training purposes, and it has been used in more than 1,000 studies.

The original SCID was designed for application in both research and clinical settings. Recently, the SCID has been split into two distinct versions: the Research Version and the Clinician Version. The Research Version covers more disorders, subtypes, and course specifiers than the Clinician Version and, therefore, takes longer to complete. The benefit, however, is that it provides for a wealth of diagnostic data that is particularly valued by clinical researchers. The research version is distributed by the Biometrics Research Department of the New York State Psychiatric Institute (http://nyspi.org).

The Clinician Version of the SCID (SCID-CV; First, Spitzer, Gibbon, & Williams, 1997a) is designed for use in clinical settings. It has been trimmed to encompass only those *DSM-IV* disorders that are most typically seen in clinical practice and can further be abbreviated on a module-by-module basis. The SCID-CV contains six self-contained modules of major diagnostic categories (Mood Episodes, Psychotic Symptoms, Psychotic Disorders, Mood Disorders, Substance Use Disorders, and Anxiety and Other Disorders).

The modular design of the SCID represents a major strength of the instrument, because administration can be customized easily to meet the unique needs of the user. For example, the SCID can be shortened or lengthened to include only those categories of interest, and the order of modules can be altered. The format and sequence of the SCID was designed to approximate the flowcharts and decision trees followed by experienced diagnostic interviewers. The SCID begins with an open-ended overview portion, during which the development and history of the present psychological disturbance are elicited and tentative diagnostic hypotheses are generated. Then the SCID systematically presents modules that allow for assessment of specific disorders and symptoms. Most disorders are evaluated for two time periods: current (meets criteria for the past month) and lifetime (ever met criteria).

Consistent with its linkage with *DSM-IV*, formal diagnostic criteria are included in the SCID booklet, thus permitting interviewers to see the exact criteria to which the SCID questions pertain. This unique feature makes the SCID an outstanding training tool for clinicians because it facilitates the learning of diagnostic criteria and presents excellent questions to assess the criteria. The SCID has many open-ended prompts that encourage respondents to elaborate freely about their symptoms. At times, open-ended prompts are followed by closed-ended questions to clarify fully a particular symptom. Although the SCID provides structure to cover criteria for each disorder, its semistructured format provides significant latitude for interviewers to restate questions, ask for further clarification, probe, and challenge if the initial prompt was misunderstood by the interviewee or clarification is needed to rate a symptom. SCID interviewers are encouraged to use all sources of information about a respondent, and gentle challenging of the respondent is encouraged if discrepant information is suspected.

During administration, each symptom is rated as either absent (or below threshold) or present (and clinically significant). A question mark (?) denotes that inadequate information was obtained to code the symptom. The SCID flowchart instructs interviewers to skip-out a particular diagnostic section when essential symptoms are judged to be below threshold or absent. These skip-outs result in decreased time of administration as well as the skipping of items with no diagnostic significance. Administration of the SCID is typically completed in one session and takes from 45 to 90 minutes. Once administration is completed, all current and past disorders for which criteria are met are listed on a Diagnostic Summary sheet.

The SCID is optimally administered by trained clinicians. Because of the semistructured format of the SCID, proper administration often requires that interviewers restate or clarify questions in ways that are sometimes not clearly outlined in the manual to judge accurately if a particular diagnostic criterion has been met. The task requires that SCID assessors have a working knowledge of psychopathology, *DSM-IV* diagnostic criteria, and basic interviewing skills. Standard procedures for training to use the SCID include carefully reading the SCID Users Guide (First, Spitzer, Gibbon, & Williams, 1997b), reviewing the SCID administration booklet and score sheet, viewing SCID videotape training materials that are available from the SCID authors, and conducting role-played practice administrations with extensive feedback discussions. Next, trainees may administer the SCID to representative participants who are jointly rated so that a discussion about sources of disagreements can ensue. In research settings, a formal reliability study is advantageous. Reliability and validity of the SCID in adult populations with diverse disorders has been evaluated in several investigations, with generally excellent results among widely varied participant samples and experimental designs (First & Gibbon, 2004; Segal, Hersen, & Van Hasselt, 1994).

Overall, the SCID is a widely used and respected assessment instrument. It has been translated into 12 languages and has been applied successfully in research studies and clinical practice in many countries. Computer-assisted clinician-administered versions of the SCID-CV and SCID Research Version are available. A self-administered computerized screening version of the SCID, called the SCID-Screen-PQ, is also available, but it does not produce final diagnoses. Rather, likely diagnoses are further evaluated by a full SCID interview or a clinical evaluation. For more information on the SCID, visit the SCID website (www.scid4.org).

## SEMISTRUCTURED INTERVIEWS FOR AXIS II

*Diagnostic Interview for Personality Disorders*   The Diagnostic Interview for *DSM-IV* Personality Disorders (DIPD-IV; Zanarini, Frankenburg, Sickel, & Yong, 1996) is a semistructured interview designed to assess the presence or absence of the 10 standard *DSM-IV* personality disorders as well as depressive personality disorder and passive-aggressive personality disorder in the *DSM-IV* appendix. Prior to personality disorder assessment, a full screening for Axis I disorders is recommended. Additionally, an assessment of the respondent's general functioning (e.g., in the domains of work, school, and social life) is advised before administration of the DIPD-IV (Zanarini et al., 1996).

The interview is conducted on a disorder-by-disorder basis. The interview contains 108 sets of questions, each designed to assess a specific *DSM-IV* personality disorder diagnostic criterion. The *DSM-IV* criterion is provided in bold below each set of questions for easy cross-reference. The initial question for each criterion typically has a yes-no format that is followed by open-ended questions to explore more fully clients' experiences. Clients are informed that the interview pertains to the past 2 years of their life and that the interviewer wants to learn about the thoughts, feelings, and behaviors that have been typical for them during the 2-year period. Whereas clients are the sole source of information for rating most of the diagnostic criteria, behavior exhibited during the interview is valued and may override client self-report if there are contradictions. The administrator is encouraged to probe further if responses appear incomplete or untrue.

Each diagnostic criterion is rated on the following scale: "0" indicates absent or clinically insignificant, "1" indicates present but of uncertain clinical significance, "2" indicates present and clinically significant, and "NA" indicates not applicable. After all 108 criteria are evaluated, final categorical diagnosis for each personality disorder is made based on the number of criteria met. The final output is recorded as

"2" indicating "yes" or met full criteria, "1" indicating "subthreshold" (one less than required number of criteria), or "0" indicating "no."

Information about administration and scoring of the DIPD-IV is relatively sparse, at least compared to the other Axis II interviews. Training requirements include at minimum a bachelor's degree, at least 1 year of clinical experience with personality-disordered clients, and several training interviews in which the person observes skilled administrators and then administers the interview. Training tapes and workshops are available, as is a Spanish version. Administration time is typically about 90 minutes. Most notably, the DIPD-IV has been chosen as the primary diagnostic measure for personality disorders in the Collaborative Longitudinal Personality Disorders Study, which is a large, multisite, prospective naturalistic longitudinal study of personality disorders and comorbid mental health problems. For further information on the DIPD-IV, contact Dr. Mary C. Zanarini (zanarini@mclean.harvard.edu).

*International Personality Disorder Examination*   The International Personality Disorder Examination (IPDE; Loranger, 1999) is an extensive, semistructured diagnostic interview administered by experienced clinicians to evaluate personality disorders for both the *DSM-IV* and the *International Classification of Diseases, 10th edition* (*ICD-10*) classification systems. The IPDE was developed within the Joint Program for the Diagnosis and Classification of Mental Disorders of the World Health Organization and U.S. National Institutes of Health aimed at producing a standardized assessment instrument to measure personality disorders on a worldwide basis. As such, the IPDE is the only personality disorder interview based on worldwide field trials. The IPDE manual contains the interview questions to assess either the 11 *DSM-IV* or the 10 *ICD-10* personality disorders. The two IPDE modules (*DSM-IV* and *ICD-10*) contain both a self-administered screening questionnaire and a semistructured interview booklet with scoring materials.

The screening questionnaire is a self-administered form that contains 77 *DSM-IV* or 59 *ICD-10* items written at a fourth-grade reading level. Items are answered either "true" or "false," and the questionnaire is typically completed in about 15 minutes. The clinician can quickly score the questionnaire and identify those respondents whose scores suggest the presence of a personality disorder. Subsequently, the IPDE clinical interview is administered.

The IPDE interview modules (for either the *DSM-IV* or *ICD-10* systems) contain questions, each reflecting a personality disorder criterion, that are grouped into six thematic headings: work, self, interpersonal relationships, affects, reality testing, and impulse control (Loranger, 1999). Because disorders are not covered on a one-by-one basis, the intent of the evaluation is less transparent, similar to the SIDP-IV. At the beginning of each section, open-ended inquiries are provided to enable a smooth transition from the previous section and to encourage respondents to elaborate about themselves in a less structured fashion. Then, specific questions are asked to evaluate each personality disorder criterion. For each question, the corresponding personality disorder and the specific diagnostic criterion are identified with specific scoring guidelines.

Respondents are encouraged to report their typical or usual functioning, rather than their personality functioning during times of episodic psychiatric illness. The IPDE requires that a trait be prominent during the last 5 years to be considered a part of the respondent's personality. Information about age of onset of particular behaviors is explored to determine if a late-onset diagnosis (after age 25 years) is appropriate. When a respondent acknowledges a particular trait, interviewers follow up by asking for examples and anecdotes to clarify the trait or behavior, gauge the impact of the trait on the person's functioning, and fully substantiate the rating. Such probing requires significant clinical judgment and knowledge on the part of interviewers about each criterion. Items may also be rated based on observation of the respondent's behavior during the session, and this too requires a certain level of clinical expertise. To supplement self-report, an interview of informants is encouraged. Clinical judgment is needed to ascertain which source is more reliable if inconsistencies arise.

Each criterion is rated on a scale with the following definitions: "0" indicates that the behavior or trait is absent or within normal limits, "1" refers to exaggerated or accentuated degree of the trait, "2" signifies criterion level or pathological, and "?" indicates the respondent refuses or is unable to answer. Comprehensive item-by-item scoring guidelines are provided in the manual (Loranger, 1999). At the end of the interview, the clinician records the scores for each response on the appropriate IPDE Answer Sheet. Ratings are then collated either by hand or computer. The ultimate output is quite extensive, including presence or absence of each criterion, number of criteria met for each personality disorder, a dimensional score (sum of individual scores for each criterion for each disorder), and a categorical diagnosis (definite, probable, or negative) for each personality disorder (Loranger, 1999). Such comprehensive output is often of value to clinical researchers.

The IPDE is intended to be administered by experienced clinicians who have also received specific training in the use of the IPDE. Such training typically involves a workshop with demonstration videotapes, discussions, and practice. Average administration time is 90 minutes for the interview, which can be reduced by using the screening questionnaire (omitting interview items associated with unlikely personality disorders). Because the IPDE has been selected by the WHO for international application, it has been translated into numerous languages to facilitate cross-cultural research. Ample evidence of reliability and validity of the IPDE has been documented (Loranger et al., 1994; Loranger, 1999). Because of the instrument's ties to the *DSM-IV* and *ICD-10* classification systems and adoption by the WHO, the IPDE is widely used for international and cross-cultural investigations of personality disorders.

*Structured Clinical Interview for* DSM-IV *Axis II Personality Disorders*   To complement the Axis I version of the SCID, a version focusing on Axis II personality disorders according to *DSM-IV* has been developed, and it is called the Structured Clinical Interview for *DSM-IV* Axis II Personality Disorders (SCID-II; First et al., 1997). The SCID-II has a similar semistructured format as the SCID Axis I version, but it covers the 10 standard *DSM-IV* Axis II personality disorders, as well as depressive personality disorder and passive-aggressive personality disorder (which are listed as disorders to be studied further in an appendix of the *DSM-IV*).

For comprehensive assessment, the SCID-II may be easily used in conjunction with the Axis I SCID that would be administered prior to personality disorder assessment. This is encouraged so that the respondent's present mental state can be considered when judging accuracy of self-reported personality traits. The basic structure and conventions of the SCID-II closely resemble those of the SCID-I. An additional feature of the SCID-II is that it includes a 119-item self-report screening component called the Personality Questionnaire that may be administered prior to the interview portion and takes about 20 minutes. The purpose of the Personality Questionnaire is to reduce overall administration time, because only those items that are scored in the pathological direction are further evaluated during the structured interview portion.

During the structured interview component, the pathologically endorsed screening responses are further pursued to determine whether symptoms are actually experienced at clinically significant levels. Here, the respondent is asked to elaborate about each suspected personality disorder criteria and specified prompts are provided. Like the Axis I SCID, the *DSM-IV* diagnostic criteria are printed on the interview page for easy review, and responses are coded as follows: "?" indicates inadequate information, "1" indicates absent or false, "2" indicates subthreshold, and "3" indicates threshold or true. Each personality disorder is assessed completely, and diagnoses are completed before proceeding to the next disorder. The modular format permits researchers and clinicians to tailor the SCID-II to their specific needs and reduce administration time. Clinicians who administer the SCID-II are expected to use their clinical judgment to clarify responses, gently challenge inconsistencies, and ask for additional information as required to rate accurately each criterion. Collection of diagnostic information from ancillary sources is permitted. Complete administration of the SCID-II typically takes less than 60 minutes.

Training requirements and interviewer qualifications are similar to that of the Axis I SCID. There is no Clinician Version of the SCID-II. Psychometric properties of the SCID-II are strong, and interested readers are referred to First and Gibbon (2004) for a comprehensive review. Given the extensive coverage of the personality disorders, modular approach, and strong operating characteristics, the SCID-II should remain a popular and effective tool for personality disorder assessment. The SCID-II website is the same as for the Axis I SCID and can be accessed at www .scid4.org.

*Structured Interview for* DSM-IV *Personality*   The Structured Interview for *DSM-IV* Personality (SIDP-IV; Pfohl, Blum, & Zimmerman, 1997) is a comprehensive semi-structured diagnostic interview for *DSM-IV* personality disorders. It covers 14 *DSM-IV* Axis II diagnoses, including the 10 standard personality disorders, self-defeating personality disorder, depressive personality disorder, negativistic personality disorder, and mixed personality disorder. Prior to the SIDP-IV structured interview, a full evaluation of current mental state or Axis I conditions is required (Pfohl et al., 1997). This is not surprising given that self-report of enduring personality characteristics can be seriously compromised in a respondent who is experiencing acute psychopathology. Indeed, the aim of all personality assessment measures is to rate the respondent's typical, habitual, and lifelong personal functioning rather than acute or temporary states.

Interestingly, the SIDP-IV does not cover *DSM* personality categories on a disorder-by-disorder basis. Rather, *DSM-IV* personality disorder criteria are reflected in items that are grouped according to 10 topical sections that reflect a different dimension of personality functioning. These sections include interests and activities, work style, close relationships, social relationships, emotions, observational criteria, self-perception, perception of others, stress and anger, and social conformity. These categories are not scored; rather, they reflect broad areas of personal functioning under which personality disorder items can logically be subsumed (Pfohl et al., 1997).

Each SIDP-IV question corresponds to a unique *DSM-IV* Axis II criterion, except that one item addresses two criteria. An attractive feature is that the specific *DSM-IV* criterion associated with each question is provided for interviewers to view easily. All questions are administered, and there are no skip-out options. Most questions are conversational in tone and open-ended to encourage respondents to talk about their *usual* behaviors and long-term functioning. In fact, respondents are specifically instructed to focus on their typical or habitual behavior when addressing each item and are prompted to "remember what you are like when you are your usual self." Based on client responses, each criterion is rated on a scale with four anchor points. A rating of "0" indicates that the criterion was not present, "1" corresponds to a subthreshold level where there is some evidence of the trait but it is not sufficiently prominent, "2" refers to the criterion being present for most of the last 5 years, and "3" signifies a strongly present and debilitating level. The SIDP-IV requires that a trait be prominent for most of the last 5 years to be considered a part of the respondent's personality. This 5-year rule helps ensure that the particular personality characteristic is stable and of long duration, as required by the General Diagnostic Criteria for a Personality Disorder described in *DSM-IV*.

A strong point of the organizational format by personality dimensions (rather than by disorders) is that data for specific diagnoses are minimized until final ratings have been collated on the summary sheet. This feature can potentially reduce interviewer biases, such as the halo effect or changing thresholds, if it is obvious that a respondent needs to meet one additional criterion to make the diagnosis. This topical organization also makes the interview's intent less transparent compared to the disorder-by-disorder approach of some other interviews.

Significant clinical judgment is required to properly administer the SIDP-IV, because interviewers are expected to ask additional questions to clarify client responses when necessary. Also, data are not limited to self-report; rather, chart records and significant others such as relatives and friends who know the client well should be consulted when available, and a standard informed consent is included for informant interviews. Such collateral information is particularly prized when evaluating personality-disordered individuals who may lack insight into their own maladaptive personality traits and distort facts about their strengths and limitations. Moreover, informants can also provide diagnostic data that can help resolve the state/trait distinction about specific criterion behaviors.

If discrepancies between sources of information are noted, interviewers must consider all data and use their own judgment to determine the veracity of each source. Making this distinction can be one of the challenges faced by SIDP-IV administrators. Given multiple sources of diagnostic data, final ratings are made after all sources of information are considered. Such ratings are then transcribed onto a summary sheet that lists each criterion organized by personality disorder, and formal diagnoses are assigned. As required by the *DSM*, diagnoses are made only if the minimum number of criteria (or threshold) has been met for that particular disorder.

Minimum qualifications for competent administration consist of an interviewer with an undergraduate degree in the social sciences and 6 months' experience with diagnostic interviewing. Moreover, an additional month of specialized training and practice with the SIDP is required to become a competent interviewer (Pfohl et al., 1997). Administrators are required to possess an understanding of manifest psychopathology and the typical presentation and course of Axis I and Axis II disorders. Training tapes and workshop information are available from the instrument authors. The SIDP typically requires 60 to 90 minutes for the client interview, 20 minutes for interview of significant informants, and approximately 20 minutes to fill out the summary score sheet. Studies documenting the strong psychometric properties of the SIDP are plentiful, and they are summarized in the manual for the instrument (Pfohl et al., 1997).

## SUMMARY AND CONCLUSIONS

This chapter highlights the fact that structured and semistructured interviews have greatly facilitated psychiatric diagnosis, objective measurement of symptoms, *DSM-IV-TR* classification, and problem clarification in a diverse range of clinical and research settings. Reliability of diagnosis is much improved with the use of structured interviews compared to the nonstandardized approach that is common in clinical practice, and improved reliability provides the foundation for enhanced validity of diagnosis. Given the field's recent emphasis on empirically supported psychotherapeutic interventions and processes (e.g., Barlow, 2008; Castonguay & Beutler, 2006; McHugh & Barlow, 2010), we hope that a concomitant focus on clinically relevant, standardized, objective, and validated assessment procedures will be realized as well. Structured and semistructured interviews play an important role in the advancement of the science of clinical psychology.

This chapter provided a broad overview of the basic issues surrounding structured and semistructured interviews, and it described many interviews available to clinicians and researchers. We hope that this information enables clinicians and researchers to choose instruments that will most appropriately suit their needs. Finally, we are aware that with the looming publication of *DSM-5*, it is likely that the major structured and semistructured interviews described in this chapter will need to undergo significant revisions to match the diagnostic changes that will likely occur for many diagnostic categories. As such, this is an exciting time for researchers and clinicians who use structured and semistructured interviews.

## REFERENCES

American Psychiatric Association. (1994). *Diagnostic and statistical manual of mental disorders* (4th ed.). Washington, DC: Author.

American Psychiatric Association. (2000). *Diagnostic and statistical manual of mental disorders* (4th ed., text revision). Washington, DC: Author.

Barlow, D. H. (Ed.). (2008). *Clinical handbook of psychological disorders: A step-by-step treatment manual* (4th ed.). New York, NY: Guilford Press.

Brown, T. A., DiNardo, P. A., & Barlow, D. H. (1994a). *Anxiety Disorders Interview Schedule for DSM-IV (ADIS-IV)*. Albany, NY: Graywind Publications.

Brown, T. A., DiNardo, P. A., & Barlow, D. H. (1994b). *Anxiety Disorders Interview Schedule for DSM-IV: Adult and lifetime version, clinician manual*. Albany, NY: Graywind Publications.

Castonguay, L. G., & Beutler, L. E. (Eds.). (2006). *Principles of therapeutic change that work*. New York, NY: Oxford University Press.

Compton, W. M., & Cottler, L. B. (2004). The Diagnostic Interview Schedule (DIS). In M. Hilsenroth & D. L. Segal (Eds.), *Personality assessment*. Volume 2 in M. Hersen (Ed.-in-Chief), *Comprehensive handbook of psychological assessment* (pp. 153–162). Hoboken, NJ: John Wiley & Sons.

Coolidge, F. L., & Segal, D. L. (1998). Evolution of the personality disorder diagnosis in the Diagnostic and Statistical Manual of Mental Disorders. *Clinical Psychology Review, 18*, 585–599.

Coolidge, F. L., & Segal, D. L. (2010a). Reliability. In I. Weiner & W. E. Craighead (Eds.), *The Corsini encyclopedia of psychology and behavioral science* (4th ed., pp. 1448–1449). Hoboken, NJ: John Wiley & Sons.

Coolidge, F. L., & Segal, D. L. (2010b). Validity. In I. Weiner & W. E. Craighead (Eds.), *The Corsini encyclopedia of psychology and behavioral science* (4th ed., pp. 1826–1828). Hoboken, NJ: John Wiley & Sons.

DiNardo, P. A., Brown, T. A., & Barlow, D. H. (1994). *Anxiety Disorders Interview Schedule for DSM-IV: Lifetime version (ADIS-IV-L)*. Albany, NY: Graywind Publications.

Endicott, J., & Spitzer, R. L. (1978). A diagnostic interview: The schedule for affective disorders and schizophrenia. *Archives of General Psychiatry, 35*, 837–844.

First, M. B., & Gibbon, M. (2004). The Structured Clinical Interview for DSM-IV Axis I Disorders (SCID-I) and the Structured Clinical Interview for DSM-IV Axis II Disorders (SCID-II). In M. Hilsenroth & D. L. Segal (Eds.), *Personality assessment*. Volume 2 in M. Hersen (Ed.-in-Chief), *Comprehensive handbook of psychological assessment* (pp. 134–143). Hoboken, NJ: John Wiley & Sons.

First, M. B., Gibbon, M., Spitzer, R. L., Williams, J. B. W., & Benjamin, L. S. (1997). *Structured Clinical Interview for DSM-IV Axis II Personality Disorders (SCID-II)*. Washington, DC: American Psychiatric Press.

First, M. B., Spitzer, R. L., Gibbon, M., & Williams, J. B. W. (1997a). *Structured Clinical Interview for DSM-IV Axis I Disorders: Clinician version (SCID-CV)*. Washington, DC: American Psychiatric Press.

First, M. B., Spitzer, R. L., Gibbon, M., & Williams, J. B. W. (1997b). *User's guide to the Structured Clinical Interview for DSM-IV Axis I Disorders: Clinician version (SCID-CV)*. Washington, DC: American Psychiatric Press.

Grisham, J. R., Brown, T. A., & Campbell, L. A. (2004). The Anxiety Disorders Interview Schedule for DSM-IV (ADIS-IV). In M. J. Hilsenroth & D. L. Segal (Eds.), *Personality assessment*. Volume 2 in M. Hersen (Ed.-in-Chief), *Comprehensive handbook of psychological assessment* (pp. 163–177). Hoboken, NJ: John Wiley & Sons.

Loranger, A. W. (1999). *International Personality Disorder Examination (IPDE)*. Odessa, FL: Psychological Assessment Resources.

Loranger, A. W., Sartorius, N., Andreoli, A., Berger, P., Buchheim, P., Channabasavanna, S. M., . . . Regier, D. A. (1994). The International Personality Disorder Examination: The World Health Organization/Alcohol, Drug Abuse, and Mental Health Administration international pilot study of personality disorders. *Archives of General Psychiatry, 51*, 215–224.

McHugh, R. K., & Barlow, D. H. (2010). The dissemination and implementation of evidence-based psychological treatments. *American Psychologist, 65*, 73–84.

Pfohl, B., Blum, N., & Zimmerman, M. (1997). *Structured Interview for DSM-IV Personality.* Washington, DC: American Psychiatric Press.

Robins, L. N., Cottler, L. B., Bucholz, K. K., Compton, W. M., North, C. S., & Rourke, K. (2000). *Diagnostic Interview Schedule for DSM-IV (DIS-IV).* St. Louis, MO: Washington University School of Medicine.

Rogers, R. (2001). *Handbook of diagnostic and structured interviewing.* New York, NY: Guilford Press.

Rogers, R. (2003). Standardizing DSM-IV diagnoses: The clinical applications of structured interviews. *Journal of Personality Assessment, 81*, 220–225.

Rogers, R., Jackson, R. L., & Cashel, M. (2004). The Schedule for Affective Disorders and Schizophrenia (SADS). In M. Hilsenroth & D. L. Segal (Eds.), *Personality assessment.* Volume 2 in M. Hersen (Ed.-in-Chief), *Comprehensive handbook of psychological assessment* (pp. 144–152). Hoboken, NJ: John Wiley & Sons.

Segal, D. L. (2010). Diagnostic and statistical manual of mental disorders (DSM-IV-TR). In I. Weiner & W. E. Craighead (Eds.), *The Corsini encyclopedia of psychology and behavioral science* (4th ed., pp. 495–497). Hoboken, NJ: John Wiley & Sons.

Segal, D. L., & Coolidge, F. L. (2001). Diagnosis and classification. In M. Hersen & V. B. Van Hasselt (Eds.), *Advanced abnormal psychology* (2nd ed., pp. 5–22). New York, NY: Kluwer Academic/Plenum.

Segal, D. L., Coolidge, F. L., & Rosowsky, E. (2006). *Personality disorders and older adults: Diagnosis, assessment, and treatment.* Hoboken, NJ: John Wiley & Sons.

Segal, D. L., & Hersen, M. (Eds.). (2010). *Diagnostic interviewing* (4th ed.). New York, NY: Springer.

Segal, D. L., Hersen, M., & Van Hasselt, V. B. (1994). Reliability of the Structured Clinical Interview for DSM-III-R: An evaluative review. *Comprehensive Psychiatry, 35*, 316–327.

Segal, D. L., Maxfield, M., & Coolidge, F. L. (2008). Diagnostic interviewing. In M. Hersen & A. M. Gross (Eds.), *Handbook of clinical psychology, Volume 1: Adults* (pp. 371–394). Hoboken, NJ: John Wiley & Sons.

Segal, D. L., Qualls, S. H., & Smyer, M. A. (2011). *Aging and mental health* (2nd ed.). Hoboken, NJ: John Wiley & Sons.

Summerfeldt, L. J., Kloosterman, P. H., & Antony, M. M. (2010). Structured and semistructured diagnostic interviews. In M. M. Antony & D. H. Barlow (Eds.), *Handbook of assessment and treatment planning for psychological disorders* (2nd ed., pp. 95–140). New York, NY: Guilford Press.

Widiger, T. A., & Samuel, D. B. (2005). Evidence based assessment of personality disorders. *Psychological Assessment, 17*, 278–287.

Widiger, T. A., & Trull, T. J. (2007). Plate tectonics in the classification of personality disorder: Shifting to a dimensional model. *American Psychologist, 62*, 71–83.

Zanarini, M. C., Frankenburg, F. R., Sickel, A. E., & Yong, L. (1996). *The Diagnostic Interview for DSM-IV Personality Disorders (DIPD-IV).* Belmont, MA: McLean Hospital.

# CHAPTER 4

# Impact of Race and Ethnicity on the Expression, Assessment, and Diagnosis of Psychopathology

SUSAN TINSLEY LI, SANDRA JENKINS, and SOPHIA GREWAL

THIS CHAPTER PROVIDES an overview and framework for understanding race and ethnicity as factors that affect adult psychopathology. Of primary interest is the assessment and diagnosis of psychopathology in diverse individuals that is responsible, responsive, and knowledgeable with respect to the unique issues that nondominant individuals bring to the mental health arena. The chapter is organized into three sections. In the first section, we address multicultural competency. The second section includes considerations for assessment with diverse individuals. The final section focuses specifically on the process of diagnosis with ethnic minorities while attempting to identify common concerns and pitfalls.

Competent and ethical multicultural diagnosis continues to be a daunting and dubious endeavor even after three decades of changes in philosophy, instrumentation, and research methods. Starting in the 1950s and 1960s, social forces such as the civil rights, women's, and gay/lesbian movements have exerted considerable pressure on mental health professionals to reexamine the state of fair, humane, competent, and equitable treatment practices. As a result of these influences there was a momentous increase in multicultural research in psychology. The early 2000s were marked by a significant increase in writings regarding multicultural/cross-cultural assessment in neuropsychology (Fletcher-Janzen, Strickland, & Reynolds, 2000), general multicultural assessment (Suzuki & Ponterotto, 2007), and personality assessment (Dana, 2000).

Other forces, notably demographic and economic forces, have been major factors in the ongoing efforts to reevaluate the appropriateness of traditional mainstream standards for multicultural practice. The United States is rapidly undergoing a redistribution of racial and ethnic populations. By the middle of the current century it is projected that the composition of the United States will be 13.3% foreign-born; Caucasians 52.8%; African Americans 14.7%; Hispanics 24.5%; Asians/Pacific Islanders 9.3%, and Native Americans 1.1%. Other projections suggest that visible minority groups will make up more than half of the U.S. population before mid-century (Dana, 1996; Stuart, 2004; Sue, Arredondo, & McDavis, 1992). These transitions are because of worldwide immigration patterns and differences in birth rates (Chui, 1996). In some states, such as California, New Mexico, Hawaii, and the District of Columbia, the transition has already occurred and minorities are no longer statistical minorities. These changing demographics are reflected in the 2010 census data, which show increases in non-Caucasian populations in the United States that range from 2 to 8 times the percentage increases from 2000 to 2010 for Caucasians (U.S. Census Bureau, 2011). The largest increases are found for Latino and Asian populations, which increased 43% and 43.3%, respectively, in the last 10 years.

Demographic and social change pressures have propelled the philosophy that mental health has an inherent cultural component (Good, 1996). Cultural dimensions affect the expressions of different symptoms, the uniformity of psychological constructs, and the validity of assessment instruments. The main thrust of post-1960s mental health standards has been to identify the need for culturally sensitive and culturally relative diagnosis and treatment. In response to the addition of culture as a moderator variable, psychological and psychiatric associations revised their guidelines for practice to include competency and appropriate practice with ethnic minority groups.

## MULTICULTURAL COMPETENCY

When considering the need for multicultural competency, the mandate is clear. Researchers and clinicians are called upon to work with and serve a variety of individuals, groups, and families that differ significantly from the population on which the prevailing measures and diagnostic systems are based. Recognizing the need for change, the American Psychological Association (APA) has issued a set of guidelines that outline areas in which psychologists are called upon to gain cultural competency (APA, 2002b). *The Guidelines on Multicultural Education, Training, Research, Practice, and Organizational Change for Psychologists* build upon the work of authors such as Sue and Sue (2007) and Arredondo et al. (1996), who were instrumental in originally conceptualizing the components of multicultural competency, such as clinician awareness and attitudes, knowledge, and skills.

The six APA guidelines cover the broad array of roles and settings in which psychologists encounter diverse individuals. The guidelines are less restrictive than mandated requirements such as those provided in the APA ethics code (APA, 2002a), but they are also expected to be viewed as "strongly encouraged" rather than as purely aspirational goals. It is incumbent on the professional to personally drive the movement toward greater competency in the domains in which the professional functions. Unlike previous clinical service–oriented guidelines, these guidelines also address research and organizational change in addition to clinical competency (Resnick, 2006). Three guidelines specifically focus on the clinician, including the clinician's attitudes, beliefs, and biases (guideline 1), recognition of the importance of cultural competency (guideline 2), and responsibility to provide culturally competent services (guideline 5). Guidelines 4 and 6, respectively, address the importance of conducting culturally competent research and the importance of cultural competence within organizations and involvement in organizational policy. Guideline 3 is directed toward educators and focuses on the importance of diversity in a clinician's education. Together, these guidelines lay a foundation for responsible research and practice with ethnic and racial minorities.

## MULTICULTURAL CONSIDERATIONS

Diagnosis and assessment with racial and ethnic minority individuals requires knowledge of key considerations that impact these processes. Multicultural considerations include ethnic identity of the individual, level of acculturation, psychological mindedness, and willingness to access mental health services. Table 4.1 provides a list and examples of some cultural issues that can impact diagnosis and assessment.

Although this list is not comprehensive, it includes many of the typical areas of content covered in general human diversity courses. In the move toward integrating diversity within courses on psychopathology and assessment, these areas must become integrated into competent diagnosis and assessment. For example,

**Table 4.1**
Multicultural Considerations

**Ethnic identity**

Examples: Affirmation and belonging; ethnic pride; self, group, and other orientation as appreciating or deprecating; stages of development

**Acculturation**

Examples: Immigration/generational status; behavioral versus attitudinal acculturation; acculturative stress

**Beliefs about illness**

Examples: Beliefs about the origin and cause of disease; amount of external control; acceptability of distress, pain, or mental illness

**Manifestation of symptoms**

Examples: Emotional expressivity, somatization, and definition of pathology

**Norms/values within the culture and worldview**

Examples: Collectivism, familism

**Resiliency and natural sources of protection**

Examples: Elicitation of individual, family, and cultural strengths/competencies

**Need for systemic involvement**

Examples: Information as viewed by the client, the family, the community, and by professionals; level of distress and perceived functioning as reported by multiple systems

**Orientation to mental health services**

Examples: Cultural perception of outside intervention; familiarity with mental health services; issues of underutilization; trust, shame, stigma, and knowledge about potential treatments; use of traditional providers and alternative treatments

**Nature of reporting**

Examples: Use of stories; brief versus extended answers; cultural proscriptions against disclosure; verbal and nonverbal behaviors; other forms of expression such as art, poetry, music, play, and drawings; cultural responses to Likert scales differences in the manifestation of symptoms for dominant and nondominant individuals can ultimately affect the selection of appropriate measures and the diagnoses given. Consider the following true case example:

> Ms. N is a 19-year-old Vietnamese immigrant who was admitted to the inpatient unit at the state hospital for psychotic symptoms. Upon entering the day room, the examiner (who was also of Asian descent) approached the patient and greeted her. The patient immediately fell to her knees, prostrated herself, and began praying to the examiner as if she were one of her ancestors. Ms. N would not return to her chair or stand as requested, but continued to remain on her knees throughout the encounter.

This situation raises several issues to be considered. Germane to accurate diagnosis of Ms. N is her level of acculturation, her beliefs about illness, and the way in which she is manifesting symptoms. The function of her behaviors and how normative these are within her cultural context will impact the severity of the diagnosis given and whether a diagnosis of psychosis is truly warranted.

## ASSESSMENT

One of the major issues in effective assessment of racial and ethnic minorities is identifying the appropriate measures that should be used with a given individual or population (Knight, Roosa, & Umma-Taylor, 2009; Wong, Strickland, Fletcher-Janzen, Ardila, & Reynolds, 2000). Standard 9.02 of the American Psychological Association Ethics Code (APA, 2002a) emphasizes using instruments that have established reliability and validity for use with members of the population tested. Although there is no doubt that using measures validated for a given population is appropriate and best practice, there are several difficulties in meeting this standard. Rarely are clinical instruments standardized on members of ethnic and racial groups with the same rigor applied to the dominant Caucasian group. Even when diverse individuals are included within the standardization sample, a careful review of the manual frequently reveals that the actual numbers within each group is small and unlikely to be representative. Although some authors have issued a call for test developers to provide better standardization (e.g., Okazaki & Sue, 2000), other authors have pointed out the unlikelihood of such a change occurring and the impossibility of ever standardizing a test on all of the myriad of ethnic groups on which the test will eventually be used (Hays, 2007). Thus, it becomes incumbent on the examiner to understand the limitations of assessment measures when used with ethnic and racial minorities and to be familiar with the areas of knowledge necessary for competency.

### CROSS-CULTURAL MEASUREMENT EQUIVALENCE

Fundamental to the assessment enterprise are issues of validity and reliability. In the realm of diversity assessment, reliability and validity are linked to questions of cross-cultural measurement equivalence. The literature on cross-cultural measurement equivalence has grown substantially in the last 20 years, such that a set of key terms and statistical techniques has been identified and associated with quality work in this area. At a fundamental level, the goal of measurement equivalence studies is to determine if a particular instrument is valid for use with a population on which the measure was not initially developed or standardized. Knight et al. (2009), Allen and Walsh (2000), and Nichols, Padilla, and Gomez-Maqueo (2000) have defined a similar set of guidelines for determining measurement equivalence that include linguistic or translation equivalence, conceptual equivalence, and psychometric equivalence (see also Arnold & Matus, 2000; Byrne et al., 2009).

Linguistic/translation equivalence involves the accuracy of the translation and whether diverse individuals have a similar understanding of words or phrases used in the instrument. There is a standard for appropriate translation of a measure that involves both forward and back translation (e.g., Butcher, 1996). A poor-quality translation is easily detected by the absence of back translation in the development process, or by using untrained translators who are not fully bilingual (i.e., are not fully proficient in both languages, but show limited or partial bilingualism). Despite the presence of this standard, there continue to be translations of measures by untrained individuals without adequate education in both languages.

Of greatest concern to assessment is the notion of conceptual equivalence or whether the underlying construct holds the same meaning across groups. Do dominant and nondominant individuals give equivalent meaning to the construct, such that psychosis or psychotic thought processes are the same concept in both groups? A common example of difficulty is when one group defines specific behaviors as mental illness or psychopathology while another group views the same behaviors as normative and not associated with a cluster of diagnostic symptoms.

Once the translation phase is complete and there is reasonable certainty that the constructs are equivalent across groups, additional steps are required to determine whether there is psychometric equivalence. Using configural invariance, scalar equivalence, metric equivalence, and item equivalence, psychometric equivalence addresses the issue of whether the instrument measures the same attribute among people from different groups. Statistical procedures for determining the psychometric equivalence of measures have been outlined by various authors and continue to be developed (Hui & Triandis, 1985; Kankaras & Moors, 2010; Knight & Hill, 1998; Vandenberg & Lance, 2000). Debate exists as to whether differences at the item level appear at the scale level (Bruno, 2003) and the best way to establish equivalence. However, the ultimate goal of psychometric equivalence studies is the same. A well-validated and reliable measure should manifest the same psychometric properties across groups so that conclusions based on the measure are not biased. For example, can a clinical cutoff score for one population be used in the second population without resulting in greater misclassification such as increased false positives and false negatives? Do dominant and nondominant individuals respond to a Likert scale in similar ways? As Orlando and Marshall (2002) found when evaluating a PTSD scale for use with Latinos, nondominant groups often do not use standard response categories in the same fashion as Caucasians on whom the scale was developed. There is evidence that Latino individuals may be more prone to utilizing specific response styles when answering questions on traditional Likert-type scales (Hui & Triandis, 1989; Marin, Gamba, & Marin, 1995). These response styles, termed extreme response and acquiescence response, introduce measurement error and can bias self-report data (Weijters, Geuens, & Schillewaert, 2010). Thus, cultural factors influence how individuals respond to questionnaires and whether they are likely to use the upper- or lower-extreme values of a rating scale (Arce-Ferrer, 2006).

Examples of well-conducted measurement equivalence studies come from the depression literature. Cross-cultural measurement equivalence has been a focus of attention for researchers interested in measures of symptomatology and depression for Caucasians and Latinos (Crockett, Randall, Shen, Russell, & Driscoll, 2005; Knight, Virdin, Ocampo, & Roosa, 1994; Posner, Stewart, Marin, & Perez-Stable, 2001). Posner et al. (2001) found a lack of both configural and metric equivalence for the Center for Epidemiological Studies Depression Scale (CES-D) among Latino males. However, the measure was found to be more appropriate for Latino females. Crockett et al. (2005) reported mixed evidence for the equivalence of the CES-D across Caucasian, Mexican-American, Cuban, and Puerto Rican adolescents. Better psychometric properties were found for 10-item short versions of the CES-D with Mexican immigrants (Grzywacz, Hovey, Seligman, Arcury, & Quandt, 2006).

Crockett et al.'s findings indicated that the CES-D would likely underestimate depression in 1% to 2% of youths and could result in greater risk of misclassification with particular Latino subgroups (i.e., Cuban and Puerto Rican) because of differences in the nature of symptoms expressed. Another depression instrument, the Beck Depression Inventory, has shown promising results in a college sample of acculturated Latino students, but has not been validated for use with older or less-acculturated samples who are likely to show greater differences (Contreras, Fernandez, Malcarne, Ingram, & Vaccarino, 2004). Furthermore, differential item functioning has been found for a Spanish translation of the Beck Depression Inventory when used with a Latino medical sample (Azocar, Arean, Miranda, & Munoz, 2001).

Measurement studies such as Posner et al. (2001) have important implications for the assessment of symptomatology and establishing the prevalence of psychopathology in racial and ethnic minorities. More research is needed to establish measurement equivalence for instruments most frequently used by psychologists for diagnostic purposes. For widely adopted psychopathology measures such as the MMPI-2 and PAI, there is modest availability of writings with regard to the use of this measure across cultures (Carbonell, 2000; Fernandez, Boccaccini, & Noland, 2008; Nichols et al., 2000; Okazaki & Sue, 2000), but for most clinical assessment tools, the evidence is lacking.

Given the dearth of instruments for which equivalence has been established, researchers and clinicians are left to determine how to ensure responsible and ethical assessment of racial and ethnic minorities. At a basic level, competent interpretation is emphasized. Standards 9.02 and 9.06 of the APA Ethics Code (APA, 2002a) state that if validity and reliability of a measure have not been established, then strengths and limitations of the results and subsequent interpretations need to be described to account for cultural differences. However, these standards only address the outcome of the assessment and not the process. Guidance for how to modify the assessment process for diverse individuals exist in the multicultural assessment literature.

## MODELS OF MULTICULTURAL ASSESSMENT

The proliferation of research has led to several multicultural assessment models to guide the evaluation of ethnic and racial minorities. These models build upon the multicultural considerations previously presented and attempt to outline the process of assessment with racial and ethnic minorities. For example, Dana (1998, 2000, 2005) developed a Multicultural Assessment-Intervention Process Model (MAIP) for research and practice with multicultural populations. The model includes an elaborate flowchart in which the answers to seven questions lead the reader through a series of decision points to arrive at a diagnostic formulation and intervention appropriate to that individual.

Through the process of answering the seven questions (see Table 4.2), the evaluator addresses the individual's cultural orientation, evaluates the availability of etic (i.e., universal) and emic (i.e., culture-specific) instruments, assesses the appropriateness of using standard norms, considers the need for a culture-specific orientation, and determines whether a diagnosis is truly necessary. The final diagnostic formulation that results from the flowchart can range from a universal diagnostic formulation to a standard Caucasian diagnostic formulation to a combined formulation with both standard Caucasian and culture-specific elements.

**Table 4.2**
Models of Multicultural Assessment

| Grieger & Ponterotto's Six-Step Applied Assessment Framework (Ponterotto, Gretchen, & Chauhan, 2001) | Dana's Multicultural Assessment-Intervention Process Model (MAIP) (Dana, 1998, 2000, 2005) | Morris's Culturally Sensitive Assessment and Treatment Model (Morris, 2000) |
|---|---|---|
| 1. Client's level of psychological mindedness<br>2. Family's level of psychological mindedness<br>3. Client's and family's attitudes toward helping and counseling<br>4. Client's level of acculturation<br>5. Family's level of acculturation<br>6. Family's attitude toward acculturation | 1. Is an etic (universal) instrument available?<br>2. What is the individual's cultural orientation?<br>3. Is a clinical diagnosis necessary?<br>4. Is there an emic (culture-specific) instrument available?<br>5. Can Anglo or standard norms be used?<br>6. Is there cross-cultural interaction stress such that a culture-specific conceptualization is required?<br>7. Is a diagnosis necessary? | 1. Worldview—Predominant Eurocentric to predominantly ethnic<br>2. Racial Identity<br>3. Treatment Goals—Individual goals versus cultural goals or some balance of both<br>4. Assessment Measures—Standard measures, modified measures, or culture-specific measures<br>5. Conceptual Synthesis—Monocultural American to cross-cultural to monocultural ethnic<br>6. Intervention Strategies—Universal strategies, combined, or culture-specific strategies<br>7. Diagnosis—Appropriate, appropriate with clarification, or inappropriate |

The formulation is considered to directly impact any interventions chosen. Interventions may be culture-universal, culture-general, a combination of culture-general and culture-specific, culture-specific, or identity-specific, depending on the answers to the seven questions.

The emphasis on the consideration of client characteristics found in Dana's (2000) model and the range of outcomes possible for each individual (i.e., specific to universal) is reflected in other models of cross-cultural assessment, such as Grieger and Ponterotto's Six-Step Applied Assessment Framework (Burkhard & Ponterotto, 2007; Ponterotto, Gretchen, & Chauhan, 2001) and Morris's (2000) Culturally Sensitive Assessment and Treatment Model. Detailed steps for each of these models are listed in Table 4.2. Other writers such as Gopaul-McNicol and Armour-Thomas (2002) have addressed topics such as report writing and testing the limits with diverse individuals in addition to considering individual aspects of cultural orientation.

## SYMPTOM EXPRESSION AND DIAGNOSIS

The manner in which an individual describes their psychological distress varies from person to person. However, the current diagnostic system (American Psychiatric Association, 2000) assumes some commonalities across symptom clusters. The problem with this assumption is that research defining those symptom clusters was largely based on Caucasian-American individuals. Consequently, experiences of psychological distress by individuals from nondominant cultures may not be captured in the diagnostic descriptions, and, conversely, symptoms linked to pathology in dominant individuals may not be indicative of pathology for some individuals from nondominant cultures. Draguns and Tanaka-Matsumi (2003) suggested that symptom expression may vary according to various cultural dimensions (Hofstede, 2001) such as an individualistic or collectivistic orientation. For example, people from more individualistic cultures may be more likely to express psychological distress and dysfunction through symptoms of "guilt, alienation, and loneliness" (p. 768), whereas people from more collectivistic cultures may be more likely to describe symptoms of "unrewarding personal relationships, social rejection, and shame" (p. 768). These general themes may be helpful when determining whether self-reported experiences are part of a pathological or culturally concordant process (see also Diaz et al., 2009; Fields, 2010; Mackin, Targum, Kalali, Rom, & Young, 2006).

### SOMATIZATION ACROSS CULTURES

According to the U.S. Department of Health and Human Services (U.S. DHHS) in *Mental Health: Culture, Race, and Ethnicity—A Supplement to Mental Health: A Report of the Surgeon General* (2001), somatization is a common presentation of distress across all cultures; however, the type and frequency of bodily symptoms expressed may vary. For example, Latinos and Caucasians may report abdominal problems (e.g., stomachache or chest pains), Asians may report vestibular problems (e.g., feeling dizzy or having trouble seeing clearly), and Africans may report burning sensations in their extremities (U.S. DHHS, 2001). Although there is a general tendency toward somatization across all cultures, ethnic minority individuals in the United States are likely to express distress through bodily symptoms for two primary reasons: (1) as compared to Caucasians, there is a higher level of stigma associated with mental illness, and (2) there is less of a distinction between mind and body among ethnic minorities (U.S. DHHS, 2001).

There are also specific instances under which the tendency to somaticize distress is more likely. For example, the context of talking to a mental health worker may increase the likelihood that a Chinese individual will express bodily symptoms rather than affective symptoms. African Americans tend to express mild somatic symptoms more frequently than Caucasians. Specific subgroups of the Latino population are more likely than others to report bodily symptoms as an expression of mental distress. Puerto Ricans tend to somaticize more than Mexican Americans, and Mexican-American women more than 40 years old tend to somaticize more than Caucasians. Allen, Gara, Escobar, Waitzkin, and Silver (2001) found a significant rate of somatization in a sample of adults from a primary care setting in which 64% of the participants were of Latino descent. Somatization was associated with higher rates of depression and anxiety in this group. In sum, somatization of psychological distress occurs across cultures, and yet culture sets the parameters for how people report these bodily symptoms.

It is important to note that not all studies have reported the same patterns of increased somatization for ethnic minorities. Zhang and Snowden (1999) reported data from a multicity study of 18,152 community residents in which they did not find increased somatization among Hispanic and Asian Americans as compared to Caucasians. In fact, they found that although Hispanic Americans reported similar rates of somatic symptoms as Caucasians, Asian Americans actually reported significantly fewer somatic symptoms than Caucasians. Consistent with the Surgeon General's report (U.S. DHHS, 2001), however, Zhang and Snowden found that African Americans reported more somatic symptoms than Caucasians.

## INFLUENCE OF LANGUAGE

Another influence on symptom expression is the language of discourse (Acevedo, Reyes, Annett, & Lopez, 2003; Diaz et al., 2009). Malgady and Constantino (1998) examined the influence of language by experimentally varying the language spoken during the interview using Hispanic clinicians. They found that severity of psychopathology (as measured by the Brief Psychiatric Rating Scale) was highest in the bilingual condition, followed by the Spanish-speaking condition, and then the English-speaking condition. According to the results of this study, there was a tendency for clinicians to rate Latino clients speaking Spanish or Spanish and English as having more severe psychopathology and as functioning less well than Latino clients speaking English only. Malgady and Constantino aptly noted that "what remains to be determined is whether or not this is bias in the form of overly pathologizing on the clinicians' part or whether they are more sensitive to patients' presenting symptoms" (p. 125). Regardless, there appears to be an important effect of language on diagnosis.

## PATHOLOGICAL VERSUS NONPATHOLOGICAL SYMPTOMS

Classical training in diagnosis emphasizes certain behaviors and symptoms as indicators of pathological processes. However, cultural differences in belief systems, values, and experiences shape the extent to which behaviors are or are not part of a pathological process. The most obvious examples are paranoid ideation and hallucinations, which are often quickly labeled as psychosis in the dominant U.S. culture and, therefore, part of a pathological process. However, this may not be the case for nondominant individuals for whom the specific symptoms may be more normative. Sharpley, Hutchinson, McKenzie, and Murray (2001) described how a paranoid attributional style among African and African-Caribbean individuals in the United Kingdom resulted not from an inherent biological pathology but was based on "their experience of social disadvantage and racial discrimination in the United Kingdom." This experience results in (1) a need to question self-perception and identity, and (2) more threat in their everyday social life (Sharpley et al., 2001, p. 65). Researchers in the United States have come to similar conclusions regarding the relationship of paranoia to social disadvantage and attributional style among ethnic minorities. Whaley (1998) found that paranoia and mistrust were associated not only with African Americans but with many different groups who have experienced powerlessness, such as women, people of low socioeconomic status, and people with less education. He, like Sharpley et al. (2001), purported that paranoia and mistrust were related to attributional style:

> If people live in an environment in which they experience powerlessness in the face of victimization, then paranoia serves a self-protective function. People can protect their self-esteem and prevent depression associated with experiences of failure, when they can attribute that failure to the power of external others. (p. 328)

### SYMPTOM EXPRESSION AND DIAGNOSIS

Psychotic disorders are noted to be overdiagnosed among African Americans and others when a diagnosis of depression (or no diagnosis) may be more accurate (Whaley, 1998). He argued that paranoia among African Americans may be less often part of a psychotic, pathological spectrum and more often part of a normal experience of an oppressed individual. The explanations put forth by these authors further illustrate the tendency for an overemphasis on pathological explanations among dominant-culture individuals when diagnosing and evaluating nondominant individuals. Besides paranoia, another symptom that can often be mistaken as inherently pathological is hallucinations. Geltman and Chang (2004) interviewed Caribbean Latinos (85% of whom were from Puerto Rico or the Dominican Republic) receiving outpatient mental health treatment and found that 46% of them reported some experience of hallucinations. Furthermore, they found that "hallucinations were not associated with clinical variables including neurological illness, history of head trauma, mood disorders, and current or prior substance abuse" (Geltman & Chang, 2004, p. 154). Draguns and Tanaka-Matsumi (2003) reviewed the literature on hallucinations across cultures and stated that many aspects of hallucinations are culturally determined, such as the definition of the experience as pathological or not and the sensory modality through which they are most commonly experienced.

These authors suggested that determining whether the hallucinations are a symptom of pathology or part of a culturally concordant experience includes assessment of environmental effects, factors, and settings before and after the experience. "Like any other behavior, hallucinations become a symptom when they are so labeled" (Draguns & Tanaka-Matsumi, 2003, p. 765). In summary, paranoid ideation and hallucinations are examples of two symptoms that may lead to misdiagnosis owing to differences in conceptualizations across cultures.

## Role of Stereotypes, Biases, and the Clinician's Culture

Different prevalence of symptom clusters among various ethnic groups create questions about the role of stereotypes, biases, and Eurocentric training of clinicians. For example, Minsky, Vega, Miskimen, Gara, and Escobar (2003) attributed the higher rates of depression in Latinos to "cultural variances in characteristic symptom clusters typically used by clinicians as a template for assigning a diagnosis in a treatment setting" (p. 643). Furthermore, Gonzales et al. (1997) stated that clinicians tended to restrict their diagnoses of Mexican Americans to a fraction of the disorders represented in the *DSM*. They hypothesized that this restriction may be based on clinicians' interpretation of the idiom of distress displayed by Mexican Americans or possibly the clinicians' stereotypes of Mexican American patients. Biases not only affect the diagnoses of ethnic minority individuals, but they may also lead to underdiagnosis of dominant individuals.

There are numerous examples of how stereotypes can influence clinician judgments. In one experimental study (Abreu, 1999), stereotypes of African Americans, unrelated to psychopathology, were primed prior to giving clinicians a vignette. There was an interaction between years of clinician experience and the race of the individual in the vignette, such that more experienced clinicians gave more pathological interpretations of the vignette when the individual in the vignette was revealed to be African American (versus when the race of the individual in the vignette was not disclosed). Abreu hypothesized that the potentially racially based "clinical schemas [of the experienced clinicians] may be the source of biases in clinical judgment" (p. 392).

In their article on the role of health care providers in maintaining racial and ethnic disparities in access to services, van Ryn and Fu (2003) summarized the impact of social cognition research for providers:

> It is both difficult and painful for many of us to accept the massive evidence that social categories automatically and unconsciously influence the way we perceive people and, in turn, influence the way in which we interpret their behavior and behave toward them. However, given that this type of strategy is common to all humans in all cultures and is more likely to be used in situations that tax cognitive resources (e.g., time pressure), the expectation that providers will be immune is unrealistic. (p. 250)

Consequently, extra care is needed to improve diagnostic accuracy and how mental health professionals view themselves and the individuals they interview. Clinicians must consider which stereotypes they use in categorization (e.g., a stereotype of what psychosis looks like, a stereotype of what a "normal" African American looks like, etc.) and the possible alternative explanations that exist for the observed behavior.

DIAGNOSIS

The purpose of diagnosis is to understand the cause or reasons for a behavior or syndrome of behaviors that are symptoms of disordered functioning. The etiology and extent of pathology is at the center of effective and adequate treatment strategies. Diagnosis is essential for correctly identifying particular disorders and subsequently, selecting the proper treatment approaches. Because diagnosis precedes treatment, the diagnosis often determines the treatment, or lack of treatment, that will follow. It is, therefore, imperative for psychologists to accurately interpret and integrate cultural variables into diagnostic procedures in order to provide competent and ethical mental health services to minorities or nonmainstream clients.

In 1994 the APA used a large and diverse group of mental health professionals who revised the *Diagnostic and Statistical Manual, 4th edition* (*DSM-IV*) to include cultural constructs as components of standard diagnostic practice. Axis V of the *DSM-IV* is used to incorporate social problems including racial discrimination. Appendix I of the *DSM-IV* provides a glossary of "culturebound syndromes" that are common in specific cultural groups but may be unknown in the mainstream culture.

For several decades psychologists and psychiatrists have debated the merits and pitfalls of the diagnostic process, including the use of diagnostic categories. After five revisions of the *DSM*, questions of reliability, utility, validity, empirical and theoretical underpinnings, and so forth have been addressed to a suitable level of professional agreement. The debates, however, continue. Questions concerning biopsychosocial rather than medical models and nomenclature, plus indications that inclusion or exclusion of some diagnostic disorders are subject to the political views of the times, continue to be areas of dispute (Alarcon et al., 2009; Nathan, 1998). Culture has been given a place at the table, and for the *DSM-V*, the convening of the Gender and Cross-Cultural Study Group should address some of the issues in cross-cultural diagnosis (American Psychiatric Association, 2010)

Yet, despite these reforms and revisions, there is reason to believe that many clinicians are conducting cross-racial and cross-cultural assessments that arrive at diagnoses that are often inconsistent with the standards for ethical practice. Evidence shows that minorities are often misdiagnosed or that diagnoses are often determined by mainstream cultural norms, rather than the appropriate cultural criteria for the individual client. Both Type I (diagnose presence of pathology when there is none) and Type II (diagnose no pathology when pathology is present) errors are cited in the literature (Gasquoine, 2001; Ridley, Li, & Hill, 1998).

Much of the research shows that African Americans and Hispanics are misdiagnosed as schizophrenic, when the more probable diagnosis would be bipolar disorder. In particular, African Americans are more often given the diagnosis of paranoid schizophrenia than Caucasians with similar symptoms, and in some cases, paranoid schizophrenia is the most frequent diagnosis given to African Americans. For Hispanics the research results are mixed and contradictory. Solomon (1992) reports that more Puerto Ricans are diagnosed schizophrenic than any other group, including other Hispanics. Chui (1996) asserts that Hispanics receive a diagnosis of schizophrenia less often than African Americans and Caucasians, but they more often receive diagnoses of other mental illnesses. In any case, when minorities are diagnosed with psychotic or affective disorders they are more likely to be viewed as chronic, rather than acute, disorders as compared to Caucasians with the same diagnoses. Likewise, assessments of dangerousness follow a racial bias pattern. Potential for violence and levels of dangerousness are repeatedly overestimated for African American inpatients and African American prison inmates (Good, 1996; Wood, Garb, Lilienfeld, & Nezworski, 2002).

Founded upon biased and culturally incompetent diagnoses, treatment discrepancies also follow distinct racial patterns. Minorities are typically overmedicated as compared to Caucasians (Wood et al., 2002). Hispanics, however, are less likely than African Americans and Caucasians to be medicated. African American inpatients are less often referred for individual and group psychotherapy treatments, and are discharged earlier than Caucasians.

Currently, minorities represent the fastest growing segment of the workforce in the United States (U.S. Bureau of Labor Statistics, 2011) As the ethnic and racial composition of the United States changes, educational systems are under increasing pressure to conduct culturally fair academic assessments and cognitive diagnoses of minority individuals (Taylor, 1994). Since 1967, U.S. courts have had to deal with the problem of significant overrepresentation of minorities in classes designated for mentally retarded students. Out of these court decisions have come new requirements for testing and diagnosing of mental abilities, especially for individuals for whom English is a second language (Figueroa, 1979; Mercer, 1979). However, intellectual assessment and subsequent diagnosis of adult clients continues to be an area of concern and debate. Diagnosing cognitive impairment in ethnic and racial minorities is a tricky endeavor laden with social implications. It is further complicated by the lack of well-standardized intellectual assessment instruments with high validity across cultural groups. For example, Renteria (2005) conducted a standardization of the WAIS-TEA, the Spanish version of the WAIS-III normed in Spain, on an urban sample of Mexican Americans. Overall, internal-consistency reliabilities for the IQ scores were all lower than those reported in Caucasian samples, and level of acculturation had a significant effect on IQ scores. Furthermore, many of the individuals in this community-based sample scored in the borderline range of intellectual ability. Thus, differences in test scores, as a result of a less valid and reliable measure and inaccurate interpretation practices, could lead to potentially inaccurate cognitive diagnostic conclusions.

Another interesting finding of Renteria's (2005) study was that the participants performed equally on measures of performance and verbal abilities. This is in contrast to the common practice of using performance tests rather than verbal tests under the assumption that they are a better indicator of intellectual ability. In fact, the performance IQ score of an individual who is tested in English (when English is not the first language) may still underestimate the individual's true intellectual ability.

The previous sections have raised a myriad of issues with regard to accurate assessment, differences in symptom expression, and diagnostic considerations with ethnic and racial minorities. A case study is provided to illustrate some of the issues involved in multicultural assessment and diagnosis, specifically with a Latino male client.

CASE STUDY

Mr. A is a 47-year-old Mexican-American male referred for evaluation following a right cerebral vascular injury. Prior to his stroke, Mr. A was regularly employed as a maintenance worker in the local school district. Mr. A has not worked since the stroke and currently requires help from his wife with dressing and some self-care activities due to left-sided hemiparesis. Mr. A is only able to drive during daylight hours due to left-sided visual neglect.

Results from Mr. A's evaluation indicated general intellectual functioning in the low average range, with significantly poorer visual-spatial than verbal skills. During the evaluation, Mr. A's mood was dysphoric and his affect was constricted. Mr. A was reported to have exhibited significant personality changes following the stroke, and by his own report, he is experiencing a high degree of frustration with the recovery process.

Of significant consideration is the impact of cultural values on his ability to cope with a disabling condition and the loss of masculine roles. Mr. A was the primary economic source for his family in a traditional household. Cultural values such as machismo and familism that are common Latino values affect his current views of his limitations (U.S. DHHS, 2001; Santiago-Rivera, Arredondo, & Gallardo-Cooper, 2002).

The evaluation of Mr. A requires an analysis of cultural elements. Using Dana's (2000) model, one would need to ascertain Mr. A's cultural orientation, determine what assessment measures were available, and decide whether a diagnosis was necessary. In Mr. A's case, a diagnosis was required for Social Security benefits due to his disability. Thus, it was important to complete a comprehensive evaluation and arrive at an accurate diagnosis.

In regards to his intellectual evaluation, Mr. A's intellectual test scores must be viewed with caution. A review of the literature has revealed that the WAIS-III has not been standardized with Spanish-speaking Mexican-American individuals in the United States and may underestimate or produce unreliable intellectual ability estimates (Renteria, 2005). When evaluating Mr. A's emotional functioning, several difficulties are encountered. In terms of specific measures to assess personality and mood, several of the widely used measures have both strengths and limitations. Although the validity of the MMPI-2 has been investigated with Latino populations, Latino individuals often produce invalid profiles on the MMPI-2 (Carbonell, 2000). Carbonell (2000) notes that the MMPI-2 "continues to have great potential for clinical misuse" (p. 563) and should be used with caution with Latinos.

Mr. A was also reported to have personality changes following his stroke and is a likely candidate for depressive symptoms. However, as noted earlier, depression scales such as the CES-D are problematic when evaluating depression in Latino males (Posner et al., 2001). As Uomoto and Wong (2000) point out, "in the rehabilitation setting, cultural sensitivity to the evaluation of mood is necessary to fairly evaluate the efficacy of interventions for depression in the multicultural patient" (p. 180).

Overall, the assessment of Mr. A's cognitive and emotional functioning is complicated by the lack of well-validated, reliable measures for his ethnic group. As is often encountered in the assessment of ethnic and racial minorities, there is no "right" instrument available to best answer the question of interest. Alternatively, as noted in the APA guidelines, how the instrument is used and interpreted become primary concerns. In summary, successful evaluation and diagnosis of Mr. A requires expertise in knowledge of multicultural considerations for Mr. A's cultural group and an awareness of the strengths and limitations of the evaluation measures and diagnostic systems available.

## CLINICAL APPLICATION

Does culture always impact the diagnosis of psychopathology? Although the obvious answer is "yes," it does so in varying ways and to varying degrees. In this next section, we present two cases. One in which cultural issues were present yet did not substantially affect the final diagnosis (Case: Tesfaye) and one in which cultural concerns altered the clinician's approach to the case (Case: Marva).

### CASE EXAMPLE: TESFAYE

Tesfaye was a 24-year-old Ethiopian-American female who was referred to therapy by a spiritual leader due to anxiety symptoms and a history of trauma. Tesfaye was sexually abused by a family friend when she was between the ages of 4 and 6 years old, and due to this early childhood trauma, she had never had an intimate relationship. She experienced significant anxiety related to interactions with men and was in constant fear that she may be physically or sexually attacked at any minute. She reported both behavioral and experiential avoidance as a result of these fears. Tesfaye also reported difficulty with motivation and decision making. She had trouble making everyday decisions and became overwhelmed with even the simplest of tasks. During her initial sessions, her therapist attempted to gather information regarding her history, symptomatology, and cultural influences.

Tesfaye's parents left Ethiopia together and settled in the Midwest before she was born; thus, she and her siblings were born and raised in the United States and were bilingual. Tesfaye reported a strained relationship with her parents that had persisted throughout her childhood and into her adulthood. She reported a history of verbal and emotional abuse from parents, who struggled to fit into mainstream American culture. Her father was especially strict on her siblings and herself while growing up, and Tesfaye was quite fearful of him as a child and adolescent. She was expected to be obedient and respectful at all times. She stated that her relationship with her family became even more troubled when, at the age of 20, she moved out of their home and across the country to the Pacific Northwest. Even Tesfaye's brothers, who were still living at home with their parents, disagreed with her decision to move out. Tesfaye had limited contact with her family upon the commencement of her therapy sessions, with only occasional phone calls to her mother.

Tesfaye's therapist used the following assessment measures in the initial stages of therapy: an Anxiety Disorder Interview Schedule (ADIS) to clarify anxiety diagnoses, the MMPI-2, the Beck Depression Inventory, the Beck Hopelessness Scale, the Beck Anxiety Inventory, and the Penn State Worry Questionnaire. These assessments revealed that Tesfaye met criteria for Posttraumatic Stress Disorder, Generalized Anxiety Disorder, and Major Depressive Disorder. Tesfaye's therapist, who was also a visible ethnic minority, spent time during their feedback session discussing the impact of Tesfaye's ethnic background on her diagnoses, as well as the impact of her minority status on her symptomatology. She also inquired what it was like to be an Ethiopian-American female living in a predominantly Caucasian city in the Pacific Northwest. Tesfaye expressed relief at the therapist's willingness to engage in this conversation and revealed that all of her close friends were Caucasian; thus, she had never had the opportunity to discuss such cultural differences and influences with anyone in the past.

Although having this discussion related to racial and cultural influences was a valuable experience for Tesfaye, these variables did not directly impact her diagnoses or treatment. The therapist proceeded with an empirically based treatment for PTSD, which Tesfaye responded to quite favorably. By the end of her treatment, Tesfaye was no longer experiencing worries or fears related to being attacked, no longer reported depressive symptomatology, and even reported a significant improvement in her relationship with her parents. Tesfaye had enrolled in classes to further her education and was no longer debilitated by her anxiety and depressive symptoms.

## CASE EXAMPLE: MARVA

Marva was a 32-year-old African-American woman who was referred to an African-American psychologist for a comprehensive psychological assessment because her state welfare case worker was concerned that she could not hold a regular job. Marva had two young children by a man who had deserted her and his kids. There was some concern that she was using drugs and seeing men who might be abusive and involved with criminal activities in the community. Marva had not been able to find a job, and she was living in a state-supported low-income housing project. Previously she had not managed to keep jobs that she had been assisted to find.

The state was considering removing her children from her custody and wanted a psychological evaluation to use as evidence that she either could, or could not, be a fit mother. Specifically, the case worker wanted an evaluation that would address her "lack of follow-through" with the state objectives and plans for her to find employment, her lack of motivation to maintain a job, her seeming resistance to the concerns that she was incapable of providing for her children, and her poor choices in the men she became involved with. Her case worker had the impression that Marva was hostile, rude, and not honest about her involvement with men and drugs. The state had some concerns about the racial and cultural issues involved in making a fair assessment, so an African-American female psychologist was asked to conduct the assessment.

Marva came to the assessment appointment on time, but she said she was not feeling well and didn't want to stay long. When she was told that the assessment process might take as long as four to six hours, she protested that she didn't think she could do that much. Marva also stated that she didn't know why the state was concerned about her ability to parent, thus, there was no reason for the assessment. She did, however, agree to complete the assessment work if it could be done in a sequence of shorter sessions, so she would not have to endure a period of four hours or longer. The examiner agreed to conduct the evaluation over two to three sessions.

During the two interview periods, Marva said that she was the middle child of three children. Her family had come from the Southeast to the Northwest when she was 5 years old. Overall, she reported that her family had struggled with poverty and job opportunities. Her parents had broken up, and she lived off and on with her father and stepmother. She stated that she was treated very badly by her stepmother, who would burn her with a lighter and beat her. She didn't have any friends growing up, and she wasn't allowed to play with other children or go outside. She said she felt like "the child in the window." Her grandmother called her mother when she realized she was being mistreated by her stepmother, and her mother came and got her. In addition to abuse from her stepmother, her nephew, who was 2 years older, molested her sexually for 4 to 5 years during her middle childhood.

When asked about her father, she stated that she didn't know what kind of work her father had done and that she never saw him much. She said her mother was "fine" and that her parents were both "fine people." She reported that her older sister had been her "running mate" when she was growing up and that she felt closest to her maternal grandmother, who had died when she was a teenager. With some persistence and pressing from the examiner, she finally recalled many fights with her mother as an adolescent, and for a 1-year period they barely spoke. Marva reported that throughout her life she had "hated school" and had never done well. She didn't like her teachers and had dropped out of high school, but was planning to get her GED.

Marva said that she became pregnant with her first child at 18. She left home to live with her child's father because she thought "he actually cared about me," but he had abused her. After the birth of her second child, the abuse got worse, and her husband left her. She reported that for about a year she had no money to pay the bills, and about this time, she attempted suicide. She began seeing another man, but state child welfare was called because he was beating her and punching holes in the walls. She claimed she was no longer seeing him. At the same time, she denied having any current emotional problems in her life. She emphatically denied using drugs or alcohol and insisted that a meddlesome and vindictive neighbor had started that rumor out of spite. She also denied feeling depressed, anxious, or angry. She stated that her appetite and sleep patterns were "fine." She denied any problems with her children. She insisted that everything was "fine" and that she didn't know why her case worker was concerned about anything. Her basic stance was one of denial and minimal one-sentence or "yes" or "no" answers. She volunteered nothing and admitted to nothing. The basic impression was that she was refusing to fully cooperate in the best way she knew how, by denying anything that might raise any suspicions or reasons to believe that she needed further intervention or interference from the state case worker.

The evaluation included the WAIS, the MMPI, and the Bender-Gestalt. During the administration of the WAIS, Marva stated that she knew she would "not do well on this test." She was clearly intimidated and hesitated to answer the questions. She sighed and behaved in a defeated and angry manner. She said she was not "going to get the answers right" and she didn't want to do any of the tests. The psychologist tried to encourage her and support her in making an effort. With some encouragement she did complete the WAIS, and her attitude improved over the course of the process, but she remained convinced that she had done poorly and that she had essentially failed to make a positive impression.

Despite her apprehensions, her WAIS results showed that she was able to function well in most everyday situations but would likely experience problems in academic or unusually stressful situations. She would be able to learn basic parenting skills and could also be expected to complete most job training programs. She needed remedial education help in math and reading skills. The MMPI profile showed that she endorsed extreme symptoms of anxiety, depression, social isolation, paranoid ideations, and thought disturbance. She expressed extremely poor self-confidence and was clearly "at the end of her rope" in coping with her life problems. However, there was no evidence that the extreme elevations were due to psychosis or poor reality testing, but rather to chronic underlying anxieties.

When Marva returned to complete the final interview, the examiner had spent that interim time considering Marva's level of cooperation and her resistance to the assessment process. It was clear that she had not made her best effort and that this attitudinal stance was affecting her performance and, therefore, compromising the ultimate outcome of the evaluation. It was not clear if her true abilities were being accurately reflected in her test scores. In fact, her attitude made it entirely possible that the testing was, to some extent, invalid. The examiner decided that it was necessary to have a discussion about their working relationship and to open a dialogue about Marva's resistance to the process and the possible barriers created by her attitude to arriving at a valid assessment.

Marva sat silently for awhile considering how to respond to the examiner. She then said that she had only done this because her case worker had insisted, and she didn't want to get into more trouble. She stated that none of this was her idea, and she didn't think it mattered what she thought about anything. She clearly felt resentful that the assessment had been imposed upon her, which she took as a sign of a lack of respect for her feelings and wishes. Moreover, she was concerned that she was not going to get a fair evaluation. When the examiner asked her to say why she assumed this, she looked around the office and said, "Look at all of your degrees and things." She then said, "You are not like me. I grew up very poor, we didn't have much. We never had much. I didn't go to school really. I'm not educated like you. Can someone like you understand someone like me?"

The examiner considered this to be a legitimate question. Could the examiner understand someone like Marva enough to feel confident that she would not come to biased conclusions in her report and recommendations to the state? Had the client received a fair and impartial assessment? These questions posed a significant validity consideration. The examiner decided that, in fact, there were significant differences in life experiences and lifestyles such that she could not feel confident in her ability to fully comprehend the client's life adaptations, choices, and decision making. What should be done? The examiner decided that the best way to avoid the intrusions of biases into her report would be to keep summaries and recommendations strictly behaviorally oriented. This approach would likely allow for as much objectivity as possible, in order to avoid an unfair assessment and subsequent judgment on the state's part with regard to the child custody question.

As has been said, multicultural assessment can be daunting. Several variables, such as ethnic heritages, social class, gender, and education levels, can combine to make cross-cultural situations especially complex. Cultural, political, and economic histories contribute to client test-taking attitudes, expectations, and behavioral responses during the assessment process. When variables such as ethnic minority membership, low income, and low education levels are combined, assessment outcomes can be significantly influenced by the biases of the examiner. In addition, both the examiner and the client may, consciously or unconsciously, assume stereotypic attitudes, stances, and behaviors during the assessment process, subsequently shaping and affecting assessment outcomes. Obviously, it is crucial that examiner biases are not allowed to slant assessment procedures, outcomes, or treatment recommendations. Examiners must distinguish between a fair versus biased interpretation of data and offer unbiased answers to referral questions. Unless this occurs, practitioners cannot avoid placing already socially disadvantaged clients into further disadvantaged situations.

In order to avoid Type I and Type II errors, the evaluator must sort through and consider how each of these variables contributes to the collection and interpretation of test data and address the referral questions accurately and appropriately in light of the effects of multicultural variables. Referral questions and recommendations for treatment must be addressed by taking into account cultural differences, but not to the extent those interpretations and conclusions are determined by them. In other words, cultural differences and norms need to be viewed as variables that speak to the history, identity, values, and goals of the client, but do not explain everything fully. Individual differences are also important, such as individual personality development, social skills, and intellectual capacities that are often the subject of assessment procedures.

The cultural background of the assessor can make quite a difference with some bias obstacles to fair and impartial assessment, but not necessarily so. Members of the same ethnic and cultural groups typically have fewer problems with mutual recognition of appropriate behavioral norms and social expectations and often share similar interpersonal styles. Yet, when variables such as social class and educational backgrounds come into play, as they often do in professional settings, some bias errors become more likely. Thus, the extent to which the examiner has been adequately trained and the extent to which they are competent to sort through group and individual variables, as well as recognize the possible impact of their own biases, is the key to accuracy in multicultural assessments.

As noted in the preceding cases, diagnoses are differentially affected by culture, and it is the clinician's responsibility to evaluate the appropriateness of the diagnosis. Fields (2010) highlights the potential errors that can result when culture is and is not taken into account. Earlier, we referred to Type I and Type II errors in the context of the presence or absence of psychopathology. In Fields's (2010) framework, a Type I error occurs when the clinician concludes that culture explains the client's symptomatology or is a strong factor in the diagnosis when it is not a main concern, and thus a clinical error is made. Conversely, when a Type II error is made, the clinician fails to recognize the contribution of culture to the diagnosis when in fact the cultural factors are more relevant than the clinician realizes. As with any clinical decision-making model, the clinician strives to maximize the true positives, or the number of times the clinician is correct about the contribution of culture to the diagnosis. However, clinical decision making is a complex enterprise that is further complicated when culture is considered (Galanter & Jensen, 2009; Hulme, 2010).

In real life, a dualistic framework (i.e., yes/no) is rarely reflected in the true situation of the client. The contribution of culture is more likely to be a question of relative contribution or the degree to which culture is a consideration than that it clearly is or is not a concern. Clinicians most frequently operate in this gray area, which creates difficulty for decision making. An important concept to be added to the process of multicultural diagnosis is the idea of *diagnostic fit*. Culture can both exacerbate and ameliorate symptoms of psychopathology. Various clients may clearly meet some diagnostic criteria but not others. How can this information be captured in clinical diagnostic decision making in a way that is useful for both the current clinician and future treating professionals? Particularly in cases where the client's intake specialist is a different individual from the therapist, a diagnostic fit index would enable the clinician to have a basis or a reference point from which to proceed with treatment.

For example, in the case of Tesfaye, whom we described, the diagnostic fit was quite high. The cultural issues were present and important to consider, but they did not substantially change the diagnosis. An evidence-based practice could be applied in this case with good confidence that the treatment would be successful and appropriate. Using a model similar to the GAF scale in which anchors are provided with various descriptors of functioning at each demarcation, we recommend a diagnostic fit index in which high scores indicate good fit to the *DSM-IV* diagnostic system and low scores indicate poor fit.

The case of Marva had much poorer fit to the traditional *DSM* nosological system. The cultural issues substantially affected the client's symptomatology, and biases in the examiner needed to be considered. In this case, a diagnostic fit index could provide an indicator of the degree to which the *DSM* multiaxial system was an appropriate conceptualization of the client's symptomatology.

In the next sections we describe some of the common problems in diagnosis with ethnic and racial minorities and our recommendations to further address multicultural competency among mental health professionals.

## COMMON PROBLEMS IN ASSESSMENT, DIAGNOSIS, AND TREATMENT WITH ETHNIC AND RACIAL MINORITIES

There are many reasons for deficiencies in diagnoses and treatment. The current empirical findings are reviewed as follows:

1. *Assessment strategies and procedures are flawed.* A common problem is test instruments that yield information that is often inadequate or misleading when used with cultural minorities because test validity and reliability were normed for the mainstream culture (Dana, 1996). Poor validity, poor equivalence of constructs (a construct does not have a shared meaning in the different cultures), and instrument bias have all been identified as factors contributing to flawed diagnostic results (Bhui, Mohamud, Warfa, Craig, & Stansfeld, 2003;

Constantine, 1998; Vijver & Phalet, 2004). In addition, when language barriers are not adequately addressed, there can be misinterpretations of test results. This can be especially true in cognitive evaluations and neuropsychological testing and forensic work (Echemendia, 2004; Gasquoine, 2001; Wood et al., 2002). Other client variables, such as income level and education level, will also affect test outcomes unless these variables are incorporated into the selection of test instruments and interviewing approaches. In addition, trends in managed care restrict the amount of time and money allotted for assessment services. This can lead to additional flaws because of a tendency to select tests for their time and effort utility rather than for their cultural appropriateness (Ridley et al., 1998; Wood et al., 2002).

2. *Symptoms are experienced and expressed differently in different cultures.* As previously discussed, different expressions and presentations can suggest different diagnostic impressions in different cultures. Symptoms of depression, dissociation, and somatic versus affective presentations are subject to learned cultural norms (Frey & Roysicar, 2004; Nelson-Jones, 2002). Mainstream clinicians, using mainstream cultural norms, can make assessment and diagnostic mistakes when observing and interviewing clients from different cultural groups.

3. *There is a lack of knowledge about different cultural norms, behaviors, and values.* This problem is most often cited as the major obstruction to competent cross-cultural diagnosis. Many problems can be mitigated when clinicians have ample knowledge of the cultural norms as presented by the client being evaluated. Many minorities have little experience with mainstream professionals or how and why an evaluation is conducted. People who are knowledgeable about the professional norms will answer questions differently and provide different information, as well as establish different overall impressions, than will persons who lack this knowledge. Culture can also determine the client's responsiveness during an evaluation session (Parron, 1997). African Americans are taught to be wary of the motives and judgment calls of professionals, whereas Asian Americans are taught to be respectful of and cooperative with authority figures. If clinicians are unfamiliar with these cultural patterns, mistaken notions about the client's diagnostic picture become commonplace.

4. *Clinicians can be biased.* Many psychologists and psychiatrists do not consider their own racial and cultural biases when conducting an assessment from which they derive a diagnostic conclusion. In effect, they can see what they already believe to be true: for example, African Americans are socially prone to delinquent behavior, rather than this particular African American individual is acting out deeper problems with symptoms of stress, depression, or PTSD. Or, African Americans and Hispanics are generally more disturbed and functioning at a lower level than most Caucasians. The upshot is minorities receive more serious diagnoses and fewer referrals for psychotherapy treatments (Kwan, 2001; Laszloffy & Hardy, 2000; Solomon, 1992; Trierweiler, Muroff, Jackson, Neighbors, & Munday, 2005; Whaley, 1997).

5. *Different ethnic/racial/cultural groups are numerous and not homogenous.* Within-group differences can be greater than between-group differences. This can be especially true when other variables such as education, income, levels of acculturation, differences among subgroups (such as Asian Americans and

Hispanic Americans), length of time in the second culture, and amount of intercultural contact are taken into account. It can become daunting to acquire sufficient knowledge of all of the different cultural and subcultural groups to become a competent cross-cultural diagnostician. How to sort through all of the variables, especially compounding variables of race, gender, age, education, sexuality, in order to arrive at an accurate case formulation for the individual client has been an ongoing problem. Multiple variables notwithstanding, the aim of successful diagnosis is to derive a comprehensive portrayal of the nature of the problems and suggest an adequate treatment strategy. In order to do this successfully, clinicians need to master a comprehensive, systematic methodology to sort through and integrate the group versus individual variables. Thus far, this methodology is in a formative stage and has not been applied consistently (Arbona, 1998).

6. *There is a lack of a sufficient scientific evidence base.* Much of the literature points to the need for further research to develop adequate models for cross-cultural assessment and diagnosis. Debates are ongoing about the nature of cultural variables and their impact on individual client diagnosis (Alarcon, 2009; Spengler, 1998). Questions of racial identity formation, political forces, and levels of acculturation continue to lack adequate empirically based norms that should be applied to the administration and interpretation procedures of diagnostic testing and interviewing.

7. *Some professionals lack adequate training.* It is likely that most of the problems with competent multicultural diagnosis are because of inadequate training. Many degree programs now have a course or courses in cross-cultural or multicultural practice, but it is still not known how many schools include these training programs. Moreover, the quality of the existing training programs and the competency outcomes of the training have not been systematically investigated (Ponterotto, Rieger, Barrett, & Sparks, 1994).

## SUMMARY

Much work is needed to bring multicultural diagnostic procedures into the 21st century. Trends in misdiagnosis and inadequate treatment decisions raise ethical concerns about unfair, as well as incompetent, professional practices. The mental health services needs of minorities are frequently mismanaged, and these regrettable prevailing outcomes have been well documented for at least three decades. If these trends continue, we are essentially establishing separate and unequal mental health services systems in the United States.

What are some of the changes in professional practice that need to be in place before this century reaches the midpoint and demographic forces begin to exacerbate the situation? We suggest four possible changes that need to be implemented as soon as possible. First, we suggest that a large-scale measurement equivalence undertaking supported by federal agencies such as the National Institute of Mental Health is needed that could result in a set of robust measures recognized by the professional community as meeting the basic requirements of equivalency. This would be a significant advancement for the individual clinician or researcher to be able to rely on an established set of cross-culturally validated measures.

The fact that multicultural diagnosis is exceedingly difficult to do, let alone do well, has been widely acknowledged. Competent and responsible cross-cultural diagnosis requires years of training to master the knowledge base and refined skills required. One or two courses in graduate school are simply not sufficient to meet the demands and standards of ethical practice. Given the wide range of diversity in our society, our second suggestion asserts that it may be time to require additional postdoctoral training for all professionals conducting cross-cultural diagnostic evaluations. As such, professionals could receive certification verifying their competence levels by attending training seminars and continuing education workshops.

Third, responsible assessment allows for the fact that valid results are often difficult to achieve. When the cultural gaps between clinician and client are broad and the client is not well educated or is from a low-income background, results can be particularly dubious. It should become allowable to make a diagnostic call that recognizes the possible long-term risks present in that situation. A diagnosis of "Due to the extent and degree of cultural differences, no reliable diagnosis is possible at this time" should be included in the *DSM-5*.

Fourth, at a minimum, individuals who work with racial and ethnic minorities should consider establishing a personal plan for competent assessment and diagnosis. Elements of that plan may include researching the literature and staying abreast of new developments. In Table 4.3, we describe some of the components of a plan for competency, including consultation, specialty training, and increased direct knowledge of the population.

Misdiagnosis of minorities can lead to biased distortions, mismanagement of treatment, poor predictive validity, and gross injustices in delivery of adequate mental health services. Competent assessment, diagnosis, and treatment for all individuals and groups should be the goal for mental health professionals across the field. By taking into account the considerations raised in this chapter, researchers and clinicians will view psychopathology among racial and ethnic minorities in a different light with fuller attention to the unique challenges inherent in multicultural assessment and diagnosis.

**Table 4.3**

Establishing a Plan for Competent Assessment and Diagnosis

1. *Consult the literature.* Review recent literature in both specialty journals as well as established journals to determine tests with more or less evidence or particular diagnostic recommendations with the group of interest.
2. *Seek specialty training.* Investigate opportunities for specialty classes, workshops, and trainings in how profiles/scores or diagnostic symptoms vary in the group of interest.
3. *Gain direct knowledge and exposure to the culture.* Immerse in cultures and communities that are representative of the individuals with whom you are likely to encounter. By attending activities and celebrations within the community, reading local and community newspapers, and volunteering at local community agencies, you will develop better hypotheses of how assessments and diagnoses are likely to be affected.
4. *Seek consultation/supervision.* Consult with a recommended expert who is familiar with the community. Use professional networks to identify an expert in assessment and diagnosis for the particular group. Engage a mentor who is culturally competent.

# REFERENCES

Abreu, J. M. (1999). Conscious and nonconscious African American stereotypes: Impact on first impression and diagnostic ratings by therapists [Electronic version]. *Journal of Consulting & Clinical Psychology, 67*(3), 387–393.

Acevedo, M. C., Reyes, C. J., Annett, R. D., & Lopez, E. M. (2003). Assessing language competence: Guidelines for assisting persons with limited English proficiency in research and clinical settings. *Multicultural Counseling and Development, 31*, 192–204.

Alarcon, R. D. (2009). Culture, cultural factors and psychiatric diagnosis: Review and projections. *World Psychiatry, 8*, 131–139.

Alarcon, R. D., Becker, A. E., Lewis-Fernandez, R., Like, R. C., Desai, P., Foulks, E., . . . Primm, A. for the Cultural Psychiatry Committee of the Group for the Advancement of Psychiatry (2009). Issues for DSM-V: The Role of Culture in Psychiatric Diagnosis. *Journal of Nervous and Mental Disease, 197*, 559–560.

Allen, J., & Walsh, J. A. (2000). A construct-based approach to equivalence: Methodologies for cross-cultural/multicultural personality assessment research. In R. H. Dana (Ed.), *Handbook of cross-cultural and multicultural personality assessment* (pp. 63–85). Mahwah, NJ: Erlbaum.

Allen, L. A., Gara, M. A., Escobar, J. I., Waitzkin, H., & Silver, R. C. (2001). Somatization: A debilitating syndrome in primary care. *Psychosomatics, 42*, 63–67.

American Psychiatric Association. (2000). *Diagnostic and statistical manual of mental disorders* (4th ed., text revision). Washington, DC: Author.

American Psychiatric Association (2010). *American Psychiatric Association DSM-5 development: Gender and cross-cultural issues*. Retrieved July 10, 2011 from www.dsm5.org/MeetUs/Pages/GenderandCross-CulturalIssues.aspx

American Psychological Association. (2002a). *Ethical principles of psychologists and code of conduct*. Washington, DC: Author.

American Psychological Association. (2002b). *Guidelines on multicultural education, training, research, practice, and organization change for psychologists*. Washington, DC: Author.

Arbona, C. (1998). Psychological assessment: Multicultural or universal? *The Counseling Psychologist, 26*, 911–921.

Arce-Ferrer, A. J. (2006). An investigation into the factors influencing extreme-response style: Improving meaning of translated and culturally adapted rating scales. *Educational and Psychological Measurement, 66*, 374–392. doi: 10.1177/0013164405278575

Arnold, B. R., & Matus, Y. E. (2000). Test translation and cultural equivalence methodologies for use with diverse populations. In I. Cuellar & F. A. Paniagua (Eds.), *Handbook of multicultural mental health* (pp. 121–136). San Diego, CA: Academic Press.

Arredondo, P., Toporek, R., Pack Brown, S., Jones, J., Locke, D. C., Sanchez, J., & Stadler, H. (1996). Operationalization of the multicultural counseling competencies. *Journal of Multicultural Counseling and Development, 24*, 42–78.

Azocar, F., Arean, P., Miranda, J., & Munoz, R. F. (2001). Differential item functioning in a Spanish translation of the Beck Depression Inventory. *Journal of Clinical Psychology, 57*, 355–365.

Bhui, K., Mohamud, S., Warfa, N., Craig, T. J., & Stansfeld, S. A. (2003). Cultural adaptation of mental health measures: Improving the quality of clinical practice and research. *British Journal of Psychiatry, 183*, 184–186.

Bruno, Z. (2003). Does item-level DIF manifest itself in scale-level analyses? Implications for translating language tests. *Language Testing, 20*, 136–147.

Burkhard, A. W., & Ponterotto, J. G. (2007). Cultural identity, racial identity, and the multicultural personality. In L. A. Suzuki, & J. G. Ponterotto (Eds.), *Handbook of multicultural assessment: Clinical psychological and education applications* (3rd ed., pp. 52–72). San Francisco, CA: Jossey-Bass.

Butcher, J. N. (1996). Translation and adaptation of the MMPI-2 for international use. In J. N. Butcher (Ed.), *International adaptations of the MMPI-2* (pp. 3–46). Minneapolis: University of Minnesota Press.

Byrne, B. M., Oakland, T., Leong, F. T. L., van de Vijver, F. J. R., Hambleton, R. K., & Cheung, F. M. (2009). A critical analysis of cross-cultural research and testing practices: Implications for improved education and training in psychology. *Training and Education in Professional Psychology*, 3(2), 94–105.

Carbonell, S. I. (2000). An assessment practice with Hispanics in Minnesota. In R. H. Dana (Ed.), *Handbook of cross-cultural and multicultural personality assessment* (pp. 547–572). Mahwah, NJ: Erlbaum.

Chui, T. L. (1996). Problems caused for mental health professionals worldwide by increasing multicultural populations and proposed solutions [Electronic version]. *Journal of Multicultural Counseling & Development*, 24, 129–140.

Constantine, M. G. (1998). Developing competence in multicultural assessment: Implications for counseling psychology training and practice. *The Counseling Psychologist*, 26, 922–929.

Contreras, S., Fernandez, S., Malcarne, V. L., Ingram, R. E., & Vaccarino, V. R. (2004). Reliability and validity of the Beck Depression and Anxiety inventories in Caucasian Americans and Latinos. *Hispanic Journal of Behavioral Sciences*, 26, 446–462.

Crockett, L. J., Randall, B. A., Shen, Y.-L., Russell, S. T., & Driscoll, A. K. (2005). Measurement equivalence of the center for epidemiological studies depression scale for Latino and Anglo adolescents: A national study. *Journal of Consulting and Clinical Psychology*, 73, 47–58.

Dana, R. H. (1996). Culturally competent assessment practice in the United States. *Journal of Personality Assessment*, 66, 472–487.

Dana, R. H. (1998). *Understanding cultural identity in intervention and assessment.* Thousand Oaks, CA: Sage.

Dana, R. H. (2000). *Handbook of cross-cultural and multicultural personality assessment.* Mahwah, NJ: Erlbaum.

Dana, R. H. (2005). *Multicultural assessment: Principles, applications, and examples.* Mahwah, NJ: Erlbaum.

Diaz, E., Miskemen, T., Vega, W. A., Gara, M., Wilson, D. R., Lesser, I., . . . Starkowski, S. (2009). Inconsistencies in diagnosis and symptoms among bilingual and English-speaking Latinos and Euro-Americans. *Psychiatric Services*, 60(10), 1379–1382.

Draguns, J. G., & Tanaka-Matsumi, J. (2003). Assessment of psychopathology across and within cultures: Issues and findings [Electronic version]. *Behaviour Research and Therapy*, 41, 755–776.

Echemendia, R. J. (2004). Cultural diversity and neuropsychology: An uneasy relationship in a time of change. *Applied Neuropsychology*, 11, 1–3.

Fernandez, K., Boccaccini, M. T., & Noland, R. M. (2008). Detecting over- and underreporting of psychopathology with the Spanish-language personality assessment inventory: Findings from a simulation study with bilingual speakers. *Psychological Assessment*, 20(2), 189–194. doi: 10.1037/1040–3590.20.2.189

Fields, A. J. (2010). Multicultural research and practice: Theoretical issues and maximizing cultural exchange. *Professional Psychology*, 41, 196–201.

Figueroa, R. A. (1979). The system of multicultural pluralistic assessment. *School Psychology Digest*, 8, 28–36.

Fletcher-Janzen, E., Strickland, T. L., & Reynolds, C. R. (2000). *Handbook of cross-cultural neuropsychology.* New York, NY: Kluwer.

Frey, L., & Roysicar, G. (2004). Effects of acculturation and worldview for white American, South American, South Asian, and Southeast Asian students. *International Journal for the Advancement of Counseling, 26,* 229–248.

Galanter, C. A., & Jensen, P. S. (2009). Diagnostic decision making. In C. A. Galanter and P. S. Jensen (Eds.), *DSM-IV-TR casebook and treatment guide for child mental health* (pp. 553–572). Arlington, VA: American Psychiatric Publishing.

Gasquoine, P. G. (2001). Research in clinical neuropsychology with Hispanic and American participants: A review. *The Clinical Neuropsychologist, 15,* 2–12.

Geltman, D., & Chang, G. (2004). Hallucinations in Latino psychiatric outpatients: A preliminary investigation [Electronic version]. *General Hospital Psychiatry, 26*(2), 152–157.

Gonzales, M., Castillo-Canez, I., Tarke, H., Soriano, F., Garcia, P., & Velasquez, R. J. (1997). Promoting the culturally sensitive diagnosis of Mexican Americans: Some personal insights. *Journal of Multicultural Counseling & Development, 25*(2), 156–161.

Good, B. J. (1996). Culture and *DSM-IV*: Diagnosis, knowledge and power. *Culture, Medicine and Psychiatry, 20,* 127–132.

Gopaul-McNicol, S., & Armour-Thomas, E. (2002). *Assessment and culture: Psychological tests with minority populations.* San Diego, CA: Academic Press.

Grzywacz, J. G., Hovey, J. D., Seligman, L. D., Arcury, T. A., & Quandt, S. A. (2006). Evaluating short-form versions of the CES-D for measuring depressive symptoms among immigrants from Mexico. *Hispanic Journal of Behavioral Sciences, 28*(3), 404–424.

Hays, P. A. (2007). *Addressing cultural complexities in practice: Assessment, diagnosis, and therapy* (2nd ed.). Washington, DC: American Psychological Association.

Hofstede, G. (2001). *Culture's consequences: Comparing values, institutions, and organizations across nations* (2nd ed.). Thousand Oaks, CA: Sage.

Hui, C. H., & Triandis, H. C. (1985). Measurement in cross-cultural psychology. *Journal of Cross-Cultural Psychology, 16,* 131–152.

Hui, C., & Triandis, H. (1989). Effects of culture and response format on extreme response style. *Journal of Cross-Cultural Psychology, 20,* 296–309.

Hulme, P. A. (2010). Cultural considerations in evidenced-based practice. *Journal of Transcultural Nursing, 21,* 271–280.

Kankaras, M., & Moors, G. (2010). Researching measurement equivalence in cross-cultural studies. *Psihologija, 43*(2), 121–136. doi: 10.2298/PSI1002121K

Knight, G. P., & Hill, N. (1998). Measurement equivalence in research involving minority adolescents. In V. C. McLoyd & L. Steinberg, (Eds.), *Studying minority adolescents: Conceptual, methodological, and theoretical issues* (pp. 183–210). Mahwah, NJ: Erlbaum.

Knight, G. P., Roosa, M. W., & Umma-Taylor, A. J. (2009). Studying ethnic minority and economically disadvantaged populations: Methodological challenges and best practices. *Measurement and measurement equivalence issues* (pp. 97–134). Washington, DC: American Psychological Association.

Knight, G. P., Virdin, L. M., Ocampo, K. A., & Roosa, M. (1994). An examination of the crossethnic equivalence of measures of negative life events and mental health among Hispanic and Anglo American children. *American Journal of Community Psychology, 22,* 767–783.

Kwan, K. K. (2001). Models of racial and ethnic identity development: Delineation of practice implications. *Journal of Mental Health Counseling, 23,* 269–277.

Laszloffy, T. A., & Hardy, K. V. (2000). Uncommon strategies for a common problem: Addressing racism in family therapy. *Family Process, 39*(1), 35–50.

Mackin, P., Targum, S. D., Kalali, A., Rom, D., & Young, A. H. (2006). Culture and assessment of manic symptoms. *British Journal of Psychiatry, 189*, 379–380. doi: 10.1192/bjp. bp.105.01392010.1192/bjp.bp.105.013920

Malgady, R. G., & Constantino, G. (1998). Symptom severity in bilingual Hispanics as a function of clinician ethnicity and language of interview [Electronic version]. *Psychological Assessment, 10*(2), 120–127.

Marin, G., Gamba, R., & Marin, B. (1995). Extreme response style and acquiescence among Hispanics. *Journal of Cross-Cultural Psychology, 23*, 498–509.

Mercer, J. R. (1979). In defense of racially and culturally non-discriminatory assessment. *School Psychology Digest, 8*, 89–115.

Minsky, S., Vega, W., Miskimen, T., Gara, M., & Escobar, J. (2003). Diagnostic patterns in Latino, African American, and European American psychiatric patients. *Archives of General Psychiatry, 60*(6), 637–644.

Morris, E. F. (2000). Assessment practices with African Americans: Combining standard assessment measures within an Africentric orientation. In R. H. Dana (Ed.), *Handbook of cross-cultural and multicultural personality assessment* (pp. 573–603). Mahwah, NJ: Erlbaum.

Nathan, P. E. (1998). The *DSM-IV* and its antecedents: Enhancing syndromal diagnosis. In J. Barron (Ed.), *Making diagnosis meaningful: Enhancing evaluation and treatment of psychological disorders* (pp. 2–27). Washington, DC: American Psychological Association.

Nelson-Jones, R. (2002). Diverse goals for multicultural counseling and therapy. *Counseling Psychology Quarterly, 15*, 133–143.

Nichols, D. S., Padilla, J., & Gomez-Maqueo, E. L. (2000). Issues in the cross-cultural adaptation and use of the MMPI-2. In R. H. Dana (Ed.), *Handbook of cross-cultural and multicultural personality assessment*. Mahwah, NJ: Erlbaum.

Okazaki, S., & Sue, S. (2000). Implications of test revisions for assessment with Asian Americans. *Psychological Assessment, 12*, 272–280.

Orlando, M., & Marshall, G. N. (2002). Differential item functioning in a Spanish translation of the PTSD checklist: Detection and evaluation of impact. *Psychological Assessment, 14*, 50–59.

Parron, D. L. (1997). The fusion of cultural horizons: Cultural influences on the assessment of psychopathology on children. *Applied Development Science, 1*, 156–159.

Ponterotto, J. G., Gretchen, D., & Chauhan, R. V. (2001). Cultural identity and multicultural assessment: Quantitative and qualitative tools for the clinician. In L. A. Suzuki, J. G. Ponterotto, & P. J. Meller (Eds.), *Handbook of multicultural assessment: Clinical psychological and education applications* (2nd ed., pp. 67–99). Thousand Oaks, CA: Sage.

Ponterotto, J. G., Rieger, B. P., Barrett, A., & Sparks, R. (1994). Assessing multicultural counseling competence: A review of instrumentation. *Journal of Counseling & Development, 72*, 316–322.

Posner, S. F., Stewart, A. L., Marin, G., & Perez-Stable, E. J. (2001). Factor variability of the Center for Epidemiological Studies Depression Scale (CES-D) among urban Latinos. *Ethnicity & Health, 6*, 137–144.

Renteria, L. (2005). Validation of the Spanish language Wechsler Adult Intelligence Scale (3rd Edition) in a sample of American, urban, Spanish speaking Hispanics. Unpublished doctoral dissertation. Chicago, IL: Loyola University.

Resnick, J. L. (2006). Strategies for implementation of the multicultural guidelines in university and college counseling centers. *Professional Psychology: Research and Practice, 37*(1), 14–20. doi: 10.1037/0735-7028.37.1.14

Ridley, C. R., Li, L. C., & Hill, C. L. (1998). Multicultural assessment: Reexamination, reconceptualization, and practical application. *The Counseling Psychologist, 26*, 827–910.

Santiago-Rivera, A. L., Arredondo, P., & Gallardo-Cooper, M. (2002). *Counseling Latinos and la familia: A practical guide.* Thousand Oaks, CA: Sage.

Sharpley, M., Hutchinson, G., McKenzie, K., & Murray, R. M. (2001). Understanding the excess of psychosis among the African-Caribbean population in England [Electronic version]. *British Journal of Psychiatry, 178*(40), 60–68.

Solomon, A. (1992). Clinical diagnosis among diverse populations: A multicultural perspective. *Families in Society: The Journal of Contemporary Human Services, 73*, 371–377.

Spengler, P. M. (1998). Multicultural assessment and a scientist-practitioner model of psychological assessment. *The Counseling Psychologist, 26*, 930–938.

Stuart, R. B. (2004). Twelve practical suggestions for achieving multicultural competence. *Professional Psychology: Research and Practice, 35*, 3–9.

Sue, D. W., Arredondo, P., & McDavis, R. J. (1992). Multicultural counseling competencies and standards: A call to the profession. *Journal of Multicultural Counseling & Development, 20*, 64–88.

Sue, D. W., & Sue, D. (2007). *Counseling the culturally diverse: Theory and practice* (5th ed.). Hoboken, NJ: John Wiley & Sons.

Suzuki, L. A., & Ponterotto, J. G. (2007). *Handbook of multicultural assessment: Clinical psychological and education applications* (3rd ed.). San Francisco, CA: Jossey-Bass.

Taylor, T. R. (1994). A review of three approaches to cognitive assessment, and a proposed integrated approach based on a unifying theoretical framework [Electronic version]. *South African Journal of Psychology, 24*, 184–207.

Trierweiler, S. J., Muroff, J. R., Jackson, J. S., Neighbors, H. W., & Munday, C. (2005). Clinician race, situational attributions, and diagnoses of mood versus schizophrenia disorders. *Cultural Diversity and Ethnic Minority Psychology, 11*(4), 351–364. doi: 10.1037/1099–9809.11.4.351

Uomoto, J. M., & Wong, T. M. (2000). Multicultural perspectives on the neuropsychology of brain injury assessment and rehabilitation. In E. Fletcher-Janzen, T. L. Strickland, & C. R. Reynolds (Eds.), *Handbook of cross-cultural neuropsychology* (pp. 169–184). New York, NY: Kluwer.

U.S. Bureau of Labor Statistics. (2011). *Working in the 21st century.* Retrieved July 10, 2011, from www.bls.gov/opub/working/home.htm

U.S. Census Bureau. (2011). *2010 Census data: 2010 census demographic profiles.* Retrieved July 10, 2011, from http://2010.census.gov/2010census/data/

U.S. Department of Health and Human Services (U.S. DHHS). (2001). *Mental health: Culture, race, and ethnicity—A supplement to mental health: A report of the Surgeon General.* Rockville, MD: Substance Abuse and Mental Health Services Administration, Center for Mental Health Services.

Vandenberg, R. J., & Lance, C. E., (2000). A review and synthesis of the measurement invariance literature: Suggestions, practices, and recommendations for organizational research. *Organizational Research Methods, 3*, 4–70.

van Ryn, M., & Fu, S. S. (2003). Paved with good intentions: Do public health and human service providers contribute to racial/ethnic disparities in health? [Electronic version]. *American Journal of Public Health, 93*(2), 248–255.

Vijver, F., & Phalet, K. (2004). Assessment in multicultural groups: The role of acculturation. *Applied Psychology: An International Review, 53*, 215–236.

Weijters, B., Geuens, M., & Schillewaert, N. (2010). The individual consistency of acquiescence and extreme response style in self-report questionnaires. *Applied Psychological Measurement*, *34*, 105–121.

Whaley, A. L. (1997). Ethnicity/race, paranoia, and psychiatric diagnoses: Clinician bias versus sociocultural differences. *Journal of Psychopathology and Behavioral Assessment*, *19*, 1–20.

Whaley, A. L. (1998). Cross-cultural perspective on paranoia: A focus on the black American experience [Electronic version]. *Psychiatric Quarterly*, *69*(4), 325–343.

Wong, T. M., Strickland, T. L., Fletcher-Janzen, E., Ardila, A., & Reynolds, C. R. (2000). Theoretical and practical issues in the neuropsychological assessment and treatment of culturally dissimilar patients. In E. Fletcher-Janzen, T. L. Strickland, & C. R. Reynolds (Eds.), *Handbook of cross-cultural neuropsychology* (pp. 3–18). New York, NY: Kluwer.

Wood, J. M., Garb, H. N., Lilienfeld, S. O., & Nezworski, M. T. (2002). Clinical assessment. *Annual Review of Psychology*, *53*, 519–543.

Zhang, A. Y., & Snowden, L. R. (1999). Ethnic characteristics of mental disorders in five U. S. communities. *Cultural Diversity and Ethnic Minority Psychology*, *5*, 134–146.

# PART II

## SPECIFIC DISORDERS

# CHAPTER 5

# Delirium, Dementia, and Amnestic and Other Cognitive Disorders (Neurocognitive Disorders)

GERALD GOLDSTEIN

## INTRODUCTION AND RECENT DEVELOPMENTS

Most of the neurological disorders of mankind are ancient diseases, and developments in treatment and cure have been painfully slow. However, we continue to learn more about these disorders, and in previous versions of this chapter (Goldstein, 1997, 2007) we commented on major new events that took place during recent years that represented highly substantive developments. A new disorder, AIDS dementia, had appeared, and the marker for the Huntington's disease gene had been discovered. At the time of the 1997 writing, it was mentioned that a still mysterious and controversial disorder appeared, sustained by military personnel during the war with Iraq in the Persian Gulf area, popularly known as the Gulf War syndrome. An aspect of this syndrome has been said to involve impaired brain function (Goldstein, 2011; Goldstein, Beers, Morrow, Shemansky, & Steinhauer, 1996). Gulf War syndrome remains far from fully understood, but increased knowledge, particularly involving the roles of infections and toxins, has been acquired (Parkhurst & Guilmette, 2009). A more readily understood condition emerging from the Gulf and Afghanistan Wars is the blast injuries caused largely by roadside bombs. These injuries appeared to have different characteristics from those associated with the open or closed head injuries associated with previous wars and accidents in civilian life (Belanger, Kretzmer, Vanderploeg, & French, 2010).

Another consequence of the Gulf and Afghanistan Wars has been a reconsideration of the problem of mild traumatic brain injury (mTBI), often called *concussion*. Concussion is a common sports injury, but it also appears to be a common consequence of sustaining a blast injury. It is sometimes complicated by its association with posttraumatic stress disorder (PTSD) acquired in reaction to the injury, and diagnostic difficulties have been created regarding whether the victim sustained brain injury, developed PTSD, or both. It was commonly accepted that concussion was a self-limiting disorder, and that essentially full recovery could be expected within no more than 90 days. Recently, however, it has been observed that some individuals with histories of concussion do not fully recover during that period and continue to have complaints of cognitive problems, notably in attention, memory, and organizational abilities. Individuals with multiple concussions appear to experience a cumulative effect.

Initially, these symptoms were attributed to stress, but neuroimaging studies using advanced technologies have found that identifiable brain damage may result from concussion, involving the upper brainstem, base of the frontal lobe, hypothalamic-pituitary axis, medial temporal lobe, fornix, and corpus callosum. Bigler (2008) has written a review of this area, employing the phrase "persistent post-concussive syndrome" to describe this condition. Substantial support for the neurological basis for this disorder comes from use of a technology that was just beginning its development and widespread use at the last writing, called *diffusion tensor imaging* (DTI). DTI is an MRI-related procedure that tracks axonal white matter, identifying misalignments.

In the Gulf War, concussion and more serious trauma was associated with blast injuries sustained mainly as a result of roadside bombing. Blast injuries remain a controversial area, with some authorities claiming they are no different from the commonly accepted types of brain injury (Hoge et al., 2008; Wilk et al., 2010), but with others claiming they are a unique from of trauma not identified previously. The matter is further complicated by the fact that the bombs used were sometimes loaded with depleted uranium or possibly infectious agents. Thus, the understanding of head injury has changed since the last writing, with the development of methods that can detect persistent neurological consequences of concussion producing a new diagnosis called persistent postconcussive syndrome, and the problem of blast injury, which is still under intensive investigation. The interaction between head injury and the stress often associated with the event producing it, often eventuating in PTSD, is also a major area of investigation.

## PROPOSED CHANGES IN *DSM-5*

We also commented on the substantial change in how organic mental disorders are classified by psychiatry, reflected in the most recent *Diagnostic and Statistical Manual of Mental Disorders* (*DSM-IV*; American Psychiatric Association [APA], 1994). Since the last writing, there have been no changes in the formal classification system, as *DSM-5* has not yet arrived. Although *DSM-5* has not appeared as yet, preliminary reports indicate that there may be substantial changes from *DSM-IV* in terminology and content. The phrase Delirium, Dementia, Amnestic, and other Cognitive Disorders used in *DSM-IV* as the diagnostic category may be replaced by the phrase Neurocognitive Disorders. The term *delirium* will be kept as part of a set of three major subcategories: Major Neurocognitive Disorder, Minor Neurocognitive Disorder, and Delirium. The term *dementia* may be entirely eliminated, as may be several diagnoses including Cognitive Disorder Not Otherwise Specified, Amnestic Disorders, and Dementia of the Alzheimer Type or Due to a General Medical Condition. The diagnosis of Vascular Dementia will also be eliminated. As the replacement, the major and minor disorders will be classified into several subtypes including

Alzheimer's disease and several other disorders for which criteria have not yet been developed. They include vascular cognitive impairment and dementia, frontotemporal lobar degeneration, dementia with Lewy bodies, Huntington's disease, Parkinson's disease, and traumatic brain injuries, possibly in addition to other disorders not yet specified. Draft criteria for the Alzheimer's disease subtype have been written and include meeting criteria for Major or Minor Neurocognitive Disorder, early and prominent impairment in memory, deficits in at least one other domain in the case of the Major form of the disorder, a course of gradual onset and continuing cognitive decline, and a ruling out of the condition being attributable to other disorders. Behavior disturbance, notably psychosis and depression, will be diagnosed, as will domains of impairment such as attention and learning and memory. In the case of Alzheimer's disease, the diagnosis may indicate whether it occurs with or without behavioral disturbance. Separate criteria for psychosis and depression have been proposed.

There has been some reconceptualization of the concept of vascular dementia. Although the diagnosis continues to be used, there is substantial evidence that there is a great deal of overlap with Alzheimer's disease. Autopsy studies often show that there is evidence of vascular pathology in individuals diagnosed with Alzheimer's disease, and the reverse is also true. It has been suggested that cardiovascular illness may be a risk factor for Alzheimer's disease. Moreover, there appears to have been an increased focus of interest in the specific vascular disorders, including heart failure, stroke, and arteriovenous malformations, each of which has different cognitive consequences (Festa, 2010; Lantz, Lazar, Levine, & Levine, 2010; Pavol, 2010).

Another important proposed change is elimination of the term *mental retardation*, which is replaced by *intellectual disability*. This new term is felt to reflect more accurately the nature of the disorder and corrects for the demeaning connotations of the term *mental retardation*. This change has already been widely accepted.

In this author's judgment, the major developments over the past years continue to be technological in nature. Increasingly sophisticated techniques have been developed to image the brain, not only structurally as in an X-ray but also functionally. We now have very advanced capacities to image brain activity while the individual is engaging in some form of behavior. At present, functional magnetic resonance imaging (fMRI) is the most widely used of these procedures. It involves performing magnetic resonance imaging while the individual is given tasks to perform and recording changes in brain activity. Thus, for example, it is possible to observe increased activity in the language area of the brain while the person is performing a language task.

New developments have also appeared regarding techniques used to make a pathological diagnosis of Alzheimer's disease in a living person. Previously, the diagnosis could only be made at autopsy. Now there is a neuroimaging procedure that can visualize neurochemical changes in the brain that can make a specific diagnosis. It involves an amyloid-imaging positron emission tomography (PET) tracer called Pittsburgh Compound B that detects amyloid in the brain. Amyloid is known to be central to the pathogenesis of Alzheimer's disease (Fagan et al., 2005; Klunk et al., 2004). There have been advances in the genetics of Alzheimer's disease, with great interest in the apolipoprotein E epsilon 4 allele (APOE4) that appears to be associated with age of onset of the disorder. There has also been substantial interest in mild cognitive impairment (MCI), the mild cognitive deficits that frequently appear in elderly people. The question raised has involved whether occurrence of MCI results in conversion to Alzheimer's disease. Degree of deficits noted on neuropsychological testing has been found to be significantly associated with conversion to Alzheimer's disease, thereby constituting a significant risk factor.

Other developments have been more incremental, with increases in our understanding of the Gulf War syndrome and neurodevelopmental disorders, notably autism. The changes in *DSM-IV* have essentially codified the abandonment of the traditional distinction made in psychopathology between the so-called organic and functional disorders. The latter type of disorder was generally viewed as a reaction to some environmental or psychosocial stress, or as a condition in which the presence of a specific organic etiological factor is strongly suspected, but not proven. The anxiety disorders would be an example of the first alternative, and schizophrenia would be an example of the second. The organic mental disorders are those conditions that can be more or less definitively associated with temporary or permanent dysfunction of the brain. Thus, individuals with these illnesses are frequently described as "brain-damaged" patients or patients with "organic brain syndromes." It is clear that recent developments in psychopathological research and theory have gone a long way toward breaking down this distinction, and it is becoming increasingly clear that many of the schizophrenic, mood, and attentional disorders have their bases in some alteration of brain function. Perhaps most recently, the significance of brain function for several developmental disorders, notably autism and related pervasive developmental disorders, has been recognized and emphasized. Psychiatric classification has therefore dropped use of the word *organic* to describe what was formerly called the *organic mental disorders*.

The word was initially replaced by several terms: *delirium, dementia, amnesia, cognitive disorders,* and *mental disorders due to a general medical condition,* and will apparently be replaced again with the phrase Major or Minor Neurocognitive Disorder. Nevertheless, the clinical phenomenology, assessment methods, and treatment management procedures associated with patients generally described as brain damaged are sufficiently unique that the traditional functional versus organic distinction is probably worth retaining for certain purposes. Brain-damaged patients have clinical phenomenologies, symptoms, courses, and outcomes that are quite different from those of patients with other psychopathological disorders. However, in order to delineate the subject matter of this chapter as precisely as possible, we would nevertheless prefer to say that we will be concerned with individuals having structural brain damage rather than with organic patients.

The theoretical approach taken here will be neuropsychological in orientation, in that it will be based on the assumption that clinical problems associated with brain damage can be understood best in the context of what is known about the relationships between brain function and behavior. Thus, attempts will be made to expand our presentation beyond the descriptive psychopathology of *DSM-IV* (APA, 1994) in the direction of attempting to provide some material related to basic brain-behavior mechanisms. There are many sources of brain dysfunction, and the nature of the source has a great deal to do with determining behavioral consequences: morbidity and mortality. Thus, a basic grasp of key neuropathological processes is crucial to understanding the differential consequences of brain damage. Furthermore, it is important to have some conceptualization of how the brain functions. Despite great advances in neuroscience, we still do not know a great deal about this matter yet, and so it remains necessary to think in terms of brain models or conceptual schema concerning brain function. However, we have learned a great deal about the genetics and neurochemistry of how memories and other cognitive abilities are preserved in brain tissue. There are several neuropsychological models and hypotheses concerning memory in particular, portions of which have been supported by neurochemical and neurophysiological research.

In recent years, knowledge of the neurological systems important for such areas as memory and language has been substantially expanded. For example, it seems clear now that there are several separate memory systems located in different areas of the brain, notably the hippocampus, the amygdala, the neocortex, and the cerebellum. Each system interacts with the others but supports a different form of memory, such as immediate recall, remote recall, and the brief storage of information during ongoing cognitive activity known as working memory (Baddeley, 1986).

In recognition of the complexities involved in relating structural brain damage to behavioral consequences, the field of clinical neuropsychology has emerged as a specialty area within psychology. Clinical neuropsychological research has provided specialized instruments for assessment of brain-damaged patients and a variety of rehabilitation methods aimed at remediation of neuropsychological deficits. This research has also pointed out that brain damage, far from being a single clinical entity, actually represents a wide variety of disorders.

Initially, neuropsychologists were strongly interested in the relationship between localization of the brain damage and behavioral outcome. In recent years, however, localization has come to be seen as only one determinant of outcome, albeit often a very important one. Other considerations include such matters as the individual's current age, the individual's age when the brain damage was acquired, the premorbid personality and level of achievement, and the type of pathological process producing the brain dysfunction. Furthermore, neuropsychologists are now cognizant of the possible influence of various nonorganic factors on their assessment methods, such as educational level, socioeconomic status, and mood states. There has been an increasing interest in sociocultural aspects of neuropsychological assessment, particularly with reference to research and testing in cultures throughout the world that are experiencing significant effects of some brain disease, such as AIDS dementia (Heaton, 2006). Thus, this chapter presents concepts of brain dysfunction in historical and contemporary perspectives, the various causes of brain dysfunction, and the clinical phenomenology of several syndromes associated with brain damage in relation to such factors as localization, age of the individual, age of the lesion, and pathological process.

## CHANGING VIEWS OF BRAIN FUNCTION AND DYSFUNCTION

Concepts of how mental events are mediated have evolved from vague philosophical speculations concerning the "mind-body problem" to rigorous scientific theories supported by objective experimental evidence. We may recall from studies of the history of science that it was not always understood that the "mind" was in the brain, and mental events were thought to be mediated by other organs of the body. Boring (1950) indicates that Aristotle thought that the mind was in the heart.

Once the discovery was made that it was in the brain, scientists turned their interest to how the brain mediates behavior, thus ushering in a line of investigation that to this day is far from complete. Two major methodologies were used in this research: direct investigations of brain function through lesion generation or brain stimulation in animal subjects, and studies of patients who had sustained brain damage, particularly localized brain damage. The latter method, with which we will be mainly concerned here, can be reasonably dated back to 1861 when Paul Broca produced his report (1861) on the case of a patient who had suddenly developed speech loss. An autopsy done on this patient revealed that he had sustained an extensive infarct in the area of the third frontal convolution of the left cerebral hemisphere. Thus, an important center in the brain for speech had been discovered, but perhaps more significantly, this case produced what many would view as the first reported example of a neuropsychological or brain-behavior relationship in a human. Indeed, to this day, the third frontal convolution of the left hemisphere is known as Broca's area, and the type of speech impairment demonstrated by the patient is known as Broca's aphasia.

Following Broca's discovery, much effort was devoted to relating specific behaviors to discrete areas of the brain. Wernicke made the important discovery that the area that mediates the comprehension as opposed to the expression of speech is not Broca's area but in a more posterior region in the left temporal lobe: the superior temporal gyrus. Other investigators sought to localize other language, cognitive, sensory, and motor abilities in the tradition of Broca and Wernicke, some using animal lesion and stimulation methods and others clinical autopsy investigations of human brain-damaged patients. Various syndromes were described, and centers or pathways whose damage or disconnection produced these syndromes were suggested. These early neuropsychological investigations not only provided data concerning specific brain-behavior relationships, but also explicitly or implicitly evolved a theory of brain function, now commonly known as *classical localization theory*. In essence, the brain was viewed as consisting of centers for various functions connected by neural pathways. In human subjects, the presence of these centers and pathways was documented through studies of individuals who had sustained damage to either a center or the connecting links between one center and another such that they became disconnected. To this day, the behavioral consequences of this latter kind of tissue destruction are referred to as a *disconnection syndrome* (Geschwind, 1965). For example, there are patients who can speak and understand, but who cannot repeat what was just said to them. In such cases, it is postulated that there is a disconnection between the speech and auditory comprehension centers.

From the beginnings of the scientific investigation of brain function, not all investigators advocated localization theory. The alternative view is that rather than functioning through centers and pathways, the brain functions as a whole in an integrated manner. Views of this type are currently known as mass action, holistic, or organismic theories of brain function. Although we generally think of holistic theory as a reaction to localization theory, it actually can be seen as preceding localization theory, in that the very early concepts of brain function proposed by

Galen and Descartes can be understood as holistic in nature. However, what is viewed as the first scientific presentation of holistic theory was made in 1824 by Flourens. Flourens (1824) proposed that the brain might have centers for special functions (action propre), but there is a unity to the system as a whole (action commune), and this unity dominates the entire system. Boring (1950) quotes Flourens's statement, "Unity is the great principle that reigns; it is everywhere, it dominates everything." The legacy of holistic theory has come down to us from Flourens through the neurologist Hughlings Jackson, who proposed a distinction between primary and secondary symptoms of brain damage. Primary symptoms are the direct consequences of the insult to the brain itself, while the secondary symptoms are the changes that take place in the unimpaired stratum. Thus, a lesion produces changes not only at its site but also throughout the brain.

In contemporary neuropsychology the strongest advocates of holistic theory were Kurt Goldstein, Martin Scheerer, and Heinz Werner. Goldstein and Scheerer (1941) are best known for their distinction between abstract and concrete behavior, their description of the "abstract attitude," and the tests they devised to study abstract and concrete functioning in brain-damaged patients. Their major proposition was that many of the symptoms of brain damage could be viewed not as specific manifestations of damage to centers or connecting pathways but as some form of impairment of the abstract attitude. The abstract attitude is not localized in any region of the brain but depends upon the functional integrity of the brain as a whole. Goldstein (1959) describes the abstract attitude as the capacity to transcend immediate sensory impressions and consider situations from a conceptual standpoint. Generally, it is viewed as underlying such functions as planning, forming intentions, developing concepts, and separating ourselves from immediate sensory experience. The abstract attitude is evaluated objectively primarily through the use of concept formation tests that involve sorting or related categorical abilities. In language it is evaluated by testing the patient's ability to use speech symbolically. Often this testing is accomplished by asking the patient to produce a narrative about some object that is not present in the immediate situation.

Heinz Werner and various collaborators applied many of Goldstein's concepts to studies of brain-injured and intellectually disabled children (e.g., Werner & Strauss, 1942). His analyses and conceptualizations reflected an orientation toward Gestalt psychology and holistic concepts, dealing with such matters as figure-ground relationships and rigidity. Halstead (1947) made use of the concept of the abstract attitude in his conceptualizations of brain function, but in a modified form. Like most contemporary neuropsychologists, Halstead viewed abstraction as one component domain, or factor, in cognitive function among many, and did not give it the central role attributed to it by Goldstein and his followers. Correspondingly, rather than adhering to an extreme position concerning the absence of localization, Halstead provided evidence to suggest that the frontal lobes were of greater importance in regard to mediation of abstract behavior than were other regions of the brain. Goldstein (1936) also came to accept the view that the frontal lobes were particularly important in regard to mediation of the abstract attitude.

The notion of a nonlocalized generalized deficit underlying many of the specific behavioral phenomena associated with brain damage has survived to some extent in contemporary neuropsychology, but in a greatly modified form. Similarly, some aspects of classical localization theory are still with us, but also with major changes (Mesulam, 1985). None of the current theories accepts the view that there is no localization of function in the brain, and correspondingly, none of them would deny that some behaviors cannot be localized to some structure or group of structures. This synthesis is reflected in several modern concepts of brain function, the most explicit one probably being that of Luria (1973). Luria has developed the concept of functional systems as an alternative to both strict localization and mass action theories. Basically, a functional system consists of several elements involved in the mediation of some complex behavior. For example, there may be a functional system for auditory comprehension of language. The concept of pluripotentiality is substituted for Lashley's (1960) older concept of equipotentiality. Equipotentiality theory suggests that any tissue in a functional area can carry out the functions previously mediated by destroyed tissue. Pluripotentiality is a more limited concept suggesting that one particular structure or element may be involved in many functional systems. Thus, no structure in the brain is only involved in a single function. Depending upon varying conditions, the same structure may play a role in several functional systems.

Current neuropsychological thought reflects some elements of all of the general theories of brain function briefly outlined in the preceding paragraphs. In essence, it is thought that the brain is capable of highly localized activity directed toward control of specific behaviors, but also of mediating other behaviors through means other than geographically localized centers. Indeed, since the discovery of the neurotransmitters (chemical substances that appear to play an important role in brain function), there appears to have been a marked change in how localization of function is viewed. To some authorities at least, localization is important only because the receptor sites for specific neurotransmitters appear to be selectively distributed in the brain. Neuroscientists now tend to think not only in terms of geographical localization but of neurochemical localization as well.

With regard to clinical neuropsychology, however, the main point seems to be that there are both specific and nonspecific effects of brain damage. Evidence for this point of view has been presented most clearly by Teuber and his associates (Teuber, 1959) and by Satz (1966). The Teuber group was able to show that patients with penetrating brain wounds that produced very focal damage had symptoms that could be directly attributed to the lesion site, but they also had other symptoms that were shared by all patients studied, regardless of their specific lesion sites. For example, a patient with a posterior lesion might have an area of cortical blindness associated with the specific lesion site in the visual projection areas, but he or she might also have difficulties in performing complex nonvisual tasks, such as placing blocks into a formboard while blindfolded. Most of Teuber's patients had difficulty with formboard type and other complex tasks regardless of specific lesion site. In clinical settings we may see brain-damaged patients with this combination of specific and nonspecific symptoms as well as patients with only nonspecific symptoms. One of the difficulties with early localization theory is that investigators tended to be unaware of the problem of nonspecific symptoms and so only reported the often more dramatic specific symptoms.

An old principle of brain function in higher organisms that has held up well and that is commonly employed in clinical neuropsychology involves contralateral control; the right half of the brain controls the left side of the body and vice versa. Motor, auditory, and somatosensory fibers cross over at the base of the brain and thus control the contralateral side of the body. In the case of vision, the crossover is atypical. The optic nerve enters a structure called the *optic chiasm*, at which point fibers coming from the outer or temporal halves of the retinas go to the ipsilateral side of the brain, while fibers from the inner or nasal halves cross over and go the contralateral cerebral hemispheres. However, the pattern is thought to be complete, and all fibers coming from a particular hemiretina take the same course. In the case of somesthesis, hearing, and motor function, the crossover is not complete, but the majority of fibers do cross over. Thus, for example, most of the fibers from the right auditory nerve find their way to the left cerebral hemisphere. The contralateral control principle is important for clinical neuropsychology because it explains why patients with damage to one side of the brain may become paralyzed only on the opposite side of their body or may develop sensory disturbances on that side. We see this condition most commonly in individuals who have had strokes, but it is also seen in some patients who have open head injuries or who have brain tumors.

Although aphasia, or impaired communicative abilities as a result of brain damage, was recognized before Broca (Benton & Joynt, 1960), it was not recognized that it was associated with destruction of a particular area of one side of the brain. Thus, the basic significance of Broca's discovery was not the discovery of aphasia, but of cerebral dominance. *Cerebral dominance* is the term that has been commonly employed to denote the fact that the human brain has a hemisphere that is dominant for language and a nondominant hemisphere. In most people, the left hemisphere is dominant, and left hemisphere brain damage may lead to aphasia. However, some individuals have dominant right hemispheres, while others do not appear to have a dominant hemisphere. What was once viewed as a strong relationship between handedness and choice of dominant hemisphere has not held up in recent studies. But the answers to questions regarding why the left hemisphere is dominant in most people and why some people are right dominant or have no apparent dominance remain unknown. In any event, it seems clear that for individuals who sustain left hemisphere brain damage, aphasia is a common symptom, while aphasia is a rare consequence of damage to the right hemisphere.

Following Broca's discovery, other neuroscientists discovered that just as the left hemisphere has specialized function in the area of language, the right hemisphere also has its own specialized functions. These functions seem to relate to nonverbal abilities such as visual-spatial skills, perception of complex visual configurations, and, to some extent, appreciation of nonverbal auditory stimuli such as music. Some investigators have conceptualized the problem in terms of sequential as opposed to simultaneous abilities. The left hemisphere is said to deal with material in a sequential, analytic manner, while the right hemisphere functions more as a detector of patterns or configurations (Dean, 1986). Thus, while patients with left hemisphere brain damage tend to have difficulty with language and other activities that involve sequencing, patients with right hemisphere brain damage have difficulties with such tasks as copying figures and producing constructions, because such tasks involve either perception or synthesis of patterns. In view of these findings regarding specialized functions of the right hemisphere, many neuropsychologists now prefer to use the expression *functional asymmetries of the cerebral hemispheres* rather than *cerebral dominance*. The former terminology suggests that one hemisphere does not really dominate or lead the other. Rather, each hemisphere has its own specialized functions.

Since the appearance of the first version of this chapter, it would probably be fair to say that a third major methodology has been added to the study of brain function, in addition to animal and human lesion studies. It derives from neuroradiology but has become far more advanced than the films of the skull that we looked at in the past, and even beyond the earlier development of the computed tomography (CT) scan. It is now possible to directly observe numerous aspects of brain function in living individuals while they are engaged in some targeted activity. The two most widely used procedures to do this are PET and fMRI. Using different technologies, these procedures can detect changes when the brain is behaviorally activated. It has become possible to elicit very specific activity in relation to specific stimuli. Language tasks might activate areas in the language zone of the brain in the left temporal lobe. Conceptual activities, such as doing a sorting test, will activate portions of the frontal lobes. It is now also possible to track conduction from one structure to another while some complex behavior is being performed, such as listening to a word and saying what it is. These methods are known as *online procedures* because the individual is having recordings made at the same time as the behavior is performed.

A second new development is magnetic resonance spectroscopy (MRS). MRS uses MRI technology, but instead of producing a visualization of brain structure or activity, it generates a chemical profile of the brain. While the individual lies under the magnet, a surface coil placed around the head generates various chemical spectra that provide data about underlying tissue at a microbiological level. In the brain, the phosphorous spectrum produces information about brain metabolism based on the activity of phospholipids that exist in cell membranes. The hydrogen spectrum is most often used to determine the level of a substance called N-Acetyl Aspartate (NAA). NAA level has been found to be associated with integrity of neurons and thus provides an index of neuronal loss, deterioration, or maldevelopment. We therefore have a way of examining brain tissue at a molecular biological level in a living individual. PET, fMRI, and MRS have substantially advanced our capability of assessing brain function. Diffusion Tensor Imaging (DTI) is an MRI-related technique that can evaluate misalignment of axonal white matter as may be found with head injury or some developmental disorders. It evaluates anisotropy associated with diffusion of water mainly in white matter.

## DESCRIPTION OF THE DISORDER

### NEUROPATHOLOGICAL CONSIDERATIONS

Localization alone is an important determinant of the behavioral outcomes of brain damage, but there are numerous other considerations. Although age, sociocultural, and personality factors make their contributions, perhaps the most important matter is the type of brain damage. Some would argue that neuropsychological assessment is rarely the best method of determining type of brain damage, because other techniques such as the CT scan, cerebral blood flow studies, and MRI are more adequate for that purpose. The point may be well taken, but the problem remains that different types of lesions produce different behavioral outcomes even when they involve precisely the same areas of the brain. Thus, the clinician should be aware that the assessment methodology used may not be the best one to meet some specific diagnostic goal, and it is often necessary to use a variety of methods coming from different disciplines to arrive at an adequate description of the patient's condition. In the present context, an adequate description generally involves identification of the kind of brain damage the patient has as well as its location. In order to point out the implications of this principle, it is necessary to provide a brief outline of the types of pathology that involve the brain and their physical and behavioral consequences.

The brain may incur many of the illnesses that afflict other organs and organ systems. It may be damaged by trauma or it may become infected. The brain can become cancerous or can lose adequate oxygen through occlusion of the blood vessels that supply it. The brain can be affected through acute or chronic exposure to toxins, such as carbon monoxide or other poisonous substances. Nutritional deficiencies can alter brain function just as they alter the function of other organs and organ systems. The brain may mature abnormally during pregnancy for various reasons, producing different developmental disorders. Aside from these general systemic and exogenous factors, there are diseases that more or less specifically have the central nervous system as their target. These conditions, generally known as degenerative and demyelinating diseases, include Huntington's disease, multiple sclerosis, Parkinson's disease, and disorders associated with aging. From the point of view of neuropsychological considerations, it is useful to categorize the various disorders according to temporal and topographical parameters. Thus, certain neuropathological conditions are static and do not change substantially; others are slowly progressive; and some are rapidly progressive. With regard to topography, certain conditions tend to involve focal, localized disease, others multifocal lesions, and still others diffuse brain damage without specific localization. Another very important consideration has to do with morbidity and mortality. Some brain disorders are more or less reversible, some are static and do not produce marked change in the patient over lengthy periods, while some are rapidly or slowly progressive, producing increasing morbidity and eventually leading to death. Thus, some types of brain damage produce a stable condition with minimal changes, some types permit substantial recovery, and other types are in actuality terminal illnesses. It is therefore apparent that the kind of brain disorder the patient suffers from is a crucial clinical consideration in that it has major implications for treatment, management, and planning.

## HEAD TRAUMA

Although the skull affords the brain a great deal of protection, severe blows to the head can produce temporary brain dysfunction or permanent brain injury. The temporary conditions, popularly known as concussions, are generally self-limiting and involve a period of confusion, dizziness, and perhaps double vision. However, there seems to be complete recovery in most cases. In concussion, the brain is not thought to be permanently damaged, but there are exceptions. More serious trauma is generally classified as closed or open head injury. In closed head injury, which is more common, the vault of the skull is not penetrated, but the impact of the blow crashes the brain against the skull and thus may create permanent structural damage. A commonly occurring type of closed head injury is the subdural hematoma, in which a clot of blood forms under the dura (one of the protective layers on the external surface of the brain). These clots produce pressure on the brain that may be associated with clear-cut neurological symptoms. They may be removed surgically, but even when that is done there may be persistent residual symptoms of a localized nature, such a weakness of one side of the body. In the case of open head injury, the skull is penetrated by a missile of some kind. Open head injuries occur most commonly during wartime as a result of bullet wounds. They sometimes occur as a result of vehicular or industrial accidents, if some rapidly moving object penetrates the skull. Open head injuries are characterized by the destruction of brain tissue in a localized area. There are generally thought to be more remote effects as well, but usually the most severe symptoms are likely to be associated with the track of the missile through the brain. Thus, an open head injury involving the left temporal lobe could produce aphasia, while similar injury to the back of the head could produce a visual disturbance.

A major neuropsychological difference between open and closed head injury is that while the open injury typically produces specific, localized symptoms, the closed head injury, with the possible exception of subdural hematoma, produces diffuse dysfunction without specific focal symptoms. In both cases, some of these symptoms may disappear with time, while others may persist. There is generally a sequence of phases that applies to the course of both closed and open head injury. Often, the patient is initially unconscious and may remain that way for an extremely varying amount of time, ranging from minutes to weeks or months. After consciousness is regained, the patient generally goes through a so-called acute phase, during which there may be confusion and disorientation.

Very often a condition called posttraumatic amnesia is present, in which the patient cannot recall events that immediately preceded the trauma up to the present time. Research has shown that the length of time spent unconscious as well as the length of posttraumatic amnesia are reasonably accurate prognostic signs; the longer either persists, the worse the prognosis. During this stage, seizures are common, and treatment with anticonvulsant drugs is often necessary. When the patient emerges from this acute phase, the confusion diminishes, amnesia may persist but may not be as severe as previously, the seizures may abate, and one gets a better picture of what the long-term outcome will be. The range of variability here is extremely wide, extending from patients remaining in persistent vegetative state to essentially complete recovery of function. In general, the residual difficulties of the head trauma patient, when they are significant, represent a combination of cognitive and physical symptoms. With regard to the latter, these patients are often more or less permanently confined to wheelchairs because of partial paralysis. Frequently there are sensory handicaps such as partial loss of vision or hearing.

Trauma to the head can do damage not only to the brain but to other parts of the head as well, such as the eyes and ears. Additionally, there is sometimes substantial disfigurement in the form of scars, some of which can be treated with cosmetic surgery. The cognitive residual symptoms of head trauma are extremely varied, because they are associated with whether the injury was open head or closed head and if there was clear tissue destruction. Most often, patients with closed head injury have generalized intellectual deficits involving abstract reasoning ability, memory, and judgment. Sometimes, marked personality changes are noted, often having the characteristic of increased impulsiveness and exaggerated affective responsivity. Patients suffering from the residual of open head injury may have classic neuropsychological syndromes such as aphasia, visual-spatial disorders, and specific types of memory or perceptual disorders. In these cases, the symptoms tend to be strongly associated with the lesion site. For example, a patient with left hemisphere brain damage may have an impaired memory for verbal material such as names of objects, whereas the right hemisphere patient may have an impaired memory for nonverbal material such as pictures or musical compositions. In these cases there is said to be both modality (e.g., memory) and material (e.g., verbal stimuli) specificity. Head trauma is generally thought to be the most frequently seen type of brain damage in adolescents and young adults. It, therefore, generally occurs in a reasonably healthy brain. When the combination of a young person with a healthy brain exists, the prognosis for recovery is generally good if the wound itself is not devastating in terms of its extent or the area of the brain involved. For practical purposes, residual brain damage is a static condition that does not generate progressive changes for the worse. Although there is some research evidence (Walker, Caveness, & Critchley, 1969) that following a long quiescent phase, head-injured individuals may begin to deteriorate more rapidly than normal when they become elderly, and there is some evidence that brain injury may be a risk factor for Alzheimer's disease (Lye & Shores, 2000). However, head-injured individuals may nevertheless have many years of productive functioning. There has been a strong interest in outcome following mild head injury (Levin, Eisenberg, & Benton, 1989), as well as in the specific problems associated with head injury in children (Noggle & Pierson, 2010). It has been frequently pointed out in recent years that trauma is the major cause of death in children, and head trauma among children is not uncommon. Most recently, a marked interest has developed in sports injuries (e.g., Schatz et al., 2006), with most studies assessing athletes shortly after sustaining a concussion and evaluating future outcome.

Since the Persian Gulf War era, there has been a substantial increase in the study of head injury, particularly head injuries sustained by veterans, and more specifically by those who had blast injuries or concussions. Thus far, the results are mixed and the characteristics of persistent postconcussion syndrome and its association with PTSD are far from fully understood. While standard neuroimaging procedures are typically normal following concussion, studies with DTI show some abnormal findings, as reviewed in Bigler (2008). However, in an individual study by Levin et al. (2010), there were no consequential findings with DTI, with head-injured subjects showing normal functional anisotropy, suggesting the absence of axonal misalignment. Wilk et al. (2010) found no or inconsistent association between self-reported concussion and the presence of persistent postconcussive symptoms. However, Mayer et al. (2010) did report finding white matter abnormalities based upon DTI studies in patients with mild TBI. The roles of PTSD and depression as mediators of these associations have been stressed (Belanger et al., 2010).

## BRAIN TUMORS

Cancer of the brain is a complex area, particularly as cancer in general continues to be incompletely understood. However, the conventional distinction between malignant and nonmalignant tumors is a useful one for the brain as it is for other organs and organ systems. Thus, some brain tumors are destructive, rapidly progressive, and essentially untreatable. Generally, these tissue structures are known as *intrinsic tumors* because they directly infiltrate the parenchyma of the brain. The most common type is a class of tumor that is known as *glioma*. Other types of tumors grow on the external surface of the brain and produce symptoms through the exertion of pressure on brain tissue. This type of tumor is described as being extrinsic, and the most common type is called a *meningioma*. Aside from these two types, there are metastases in which tumors have spread to the brain from some other organ of the body, often the lung. The extrinsic tumors are often treatable surgically, but metastases are essentially untreatable. The clinical symptoms of tumor include headache that frequently occurs at night or on awakening, seizures, and vomiting. There are often progressive cognitive changes, perhaps beginning with some degree of confusion and poor comprehension and progressing to severe dementia during the terminal stages. Because tumors often begin in quite localized areas of the brain, the symptoms associated with them tend to be dependent upon the particular location affected. For example, there is a large literature on frontal lobe tumors in which impairment of judgment, apathy, and general loss of the ability to regulate and modulate behavior are the major symptoms (Berg, 1998). As in the case of head injury, patients with left hemisphere tumors may develop aphasia, whereas patients with right hemisphere tumors may have visual-spatial disorders as their most prominent symptoms. The difference from head injury is that short of surgical intervention, the severity of symptoms increases with time, sometimes at a very slow and sometimes at a very rapid rate, depending upon the type of tumor.

On rare occasions, the clinical neuropsychologist, neurologist, or psychiatrist may see patients with tumors that affect particular structures in the brain, thereby generating characteristic syndromes. Among the most common of these are the cranial pharyngiomas, the pituitary adenomas, and the acoustic neuromas. The cranial pharyngiomas are cystic growths that lie near the pituitary gland and often depress the optic chiasm so that the primary symptoms may involve delayed development in children and waning libido and amenorrhea in adults, in combination with weakening of vision. The pituitary adenomas are similar in location, but the visual loss is often more prominent, frequently taking the form of what is called a *bitemporal hemianopia*: a loss of vision in both peripheral fields. The acoustic neuromas are tumors of the auditory nerve and thereby produce hearing loss as the earliest symptom. However, because the auditory nerve also has a vestibular component, there may be progressive unsteadiness of gait and dizziness. Clinicians may also see patients who have had surgically treated tumors. When these patients demonstrate residual neuropsychological symptoms, they look like patients with histories of open head injury. Perhaps that is because the brain lesion has, in a manner of speaking, been converted from a mass of abnormal tissue to a stable, nonmalignant wound. When neurosurgery has been successful, the changes are often rapid and very substantial. One is normally concerned about recurrence, and these patients should remain under continued medical care. There is concern about the cognitive effects of cancer treatment in the form of radiotherapy and chemotherapy, with reports of cognitive dysfunction being produced by these treatments (Correa, 2010). However, successful surgical or other treatment may leave the patient with many years of productive life.

BRAIN MALFORMATIONS AND EARLY-LIFE BRAIN DAMAGE

Perhaps nowhere in the neurocognitive disorders is the type of lesion issue as significant as it is in the case of the developmental disorders of brain function. The crux of the matter here is that there is a great deal of difference between destruction of function already acquired and destruction of the brain mechanisms needed to acquire that function before it has been developed. Thus, the consequences of being born with an abnormal brain or acquiring brain damage during the early years of life may be quite different from the consequences of acquiring brain damage as an adult. On the positive side, the young brain generally has greater plasticity than the older brain, and it is somewhat easier for preserved structures to take over functions of impaired structures. On the negative side, however, when the brain mechanisms usually involved in the acquisition of some function are absent or impaired, that function is often not learned or not learned at a normal level. Although the relationship between age and consequences of brain damage remains an intensively researched area (Baron & Gioia, 1998), for practical purposes it can be said that there is a population of individuals born with abnormal brain function, or who have sustained structural brain damage at or shortly after birth, who go on to have developmental histories of either generalized or specific cognitive subnormality. Those with generalized deficit, when it is sufficiently severe, are frequently described with a variety of terms, such as *minimal brain damage, learning disability*, and *attention deficit-hyperactivity disorder*.

The developmental disorders represent a type of condition in which the distinction made in the *DSM* system between child and adult disorders is not particularly pertinent. The planners of *DSM-5* have noted this situation by saying in regard to the adult neurocognitive disorders:

> The differing characteristics of these disorders are that their core or primary deficits are in cognition and that these deficits represent a decline from a previously attained level of cognitive functioning; the latter feature distinguishes them from the neurodevelopmental disorders in which a neurocognitive deficit is present at birth or interferes with development. However, it is possible to develop a neurocognitive disorder superimposed on a neurodevelopmental disorder, for example Alzheimer's disease in a patient with mental retardation associated with Down syndrome. (APA, 2010)

One common subclass of this specific group consists of children who fail to learn to read normally despite adequate educational opportunity and average intelligence. These children are described as having dyslexia or developmental dyslexia. A related rare condition is developmental amnesia, or global anterograde amnesia, in which there is exceptionally poor development of episodic memory in the context of otherwise normal cognitive abilities (Vargha-Khadem et al., 1997).

With regard to neuropathological considerations, several types of brain disorder may occur during the prenatal period. Some of them are developmental in nature in the sense that either the brain or the skull does not grow normally during gestation. When the skull is involved, the brain is damaged through the effects of pressure on it. Sometimes a genetic factor is present, as is clearly the case with Down syndrome. Sometimes poor prenatal care is the responsible agent, with fetal alcohol syndrome perhaps being an extreme case of this condition. Sometimes an infection acquired during pregnancy, notably rubella (German measles), can produce a course of development of severe intellectual dysfunction during gestation. Probably most often, however, the causes of the developmental abnormality are unknown.

There is now a field of behavioral toxicology that deals with the matter of environmental hazards that impact cognitive function. The major consideration has to do with the problem of mothers living in a toxic environment, particularly while they are pregnant. A major toxin is methylmercury, and there is an extensive literature on the effects of methylmercury exposure obtained through eating certain kinds of fish on cognitive development of children who are exposed to this toxin during gestation (reviewed in Shemansky and Goldstein, 2011). These studies have found demonstrable impaired development of intelligence associated with this toxic exposure. This condition is geographically regional and occurs mainly in areas in which seafood, particularly pilot whale meat, contains high methylmercury levels. Thus, it now seems well established that environmental hazards that sometimes produce toxic exposure to children during embryonic development can result in developmental abnormalities of brain function.

Damage to the brain can also occur as the result of a traumatic birth. Such conditions as cerebral anoxia, infection, and brain dysfunction associated with such ongoing conditions as malnutrition or exposure to toxic substances are the major agents. Children have strokes and brain tumors, but they are quite rare. In essence, brain damage can occur in the very young before, during, and after birth. Although the neuropathological distinction among the various disorders is quite important, the life span development of individuals from all three categories shares some common characteristics. And retrospectively, it is often difficult to identify the responsible agent in the school-age child or adult. Thus, it is sometimes useful to think in terms of some general concept, such as perinatal or early-life brain damage, rather than to attempt to specifically relate a particular developmental course or pattern of functioning to a single entity.

Early-life brain damage is usually a static condition in the sense that the lesion itself does not change, but it may have varying consequences throughout life. During the preschool years, the child may not achieve the generally accepted landmarks, such as walking and talking at the average times. In school, these children often do not do well academically and may be either poor learners in general or have specific disabilities in such areas as reading, arithmetic, or visual-spatial skills. These academic difficulties may be accompanied by some form of behavior disorder, often manifested in the form of hyperactivity or diminished attentional capacity. During adulthood, it is often found that these individuals do not make satisfactory vocational adjustments, and many researchers now feel that they are particularly vulnerable to certain psychiatric disorders, notably alcoholism (Tarter, 1976) or schizophrenia (Green, 1998).

We would note that, although this volume does not address child psycho-pathology, several disorders may be classed as organic mental, or neurocognitive, disorders that begin during childhood but persist into adulthood. There is growing evidence (Katz, Goldstein, & Beers, 2001; Spreen, 1987) that learning disability frequently persists into adulthood. Autism, which is now generally viewed as a neurobehavioral disorder (Minshew, 1996), also generally persists into adulthood. A study (Rumsey & Hamburger, 1988) that followed up some of Kanner's (1943) original cases demonstrated the persistence of neuropsychological deficit in these autistic adults. Since this pioneering study of Rumsey and Hamburger, there has been a rapidly growing literature concerning neuropsychological aspects of autism using a wide variety of tests, experimental procedures, and theoretical frameworks (Katz, Goldstein, & Beers, 2001). These studies are now often done in association with use of various neuroimaging procedures, providing rather definitive evidence of brain abnormalities in individuals with autism. For example, head circumference is larger in individuals with autism than in typically developing individuals (Griebling, Williams, Goldstein, & Minshew, 2011).

## DISEASES OF THE CIRCULATORY SYSTEM

Current thinking about the significance of vascular disease has changed from the time when it was felt that cerebral arteriosclerosis or "hardening of the arteries" was the major cause of generalized brain dysfunction in the middle-aged and elderly. Although this condition is less common than was once thought, the status of the heart and the blood vessels are significantly related to the intactness of brain function. Basically, the brain requires oxygen to function, and oxygen is distributed to the brain through the cerebral blood vessels. When these vessels become occluded, circulation is compromised and brain function is correspondingly impaired. This impairment occurs in several ways, perhaps the most serious and abrupt being stroke. A stroke is a sudden total blockage of a cerebral artery caused by blood clot or a hemorrhage. The clot may be a thrombosis formed out of atherosclerotic plaque at branches and curves in the cerebral arteries or an embolism, which is a fragment that has broken away from a thrombus in the heart that has migrated to the brain. Cerebral hemorrhages are generally fatal, but survival from thrombosis or embolism is not at all uncommon. Following a period of stupor or unconsciousness, the most common and apparent postacute symptom is hemiplegia—paralysis of one side of the body. There is also a milder form of stroke known as a transient ischemic attack (TIA), which is basically a temporary, self-reversing stroke that does not produce severe syndromes, or may be essentially asymptomatic. The phrase "silent stroke" or "silent cerebral infarction" is used when stroke-type neuropathology is detected by MRI or related procedures, but there are no apparent symptoms (Das et al., 2008).

A somewhat different picture emerges in another cerebral vascular disorder called vascular dementia in *DSM-IV* (APA, 1994). As opposed to the abruptly rapid onset seen in stroke, vascular dementia is a progressive condition based on a history of small strokes associated with hypertension. Patients with vascular dementia experience a stepwise deterioration of function, with each small stroke making the dementia worse in some way. There are parallels between vascular dementia and the older concept of cerebral arteriosclerosis in that they both relate to the role of generalized cerebral vascular disease in producing progressive brain dysfunction. However, vascular dementia is actually a much more precisely defined syndrome that, although not rare, is not extremely common either. Many patients who used to be diagnosed as having cerebral arteriosclerosis would now be diagnosed as having one of the degenerative diseases associated with the presenile or senile period of life.

Other relatively common cerebrovascular disorders are associated with aneurysms and other vascular malformations in the brain. An aneurysm is an area of weak structure in a blood vessel that may not produce symptoms until it balloons out to the extent that it creates pressure effects or it ruptures. A ruptured aneurysm is an extremely serious medical condition in that it may lead to sudden death. However, surgical intervention in which the aneurysm is ligated is often effective. Arteriovenous malformations are congenitally acquired tangles of blood vessels. They may be asymptomatic for many years, but they can eventually rupture and hemorrhage. They may appear anywhere in the brain, but commonly they occur in the posterior half. The symptoms produced, when they occur, may include headache and neurological signs associated with the particular site.

There are major neuropsychological differences between the individual with a focal vascular lesion, most commonly associated with stroke, and the patient with generalized vascular disease such as vascular dementia. The stroke patient is not only characterized by the hemiplegia or hemiparesis, but sometimes by an area of blindness in the right or left visual fields and commonly by a pattern of behavioral deficits associated with the hemisphere of the brain affected and the locus within that hemisphere. If the stroke involves a blood vessel in the left hemisphere, the patient will be paralyzed or weak on the right side of the body, the area of blindness, if present, will involve the right field of vision, and there will frequently be aphasia. Right hemisphere strokes may produce left-sided weakness or paralysis and left visual field defects but no aphasia. Instead, a variety of phenomena may occur. The patient may acquire a severe difficulty with spatial relations—a condition known as *constructional apraxia*. The ability to recognize faces or to appreciate music may be affected. A phenomenon known as *unilateral neglect* may develop, in which the patient does not attend to stimuli in the left visual field, although it may be demonstrated that basic vision is intact. Sometimes affective changes occur in which the patient denies that he or she is ill and may even develop euphoria.

In contrast with this specific, localized symptom picture seen in the stroke patient, the individual with vascular dementia or other generalized cerebral vascular disease has quite a different set of symptoms. Generally, there is no unilateral paralysis, no visual field deficit, no gross aphasia, and none of the symptoms characteristic of patients with right hemisphere strokes. Rather, there is a picture of generalized intellectual, and to some extent physical, deterioration. If weakness is present, it is likely to affect both sides of the body, and typically there is general diminution of intellectual functions including memory, abstraction ability, problem-solving ability, and speed of thought and action. In the case of the patient with vascular dementia, there may be localizing signs, but there would tend to be several of them, and they would not point to a single lesion in one specific site.

The more common forms of cerebral vascular disease are generally not seen until at least middle age, and for the most part are diseases of the elderly. Clinically significant cerebral vascular disease is often associated with a history of generalized cardiovascular or other systemic diseases, notably hypertension and diabetes. Some genetic or metabolic conditions promote greater production of atheromatous material than is normal, and some people are born with arteriovenous malformations or aneurysms, placing them at higher than usual risk for serious cerebral vascular disease. When a stroke is seen in a young adult, it is usually because of an aneurysm or other vascular malformation. Most authorities agree that stroke is basically caused by atherosclerosis, and so genetic and acquired conditions that promote atherosclerotic changes in blood vessels generate risk of stroke. With modern medical treatment there is a good deal of recovery from stroke with substantial restoration of function. However, in the case of the diffuse disorders, there is really no concept of recovery because they tend to be slowly progressive. The major hope is to minimize the risk of future strokes, through such means as controlling blood pressure and weight.

An area of particular interest is the long-term effects of hypertension on cerebral function, as well as the long-term effects of antihypertensive medication. Reviews written some time ago (Elias & Streeten, 1980; King & Miller, 1990) have demonstrated that hypertension in itself, as well as antihypertensive medication, can impair cognitive function, but there are no definite conclusions in this area as yet, with studies reporting mixed as well as benign outcomes associated with prudent use of the newer antihypertensive medications (Goldstein, 1986).

## DEGENERATIVE AND DEMYELINATING DISEASES

The degenerative and demyelinating diseases constitute a variety of disorders that have several characteristics in common but that are also widely different from each other in many ways. What they have in common is that they specifically attack the central nervous system, they are slowly progressive and incurable, and while they are not all hereditary diseases, they appear to stem from some often unknown but endogenous defect in physiology. Certain diseases, once thought to be degenerative, have been found not to be so, or are thought not to be so at present. For example, certain dementias have been shown to be caused by so-called slow viruses, while multiple sclerosis, the major demyelinating disease, is strongly suspected of having a viral etiology. Thus, in these two examples, the classification would change from degenerative to infectious disease.

The term *degenerative disease* means that for some unknown reason the brain or the entire central nervous system gradually wastes away. In some cases, this wasting, or atrophy, resembles what happens to the nervous system in very old people, but substantially earlier than the senile period, perhaps as early as the late forties. The previously made distinction between presenile and senile dementia is not currently used much, apparently based upon the understanding that it is the same disease, most often Alzheimer's disease, but the research literature continues to be controversial, showing some important neurobiological differences between those who demonstrate presence of the disease before or during late life. *DSM-IV* does make a distinction within dementia of the Alzheimer's type between early-onset (65 years or younger) and late-onset (older than age 65) subtypes. Senile dementia is generally diagnosed in elderly individuals when the degree of cognitive deficit is substantially greater than one would expect with normal aging. In other words, not all old people become significantly demented before death. Most of those who do, but who do not have another identifiable disease of the central nervous system, are generally thought to have Alzheimer's disease. Indeed, Alzheimer's disease is now thought to account for more senile dementia than does vascular disease. There is another disorder related to Alzheimer's disease called Pick's disease, but it is difficult to distinguish from Alzheimer's disease in living individuals. The distinction only becomes apparent on autopsy, as the neuro-pathological changes in the brain are different. Within psychiatry, there is no longer an attempt to differentiate clinically among Alzheimer's, Pick's, and some rarer degenerative diseases. *DSM-IV* describes them with the single phrase Dementia of the Alzheimer's Type. However, efforts have been made to refine the diagnosis of dementia.

Another frequently occurring degenerative disease found in younger adults is called Huntington's chorea or Huntington's disease. The disease is characterized by progressive intellectual deterioration and a motor disorder involving gait disturbance and involuntary jerky, spasmodic movements. It has definitely been established as a hereditary disorder, and there is a 50% chance of acquiring the disease if an individual is born to a carrier of the gene for it. Symptoms may begin to appear during the second or third decade, and survival from the time of appearance of symptoms is generally about 8 years. The intellectual deterioration is characterized by progressively profound impairment of memory, with most cognitive functions eventually becoming involved. There is often a speech articulation difficulty because of the loss of control of the musculature involved in speech.

Although much is still not known about the degenerative disorders, much has been discovered in recent years. The major discovery was that Alzheimer's and Huntington's disease are apparently based on neurochemical deficiencies. In the case of Alzheimer's disease, the deficiency is thought to be primarily the group of substances related to choline, one of the neurotransmitters. The disease process itself is characterized by progressive death of the choline neurons—the cells that serve as receptor sites for cholinergic agents. Huntington's disease is more neuro-chemically complex because three neurotransmitters are involved: choline, GABA, and substance P. The reasons for these neurochemical deficiency states remain unknown, but the states themselves have been described, and treatment efforts have been initiated based on this information. For example, some Alzheimer's patients have been given choline or lecithin, a substance related to choline, and other newer drugs such as Aricept, in the hope of slowing down the progression of the illness. As indicated previously, the genetic marker for Huntington's disease has been discovered.

Most recently, an extensive literature has developed around progressive dementias that resemble but are pathologically or behaviorally different from Alzheimer's disease. One group is now known as prion diseases. Prions are proteins that are infectious and can transmit biological information. They are apparently associated with Creutzfeldt-Jakob disease, a progressive dementia. A condition has been identified known as frontotemporal dementia in which there is specific impairment of social judgment, decision making, and particular language and memory skills. There is a related condition called semantic dementia in which there is specific impairment of semantic memory. Lewy body dementia is a condition that has a different pathology from Alzheimer's disease, being associated more with Parkinson's disease (Becker, Farbman, Hamilton, & Lopez, 2011; McKeith et al., 2004). The major symptoms are variations in alertness, recurrent hallucinations, and Parkinsonian symptoms (e.g., tremor, rigidity). Lewy bodies are intraneuron inclusion bodies first identified in the substantia nigra of patients with Parkinson's disease.

Multiple sclerosis is the most common of the demyelinating diseases and is described as such because its pathology involves progressive erosion of the myelin sheaths that surround fibers in the central nervous system. Both the brain and the spinal cord are involved in this illness. Nerve conduction takes place along the myelin sheaths and, therefore, cannot occur normally when these sheaths erode. This abnormality leads to motor symptoms such as paralysis, tremor, and loss of coordination, but there are characteristic changes in vision if the optic nerve is involved, and in cognitive function. Obviously, cognitive skills that involve motor function tend to be more impaired than those that do not. Until its final stages, multiple sclerosis does not have nearly as devastating an effect on cognitive function as do the degenerative diseases. The crippling motor disorder may be the only apparent and significantly disabling symptom for many years. Less often, but not infrequently, progressive loss of vision also occurs. Multiple sclerosis acts much like an infectious disease, and some authorities feel that it is, in fact, caused by some unknown viral agent. There has been a particular interest in the Epstein-Barr virus, also called human herpesvirus 4 (Farrell et al., 2009). Symptoms generally appear during young adulthood and may be rapidly or slowly progressive, leading some authorities to differentiate between acute and chronic multiple sclerosis. Individuals with this disorder may live long lives; there are sometimes lengthy periods during which no deterioration takes place. Sometimes temporary remission of particular symptoms is seen in the so-called relapsing-remitting form of multiple sclerosis. There have been extensive neuropsychological studies of multiple sclerosis (reviewed in Allen et al., 1998), and a particular interest in differences between relapsing-remitting and chronic/progressive forms of the disease (Heaton et al., 1985).

## ALCOHOLISM

The term *alcoholism* in the context of central nervous system function involves not only the matter of excessive consumption of alcoholic beverages, but also a complex set of considerations involving nutritional status, related disorders such as head trauma, physiological alterations associated with the combination of excessive alcohol consumption and malnutrition, and possible genetic factors. What is frequently observed in long-term chronic alcoholism is a pattern of deterioration of intellectual function not unlike what is seen in patients with degenerative dementia of the Alzheimer's type. However, it is not clear that the deteriorative process is specifically associated with alcohol consumption per se. Thus, while some clinicians use the term *alcoholic dementia*, this characterization lacks sufficient specificity, as it is rarely at all clear that the observed dementia is in fact solely a product of excessive use of alcohol. Looking at the matter in temporal perspective, there first of all may be a genetic propensity for the acquisition of alcoholism that might ultimately have implications for central nervous system function (Goodwin, 1979). Second, Tarter (1976) has suggested that there may be an association between having minimal brain damage or a hyperactivity syndrome as a child and the acquisition of alcoholism as an adult. These two considerations suggest the possibility that at least some individuals who eventually become alcoholics may not have completely normal brain function anteceding the development of alcoholism. Third, during the course of becoming chronically alcoholic, dietary habits tend to become poor, and multiple head injuries may be sustained as a result of fights or accidents. As the combination of excessive alcohol abuse and poor nutrition progresses, major physiological changes may occur, particularly in the liver, and to some extent in the pancreas and gastrointestinal system. Thus, the dementia seen in long-term alcoholic patients may well involve a combination of all of these factors in addition to the always-present possibility of other neurological complications.

The majority of alcoholics who develop central nervous system complications manifest it in the form of general deterioration of intellectual abilities, but some develop specific syndromes. The most common of these is the Wernicke-Korsakoff syndrome, which begins with the patient going into a confusional state, accompanied by difficulty in walking and controlling eye movements, and by polyneuritis, a condition marked by pain or loss of sensation in the arms and legs. The latter symptoms may gradually disappear, but the confusional state may evolve into a permanent, severe amnesia. When this transition has taken place, the patient is generally described as having Korsakoff's syndrome or alcohol amnestic disorder, and is treated with large dosages of thiamine, because the etiology of the disorder appears to be a thiamine deficiency rather than a direct consequence of alcohol ingestion. Data reported previously (Blass & Gibson, 1977) that the thiamine deficiency must be accompanied by an inborn metabolic defect related to an enzyme that metabolizes thiamine and is associated with thiamine transport genes (Guerrini, Thomson, & Gurling, 2009). It should be noted that the amnesic and intellectual disorders found in chronic alcoholics are permanent and present even when the patient is not intoxicated. The acute effects of intoxication or withdrawal (e.g., delirium tremens [DTs]) are superimposed on these permanent conditions. These disorders are also progressive as long as the abuse of alcohol and malnutrition persist. Other than abstinence and improved nutrition, there is no specific treatment. Even thiamine treatment for the Korsakoff patient does not restore memory; it is used primarily to prevent additional brain damage.

It is probably fair to say that a major interest in recent years has been the genetics of alcoholism. Findings have been impressive thus far, and there is a growing, probably well-justified, belief that the presence in an individual of a positive family history of alcoholism puts that individual at increased risk for becoming alcoholic, if exposed to alcoholic beverages. The research done has been broad-ranging, including extensive family adoption studies (Goodwin et al., 1973); neuropsychological studies of relatives (Schaeffer, Parsons & Yohman, 1984) and children of alcoholics (Tarter et al., 1984); psychophysiological studies, emphasizing brain event–related potentials in siblings (Steinhauer, Hill, & Zubin, 1987) and children (Begleiter, Porjesz, Bihari, & Kissin, 1984) of alcoholics; and laboratory genetic studies. In summary, an extensive effort is being made to find biological markers of alcoholism (Hill, Steinhauer, & Zubin, 1987) and to determine the transmission of alcoholism in families. At this point in research, several susceptibility genes have been identified (Hill et al., 2004). One reasonable assumption is that alcoholism is a heterogeneous disorder, and there may be both hereditary and nonhereditary forms of it (Cloninger, Bohman, & Sigvardsson, 1981).

TOXIC, INFECTIOUS, AND METABOLIC ILLNESSES

The brain may be poisoned by exogenous or endogenous agents or it may become infected. Sometimes these events occur with such severity that the person dies, but more often, the individual survives with a greater or lesser degree of neurological dysfunction. Beginning with the exogenous toxins, we have already discussed the major one: alcohol. However, excessive use of drugs such as bromides and barbiturates may produce at least temporary brain dysfunction. This temporary condition, called delirium in *DSM-IV*, is basically a loss of capacity to maintain attention with corresponding reduced awareness of the environment. Tremors and lethargy may be accompanying symptoms. Delirium is reversible in most cases but may evolve into a permanent dementia or other neurological disorder.

In psychiatric settings a fairly frequently seen type of toxic disorder is carbon monoxide poisoning. This disorder and its treatment are quite complex, because it usually occurs in an individual with a major mood or psychotic disorder who attempted to commit suicide by inhaling car fumes in a closed garage. The brain damage sustained during the episode may often be permanent, resulting in significant intellectual and physical dysfunction in addition to the previously existing psychiatric disorder. Other toxic substances that may affect central nervous system function include certain sedative and hypnotic drugs, plant poisons, heavy metals, and toxins produced by certain bacteria, leading to such conditions as tetanus and botulism. The specific effects of these substances themselves, as well as of whether exposure is acute (as in the case of tetanus or arsenic poisoning) or chronic (as in the case of addiction to opiates and related drugs), are often crucial.

Many brain disorders are associated with inborn errors of metabolism. In some way a fault in metabolism produces a detrimental effect on the nervous system, generally beginning in early life. There are so many of these disorders that we will only mention two of the more well-known ones as illustrations. The first is phenylketonuria (PKU). PKU is an amino acid uria, a disorder that involves excessive excretion of an amino acid into the urine. It is genetic and, if untreated, can produce intellectual disability accompanied by poor psychomotor development and hyperactivity. The treatment involves a diet low in a substance called phenylalanine. The second disorder is Tay-Sachs disease. The enzyme abnormality here is a deficiency in a substance called hexasaminidase A, which is important for the metabolism of protein and polysaccharides. It is hereditary, occurs mainly in Jewish children, and is present from birth. The symptoms are initially poor motor development and progressive loss of vision, followed by dementia, with death usually occurring before age five. These two examples illustrate similarity in process, which is basically an inherited enzyme deficiency, but variability in outcome. PKU is treatable, with a relatively favorable prognosis, whereas Tay-Sachs is a rapidly progressive, incurable terminal illness.

Bacterial infections of the brain are generally associated with epidemics but sometimes are seen when there are no epidemics at large. They are generally referred to as encephalitis, when the brain is infected, or meningitis, when the infection is in the membranous tissue that lines the brain, known as the *meninges*. Infections, of course, are produced by microorganisms that invade tissue and produce inflammation. During the acute phase of the bacterial infections, the patient may be quite ill, and survival is an important issue. Headaches, fever, and a stiff neck are major symptoms. There may be delirium, confusion, and alterations in state of consciousness ranging from drowsiness, through excessive sleeping, to coma. Some forms of encephalitis were popularly known as "sleeping sickness." Following the acute phase of bacterial infection, the patient may be left with residual neurological and neuropsychological disabilities and personality changes. Sometimes infections are local, and the patient is left with neurological deficits that correspond with the lesion site. The irritability, restlessness, and aggressiveness of postencephalitic children are mentioned in the literature. Jervis (1959) described them as overactive, restless, impulsive, assaultive, and wantonly destructive.

Neurosyphylis is another type of infection that has a relatively unique course. Most interesting, aside from the progressive dementia that characterizes this disorder, are the major personality changes involving the acquisition of delusions and a tendency toward uncritical self-aggrandizement. Although neurosyphilis or general paresis played a major role in the development of psychiatry, it is now a relatively rare disease and is seldom seen in clinical practice. Similarly, the related neurosyphilitic symptoms, such as tabes dorsalis and syphilitic deafness, are also rarely seen.

The incidence and perhaps the interest in the bacterial infections and neurosyphilis have diminished, but interest in viral infections has increased substantially during recent years. There are perhaps four reasons for this phenomenon: (1) Jonas Salk's discovery that poliomyelitis was caused by a virus and could be prevented by vaccination; (2) the recent increase in the incidence of herpes simplex, which is a viral disorder; (3) the appearance of AIDS; and (4) the discovery of the "slow viruses." The latter two reasons are probably of greatest interest in the present context. With regard to the slow viruses, it has been discovered that certain viruses have a long incubation period and may cause chronic degenerative disease, resembling Alzheimer's disease in many ways. Thus, some forms of dementia may be produced by a transmittable agent. One of these dementias appears to be a disease known as *kuru*, and another is known as Creutzfeldt-Jakob disease. Recently, there has been an outbreak of a related disorder called mad cow disease, or bovine spongiform encephalopathy (Balter, 2001). The importance of the finding is that the discovery of infection as the cause of disease opens the possibility of the development of preventive treatment in the form of a vaccine. AIDS dementia is another form of viral encephalopathy. It is a consequence of human immunovirus (HIV) infection and apparently represents an illness that has not appeared on the planet previously. It has been characterized as a progressive subcortical dementia of the type seen in patients with Huntington's disease and other neurological disorders in which the major neuropathology is in the subcortex. The syndrome has not been completely described, but there is substantial evidence of neuropsychological abnormalities. The first papers in this area appeared circa 1987, with the best-known study being that of

Grant et al. (1987). A review is contained in Bornstein, Nasrallah, Para, and Whitacre (1993), and recent updates have been provided by Heaton (2006) and Woods et al. (2009).

EPILEPSY

Despite the usual manner in which this condition is described, epilepsy is really a symptom of many diseases and not really a disease in itself. Patients are generally diagnosed as epileptics when seizures are the major or only presenting symptoms and the cause cannot be determined. However, seizures are commonly associated with diagnosable disorders such as brain tumors, alcoholism, or head trauma. Furthermore, the view that epilepsy means that the patient has "fits" or episodes of falling and engaging in uncontrolled, spasmodic movements is also not completely accurate. These fits or convulsions do represent one form of epilepsy, but there are other forms as well. Several attempts have been made to classify epilepsy into subtypes, and we will mention only the most recent one generally accepted by neurologists (Gastaut, 1970).

The major distinction made is between generalized and partial seizures. In the case of the generalized seizures, there is a bilaterally symmetrical abnormality of brain function, with one of two things generally happening. One is a massive convulsion with a sequence of spasmodic movements and jerking, whereas the other is a brief abrupt loss of consciousness with little in the way of abnormal motor activity. There may be some lip smacking or involuntary movements of the eyelids. The former type used to be called a grand mal seizure, whereas the latter type was called a petit mal seizure or absence. The partial seizures may have what is described as a simple or complex symptomatology. In the simple case, the seizure may be confined to a single limb and may involve either motor or sensory function. When motor function is involved, there is often a turning movement of the head, accompanied by contractions of the trunk and limbs. There is a relatively rare form of this disorder called a Jacksonian motor seizure, in which the spasmodic movements spread from the original site to the entire side of the body. The phenomenon is referred to as a *march*. In the case of sensory seizures, the epileptic activity may consist of a variety of sensory disorders, such as sudden numbness, a "pins and needles" feeling, seeing spits of light, or even a buzzing or roaring in the ears.

The complex partial seizures involve confused but purposeful-appearing behavior followed by amnesia for the episode. In this condition, sometimes known as temporal lobe or psychomotor epilepsy, the patient may walk around in a daze, engage in inappropriate behavior, or have visual or auditory hallucinations. From this description, it is clear that not all seizures involve massive motor convulsions. What all of these phenomena have in common is that they are based on a sudden, abrupt alteration of brain function. The alteration is produced by an excessive, disorganized discharge of neurons. Thus, if one were looking at an epileptic individual's brain waves on an electroencephalograph (EEG), if a seizure occurred, there would be a sudden and dramatic alteration in the characteristics of the EEG. The presence and particular pattern of these alterations are often used to identify and diagnose various forms of epilepsy.

The question of whether there is an association between epilepsy and intellectual impairment is a complex one. According to Klove and Matthews (1974), individuals having complex partial (temporal lobe) seizures demonstrate little in the way of intellectual impairment. However, individuals with generalized seizures of unknown etiology that appear early in life are likely to have significant intellectual deficit. The matter is also complicated by the cause of the seizure. If an individual has seizures related to a brain tumor, it is likely that the neuropsychological deficits generally associated with the lesion sites involved can be expected to appear as well as the seizures. The question of intellectual deficit seems to arise primarily in the case of individuals who are just epileptic and have no other apparent neurological signs or symptoms. This condition is known as recurrent seizures of unknown cause or as idiopathic epilepsy. Our tentative answer to the question appears to be that there is a higher probability of significant intellectual deficit when the disorder involves generalized seizures and appears early in life.

The mental health practitioner should be aware that, although epilepsy is an eminently treatable disorder through the use of a variety of anticonvulsant medications, the epileptic patient might have many difficulties of various types. There still appears to be some degree of social stigma attached to the disorder, either in the form of superstitious beliefs or the inaccurate stereotype that epileptics tend to be violent or impulsive people. More realistically, epileptics do have difficulties with such matters as obtaining driver's licenses or insurance coverage that allows them to work around potentially hazardous equipment. It is possible that during a complex partial seizure an individual can perform an antisocial act over which he or she honestly has no control and cannot remember. Epileptic seizures may be symptoms of some life-threatening illness. Children with petit mal epilepsy may have school difficulties because of their momentary lapses of consciousness. Individuals with motor seizures may injure their heads during the seizure and produce additional brain dysfunction through trauma. Thus, the epileptic may have many problems in living that are not experienced by the nonepileptic, and epileptics frequently may be assisted through an understanding of the nature of the condition and counseling and support in coping with it.

Myslobodsky and Mirsky (1988) have edited an extensive work on petit mal epilepsy that covers its genetic, neurophysiological, neuropsychological, metabolic, and electrophysiological aspects. There is a growing interest in psychosocial aspects of epilepsy. Having seizures clearly produces an impact on one's environment, and people in the environment may maintain the older superstitions and false beliefs about epilepsy. Furthermore, modifications of behavior in epileptics may be largely biologically determined because of the cerebral dysfunction associated with the disorder. Dodrill (1986) has reviewed the extensive literature on psychosocial consequences of epilepsy, providing a useful outline of the types of psychosocial difficulties epileptics commonly experience, the relationship between psychosocial and neuropsychological function, and treatment-related issues.

## SOME COMMON SYNDROMES

In this section we will provide descriptions of the more commonly occurring disorders associated with structural brain damage. It is clear that what is common in one setting may be rare in another. Thus, we will focus on what is common in an adult neuropsychiatric setting. The neuropsychological syndromes found in childhood are often quite different from what is seen in adults and deserve separate treatment. Furthermore, the emphasis will be placed on chronic rather than acute syndromes because, with relatively rare exceptions, the psychologist and psychiatrist encounter the former type far more frequently than the latter. However, initially acute conditions such as stroke that evolve into chronic conditions will be dealt with in some detail.

Thus far, we have viewed matters from the standpoints of general concepts of brain function and of neuropathological processes. Now we will be looking at the behavioral manifestations of the interaction between various brain mechanisms and different types of pathology. It is useful to view these manifestations in the form of identified patterns of behavioral characteristics that might be described as neuropsychological syndromes. Although there are admittedly other ways of describing and classifying neuropsychological deficit, the syndrome approach has the advantage of providing rather graphic phenomenological descriptions of different kinds of brain-damaged patients. However, it runs the risk of suggesting that every brain-damaged patient can be classified as having some specific, identifiable syndrome— something that is not at all true. It is, therefore, important to keep in mind that we are discussing classic types of various disorders that are in fact seen in some actual patients. However, many brain-damaged patients do not have classic-type syndromes, their symptomatology reflecting an often complex combination of portions of several syndromes.

Heilman and Valenstein (2003), in the way in which they outlined their clinical neuropsychology text, have suggested a useful and workable classification of syndromes. There are first of all the communicative disorders, which may be subdivided into aphasia and the specialized language or language-related disorders, including reading impairment (alexia), writing disorders (agraphia), and calculation disorders (acalculia). Second, there are the syndromes associated with some aspect of perception or motility. These include the perception of one's body (the body schema disturbances), the various visual-spatial disorders (which may involve perception, constructional abilities, or both), the gnostic disorders (impairment of visual, auditory, and tactile recognition), the neglect syndromes, and the disorders of skilled and purposeful movement, called apraxias. Third, there are the syndromes that primarily involve general intelligence and memory-dementia and the amnesic disorders. Associated with this latter type are the relatively unique syndromes associated with damage to the frontal lobes. These three general categories account for most of the syndromes seen in adults, and our discussion here will be limited to them.

*The Communicative Disorders*   In general, aphasia and related language disorders are associated with unilateral brain damage to the dominant hemisphere, which in most individuals is the left hemisphere. Most aphasias result from stroke, but they can be acquired on the basis of left hemisphere head trauma or from brain tumor. Whereas the definition has changed over the years, the most current one requires the presence of impairment of communicative ability associated with focal, structural brain damage. Thus, the term is not coextensive with all disorders of communicative ability and does not include, for example, the language disorders commonly seen in demented individuals with diffuse brain damage. The study of aphasia has in essence become a separate area of scientific inquiry, having its own literature and several theoretical frameworks. The term *aphasia* does not convey a great deal of clinically significant information, because the various subtypes are quite different from each other.

Numerous attempts have been made to classify the aphasias, and there is no universally accepted system. Contemporary theory indicates that perhaps the most useful major distinction is between fluent and nonfluent aphasias. To many authorities, this distinction is more accurate than the previously more commonly made one between expressive and receptive aphasias. The problem is that people with aphasia with primarily expressive problems do not generally have normal language comprehension, and it is almost always true that people with aphasia with major speech comprehension disturbances do not express themselves normally. However, there are individuals with aphasia who talk fluently and others whose speech is labored, very limited, and halting, if present at all in a meaningful sense. In the case of the former group, while speech is fluent, it is generally more or less incomprehensible because of a tendency to substitute incorrect words for correct ones; a condition known as *verbal paraphasia*. However, the primary disturbance in these patients involves profoundly impaired auditory comprehension. This combination of impaired comprehension and paraphasia is generally known as Wernicke's aphasia. The responsible lesion is generally in the superior gyrus of the left temporal lobe. In nonfluent aphasia, comprehension is generally somewhat better, but speech is accomplished with great difficulty and is quite limited. This condition is generally known as Broca's aphasia, the responsible lesion being in the lower, posterior portion of the left frontal lobe (i.e., Broca's area). Several other types of aphasia are relatively rare and will not be described here. However, it is important to point out that most aphasias are mixed, having components of the various pure types. Furthermore, the type of aphasia may change in the same patient, particularly during the course of recovery.

The disorders of reading, writing, and calculation may also be divided into subtypes. In the case of reading, our interest here is in the so-called acquired alexias, in which an individual who was formerly able to read has lost that ability because of focal, structural brain damage. The ability to read letters, words, or sentences may be lost. Handwriting disturbances, or agraphia, might involve a disability in writing words from dictation or a basic disability in forming letters. Thus, some agraphic patients can write, but with omissions and distortions relative to what was dictated. However, some can no longer engage in the purposive movements needed to form letters. Calculation disturbances, or acalculias, are also of several types. The patient may lose the ability to read numbers, to calculate even if the numbers can be read, or to arrange numbers in a proper spatial sequence for calculation. The various syndromes associated with communicative disorders, while sometimes existing in pure forms, often merge together. For example, alexia is frequently associated with Broca's aphasia, and difficulty with handwriting is commonly seen in patients with Wernicke's aphasia. However, there is generally a pattern in which there is a clear primary disorder, such as impaired auditory comprehension, with other disorders, such as difficulty with reading or writing, occurring as associated defects. Sometimes rather unusual combinations occur, as in the case of the syndrome of alexia without agraphia. In this case, the patient can write but cannot read, often to the extent that the patient cannot read what she or he just wrote. Based upon recent research, we would add that academic deficits that are not the product of brain damage acquired during adulthood, nor of inadequate educational opportunity, are frequently seen in adults. Rather, people with these deficits have developmentally based learning disabilities that they never outgrew. The view that learning disability is commonly outgrown has been rejected by most students of this area (Katz, Goldstein, & Beers, 2001).

*Disorders of Perception and Motility*    The disorders of perception can involve perception of one's body as well as perception of the external world. In the case of the external world, the disorder can involve some class of objects or some geographic location. The disorders of motility to be discussed here will not be primary losses of motor function as in the cases of paralysis or paresis, but losses in the area of the capacity to perform skilled, purposive acts. The set of impairments found in this area is called apraxia. There is also the borderline area in which the neuro-psychological defect has to do with the coordination of a sense modality, usually vision, and purposive movement. These disorders are sometimes described as impairment of constructional or visual-spatial relations ability. In some patients the primary difficulty is perceptual, whereas in others it is mainly motoric. The body schema disturbances most commonly seen are of three types. The first has to do with the patient's inability to point to his or her own body parts on command. The syndrome is called autotopognosia, meaning lack of awareness of the surface of one's body. A more localized disorder of this type is finger agnosia, in which, while identification of body parts is otherwise intact, the patient cannot identify the fingers of his or her own hands, or the hands of another person. Finger agnosia has been conceptualized as a partial dissolution of the body schema. The third type of body schema disturbance is right-left disorientation, in which the patient cannot identify body parts in regard to whether they are on the right or left side. For example, when the patient is asked to show the right hand, he or she may become confused or show the left hand. More commonly, however, a more complex command is required to elicit this deficit, such as asking the patient to place the left hand on the right shoulder. The traditional thinking about this disorder is that both finger agnosia and right-left disorientation are part of a syndrome, the responsible brain damage being in the region of the left angular gyrus. However, Benton (1985) has pointed out that the matter is more complicated than that, and the issue of localization involves the specific nature of these defects in terms of the underlying cognitive and perceptual processes affected.

The perceptual disorders in which the difficulty is in recognition of some class of external objects are called gnostic disorders or agnosias. These disorders may be classified with regard to modality and verbal or nonverbal content. Thus, one form of the disorder might involve visual perception of nonverbal stimuli, and would be called visual agnosia. By definition, an agnosia is present when primary function of the affected modality is intact, but the patient cannot recognize or identify the stimulus. For example, in visual agnosia, the patient can see but cannot recognize what he or she has seen. In order to assure oneself that visual agnosia is present, it should be determined that the patient can recognize and name the object in question when it is placed in his or her hand, so that it can be recognized by touch, or when it produces some characteristic sound, so that it can be recognized by audition. The brain lesions involved in the agnosias are generally in the association areas for the various perceptual modalities. Thus, visual agnosia is generally produced by damage to association areas in the occipital lobes. When language is involved, there is obviously a great deal of overlap between the agnosias and the aphasias. For example, visual-verbal agnosia can really be viewed as a form of alexia. In these cases, it is often important to determine through detailed testing whether the deficit is primarily a disturbance of perceptual recognition or a higher-level conceptual disturbance involving language comprehension. There is a wide variety of gnostic disorders reported in the literature involving such phenomena as the inability to recognize faces, colors, or spoken words. However, they are relatively rare conditions, and when present they may only persist during the acute phase of the illness. In general, agnosia has been described as "perception without meaning," and it is important to remember that it is quite a different phenomenon from what we usually think of as blindness or deafness.

Sometimes a perceptual disorder does not involve a class of objects but a portion of geographic space. The phenomenon itself is described by many terms, the most frequently used ones being *neglect* and *inattention*. It is seen most dramatically in vision, where the patient may neglect the entire right or left side of the visual world. It also occurs in the somatosensory modality, in which case the patient may neglect one side or the other of his or her body. Neglect can occur on either side, but it is more common on the left side, because it is generally associated with right hemisphere brain damage. In testing for neglect, it is often useful to employ the method of double stimulation, for example, in the form of simultaneous finger wiggles in the areas of the right and left visual fields. Typically, the patient may report seeing the wiggle in the right field but not in the left. Similarly, when the patient with neglect is touched lightly on the right and left hand at the same time, he or she may report feeling the touch in only one hand or the other. As in the case of the gnostic disorders, neglect is defined in terms of the assumption of intactness of the primary sensory modalities. Thus, the patient with visual neglect should have otherwise normal vision in the neglected half field, while the patient with tactile neglect should have normal somatosensory function. Clinically, neglect may be a symptom of some acute process and should diminish in severity or disappear as the neuropathological condition stabilizes. For example, visual neglect of the left field is often seen in individuals who have recently sustained right hemisphere strokes, but it can be expected to disappear as the patient recovers.

The apraxias constitute a group of syndromes in which the basic deficit involves impairment of purposive movement occurring in the absence of paralysis, weakness, or unsteadiness. For some time, the distinction has been made among three major types of apraxia: ideomotor, limb-kinetic, and ideational. In ideomotor apraxia, the patient has difficulty in performing a movement to verbal command. In the case of limb-kinetic apraxia, movement is clumsy when performed on command or when the patient is asked to imitate a movement. In ideational apraxia, the difficulty is with organizing the correct motor sequences in response to language. In other words, it may be viewed as a disability in regard to carrying out a series of acts. In addition, there are facial apraxias, in which the patient cannot carry out facial movements to command. These four types are thought to involve different brain regions and different pathways. However, they are all generally conceptualized as a destruction or disconnection of motor engrams or traces that control skilled, purposive movement. Certain of the visual-spatial disorders are referred to as apraxias, such as constructional or dressing apraxia, but they are different in nature from the purer motor apraxias described above.

The basic difficulty the patient with a visual-spatial disorder has relates to comprehension of spatial relationships, and in most cases, coordination between visual perception and movement. In extreme cases, the patient may readily become disoriented and lose his or her way when going from one location to another. However, in most cases, the difficulty appears to be at the cognitive level and may be examined by asking the patient to copy figures or solve jigsaw or block design type puzzles. Patients with primarily perceptual difficulties have problems in localizing points in space, judging direction, and maintaining geographic orientation, as tested by asking the patient to describe a route or use a map. Patients with constructional difficulties have problems with copying and block building. So-called dressing apraxia may be seen as a form of constructional disability in which the patient cannot deal effectively with the visual-spatial demands involved in such tasks as buttoning clothing. Whereas visual-spatial disorders can arise from lesions found in most parts of the brain, they are most frequently seen, and seen with the greatest severity, in patients with right hemisphere brain damage. Generally, the area that will most consistently produce the severest deficit is the posterior portion of the right hemisphere. In general, while some patients show a dissociation between visual-spatial and visual-motor or constructional aspects of the syndrome of constructional apraxia, most patients have difficulties on both purely perceptual and constructional tasks.

*Dementia*   Dementia is probably the most common form of major neurocognitive disorder. There are several types of dementia, but they all involve usually slowly progressive deterioration of intellectual function. The deterioration is frequently patterned, with loss of memory generally being the first function to decline, and other abilities deteriorating at later stages of the illness. One major class of dementia consists of those disorders that arise during late life, either during late middle age or old age. *DSM-IV* makes this distinction with the terms *early onset* and *late onset* in place of the previously used terms *presenile* and *senile*. As the terms are used now, dementia may occur at any age. In children it is differentiated from intellectual disability on the basis of the presence of deterioration from a formerly higher level. Dementia may result from head trauma or essentially any of the neuropathological conditions discussed previously. One common cause of dementia appears to be alcoholism and the nutritional disorders that typically accompany it. A specific type of dementia that generally appears before the presenile period is Huntington's disease.

The term *dementia*, when defined in the broad way suggested here, is not particularly useful and does not really provide more information than do such terms as *organic brain syndrome* or *chronic brain syndrome*. However, when the term is used in a more specific way, it becomes possible to point out specific characteristics that may be described as syndromes. This specificity may be achieved by defining the dementias as those disorders in which, for no exogenous reason, the brain begins to deteriorate and continues to do so until death. *DSM-IV* describes these conditions as dementia of the Alzheimer's type, because the most common type of progressive degenerative dementia is Alzheimer's disease. As indicated earlier, a diagnostic method has recently become available to specifically diagnose Alzheimer's disease in the living patient. Its presence also becomes apparent on examination of the brain at autopsy.

Clinically, the course of the illness generally begins with signs of impairment of memory for recent events, followed by deficits in judgment, visual-spatial skills, and language. The language deficit has become a matter of particular interest, perhaps because the communicative difficulties of dementia patients are becoming increasingly recognized. Generally, the language difficulty does not resemble aphasia, but can perhaps be best characterized as an impoverishment of speech, with word-finding difficulties and progressive inability to produce extended and comprehensible narrative speech. Basically the same finding was noted in the descriptive writing of Alzheimer's disease patients (Neils, Boller, Gerdeman, & Cole, 1989). The patients wrote shorter descriptive paragraphs than did age-matched controls, and they also made more handwriting errors of various types. The end state of dementia is generalized, severe intellectual impairment involving all areas, with the patient sometimes surviving for various lengths of time in a persistent vegetative state. The progressive dementia seen in Huntington's disease also involves significant impairment of memory, with other abilities becoming gradually affected through the course of the illness. However, it differs from Alzheimer's disease in that it is accompanied by the choreic movements described earlier and by the fact that the age of onset is substantially earlier than is the case for Alzheimer's disease. Because of the chorea, there is also a difficulty in speech articulation frequently seen, which is not the case for Alzheimer's patients.

A form of dementia that does not have an unknown etiology but that is slowly progressive has been described as vascular dementia. This disorder is known to be associated with hypertension and a series of strokes, with the end result being substantial deterioration. However, the course of the deterioration is not thought to be as uniform as is the case in Alzheimer's disease, but rather is generally described as stepwise and patchy. The patient may remain relatively stable between strokes, and the symptomatology produced may be associated with the site of the strokes. It may be mentioned that whereas these distinctions between vascular and Alzheimer's type dementia are clearly described, in individual patients it is not always possible to make a definitive differential diagnosis. Even such sophisticated radiological methods as the CT scan and MRI do not always contribute to the diagnosis.

During the bulk of the course of the illness, the dementia patient will typically appear as confused, possibly disoriented, and lacking in the ability to recall recent events. Speech may be very limited, and if fluent, likely to be incomprehensible. Thus, these patients do not have the specific syndromes of the type described previously surrounded by otherwise intact function. Instead, the deficit pattern tends to be global in nature, with all functions more or less involved. Some investigators have attempted to identify syndromal subtypes, with some having more deficit in the area of abstraction and judgment, some in the area of memory, and some in regard to affect and personality changes. This typology has recently received support from studies delineating frontotemporal dementia, semantic dementia, and Lewy body dementia as separate entities, but most patients have difficulties with all three areas. Although there are some treatable dementias, particularly dementias associated with endocrine disorders or normal pressure hydrocephalus, there is no curative treatment for Alzheimer's type dementia. Current research offers the hope that pharmacological treatment may eventually be able to ameliorate the course of Alzheimer's disease, but thus far no such effective treatment is available.

As indicated, frontal lobe or frontotemporal dementia has been proposed as a separate disorder. It is only diagnosed when Alzheimer's disease has been ruled out, and the patient must have symptoms that can be characterized as forming a "frontal lobe syndrome" (Rosenstein, 1998). The generic term commonly used to characterize the behaviors associated with this syndrome is *executive dysfunction*, a concept originally introduced by Luria (1966). Executive function is progressively impaired, and personality changes involving either apathy and indifference or childishness and euphoria occur. Compared with patients with Alzheimer's disease, frontal dementia patients have greater impairment of executive function but relatively better memory and visuoconstructional abilities. The outstanding features all may be viewed as relating to impaired ability to control, regulate, and program behavior. This impairment is manifested in numerous ways, including poor abstraction ability, impaired judgment, apathy, and loss of impulse control. Language is sometimes impaired, but in a rather unique way. Rather than having a formal language disorder, the patient loses the ability to control behavior through language. There is also often a difficulty with narrative speech that has been interpreted as a problem in forming the intention to speak or in formulating a plan for a narrative. Such terms as lack of insight or of the ability to produce goal-oriented behavior are used to describe the frontal lobe patient. In many cases, these activating, regulatory, and programming functions are so impaired that the outcome looks like a generalized dementia with implications for many forms of cognitive, perceptual, and motor activities. Frontal dementia may occur as a result of several processes, such as head trauma, tumor, or stroke, but the syndrome produced is more or less the same.

## AMNESIA

Whereas some degree of impairment of memory is a part of many brain disorders, there are some conditions in which loss of memory is clearly the most outstanding deficit. When the loss of memory is particularly severe and persistent, and other cognitive and perceptual functions are relatively intact, the patient can be described as having an amnesic syndrome. Dementia patients are often amnesic, but their memory disturbance is embedded in significant generalized impairment of intellectual and communicative abilities. The amnesic patient generally has normal language and may be of average intelligence. As in the case of aphasia and several of the other disorders, there is more than one amnesic syndrome. The differences among them revolve around what the patient can and cannot remember. The structures in the brain that are particularly important for memory are the limbic system, especially the hippocampus, and certain brainstem structures, including the mammilary bodies and the dorsomedial nucleus of the thalamus.

There are many systems described in the literature for distinguishing among types of amnesia and types of memory. With regard to the amnesias, perhaps the most basic distinction is between anterograde and retrograde amnesia. Anterograde amnesia involves the inability to form new memories from the time of the onset of the illness producing the amnesia, whereas retrograde amnesia refers to the inability to recall events that took place before the onset of the illness. This distinction dovetails with the distinction between recent and remote memory. It is also in some correspondence with the distinction made between short-term and long-term memory in the experimental literature. However, various theories define these terms somewhat differently, and perhaps it is best to use the more purely descriptive terms *recent* and *remote memory* in describing the amnesic disorders. It then can be stated that the most commonly appearing amnesic disorders involve dramatic impairment of recent memory with relative sparing of remote memory. This sparing becomes greater as the events to be remembered become more remote. Thus, most amnesic patients can recall their early lives, but they may totally forget what occurred during the last several hours. This distinction between recent and remote memory possibly aids in explaining why most amnesic patients maintain normal language function and average intelligence. In this respect, an amnesic disorder is not so much an obliteration of the past as it is an inability to learn new material.

Probably the most common type of relatively pure amnesic disorder is alcoholic Korsakoff's syndrome. These patients, while often maintaining average levels in several areas of cognitive function, demonstrate a dense amnesia for recent events with relatively well-preserved remote memory. Alcoholic Korsakoff's syndrome has been conceptualized by Butters and Cermak (1980) as an information-processing defect in which new material is encoded in a highly degraded manner leading to high susceptibility to interference. Butters and Cermak (1980), as well as numerous other investigators, have accomplished detailed experimental studies of alcoholic Korsakoff's patients in which the nature of their perceptual, memory, and learning difficulties has been described in detail. The results of this research aid in explaining numerous clinical phenomena noted in Korsakoff's patients, such as their capacity to perform learned behaviors without recall of when or if those behaviors were previously executed, or their tendency to confabulate or "fill in" for the events of the past day that they do not recall. It may be noted that while confabulation was once thought to be a cardinal symptom of Korsakoff's syndrome, it is only seen in some patients.

Another type of amnesic disorder is seen when there is direct, focal damage to the temporal lobes, and most important, to the hippocampus. These temporal lobe or limbic system amnesias are less common than Korsakoff's syndrome, but they have been well studied because of the light they shed on the neuropathology of memory. These patients share many of the characteristics of Korsakoff's patients but have a much more profound deficit in regard to basic consolidation and storage of new material. When Korsakoff's patients are sufficiently cued and given enough time, they can learn. Indeed, sometimes they can demonstrate normal recognition memory. However, patients with temporal lobe amnesias may find it almost impossible to learn new material under any circumstances.

In some cases, amnesic disorders are modality specific. If one distinguishes between verbal and nonverbal memory, the translation can be made from the distinction between language and nonverbal abilities associated with the specialized functions of each cerebral hemisphere. It has in fact been reported that patients with unilateral lesions involving the left temporal lobe may have memory deficits for verbal material only, while right temporal patients have corresponding deficits for nonverbal material. Thus, the left temporal patient may have difficulty with learning word lists, while the right temporal patient may have difficulty with geometric forms. In summary, whereas there are several amnesic syndromes, they all have in common the symptom of lack of ability to learn new material following the onset of the illness. Sometimes the symptom is modality specific, involving only verbal or nonverbal material, but more often than not it involves both modalities. There are several relatively pure types of amnesia, notably Korsakoff's syndrome, but memory difficulties are cardinal symptoms of many other brain disorders, notably the progressive dementias and certain disorders associated with infection. For example, people with Herpes encephalitis frequently have severely impaired memories, but they have other cognitive deficits as well.

## ALTERNATIVE DESCRIPTIVE SYSTEMS

As has been indicated, not all clinicians or researchers associated with brain-damaged patients have adopted the neuropsychologically oriented syndrome approach briefly described in the preceding sections. There are many reasons for the existence of these differing views, some of them methodological and some substantive in nature. The methodological issues largely revolve around the operations used by investigators to establish the existence of a syndrome. Critics suggest that syndromes may be established on the basis of overly subjective inferences as well as on incomplete examinations. The alternative method proposed is generally described as a dimensional approach in which, rather than attempting to assign patients to categories, they are measured on a variety of neuropsychologically relevant dimensions such as intellectual function, language ability, and memory. Advocates of this approach are less concerned with determining whether the patient has a recognizable syndrome and more involved with profiling the patient along several continuous dimensions and relating that profile to underlying brain mechanisms. Rourke and Brown (1986) have clarified this issue in a full discussion of similarities and differences between behavioral neurology and clinical neuropsychology. Using a dimensional philosophy, there is no need to develop a classification system except perhaps in terms of certain characteristic profiles. For purposes of providing an overview of the descriptive phenomenology of structural brain damage, however, substantive matters probably are of more relevance.

In essence, the disciplines of neurology, neuropsychology, and psychiatry have all developed descriptive classificatory systems that differ in many respects. We have already discussed the ways in which brain damage is described and classified by neurologists and neuropsychologists. However, the psychiatric descriptions are also quite important, because they point to problems not uncommonly seen in brain-damaged patients that are not always clearly identifiable in the neurological and neuropsychological systems. There is an area of overlap in regard to dementia and the amnesias, but *DSM-III, DSM-III-R,* and *DSM-IV* contain several categories that are not clearly defined neurologically or neuropsychologically. However, there has been a major reorganization of the categorization of these disorders in *DSM-IV,* largely revolving around an abandonment of the term *organic.* In general, what was previously characterized as an organic disorder, such as organic delusional syndrome, is now characterized as a mental disorder due to a general medical condition. Thus, the closest diagnosis to "organic delusional syndrome" would be "psychotic disorder due to a general medical condition," and the diagnostic criteria are listed under the heading "Schizophrenia and Other Psychotic Disorders." Patients with this disorder have delusional beliefs or hallucinations while in a normal state of consciousness as the primary symptoms. It must be established that the delusions have an organic basis and the patient is not actually delusional because of a paranoid or schizophrenic disorder. The neurological basis for this syndrome is varied, and may involve drug abuse, right hemisphere brain damage, or in some cases Huntington's disease or other dementias. This diagnosis incorporates what was previously described as organic hallucinosis. Delusions or hallucinations are specified as the predominant symptom. Other mental disorders due to a general medical condition include disorders of mood, anxiety, sexual dysfunction, sleep, and catatonic disorder. *DSM-IV* also contains a category of personality change due to a general medical condition. Such changes may be classified as disinhibited, aggressive, paranoid, other, or combined. The personality changes noted often involve increased impulsiveness, emotional lability, or apathy. Perhaps these are really mainly frontal lobe syndromes, but the syndrome may also be seen in conjunction with temporal lobe epilepsy. In *DSM-IV,* the specific medical condition, if known, becomes a part of the diagnosis.

*DSM-IV* also classifies under the organic mental disorders substance-induced delirium and persisting dementia. Delirium may be associated with intoxication or withdrawal. If cognitive symptoms persist beyond the period of delirium, intoxication, or withdrawal, the diagnosis of substance-induced persisting dementia is made. The specific substance or substance combination is indicated if known. Thus, for example, one can make the diagnosis of alcohol-induced persisting dementia. Typically, delirium is an acute phenomenon and does not persist beyond a matter of days. However, delirium, notably when it is associated with alcohol abuse, may eventually evolve into permanent disorders in the form of persistent dementia. The behavioral correlates of delirium generally involve personality changes such as euphoria, agitation, anxiety, hallucinations, and depersonalization. The more permanent cognitive changes might include impairment of memory and inability to concentrate. Within the context of psychopathology, the commonality between these conditions and those related to more permanent, structural brain damage is that they all have an identified or presumed organic basis and are therefore distinct from the functional psychiatric disorders. The phraseology used throughout the Delirium, Dementia, and Amnestic and Other Cognitive Disorders section of *DSM-IV* is, "There is evidence, from the history, physical examination, or laboratory findings of" the presence of the disorder under consideration; for example, "that the deficits are etiologically related to the persisting effects of substance abuse."

With regard to *DSM-5*, the draft criteria for what is termed the Alzheimer's disease subtype of Major or Minor Neurocognitive Disorders have appeared, but work on the other subtypes is still in progress at this writing. Apparently there are plans for developing subtype criteria for frontotemporal lobar degeneration, Huntington's disease, traumatic brain injury, and other types of dementia.

Psychiatrically based categorization can perhaps be most productively viewed as supplemental to the type of neuropsychological system used by Heilman and Valenstein (2003), rather than as an alternative to it. It plays a major role in describing the noncognitive kinds of symptomatology that are often associated with structural brain damage, particularly for those cases in which these personality, mood, and affective changes are the predominant symptoms. These considerations are of the utmost clinical importance, because the failure to recognize the organic basis for some apparently functional symptom such as a personality change may lead to the initiation of totally inappropriate treatment or the failure to recognize a life-threatening physical illness.

Although alterations in brain function can give rise to symptoms that look like functional personality changes, the reverse can also occur. That is, a nonorganic personality change, notably the acquisition of a depression, can produce symptoms that look like they have been produced by alterations in brain function. The term generally applied to this situation is *pseudodementia*, and it is most frequently seen in elderly people who become depressed. The concept of pseudodementia or depressive pseudodementia is not universally accepted, but it is not uncommon to find elderly patients diagnosed as demented when in fact the symptoms of dementia are actually produced by depression. The point is proven when the symptoms disappear or diminish substantially after the depression has run its course, or the patient is treated with antidepressant medication. Wells (1979, 1980) has pointed out that this differential diagnosis is a difficult one to make, and it cannot be accomplished satisfactorily with the usual examinational, laboratory, and psychometric methods. He suggests that perhaps the most useful diagnostic criteria are clinical features. For example, patients with pseudodementia tend to complain about their cognitive losses, whereas patients with dementia tend not to complain. In a more recent formulation, Caine (1986) pointed to the many complexities of differential diagnosis in the elderly, referring in particular to the abundant evidence for neuropsychological deficits in younger depressed patients, and to the not uncommon coexistence of neurological and psychiatric impairments in the elderly.

In recent years there has been substantial rethinking about the concept of pseudodementia in the direction of characterizing it as a neurobiological disorder associated with demonstrable changes in brain structure. Clinicians have observed that depression may sometimes be the first indicator of Alzheimer's disease, and Nussbaum (1994), based on an extensive review of the literature, concluded that pseudodementia or late-life depression has a neurological substrate involving subcortical structures and the frontal lobes. He indicated that the probable pathology is leukoaraiosis, diminution in the density of white matter, which particularly involves the subcortex in this disorder. Leukoaraiosis is frequently seen in the MRIs of elderly depressed individuals.

## EPIDEMIOLOGY

The epidemiology of delirium, dementia, and amnestic and other neurocognitive disorders varies with the underlying disorder, and so is unlike what is the case for most of the other diagnostic categories in *DSM-IV*. Here, we will only sample from those disorders in which epidemiological considerations are of particular interest. There are some exceptionally interesting and well-documented findings for multiple sclerosis, in which prevalence is directly related to latitude in which one resides; the farther from the equator, the higher the prevalence (Koch-Henriksen & Sørensen, 2010). Further study of this phenomenon has tended to implicate an environmental rather than an ethnic factor.

The epidemiology of head trauma has been extensively studied, with gender, age, and social class turning out to be important considerations. Head trauma has a higher incidence in males than in females (274 per 100,000 in males and 116 per 100,000 in females in one study; Levin, Benton, & Grossman, 1982). It is related to age, with risk peaking between ages 15 and 24, and occurs more frequently in individuals from lower social classes. Alcohol is a major risk factor, but marital status, preexisting psychiatric disorder, and previous history of head injury have also been implicated. The major causes of head injury are motor vehicle accidents, falls, assaults, and recreational or work activities, with motor vehicle accidents clearly being the major cause (50% to 60%; Smith, Barth, Diamond, & Giuliano, 1998).

The epidemiology of Huntington's disease has also been extensively studied. The disease is transmitted as an autosomal dominant trait, and the marker for the gene has been located on the short arm of chromosome 4 (Gusella et al., 1983). Prevalence estimates vary between 5 and 7 per 100,000. There are no known risk factors for acquiring the disorder, the only consideration being having a parent with the disease. If that is the case, the risk of acquiring the disorder is 50%. A test is now available to detect carriers of the defective gene, and its availability and usage may eventually reduce the prevalence of Huntington's disease.

There is a great interest in the epidemiology of Alzheimer's disease, because the specific cause of the disease is not fully understood, and prevention of exposure to risk factors for Alzheimer's disease and related disorders remains a possibility. General health status considerations do not appear to constitute risk factors, but some time ago there were beliefs that a transmissible infective agent existed, and that exposure to aluminum might be a risk factor. The aluminum hypothesis has largely been discarded. It now seems well established that an infective agent is responsible in the case of a rare form of dementia called Creutzfeldt-Jakob disease, but Alzheimer's disease is apparently not associated with infection. Recently, it has been reported that Creutzfeldt-Jakob disease resembles mad cow disease, and it is thought that a risk factor may be eating beef from cattle possibly exposed to mad cow disease. Recently, episodes of head trauma have been implicated as a possible risk factor for Alzheimer's disease (Lye & Shores, 2000). A reasonably solid genetic association involving chromosome 21 trisomy has been formed between what appears to be an inherited form of Alzheimer's disease and Down syndrome.

Much of the epidemiology of the organic mental disorders merges with general considerations regarding health status. Cardiovascular risk factors such as obesity and hypertension put one at greater than usual risk for stroke. Smoking is apparently a direct or indirect risk factor for several disorders that eventuate in brain dysfunction. The diagnosis of dementia associated with alcoholism is now relatively widely accepted, although it was controversial at one time. Alcohol most clearly, and perhaps several other abused substances, make for significant risk factors.

In some cases, the crucial risk factor is provided not by the individual, but by the mother of the individual during pregnancy. Existence of fetal alcohol syndrome is well established, and the evidence for association between birth defects and other forms of substance abuse during pregnancy is increasing. Up until recently, the risk of acquiring brain disease by infection had diminished substantially, but that situation has changed markedly with the appearance of human immunodeficiency virus, or HIV-1 infection, or acquired immunodeficiency syndrome (AIDS) dementia (Bornstein et al., 1993; Grant et al., 1987; van Gorp et al., 1989; Woods et al., 2009). It has become increasingly clear that AIDS is frequently transmitted to children during pregnancy or in association with breast feeding. New anti-infection medication is in actual use or in the process of going through extensive clinical trials, and there is great promise of effectiveness.

In summary, the prevalence and incidence of the organic mental disorders vary substantially, ranging from very rare to common diseases. Number of risk factors also varies, ranging from complete absence to a substantial number of them. The genetic and degenerative diseases, notably Huntington's and Alzheimer's disease, possess little in the way of risk factors, and there is not much that can be done to prevent their occurrence. The development of a test for risk of transmitting Huntington's disease has opened up the admittedly controversial and complex matter of genetic counseling. On the other hand, such disorders as dementia associated with alcoholism, and perhaps stroke, are preventable by good health maintenance. Indeed, the incidence of major stroke has declined in recent years.

## COURSE AND PROGNOSIS

Course and prognosis for delirium, dementia, and amnestic and other neurocognitive disorders also vary with the underlying disorder. We will review the basic considerations here by first introducing some stages of acceleration and development. Then we will provide examples of disorders that have courses and prognoses consistent with various acceleration and developmental combinations. The acceleration stages are steady state, slow, moderate, and rapid. The developmental stages are the perinatal period, early childhood, late childhood and adolescence, early adulthood, middle age, and old age. The acceleration stages have to do with the rate of progression of the disorder, while the developmental stages characterize the age of onset of symptoms.

Intellectual disability would be a disorder with a course involving onset during the perinatal period and steady-state acceleration. Intellectual disability is one of those disorders in which there is little if any progression of neuropathology, but there may be a slowly progressive disability because of increasing environmental demands for cognitive abilities that the individual does not possess. Other developmental disorders, such as specific learning disability, do not have their onsets during the perinatal period but rather during early childhood when academic skills are first expected to be acquired.

In contrast to these disorders, stroke is typically characterized by onset during middle age. The acceleration of the disorder is first extremely rapid and then slows down, gradually reaching steady state. Thus, the stroke patient, at the time of the stroke, becomes seriously ill very rapidly, and this is followed by additional destructive processes in the brain. Assuming a good outcome, a gradual recovery period follows, and there is restoration of the brain to a relatively normal steady state. On the other hand, malignant brain tumors that also tend to appear during middle age progress rapidly and do not decelerate unless they are successfully surgically removed.

The progressive dementias generally appear during middle or old age and accelerate slowly or moderately. Huntington's disease generally progresses less rapidly than Alzheimer's disease, and so the Huntington's patient may live a long life with his or her symptoms. Head trauma is a disorder that may occur at any age, but once the acute phase of the disorder is over, the brain typically returns to a steady state. Thus, the head trauma patient, if recovery from the acute condition is satisfactory, may have a normal life expectancy with an often dramatic picture of deterioration immediately following the trauma until completion of resolution of the acute phase followed by substantial recovery. However, degree of residual disability may vary widely.

Briefly summarizing these considerations from a developmental standpoint, the most common organic mental disorder associated with the perinatal period is intellectual disability and its variants. During early childhood, the specific and pervasive developmental disorders begin to appear. Head trauma typically begins to appear during late childhood and adolescence, and incidence peaks during young adulthood. Systemic illnesses, notably cardiovascular, cardiopulmonary, and neoplastic disease, most commonly impact negatively on brain functions during middle age. Dementia associated with alcoholism also begins to appear during early middle age. The progressive degenerative dementias are largely associated with old age.

With regard to acceleration, following the time period surrounding the acquisition of the disorder, developmental, vascular, and traumatic disorders tend to be relatively stable. Malignant tumors and certain infectious disorders may be rapidly progressive, and the degenerative disorders progress at a slow to moderate pace. Although the connotation of the term *progressive* is progressively worse, not all of the neurocognitive disorders remain stable or get worse. There is recovery of certain disorders as a natural process or with the aid of treatment. In the case of head trauma, there is a rather typical history of initial unconsciousness, lapsing into coma for a varying length of time, awakening, a period of memory loss and incomplete orientation called posttraumatic amnesia, and resolution of the amnesia. Rehabilitation is often initiated at some point in this progression, sometimes beginning while the patient is still in a coma. The outcome of this combination of spontaneous recovery and rehabilitation is rarely, if ever, complete return to preinjury status, but often allows for a return to productive living in the community. Recovery from stroke is also common, and many poststroke patients can return to community living. Among the most important prognostic indicators for head trauma are length of time in coma and length of posttraumatic amnesia. General health status is a good predictor for stroke outcome and potential for recurrence. Patients who maintain poor cardiac status, hypertension, inappropriate dietary habits, or substance abuse are poorer candidates for recovery than are poststroke patients who do not have these difficulties. Some patients, particularly those with chronic, severe hypertension, may have multiple strokes, resolving into a vascular dementia.

There is increasing evidence that rehabilitation of head trauma may often have beneficial effects over and above spontaneous recovery. With regard to the developmental disorders, enormous efforts have been made in institutional and school settings to provide appropriate educational remediation for developmentally disabled children, often with some success. Effective treatment at the time of onset of acute disorder also has obvious implications for prognosis. Use of appropriate medications and management following trauma or stroke, and the feasibility and availability of neurosurgery, are major considerations. Tumors can be removed, aneurysms can be repaired, and increased pressure can be relieved by neurosurgeons. These interventions during the acute phase of a disorder are often mainly directed toward preservation of life, but they also have important implications for the outcomes of surviving patients.

## FAMILIAL AND GENETIC PATTERNS

The organic mental disorders are based on some diseases of known genetic origin, some diseases in which a genetic or familial component is suspected, and some that are clearly acquired disorders. It is well established that Huntington's disease and certain forms of intellectual disability, notably Down syndrome, are genetic disorders. There appears to be evidence that there is a hereditary form of Alzheimer's disease, although the genetic contribution to Alzheimer's disease in general is not fully understood. A relatively rare genetic subtype has been identified consisting of patients who develop psychosis (DeMichele-Sweet & Sweet, 2010). The great majority of individuals with this subtype and other individuals with Alzheimer's disease have a gene on chromosome 14 called Apolipoprotein E that promotes development of the amyloid plaques that constitute the major brain pathology associated with the disease. Whether multiple sclerosis has a genetic component remains under investigation, although it is clearly not a hereditary disorder like Huntington's disease.

Of great recent interest is the role of genetics in the acquisition of alcoholism, and subsequently dementia associated with alcoholism or alcohol amnestic disorder. Evidence suggests that having an alcoholic parent places one at higher than average risk for developing alcoholism. The specific genetic factors are far from understood, but the association in families appears to be present. Whether having a family history of alcoholism increases the risk of acquiring dementia associated with alcoholism is not clear, but it has been shown that nonalcoholic sons of alcoholic fathers do more poorly on some cognitive tests than do matched controls. The matter is substantially clearer in the case of alcohol amnestic disorder of Korsakoff's syndrome. A widely cited study by Blass and Gibson (1977) showed acquisition of Korsakoff's syndrome is dependent upon the existence of a genetic defect in a liver enzyme called transketolase in combination with a thiamine deficiency.

Other genetic and familial factors associated with the organic mental disorders relate largely to the genetics of underlying systemic disorders. Thus, the genetics of cancer might have some bearing on the likelihood of acquiring a brain tumor, while the genetics of the cardiovascular system might have some bearing on the risk for stroke. Disorders such as hypertension and diabetes appear to run in families and have varying incidences in different ethnic groups. Ethnic specificity is sometimes quite precise (but this is rare), as in the case of Tay-Sachs disease, a degenerative disorder of early childhood that is found almost exclusively in Eastern European Jews.

## SUMMARY

The diagnostic category of delirium, dementia, and amnestic and other cognitive disorders—formerly known as organic mental disorders and probably to be known in the future as neurocognitive disorders—comprises many conditions in which behavioral changes may be directly associated with some basis in altered brain function. Although the general diagnostic term *organic brain syndrome* has commonly been used to describe these conditions, the wide variability in the manifestations of brain dysfunction makes this term insufficiently precise in reference to clinical relevance, and it has been abandoned. It was pointed out that the variability is attributable to several factors, including the following considerations: (1) the location of the damage in the brain, (2) the neuropathological process producing the damage, (3) the length of time the brain damage has been present, (4) the age and health status of the individual at the time the damage is sustained, and (5) the individual's premorbid personality and level of function.

The neuropsychological approach to the conceptualization of these disorders has identified behavioral parameters along which the manifestations of brain dysfunction can be described and classified. The most frequently considered dimensions are intellectual function, language, attention, memory, visual spatial skills, perceptual skills, and motor function. Some important concepts related to brain function and brain disorders include the principle of contralateral control of perceptual and motor functions and functional hemisphere asymmetries. In addition, studies of brain-damaged patients have shown that particular structures in the brain mediate relatively discrete behaviors. Neurologists and neuropsychologists have identified several syndromes in such areas as language dysfunction, memory disorder, and general intellectual impairment. It was pointed out that there are also major variations in the courses of neurocognitive disorders. Some are transient, leaving little or no residual; some are permanent but not progressive; others are either slowly or rapidly progressive. Whereas these disorders most profoundly and commonly involve impairment of cognitive, perceptual, and motor skills, sometimes personality changes of various types are the most prominent symptoms. More often than not, personality and affective changes appear in brain-damaged patients along with their cognitive, perceptual, and motor disorders. Thus, a mood disorder or such symptoms as delusions and hallucinations may be sequelae of brain damage for various reasons.

During the years spanning the writing of the various editions of this chapter, there have been several major developments in the area of what was originally called the organic mental disorders. There has been the appearance of at least one new disorder, AIDS dementia, major discoveries in the genetics of Huntington's disease and alcoholism, enormous developments in the technology of neuroimaging, growth of a field of neurotoxicology producing knowledge about the epidemiology of neurodevelopmental disorders in particular, and a reconceptualization by psychiatry of the previously held distinction between functional and organic disorders. The work in neuroimaging is particularly exciting, because it goes beyond obtaining more refined pictures of the brain and now allows us to observe the working of the brain during ongoing behavior through fMRI, and to examine the molecular biology of brain function through MRS.

## REFERENCES

Allen, D. N., Sprenkel, D. G., Heyman, R. A., Schramke, C. J., & Heffron, N. E. (1998). Evaluation of demyelinating and degenerative disorders. In G. Goldstein, P. D. Nussbaum, & S. R. Beers (Eds.), *Neuropsychology* (pp. 187–208). New York, NY: Plenum Press.

American Psychiatric Association. (1994). *Diagnostic and statistical manual of mental disorders* (4th ed.). Washington, DC: Author.

American Psychiatric Association. (2010). *Proposed revision/APA DSM-V*. Arlington, VA: American Psychiatric Association.

Baddeley, A. (1986). *Working memory*. New York, NY: Oxford University Press.

Balter, M. (2001). Genes and disease: Immune gene linked to vCJD susceptibility. *Science, 294*, 1438–1439.

Baron, I. S., & Gioia, G. A. (1998). Neuropsychology of infants and young children. In G. Goldstein, P. D. Nussbaum, & S. R. Beers (Eds.), *Neuropsychology* (pp. 9–34). New York, NY: Plenum Press.

Becker, J. T., Farbman, E. S., Hamilton, R. L., & Lopez, O. L. (2011). Dementia with Lewy bodies. In G. Goldstein, T. M. Incagnoli, & A. E. Puente, (Eds.), *Contemporary neurobehavioral syndromes* (pp. 111–129). New York, NY: Psychology Press.

Begleiter, H., Porjesz, B., Bihari, B., & Kissin, B. (1984). Event-related potentials in boys at high risk for alcoholism. *Science, 225*, 1493–1496.

Belanger, H. G., Kretzmer, T., Vanderploeg R. D., & French, L. M. (2010). Symptom complaints following combat-related traumatic brain injury: Relationship to traumatic brain injury severity and posttraumatic stress disorder. *Journal of the International Neuropsychological Society, 16*, 194–199.

Benton, A. (1985). Body schema disturbances: Finger agnosia and right-left disorientation. In K. M. Heilman & E. Valenstein (Eds.), *Clinical neuropsychology* (2nd ed., pp. 115–129). New York, NY: Oxford University Press.

Benton, A. L., & Joynt, R. J. (1960). Early descriptions of aphasia. *Archives of Neurology, 3*, 205–222.

Berg, R. A. (1998). Evaluation of neoplastic processes. In G. Goldstein, P. D. Nussbaum, & S. R. Beers (Eds.), *Neuropsychology* (pp. 248–269). New York, NY: Plenum Press.

Bigler, E. D. (2008). Neuropsychology and clinical neuroscience of persistent post-concussive syndrome. *Journal of the International Neuropsychological Society, 14*, 1–22.

Blass, J. P., & Gibson, G. E. (1977). Abnormality of a thiamine-requiring enzyme in patients with Wernicke-Korsakoff syndrome. *The New England Journal of Medicine, 297*, 1367–1370.

Boring, E. G. (1950). *A history of experimental psychology* (2nd ed.). New York, NY: Appleton-Century-Crofts.

Bornstein, R. A., Nasrallah, H. A., Para, M. F., & Whitacre, C. C. (1993). Neuropsychological performance in symptomatic and asymptomatic HIV infection. *AIDS, 7,* 519–524.

Broca, P. (1861). Perte de la parole. Ramollissement chronique et destruction partielle du lobe anterieur gauche du cerveau. [Loss of the word. Chronic softening and partial destruction of the left frontal lobe of the brain.] *Bulletin de la Société Anthropologique, 2,* 235–238.

Butters, N., & Cermak, L. S. (1980). *Alcoholic Korsakoff's syndrome.* New York, NY: Academic Press.

Caine, E. D. (1986). The neuropsychology of depression: The pseudodementia syndrome. In I. Grant & K. M. Adams (Eds.), *Neuropsychological assessment of neuropsychiatric disorders* (pp. 221–243). New York, NY: Oxford University Press.

Cloninger, C. R., Bohman, M., & Sigvardsson, S. (1981). Inheritance of alcohol abuse: Cross-fostering analysis of adopted men. *Archives of General Psychiatry, 38,* 861–868.

Correa, D. D. (2010). Neurocognitive function in brain tumors. *Current Neurology and Neuroscience Reports, 10,* 232–239.

Das, R. R., Seshadri, S., Beiser, A. S., Kelly-Hayes, M., Au, R., Himali, J. J., . . . Wolf, P. A. (2008). Prevalence and correlates of silent cerebral infarcts in the Framingham offspring study. *Stroke, 39,* 2929–2935.

Dean, R. S. (1986). Lateralization of cerebral functions. In D. Wedding, A. M. Horton Jr., & J. Webster (Eds.), *The neuropsychology handbook: Behavioral and clinical perspectives* (pp. 80–102). New York, NY: Springer.

DeMichele-Sweet, M. A., & Sweet, R. A. (2010). Genetics of psychosis in Alzheimer's disease: A review. *Journal of Alzheimer's Disease, 19,* 761–780.

Dodrill, C. B. (1986). Psychosocial consequences of epilepsy. In S. B. Filskov & T. J. Boll (Eds.), *Handbook of clinical neuropsychology,* Vol. 2 (pp. 338–363). New York, NY: John Wiley & Sons.

Elias, M. F., & Streeten, D.H.P. (1980). *Hypertension and cognitive processes.* Mount Desert, ME: Beech Hill.

Fagan, A. M., Mintun, M. A., Mach, R. H., Lee, S. Y., Dence, C. S., Shah, A. R., . . . Holtzman, D. M. (2005). Inverse relation between in vivo amyloid imaging load and cerebrospinal fluid A beta42 in humans. *Annals of Neurology, 59,* 512–519.

Farrell, R. A., Antony, D., Wall, G. R., Clark, D. A., Fisniku, L., Swanton, J., . . . Giovannoni, G. (2009). Humoral immune response to EBV in multiple sclerosis is associated with disease activity on MRI. *Neurology, 73,* 32–38.

Festa, J. R. (2010). Cognitive dysfunction in heart failure. *Division of Clinical Neuropsychology Newsletter, 28,* 3–9.

Flourens, M. J. P. (1824). *Recherches experimentales sur les proprietes et les fonctions du systeme nerveux dans les animaux vertebres.* [Experimental research on the properties and functions of the nervous system in vertebrate animals.] Paris, France: Crevot.

Gastaut, H. (1970). Clinical and electroencephalographical classification of epileptic seizures. *Epilepsia, 11,* 102–103.

Geschwind, N. (1965). Disconnection syndromes in animals and man. *Brain, 88,* 237–294.

Goldstein, G. (1986, February). Neuropsychological effects of five antihypertensive agents. Poster session presented at the annual meeting of the International Neuropsychological Society, Denver, CO.

Goldstein, G. (1997). Delirium, dementia, and amnestic and other cognitive disorders. In S. M. Turner & M. Hersen (Eds.), *Adult psychopathology and diagnosis* (3rd ed., pp. 89–127). New York, NY: John Wiley & Sons.

Goldstein, G. (2007). Delirium, dementia, and amnestic and other cognitive disorders. In M. Hersen, S. M. Turner, & D. C. Beidel (Eds.), *Adult psychopathology and diagnosis* (5th ed., pp. 125–165). Hoboken, NJ: John Wiley & Sons.

Goldstein, G. (2011). Persian Gulf and other "deployment" syndromes. In G. Goldstein, T. M. Incagnoli, & A. E. Puente (Eds.), *Contemporary neurobehavioral syndromes* (pp. 131–150). New York, NY: Psychology Press.

Goldstein, G., Beers, S. R., Morrow, L. A., Shemansky, W. J., & Steinhauer, S. R. (1996). A preliminary neuropsychological study of Persian Gulf veterans. *Journal of the International Neuropsychological Society, 2,* 368–371.

Goldstein, K. (1936). The significance of the frontal lobes for mental performance. *Journal of Neurology and Psychopathology, 17,* 27–40.

Goldstein, K. (1959). Functional disturbances in brain damage. In S. Arieti (Ed.), *American handbook of psychiatry.* New York, NY: Basic Books.

Goldstein, K., & Scheerer, M. (1941). Abstract and concrete behavior: An experimental study with special tests. *Psychological Monographs, 53* (2, Whole No. 239).

Goodwin, D. W. (1979). Alcoholism and heredity: A review and hypothesis. *Archives of General Psychiatry, 36,* 57–61.

Goodwin, D. W., Schulsinger, F., Hermansen, L., Guze, S. B., & Winokur, G. (1973). Alcohol problems in adoptees raised apart from alcoholic biological parents. *Archives of General Psychiatry, 28,* 238–243.

Grant, I., Atkinson, J. H., Hesselink, J. R., Kennedy, C. J., Richman, D. D., Spector, S. A., & McCutchan, J. A. (1987). Evidence for early central nervous system involvement in the acquired immunodeficiency syndrome (AIDS) and other human immunodeficiency virus (HIV) infections. *Annals of Internal Medicine, 107,* 828–836.

Green, M. F. (1998). *Schizophrenia from a neurocognitive perspective.* Boston, MA: Allyn and Bacon.

Griebling, J., Williams, D. L., Goldstein, G., & Minshew, N. J. (2011). Reconceptualization of autism and autism spectrum disorders as neurodevelopmental disorders. In G. Goldstein, T. M. Incagnoli, & A. E. Puente (Eds.), *Contemporary neurobehavioral syndromes* (pp. 33–70). New York, NY: Psychology Press.

Guerrini, I., Thomson, A. D., & Gurling, H. M. (2009). Molecular genetics of alcohol-related brain damage. *Alcohol and Alcoholism, 44,* 166–170.

Gusella, J. F., Wexler, N. S., Conneally, P. M., Naylor, S. L., Anderson, M. A., Tanzi, R. E., . . . Martin, J. B. (1983). A polymorphic DNA marker genetically linked to Huntington's disease. *Nature, 306,* 234–238.

Halstead, W. C. (1947). *Brain and intelligence.* Chicago, IL: University of Chicago Press.

Heaton, R. K. (2006, February 1–4). Presidential address given at the annual meeting of the International Neuropsychological Society, Boston, MA.

Heaton, R. K., Nelson, L. M., Thompson, D. S., Burks, J. S., & Franklin, G. M. (1985). Neuropsychological findings in relapsing-remitting and chronic-progressive multiple sclerosis. *Journal of Consulting and Clinical Psychology, 53,* 103–110.

Heilman, K. M., & Valenstein, E. (Eds.). (2003). *Clinical neuropsychology* (4th ed.). New York, NY: Oxford University Press.

Hill, S. Y., Shen, S., Zezza, N., Hoffman, E. K., Perlin, M., & Alan, W. (2004). A genome wide search for alcoholism susceptibility genes. *American Journal of Medical Genetics B: Neuropsychiatric Genetics, 128,* 102–113.

Hill, S. Y., Steinhauer, S. R., & Zubin, J. (1987). Biological markers for alcoholism: A vulnerability model conceptualization. In C. Rivers (Ed.), *Nebraska symposium on motivation, Vol. 34: Alcohol and addictive behavior* (pp. 207–256). Lincoln: University of Nebraska Press.

Hoge, C. W., McGurk, D., Thomas, J. J., Cox, A.L., Engel, C. C., & Castro, C. A. (2008). Mild traumatic brain injury in U.S. soldiers returning from Iraq. *New England Journal of Medicine, 358,* 453–463.

Jervis, G. A. (1959). The mental deficiencies. In S. Arieti (Ed.), *American handbook of psychiatry* (Vol. 4, pp. 1289–1314). New York, NY: Basic Books.

Kanner, L. (1943). Autistic disturbances of affective contact. *Nervous Child, 2,* 217–250.

Katz, L. J., Goldstein, G., & Beers, S. R. (2001). *Learning disabilities in older adolescents and adults.* New York, NY: Kluwer Academic/Plenum.

King, H. E., & Miller, R. E. (1990). Hypertension: Cognitive and behavioral considerations. *Neuropsychology Review, 1,* 31–73.

Klove, H., & Matthews, C. G. (1974). Neuropsychological studies of patients with epilepsy. In R. M. Reitan & L. A. Davison (Eds.), *Clinical neuropsychology: Current status and applications* (pp. 237–265). New York, NY: Winston-Wiley.

Klunk, W. E., Engler, H., Nordberg, A., Wang, Y., Blomqvist, G., Holt, D. P., . . . Långström, B. (2004). Imaging brain amyloid in Alzheimer's disease with Pittsburgh Compound-B. *Annals of Neurology, 5,* 306–319.

Koch-Henriksen, N., & Sørensen, P. S. (2010). The changing demographic pattern of multiple sclerosis epidemiology. *Lancet Neurology, 9,* 520–532.

Lantz, E. R., Lazar, R. M., Levine, R., & Levine, J. (2010). Cerbrovascular anomalies: Brain AVMSs and cerebral aneurysms and brain arteriovenous malformations. *Division of Clinical Neuropsychology Newsletter, 28,* 17–23.

Lashley, K. S. (1960/1950). In search of the engram. In F. A. Beach, D. O. Hebb, C. T. Morgan, & H. W. Nissen (Eds.), *The neuropsychology of Lashley* (pp. 478–505). New York, NY: McGraw-Hill.

Levin, H. S., Benton, A. L., & Grossman, R. G. (1982). *Neurobehavioral consequences of closed head injury.* New York, NY: Oxford University Press.

Levin, H. S., Eisenberg, H. M., & Benton, A. L. (1989). *Mild head injury.* New York, NY: Oxford University Press.

Levin, H. S., Wilde, E., Troyanskaya, M., Petersen, N. J., Scheibel, R., Newsome, M., . . . Li, X. (2010). Diffusion tensor imaging of mild to moderate blast-related traumatic brain injury and its sequelae. *Journal of Neurotrauma, 27,* 683–694.

Luria, A. R. (1966). *Higher cortical functions in man* (B. Haigh, Trans.) New York, NY: Basic Books.

Luria, A. R. (1973). *The working brain.* New York, NY: Basic Books.

Lye, T. C., & Shores, E. A. (2000). Traumatic brain injury as a risk factor for Alzheimer's disease: A review. *Neuropsychology Review, 10,* 115–129.

Mayer, A. R., Ling, J., Manell, M. V., Gasparovic, C., Phillips, J. P., Doezema, D., . . . Yeo, R. A. (2010). A prospective diffusion tensor imaging study in mild traumatic brain injury. *Neurology, 74,* 643–650.

McKeith, I., Mintzer, J., Aarsland, D., Burn, D., Chiu, H., Cohen-Mansfield, J., . . . Reid, W.; International Psychogeriatric Association Expert Meeting on DLB. (2004). Dementia with Lewy bodies. *Lancet Neurology, 3,* 19–28.

Mesulam, M. M. (1985). *Principles of behavioral neurology.* Philadelphia, PA: F. A. Davis.

Minshew, N. J. (1996). Autism. In B. O. Berg (Ed.), *Principles of child neurology* (pp. 1713–1730). New York, NY: McGraw-Hill.

Myslobodsky, M. S., & Mirsky, A. F. (1988). *Elements of petit mal epilepsy.* New York, NY: Peter Lang.

Neils, J., Boller, F., Gerdeman, B., & Cole, M. (1989). Descriptive writing abilities in Alzheimer's disease. *Journal of Clinical and Experimental Neuropsychology, 11,* 692–698.

Noggle, C. A., & Pierson, E. E. (2010). Pediatric TBI: Prevalence and functional ramifications. *Applied Neuropsychology, 17,* 81–82.

Nussbaum, P. D. (1994). Pseudodementia: A slow death. *Neuropsychology Review, 4,* 71–90.

Parkhurst, M. A., & Guilmette, R. A. (2009). Overview of the Capstone depleted uranium study of aerosols from impact with armored vehicles: Test setup and aerosol generation, characterization, and application in assessing dose and risk. *Health Physics, 96,* 207–220.

Pavol, M. (2010). Neuropsychology of ischemic stroke. *Division of Clinical Neuropsychology Newsletter, 28,* 12–16.

Rosenstein, L. D. (1998). Differential diagnosis of the major progressive dementias and depression in middle and late adulthood: A summary of the literature of the early 1990s. *Neuropsychology Review, 8,* 109–167.

Rourke, B. P., & Brown, G. G. (1986). Clinical neuropsychology and behavioral neurology: Similarities and differences. In S. B. Filskov & T. J. Boll (Eds.), *Handbook of clinical neuropsychology* (Vol. 2, pp. 3–18). New York, NY: John Wiley & Sons.

Rumsey, J. M., & Hamburger, S. D. (1988). Neuropsychological findings in high-functioning men with infantile autism, residual state. *Journal of Clinical and Experimental Neuropsychology, 10,* 201–221.

Satz, P. (1966). Specific and nonspecific effects of brain lesions in man. *Journal of Abnormal Psychology, 71,* 65–70.

Schaeffer, K. W., Parsons, O. A., & Yohman, J. R. (1984). Neuropsychological differences between male familial and nonfamilial alcoholics and nonalcoholics. *Alcoholism: Clinical and Experimental Research, 8,* 347–351.

Schatz, P., Pardini, J. F., Lovell, M. R., Collins, M. W., & Podell, K. (2006). Sensitivity and specificity of the ImPACT Test Battery for concussion in athletes. *Archives of Clinical Neuropsychology, 21,* 91–99.

Shemansky, W. J., & Goldstein, G. (2011). Behavioral toxicological disorders. In G. Goldstein, T. M. Incagnoli, & A. E. Puente (Eds.), *Contemporary neurobehavioral syndromes* (pp. 195–218). New York, NY: Psychology Press.

Smith, R. J., Barth, J. T., Diamond, R., & Giuliano, A. J. (1998). Evaluation of head trauma. In G. Goldstein, P. D. Nussbaum, & S. R. Beers (Eds.), *Neuropsychology* (pp. 135–170). New York, NY: Plenum Press.

Spreen, O. (1987). *Learning disabled children growing up: A follow-up into adulthood.* Lisse, The Netherlands: Swets & Zeitlinger.

Steinhauer, S. R., Hill, S. Y., & Zubin, J. (1987). Event related potentials in alcoholics and their first-degree relatives. *Alcoholism, 4,* 307–314.

Tarter, R. E. (1976). Neuropsychological investigations of alcoholism. In G. Goldstein & C. Neuringer (Eds.), *Empirical studies of alcoholism* (pp. 231–256). Cambridge, MA: Ballinger.

Tarter, R. E., Hegedus, A., Goldstein, G., Shelly, C., & Alterman, A. I. (1984). Adolescent sons of alcoholics: Neuropsychological and personality characteristics. *Alcoholism: Clinical and Experimental Research, 8,* 216–222.

Teuber, H.-L. (1959). Some alterations in behavior after cerebral lesions in man. In A. D. Bass (Eds.), *Evolution of nervous control from primitive organisms to man.* Washington, DC: American Association for the Advancement of Science.

Van Gorp, W. G., Miller, E. N., Satz, P., & Visscher, B. (1989). Neuropsychological performance in HIV-1 immunocompromised patients: A preliminary report. *Journal of Clinical and Experimental Neuropsychology, 11,* 763–773.

Vargha-Khadem, F., Gadian, D. G., Watkins, K. E., Connelly, A., Van Paesschen, W. P., & Mishkin, M. (1997). Differential effects of early hippocampal pathology on episodic and semantic memory. *Science, 277,* 376–380.

Walker, A. E., Caveness, W. F., & Critchley, M. (Eds.). (1969). *Late effects of head injury.* Springfield, IL: Charles C. Thomas.

Wells, C. E. (1979). Pseudodementia. *American Journal of Psychiatry, 136*, 895–900.

Wells, C. E. (1980). The differential diagnosis of psychiatric disorders in the elderly. In J. O. Cole & J. E. Barrett (Eds.), *Psychopathology in the aged* (pp. 19–31). New York, NY: Raven Press.

Werner, H., & Strauss, A. (1942). Experimental analysis of the clinical symptom "perseveration" in mentally retarded children. *American Journal of Mental Deficiency, 47*, 185–188.

Wilk, J. E., Thomas, J. L., McGurk, D. M., Riviere, L. A., Castro, C. A., & Hoge, C. W. (2010). Mild traumatic brain injury (concussion) during combat: Lack of association of blast mechanism with persistent postconcussive symptoms. *Journal of Head Trauma Rehabilitation, 25*, 9–14.

Woods, S. P, Carey, C. L., Iudicello, J. E., Letendre, S. L., Fennema-Notestine, C. & Grant, I. (2009). Neuropsychological aspects of HIV infection. In I. Grant & K. M. Adams (Eds.), *Neuropsychological assessment of neuropsychiatric and neuromedical disorders* (3rd ed., pp. 366–397). New York, NY: Oxford University Press.

# CHAPTER 6

# Substance-Related Disorders: Alcohol

ERIC F. WAGNER, MICHELLE M. HOSPITAL, MARK B. SOBELL, and LINDA C. SOBELL

## DESCRIPTION OF THE DISORDER

This chapter addresses diagnostic and assessment issues across the continuum of individuals suffering with alcohol problems, ranging from "misusers" to those who are severely dependent on alcohol. Although scientific study and clinical treatment historically focused on individuals who were severely dependent on alcohol, it is now widely recognized that such persons constitute a minority of the public suffering with alcohol problems. Epidemiological studies reveal that individuals with less serious alcohol problems outnumber those with severe alcoholism (Curry, Ludman, Grothaus, Gilmore, & Donovan, 2002; Institute of Medicine, 1990; World Health Organization, 2004). This recognition has led to increased research on and clinical attention to individuals with less severe alcohol problems, as well as the widespread acknowledgment that alcohol use problems lie along a continuum.

Current views about alcohol use problems are a grafting of concepts derived from research, clinical anecdotes, and common wisdom. Over the past century, public opinion has softened from viewing those who suffer with alcohol problems as moral reprobates to being victims of a disease. In the United States, the view that alcohol problems are a medical disorder became dominant in the mid-1900s with the rise of Alcoholics Anonymous (AA), the seminal work of E. M. Jellinek, and the proclamation by the American Medical Association that alcoholism is a disease. The embracing of the disease concept was intended to shift responsibility for dealing with alcohol problems from the criminal justice system to the health care system.

Alcoholics Anonymous, the ubiquitous mutual help approach that emerged in the 1930s, viewed alcoholism as a biological aberration—an "allergy" to alcohol (i.e., with repeated exposure to alcohol, alcoholics would quickly become physically dependent to the substance, and once dependent they would continue to drink to avoid withdrawal symptoms). To explain relapse, AA stated that alcoholics had an "obsession" to drink like normal drinkers. In addition, alcoholism was thought to be a progressive disorder (i.e., if alcoholics continued to drink, their problem would inevitably worsen), and persons who were mildly dependent on alcohol were thought to be in the "early stages" of developing alcoholism. Consequently, even

197

those with mild problems were viewed as needing the same treatment as those who were severely dependent.

E. M. Jellinek, a scientist, attempted to bridge the gap between lay views and the evidence in support of the disease concept. He and others felt that the medical profession should be responsible for treating alcohol abusers (Bacon, 1973). Although he alluded to genetic components, he did not speculate as to why some drinkers develop alcohol problems but others do not. Jellinek did postulate that alcoholics: (a) use alcohol to cope with emotional problems; (b) over time develop tolerance to alcohol, thereby leading to increased consumption to achieve desired effects; and (c) eventually develop "loss of control," where even small amounts of alcohol would initiate physical dependence and trigger more drinking (Jellinek, 1960). Finally, Jellinek proposed that there were many types of alcohol problems, including gamma alcoholism, which he felt was the most common type in the United States and a progressive disorder.

Over the past half century, considerable research has refuted these traditional conceptualizations. Although some individuals may be genetically predisposed to develop alcohol problems, a large proportion of individuals with alcohol problems do not have this positive family history, and a large proportion of individuals with a positive family history for alcohol use disorders do not have alcohol problems (Dahl et al., 2005; Humphreys, 2009). Research shows that social and cultural factors play a large role in the development of alcohol problems (Hendershot, MacPherson, Myers, Carr, & Wall, 2005; Miles, Silberg, Pickens, & Eaves, 2005; Penninkilampi-Kerola, Kaprio, Moilanen, & Rose, 2005). Moreover, in most cases of alcohol problems, the natural history of the disorder is not progressive (Dawson, 1996; Institute of Medicine, 1990); rather, it includes periods of alcohol problems of varying severity separated by periods of either nondrinking or drinking limited quantities without problems (Cahalan, 1970; King & Tucker, 2000). Also, natural history studies have found that recovery from alcohol problems in the absence of treatment is more prevalent than once thought (Bischof et al., 2003; Dawson et al., 2005; Klingemann et al., 2001; Klingemann, Sobell, & Sobell, 2009; Mohatt et al., 2007; Sobell, Cunningham, & Sobell, 1996; Sobell, Ellingstad, & Sobell, 2000).

With regard to loss of control, research has demonstrated that even in very severe cases, physical dependence is not initiated by a small amount of drinking (Marlatt, 1978; Pattison, Sobell, & Sobell, 1977); other factors, such as conditioned cues (Niaura et al., 1988) and positive consequences of drinking (Orford, 2001), are necessary to explain why some people continue drinking despite having repeatedly suffered adverse consequences (Humphreys, 2009). Finally, considerable research shows that mildly dependent alcohol abusers respond well to brief interventions, often by reducing their drinking to nonproblematic levels rather than ceasing their drinking (Bien, Miller, & Tonigan, 1993; Cunningham, Wild, Cordingley, van Mierlo, & Humphreys, 2010; Hester, Delaney, Campbell, & Handmaker, 2009; Sobell & Sobell, 1993; Sobell & Sobell, 1995).

## CLINICAL PICTURE

Unless the reasons for stopping drinking are extremely compelling, individuals with alcohol problems are very ambivalent about ending their alcohol use. Alchohol use is widespread in our society, and even those with severe alcohol dependence like the subjective experience of drinking. For individuals at the less severe end of the alcohol problem continuum, ambivalence can be very pronounced as the decision to stop or reduce drinking is based on probable risks rather than certain consequences. Failure to recognize this commonplace and logical ambivalence about stopping drinking can seriously compromise the success of the assessment and treatment process.

Traditional conceptualizations assert that individuals with alcohol problems will present in denial; that is, they will fail to recognize that their drinking is a problem (Nowinski, Baker, & Carroll, 1992). In response, traditional interventions attempt to confront and break through the denial. The rationale is that this procedure is consistent with the first step of AA (i.e., recognizing that one is powerless over alcohol; Nowinski et al., 1992). However, being confronted and labeled as alcoholic often elicits resentment, retaliation, and resistance to intervention. Stated simply, a confrontational approach to assessment and treatment can cause otherwise receptive clients to deny that they have an alcohol problem. An alternative approach concentrates on the ambivalence and avoids the use of confrontation, labeling, or other tactics that provoke defensiveness and resistance. This alternative nonthreatening, nonconfrontational style of interviewing is called motivational interviewing (MI; Miller & Rollnick, 1991, 2002; Substance Abuse and Mental Health Services Administration, 1999), which has grown immensely in popularity over the past two decades. Several randomized controlled trials (RCTs) of brief interventions using MI principles have found clinical significant improvements among individuals with alcohol problems (Bien et al., 1993; Burke, Arkowitz, & Menchola, 2003; Copeland, Blow, & Barry, 2003; Heather, 1990; Rubak, Sandbaek, Lauritzen, & Christensen, 2004; Sobell & Sobell, 1993), which has led MI to becoming accepted as an empirically supported treatment approach for alcohol problems.

## DIAGNOSTIC CONSIDERATIONS

Diagnostic formulations play an integral role in decisions about treatment goals and intensities, and are a requirement of insurance and clinical recording. An accurate diagnosis defines the problem in a way that can be communicated and understood by clinicians and researchers. A diagnostic formulation coupled with an assessment provides an initial understanding of the problem as well as a foundation for initial treatment planning. The two major diagnostic classifications of mental disorders are the *Diagnostic and Statistical Manual of Mental Disorders* (*DSM*) and the Mental Disorder Section of the *International Classification of Diseases* (*ICD*). The first *DSM* (*DSM-I*) was published in 1952 by the American Psychiatric Association and was a variant of the *ICD-6*. Over the past few decades, changes in the *DSM* alcohol use disorder classification criteria have reflected both the state of knowledge and contemporary attitudes. For example, while the *DSM-III-R* viewed alcohol dependence as a graded phenomenon ranging from mild (enough consequences to meet criteria but no major withdrawal symptoms) to severe (several negative consequences and withdrawal symptoms), the *DSM-IV* separates psychological from physiological dependence by making physical dependence a specifier rather than a central symptom. Presently, we are on the verge of having a *DSM-5*; the proposed *DSM-5* diagnostic approach to alcohol use problems is reviewed later in this chapter.

Several common clinical features of alcohol use disorders complicate their diagnosis and treatment. First, there is a high prevalence of co-occurring psychiatric disorders among individuals with alcohol problems (National Survey on Drug Use and Health [NSDUH], 2004, 2006, 2007; Nunes, Selzer, Levounis, & Davies, 2010). Psychiatric disorders with an exceptionally high co-occurrence with alcohol disorders include mood disorders such as depression, anxiety disorders, schizophrenia, and personality disorders such as antisocial personality disorder and borderline personality disorder. Given the frequent co-occurrence with psychiatric disorders, diagnostic formulation with alcohol disorders must assess three things: (1) the extent and nature of the alcohol problem; (2) the extent and nature of psychiatric disorders; and, (3) and the extent and nature of interaction between alcohol problems and psychiatric problems (Boden & Moos, 2009; Mack, Harrington, & Frances, 2010). Ideally, individuals should be alcohol free for several weeks in order to accurately assess for co-occurring psychiatric diagnoses, because active alcohol use can mask or exacerbate psychiatric symptoms (Schuckit, 1995).

Several studies have shown that people with alcohol use problems with co-occurring psychiatric problems have poorer treatment outcomes than people with alcohol use problems without co-occurring psychiatric problems (Le Fauve et al., 2004; Nunes et al., 2010). Although an integrated treatment approach involving additional and specialized counseling is often suggested for clients who have co-occurring disorders (Steele & Rechberger, 2002), there is a lack of empirical data about whether ancillary counseling improves treatment outcomes among individuals with a dual diagnosis of alcohol and psychiatric disorders (Assanangkornchai & Srisurapanont, 2007; Baigent, 2005; Echeburúa, Bravo de Medina, & Aizpiri, 2007; Le Fauve et al., 2004; Trull, Jahng, Tomko, Wood, & Sher, 2010; Whicher & Abou-Saleh, 2009).

Second, many individuals with alcohol disorders also have problems with the use of other substances. For people with alcohol problems who use other drugs including nicotine, it is important to gather a comprehensive profile of all types of psychoactive substance use and substance use problems. Over the course of an intervention, drug use patterns may change (e.g., decreased alcohol use, increased smoking; decreased alcohol use, increased cannabis use). Furthermore, alcohol abusers who use other drugs may experience pharmacological synergism (i.e., a multiplicative effect of similarly acting drugs taken concurrently) and/or cross-tolerance (i.e., lessened drug effect because of past heavy use of pharmacologically similar drugs), both of which must be considered when treating those with alcohol problems who use other drugs. The foregoing speaks to important differences between the treatment of individuals with alcohol use problems only and of individuals who have other substance use problems in addition to their alcohol use problems (Batki et al., 2009; González-Pinto et al., 2010; Pakula, Macdonald, & Stockwell, 2009; Shillington & Clapp, 2006).

Third, people with an alcohol use disorder who drink alcohol daily and in large quantities are likely to experience withdrawal symptoms when access to alcohol is restricted. These symptoms can range from minor withdrawal symptoms (e.g., psychomotor agitation) to, in the most severe cases, delirium tremens (DTs). A history of past withdrawal symptoms, coupled with reports of recent heavy ethanol consumption, can alert clinicians that withdrawal symptoms are likely to occur upon cessation of drinking; such symptoms can be successfully managed with medical interventions. Moreover, some research suggests that severity of alcohol dependence may interact with response to treatment goals; different treatment intensities may be the most appropriate treatment with different levels of dependence (e.g., mild vs. severe), consistent with client-treatment matching (Babor & Del Boca, 2003; McKay, 2009). Thus, important diagnostic goals when assessing individuals with alcohol problems are to determine the severity of the problem and whether withdrawal symptoms are likely to occur when drinking is reduced.

## EPIDEMIOLOGY

Next to caffeine, alcohol is the second most used psychoactive substance (Adams, Martinez & Vickerie, 2009). The World Health Organization (WHO, 2004) estimates that approximately 2 billion people worldwide consume alcoholic beverages and 76.3 million people have diagnosable alcohol use disorders. The global burden related to alcohol consumption, both in terms of (a) morbidity and mortality and (b) economic and social costs, is considerable. Worldwide, it has been estimated that alcohol causes 1.8 million deaths (3.2% of total) and a loss of 58.3 million (4% of total) of Disability-Adjusted Life Years (DALY) (WHO, 2004). High-level, long-term, chronic drinking dramatically increases the risk for more than 60 diseases (English & Holman, 1995; Gutjahr, Gmel, & Rehm, 2001; Ridolfo & Stevenson, 2001; Single, Robson, Rehm, & Xi, 1999). Alcohol use problems play a causal role in 20% to 30% of esophageal cancer, liver cancer, cirrhosis of the liver, homicide, epileptic seizures, and motor vehicle accidents worldwide (WHO, 2004). Acute intoxication from drinking is associated with motor vehicle traffic accidents, homicide and unintentional or intentional injury, falls, and poisonings (WHO, 2004). Moreover, alcohol consumption is linked to many harmful consequences for the individual drinker, the drinker's immediate environment, and society as a whole. Alcohol-related social consequences include traffic accidents, workplace-related problems, family and domestic problems, and interpersonal violence (Klingemann & Gmel, 2001).

The National Institute on Alcohol Abuse and Alcoholism (NIAAA) surveyed a representative sample of 42,862 American adults in the National Longitudinal Alcohol Epidemiologic Survey (Grant, 1997). It was found that the lifetime prevalence of alcohol dependence was 13.3%, and the past year prevalence was 4.4%. Men were more likely than women to use alcohol and to have alcohol use disorders. NIAAA conducted a second survey of a representative sample of 43,093 Americans in the National Epidemiologic Survey on Alcohol and Related Conditions (Stinson et al., 2005) and found the 12-month prevalence of alcohol use disorders to be only 7.35%, and of comorbid alcohol and substance use disorders to be 1.10%. In terms of the stability of diagnoses, Hasin, Grant, and Endicott (1990) found that of those individuals originally diagnosed as alcohol dependent, 46% were still classified as dependent 4 years later, 15% were classified as having alcohol abuse, and 39% could not be diagnosed with an alcohol problem. Similarly, in a national survey, Dawson (1996) found that among 4,585 adults who previously had met criteria for a *DSM-IV* diagnosis of alcohol dependence, 28% still met the criteria for alcohol abuse or dependence, 22% were abstinent, and 50% could not be diagnosed as having an alcohol problem. As compared to people who had not been in treatment, treated individuals were more likely to be abstinent (39% vs. 16%), whereas those who had not been treated were more likely to be drinking asymptomatically (58% vs. 28%). In another national survey, Dawson (2000) reported that frequency of intoxication had the strongest association with the probability of having a diagnosable alcohol use disorder, followed by the frequency of drinking five drinks per day. These findings underscore that alcohol problems are not necessarily progressive.

From the standpoint of symptom-based prevalence, the ratio of problem drinkers to severely dependent drinkers is a function of the definitions used and the populations sampled. Regardless of the definitions, on a problem severity continuum the population of persons with identifiable problems but no severe signs of dependence is much larger than the population with severe dependence. Problem drinkers constitute 15% to 35% of individuals in the adult population, whereas severely dependent drinkers account for 3% to 7% (Hilton, 1991; Institute of Medicine, 1990). Moreover, the prevalence of alcohol abuse is approximately twice the prevalence of alcohol dependence (Harford, Grant, Yi, & Chen, 2005).

Drinking problems are not distributed equally across sociodemographic groups. Males continue to outnumber females (National Institute on Alcohol Abuse and Alcoholism [NIAAA], 2005), though the gender gap in alcohol use disorders has been narrowing since the Vietnam War (Grant, 1997). Besides gender differences in prevalence, problem drinking tends to occur later in life for women (NIAAA, 2005). Alcohol-related problems also appear to be inversely related to age, with the highest problem rates occurring for those 18 to 29 years of age (Fillmore, 1988; NIAAA, 2000; Robins & Regier, 1991; SAMHSA, 2004). Marital status also is related to problem drinking, with single individuals experiencing more physiological symptoms of dependence and more psychosocial problems than those who are married (Hilton, 1991; SAMHSA, 2006). Specifically, alcohol abuse or dependence is more prevalent among adults who have never married (16.0%) than among adults who are divorced or separated (10.0%), married (4.6%), or widowed (1.3%) (SAMHSA, 2006).

Even though epidemiological studies provide information on ethnic and racial differences in relation to alcohol use and abuse, the methods used for categorizing respondents' cultural/ethnic backgrounds have been rudimentary. Consequently, data on ethnic differences must be considered preliminary. That said, across ethnic/racial groups, national epidemiological studies consistently document ethnic variation in drinking, alcohol use disorders, alcohol use, and treatment engagement and retention (Chartier & Caetano, 2010). Compared with other ethnic groups, (a) Native Americans and Hispanics report higher rates of high-risk drinking; (b) Native Americans and Whites have a greater risk for alcohol use disorders; (c) Native Americans, Hispanics, and Blacks experience more severe drinking-related consequences; and (d) Hispanic problem drinkers are less likely to enter and stay in treatment. Moreover, among alcohol-dependent drinkers, Blacks and Hispanics are more likely to demonstrate recurrent or persistent alcohol dependence. Among Asian Americans, alcohol problem rates are generally lower than among other ethnic and cultural groups (Galvan & Caetano, 2003; Makimoto, 1998; NIAAA, 1993). However, some evidence suggests that Asian Americans of mixed ethnic heritage may be at elevated risk for alcohol use problems (Price, Risk, Wong, & Klingle, 2002). Both Asian cultural norms and physiological sensitivity to alcohol appear to influence the likelihood of alcohol use problems among Asian American groups (Clark & Hesselbrock, 1988).

## PSYCHOLOGICAL AND BIOLOGICAL ASSESSMENT

A thorough and careful assessment is critical to the development of meaningful treatment plans, including an accurate diagnosis of alcohol use and other concurrent disorders. Assessment serves several critical functions; it provides clinicians with (a) an in-depth picture of a person's alcohol use, problem severity, and related consequences—this picture can be used to develop an individualized treatment plan tailored to the needs of each client; (b) an objective process by which to gauge treatment progress; and (c) empirical feedback about how a treatment plan already in place could be improved. The depth and intensity of an assessment will be related to problem severity, the complexity of the presenting case, and the specific interests of the clinician and/or researcher conducting the assessment. The instruments and methods described in this chapter can be used clinically to gather information that is relevant to the assessment and treatment planning process. The implications of assessment data for treatment issues, such as drinking goals and treatment intensity, show how the clinical interview can significantly impact on treatment.

### CRITICAL ISSUES IN ASSESSMENT

In the alcohol field, most research and clinical information is obtained through retrospective self-reports. Clients are asked to recount their use of alcohol and any alcohol-related negative consequences over a specified period or time, such as the past month, 90 days, or year. Research has confirmed that alcohol abusers' self-reports are generally accurate if clients are interviewed in clinical or research settings, when they are alcohol free (i.e., there is no alcohol in their system), and when they are given assurances of confidentiality. Self-reports are prone to some degree of inaccuracy, however, due to recall biases, social desirability biases, misinterpretation of questions, and the like. One way to confirm the accuracy of self-reports is to obtain overlapping information from sources such as chemical tests, collateral reports, and official records. Data from different sources are then compared and contrasted, and conclusions as to the presenting problems are based on a convergence of information. When the measures converge, one can have confidence in the accuracy of the reports.

Getting accurate information during the assessment of alcohol use problems is essential to the success of treatment. Information gathered through the assessment process can be used to provide feedback to clients to enhance their commitment to change. In order to make the assessment and feedback about the assessment most beneficial to clients, they should be delivered in a nonconfrontational manner using principles of motivational interviewing (Sobell & Sobell, 2008). Readers desiring a comprehensive description of how to do motivational interviewing and how to use advice/feedback from an assessment are referred to excellent publications by the Substance Abuse and Mental Health Services Administration (1999), the National Institute on Alcohol Abuse and Alcoholism (2003, 2005), and the American Psychological Association (Sobell & Sobell, 2008).

With respect to the length of an assessment, the breadth and depth of an assessment for alcohol use disorders will vary due to heterogeneity in alcohol problem severity across clients. Because persons with less severe alcohol problems often respond well to a brief intervention, an assessment that is longer than the intervention makes little sense (see Dunn et al., 2010). In contrast, severely dependent alcohol abusers may require a more intensive assessment covering such areas as organic brain dysfunction, psychiatric comorbidity, social needs, and medical status (e.g., liver function). Ultimately, an assessment should be based on clinical judgment and the client's needs. The next section describes different assessment areas and reviews relevant assessment instruments, scales, and questionnaires that can be used for assessing alcohol use and abuse. Only instruments that have sound psychometric properties and clinical utility are discussed. With respect to selecting an appropriate instrument for clinical or research purposes, it is helpful to ask, "What will I learn from using the instrument that I would not otherwise know from a routine clinical interview?"

## ALCOHOL USE

Assessing alcohol consumption involves measuring the quantity and frequency of past and present use. When choosing an instrument to assess drinking, level of precision and time frame are key considerations. Two major dimensions along which measures differ are (1) whether they gather summarized information (e.g., "How many days per week on average do you drink any alcohol?") versus specific information (e.g., "How many drinks did you have on each day of the past month?") and (2) whether the information is recalled retrospectively or recorded in real time as it occurs. Specific measures are preferred over summary measures for pretreatment and within-treatment assessments because they provide (a) information about patterns of drinking and (b) opportunities to inquire about events associated with problem drinking that are not possible using summary data (e.g., "What was happening on Friday when you had 12 drinks?").

In terms of key instruments, there are four long-established approaches to assessing alcohol consumption: (1) Lifetime Drinking History (LDH; Skinner & Sheu, 1982; Sobell & Sobell, 1995; Sobell, Toneatto, & Sobell, 1994); (2) Quantity-Frequency methods (QF; Room, 1990; Skinner & Sheu, 1982; Sobell & Sobell, 1995); (3) Timeline Followback (TLFB; APA, 2000b; Sobell & Sobell, 1992, 1995, 2000); and (4) Self-Monitoring (SM; Sobell, Bogardis, Schuller, Leo, & Sobell, 1989; Sobell & Sobell, 1995). The first three are retrospective estimation methods (i.e., they obtain information about alcohol use after it has occurred). The TLFB can also be used in treatment as an advice-feedback tool to help increase clients' motivation to change (Sobell & Sobell, 1995). The fourth method, self-monitoring, asks clients to record their drinking at or about the same time that it occurred. The self-monitoring approach possesses several clinical advantages: (a) it provides feedback about treatment effectiveness; (b) it identifies situations that pose a high risk of relapse; and (c) it gives outpatient clients an opportunity to discuss their drinking that occurred since the previous session. Because several reviews have detailed the advantages and disadvantages of these drinking instruments, readers interested in the use of these instruments are referred to the primary source articles listed for each approach.

ALCOHOL USE CONSEQUENCES

One of the key defining characteristics of a *DSM-IV* diagnosis is alcohol-related consequences. Several short self-administered scales have been developed to assess alcohol-related psychosocial consequences and dependence symptoms: (1) Alcohol Use Disorders Identification Test (AUDIT; Saunders, Aasland, Babor, De La Fuente, & Grant, 1993); (2) Severity of Alcohol Dependence Questionnaire (SADQ; Stockwell, Murphy, & Hodgson, 1983; Stockwell, Sitharthan, McGrath, & Lang, 1994); (3) Alcohol Dependence Scale (ADS; Skinner & Allen, 1982); and (4) Short Alcohol Dependence Data Questionnaire (SADD; Raistrick, Dunbar, & Davidson, 1983). These scales take about 5 minutes to administer and range from 10 to 25 items in length. Although several scales are used for brief screening and identification of harmful and hazardous alcohol use, the AUDIT stands out for its psychometric characteristics, convenience, and cross-cultural validation. The AUDIT, developed as a multinational WHO project, is a brief screening test for the early detection of harmful and hazardous alcohol use in primary health care settings (Saunders et al., 1993). The 10 questions are scored based on the frequency of the experience (i.e., from 0 "never" to 4 "daily"). The AUDIT has been shown to be as good as or better than other screening tests (e.g., CAGE, MAST, ADS) in identifying individuals with probable alcohol problems (Barry & Fleming, 1993; Fleming, Barry, & MacDonald, 1991). According to the authors, the differences between the AUDIT and most other screening tests are that it (a) detects drinkers along the entire severity continuum from mild to severe; (b) emphasizes hazardous consumption and frequency of intoxication compared with drinking behavior and adverse consequences; (c) uses a time frame that asks questions about current (i.e., past year) and lifetime use; and (d) avoids using a "yes/no" format and instead uses Likert rating scales to reduce face validity.

CO-OCCURRING DISORDERS

As reviewed earlier, a substantial number of people with alcohol problems have co-occurring psychiatric problems. Although several diagnostic interviews and scales exist for assessing psychiatric comorbidity among individuals with alcohol disorder, the comprehensiveness of these assessments will vary depending on the resources available, specificity of the information required, treatment setting, and the assessor's skill level. Several brief and widely available questionnaires can assess for symptoms of co-occurring disorders. These instruments include (1) the Beck Depression Inventory (Beck, Steer, & Garbin, 1988); (2) the Beck Anxiety Inventory (Beck, Epstein, Brown, & Steer, 1988); (3) the Hamilton Rating Scale for Depression (Hamilton, 1960); and (4) the Symptom Checklist-90-R (Derogatis, 1983). For brief descriptions of the clinical utility of these instruments with individual with alcohol use disorders, readers are referred to two reviews (Carey & Correia, 1998; Sobell et al., 1994). Personality tests, especially objective tests rather than projective tests, also have clinical utility in assessing psychiatric disorder among individuals with alcohol use disorder. Prominent examples of objective personality tests include the Minnesota Multiphasic Personality Inventory–2 (Hathaway & McKinley, 1989 [revised 2001]) and the Millon Clinical Multiaxial Inventory–III (Millon, Millon, Davis, & Grossman, 2006).

## High-Risk Situations and Self-Efficacy

Because relapse rates among individuals treated for alcohol problems are extremely high, the assessment of high-risk situations for drinking has long been recognized as important at assessment and during treatment (Marlatt & Gordon, 1985; Sobell & Sobell, 1993). The Situational Confidence Questionnaire (SCQ-39) assesses self-efficacy to resist drinking by asking clients to rate their self-efficacy across a variety of situations on a scale ranging from 100% confident to 0% confident. The SCQ-39 can be completed in less than 20 minutes and contains eight subscales (e.g., unpleasant emotions, pleasant emotions, testing personal control) based on the classic relapse research by Marlatt and Gordon (Marlatt & Gordon, 1985). For clinical purposes, the Brief SCQ (BSCQ), a variant of the SCQ that is easy to score and interpret, was developed and consists of eight items that represent the eight subscales (Breslin, Sobell, Sobell, & Agrawal, 2000). Although the BSCQ can be used clinically to enhance treatment planning, it only identifies generic situations and problem areas. To examine clients' individual high-risk situations or areas where they lack self-confidence, clinicians should explore in depth specific high-risk situations with clients. For example, clients can be asked to describe their two or three highest-risk situations for alcohol use in the past year, with attention to the similarities and differences across the situations. Another instrument for measuring self-efficacy to resist substance use is the Drug-Taking Confidence Questionnaire–8 (DTCQ-8; Sklar & Turner, 1999), an eight-item questionnaire similar to the BSCQ but applicable across a variety of different substance use disorders.

## Neuropsychological Functioning

Numerous neurophysiological and neuropsychological studies have identified negative consequences from both acute and chronic alcohol consumption in areas of brain functioning, including attention, auditory working memory, verbal processing, abstraction/cognitive flexibility, psychomotor function, immediate memory, delayed memory, reaction time, and spatial processing (Lyvers, 2000; Oscar-Berman & Marinkovic, 2007). Moreover, it is well documented that individuals with alcohol use disorder are at elevated risk for neuropsychological problems, which may be barriers to treatment success if they are not identified and addressed. Thus, a comprehensive alcohol use disorders assessment should include neuropsychological screening. Multiple screening tests are available for measuring neuropsychological functioning, but the most widely used include (a) the Digit Span, Letter Number Sequencing, and Similarities subscales from the Wechsler Adult Intelligence Scale (WAIS-III; Wechsler, 1997a); (b) the Trail Making Test (Davies, 1968); (c) the Wisconsin Card Sorting Test-64 (Kongs, Thompson, Iverson, & Heaton, 2000); and (d) the Spatial Span subscale from the Wechsler Memory

Scale (WMS-III; Wechsler, 1997b). These screening tests are relatively easy and quick to administer (e.g., about 5 minutes) and are highly sensitive to alcohol-related brain dysfunction. For a good overview of neuropsychological assessment with individuals with alcohol use disorder, interested readers are referred to Allen, Strauss, Leany, and Donohue (2008).

BARRIERS TO CHANGE

In developing a treatment plan, it is helpful to anticipate possible barriers that clients might encounter with respect to changing their behavior. Barriers can be both motivational and practical. If an individual is not motivated to change, there is little reason to expect that change will occur. Because many alcohol abusers are coerced into treatment (e.g., courts, significant others), such individuals might not have a serious interest in changing (Cunningham, Sobell, Sobell, & Gaskin, 1994). Thus, it is important to evaluate a client's motivation for and commitment to change. According to Miller and Rollnick (1991), "motivation is a state of readiness or eagerness to change, which may fluctuate from one time or situation to another. This state is one that can be influenced" (p. 14). Thus, rather than a trait, motivation is a state that can be influenced by several variables, one of which is the therapist.

An easy way to assess readiness to change is to use a Readiness Ruler (see p. 139; SAMHSA, 1999). The Readiness Ruler asks clients to indicate their readiness to change using a 5-point scale ranging from "not ready to change" to "unsure" to "very ready to change." The ruler has face validity, is user friendly, and takes only a few seconds to complete. For a detailed description of methods for increasing motivation for change, readers are referred to two excellent resources (Miller & Rollnick, 2002; SAMHSA, 1999). Environmental factors can also present formidable obstacles to change. For example, individuals in an environment where alcohol is readily available and where there are many cues to drink might find it difficult to abstain. For some individuals, social avoidance strategies (e.g., avoiding bars, no alcohol in the house) might be the only effective alternative. Finally, clinicians should attend to individual barriers that can also affect a person's ability to enter and complete treatment (e.g., child care, transportation, inability to take time off from work, unwillingness to adopt an abstinence goal) (Schmidt & Weisner, 1995).

BIOCHEMICAL MEASURES

Both unintentional and intentional recall biases can lead to inaccuracies in the self-report measurement of alcohol use. The use of alcohol, tobacco, and other drugs can be detected in different bodily fluids (e.g., breath, blood, urine, hair, saliva) and by several biochemical detection methods. In situations where there are concerns about the validity of self-reports (e.g., drug use among criminal offenders), a convergent validity approach relying on biochemical measures is often employed. Although there has been a tendency to consider biochemical measures as "gold standards" that are superior to self-reports, it is important to note that biochemical measures can suffer from validity and implementation problems. In fact, in some settings, self-reports may be superior to certain biochemical measures

(Gmel, Wicki, Rehm, & Heeb, 2008). Moreover, issues of self-report accuracy take on different meanings for clinical versus research purposes, where different levels of reporting precision are required. For example, clinicians do not routinely have to obtain information to confirm their clients' alcohol use unless the situation warrants it. However, in clinical trials, researchers typically choose to verify their clients' self-reports using biochemical or other alternative measures (e.g., collateral reports).

Urinalysis can provide qualitative (i.e., which substances are currently in the body) and quantitative (i.e., how much of a substance is currently in the body) information. The detection of alcohol in the urine typically uses ethyl glucuronide (EtG), a direct metabolite of ethanol alcohol. EtG is present in the urine roughly 80 hours after alcohol has been metabolized. Given its relatively high reliability and sensitivity, and low expense, EtG testing is often used in situations where alcohol consumption is prohibited, such as by the military or in recovering alcoholic patients. However, all urine tests have limitations. Urinalyses cannot specify when a drug was taken. Rather, it only provides evidence of whether consumption occurred and the amount of drug or the drug's metabolite in the system at the time of testing. Moreover, urine tests are not able to distinguish between alcohol absorbed into the body from the actual consumption of alcohol versus exposure to any of the many common commercial and household products containing alcohol. A final problem with urine testing is the urine specimen itself, which can be embarrassing to obtain, be adulterated or substituted, and present a biological hazard during shipping and disposal.

Breath and hair analysis can also provide reliable information on alcohol use. A breath analyzer will yield reasonably accurate readings of a person's blood alcohol concentration (BAC), which is measured indirectly by analyzing the amount of alcohol in one's breath. Breath alcohol testers are noninvasive, inexpensive, easy to use, portable, and provide an immediate determination of BAC. Several portable testers differing in cost and precision are commercially available. Although they are relatively robust measures of BAC, breath analyzers can produce false readings due to tobacco smoke, recent drinking, a person's breathing rate, or equipment or operator error. Hair analysis tests whether two markers of alcohol use, ethyl glucuronide (EtG) and fatty acid ethyl esters (FAEEs), are present. Only scalp hair can be used, and a sample approximately the diameter of a pencil and about 1.5 inches long is required. Hair analysis is relatively noninvasive and highly accurate, and it can provide a history of alcohol consumption for up to several years. Moreover, hair samples are nearly impossible to adulterate and are highly stable and transportable. Despite these advantages, hair analysis is several times more expensive than urine analysis, and it will not work if a person has very short hair or a shaved head.

Liver function problems are highly prevalent in alcoholics (Lucey, Mathurin, & Morgan, 2009), so physicians routinely assess hepatic dysfunction when presented with a patient with chronic drinking problems. Elevated liver enzymes, which indicate liver dysfunction, are seen among alcohol-dependent drinkers. However, most problem drinkers (i.e., those who are not severely dependent on alcohol) do not show elevations on liver function tests (Sobell, Agrawal, & Sobell, 1999). In addition, alcohol-dependent women, more than alcoholic men, are likely to demonstrate hepatic dysfunction (Wagnerberger, Schafer, Schwarz, Bode, & Parlesak, 2008). Cirrhosis, which is permanent and nonreversible cellular liver damage (Maher, 1997), occurs typically among only those with the heaviest drinking patterns. Unlike assessment of acute hepatic dysfunction, which can be done through a blood test, cirrhosis must be diagnosed through a liver biopsy.

## ETIOLOGICAL CONSIDERATIONS

### Behavioral Genetics and Molecular Genetics

Risk for alcohol use disorder involves genetic influences and environmental influences to an approximately equal extent (Enoch, Schuckit, Johnson, & Goldman, 2003; Knopik et al., 2004; Schuckit, 2000). Close relatives of persons with alcohol problems, adopted-away children of men and women with alcohol problems, and identical twins whose parents had alcohol problems all have been found to demonstrate a much higher likelihood of experiencing alcohol use problems than the general population (Foroud, Edenberg, & Crabbe, 2010). Several endophenotypes—or subconditions that increase the risk for a disorder—have been identified in regard to alcohol problems, and these endophenotypes appear to have strong genetic influences (Puls & Gallinat, 2008; Schuckit, 2000). The absence or limited production of alcohol-metabolizing enzymes (most common among Asians), low response level to alcohol (i.e., needing a greater number of drinks to have an effect), low amplitude of the P300 wave component of event-related potentials, and low alpha activity and voltage on electroencephalograms all are associated with an increased risk of drinking problems, and all have strong genetic influences.

In regard to specific genes, the genes encoding two alcohol-metabolizing enzymes—alcohol dehydrogenase (ADH) and aldehyde dehydrogenase (ALDH)—appear to have the strongest relation to alcohol use disorder; other gene variants associated with alcohol use disorder demonstrate much weaker relations (Foroud et al., 2010). In terms of mechanisms of action, the genetic variants associated with alcohol use disorder affect the metabolism and pharmacokinetics of alcohol, as well as the subjective response to alcohol (Heath and Martin, 1991; Ray, MacKillop, & Monti, 2010; Viken, Rose, Morzorati, Christian, & Li, 2003). Although genetic studies have documented genetic influences on the risk of alcohol problems in men, this has occurred less so with women (McGue, 1999; Prescott, 2002). In a notable exception, Hardie, Moss, and Lynch (2008) found provisional support for gender differences in heritability with regard to specific symptoms of alcohol use problems. Despite the strong association between genetic risk and the development of alcohol use disorder, it is important to remember that a wide array of environmental influences condition whether and how that risk is expressed (Johnson, van den Bree, Gupman, & Pickens, 1998).

### Neuroanatomy and Neurobiology

Multiple biological and physiological systems are impacted by and appear to influence alcohol consumption. As reviewed earlier, biological factors found to be associated with the development of alcohol problems include the absence or limited production of alcohol-metabolizing enzymes, low level of response to alcohol (i.e., needing more drinks to have an effect), low amplitude of the P300 wave component of event-related potentials, and low alpha activity and voltage on electroencephalograms. These factors all substantially raise the likelihood that an individual will develop alcohol problems, but none, alone or in combination, is a sufficient or necessary determinant of alcohol abuse or dependence.

In addition, two other biological systems are currently receiving considerable research attention. The hypothalamic-pituitary-adrenal (HPA) axis is a hormone system that plays a central role in the body's response to stress. Alcohol consumption has been shown to stimulate the HPA axis system, and several studies suggest that individuals who demonstrate greater HPA activity in response to various stimuli may find alcohol consumption more reinforcing than individuals who demonstrate lower HPA activity (Gianoulakis, 1998; Kiefer, Jahn, Schick, & Wiedemann, 2002). However, it is important to note that there are large individual differences in the response of the HPA axis to either stress or alcohol, and HPA dysfunction may play a role in only a subgroup of individuals with alcohol use problems (Sillaber & Henniger, 2004). The endogenous opioid system plays a central role in various physiological processes, including pain relief, euphoria, and the rewarding and reinforcing effect of psychoactive substances (Volkow, 2010). Alcohol consumption also stimulates the endogenous opioid system, and it appears that endogenous opioids help mediate the reinforcing effects of alcohol (Gianoulakis, 1998; Le Merrer, Becker, Befort, & Kieffer, 2009). Specifically, alcohol consumption increases dopamine in the nucleus accumbens (NAc), which may account for some of its reinforcing effects among some individuals. As with HPA, the endogenous opioid system may be most influential among a subgroup of individuals with alcohol use problems (Volkow, 2010).

### LEARNING, MODELING, AND LIFE EVENTS

Learning theory, as applied to alcohol use, assumes that drinking is largely learned and that basic learning principles guide the acquisition, maintenance, and modification of drinking behavior (Carroll, 1999). Classical conditioning models posit that the development of a drinking problem occurs largely through the pairing of conditioned stimuli, such as locations or people, with the unconditioned stimulus of alcohol (Hesselbrock, Hesselbrock, & Epstein, 1999). Through repeated pairings with alcohol, the conditioned stimuli come to elicit a conditioned response, which is manifested in craving for alcohol. Tolerance to alcohol also has been explained using a classical conditioning model, where the conditioned stimuli come to elicit a conditioned compensatory response (i.e., an opposite reaction to the initial drug effects) that resembles the unconditioned compensatory response elicited by alcohol consumption (Sherman, Jorenby, & Baker, 1988; Wikler, 1973). Operant conditioning models assume that alcohol consumption is governed by its reinforcing effects, including physiological and phenomenological changes in response to drinking, the social consequences of drinking, and/or the avoidance or cessation of withdrawal symptoms (Hesselbrock et al., 1999). In summary, learning models may explain how drinking problems may develop and provide guidance in the design of interventions designed to modify drinking.

An especially influential variable in alcohol use and abuse that appears to be governed by basic learning principles is alcohol expectancies. Alcohol expectancies are the effects (positive and negative) attributed to alcohol that an individual anticipates experiencing when drinking (Goldman, Del Boca, & Darkes, 1999). Expectancies appear to develop early in life, are consistent across gender, and are learned according to social learning principles, including classical conditioning, operant conditioning, and modeling (Hesselbrock et al., 1999). In several different studies, alcohol expectancies have been shown to be highly related to adult and adolescent drinking practices, including drinking problems and relapse to drinking following a period of abstinence (Marlatt & Witkiewitz, 2005; Witkiewitz & Marlatt, 2007).

Research on the modeling of alcohol consumption emerged from Bandura's (1969) social learning theory, which posits that modeling influences the acquisition and performance of a variety of social behaviors. Caudill and Marlatt (1975) were among the first to experimentally study the influence of social modeling on drinking behavior, and they found that participants exposed to a heavy drinking model (a research confederate) consumed significantly more wine than participants exposed to a light drinking or no model. Collins and Marlatt (1981) reviewed the research in 1981 and concluded that modeling was a powerful influence on drinking that occurred regardless of study setting or moderating variables (e.g., gender, age). More recently, Quigley and Collins (1999) performed a meta-analysis on published studies concerning the modeling of alcohol consumption and found "a definitive effect" of modeling on drinking behavior. Large effect sizes for both amount of alcohol consumed and BAC were documented. Modeling effects appear to be particularly influential among underage and young adult drinkers (Ennett et al., 2008).

For centuries, stress from life events has been thought to be related to alcohol consumption, and drinking has been seen as relieving stress (Sayette, 1999). The relationship between drinking and stress can be traced to the sociological literature of the 1940s and the emergence of the tension-reduction hypothesis in the 1950s (Pohorecky, 1991). The tension-reduction hypothesis proposes that (a) alcohol consumption will reduce stress under most circumstances, and (b) people will be motivated to drink in times of stress. This hypothesis forms the basis of current research about the relationship between drinking and stress (Sayette, 1999). Although studies indicate that drinking can reduce stress related to life events in certain people and under certain circumstances, the relationship between drinking and life events is far more complex than originally thought. Individual differences, including a family history of alcohol problems, certain personality traits (e.g., impulsivity), extent of self-consciousness, level of cognitive functioning, gender, and situational factors including distraction and the timing of drinking and stress, have all been shown to be important moderators of the degree to which alcohol will reduce the subjective, behavioral, neurochemical, and immunological consequences of stress (Fox, Bergquist, Gu, & Sinha, 2010; Hussong, Hicks, Levy, & Curran, 2001; Sayette, 1999).

## COGNITIVE INFLUENCES

An extensive literature exists regarding the role of cognitive influences on alcohol use. Among the earliest cognitive models of alcohol use is Hull's (1981) Self-Awareness

Model. This model proposes that alcohol interferes with the process of encoding information, which subsequently decreases self-awareness by preventing the encoding of failures or poor evaluative feedback. Furthermore, the Self-Awareness Model postulates that people drink to reduce self-evaluative forms of stress. While influential in stimulating research on cognitive influences on alcohol use problems, empirical evidence in support of the Self-Awareness Model has been inconsistent (Bacon & Ham, 2010), and other cognitive models subsequently have been proposed. The Attentional Allocation Model and Appraisal Disruption Model are especially notable.

Steele and Josephs' (1988, 1990; Josephs & Steele, 1990) Attentional Allocation Model proposes that alcohol consumption reduces an individual's capacity for controlled and effortful information processing and for paying attention. Alcohol consumption results in "alcohol myopia," where attention is focused only on cues that are immediately salient and require little effortful processing. Depending on how attention is focused during intoxication (e.g., on a distraction or on current stressors), attention allocation can account for both increases and decreases in perceived stress and subjective well-being from drinking. Sayette's (1993) Appraisal-Disruption Model includes aspects of both the Self-Awareness Model and the Attention-Allocation Model, but it uniquely proposes that alcohol interferes with cognitive processing at the level of appraisal, which occurs early in information processing and involves the determination of the personal valence and relevance of stimuli and cues. The Appraisal-Disruption Model focuses on alcohol's effects on information organization, as opposed to self-awareness or attentional allocation, and includes a temporal dimension (i.e., before or during intoxication) in predicting how cue appraisal will influence drinking and its subjective consequences.

## SEX AND RACIAL-ETHNIC CONSIDERATIONS

Whenever and wherever women's and men's alcohol use has been measured, results show that women drink less than men, and women's drinking leads to fewer social problems than men's drinking (NIAAA, 2005; Wilsnack, Vogeltanz, Wilsnack, & Harris, 2000). However, few studies go beyond demonstrating that men use and have problems with alcohol more than women do, and currently both biological and social-structural theoretical explanations exist for these gender differences (Wilsnack et al., 2000). The biological explanations emphasize gender differences in the metabolism of alcohol, and the social-structural explanations emphasize gender differences in social roles, and how these differences may influence drinking behavior. In regard to biological explanations, several animal studies have documented gender differences in alcohol metabolism, and it appears that hormonal differences between the sexes may modulate these differences (Smith & Lin, 1996). Moreover, women are more susceptible to alcoholic liver injury than are men, and this appears to be the result of less metabolism of alcohol in the stomach, and thus greater exposure to high alcohol concentrations (Frezza et al., 1990; Moack & Anton, 1999; Morgan, 1994; Schenker, 1997). Whereas research has suggested that women's reproductive functioning influences alcohol metabolism, evidence is mixed regarding how menstrual cycle phase may affect alcohol consumption, metabolism, and self-estimates of blood alcohol levels

(Jensvold, 1996). Although one study has suggested that the use of oral contraceptives results in decreased alcohol metabolism, and thus increased alcohol effects (Jones & Jones, 1976), another study found no effect of oral contraceptives on alcohol metabolism (Hobbes, Boutagy, & Shenfield, 1985).

In regard to social-structural explanations, some investigators have examined how women's social roles vis-à-vis alcohol may explain lower rates of alcohol use and abuse among women than men. Cross-culturally, women's drinking has been more socially restricted than their male counterparts, primarily because it may negatively affect women's social behavior and responsibilities (Wilsnack et al., 2000). Consistent with this perspective, there is evidence that social influences play a greater role in women's than men's drinking. For example, partners' heavy drinking has a greater influence on female problem drinking than on male problem drinking (Gomberg, 1994), and there is more marital disruption (i.e., never married, divorced or separated, widowed) among females (Gomberg, 1995). Moreover, a recent study indicates that the types of problems experienced by women with alcohol use disorder differ from those experienced by men with alcohol use disorder. Nichol, Krueger, and Iacono (2007) found that one-third of the symptoms typically used to diagnose alcohol problems concerned problems experienced almost exclusively by males (e.g., fighting while drinking). In addition, depression appears to be particularly associated with women's drinking and drinking problems (Conner, Pinquart, & Gamble, 2009; Nichol et al., 2007). This speaks to the need for more sensitive indices for detecting drinking problems among women, with an emphasis on depressed affect. In sum, it appears that both biological and social-structural explanations may be needed to account for gender differences in alcohol use and abuse.

Regarding race and ethnicity, epidemiological studies show that alcohol use, morbidity, and mortality vary by race/ethnicity in seemingly paradoxical ways. For example, African Americans and some Hispanic/Latino groups have lower overall rates of alcohol involvement than do non-Latino whites, yet these groups demonstrate higher rates of alcohol-related morbidity and mortality than do non-Latino whites (Caetano, 2003; Gilliland, Becker, Samet, & Key, 1995; Lee, Markides, & Ray, 1997). This paradox may result from ethnic/racial variations in the processes by which alcohol use can lead to alcohol problems. For example, the accelerated progression from use to problem use seen among these minority populations could result from socioeconomic polarization, criminal justice problems, or the lack of appropriate treatment options. Compared with other ethnic groups, (a) Native Americans and Hispanics report higher rates of high-risk drinking; (b) Native Americans and Whites have a greater risk for alcohol use disorders; (c) Native Americans, Hispanics, and Blacks experience more severe drinking-related consequences; and (d) Hispanic problem drinkers are less likely to enter and stay in treatment (Chartier & Caetano, 2010). Moreover, among alcohol-dependent drinkers, Blacks and Hispanics are more likely to demonstrate recurrent or persistent alcohol dependence. Additional factors that may affect how race and ethnicity are associated with the progression to alcohol problems, as well as with response to alcohol abuse treatment, include perceived discrimination and cultural mistrust for African Americans, and acculturation stress, nativity, and immigration history for Hispanics/Latinos.

## COURSE AND PROGNOSIS

Based largely on Jellinek's work on the progression of alcoholism (Jellinek, 1952), mid-20th-century thinking about the course of alcohol problems was that such problems develop in early adulthood (i.e., 20 to 30 years of age) and increase in severity over the course of several years. As noted earlier in this chapter, the notion of progressivity in alcohol problems has not been supported by research, although some alcohol problems do worsen over time. Research also shows that alcohol problems can occur at any age (Atkinson, 1994; Schonfeld & Dupree, 1991; Schuckit & Smith, 2011; Wilsnack, Klassen, Schur, & Wilsnack, 1991). The temporal pattern can be variable, with problems sometimes remitting, worsening, or improving (Cahalan & Room, 1974; Dawson, 1996; DeLucchi & Kaskutas, 2010; Hasin et al., 1990; Mandell, 1983). If an individual is experiencing alcohol problems at one point, it is not possible to predict that in the absence of treatment the problem will worsen. It has been found, however, that men whose alcohol problems are severe are likely to continue to worsen over time if they continue to drink (Fillmore & Midanik, 1984). More recent research indicates that gender differences in the course of alcohol use and alcohol use problems are decreasing among younger cohorts, while gender differences in time from first use to dependence are increasing, with an accelerated time to dependence among men (Keyes, Martins, Blanco, & Hasin, 2010).

Alcohol problems have been characterized as a recurrent disorder (Polich, Armor, & Braiker, 1981). This characteristic has given the disorder a reputation as difficult to treat and seldom cured. Recent research, however, has found that the probability of relapse in persons who have been in remission for several years is low (Finney & Moos, 1991; Schuckit & Smith, 2011; Sobell, Sobell, & Kozlowksi, 1995). Clinically, the high likelihood of recurrence has led to relapse prevention procedures (Marlatt & Gordon, 1985). Such procedures include advising clients that setbacks may occur during recovery from the disorder, and that they should use these setbacks as learning experiences to prevent future relapses, rather than as evidence that recovery is impossible. Moreover, a recent 16-year-long study of individuals treated for alcohol problems found predictors of long-term success to include first-year post-treatment engagement in AA, reduced depressive symptoms, improved stress coping, and enhanced social support for nondrinking (McKellar, Ilgen, Moos, & Moos, 2008). Finally, the presence of co-occurring psychiatric disorder(s) is associated with a more guarded prognosis for recovery among individuals treated for alcohol use disorders (Baigent, 2005; Le Fauve et al., 2004; Modesto-Lowe & Kranzler, 1999).

## LOOKING AHEAD TO DSM-5

The *DSM-5* Substance-Related Work Group has proposed new alcohol use disorder diagnostic criteria (see www.dsm5.org/ProposedRevisions/Pages/Substance-RelatedDisorders.aspx). The work group concluded that the overuse of the terms "addiction" and "dependence" has confused the diagnosis and treatment of people with alcohol use disorders and resulted in patients with normal tolerance and withdrawal being labeled as "addicts." Accordingly, in the proposed *DSM-5* criteria, the word "dependence" will be limited to physiological dependence, and alcohol use problems will be diagnosed on a severity continuum, and as with or without alcohol dependence. Moreover, the presence of tolerance and withdrawal symptoms will no longer count as symptoms for the diagnosis of alcohol use disorder.

## CASE STUDY

The following case study provides an example of a typical client presenting for outpatient treatment of alcohol use problems.

### CASE IDENTIFICATION

The patient is a 27-year-old white, single male who voluntarily entered treatment at the Guided Self-Change (GSC) Clinic at the Addiction Research Foundation (Toronto, Canada). Guided Self-Change treatment, a motivationally based cognitive-behavioral intervention, emphasizes helping clients to help themselves (Sobell & Sobell, 1993). The intervention includes an assessment, four semistructured sessions, and an aftercare component. In addition, clients are given an opportunity to request additional sessions. The GSC treatment intervention has been evaluated in several clinical trials (Sobell & Sobell, 1998).

### PRESENTING COMPLAINTS

The patient was in his last year of graduate school and was planning to pursue a postdoctoral fellowship in the coming year. He reported seeking treatment because of "hitting a personal rock bottom" and an "ultimatum from my girlfriend." The client reported that 2 years prior to treatment, the frequency and quantity of his drinking had increased and that he had tried to cut down and stop without success. He also reported that his university friends and colleagues drank heavily after seminars, and that he perceived there was a "stigma" attached to people who left after a few drinks. He noted that he felt pressured to drink when others around him drank. At treatment entry, he reported he was "extremely ready" to take action to change his drinking, and at the assessment he stated, "I've started working on my problem, but I need some help." When asked why he decided to seek treatment, he stated:

> *A series of events which started with increased drinking, behavioral change, fights when I was intoxicated, or "drunk" for a better word, breakups with friends, stupid arguments with friends, arguments with girlfriends—Just a lot of bad times and a lot of problems. I usually go for maybe two or three weeks and say "I'm positively not going to have anything to drink," but when I would say "Okay, well I can handle this now," it seemed to get worse, so I thought it's time to talk to somebody about it.*

### HISTORY

Although he reported drinking heavily for 8 years, he felt that his drinking had only been a problem for the last 4 years. His score on the Alcohol Dependence Scale (ADS; Skinner & Allen, 1982) was 11 and on the Drug Abuse Screening Test (DAST-20; Skinner, 1982) was 1. An ADS score of 11 is in the first quartile for ADS norms and is reflective of someone who has a mild alcohol problem. A DAST-20 score of 1 suggests no current drug problem. The patient also reported no current use of prescription medications or other psychoactive substances, including nicotine. He reported no current health problems or past treatment for mental health or substance use problems. He also reported never having attended self-help group meetings (e.g., AA) and had no prior alcohol-related hospitalizations or arrests. He reported no morning drinking in the past year, and in terms of family history, reported that his father had had a problem with alcohol. He reported experiencing several alcohol-related consequences in the 6 months prior to the assessment (e.g., fights in bars, personal problems, verbally abusive, spending too much money on alcohol). He reported that his highest-risk situations for problem drinking were when he was home alone, bored and stressed, and when with friends after work at seminars. He also reported that on about half the days when he drank alcohol, it was when he was alone. Although this was his first treatment experience, he reported several prior attempts to quit or reduce his alcohol use.

ASSESSMENT

At the assessment, his subjective evaluation of the severity of his alcohol problem was "major," and he rated the overall quality of his life as "very unsatisfactory." Self-report of his drinking in the past year using the Timeline Followback assessment (LaBrie, Pedersen, & Earleywine, 2005; Sobell & Sobell, 1992) was (1) abstinence: 59% of the days; (2) drinks per drinking day: 4.5 standard drinks (SDs; 1 SD = 13.6 g of absolute ethanol); (3) average weekly consumption: 13 SDs; (4) highest single drinking day in the past year: 14 SDs; (5) low consumption days (1–3 SDs): 42% of all days; (6) heavy consumption: 22% of all days (20% = 4–9 SDs, 2% were 10 SDs). When shown the personalized feedback based on his self-reports of drinking (Sobell & Sobell, 1996; Sobell & Sobell, 1998; SAMHSA, 1999), he said: "I'm a little alarmed. More than a little alarmed, but I'm alarmed that I'm at the high end, but I know, I, that's why I'm here. The other part that alarms me is that most of the people I know, I would put them in that." Based on the assessment interview, this patient met the criteria for a *DSM-IV* diagnosis of alcohol dependence (American Psychiatric Association, 2000a); however, on a continuum of alcohol problems, the severity of his problem would be evaluated as mild.

## SUMMARY

Conceptualizations of alcohol problems have improved markedly over the past three decades, affecting research and practice in regard to alcohol use disorders and their treatment. In particular, it is now recognized that severely dependent alcoholics represent only a small proportion of individuals suffering with alcohol problems. A one-size-fits-all approach is no longer appropriate for all individuals with alcohol problems, and residential treatment has fallen out of favor. The concept that alcohol problems can be scaled along a continuum of severity has major implications for assessment and treatment. For example, less severely dependent alcohol abusers can benefit from brief treatment, preceded by a brief assessment. The idea of a continuum of severity suggests that treatment for alcohol problems should be provided using a stepped-care model where the first treatment is the least intensive, costly, and invasive, has demonstrated effectiveness, and is appealing and engaging to consumers. If treatment is not successful, then it can be stepped up to include longer, more intensive, or different components.

Assessment of alcohol problems is critical to good treatment planning and is a process that carries on throughout treatment. Besides using sound psychometric assessments instruments, the instruments should be clinically useful. Several important issues also need to be addressed at assessment. Tantamount among these is the assessment of co-occurring psychiatric disorders and other drug and nicotine use. Although many people with alcohol problems voluntarily seek treatment, many are coerced to seek treatment (e.g., by the courts, significant others, employers). In this regard, they often exhibit resistance and a lack of commitment to change. Motivational enhancement techniques and a motivational interviewing style can be used to decrease patients' resistance and increase their commitment to change. Lastly, although alcohol problems can be treated successfully, there is still a high rate of relapse that must be addressed in treatment, but recurrence of problems should not be taken as an indication that the disorder is worsening, because there is now abundant data showing that alcohol problems are not necessarily progressive.

## REFERENCES

Adams, P. F., Martinez, M. E., & Vickerie, J. L. (2009) Summary health statistics for the U.S. population: National health interview survey. National Center for Health Statistics. *Vital Health Stat, 10*, 248.

Allen, D. N., Strauss, G. P., Leany, B. D., & Donohue, B. (2008). Neuropsychological assessment of individuals with substance use disorders. In A. M. Horton, Jr. & D. Wedding (Eds.), *The neuropsychology handbook* (3rd ed., pp. 705–728). New York, NY: Springer.

American Psychiatric Association. (2000a). *Diagnostic and statistical manual of mental disorders* (4th ed., rev.). Washington, DC: Author.

American Psychiatric Association. (2000b). *Handbook of psychiatric measures.* Washington, DC: Author.

Assanangkornchai, S., & Srisurapanont, M. (2007). The treatment of alcohol dependence. *Current Opinion in Psychiatry, 20*(3), 222–227.

Atkinson, R. M. (1994). Late onset problem drinking in older adults. *International Journal of Geriatric Psychiatry, 9*, 321–326.

Babor, T., & Del Boca, F. (2003). *Treatment matching in alcoholism.* New York, NY: Cambridge University Press. Retrieved from PsycINFO database.

Bacon, A. K., & Ham, L. S. (2010). Attention to social threat as a vulnerability to the development of comorbid social anxiety disorder and alcohol use disorders: An avoidance-coping cognitive model. *Addictive Behaviors, 35*, 925–939.

Bacon, S. D. (1973). The process of addiction to alcohol: Social aspects. *Quarterly Journal of Studies on Alcohol, 34*, 1–27.

Baigent, M. F. (2005). Understanding alcohol misuse and comorbid psychiatric disorders. *Current Opinion in Psychiatry, 18*, 223–228.

Bandura, A. (1969). *Principles of behavior modification.* New York, NY: Holt, Rinehart & Winston.

Barry, K. L., & Fleming, M. F. (1993). The Alcohol Use Disorders Identification Test (AUDIT) and the SMAST-13: Predictive validity in a rural primary care sample. *Alcohol and Alcoholism, 28*, 33–42.

Batki, S. L., Meszaros, Z. S., Strutynski, K., Dimmock, J. A., Leontieva, L., Ploutz-Snyder, R., . . . Drayer, R. A. (2009). Medical comorbidity in patients with schizophrenia and alcohol dependence. *Schizophrenia Research, 107*(2), 139–146.

Beck, A. T., Epstein, N., Brown, G., & Steer, R. A. (1988). An inventory for measuring clinical anxiety: Psychometric properties. *Journal of Consulting and Clinical Psychology, 56,* 893–897.

Beck, A. T., Steer, R. A., & Garbin, M. G. (1988). Psychometric properties of the Beck Depression Inventory: Twenty-five years of evaluation. *Clinical Psychology Review, 8,* 77–100.

Bien, T. H., Miller, W. R., & Tonigan, J. S. (1993). Brief interventions for alcohol problems: A review. *Addiction, 88,* 315–336.

Bischof, G., Rumpf, H. J., Hapke, U., Meyer, C., & John, U. (2003). Types of natural recovery from alcohol dependence: A cluster analytic approach. *Addiction,* 98 (12), 1737–1746.

Boden, M. T., & Moos, R. (2009) Dually diagnosed patients' responses to substance use disorder treatment. *Journal of Substance Abuse Treatment, 37*(4), 335–345.

Breslin, F. C., Sobell, L. C., Sobell, M. B., & Agrawal, S. (2000). A comparison of a brief and long version of the Situational Confidence Questionnaire. *Behaviour Research and Therapy, 38,* 1211–1220.

Burke, B. L., Arkowitz, H., & Menchola, M. (2003). The efficacy of motivational interviewing: A meta-analysis of controlled clinical trials. *Journal of Consulting and Clinical Psychology, 71,* 5843–5861.

Caetano, R. (2003). Alcohol-related health disparities and treatment related epidemiological findings among whites, blacks, and Hispanics in the United States. *Research Society on Alcoholism, 27,* 1337–1339.

Cahalan, D. (1970). *Problem drinkers: A national survey.* San Francisco, CA: Jossey-Bass.

Cahalan, D., & Room, R. (1974). *Problem drinking among American men.* Piscataway, NJ: Rutgers University, Rutgers Center of Alcohol Studies.

Carey, K. B., & Correia, C. J. (1998). Severe mental illness and addictions: Assessment considerations. *Addictive Behaviors, 23,* 735–748.

Carroll, K. M. (1999). Behavioral and cognitive behavioral treatments. In B. S. McCrady & E. E. Epstein (Eds.), *Addictions: A comprehensive guidebook* (pp. 250–267). New York, NY: Oxford University Press.

Caudill, B. D., & Marlatt, G. A. (1975). Modeling influences in social drinking: An experimental analogue. *Journal of Clinical & Consulting Psychology, 43,* 405–415.

Chartier, K., & Caetano, R. (2010). Ethnicity and health disparities in alcohol research. *Alcohol Research & Health, 33*(1), 152–160.

Clark, W. B., & Hesselbrock, M. A. (1988). A comparative analysis of U.S. and Japanese drinking patterns. In T. Harford & L. Towle (Eds.), *Cultural influences and drinking patterns: A focus on Hispanic and Japanese populations* (pp. 79–98) (NIA Research Monograph No. 19). Washington DC: U.S. Government Printing Office.

Collins, R. L., & Marlatt, G. A. (1981). Social modeling as a determinant of drinking behavior: Implications for prevention and treatment. *Addictive Behaviors, 6,* 233–239.

Conner, K. R., Pinquart, M., & Gamble, S. A. (2009). Meta-analysis of depression and substance use among individuals with alcohol use disorders. *Journal of Substance Abuse Treatment, 37* (2), 127–137.

Copeland, L. A., Blow, F. C., & Barry, K. L. (2003). Health care utilization by older alcohol using veterans: Effects of a brief intervention to reduce at-risk drinking. *Health Education and Behavior, 30,* 305–321.

Cunningham, J. A., Sobell, L. C., Sobell, M. B., & Gaskin, J. (1994). Alcohol and drug abusers' reasons for seeking treatment. *Addictive Behaviors, 19,* 691–696.

Cunningham, J. A., Wild, T. C., Cordingley, J., van Mierlo, T., & Humphreys, K. (2010). Twelve month follow-up results from a randomized controlled trial of a brief personalized feedback intervention for problem drinkers. *Alcohol and Alcoholism, 45,* 258–262.

Curry, S. J., Ludman, E., Grothaus, L., Gilmore, T., & Donovan, D. (2002) At-risk drinking among patients in an occupational medicine clinic. *Alcohol & Alcoholism, 37*(3), 289–294.

Dahl, J. P., Doyle, G. A., Oslin, D. W., Buono, R. J., Ferraro, T. N., Lohoff, F. W., & Berrettini, W. H. (2005). Lack of association between single nucleotide polymorphisms in the cortico-trophin releasing hormone receptor 1 (CRHR1) gene and alcohol dependence. *Journal of Psychiatric Research, 39*, 475–479.

Davies, A. D. M. (1968). The influence of age on trail making test performance. *Journal of Clinical Psychology, 24*, 96–98.

Dawson, D. A. (1996). Correlates of past-year status among treated and untreated persons with former alcohol dependence: United States,1992. *Alcoholism: Clinical and Experimental Research, 20*, 771–779.

Dawson, D. A. (2000). Drinking patterns among individuals with and without *DSM-IV* alcohol use disorders. *Journal of Studies on Alcohol, 61*, 111–120.

Dawson, D. A., Grant, B. F., Stinson, F. S., Chou, P. S., Huang, B., & Ruan, W. J. (2005). Recovery from *DSM-IV* alcohol dependence: United States, 2001–2002. *Addiction, 100*, 281–292.

Delucchi, K. L., & Kaskutas, L. A. (2010). Following problem drinkers over eleven years: Understanding changes in alcohol consumption. *Journal of Studies on Alcohol and Drugs, 71*, 831–836.

Derogatis, L. R. (1983). *SCL-90 Revised Version Manual-1*. Baltimore, MD: Johns Hopkins University, School of Medicine.

Dunn, C., Huber, A., Estee, S., Krupski, A., O'Neil, S., Malmer, D., & Ries, R. (2010). *Screening, brief intervention, and referral to treatment for substance abuse: Bringing Substance abuse counseling to acute medical care*. Olympia, WA: Department of Social and Health Services.

Echeburúa, E., Bravo de Medina, R., & Aizpiri, J. (2007). Comorbidity of alcohol dependence and personality disorders: A comparative study. *Alcohol & Alcoholism, 42*, 618–622.

English, D., & Holman, D. (1995). *The quantification of drug-caused mortality in Australia, 1992*. Canberra, Australia: Commonwealth Department of Human Services and Health.

Ennett, S. T., Foshee, V. A., Bauman, K. E., Hussong, A., Cai, L., Reyes, H. L. M., . . . DuRant, R. (2008). The social ecology of adolescent alcohol misuse. *Child Development, 79*(6), 1777–1791.

Enoch, M. A., Schuckit, M. A., Johnson, B. A., & Goldman, D. (2003). Genetics of alcoholism using intermediate phenotypes. *Alcoholism: Clinical and Experimental Research, 27*, 169–176.

Fillmore, K. M. (1988). Alcohol use across the life course: *A critical review of 70 years of international longitudinal research*. Toronto, Ontario: Addiction Research Foundation.

Fillmore, K. M., & Midanik, L. (1984). Chronicity of drinking problems among men: A longitudinal study. *Journal of Studies on Alcohol, 45*, 228–236.

Finney, J. W., & Moos, R. H. (1991). The long-term course of treated alcoholism, I: Mortality, relapse and remission rates and comparisons with community controls. *Journal of Studies on Alcohol, 52*, 44–54.

Fleming, M. F., Barry, K. L., & MacDonald, R. (1991). The Alcohol Use Disorders Identification Test (AUDIT) in a college sample. *International Journal of Addictions, 26*, 1173–1185.

Foroud, T., Edenberg, H. J., & Crabbe, J. C. (2010). Who is at risk for alcoholism? *Alcohol Research & Health, 33*(1), 64–75.

Fox, H. C., Bergquist, K. L., Gu, P., & Sinha, R. (2010). Interactive effects of cumulative stress and impulsivity on alcohol consumption. *Alcoholism: Clinical and Experimental Research, 34*(8), 1376–1385.

Frezza, M., di Padova, C., Pozzato, G., Terpin, M., Baraona, E., & Lieber, C. S. (1990). High blood alcohol levels in women: The role of decreased gastric alcohol dehydrogenase activity and first-pass metabolism. [see comments]. [erratum appears in *N Engl J Med* 1990 Aug 23; 323 (8): 553; *N Engl J Med* 1990 May 24; 322 (21):1540]. *New England Journal of Medicine, 322*, 95–99.

Galvan, F. H., & Caetano, R. (2003). Alcohol use and related problems among ethnic minorities in the United States. *Alcohol Research & Health*, 27(1), 87–94.

Gianoulakis, C. (1998). Alcohol seeking behavior: The roles of the hypothalamic-pituitaryadrenal axis and the endogenous opioid system. *Alcohol Health and Research World*, 22, 202–210.

Gilliland, F. D., Becker, T. M., Samet, J. M., & Key, C. R. (1995). Trends in alcohol-related mortality among New Mexico's American Indians, Hispanics, and non-Hispanic whites. *Alcoholism: Clinical and Experimental Research*, 19, 1572–1577.

Gmel, G., Wicki, M., Rehm, J., & Heeb, J.-L. (2008). Estimating regression to the mean and true effects of an intervention in a four-wave panel study. *Addiction*, 103(1), 32–41.

Goldman, M. S., Del Boca, F. K., & Darkes, J. (1999). Alcohol expectancy theory: The application of cognitive neuroscience. In K. E. Leonard & H. T. Blane (Eds.), *Psychological theories of drinking and alcoholism* (2nd ed., pp. 203–246). New York, NY: Guilford Press.

Gomberg, E. S. L. (1994). Risk factors for drinking over a woman's life span. *Alcohol Health and Research World*, 18, 220–227.

Gomberg, E. S. L. (1995). Older women and alcohol. In M. Galanter (Ed.), *Recent developments in alcoholism* (Vol. 12, pp. 61–70). New York, NY: Plenum Press.

González-Pinto, A., Alberich, S., Barbeito, S., Alonso, M., Vieta, E., Martínez-Arán, A., . . . López, P. (2010). Different profile of substance abuse in relation to predominant polarity in bipolar disorder: The Vitoria long-term follow-up study. *Journal of Affective Disorders*, 124(3), 250–255.

Grant, B. F. (1997). Prevalence and correlates of alcohol use and *DSM-IV* alcohol dependence in the United States: Results of the National Longitudinal Alcohol Epidemiologic Survey. *Journal of Studies on Alcohol*, 58, 464–473.

Gutjahr, E., Gmel, G., & Rehm, J. (2001). Relation between average alcohol consumption and disease: An overview. *European Addiction Research*, 7(3), 117–127.

Hamilton, M. (1960). A rating scale for depression. *Journal of Neurology, Neurosurgery and Psychiatry*, 23, 56–62.

Hardie, T. L., Moss, H. B., & Lynch, K. G. (2008). Sex differences in the heritability of alcohol problems. *The American Journal on Addictions*, 17, 319–327.

Harford, T. C., Grant, B. F., Yi, H., & Chen, C. M. (2005). Patterns of *DSM-IV* alcohol abuse and dependence criteria among adolescents and adults: Results from the 2001 National Household Survey on Drug Abuse. *Alcoholism: Clinical and Experimental Research*, 29, 810–828.

Hasin, D. S., Grant, B., & Endicott, J. (1990). The natural history of alcohol abuse: Implications for definitions of alcohol use disorders. *American Journal of Psychiatry*, 147, 1537–1541.

Hathaway, S. R., & McKinley, J. C. (1989). *The Minnesota Multiphasic Personality Inventory*. Restandardized by J. N. Butcher, W. G. Dahlstrom, J. R. Graham, A. Tellegen, & B. Kaemmer. (2001). Minneapolis: University of Minnesota Press.

Heath, A. C., & Martin, N. G. (1991). Intoxication after an acute dose of alcohol: An assessment of its association with alcohol consumption patterns by using twin data. *Alcoholism: Clinical and Experimental Research*, 15, 122–128.

Heather, N. (1990). *Brief intervention strategies*. New York, NY: Pergamon Press.

Hendershot, C. S., MacPherson, L., Myers, M. G., Carr, L. G., & Wall, T. L. (2005). Psychosocial, cultural and genetic influences on alcohol use in Asian American youth. *Journal of Studies on Alcohol*, 66, 185–195.

Hesselbrock, M. N., Hesselbrock, V. M., & Epstein, E. E. (1999). Theories of etiology of alcohol and other drug use disorders. In B. S. McCrady & E. E. Epstein (Eds.), *Addictions: A comprehensive guidebook* (pp. 50–72). New York, NY: Oxford University Press.

Hester, R. K., Delaney, H. D., Campbell, W., & Handmaker, N. (2009). A web application for moderation training: Initial results of a randomized clinical trial. *Journal of Substance Abuse Treatment*, 37(3), 266–276.

Hilton, M. E. (1991). Trends in U.S. drinking patterns: Further evidence from the past twenty years. In W. B. Clark & M. E. Hilton (Eds.), *Alcohol in America* (pp. 121–138). Albany: State University of New York Press.

Hobbes, J., Boutagy, J., & Shenfield, G. M. (1985). Interactions between ethanol and oral contraceptive steroids. *Clinical Pharmacology & Therapeutics, 38,* 371–380.

Hull, J. G. (1981). A self-awareness model of the causes and effects of alcohol consumption. *Journal of Abnormal Psychology, 90*(6), 586–600.

Humphreys, K. (2009). Searching where the light is worse: Overemphasizing genes and underplaying environment in the quest to reduce substance misuse. *Clinical Pharmacology and Therapeutics, 85,* 357–358.

Hussong, A. M., Hicks, R. E., Levy, S. A., & Curran, P. J. (2001). Specifying the relations between affect and heavy alcohol use among young adults. *Journal of Abnormal Psychology, 110*(3), 449–461.

Institute of Medicine. (1990). *Broadening the base of treatment for alcohol problems.* Washington, DC: National Academy Press.

Jellinek, E. M. (1952). Phases of alcohol addiction. *Quarterly Journal of Studies on Alcohol, 13,* 673–684.

Jellinek, E. M. (1960). *The disease concept of alcoholism.* New Brunswick, NJ: Hillhouse Press.

Jensvold, M. F. (1996). Nonpregnant reproductive age women, Part I: The menstrual cycle and psychopharmacology. In M. F. Jensvold, U. Halbreich, & J. A. Hamilton (Eds.), *Psychopharmacology and women: Sex, gender, and hormones* (pp. 139–169). Washington, DC: American Psychiatric Press.

Johnson, E. O., van den Bree, M., Gupman, A. E., & Pickens, R. W. (1998). Extension of a typology of alcohol dependence based on relative genetic and environmental loading. *Alcoholism: Clinical and Experimental Research, 22,* 1421–1429.

Jones, B. M., & Jones, M. K. (1976). Male and female intoxication levels for three alcohol doses, or do women really get higher than men? *Alcohol Technical Reports, 5,* 11–14.

Josephs, R. A., & Steele. C. M. (1990). The two faces of alcohol myopia: Attentional mediation of psychological stress. *Journal of Abnormal Psychology, 99,* 115–126.

Keyes, K. M., Martins, S. S., Blanco, C., & Hasin, D. S. (2010). Telescoping and gender differences in alcohol dependence: New evidence from two national surveys. *American Journal of Psychiatry, 167,* 969–976.

Kiefer, F., Jahn, H., Schick, M., & Wiedemann, K. (2002). Alcohol self-administration, craving and HPA-axis activity: An intriguing relationship. *Psychopharmacology, 164,* 239–240.

King, M. P., & Tucker, J. A. (2000). Behavior change patterns and strategies distinguishing moderation drinking and abstinence during the natural resolution of alcohol problems without treatment. *Psychology of Addictive Behaviors, 14,* 48–55.

Klingemann, H., & Gmel, G. (Eds.). (2001). *Mapping the social consequences of alcohol consumption.* Dordrecht, The Netherlands: Kluwer Academic.

Klingemann, H. K., Sobell, L. C., Barker, J., Blomquist, J., Cloud, W., Ellinstad, D., . . . Tucker, J. (2001). *Promoting self-change from problem substance use: Practical implications for policy, prevention and treatment.* Boston, MA: Kluwer Academic.

Klingemann, H., Sobell, M. B., & Sobell, L. C. (2009). Continuities and changes in self-change research. *Addiction, 105,* 1510–1518.

Knopik, V. S., Heath, A. C., Madden, P. A. F., Bucholz, K. K., Slutske, W. S., Nelson, E. C., . . . Martin, N. G. (2004). Genetic effects on alcohol dependence risk: Re-evaluating the importance of psychiatric and other heritable risk factors. *Psychological Medicine, 34,* 1519–1530.

Kongs, S. K., Thompson, L. L., Iverson, G. L., & Heaton, R. K. (2000). Wisconsin Card Sorting Test - 64 card version: Professional manual. Odessa, Ukraine: Psychological Assessment Resources.

LaBrie, J., Pedersen, E., & Earleywine, M. (2005). A group-administered timeline followback assessment of alcohol use. *Journal of Studies on Alcohol, 66,* 693–697.

Lee, D. J., Markides, K. S., & Ray, L. A. (1997). Epidemiology of self-reported past heavy drinking in Hispanic adults. *Ethnicity & Health, 2,* 77–88.

Le Fauve, C. E., Litten, R. Z., Randall, C. L., Moak, D. H., Salloum, I. M., & Green, A. I. (2004). Pharmacological treatment of alcohol abuse/dependence with psychiatric comorbidity. *Alcoholism: Clinical and Experimental Research, 28,* 302–312.

Le Merrer, J., Becker, J. A., Befort, K., & Kieffer, B. L. (2009). Reward processing by the opioid system in the brain. *Physiological Research, 89,* 1379–1412.

Lucey, M. R., Mathurin, P., & Morgan, T. R. (2009). Alcoholic hepatitis. *New England Journal of Medicine, 360,* 2758–2769.

Lyvers, M. (2000). "Loss of control" in alcoholism and drug addiction: A neuroscientific interpretation. *Experimental and Clinical Psychopharmacology, 8,* 225–249.

Mack, A. H., Harrington, A. L., & Frances, R. J. (2010). *Clinical manual for treatment of alcoholism and addictions.* Arlington, VA: American Psychiatric.

Maher, J. J. (1997). Exploring alcohol's effects on liver function. *Alcohol Health and Research World, 21,* 5–12.

Makimoto, K. (1998). Drinking patterns and drinking problems among Asian-Americans and Pacific Islanders. *Alcohol Health & Research World, 22*(4), 270–275.

Mandell, W. (1983). Types and phases of alcohol dependence. In M. Galanter (Ed.), *Recent developments in alcoholism* (Vol. 3, pp. 415–448). New York, NY: Plenum Press.

Marlatt, G. A. (1978). *Craving for alcohol, loss of control, and relapse.* New York, NY: Plenum Press.

Marlatt, G. A., & Gordon, J. R. (1985). *Relapse prevention.* New York, NY: Guilford Press.

Marlatt, G. A., & Witkiewitz, K. (2005). Relapse prevention for alcohol and drug problems. In G. A. Marlatt & D. M. Donovan (Eds.), *Relapse prevention: Maintenance strategies in the treatment of addictive behaviors* (2nd ed., pp. 1–44). New York, NY: Guilford Press.

McGue, M. (1999). Behavioral genetic models of alcoholism and drinking. In K. E. Leonard & H. T. Blane (Eds.), *Psychological theories of drinking and alcoholism* (2nd ed., pp. 372–421). New York, NY: Guilford Press.

McKay, J. R. (2009). Initial attempts to individualize treatment for substance use disorders (pp. 93–103). American Psychological Association. Retrieved from http://search.proquest.com/docview/621990176?accountid=10901

McKellar, J., Ilgen, M., Moos, B. S., & Moos, R. (2008). Predictors of changes in alcohol-related self-efficacy over 16 years. *Journal of Substance Abuse Treatment, 35,* 148–155.

Miles, D. R., Silberg, J. L., Pickens, R. W., & Eaves, L. J. (2005). Familial influences on alcohol use in adolescent female twins: Testing for genetic and environmental interactions. *Journal of Studies on Alcohol, 66,* 445–451.

Miller, W. R., & Rollnick, S. (1991). *Motivational interviewing: Preparing people to change addictive behavior.* New York, NY: Guilford Press.

Miller, W. R., & Rollnick, S. (2002). *Motivational interviewing: Preparing people for change* (2nd ed.). New York, NY: Guilford Press.

Millon, T., Millon, C., Davis, R., & Grossman, S. (2006). *Millon Clinical Multiaxial Inventory-III* (MCMI-III). San Antonio, TX: Pearson.

Moack, D. H., & Anton, R. F. (1999). Alcohol. In B. S. McCrady & E. E. Epstein (Eds.), *Addictions: A comprehensive guidebook* (pp. 75–94). New York, NY: Oxford University Press.

Modesto-Lowe, V., & Kranzler, H. R. (1999). Diagnosis and treatment of alcohol-dependent patients with comorbid psychiatric disorders. *Alcohol Health and Research World, 23,* 144–149.

Mohatt, G. V., Rasmus, S. M., Thomas, L., Allen, J., Hazel, K., & Marlatt, G. A. (2007). Risk, resilience, and natural recovery: A model of recovery from alcohol abuse for Alaska natives. *Addiction, 103*, 205–215.

Morgan, M. Y. (1994). The prognosis and outcome of alcoholic liver disease. *Alcohol and Alcoholism* (Suppl. 2), 335–343.

National Institute on Alcohol Abuse and Alcoholism (NIAAA). (1993). *Eighth special report to the U.S. Congress on alcohol and health*. NIH Pub. No. 94–3699. Washington, DC: U.S. Government Printing Office.

National Institute on Alcohol Abuse and Alcoholism (NIAAA). (2000). *Tenth special report to the U.S. Congress on alcohol and health*. REP 023. Washington, DC: U.S. Government Printing Office.

National Institute on Alcohol Abuse and Alcoholism (NIAAA). (2003). *Assessing alcohol problems: A guide for clinicians and researchers* (2nd ed.). J. P. Allen & V. B. Wilson (Eds.). NIH Pub. No. 03–3745. Bethesda, MD: National Institute on Alcohol Abuse and Alcoholism.

National Institute on Alcohol Abuse and Alcoholism (NIAAA). (2005). *Alcohol: A women's health issue*. NIH Pub. No. 03-4956. Bethesda, MD: National Institute on Alcohol Abuse and Alcoholism.

National Survey on Drug Use and Health (NSDUH). (2004). *Women with Co-occurring serious mental illness and a substance use disorder*. Rockville, MD: U.S. Department of Health and Human Services.

National Survey on Drug Use and Health (NSDUH). (2006). *Serious psychological distress and substance use among young adult males*. Rockville, MD: U.S. Department of Health and Human Services.

National Survey on Drug Use and Health (NSDUH). (2007). *Co-occurring major depressive episode (MDE) and alcohol use disorder among adults*. Rockville, MD: U.S. Department of Health and Human Services.

Niaura, R. S., Rohsenow, D. J., Binkoff, J. A., Monti, P. M., Abrams, D. A., & Pedraza, M. (1988). Relevance of cue reactivity to understanding alcohol and smoking relapse. *Journal of Abnormal Psychology, 97*, 133–152.

Nichol, P. E., Krueger, R. F., & Iacono, W. G. (2007). Investigating gender differences in alcohol problems: A latent trait modeling approach. *Alcoholism: Clinical and Experimental Research, 31* (5), 783–794.

Nowinski, J., Baker, S. C., & Carroll, K. (1992). *Twelve step facilitation therapy manual* (Project MAT CH Monograph Vol. 1). Rockville, MD: National Institute on Alcohol Abuse and Alcoholism.

Nunes, E.V., Selzer, J., Levounis, P., & Davies, C. (2010). *Substance dependence and co-occurring psychiatric disorders: Best practices for diagnosis and clinical treatment*. New York, NY: Civic Research Institute.

Orford, J. (2001). Addiction as excessive appetite. *Addiction, 96*, 15–31.

Oscar-Berman, M., & Marinkovic, K. (2007). Effects of alcoholism on neurocognition. In A. D., Kalechstein & W. G. van Gorp (Eds.), *Neuropsychological consequences of substance abuse* (pp. 43–73). New York, NY: Taylor & Francis.

Pakula, B., Macdonald, S., & Stockwell, T. (2009). Settings and functions related to simultaneous use of alcohol with marijuana or cocaine among clients in treatment for substance abuse. *Substance Use & Misuse, 44*(2), 212–226.

Pattison, E. M., Sobell, M. B., & Sobell, L. C. (1977). *Emerging concepts of alcohol dependence*. New York, NY: Springer.

Penninkilampi-Kerola, V., Kaprio, J., Moilanen, I., & Rose, R. J. (2005). Co-twin dependence modifies heritability of abstinence and alcohol use: A population-based study of Finnish twins. *Twin Research and Human Genetics, 8,* 232–244.

Pohorecky, L. A. (1991). Stress and alcohol interaction: An update of human research. *Alcoholism: Clinical and Experimental Research, 15,* 438–459.

Polich, J. M., Armor, D. J., & Braiker, H. B. (1981). *The course of alcoholism: Four years after treatment.* New York, NY: John Wiley & Sons.

Prescott, C. A. (2002). Sex differences in the genetic risk for alcoholism. *Alcohol Research & Health, 26*(4), 264–273.

Price, R. K., Risk, N. K., Wong, M. W., & Klingle, R. S. (2002). Substance use and abuse in Asian American and Pacific Islanders (AAPIs): Preliminary results from four national epidemiologic Studies. *Public Health Reports, 17,* S39–S50.

Puls, I., & Gallinat, J. (2008). The concept of endophenotypes in psychiatric diseases meeting the expectations? *Pharmacopsychiatry, 41*(1), S37–S43.

Quigley, B. M., & Collins, R. L. (1999). The modeling of alcohol consumption: A meta-analytic review. *Journal of Studies on Alcohol, 60,* 90–98.

Raistrick, D., Dunbar, G., & Davidson, R. (1983). Development of a questionnaire to measure alcohol dependence. *British Journal of Addiction, 78,* 89–95.

Ray, L. A., MacKillop, J., & Monti, P. M. (2010). Subjective responses to alcohol consumption as endophenotypes: Advancing behavioral genetics in etiological and treatment models of alcoholism. *Substance Use & Misuse, 45,* 1742–1765.

Ridolfo, B., & Stevenson, C., (2001). *The quantification of drug-caused mortality and morbidity in Australia.* Canberra, Australia: Australian Institute of Health and Welfare.

Robins, L. N., & Regier, D. A. (1991). *Psychiatric disorders in America: The Epidemiologic Catchment Area study.* New York, NY: Free Press.

Room, R. (1990). *Measuring alcohol consumption in the United States: Methodsand rationales.* New York, NY: Plenum Press.

Rubak, S., Sandbaek, A., Lauritzen, T., & Christensen, B. (2004). Motivational interviewing: A systematic review and meta-analysis. *British Journal of General Practice, 55,* 305–312.

Saunders, J. B., Aasland, O. G., Babor, T. F., De La Fuente, J. R., & Grant, M. (1993). Development of the Alcohol Use Disorders Identification Test (AUDIT): WHO collaborative project on early detection of persons with harmful alcohol consumption—II. *Addiction, 88,* 791–804.

Sayette, M. A. (1993). An appraisal-disruption model of alcohol's effects on stress responses in social drinkers. *Psychological Bulletin, 114*(3), 459–476.

Sayette, M. A. (1999). Does drinking reduce stress? *Alcohol Health and Research World, 23,* 250–255.

Schenker, S. (1997). Medical consequences of alcohol abuse: Is gender a factor? *Alcoholism: Clinical and Experimental Research, 21,* 179–181.

Schmidt, L., & Weisner, C. (1995). *The emergence of problem-drinking women as a special population in need of treatment.* New York, NY: Plenum Press.

Schonfeld, L., & Dupree, L. W. (1991). Antecedents of drinking for early-onset and late-onset elderly alcohol abusers. *Journal of Studies on Alcohol, 52,* 587–592.

Schuckit, M. A. (1995). *Drug and alcohol abuse: A clinical guide to diagnosis and treatment* (4th ed.). New York, NY: Plenum Press.

Schuckit, M. A. (2000). Genetics of the risk for alcoholism. *American Journal on Addictions, 9,* 103–112.

Schuckit, M. A., & Smith, T. L. (2011). Onset and course of alcoholism over 25 years in middle class men. *Drug and Alcohol Dependence, 113,* 21–28.

Sherman, J. E., Jorenby, D. E., & Baker, T. B. (1988). Classical conditioning with alcohol: Acquired preferences and aversions, tolerance, and urges/cravings. In. C. D. Chaudron & D. A. Wilkinson (Eds.), *Theories on alcoholism* (pp. 173–237). Toronto, Canada: Addiction Research Foundation.

Shillington, A. M., & Clapp, J. D. (2006). Heavy alcohol use compared to alcohol and marijuana use: Do college students experience a difference in substance use problems? *Journal of Drug Education, 36*(1), 91–103.

Sillaber, I., & Henniger, M. S. H. (2004). Stress and alcohol drinking. *Annals of Medicine, 36*(8), 596–605.

Single, E., Robson, L., Rehm, J., & Xi, X. (1999). Morbidity and mortality attributable to alcohol, tobacco, and illicit drug use. *Canada American Journal of Public Health, 89*, 385–390.

Skinner, H. A. (1982). The drug abuse screening test. *Addictive Behaviors, 7*, 363–371.

Skinner, H. A., & Allen, B. A. (1982). Alcohol dependence syndrome: Measurement and validation. *Journal of Abnormal Psychology, 91*, 199–209.

Skinner, H. A., & Sheu, W. J. (1982). Reliability of alcohol use indices: The Lifetime Drinking History and the MAST. *Journal of Studies on Alcohol, 43*, 1157–1170.

Sklar, S. M., & Turner, N. E. (1999). A brief measure for the assessment of coping self-efficacy among alcohol and other drug users. *Addiction, 94*, 723–729.

Smith, M., & Lin, K.-M. (1996). Gender and ethics differences in the pharmacogenetics of psychotropics. In M. F. Jensvold, U. Halbreich, & J. A. Hamilton (Eds.), *Psychopharmacology and women: Sex, gender, and hormones* (pp. 121–136). Washington, DC: American Psychiatric Press.

Sobell, L. C., Agrawal, S., & Sobell, M. B. (1999). Utility of liver function tests for screening "alcohol abusers" who are not severely dependent on alcohol. *Substance Use & Misuse, 34*, 1723–1732.

Sobell, L. C., Cunningham, J. A., & Sobell, M. B. (1996). Recovery from alcohol problems with and without treatment: Prevalence in two population surveys. *American Journal of Public Health, 86*, 966–972.

Sobell, L. C., Ellingstad, T. P., & Sobell, M. B. (2000). Natural recovery from alcohol and drug problems: Methodological review of the research with suggestions for future directions. *Addiction, 95*, 749–764.

Sobell, L. C., & Sobell, M. B. (1992). Timeline follow-back: A technique for assessing self reported alcohol consumption. In R. Z. Litten & J. Allen (Eds.), *Measuring alcohol consumption: Psychosocial and biological methods* (pp. 41–72). Totowa, NJ: Humana Press.

Sobell, L. C., & Sobell, M. B. (1995). Alcohol consumption measures. In J. P. Allen & M. Columbus (Eds.), *Assessing alcohol problems: A guide for clinicians and researchers* (pp. 55–73). Rockville, MD: National Institute on Alcohol Abuse and Alcoholism.

Sobell, L. C., & Sobell, M. B. (1996). *Alcohol Timeline Followback (TLFB) Users' Manual.* Toronto, Canada: Addiction Research Foundation.

Sobell, L. C., & Sobell, M. B. (2000). Alcohol Timeline Followback (TLFB). In American Psychiatric Association (Ed.), *Handbook of psychiatric measures* (pp. 477–479). Washington, DC: Author.

Sobell, L. C., & Sobell, M. B. (2008). *Assessing alcohol problems using motivational interviewing.* APA Psychotherapy Video Series. Washington, DC: American Psychological Association.

Sobell, L. C., Toneatto, T., & Sobell, M. B. (1994). Behavioral assessment and treatment planning for alcohol, tobacco, and other drug problems: Current status with an emphasis on clinical applications. *Behavior Therapy, 25*, 533–580.

Sobell, M. B., Bogardis, J., Schuller, R., Leo, G. I., & Sobell, L. C. (1989). Is self-monitoring of alcohol consumption reactive? *Behavioral Assessment, 11*, 447–458.

Sobell, M. B., & Sobell, L. C. (1993). *Problem drinkers: Guided self-change treatment*. New York, NY: Guilford Press.

Sobell, M. B., & Sobell, L. C. (1995). Controlled drinking after 25 years: How important was the great debate? *Addiction, 90*, 1149–1153.

Sobell, M. B., & Sobell, L. C. (1998). Guiding self-change. In W. R. Miller & N. Heather (Eds.), *Treating addictive behaviors* (2nd ed., pp. 189–202). New York, NY: Plenum Press.

Sobell, M. B., Sobell, L. C., & Kozlowksi, L. T. (1995). Dual recoveries from alcohol and smoking problems. In J. B. Fertig & J. A. Allen (Eds.), *Alcohol and tobacco: From basic science to clinical practice* (NIA Research Monograph No. 30, pp. 207–224). Rockville, MD: National Institute on Alcohol Abuse and Alcoholism.

Steele, C. M., & Josephs, R. A. (1988). Drinking your troubles away, II: An attention allocation model of alcohol's effect on psychological stress. *Journal of Abnormal Psychology, 97*(2), 196–205.

Steele, C. M., & Josephs, R. A. (1990). Alcohol myopia: Its prized and dangerous effects. *The American Psychologist, 45*(8), 921–933.

Steele, L. D., & Rechberger, E. (2002). Meeting the treatment needs of multiple diagnosed consumers. *Journal of Drug Issues, 32*(3), 811–823.

Stinson, F. S., Grant, B. F., Dawson, D. A., Ruan, W. J., Huang, B., & Saha, T. (2005). Comorbidity between *DSM-IV* alcohol and specific drug use disorders in the United States: Results from the National Epidemiologic Survey on Alcohol and Related Conditions. *Drug and Alcohol Dependence, 80*, 105–116.

Stockwell, T., Murphy, D., & Hodgson, R. (1983). The Severity of Alcohol Dependence Questionnaire: Its use, reliability and validity. *British Journal of Addiction, 78*, 145–155.

Stockwell, T., Sitharthan, T., McGrath, D., & Lang, E. (1994). The measurement of alcohol dependence and impaired control in community samples. *Addiction, 89*, 167–174.

Substance Abuse and Mental Health Services Administration (SAMHSA). (1999). *Enhancing motivation for change in substance abuse treatment*. Treatment Improvement Protocol Series. Rockville, MD: U.S. Department of Health and Human Services.

Substance Abuse and Mental Health Services Administration (SAMHSA). (2004). *Results from the 2003 National Survey on Drug Use and Health: National findings*. Office of Applied Studies, NSDUH Series H-25, DHHS Publication No. SMA 04-3964. Rockville, MD: U.S. Department of Health and Human Services.

Substance Abuse and Mental Health Services Administration (SAMHSA). (2006). *Results from the 2003 National Survey on Drug Use and Health: National findings—Alcohol dependence or abuse: 2002, 2003, and 2004*. Rockville, MD: U.S. Department of Health and Human Services.

Trull, T. J., Jahng, S., Tomko, R. L., Wood, P. K., & Sher, K. J. (2010). Revised NESARC personality disorder diagnoses: Gender, prevalence, and comorbidity with substance dependence disorders. *Journal of Personality Disorders 24*(4), 412–426.

Viken, R. J., Rose, R. J., Morzorati, S. L., Christian, J. C., & Li, T.-K. (2003). Subjective intoxication in response to alcohol challenge: Heritability and covariation with personality, breath alcohol level, and drinking history. *Alcoholism: Clinical and Experimental Research, 27*(5), 795–803.

Volkow, N. L. (2010). Opioid-dopamine interactions: Implications for substance use disorders and their treatment. *Biological Psychiatry, 68*, 685–686.

Wagnerberger, S., Schafer, C., Schwarz, E., Bode, C., & Parlesak, A. (2008). Is nutrient intake a gender-specific cause for enhanced susceptibility to alcohol-induced liver disease in women? *Alcohol & Alcoholism, 43*(1), 9–14.

Wechsler, D. (1997a). *Wechsler Adult Intelligence Scale* (3rd ed., WAIS-III). San Antonio, TX: The Psychological Corporation.

Wechsler, D. (1997b). *WAIS-III WMS-III Technical Manual*. San Antonio, TX: The Psychological Corporation.

Whicher, E. V., & Abou-Saleh, M. (2009). Service development: Developing a service for people with dual diagnosis. *Mental Health and Substance Use: Dual Diagnosis, 2*(3), 226–234.

Wikler, A. (1973). Dynamics of drug dependence. *Archives of General Psychiatry, 28*, 611–616.

Wilsnack, R. W., Vogeltanz, N. D., Wilsnack, S. C., & Harris, T. R. (2000). Gender differences in alcohol consumption and adverse drinking consequences: Cross-cultural patterns. *Addiction, 95*, 251–265.

Wilsnack, S. C., Klassen, A. D., Schur, B. E., & Wilsnack, R. W. (1991). Predicting onset and chronicity of women's problem drinking: A five-year longitudinal analysis. *American Journal of Public Health, 81*, 305–318.

Witkiewitz, K., & Marlatt, G. A. (2007). Overview of relapse prevention. In K. A. Witkiewitz & G. A. Marlatt (Eds.), *Therapist's guide to evidence-based relapse prevention* (pp. 3–17). San Diego, CA: Elsevier Academic Press.

World Health Organization. (2004). *Global Status on Alcohol 2004*. Geneva, Switzerland: WHO, Department of Mental Health and Substance Abuse.

# CHAPTER 7

# Psychoactive Substance Use Disorders: Drugs

STACEY B. DAUGHTERS, JORDANA L. HEMBERG, and JESSICA M. RICHARDS

## DESCRIPTION OF THE DISORDER

Illicit drug use is a prevalent and pervasive issue in the United States and, as a result, substance use disorders (SUDs) incur major costs to individuals, families, and society at large. In 2008 approximately 8.9% (22.2 million) of Americans age 12 or older were classified with substance dependence or abuse in the past year, and these estimates have remained constant over the past 7 years (SAMHSA, 2009a). The financial burden on society is estimated to be $484 billion annually in substance use–related treatment and prevention, health care expenditures, lost wages, reduced job production, accidents, and crime. In addition to the substantial economic cost of substance use, SUDs are associated with engagement in multiple health-compromising and risk-taking behaviors (e.g., condom nonuse, multiple partners, impulsive spending, driving while intoxicated) that contribute to the significant public health costs associated with SUDs (Office of National Drug Control Policy [ONDCP], 2004).

## CLINICAL PICTURE

SUDs can result from abuse of a single drug or multiple substances. Commonly, drugs of abuse are grouped based on categories that vary in their physiological and behavioral effects. In this section we discuss the different drug categories, including street and slang names, physiological and psychological effects of each category, and the withdrawal symptoms that occur as tolerance and dependence develop. Interested readers are referred to Julien (2004) for an extensive review.

Cannabinoids, such as marijuana and hashish (street names include dope, pot, weed, grass, hash), produce mild euphoria, sedation, enhanced sensory perception, increased appetite and pulse, psychomotor impairment, and confusion. Tolerance can occur with habitual use, and discontinuation of use can result in uncomfortable withdrawal effects including anxiety, depression, irritability, and insomnia. Alternatively, hallucinogens, which include LSD (acid, blotter), mescaline (buttons, peyote, mesc), and psilocybin (magic mushrooms, shrooms), create an altered state of consciousness, detachment from self and environment, and dissociative symptoms. Hallucinogens are not physically addictive; however, LSD and mescaline produce negative physiological reactions such as increased body temperature, blood pressure, and heart rate. Psychologically, hallucinogen use can result in persistent mental disorders characterized by panic attacks and psychosis.

Both cannabinoids and hallucinogens are illegal street drugs, but central nervous system (CNS) depressants, including alcohol, benzodiazepines (e.g., alprazolam [Xanax], diazepam [Valium], lorazepam [Ativan], clonazepam [Klonopin]; benzos, xannies), and barbiturates (Seconal, Amytal, Phenobarbital; reds, yellows, yellow jackets, barbs) are legal substances that can be obtained with a doctor's prescription. With low or moderate doses, they produce euphoria and disinhibition as well as decreased respiration, pulse, and blood pressure. At higher doses, confusion, impaired judgment, coordination, and memory loss occur. CNS depressants are particularly dangerous when combined because this increases the risk of respiratory depression and arrest. With long-term use, tolerance occurs and discontinuation of use can cause symptoms ranging from anxiety, insomnia, nausea, and muscle tension to more severe symptoms such as seizures, hallucinations, and psychosis.

Opioids are often prescribed for pain relief (e.g., codeine, fentanyl, oxycodone), but these drugs are also commonly abused. Other drugs in this category include opium (big O, tar) and heroin (dope, H, junk, smack). The effects of intoxication include euphoria, sedation, drowsiness, confusion, nausea, constipation, and respiratory depression. High doses of opioids can lead to coma and death. With prolonged use, tolerance occurs and, in the absence of the drug, users experience craving, sweating, fever, diarrhea, vomiting, and pain.

Unlike CNS depressants and opiates, stimulants increase respiration, heart rate, and blood pressure, and decrease appetite. Stimulant intoxication produces euphoria, mental alertness, and increased energy. Impulsive behavior, aggressiveness, anxiety, and irritability are also common features experienced by users. Additionally, prolonged use or high doses of stimulants can result in stimulant-induced psychosis. Due to the stress placed on the cardiovascular system, stimulant use can cause cardiac arrest, stroke, and death. Stimulants include cocaine (crack, coke, blow, yayo), methamphetamine (meth, speed, crystal, crank), MDMA (ecstasy, E, X, Adam), amphetamines (Adderall, Dexedrine; speed), and methylphenidate (Ritalin, vitamin R). Nicotine, found in cigarettes, cigars, and smokeless tobacco (snuff, dip, spit) is also a stimulant. Tolerance occurs quickly and can often lead to dependence. Withdrawal symptoms include anxiety, anhedonia, irritability, insomnia, and depression.

Dissociative anesthetics, such as ketamine (Special K, vitamin K) and PCP (angel dust, hog, love boat, sherms), create a dream-like state, euphoria, numbness, increased heart rate and blood pressure, and impaired memory and motor function. At high doses, ketamine can cause delirium, respiratory depression, and arrest. PCP use can result in panic, aggression, depression, and violence. Users of dissociative anesthetics quickly experience increasing tolerance, and a permanent tolerance may develop after several months of use. Although tolerance occurs, these drugs do not appear to have withdrawal symptoms or dependence.

Inhalants include a range of solvents (glues, paint thinners, gasoline), gases (propane, butane, aerosol propellants, nitrous oxide; laughing gas, whippets), nitrates (isobutyl, isoamyl; poppers, snappers), and aerosols (hair spray, spray paint). Inhalants are "huffed" through the nose and mouth and enter the lungs and subsequently the bloodstream rather quickly. The effects of intoxication include loss of motor skills and inhibition, slurred speech, headache, nausea, wheezing, and loss of consciousness. Extended use can lead to muscle weakness, memory impairment, depression, damage to the nervous and cardiovascular systems, and sudden death. There is little known about tolerance, withdrawal, and dependence in relation to inhalants.

In summary, once an SUD is present, the withdrawal experience from different substances varies by the class of drug. In general, common psychological features of withdrawal involve symptoms of depression and anxiety. Although the physical symptoms of withdrawal can be difficult to tolerate, they are often short lived.

## DIAGNOSTIC CONSIDERATIONS

The *Diagnostic and Statistical Manual* (*DSM-IV-TR*; APA, 2000) provides a comprehensive classification system for the assessment and subsequent diagnosis of substance abuse and dependence. The *DSM-IV-TR* diagnostic criteria for *substance abuse* require evidence of a maladaptive pattern of substance use with clinically significant levels of impairment or distress. Impairment in this case is defined as an inability to meet major role obligations, leading to reduced functioning in one or more major life areas, risk-taking behavior, an increase in the likelihood of legal problems due to possession, and exposure to hazardous situations. Within the *DSM*, substance abuse is treated as a residual category, such that it can only be met without the presence of current substance dependence.

The *DSM-IV-TR* diagnostic criteria for *substance dependence* specifies a maladaptive pattern of substance use leading to clinically significant impairment or distress as manifested by three (or more) problems occurring at any time in the same 12-month period. These problems include (a) taking the substance in larger amounts or over a longer period than intended; (b) a persistent desire or unsuccessful efforts to cut down or control substance use; (c) spending a great deal of time in activities necessary to obtain (e.g., visiting multiple doctors or driving long distances), use (e.g., chain smoking), or recover (e.g., recovering from a hangover) from the effects of substance use; (d) reduction in important social, occupational, or recreational activities; and (e) continued use despite knowledge of having a persistent or recurrent psychological or physical problem that is caused or exacerbated by use of the substance. Additional symptoms of dependence are tolerance, defined as either a need for increasing amounts of the substance in order to achieve intoxication or desired effect, or markedly diminished effect with continued use of the same amount; and withdrawal, which is manifested by physical or psychological symptoms characteristic for a particular substance (APA, 2000). It is expected there will be significant changes to the abuse and dependence sections in the upcoming *DSM-5*.

Another system, the *International Classification of Diseases, 10th Revision* (*ICD-10*; WHO, 1994), is considered the international standard diagnostic classification system for all general epidemiological and many health management purposes, including the analysis of the general health situation of population groups and monitoring of the incidence and prevalence of diseases in relation to social, biological, and interpersonal variables. Although the *DSM* and *ICD* have very similar definitions of substance dependence, the two systems have had different paradigms for less severe forms of maladaptive substance use that overlap only partially. Consider the example of a diagnosis of substance abuse (in the *DSM-IV*) and the corresponding diagnosis of harmful use (in the *ICD-10*). As pointed out previously, the *DSM-IV* defines substance abuse as a residual category that can only be applied in the absence of substance dependence; however, this is not the case for harmful use in the *ICD-10*. Furthermore, the *DSM-IV* characterizes substance abuse by negative legal and social consequences of recurrent or continued use, whereas the *ICD-10* includes a category for harmful use (a nonresidual category), which requires demonstrable physical or psychological harm. The emphasis on physical or psychological harm (rather than legal and social) in the *ICD-10* stems from a need for developing criteria that can be applied uniformly across different countries and cultures.

Substance use disorders co-occur with the majority of adult *DSM-IV-TR* Axis I and II disorders. National epidemiological data suggest that among individuals with any SUD, the prevalence for any mood or anxiety disorder is 40.9% and 29.9% respectively (Conway, Compton, Stinson, & Grant, 2006). Mood and anxiety disorders are the most common comorbidities, followed by antisocial personality disorder (Jane-Llopis & Matysina, 2006) and schizophrenia-spectrum disorders (Kushner, Abrams, & Borchardt, 2000). Among Axis II disorders, borderline and antisocial personality disorders have the highest rates of co-occurrence with SUDs, with estimates ranging from 5% to 32% and 14% to 69%, respectively (e.g., Goldstein et al., 2007; Trull, Sher, Minks-Brown, Durbin, & Burr, 2000). In fact, estimates from the Epidemiologic Catchment Area (ECA) Survey suggest that SUDs are more strongly associated with antisocial personality disorder than with any other Axis I disorder (Regier et al., 1993). Additionally, prevalence of disorders differs by substance. For example, among individuals with lifetime opioid abuse or dependence, nearly 50% met the criteria for an Axis II disorder (Grella, Karno, Warda, Niv, & Moore, 2009). These statistics are particularly alarming given that individuals with co-occurring disorders generally have worse treatment outcomes (e.g., noncompliance and relapse), higher rates of suicidal ideation, distorted perception and cognition, social exclusion, aggression, and homelessness (Horsfall, Cleary, Hunt, & Walter, 2009). The causal direction of co-occurring conditions is mixed, with some evidence of mental disorders predicting the onset of SUDs, while other studies have found that SUDs predict later mental illness (Kessler, 2004; NIDA, 2009).

## EPIDEMIOLOGY

Approximately 20.1 million (8%) Americans aged 12 or older report illicit drug use in the past month, of which 57.3% report using only marijuana and 42.7% report illicit drug use other than marijuana (SAMHSA, 2009b). Specific populations are more vulnerable to initiation and continued illicit drug use. In particular, youth and young adults are a special population of interest, because early use increases the likelihood of future substance use problems. Data from the Monitoring the Future Study indicates that although use of several drugs (including inhalants, ecstasy, and amphetamines) has declined over the past decade, within the past 2 years, marijuana use has increased. Approximately 12% of 8th graders, 27% of 10th graders, and 33% of 12th graders reported marijuana use in the past year. Respectively, about 15%, 29%, and 37% reported using any illicit drug in the past year (Johnston, O'Malley, Bachman, & Schulenberg, 2010).

In 2007, there were more than 1.8 million admissions to treatment, with the majority of these admissions being for alcohol only or alcohol and a secondary substance (SAMHSA, 2009b). Among the different treatment settings available, most admissions were in ambulatory care (62.3%), which is made up of outpatient (49.4%), intensive outpatient (10.6%), and detoxification (2.2%). Additionally, 18% of admissions entered residential treatment, with the majority in short-term treatment (less than 31 days), and 19.7% of admissions were for short detoxification (24-hour service) (SAMHSA, 2009b).

## PSYCHOLOGICAL AND BIOLOGICAL ASSESSMENT

Several variables need to be considered when determining the best method of assessment for patients with substance use problems. It is important to determine if the goal of the assessment is to screen for potential substance use problems, to determine if an individual meets diagnostic criteria for an SUD, to develop treatment goals and a treatment plan, or to assess treatment outcome. Outlined in Table 7.1 are commonly used psychological measures for screening, diagnosis, treatment planning, and posttreatment outcome measurement.

Given the high rate of comorbidity between SUD and other Axis I disorders, patients often present to treatment for problems other than drug dependence. As such, screening measures are useful for identifying SUDs in other settings. Several diagnostic instruments are available for use in both research and clinical settings, with advantages and disadvantages inherent in each instrument with regard to administration, cost, and interviewer qualification and training requirements.

Once a substance use problem or diagnosis is established, it is important to assess how the patient's level of substance use has affected other life areas (e.g., social and occupational functioning) in order to develop appropriate treatment goals and a treatment plan. Additional assessment techniques are utilized prior to and during treatment to target processes such as treatment planning, utilization of services, and goal attainment. It has been suggested that assessing one's readiness for change prior to developing a treatment plan will improve treatment outcomes (DiClemente & Prochaska; 1998). Accordingly, the transtheoretical model (TTM) argues that the individual moves through five stages when changing behaviors: precontemplation, contemplation, preparation, action, and maintenance.

Functional analysis often is used in substance use treatment to help patients effectively problem-solve ways to reduce the probability of future drug use. Within this model, an analysis of the antecedents and consequences of drug use is used to develop alternative cognitive and behavioral skills to reduce the risk of future drug use. Working together, the therapist and patient identify high-risk situations and the (1) trigger for that situation, (2) thoughts during that situation, (3) feelings

**Table 7.1**

Instruments for the Screening and Diagnosis of Substance Use Disorders

| Instrument | Summary | Method of Administration | Population |
|---|---|---|---|
| **Screening** | | | |
| Alcohol Use Disorders Identification Test (AUDIT; Saunders, Aasland, & Babor, 1993) | Developed by WHO, the AUDIT screens for increased risk for hazardous drinking, and can identify problem drinking and dependence. | Interview, self-administered and computerized versions. | Adults; Validated cross-culturally; translated into many languages |
| Drug Use Disorders Identification Test (DUDIT; Stuart, Moore, & Kahler, 2003) | An 11-item measure to screen for drug-related problems across the following drug classes: cannabis, cocaine, hallucinogens, stimulants, sedatives, and opiates. | Self-report | Adults |
| CAGE (Cooney, Zweben, & Fleming, 1995) | Consists of 4 questions used to screen for a substance use problem. Each "have you ever?" question can be answered either "YES" or "NO," and each positive response gets 1 point. A score of 1 of 4 indicates "possible," and 2 detects most cases of substance misuse. However, may not be sensitive enough to capture binge drinkers. | Interview | Adults; Adolescents |
| Drug Abuse Screening Test (DAST; Skinner, 1982) | Focuses on lifetime severity of drug abuse and its consequences and provides an index of drug use severity. Covers a variety of consequences related to drug use without specifying drug type, alleviating the necessity of using different instruments specific to each drug. | Interview or self-administered | Adults |
| MCMI-III (Millon & Meagher, 2004) | Short 14-item drug dependence scale. High scores on this scale suggest a recurrent or recent history of drug abuse, a tendency to have poor impulse control, and an inability to manage the consequences of drug use and impulsive behavior. | Self-report | Adults |
| Addiction Potential Scale (APS) of the MMPI-2 (Weed, Butcher, & McKenna, 1992) | This measure does not directly assess substance use behavior, but was designed to identify personality characteristics and lifestyle patterns that are associated with substance abuse. | Self-report | Adults |

| Instrument | Description | Administration | Population |
| --- | --- | --- | --- |
| Simple Screening Instrument for Substance Abuse (SSI-SA; SAMHSA, 2005) | The SSI-SA screens for five domains of substance use including substance consumption, preoccupation and loss of control, adverse consequences, problem recognition, and tolerance and withdrawal. | Interview or self-administered | Adults; Co-occurring disorders |
| Alcohol, Smoking, and Substance Involvement Screening Test (ASSIST; Ali et al., 2002) | Developed by WHO, the ASSIST uses 8 questions to screen for tobacco, alcohol, and illicit drug use. Additional items assess problems related to substance use, the risk of current or future harm, level of dependence, and method of use (e.g., needle injection). | Interview or self-administered | Adults |

**Diagnostic Status**

| Instrument | Description | Administration | Population |
| --- | --- | --- | --- |
| Structured Clinical Interview for DSM-IV-TR (SCID; First, Spitzer, Gibbon, & Williams, 1997) | The SCID is a precise method for identifying substance dependence and abuse and is the most frequently used instrument in clinical trials. In addition to guidelines for general substance dependence and abuse, the interview assesses for dependence and abuse of 11 classes of drugs, including alcohol, amphetamines, caffeine, cannabis, cocaine, hallucinogens, inhalants, nicotine, opioids, phencyclidine (PCP), and sedatives, hypnotics, or anxiolytics. | Interview; Clinician administered | Adults; Adolescents |
| Substance Dependence Severity Scale (SDSS; Miele et al., 2000) | Assesses both the frequency and severity of symptoms. For each symptom, the SDSS measures total number of days a symptom occurred, usual severity of the symptom, and worst severity of the symptom over a 30-day time frame. | Interview; Clinician-administered | Adults; Adolescents |
| Diagnostic Interview Schedule for DSM-IV (DIS-IV; Robins, Helzer, Croughan, & Ratcliff, 1981) | Structured interview that assesses for the presence DSM-IV lifetime and past 12-month history of symptoms across 11 drug classes. The DIS-IV has demonstrated good reliability and validity and can be administered by a lay interviewer. | Interview | Adults |
| Composite International Diagnostic Interview-Second Edition (CIDI-2; Kessler & Ustun, 2004) | Structured interview that provides lifetime diagnoses for past and current substance use disorders according to both the DSM-IV and ICD-10. An SUD diagnosis from the CIDI has demonstrated good reliability and validity and can be administered by a lay interviewer in approximately 20 to 30 minutes. | Interview | Adults; Adolescents |

(continued)

**Table 7.1**
*(Continued)*

| Instrument | Summary | Method of Administration | Population |
|---|---|---|---|
| **Treatment Planning and Outcome** | | | |
| Addiction Severity Index (ASI; McLellan et al., 1992) | The most comprehensive and widely used measure. The ASI assesses drug and alcohol use in the context of 7 domains: medical status, employment status, family history, legal status, psychiatric status, and family and social relationships. It identifies problem areas in need of targeted intervention and is often used in clinical settings for treatment planning and outcome evaluation. | Interview or self-report | Adults |
| Drug Use Screening Inventory (DUSI; Tarter, 1991) | Measures the severity of drug and alcohol problem in 10 psychosocial and psychiatric domains: behavior patters, drug consequences, health status, psychiatric disorder, social competency, family system, school performance, work adjustments, recreation, and peer relationships. A "lie scale" is built in to ensure truthfulness and increase reliability by identifying inconsistencies. | Interview or self-report | Adults; Adolescents |
| Inventory of Drug Use Consequences (InDUC; Tonigan & Miller, 2002) | An inventory of alcohol-related consequences. The InDUC is distinct from screening instruments in that it measures adverse consequences of substance use including items referring to pathological use practices (e.g., rapid use), items reflecting dependence symptoms (e.g., craving), and items concerning help seeking (e.g., Narcotics Anonymous). Includes five scales including impulse control, social responsibility, and physical, interpersonal, and intrapersonal domains. | Self-report | Adults |
| Timeline Followback (TLFB; Fals-Stewart, O'Farrell, & Freitas, 2000) | Assesses recent substance use by asking the client to retrospectively report use in a defined period prior to the interview date. In addition to capturing use, the TLFB can also identify frequency of use. | Interview or self-report | Adults; Adolescents |
| Form 90D (Westerberg, Tonigan, & Miller, 1998) | Using a calendar, this semi-structured interview captures substance use for the past 90 days. | Clinician-administered | Adults; Adolescents |

## Motivation and Treatment Readiness

| | | | |
|---|---|---|---|
| University of Rhode Island Change Assessment (URICA; McConnaughy, Prochaska, & Velicer, 1983) | Measures the Stages Of Change (Precontemplation, Contemplation, Action and Maintenance) using a 5-point Likert scale. Assesses readiness to change when clients enter treatment. | Self-report | Adults; Co-occurring disorders |
| Stages of Change Readiness and Treatment Eagerness Scale (SOCRATES; Miller & Tonigan, 1996) | Scale used to assess motivation for change, in relation to alcohol and drug use, using three factoria ly-derived scores: Recognition, Ambivalence, and Taking Steps. | Self-report | Adults |
| Readiness to Change Questionnaire (RTCQ; Rollnick, Heather, Gold, & Hall, 1992) | Uses Stages of Change Model to assign substance users to three stages: precontemplation, contemplation, and action. | Interview | Adults; Adolescents |

experienced in response to the trigger and thoughts, (4) drug use behavior, and (5) positive and negative consequences of drug use. After analyzing this behavior chain, the therapist and patient then develop strategies for altering thoughts and behaviors when faced with those same situations. Those interested in the use of functional analysis in treatment are directed to Monti, Kadden, Rohsenhow, Cooney, and Abrams (2002) or the National Institutes for Drug Abuse online publications *A Community Reinforcement Approach: Treating Cocaine Addiction.*

Outcome assessments should include a wide range of dimensions beyond substance use behavior, including changes in social, occupational, and psychological functioning. As such, it is ideal to readminister comprehensive measures such as the *Addiction Severity Index*, *Drug Use Screening Inventory*, and *Inventory of Drug Use Consequences* (see Table 7.1). In addition, self-report and biological indicators can be used to determine return to drug use, drug use behavior, and psychiatric symptoms.

The following is a brief overview of recent trends in the biological assessment of substance use (see Wolff, 2006, for an extensive review). Although recent work has identified cutting-edge technologies for biological testing of substance use, *urinalysis* remains the preferred method of detection for several reasons. First, because urinalysis has been used historically, it is well-known and many of the problems associated with it have been addressed. Second, urine contains high concentrations of the target drug or its metabolites. Third, it is inexpensive and may be acquired in a minimally invasive manner as compared to other biological approaches. Self-contained urine-based testing kits that can reliably detect the most commonly used psychoactive substances are becoming increasingly available, which allow practitioners and researchers to conduct on-site testing across a wide range of settings. Finally, recently developed quantitative and semi-quantitative tests are more sensitive to changes in the pattern, frequency, and amount of use (Preston, Silverman, Schuster, & Charles, 2002). Thus, in addition to indicating the presence or absence of a drug, quantitative urinalysis can be useful in detecting initial efforts to reduce drug use and monitoring the effects of treatments.

While urinalysis has several advantages and obvious clinical utility, several limitations remain. Urine can only indicate drug use in the past 3 days (except for cannabis, methadone, and diazepam), thereby increasing the reliance on self-report for longer-term follow-up periods. In addition, urine is easily adulterated by using chemicals such as bleach, vinegar, or liquid soap, and can be easily diluted by using old urine or someone else's urine. Conversely, over-the-counter medications and certain foods can produce positive test results in the absence of illicit drug use. As such, careful attention to detail and procedures are needed to ensure accurate collection, and positive tests may need additional confirmation.

*Blood* collection is another method that can detect very recent drug use and is considered an ideal method for assessing quantitative levels when accuracy is the primary criterion for measure selection. However, blood often is not collected due to its invasive nature, reliance on trained personnel, and the potential risks of spreading infections such as HIV and hepatitis. *Saliva* is the only body fluid that can be used as a substitute for blood, as drug concentration levels are comparable. Saliva collection has the advantage of being easy to obtain and is cost-effective because, similar to urinalysis, self-contained testing kits are widely available that eliminate the need for trained personnel and off-site testing. One collection procedure often utilized is the sallivete-sampling device. It consists of a cotton wool swab, which is placed in the patients' buccal cavity for saliva collection by absorption. Drawbacks to saliva collection include difficulty collecting an adequate amount for drug detection and the possible contamination of the oral cavity as a result of oral, intranasal, and smoking drug use.

*Hair* testing has been developed and theorized to have the potential benefits of drug detection over a longer period of time as is possible with the aforementioned methods. However, quality control criteria and standard laboratory methods have yet to be established. In addition, evidence indicates that drug detection may differentially appear in darker hair, leading to a bias toward missing drug use in blonde individuals and differentially detecting it in people with black hair. In addition, hair is sensitive to smoke in the air, resulting in a false positive for individuals who abstain yet are surrounded by people who have smoked drugs.

## ETIOLOGICAL CONSIDERATIONS

### BEHAVIORAL GENETICS AND MOLECULAR GENETICS

*Behavioral Genetics* Findings from twin, adoption, and family studies suggest that genetic factors account for a significant portion of the variance in liability for substance use disorders. Indeed, SUDs are some of the most highly heritable psychiatric disorders, with heritability estimates ranging from 0.39 for hallucinogens to 0.72 for cocaine (Goldman, Oroszi, & Ducci, 2005). The magnitude of genetic influence on substance use varies over the course of development, beginning with a negligible amount of genetic influence during early adolescence that increases over time until it stabilizes by age 35 to 40 (Kendler, Schmitt, Aggen, & Prescott, 2008). It also appears that the majority of the genetic vulnerability for SUDs can be accounted for by shared genetic influences that are common across drug classes (Agrawal, Neale, Prescott, & Kendler, 2004; True et al., 1999; Tsuang et al., 1998). For SUDs that are highly comorbid, such as alcohol and nicotine dependence, a common genetic factor for alcohol use and smoking accounts for approximately 45% of the genetic variance in heavy alcohol use and 35% of the genetic variance in heavy smoking (Swan, Carmelli, & Cardon, 1997). These findings point to significance of genetic factors in addiction liability, as well as the importance of studying genes that are involved in neurobiological substrates that are common across substance use disorders.

*Molecular Genetics* More recent work has focused on the extent to which specific genetic polymorphisms (variations in DNA structure) contribute to one's vulnerability for an SUD. The strongest and most consistent single-gene effects on SUD vulnerability are largely specific to Asian populations, including polymorphisms in the aldehyde (ALDH) and alcohol dehydrogenase (ADH) genes, which code for enzymes involved in alcohol metabolism (Wolff, 1972). Individuals who carry one or more of these alleles are less likely to become alcohol dependent (reviewed by Uhl, Drgon, Johnson, & Liu, 2009), and the protective effects of these genes appear to be additive (Thomasson et al., 1991).

Also significantly associated with substance dependence are γ-aminobutyric acid (GABA) receptor genes on chromosome 4. Convergent evidence suggests that polymorphisms, specifically in GABRA2, are associated with alcohol dependence (Covault et al., 2004; Edenberg et al., 2004; Fehr et al., 2006; Lappalainen et al., 2005; Soyka et al., 2008), nicotine dependence, cannabis use, and polysubstance abuse (Agrawal et al., 2008a; Agrawal et al., 2008b; Drgon, D'Addario, & Uhl, 2006). Evidence from recent genome wide association studies (GWAS) has converged to implicate a cluster of nicotinic acetylcholine receptor (nAChR) subunit genes in nicotine dependence, as well as dependence on other substances. For example, variants in CHRNA4 and the CHRNA5/A3/B4 cluster have been associated with nicotine dependence across populations, as well as subjective response to smoking (Berrettini et al., 2008; Feng et al., 2004; Hutchison et al., 2007; Li et al., 2005; Saccone et al., 2007; Weiss et al., 2008). Meta-analytic approaches have provided convergent evidence for the role of nAChR subunit genes, including CHRNA3 and CHRNA5, in smoking initiation and smoking quantity (Liu et al., 2010; Thorgeirsson et al., 2010; Tobacco and Genetics Consortium, 2010), alcohol dependence (Wang et al., 2009), and cocaine dependence (Grucza et al., 2008); however, the effect on cocaine dependence is opposite to that seen in nicotine dependence.

Additional genes that increase the risk of SUDs include polymorphisms in dopamine receptor genes that play a role in reward and reinforcement behavior (Blum et al., 2000). A meta-analysis including 55 studies confirmed the A1$^+$ allele of DRD2 as a marker of substance use and severe substance misuse (Young, Lawford, Nutting, & Noble, 2004). Similarly, a polymorphism in the DAT1 gene has been associated with cocaine abuse (Guindalini et al., 2006) and alcohol dependence (Samochowiec et al., 2006). Recent meta-analyses provide additional support for the involvement of both genes in substance dependence across drug classes (reviewed by Li & Burmeister, 2009), suggesting that genes encoding for dopaminergic functioning may modulate SUD liability to a variety of substances.

*Gene-Environment Interactions* Beyond examining genetic factors in isolation, environmental risk factors have been shown to interact with genes to contribute to the development of SUDs. For example, individuals with the A1 allele of the DRD2 gene who also report high levels of stress are at the greatest risk of alcohol dependence (Bau, Almeida, & Hutz, 2000; Madrid, MacMurray, Lee, Anderson, & Comings, 2001). Similarly, Blomeyer and colleagues (2008) found that adolescents with the C allele of a single nucleotide polymorphism (SNP) in CHRNA1 were at an increased risk of alcohol use and heavy drinking, but only if they also experienced three or more negative life events. Additionally, polymorphisms in the monoamine oxidase A (MAOA) gene interact with childhood maltreatment in predicting alcohol use problems (Ducci et al., 2007; Nilsson et al., 2007; Nilsson et al., 2008). Related to smoking outcomes, one recent study found that an SNP in CHRNA5 increased the risk of nicotine dependence, but only among individuals who reported low levels of parental monitoring during early adolescence; however, parental monitoring did not moderate the effect of an SNP in CHRNA3 on nicotine dependence (Chen et al., 2009). Taken together, genetic risk factors for substance use may be moderated by environmental variables, suggesting that as genetic researchers continue to incorporate environmental measures into their studies, additional gene-environment interactions may be revealed.

NEUROANATOMY AND NEUROBIOLOGY

Several neurobiological models have been proposed to explain how chronic substance use contributes to development of SUDs and vulnerability to relapse, with a great deal of emphasis placed on the role of neuroadaptive changes that take place in brain reward and stress circuits over the course of chronic drug use (e.g., Koob & LeMoal, 2001, 2008; Li & Sinha, 2008; Robinson & Berridge, 1993, 2001; Wise, 1980, 2002). The following sections will discuss neurobiological mechanisms that increase liability to substance use across drug classes, as well as the neurobiological changes that contribute to development and maintenance of SUDs.

*Brain Reward Circuits*   One pharmacological effect that is common to all drugs of abuse is increased activation in the mesocorticolimbic dopamine pathway of the brain (Di Chiara et al., 2004; Wise, 1996). Dopamine neurons project from the ventral tegmental area (VTA) to the ventral striatum and prefrontal cortex (PFC), and dopaminergic functioning in these regions is believed to be a key component of the brain reward systems, which are critical for the reinforcing properties of drugs. Human neuroimaging studies show that acute administration of nearly all drugs of abuse leads to increased activation in mesolimbic dopaminergic regions, and that this activation correlates with subjective ratings of high or euphoria and craving. However, chronic drug administration and acute withdrawal are associated with alterations in this pathway, characterized by decreases in extracellular dopamine, reduced D2 receptor availability, and reduced dopamine transmission in frontal and ventral striatal regions (for detailed reviews, see Koob & LeMoal, 2008; Sinha, 2008; Volkow, Fowler, & Wang, 2002). Based on this evidence, some researchers have suggested that neuroadaptive changes that take place in dopaminergic circuits over the course of chronic drug use may underlie the aversive affective symptoms that are common during withdrawal, which may drive individuals to relapse to drug use in order to escape this aversive state (Koob & LeMoal, 1997, 2008). As such, alterations in dopaminergic functioning appears to be an important neurobiological mechanism underlying the development and maintenance of addictive disorders.

*Brain Stress Circuits*   The hypothalamic-pituitary-adrenal (HPA) axis and its primary hormone, cortisol, plays a central role in mediating the body's response to stress and is extremely sensitive to inputs from the limbic system and prefrontal cortex, two brain areas that are important for modulating reinforcement and motivational processes (e.g., Li & Sinha, 2008). In animal models of substance use, evidence suggests that rats with elevated HPA axis reactivity to stress show greater self-administration of addictive substances (Piazza, Deminiere, Le Moal, & Simon, 1989, 1990; Piazza, Derouche, Rouge-Pont, & Le Moal, 1998; Piazza et al., 1991; Piazza et al., 1996), and administration of exogenous corticosteroids to rats that were low-level responders led to an increased risk that these rats would begin to self-administer amphetamines (Piazza et al., 1991). Evidence also suggests that HPA axis activation, and subsequent release of ACTH and cortisol in response to stress, is associated with increased dopaminergic neurotransmission in mesolimbic reward circuits (Dunn, 1988; Kalivas & Duffy, 1989; Piazza & Le Moal, 1996; Prasad, Sorg, Ulibarri, & Kalivas, 1995; Thierry, Tassin, Blanc, & Glowinski, 1976), suggesting that reactivity in brain stress circuits plays an important role in both substance use liability and drug reinforcement.

*Neuroadaptation in Reward and Stress Circuitry* Neurobiological models of drug addiction hypothesize that reward and stress circuits in the brain become dysregulated in response to chronic drug use, and this dysregulation contributes to the establishment of a "negative affect" or psychologically distressed state during abstinence, which increases the reinforcing effects of drugs and thus vulnerability to relapse following cessation (Koob, 2009; Koob & Le Moal, 2001, 2008). Specifically, when reward pathways (i.e., the mesocorticolimbic dopamine system discussed previously) are activated by drug administration, opposing antireward systems (i.e., brain stress systems localized in the central nucleus of the amygdala and the bed nucleus of the stria terminalis) are recruited to limit reward function and maintain homeostasis. Over the course of chronic drug administration, neuroadaptive changes occur in response to the excessive utilization of brain reward systems, including subsequent decreases in activation of brain reward systems and increases in the opposing brain stress circuits. Such combination of depressed reward circuits and elevated antireward circuits is hypothesized to be the driving force motivating continued drug-seeking behavior (Koob & Le Moal, 2008). Furthermore, elevated brain stress activation is hypothesized to reduce an individual's ability to adapt or cope with additional stressors during abstinence, thereby driving vulnerability to stress-induced relapse. This is in line with the negative reinforcement theory of addiction, which states that the motivation for substance use is the reduction or avoidance of negative emotional states (Baker, Piper, McCarthy, Majeskie, & Fiore, 2004). Indeed, evidence indicates that a behavioral proxy of negative reinforcement, namely distress tolerance, is associated with an increased frequency of substance use and poor substance use outcomes (Brandon et al., 2003; Brown, Lejuez, Kahler, & Strong, 2002; Daughters et al., 2005a; Daughters et al., 2005b; Quinn, Brandon, & Copeland, 1996). Taken together, neurobiological models suggest that chronic drug use is associated with neuroadaptive changes, including decreases in reward system activation and increases in antireward system functioning, which may maintain compulsive drug-seeking behaviors, even after protracted periods of abstinence.

### LEARNING, MODELING, AND LIFE EVENTS

Theories of learning and conditioning have been utilized to understand the development and maintenance of SUDs, and as a result, studies have been conducted in laboratory animals and humans that support the notion of drugs as reinforcers (for a review, see Higgins, Heil, & Lussier, 2004), with drug use theorized to be a form of operant behavior influenced by antecedents and consequences. Drug self-administration studies with humans have been used to examine the influence of nondrug reinforcers on heroin and cocaine use (Comer, Collins, & Fischman, 1997; Greenwald & Steinmiller, 2009; Higgins et al., 1994). In each study, the choice of using either cocaine or heroin decreased in an orderly and graded function of increasing value of a monetary option. Specifically, as the nondrug reinforcer increased in value, drug use decreased, suggesting the power of alternative reinforcers in affecting drug use.

Taking this approach a step further, the behavioral economics perspective proposes that the reinforcing value of drug use is critically influenced by the environmental context of other available reinforcers. Accordingly, research has revealed a relationship between degree of substance use and engagement in substance-free activities. High rates of drug use are most likely in contexts without substance-free sources of reinforcement, and drug use will generally decrease if access to alternative reinforcers is increased (Higgins, Heil, & Lussier, 2004). In a comprehensive review of the literature, Carroll (1996) concludes that the availability of nondrug alternative reinforcers reliably reduces drug use in animals and humans across a variety of drug types, routes of administration, and types of alternative reinforcers. Although the majority of research in this area has focused on alcohol use (e.g., Correia, Benson, & Carey, 2005), findings have also been demonstrated among illicit drug users (Van Etten, Higgins, Budney, & Badger, 1998). Taken together, individuals with fewer alternative behavioral choices will be more likely to develop an SUD. Additionally, clinical research has reported positive outcomes for treatments developed based upon reinforcement theories such as contingency management (e.g., Prendergast, Podus, Finney, Greenwell, & Roll, 2006), behavioral activation (Daughters et al., 2008), and a community reinforcement approach (e.g., Abbott, 2009).

In addition to behavioral theories of addiction, research has evidenced an association between stressful life events and substance use. Chronic stress has been identified as a contributor to both substance use initiation and maintenance (Fox & Sinha, 2009). Adolescent exposure to stressful life events, such as parental alcoholism or financial difficulty, has been shown to increase emotional and behavioral problems that intensify the risk for developing an SUD (King & Chassin, 2007). Furthermore, populations dealing with chronic stress, including emotional stressors ranging from violence and loss to trauma, poor social support, and interpersonal conflict, have evidenced higher vulnerability to SUDs (Sinha, 2008).

## COGNITIVE INFLUENCES

*Expectancies*  Turning to research emphasizing the role of cognition, social learning theories (Bandura, 1977) emphasize the role of a biased belief system in maintaining substance use. These theories posit that positive expectancies for engaging in drug use, coupled with minimal negative expectancies and poor self-efficacy beliefs as to one's ability to cope without drugs, leads to the development and maintenance of SUDs. Specifically, substance use expectancies are an individual's beliefs about the consequences of substance use (e.g., "I expect to feel good if I use marijuana"). The beliefs and attitudes that drive substance use expectancies are generated from a range of sources, such as the perception of use, actual experiences, social norms, and peer influence (Hayaki et al., 2010). Empirical evidence indicates that there is a relationship between positive expectancies and substance use (McCusker, 2001). For example, in a community sample of cocaine users, the expectation that use would increase physical and social pleasure was positively associated with frequency of cocaine use (Hayaki, Anderson, & Stein, 2008). Furthermore, positive expectancies have predicted the initiation and maintenance of alcohol consumption, the onset of drinking problems, and in some studies, emergence and persistence of alcohol dependence (Jones, Corbin, & Fromme, 2001). Conversely, research has also highlighted the role of negative expectancies, particularly as a predictive tool for continued abstinence following treatment (McCusker, 2001). Negative expectancies (e.g., "If I drink alcohol, I will lose control") also act as motivation to limit substance use (Oei & Morawska, 2004).

*Executive Functioning*   Executive functioning is implicated in behavior regulation and control, and includes the constructs of impulsivity, decision making, and attentional bias. Across studies, impulsivity has been associated with the initiation and continued use of substances (de Wit, 2009; Field, Schoenmakers, & Wiers, 2008; Johnson, Bickel, Moore, Badger, & Budney, 2010; Petry & Casarella, 1999). Drug use also causes neuronal changes that alter a person's ability to choose nonrisky alternative behaviors, though others argue that the decision-making mechanism is already weak in individuals who are prone to addiction (Bechara, 2005). For instance, using the Game of Dice Task (Brand et al., 2004), Brand and colleagues (2008) found subjects with opiate dependence exhibited a preference for decisions that led to more negative long-term consequences and made riskier choices compared to matched controls (Brand, Roth-Bauer, Driessen & Markowitsch, 2008). The relationship between attentional bias and SUDs has demonstrated that illicit drug users attend more to drug-related stimuli (Costantinou et al., 2010; Hester, Dixon, & Garavan, 2006; McCusker & Gettings, 1997), and a stronger attentional bias is associated with heavier substance use (Stacey & Wiers, 2010).

## Sex and Racial-Ethnic Considerations

*Sex Differences*   Existing research has demonstrated that women differ from men in their pathways into drug addiction. Compared to men, women are less likely to have an SUD, and onset of their substance abuse tends to be later in life. Yet women become dependent at a quicker rate and experience more severe consequences of drug use over shorter periods of time (e.g., Hser, Huang, Teruya, & Anglin, 2004). This accelerated development to dependence has been termed *telescoping*, and this trend has been consistently documented (Greenfield, Back, Lawson, & Brady, 2010). For women the pathway into drug use is often relationship-based; for instance, women are more likely to initiate and continue substance use in the context of an intimate partner relationship (Frajzyngier et al., 2007; Tuchman, 2010), and following treatment, women's drug use is more likely to be influenced by their partner's continued substance use, compared to men (Grella, Scott, Foss, & Dennis, 2008). Furthermore, women with SUDs are also more likely than men with SUDs to have a partner who uses illegal drugs (Westermeyer & Boedicker, 2000).

With regard to treatment, co-occurring psychiatric disorders are more common among women and also create a barrier to treatment. As indicated in a review by Greenfield and colleagues (2007), females have higher rates of SUDs and specifically eating disorders, mood and anxiety disorders, and posttraumatic stress disorder, which subsequently make it difficult for them to find appropriate treatment to manage both disorders. Gender differences in stress reactivity may be one important mechanism underlying these differences. Fox and Sinha (2009), in a review, reported that compared to substance-abusing men, women may experience increased emotional sensitivity to changes in the stress system, and the resulting neuroadaptations in autonomic function and affect may alter vulnerability to co-occurring disorders, possible relapse, and treatment outcome.

Women also face unique barriers to treatment engagement that may explain women's reduced likelihood to enter treatment relative to men. For instance, barriers relating to child-rearing responsibilities, including limited access to child care services, as well as society's punitive attitude toward substance abuse by women as child bearers, present just some of the major treatment barriers for women suffering from SUDs (e.g., Greenfield et al., 2007). Moreover, women also differ from men in their response to treatment. Data on this topic has proven to be somewhat conflicting: Whereas some researchers have reported that women are more likely than men to drop out of substance abuse treatment (King & Canada, 2004), others have proposed a complex interaction of gender and treatment modality (e.g., methadone versus drug-free programs; Joe, Simpson, & Broome, 1999; McCaul, Svikis, & Moore, 2001; Simpson, Joe, Rowan-Szal, & Greener, 1997). There is also evidence that women are more likely than men to complete treatment (Hser et al., 2004). The reasons underlying these discrepancies are unknown, but they suggest a fruitful avenue for future research.

*Racial-Ethnic Differences*   Studies suggest that there are unique risks and needs among minority drug users. For instance, racial-ethnic minorities who reside in inner-city areas are particularly vulnerable to drug use and risky sexual behavior as a result of higher levels of poverty, violence, general risk practices, and availability of street drugs (e.g., Avants, Marcotte, Arnold, & Margolin, 2003). Importantly, there are great racial-ethnic disparities in access and utilization of treatment services, and evaluations of the substance abuse treatment system have shown that racial-ethnic minorities are underserved (Marsh, Cao, Guerro, & Shin, 2009). Aside from Asian Americans, all racial groups have a larger treatment gap than Whites (Schmidt & Mulia, 2009), and among treatment-seeking individuals, African Americans and Hispanics are more likely than Whites to report unmet needs (Wells, Klap, Koike, & Sherbourne, 2001).

As with other health care access issues, racial-ethnic differences in accessing substance abuse treatment services may result from underlying differences in barriers to care. Factors such as perceived discrimination, prior negative experiences associated with services, and limited knowledge of available services may provide a better understanding of why there is an unmet need among those who perceive need for substance abuse treatment in minority groups (Grella, Karno, Warda, Moore, & Niv, 2009), and data indicate that Whites experience half the rate of barriers compared to African Americans and Hispanics (Perron et al., 2009). Looking beyond access and utilization of treatment, treatment outcome studies suggest mixed findings when exploring racial-ethnic minorities compared to Whites. Some data indicate that members of minority groups are less likely to complete and/or seek treatment, receive fewer treatment services, and are less likely to achieve recovery (Jerrell & Wilson, 1997; Rebach, 1992). However, research reports indicate that minority clients do not differ from nonminority clients in their response to treatment (e.g., Pickens & Fletcher, 1991) and in treatment outcomes (Niv, Pham, & Hser, 2009).

## COURSE AND PROGNOSIS

By the 12th grade, more than 47% of adolescents have used an illicit substance (Johnston, O'Malley, Bachman, & Schulenberg, 2009). The most common substances used by adolescents include tobacco, cannabis, and alcohol (SAMHSA, 2009a). It should be noted that although many adolescents may experiment with drugs, most do not progress to abuse or dependence (Newcomb & Richardson, 1995). There is an ongoing debate about the development and progression of substance use among adolescents. Some researchers subscribe to the "gateway theory," which hypothesizes that for adolescents, there is a distinct sequential pattern of substance use, beginning with licit substances (i.e., tobacco, alcohol) and progressing to illicit substance (e.g., marijuana) and finally advancing through a hierarchy of illicit substances (e.g., cocaine, heroin; Kandel, Yamaguchi, & Chen, 1992). However, more recent research finds that adolescent substance use does not always evidence a temporal sequence from licit to illicit substances, and the choice of substance used by adolescents is a function of contextual variables (e.g., availability, parental supervision) more than a normative sequential order (Tarter, Vanyukov, Kirisci, Reynolds, & Clark, 2006).

Although there are conflicting hypotheses as to adolescent use and progression, research has consistently evidenced similar risk factors for the development of substance dependence. Two primary risk factors include age of initiation and frequency of use during adolescence (Behrendt, Wittchen, Hofler, Lieb, & Beesdo, 2009; Degenhardt et al., 2009; King & Chassin, 2007). Age of initiation increases risk in part because earlier age of substance use allows for greater exposure to the substance. Considering that adolescence is a time of substantial neurological development, the adolescent brain may be particularly susceptible to substance abuse and addiction (Winters & Lee, 2008). In addition, drug-related problems (i.e., some symptoms of an SUD without meeting full diagnostic criteria) in adolescence significantly predict a future SUD, elevated levels of depression, and antisocial and borderline personality disorder symptoms by age 24 (Rohde, Lewinsohn, Kahler, Seeley, & Brown, 2001).

Once an SUD is present, recovery is notoriously difficult, even with exceptional treatment resources. For those who receive treatment, the next challenge is staying in treatment. Treatment dropout rates range up to 50% (SAMHSA, 2007). Such high rates of premature treatment termination are of concern, because time in treatment is related to positive outcomes (e.g., Garner, Godley, Funk, Lee, & Garnick, 2010; Simpson, Joe, & Brown, 1997). As for relapse rates, estimates suggest that 90% of heroin- and cocaine-dependent users experience at least one relapse within the 4 years after treatment, with many relapsing considerably sooner. Furthermore, of the patients admitted to the U.S. public treatment system in 2007, approximately 57% were re-entering treatment (Office of Applied Studies, 2009). Retrospective and prospective treatment studies report that most participants initiate three to four episodes of treatment over multiple years before attaining abstinence (Hser et al., 1998), and as many as 80% transition between treatment, recovery, using, and incarceration at least once over a 4-year follow-up period (Grella, Scott, Foss, & Dennis, 2008).

Treatment outcomes are dependent on a variety of factors, including individual characteristics and life problems, severity of addiction and drug use, aptness of treatment and linkage to services to treat other problems, and the quality of the transaction between the individual and the treatment program (NIDA, 2009). As previously stated, better treatment outcomes are related to length of stay, and for residential/inpatient and outpatient programs, treatment participation of 90 days or longer is recommended for sustaining recovery and positive results (NIDA, 2009). However, 90 days of treatment is not always feasible (i.e., lack of insurance and prohibitive cost). Historically, persons with SUDs receive a traditional acute treatment approach involving assessment, treatment, and discharge all within a short time frame (i.e., 28 days or 2 months), with the supposition that the patient is cured and will be able to maintain abstinence following the single treatment episode (Dennis & Scott, 2007).

However, recent literature addresses SUDs as a chronic condition, analogous to other chronic medical diseases. For example, McLellan and colleagues (2000) illustrate the similarities in genetic heritability, environmental factors, and personal choice within addiction and other medical conditions with chronic care treatment (e.g., type 2 diabetes mellitus, hypertension, and asthma). Of note, they found that treatment compliance for individuals with an SUD is no better than adherence rates to prescribed treatments for these other medically accepted chronic diseases (McLellan, Lewis, O'Brien, & Kleber, 2000). Similar to chronic diseases such as diabetes and congestive heart failure, there is no cure for addiction, and multiple relapses are common (Saitz, Larson, LaBelle, Richardson, & Samet, 2008); therefore, adjusting treatment to involve a continuum of care may improve long-term outcomes for people with SUDs.

## LOOKING AHEAD TO *DSM-5*

Several recommendations have been made for modifying the *DSM* criteria for SUDs in the upcoming *DSM-5*. Interested readers are referred to the 2006 special issue in *Addiction*, as well as Martin, Chung, and Langenbucher (2008), for a comprehensive review. Taken together, two of the key issues in consideration include removing *substance abuse* as a separate diagnosis and adopting both a categorical and dimensional diagnostic system.

An inherent issue with the diagnosis of substance abuse is that a diagnosis of dependence precludes abuse, suggesting that a diagnosis of dependence is more severe than abuse. However, the *DSM-IV-TR* inconsistently implies that abuse and dependence are distinct factors. A large amount of data supports this inconsistency, calling for further evaluation of the clinical utility of the abuse diagnosis. These data include a lack of consistent variability in the ratio of abuse to dependence diagnoses, factor, and latent class analyses, indicating a single dimension of substance problems, and abuse and dependence failing to demonstrate distinct predictive validity, distinguish age of onset, or differentiate prevalence and severity (Martin et al., 2008).

Diagnostic criteria in the *DSM-IV-TR* present SUDs using a categorical model, although many researchers and clinicians argue for the implementation of a dimensional model. For planning health care needs and reporting to insurance companies, assigning defined categories for abuse and dependence meets a clinical need. However, by using a categorical model, some people with dependence symptoms who are "diagnostic orphans" are not captured using this method of identifying dependence (Saunders, 2006). Some have argued that a combination or hybrid of the categorical and dimensional models would best represent the nature of the disorder, specifically including a dimension component for symptoms (Helzer, van den Brink, & Guth, 2006; Muthen, 2006). In addition, the *DSM* utilizes the same criterion equally for all symptoms, regardless of severity. As such, implementing severity rankings and incorporating this into the overall diagnosis (either dimensionally or categorically) is a potential modification in the *DSM-5*.

## CASE STUDY

### CASE IDENTIFICATION

The patient (John) is a 45-year-old African American male who entered treatment voluntarily at an urban residential substance use treatment center.

### PRESENTING COMPLAINTS

John reports that he relapsed to substance use 8 months ago, and his primary drug of choice is crack/cocaine accompanied by frequent alcohol use. He reports that he had success in treatment for the first time after he was released from prison 4 years ago, and he would like to try and get back on track, as he has hit a low point in the past few months. At the time of treatment entry, John reports no stable living arrangement and had recently been splitting time at the homes of his friends, ex-girlfriend, and uncle. He has four children between the ages of 10 and 27, with three separate women, and has intermittent contact with each of them. He reports that a fifth child, his oldest son, was murdered 5 months ago in a drug-related incident. In his current environment, he reports spending most of his time with old friends, who he reestablished a relationship with after he was laid off from his job 9 months ago.

### HISTORY

John was raised by his mother and never met his father. He reports an extensive family history of substance use, including heroin and crack/cocaine use in his mother, who passed away 10 years ago. John dropped out of high school after the 10th grade. Between the ages of 18 and 40, he was arrested and spent time in prison multiple times for charges related to theft and possession of cocaine. He was released from his last prison term at the age of 41. He has worked primarily as an assistant electrician over the course of his life, but he refused to provide additional details regarding his employment history. His most stable employment history has been during the past 4 years after completing a court-mandated treatment at a residential substance use treatment facility. He reports that he was committed to "turning my life around" at this time, and he successfully remained abstinent until approximately 6 months ago.

### ASSESSMENT

The SCID-IV and Addiction Severity Index were administered to determine Axis I psychopathology, including substance abuse and dependence, substance use history and severity, environmental strengths and stressors, legal issues, and psychiatric symptoms. During the interview, John displayed psychomotor retardation, clear thought processes, and no obvious perceptual abnormalities. His speech volume and tone were within normal limits, yet his speech rate was somewhat slower than normal. Based on this assessment, John met criteria for current crack/cocaine dependence, alcohol abuse, and major depressive disorder (MDD). He reported past crack/cocaine and alcohol dependence beginning at age 17. His MDD symptoms include depressed mood most of the day, nearly every day, markedly diminished interest in almost all activities, feelings of worthlessness and excessive guilt, and a diminished ability to think or concentrate. After a careful assessment of the timeline of his symptoms, it was concluded that his MDD is not substance induced, as his symptoms preceded the onset of his relapse to substance use. Furthermore, these symptoms preceded the death of his son and have persisted for longer than 2 months, and therefore are not classified as bereavement.

The assessment of legal issues indicated that he is no longer on probation with the court system and entered treatment voluntarily. John evidenced difficulty in identifying strengths, but with some additional probing he was able to acknowledge potential support from his uncle and sister, as well as the importance of his spirituality. He reports that his Narcotics Anonymous (NA) sponsor was a source of support but moved away from the area about a year ago. He stopped attending NA meetings around that time.

It was determined that a functional analysis to identify the antecedents and consequences of his substance use and depression would provide the most useful information for treatment planning. First, following the loss of his job, he reported that he had a lot of free time and got bored easily. He felt worthless that he couldn't find a job and often ruminated over the guilt he felt about his choices in life and his inability to provide for his family. He contacted his old friends, which was soon followed by cocaine and alcohol use. He also reported feeling lonely, guilty, and worthless following the loss of his son, and drug use helped him "get rid of" these feelings, although they would always resurface when he was sober, leading to a cycle of negative reinforcement. Finally, he reported intensifying feelings of sadness and shame that he had used crack/cocaine and alcohol again given how much progress he had made following his release from prison. He felt that he had let his family down, as he was just starting to reestablish relationships with his children before his relapse. Taken together, it appeared that a lack of drug-free reinforcements following loss of his job was strongly associated with his relapse to substance use. This was soon thereafter compounded by the negative feelings about the loss of his son, leading to substance dependence and a cycle of negative reinforcement.

## SUMMARY

Substance use problems are complex, and a comprehensive understanding requires knowledge of biological, genetic, neural, behavioral, and cognitive factors. This chapter provided an overview of current practices and cutting-edge advancements for understanding and assessing drug-specific SUDs. Although much work is still needed, great progress has been made in understanding development of SUDs, with greatest promise evident in approaches that consider the interactive influence of these factors. Additionally, clear advancements have been made in both initial as well as ongoing assessment using self-report, interview, behavioral, and biological methods. Also of great promise is the greater attention to neurobiological, genetic, gender, and diversity issues when considering vulnerabilities to developing SUDs, as well as barriers to assessment and proper treatment. Looking forward, *DSM-5* is likely to address limitations in *DSM-IV-TR*, thereby increasing the reliability and validity of the *DSM* diagnosis system. In summary, although challenges of understanding and assessing SUDs continue to grow, it is clear that the field has evidenced important advancements aimed at addressing these challenges.

## REFERENCES

Abbott, P. J. (2009). A review of the community reinforcement approach in the treatment of opioid dependence. *Journal of Psychoactive Drugs, 41*(4), 379–385.

Agrawal, A., Neale, M. C., Prescott, C. A., & Kendler K. S. (2004). A twin study of early cannabis use and subsequent use and abuse/dependence of other illicit drugs. *Psychological Medicine, 34*, 1227–1237.

Agrawal, A., Pergadia, M. L., Saccone, S. F., Hinrichs, A. L., Lessov-Schlaggar, C. N., Saccone, N., . . . Madden, P. A. (2008a). Gamma-aminobutyric acid receptor genes and nicotine dependence: Evidence for association from a case-control study. *Addiction, 103*(6), 1027–1038.

Agrawal, A., Pergadia, M. L., Saccone, S. F., Lynskey, M. T., Wang, J. C., Martin, N. G., . . . Madden, P. A. (2008b). An autosomal linkage scan for cannabis use disorders in the nicotine addiction genetics project. *Archives of General Psychiatry, 65*(6), 713–721.

Ali, R., Awwad, E., Babor, T. F., Bradley, F., Butau, T., Farrell, M., . . . Vendetti, J. (2002). The Alcohol, Smoking and Substance Involvement Screening Test (ASSIST): Development, reliability and feasibility. *Addiction, 97*(9), 1183–1194.

American Psychiatric Association (APA). (2000). *Diagnostic and Statistical Manual of Mental Disorders* (4th ed., text revision, DSM-IV). Washington, DC: Author.

Avants, S. K., Marcotte, D., Arnold, R., & Margolin, A. (2003). Spiritual beliefs, world assumptions, and HIV risk behavior among heroin and cocaine users. *Psychology of Addictive Behaviors, 17*(2), 159–162.

Baker, T. B., Piper, M. E., McCarthy, D. E., Majeskie, M. R., & Fiore, M. C. (2004). Addiction motivation reformulated: An affective processing model of negative reinforcement. *Psychological Review, 111*(1), 33–51.

Bandura, A. (1977). *Social learning theory.* Oxford, England: Prentice-Hall.

Bau, C. H. D., Almeida, S., & Hutz, M. H. (2000). The Taq1 A1 allele of the dopamine D2 receptor gene and alcoholism in Brazil. *American Journal of Medical Genetics, 96*, 302–306.

Bechara, A. (2005). Decision making, impulse control and loss of willpower to resist drugs: A neurocognitive perspective. *Nature Neuroscience, 8*(11), 1458–1463.

Behrendt, S., Wittchen, H.-U., Hofler, M., Lieb, R., & Beesdo, K. (2009). Transitions from first substance use to substance use disorders in adolescence: Is early onset associated with rapid escalation? *Drug and Alcohol Dependence, 99*, 68–78.

Berrettini, W., Yuan, X., Tozzi, F., Song, K., Francks, C., Chilcoat, H., . . . Mooser, V. (2008). Alpha-5/alpha-3 nicotinic receptor subunit alleles increase risk for heavy smoking. *Molecular Psychiatry, 13*, 368–373.

Blomeyer, D., Treutlein, J., Esser, G., Schmidt, M., Schumann, G., & Laucht, M. (2008). Interaction between CRHR1 gene and stressful life events predicts adolescent heavy alcohol use. *Biological Psychiatry, 63*, 146–151.

Blum, K., Braverman, E. R., Holder, J. M., Lubar, J. F., Monastra, V. J., Miller, D., . . . Comings, D. (2000). Reward deficiency syndrome: A biogenetic model for the diagnosis and treatment of impulsive, addictive, and compulsive behaviors. *Journal of Psychoactive Drugs, 32*(Suppl.), 1–68.

Brand, M., Labudda, K., Kalbe, E., Hilker, R., Emmans, D., Fuchs, G., . . . Markowitsch, H. J. (2004). Decision-making impairments in patients with Parkinson's disease. *Behavioral Neurology, 15*, 77–85.

Brand, M., Roth-Bauer, M., Driessen, M., & Markowitsch, H. J. (2008). Executive functions and risky decision-making in patients with opiate dependence. *Drug and Alcohol Dependence, 97*, 64–72.

Brandon, T. H., Herzog, T. A., Juliano, L. M., Irvin, J. E., Lazev, A. B., & Simmons, V. N. (2003). Pretreatment task-persistence predicts smoking cessation outcome. *Journal of Abnormal Psychology, 112*, 448–456.

Brown, R. A., Lejuez, C. W., Kahler, C. W., & Strong, D. (2002). Distress tolerance and duration of past smoking cessation attempts. *Journal of Abnormal Psychology, 111*, 180–185.

Carroll, M. E. (1996). Reducing drug abuse by enriching the environment with alternative nondrug reinforcers. In L. Green & J. H. Kagel, *Advances in behavioral economics, Vol. 3: Substance use and abuse*. Westport, CT: Ablex.

Center for Substance Abuse Treatment. *Substance Abuse Treatment for Persons With Co-Occurring Disorders*. Treatment Improvement Protocol (TIP) Series, Number 42. Appendix H: Screening Instruments, pp. 497–512. Rockville, MD: Substance Abuse and Mental Health Services Administration, 2005.

Chen, L. S., Johnson, E. O., Breslau, N., Hatsukami, D., Saccone, N. L., Grucza, R. A., . . . (Bierut, L. J. (2009). Interplay of genetic risk factors and parent monitoring in risk for nicotine dependence. *Addiction, 104*(10), 1731–1740.

Comer, S. D., Collins, E. D., & Fischman, M. W. (1997). Choice between money and intranasal heroin in morphine-maintained humans. *Behavioural Pharmacology, 8*(8), 677–690.

Conway, K. P., Compton, W., Stinson, F. S., & Grant, B. F. (2006). Lifetime comorbidity of DSM-IV mood and anxiety disorders and specific drug use disorders: Results from the National Epidemiologic Survey on Alcohol and Related Conditions. *Journal of Clinical Psychiatry, 67*(2), 247–257.

Cooney, N. L., Zweben, A., & Fleming, M. F. (1995). Handbook of alcoholism treatment approaches. In R. K. Hester & W. R. Miller (Eds.), *Effective alternatives* (2nd ed., pp. 45–60). Needham Heights, MA: Allyn & Bacon.

Correia, C. J., Benson, T. A., & Carey, K. B. (2005). Decreased substance use following increases in alternative behaviors: A preliminary investigation. *Psychology of Addictive Behaviors, 30*(1), 19–27.

Costantinou, N., Morgan, C. J. A., Battistella, S., O'Ryan, D., Davis, P., & Curran, H. V. (2010). Attentional bias, inhibitory control and acute stress in current and former opiate addicts. *Drug and Alcohol Dependence, 109*, 220–225.

Covault, J., Gelernter, J., Hesselbrock, V., Nellissery, M., & Kranzler, H. R. (2004). Allelic and haplotypic association of GABRA2 with alcohol dependence. *American Journal of Medical Genetics Part B: Neuropsychiatric Genetics, 129B*(1), 104–109.

Daughters, S. B., Braun, A. R., Sargeant, M. N., Reynolds, E. K, Hopko, D. R., Blanco, C., & Lejuez, C. W. (2008). Effectiveness of a brief behavioral treatment for inner-city illicit drug users with elevated depressive symptoms: The Life Enhancement Treatment for Substance Use (LETS ACT!). *The Journal of Clinical Psychiatry, 69*, 122–129.

Daughters, S. B., Lejuez, C. W., Bornovalova, M. A., Kahler, C., Strong, D. R., & Brown, R. (2005a). Distress tolerance as a predictor of early treatment dropout in a residential substance abuse treatment facility. *Journal of Abnormal Psychology, 114*, 729–734.

Daughters, S. B., Lejuez, C. W., Kahler, C., Strong, D., & Brown, R. (2005b). Psychological distress tolerance and duration of most recent abstinence attempt among residential treatment seeking substance abusers. *Psychology of Addictive Behaviors, 19*, 208–211.

Degenhardt, L., Chiu, W. T., Conway, K., Dierker, L., Glantz, M., Kalaydjian, A., . . . Kessler, R. C. (2009). Does the "gateway" matter? Associations between the order of drug use initiation and the development of drug dependence in the National Comorbidity Study replication. *Psychological Medicine, 39*, 157–167.

Dennis, M., & Scott, C. K. (2007). Managing addiction as a chronic condition. *Addiction Science and Clinical Practice, 4*(1), 56–57.

de Wit, H. (2009). Impulsivity as a determinant and consequence of drug use: A review of underlying processes. *Addiction Biology, 14*(1), 22–31.

Di Chiara, G., Bassareo, V., Fenu, S., De Luca, M. A., Spina, L., Cadoni, C., . . . Lecca, D. (2004). Dopamine and drug addiction: The nucleus accumbens shell connection. *Neuropharmacology, 47*(Suppl. 1), 227–241.

DiClemente, C. C., & Prochaska, J. O. (1998). Toward a comprehensive, transtheoretical model of change: Stages of change and addictive behaviors. In W. R. Miller & N. Heather (Eds.), *Treating addictive behaviors* (2nd ed., pp. 3–24). New York, NY: Plenum Press.

Drgon, T., D'Addario, C., & Uhl, G. R. (2006). Linkage disequilibrium, haplotype and association studies of a chromosome 4 GABA receptor gene cluster: Candidate gene variants for addictions. *American Journal of Medical Genetics Part B: Neuropsychiatric Genetics, 141B*(8), 854–860.

Ducci, F., Enoch, M., Hodgkinson, C., Xu, K., Catena, M., Robin R. W., & Goldman, D. (2007). Interaction between a functional MAOA locus and childhood sexual abuse predicts alcoholism and antisocial personality disorder in adult women. *Molecular Psychiatry, 1*, 1–14.

Dunn, A. (1988). Stress related activation of cerebral dopaminergic systems. *Annals of the New York Academy of Sciences, 537*, 188–205.

Edenberg, H. J., Dick, D. M., Xuei, X., Tian, H., Almasy, L., Bauer, L. O., . . . Begleiter, H. (2004). Variations in GABRA2, encoding the α2 subunit of the GABAA receptor, are associated with alcohol dependence and with brain oscillations. *The American Journal of Human Genetics, 74*(4), 705–714.

Fals-Stewart, W., O'Farrell, T. J., & Freitas, T. T. (2000). The timeline followback reports of psychoactive substance use by drug-abusing patients: Psychometric properties. *Journal of Consulting and Clinical Psychology, 68*(1), 134–144.

Fehr, C., Sander, T., Tadic, A., Lenzen, K. P., Anghelescu, I., Klawe, C., . . . Szegedi, A. (2006). Confirmation of association of the GABRA2 gene with alcohol dependence by subtype-specific analysis. *Psychiatric Genetics, 16*(1), 9–17.

Feng, Y., Niu, T., Xing, H., Xu, X., Chen, C., Peng, S., . . . Xu, X. (2004). A common haplotype of the nicotine acetylcholine receptor α4 subunit gene is associated with vulnerability to nicotine addiction in men. *American Journal of Human Genetics, 75*, 112–121.

Field, M., Schoenmakers, T., & Wiers, R. W. (2008). Cognitive processes in alcohol binges: A review and research agenda. *Current Drug Abuse Reviews, 1*, 263–279.

First, M. B., Spitzer, R. L., Gibbon M., & Williams, J. B. W. (1997). *Structured clinical interview for DSM-IV Axis I disorders—Clinician version (SCID-CV)*. Washington, DC: American Psychiatric Press.

Fox, H. C., & Sinha, R. (2009). Sex differences in drug-related stress-system changes: Implications for treatment in substance abusing women. *Harvard Review of Psychiatry, 17,* 103–119.

Frajzyngier, V., Neaigus, A., Gyarmathy, V. A., Miller, M., & Friedman, S. R. (2007). Gender differences in injections risk behaviors at the first injection episode. *Drug and Alcohol Dependence, 89,* 145–152.

Garner, B., Godley, M., Funk, R., Lee, M., & Garnick, D. (2010). The Washington Circle continuity of care performance measure: Predictive validity with adolescents discharged from residential treatment. *Journal of Substance Abuse Treatment, 38*(1), 3–11.

Goldman, D., Oroszi, G., & Ducci, F. (2005). The genetics of addictions: Uncovering the genes. *Nature Reviews Genetics, 6,* 521–532.

Goldstein, R., Compton, W. M., Pulay, A. J., Ruana, W. J., Pickering, R. P., Stinson, F. S., & Grant, B. F. (2007). Antisocial behavioral syndromes and DSM-IV drug use disorders in the United States: Results from the National Epidemiologic Survey on Alcohol and Related Conditions. *Drug and Alcohol Dependence, 90,* 145–158.

Greenfield, S., Back, S., Lawson, K., & Brady, K. (2010). Substance abuse in women. *Psychiatric Clinics of North America, 33*(2), 339–355.

Greenfield, S., Brooks, A., Gordon, S., Green, C., Kropp, F., McHugh, R., . . . Miele, G. M. (2007). Substance abuse treatment entry, retention, and outcome in women: A review of the literature. *Drug and Alcohol Dependence, 86*(1), 1–21.

Greenwald, M. K., & Steinmiller, C. L. (2009). Behavioral economic analysis of opioid consumption in heroin-dependent individuals: Effects of alternative reinforcer magnitude and post-session drug supply. *Drug and Alcohol Dependence, 104,* 84–93.

Grella, C. E., Karno, M. P., Warda, U. S., Moore, M. D., & Niv, N. (2009). Perceptions of need and help received for substance dependence in a national probability survey. *Psychiatric Services, 60,* 1068–1074.

Grella, C. E., Karno, M. P., Warda, U. S., Niv, N., & Moore, A. A. (2009). Gender and comorbidity among individuals with opioid use disorders in the NESARC Study. *Addictive Behaviors, 34*(6–7), 498–504.

Grella, C. E., Scott, C. K., Foss, M. A., & Dennis, M. L. (2008). Gender similarities and differences in the treatment, relapse and recovery cycle. *Evaluation Review, 32,* 113–137.

Grucza, R. A., Wang, J. C., Stitzel, J. A., Hinrichs, A. L., Saccone, S. F., Saccone, N. L., . . . Bierut, L. J. (2008). A risk allele for nicotine dependence in CHRNA5 is a protective allele for cocaine dependence. *Biological Psychiatry, 64*(11), 922–929.

Guindalini, C., Howard, M., Haddley, K., Laranjeira, R., Collier, D., Ammar, N., . . . Breen, G. (2006). A dopamine transporter gene functional variant associated with cocaine abuse in a Brazilian sample. *Proceedings of the National Academy of Sciences of the United States of America, 103*(12), 4552–4557.

Hayaki, J., Anderson, B. J., & Stein, M. D. (2008). Drug use expectancies among non-abstinent community cocaine users. *Drug and Alcohol Dependence, 94,* 109–115.

Hayaki, J., Hagerty, C. E., Herman, D. S., de Dios, M. A., Anderson, B. J., & Stein, M. D. (2010). Expectancies and marijuana use frequency and severity among young females. *Addictive Behaviors, 35,* 995–1000.

Helzer, J. E., van den Brink, W., & Guth, S. E. (2006). Should there be both categorical and dimensional criteria for the substance use disorders in *DSM-V? Addiction,101*(1), 17–22.

Hester, R., Dixon, V., & Garavan, H. (2006). A consistent attentional bias for drug-related material in active cocaine users across word and picture versions of the emotional Stroop task. *Drug and Alcohol Dependence, 81,* 251–257.

Higgins, S. T., Budney, A. J., Bickel, W. K., Foerg, F. E., Donham, R., & Badger, G. J. (1994). Incentives improve outcome in outpatient behavioral treatment of cocaine dependence. *Archives of General Psychiatry, 51*(7), 568–576.

Higgins, S. T., Heil, S. H., & Lussier, J. P. (2004). Clinical implications of reinforcement as a determinant of substance use disorders. *Annual Review of Psychology, 55*, 431–461.

Horsfall, J., Cleary, M., Hunt, G. E., & Walter, G. (2009). Psychosocial treatments for people with co-occurring severe mental illnesses and substance use disorders (dual diagnosis): A review of empirical evidence. *Harvard Review of Psychiatry, 17*(1), 24–34.

Hser, Y. I., Huang, Y. C., Teruya, C., & Anglin, M. D., (2004). Gender differences in treatment outcomes over a three-year period: A PATH model analysis. *Journal of Drug Issues 34*(2), 419–439.

Hser, Y., Maglione, M., Polinsky, M., & Anglin, M. (1998). Predicting drug treatment entry among treatment-seeking individuals. *Journal of Substance Abuse Treatment, 15*(3), 213–220.

Hutchison, K. E., Allen, D. L., Filbey, F. M., Jepson, C., Lerman, C., Benowitz, N. L., . . . Haughey, H. M. (2007). CHRNA4 and tobacco dependence: From gene regulation to treatment outcome. *Archives of General Psychiatry, 64*, 1078–1086.

Jane-Llopis, E., & Matysina, I. (2006). Mental health and alcohol, drugs and tobacco: A review of the comorbidity between mental disorders and the use of alcohol, tobacco and illicit drugs. *Drug and Alcohol Review, 25*, 515–536.

Jerrell, J. M., & Wilson, J. L. (1997). Ethnic differences in the treatment of dual mental and substance disorders. *Journal of Substance Abuse Treatment, 14*(2), 133.

Joe, G. W., Simpson, D. D., & Broome, K. M. (1999). Retention and patient engagement models for different treatment modalities in DATOS. *Drug and Alcohol Dependence, 57*, 113–125.

Johnson, M. W., Bickel, W. K., Moore, B. A., Badger, G. J., & Budney, A. J. (2010). Delay discounting in current and former marijuana-dependent individuals. *Experimental and Clinical Psychopharmacology, 18*(1), 99–107.

Johnston, L. D., O'Malley, P. M., Bachman, J. G., & Schulenberg, J. E. (2009). *Monitoring the Future national survey results on drug use, 1975- 2008. Volume I: Secondary school students* (NIH Publication No. 09-7402). Bethesda, MD: National Institute on Drug Abuse.

Johnston, L. D., O'Malley, P. M., Bachman, J. G., & Schulenberg, J. E. (2010). *Monitoring the Future national results on adolescent drug use: Overview of key findings, 2009* (NIH Publication No. 10-7583). Bethesda, MD: National Institute on Drug Abuse.

Jones, B. T., Corbin, W., & Fromme, K. (2001). A review of expectancy theory and alcohol consumption. *Addiction, 96*, 57–72.

Julien, R. M. (2004). *A primer of drug action: A comprehensive guide to the actions, uses, and side effects of psychoactive drugs.* New York, NY: Worth.

Kalivas, P. W., & Duffy, P. (1989). Similar effects of daily cocaine and stress on mesocorticolimbic dopamine neurotransmission in the rat. *Biological Psychiatry, 25*(7), 913–928.

Kandel, D. B., Yamaguchi, K., & Chen, K. (1992). Stages of progression in drug involvement from adolescence to adulthood: Further evidence for the gateway theory. *Journal of Studies on Alcohol, 53*(5), 447–457.

Kendler, K. S., Schmitt, E., Aggen, S. H., & Prescott, C. A. (2008). Genetic and environmental influences on alcohol, caffeine, cannabis, and nicotine use from early adolescence to middle adulthood. *Archives of General Psychiatry, 65*(6), 674–682.

Kessler, R. C. (2004). The epidemiology of dual diagnosis. *Biological Psychology, 56*, 730–737.

Kessler, R. C., & Ustun, T. B. (2004). The World Mental Health (WMH) survey initiative version of the World Health Organization (WHO) Composite International Diagnostic Interview (CIDI). *International Journal of Methods in Psychiatric Research, 13*(2), 93–121.

King, A. C., & Canada, S. A., (2004). Client-related predictors of early treatment drop-out in a substance abuse clinic exclusively employing individual therapy. *Journal of Substance Abuse Treatment*, 26, 189–195.

King, K. M., & Chassin, L. (2007). A prospective study of the effects of age of initiation of alcohol and drug use on young adult substance dependence. *Journal of Studies on Alcohol and Drugs*, 68(20), 256–265.

Koob, G. F. (2009). Neurobiological substrates for the dark side of compulsivity in addiction. *Neuropharmacology*, 56(Suppl. 1), 18–31.

Koob, G. F., & Le Moal, M. (1997). Drug abuse: Hedonic homeostatic dysregulation. *Science*, 278, 52–58.

Koob, G., & Le Moal, M. (2001). Drug addiction, dysregulation of reward, and allostasis. *Neuropsychopharmacology*, 24, 97–129.

Koob, G. F., & Le Moal, M. (2008). Addiction and the brain antireward system. *Annual Review of Psychology*, 59, 29–53.

Kushner, M. G., Abrams, K., & Borchardt, C. (2000). The relationship between anxiety disorders and alcohol use disorders: A review of major perspectives and findings. *Clinical Psychology Review*, 20, 149–171.

Lappalainen, J., Krupitsky, E., Remizov, M., Pchelina, S., Taraskina, A., Zvartau, E., . . . Gelernter, J. (2005). Association between alcoholism and γ-amino butyric acid α2 receptor subtype in a Russian population. *Alcoholism: Clinical and Experimental Research*, 29(4), 493–498.

Li, C. R., & Sinha, R. (2008). Inhibitory control and emotional stress regulation: Neuroimaging evidence for frontal-limbic dysfunction in psycho-stimulant addiction. *Neuroscience and Biobehavioral Reviews*, 32(3), 581–597.

Li, M. D., Beuten, J., Ma, J. Z., Payne, T. J., Lou, X. Y., Garcia, V., . . . Elston, R. C. (2005). Ethnic- and gender-specific association of the nicotinic acetylcholine receptor α4 subunit gene (CHRNA4) with nicotine dependence. *Human Molecular Genetics*, 14, 1211–1219.

Li, M. D., & Burmeister, M. (2009). New insights into the genetics of addiction. *Nature Reviews Genetics*, 10, 225–231.

Liu, J. Z., Tozzi, F., Waterworth, D. M., Pillai, S. G., Muglia, P., Middleton, L., . . . Marchini, J. (2010). Meta-analysis and imputation refines the association of the 15q25 with smoking quantity. *Nature Genetics*, 42, 436–440.

Madrid, G. A., MacMurray, J., Lee, J. W., Anderson, B. A., & Comings, D. E. (2001). Stress as a mediating factor in the association between the DRD2 taq1 polymorphism and alcoholism. *Alcohol*, 23, 117–122.

Marsh, J. C., Cao, D., Guerro, E., & Shin, H.-C. (2009). Need-service matching in substance abuse treatment: Racial/ethnic differences. *Evaluation and Program Planning*, 32, 43–51.

Martin, C. S., Chung, T., & Langenbucher, J. W. (2008). How should we revise diagnostic criteria for substance use disorders in the DSM-V? *Journal of Abnormal Psychology*, 117(3), 561–575.

McCaul, M. E., Svikis, D. S., & Moore, R. D. (2001). Predictors of outpatient treatment retention: Patient versus substance use characteristics. *Drug and Alcohol Dependence*, 62, 9–17.

McConnaughy, E. A., Prochaska, J. O., & Velicer, W. F. (1983). Stages of change in psychotherapy: Measurement and sample profiles. *Psychotherapy: Theory, Research & Practice*, 20(3), 368–375.

McCusker, C. G. (2001). Cognitive biases and addiction: An evolution in theory and method. *Addiction*, 96(1), 47–56.

McCusker, C. G., & Gettings, B. (1997). Automaticity of cognitive biases in addictive behaviours: Further evidence with gamblers. *British Journal of Clinical Psychology*, 36(4), 543–554.

McLellan, A. T., Kushner H., Metzger, D., Peters, R., Smith, I., & Grissom, G., (1992). The fifth edition of the Addiction Severity Index. *Journal of Substance Abuse Treatment, 9*(3), 199–213.

McLellan, A. T., Lewis, D. C., O'Brien, C. P., & Kleber, H. D. (2000). Drug dependence, a chronic medical illness: Implications for treatment, insurance and outcome evaluation. *Journal of the American Medical Association, 28*(13), 1689–1695.

Miele, G., Carpenter, K., Cockerham, M., Trautman, K., Blaine, J., & Hasin, D. (2000). Substance Dependence Severity Scale (SDSS): Reliability and validity of a clinician-administered interview for DSM-IV substance use disorders. *Drug and Alcohol Dependence, 59*(1), 63–75. doi:10.1016/S0376-8716(99)00111-8

Miller, W. R., & Tonigan, J. S. (1996). Assessing drinkers' motivations for change: The Stages of Change Readiness and Treatment Eagerness Scale (SOCRATES). *Psychology of Addictive Behaviors, 10*(2), 81–89.

Millon, T., & Meagher, S. E., (2004). The Millon Clinical Multiaxial Inventory-III (MCMI-III). In M. J. Hilsenroth & D. L. Segal (Eds.), *Comprehensive handbook of psychological assessment, Vol. 2: Personality assessment* (pp. 108–121). Hoboken, NJ: John Wiley & Sons.

Monti, P. M., Kadden, R. M., Rohsenhow, D. J., Cooney, N. L., & Abrams, D. B. (2002). *Treating alcohol dependence: A coping skills training guide* (2nd ed.). New York, NY: Guilford Press.

Muthen, B. (2006). Should substance use disorders be considered as categorical or dimensional? *Addiction, 101*(1), 6–16.

National Institutes for Drug Abuse (NIDA). (2005). *Drug abuse and addiction: One of America's most challenging public health problems.* Retrieved from http://archives.drugabuse.gov/about/welcome/aboutdrugabuse/magnitude/

Newcomb, M. D., & Richardson, M. A. (1995). In M. Hersen & R. T. Ammerman (Eds.), *Advanced abnormal child psychology* (pp. 411–431). Hillsdale, NJ: Erlbaum.

Nilsson, K. W., Sjöberg, R. L., Wargelius, H., Leppert, J., Lindström, L., & Oreland L. (2007). The monoamine oxidase A (MAO-A) gene, family function and maltreatment as predictors of destructive behaviour during male adolescent alcohol consumption. *Addiction, 102,* 389–398.

Nilsson, K. W., Wargelius, H., Sjöberg, R. L., Leppert, J., & Oreland L. (2008). The MAO-A gene, platelet MAO-B activity and psychosocial environment in adolescent female alcohol related problem behaviour. *Drug and Alcohol Dependence, 93,* 51–62.

Niv, N., Pham, R., & Hser, Y. (2009). Racial and ethnic differences in substance abuse service needs, utilization, and outcomes in California. *Psychiatric Services, 60*(10), 1350–1356.

Oei, T. P. S., & Morawska, A. (2004). A cognitive model of binge drinking: The influence of alcohol expectancies and drinking refusal self-efficacy. *Addictive Behaviors, 29,* 159–179.

Office of Applied Studies (2009). *Results from the 2008 survey on drug use and health: National findings.* Rockville, MD: Substance Abuse and Mental Health Services Administration, Department of Health and Human Services.

Office of National Drug Control Policy (ONDCP). (2004). *The economic costs of drug abuse in the United States, 1992–2002.* Washington, DC: Executive Office of the President (Publication No. 207303).

Perron, B. E., Mowbray, O. P., Glass, J. E., Delva, J., Vaughn, M. G., & Howad, M. O. (2009). Differences in service utilization and barriers among Blacks, Hispanics, and Whites with drug use disorders. *Substance Abuse Treatment, Prevention, and Policy,* doi:10.1186/1747-597X-4-3

Petry, N. M., & Casarella, T. (1999). Excessive discounting of delayed rewards in substance abusers with gambling problems. *Drug and Alcohol Dependence, 56,* 25–32.

Piazza, P. V., Deminiere, J. M., Le Moal, M., & Simon, H. (1989). Factors that predict individual vulnerability to amphetamine self-administration. *Science, 245,* 1511–1513.

Piazza, P. V., Deminiere, J. M., Le Moal, M., & Simon, H. (1990). Stress- and pharmacologically-induced behavioral sensitization increases vulnerability to acquisition of amphetamine self-administration. *Brain Research, 514*(1), 22–26.

Piazza, P. V., Derouche, V., Rouge-Pont, F., & Le Moal, M. (1998). Behavioral and biological factors associated with individual vulnerability to psychostimulant abuse. *NIDA Research Monographs, 169*, 105–133.

Piazza, P. V., & Le Moal, M. L. (1996). Pathophysiological basis of vulnerability to drug abuse: Role of an interaction between stress, glucocorticoids, and dopaminergic neurons. *Annual Review of Pharmacology and Toxicology, 36*, 359–378.

Piazza, P. V., Maccari, S., Deminiere, J. M., Le Moal, M., Mormede, P., & Simon, H. (1991). Corticosterone levels determine individual vulnerability to amphetamine self-administration. *Proceedings of the National Academy of Sciences of the United States of America, 88*(6), 2088–2092.

Piazza, P. V., Marinelli, M., Rougé-Pont, F., Deroche, V., Maccari, S., Simon, H., & Le Moal, M. (1996). Stress, glucocorticoids, and mesencephalic dopaminergic neurons: A pathophysiological chain determining vulnerability to psychostimulant abuse. *NIDA Research Monograph, 163*, 277–299.

Pickens, R., & Fletcher, B. (1991). Overview of treatment issues. In R. Pickens, C. Leukefeld, & C. Schuster (Eds.), *Improving drug abuse treatment* (pp. 1–19). National Institute on Drug Abuse (NIDA) Research Monograph No. 106 Rockville, MD: NIDA.

Prasad, B., Sorg, B., Ulibarri, C., & Kalivas, P. (1995). Sensitization to stress and psychostimulants: Involvement of dopamine transmission versus the HPA axis. *Annals of the New York Academy of Science, 771*, 617–625.

Prendergast, M., Podus, D., Finney, J., Greenwell, L., & Roll, J. (2006). Contingency management for treatment of substance use disorders: a meta-analysis. *Addiction, 101*(11), 1546–1560.

Preston, K. L., Silverman, K., Schuster, C., & Charles, R. (2002). Assessment of cocaine use with quantitative urinalysis and estimation of new uses. *Addiction, 92*(6), 717–727.

Quinn, E. P., Brandon, T. H., & Copeland, A. L. (1996). Is task persistence related to smoking and substance abuse? The application of learned industriousness theory to addictive behaviors. *Experimental & Clinical Psychopharmacology, 4*, 186–190.

Rebach, H. (1992). Alcohol and drug use among ethnic minorities. In J. Trimble, C. Bolek, & S. Niemcryk (Eds.), *Ethnic and multicultural drug abuse: Perspective on current research* (pp. 23–57). New York, NY: Haworth Press.

Regier, D. A., Farmer, M. E., Rae, D. S., Myers, J. K., Kramer, M., Robins, L. N., . . . Locke, B. Z. (1993). One-month prevalence of mental disorders in the United States and sociodemographic characteristics: The Epidemiologic Catchment Area program. *Acta Psychiatrica Scandinavica, 88*, 35–47.

Robins, L., Helzer, J., Croughan, J., & Ratcliff, K. (1981). National Institute of Mental Health diagnostic interview schedule: Its history, characteristics, and validity. *Archives of General Psychiatry, 38*(4), 381–389.

Robinson, T. E., & Berridge, K. C. (1993). The neural basis of drug craving: An incentive-sensitization theory of addiction. *Brain Research Reviews, 18*(3), 247–291.

Robinson, T. E., & Berridge, K. C. (2001). Incentive-sensitization and addiction. *Addiction, 96*, 103–114.

Rohde, P., Lewinsohn, P. M., Kahler, C. W., Seeley, J. R., & Brown, R. A. (2001). Natural course of alcohol use disorders from adolescence to young adulthood. *Journal of the American Academy of Child & Adolescent Psychiatry, 40*(1), 83–90.

Rollnick, S., Heather, N., Gold, R., & Hall, W. (1992). Development of a short "readiness to change" questionnaire for use in brief, opportunistic interventions among excessive drinkers. *British Journal of Addiction, 87*(5), 743–754.

Saccone, S. F., Hinrichs, A. L., Saccone, N. L., Chase, G. A., Konvicka, K., Madden, P. A. F., . . . Bierut, L. J. (2007). Cholinergic nicotinic receptor genes implicated in a nicotine dependence association study targeting 348 candidate genes with 3713 SNPs. *Human Molecular Genetics*, *16*(1), 36–49.

Saitz, R., Larson, M. J., LaBelle, C., Richardson, J., & Samet, J. H. (2008). The case for chronic disease management for addiction. *Journal of Addiction Medicine*, *2*(2), 55–65.

Samochowiec, J., Kucharska-Mazur, J., Grzywacz, A., Jablonski, M., Rommelspacher, H., Samochowiec, A., . . . Pelka-Wysiecka, J. (2006). Family-based and case-control study of DRD2, DAT, 5HTT, COMT genes polymorphisms in alcohol dependence. *Neuroscience Letters*, *410*(1), 1–5.

Saunders, J. (2006). Substance dependence and non-dependence in the *Diagnostic and Statistical Manual of Mental Disorders* (DSM) and *International Classification of Diseases* (ICD): Can identical conceptualization be achieved? *Addiction*, *101*(1), 48–58.

Saunders, J. B., Aasland, O. G., & Babor T. F. (1993). Development of the Alcohol Use Disorders Identification Test (AUDIT): WHO collaborative project on early detection of persons with harmful alcohol consumption: II. *Addiction*, *88*(6), 791–804.

Schmidt, L. A., & Mulia, N. (2009). Racial and ethnic disparities in AOD treatment. Robert Wood Johnson Foundation's Substance Abuse Policy Research Program. Retrieved July 15, 2010 from http://saprp.org/knowledgeassets/knowledge_detail.cfm?KAID=11

Simpson, D. D., Joe, G. W., & Brown, B. S. (1997). Treatment retention and follow-up outcomes in the drug abuse treatment outcome study (DATOS). *Psychology of Addictive Behaviors*, *11*(4), 294–307.

Simpson, D. D., Joe, G. W., Rowan-Szal, G. R., & Greener, J. (1997). Drug abuse treatment process components that improve retention. *Journal of Substance Abuse Treatment*, *14*(6), 565–572.

Sinha, R. (2008). Chronic stress, drug use, and vulnerability to addiction. *Annals of the New York Academy of Sciences*, *1141*, 105–130.

Skinner, H. A. (1982). The drug abuse screening test. *Addictive Behaviors*, *7*(4), 363–371.

Soyka, M., Preuss, U. W., Hesselbrock, V., Zill, P., Koller, G., & Bondy, B. (2008). GABA-A2 receptor subunit gene (GABRA2) polymorphisms and risk for alcohol dependence. *Journal of Psychiatric Research*, *42*(3), 184–191.

Stacey, A., & Wiers, R. (2010). Implicit cognition and addiction: A tool for explaining paradoxical behavior. *Annual Review of Clinical Psychology*, *6*, 551–575.

Stuart, G. L., Moore, T. M., & Kahler, C. W. (2003). Substance abuse and relationship violence among men court-referred to batterers' intervention programs. *Substance Abuse*, *24*(2), 107–122.

Substance Abuse and Mental Health Services Administration (SAMHSA), Center for Substance Abuse Treatment. (1994). *Simple screening instruments for outreach for alcohol and other drug abuse and infectious diseases: Treatment improvement protocol (TIP) series 11.* (DHHS Publication No. SMA 94-2094). Rockville, MD: Author.

Substance Abuse and Mental Health Services Administration (SAMHSA), Office of Applied Studies. (2007). *Results from the 2006 national survey on drug use and health: National findings.* (NSDUH Series H-32, DHHS Publication No. SMA 07-4293). Rockville, MD: Author.

Substance Abuse and Mental Health Services Administration (SAMHSA), Office of Applied Studies. (2009a). *Results from the 2008 national survey on drug use and health: National findings.* (NSDUH Series H-36, HHS Publication No. SMA 09-4434). Rockville, MD: Author.

Substance Abuse and Mental Health Services Administration (SAMHSA), Office of Applied Studies. (2009b). *Treatment Episode Data Set (TEDS) Highlights—2007 national admissions to substance abuse treatment services*. OAS Series #S-45, HHS Publication No. (SMA) 09-4360, Rockville, MD: Author.

Swan, G. E., Carmelli, D., & Cardon, L. R. (1997). Heavy consumption of cigarettes, alcohol and coffee in male twins. *Journal of Studies on Alcohol, 58*, 182–190.

Tarter, R. (1991). The Drug Use Screening Inventory: Its applications in the evaluation and treatment of alcohol and other drug abuse. *Alcohol Health and Research World, 15*, 65.

Tarter, R. E., Vanyukov, M., Kirisci, L., Reynolds, M., & Clark, D. B. (2006). Predictors of marijuana use in adolescents before and after licit drug use: Examination of the gateway hypothesis. *American Journal of Psychiatry, 163*, 2134–2140.

Thierry, A. M., Tassin, J. P., Blanc, G., & Glowinski, J. (1976). Selective activation of the mesocortical dopamine system by stress. *Nature 263*, 242–244.

Thomasson, H. R., Edenberg, H. J., Crabb, D. W., Mai, X. L., Jerome, R. E., Li, T.-K., . . . Yin, S. J. (1991). Alcohol and aldehyde dehydrogenase genotypes and alcoholism in Chinese men. *American Journal of Human Genetics, 48*(4), 677–681.

Thorgeirsson, T. E., Gudbjartsson, D. F., Surakka, I., Vink, J. M., Amin, N., Geller, F., . . . Stefansson, K. (2010). Sequence variants at CHRNB3-CHRNA6 and CYP2A6 affect smoking behavior. *Nature Genetics, 42*, 448–453.

Tobacco and Genetics Consortium. (2010). Genome-wide meta-analyses identify multiple loci associated with smoking behavior. *Nature Genetics, 42*, 366–368.

Tonigan, J. S., & Miller, W. R. (2002). The inventory of drug use consequences (InDUC): Test-retest stability and sensitivity to detect change. *Psychologically Addictive Behavior, 16*(2), 165–168.

True, W. R., Xian, H., Scherrer, J. F., Madden, P. A. F., Bucholz, K. K., Heath, A. C., . . . Tsuang, M. (1999). Common genetic vulnerability for nicotine and alcohol dependence in men. *Archives of General Psychiatry, 56*, 655–661.

Trull, T. J., Sher, K. J., Minks-Brown, C., Durbin, J., & Burr, R. (2000). Borderline personality disorder and substance use disorders: A review and integration. *Clinical Psychology Review, 20*, 235–253.

Tsuang, M. T., Lyons, M. J., Meyer, J. M., Doyle, T., Eisen, S. A., Goldberg J., . . . Eaves, L. (1998). Co-occurrence of abuse of different drugs in men: The role of drug-specific and shared vulnerabilities. *Archives of General Psychiatry, 55*, 967–972.

Tuchman, E. (2010). Women and addiction: The importance of gender issues in substance abuse research. *Journal of Addictive Diseases, 29*(2), 127–138.

Uhl, G. R., Drgon, T., Johnson, C., & Liu, Q. R. (2009). Addiction genetics and pleiotropic effects of common haplotypes that make polygenic contributions to vulnerability to substance dependence. *Journal of Neurogenetics, 23*(3), 272–282.

Van Etten, M. L., Higgins, S. T., Budney, A. J., & Badger, G. J. (1998). Comparison of the frequency and enjoyability of pleasant events in cocaine abusers vs. non-abusers using a standardized behavioral inventory. *Addiction, 93*(11), 1669–1680.

Volkow, N. D., Fowler, J. S., & Wang, G. J. (2002). Role of dopamine in drug reinforcement and addiction in humans: Results from imaging studies. *Behavioral Pharmacology, 13*, 355–366.

Wang, J. C., Grucza, R., Cruchaga, C., Hinrichs, A. L., Bertelsen, S., Budde, J. P., . . . Goate, A. M. (2009). Genetic variation in the CHRNA5 gene affects mRNA levels and is associated with risk for alcohol dependence. *Molecular Psychiatry, 14*(5), 501–510.

Weed, N. C., Butcher, J. N., & McKenna, T. (1992) New measures for assessing alcohol and drug abuse with the MMPI-2: The APS and AAS. *Journal of Personality Assessment, 58*(2), 389–404.

Weiss, R. B., Baker, T. B., Cannon, D. S., von Niederhausern, A., Dunn, D. M., Matsunami, N., . . . Leppert, M. F. (2008). A candidate gene approach identifies the CHRNA5-A3-B4 region as a risk factor for age-dependent nicotine addiction. *PLoS Genetics, 4*(7): e1000125. doi: 10.1371/journal.pgen.1000125

Wells, K., Klap, R., Koike, A., & Sherbourne, C. (2001). Ethnic disparities in unmet need for alcoholism, drug abuse, and mental health care. *American Journal of Psychiatry, 158,* 2027–2032.

Westerberg, V. S., Tonigan, J. S., & Miller, W. R. (1998). Reliability of Form 90D: An instrument for quantifying drug use. *Substance Abuse, 19,* 179–189.

Westermeyer, J., & Boedicker, A. E. (2000). Course, severity, and treatment of substance abuse among women verses men. *American Journal of Drug and Alcohol Abuse, 26*(4), 523–535.

Winters, K. C., & Lee, C. S. (2008). Likelihood of developing an alcohol and cannibis use disorder during youth: Association with recent use and age. *Drug and Alcohol Dependence, 92,* 239–247.

Wise, R. A. (1980). The dopamine synapse and the notion of "pleasure centers" in the brain. *Trends in Neuroscience, 3*(4), 91–95.

Wise, R. A. (1996). Neurobiology of addiction. *Current Opinions in Neurobiology, 6*(2), 243–251.

Wise, R. A. (2002). Brain reward circuitry. *Neuron, 36*(2), 229–240.

Wolff, K. (2006). Biological markers of drug use. *Psychiatry, 5*(12), 439–441.

Wolff, P. H. (1972). Ethnic differences in alcohol sensitivity. *Science, 175*(20), 449–450.

World Health Organization (WHO). (1994). *International Classification of Diseases and related health.* Geneva, Switzerland: Author.

Young, R. M., Lawford, B. R., Nutting, A., & Noble, E. P. (2004). Advances in molecular genetics and the prevention and treatment of substance misuse: Implications of association studies of the A1 allele of the D2 dopamine receptor gene. *Addictive Behavior, 29*(7), 1275–1294.

# CHAPTER 8

# Schizophrenia

DENNIS R. COMBS, KIM T. MUESER, and MARISELA M. GUTIERREZ

## INTRODUCTION

Schizophrenia is the most debilitating and costly of all adult psychiatric illnesses. Despite the recent trend toward community-oriented treatment, about 25% of all psychiatric hospital beds are occupied by persons with schizophrenia. The costs of treating schizophrenia are significant in terms of both financial and personal costs. It was estimated that the fiscal cost of schizophrenia in the United States was $62.7 billion in 2002 (Wu et al., 2005) and $6.85 billion in Canada in 2004 (Goeree et al., 2005). About one-third (roughly 22.7 billion) of the U.S. dollars spent on schizophrenia is directed to the treatment and medical needs of this population. Despite the economic costs, the impact on the person's social and occupational functioning over a lifetime may be even more devastating (Knapp, Mangalore, & Simon, 2004). In fact, the largest indirect cost associated with schizophrenia is the loss of productivity over the lifetime. The burden of schizophrenia places the disorder as one of the top 10 most disabling conditions in the world in terms of illness-adjusted life years (Mueser & McGurk, 2004; Murray & Lopez, 1996). Even when persons with schizophrenia receive optimal treatments, many continue to experience substantial impairments throughout most of their lives.

Since schizophrenia was first described more than 100 years ago, the nature of the disorder has been hotly debated, and public misconceptions about it have been commonplace. In recent years, there has been a growing consensus among clinicians and researchers to more rigorously define the psychopathology and diagnostic features of this disorder. Once referred to as a "wastebasket diagnosis," the term *schizophrenia* is now used to describe a specific clinical syndrome. Current arguments about the disorder have focused on the validity of the diagnostic category of schizophrenia, and alternative models argue that it is more beneficial to focus on psychotic symptoms (e.g., paranoia, hallucinations, and delusions) (Bentall, Jackson, & Pilgrim, 1988). Nonetheless, an understanding of the core clinical features of schizophrenia is necessary for diagnosis and treatment planning. After many years of struggling to improve the long-term course of schizophrenia, there is now abundant evidence that combined pharmacological and psychosocial interventions can have a major impact on improving functioning. This chapter provides an up-to-date review of schizophrenia, with a particular focus on the psychopathology of the illness and its impact on other domains of functioning.

## DESCRIPTION OF THE DISORDER

Schizophrenia is characterized by impairments in social functioning, including difficulty establishing and maintaining interpersonal relationships, problems working or fulfilling other instrumental roles (e.g., student, homemaker, employee), and difficulties caring for oneself (e.g., poor grooming and hygiene). These problems in daily living, in the absence of significant impairment in intellectual functioning, are the most distinguishing characteristics of schizophrenia and are a necessary criterion for its diagnosis according to most diagnostic systems (e.g., American Psychiatric Association [APA], 2000). Consequently, many individuals with the illness depend on others to meet their daily living needs. For example, estimates suggest that between 25% and 60% of persons with schizophrenia live with relatives, and an even higher percentage rely on relatives for caregiving (Goldman, 1982; Torrey, 2001). Time spent providing support and care for a person with schizophrenia can be substantial (with reports as high as 6 to 9 hours per day for some families; Magliano et al., 1998). It appears that the emotional and physical burden on caregivers is found across cultures (Breitborde, Lopez, Chang, Kopelowicz, & Zarate, 2009; Huang, Hung, Sun, Lin, & Chen, 2009; Zahid & Ohaeri, 2010). Individuals without family support typically rely on mental health, residential, and case management services to get their basic needs met. In the worst-case scenario, persons with schizophrenia who have insufficient contact with relatives and who fall between the cracks of the social service delivery system end up in jail (Torrey et al., 1992) or become homeless, with between 10% and 20% of homeless persons having schizophrenia (Susser, Stuening, & Conover, 1989).

In addition to the problems of daily living that characterize schizophrenia, individuals with the illness experience a range of different symptoms. The most common symptoms include positive symptoms (e.g., hallucinations, delusions, disorganization), negative symptoms (e.g., social withdrawal, apathy, anhedonia, poverty of speech), cognitive impairments (e.g., memory difficulties, planning ability, abstract thinking), and problems with mood (e.g., depression, anxiety, anger). The specific nature of these symptoms is described in greater detail in the following section titled "Clinical Picture." The symptoms of schizophrenia appear to account for some, but not all, of the problems in social functioning (Glynn, 1998).

The various impairments associated with schizophrenia tend to be long term, punctuated by fluctuations in severity (i.e., relapse) over time. For this reason, schizophrenia has a broad impact on the family, and individuals are often impeded from pursuing personal life goals. Despite the severity of the disorder, advances in the treatment of schizophrenia provide solid hope for improving the outcome.

## CLINICAL PICTURE

Most studies on the dimensions of schizophrenia agree on at least three major groups of symptoms (Liddle, 1987; Mueser, Curran, & McHugo, 1997; Van Der Does,

Dingemans, Linszen, Nugter, & Scholte, 1993), including positive symptoms, negative symptoms, and cognitive impairments. Positive symptoms refer to thoughts, sensory experiences, and behaviors that are present in persons with the disorder but are ordinarily absent in persons without the illness. Common examples of positive symptoms include hallucinations (e.g., hearing voices, seeing visions), delusions (e.g., believing that people are persecuting the person), and bizarre, disorganized behavior (e.g., maintaining a peculiar posture for no apparent reason, wearing multiple layers of clothes). Persecutory delusions (i.e., belief that some entity, group, or person has clear ongoing or future intentions to harm the person) are the most common type of delusion found in schizophrenia (Appelbaum, Robbins, & Roth, 1999; as reviewed in Bentall et al., 2001). About 75% of persons with schizophrenia report hallucinations (Cutting, 1995). Auditory hallucinations are the most common form and are frequently derogatory, negative, or abusive, although some can be benevolent, comforting, and kind (Chadwick & Birchwood, 1995; Copolov, Mackinnon, & Trauer, 2004; Cutting, 1995). Less frequent, but more specific to schizophrenia, are voices that keep a running commentary on the person's actions or consist of two or more voices having a conversation. Auditory hallucinations can range from inaudible sounds (buzzing sounds, noises, muffled speech) or clearly perceived voices of either gender and can occur intermittently or on a continuous basis. It has been assumed that visual hallucinations were infrequent in schizophrenia and were more reflective of a medical condition (prevalence of 10% to 15% in schizophrenia), but recent evidence suggests that these symptoms are more common than initially believed, especially in more severe forms of the disorder (Bracha, Wolkowitz, Lohr, Karson, & Bigelow, 1989; Mueser, Bellack, & Brady, 1990).

Negative symptoms, conversely, refer to the absence or diminution of cognitions, feelings, or behaviors that are ordinarily present in persons without the illness. Common negative symptoms include blunted or flattened affect (e.g., diminished facial expressiveness), poverty of speech (i.e., diminished verbal communication), anhedonia (i.e., inability to experience pleasure), apathy, psychomotor retardation (e.g., slow rate of speech), and physical inertia. The positive symptoms of schizophrenia tend to fluctuate over the course of the disorder and are often in remission between episodes of the illness. In addition, positive symptoms tend to be responsive to the effects of antipsychotic medication (Kane & Marder, 1993). In contrast, negative symptoms and cognitive impairments tend to be stable over time and are less responsive to antipsychotic medications (Greden & Tandon, 1991). However, there is some evidence that atypical antipsychotic medications, such as clozapine, risperidone, and olanzapine, have a beneficial impact on negative symptoms and cognitive functioning (Breier, 2005; Green et al., 1997; Tollefson & Sanger, 1997; Wahlbeck, Cheine, Essali, & Adams, 1999).

Aside from the core symptoms of schizophrenia, many persons with schizophrenia experience negative emotions (e.g., depression, anxiety, and anger) as a consequence of their illness (Freeman & Garety, 2003). Depression is quite common (estimated comorbidity rate of 45%; Leff, Tress, & Edwards, 1988) among people with schizophrenia and has been associated with poor outcomes (e.g., increased hospital use, lower employment rates) and suicidal tendencies (Sands & Harrow, 1999). Depressive symptoms can occur during all phases of the illness (prepsychotic, prodrome, acute, and remission), but they tend to attenuate as the active psychotic symptoms remit (Birchwood, Iqbal, Chadwick, & Trower, 2000). In addition, it was generally estimated that approximately 10% of the persons with this illness die from suicide (Bromet, Naz, Fochtmann, Carlson, & Tanenberg-Karant, 2005; Drake, Gates, Whitaker, & Cotton, 1985; Jobe & Harrow, 2005; Roy, 1986), but recent research examining suicide rates has lowered this estimate to around 4.0% to 5.6% (Inskip, Harris, & Barraclough, 1998; Palmer, Pankratz, & Bostwick, 2005). Risk of suicide is greater in the presence of mood symptoms and substance use, if previous suicide attempts were made, during the initial onset of the disorder (Hawton, Sutton, Haw, Sinclair, & Deeks, 2005; first psychotic episode; rates 11% to 26%, as reviewed in Malla & Payne, 2005), and in time immediately preceding and following inpatient hospitalization (Qin & Nordentoft, 2005). Anxiety is also common in schizophrenia (estimated comorbidity rate of 43%) and is a frequent precursor to psychosis (Argyle, 1990; Braga, Mendlowicz, Marrocos, & Figueria, 2005; Cosoff & Hafner, 1998; Penn, Hope, Spaulding, & Kucera, 1994; Tien & Eaton, 1992). Specifically, there is evidence for the role of anxiety in both the formation and maintenance of persecutory delusions (threat beliefs) as well as hallucinations (Freeman et al., 2002; Freeman & Garety, 2003). Finally, anger, hostility, and social avoidance may also be present, especially when the person is paranoid (Bartels, Drake, Wallach, & Freeman, 1991; Freeman, Garety, & Kuipers, 2001; Gay & Combs, 2005). Interestingly, as paranoia increases, so does the tendency to perceive ambiguous interactions in a negative, threatening manner (Combs & Penn, 2004; Freeman et al., 2005).

In addition to the positive symptoms and negative emotions commonly present in schizophrenia, individuals with this diagnosis often have comorbid substance use disorders. Epidemiological surveys have repeatedly found that persons with psychiatric disorders are at increased risk for alcohol and drug abuse (Mueser et al., 1990; Mueser, Yarnold, & Bellack, 1992). This risk is highest for persons with the most severe psychiatric disorders, including schizophrenia and bipolar disorder. For example, individuals with schizophrenia are more than four times as likely to have a substance abuse disorder than are individuals in the general population (Regier et al., 1990). In general, approximately 50% of all persons with schizophrenia have a lifetime history of substance use disorder, and 25% to 35% have a recent history of such a disorder (Mueser, Bennett, & Kushner, 1995). The presence of comorbid substance-use disorders in schizophrenia has consistently been found to be associated with a worse course of the illness, including increased vulnerability to relapses and hospitalizations, housing instability and homelessness, violence, economic family burden, and treatment noncompliance (Drake & Brunette, 1998). For these reasons, the recognition and treatment of substance use disorders in persons with schizophrenia is crucial to the overall management of the illness.

Another important clinical feature of schizophrenia is lack of insight and compliance with treatment (Amador & Gorman, 1998; Amador, Strauss, Yale, & Gorman, 1991). Many individuals with schizophrenia have little or no insight into the fact that they have a psychiatric illness or even that they have any problems at all. This denial of illness can lead to noncompliance with recommended treatments, such as psychotropic medications and psychosocial therapies (McEvoy et al., 1989). Furthermore, fostering insight into the illness is a difficult and often impossible task with these persons.

Noncompliance with treatment is a related problem, but it can also occur because of the severe negativity often present in the illness, independent of poor insight. Problems with paranoia and distrust may contribute to noncompliance. Some persons may believe medications or treatment providers are dangerous to them. Furthermore, the side effects of some medications (e.g., sedation, dry mouth, motor side effects), particularly the conventional antipsychotics, are unpleasant and can also lead to noncompliance. Medication noncompliance increases the risk of relapse, and between 50% to 75% of individuals who discontinue their medication will relapse within 1 year. Therefore, treatment compliance is a major concern to clinical treatment providers (Buchanan, 1992). It has been argued that the newer atypical antipsychotics may lead to higher rates of compliance owing to better side effect profiles (Breier, 2005). However, a recent study of 63,000 individuals with schizophrenia in the Veteran's Affairs medical system found widespread noncompliance (compliance measured in terms of filling needed prescriptions) across both conventional and atypical antipsychotics (Valenstein et al., 2004). Strategies for enhancing compliance involve helping the person become a more active participant in treatment, identifying personal goals of treatment that have high relevance for that individual, and helping the person integrate strategies for taking medications into the daily routines (Azrin & Teichner, 1998; Corrigan, Liberman, & Engle, 1990; Kemp, Hayward, Applewhaite, Everitt, & David, 1996; Kemp, Kirov, Everitt, Hayward, & David, 1998).

People with schizophrenia are sometimes assumed to be violent or otherwise dangerous. Indeed, rates of violence have been found to be relatively higher in people with schizophrenia and other severe mental illnesses compared to the general population (Hodgins, Mednick, Brennan, Schulsinger, & Engberg, 1996; Swanson, Holzer, Ganju, & Jono, 1990). However, a more accurate comparison may be to examine the rates of violence between schizophrenia with other psychiatric disorders. Data from the MacArthur Risk Assessment Study found that the actual rates of violence for persons with schizophrenia was 8% for the first 20 weeks following discharge (most violent events occur in the first 20 weeks) and 14% over the course of a 1-year period (Monahan et al., 2001). In comparison, the rates of violence for persons with schizophrenia were actually lower than those for persons with depression and bipolar disorder for the same time period. A prospective study of violent behaviors in females with severe mental illness reported a prevalence rate of 17% over a 2-year period (Dean et al., 2006). Rates vary widely depending upon source of information (e.g., self-report vs. collateral reports), definition of violence, population studied (e.g., inpatients vs. outpatients), and where the research takes place (e.g., country). However, it should be emphasized that the majority of people with schizophrenia and other mental illnesses are not violent (Swanson, 1994). When violence does occur, it is often associated with substance abuse (Steadman et al., 1998) or the combination of substance abuse and medication noncompliance (Swartz et al., 1998). Other factors such as psychopathy (Nolan, Volavka, Mohr, & Czobor, 1999) or antisocial personality disorder (Hodgins & Côté, 1993, 1996) also have been implicated. Finally, targets of violence tend to be family members or friends rather than strangers, which is not unexpected given that most persons with schizophrenia rely heavily on family members for support (Steadman et al., 1998).

Although there is an increased rate of violence in schizophrenia, people with schizophrenia are much more likely to be the victims of violence and violent crime (Hiday, Swartz, Swanson, Borum, & Wagner, 1999). About 34% to 53% of individuals with severe mental illness report childhood sexual or physical abuse (Greenfield, Strakowski, Tohen, Batson, & Kolbrener, 1994; Jacobson & Herald, 1990; Rose, Peabody, & Stratigeas, 1991; Ross, Anderson, & Clark, 1994), and 43% to 81% report some type of victimization over their lives (Carmen, Rieker, & Mills, 1984; Hutchings & Dutton, 1993; Jacobson, 1989; Jacobson & Richardson, 1987; Lipschitz et al., 1996). Two recent surveys of a large number of people with severe mental illness found high rates of severe physical or sexual assault in the past year (Goodman et al., 2001; Silver, Arseneault, Langley, Caspi, & Moffitt, 2005). These numbers are striking compared to estimates of the general population, in which 0.3% of women and 3.5% of men reported assault in the past year (Tjaden & Thoennes, 1998). Studies of the prevalence of interpersonal trauma in women with severe mental illness indicate especially high vulnerability to victimization, with rates ranging as high as 77% to 97% for episodically homeless women (Davies-Netzley, Hurlburt, & Hough, 1996; Goodman, Dutton, & Harris, 1995).

The prevalence of posttraumatic stress disorder (PTSD) among people with schizophrenia and other severe mental illnesses in various samples has ranged from 29% to 43% (Cascardi, Mueser, DeGirolomo, & Murrin, 1996; Craine, Henson, Colliver, & MacLean, 1988; Mueser et al., 1998; Mueser et al., 2004; Switzer et al., 1999), but has been as low as 3.8% (Braga, Mendlowicz, Marrocos, & Figueira, 2005). These current rates of PTSD are far in excess of the lifetime prevalence of PTSD in the general population, with estimates ranging between 8% and 12% (Breslau, Davis, Andreski, & Peterson, 1991; Kessler, Sonnega, Bromet, Hughes, & Nelson, 1995; Resnick, Kilpatrick, Dansky, Saunders, & Best, 1993). Thus, interpersonal violence is so common in the serious mental illness population that it must sadly be considered a normative experience (Goodman, Dutton, & Harris, 1997).

## DIAGNOSTIC CONSIDERATIONS

The diagnostic criteria for schizophrenia are fairly similar across a variety of different diagnostic systems. In general, the diagnostic criteria specify some degree of social impairment, combined with positive and negative symptoms lasting a significant duration (e.g., 6 months or more). The diagnostic criteria for schizophrenia according to *DSM-IV-TR* (APA, 2000) are summarized in Table 8.1.

The diagnosis of schizophrenia requires a clinical interview with the patient, a thorough review of all available records, and standard medical evaluations to rule out the possible role of organic factors (e.g., CAT scan to rule out a brain tumor). In addition, because many persons with schizophrenia are poor historians or may not provide accurate accounts of their behavior, information from significant others, such as family members, is often critical to establish a diagnosis of schizophrenia. The use of family and other informants is especially important in the assessment of prodromal and prepsychotic states. Because of the wide variety of symptoms characteristic of schizophrenia and variations in interviewing style and format across different clinical interviewers, the use of structured clinical interviews, such as the Structured Clinical Interview for *DSM-IV* (SCID; First, Spitzer, Gibbon, &

**Table 8.1**

*DSM-IV-TR* Criteria for the Diagnosis of Schizophrenia

A. Presence of at least two of the following characteristic symptoms in the active phase for at least 1 month (unless the symptoms are successfully treated):

1. Delusions

2. Hallucinations

3. Disorganized speech (e.g., frequent derailment or incoherence)

4. Grossly disorganized or catatonic behavior

5. Negative symptoms (i.e., affect flattening, alogia, or avolition)

*Note:* Only one of these symptoms is required if delusions are bizarre or hallucinations consist of a voice keeping up a running commentary on the person's behavior or thoughts, or two or more voices conversing with each other.

B. *Social/occupational dysfunction:* For a significant proportion of the time from the onset of the disturbance, one or more areas of functioning, such as work, interpersonal relations, or self-care, is markedly below the level achieved prior to the onset (or, when the onset is in childhood or adolescence, failure to achieve expected level of interpersonal, academic, or occupational achievement).

C. *Duration:* Continuous signs of the disturbance persist for at least 6 months. This 6-month period must include at least 1 month of symptoms that meet criterion A (i.e., active-phase symptoms) and may include periods of prodromal or residual symptoms. During these prodromal or residual periods, the signs of the disturbance may be manifested by only negative symptoms or by two or more symptoms listed in criterion A present in an attenuated form (e.g., odd beliefs, unusual perceptual experiences).

D. *Schizoaffective and mood disorders exclusion:* Schizoaffective disorder and mood disorder with psychotic features have been ruled out because either (1) no major depressive or manic episodes have occurred concurrently with the active-phase symptoms, or (2) if mood episodes have occurred during active-phase symptoms, their total duration has been brief relative to the duration of the active and residual periods.

E. *Substance/general medical condition exclusion:* The disturbance is not owing to the direct effects of a substance (e.g., drugs of abuse, medication) or a general medical condition.

Williams, 1996) can greatly enhance the reliability and validity of psychiatric diagnosis. Structured clinical interviews have two main advantages over more open clinical interviews. First, structured interviews provide definitions of the key symptoms, agreed upon by experts, thus making explicit the specific symptoms required for diagnosis. Second, by conducting the interview in a standardized format, including a specific sequence of asking questions, variations in interviewing style are minimized, thus enhancing the comparability of diagnostic assessments across different clinicians. The second point is especially crucial considering that most research studies of schizophrenia employ structured interviews to establish diagnoses. It is important that interviewers are properly trained and interrater reliability with a criterion-trained or expert rater is established before the use of structured interviews are initiated. If the findings of clinical research studies are to be generalized into clinical practice, efforts must be taken to ensure the comparability of the patient populations and the assessment techniques employed.

The symptoms of schizophrenia overlap with many other psychiatric disorders. Establishing a diagnosis of schizophrenia requires particularly close consideration of four other overlapping disorders: substance use disorders, affective disorders, schizoaffective disorder, and delusional disorder. We discuss issues related to each of these disorders and the diagnosis of schizophrenia in the following sections.

SUBSTANCE USE DISORDERS

Substance use disorder, such as alcohol dependence or drug abuse, can either be a differential diagnosis to schizophrenia or a comorbid disorder (i.e., the individual can have both schizophrenia and a substance use disorder). With respect to differential diagnosis, substance use disorders can interfere with a clinician's ability to diagnosis schizophrenia and can lead to misdiagnosis if the substance abuse is covert, denied, or not reported accurately (Corty, Lehman, & Myers, 1993; Kranzler et al., 1995). Psychoactive substances, such as alcohol, marijuana, cocaine, and amphetamine, can produce symptoms that mimic those found in schizophrenia, such as hallucinations, delusions, and social withdrawal (Schuckit, 1995). In those cases in which the substance is involved in the etiology of psychosis, a diagnosis of substance-induced psychotic disorder would be appropriate. Further complicating matters, the use of these substances can exacerbate psychotic symptoms and in many cases lead to a return of acute psychosis. Because the diagnosis of schizophrenia requires the presence of specific symptoms in the absence of identifiable organic factors, schizophrenia can only be diagnosed in persons with a history of substance use disorder by examining the individual's functioning during sustained periods of abstinence from drugs or alcohol. When such periods of abstinence can be identified, a reliable diagnosis of schizophrenia can be made. However, persons with schizophrenia who have a long history of substance abuse, with few or no periods of abstinence, are more difficult to assess. For example, in a sample of 461 individuals admitted to a psychiatric hospital, a psychiatric diagnosis could not be confirmed nor ruled out because of history of substance abuse in 71 persons (15%; Lehman, Myers, Dixon, & Johnson, 1994).

Substance use disorder is the most common comorbid diagnosis for persons with schizophrenia. Because substance abuse can worsen the course and outcome of schizophrenia, recognition and treatment of substance abuse in schizophrenia is a critical goal of treatment. The diagnosis of substance abuse in schizophrenia is complicated by several factors. Substance abuse, as in the general population, is often denied because of social and legal sanctions (Galletly, Field, & Prior, 1993; Stone, Greenstein, Gamble, & McLellan, 1993), a problem that may be worsened in this population because of a fear of losing benefits. Denial of problems associated with substance abuse, a core feature of primary substance use disorders, may be further heightened by psychotic distortions and cognitive impairments present in schizophrenia. Furthermore, the criteria used to establish a substance use disorder in the general population are less useful for diagnosis in schizophrenia (Corse, Hirschinger, & Zanis, 1995). For example, the common consequences of substance abuse in the general population of loss of employment, driving under the influence of alcohol, and relationship problems are less often experienced by people with schizophrenia, who are often unemployed, do not own cars, and have limited interpersonal relationships. Rather, persons with schizophrenia more often experience increased symptoms and rehospitalizations, legal problems, and housing instability because of substance abuse (Drake & Brunette, 1998).

Individuals with schizophrenia tend to use smaller quantities of drugs and alcohol (Cohen & Klein, 1970; Crowley, Chesluk, Dilts, & Hart, 1974; Lehman et al., 1994) and rarely develop the full physical dependence syndrome that is often present in persons with a primary substance use disorder (Corse et al., 1995; Drake et al., 1990; Test, Wallisch, Allness, & Ripp, 1989) or show other physical consequences of alcohol such as stigmata (Mueser et al., 1999). Even very low scores on instruments developed for the primary substance use disorder population, such as the Addiction Severity Inventory, may be indicative of substance use disorder in persons with schizophrenia (Appleby, Dyson, Altman, & Luchins, 1997; Corse et al., 1995; Lehman, Myers, Dixon, & Johnson, 1996). Because of the difficulties in using existing measures of substance abuse for people with schizophrenia and other severe mental illnesses, a screening tool was developed specifically for these populations: the Dartmouth Assessment of Lifestyle Instrument (DALI; Rosenberg et al., 1998). The DALI is an 18-item questionnaire that has high classification accuracy for current substance use disorders of alcohol, cannabis, and cocaine for people with severe mental illness.

Despite the difficulties involved in assessing comorbid substance abuse in persons with schizophrenia, recent developments in this area indicate that if appropriate steps are taken, reliable diagnoses can be made (Drake, Rosenberg, & Mueser, 1996; Maisto, Carey, Carey, Gordon, & Gleason, 2000). The most critical recommendations for diagnosing substance abuse in schizophrenia include (1) maintain a high index of suspicion of current substance abuse, especially if a person has a past history of substance abuse; (2) use multiple assessment techniques, including self-report instruments, interviews, clinician reports, reports of significant others, and biological assays for the presence of substances, which are routinely collected on admission to inpatient treatment; and (3) be alert to signs that may be subtle indicators of the presence of a substance use disorder, such as unexplained symptom relapses, familial conflict, money management problems, and sudden depression or suicidality. Once a substance use disorder has been diagnosed, integrated treatment that addresses both the schizophrenia and the substance use disorder (co-occurring disorders) is necessary to achieve a favorable clinical outcome (Drake, Mercer-McFadden, Mueser, McHugo, & Bond, 1998).

## Mood Disorders

Schizophrenia overlaps more prominently with the major mood disorders than any other psychiatric disorder. The differential diagnosis of schizophrenia from mood disorders is critical, because the disorders respond to different treatments, particularly pharmacological interventions. Two different mood disorders can be especially difficult to distinguish from schizophrenia: bipolar disorder and major depression. The differential diagnosis of these disorders from schizophrenia is complicated by the fact that mood symptoms are frequently present in all phases of schizophrenia (prodrome, acute, and remission), and psychotic symptoms (e.g., hallucinations, delusions) may be present in persons with severe mood disorders (APA, 2000; Pope & Lipinski, 1978). The crux of making a differential diagnosis between schizophrenia and a major mood disorder is determining whether psychotic symptoms are present in the absence of mood symptoms. If there is strong evidence that psychotic symptoms persist even when the person is not experiencing symptoms of mania or depression, then the diagnosis is either schizophrenia or the closely related disorder of schizoaffective disorder (discussed in the following section). If, on the other hand, symptoms of psychosis are present only during a mood episode, but disappear when the person's mood is stable, then the appropriate diagnosis is either major depression or bipolar disorder. For example, it is common for people with bipolar disorder to have hallucinations and delusions during the height of a manic episode, but for these psychotic symptoms to remit when the person's mood becomes stable again. Similarly, persons with major depression often experience hallucinations or delusions during a severe depressive episode, which subside as their mood improves. If the patient experiences chronic mood problems, meeting criteria for manic, depressive, or mixed episodes, it may be difficult or impossible to establish a diagnosis of schizophrenia, because there are no sustained periods of stable mood.

SCHIZOAFFECTIVE DISORDER

Schizoaffective disorder is a diagnostic entity that overlaps with both the mood disorders and schizophrenia (APA, 2000). Three conditions must be met for a person to be diagnosed with schizoaffective disorder: (1) the person must meet criteria for a mood episode (i.e., a 2-week period in which manic, depressive, or mixed mood features are present to a significant degree); (2) the person must also meet criteria for the symptoms of schizophrenia during a period when that person is not experiencing a mood syndrome (e.g., hallucinations or delusions in the absence of manic or depressive symptoms); and (3) the mood episode must be present for a substantial period of the person's psychiatric illness (i.e., a person who experiences brief, transient mood states and who is chronically psychotic and has other long-standing impairments would be diagnosed with schizophrenia, rather than schizoaffective disorder); see Table 8.2.

Schizoaffective disorder and major mood disorder are frequently mistaken for one another because it is incorrectly assumed that schizoaffective disorder simply requires the presence of both psychotic and mood symptoms at the same time. Rather, as described in the preceding section, if psychotic symptoms always coincide with mood symptoms, the person has a mood disorder, whereas if

**Table 8.2**
*DSM-IV-TR* Criteria for the Diagnosis of Schizoaffective Disorder

A. An uninterrupted period of illness during which at some time there is either a major depressive episode (which must include depressed mood) or manic episode concurrent with symptoms that meet criterion A of schizophrenia.

B. During the same period of illness, there have been delusions or hallucinations for at least 2 weeks in the absence of prominent mood symptoms.

C. Symptoms meeting the criteria for a mood disorder are present for a substantial portion of the total duration of the active and residual periods of the illness.

D. The disturbance is not owing to the direct effects of a substance (e.g., drugs of abuse, medication) or a general medical condition.

psychotic symptoms are present in the absence of a mood episode, the person meets criteria for either schizoaffective disorder or schizophrenia. Thus, schizoaffective disorder requires longitudinal information about the relationship between mood and psychosis to make a diagnosis. This information is often obtained from the individual but is subject to memory and self-reporting biases (poor insight, or lack of awareness of mood states). The distinction between schizophrenia and schizoaffective disorder can be more difficult to make, because judgment must be made as to whether the affective symptoms have been present for a substantial part of the person's illness. Decision rules for determining the extent to which mood symptoms must be present to diagnose a schizoaffective disorder have not been clearly established.

Although the differential diagnosis between schizophrenia and schizoaffective disorder is difficult to make, the clinical implications of this distinction are less important than between the mood disorders and either schizophrenia or schizoaffective disorder. Research on family history and treatment response suggest that schizophrenia and schizoaffective disorder are similar disorders and respond to the same interventions (Kramer, et al., 1989; Levinson & Levitt, 1987; Levinson & Mowry, 1991; Mattes & Nayak, 1984). In fact, many studies of schizophrenia routinely include persons with schizoaffective disorder and find few differences. Therefore, the information provided in this chapter on schizophrenia also pertains to schizoaffective disorder, and the differential diagnosis between the two disorders is not of major importance from a clinical perspective.

DELUSIONAL DISORDER

Delusions can be found in schizophrenia, schizoaffective disorder, severe mood disorders, organic conditions, and delusional disorder and are a nonspecific symptom in many cases. Persons with delusional disorder develop fixed, nonbizarre delusions and do not show the other symptoms of schizophrenia (auditory hallucinations, disorganization, negative symptoms). The delusion may lead to problems with others, but in general the person has good social, educational, and occupational functioning. Tactile and olfactory hallucinations can be present and will usually be incorporated into the delusional belief. Delusional disorder is more common in females (3:1 female to male ratio) and has a later age of onset (mean age of 40; Evans, Paulsen, Harris, Heaton, & Jeste, 1996; Manschreck, 1996; Yamada, Nakajima, & Noguchi, 1998). Delusional disorder accounts for 1% to 4% of all inpatient admissions and is relatively rare in clinical practice (Kendler, 1982). The differential diagnosis between delusional disorder and schizophrenia is based on the presence of nonbizarre delusions and absence of other symptoms of schizophrenia. Nonbizarre delusions are based on events or situations that could occur in real life but are highly improbable and lack supporting evidence (Sedler, 1995). Examples of nonbizarre delusions include being watched, followed, spied upon, harassed, loved, or poisoned. In contrast, bizarre delusions involve mechanisms not believed to exist in an individual's culture, such as beliefs of thought insertion, control, and broadcasting. In reality, the distinction between nonbizarre and bizarre beliefs is highly subjective and difficult (Junginger, Barker, & Coe, 1992; Sammons, 2005). Many persons with delusions will provide convincing arguments that their beliefs are true, and a decision on whether the belief is plausible must often be made with very little corroborating evidence (Flaum, Arndt, & Andreasen, 1991; Jones, 1999). An examination of the person's history, premorbid and current functioning, and symptom profile can be useful in distinguishing delusional disorder from schizophrenia. A structured interview, such as the SCID, can be useful in assessing delusional beliefs along with the other symptoms of schizophrenia.

## EPIDEMIOLOGY

It is estimated that approximately 2.2 million persons in the United States have schizophrenia at any given time (Narrow, Rae, Robins, & Regier, 2002; Torrey, 2001). It is believed that 51 million persons have schizophrenia worldwide. The annual incidence of new cases of schizophrenia ranges from 8 to 40 per 100,000 persons (Jablensky, 2000; McGrath et al., 2004, as cited in Tandon, Keshavan, & Nasrallah, 2008a). Point prevalence for any given time period ranges between 3% to 7% per 1,000 persons, with some estimates as high as 10% (Goldner, Hsu, Waraich, & Somers, 2002; Jablensky, 2000; Saha, Chant, Welham, & McGrath, 2005). The lifetime risk for developing schizophrenia appears to be about 0.7% on average (see Saha et al., 2005, as reviewed in Tandon et al., 2008b).

In general, the prevalence of schizophrenia is believed to be remarkably stable across a wide range of different populations and cultures (Crow, 2008; Saha, Welham, Chant, & McGrath, 2006; Tandon et al., 2008a). There has been little difference in the rates of schizophrenia according to gender, race, religion, or level of industrialization (Jablensky, 1999). Similar incidence rates and symptom patterns were found across 10 countries in a study sponsored by the World Health Organization (WHO; Jablensky et al., 1992). However, a more recent review of prevalence studies showed considerable heterogeneity in the rates of schizophrenia among different countries that may be partly owing to variations in diagnostic criteria (Goldner et al., 2002). Furthermore, there is evidence that schizophrenia is more heavily concentrated in urban areas of industrialized countries and, in fact, persons from developing countries may have a better prognosis and course of illness (Jablensky, 2000; Jablensky et al., 2000; Peen & Dekker, 1997; Takei, Sham, O'Callaghan, Glover, & Murray, 1995; Torrey, Bowler, & Clark, 1997). This increased risk appears to be related not only to the likelihood of people with schizophrenia drifting to urban areas, but to being born in urban areas as well, which suggests that "urbanicity" has an effect on schizophrenia (Torrey et al., 1997).

Because schizophrenia frequently has an onset during early adulthood when important educational, social, and occupational milestones are often achieved, persons with the illness are especially affected in that they are less likely to marry or remain married, particularly males (Eaton, 1975; Munk-Jørgensen, 1987), and they are less likely to complete higher levels of education (Kessler, Foster, Saunders, & Stang, 1995) and have problems in occupational performance (Marwaha & Johnson, 2004). In terms of employment rates, only 14% to 20% of persons with schizophrenia hold competitive employment despite reporting a desire to work (Mueser, Salyers, & Mueser, 2001; Rosenheck et al., 2006). It has long been known that there is an association between poverty and schizophrenia, with people belonging to lower socioeconomic classes more likely to develop the disorder (Hollingshead & Redlich, 1958; Salokangas, 1978).

Historically, two theories have been advanced to account for this association. The social drift hypothesis postulates that the debilitating effects of schizophrenia on capacity to work result in a lowering of socioeconomic means, and hence poverty (Aro, Aro, & Keskimäki, 1995). The environmental stress hypothesis proposes that the high levels of stress associated with poverty precipitate schizophrenia in some individuals who would not otherwise develop the illness (Bruce, Takeuchi, & Leaf, 1991). Recently, attention has been aimed at different ethnic and migratory groups, such as second-generation Afro-Caribbeans living in the United Kingdom, who show higher incidence rates of schizophrenia (Boydell et al., 2001; Cantor-Graae & Selten, 2005). It is believed that being a minority in a potentially hostile social environment where racism and discrimination are present may lead to increased stress and potentially higher rates of symptoms (Clark, Anderson, Clark, & Williams, 1999; Combs et al., 2006). Both of these explanations may be partly true, and longitudinal research on changes in socioeconomic class status (SES) and schizophrenia provide conflicting results. For example, Fox (1990) reanalyzed data from several longitudinal studies and found that after controlling for initial levels of socioeconomic class, downward drift was not evident. Furthermore, Samele et al. (2001) found that a downward drift in occupational functioning over a 2-year period was not linked to illness course or prognosis. However, Dohrenwend et al. (1992) did find evidence for social drift, even after controlling for socioeconomic class. Also, it is possible that SES level may interact with gender, as males from higher SES homes show poorer clinical outcomes (Parrott & Lewine, 2005). Thus, more work is needed to sort out the relationships between SES and schizophrenia.

## PSYCHOLOGICAL AND BIOLOGICAL ASSESSMENT

Diagnostic assessment provides important information about the potential utility of interventions for schizophrenia (e.g., antipsychotic medications). However, assessment does not end with a diagnosis. It must be supplemented with additional psychological and biological assessments.

### PSYCHOLOGICAL ASSESSMENT

A wide range of different psychological formulations have been proposed for understanding schizophrenia. For example, there are extensive writings about psychodynamic and psychoanalytic interpretations of schizophrenia. Although this work has made contributions to the further development of these theories, these formulations do not appear to have improved the ability of clinicians to understand persons with this disorder or led to more effective interventions (Mueser & Berenbaum, 1990). Therefore, the use of projective assessment techniques based on psychodynamic concepts of personality, such as the Rorschach and Thematic Apperception Test, is not considered here.

One of the primary areas to assess is severity of psychotic symptoms, because treatment progression is mainly judged by a reduction of symptoms (Andreasen et al., 2005). This includes an assessment of positive and negative symptoms and general psychopathology due to the high comorbidity with anxiety and mood disorders. Measures such as the Positive and Negative Syndrome Scale (PANNS; Kay, Fiszbein, & Opler, 1987), the Brief Psychiatric Rating Scale (BPRS; Overall & Gorham, 1962), and the Psychotic Rating Scale (PSYRATS; Haddock et al., 1999) have been frequently used in schizophrenia research and have good psychometric properties. Scales specific to positive (Scale for the Assessment of Positive Symptoms; Andreasen & Olsen, 1982) and negative symptoms (Scale for the Assessment of Negative Symptoms; Andreasen, 1982) can be used for a more in-depth and detailed assessment of these areas. There are also self-report and interview-based measures of insight available as well (see Amador & David, 2004). Commonly, these symptom measures are used in conjunction with a structured diagnostic interview in the assessment of schizophrenia.

As noted earlier, schizophrenia is often associated with a variety of neuropsychological impairments. Core areas to assess in terms of cognitive functioning are verbal and visual learning and memory, working memory, attention/vigilance, abstract reasoning/executive functioning, speed of information processing, and social cognition. These areas are part of the National Institute of Mental Health—Measurement and Treatment Research to Improve Cognition in Schizophrenia cognitive battery (NIMH-MATRICS; Green et al., 2004). Having information on cognitive functioning in these areas will aid in examining the beneficial effects of antipsychotic medication on cognition. It also is important to consider the generalization of these impairments to different situations (i.e., transfer of training problems). Thus, assessment needs to be conducted in the environments in which the skills are to be used in order to provide a more ecologically valid assessment. For example, successful employment interventions incorporate assessment on the job on an ongoing basis rather than extensive prevocational testing batteries that do not generalize to real-world settings (Bond, 1998; Drake & Becker, 1996). Similarly, when assessing independent living skills, it is important that these be measured directly in the living environment of the patient or in simulated tests (Wallace, Liberman, Tauber, & Wallace, 2000).

A great deal of research has been done on the functional assessment of social skills in people with schizophrenia. Social skills refer to the individual behavioral components, such as eye contact, voice loudness, and the specific choice of words, which in combination are necessary for effective communication with others (Mueser & Bellack, 1998). As previously described, poor social competence is a hallmark of schizophrenia. Although not all problems in social functioning are the consequence of poor social skill, many social impairments appear to be related to skill deficits (Bellack, Morrison, Wixted, & Mueser, 1990b).

Several different strategies can be used to assess social competence. Clinical interviews can be a good starting place for identifying broad areas of social dysfunction. These interviews can focus on answering questions such as: Is the patient lonely? Would the patient like more or closer friends? Is the patient able to stand up for his or her rights? and Is the patient able to get others to respond positively to him or her? Patient interviews are most informative when combined with interviews with significant others, such as family members and clinicians who are familiar with the nature and quality of the patient's social interactions, as well as naturalistic observations of the patient's social interactions. The combination of these sources of information is useful for identifying specific areas in need of social skills training.

One strategy for assessing social skills that yields the most specific type of information is role-play assessments. Role plays usually involve brief simulated social interactions between the person and a confederate taking the role of an interactive partner. During role plays, individuals are instructed to act as though the situation were actually happening in real life. Role plays can be as brief as 15 to 30 seconds to assess skill areas such as initiating conversations, or they can be as long as several minutes to assess skills such as problem-solving ability. Role plays can be audiotaped or videotaped and later rated on specific dimensions of social skill. Alternatively, role playing can be embedded into the procedures of social skills training, in which persons with schizophrenia practice targeted social skills in role plays, followed by positive and corrective feedback and additional role-play rehearsal. In the latter instance, the assessment of social skills is integrated into the training of new skills, rather than preceding skills training.

A commonly used assessment measure for social skill is the Maryland Assessment of Social Competence (MASC; Bellack & Thomas-Lohrman, 2003). The MASC is a structured role-play assessment that consists of four 3-minute interactions. Following each role play, ratings on verbal and nonverbal skill and effectiveness are made, thus allowing the clinician to examine social skill across different situations and contexts.

Recent research on the reliability and validity of social skill assessments, and the benefits of social skills training for persons with schizophrenia, has demonstrated the utility of the social skills construct. Persons with schizophrenia have consistently been found to have worse social skills than persons with other psychiatric disorders (Bellack, Morrison, Wixted, & Mueser, 1990b; Bellack, Mueser, Wade, Sayers, & Morrison, 1992; Mueser, Bellack, Douglas, & Wade, 1991b), and approximately half of the persons with schizophrenia demonstrate stable deficits in basic social skills compared to the nonpsychiatric population (Mueser, Bellack, Douglas, & Morrison, 1991a). In the absence of skills training, social skills tend to be stable over periods of time as long as 6 months to 1 year (Mueser et al., 1991a). Social skill in persons with schizophrenia is moderately correlated with level of premorbid social functioning, current role functioning, and quality of life (Mueser, Bellack, Morrison, & Wixted, 1990). Social skills tend to be associated with negative symptoms (Appelo et al., 1992; Bellack et al., 1990b; Lysaker, Bell, Zito, & Bioty, 1995; Penn, Mueser, Spaulding, Hope, & Reed, 1995), but not with positive symptoms (Mueser, Douglas, Bellack, & Morrison, 1991; Penn et al., 1995). Furthermore, role-play assessments of social skill are also strongly related with social skill in more natural contexts, such as interactions with significant others (Bellack, Morrison, Mueser, Wade, & Sayers, 1990a). Persons with schizophrenia show a wide range of impairments in social skills, including areas such as conversational skill, conflict resolution, assertiveness, and problem solving (Bellack, Sayers, Mueser, & Bennett, 1994; Douglas & Mueser, 1990). Thus, ample research demonstrates that social skills are impaired with persons with schizophrenia, tend to be stable over time in the absence of intervention, and are strongly related to other measures of social functioning. Furthermore, there is growing evidence supporting the efficacy of social skills training for schizophrenia (Bellack, 2004; Heinssen, Liberman, & Kopelowicz, 2000).

The broadest area of psychological assessment is community functioning, and improvement in this area is linked to the concept of recovery (see "Course and Prognosis"). Persons with schizophrenia show not only poor social skills but also poor adaptive functioning in the community. Ideally, treatment programs should aim to improve the person's quality of life and satisfaction. Independent living skills, quality of life, and social functioning may need to be assessed in order to examine the person's current functional capacity level. The Social Functioning Scale (Birchwood, Smith, Cochrane, Wetton, & Copstake, 1990) and UCSD Performance-Based Skills Assessment (UPSA; Patterson, Goldman, McKibbin, Hughs, & Jeste, 2001) are widely used measures of adaptive and community functioning.

## FAMILY ASSESSMENT

The assessment of family functioning has high relevance in schizophrenia for two reasons. First, Expressed Emotion (EE), which refers to the presence of hostile, critical, or emotionally overinvolved attitudes and behaviors on the part of close relatives of persons with schizophrenia, is an important stressor that can increase the chance of relapse and rehospitalization (Butzlaff & Hooley, 1998). Second, caring for an individual with a psychiatric illness can lead to a significant burden on relatives (Webb et al., 1998), which ultimately can threaten their ability to continue to provide emotional and material support to the individual. Family burden has its own negative consequences and can be related to EE and the ability of the family to care for the person with schizophrenia. Thus, a thorough assessment of these family factors is important in order to identify targets for family intervention. Several specific methods can be used to assess a negative emotional climate in the family and the burden of the illness. Interviews with individual family members, including the person with schizophrenia, as well as with the entire family, coupled with observation of more naturalistic family interactions, can provide invaluable information about the quality of family functioning. The vast majority of research on family EE has employed a semistructured interview with individual family members, the Camberwell Family Interview (Leff & Vaughn, 1985). This instrument is primarily a research instrument, and it is too time-consuming to be used in clinical practice. Alternatives to the Camberwell Family Interview have been proposed (e.g., Magaña et al., 1986), although none has gained widespread acceptance yet. Several studies have successfully employed the Family Environment Scale (Moos & Moos, 1981), a self-report instrument completed by family members, which has been found to be related to symptoms and outcome in patients with schizophrenia (Halford, Schweitzer, & Varghese, 1991).

Many instruments have been developed for the assessment of family burden. The most comprehensive instrument, with well-established psychometric properties, is the Family Experiences Interview Schedule (Tessler & Gamache, 1995). This measure provides information regarding both dimensions of subjective burden (e.g., emotional strain) and objective burden (e.g., economic impact), as well as specific areas in which the burden is most severe (e.g., household tasks). The importance of evaluating family functioning is supported by research demonstrating clinical benefits of family intervention for schizophrenia. Numerous controlled studies of family treatment for schizophrenia have shown that family intervention has a significant impact on reducing relapse rates and rehospitalizations (Dixon et al., (2001; Pitschel-Walz, Leucht, Bäuml, Kissling, & Engel, 2001). The critical elements shared across different models of family intervention are education about schizophrenia, the provision of ongoing support, improved communication skills, and a focus on helping all family members improve the quality of their lives (Dixon & Lehman, 1995; Glynn, 1992; Lam, 1991).

## BIOLOGICAL ASSESSMENT

Biological assessments are becoming more common in the clinical management of schizophrenia. For diagnosis, biological assessments may be used to rule out possible organic factors such as a tumor, stroke, or covert substance abuse. Urine and blood specimens are sometimes obtained in order to evaluate the presence of substance abuse. Similarly, blood samples may be obtained in order to determine whether the person is compliant with the prescribed antipsychotic medication, although the specific level of medication in the blood has not been conclusively linked to clinical response. Blood levels may also be monitored to ensure appropriate levels of mood stabilizers (e.g., lithium). Some newer medications (e.g., Clozaril) also require ongoing blood tests to detect very rare, but potentially lethal, blood disorders (Alvir, Lieberman, & Safferman, 1995; Young, Bowers, & Mazure, 1998). Client participation in this type of medical monitoring is crucial when using these medications.

Biological measures are sometimes used to characterize impairments in brain functioning associated with schizophrenia, although these assessments are expensive and do not have clear implications for treatment of the illness at this time. In addition, many clinicians do not have access to imaging technology, and its use has been specific to research settings. In terms of brain function and structure, computerized axial tomography (CAT) scans indicate that between one-half and two-thirds of all persons with schizophrenia display enlarged cerebral ventricles, particularly the lateral and third ventricles, which is indicative of cortical atrophy (Liddle, 1995). Magnetic resonance imaging (MRI) studies have found structural changes and a reduction in gray matter volumes in the prefrontal, superior temporal, amygdala, hippocampus, and thalamus (Lawrie & Abukmeil, 1998; Wright et al., 2000). These findings have also been found in first-episode and nonill relatives as well and may be a pathophysiological marker for the disorder (Fannon et al., 2000; McDonald et al., 2002). These gross structural impairments in brain functioning, such as enlarged ventricles, tend to be associated with a wide range of neuropsychological impairments and negative symptoms often present in schizophrenia (Andreasen, Flaum, Swayze, Tyrrell, & Arndt, 1990; Buchanan et al., 1993; Merriam, Kay, Opler, Kushner, & van Praag, 1990). In addition, positron emission tomography (PET) and single photon emission computerized tomography (SPECT) have shown reduced metabolism and blood flow in several of the prefrontal and temporal cortex and abnormal activation of the thalamus (Kindermann, Karimi, Symonds, Brown, & Jeste, 1997; Liddle, 1997; McClure, Keshavan, & Pettegrew, 1998; Miyamoto et al., 2003). Functional MRI (fMRI) studies have found less activation in the prefrontal cortex and anterior cingulate cortex during working memory tasks (Carter, MacDonald, Ross, & Stenger, 2001; Perlstein, Carter, Noll, & Cohen, 2001). Finally, diffuse tensor imaging methods, which assess the integrity of white matter pathways in the brain, have found problems in myelinated neurons in the prefrontal lobes specifically and in the connections between the frontal, temporal, and parietal lobes (Burns et al., 2003; Lim et al., 1998).

To date, most of the advances in the treatment of schizophrenia have been in psychopharmacology. Biological assessments are still not useful for diagnosing the illness or for guiding treatment. However, the clinical utility of biological assessment is likely to increase in the years to come as advances continue to be made in the understanding of the biological roots of schizophrenia.

## ETIOLOGICAL CONSIDERATIONS

### BEHAVIORAL GENETICS AND MOLECULAR GENETICS

The etiology of schizophrenia has been a topic of much debate over the past 100 years. Kraepelin (1919/1971) and Bleuler (1911/1950) clearly viewed the illness as having a biological origin. However, from the 1920s to the 1960s, alternative theories gained prominence, speculating that the disease was the result of disturbed family interactions (Bateson, Jackson, Haley, & Weakland, 1956). Psychogenic theories of the etiology of schizophrenia, positing that the illness was psychological in nature rather than biological, played a dominant role in shaping the attitudes and behavior of professionals toward persons with schizophrenia and their relatives (Fromm-Reichmann, 1950; Searles, 1965). These theories have not been supported empirically (Jacob, 1975; Waxler & Mishler, 1971). Moreover, in many cases, psychogenic theories fostered poor relationships between mental health professionals and relatives (Terkelsen, 1983), which have only begun to mend in recent years (Mueser & Glynn, 1999). For more than a century, clinicians have often noted that schizophrenia tends to "run in families." However, the clustering of schizophrenia in family members could reflect learned behavior that is passed on from one generation to the next, rather than predisposing biological factors.

In the 1950s and 1960s, two paradigms were developed for evaluating the genetic contributions to the illness. The first approach, the high-risk paradigm, involves examining the rate of schizophrenia in adopted-away or biological offspring of mothers with schizophrenia. If the rate of schizophrenia in children of biological parents with schizophrenia is higher than in the general population, then even in the absence of contact with those parents, a role for genetic factors in developing the illness is supported. The second approach, the monozygotic/dizygotic twin paradigm, involves comparing the concordance rate of schizophrenia in identical twins (monozygotic) compared to fraternal twins (dizygotic). Because monozygotic twins share the exact same gene pool, whereas dizygotic twins share only approximately half their genes, a higher concordance rate of schizophrenia among monozygotic twins than dizygotic twins, even reared in the same environment, would support a role for genetic factors in the etiology of schizophrenia.

Over the past 30 years, numerous studies employing either the high-risk or twin paradigm have been conducted examining the role of genetic factors in schizophrenia. There has been almost uniform agreement across studies indicating that the risk of developing schizophrenia in biological relatives of persons with schizophrenia is greater than in the general population, even in the absence of any contact between the relatives (Kendler & Diehl, 1993). Thus, support exists for the role of genetic factors in the etiology of at least some cases of schizophrenia. For example, the odds of developing schizophrenia if one parent has the disorder is 13% and rises to about 50% if both parents have the disorder, compared to only 1% risk in the general population (Gottesman, 1991, 2001; McGuffin, Owen, & Farmer, 1995). Similarly, the concordance rate of one identical twin developing schizophrenia if his or her co-twin also has schizophrenia is between 25% and 50%, compared to about 6% and 15% for fraternal twins (Cardno et al., 1999; Faraone & Tsuang, 1985; Torrey, 1992; Walker, Downey, & Caspi, 1991). It also appears that the risk of developing schizophrenia is greater in more severe types of schizophrenia (average 20% for disorgranized and catatonic types; see Gottesman & Shields, 1982).

The fact that identical twins do not have a 100% concordance rate of schizo-phrenia (heritability rates = 0.80 on average), as might be expected if the disorder were purely genetic, has raised intriguing questions about the etiology of schizo-phrenia. In a review of 40 studies on genetic risk, it was found that 80% of persons with psychotic symptoms do not have a single parent with the disorder, and 60% have a negative family history (Gottesman, 2001). It is likely that the development of schizophrenia results from an interaction between genetic and environmental factors. The results of a series of longitudinal studies support this case. Tienari (1991; Tienari et al., 1987, 2004) compared the likelihood of developing schizo-phrenia in three groups of children raised by adoptive families. Two groups of children had biological mothers with schizophrenia, and the third group had biological mothers with no psychiatric disorder. The researchers divided the adoptive families of the children into two broad groups based on the level of disturbance present in the family: healthy adoptive families and disturbed adop-tive families. Follow-up assessments were conducted to determine the presence of schizophrenia and other severe psychiatric disorders in the adopted children raised in all three groups. The researchers found that biological children of mothers with schizophrenia who were raised by adoptive families with high levels of disturbance were significantly more likely to develop schizophrenia or another psychotic disorder (46%) than either similarly vulnerable children raised in fami-lies with low levels of disturbance (5%) or children with no biological vulnerability raised in either disturbed (24%) or healthy (3%) adoptive families. This study raises the intriguing possibility that some cases of schizophrenia develop as a result of the interaction between biological vulnerability and environmental stress.

Although families do not cause schizophrenia, there are important interactions between the family and person with schizophrenia that deserve consideration. First, as previously mentioned, it has repeatedly been found that critical attitudes and high levels of emotional overinvolvement (Expressed Emotion [EE]) on the part of the relatives toward the individual with schizophrenia are strong predictors of the likelihood that persons with schizophrenia will relapse and be rehospitalized

(Butzlaff & Hooley, 1998). The importance of family factors is underscored by the fact that the severity of persons' psychiatric illness or their social skill impairments is not related to family EE (Mueser et al., 1993). Rather, family EE seems to act as a stressor, increasing the vulnerability of persons with schizophrenia to relapse.

A second important family consideration is the amount of burden on relatives caring for a mentally ill person. Family members of persons with schizophrenia typically experience a wide range of negative emotions related to coping with the illness, such as anxiety, depression, guilt, and anger (Hatfield & Lefley, 1987, 1993; Oldridge & Hughes, 1992). Burden is even associated with negative health consequences for relatives (Dyck, Short, & Vitaliano, 1999). Family burden may be related to levels of EE, ability to cope with the illness, and ultimately the ability of the family to successfully monitor and manage schizophrenia in a family member (Mueser & Glynn, 1999). Thus, EE and family burden are important areas for assessment and intervention. Finally, researchers have been interested in discovering genes and chromosomal areas involved in schizophrenia. Current research has focused on nine chromosomes (i.e., most important appear to be areas 8p and 22q) and seven candidate genes, which may be important in schizophrenia (see Harrison & Owen, 2003). In particular, researchers are interested in identifying genes found across family members with the disorder (linkage studies) or directly related to the underlying pathophysiology of schizophrenia (e.g., genes that affect neurotransmitter functioning such as dopamine, serotonin, or glutamate). This area of research has been hampered by the lack of independent replication of these genetic markers. The exact mechanism for genetic transmission of the disorder is unknown, but it appears that schizophrenia does not follow a Mendelian single gene pattern of inheritance. It is more likely that schizophrenia is a polygenetic condition or that it arises from an interaction of multiple genes, which increase the susceptibility to the disorder (Craddock, O' Donovan, & Owen, 2006; Miyamoto et al., 2003). Regardless, genes and gene-environment interactions are estimated to account for 80% of the risk for schizophrenia, according to a review of the literature (as reviewed in Tandon et al., 2008b).

## Neuroanatomy and Neurobiology

Although there is clear evidence that genetic factors can play a role in the development of schizophrenia, there is also a growing body of evidence pointing to the influence of other biological, nongenetic factors playing a critical role. For example, obstetric complications, maternal exposure to the influenza virus, and other environmental-based insults to the developing fetus (e.g., maternal starvation) are all associated with an increased risk of developing schizophrenia (Geddes & Lawrie, 1995; Kirch, 1993; Rodrigo, Lusiardo, Briggs, & Ulmer, 1991; Susser & Lin, 1992; Susser et al., 1996; Takei et al., 1996; Thomas et al., 2001; Torrey, Bowler, Rawlings, & Terrazas, 1993). Thus, there is a growing consensus that the etiology of schizophrenia may be heterogeneous, with genetic factors playing a role in the development of some cases and early environmental-based factors playing a role in the development of other cases. This heterogeneity may account for the fact that the genetic contribution to schizophrenia has consistently been found to be lower than the genetic contribution to bipolar disorder (Goodwin & Jamison, 1990). Other biological and physiological factors include alterations in brain chemistry and structure.

Pharmacological research has identified many neurochemical changes associated with schizophrenia. By far, the neurotransmitter most commonly implicated in the onset of schizophrenia is dopamine. The dopamine hypothesis proposes that alterations in levels of dopamine are responsible for the symptoms of schizophrenia. Originally, this hypothesis was based on findings that substances that increase dopamine (e.g., levadopa used to treat Parkinson's disease) increase psychotic symptoms, and substances that decrease dopamine reduce psychotic symptoms. Current versions of this hypothesis suggest that an overabundance of dopamine in certain limbic areas of the brain may be responsible for positive symptoms, whereas a lack of dopamine in cortical areas may be responsible for negative symptoms (Davis, Kahn, Ko, & Davidson, 1991; Moore, West, & Grace, 1999). Other neurochemicals also appear to be implicated in schizophrenia. In particular, serotonin may directly or indirectly (e.g., by mediating dopamine) affect symptoms of schizophrenia, because several of the newer antipsychotic medications impact serotonin levels (Lieberman et al., 1998). In addition, glutamate and GABA may be altered in schizophrenia (Pearlson, 2000).

As discussed in the section "Biological Assessment," abnormalities in several brain structures have also been identified. In particular, enlarged ventricles and decreased brain volume and blood flow to cortical areas have been associated with a wide range of cognitive impairments and negative symptoms of schizophrenia (Andreasen et al., 1990; Buchanan et al., 1993; Merriam et al., 1990).

LEARNING, MODELING, AND LIFE EVENTS

Although schizophrenia is broadly accepted to be a biologically based disorder and not a learned one, learning and modeling may play a role in the course, outcome, and symptom expression of the disorder. In terms of symptom expression, there is empirical support for the role of operant conditioning in delusions and hallucinations (e.g., hallucinations increase when reinforced). Furthermore, research has shown that psychotic behavior can be modified using differential reinforcement (i.e., attention for any other behavior besides the expression of delusional statements) or punishment principles (Schock, Clay & Cipani, 1998; Jimenez, Todman, Perez, Godoy, & Landon-Jimenez, 1996). However, these processes are probably more relevant for the maintenance of psychotic symptoms than for etiology. Haynes (1986) proposed a behavioral model of paranoia in which suspiciousness partially stems from the reinforcement of paranoid statements and parental modeling, but this theory has been largely untested. As described in the following section, the stress-vulnerability model of schizophrenia posits that coping skills mediate the noxious effects of stress on psychobiological vulnerability on symptoms and relapses (Liberman et al., 1986; Nuechterlein & Dawson, 1984). Coping skills, such as social skills for developing and maintaining close relationships with others and strategies for managing negative emotions and distorted thinking processes, can be acquired either naturalistically through access to good role models (e.g., family, friends) or through social learning-based programs, such as social skills training (Bellack, Mueser, Gingerich, & Agresta, 1997) or cognitive-behavior therapy (Chadwick & Birchwood, 1995; Fowler, Garety, & Kuipers, 1995). Thus, improving coping skills, as well as other life skills, through the systematic application of social learning methods is a common treatment goal in schizophrenia.

Although stressful life events alone are not the cause of schizophrenia, some theories hypothesize that life events may contribute to the development of the disorder and can play an important role in the course of schizophrenia. The stress-vulnerability model (Liberman et al., 1986; Zubin & Spring, 1977) assumes that symptom severity and related impairments of psychiatric disorders such as schizophrenia have a biological basis (psychobiological vulnerability) determined by a combination of genetic and early environmental factors. This vulnerability can be decreased by medications and worsened by substance use disorder. Stress, including discrete events such as traumas and exposure to ongoing conditions such as a hostile environment, can impinge on vulnerability, precipitating relapses and worse outcomes. Finally, coping resources, such as coping skills or the ability to obtain social support, can minimize the effects of stress on relapse and the need for acute care.

As described earlier, Expressed Emotion represents a stressful familial environment that may increase relapse and hospitalization in people with schizophrenia. In addition, in the "Clinical Picture" section, we discussed that people with schizophrenia are often the targets of violence and have frequently been exposed to physical and/or sexual assault. Exposure to traumatic events may lead to post-traumatic strees disorder (PTSD), a condition characterized by reliving the traumatic experience (e.g., nightmares, intrusive memories), avoidance of people, places, and things that remind the person of the event, and increased arousal symptoms (e.g., irritability, sleep problems). Exposure to trauma and the presence of PTSD are likely to worsen the course of schizophrenia and complicate treatment (Mueser, Rosenberg, Goodman, & Trumbetta, 2002). For example, research shows that both discrete stressors (e.g., life events) and exposure to a stressful environment can worsen psychotic disorders (Butzlaff & Hooley, 1998). PTSD is also associated with substance abuse (Chilcoat & Breslau, 1998), which, as described earlier, can have severe consequences for people with schizophrenia.

## COGNITIVE INFLUENCES

Cognitive impairments refer to difficulties in verbal and visual learning and memory, working memory, attention/vigilance, abstract reasoning/executive functioning (i.e., understanding a concept, planning, organizing), and speed of information processing (Green et al., 2004). These cognitive deficits have been observed in unmedicated, medicated, first-episode, remitted, and high-risk children prior to developing the disorder. Thus, cognitive impairments are so commonplace that they are now considered a core feature of schizophrenia (Palmer et al., 1997; Wilk et al., 2005). A recent meta-analysis of cognitive performance found that normal controls without a history of schizophrenia perform consistently better (about 1 standard deviation) than persons with schizophrenia on most cognitive tasks, which suggests that a generalized cognitive deficit is present (Heinrichs, 2005). These deficits also appear to be relatively stable over time and do not appear to reflect a progressive deterioration (Heaton et al., 2001). These cognitive impairments may interfere with the person's ability to focus for sustained periods on work or recreational pursuits, interact effectively with others, perform basic activities of daily living, or participate in conventional psychotherapeutic interventions (Bellack, Gold, & Buchanan, 1999; Brekke, Raine, Ansel, Lencz, & Bird, 1997; Green et al., 2000; Sevy & Davidson, 1995; Velligan et al., 1997). Cognitive impairments also result in difficulties with generalizing training or knowledge to other areas (i.e., transfer of training problems) (Mueser et al., 1991b; Smith, Hull, Romanelli, Fertuck, & Weiss, 1999). Thus, many rehabilitative efforts focus on teaching persons with schizophrenia directly in the environment in which skills will be used or involve specialized teaching methods, such as errorless learning procedures (Kern, Liberman, Kopelowicz, Mintz, & Green, 2002).

In addition to cognitive deficits, it has become apparent that impairments in social cognition (defined as the way people perceive, interpret, and understand social information) are also found in schizophrenia (Penn, Corrigan, Bentall, Racenstein, & Newman, 1997). Deficits in emotion and social cue perception, problems inferring the intentions and motivations of others (Theory of Mind), and impairments in social knowledge and schemata have all been found in schizophrenia (Brune, 2005; Corrigan & Penn, 2001; Edwards, Jackson, & Pattison, 2002). More specifically, persons with persecutory delusions exhibit an attributional style in which they tend to blame others rather than situations for negative events (e.g., personalizing attributional style; see Garety & Freeman, 1999). Deficits in social cognition appear to be independent from nonsocial cognition (e.g., memory, attention) in that they predict incremental variance in social functioning and social skill and may arise from distinct brain structures involved in social information processing (Penn, Combs, & Mohamed, 2001; Penn et al., 1997; Pinkham, Penn, Perkins, & Lieberman, 2003). The exact nature of the relationship between social cognition and cognitive functioning is unclear, but social cognition appears to be important in the social functioning of persons with schizophrenia (Green, Oliver, Crawley, Penn, & Silverstein, 2005).

## SEX AND RACIAL-ETHNIC CONSIDERATIONS

Several issues related to gender are important for understanding the psychopathology in the course of schizophrenia. As described in the section on course and prognosis, women tend to have a milder overall course and later onset of schizophrenia than do men. The net consequence of this is that, although similar numbers of men and women have schizophrenia, men are more likely to receive treatment for the disorder. In fact, most research on the treatment of schizophrenia is conducted on samples ranging from 60% to 100% male.

Because treatment studies usually sample persons with schizophrenia who are currently receiving treatment, often inpatient treatment, the efficacy of widely studied psychosocial interventions, such as social skills training and family therapy, has been less adequately demonstrated in women. For example, some research suggests that social skills training may be more helpful to men than to women (Mueser, Levine, Bellack, Douglas, & Brady, 1990; Schaub, Behrendt, Brenner, Mueser, & Liberman, 1998; Smith et al., 1997). There is a need for more research on the effects of treatments for women with schizophrenia. At the same time, further consideration needs to be given to the different needs of women with this illness.

For example, women with schizophrenia are much more likely than men to marry and have children. It is crucial, therefore, that psychosocial interventions be developed to address the relationship, family planning, and parenting needs of women with schizophrenia (Apfel & Handel, 1993; Brunette & Dean, 2002; Coverdale & Grunebaum, 1998).

Another issue related to gender in need of further consideration is exposure to trauma. As described earlier, people with schizophrenia are at risk for being the victims of violence. Although both men and women with schizophrenia report histories of abuse and assault, women report more sexual assault (Goodman et al., 2001; Mueser et al., 1998). Furthermore, in the general population, women are more likely to be abused than men, are more likely to sustain injuries, and are more likely to be economically dependent upon perpetrators of domestic violence. Thus, there is a particular need to recognize and address trauma in the lives of women with schizophrenia. Accurate detection of trauma is further complicated by the fact that most severely mentally ill persons who have been physically or sexually assaulted deny that they have been abused (Cascardi et al., 1996). The development of programs that address both the causes of domestic violence and their sequelae, especially for women with schizophrenia, is a priority in this area (Harris, 1996; Rosenberg et al., 2001).

Research on the relationships between race, ethnicity, and severe psychiatric disorders demonstrates that cultural factors are critical to understanding how persons with schizophrenia are perceived by others in their social milieu, as well as the course of the illness. Although the prevalence of schizophrenia is comparable across different cultures, several studies have shown that course of the illness is more benign in developing countries compared to industrialized nations (Lo & Lo, 1977; Murphy & Raman, 1971; Sartorius et al., 1986). Westermeyer (1989) has raised questions about the comparability of clinical samples in cross-cultural studies, but a consensus remains that the course of schizophrenia tends to be milder in non-industrialized countries (Jablensky, 1989).

A variety of different interpretations has been offered to account for the better prognosis of schizophrenia in some cultures (Lefley, 1990). It is possible that the strong stigma and social rejection that results from serious mental illness and poses an obstacle to the ability of persons with schizophrenia to cope effectively with their disorder and assimilate into society (Fink & Tasman, 1992) is less prominent in some cultures (Parra, 1985). Greater cultural, familial, and societal acceptance of the social deviations present in schizophrenia may enable these persons to live less stressful and more productive lives. This may be especially true for Hispanic families, who show less expressed emotion as compared to White families (Dorian, Garcia, Lopez, & Hernandez, 2008; Lopez et al., 2009). Hispanic families are typically characterized as more accepting and less blaming of persons with schizophrenia (Kymalainen & Weisman de Mamani, 2008). This is important given the link between EE and relapse and, in fact, lower rates of relapse have been found in minority families (Aguilera, Lopez, Breitborde, Kopelowicz, & Zarate, 2010). Cultures with a stronger degree of family ties, in particular, may be less vulnerable to the effects of mental illness (Lin & Kleinman, 1988). For example, Liberman (1994) has described how the strong functional ties of seriously mentally ill persons to their families and work foster the reintegration of persons with schizophrenia back into Chinese society following psychiatric hospitalization. In contrast, until recently, families of persons with schizophrenia in many Western societies were viewed by mental health professionals as either irrelevant, or worse, as causal agents in the development of the illness (Lefley, 1990; Mueser & Glynn, 1999), thus precluding them from a role in psychiatric rehabilitation. Furthermore, the use of other social supports may vary across different ethnic groups or cultures, such as the importance of the church to the African American community and its potential therapeutic benefits (Griffith, Young, & Smith, 1984; Lincoln & Mamiya, 1990).

Some have hypothesized that different cultural interpretations of the individual's role in society and of the causes of mental illness may interact to determine course and outcome. Estroff (1989) has suggested that the emphasis on the self in Western countries, compared to a more family or societally based identification, has an especially disabling effect on persons with schizophrenia, whose sense of self is often fragile or fragmented. Another important consideration is the availability of adaptive concepts for understanding mental illness. For example, *espiritismo* in Puerto Rican culture is a system of beliefs involving the interactions between the invisible spirit world and the visible world, in which spirits can attach themselves to persons (Comas-Díaz, 1981; Morales-Dorta, 1976). Spirits are hierarchically ordered in terms of their moral perfection, and the practice of *espiritismo* is guided by helping individuals who are spiritually ill to achieve higher levels of this perfection. Troubled persons are not identified as sick, nor are they blamed for their difficulties; in some cases, symptoms such as hallucinations may be interpreted favorably as signs that the person is advanced in his or her spiritual development, resulting in some prestige (Comas-Díaz, 1981). Thus, certain cultural interpretations of schizophrenia may promote more acceptance of persons who display the symptoms of schizophrenia, as well as avoiding the common assumption that these phenomenological experiences are the consequence of a chronic, unremitting condition.

Understanding different cultural beliefs, values, and social structures can have important implications for the diagnosis of schizophrenia. Religious practices and beliefs may complicate diagnosis. For example, high levels of religiosity have been found in people with schizophrenia (Brewerton, 1994). Without a clear understanding of the religious and cultural background, patients may be misdiagnosed (May, 1997). Ethnic groups may differ in their willingness to report symptoms, as illustrated by one study that reported that African American persons were less likely than Hispanics or non-Hispanic whites to report symptoms (Skilbeck, Acosta, Yamamoto, & Evans, 1984). Several studies have shown that ethnic differences in diagnosis vary as a function of both the client's and the interviewer's ethnicity (Baskin, Bluestone, & Nelson, 1981; Loring & Powell, 1988). Misdiagnosis of mood disorders as schizophrenia is the most common problem with the diagnosis of ethnic minorities in the United States (e.g., Jones, Gray, & Parsons, 1981, 1983). Other studies have found that African Americans are more likely than Whites to be inappropriately diagnosed with paranoid schizophrenia, which has been viewed as a clinician bias in the interpretation of mistrust (Adams, Dworkin, & Rosenberg, 1984; Combs, Penn, & Fenigstein, 2002; Combs et al., 2006; Whaley, 1997, 2001). Alternatively, this finding may also represent the effects of stress and poverty in the development of schizophrenia given the numbers of minorities who live in poverty (Bruce, Takeuchi, & Leaf, 1991; as discussed in "Epidemiology"). Knowledge of cultural norms appears critical to avoid the possible misinterpretation of culturally bound beliefs, experiences, and practices when arriving at a diagnosis.

Cultural differences are also critical in the treatment of schizophrenia, both with respect to service utilization and the nature of treatment provided. There is a growing body of information documenting that ethnic groups differ in their use of psychiatric services. Several studies have indicated that Hispanics and Asian Americans use fewer psychiatric services than non-Hispanic whites, whereas blacks use more emergency and inpatient services (Cheung & Snowden, 1990; Hough et al., 1987; Hu, Snowden, Jerrell, & Nguyen, 1991; Padgett, Patrick, Burns, & Schlesinger, 1994; Sue, Fujino, Hu, Takeuchi, & Zane, 1991). Aside from cultural-based practices that may cause some individuals to seek assistance outside the mental health system (e.g., practitioners of santeria; González-Wippler, 1992), access to and retention in the mental health system may be influenced by the proximity of mental health services (Dworkin & Adams, 1987) and by the ethnicity of treatment providers. Sue et al. (1991) reported that matching clinician and client ethnicity resulted in higher retention of ethnic minorities in mental health services. Increasing access to needed services for racial/ethnic minorities may require a range of strategies, including ensuring that services are available in the communities where clients live, working with the natural social supports in the community, awareness of relevant cultural norms, and adequate representation of ethnic minorities as treatment providers.

Cultural factors may have an important bearing on psychotherapeutic treatments provided for schizophrenia. Sue and Sue (1990) have described the importance of providing psychotherapy driven by goals that are compatible with clients' cultural norms. This requires both knowledge of subcultural norms and familiarity with the other social support mechanisms typically available to those individuals. Interventions developed for one cultural group may need substantial modification to be effective in other groups. For example, Telles et al. (1995) reported that behavioral family therapy, which has been found to be effective at reducing relapse in schizophrenia for samples of non-Hispanic white and African American individuals (Mueser & Glynn, 1999), was significantly less effective for Hispanic Americans (of Mexican, Guatemalan, and Salvadoran descent) with low levels of acculturation than for more acculturated individuals. In addition, behavioral family therapy has been found to be effective when implemented in Spain and China (Montero et al., 2001; Xiong et al., 1994; Zhang, Wang, Li, & Phillips, 1994). These findings underscore the importance of tailoring psychosocial interventions to meet the unique needs of clients from different cultural backgrounds.

A final cultural factor is stigma—that is, negative attitudes that lead to prejudice and discrimination against people with schizophrenia. Although stigma can be present for a variety of disabilities, attitudes toward people with serious mental illness tend to be more negative (Corrigan & Penn, 1999). Stigma may stem from characteristics of the disorder itself, such as poor social skills, bizarre behavior, and unkempt appearance, and stigma may develop and be maintained through negative media portrayals and myths (e.g., dangerousness, unpredictability) (Farina, 1998). Stigma and discrimination can greatly undermine the person's ability to recover from the effects of schizophrenia and integrate into society. For example, people with serious mental illness identify role functioning, such as employment, developing and maintaining friendships and intimate relationships, and regular activities as critical to their recovery (Uttaro & Mechanic, 1994). However, many studies have shown that these are the very areas most affected by stigma (Farina, 1998). Much is being done to try to reduce stigma associated with schizophrenia and other mental illness. In particular, strategies that involve active education and increased contact with people with mental illness (best if same status and background) may be most effective for eradicating this serious problem (Corrigan & Penn, 1999).

## COURSE AND PROGNOSIS

Schizophrenia usually has an onset in late adolescence or early adulthood, most often between the ages of 16 and 25. However, there is evidence that signs of the disorder are present long before the clinical symptoms of psychosis appear. Children who later develop schizophrenia show impairments in sociability, emotional expressiveness (less positive and more negative facial expressions), and neuromotor functioning (Schiffman et al., 2004; Walker, Grimes, Davis, & Smith, 1993). Data from the New York High-Risk Project, which followed a cohort of children at high risk for schizophrenia, found that deficits in verbal memory, attentional vigilance, and gross motor skills in childhood (ages 7 to 12) predicted the development of schizophrenia later in life (Erlenmeyer-Kimling et al., 2000). Some individuals display a maladaptive pattern of behaviors, including disruptive behavior, problems in school, poor interpersonal relationships, and impulsivity (Amminger et al., 1999; Baum & Walker, 1995; Fuller et al., 2002; Hans, Marcus, Henson, Auerbach, & Mirsky, 1992). Similarly, symptoms of conduct disorder in childhood, such as repeated fighting, truancy, and lying, have been found to be predictive of the later development of schizophrenia (Asarnow, 1988; Cannon et al., 1993; Neumann, Grimes, Walker, & Baum, 1995; Robins, 1966; Robins & Price, 1991; Rutter, 1984; Watt, 1978). However, other persons with schizophrenia display no unusual characteristics in their premorbid functioning or competence (Zigler & Glick, 1986). The signs of schizophrenia in childhood may be subtle, irregular, and gradual in onset, but they become increasingly more apparent as adolescence approaches (Dworkin et al., 1991).

Prior to the emergence of schizophrenia, many persons enter a prodromal period of the illness, which is characterized by changes in mood and behavior (Yung & McGorry, 1996). The prodrome is an intensification of the core features of the disorder that can last up to 5 years. Prodromal symptoms are subclinical or attenuated symptoms that fail to reach the threshold for a clinical diagnosis but become increasingly apparent to others. Disruptions in sleep, anxiety, depression, aggression/irritability, paranoia, and odd beliefs are common in the prodromal phase (Häfner, Maurer, Trendler, an der Heiden, & Schmidt, 2005; Malla & Payne, 2005; Norman, Scholten, Malla, & Ballageer, 2005; Yung & McGorry, 1996). Social isolation, withdrawal, changes in role functioning, and avolition may be present during this stage as well.

The initial emergence of clinical symptoms (first-episode or first break) is a crucial time for treatment and intervention (Lincoln & McGorry, 1995). It is widely believed that the earlier antipsychotic medications are initiated, the better the long-term outcome becomes (Penn, Waldheter, Perkins, Mueser, & Lieberman, 2005). In fact, a critical time for treatment appears to be during the first 5 years of the disorder (Malla, Norman, & Joober, 2005). This finding, combined with the efficacy of antipsychotic medications (50% show remission after 3 months and 80% show remission at 1 year; as reviewed in Penn et al., 2005) in first-episode individuals, makes early intervention programs a crucial aspect of treatment. Unfortunately, even after symptom remission is attained, most individuals with schizophrenia still have deficits in social, vocational, and community functioning (Tohen et al., 2000). Negative symptoms in first-episode individuals have been linked to poor cognitive functioning and longer durations of untreated psychosis (Malla & Payne, 2005).

It is extremely rare for the first onset of schizophrenia to occur before adolescence (e.g., before the age of 12), with most diagnostic systems considering childhood-onset schizophrenia to be a different disorder than adolescent or adult onset (APA, 2000). More common than childhood schizophrenia, but nevertheless rare in the total population of persons with schizophrenia, are individuals who develop the illness later in life, such as after the age of 40 (late-onset schizophrenia) or after the age of 60 (very-late-onset schizophrenia) (Cohen, 1990; Howard, Rabins, Seeman, Jeste, & the International Late-Onset Schizophrenia Group, 2000). It is estimated that approximately 23% of individuals with schizophrenia develop symptoms after the age of 40 (Harris & Jeste, 1988). Late-onset schizophrenia is more common in women, and there is evidence of better social, educational, and occupational functioning as compared to early-onset schizophrenia (Howard et al., 2000). Late-onset schizophrenia is more likely to involve positive symptoms (visual, tactile, and olfactory hallucinations; persecutory delusions) and less likely to involve formal thought disorder or negative symptoms (Bartels, Mueser, & Miles, 1998). Late-onset schizophrenia is further complicated by the lack of clear-cut distinguishing characteristics that discriminate this disorder from a variety of other disorders that develop later in old age such as dementia (Howard, Almeida, & Levy, 1994). Thus, it is important to emphasize that the symptoms of schizophrenia can arise at any point in life and are a developmental phenomenon. The onset, course, and prognosis of the illness are closely tied to gender (Haas & Garratt, 1998). Women tend to have later age of onset of the illness (average onset is between 25 to 29 years), spend less time in hospitals, have fewer negative symptoms, demonstrate less cognitive impairment, and have better social competence and social functioning than men with the illness (Goldstein, 1988; Häfner et al., 1993; Leung & Chue, 2000; Mueser, Bellack, Morrison, & Wade, 1990; Salem & Kring, 1998). The benefits experienced by women do not appear to be explained by societal differences in tolerance for deviant behavior. A variety of different hypotheses have been advanced to account for the superior outcome of women with schizophrenia (e.g., role of estrogen on dopamine receptors, more adaptive coping with socioenvironmental stressors, improved social networks and competence [Castle & Murray, 1991; Flor-Henry, 1985; Halari et al., 2004]), but no single theory has received strong support.

In general, the onset of schizophrenia can be described as either gradual or acute. The gradual onset of schizophrenia can take place over many months or years, and it may be difficult for family members and others to clearly distinguish onset of the illness (prepsychotic and prodromal signs). In other cases, the symptoms develop rapidly over a period of a few weeks with dramatic and easily observed changes occurring over this time. People with acute onset of schizophrenia have a somewhat better prognosis than those with a more insidious illness (Fenton & McGlashan, 1991; Kay & Lindenmayer, 1987).

Although schizophrenia is a long-term and severe psychiatric illness, there is considerable interindividual variability in the course and outcome of the illness over time (Marengo, 1994). Generally, though, once schizophrenia has developed, the illness usually continues to be present at varying degrees of severity throughout most of the person's life. Schizophrenia is usually an episodic illness with periods of acute symptom exacerbation (i.e., relapse) requiring more intensive, often inpatient, treatment interspersed by periods of higher functioning between episodes (i.e., remission). Preventing relapse is a significant clinical concern, because each relapse leads to more persistent symptoms and greater cognitive and psychosocial impairment. Although most persons with schizophrenia live in the community, it is comparatively rare, at least in the short term, for individuals to return to their premorbid levels of functioning between episodes. Remission is the reduction of active symptoms to nonproblematic, less severe levels (Andreasen et al., 2005). Recovery is much broader and includes both symptom remission and an improvement in social, community, occupational, and adaptive functioning. Recovery is also largely based on consumer perceptions of improvement. A recent review of 10 longitudinal studies on outcome in schizophrenia, some of which followed individuals for more than 20 years, reported that between 21% and 57% of persons with schizophrenia showed periodic episodes of recovery (improved symptoms; greater social, educational, and occupational functioning; Jobe & Harrow, 2005). In fact, some of these individuals showed extended periods of recovery without mental health treatment (Harrow, Grossman, Jobe, & Herbener, 2005; Jobe & Harrow, 2005).

Some general predictors of the course and outcome of schizophrenia have been identified, such as premorbid functioning, but overall, the ability to predict outcome is rather poor (Avison & Speechley, 1987; Tsuang, 1986). The primary reason for this is that symptom severity and functioning are determined by the dynamic interplay between biological vulnerability, environmental factors, and coping skills (Nuechterlein & Dawson, 1984; Liberman et al., 1986). Factors such as compliance with medication (Buchanan, 1992), substance abuse (Drake, Osher, & Wallach, 1989), exposure to a hostile or critical environment (Butzlaff & Hooley, 1998), the availability of psychosocial programming (Bellack & Mueser, 1993), and assertive case management and outreach (Mueser, Bond, Drake, & Resnick, 1998; Mueser, Drake, & Bond, 1997; Phillips et al., 2001; Quinlivan et al., 1995) are all environmental factors that in combination play a large role in determining outcome.

The importance of environmental factors and rehabilitation programs in determining the outcome of schizophrenia is illustrated by two long-term outcome studies conducted by Harding and associates (DeSisto, Harding, McCormick, Ashikaga, & Brooks, 1995; Harding, Brooks, Ashikaga, Strauss, & Breier, 1987a, 1987b). The first study was conducted in Vermont, which had a highly developed system of community-based rehabilitation programs for persons with severe mental illness. Persons with schizophrenia in this study demonstrated surprisingly positive outcomes (60% recovery rate) over the 20- to 40-year follow-up period. In contrast, similar individuals in Maine, where more traditional hospital-based treatment programs existed, fared substantially worse over the long-term course of their illness. Thus, the outcome of most cases of schizophrenia is not predetermined by specific biological factors, but rather is influenced by the interaction between biological and environmental factors.

In summary, the prognosis of schizophrenia is usually considered poor to fair, and there is general agreement that it is worse than for other major psychiatric disorders, such as bipolar disorder or major depression (Jobe & Harrow, 2005). Despite the widespread acceptance that schizophrenia is usually a lifelong disability, recent research on the long-term outcome of schizophrenia has challenged this assumption. Many persons with schizophrenia can attain symptom remission and recovery with the appropriate pharmacological and psychosocial treatment (Ciompi, 1980; Harding et al., 1987a, 1987b; Harrow, Grossman, Jobe, & Herbener, 2005).

## LOOKING AHEAD TO *DSM-5*

The proposed changes in the Schizophrenia and Other Psychotic Disorders section of the *DSM-5* (estimated publication date of 2013) are relatively minor in scope. Only two disorders, schizophrenia and schizoaffective disorder, have revised diagnostic criteria. The proposed changes are only tentative at this point in time pending final confirmation of the *DSM-5* work and task force groups and subsequent field trials. Changes to schizophrenia include the presence of two or more of the following symptoms for 1 month: (1) delusions, (2) hallucinations, (3) disorganized speech, (4) catatonia, and/or (5) negative symptoms (either restricted affect or avolition/asociality). Participants must have at least one symptom from numbers 1 to 3. The previous inclusion of disorganized behavior in the *DSM-IV-TR* (criterion A.4) has been removed and replaced with catatonia. This change was due to the overlap between disorganized speech and behaviors into a behavioral cluster that reflects disorganization. Negative symptoms now reflect two core dimensions of emotional restriction and avolition/asociality, because these two symptoms groups appear more distinguishable in schizophrenia. The classic subtypes of schizophrenia, such as paranoid, catatonic, disorganized, undifferentiated, and residual, may be eliminated because these have proven less useful in treatment and research. In the *DSM-5*, a person will only receive a diagnosis of schizophrenia without a focus on subtype characteristics.

Changes to schizoaffective disorder include an emphasis on the presence of major mood episodes, such as major depressive, manic, or mixed mood episodes, along with the symptoms of psychosis to enhance its differentiation from schizophrenia (e.g., mood symptoms if present are minimal). The symptoms of a major mood episode must be present for a majority of the total duration of illness (more than 50% of the time) and present for 2 weeks in the absence of delusions and hallucinations. Thus, schizoaffective disorder is conceptualized as the sequential presence of psychosis and major mood episodes, unlike bipolar disorder with psychotic features in which the symptoms co-occur at the same time. These changes were made to improve the reliability of the diagnosis and to emphasize the presence of major mood impairments along with psychosis.

One of the new features added to the Schizophrenia and Other Psychotic Disorders section includes the rating of core symptoms on a dimensional scale. This addition stemmed from research that psychosis symptoms do not appear to be entirely categorical and are better viewed on a continuum. As part of the diagnostic interview, the clinician can rate the severity of the following symptoms on a scale of 0 (not present) to 4 (present and severe) for hallucinations, delusions, disorganization, abnormal psychomotor behavior, restricted affect, avolition, impaired cognition, depression, and mania. These symptoms are to be rated for the past month. These ratings can be used to assess prognosis and treatment response over time.

There are several psychotic disorders that are recommended for elimination in *DSM-5*, and two new disorders are recommended for possible inclusion as major psychotic disorders or in the appendix for further study. Possible new additions include attenuated psychotic symptoms syndrome and a catatonia specifier. Attenuated psychotic symptoms syndrome is based on the presence of (1) delusions, (2) hallucinations, or (3) disorganized speech. These attenuated symptoms are present for at least 1 month and occur at least one time per week in that month. The symptoms are of such severity that they cannot be ignored or discounted, and there is a general progression of symptoms over the course of a year. Intact reality testing is present in these persons. The symptoms lead to distress, disability, or treatment-seeking behaviors. This diagnostic category essentially reflects those persons (mainly adolescents) who are at high risk for developing the disorder and who are showing early signs of psychotic illness. Consistent with research on first-episode psychosis, the earlier treatment is begun, the better the long-term outcome and a formal recognition of these persons in the *DSM-5* may be warranted. The catatonia specifier can be applied to psychotic or mood disorders or as a result from a general medical condition when the symptoms of catatonia are present and prominent. Shared psychotic disorder and the schizophrenia subtypes (see previous discussion) are recommended for elimination in the *DSM-5*. Persons with shared psychotic disorder will also meet the criteria for delusional disorder, so the use of an additional diagnostic category is not needed. Also, there is little research evidence on the etiology and symptoms of shared psychotic disorder, and most of the data comes from case studies.

## CASE STUDY

### CASE IDENTIFICATION

Isaac is a 30-year-old, never-married man who lives independently and receives Social Security Supplemental Income because of impaired functioning due to schizophrenia, which developed approximately 10 years ago. Isaac maintains close contact with his parents, who live in the same town, and has occasional contact with his two older brothers and a younger sister. Isaac receives outpatient treatment at his local community mental health center, including antipsychotic medications, involvement in a group program aimed at teaching him how to manage his illness, and participation in a supported employment program that helps him maintain a part-time competitive job at a local grocery store.

## PRESENTING COMPLAINTS

Isaac is dissatisfied with several areas of his life that are the focus of treatment. Although medication significantly reduced many of his paranoid symptoms, he continues to have suspicious thoughts in some social situations and feels anxious around other people. He has few friends, none of them women, and he would like to have more friends, including a girlfriend. Although his hygiene is generally good, when his psychotic symptoms increase, he becomes more disheveled, smokes more cigarettes, and becomes agitated. In addition to Isaac's mild paranoia and social anxiety, his social skills are not strong. For example, Isaac maintains poor eye contact and speaks in a low tone of voice when talking with other people, he rarely smiles spontaneously, and he has difficulty coming up with interesting conversational topics. Isaac is also dissatisfied with not completing his college degree because his three siblings have all graduated college, but he doesn't want to return to school until he has proved to himself that he can hold down his part-time job. He has a very low energy level and sometimes has trouble following through regularly on his goals, including his part-time job. Isaac recognizes that he has problems and needs help, but he lacks basic insight into his psychiatric disorder, and he does not believe he has schizophrenia. Isaac also does not like having to take medications, partly because of the weight gain he has experienced from his antipsychotic medication. He periodically stops taking his medications when he feels better, which often leads to relapses in his symptoms, a deterioration in functioning, and sometimes rehospitalization.

## HISTORY

Isaac first began to experience psychiatric problems 10 years ago. During the summer before his junior year in college, he was working in a busy office. He became increasingly concerned that his office mates were "out to get him" and that there was an intricate plot to discredit him. He also believed that his coworkers were secretly communicating with each other about him through certain facial expressions, choice of clothing, and the configuration of items on their desks. As his paranoia escalated, he became more disorganized in his thinking and behavior, he was less able to take care of his daily activities, and he experienced increased difficulties performing his job because of a combination of difficulties with attention and fear of his coworkers, and he eventually stopped coming to work. Isaac began to believe he was dying and attributed a variety of factors that were playing a role in his demise, including being poisoned by indoor air pollution. Isaac moved back home with his parents and informed them that he would not be returning to school in the fall. As a result of Isaac's symptoms, combined with the deterioration in his ability to take care of himself and meet role expectations at work and school, his parents took him to a mental health professional, who arranged for him to be hospitalized due to the extent of his functional impairment.

During this hospitalization, Isaac was first diagnosed with provisional schizo-phreniform disorder and treated with antipsychotic medication. Isaac benefited from his treatment, and his most flagrant symptoms improved substantially, including his belief that others were plotting against him. He was discharged after a 4-week period and referred to his local community mental health center for follow-up treatment and rehabilitation. Although Isaac's symptoms were improved, he continued to have impairments in his functioning, including his self-care skills, limited social relationships, and decreased ability to work or attend school in his previous capacity. When these impairments in psychosocial functioning had persisted for 6 months, his diagnosis was changed to schizophrenia.

Although Isaac continued to have symptoms and impairments of schizophrenia since he first developed the disorder 10 years ago, he also made some positive steps toward improving the quality of his life, with the help of his treatment team and his family. After several years of living at home, Isaac moved out 2 years ago to his own apartment. Isaac has been able to live on his own with the support of his family members and his case manager, who coordinates his care with Isaac's treatment team. At first when Isaac moved back home, there was a significant amount of tension in the household, as his parents and younger sister did not understand the nature of his illness and were upset by his occasionally disruptive living habits, such as staying up much of the night. With the help of a clinician who worked with Isaac and his family for 15 months after he returned home, his family was able to learn more about schizophrenia, the principles of its treatment, and strategies for solving problems together.

Last, after attending a local day treatment program, Isaac became interested in working. The mental health center where he receives his treatment had a supported employment program in which an employment specialist was assigned to Isaac to help him find a job in his area of interest and to provide supports to help him keep that job. Isaac said that he was interested in working with animals, so his employment specialist helped him get a part-time job at a local pet store, where he cares for the animals, feeds them, and cleans their cages. Isaac has kept this job for almost 2 years; on two occasions he has had to take some time off when he had a relapse of his symptoms and had to return to the hospital. Isaac's employment specialist arranged with his employer for him to be able to return to his job when he had recovered from his relapse. Isaac's case manager and employment specialist also worked together to motivate Isaac to participate in a program designed to teach him more about his psychiatric disorder and how to manage it in collaboration with others, in order to achieve his recovery goal of returning to school and completing his college degree.

### ASSESSMENT

A diagnosis of schizophrenia was confirmed using the Structured Interview for *DSM-IV-TR* (SCID). Many of the symptoms described in this vignette are highlighted in *DSM-IV-TR* criteria for schizophrenia (see "Diagnostic Considerations" and Table 8.1). Regarding the A criteria, Isaac clearly experienced three "characteristic symptoms," including delusions (e.g., his beliefs about his coworkers and being poisoned by air pollution), disorganized speech and behavior, and negative symptoms (e.g., flattened affect, apathy). In terms of the B criteria, Isaac has experienced clear impairments in his social and occupational functioning—at the time of diagnosis, he was no longer able to care for himself or go to work, and he had dropped out of school. The duration criteria of *DSM-IV-TR* were met because these difficulties lasted longer than 6 months. In addition, with respect to the D and E diagnostic criteria for schizophrenia, other diagnoses were ruled out (e.g., mood disorders, substance abuse, developmental disorders). In addition to illustrating some of the symptoms and characteristic impairments of schizophrenia, this vignette illustrates that people with this illness are often able to lead rewarding and productive lives, usually with help of pharmacological and psychological treatment, as well as social supports, despite continued symptoms and impairment due to the illness.

## SUMMARY

Schizophrenia is a severe, long-term psychiatric illness characterized by impairments in social functioning, the ability to work, self-care skills, positive symptoms (hallucinations, delusions), negative symptoms (social withdrawal, apathy), and cognitive impairments. Schizophrenia is a relatively common illness, afflicting approximately 1% of the population, and tends to have an episodic course over the lifetime, with symptoms gradually improving over the long term. Most evidence indicates that schizophrenia is a biological illness that may be caused by a variety of factors, such as genetic contributions and early environmental influences (e.g., insults to the developing fetus). Despite the biological nature of schizophrenia, environmental stress can either precipitate the onset of the illness or symptom relapses. Schizophrenia can be reliably diagnosed with structured clinical interviews, with particular attention paid to the differential diagnosis of affective disorders. There is a high comorbidity of substance use disorders in persons with schizophrenia, which must be treated if positive outcomes are to accrue. Psychological assessment of schizophrenia is most useful when it focuses on behavioral, rather than dynamic, dimensions of the illness. Thus, assessments and interventions focused on social skill deficits and family functioning have yielded promising treatment results. Biological assessments are useful at this time primarily for descriptive rather than clinical purposes. Finally, there are a great many issues related to gender and racial or ethnic factors that remain unexplored. Although schizophrenia remains one of the most challenging psychiatric illnesses to treat, substantial advances have been made in recent years in developing reliable diagnostic systems, understanding the role of various etiological factors, development of effective pharmacological and psychosocial treatments, and the identification of factors that mediate the long-term outcome of the illness, such as stress and substance abuse. These developments bode well for the ability of researchers and clinicians to continue to make headway in treating this serious illness.

## REFERENCES

Adams, G. L., Dworkin, R. J., & Rosenberg, S. D. (1984). Diagnosis and pharmacotherapy issues in the care of Hispanics in the public sector. *The American Journal of Psychiatry, 141*, 970–974.

Aguilera, A., Lopez, S. R., Breitborde, N. J. K., Kopelowicz, A., & Zarate, R. (2010). Expressed emotion and sociocultural moderation in the course of schizophrenia. *Journal of Abnormal Psychology, 119*, 875–885.

Alvir, J. M. J., Lieberman, J. A., & Safferman, A. Z. (1995). Do white-cell count spikes predict agranulocytosis in clozapine recipients? *Psychopharmacology Bulletin, 31*, 311–314.

Amador, X. F., & David, A. (2004). *Insight and psychosis: Awareness of illness in schizophrenia and related disorders.* New York, NY: Oxford University Press.

Amador, X. F., & Gorman, J. M. (1998). Psychopathologic domains and insight in schizophrenia. *The Psychiatric Clinics of North America, 21*, 27–42.

Amador, X. F., Strauss, D., Yale, S., & Gorman, J. M. (1991). Awareness of illness in schizophrenia. *Schizophrenia Bulletin, 17*, 113–132.

American Psychiatric Association. (2000). *Diagnostic and statistical manual of mental disorders* (4th ed., text revision; DSM-IV-TR). Washington, DC: Author.

Amminger, G. P., Pape, S., Rock, D., Roberts, S. A., Ott, S. L., Squires-Wheeler, E., . . . Erlenmeyer-Kimling, L. (1999). Relationship between childhood behavioral disturbance and later schizophrenia in the New York high-risk project. *The American Journal of Psychiatry, 156*, 525–530.

Andreasen, N. C. (1982). Negative symptoms in schizophrenia: Definition and reliability. *Archives of General Psychiatry, 39*, 784–788.

Andreasen, N. C., Carpenter, W. T., Kane, J. M., Lasser, R. A., Marder, S. R., & Weinberger, D. R. (2005). Remission in schizophrenia: Proposed criteria and rational for consensus. *The American Journal of Psychiatry, 162*, 441–449.

Andreasen, N. C., Flaum, M., Swayze, II, V. W., Tyrrell, G., & Arndt, S. (1990). Positive and negative symptoms in schizophrenia: A critical reappraisal. *Archives of General Psychiatry, 47*, 615–621.

Andreasen, N. C., & Olsen, S. (1982). Negative versus positive schizophrenia: Definition and validation. *Archives of General Psychiatry, 39*, 784–788.

Apfel, R. J., & Handel, M. H. (1993). *Madness and loss of motherhood: Sexuality, reproduction, and long-term mental illness.* Washington, DC: American Psychiatric Press.

Appelbaum, P. S., Robbins, P. C., & Roth, L. H. (1999). Dimensional approach to delusions: Comparison across types and diagnoses. *American Journal of Psychiatry, 156*, 1938–1943.

Appelo, M. T., Woonings, F. M. J., van Nieuwenhuizen, C. J., Emmelkamp, P. M. G., Sloof, C. J., & Louwerens, J. W. (1992). Specific skills and social competence in schizophrenia. *Acta Psychiatrica Scandinavica, 85*, 419–422.

Appleby, L., Dyson, V., Altman, E., & Luchins, D. (1997). Assessing substance use in multi-problem patients: Reliability and validity of the Addiction Severity Index in a mental hospital population. *Journal of Nervous and Mental Disease, 185*, 159–165.

Argyle, N. (1990). Panic attacks in chronic schizophrenia. *British Journal of Psychiatry, 157*, 430–433.

Aro, S., Aro, H., & Keskimäki, I. (1995). Socio-economic mobility among patients with schizophrenia or major affective disorder: A 17-year retrospective follow-up. *British Journal of Psychiatry, 166*, 759–767.

Asarnow, J. R. (1988). Children at risk for schizophrenia. Converging lines of evidence. *Schizophrenia Bulletin, 14*, 613–631.

Avison, W. R., & Speechley, K. N. (1987). The discharged psychiatric patient: A review of social, social-psychological, and psychiatric correlates of outcome. *American Journal of Psychiatry, 144*, 10–18.

Azrin, N. H., & Teichner, G. (1998). Evaluation of an instructional program for improving medication compliance for chronically mentally ill outpatients. *Behaviour Research and Therapy, 36*, 849–861.

Bartels, S. J., Drake, R. E., Wallach, M. A., & Freeman, D. H. (1991). Characteristic hostility in schizophrenic outpatients. *Schizophrenia Bulletin, 17*, 163–171.

Bartels, S. J., Mueser, K. T., & Miles, K. M. (1998). Schizophrenia. In M. Hersen and V. B. Van Hasselt (Eds.), *Handbook of clinical geropsychology* (pp. 173–194). New York, NY: Plenum Press.

Baskin, D., Bluestone, H., & Nelson, M. (1981). Ethnicity and psychiatric diagnosis. *Journal of Clinical Psychology, 37*, 529–537.

Bateson, G., Jackson, D. D., Haley, J., & Weakland, J. (1956). Toward a theory of schizophrenia. *Behavioral Science, 1*, 251–264.

Baum, K. M., & Walker, E. F. (1995). Childhood behavioral precursors of adult symptom dimensions in schizophrenia. *Schizophrenia Research, 16*, 111–120.

Bellack, A. S. (2004). Skills training for people with severe mental illness. *Psychiatric Rehabilitation Journal, 27*, 375–391.

Bellack, A. S., Gold, J. M., & Buchanan, R. W. (1999). Cognitive rehabilitation for schizophrenia: problems, prospects, and strategies. *Schizophrenia Bulletin, 25*, 257–74.

Bellack, A. S., Morrison, R. L., Mueser, K. T., Wade, J. H., & Sayers, S. L. (1990a). Role play for assessing the social competence of psychiatric patients. *Psychological Assessment, 2*, 248–255.

Bellack, A. S., Morrison, R. L., Wixted, J. T., & Mueser, K. T. (1990b). An analysis of social competence in schizophrenia. *British Journal of Psychiatry, 156*, 809–818.

Bellack, A. S., & Mueser, K. T. (1993). Psychosocial treatment for schizophrenia. *Schizophrenia Bulletin, 19*, 317–336.

Bellack, A. S., Mueser, K. T., Gingerich, S., & Agresta, J. (1997). *Social skills training for schizophrenia: A step-by-step guide.* New York, NY: Guilford Press.

Bellack, A. S., Mueser, K. T., Wade, J. H., Sayers, S. L., & Morrison, R. L. (1992). The ability of schizophrenics to perceive and cope with negative affect. *British Journal of Psychiatry, 160*, 473–480.

Bellack, A. S., Sayers, M., Mueser, K. T., & Bennett, M. (1994). An evaluation of social problem solving in schizophrenia. *Journal of Abnormal Psychology, 103*, 371–378.

Bellack, A. S., & Thomas-Lohrman, S. (2003). *Maryland assessment of social competence.* Unpublished assessment manual, Baltimore.

Bentall, R. P., Corcoran, R., Howard, R., Blackwood, N., & Kinderman, P. (2001). Persecutory delusions: A review and theoretical integration. *Clinical Psychology Review, 21*, 1143–1192.

Bentall, R. P., Jackson, H. F., & Pilgrim D. (1988). Abandoning the concept of schizophrenia: Some implications of validity arguments for psychological research into psychotic phenomena. *British Journal of Clinical Psychology, 27*, 156–169.

Birchwood, M., Iqbal, Z., Chadwick, P., & Trower, P. (2000). Cognitive approach to depression and suicidal thinking in psychosis I: Ontogeny of post-psychotic depression. *British Journal of Psychiatry, 177*, 516–521.

Birchwood, M., Smith, J., Cochrane, R., Wetton, S., & Copstake, S. (1990). The social functioning scale: The development and validation of a new scale of social adjustment for the use in family intervention programmes with schizophrenic patients. *British Journal of Psychiatry, 157*, 853–859.

Bleuler, E. (1911/1950). *Dementia praecox or the group of schizophrenias.* New York, NY: International Universities Press.

Bond, G. R. (1998). Principles of the individual placement and support model: Empirical support. *Psychiatric Rehabilitation Journal, 22*, 11–23.

Boydell, J., van Os, J., McKenzie, K., Allardyce, J., Goel, R., McCreadie, R. G., & Murray, R. M. (2001). Incidence of schizophrenia in ethnic minorities in London: Ecological study into interactions with environment. *British Medical Journal, 323*, 1336–1338.

Bracha, H. S., Wolkowitz, O. M., Lohr, J. B., Karson, C. N., & Bigelow, L. B. (1989). High prevalence of visual hallucinations in research subjects with chronic schizophrenia. *The American Journal of Psychiatry, 146*, 526–528.

Braga, R. J., Mendlowicz, M. V., Marrocos, R. P., & Figueria, I. L. (2005). Anxiety disorders in outpatients with schizophrenia: Prevalence and impact on the subjective quality of life. *Journal of Psychiatric Research, 39*, 409–414.

Breier, A. (2005). Developing drugs for cognitive impairment in schizophrenia. *Schizophrenia Bulletin, 31*, 816–822.

Breitborde, N. J. K., Lopez, S. R., Chang, C., Kopelowicz, A., & Zarate, R. (2009). Emotional over-involvement can be deleterious for caregivers' health: Mexican Americans caring for a relative with schizophrenia. *Social Psychiatry and Psychiatric Epidemiology, 44*, 716–723.

Brekke, J. S., Raine, A., Ansel, M., Lencz, T., & Bird, L. (1997). Neuropsychological and Psychophysiological correlates of psychosocial functioning in schizophrenia. *Schizophrenia Bulletin, 23*, 19–28.

Breslau, N., Davis, G. C., Andreski, P., & Peterson, E. (1991). Traumatic events and post-traumatic stress disorder in an urban population of young adults. *Archives of General Psychiatry, 48*, 216–222.

Brewerton, T. D. (1994). Hyperreligiosity in psychotic disorders. *Journal of Nervous and Mental Disease, 182*, 302–304.

Bromet, E. J., Naz, B., Fochtmann, L. J., Carlson, G. A., & Tanenberg-Karant, M. (2005). Long-term diagnostic stability and outcome in recent first-episode cohort studies of schizophrenia. *Schizophrenia Bulletin, 31*, 639–649.

Bruce, M. L., Takeuchi, D. T., & Leaf, P. J. (1991). Poverty and psychiatric status: Longitudinal evidence from the New Haven Epidemiologic Catchment Area Study. *Archives of General Psychiatry, 48*, 470–474.

Brune, M. (2005). "Theory of mind" in schizophrenia: A review of the literature. *Schizophrenia Bulletin, 31*, 21–42.

Brunette, M. F., & Dean, W. (2002). Community mental health care of women with severe mental illness who are parents. *Community Mental Health Journal, 38*, 153–165.

Buchanan, A. (1992). A two-year prospective study of treatment compliance in patients with schizophrenia. *Psychological Medicine, 22*, 787–797.

Buchanan, R. W., Breier, A., Kirkpatrick, B., Elkashef, A., Munson, R. C., Gellad, F., & Carpenter, W. T. (1993). Structural abnormalities in deficit and nondeficit schizophrenia. *American Journal of Psychiatry, 150*, 59–65.

Burns, H., Job, M., Bastin, M. E., Whalley, H., Macgillivray, T., Johnstone, E. C., & Lawrie, S. M. (2003). Structural disconnectivity in schizophrenia: A diffusion tensor magnetic resonance imaging study. *British Journal of Psychiatry, 182*, 439–443.

Butzlaff, R. L., & Hooley, J. M. (1998). Expressed emotion and psychiatric relapse: A meta-analysis. *Archives of General Psychiatry, 55*, 547–552.

Cannon, T. D., Mednick, S. A., Parnas, J., Schulsinger, F., Praestholm, J., & Vestergaard, A. (1993). Developmental brain abnormalities in the offspring of schizophrenic mothers. *Archives of General Psychiatry, 50*, 551–564.

Cantor-Graae, E., & Selten, J. P. (2005). Schizophrenia and migration: A meta-analysis and review. *American Journal of Psychiatry, 162*, 12–24.

Cardno, A., Marshall, E. J., Coid, B., Macdonald, A. M., Ribchester, T. R., Davies, N. J., . . . Murray, R. M. (1999). Heritability estimates for psychotic disorders: The Maudsley twin psychosis series. *Archives of General Psychiatry, 56*, 162–168.

Carmen, E., Rieker, P. P., & Mills, T. (1984). Victims of violence and psychiatric illness. *American Journal of Psychiatry, 141*, 378–383.

Carter, C. S., MacDonald, A. W., Ross, L. L., & Stenger, V. A. (2001). Anterior cingulated cortex activity and impaired self-monitoring of performance in patients with schizophrenia: An event related fMRI study. *American Journal of Psychiatry, 158,* 1423–1428.

Cascardi, M., Mueser, K. T., DeGirolomo, J., & Murrin, M. (1996). Physical aggression against psychiatric inpatients by family members and partners: A descriptive study. *Psychiatric Services, 47,* 531–533.

Castle, D. J., & Murray, R. M. (1991). The neurodevelopmental basis of sex differences in schizophrenia [Editorial]. *Psychological Medicine, 21,* 565–575.

Chadwick, P., & Birchwood, M. (1995). The omnipotence of voices II: The beliefs about voices questionnaire. *British Journal of Psychiatry, 166,* 773–776.

Cheung, F. K., & Snowden, L. R. (1990). Community mental health and ethnic minority populations. *Community Mental Health Journal, 26,* 277–289.

Chilcoat, H. D., & Breslau, N. (1998). Posttraumatic stress disorder and drug disorders: Testing causal pathways. *Archives of General Psychiatry, 55,* 913–917.

Ciompi, L. (1980). Catamnestic long-term study of life and aging in chronic schizophrenic patients. *Schizophrenia Bulletin, 6,* 606–618.

Clark, R., Anderson, N. B., Clark, V. R., & Williams, D. R. (1999). Racism as a stressor for African Americans. *American Psychologist, 54,* 805–816.

Cohen, C. I. (1990). Outcome of schizophrenia into later life: An overview. *The Gerontologist, 30,* 790–797.

Cohen, M., & Klein, D. F. (1970). Drug abuse in a young psychiatric population. *American Journal of Orthopsychiatry, 40,* 448–455.

Comas-Díaz, L. (1981). Puerto Rican espiritismo and psychotherapy. *American Journal of Orthopsychiatry, 51,* 636–645.

Combs, D. R., & Penn, D. L. (2004). The role of sub-clinical paranoia on social perception and behavior. *Schizophrenia Research, 69,* 93–104.

Combs, D. R., Penn, D. L., Cassisi, J., Michael, C. O., Wood, T. D., Wanner, J., & Adams, S. D. (2006). Perceived racism as a predictor of paranoia among African Americans. *Journal of Black Psychology, 32*(1), 87–104.

Combs, D. R., Penn, D. L., & Fenigstein, A. (2002). Ethnic differences in sub-clinical paranoia: An expansion of norms of the paranoia scale. *Cultural Diversity & Ethnic Minority Psychology, 8,* 248–256.

Copolov, D. L., Mackinnon, A., & Trauer, T. (2004). Correlates of the affective impact of auditory hallucinations in psychotic disorders. *Schizophrenia Bulletin, 30,* 163–171.

Corrigan, P. W., Liberman, R. P., & Engle, J. D. (1990). From noncompliance to collaboration in the treatment of schizophrenia. *Hospital and Community Psychiatry, 41,* 1203–1211.

Corrigan, P. W., & Penn, D. L. (1999). Lessons from social psychology on discrediting psychiatric stigma. *American Psychologist, 54,* 765–776.

Corrigan, P. W., & Penn, D. L. (2001). *Social cognition in schizophrenia.* Washington, DC: American Psychological Association.

Corse, S. J., Hirschinger, N. B., & Zanis, D. (1995). The use of the Addiction Severity Index with people with severe mental illness. *Psychiatric Rehabilitation Journal, 19,* 9–18.

Corty, E., Lehman, A. F., & Myers, C. P. (1993). Influence of psychoactive substance use on the reliability of psychiatric diagnosis. *Journal of Consulting and Clinical Psychology, 61,* 165–170.

Cosoff, S. J., & Hafner, R. J. (1998). The prevalence of comorbid anxiety in schizophrenia, schizoaffective disorder, and bipolar disorder. *Australian and New Zealand Journal of Psychiatry, 32,* 67–72.

Coverdale, J. H., & Grunebaum, H. (1998). Sexuality and family planning. In K. T. Mueser and N. Tarrier (Eds.), *Social functioning in schizophrenia* (pp. 224–237). Boston, MA: Allyn and Bacon.

Craddock, N., O'Donovan, M. C., & Owen, M. J. (2006). Genes for schizophrenia and bipolar disorder? Implications for psychiatric nosology. *Schizophrenia Bulletin, 32*, 9–16.

Craine, L. S., Henson, C. E., Colliver, J. A., & MacLean, D. G. (1988). Prevalence of a history of sexual abuse among female psychiatric patients in a state hospital system. *Hospital and Community Psychiatry, 39*, 300–304.

Crow, T. (2008). The "big bang" theory of the origin of psychosis and the faculty of language. *Schizophrenia Research, 102*, 31–52.

Crowley, T. J., Chesluk, D., Dilts, S., & Hart, R. (1974). Drug and alcohol abuse among psychiatric admissions. *Archives of General Psychiatry, 30*, 13–20.

Cutting, J. (1995). Descriptive psychopathology. In S. R. Hirsch & D. R. Weinberger (Eds.), *Schizophrenia.* New York, NY: Cambridge University Press.

Davies-Netzley, S., Hurlburt, M. S., & Hough, R. (1996). Childhood abuse as a precursor to homelessness for homeless women with severe mental illness. *Violence and Victims, 11*, 129–142.

Davis, K. L., Kahn, R. S., Ko, G., & Davidson, M. (1991). Dopamine in schizophrenia: A review and reconceptualization. *American Journal of Psychiatry, 148*, 1474–1486.

Dean, K., Walsh, E., Moran, P., Tyrer, P., Creed, F., Byford, S., . . . Fahy, T. (2006). Violence in women with psychosis in the community: A prospective study. *British Journal of Psychiatry, 188*, 264–270.

DeSisto, M. J., Harding, C. M., McCormick, R. V., Ashikaga, T., & Brooks, G. W. (1995). The Maine and Vermont three-decade studies of serious mental illness: I. Matched comparison of cross-sectional outcome. *British Journal of Psychiatry, 167*, 331–342.

Dixon, L. B., & Lehman, A. F. (1995). Family interventions for schizophrenia. *Schizophrenia Bulletin, 21*, 631–643.

Dixon, L. B., McFarlane, W., Lefley, H., Lucksted, A., Cohen, C., Falloon, I., . . . Sondheimer, D. (2001). Evidence-based practices for services to family members of people with psychiatric disabilities. *Psychiatric Services, 52*, 903–910.

Dohrenwend, B. R., Levav, I., Shrout, P. E., Schwartz, S., Naveh, G., Link, B. G., . . . Stueve, A (1992). Socioeconomic status and psychiatric disorders: The causation-selection issue. *Science, 255*, 946–952.

Dorian, M., Garcia, J. I. R., Lopez, S. R., & Hernandez, B. (2008). Acceptance and expressed emotion in Mexican American caregivers of relatives with schizophrenia. *Family Process, 47*, 215–228.

Douglas, M. S., & Mueser, K. T. (1990). Teaching conflict resolution skills to the chronically mentally ill: Social skills training groups for briefly hospitalized patients. *Behavior Modification, 14*, 519–547.

Drake, R. E., & Becker, D. R. (1996). The individual placement and support model of supported employment. *Psychiatric Services, 47*, 473–475.

Drake, R. E., & Brunette, M. F. (1998). Complications of severe mental illness related to alcohol and drug use disorders. In M. Galanter (Ed.), *Recent developments in alcoholism, Vol. 14: The consequences of alcoholism* (pp. 285–299). New York, NY: Plenum Press.

Drake, R. E., Gates, C., Whitaker, A., & Cotton, P. G. (1985). Suicide among schizophrenics: A review. *Comprehensive Psychiatry, 26*, 90–100.

Drake, R. E., Mercer-McFadden, C., Mueser, K. T., McHugo, G. J., & Bond, G. R. (1998). Review of integrated mental health and substance abuse treatment for patients with dual disorders. *Schizophrenia Bulletin, 24*, 589–608.

Drake, R. E., Osher, F. C., Noordsy, D. L., Hurlbut, S. C., Teague, G. B., & Beaudett, M. S. (1990). Diagnosis of alcohol use disorders in schizophrenia. *Schizophrenia Bulletin, 16*, 57–67.

Drake, R. E., Osher, F. C., & Wallach, M. A. (1989). Alcohol use and abuse in schizophrenia: A prospective community study. *Journal of Nervous and Mental Disease, 177*, 408–414.

Drake, R. E., Rosenberg, S. D., & Mueser, K. T. (1996). Assessment of substance use disorder in persons with severe mental illness. In R. E. Drake & K. T. Mueser (Eds.), *Dual diagnosis of major mental illness and substance abuse disorder, II: Recent research and clinical implications, Vol. 70: New directions in mental health services* (pp. 3–17). San Francisco, CA: Jossey-Bass.

Dworkin, R. J., & Adams, G. L. (1987). Retention of Hispanics in public sector mental health services. *Community Mental Health Journal, 23,* 204–216.

Dworkin, R. H., Bernstein, G., Kaplansky, L. M., Lipsitz, J. D., Rinaldi, A., Slater, S. L., . . . Erlenmeyer-Kimling, L. (1991). Social competence and positive and negative symptoms: A longitudinal study of children and adolescents at risk for schizophrenia and affective disorder. *American Journal of Psychiatry, 148,* 1182–1188.

Dyck, D. G., Short, R., & Vitaliano, P. P. (1999). Predictors of burden and infectious illness in schizophrenia caregivers. *Psychosomatic Medicine, 61,* 411–419.

Eaton, W. W. (1975). Marital status and schizophrenia. *Acta Psychiatrica Scandinavica, 52,* 320–329.

Edwards, J., Jackson, H. J., & Pattison, P. E. (2002). Emotion recognition via facial expression and affective prosody in schizophrenia: A methodological review. *Clinical Psychology Review, 22,* 789–832.

Erlenmeyer-Kimling, L., Rock, D., Roberts, S. A., Janal, M., Kestenbaum, C., Cornblatt, B., . . . Gottesman, I. I. (2000). Attention, memory, and motor skills as childhood predictors of schizophrenia-related psychoses: The New York High-Risk Project. *American Journal of Psychiatry, 157,* 1416–1422.

Estroff, S. E. (1989). Self, identity, and subjective experiences of schizophrenia: In search of the subject. *Schizophrenia Bulletin, 15,* 189–196.

Evans, J. D., Paulsen, J. S., Harris, M. J., Heaton, R. K., & Jeste, D. V. (1996). A clinical and neuropsychological comparison of delusional disorder and schizophrenia. *The Journal of Neuropsychiatry and Clinical Neurosciences, 8,* 281–286.

Fannon, D., Chitnis, X., Doku, V., Tennakoon, L., Ó'Ceallaigh, S., Soni, W., . . . Sharma, T. (2000). Features of structural brain abnormality detected in early first episode psychosis. *American Journal of Psychiatry, 157,* 1829–1834.

Faraone, S. V., & Tsuang, M. T. (1985). Quantitative models of the genetic transmission of schizophrenia. *Psychological Bulletin, 98,* 41–66.

Farina, A. (1998). Stigma. In K. T. Mueser & N. Tarrier (Eds.), *Handbook of social functioning in schizophrenia* (pp. 247–279). Boston, MA: Allyn & Bacon.

Fenton, W. S., & McGlashan, T. H. (1991). Natural history of schizophrenia subtypes, II: Positive and negative symptoms and long term course. *Archives of General Psychiatry, 48,* 978–986.

Fink, P. J., & Tasman, A. (Eds.). (1992). *Stigma and mental illness.* Washington, DC: American Psychiatric Press.

First, M. B., Spitzer, R. L., Gibbon, M., & Williams, J. B. W. (1996). *Structured clinical interview for Axes I and II DSM-IV Disorders—Patient Edition (SCID-I/P).* New York: Biometrics Research Department, New York State Psychiatric Institute.

Flaum, M., Arndt, S., & Andreasen, N. C. (1991). The reliability of ''bizarre'' delusions. *Comparative Psychiatry, 32,* 59–65.

Flor-Henry, P. (1985). Schizophrenia: Sex differences. *Canadian Journal of Psychiatry, 30,* 319–322.

Fowler, D., Garety, P., & Kuipers, E. (1995). *Cognitive behaviour therapy for psychosis: Theory and practice.* Chichester, England: John Wiley & Sons.

Fox, J. W. (1990). Social class, mental illness, and social mobility: The social selection-drift hypothesis for serious mental illness. *Journal of Health and Social Behavior, 31,* 344–353.

Freeman, D., & Garety, P. A. (2003). Connecting neurosis and psychosis: The direct influence of emotion on delusions and hallucinations. *Behaviour Research and Therapy, 41,* 923–947.

Freeman, D., Garety, P. A., Bebbington, P. E., Slater, M., Kuipers, E., Fowler, D., . . . Dunn, G., (2005). The psychology of persecutory ideation, II: A virtual reality experimental study. *Journal of Nervous and Mental Disease, 193*, 309–315.

Freeman, D., Garety, P. A., & Kuipers, E. (2001). Persecutory delusions: Developing the understanding of belief maintenance and emotional distress. *Psychological Medicine, 31*, 1293–1306.

Freeman, D., Garety, P. A., Kuipers, E., Fowler, D., & Bebbington, P. E. (2002). A cognitive model of persecutory delusions. *British Journal of Clinical Psychology, 41*, 331–347.

Fromm-Reichmann, F. (1950). *Principles of intensive psychotherapy.* Chicago, IL: University of Chicago Press.

Fuller, R., Nopoulos, P., Arndt, S., O'Leary, D., Ho, B., & Andreasen, N. C. (2002). Longitudinal assessment of premorbid cognitive functioning in patients with schizophrenia through examination of standardized scholastic test performance. *The American Journal of Psychiatry, 159*, 1183–1189.

Galletly, C. A., Field, C. D., & Prior, M. (1993). Urine drug screening of patients admitted to a state psychiatric hospital. *Hospital and Community Psychiatry, 44*, 587–589.

Garety, P. A., & Freeman, D. (1999). Cognitive approaches to delusions: A critical review of theories and evidence. *British Journal of Clinical Psychology, 38*, 113–154.

Gay, N. W., & Combs, D. R. (2005). Social behaviors in persons with and without persecutory delusions. *Schizophrenia Research, 80*, 2–3.

Geddes, J. R., & Lawrie, S. M. (1995). Obstetric complications and schizophrenia: A meta-analysis. *British Journal of Psychiatry, 167*, 786–793.

Glynn, S. M. (1992). Family-based treatment for major mental illness: A new role for psychologists. *The California Psychologist, 25*, 22–23.

Glynn, S. M. (1998). Psychopathology and social functioning in schizophrenia. In K. T. Mueser & N. Tarrier (Eds.), *Handbook of social functioning in schizophrenia* (pp. 66–78). Boston, MA: Allyn & Bacon.

Goeree, R., Farahati, F., Burke, N., Blackhouse, G., O'Reilly, D., Pyne, J., & Tarride, J. E. (2005). The economic burden of schizophrenia in Canada in 2004. *Current Medical Research & Opinion, 21*, 2017–2028.

Goldman, H. H. (1982). Mental illness and family burden: A public health perspective. *Hospital and Community Psychiatry, 33*, 557–560.

Goldner, E. M., Hsu, L., Waraich, P., & Somers, J. M. (2002). Prevalence and incidence studies of schizophrenic disorders: A systematic review of the literature. *Canadian Journal of Psychiatry, 47*, 833–843.

Goldstein, J. M. (1988). Gender differences in the course of schizophrenia. *American Journal of Psychiatry, 146*, 684–689.

González-Wippler, M. (1992). *Powers of the orishas: Santeria and the worship of saints.* New York, NY: Original Publications.

Goodman, L. A., Dutton, M. A., & Harris, M. (1995). Physical and sexual assault prevalence among episodically homeless women with serious mental illness. *American Journal of Orthopsychiatry, 65*, 468–478.

Goodman, L. A., Dutton, M. A., & Harris, M. (1997). The relationship between violence dimensions and symptom severity among homeless, mentally ill women. *Journal of Traumatic Stress, 10*, 51–70.

Goodman, L. A., Salyers, M. P., Mueser, K. T., Rosenberg, S. D., Swartz, M., Essock, S. M., . . . the 5 Site Health and Risk Study Research Committee. (2001). Recent victimization in women and men with severe mental illness: Prevalence and correlates. *Journal of Traumatic Stress, 14*, 615–632.

Goodwin, F. K., & Jamison, K. R. (1990). *Manic-depressive illness.* New York, NY: Oxford University Press.

Gottesman, I. I. (1991). *Schizophrenia genesis: The origins of madness.* New York, NY: Freeman.

Gottesman, I. I. (2001). Psychopathology through a life span-genetic prism. *American Psychologist, 56,* 867–878.

Gottesman, I. I., & Shields, J. (1982). *Schizophrenia: The epigenetic puzzle.* New York, NY: Cambridge University Press.

Greden, J. F., & Tandon, R. (Eds.). (1991). *Negative schizophrenic symptoms: Pathophysiology and clinical implications.* Washington, DC: American Psychiatric Press.

Green, M. F., Kern, R. S., Braff, D. L., & Mintz, J. (2000). Neurocognitive deficits and functional outcome in schizophrenia: Are we measuring the "right stuff"? *Schizophrenia Bulletin, 26,* 119–136.

Green, M. F., Marshall, B. D., Jr., Wirshing, W. C., Ames, D., Marder, S. R., McGurk, S., . . . Mintz, J. (1997). Does Risperidone improve verbal working memory in treatment-resistant schizophrenia? *American Journal of Psychiatry, 154,* 799–804.

Green, M. F., Nuechterlein, K. H., Gold, J. M., Barch, D. M., Cohen, J., Essock, S., . . . Marder, S. R. (2004). Approaching a consensus battery for clinical trials in schizophrenia: The NIMH-MATRI CS conference to select cognitive domains and test criteria. *Biological Psychiatry, 56,* 301–307.

Green, M. F., Olivier, B., Crawley, J. N., Penn, D. L., & Silverstein, S. (2005). Social cognition in schizophrenia: Recommendations from the measurement and treatment research to improve cognition in schizophrenia new approaches conference. *Schizophrenia Bulletin, 31,* 882–887.

Greenfield, S. F., Strakowski, S. M., Tohen, M., Batson, S. C., & Kolbrener, M. L. (1994). Childhood abuse in first-episode psychosis. *British Journal of Psychiatry, 164,* 831–834.

Griffith, E. E. H., Young, J. L., & Smith, D. L. (1984). An analysis of the therapeutic elements in a black church service. *Hospital and Community Psychiatry, 35,* 464–469.

Haas, G. L., & Garratt, L. S. (1998). Gender differences in social functioning. In K. T. Mueser & N. Tarrier (Eds.), *Handbook of social functioning in schizophrenia* (pp. 149–180). Boston, MA: Allyn and Bacon.

Haddock, G., McCarron, J., Tarrier, N., & Faragher, E. B. (1999). Scales to measure dimensions of hallucinations and delusions: The psychotic symptom rating scales (PSYRAT S). *Psychological Medicine, 29*(4), 879–889.

Häfner, H., Maurer, K., Trendler, G., an der Heiden, W., & Schmidt, M. (2005). The early course of schizophrenia and depression. *European Archives of Psychiatry and Clinical Neuroscience, 255,* 167–173.

Häfner, H., Riecher-Rössler, A., an der Heiden, W., Maurer, K., Fätkenheuer, B., & Löffler, W. (1993). Generating and testing a causal explanation of the gender difference in age at first onset of schizophrenia. *Psychological Medicine, 23,* 925–940.

Halari, R., Kumari, V., Mehorotra, R., Wheeler, M., Hines, M., & Sharma, T. (2004). The relationship of sex hormones and cortisol with cognitive functioning in schizophrenia. *Journal of Pharmacology, 18,* 366–374.

Halford, W. K., Schweitzer, R. D., & Varghese, F. N. (1991). Effects of family environment on negative symptoms and quality of life on psychotic patients. *Hospital and Community Psychiatry, 42,* 1241–1247.

Hans, S. L., Marcus, J., Henson, L., Auerbach, J. G., & Mirsky, A. F. (1992). Interpersonal behavior of children at risk for schizophrenia. *Psychiatry, 55,* 314–335.

Harding, C. M., Brooks, G. W., Ashikaga, T., Strauss, J. S., & Breier, A. (1987a). The Vermont longitudinal study of persons with severe mental illness, I: Methodology, study sample, and overall status 32 years later. *American Journal of Psychiatry, 144,* 718–726.

Harding, C. M., Brooks, G. W., Ashikaga, T., Strauss, J. S., & Breier, A. (1987b). The Vermont longitudinal study of persons with severe mental illness, II: Long-term outcome of subjects who retrospectively met *DSM-II* criteria for schizophrenia. *American Journal of Psychiatry, 144*, 727–735.

Harris, M. (1996). Treating sexual abuse trauma with dually diagnosed women. *Community Mental Health Journal, 32*, 371–385.

Harris, M. J., & Jeste, D. V. (1988). Late-onset schizophrenia: An overview. *Schizophrenia Bulletin, 14*, 39–45.

Harrison, P. J., & Owen, M. J. (2003). Genes for schizophrenia: Recent findings and their pathophysiological implications. *The Lancet, 361*, 417–419.

Harrow, M., Grossman, L. S., Jobe, T. H., & Herbener, E. S. (2005). Do patients with schizophrenia ever show periods of recovery? A 15-year multi-follow-up study. *Schizophrenia Bulletin, 31*, 723–734.

Hatfield, A. B., & Lefley, H. P. (Eds.). (1987). *Families of the mentally ill: Coping and adaptation.* New York, NY: Guilford Press.

Hatfield, A. B., & Lefley, H. P. (Eds.). (1993). *Surviving mental illness: Stress, coping, and adaptation.* New York, NY: Guilford Press.

Hawton, K., Sutton, L., Haw, C., Sinclair, J., & Deeks, J. J. (2005). Schizophrenia and suicide: Systematic review of risk factors. *British Journal of Psychiatry, 187*, 9–20.

Haynes, S. (1986). Behavioral model of paranoid behaviors. *Behavior Therapy, 17*, 266–287.

Heaton, R. K., Gladsjo, J. A., Palmer, B. W., Kuck, J., Marcotte, T. D., & Jeste, D. V. (2001). Stability and course of neuropsychological deficits in schizophrenia. *Archives of General Psychiatry, 58*, 24–32.

Heinrichs, R. W. (2005). The primacy of cognition in schizophrenia. *American Psychologist, 60*, 229–242.

Heinssen, R. K., Liberman, R. P., & Kopelowicz, A. (2000). Psychosocial skills training for schizophrenia: Lessons from the laboratory. *Schizophrenia Bulletin, 26*, 21–46.

Hiday, V. A., Swartz, M. S., Swanson, J. W., Borum, R., & Wagner, H. R. (1999). Criminal victimization of persons with severe mental illness. *Psychiatric Services, 50*, 62–68.

Hodgins, S., & Côté, G. (1993). Major mental disorder and antisocial personality disorder: A criminal combination. *Bulletin of the American Academy of Psychiatry Law, 21*, 155–160.

Hodgins, S., & Côté, G. (1996). Schizophrenia and antisocial personality disorder: A criminal combination. In L. B. Schlesinger (Ed.), *Explorations in criminal psychopathology: Clincal syndromes with forensic implications* (pp. 217–237). Springfield, IL: Charles C. Thomas.

Hodgins, S., Mednick, S. A., Brennan, P. A., Schulsinger, F., & Engberg, M. (1996). Mental disorder and crime: Evidence from a Danish birth cohort. *Archives of General Psychiatry, 53*, 489–496.

Hollingshead, A. B., & Redlich, F. C. (1958). *Social class and mental illness: A community study.* New York, NY: John Wiley & Sons.

Hough, R. L., Landsverk, J. A., Karno, M., Burnam, A., Timbers, D. M., Escobar, J. I., & Regier, D. A. (1987). Utilization of health and mental health services by Los Angeles Mexican Americans and non-Hispanic whites. *Archives of General Psychiatry, 44*, 702–709.

Howard, R., Almeida, O., & Levy R. (1994). Phenomenology, demography and diagnosis in late paraphrenia. *Psychological Medicine, 24*, 397–410.

Howard, R., Rabins, P. V., Seeman, M. V., Jeste, D. V., & the International Late-Onset Schizophrenia Group (2000). Late-onset schizophrenia and very-late-onset schizophrenia-like psychosis: An international consensus. *American Journal of Psychiatry, 157*, 172–178.

Hu, T., Snowden, L. R., Jerrell, J. M., & Nguyen, T. D. (1991). Ethnic populations in public mental health: Services choices and level of use. *American Journal of Public Health, 81*, 1429–1434.

Huang, X. Y., Hung, B. J., Sun, F. K., Lin, J. D., & Chen, C. C. (2009). The experiences of carers in Taiwanese culture who have long-term schizophrenia in their families: A phenomenological study. *Journal of Psychiatric and Mental Health Nursing, 16*, 874–883.

Hutchings, P. S., & Dutton, M. A. (1993). Sexual assault history in a community mental health center clinical population. *Community Mental Health Journal, 29*, 59–63.

Inskip, H. M., Harris, E. C., & Barraclough, B. (1998). Lifetime risk of suicide for affective disorder, alcoholism, and schizophrenia. *British Journal of Psychiatry, 172*, 35–37.

Jablensky, A. (1989). Epidemiology and cross-cultural aspects of schizophrenia. *Psychiatric Annals, 19*, 516–524.

Jablensky, A. (1999). Schizophrenia: Epidemiology. *Current Opinion in Psychiatry, 12*, 19–28.

Jablensky, A. (2000). Epidemiology of schizophrenia: The global burden of disease and disability. *European Archives of Psychiatry and Clinical Neuroscience, 250*, 274–285.

Jablensky, A., McGrath, J., Herman, H., Castle, D., Gureje, O., Evans, M., . . . Harvey, C. (2000). Psychotic disorders in urban areas: An overview of the study on low prevalence disorders. *Australian and New Zealand Journal of Psychiatry, 34*, 221–236.

Jablensky, A., Sartorius, N., Ernberg, G., Anker, M., Korten, A., & Cooper, J. E. (1992). Schizophrenia: Manifestations, incidence, and course in different cultures—A World Health Organizationten country study. *Psychological Medical Monograph Supplement, 20*, 1–97.

Jacob, T. (1975). Family interaction in disturbed and normal families: A methodological and substantive review. *Psychological Bulletin, 82*, 33–65.

Jacobson, A. (1989). Physical and sexual assault histories among psychiatric outpatients. *American Journal of Psychiatry, 146*, 755–758.

Jacobson, A., & Herald, C. (1990). The relevance of childhood sexual abuse to adult psychiatric inpatient care. *Hospital and Community Psychiatry, 41*, 154–158.

Jacobson, A., & Richardson, B. (1987). Assault experiences of 100 psychiatric inpatients: Evidence of the need for routine inquiry. *American Journal of Psychiatry, 144*, 508–513.

Jimenez, J. M., Todman, M., Perez, M., Godoy, J. F., & Landon-Jimenez, D. V. (1996). The behavioral treatment of auditory hallucinatory responding of a schizophrenic patient. *Journal of Behavioral Therapy and Experimental Psychiatry, 27*, 299–310.

Jobe, T. H., & Harrow, M. (2005). Long-term outcome of patients with schizophrenia: A review. *Canadian Journal of Psychiatry, 50*, 892–900.

Jones, B. E., Gray, B. A., & Parsons, E. B. (1981). Manic-depressive illness among poor urban blacks. *American Journal of Psychiatry, 138*, 654–657.

Jones, B. E., Gray, B. A., & Parsons, E. B. (1983). Manic-depressive illness among poor urban Hispanics. *American Journal of Psychiatry, 140*, 1208–1210.

Jones, E. (1999). The phenomenology of abnormal belief. *Philosophy, Psychiatry, and Psychology, 6*, 1–16.

Junginger, J., Barker, S., & Coe, D. (1992). Mood theme and bizarreness of delusions in schizophrenia and mood psychosis. *Journal of Abnormal Psychology, 101*, 287–292.

Kane, J. M., & Marder, S. R. (1993). Psychopharmacologic treatment of schizophrenia. *Schizophrenia Bulletin, 19*, 287–302.

Kay, S. R., Fiszbein, A., & Opler, L. A. (1987). The positive and negative syndrome scale (PANSS) for schizophrenia. *Schizophrenia Bulletin, 13*, 261–276.

Kay, S. R., & Lindenmayer, J. (1987). Outcome predictors in acute schizophrenia: Prospective significance of background and clinical dimensions. *Journal of Nervous and Mental Disease, 175*, 152–160.

Kemp, R., Hayward, P., Applewhaite, G., Everitt, B., & David, A. (1996). Compliance therapy in psychotic patients: Randomised controlled trial. *British Medical Journal, 312*, 345–349.

Kemp, R., Kirov, G., Everitt, B., Hayward, P., & David, A. (1998). Randomised controlled trial of compliance therapy. 18-month follow-up. *British Journal of Psychiatry, 173,* 271–272.

Kendler, K. S. (1982). Demography of paranoid psychosis (delusional disorder): A review and comparison with schizophrenia and affective illness. *Archives of General Psychiatry, 39,* 890–902.

Kendler, K. S., & Diehl, S. R. (1993). The genetics of schizophrenia. *Schizophrenia Bulletin, 19,* 261–285.

Kern, R. S., Liberman, R. P., Kopelowicz, A., Mintz, J., & Green, M. F. (2002). Applications of errorless learning for improving work performance in persons with schizophrenia. *American Journal of Psychiatry, 159,* 1921–1926.

Kessler, R. C., Foster, C. L., Saunders, W. B., & Stang, P. E. (1995). Social consequences of psychiatric disorders, I: Educational attainment. *American Journal of Psychiatry, 152,* 1026–1032.

Kessler, R. C., Sonnega, A., Bromet, E., Hughes, M., & Nelson, C. B. (1995). Posttraumatic stress disorder in the national comorbidity survey. *Archives of General Psychiatry, 52,* 1048–1060.

Kindermann, S. S., Karimi, A., Symonds, L., Brown, G. G., & Jeste, D. V. (1997). Review of functional magnetic resonance imaging in schizophrenia. *Schizophrenia Research, 27,* 143–156.

Kirch, D. G. (1993). Infection and autoimmunity as etiologic factors in schizophrenia: A review and reappraisal. *Schizophrenia Bulletin, 19,* 355–370.

Knapp, M., Mangalore, R., & Simon, J. (2004). The global costs of schizophrenia. *Schizophrenia Bulletin, 30,* 279–293.

Kraepelin, E. (1971). *Dementia praecox and paraphrenia* (R. M. Barclay, Trans.). New York, NY: Robert E. Krieger. (Original work published 1919.)

Kramer, M. S., Vogel, W. H., DiJohnson, C., Dewey, D. A., Sheves, P., Cavicchia, S., . . . Kimes, I. (1989). Antidepressants in "depressed" schizophrenic inpatients. *Archives of General Psychiatry, 46,* 922–928.

Kranzler, H. R., Kadden, R. M., Burleson, J. A., Babor, T. F., Apter, A., & Rounsaville, B. J. (1995). Validity of psychiatric diagnoses in patients with substance use disorders: Is the interview more important than the interviewer? *Comprehensive Psychiatry, 36,* 278–288.

Kymalainen, J. A., & Weisman de Mamani, A. G. (2008). Expressed emotion, communication deviance, and culture in families of patients with schizophrenia: A review of the literature. *Cultural Diversity and Ethnic Minority Psychology, 14,* 85–91.

Lam, D. H. (1991). Psychosocial family intervention in schizophrenia: A review of empirical studies. *Psychological Medicine, 21,* 423–441.

Lawrie, S. M., & Abukmeil S. S. (1998). Brain abnormality in schizophrenia: A systematic and quantitative review of volumetric magnetic resonance imaging studies. *British Journal of Psychiatry, 172,* 110–120.

Leff, J., Tress, K., & Edwards, B. (1988). The clinical course of depressive symptoms in schizophrenia. *Schizophrenia Research, 1,* 25–30.

Leff, J., & Vaughn, C. (1985). *Expressed emotion in families: Its significance for mental illness.* New York, NY: Guilford Press.

Lefley, H. P. (1990). Culture and chronic mental illness. *Hospital and Community Psychiatry, 41,* 277–286.

Lehman, A. F., Myers, C. P., Dixon, L. B., & Johnson, J. L. (1994). Defining subgroups of dual diagnosis patients for service planning. *Hospital and Community Psychiatry, 45,* 556–561.

Lehman, A. F., Myers, C. P., Dixon, L. B., & Johnson, J. L. (1996). Detection of substance use disorders among psychiatric inpatients. *The Journal of Nervous and Mental Disease, 184,* 228–233.

Leung, A., & Chue, P. (2000). Sex differences in schizophrenia: A review of the literature. *Acta Psychiatrica Scandinavica, 401,* 3–38.

Levinson, D. F., & Levitt, M. M. (1987). Schizoaffective mania reconsidered. *The American Journal of Psychiatry, 144,* 415–425.

Levinson, D. F., & Mowry, B. J. (1991). Defining the schizophrenia spectrum: Issues for genetic linkage studies. *Schizophrenia Bulletin, 17,* 491–514.

Liberman, R. P. (1994). Treatment and rehabilitation of the seriously mentally ill in China: Impressions of a society in transition. *American Journal of Orthopsychiatry, 64,* 68–77.

Liberman, R. P., Mueser, K. T., Wallace, C. J., Jacobs, H. E., Eckman, T., & Massel, H. K. (1986). Training skills in the psychiatrically disabled: Learning coping and competence. *Schizophrenia Bulletin, 12,* 631–647.

Liddle, P. F. (1987). Schizophrenic syndromes, cognitive performance and neurological dysfunction. *Psychological Medicine, 17,* 49–57.

Liddle, P. F. (1995). Brain imaging. In S. R. Hirsch & D. R. Weinberger (Eds.), *Schizophrenia* (pp. 425–439). Cambridge, MA: Blackwell Science.

Liddle, P. F. (1997). Dynamic neuroimaging with PET, SPET or fMRI. *International Review of Psychiatry, 9,* 331–337.

Lieberman, J. A., Mailman, R. B., Duncan, G., Sikich, L., Chakos, M., Nichols, D. E., & Kraus, J. E. (1998). A decade of serotonin research: Role of serotonin in treatment of psychosis. *Biological Psychiatry, 44,* 1099–1117.

Lim, K. O., Hedehus, M., de Crespigny, A., Menon, V., & Moseley, M. (1998). Diffusion tensor imaging of white matter tracts in schizophrenia. *Biological Psychiatry, 43* (Suppl. 8S), 11S.

Lin, K.-M., & Kleinman, A. M. (1988). Psychopathology and clinical course of schizophrenia: A cross-cultural perspective. *Schizophrenia Bulletin, 14,* 555–567.

Lincoln, C. V., & McGorry, P. (1995). Who cares? Pathways to psychiatric care for young people experiencing a first episode of psychosis. *Psychiatric Services, 46,* 1166–1171.

Lincoln, E. C., & Mamiya, L. H. (1990). *The black church in the African American experience.* Durham, NC: Duke University Press.

Lipschitz, D. S., Kaplan, M. L., Sorkenn, J. B., Faedda, G. L., Chorney, P., & Asnis, G. M. (1996). Prevalence and characteristics of physical and sexual abuse among psychiatric outpatients. *Psychiatric Services, 47,* 189–191.

Lo, W. H., & Lo, T. (1977). A ten-year follow-up study of Chinese schizophrenics in Hong Kong. *British Journal of Psychiatry, 131,* 63–66.

Lopez, S. R., Ramirez Garcia, J. I., Ullman, J. B., Kopelowicz, A., Jenkins, J., Breitborde, N. J. K., & Placencia, P. (2009). Cultural variability in the manifestation of expressed emotion. *Family Process, 48,* 179–194.

Loring, M., & Powell, B. (1988). Gender, race, and *DSM-II*: A study of the objectivity of psychiatric diagnostic behavior. *Journal of Health and Social Behavior, 29,* 1–22.

Lysaker, P. H., Bell, M. D., Zito, W. S., & Bioty, S. M. (1995). Social skills at work: Deficits and predictors of improvement in schizophrenia. *Journal of Nervous and Mental Disease, 183,* 688–692.

Magaña, A. B., Goldstein, M. J., Karno, M., Miklowitz, D. J., Jenkins, J., & Falloon, I. R. H. (1986). A brief method for assessing expressed emotion in relatives of psychiatric patients. *Psychiatry Research, 17,* 203–212.

Magliano, L., Fadden, G., Madianos, M., de Almeida, J. M., Held, T., Guarneri, M., . . . Maj, M. (1998). Burden on the families of patients with schizophrenia: Results of the BIOMED I study. *Social Psychiatry and Psychiatric Epidemiology, 33,* 405–412.

Maisto, S. A., Carey, M. P., Carey, K. B., Gordon, C. M., & Gleason, J. R. (2000). Use of the AU DIT and the DAST-10 to identify alcohol and drug use disorders among adults with a severe and persistent mental illness. *Psychological Assessment, 12,* 186–192.

Malla, A. K., Norman, R. M. G., & Joober, R. (2005). First-episode psychosis, early intervention, and outcome: What haven't we learned? *Canadian Journal of Psychiatry, 50,* 881–891.

Malla, A., & Payne, J. (2005). First-episode psychosis: Psychopathology, quality of life, and functional outcome. *Schizophrenia Bulletin, 31,* 650–671.

Manschreck, T. C. (1996). Delusional disorder: The recognition and management of paranoia. *The Journal of Clinical Psychiatry, 57,* 32–38.

Marengo, J. (1994). Classifying the courses of schizophrenia. *Schizophrenia Bulletin, 20,* 519–536.

Marwaha, S., & Johnson, S. (2004). Schizophrenia and employment: A review. *Social Psychiatry and Psychiatric Epidemiology, 39,* 337–349.

Mattes, J. A., & Nayak, D. (1984). Lithium versus fluphenazine for prophylaxis in mainly schizophrenic schizoaffectives. *Biological Psychiatry, 19,* 445–449.

May, A. (1997). Psychopathology and religion in the era of "enlightened science": A case report. *European Journal of Psychiatry, 11,* 14–20.

McClure, R. J., Keshavan, M. S., & Pettegrew, J. W. (1998). Chemical and physiologic brain imaging in schizophrenia. *Psychiatric Clinics of North America, 21,* 93–122.

McDonald, C., Grech, A., Toulopoulou, T., Schulze, K., Chapple, B., Sham, P., . . . Murray, R. M. (2002). Brain volumes in familial and non-familial schizophrenic probands and their unaffected relatives. *American Journal of Medical Genetics and Neuropsychiatric Genetics, 114,* 616–625.

McEvoy, J. P., Freter, S., Everett, G., Geller, J. L., Appelbaum, P., Apperson, L. J., & Roth, L. (1989). Insight and the clinical outcome of schizophrenic patients. *The Journal of Nervous and Mental Disease, 177,* 48–51.

McGrath, J., Saha, S., Welham, J., El Saadi, O., MacCauley, C., & Chant, D. (2004). A systematic review of the incidence of schizophrenia: The distribution and the influence of sex, urbanicity, migrant status, and methodology. *BMC. Medicine, 2,* 13.

McGuffin, P., Owen, M. J., & Farmer, A. E. (1995). Genetic basis of schizophrenia. *The Lancet, 346,* 678–682.

Merriam, A. E., Kay, S. R., Opler, L. A., Kushner, S. F., & van Praag, H. M. (1990). Neurological signs and the positive-negative dimension in schizophrenia. *Biological Psychiatry, 28,* 181–192.

Miyamoto, S., LaMantia, A. S., Duncan, G. E., Sullivan, P., Gilmore, J. H., & Lieberman, A. (2003). Recent advances in the neurobiology of schizophrenia. *Molecular Interventions, 3,* 27–39.

Monahan, J., Steadman, H. J., Silver, E., Appelbaum, P. S., Robbins, P. C., Mulvey, E. P., . . . Banks, S. (2001). *Rethinking risk assessment: The MacArthur study of mental disorder and violence.* New York, NY: Oxford University Press.

Montero, I., Asencio, A., Hernández, I., Masanet, M. J., Lacruz, M., Bellver, F., . . . Ruiz, I. (2001). Two strategies for family intervention in schizophrenia. A randomized trial in a Mediterranean environment. *Schizophrenia Bulletin, 27,* 661–670.

Moore, H., West, A. R., & Grace, A. A. (1999). The regulation of forebrain dopamine transmission: Relevance to the pathophysiology and psychopathology of schizophrenia. *Biological Psychiatry, 46,* 40–55.

Moos, R. H., & Moos, B. S. (1981). *Family environment scale manual.* Palo Alto, CA: Consulting Psychologists Press.

Morales-Dorta, J. (1976). *Puerto Rican espiritismo: Religion and psychotherapy.* New York, NY: Vantage Press.

Mueser, K. T., & Bellack, A. S. (1998). Social skills and social functioning. In K. T. Mueser and N. Tarrier (Eds.), *Handbook of social functioning in schizophrenia* (pp. 79–96). Boston, MA: Allyn and Bacon.

Mueser, K. T., Bellack, A. S., & Brady, E. U. (1990). Hallucinations in schizophrenia. *Acta Psychiatrica Scandinavica, 82,* 26–29.

Mueser, K. T., Bellack, A. S., Douglas, M. S., & Morrison, R. L. (1991a). Prevalence and stability of social skill deficits in schizophrenia. *Schizophrenia Research, 5,* 167–176.

Mueser, K. T., Bellack, A. S., Douglas, M. S., & Wade, J. H. (1991b). Prediction of social skill acquisition in schizophrenic and major affective disorder patients from memory and symptomatology. *Psychiatry Research, 37,* 281–296.

Mueser, K. T., Bellack, A. S., Morrison, R. L., & Wade, J. H. (1990). Gender, social competence, and symptomatology in schizophrenia: A longitudinal analysis. *Journal of Abnormal Psychology, 99,* 138–147.

Mueser, K. T., Bellack, A. S., Morrison, R. L., & Wixted, J. T. (1990). Social competence in schizophrenia: Premorbid adjustment, social skill, and domains of functioning. *Journal of Psychiatric Research, 24,* 51–63.

Mueser, K. T., Bellack, A. S., Wade, J. H., Sayers, S. L., Tierney, A., & Haas, G. (1993). Expressed emotion, social skill, and response to negative affect in schizophrenia. *Journal of Abnormal Psychology, 102,* 339–351.

Mueser, K. T., Bennett, M., & Kushner, M. G. (1995). Epidemiology of substance use disorders among persons with chronic mental illnesses. In A. Lehman & L. Dixon (Eds.), *Double jeopardy: Chronic mental illness and substance abuse* (pp. 9–25). Chur, Switzerland: HarwoodAcademic.

Mueser, K. T., & Berenbaum, H. (1990). Psychodynamic treatment of schizophrenia: Is there a future? *Psychological Medicine, 20,* 253–262.

Mueser, K. T., Bond, G. R., Drake, R. E., & Resnick, S. G. (1998). Models of community care for severe mental illness: A review of research on case management. *Schizophrenia Bulletin, 24,* 37–74.

Mueser, K. T., Curran, P. J., & McHugo, G. J. (1997). Factor structure of the Brief Psychiatric Rating Scale in schizophrenia. *Psychological Assessment, 9,* 196–204.

Mueser, K. T., Douglas, M. S., Bellack, A. S., & Morrison, R. L. (1991). Assessment of enduring deficit and negative symptom subtypes in schizophrenia. *Schizophrenia Bulletin, 17,* 565–582.

Mueser, K. T., Drake, R. E., & Bond, G. R. (1997). Recent advances in psychiatric rehabilitation for patients with severe mental illness. *Harvard Review of Psychiatry, 5,* 123–137.

Mueser, K. T., & Glynn, S. M. (1999). *Behavioral family therapy for psychiatric disorders* (2nd ed.). Oakland, CA: New Harbinger.

Mueser, K. T., Goodman, L. B., Trumbetta, S. L., Rosenberg, S. D., Osher, F. C., Vidaver, R., . . . Foy, D. W. (1998). Trauma and posttraumatic stress disorder in severe mental illness. *Journal of Consulting and Clinical Psychology, 66,* 493–499.

Mueser, K. T., Levine, S., Bellack, A. S., Douglas, M. S., & Brady, E. U. (1990). Social skills training for acute psychiatric patients. *Hospital and Community Psychiatry, 41,* 1249–1251.

Mueser, K. T., & McGurk, S. R. (2004). Schizophrenia. *The Lancet, 363,* 2063–2072.

Mueser, K. T., Rosenberg, S. D., Drake, R. E., Miles, K. M., Wolford, G., Vidaver, R., & Carrieri, K. (1999). Conduct disorder, antisocial personality disorder, and substance use disorders in schizophrenia and major affective disorders. *Journal of Studies on Alcohol, 60,* 278–284.

Mueser, K. T., Rosenberg, S. D., Goodman, L. A., & Trumbetta, S. L. (2002). Trauma, PTSD, and the course of schizophrenia: An interactive model. *Schizophrenia Research, 53,* 123–143.

Mueser, K. T., Salyers, M. P., & Mueser, P. R. (2001). A prospective analysis of work in schizophrenia. *Schizophrenia Bulletin, 27,* 281–296.

Mueser, K. T., Salyers, M. P., Rosenberg, S. D., Goodman, L. A., Essock, S. M., Osher, F. C., . . . the 5 Site Health & Risk Study Research Committee. (2004). Interpersonal trauma and posttraumatic stress disorder in patients with severe mental illness: Demographic, clinical, and health correlates. *Schizophrenia Bulletin, 30,* 45–57.

Mueser, K. T., Yarnold, P. R., & Bellack, A. S. (1992). Diagnostic and demographic correlates of substance abuse in schizophrenia and major affective disorder. *Acta Psychiatrica Scandinavica, 85,* 48–55.

Mueser, K. T., Yarnold, P. R., Levinson, D. F., Singh, H., Bellack, A. S., Kee, K., . . . Yadalam, K. Y. (1990). Prevalence of substance abuse in schizophrenia: Demographic and clinical correlates. *Schizophrenia Bulletin, 16,* 31–56.

Munk-Jørgensen, P. (1987). First-admission rates and marital status of schizophrenics. *Acta Psychiatrica Scandinavica, 76,* 210–216.

Murphy, H. B. M., & Raman, A. C. (1971). The chronicity of schizophrenia in indigenous tropical peoples. *British Journal of Psychiatry, 118,* 489–497.

Murray, C. J. L., & Lopez, A. D. (Eds.). (1996). *The global burden of disease and injury series, Vol. I: A comprehensive assessment of mortality and disability from diseases, injuries, and risk factors in 1990 and projected to 2020.* Cambridge, MA: Harvard University Press.

Narrow, W. E., Rae, D. S., Robins, L. N., & Regier, D. A. (2002). Revised prevalence estimates of mental disorders in the United States. *Archives of General Psychiatry, 59,* 115–123.

Neumann, C. S., Grimes, K., Walker, E., & Baum, K. (1995). Developmental pathways to schizophrenia: Behavioral subtypes. *Journal of Abnormal Psychology, 104,* 558–566.

Nolan, K. A., Volavka, J., Mohr, P., & Czobor, P. (1999). Psychopathy and violent behavior among patients with schizophrenia or schizoaffective disorder. *Psychiatric Services, 50,* 787–792.

Norman, R. M., Scholten, D. J., Malla, A. K., & Ballageer, T. (2005). Early signs in schizophrenia spectrum disorders. *The Journal of Nervous and Mental Disease, 193,* 17–23.

Nuechterlein, K. H., & Dawson, M. E. (1984). A heuristic vulnerability/stress model of schizophrenic episodes. *Schizophrenia Bulletin, 10,* 300–312.

Oldridge, M. L., & Hughes, I. C. T. (1992). Psychological well-being in families with a member suffering from schizophrenia. *British Journal of Psychiatry, 161,* 249–251.

Overall, J. E., & Gorham, D. R. (1962). The brief psychiatric rating scale. *Psychological Reports, 10,* 799–812.

Padgett, D. K., Patrick, C., Burns, B. J., & Schlesinger, H. J. (1994). Women and outpatient mental health services: Use by black, Hispanic, and white women in a national insured population. *The Journal of Mental Health Administration, 21,* 347–360.

Palmer, B. W., Heaton, R. K., Paulsen, J. S., Kuck, J., Braff, D., Harris, M. J., . . . Jeste, D. V. (1997). Is it possible to be schizophrenic yet neuropsychologically normal? *Neuropsychology, 11,* 437–446.

Palmer, B. A., Pankratz, V. S., & Bostwick, J. M. (2005). The lifetime risk of suicide in schizophrenia: A reexamination. *Archives of General Psychiatry, 62,* 247–253.

Parra, F. (1985). Social tolerance of the mentally ill in the Mexican American community. *International Journal of Social Psychiatry, 31,* 37–47.

Parrott, B., & Lewine, R. (2005). Socioeconomic status of origin and the clinical expression of schizophrenia. *Schizophrenia Research, 75,* 417–424.

Patterson, T. L., Goldman, S., McKibbin, C. L., Hughs, T., & Jeste, D. (2001). UCSD performance-based skills assessment: Development of a new measure of everyday functioning for severely mentally ill adults. *Schizophrenia Bulletin, 27,* 235–245.

Pearlson, G. D. (2000). Neurobiology of schizophrenia. *Annals of Neurology, 48,* 556–566.

Peen, J., & Dekker, J. (1997). Admission rates for schizophrenia in the Netherlands: An urban/rural comparison. *Acta Psychiatrica Scandinavica, 96,* 301–305.

Penn, D. L., Combs, D. R., & Mohamed, S. (2001). Social cognition and social functioning in schizophrenia. In P. W. Corrigan & D. L. Penn (Eds.), *Social cognition and schizophrenia* (pp. 97–122). Washington, DC: American Psychological Association.

Penn, D. L., Corrigan, P. W., Bentall, R. P., Racenstein, J. M., & Newman, L. (1997). Social cognition in schizophrenia. *Psychological Bulletin, 121,* 114–132.

Penn, D., Hope, D. A., Spaulding, W. D., & Kucera, J. (1994). Social anxiety in schizophrenia. *Schizophrenia Research, 11,* 277–284.

Penn, D. L., Mueser, K. T., Spaulding, W. D., Hope, D. A., & Reed, D. (1995). Information processing and social competence in chronic schizophrenia. *Schizophrenia Bulletin, 21,* 269–281.

Penn, D. L., Waldheter, E. J., Perkins, D. O., Mueser, K. T., & Lieberman, J. A. (2005). Psychosocial treatment for first-episode psychosis: A research update. *American Journal of Psychiatry, 162,* 2220–2232.

Perlstein, W. M., Carter, C. S., Noll, D. C., & Cohen, J. D. (2001). Relation of prefrontal cortex dysfunction to working memory and symptoms of schizophrenia. *American Journal of Psychiatry, 158,* 1105–1113.

Phillips, S. D., Burns, B. J., Edgar, E. R., Mueser, K. T., Linkins, K. W., Rosenheck, R. A., . . . Herr, E. C. M. (2001). Moving assertive community treatment into standard practice. *Psychiatric Services, 52,* 771–779.

Pinkham, A., Penn, D., Perkins, D., & Lieberman, J. (2003). Implications for the neural basis of social cognition for the study of schizophrenia. *The American Journal of Psychiatry, 160,* 815–824.

Pitschel-Walz, G., Leucht, S., Bäuml, J., Kissling, W., & Engel, R. R. (2001). The effect of family interventions on relapse and rehospitalization in schizophrenia: A meta-analysis. *Schizophrenia Bulletin, 27,* 73–92.

Pope, H. G., & Lipinski, J. F. (1978). Diagnosis in schizophrenia and manic-depressive illness. *Archives of General Psychiatry, 35,* 811–828.

Qin, P., & Nordentoft, M. (2005). Suicide risk in relation to psychiatric hospitalization: Evidence based on longitudinal registers. *Archives of General Psychiatry, 62,* 427–432.

Quinlivan, R., Hough, R., Crowell, A., Beach, C., Hofstetter, R., & Kenworthy, K. (1995). Service utilization and costs of care for severely mentally ill clients in an intensive case management program. *Psychiatric Services, 46,* 365–371.

Regier, D. A., Farmer, M. E., Rae, D. S., Locke, B. Z., Keith, S. J., Judd, L. L., & Goodwin, F. K. (1990). Comorbidity of mental disorders with alcohol and other drug abuse. *Journal of the American Medical Association, 264,* 2511–2518.

Resnick, H. S., Kilpatrick, D. G., Dansky, B. S., Saunders, B. E., & Best, C. L. (1993). Prevalence of civilian trauma and post-traumatic stress disorder in a representative national sample of women. *Journal of Consulting and Clinical Psychology, 61,* 984–991.

Robins, L. N. (1966). *Deviant children grown up.* Huntington, NY: Krieger.

Robins, L. N., & Price, R. K. (1991). Adult disorders predicted by childhood conduct problems: Results from the NIMH Epidemiologic Catchment Area project. *Psychiatry, 54,* 116–132.

Rodrigo, G., Lusiardo, M., Briggs, G., & Ulmer, A. (1991). Differences between schizophrenics born in winter and summer. *Acta Psychiatrica Scandinavica, 84,* 320–322.

Rose, S. M., Peabody, C. G., & Stratigeas, B. (1991). Undetected abuse among intensive case management clients. *Hospital and Community Psychiatry, 42*, 499–503.

Rosenberg, S. D., Drake, R. E., Wolford, G. L., Mueser, K. T., Oxman, T. E., Vidaver, R. M., . . . Luckoor, R. (1998). Dartmouth assessment of lifestyle instrument (DALI): A substance use disorder screen for people with severe mental illness. *The American Journal of Psychiatry, 155*, 232–238.

Rosenberg, S. D., Mueser, K. T., Friedman, M. J., Gorman, P. G., Drake, R. E., Vidaver, R. M., . . . Jankowski, M. K. (2001). Developing effective treatments for posttraumatic disorders: A review and proposal. *Psychiatric Services, 52*, 1453–1461.

Rosenheck, R., Leslie, D., Keefe, R., McEvoy, J., Swartz, M., Perkins, D., . . . Lieberman, J. (2006). Barriers to employment for people with schizophrenia. *The American Journal of Psychiatry, 163*, 411–417.

Ross, C. A., Anderson, G., & Clark, P. (1994). Childhood abuse and the positive symptoms of schizophrenia. *Hospital and Community Psychiatry, 45*, 489–491.

Roy, A. (Ed.) (1986). *Suicide.* Baltimore, MD: Williams and Wilkins.

Rutter, M. (1984). Psychopathology and development, I: Childhood antecedents of adult psychiatric disorder. *Australian and New Zealand Journal of Psychiatry, 18*, 225–234.

Saha, S., Chant, D., Welham, J., & McGrath, J. (2005). A systematic review of the prevalence of schizophrenia. *Public Library of Science, 2*, e141.

Saha, S., Welham, J., Chant, D., & McGrath, J. (2006). Incidence of schizophrenia does not vary with economic status of the country. *Social Psychiatry and Psychiatric Epidemiology, 41*, 338–340.

Salem, J. E., & Kring, A. M. (1998). The role of gender in the reduction of etiologic heterogeneity in schizophrenia. *Clinical Psychology Review, 18*, 795–819.

Salokangas, R. K. R. (1978). Socioeconomic development and schizophrenia. *Psychiatria Fennica*, 103–112.

Samele, C., van Os, J., McKenzie, K., Wright, A., Gilvarry, C., Manley, C., . . . Murray, R. (2001). Does socioeconomic status predict course and outcome in patients with psychosis? *Social Psychiatry and Psychiatric Epidemiology, 36*, 573–581.

Sammons, M. T. (2005). Pharmacotherapy for delusional disorder and associated conditions. *Professional Psychology: Research and Practice, 36*, 476–479.

Sands, J. R., & Harrow, M. (1999). Depression during the longitudinal course of schizophrenia. *Schizophrenia Bulletin, 25*, 157–171.

Sartorius, N., Jablensky, A., Korten, A., Ernberg, G., Anker, M., Cooper, J. E., & Day, R. (1986). Early manifestations and first-contact incidence of schizophrenia in different cultures. *Psychological Medicine, 16*, 909–928.

Schaub, A., Behrendt, B., Brenner, H. D., Mueser, K. T., & Liberman, R. P. (1998). Training schizophrenic patients to manage their symptoms: Predictors of treatment response to the German version of the symptom management module. *Schizophrenia Research, 31*, 121–130.

Schiffman, J., Walker, E., Ekstrom, M., Schulsinger, F., Sorensen, H., & Mednick, S. (2004). Childhood videotaped social and neuromotor precursors of schizophrenia: A prospective investigation. *The American Journal of Psychiatry, 161*, 2021–2027.

Schock, K., Clay, C., & Cipani, E. (1998). Making sense of schizophrenic symptoms: Delusional statements and behavior may be functional in purpose. *Journal of Behavior Therapy and Experimental Psychiatry, 29*, 131–141.

Schuckit, M. A. (1995). *Drug and alcohol abuse: A clinical guide to diagnosis and treatment* (Critical issues in psychiatry) (4th ed.). New York, NY: Plenum Press.

Searles, H. (1965). *Collected papers on schizophrenia and related subjects.* New York, NY: International Universities Press.

Sedler, M. J. (1995). Understanding delusions. *The Psychiatric Clinics of North America, 18,* 251–262.

Sevy, S., & Davidson, M. (1995). The cost of cognitive impairment in schizophrenia. *Schizophrenia Research, 17,* 1–3.

Silver, E., Arseneault, L., Langley, J., Caspi, A., & Moffitt, T. E. (2005). Mental disorder and violent victimization in a total birth cohort. *American Journal of Public Health, 95,* 2015–2021.

Skilbeck, W. M., Acosta, F. X., Yamamoto, J., & Evans, L. A. (1984). Self-reported psychiatric symptoms among black, Hispanic, and white outpatients. *Journal of Clinical Psychology, 40,* 1184–1189.

Smith, T. E., Hull, J. W., Anthony, D. T., Goodman, M., Hedayat-Harris, A., Felger, T., . . . Romanelli, S. (1997). Post-hospitalization treatment adherence of schizophrenic patients: Gender differences in skill acquisition. *Psychiatry Research, 69,* 123–129.

Smith, T. E., Hull, J. W., Romanelli, S., Fertuck, E., & Weiss, K. A. (1999). Symptoms and neurocognition as rate limiters in skills training for psychotic patients. *The American Journal of Psychiatry, 156,* 1817–1818.

Steadman, H. J., Mulvey, E. P., Monahan, J., Robbins, P. C., Appelbaum, P. S., Grisso, T., . . . Silver, E. (1998). Violence by people discharged from acute psychiatric inpatient facilities and by others in the same neighborhoods. *Archives of General Psychiatry, 55,* 393–401.

Stone, A., Greenstein, R., Gamble, G., & McLellan, A. T. (1993). Cocaine use in chronic schizophrenic outpatients receiving depot neuroleptic medications. *Hospital and Community Psychiatry, 44,* 176–177.

Sue, D. W., & Sue, D. C. (1990). *Counseling the culturally different: Theory and practice* (2nd ed.). New York, NY: John Wiley & Sons.

Sue, S., Fujino, D. C., Hu, L.-T., Takeuchi, D. T., & Zane, N. W. S. (1991). Community mental health services for ethnic minority groups: A test of the cultural responsiveness hypothesis. *Journal of Consulting and Clinical Psychology, 59,* 533–540.

Susser, E., & Lin, S. (1992). Schizophrenia after prenatal exposure to the Dutch Hunger Winter of 1944–1945. *Archives of General Psychiatry, 49,* 983–988.

Susser, E., Neugebauer, R., Hoek, H. W., Brown, A. S., Lin, S., Labovitz, D., & Gorman, J. M. (1996). Schizophrenia after prenatal famine: Further evidence. *Archives of General Psychiatry, 53,* 25–31.

Susser, E., Struening, E. L., & Conover, S. (1989). Psychiatric problems in homeless men: Lifetime psychosis, substance use, and current distress in new arrivals at New York City shelters. *Archives of General Psychiatry, 46,* 845–850.

Swanson, J. W. (1994). Mental disorder, substance abuse, and community violence: An epidemiological approach. In J. Monahan & H. Steadman (Eds.), *Violence and mental disorder: Developments in risk assessment* (pp. 101–136). Chicago, IL: University of Chicago Press.

Swanson, J. W., Holzer, C. E., Ganju, V. K., & Jono, R. T. (1990). Violence and psychiatric disorder in the community: Evidence from the Epidemiologic Catchment Area Surveys. *Hospital and Community Psychiatry, 41,* 761–770.

Swartz, M. S., Swanson, J. W., Hiday, V. A., Borum, R., Wagner, H. R., & Burns, B. J. (1998). Violence and severe mental illness: The effects of substance abuse and nonadherence to medication. *The American Journal of Psychiatry, 155,* 226–231.

Switzer, G. E., Dew, M. A., Thompson, K., Goycoolea, J. M., Derricott, T., & Mullins, S. D. (1999). Posttraumatic stress disorder and service utilization among urban mental health center clients. *Journal of Traumatic Stress, 12,* 25–39.

Takei, N., Mortensen, P. B., Klaening, U., Murray, R. M., Sham, P. C., O'Callaghan, E., & Munk-Jørgensen, P. (1996). Relationship between in utero exposure to influenza epidemics and risk of schizophrenia in Denmark. *Biological Psychiatry, 40,* 817–824.

Takei, N., Sham, P. C., O'Callaghan, E., Glover, G., & Murray, R. M. (1995). Schizophrenia: Increased risk associated with winter and city birth—A case-control study in 12 regions within England and Wales. *Journal of Epidemiology and Community Health, 49,* 106–109.

Tandon, R., Keshavan, M.S., & Nasrallah, H.A. (2008a). Schizophrenia "just the facts": What we know in 2008, Part 1: Overview. *Schizophrenia Research, 100,* 4–19.

Tandon, R., Keshavan, M. S., & Nasrallah, H. A. (2008b). Schizophrenia "just the facts": What we know in 2008, Part 2: Epidemiology and etiology. *Schizophrenia Research, 102,* 1–18.

Telles, C., Karno, M., Mintz, J., Paz, G., Arias, M., Tucker, D., & Lopez, S. (1995). Immigrant families coping with schizophrenia: Behavioral family intervention v. case management with a low-income Spanish-speaking population. *British Journal of Psychiatry, 167,* 473–479.

Terkelsen, K. G. (1983). Schizophrenia and the family, II: Adverse effects of family therapy. *Family Process, 22,* 191–200.

Tessler, R., & Gamache, G. (1995). *Evaluating family experiences with severe mental illness*: To be used in conjunction with the Family Experiences Interview Schedule (FEI S): The Evaluation Center @ HSRI toolkit. Cambridge, MA: The Evaluation Center.

Test, M. A., Wallisch, L. S., Allness, D. J., & Ripp, K. (1989). Substance use in young adults with schizophrenic disorders. *Schizophrenia Bulletin, 15,* 465–476.

Thomas, H. V., Dalman, C., David, A. S., Gentz, J., Lewis, G., & Allebeck, P. (2001). Obstetric complications and risk of schizophrenia: Effect of gender, age at diagnosis and maternal history of psychosis. *British Journal of Psychiatry, 179,* 409–414.

Tien, A. Y., & Eaton, W. W. (1992). Psychopathologic precursors and sociodemographic risk factors for the schizophrenia syndrome. *Archives of General Psychiatry, 49,* 37–46.

Tienari, P. (1991). Interaction between genetic vulnerability and family environment: The Finnish Adoptive Family Study of schizophrenia. *Acta Psychiatrica Scandinavica, 84,* 460–465.

Tienari, P., Sorri, A., Lahti, I., Naarala, M., Wahlberg, K., Moring, J., . . . Wynne, L. C. (1987). Genetic and psychosocial factors in schizophrenia: The Finnish Adoptive Family Study. *Schizophrenia Bulletin, 13,* 477–484.

Tienari, P., Wynne, L. C., Sorri, A., Lahti, I., Lasky, K., Moring, J., . . . Wahlberg, K. (2004). Genotype-environment interaction in schizophrenia spectrum disorder. *British Journal of Psychiatry, 184,* 216–222.

Tjaden, P., & Thoennes, N. (1998, November). *Prevalence, incidence, and consequences of violence against women: Findings from the National Violence against Women Survey* (Research in Brief). Washington, DC: U.S. Department of Justice, National Institute of Justice.

Tohen, M., Strakowski, S. M., Zarate, C., Hennen, J., Stoll, A. L., Suppes, T., . . . Baldessarini, R. J. (2000). The McLean-Harvard first episode project: Six month symptomatic and functional outcome in affective and nonaffective psychosis. *Biological Psychiatry, 48,* 467–476.

Tollefson, G. D., & Sanger, T. M. (1997). Negative symptoms: A path analytic approach to a double-blind, placebo- and haloperidol-controlled clinical trial with olanzapine. *American Journal of Psychiatry, 154,* 466–474.

Torrey, E. F. (1992). Are we overestimating the genetic contribution to schizophrenia? *Schizophrenia Bulletin, 18,* 159–170.

Torrey, E. F. (2001). *Surviving schizophrenia* (4th ed.). New York, NY: HarperCollins.

Torrey, E. F., Bowler, A. E., & Clark, K. (1997). Urban birth and residence as risk factors for psychoses: An analysis of 1880 data. *Schizophrenia Research, 25,* 169–176.

Torrey, E. F., Bowler, A. E., Rawlings, R., & Terrazas, A. (1993). Seasonality of schizophrenia and stillbirths. *Schizophrenia Bulletin, 19*, 557–562.

Torrey, E. F., Stieber, J., Ezekiel, J., Wolfe, S. M., Sharfstein, J., Noble, J. H., & Flynn, L. M. (1992). *Criminalizing the seriously mentally ill: The abuse of jails as mental hospitals.* Joint Report of the National Alliance of the Mentally Ill. Washington, DC: Public Citizen's Health Research Group.

Tsuang, M. T. (1986). Predictors of poor and good outcome in schizophrenia. In L. Erlenmeyer-Kimling & N. E. Miller (Eds.), *Life-span research on the prediction of psychopathology.* Hillsdale, NJ: Erlbaum.

Uttaro, T., & Mechanic, D. (1994). The NAMI consumer survey analysis of unmet needs. *Hospital and Community Psychiatry, 45*, 372–374.

Valenstein, M., Blow, F. C., Copeland, L. A., McCarthy, J. F., Zeber, J. E., Gillon, L., . . . Stavenger, T. (2004). Poor antipsychotic adherence among patients with schizophrenia: Medication and patient factors. *Schizophrenia Bulletin, 30*, 255–264.

Van Der Does, A. J. W., Dingemans, P. M. A. J., Linszen, D. H., Nugter, M. A., & Scholte, W. F. (1993). Symptom dimensions and cognitive and social functioning in recent-onset schizophrenia. *Psychological Medicine, 23*, 745–753.

Velligan, D. I., Mahurin, R. K., Diamond, P. L., Hazleton, B. C., Eckert, S. L., & Miller, A. L. (1997). The functional significance of symptomatology and cognitive function in schizophrenia. *Schizophrenia Research, 25*, 21–31.

Wahlbeck, K., Cheine, M., Essali, A., & Adams, C. (1999). Evidence of clozapine's effectiveness in schizophrenia: A systematic review and meta-analysis of randomized trials. *The American Journal of Psychiatry, 156*, 990–999.

Walker, E., Downey, G., & Caspi, A. (1991). Twin studies of psychopathology: Why do the concordance rates vary? *Schizophrenia Research, 5*, 211–221.

Walker, E. F., Grimes, K. E., Davis, D. M., & Smith, A. J. (1993). Childhood precursors of schizophrenia: Facial expressions of emotion. *The American Journal of Psychiatry, 150*, 1654–1660.

Wallace, C. J., Liberman, R. P., Tauber, R., & Wallace, J. (2000). The Independent Living Skills Survey: A comprehensive measure of the community functioning of severely and persistently mentally ill individuals. *Schizophrenia Bulletin, 26*, 631–658.

Watt, N. F. (1978). Patterns of childhood social development in adult schizophrenics. *Archives of General Psychiatry, 35*, 160–165.

Waxler, N. E., & Mishler, E. G. (1971). Parental interaction with schizophrenic children and well siblings. *Archives of General Psychiatry, 25*, 223–231.

Webb, C., Pfeiffer, M., Mueser, K. T., Mensch, E., DeGirolomo, J., & Levenson, D. F. (1998). Burden and well-being of caregivers for the severely mentally ill: The role of coping style and social support. *Schizophrenia Research, 34*, 169–180.

Westermeyer, J. (1989). Psychiatric epidemiology across cultures: Current issues and trends. *Transcultural Psychiatric Research Review, 26*, 5–25.

Whaley, A. L. (1997). Ethnicity, race, paranoia, and psychiatric diagnoses: Clinician bias versus socio-cultural differences. *Journal of Psychopathology and Behavioral Assessment, 19*, 1–20.

Whaley, A. L. (2001). Cultural mistrust: An important psychological construct for diagnosis and treatment of African-Americans. *Professional Psychology: Research and Practice, 32*, 555–562.

Wilk, C. M., Gold, J. M., McMahon, R. P., Humber, K., Iannone, V. N., & Buchanan, R. W. (2005). No, it is not possible to be schizophrenic yet neuropsychologically normal. *Neuropsychology, 6*, 778–786.

Wright, I. C., Rabe-Hesketh, S., Woodruff, P. W. R., David, A. S., Murray, R. M., & Bullmore, E. T. (2000). Meta-analysis of regional brain volumes in schizophrenia. *The American Journal of Psychiatry, 157*, 16–25.

Wu, E. Q., Birnbaum, H. G., Shi, L., Ball, D. E., Kessler R. C., Moulis, M., & Aggarwal, J. (2005). The economic burden of schizophrenia in the United States in 2002. *The Journal of Clinical Psychiatry, 66*, 1122–1129.

Xiong, W., Phillips, M. R., Hu, X., Ruiwen, W., Dai, Q., Kleinman, J., & Kleinman, A. (1994). Family-based intervention for schizophrenic patients in China: A randomised controlled trial. *British Journal of Psychiatry, 165*, 239–247.

Yamada, N., Nakajima, S., & Noguchi, T. (1998). Age at onset of delusional disorder is dependent on the delusional theme. *Acta Psychiatrica Scandinavica, 97*, 122–124.

Young, C. R., Bowers, M. B., & Mazure, C. M. (1998). Management of the adverse effects of clozapine. *Schizophrenia Bulletin, 24*, 381–390.

Yung, A. R., & McGorry, P. D. (1996). The initial prodrome in psychosis: Descriptive and qualitative aspects. *The Australian and New Zealand Journal of Psychiatry, 30*, 587–599.

Zahid, M. A., & Ohaeri, J. U. (2010). Relationship of family caregiver burden with quality of care and psychopathology in a sample of Arab subjects with schizophrenia. *BMC Psychiatry, 10*, 71.

Zhang, M., Wang, M., Li, J., & Phillips, M. R. (1994). Randomised-control trial of family intervention for 78 first-episode male schizophrenic patients: An 18-month study in Suzhou, Jiangsu. *British Journal of Psychiatry, 165*, 96–102.

Zigler, E., & Glick, M. (1986). *A developmental approach to adult psychopathology*. New York, NY: John Wiley & Sons.

Zubin, J., & Spring, B. (1977). Vulnerability: A new view of schizophrenia. *Journal of Abnormal Psychology, 86*, 103–123.

# CHAPTER 9

# Mood Disorders: Depressive Disorders

LEILANI FELICIANO, BRENNA N. RENN, and PATRICIA A. AREÁN

## DESCRIPTION OF THE DISORDER

### OVERVIEW

Depressive disorders are among the most common psychiatric disorders occurring in both younger and older adults (Waraich, Goldner, Somers, & Hsu, 2004). They are characterized by feelings of sadness, lack of interest in formerly enjoyable pursuits, sleep and appetite disturbances, feelings of worthlessness, and at times thoughts of death and dying. In older adults, depressive disorders may present differently, with less reported sadness and depression and more somatic complaints (Hybels, Blazer, Pieper, Landerman, & Steffens, 2009).

All depressive disorders are extremely debilitating and negatively impact the quality of life of those afflicted. At the beginning of this millennium, depressive disorders were second only to heart disease as the illness most responsible for poor quality of life and disability (Pincus & Pettit, 2001). By the year 2030, Major Depressive Disorder is predicted to be among the leading causes of disability globally, comparable to heart disease and second only to HIV/AIDS (Mathers & Loncar, 2006). Depression is also associated with increased suicide risk. In a recent cross-national sample of 17 countries, individuals with a mood disorder had an odds ratio of 3.4 to 5.9 over that of individuals without a mood disorder, even after controlling for such factors as age, education, and relationship status (Nock et al., 2008). In terms of suicide completion, early statistics indicated that 15% of people with major depression completed suicide (Guze & Robins, 1970), although recent estimates are more conservative and place the lifetime risk of completed suicide between 2.2% (Bostwick & Pankratz, 2000) and 4.2% (Coryell & Young, 2005) in individuals with depressive disorders. Comorbid substance use and personality disorders (borderline personality disorder in particular) increase the risk of attempted and completed suicide in people with depressive disorders (Bolton, Pagura, Enns, Grant, & Sareen, 2010). Fortunately, depressive disorders can be treated successfully with psychotherapy, antidepressant medication, or both

(Norman & Burrows, 2007). The research on these disorders continues to grow, and we know quite a bit about how depressive disorders are presented, their etiology, and their course and prognosis. The purpose of this chapter is to describe the depressive disorders, discuss their prevalence and effects on people who have these disorders, examine the best methods for assessing depressive disorders, and present the latest research on their etiology.

## DIAGNOSIS AND DESCRIPTION

According to the fourth edition of the *Diagnostic and Statistical Manual of Mental Disorders, Text Revision* (*DSM-IV-TR*; American Psychiatric Association, 2000), depressive disorders include three categories of illnesses: Major Depressive disorder (MDD), Dysthymic Disorder, and Depressive Disorder Not Otherwise Specified (depression NOS). As outlined in Table 9.1, all three categories share common symptoms and clinical features. First, all three disorders consist of mood symptoms, which include feeling sad, empty, worried, and irritable. Second, these disorders are characterized by vegetative symptoms, which include fatigue, social withdrawal, and agitation.

Disturbances in sleep and appetite are also common, with lack of sleep and appetite being more typical in depression, although patients with an atypical presentation (discussed later) will complain of hypersomnia (increased sleep) or weight gain caused by frequent eating. Finally, all three disorders consist of cognitive symptoms. These include trouble concentrating; difficulty making decisions; low self-esteem; negative thoughts about oneself, the world, and others; guilt; and suicidal ideation. The degree to which these features occur and the number of symptoms present will determine which type of depressive disorder a person may be

### Table 9.1
#### Diagnostic Criteria

| Symptoms | Major Depression | Dysthymic Disorder | Depression NOS |
| --- | --- | --- | --- |
| Depression<br>Anhedonia<br>Change in appetite<br>Change in sleep<br>Agitation or slowing<br>Loss of energy<br>Decreased concentration/ trouble making decisions<br>Thoughts of death/ suicide<br>Feeling guilty or worthless | Either depressed mood or anhedonia along with at least four other symptoms must be present for no less than 2 weeks, all day nearly every day. | Two or more symptoms must be present for at least 2 years, more days than not. | Either depression or anhedonia plus two other symptoms must be present for at least 2 weeks, all day nearly every day. |

experiencing. Next we discuss each disorder to clarify how it can be distinguished from the others.

## MAJOR DEPRESSIVE DISORDER

Major Depressive Disorder (MDD) is the most serious and most widely studied depressive disorder. It is characterized by at least one major depressive episode, with no history of mania (period of intense energy, euphoria, distorted thinking, and behavioral excesses). To qualify for a major depressive episode, either depressed mood or lack of interest or pleasure in usual activities (anhedonia) must be present, most of the day, nearly every day, and the episode must last at least 2 weeks. In addition, at least five out of nine possible symptoms (listed in Table 9.1) must be present during that same period. The symptoms must be severe enough to interfere with the individual's social or occupational functioning. Major Depressive Disorder is further qualified as to its severity, chronicity, and remission status. Severity is generally determined by the degree of disability experienced by the affected person. If the person can continue to pursue obligations (work, family, and social activities), then the depression is rated as *mild*. If the person has trouble getting out of bed and can no longer engage in any obligated activities, then the depression is rated as *moderate*. If a person is thinking of death or dying; is so vegetative that he or she has not gotten out of bed, eaten, or engaged in any self-management activities; or is exhibiting psychotic behavior, then the depression is rated as *severe*. Although it is rare, an individual with depression can exhibit symptoms of *catatonia*, which is characterized by immobility, excessive motor activity, extreme negativism or mutism, and bizarre posturing. A person will be diagnosed as having MDD, *recurrent type* if there has been more than one episode of MDD. *Chronic* MDD is characterized by symptoms of MDD that can last for as long as 2 or more years. Because research has found MDD to be a recurrent disorder (single episodes are rare), if a person has had an episode of MDD but is no longer experiencing any depressive symptoms, that person is considered to be *in remission*.

MDD can be further delineated by type. The *DSM-IV* describes the concept of endogenous depression, which is subsumed under the category of *melancholic depression*. This category is characterized by lack of reactivity to pleasurable stimuli, experiencing more severe depression in the morning, and excessive guilt. Some researchers have suggested that this subtype is more typically associated with biological etiology and that it may be more responsive to psychopharmacological intervention than to psychotherapies (Andrus et al., 2011; Simons & Thase, 1992). Exogenous depression is a subtype felt to be primarily caused by stressful life events or a specific psychosocial problem. Although most researchers agree there is likely to be some genetic component to this depression as well, depression would only be expressed in the face of a major problem a person could not solve immediately (e.g., loss of employment). Typical features of exogenous depression include temporary brightening of mood in response to actual or potential positive events, weight gain, hypersomnia, a heavy feeling in arms or legs, and interpersonal sensitivity to rejection. These symptoms tend to be interpreted as suggesting a depressive disorder that is more likely to respond to psychosocial interventions than to medications (Nutt et al., 2010).

## DYSTHYMIC DISORDER

Dysthymic Disorder (dysthymia) is typically thought to be a chronic depression (lasting 2 years or more) but one that is not as severe as major depressive disorder. Unlike MDD, Dysthymic Disorder has only one typical presentation. The symptoms of Dysthymic Disorder (listed in Table 9.1) must be present for 2 years, during which time there should be no more than a 2-month period in which the person is symptom free. Additionally, no major depressive episode during the first 2 years of Dysthymic Disorder should have been present, although one could occur after the 2-year period. If MDD occurs after the 2-year period, it is commonly described as *double depression*. Symptoms of Dysthymic Disorder must not be due exclusively to other disorders (including medical conditions) or to the direct physiological effects of a substance (including medication). As in MDD, the person must not ever have met criteria for manic episode, hypomanic episode, or cyclothymic disorder. If dysthymia occurs before age 21, it is described as having *early onset*; otherwise, it is described as having *late onset*.

## DEPRESSIVE DISORDER NOT OTHERWISE SPECIFIED

This category is a catchall for depressive conditions that are provisionary and have yet to be studied in depth. This category includes *Premenstrual Dysphoric Disorder*, a mood disorder thought to be caused by hormonal fluctuations in the female menstrual cycle (with symptoms more severe than what is typically seen with premenstrual syndrome); *Minor Depressive Disorder*, depressive episodes lasting for at least 2 weeks but with fewer than the five items needed to meet criteria for major depressive episode; *Recurrent Brief Depressive Disorder*, which is characterized by repeated episodes of depression that last for less than 2 weeks; *Postpsychotic Depressive Disorder of Schizophrenia*, a depression that follows a psychotic episode; major depressive episode superimposed on psychotic or delusional disorders, *Depression that co-occurs with a psychotic disorder*; and *Depression Due to General Medical Conditions*, which is depression thought to be present but not able to be determined to be primary because of medical conditions or substance use.

## WHEN DEPRESSION IS NOT A DEPRESSIVE DISORDER

Sometimes symptoms of depression may be present but may not be diagnosed as one of the depressive disorders. People who develop depression after a significant life stressor for a short time are more likely to be suffering from an adjustment disorder rather than a mood disorder. Furthermore, a previous manic episode will also exclude a diagnosis of MDD. Finally, if the individual with depression has a medical disorder known to cause symptoms of depression (e.g., hyperthyroidism), then the symptoms are classified as depression due to a general medical condition.

Everyone experiences feelings of sadness from time to time. This is a normal experience that should not be pathologized. Depressive symptoms are considered problematic when they persist for 2 weeks or more and are accompanied by considerable difficulty managing day-to-day activities. In the next section, we provide examples of these disorders.

## CLINICAL PICTURE

Major Depressive Disorder, Dysthymic Disorder, and Depressive disorder NOS all vary to a degree in their presentation but share several features that distinguish these disorders from other mental illnesses. People with depressive disorders can be identified by their pessimism and negativistic thinking, difficulty solving even everyday problems, and lack of initiative. People with depressive disorders are also quite disabled by the illness and often report having multiple somatic symptoms.

Most people with a depressive disorder exhibit what is called *negativistic thinking*. This term was coined by Aaron Beck (Beck, 1961) and has since been used extensively to describe the cognitive style of people suffering from depressive disorders. Negativistic thinking is best described as a style of thinking that is overly pessimistic and critical. People with depression tend to expect failure and disappointment at every turn and will focus only on their past failures as a way to confirm these beliefs (Alloy et al., 2000). People with negativistic thinking also have poor self-esteem and are more likely than people without this cognitive bias to experience depressive symptoms (Verplanken, Friborg, Wang, Trafimow, & Woolf, 2007). The presence of negativistic thinking in depression is a bit of a "chicken or egg" problem: Does depression cause negativistic thinking, or does negativistic thinking cause depression? Recent research suggests that the cause of depression is more likely an imbalanced thinking style and that negativistic thinking may have a clearer association with repeated exposure to failure and disappointment. In a study by Issacowitz and Seligman (2001), people with pessimistic thinking as well as those with optimistic thinking were both at risk for developing depressive symptoms after exposure to stressful life events. In fact, optimists were at higher risk for depression than pessimists were, although pessimists tended to have more persistent depression. Therefore, objective perceptions of one's abilities, of one's environment, and of other people are likely to be more protective than overly optimistic or pessimistic styles of thinking.

Negativistic thinking is primarily responsible for why individuals with depression find it difficult to engage in and enjoy activities that once gave them pleasure, and thus social isolation is a common feature of depressive disorders (Cacioppo, Hawkley, & Thisted, 2010). Many people with a depressive disorder will report that they have stopped socializing or engaging in pleasant activities, largely because they anticipate no enjoyment from the activity (Chentsova-Dutton & Hanley, 2010). As will be discussed in the section on etiology, it is hypothesized that repeated exposure to stress will influence the reward centers of the brain; animal studies have demonstrated that repeated exposure to negative events will result in the adoption of avoidance motivation over appetitive motivation; in other words, people who experience too many negative experiences begin to anticipate that all experiences will be negative and, therefore, they will be motivated by pain reduction rather than by need for pleasure (Ho & Wang, 2010). It is important that people who have depression try to reengage in social activities. Increased social isolation puts the individual with depression at greater risk of severe depression. Several studies show that social support can offset the occurrence or worsening of depression, and thus increasing exposure to socialization is an important process in recovering from depression (Barros-Loscertales et al., 2010; Dichter, Felder, & Smoski, 2010; Jakupcak, Wagner, Paulson, Varra, & McFall, 2010; Mazzucchelli, Kane, & Rees, 2010).

People with a depressive disorder also tend to use passive coping skills, or they avoid solving problems (Nolen-Hoeksema, Larson, & Grayson, 1999). This is sometimes due to a preexisting skills deficit or to learned helplessness, a condition caused by repeated attempts and failures to cope with problems (Folkman & Lazarus, 1986). Most often, after people develop depression, they avoid proactive attempts to solve problems because they anticipate that they are not capable of implementing a successful solution (Nezu, 1986). This avoidance often results in more problems; for instance, avoiding marital problems potentially results in divorce.

A relatively recent movement, *positive psychology*, focuses on an individual's strengths (virtues) as well as any skills deficits (Sin & Lyubomirsky, 2009). Seligman and Csikszentmihalyi (2000) discuss positive psychology as an adjunct to treatment of mental health problems to provide treatment to the whole person rather than a focus on treating the depressive symptoms only. The main tenets involve putting one's strengths to work in achieving a balance of three lives: the pleasant life, the good life, and the meaningful life. Seligman and colleagues have designed and researched a series of Internet exercises designed to increase happiness and decrease suffering. For a more detailed review, see Seligman, Steen, Park, and Peterson (2005).

Many people are often surprised to discover how disabling depression can be. People who have depression will complain of somatic problems, such as fatigue, stomach upset, headaches, and joint pain (Viinamäki et al., 2000). These symptoms, coupled with the pessimism and avoidant style associated with depression, are related to the increased number of disability days reported by people with depressive disorders (Pincus & Pettit, 2001). In the National Comorbidity Study (NCS; Kessler & Frank, 1997), people with depression reported a fivefold increase in time lost from work than did those without depression. In fact, patients treated for depression incurred greater disability costs to employers than did people needing treatment for hypertension and had costs comparable to those with more severe chronic illness like diabetes (Conti & Burton, 1995; Druss, Rosenheck, & Sledge, 2000). Interestingly, costs related to treating depression are almost as great as the costs due to disability days from depression (Kessler et al., 1999), and some studies have found the treatment of depression to decrease disability days (Simon et al., 2000).

## DIAGNOSTIC CONSIDERATIONS

Although the *DSM-IV-TR* provides guidelines for the diagnosis of depressive disorders, the comorbidity of other medical and psychiatric disorders can complicate a diagnostic decision. To make an accurate diagnosis of depression, the provider must consider physical health, medications, family and personal history, and medical history. *DSM-IV-TR* includes *bereavement* as a comorbid condition, but if it is present the diagnosis may not truly be depression. The latest information from the *DSM-5* Work Group is that bereavement is no longer an exclusion criteria for a diagnosis of depression; people who are suffering from the loss of a significant other could be diagnosed with a depressive disorder, if they meet the clinical characteristics (Corruble, Falissard, & Gorwood, 2011).

## MEDICAL ILLNESS

The first important step in diagnosing depressive disorders is to have the patient get a complete physical. Depression commonly co-occurs with other mental disorders (e.g., anxiety disorders) and physical disorders (King-Kallimanis, Gum, & Kohn, 2009), which can further exacerbate distress, disability, and challenge treatment efforts. Because many medical illnesses are related to the onset of a depressive episode, at times treating both the illness and the depression is a more efficient way to effect symptom change (Gupta, Bahadur, Gupta, & Bhugra, 2006; Katon, 2003; Simon, Von Korff, & Lin, 2005; Stover, Fenton, Rosenfeld, & Insel, 2003; Trivedi, Clayton, & Frank, 2007). In endocrinological disorders like hyperthyroidism and hypothyroidism, one of the diagnostic signs is a change in affect and mood. People who are treated for these disorders experience radical changes in mood. Moreover, people with chronic illnesses like diabetes mellitus have high rates of depressive symptoms, (de Groot, Jacobson, Samson, & Welch, 1999) but not necessarily higher rates of MDD or dysthymia (Fisher, Glasgow, & Strycker, 2010; Fisher, Mullan, et al., 2010). Acute medical illnesses such as stroke (Sagen et al., 2010), Parkinson's disease (Caap-Ahlgren & Dehlin, 2001), pancreatic cancer (Jia et al., 2010; Mayr & Schmid, 2010), coronary heart disease (Kubzansky & Kawachi, 2000), and myocardial infarction (Martens, Hoen, Mittelhaeuser, de Jonge, & Denollet, 2010) are associated with depressive symptoms. Neurological findings suggest that cerebrovascular disease (particularly ischemic small-vessel disease) may be related to the onset of late-life depression (Rapp et al., 2005). Although it is unclear whether these illnesses directly cause depression or the depression is the result of the life changes brought on by the illness, recovery from these diseases (when possible) will help alleviate depressive symptoms.

## DRUG AND ALCOHOL ABUSE

The next step in establishing a diagnosis is to determine to what extent the person drinks or uses drugs. Often substance abuse or dependence disorders are strongly associated with depressive symptoms (Gunnarsdottir et al., 2000; Merikangas & Avenevoli, 2000; Ostacher, 2007). Scientists have debated whether depressive symptoms are a consequence of substance abuse and the problems related to this disorder, or whether the substance use is a means of self-medicating depressive symptoms. The psychiatric and substance abuse field is slowly moving toward the comanagement of depression and substance abuse, and while abstaining from substances does often clarify the diagnostic picture, it is often very unlikely that someone who is abusing substances and has depression will be able to abstain without treatment. Therefore, when these two conditions do present themselves, clinicians generally ascribe a dual diagnosis and attempt to untangle which disorder was apparent first through gathering a thorough diagnostic history.

In determining the best course of action regarding treatment, it is crucial to get a list of all medications (both prescribed and over-the-counter) the person uses, given that the side effects of many medications can cause or contribute to the depressive symptoms observed. This is particularly true with older adults, who are more vulnerable to the side effects of medication. For example, in a review of late-life depression, Dick, Gallagher-Thompson, and Thompson (1996) note that medications such as antihistamines, antihypertensives, some antiparkinsonian drugs, and some pain medications commonly cause symptoms of depression. In addition, diuretics, synthetic hormones, and benzodiazepines have also been noted to contribute to depressive symptomatology (Cooper, Peters, & Andrews, 1998). The higher the number of drugs the person takes, the higher the risk for medication side effects and drug-drug interactions.

## GRIEF AND BEREAVEMENT

Grief over the loss of a special person or the presence of a major life stress or change can also complicate attempts to diagnose depressive disorders. Both *uncomplicated bereavement* and *adjustment disorder* have many of the symptoms of depression, but neither was considered a mood disorder until recently when the *DSM-5* mood disorders section decided to remove bereavement as an exclusion condition for depression. This removal has created controversies in the field; grief is generally felt to be a normal reaction to loss, and while bereavement can certainly turn into depression, people who are experiencing grief generally exhibit many of the symptoms associated with depression during recovery from grief. Although it is possible that those with uncomplicated bereavement or adjustment disorder can develop a depressive disorder, little is known about the extent to which grief can develop into depression (Boelen, van de Schoot, van den Hout, de Keijser, & van den Bout, 2010; Wellen, 2010).

## DEPRESSION DUE TO OTHER PSYCHIATRIC DISORDERS

People with other psychiatric disorders can have co-occurring depressive symptoms, and thus establishing a differential rule-out for these other disorders is often important. For instance, people with anxiety disorders, particularly generalized anxiety disorder, report feelings of sadness and hopelessness (Hopko et al., 2000). When under stress, people with Axis II disorders will also report significant symptoms of depression (Petersen et al., 2002). In fact, they can become quite acutely depressed. Specifically, depressive episodes are most prevalent with avoidant, borderline, and obsessive-compulsive personality disorders (Rossi et al., 2001). Furthermore, personality disorders have an association with a longer remission onset from a depressive episode (O'Leary & Costello, 2001). In addition, depression is common in prodromal phases of schizophrenia and is a recurrent feature in bipolar disorder.

## LATE-LIFE DEPRESSION

Depression, while not a natural consequence of aging, is one of the most common mental health disorders that older adults experience. Older adults are less likely to report feeling sad or depressed (Fiske, Wetherell, & Gatx, 2009) or symptoms of guilt (Gallagher et al., 2010) and may report more memory problems (in the absence of dementia) and somatic symptoms such as fatigue, decreased appetite, and muscle pain (Kim, Shin, Yoon, & Stewart, 2002). In addition, because older adults are more likely to have chronic illnesses, the presence of physical illnesses as well as the side effects of medications taken to treat these conditions can overshadow or worsen symptoms of depression (Areán & Reynolds, 2005), which can further complicate diagnosis. In older populations, depression is also associated with increased mortality and health service usage. This association highlights the importance of early recognition, differential diagnosis, and treatment of this disabling illness.

## EPIDEMIOLOGY

The patients described in this chapter are representative of a growing number of people in the United States suffering from depressive disorders. Several large-scale epidemiological studies on mental illness have taken place in the United States. The Epidemiological Catchment Area Study (ECA) was conducted in the 1980s (Regier, 1988) and was the first to definitively determine the prevalence of psychiatric problems in the United States. The second study, called the National Comorbidity Study (NCS; Kessler, McGonagle, Zhao, et al., 1994), focused specifically on English-speaking adults between the ages of 18 and 65 and was mostly concerned with the prevalence of co-occurring *DSM-III-R* psychiatric disorders in the United States. The NCS was recently replicated in 2005 to examine the prevalence for the updated *DSM-IV* and the *International Classification of Disease, version 10* (*ICD-10*) psychiatric disorders and to provide age-of-onset estimates for mental health disorders in a representative U.S. sample (Kessler et al., 2005).

The data from these studies demonstrate that the prevalence of depressive disorders varies from population to population. The following discussion will therefore present the prevalence of depressive disorders by the different populations.

### COMMUNITY SAMPLES

The lifetime prevalence, or the number of persons who have ever experienced any type of mood disorder, is 20.8% (Kessler et al., 2005), whereas the prevalence for an episode of major depression ranges from 5.8% (Regier, 1988) to 12% (Kessler, McGonagle, Zhao, et al., 1994), in community-dwelling individuals using *DSM-III* and *DSM-III-R* diagnostic criteria. When using the *DSM-IV* criteria, the lifetime prevalence of MDD increases to 16.6% (Kessler et al., 2005). These studies also indicate that in a given 6-month period, approximately 3% to 9% of the general population will experience an episode of major depression (Kessler, McGonagle, Zhao, et al., 1994; Regier, 1988). The lifetime prevalence for Dysthymic Disorder is lower than the rates for MDD. According to the NCS and the NCS-R (Kilzieh, Rastam, Ward, & Maziak, 2010), between 2.5% and 6% of the general population has had a period of dysthymia in their lifetimes. Rates for bipolar I and II disorder were 3.9%, and rates of other depressive disorders were not available.

## PREVALENCE BY GENDER

The ECA and the NCS show differential prevalence by gender. In the ECA studies, lifetime prevalence of affective disorders for adult women average 6.6%, whereas in the NCS, prevalence is significantly higher at 21.3% (Kessler, McGonagle, Nelson, et al., 1994; Regier, 1988). The lifetime prevalence for men was 8.2% in the ECA and 12.7% in the NCS. While prevalence for depression varied between these two studies, a consistent theme emerges: More women than men report having depressive episodes. Differences between men and women have been found repeatedly throughout the world and thus appear to be accurate reflections of true differences in the prevalence of the disorder between men and women (Angold, Weissman, John, Wickramaratne, & Prusoff, 1991; Kessler, McGonagle, Nelson, et al., 1994). Although the reasons for these differences are relatively unknown, some speculate that biological differences, differences in cognitive and behavioral patterns of mood control (Nolen-Hoeksema, 2000), and social influences, including differential expectations for the two genders, account for the difference in prevalence (Kilzieh et al., 2010).

## PREVALENCE BY AGE COHORT

The NCS-R included individuals over the age of 60 and up to the age of 75, which is an improvement over the previous ECA sample (Kessler & Merikangas, 2004). However, the information on the differential prevalence rates of depression between younger and older people is limited and does not include our fastest-growing segment of the population, the old-old, age 85 and older. As Burke, Burke, Rae, and Regier (1991) pointed out, rates for all psychiatric disorders are increasing with each decade, indicating that disorders like depression may be influenced by cohort effects. With the preceding caveat in mind, it is important to highlight what is known about the prevalence of depression in older adults. The prevalence of depression among older adult populations exceeds that of any other mental disorder (Baldwin, 2000). The NCS-R reports rates of MDD for individuals over the age of 60 to be 10.6% and Dysthymic Disorder to be 1.3% (Kessler et al., 2005). However, again it is important to keep in mind that the prevalence of depression varies substantially by population studied.

## PREVALENCE IN MINORITIES

Rates of depression also vary by ethnic group. According to the NCS data, African Americans have rates of depression similar to those of the Caucasian population. Approximately 3.1% of African Americans have had an MDD episode, and 3.2% have had dysthymia (Jackson-Triche et al., 2000). However, Asian Americans have the lowest rates, with only 0.8% reporting that they had experienced a major depressive episode and 0.8% experiencing Dysthymic Disorder (Jackson-Triche et al., 2000). Hispanics were found to have an interesting presentation of prevalence that depended on immigration status. According to Alderete, Vega, Kolody, and Aguilar-Gaxiola (1999), Hispanics who recently immigrated from Latin America were less likely to have depression than Hispanics who were born and raised in the United States. Hispanics who were U.S.-born had rates of depression much like the rates of Caucasians (3.5% for MDD and 5% for dysthymia), whereas immigrants reported only half the prevalence of U.S.-born Hispanics. Although unconfirmed empirically, Vega, Kolody, Valle, and Hough (1986) believe that lower rates in immigrants result from a heartiness factor; those who are able to withstand the stress related to immigration are more likely to cope with stress related to depression.

PREVALENCE IN SPECIAL SETTINGS

Prevalence of depression in certain settings is greater than what has been found in the general community. For instance, people who have depression are more likely to seek help in primary care settings (Wagner et al., 2000). Estimates vary, but most studies indicate that minor depression is the most common depressive disorder, with as many as 25% of patients meeting diagnostic criteria (Wagner et al., 2000). Although the prevalence of depressive disorders may be high, recurrence is lower in these settings than in the community. According to van Weel-Baumgarten, Schers, van den Bosch, van den Hoogen, and Zitma (2000), patients treated in primary care medicine are less likely to suffer a relapse or remission than those treated in psychiatric settings. However, psychiatry tends to manage more severely depressed patients, and thus this finding is likely an artifact of the populations served in each setting.

Another setting with high rates for depression is the skilled nursing facility. Approximately 32% of people living in assisted living facilities experience MDD (Waraich et al., 2004), with new episodes occurring in 31.6% of patients within the first 12 months of admittance (Hoover et al., 2010). The causes for higher prevalence of depressive disorders in nursing home facilities may vary but most likely include loss of functional independence, loss of familiar surroundings, decreased access to pleasant activities or loved ones, and comorbid physical illnesses. Given the impact that depressive disorders have on rehabilitation, the high rate of these disorders in these settings is cause for concern and argues for more vigilant and proactive treatment of depression in skilled nursing facilities.

## PSYCHOLOGICAL AND BIOLOGICAL ASSESSMENT

The assessment of depression has evolved over the decades, but many issues and controversies about the most adequate means of detecting this disorder still remain. Controversies over cultural differences, age differences, and the setting in which a client is being evaluated are still under investigation. This section focuses on the strengths and weaknesses of different methods for assessing depression, ranging from screening instruments to structured clinical interviews.

ASSESSING THE INDIVIDUAL WITH DEPRESSION

The most common way to assess for depressive disorders is by conducting in-person interviews with patients. The interviewers, usually mental health professionals or trained clinic workers, ask patients questions regarding the current episode of depression, including the symptoms patients are experiencing, how long they have been experiencing them, what they think caused the depression, and what they would like to do about the depressive episode. In addition, intake clinicians will also ask about family and personal history, past and current medical history, previous psychiatric history, and the impact of the depression on day-to-day functioning. All of this information is compiled to determine whether patients have a depressive disorder, the type of disorder they have, and the degree to which they are suffering. This information is then used to determine the appropriate treatment.

Most mental health professionals use their own methods of assessment. Some will conduct an open-ended interview that is guided not by any instrumentation, but only by patients' responses to questions. Although this method is most commonly practiced, it also carries the greatest risk of misdiagnosis, particularly if the interviewer is not an expert in depressive disorders. Because of this risk, many mental health organizations prefer to use a combination of an open-ended interview with a screening instrument or a guide, such as a semi-structured interview form, to help remind clinicians to ask for all relevant information. In using a screening instrument or semistructured interview, it is imperative that the instruments chosen be highly reliable and valid. Other than a medical examination to rule out physical causes for depressive symptoms, there is no biological test to diagnose depression, so accurate diagnosis rests with clinicians and the instrumentation used to confirm a diagnosis.

## Screening Instruments

In many health settings, practitioners are concerned with identifying as many people as possible who have the disorder so that quick and effective interventions can take place. This tradition comes from medical practice, where physicians routinely conduct medical tests when they suspect a particular illness. These screening tests help the doctor determine whether further tests are needed to make a specific diagnosis. For instance, when a patient sees a doctor about symptoms of fatigue, the physician will likely order blood and urine screens to determine whether the fatigue is due to anemia, diabetes, or mononucleosis. Standardized screening instruments are used for similar purposes in mental health. Screening instruments should be highly sensitive; that is, they should detect depression in everyone with the disorder. Otherwise, their utility is limited. Once someone screens positive for depression, further assessment is required to confirm a diagnosis.

The most common mechanism for diagnosing depression in adults is through self-report measures, such as the Beck Depression Inventory (BDI; Beck, 1961; also, BDI-II; Beck, Steer, & Brown, 1996), the Center for Epidemiological Studies—Depression Scale (CES-D; Radloff, 1977), the Zung Depression Scale (Zung, 1972), the Montgomery Asberg Depression Rating Scale (MADRS-S; Montgomery & Asberg, 1979), and the Profile of Mood States (POMS; Plutchik, Platman, & Fieve, 1968). Because some of these measures contain items that are related to somatic symptoms (e.g., fatigue) and are frequently scored in a depressed direction by older adults who have acute physical or chronic illnesses (Street, O'Connor, & Robinson, 2007), some self-report measures have been designed specifically for detecting depression in older adults, such as the Geriatric Depression Scale (GDS;

Yesavage et al., 1982). These instruments are completed by the patient, who indicates the degree to which he or she has experienced symptoms over a specified period (e.g., 1 week, 2 weeks), and then the instrument is hand-scored by the person administering the scale. A patient's score on the instrument reflects the severity of depressive symptoms.

These instruments are considered cost-effective and efficient. They are useful in primary care settings in making quick diagnoses, especially when followed with a second-stage interview (Schmitz, Kruse, Heckrath, Alberti, & Tress, 1999). However, they are often too inclusive in that they tend to identify some people as having depressive symptoms who do not. They also differ in their assessments of depression and specifications within the diagnosis. For example, the BDI and the MADRS-S are equivalent in their assessment of depression, but the MADRS-S has a greater focus on core depressive symptoms than does the BDI (Svanborg & Asberg, 2001). Additionally, and of late, many health care providers are using these instruments for determining a diagnosis. An issue that arises here is that these instruments are designed to be screening devices and not diagnostic tools. Furthering the problem, research indicates that such scales may be efficient in identifying psychological distress that might then be erroneously identified as major depression (Wakefield, Baer, & Schmitz, 2010).

Because of the prevalence of depression in primary care medicine, several instruments have been created specifically for use in that environment. These instruments are meant to raise a red flag to the provider so that a more thorough assessment of depression can be conducted. The Primary Care Evaluation of Mental Disorders (PRIME-MD; Spitzer et al., 1994) is a good example. The patient completes a brief questionnaire in which two questions are red flags for depression. If the patient endorses one of the two red-flag questions, then the provider asks more specific questions to finalize the diagnosis. The PRIME-MD has satisfactory reliability and validity (Spitzer, Kroenke, & Williams, 1999). The Nine-Item Patient Health Questionnaire (PHQ-9; Spitzer, Williams, Kroenke, Hornyak, & McMurray, 2000) is a self-administered depression module adapted from the PRIME-MD. Like the PRIME-MD, it has strong internal reliability in a primary care setting (Cronbach's alpha = 0.89), excellent test-retest reliability, as well as good criterion and construct validity (Kroenke, Spitzer, & Williams, 2001). In addition, the PHQ-9 has validity in individuals of different ages and from diverse cultural backgrounds, such as Latinos, African Americans, and people of Asian descent including Thai, Korean, and Chinese, as well as individuals from Nigeria and Kenya (Adewuya et al., 2006; Diez-Quevedo, Rangil, Sanchez-Planell, Kroenke, & Spitzer, 2001; Han et al., 2008; Huang et al., 2006; Lotrakul et al., 2008; Omoro et al., 2006; Yeung et al., 2008).

Another brief self-report questionnaire for medical patients is the Beck Depression Inventory—Primary Care (BDI-PC; Beck, Guth, Steer, & Ball, 1997). This seven-item questionnaire consists of some of the same items from the full BDI and instructs the patient to rate symptoms occurring over the last 2 weeks on a 4-point scale. In research examining the BDI-PC as a screening measure for MDD, it has been shown to have high internal consistency in primary care outpatient settings (Cronbach's alpha = 0.85; Steer, Cavalieri, Leonard, & Beck, 1999) and in medical inpatients as well (Cronbach's alpha = 0.86; Beck et al., 1997; Parker,

Hilton, Hadzi-Pavlovic, & Bains, 2001). When using a cut score of 4 and greater, it yielded excellent sensitivity (97%) and specificity (99%; Steer et al., 1999). Researchers noted that an advantage of the BDI-PC is that it has not been found to be correlated with age, gender, or ethnicity/racial status (Beck et al., 1997; Winter, Steer, Jones-Hicks, & Beck, 1999).

Other structured screening instruments designed for primary care include the Hospital Anxiety and Depression Scale (HADS; Zigmond & Snaith, 1983) and the Mini-International Neuropsychiatric Interview-Screen (MINI-Screen), a shorter version of the MINI that is available and described in more detail in the following section. The HADS is used in medical and community populations as a quick screen for anxiety and depressive symptoms in patients with physical illness. In an attempt to reduce confounds of depression diagnoses in the medically unwell population, the screen does not assess somatic symptoms. However, the tradeoff is that this renders it less sensitive than other measures at screening for depression (Brennan, Worrall-Davies, McMillan, Gillbody, & House, 2010) and for detecting depression in some minority groups that tend to report more somatic symptoms than affective symptoms.

Another measure used to assess depressive symptom severity in a time-efficient manner is the Quick Inventory of Depressive symptomology (QIDS; Rush et al., 2003). The QIDS is a 16-item inventory developed to assess the nine *DSM-IV-TR* criterion symptom domains (i.e., sad mood, energy/fatigue, appetite and sleep dysfunction, etc.). The inventory is available in both self-report (QIDS-SR16) and clinician-rating forms (QIDS-C16), and both forms have demonstrated a high degree of internal consistency (Cronbach's alpha = 0.86 and 0.86 respectively) and acceptable psychometric properties (Trivedi et al., 2004).

Two additional screening measures for depression are the General Health Questionnaire (GHQ; Goldberg, 1972) and the World Health Organization's Well-Being Index (WHO-5; WHO, 1990). Both measures are used in community and nonpsychiatric clinical settings, such as primary care. The GHQ is a screening instrument used in primary care and general practice to detect psychiatric disorders. The original scale included 60 questions intended to capture the patient's somatic and psychiatric symptoms in less than 10 minutes. The test creators found a 0.80 correlation between clinical assessment and GHQ score (Goldberg & Blackwell, 1970). More recent modifications of the scale include 12-item, 20-item, 28-item, and 30-item questionnaires. The WHO-5 was adapted from the original 28-item questionnaire of quality of life in patients with diabetes. The five items chosen cover positive mood, vitality, and general interest. Although originally developed as a well-being index, the WHO-5 has been validated as a depression screening tool for use with older adults (Bonsignore, Barkow, Jessen, & Heun, 2001).

STRUCTURED AND SEMISTRUCTURED CLINICAL INTERVIEWS

Once a person screens positive for a depressive disorder, the next step is to confirm the diagnosis, preferably by using a structured or semistructured interview. As stated earlier, most people who are expert in the diagnosis of depression disorders do not need the assistance of a structured instrument. However, because experts are not always available and employing them can be quite costly, structured and semistructured interviews have been developed for use by less-experienced personnel or for use in research or facility protocols to increase consistency in assessment. To address the concerns of managed-care systems, these interviews have utility in that they increase standardization in service delivery, increase consistency in diagnosis, and allow for tracking outcomes (Rogers, 2001). The best-known instruments are the Structured Clinical Interview for *DSM-IV* and the Composite International Diagnostic Interview. Another short structured diagnostic interview is the Mini-International Neuropsychiatric Interview. The Diagnostic Interview for *DSM* (DIS) has also been used widely but has been largely replaced by the CIDI and so will not be discussed in this chapter.

*The Structured Clinical Interview for DSM-IV*   The Structured Clinical Interview for *DSM-IV* (SCID; First, Spitzer, Gibbon, & Williams, 2002) was developed for clinical research to determine the presence of *DSM-IV* disorders. It is a semistructured interview to be used by formally trained staff. Although interviewers use the instrument as a guide to structure the interview, the interviewer can also rely on his or her judgment in interpreting a patient's answers to questions. Because there is a reliance on clinical judgment, the SCID functions best when administered by a trained mental health professional.

The SCID interview is divided into three sections: (1) a historical overview of the presenting complaint; (2) a screening list to determine beforehand whether the patient has symptoms of MDD, alcohol or substance abuse, obsessive-compulsive disorder, and anxiety disorders; and (3) the different diagnostic modules to reflect all the Axis I diagnoses of *DSM-IV*. Although the SCID has been used extensively in research studies, it has only fair validity and reliability. According to the SCID's creators, this instrument has a kappa coefficient of agreement equal to only 0.31 in nonpatient samples, indicating poor validity.

The utility of the SCID compared to physician diagnoses of depression has been demonstrated (Sanchez-Villegas et al., 2008). The main advantage to the SCID is its structured nature, which decreases the amount of variation of diagnosis from clinician to clinician. However, it is still a costly instrument in that staff administering the SCID must be trained in its use and must be of a professional level. However, costs can be lowered while maintaining the effectiveness of the assessment by the use of trained research assistants rather than senior investigators to administer the test (Miller et al., 1999).

*Composite International Diagnostic Interview*   The Composite International Diagnostic Interview (CIDI) was developed by WHO for the purpose of providing a variety of diagnoses that are in accord with definitions from the *DSM-IV*. This structured clinical interview is a fully computerized interview and so is able to attain a complexity and depth of diagnosis with carefully programmed skip patterns and flowcharts. Its great advantage is that it does not require a mental health professional to administer the instrument—in fact, the CIDI can be used as a patient-only-administered instrument, although it is also common for a researcher to administer it. Because the program makes the diagnosis, the researcher giving the interview does not need to make any independent clinical judgments (Kessler & Ustun, 2004).

The obvious benefits of the CIDI are that it is computerized and thus cuts down on costs of training interviewers and of using health practitioners to make diagnoses. There are, however, some drawbacks to the use of the CIDI. One important one is that because it is computerized, certain disorders may be more difficult to diagnose because of individuals' desire to maintain secrecy or denial of mental disorders (Thornton, Russell, & Hudson, 1998). Additionally, because it is computerized, differences among individuals that the program does not account for cannot be adjusted within the interview. However, the CIDI can be a useful tool provided that it is used with a follow-up interview with a clinician.

*The Mini-International Neuropsychiatric Interview*   The Mini-International Neuropsychiatric Interview (MINI) was developed by Sheehan and colleagues (1998) to assess the most common *DSM-IV* and *ICD-10* psychiatric disorders. With a 15-minute administration time, the MINI is purported to be shorter than the typical interviews used in research settings but is more thorough than screening tests. Like the CIDI, the MINI is advantageous in that it does not require a mental health professional to administer the instrument, thus saving costs and freeing time for mental health professionals to focus on other critical issues. The interview items focus on current symptoms (except for bipolar disorder) that are most routinely asked about by clinicians. This allows for a shorter administration time than other interviews, such as the SCID, that probe for past symptomatology as well.

Research testing the validity of the clinician-rated MINI has shown good to very good concordance with other clinician-rated diagnostic interviews (SCID and the CIDI), and it has excellent inter-rater reliability (kappa > 0.79) for all diagnostic categories and good test-retest reliability (kappa > 0.63) for all diagnostic categories except simple phobia and current mania. The MINI also demonstrated very good specificity (> 0.86 with SCID; > 0.72 with CIDI) and very good positive and negative predictive values for most diagnostic categories. For more details, see Sheehan et al., 1998.

The MINI is also available in other formats, including a longer version for the academic researcher called the MINI-Plus that includes 23 psychiatric disorders (as opposed to 19); a patient-rated version for use in outpatient settings (the MINI-PR); a version for children and adolescents (the MINI-Kid); and a shorter screening instrument, the MINI-Screen (as previously discussed), for primary care. There are also multiple translated-language versions and a computerized version now available whose properties are currently being investigated.

COMMENT

Determining the presence of a depressive disorder requires skill and effort in gathering information about the depression and its potential causes. The most efficient method to determine the presence of a depressive disorder is to first screen the patient and then, if the screening is positive, to perform an in-depth interview.

ETIOLOGICAL CONSIDERATIONS

The most debated topic in depression research is etiology. To date the majority of research in this area has focused on MDD, with very little research on Dysthymic

Disorder. Depression NOS appears to be related to whatever is thought to be the comorbid cause. Most scientists now believe that depressive disorders are multi-faceted, with causes resulting from the interactions of psychological, social, and biological factors (Kendler, Thornton, & Prescott, 2001; O'Keane, 2000). For example, stressful life events have been found to increase the risk for developing depression (Kendler & Gardner, 2010; McIntosh, Gillanders, & Rodgers, 2010). However, the person's coping style, social support, and genetic makeup all mediate the impact that stress has on depression (Fountoulakis, Iacovides, Kaprinis, & Kaprinis, 2006; Vergne & Nemeroff, 2006). A person who loses his job but has good social support and coping skills will be less likely to develop depression than another unemployed person who has limited coping skills and no social support. Though depression is related to many variables, their intermingling can most clearly predict the development of depression, rather than any single factor determining the onset. Genetics, learning, and life experiences all work together to cause depression.

### FAMILIAL AND GENETIC

The most fascinating research on the etiology of depression has been the recent work on the role of genetics in mental health. With the mapping of the human genome, the prospect of clearly identifying the influence of genetics on mental health is within reach. However, with depressive disorders, the contribution of genetics may take longer to uncover than for other disorders that have already demonstrated a clear genetic and biological cause (i.e., schizophrenia). Although past evidence from twin studies has been able to demonstrate some genetic involvement in depressive disorders, those links have thus far been weak.

Historically, the principal method for studying the influence of genetics on psychopathology was to compare the concordance of depression in identical twins (MZ; monozygotic twins), who originate from the same gene and are effectively genetically identical individuals, to that of fraternal twins (DZ; dizygotic), who share only half of their genes and thus are genetically similar to siblings. Because the frequency of twin births is low, genetic researchers also observe the rates of depressive disorder in first-degree relatives (often parents and children). According to the twin studies, MZ twins have greater concordance rates for depressive disorders than do DZ twins (Englund & Klein, 1990). More recent work by Kendler and Prescott (1999) evaluated MDD in DZ and MZ twins according to gender, and estimates the odds ratios for a lifetime diagnosis of MDD to be equal to 39% and is approximately the same for male and female twins. Family studies also find that the onset of depression is more likely in people with relatives with depression than in those who do not have family members with depression (Byers et al., 2009). The rates are not that compelling, however, with relatives having only a 21% risk for developing depression (Kupfer, Frank, Carpenter, & Neiswanger, 1989). Overall, the aggregate estimated rate of heritability for depression is between 31% to 42% (Sullivan, Neale, & Kendler, 2000).

However, recent research in MZ and DZ twins suggest that there is higher heritability for all unipolar depressive disorders combined compared to MDD alone. Additionally, recurrent early-onset MDD seems to be the most heritable form of the unipolar depressive disorders, with research estimating that approximately half of first-degree relatives and one-quarter of extended relatives of individuals with recurrent, early-onset MDD suffer from at least one mood disorder (Zubenko, Zubenko, Spiker, Giles, & Kaplan, 2001). Rates of heritability for MDD, when correlated with other unipolar depressive disorders (e.g., atypical depression, Dysthymic Disorder, and Adjustment Disorder with Depressive Features), were moderately higher than heritability of MDD alone. These findings suggest that some depressive disorders (MDD, Dysthmic Disorder, and depression NOS) may be reflections of the same underlying genetic liability (Edvardsen et al., 2009).

Direct genetic comparisons are becoming a more popular method for determining genetic links to mood. These methods are considered superior to the methods discussed previously, because DNA is a specific measure that is unlikely to be modified by environmental influences. The results from twin and family studies cannot account for the impact of learning on development of depression, whereas DNA is less likely to be influenced by personal experience. Additionally, molecular genetic analysis allows for specific genetic hypotheses to be tested. DNA studies are able to compare depressed with nondepressed controls on characteristics of certain genes that are associated with neurotransmitters related to depressive disorders. Although still in its infancy, this research has been very helpful in confirming the role of genetics in the development of depressive disorders. For instance, Dikeos and colleagues (1999) studied whether the genetic location of the D3 dopamine receptor differed in patients with MDD as compared to those with no history or current MDD. The investigators observed that genotypes carrying the allele (DNA structure) associated with D3 polymorphisms were found in 75% of the MDD patients and in 50% of the controls, suggesting genetic influences in MDD. Other studies, however, have not found such robust effects (Frisch et al., 1999; Neiswanger et al., 1998; Qian et al., 1999). More recently, Green and associates (2010) demonstrated an increased risk for recurrent MDD in individuals who have a variation in a gene that provides instructions to cells for making calcium channels. These channels are an important feature of cells, as they are involved in intercellular communication and generating and transmitting electrical signals, although their exact role in brain tissue is still unclear (Splawski et al., 2004). At best, the literature on the genetics of depressive disorders suggests a propensity to develop these disorders but that this propensity can be offset by learning and environmental influences.

### NEUROANATOMY AND NEUROBIOLOGY

Over the past 5 years, there has been considerable advancement in our understanding of the neuroanatomy and biology of depression. Much research effort has gone into determining biological determinants of depression, with a specific focus on the brain structures that appear to be associated with depression, neurocircuitry, and neurotransmitters.

*Neuroanatomy and Neurocircuitry*    Research into brain regions associated with depression is ongoing, but current brain theories of depression argue that several brain systems interact to regulate mood in response to stress. Research data from functional neuroimaging (fMRI) studies, research on people with brain damage, and positron emission tomography (PET) suggest that four brain regions are associated with depression. The first is the *amygdala*, which is responsible for memory of emotional reactions to stimuli. This part of the brain interprets the emotional salience of stimuli, and when there is a threatening stimulus, it produces an emotional reaction that triggers the brain into action. Next is the *orbitofrontal cortex*, which is responsible for cognitive processing and decision making. This part of the brain is in part responsible for putting logical meaning to the stimulus and for determining what should be done about the stimulus. The *dorsolateral prefrontal cortex* is responsible for affect regulation, planning, decision making, intentionality, and social judgment. Finally, the *anterior cingulate cortex* is also involved with depression and is responsible for error detection, anticipation of tasks, motivation, and modulation of emotional responses (Koenigs & Grafman, 2009). These systems work together to help us navigate our environment, and when they work well and in concert, we are able to manage most problems that come our way. When we are faced with a problem to solve, whether it is social, financial, or environmental, these systems work together to first let us know there is a problem in the environment, to assess the degree of threat the problem presents with, to modulate our emotions in reaction to the problem, to decide among a series of potential solutions to solve the problem, and then to initiate behavior to either cope with or solve the problem. When any of these systems is not working properly, whether due to brain damage, congenital anomalies, or learned behavioral patterns, our chances for developing depression are increased. For instance, if the mood regulation systems in the dorsolateral cortex are not working properly, they fail to regulate the emotional reaction to the problem. This failure prevents the orbitofrontal cortex from being able to create an action plan to solve the problem. What results is the tendency to avoid, rather than solve, the problem or to overreact to the problem.

Several functional imaging studies are beginning to support the role these systems play in depression, but the work is still very preliminary. Additionally, because depression is a rather heterogeneous disorder (people with the same diagnosis, even history, can have a very different clinical presentation), scientists are often coming up with different explanations for how these systems work, even about which systems are most important. This is partly because the expense of conducting this research is so high, and therefore the number of research participants in these studies tends to be quite small; given the heterogeneity of the illness, it is no surprise that undersampled studies would yield heterogeneous results. Finally, although technologies such as fMRI have revolutionized the field, many scientists are now claiming that results from these experiments should be viewed with caution (Logothetis, 2008).

*Neurochemistry and Transmitters*   Clinicians initially believed that depression was caused in part by lack of the two neurotransmitters *norepinephrine* and *serotonin*. Now, however, it is known that the dysregulation rather than the deficiency of these neurotransmitters causes depression (Moore & Bona, 2001). Antidepressants to regulate the production and distribution of norepinephrine and serotonin are effective in their ability to increase the availability of receptor sites rather than increase the production of the neurotransmitters (Veenstra-VanderWeele, Anderson, & Cook, 2000). Neurotransmitters provide an important but still only partial picture of the biological origin of depression, because abnormalities in neurotransmitter regulation do not necessarily lead to a depressed mood.

*Neuroendocrinology* also adds to a more complete understanding of the biological causes of depression. Evidence points to an overabundance of *cortisol* in the systems of patients with depression. Additionally, abnormalities in thyroid functions are often related to symptoms of depression, further indicating an important role for the neuroendocrine system in depression. In a study by Ghaziuddin and colleagues (2000), neuroendocrine imbalances in adolescents with MDD as compared to their non-depressed counterparts demonstrated that depression is associated with abnormal baseline levels of prolactin as well as sharper prolactin and cortisol responses to serotonergic challenges. Evidence for such abnormalities not only yields a more complete understanding of causation but also aids in the development of more effective drug treatments.

## LEARNING AND MODELING

There is a tremendous amount of research investigating and supporting behavioral, social, and environmental influences in the development of depression. A review of this literature suggests that depressive disorders appear to be related to three psychological variables and the individual's learning history (life experiences):

1. People's cognitive appraisals of themselves, their lives, and others (Alloy et al., 2000; Beck, Rush, Shaw, & Emery, 1979)
2. Whether people proactively solve problems or avoid them (D'Zurilla & Nezu, 1999)
3. The degree to which proactive attempts to cope with stress have been successful (Folkman & Lazarus, 1988)
4. An individual's learning history could lead to the development of depressive symptoms or serve maintain depression/dysphoria

In this paradigm, people who have negative expectations about their ability to cope with problems generally acquire these expectations through past learning experience. Repeated failed attempts to solve problems (learning history), for instance, leave a person feeling hopeless and helpless, abandoning his or her usual methods for solving problems, and becoming depressed (Seligman, Weiss, Weinraub, & Schulman, 1980). These factors—cognitive attributions, coping skills, and learned helplessness—have all been found to be predictive of depression.

People with negative expectations or cognitive vulnerabilities are more likely to develop depression when faced with a stressor than are people who do not possess cognitive vulnerabilities. Grazioli and Terry (2000) found that in women with postpartum depression, both general and maternal-specific dysfunctional attitudes were associated with self-reported depression, particularly in women who had children who were found to be temperamentally difficult. Another study found that individuals with negative cognitive styles had higher lifetime prevalence of depression than people who were not cognitively vulnerable (Alloy et al., 2000). Therefore, people with negative perceptions of themselves and their environment are at risk for becoming depressed.

Coping skills have also been found to be related to depression. Most research has found that people who use active forms of coping, such as problem solving, are less likely to develop depression than are people who use passive forms of coping, such as avoidance. In fact, one study people who used an avoidant coping style were more likely to develop depression when faced with psychosocial stressors (Welch & Austin, 2001). Rumination, a repetitive pattern of thoughts and behaviors focused on one's depressed state, can also result in less effective problem solving (Donaldson & Lam, 2004).

Although coping skills deficits and cognitive style contribute to depression, the interaction of these two factors seems to have the biggest impact on the development of depression. Several studies have supported this interaction in learned helplessness. Originally, these theories were tested in animal models, where unsolvable problems were presented to animals and all attempts to solve the problem were met with unpleasant consequences, such as an electric shock. After repeated attempts to solve the problem failed, these animals would exhibit depressogenic behavior—withdrawal, acting as if they were in pain—and, even after a solution was presented to them, the animals would refuse to try the solution (Altenor, Volpicelli, & Seligman, 1979). Scientists have been able to draw a relationship between learned helplessness and depression in research with people. For instance, Swendsen (1997) found that people with high-risk attributional styles were more likely to experience depressed mood after exposure to negative stressful events.

A person's learning history may also play a role in the development of depression. Since the 1970s there has been a tremendous amount of interest in investigating the role that learning principles play in the development of depression. Ferster (1973) postulated that individuals with depression did not engage in enough activities and may even avoid activities, thus leading to insufficient reinforcement for those activities. This limited engagement in activities also results in fewer opportunities to learn through experiencing those activities (contingencies of reinforcement). Lewinsohn (1974) expanded upon this theory, emphasizing depression as being the result of low levels of reinforcement contingent upon behavior. This lack of reinforcement that a person would obtain from doing something proactive would lead to less engagement in those types of behaviors in the future, eventually leading to withdrawal and isolation. According to this model, depression results from either a decrease in pleasant events or an increase in unpleasant events and speaks to the importance of considering context in the development of depression (Jacobson, Martell, & Dimidjian, 2001). Jacobson and colleagues developed the behavioral activation model (which grew from these theories and further developed them), emphasizing that when life is less rewarding or stressful, people sometimes pull away from the world around them and find that basic routines in their life become disrupted. This disruption in routines can increase depressive symptoms and make it difficult to solve life problems effectively. In turn, this can lead to secondary problems (e.g., relationships, occupational difficulties), which maintain or further exacerbate depression. Support for these models is strong and can be found in the depression treatment literature.

## Life Events

The literature is replete with data indicating that stressful life events contribute to the development of a depressive episode. Although not everyone who faces difficult problems develops depression, it is evident that prolonged exposure to psychosocial stress can precipitate a depressive episode (Hammen, Kim, Eberhart, & Brennan, 2009). Several studies have found that most depressive episodes are preceded by a severe life event or difficulty in the 6 months before onset of the episode (Kendler & Gardner, 2010). Kapci and Cramer (2000) also found that people were more likely to develop depression when they were exposed to numerous negative life events, but only if their belief in their ability to solve problems was impaired. Thus the interaction of negative life events, coping skills, and attributions about coping skills influences whether a person will experience depression. In addition, patients with more long-term or chronic depression were more likely to report past abuse, although the causal relationship is unclear (Keitner et al., 1997).

Because depression is a multifaceted disorder, it is difficult to pinpoint the specific role life events have on the development of a depressive disorder. Most people will have to face severe life stress at some point in their lives, yet not everyone develops depression. How an individual views severe life events and the perceived control he or she feels over the situation both play an important role in determining one's vulnerability to depression. For instance, several studies find that the relationship of life events to depression is mediated by other factors such as social support, cognitive style, and coping abilities (Alloy et al., 2000; Cacioppo, Hughes, Waite, Hawkley, & Thisted, 2006). Severe life events are significantly more likely to provoke a major depressive episode in individuals without social support (Leskelä et al., 2006). Support systems give an individual external support when internal coping skills are put to the test. Without the external support, however, an individual must rely exclusively on his or her own internal resources, which under severe duress might not be entirely effective. Therefore, although negative life events do influence the occurrence of depressive disorders, the social and psychological resources available to the person facing the stressful life event generally mediate the impact on mood.

## Gender and Racial-Ethnic

Many researchers have been trying to determine the reasons for the discrepant rates of depressive disorders across gender and racial-ethnic lines. Are the reasons genetic or biological? Is it that these populations are exposed to more stress and have fewer resources to cope with stress and therefore are more vulnerable than men and nonminority groups? Or is depression presented differently across these groups, and therefore the estimates in the prevalence for depressive disorders in these populations are inaccurate? Mental health researchers are still struggling with these questions and have only been able to give a partial explanation of why the discrepancy exists.

Some theorists believe that the reason minorities have differing rates of depressive disorder is that they present their symptoms of depression differently than do Caucasians (Escalante, del Rincon, & Mulrow, 2000; Ryder et al., 2008). Many researchers have spent years trying to discern the most appropriate way to assess depression in different cultures. Although research from WHO indicates that depression is similar across cultures, how people from one culture report the symptoms and their cultural attitude about mental health (and its treatment) can cloud diagnoses. Screening instruments and scales that were developed for Caucasian populations can be problematic if they are simply translated without regard for translation bias. Additionally, many studies have found that the factor structures and reliabilities of these instruments tend to differ across ethnic groups, indicating that groups vary in their reports of depressive symptoms (Azocar, Areán, Miranda, & Munoz, 2001). For instance, lower rates of depression in Asians may be attributable to their tendency to underreport affective symptoms of depression and to rely more on somatic presentation (Ryder et al., 2008).

Others have hypothesized that the different rates of depression in ethnic groups are associated with the fact that in this country, minority groups such as African Americans and Hispanics are more likely to be impoverished and to have to cope with financial and urban stress (Alexopoulos, 2005). Studies have demonstrated that socioeconomic status and exposure to trauma related to racism, urban living, and financial strain are correlated with depression and other mental illnesses such as anxiety and substance abuse (Caron & Liu, 2010; Gottlieb, Waitzkin, & Miranda, 2011; Kiima & Jenkins, 2010; Rhodes et al., 2010). Other studies have found that the rates for depression in middle class and affluent minorities are more similar to the national rates of depression as compared to middle-class and affluent Caucasians. These studies seem to argue that in the case of minority populations, increased exposure to stress is the reason for the differing rates of depressive disorder (Olfson et al., 2000).

The differing rate of depressive disorders between men and women is an interesting yet complicated finding. Researchers initially thought that the different prevalence rates resulted from reluctance on the part of men to admit feelings of depression, as well as men's tendency to cope with stress through substance use (Shorey et al., 2011). Others suggest that the increased prevalence of depression in women is because women tend to be victims of sexual abuse and therefore suffer a significant psychosocial stressor that is not as common in men (Gaudiano & Zimmerman, 2010; Ghassemi, Sadeghi, Asadollahi, Yousefy, & Mallik, 2010; Plaza et al., 2010). Still others suggest that the willingness of women over men to seek treatment services might account for the difference in prevalence (Fikretoglu, Liu, Pedlar, & Brunet, 2010). However, because the discrepancy between men and women seems to be universal, others claim that hormonal and biological differences account for the differential prevalence rates. Whatever the differential effect, the fact remains that depression is more commonly reported in women than in men, and this issue still needs to be resolved.

## COURSE AND PROGNOSIS

Research has begun to identify variables that can predict toward better or worse course and outcome, but a great deal of uncertainty still exists. Here we present the descriptive data regarding length, severity, and prognosis of depressive disorders.

## COURSE

Beyond the basic diagnostic criteria, MDD has several delineating features. Early-onset depression tends to appear before age 20 and has a more malignant course than late-onset depression (Devanand et al., 2004; Papakostas, Crawford, Scalia, & Fava, 2007). It is also associated with a family history of depression and other mood disorders (Bergemann & Boles, 2010; Wermter et al., 2010). Late-onset depression tends to emerge in the mid-thirties and is associated with fewer recurrent episodes, comorbid personality disorders, and substance abuse disorders relative to early-onset depression (Chui, Cheung, & Lam, 2011). However, there is a much greater variation in the age of onset with depression than in disorders such as schizophrenia. Second, the course of MDD tends to be time limited. The average episode lasts 6 months, although this varies greatly from person to person (Rhebergen et al., 2010). Third, MDD tends to be a recurrent disorder. Patients who have one major depressive episode have a 36.7% chance of experiencing a second; those who have two previous episodes have a 48% chance of developing a third episode. With each additional episode, chances for another additional episode increase by approximately 15% (Seemuller et al., 2010).

Dysthymic Disorder is a more chronic, long-lasting illness. The mean duration of Dysthymic Disorder is 30 years, and almost half of those patients who have Dysthymic Disorder will develop a major depressive episode in their lifetimes (Rhebergen et al., 2010). Those with Dysthymic Disorder have been found to have worse clinical prognosis than people with either MDD or depression NOS and are as disabled as those with MDD (Griffiths, Ravindran, Merali, & Anisman, 2000). Thankfully, Dysthymic Disorder is responsive to both psychotherapy and medication treatment, at least in the short term, with some studies suggesting that the most robust intervention is a combination of psychotherapy and medication (Barrett et al., 2001). Unfortunately, few people with Dysthymic Disorder ever receive treatment. Fewer than half will ever receive any kind of mental health treatment, and those who do usually do so only after having experienced a major depressive episode (Rhebergen et al., 2010).

## PROGNOSIS

Early diagnosis and treatment with therapy, medication, or both result in a better chance of recovery from MDD, Dysthymic Disorder, and depression NOS (Rhebergen et al., 2010). The ease of recovery from depression, however, is related to several factors. Prognosis is best when the patient is facing few stressful life events (Sherrington, Hawton, Fagg, Andrew, & Smith, 2001) and has a solid support network on which to rely (Rubenstein et al., 2007). Furthermore, individuals with an initial early recovery are less likely to develop recurring symptoms. Early improvements indicate that the patient has access to coping mechanisms that allow for a quick recovery, and this often suggests an overall positive long-term prognosis. The prognosis for Dysthymic Disorder is less certain. For example, Ciechanowski and colleagues (2004) demonstrated a 50% reduction at the end of a 12-month period in depressive symptoms and functional improvement using problem-solving therapy in home-based intervention for older adults with medical illnesses, minor depression, and Dysthymic Disorder. However, Klein and colleagues (1999) found that adults with dysthymia improved at a much slower rate and were more symptomatic at a 10-year follow-up than were individuals with MDD. As of this writing, few treatment studies have demonstrated any long-lasting positive effect for any intervention for Dysthymic Disorder.

Another factor involved in the prognosis for both MDD and Dysthymic Disorder are levels of self-esteem. A higher self-esteem predicts an increasingly positive prognosis (Sherrington et al., 2001). Poor self-esteem, on the other hand, predicts a longer and more delayed recovery. The prognosis of depressive disorders is poor when they have an early onset, a premorbid personality disorder exists, and there has been a previous episode (Ryder, Quilty, Vachon, & Bagby, 2010). More intensive and extended treatment can improve the remission and maintenance of remission from MDD episodes, even with high severity of the depression, although the evidence on Dysthymic Disorder is limited.

## LOOKING AHEAD TO *DSM-5*

The diagnosis for Major Depression, Dysthymia, and Depression NOS has not changed substantially. The symptoms remain the same, as do the decision-making criteria. Major changes to the depressive disorders include the addition of a dimensional assessment within depression for other co-occurring disorders (e.g., anxiety), and *DSM-5* does propose adding a suicide assessment tool to help clinicians make a clear determination of suicide risk. The biggest and most controversial change to the Depressive Disorders section of *DSM-5* is the removal of the grief exclusion (Lamb, Pies, & Zisook, 2010; Zisook et al., 2010a; Zisook et al., 2010b). Historically, depressive symptoms after the recent loss of a loved one was considered to be a normal reaction to the loss, and therefore was not considered a mood disorder. Several studies have demonstrated that while depressive symptoms are generally common after a recent loss, the degree to which one is disabled by those symptoms is a better indicator of whether the depression is serious enough to be considered a mental illness. Proponents of the original exclusion feel that removing the exclusion pathologizes a normal reaction, whereas proponents of the removal of the exclusion feel that to ignore severe depression, regardless of its cause, is unethical, and therefore clinicians should not base the need for treatment on one exclusionary criteria. We concur that what is most important is a thorough assessment of the causes and impact of depression on individual functions; although grief is a normal reaction to loss, most people experiencing a normal reaction are able to return to work within 2 months' time and are capable of basic functioning.

## CASE STUDIES

### MAJOR DEPRESSION

*Case Identification*   R.J. was a single, 32-year-old African American woman who self-referred to mental health services for what she called depression.

*Presenting Complaints* Before seeking services, R.J. had contemplated getting gastric bypass surgery and was extremely unhappy with her employment. She was managing several large projects for the company and felt that she was the only member of her staff who was doing any work. She felt that she was not trusted to do her job, was not respected for the work she did, and was being taken for granted. She was also concerned about getting the surgery, because she would need recovery time and would be unable to care for her family members. Her symptoms included feeling depressed nearly all day, every day, for the last 12 months; feeling a lack of interest in her usual activities (in this case walking and attending a weight-loss program); and increased irritability. For the last 12 months, she reported insomnia, increased appetite, and feelings of worthlessness and hopelessness about the future. She reported feelings of guilt, believed that she was being punished, and constantly worried that she was not doing enough for her family. In addition, she reported having difficulty concentrating and making decisions. Although she had occasionally felt that she would be better off dead, she was not suicidal. She did not feel that suicide was an option and had no plan to harm herself.

*History* R.J. was the younger of two female siblings from the northwestern section of the United States. As a child, she did not have time for friends, because she was often caring for her sick mother. She was a good student but had dropped out of high school to care for her mother. Her father had left her mother and moved out of state shortly before her mother became ill. R.J. had a large extended family but acutely felt the loss of a father figure. Her uncle had problems with drugs and was incarcerated. Subsequently, she had taken on the care of her younger niece and nephews. As an adult, R.J. had success in school (she was able to achieve her GED and was successfully taking college courses) and in her work. She believed that she had suffered from depression twice before in her adult life but had always been able to overcome the depression on her own. However, she had often turned to food for comfort and was suffering from obesity. She explained that she had never sought help for her depression before because she was busy caring for her family and did not take time for herself. Furthermore, she indicated that it was not like her to talk with someone about her feelings. She believed her mother was depressed following the loss of her husband and subsequent medical problems but was unsure of these facts, because these issues were never discussed.

*Assessment* R.J. presents with several interesting issues related to depression. First, she reports having no less than nine symptoms of depression, six for more than a year; she also reports having these symptoms nearly every day and that they are impairing her ability to function at work and socially. R.J. also indicates having had two previous depression episodes that spontaneously remitted, and that her mother may have suffered from depression as well. Based on this assessment, R.J. met criteria for recurrent Major Depression and may have an endogenous form of the disorder.

## DYSTHYMIC DISORDER

*Case Identification* B.G. was a retired, 55-year-old Caucasian man who sought services for depression after a doctor recommended he talk to a mental health professional.

*Presenting Complaints* B.G. stated that for the last 3 years, he occasionally felt worthless, depressed, and irritable. He reported that some days he often found it difficult to get himself going to complete his chores for the day but would somehow manage to do so. He indicated that he was unsure of treatment, because he had "good days," but upon further probing he reported that these days were infrequent (no more than 1 or 2 days per week). Although he said he and his wife did not have marital problems, he felt guilty that she worked and he did not. The primary symptoms he complained about were occasional sadness, lack of energy, irritability, feelings of worthlessness, and guilt.

*History* B.G. was the oldest of five children in his family and was currently married with three children, all of whom were grown and living in other parts of the country. He completed high school and trade school afterward. He had been employed with one construction company his entire adult life. He was living with his wife at the time of his intake. He had no serious health problems other than chronic pain resulting from a back injury. B.G. retired because of a back injury that prevented him from performing his job. Three years ago, his wife took on a part-time job to make extra money, and B.G. began looking after the house. Prior to this visit, he had never sought mental health services, nor had he ever felt depressed.

*Assessment* B.G. presents with some classic symptoms of Dysthymic Disorder; he reports having depressed mood for more days than not for more than the required 2-year period. He denied a history of manic episodes or MDD during this 2-year period. He also met the two or more additional symptom requirement, which included such symptoms as lack of energy and low self-esteem. Although B.G. did report brief periods in which he felt "good," these symptom-free periods only occurred on average 1 to 2 days per week, and therefore he met the additional criterion of not having been symptom free for more than 2 months at a time. Based on our assessment, B.G. met criteria for a diagnosis of Dysthymic Disorder, late onset.

## DEPRESSION NOS

*Case Identification* T.J. was a 40-year-old woman who was referred by her physician for treatment of depression. According to the physician, T.J. was struggling with placing her elderly mother in a nursing home, and this struggle made her quite depressed. The provider indicated that T.J. had a recent diagnosis of hyperthyroidism and was being treated with medication.

*Presenting Complaints* T.J. stated that she had been feeling depressed for several months, ever since her mother had become more seriously ill and T.J. began trying to find a nursing home for her. Her primary complaints were depression and sadness nearly all day, every day; feeling slowed down; and trouble with concentration. She also indicated that having had a recent diagnosis of hyperthyroidism complicated matters for her and that she had been unable to take her medication regularly.

*History* T.J. was an only child who was living with her mother at the time of referral. She had a college education and had been employed as an administrative assistant for

10 years. She was divorced with no children. T.J. indicated that she had been her mother's caregiver for most of her life and that they had a "love-hate" relationship. Her mother was being verbally abusive to T.J. regarding the placement, making T.J. feel guilty. T.J. indicated that she would normally be able to let her mother's abuse roll off her back, having long ago accepted that her mother was a difficult person. However, the last 4 months were hard to cope with, even though she had a good caseworker helping her, and her mother would be placed in a pleasant assisted-living facility within the next month.

*Assessment/Treatment*    After consideration of her symptoms, T.J.'s symptoms did not appear to meet full criteria for MDD, but it was clear to the therapist that a depressive disorder was present. What was unclear was whether the depression was primary or whether her medical symptoms were the cause of the depression, thus a diagnosis of Depressive Disorder, NOS was assigned.

T.J. was encouraged to start taking her medication for hyperthyroidism and was educated about the link between the illness and depressive symptoms. T.J. and her therapist agreed to meet again in 2 weeks. At that meeting, T.J. reported that her mother had been placed in the assisted-living facility and that while she felt guilty for a few days, she found that her mother was actually quite happy at the facility. She also reported taking the medication regularly and stated she already felt much better ("like my old self"), although she was still somewhat symptomatic of depression (occasional sadness and poor energy). Now that her mother had been successfully placed, T.J. indicated that she would like to work on rebuilding her social life.

## SUMMARY

Depressive disorders are common and widely studied. Given the extent of our knowledge of MDD and Dysthymic Disorder, however, research continues to address the best means of recognizing depression, how to treat depression in different settings and in different cultures, and further clarification of the etiology of these disorders. The causes and symptoms of depressive disorders are extremely variable and intermingled. The causes include both physiological and environmental factors, and the expressions of depression vary from short, severe episodes to chronic symptomatology. Because of the immense complexity of the depressive disorders, further research will aid in the ability to tailor diagnosis and therapy to each particular manifestation and explore cross-cultural concerns in assessment and treatment.

## REFERENCES

Adewuya, A. O., Ola, B. A., & Afolabi, O. O. (2006). Validity of the patient health questionnaire (PHQ-9) as a screening tool for depression amongst Nigerian university students. *Journal of Affective Disorders, 96*(1–2), 89–93.

Alderete, E., Vega, W. A., Kolody, B., & Aguilar-Gaxiola, S. (1999). Depressive symptomatology: Prevalence and psychosocial risk factors among Mexican migrant farmworkers in California. *Journal of Community Psychology, 27*(4), 457–471.

Alexopoulos, G. S. (2005). Depression in the elderly. *Lancet, 365*(9475), 1961–1970.

Alloy, L. B., Abramson, L. Y., Whitehouse, W. G., Hogan, M. E., Tashman, N. A., Steinberg, D. L., . . . Donovan, P. (2000). The Temple-Wisconsin Cognitive Vulnerability to Depression Project: Lifetime history of axis I psychopathology in individuals at high and low cognitive risk for depression. *Journal of Abnormal Psychology, 109*(3), 403–418.

Altenor, A., Volpicelli, J. R., & Seligman, M. E. (1979). Debilitated shock escape is produced by both short- and long-duration inescapable shock: Learned helplessness versus learned inactivity. *Bulletin of the Psychomonic Society, 14*(5), 337–339.

American Psychiatric Association. (2000). *Diagnostic and Statistical Manual of Mental Disorders* (4th ed., text revision; DSM-IV-TR). Washington, DC: Author.

Andrus, B. M., Blizinsky, K., Vedell, P. T., Dennis, K., Shukla, P. K., Schaffer, D. J., . . . Redei, E. E. (2011). Gene expression patterns in the hippocampus and amygdala of endogenous depression and chronic stress models. *Molecular Psychiatry* (in press).

Angold, A., Weissman, M. M., John, K., Wickramaratne, P., & Prusoff, B. (1991). The effects of age and sex on depression ratings in children and adolescents. *Journal of the American Academy of Child and Adolescent Psychiatry, 30*(1), 67–74.

Areán, P. A., & Reynolds, C. F., 3rd. (2005). The impact of psychosocial factors on late-life depression. *Biological Psychiatry, 58*(4), 277–282.

Azocar, F., Areán, P., Miranda, J., & Munoz, R. F. (2001). Differential item functioning in a Spanish translation of the Beck Depression Inventory. *Journal of Clinical Psychology, 57*(3), 355–365.

Baldwin, R. C. (2000). Poor prognosis of depression in elderly people: Causes and actions. *Annals of Medicine, 32*(4), 252–256.

Barrett, J. E., Williams, J. W., Jr., Oxman, T. E., Frank, E., Katon, W., Sullivan, M., . . . Sengupta, A. S. (2001). Treatment of dysthymia and minor depression in primary care: A randomized trial in patients aged 18 to 59 years. *Journal of Family Practice, 50*(5), 405–412.

Barros-Loscertales, A., Ventura-Campos, N., Sanjuan-Tomas, A., Belloch, V., Parcet, M. A., & Avila, C. (2010). Behavioral activation system modulation on brain activation during appetitive and aversive stimulus processing. *Social Cognitive and Affective Neuroscience, 5*(1), 18–28.

Beck, A. T. (1961). A systematic investigation of depression. *Comprehensive Psychiatry, 2*, 163–170.

Beck, A. T., Guth, D., Steer, R. A., & Ball, R. (1997). Screening for major depression disorders in medical inpatients with the Beck Depression Inventory for Primary Care. *Behaviour Research and Therapy, 35*(8), 785–791.

Beck, A. T., Rush, A. J., Shaw, B. F., & Emery, G. (1979). *Cognitive therapy of depression*. New York, NY: Guilford.

Beck, A. T., Steer, R. A., & Brown, G. K. (1996). *Manual for the Beck Depression Inventory – II*. San Antonio, TX: Psychological Corporation/Pearson.

Bergemann, E. R., & Boles, R. G. (2010). Maternal inheritance in recurrent early-onset depression. *Psychiatric Genetics, 20*(1), 31–34.

Boelen, P. A., van de Schoot, R., van den Hout, M. A., de Keijser, J., & van den Bout, J. (2010). Prolonged grief disorder, depression, and posttraumatic stress disorder are distinguishable syndromes. *Journal of Affective Disorders, 125*(1–3), 374–378.

Bolton, J. M., Pagura, J., Enns, M. W., Grant, B., & Sareen, J. (2010). A population-based longitudinal study of risk factors for suicide attempts in major depressive disorder. *Journal of Psychiatric Research, 44*(13), 817–826.

Bonsignore, M., Barkow, K., Jessen, F., & Heun, R. (2001). Validity of the five-item WHO well-being index (WHO-5) in an elderly population. *European Archives of Psychiatry and Clinical Neuroscience, 251*, (Suppl2), II27–II31.

Bostwick, J. M., & Pankratz, V. S. (2000). Affective disorders and suicide risk: A reexamination. *American Journal of Psychiatry, 157*, 1925–1932.

Brennan, C., Worrall-Davies, A., McMillan, D., Gillbody, S., & House, A. (2010). The Hospital Anxiety and Depression Scale: A diagnositc meta-analysis of case-finding ability. *Journal of Psychosomatic Research, 69*(4), 371–378.

Burke, K. C., Burke, J. D., Jr., Rae, D. S., & Regier, D. A. (1991). Comparing age at onset of major depression and other psychiatric disorders by birth cohorts in five US community populations. *Archives of General Psychiatry, 48*(9), 789–795.

Byers, A. L., Levy, B. R., Stanislav, V. K., Bruce, M. L., Allore, H. G., Caap-Ahlgren, M., & Dehlin, O. (2009). Heritability of depressive symptoms: A case study using a multilevel approach. *International Journal of Methods in Psychiatric Research, 18*(4), 287–296.

Caap-Ahlgren, M., & Dehlin, O. (2001). Insomnia and depressive symptoms in patients with Parkinson's disease: Relationship to health-related quality of life. An interview study of patients living at home. *Archives of Gerontology and Geriatrics, 32*(1), 23–33.

Cacioppo, J. T., Hawkley, L. C., & Thisted, R. A. (2010). Perceived social isolation makes me sad: 5-year cross-lagged analyses of loneliness and depressive symptomatology in the Chicago Health, Aging, and Social Relations Study. *Psychology and Aging, 25*(2), 453–463.

Cacioppo, J. T., Hughes, M. E., Waite, L. J., Hawkley, L. C., & Thisted, R. A. (2006). Loneliness as a specific risk factor for depressive symptoms: Cross-sectional and longitudinal analyses. *Psychology and Aging, 21*(1), 140–151.

Caron, J., & Liu, A. (2010). A descriptive study of the prevalence of psychological distress and mental disorders in the Canadian population: Comparison between low-income and non-low-income populations. *Chronic Diseases in Canada, 30*(3), 84–94.

Chentsova-Dutton, Y., & Hanley, K. (2010). The effects of anhedonia and depression on hedonic responses. *Psychiatry Research, 179*(2), 176–180.

Chui, W. W., Cheung, E. F., & Lam, L. C. (2011). Neuropsychological profiles and short-term outcome in late-onset depression. *International Journal of Geriatric Psychiatry, 26*(5), 458–465.

Ciechanowski, P., Wagner, E., Schmaling, K., Schwartz, S., Williams, B., Diehr, P., . . . LoGerfo, J. (2004). Community-integrated home-based depression treatment in older adults: A randomized controlled trial. *Journal of the American Medical Association, 291*(13), 1569–1577.

Conti, D. J., & Burton, W. N. (1995). The cost of depression in the workplace. *Behavioral Health Care Tomorrow, 4*(4), 25–27.

Cooper, L., Peters, L., & Andrews, G. (1998). Validity of the Composite International Diagnostic Interview (CIDI) psychosis module in a psychiatric setting. *Journal of Psychiatric Research, 32*(6), 361–368.

Corruble, E., Falissard, B., & Gorwood, P. (2011). *DSM* bereavement exclusion for major depression and objective cognitive impairment. *Journal of Affective Disorders, 130*(1–2), 113–117.

Coryell, W., & Young, E. A. (2005). Clinical predictors of suicide in primary major depressive disorder, *Journal of Clinical Psychiatry, 66*, 412–417.

de Groot, M., Jacobson, A. M., Samson, J. A., & Welch, G. (1999). Glycemic control and major depression in patients with type 1 and type 2 diabetes mellitus. *Journal of Psychosomatic Research, 46*(5), 425–435.

Devanand, D. P., Adorno, E., Cheng, J., Burt, T., Pelton, G. H., Roose, S. P., & Sackheim, H. A. (2004). Late onset dysthymic disorder and major depression differ from early onset dysthymic disorder and major depression in elderly outpatients. *Journal of Affective Disorders, 78*(3), 259–267.

Dichter, G. S., Felder, J. N., & Smoski, M. J. (2010). The effects of Brief Behavioral Activation Therapy for Depression on cognitive control in affective contexts: An fMRI investigation. *Journal of Affective Disorders, 126*(1–2), 236–244.

Dick, L. P., Gallagher-Thompson, D., & Thompson, L. W. (1996). Cognitive-behavioral therapy. In R. T. Woods (Ed.), *Handbook of the clinical psychology of ageing* (pp. 509–544). Oxford, England: John Wiley & Sons.

Diez-Quevedo, C., Rangil, T., Sanchez-Planell, L., Kroenke, K., & Spitzer, R. L. (2001). Validation and utility of the patient health questionnaire in diagnosing mental disorders in 1003 general hospital Spanish inpatients. *Psychosomatic Medicine, 63*(4), 679–686.

Dikeos, D. G., Papadimitriou, G. N., Avramopoulos, D., Karadima, G., Daskalopoulou, E. G., Souery, D., . . . Stefanis, C. N. (1999). Association between the dopamine D3 receptor gene locus (DRD3) and unipolar affective disorder. *Psychiatric Genetics, 9*(4), 189–195.

Donaldson, C., & Lam, D. (2004). Rumination, mood and social problem-solving in major depression. *Psychological Medicine, 34*(7), 1309–1318.

Druss, B. G., Rosenheck, R. A., & Sledge, W. H. (2000). Health and disability costs of depressive illness in a major U.S. corporation. *American Journal of Psychiatry, 157*(8), 1274–1278.

D'Zurilla, T. J., & Nezu, A. M. (1999). *Problem-solving therapy: A social competence approach to clinical intervention.* New York, NY: Springer.

Edvardsen, J., Torgersen, S., Roysamb, E., Lygren, S., Skre, I., Onstad, S., & Olen, P. A. (2009). Unipolar depressive disorders have a common genotype. *Journal of Affective Disorders, 117*(1–2), 30–41.

Englund, S. A., & Klein, D. N. (1990). The genetics of neurotic-reactive depression: A reanalysis of Shapiro's (1970) twin study using diagnostic criteria. *Journal of Affective Disorders, 18*(4), 247–252.

Escalante, A., del Rincon, I., & Mulrow, C. D. (2000). Symptoms of depression and psychological distress among Hispanics with rheumatoid arthritis. *Arthritis Care and Research, 13*(3), 156–167.

Ferster, C. B. (1973). A functional analysis of depression. *American Psychologist, 28*, 857–870.

Fikretoglu, D., Liu, A., Pedlar, D., & Brunet, A. (2010). Patterns and predictors of treatment delay for mental disorders in a nationally representative, active Canadian military sample. *Medical Care, 48*(1), 10–17.

First, M. B., Spitzer, R. L., Gibbon, M., & Williams, J. B. W. (2002). *Structured clinical interview for DSM-IV-TR Axis I disorders, research version, patient edition with psychotic screen.* New York: Biometrics Research, New York State Psychiatric Institute.

Fisher, L., Glasgow, R. E., & Strycker, L. A. (2010). The relationship between diabetes distress and clinical depression with glycemic control among patients with type 2 diabetes. *Diabetes Care, 33*(5), 1034–1036.

Fisher, L., Mullan, J. T., Areán, P., Glasgow, R. E., Hessler, D., & Masharani, U. (2010). Diabetes distress but not clinical depression or depressive symptoms is associated with glycemic control in both cross-sectional and longitudinal analyses. *Diabetes Care, 33*(1), 23–28.

Fiske, A., Wetherell, J. L., & Gatz, M. (2009). Depression in older adults. *Annual Review of Clinical Psychology, 5*, 363–389.

Folkman, S., & Lazarus, R. S. (1986). Stress-processes and depressive symptomatology. *Journal of Abnormal Psychology, 95*(2), 107–113.

Folkman, S., & Lazarus, R. S. (1988). The relationship between coping and emotion: Implications for theory and research. *Social Science and Medicine, 26*(3), 309–317.

Fountoulakis, K. N., Iacovides, A., Kaprinis, S., & Kaprinis, G. (2006). Life events and clinical subtypes of major depression: a cross-sectional study. *Psychiatry Research, 143*(2–3), 235–244.

Frisch, A., Postilnick, D., Rockah, R., Michaelovsky, E., Postilnick, S., Birman, E., . . . Weizman, R. (1999). Association of unipolar major depressive disorder with genes of the serotonergic and dopaminergic pathways. *Molecular Psychiatry, 4*(4), 389–392.

Gallagher, D., Mhaolain, A. N., Greene, E., Walsh, C., Denihan, A., Bruce, I., . . . Lawlor, B. A. (2010). Late life depression: A comparison of risk factors and symptoms according to age of onset in community dwelling older adults. *International Journal of Geriatric Psychiatry, 25*(10), 981–987.

Gaudiano, B. A., & Zimmerman, M. (2010). The relationship between childhood trauma history and the psychotic subtype of major depression. *Acta Psychiatrica Scandanavica, 121*(6), 462–470.

Ghassemi, G. R., Sadeghi, S., Asadollahi, G. A., Yousefy, A. R., & Mallik, S. (2010). Early experiences of abuse and current depressive disorders in Iranian women. *East Mediterranean Health Journal, 16*(5), 498–504.

Ghaziuddin, N., King, C. A., Welch, K. B., Zaccagnini, J., Weidmer-Mikhail, E., Mellow, A. M., . . . Greden, J. F. (2000). Serotonin dysregulation in adolescents with major depression: Hormone response to meta-chlorophenylpiperazine (mCPP) infusion. *Psychiatry Research, 95*(3), 183–194.

Goldberg, D. P. (1972). *The detection of psychiatric illness by questionnaire: A technique for the identification and assessment of non-psychotic psychiatric illness.* Oxford, England: Oxford University Press.

Goldberg, D. P., & Blackwell, B. (1970). Psychiatric illness in general practice: A detailed study using a new method of case identification. *British Medical Journal, 2*, 439–443.

Gottlieb, L., Waitzkin, H., & Miranda, J. (2011). Depressive symptoms and their social contexts: A qualitative systematic literature review of contextual interventions. *International Journal of Social Psychiatry* (in press).

Grazioli, R., & Terry, D. J. (2000). The role of cognitive vulnerability and stress in the prediction of postpartum depressive symptomatology. *British Journal of Clinical Psychology, 39*(4), 329–347.

Green, E. K., Grozeva, D., Jones, I., Jones, L., Kirov, G., Caesar, S., . . . Craddock, N. (2010). The bipolar disorder risk allele at CACNA1C also confers risk of recurrent major depression and of schizophrenia. *Molecular Psychiatry, 15*, 1016–1022.

Griffiths, J., Ravindran, A. V., Merali, Z., & Anisman, H. (2000). Dysthymia: A review of pharmacological and behavioral factors. *Molecular Psychiatry, 5*(3), 242–261.

Gunnarsdottir, E. D., Pingitore, R. A., Spring, B. J., Konopka, L. M., Crayton, J. W., Milo, T., & Shirazi, P. (2000). Individual differences among cocaine users. *Addictive Behaviors, 25*(5), 641–652.

Gupta, A., Bahadur, I., Gupta, K. R., & Bhugra, D. (2006). Self-awareness of depression and life events in three groups of patients: Psychotic depression, obsessive-compulsive disorder and chronic medical illness in North India. *Indian Journal of Psychiatry, 48*(4), 251–253.

Guze, S. G., & Robins, E. (1970). Suicide and primary affective diosrders. *British Journal of Psychiatry, 117*, 437–438.

Hammen, C., Kim, E. Y., Eberhart, N. K., & Brennan, P. A. (2009). Chronic and acute stress and the prediction of major depression in women. *Depression and Anxiety, 26*(8), 718–723.

Han, C., Jo, S. A., Kwak, J. H., Pae, C. U., Steffens, D., Jo, I., & Park, M. H. (2008). Validation of the Patient Health Questionnaire-9 Korean version in the elderly population: The Ansan Geriatric study. *Comprehensive Psychiatry, 49*(2), 218–223.

Ho, Y. C., & Wang, S. (2010). Adult neurogenesis is reduced in the dorsal hippocampus of rats displaying learned helplessness behavior. *Neuroscience, 171*(1), 153–161.

Hoover, D. R., Siegel, M., Lucas, J., Kalay, E., Gaboda, D., Devanand, D. P., & Crystal, S. (2010). Depression in the first year of stay for elderly long-term nursing home residents in the U.S. A. *International Psychogeriatrics, 22*(7), 1161–1171.

Hopko, D. R., Bourland, S. L., Stanley, M. A., Beck, J. G., Novy, D. M., Averill, P. M., & Swann, A. C. (2000). Generalized anxiety disorder in older adults: Examining the relation between clinician severity ratings and patient self-report measures. *Depression and Anxiety, 12*(4), 217–225.

Huang, F. Y., Chung, H., Kroenke, K., Delucchi, K. L., & Spitzer, R. L. (2006). Using the Patient Health Questionnaire-9 to measure depression among racially and ethnically diverse primary care patients. *Journal of General Internal Medicine, 21*(6), 547–552.

Hybels, C. F., Blazer, D. G., Pieper, C. F., Landerman, L. R., & Steffens, D. C. (2009). Profiles of depressive symptoms in older adults diagnosed with major depression: Latent cluster analysis. *American Journal of Geriatric Psychiatry, 17*(5), 387–396.

Isaacowitz, D. M., & Seligman, M. E. (2001). Is pessimism a risk factor for depressive mood among community-dwelling older adults? *Behavior Research and Therapy, 39*(3), 255–272.

Jacobson, N., Martell, C., & Dimidjian, S. (2001). Behavioral activation treatment for depression: Returning to contextual roots. *Clinical Psychology: Science and Practice, 8*, 255–270.

Jackson-Triche, M. E., Greer Sullivan, J., Wells, K. B., Rogers, W., Camp, P., & Mazel, R. (2000). Depression and health-related quality of life in ethnic minorities seeking care in general medical settings. *Journal of Affective Disorders, 58*(2), 89–97.

Jakupcak, M., Wagner, A., Paulson, A., Varra, A., & McFall, M. (2010). Behavioral activation as a primary care-based treatment for PTSD and depression among returning veterans. *Journal of Traumatic Stress, 23*(4), 491–495.

Jia, L., Jiang, S. M., Shang, Y. Y., Huang, Y. X., Li, Y. J., Xie, D. R., . . . Ji, F. C. (2010). Investigation of the incidence of pancreatic cancer-related depression and its relationship with the quality of life of patients. *Digestion, 82*(1), 4–9.

Kapci, E. G., & Cramer, D. (2000). The mediation component of the hopelessness depression in relation to negative life events. *Counseling Psychology Quarterly, 13*(4), 413–423.

Katon, W. J. (2003). Clinical and health services relationships between major depression, depressive symptoms, and general medical illness. *Biological Psychiatry, 54*(3), 216–226.

Keitner, G. I., Ryan, C. E., Miller, I. W., & Zlotnick, C. (1997). Psychosocial factors and the long-term course of major depression. *Journal of Affective Disorders, 44*(1), 57–67.

Kendler, K. S., & Gardner, C. O. (2010). Dependent stressful life events and prior depressive episodes in the prediction of major depression: The problem of causal inference in psychiatric epidemiology. *Archives of General Psychiatry, 67*(11), 1120–1127.

Kendler, K. S., & Prescott, C. A. (1999). A population-based twin study of lifetime major depression in men and women. *Archives of General Psychiatry, 56*, 9–44.

Kendler, K. S., Thornton, L. M., & Prescott, C. A. (2001). Gender differences in the rates of exposure to stressful life events and sensitivity to their depressogenic effects. *American Journal of Psychiatry, 158*(4), 587–593.

Kessler, R. C., Barber, C., Birnbaum, H. G., Frank, R. G., Greenberg, P. E., Rose, R. M., . . . Wang, P. (1999). Depression in the workplace: Effects on short-term disability. *Health Affairs, 18*(5), 163–171.

Kessler, R. C., Berglund, P., Demler, O., Jin, R., Merikangas, K. R., & Walters, E. E. (2005). Lifetime prevalence and age-of-onset distributions of *DSM-IV* disorders in the National Comorbidity Survey Replication. *Archives of General Psychiatry, 62*(6), 593–602.

Kessler, R. C., & Frank, R. G. (1997). The impact of psychiatric disorders on work loss days. *Psychological Medicine, 27*(4), 861–873.

Kessler, R. C., McGonagle, K. A., Nelson, C. B., Hughes, M., Swartz, M., & Blazer, D. G. (1994). Sex and depression in the National Comorbidity Survey. II: Cohort effects. *Journal of Affective Disorders, 30*(1), 15–26.

Kessler, R. C., McGonagle, K. A., Zhao, S., Nelson, C. B., Hughes, M., Eshleman, S., . . . Kendler, K. S. (1994). Lifetime and 12-month prevalence of *DSM-II-R* psychiatric disorders in the United States. Results from the National Comorbidity Survey. *Archives of General Psychiatry, 51*(1), 8–19.

Kessler, R. C., & Merikangas, K. R. (2004). The National Comorbidity Survey Replication (NCS-R): Background and aims. *International Journal of Methods in Psychiatric Research, 13*(2), 60–68.

Kessler, R. C., & Ustun, T. B. (2004). The World Mental Health (WMH) survey initiative version of the World Health Organization (WHO) Composite International Diagnostic Interview (CIDI). *International Journal of Methods in Psychiatric Research, 13*(2), 93–121.

Kiima, D., & Jenkins, R. (2010). Mental health policy in Kenya: An integrated approach to scaling up equitable care for poor populations. *International Journal of Mental Health Systems, 4*, 19.

Kilzieh, N., Rastam, S., Ward, K. D., & Maziak, W. (2010). Gender, depression and physical impairment: An epidemiologic perspective from Aleppo, Syria. *Social Psychiatry and Psychiatric Epidemiology, 45*(6), 595–602.

Kim, J. M., Shin, I. S., Yoon, J. S., & Stewart, R. (2002). Prevalence and correlates of late life depression compared between urban and rural populations in Korea. *International Journal of Geriatric Psychiatry, 17*(5), 409–415.

King-Kallimanis, B., Gum, A. M., & Kohn, R. (2009). Comorbidity of depressive and anxiety disorders for older Americans in the national comorbidity survey-replication. *The American Journal of Geriatric Psychiatry, 17*(9), 782–792.

Klein, D. N., Schatzberg, A. F., McCullough, J. P., Keller, M. B., Dowling, F., Goodman, D., . . . Harrison, W. M. (1999). Early versus late-onset dysthymic disorder: Comparison in out-patients with superimposed major depressive episodes. *Journal of Affective Disorders, 52*(1–3), 187–196.

Koenigs, M., & Grafman, J. (2009). The functional neuroanatomy of depression: Distinct roles for ventromedial and dorsolateral prefrontal cortex. *Behavioural Brain Research, 201*(2), 239–243.

Kroenke, K., Spitzer, R. L., & Williams, J. B. W. (2001). The PHQ-9: Validity of a brief depression severity measure. *Journal of General Internal Medicine, 16*(9), 606–613.

Kubzansky, L. D., & Kawachi, I. (2000). Going to the heart of the matter: Do negative emotions cause coronary heart disease? *Journal of Psychosomatic Research, 48*(4–5), 323–337.

Kupfer, D. J., Frank, E., Carpenter, L. L., & Neiswanger, K. (1989). Family history in recurrent depression. *Journal of Affective Disorders, 17*(2), 113–119.

Lamb, K., Pies, R., & Zisook, S. (2010). The Bereavement exclusion for the diagnosis of major depression: To be, or not to be. *Psychiatry, 7*(7), 19–25.

Lebowitz, B. D., Pearson J. L., Schneider L. S., Reynolds C. F. 3rd, Alexopoulos G. S., Bruce, M. L., . . . Parmelee P. (1997). Diagnosis and treatment of depression in late life: Consensus statement update. *Journal of the American Medical Association, 278*(14), 1186–1190.

Leskelä, U., Rytsälä, H., Komulainen, E., Melartin, T., Sokero, P., Lestelä-Mielonen, P., & Isometsä, E. (2006). The influence of adversity and perceived social support on the outcomes of major depressive disorder in subjects with different levels of depressive symptoms. *Psychological Medicine, 36*(6), 779–788.

Lewinsohn, P. M. (1974). A behavioral approach to depression. In R. J. Friedman & M. M. Katz (Eds.), *The psychology of depression: Contemporary theory and research*. Oxford, England: John Wiley & Sons.

Logothetis, N. K. (2008). What we can do and what we cannot do with fMRI. *Nature, 453*(7197), 869–878.

Lotrakul, M., Sumrithe, S., Saipanish, R., Lotrakul, M., Sumrithe, S., & Saipanish, R. (2008). Reliability and validity of the Thai version of the PHQ-9. *BMC Psychiatry, 8*, 46.

Martens, E. J., Hoen, P. W., Mittelhaeuser, M., de Jonge, P., & Denollet, J. (2010). Symptom dimensions of post-myocardial infarction depression, disease severity and cardiac prognosis. *Psychological Medicine, 40*(5), 807–814.

Mathers, C. D., & Loncar, D. (2006). Projections of global mortality and burden of disease from 2002 to 2030. *PLoS Medicine, 3*(11), e442. doi: 10.1371/journal.pmed.0030442

Mayr, M., & Schmid, R. M. (2010). Pancreatic cancer and depression: Myth and truth. *BMC Cancer, 10*, 569.

Mazzucchelli, T. G., Kane, R. T., & Rees, C. S. (2010). Behavioral activation interventions for well-being: A meta-analysis. *Journal of Positive Psychology, 5*(2), 105–121.

McIntosh, E., Gillanders, D., & Rodgers, S. (2010). Rumination, goal linking, daily hassles and life events in major depression. *Clinical Psychology and Psychotherapy, 17*(1), 33–43.

Merikangas, K. R., & Avenevoli, S. (2000). Implications of genetic epidemiology for the prevention of substance use disorders. *Addictive Behaviors, 25*(6), 807–820.

Miller, N. L., Markowitz, J. C., Kocsis, J. H., Leon, A. C., Brisco, S. T., & Garno, J. L. (1999). Cost effectiveness of screening for clinical trials by research assistants versus senior investigators. *Journal of Psychiatric Research, 33*(2), 81–85.

Montgomery, S. A., & Asberg, M. (1979). A new depression scale designed to be sensitive to change. *British Journal of Psychiatry, 134*, 382–389.

Moore, J. D., & Bona, J. R. (2001). Depression and dysthymia. *Medical Clinics of North America, 85*(3), 631–644.

Neiswanger, K., Zubenko, G. S., Giles, D. E., Frank, E., Kupfer, D. J., & Kaplan, B. B. (1998). Linkage and association analysis of chromosomal regions containing genes related to neuroendocrine or serotonin function in families with early-onset, recurrent major depression. *American Journal of Medical Genetics, 81*(5), 443–449.

Nezu, A. M. (1986). Cognitive appraisal of problem solving effectiveness: Relation to depression and depressive symptoms. *Journal of Clinical Psychology, 42*(1), 42–48.

Nock, M. K., Borges, G., Bromet, E. J., Alonso, J., Angermeyer, M., Beautrais, A., . . . Williams, D. (2008). Cross-national prevalence and risk factors for suicidal ideation, plans and attempts. *The British Journal of Psychiatry, 192*, 98–105.

Nolen-Hoeksema, S. (2000). Further evidence for the role of psychosocial factors in depression chronicity. *Clinical Psychology: Science and Practice, 7*(2), 224–227.

Nolen-Hoeksema, S., Larson, J., & Grayson, C. (1999). Explaining the gender difference in depressive symptoms. *Journal of Personality and Social Psychology, 77*(5), 1061–1072.

Norman, T. R., & Burrows, G. D. (2007). Emerging treatments for major depression. *Expert Review of Neurotherapeutics, 7*(2), 203–213.

Nutt, D. J., Davidson, J. R., Gelenberg, A. J., Higuchi, T., Kanba, S., Karamustafalioglu, O., . . . Zhang, M. (2010). International consensus statement on major depressive disorder. *Journal of Clinical Psychiatry, 71*(Suppl E1), E08.

O'Keane, V. (2000). Evolving model of depression as an expression of multiple interacting risk factors. *British Journal of Psychiatry, 177*, 482–483.

O'Leary, D., & Costello, F. (2001). Personality and outcome in depression: An 18-month prospective follow-up study. *Journal of Affective Disorders, 63*(1–3), 67–78.

Olfson, M., Shea, S., Feder, A., Fuentes, M., Nomura, Y., Gameroff, M., & Weissman, M. M. (2000). Prevalence of anxiety, depression, and substance use disorders in an urban general medicine practice. *Archives of Family Medicine, 9*(9), 876–883.

Omoro, S. A., Fann, J. R., Weymuller, E. A., Macharia, I. M., Yueh, B., & Omoro, S. A. O. (2006). Swahili translation and validation of the Patient Health Questionnaire-9 depression scale in the Kenyan head and neck cancer patient population. *International Journal of Psychiatry in Medicine, 36*(3), 367–381.

Ostacher, M. J. (2007). Comorbid alcohol and substance abuse dependence in depression: Impact on the outcome of antidepressant treatment. *Psychiatric Clinics of North America, 30*(1), 69–76.

Papakostas, G. I., Crawford, C. M., Scalia, M. J., & Fava, M. (2007). Timing of clinical improvement and symptom resolution in the treatment of major depressive disorder. A replication of findings with the use of a double-blind, placebo-controlled trial of *Hypericum perforatum* versus fluoxetine. *Neuropsychobiology, 56*(2–3), 132–137.

Parker, G., Hilton, T., Hadzi-Pavlovic, D., & Bains, J. (2001). Screening for depression in the medically ill: The suggested utility of a cognitive-based approach. *Australian and New Zealand Journal of Psychiatry, 35*(4), 474–480.

Petersen, T., Hughes, M., Papakostas, G. I., Kant, A., Fava, M., Rosenbaum, J. F., & Nierenberg, A. A. (2002). Treatment-resistant depression and Axis II comorbidity. *Psychotherapy and Psychosomatics, 71*(5), 269–274.

Pincus, H. A., & Pettit, A. R. (2001). The societal costs of chronic major depression. *Journal of Clinical Psychiatry, 62*(Suppl. 6), 5–9.

Plaza, A., Garcia-Esteve, L., Ascaso, C., Navarro, P., Gelabert, E., Halperin, I., . . . Martín-Santos, R. (2010). Childhood sexual abuse and hypothalamus-pituitary-thyroid axis in postpartum major depression. *Journal of Affective Disorders, 122*(1–2), 159–163.

Plutchik, R., Platman, S. R., & Fieve, R. R. (1968). Repeated measurements in the manic depressive illness: Some methodological problems. *Journal of Psychology, 70,* 131–137.

Qian, Y., Lin, S., Jiang, S., Jiang, K., Wu, X., Tang, G., & Wang, D. (1999). Studies of the DXS7 polymorphism at the MAO loci in unipolar depression. *American Journal of Medical Genetics, 88*(6), 598–600.

Radloff, L. S. (1977). The CES-D Scale: A self-report depression scale for research in the general population. *Applied Psychological Measurement, 1*(3), 385–401.

Rapp, M. A., Dahlman, K., Sano, M., Grossman, H. T., Haroutunian, V., & Gorman, J. M. (2005). Neuropsychological differences between late-onset and recurrent geriatric major depression. *American Journal of Psychiatry, 162*(4), 691–698.

Regier, D. A. (1988). The NIMH depression awareness, recognition, and treatment program: Structure, aims, and scientific basis. *American Journal of Psychiatry, 145*(11), 1351–1357.

Rhebergen, D., Beekman, A. T., de Graaf, R., Nolen, W. A., Spijker, J., Hoogendijk, W. J., & Penninx, B. W. (2010). Trajectories of recovery of social and physical functioning in major depression, dysthymic disorder and double depression: A 3-year follow-up. *Journal of Affective Disorders, 124*(1–2), 148–156.

Rhodes, J., Chan, C., Paxson, C., Rouse, C. E., Waters, M., & Fussell, E. (2010). The impact of hurricane Katrina on the mental and physical health of low-income parents in New Orleans. *American Journal of Orthopsychiatry, 80*(2), 237–247.

Rogers, R. (2001). *Handbook of diagnostic and structured interviewing.* New York, NY: Guilford Press.

Rossi, A., Marinangeli, M. G., Butti, G., Scinto, A., Di Cicco, L., Kalyvoka, A., & Petruzzi, C. (2001). Personality disorders in bipolar and depressive disorders. *Journal of Affective Disorders, 65*(1), 3–8.

Rubenstein, L. V., Rayburn, N. R., Keeler, E. B., Ford, D. E., Rost, K. M., & Sherbourne, C. D. (2007). Predicting outcomes of primary care patients with major depression: Development of a Depression Prognosis Index. *Psychiatric Services, 58*(8), 1049–1056.

Rush, A. J., Trivedi, M. H., Ibrahim, H. M., Carmody, T. J., Arnow, B., Klein, D. N., . . . Keller, M. B. (2003). The 16-item Quick Inventory of Depressive Symptomatology (QIDS), clinician rating (QIDS-C), and self-report (QIDS-SR): A psychometric evaluation in patients with chronic major depression. *Biological Psychiatry, 54*(5), 573–583.

Ryder, A. G., Quilty, L. C., Vachon, D. D., & Bagby, R. M. (2010). Depressive personality and treatment outcome in major depressive disorder. *Journal of Personality Disorders, 24*(3), 392–404.

Ryder, A. G., Yang, J., Zhu, X., Yao, S., Yi, J., Heine, S. J., & Bagby, R. M. (2008). The cultural shaping of depression: Somatic symptoms in China, psychological symptoms in North America? *Journal of Abnormal Psychology, 117*(2), 300–313.

Sagen, U., Finset, A., Moum, T., Morland, T., Vik, T. G., Nagy, T., & Dammen, T. (2010). Early detection of patients at risk for anxiety, depression and apathy after stroke. *General Hospital Psychiatry, 32*(1), 80–85.

Sanchez-Villegas, A., Schlatter, J., Ortuno, F., Lahortiga, F., Pla, J., Benito, S., & Martinez-Gonzalez, M. A. (2008). Validity of a self-reported diagnosis of depression among participants in a cohort study using the Structured Clinical Interview for DSM-IV (SCID-I). *BMC Psychiatry, 8*, 43. doi: 10.1186/1471-244X-8-43

Schmitz, N., Kruse, J., Heckrath, C., Alberti, L., & Tress, W. (1999). Diagnosing mental disorders in primary care: The General Health Questionnaire (GHQ) and the Symptom Check List (SCL-90-R) as screening instruments. *Social Psychiatry and Psychiatric Epidemiology, 34*(7), 360–366.

Seemuller, F., Riedel, M., Obermeier, M., Bauer, M., Adli, M., Kronmuller, K., . . . Möller, H. J. (2010). Outcomes of 1014 naturalistically treated inpatients with major depressive episode. *European Neuropsychopharmacology, 20*(5), 346–355.

Seligman, M. E., & Csikszentmihalyi, M. (2000). Positive psychology. An introduction. *American Psychology, 55*(1), 5–14.

Seligman, M. E., Steen, T. A., Park, N., & Peterson, C. (2005). Positive psychology progress: Empirical validation of interventions. *American Psychology, 60*(5), 410–421.

Seligman, M. E., Weiss, J., Weinraub, M., & Schulman, A. (1980). Coping behavior: Learned helplessness, physiological change and learned inactivity. *Behavior Research and Therapy, 18*(5), 459–512.

Sheehan, D. V., Lecrubier, Y., Sheehan, K. H., Amorim, P., Janavs, J., & Weiller, E. (1998). The Mini-International Neuropsychiatric Interview (MINI): The development and validation of a structured diagnostic psychiatric interview for *DSM-IV* and *ICD-10*. *Journal of Clinical Psychiatry, 59*(Suppl. 20), 22–33; 34 57.

Sherrington, J. M., Hawton, K., Fagg, J., Andrew, B., & Smith, D. (2001). Outcome of women admitted to hospital for depressive illness: Factors in the prognosis of severe depression. *Psychological Medicine, 31*(1), 115–125.

Shorey, R. C., Sherman, A. E., Kivisto, A. J., Elkins, S. R., Rhatigan, D. L., & Moore, T. M. (2011). Gender differences in depression and anxiety among victims of intimate partner violence: The moderating effect of shame proneness. *Journal of Interpersonal Violence, 26*(9), 1834–1850.

Simon, G. E., Revicki, D., Heiligenstein, J., Grothaus, L., Von Korff, M., Katon, W. J., & Hylan, T. R. (2000). Recovery from depression, work productivity, and health care costs among primary care patients. *General Hospital Psychiatry, 22*(3), 153–162.

Simon, G. E., Von Korff, M., & Lin, E. (2005). Clinical and functional outcomes of depression treatment in patients with and without chronic medical illness. *Psychological Medicine, 35*(2), 271–279.

Simons, A. D., & Thase, M. E. (1992). Biological markers, treatment outcome, and 1-year follow-up in endogenous depression: Electroencephalographic sleep studies and response to cognitive therapy. *Journal of Consulting and Clinical Psychology, 60*(3), 392–401.

Sin, N. L., & Lyubomirsky, S. (2009). Enhancing well-being and alleviating depressive symptoms with positive psychology interventions: A practice-friendly meta-analysis. *Journal of Clinical Psychology, 65*(5), 467–487.

Spitzer, R. L., Kroenke, K., & Williams, J. B. (1999). Validation and utility of a self-report version of PRIME-MD: The PHQ primary care study. Primary Care Evaluation of Mental Disorders. Patient Health Questionnaire. *Journal of the American Medical Association, 282*(18), 1737–1744.

Spitzer, R. L., Williams, J. B., Kroenke, K., Hornyak, R., & McMurray, J. (2000). Validity and utility of the PRIME-MD patient health questionnaire in assessment of 3000 obstetric-gynecologic patients: The PRIME-MD Patient Health Questionnaire Obstetrics-Gynecology Study. *American Journal of Obstetrics and Gynecology, 183*(3), 759–769.

Spitzer, R. L., Williams, J. B., Kroenke, K., Linzer, M., deGruy, F. V., 3rd, Hahn, S. R., Brody, D., & Johnson, J. G. (1994). Utility of a new procedure for diagnosing mental disorders in primary care: The PRIME-MD 1000 study. *Journal of the American Medical Association, 272*(22), 1749–1756.

Splawski, I., Timothy, K. W., Sharpe, L. M., Decher, N., Kumar, P., Bloise, R., . . . Keating, M. T. (2004). Ca(V)1.2 calcium channel dysfunction cause a multisystem disorder including arrhythmia and autism. *Cell, 119*(1), 19–31.

Steer, R. A., Cavalieri, T. A., Leonard, D. M., & Beck, A. T. (1999). Use of the Beck Depression Inventory for Primary Care to screen for major depression disorders. *General Hospital Psychiatry, 21*(2), 106–111.

Stover, E., Fenton, W., Rosenfeld, A., & Insel, T. R. (2003). Depression and comorbid medical illness: the National Institute of Mental Health perspective. *Biological Psychiatry, 54*(3), 184–186.

Street, H., O'Connor, M., & Robinson, H. (2007). Depression in older adults: Exploring the relationship between goal setting and physical health. *International Journal of Geriatric Psychiatry, 22*(11), 1115–1119.

Sullivan, P. F., Neale, M. C., & Kendler, K. S. (2000). Genetic epidemiology of major depression: Review and meta-analysis. *The American Journal of Psychiatry, 157*(10), 1552–1562.

Svanborg, P., & Asberg, M. (2001). A comparison between the Beck Depression Inventory (BDI) and the self-rating version of the Montgomery Asberg Depression Rating Scale (MADRS). *Journal of Affective Disorders, 64*(2–3), 203–216.

Swendsen, J. D. (1997). Anxiety, depression, and their comorbidity: An experience sampling test of the Helplessness-Hopelessness Theory. *Cognitive Therapy and Research, 21*(1), 97–114.

Thornton, C., Russell, J., & Hudson, J. (1998). Does the Composite International Diagnostic Interview underdiagnose the eating disorders? *International Journal of Eating Disorders, 23*(3), 341–345.

Trivedi, M. H., Clayton, A. H., & Frank, E. (2007). Treating depression complicated by comorbid medical illness or anxiety. *Journal of Clinical Psychiatry, 68*(1), e01.

Trivedi, M. H., Rush, A. J., Ibrahim, H. M., Carmody, T. J., Biggs, M. M., Suppes, T., . . . Kashner, T. M. (2004). The Inventory of Depressive Symptomatology, Clinican Rating (IDS-C) and Self-Report (IDS-SR), and the Quick Inventory of Depressive Symptomatology, Clinican Rating (QIDS-C) and Self-Report (QIDS-SR) in public sector patients with mood disorders: A psychometric evaluation. *Psychological Medicine, 34*(1), 73–82.

van Weel-Baumgarten, E. M., Schers, H. J., van den Bosch, W. J., van den Hoogen, H. J., & Zitma, F. G. (2000). Long-term follow-up of depression among patients in the community and in family practice settings. *Journal of Family Practice, 49*(12), 1113–1120.

Veenstra-VanderWeele, J., Anderson, G. M., & Cook, E. H., Jr. (2000). Pharmacogenetics and the serotonin system: Initial studies and future directions. *European Journal of Pharmacology, 410*(2–3), 165–181.

Vega, W. A., Kolody, B., Valle, R., & Hough, R. (1986). Depressive symptoms and their correlates among immigrant Mexican women in the United States. *Social Science and Medicine, 22*(6), 645–652.

Vergne, D. E., & Nemeroff, C. B. (2006). The interaction of serotonin transporter gene polymorphisms and early adverse life events on vulnerability for major depression. *Current Psychiatry Reports, 8*(6), 452–457.

Verplanken, B., Friborg, O., Wang, C. E., Trafimow, D., & Woolf, K. (2007). Mental habits: Metacognitive reflection on negative self-thinking. *Journal of Personality and Social Psychology, 92*(3), 526–554.

Viinamäki, H., Tanskanen, A., Honkalampi, K., Koivumaa-Honkanen, H., Antikainen, R., Haatainen, K., & Hintikka, J. (2000). Effect of somatic comorbidity on alleviation of depressive symptoms. *Australian and New Zealand Journal of Psychiatry, 34*(5), 755–761.

Wagner, H. R., Burns, B. J., Broadhead, W. E., Yarnall, K. S., Sigmon, A., & Gaynes, B. N. (2000). Minor depression in family practice: Functional morbidity, co-morbidity, service utilization and outcomes. *Psychological Medicine, 30*(6), 1377–1390.

Wakefield, J. C., Baer, J. C., & Schmitz, M. F. (2010). Differential diagnosis of depressive illness versus intense normal sadness: How significant is the 'clinical significance criterion' for major depression? *Expert Review of Neurotherapeutics, 10*(7), 1015–1018.

Waraich, P., Goldner, E. M., Somers, J. M., & Hsu, L. (2004). Prevalence and incidence studies of mood disorders: A systematic review of the literature. *Canadian Journal of Psychiatry, 49*(2), 124–138.

Welch, J. L., & Austin, J. K. (2001). Stressors, coping and depression in haemodialysis patients. *Journal of Advanced Nursing, 33*(2), 200–207.

Wellen, M. (2010). Differentiation between demoralization, grief, and anhedonic depression. *Current Psychiatry Reports, 12*(3), 229–233.

Wermter, A. K., Laucht, M., Schimmelmann, B. G., Banaschweski, T., Sonuga-Barke, E. J., Rietschel, M., & Becker, K. (2010). From nature versus nurture, via nature and nurture, to gene x environment interaction in mental disorders. *European Child and Adolescent Psychiatry, 19*(3), 199–210.

Winter, L. B., Steer, R. A., Jones-Hicks, L., & Beck, A. T. (1999). Screening for major depression disorders in adolescent medical outpatients with the Beck Depression Inventory for Primary Care. *Journal of Adolescent Health, 24*(6), 389–394.

World Health Organization (WHO), Regional Office for Europe and the International Diabetes Federation, Europe. (1990). Diabetes mellitus in Europe: A problem at all ages and in all countries. A model for prevention and self care. *Giornale Italiano Diabetologia e Metabolismo, 10*, supplement.

Yesavage, J. A., Brink, T. L., Rose, T. L., Lum, O., Huang, V., Adey, M., & Leirer, V. O. (1982). Development and validation of a geriatric depression screening scale: A preliminary report. *Journal of Psychiatric Research, 17*(1), 37–49.

Yeung, A., Fung, F., Yu, S. C., Vorono, S., Ly, M., Wu, S., & Fava, M. (2008). Validation of the Patient Health Questionnaire-9 for depression screening among Chinese Americans. *Comprehensive Psychiatry, 49*(2), 211–217.

Zigmond, A. S., & Snaith, R. P. (1983). The hospital anxiety and depression scale. *Acta Psychiatrica Scandinavica, 67*(6), 361–370.

Zisook, S., Reynolds, C. F. 3rd, Pies, R., Simon, N., Lebowitz, B., Madowitz, J., . . . Shear, M. K. (2010a). Bereavement, complicated grief, and *DSM*, part 1: Depression. *Journal of Clinical Psychiatry*, *71*(7), 955–956.

Zisook, S., Simon, N. M., Reynolds, C. F. 3rd, Pies, R., Lebowitz, B., Young, I. T., . . . Shear, M. K. (2010b). Bereavement, complicated grief, and *DSM*, part 2: complicated grief. *Journal of Clinical Psychiatry*, *71*(8), 1097–1098.

Zubenko, G. S., Zubenko, W. N., Spiker, D. G., Giles, D. E., & Kaplan, B. B. (2001). Malignancy of recurrent, early-onset major depression: A family study. *American Journal of Medical Genetics*, *105*(8), 690–699.

Zung, W. W. (1972). The Depression Status Inventory: An adjunct to the Self-Rating Depression Scale. *Journal of Clinical Psychology*, *28*(4), 539–543.

# CHAPTER 10

# Bipolar Disorder

DAVID J. MIKLOWITZ and SHERI L. JOHNSON

O VER THE PAST two decades, there has been a considerable resurgence of interest in bipolar affective disorder. This resurgence is attributable in part to the availability of new pharmacological agents, disorder-specific psychosocial treatments, and data on genetic mechanisms and neurophysiological and neuro-anatomical correlates. It is also been driven by the increasing recognition that the onset of the disorder is often in childhood or adolescence.

In this chapter we review the current literature on bipolar disorder. In the initial sections we describe the disorder from the vantage points of diagnostic criteria, diagnostic controversies, epidemiology, and course and prognosis, with particular attention to developmental considerations pertinent to early-onset bipolar illness. A case study illustrates these issues.

We discuss the etiology and prognosis of bipolar disorder from both a genetic and a psychosocial viewpoint. Current etiological models view bipolar disorder as a primarily genetic illness whose onset can be elicited by environmental stressors. Although few studies have examined psychosocial stressors relevant to the onset of bipolar disorder, there is now a considerable literature on psychosocial stressors that affect the course and outcome of the disease. In the final sections, we summarize the major recent findings concerning the treatment of the disorder and offer directions for further research.

## DESCRIPTION OF THE DISORDER

### Manic, Hypomanic, Depressive, and Mixed Episodes

Bipolar disorder (BD), formerly known as manic-depressive illness, is defined by manic symptoms. According to the *Diagnostic and Statistical Manual of Mental Disorders, fourth edition* (*DSM-IV*; American Psychiatric Association [APA], 2000), people with bipolar, manic episodes experience elated, expansive, or irritable mood (or any combination of these) plus at least three (four if the mood is only irritable) of the following symptoms: decreased need for sleep; racing thoughts or flight of ideas; rapid speech; inflated self-esteem (also called grandiosity); impulsive, reckless

357

behavior (e.g., spending sprees, hypersexuality); increased energy and activity; and distractibility. These symptoms must be present for at least 1 week or interrupted by hospitalization or emergency treatment. They must also cause functional impairment. Hypomania is characterized by parallel symptoms, but the criteria specify only that the symptoms last at least 4 days and result in a distinct, observable change in functioning rather than severe impairment. Bipolar II disorder is defined by hypomanic episodes as well as depressive episodes.

Depressive episodes, when present, last for at least 2 weeks and are characterized by sad mood, loss of interest or pleasure in daily activities, and at least five of the following: insomnia or hypersomnia, psychomotor agitation or retardation, increases or decreases in weight or appetite, loss of energy, difficulty concentrating or making decisions, feelings of worthlessness, and suicidal ideation or behavior. Depression must also be associated with functional impairment. Manic or depressive episodes that are clearly related to an ingested substance or to biological treatments—including antidepressant medications—are classified as substance-induced mood disorders.

Manic and depressive episodes can occur simultaneously in a mixed episode. For example, patients can have irritable mood, distractibility, decreased need for sleep, and racing thoughts along with loss of interests, suicidal thinking, feelings of worthlessness, and psychomotor agitation. A mixed episode must last at least 1 week, and patients must fulfill the criteria for a major depressive episode and a manic episode simultaneously. As many as 40% of patients with bipolar disorder have mixed episodes at some point in their illness (Calabrese, Fatemi, Kujawa, & Woyshville, 1996).

## Bipolar Subtypes

Bipolar I disorder is defined by the presence of a single manic or mixed episode that is not substance-induced (see the following case study). In other words, patients need not have experienced a major depressive episode to be called bipolar. Rates of unipolar mania are between 25% and 33% in community samples but only about 10% in clinical samples (Depue & Monroe, 1978; Karkowski & Kendler, 1997; Kessler, Chiu, Demler, & Walters, 2005; Weissman & Myers, 1978). It would appear, however, that most patients with unipolar mania eventually develop depressive episodes. In a 20-year study of unipolar mania, 20 of 27 patients had episodes of depression at follow-up (Solomon et al., 2003).

Bipolar II disorder is characterized by major depressive episodes alternating with hypomanic episodes. About 1 in 10 bipolar II patients eventually develops a full manic or mixed episode over a 10-year follow-up, and thus converts to bipolar I disorder (Coryell et al., 1995).

Cyclothymia is a variant of bipolar disorder characterized by 2 or more years of alterations between hypomanic and depressive symptoms, but none of these alterations meet the full *DSM-IV* criteria for a hypomanic or major depressive episode. Bipolar disorder, not otherwise specified (NOS) is reserved for patients whose disorder meets the minimum number of required symptoms but not the duration requirements for a full manic, hypomanic, mixed, or depressive episode.

Many childhood-onset patients receive this diagnosis (National Institute of Mental Health, 2001).

## EPIDEMIOLOGY

### PREVALENCE OF BIPOLAR DISORDER

In the National Comorbidity Survey replication, lifetime prevalence rates were 1.0% for bipolar I disorders, 1.1% for bipolar II, and 2.4% for "subthreshold" BD (Merikangas et al., 2007). Cyclothymic disorder may affect as much as 4.2% of the general population (Regeer et al., 2004). Major depressive illness is about 4 times more prevalent than bipolar disorder (Kessler et al., 2005). The onset of mood disorders appears to be getting younger in successive birth cohorts (Rice et al., 1987; Ryan et al., 1992; Wickramaratne, Weissman, Leaf, & Holford, 1989). For example, Kessler et al. (2005) reported that the lifetime risk of bipolar I or II disorders in 18- to 29-year-olds was 22 times higher than in persons over 60. It is possible, however, that younger persons feel less stigmatized by psychiatric symptoms and are more likely than older persons to report mood disorder (notably manic) symptoms.

In a large community sample of adolescents, Lewinsohn, Klein, and Seeley (2000) reported that approximately 1% of high school students met diagnostic criteria for bipolar I or II, or cyclothymic disorder. Other estimates of bipolar disorder in children or adolescents are as high as 2% (Kessler, Avenevoli, & Ries-Merikangas, 2001).

### AGE AT ONSET

The mean age of onset of bipolar I disorder is 18.2 years, and 20.3 years for bipolar II (Merikangas et al., 2007), but there is substantial variability. Between 50% and 67% of patients develop the disease by age 18, and between 15% and 28% before age 13 (Perlis et al., 2004). A review of studies prior to 1990 revealed that the peak age at onset is between 15 and 19 years (Goodwin & Jamison, 1990). Earlier age at onset is associated with rapid cycling and other negative outcomes in adulthood (Coryell et al., 2003; Schneck et al., 2004).

### GENDER AND RACIAL-ETHNIC ISSUES

Women and men are equally likely to develop bipolar I disorder. Women, however, report more depressive episodes than men and, correspondingly, are more likely to be diagnosed with bipolar II disorder (e.g., Leibenluft, 1997; Schneck et al., 2004). Women are also more likely to meet the *DSM-IV* criteria for rapid-cycling BD, especially with repeated episodes of depression (Schneck et al., 2004).

There may be racial and ethnic biases in the diagnosis and treatment of BD. Evidence exists that, compared to Caucasian patients, African American and Puerto Rican patients are less likely to be diagnosed with psychotic forms of affective disorder and more likely to be diagnosed with schizophrenia (Garb, 1997). Many patients with psychotic affective disorder are patients with bipolar disorder.

The course of BD illness may be worse among African American patients, who are more likely to have attempted suicide and been hospitalized than Caucasian patients. One study found that adult African American patients were less likely than Caucasians to be prescribed mood stabilizers or benzodiazepines and more likely to have been given antipsychotic medications (Kupfer, Frank, Grochocinski, Houck, & Brown, 2005). African American adolescents with bipolar disorder are treated for longer periods than Caucasian adolescents with atypical antipsychotics, even after adjusting for the severity of psychotic symptoms (Patel, DelBello, Keck, & Strakowski, 2005). Moreover, African American bipolar patients are less likely than Caucasian patients to have an outpatient follow-up visit within 3 months of the initial diagnosis (Kilbourne et al., 2005). The reasons for these racial disparities are unclear.

## CLINICAL PICTURE

### PHENOMENOLOGICAL STUDIES OF THE MANIC SYNDROME

Recent studies have examined the factor structure of the manic syndrome and whether there are differences between euphoric or pure mania and irritable or aggressive mania. A principal component analysis of data from 576 diagnosed manic patients identified seven stable underlying factors: depressive mood, irritable aggression, insomnia, depressive inhibition, pure manic symptoms, emotional lability/agitation, and psychosis (Sato, Bottlender, Kleindienst, & Moller, 2002). Through cluster analysis, Sato et al. identified four phenomenological subtypes of acute mania: pure, aggressive, psychotic, and depressive-mixed mania.

The pattern of manic symptoms has been investigated in youths with bipolar disorder. A meta-analysis of seven studies examining the phenomenological characteristics of mania among children and adolescents (aged 5 to 18; Kowatch, Youngstrom, Danielyan, & Findling, 2005) found that the most common symptoms during manic episodes were increased energy, distractibility, and pressure of speech. Approximately 80% showed irritability and grandiosity, whereas 70% had the "cardinal" manic symptoms of elated mood, decreased need for sleep, or racing thoughts. Less common symptoms included hypersexuality and psychotic symptoms. Thus, most manic children showed symptoms that also characterize adult mania.

### SUICIDE

Bipolar disorder is associated with multiple threats to health and livelihood, but the most fundamental concern is the risk of suicide. Estimates suggest that rates of completed suicide in bipolar disorder are 12 to 15 times higher than in the general population (Angst, Angst, Gerber-Werder, & Gamma, 2005; Harris & Barraclough, 1997; Jamison & Baldessarini, 1999) and 4 times higher than rates among patients with recurrent major depression (Brown, Beck, Steer, & Grisham, 2000). Approximately 50% of patients attempt suicide during their lifetime, and between 15% and 20% die by suicide (Harris & Barraclough, 1997; Jamison & Baldessarini, 1999). Rates are especially high among younger, recent-onset male patients and those who have comorbid alcohol or substance abuse, social isolation, depression, significant anxiety, aggression, impulsiveness, a family history of suicide, or any combination of these (Angst et al., 2005; Fawcett, Golden, & Rosenfeld, 2000; Jamison, 2000).

FUNCTIONAL IMPAIRMENT

Many patients with bipolar disorder experience ongoing impairments in social, occupational, and familial functioning even between episodes, especially if they have unresolved depressive symptoms (Fagiolini et al., 2005). Within the first year after hospitalization, only half of the patients who recover from a manic or mixed episode demonstrate full recovery (Keck et al., 1998). Diminished work, social, and family functioning persists for up to 5 years after a manic episode (Coryell et al., 1993). Goldberg, Harrow, and Grossman (1995) found that only about one in three patients with bipolar disorder who were taking lithium had good functioning over a 4.5-year follow-up.

In a survey of 253 patients with bipolar I and II disorder, only 33% worked full-time and 9% worked part-time outside of the home. Fully 57% reported being unable to work or working only in sheltered settings (Suppes et al., 2001). Only 42% of bipolar I, manic patients showed "steady" work performance an average of 1.7 years after hospital discharge (Harrow, Goldberg, Grossman, & Meltzer, 1990). In the 6 months after a hospitalization, one-third of patients were unable to work at all, and only one in five worked at their expected level (Dion, Tohen, Anthony, & Waternaux, 1988). The disorder is also associated with high rates of family or marital distress, dysfunction, separation, divorce, and problems in the adjustment of patients' offspring (Coryell et al., 1993; Hodgins, Faucher, Zarac, & Ellenbogen, 2002; Simoneau, Miklowitz, & Saleem, 1998).

There is considerable variability in functional impairment, however. For example, there appears to be a link between BD and creativity or productivity: Many famous artists, musicians, writers, and politicians probably had the disorder (Jamison, 1993). Patients with bipolar disorder and highly creative persons without psychiatric disorder appear to have temperamental commonalities, such as openness to new experiences and novelty seeking (Nowakowska, Strong, Santosa, Wang, & Ketter, 2005). Children diagnosed with bipolar disorder and children who are the offspring of bipolar parents scored higher than healthy control children on a creativity index (Simeonova, Chang, Strong, & Ketter, 2005). Interestingly, the unaffected family members of patients with bipolar disorder demonstrate higher accomplishment and creativity than do their affected relatives (Johnson, 2005b; Richards, Kinney, Lunde, Benet, & Merzel, 1988).

COURSE AND PROGNOSIS

Virtually all patients with bipolar disorder have illness recurrences. The rates of recurrence, even when patients are treated with mood stabilizers, average 37% in 1 year, 60% over 2 years, and 73% over 5 years (Gitlin, Swendsen, Heller, & Hammen, 1995). Approximately one in five patients meets criteria for rapid cycling, defined by four or more distinct episodes of mania, hypomania, mixed, or depressive disorder within 1 year (Schneck et al., 2004). Biological and psychosocial factors that predict illness recurrences are discussed further in the next section.

Even more significant are the persistent, mild-to-moderate residual symptoms that most patients experience between episodes, even when undergoing pharmacotherapy (Judd et al., 2002; Keller, Lavori, Coryell, Endicott, & Mueller, 1993; Post et al., 2003). Over a 13-year follow-up, subsyndromal symptoms were present during approximately half the weeks of follow-up (Judd et al., 2002). These symptoms were almost exclusively depressive rather than manic. A study of children with bipolar I, II, and NOS disorders observed similar patterns of residual symptoms over a 15-month follow-up (Birmaher et al., 2009). Indeed, one of the most formidable issues in the treatment of the disorder is the stabilization of depressive symptoms (e.g., Perlis et al., 2006).

## Psychosocial Predictors of the Course of Bipolar Disorder

By the end of the 1980s, researchers began to acknowledge that biological and genetic models of BD did not explain the enormous heterogeneity in the course of the illness over time (Prien & Potter, 1990). This recognition contributed to a renewed emphasis on psychosocial predictors in the course of the disorder. For example, Ellicott, Hammen, Gitlin, Brown, and Jamison (1990) found that BD patients with high life-events-stress scores were at 4.5 times greater risk for relapse in a 2-year follow-up than patients with medium or low life-events-stress scores. Miklowitz, Goldstein, Nuechterlein, Snyder, and Mintz (1988) found that BD I manic patients who returned after a hospitalization to families rated high on expressed emotion (EE) attitudes (criticism, hostility, or emotional overinvolvement) or who showed high levels of caregiver-to-patient affective negativity (criticism, hostility, or guilt induction) during face-to-face interactions were at high risk for relapse. Those whose families had both high EE and high affective negativity were highly likely to relapse within 9 months (94%), whereas those whose families rated low on both attributes were unlikely to relapse within this time frame (17%). More recently, Hillegers et al. (2004) found that negative life events predicted the onset of mood disorders among children of bipolar parents.

Although these first-generation studies established the prognostic role of psychosocial factors, they did not address how psychosocial variables influence depression versus mania. A second generation of research has examined which psychosocial variables influence the course of BD depression and which influence the course of mania.

## Psychosocial Predictors of Depression Within Bipolar Disorder

The symptomatology and neurobiology of unipolar and BD depression have many strong parallels (Cuellar, Johnson, & Winters, 2005). Given these parallels, one might expect that psychosocial predictors of unipolar depression would influence BD depression. Here, we focus on well-established predictors of unipolar depression, including negative life events (Monroe, Harkness, Simons, & Thase, 2001), low social support (Brown & Andrews, 1986), EE (Butzlaff & Hooley, 1998), neuroticism (Gunderson, Triebwasser, Phillips, & Sullivan, 1999), and negative cognitive styles (Alloy, Reilly-Harrington, Fresco, Whitehouse, & Zechmeister, 1999).

Negative life events have been perhaps the most examined predictors of bipolar depression. Fortunately, a set of BD studies have now used interview-based measures of life events. As reviewed by Johnson (2005a), three of these cross-sectional studies found that negative life events are equally common before episodes of BD depression and unipolar depression (Malkoff-Schwartz et al., 2000; Pardoen et al., 1996; Perris, 1984). Findings of prospective studies with interview-based measures also indicate that stressful life events are correlated with slow recovery from depression (Johnson & Miller, 1997) and predict increases in BD depression over several months (Johnson et al., 2008). Thus, the most methodologically rigorous studies suggest that negative life events are precipitants of bipolar depression.

Other variables involved in unipolar depression also appear to have validity as predictors of bipolar depression. For example, neuroticism (Heerlein, Richter, Gonzalez, & Santander, 1998; Lozano & Johnson, 2001), low social support (Johnson, Winett, Meyer, Greenhouse, & Miller, 1999), and family EE (Kim & Miklowitz, 2004; Yan, Hammen, Cohen, Daley, & Henry, 2004) have been found to predict increases in depressive symptoms but not manic symptoms over time. Although negative cognitive styles are often documented in BD (see Cuellar et al., 2005, for review), they (a) are most likely to be found during depression compared with well periods (Johnson & Kizer, 2002), (b) predict depression better than mania (Johnson & Fingerhut, 2004; Johnson, Meyer, Winett, & Small, 2000; but see Reilly-Harrington et al., 1999 for a counterexample), and (c) can be explained by the presence of depressive history rather than manic history (Alloy et al., 1999).

In sum, variables that influence the course of unipolar depression also influence BD depression, including negative life events, poor social support, family EE, negative cognitive styles, and low self-esteem. Few studies have examined the additive or interactive effects of these risk variables in the course of BD.

PSYCHOSOCIAL PREDICTORS OF MANIA

Compared with BD depression, less is known about the psychosocial predictors of mania. Available models highlight two sets of predictors: goal engagement and sleep/schedule disruption.

*Goal Dysregulation*   Drawing on biological models of overly sensitive reward pathways, the goal dysregulation model suggests that people with BD may show more extreme responses to rewarding stimuli (Johnson, 2005b). People with a history of mania and students who are vulnerable to mania describe themselves as more sensitive to rewards (Meyer, Johnson, & Carver, 1999; Meyer, Johnson, & Winters, 2001). People with BD place a stably high emphasis on goal pursuit, even when they are not in an episode (Johnson, Eisner & Carver, 2009). This reward sensitivity would be expected to influence reactions to life events that involve major successes. Consistent with this idea, life events involving goal attainments (such as new relationships, births of children, or career successes) predicted increases in manic symptoms but not depressive symptoms (Johnson et al., 2000; Johnson et al., 2008). Such effects were apparent even after controlling for baseline levels of manic symptoms and excluding life events that could have been caused by the patients' symptoms.

Why might attaining an important goal trigger manic symptoms? A set of studies suggest that for people with BD, cognition becomes much more positive during good moods than it does for other people. Available evidence suggests that mood states are associated with distinct positive shifts in confidence (Johnson, 2005b; Stern & Berrenberg, 1979), autobiographical recall (Eich, Macaulay, & Lam, 1997), and attention to valenced stimuli (Murphy et al., 1999). Impulsivity, or the tendency to pursue rewards without awareness of potential negative consequences, also becomes elevated as people become manic (Swann, Dougherty, Pazzaglia, Pham, & Moeller, 2004). Mood-state-dependent shifts in confidence may contribute to increased goal setting (Johnson, 2005b). In turn, investment in goal pursuit predicts increases in manic symptoms over several months (Lozano & Johnson, 2001). Building on these findings, it has been hypothesized that goal attainments may trigger increased goal engagement, which in turn may trigger manic symptoms (Johnson, 2005b).

Reward engages confidence and goal pursuit but may also bring to mind memories of failure or feelings of low self-worth (Alloy et al., 2005; Eisner, Johnson, & Carver, 2008). In one study (Miklowitz, Alatiq, Geddes, Goodwin, & Williams, 2010), remitted or partially remitted patients with BD, patients with MDD, and healthy controls unscrambled six-word strings into five-word sentences, leaving out one word. The extra word allowed the sentences to be completed in a negative, neutral, or "hyperpositive" (manic/goal-oriented) way. Under conditions of reward (a pleasing bell tone for every four sentences completed), all subjects completed more sentences than in the non-reward conditions. However, patients with BD unscrambled more negative sentences in the reward condition than did patients with MDD. Thus, a simple reward may increase the accessibility of negative thoughts among bipolar patients, consistent with earlier notions of mania as a defense against threat or low self-esteem (Adler, 1964; Lyon, Startup, & Bentall, 1999).

*Sleep and Schedule Disruption*   Experimental studies (Barbini et al., 1998) as well as longitudinal studies (Leibenluft et al., 1996) suggest that sleep deprivation is an important trigger of manic symptoms. Wehr, Sack, and Rosenthal (1987) hypothesized that sleep disruption might be one way in which life events trigger episodes of BD, noting that illness episodes are often preceded by life events interfering with the ability to sleep (e.g., transmeridian flights, childbearing). This theory was broadened by Ehlers and colleagues (Ehlers, Frank, & Kupfer, 1988; Ehlers, Kupfer, Frank, & Monk, 1993), who suggested that social disruptions to other aspects of circadian rhythms could trigger symptoms (the "social zeitgebers model"). Consistent with this idea, Jones, Hare & Evershed (2005) have documented that people with bipolar disorder demonstrate more variability in their daily schedules than do healthy controls. In two studies, Malkoff-Schwartz et al. (1998; Malkoff-Schwartz et al., 2000) found that bipolar patients reported more life events involving social-rhythm disruption (events that affect sleep or wake times, patterns of social stimulation, or daily routines) in the weeks preceding manic episodes compared to the weeks preceding depressive episodes. Thus, sleep disruptions and possibly broader schedule disruptions are important to the course of mania.

In sum, sleep or schedule disruption is proposed to trigger manic symptoms. As with research on the predictors of bipolar depression, very few longitudinal studies of sleep disruption are available. As discussed next, some of these risk factors are amenable to modification through psychosocial intervention.

TREATMENT OF BIPOLAR DISORDER: CURRENT TRENDS

Optimally, treatments for BD should involve combinations of pharmacological and psychosocial interventions. Unfortunately, in the era of managed care cost containment, drug treatments are often the only treatment provided. Perhaps as a result, the average duration of lithium treatment for patients in community settings is only 76 days (Johnson & McFarland, 1996).

*Pharmacological Treatments* Distinctions are usually made between acute pharmacological treatment and maintenance treatment. The goal of acute treatment is to stabilize an existing manic or depressive episode (for recent and thorough reviews of acute pharmacotherapy studies of adult and pediatric patients, see Goldberg, 2004, and Kowatch, Sethuraman, Hume, Kromelis, & Weinberg, 2003). Adjunctive psychotherapy is usually introduced during the post-episode stabilization phase and continued throughout maintenance treatment. The goals of adjunctive psychotherapy are to minimize residual symptoms and prevent recurrences. Untreated residual symptoms of mania or depression are prospectively associated with illness recurrences (Perlis et al., 2006).

Current pharmacotherapy algorithms for mania for adult and childhood-onset patients (e.g., Kowatch, Fristad, et al., 2005; McAllister-Williams, 2006) combine mood stabilizers (e.g., lithium carbonate, divalproex sodium, carbamazepine) with atypical antipsychotic medications (e.g., olanzapine, quetiapine, risperidone, aripiprazole, ziprasidone, and less frequently, clozapine). Adjunctive antidepressant agents are often recommended for bipolar depression. When given alone, antidepressant medications can cause manic switching and acceleration of cycles in a significant number of patients (Ghaemi, Lenox, & Baldessarini, 2001). When given with mood stabilizers, however, antidepressants do not appear to cause an increase in cycling (Altshuler et al., 2003; Sachs et al., 2007). The anticonvulsant lamotrigine is an option for many patients given its antidepressant properties and lower propensity to cause cycle acceleration (Malhi, Adams, & Berk, 2009).

Despite the clear effectiveness of many forms of pharmacotherapy, patients with BD are prone to discontinuing their medications, with as many as 60% being fully or partially noncompliant after a major episode of illness (Keck et al., 1998; Strakowski et al., 1998). Patients who discontinue their pharmacotherapy abruptly are at a high risk for recurrence and suicide attempts (Keck, McElroy, Strakowski, Bourne, & West, 1997; Strober, Morrell, Lampert, & Burroughs, 1990; Suppes, Baldessarini, Faedda, Tondo, & Tohen, 1993; Tondo & Baldessarini, 2000). For example, in a naturalistic study of adolescent BD patients followed 18 months after a hospitalization, relapse was 3 times more likely among patients who discontinued lithium than among patients who remained on it. Patients describe barriers to compliance that include missing high periods, objecting to having one's moods controlled by medications, lack of information about the disorder, or lack of social or familial supports (for review, see Colom et al., 2000).

**Table 10.1**

Key Therapeutic Elements of Psychoeducational Treatment

- Teach emotion regulation skills when challenged by stressors
- Encourage daily monitoring of moods and sleep cycles
- Enhance patient's (or family members') ability to identify and intervene early with relapses
- Track and encourage medication adherence
- Assist patient in stabilizing sleep/wake rhythms and other daily or nightly routines
- Educate family members about the disorder and enhance intrafamilial communication
- Increasing access to social and treatment supports
- Help patient acquire balanced attitudes toward the self in relation to the illness
- Encourage acceptance of the disorder

*Psychotherapy as an Adjunct to Medication Maintenance* Randomized controlled trials of psychotherapy indicate positive benefits for psychoeducational, skill-oriented, and interpersonal treatments. The modalities investigated in the trials have included individual, family, and group formats. Table 10.1 lists some of the key components of empirically supported treatments for BD. Treatments supported by at least one randomized controlled trial include individual psychoeducation (Perry, Tarrier, Morriss, McCarthy, & Limb, 1999), group psychoeducation (e.g., Colom et al., 2003; Simon et al., 2005), family-focused therapy (FFT; e.g., Miklowitz, George, Richards, Simoneau, & Suddath, 2003; Rea et al., 2003), cognitive-behavioral therapy (CBT; e.g., Lam et al., 2003), and interpersonal and social rhythm therapy (IPSRT; e.g., Frank et al., 2005) (for review, see Miklowitz & Scott, 2009).

These treatments have several elements in common. First, all include an active psychoeducational component, which often involves teaching patients (and in some cases, family members) to recognize and obtain early treatment for manic episodes before they develop fully. All emphasize medication adherence, avoiding alcohol and street drugs, and the use of skills to cope more effectively with stress triggers. They differ in the emphasis on specific strategies, including involvement of family members in psychoeducation (FFT), stabilizing sleep/wake rhythms (interpersonal and social rhythm therapy), and cognitive restructuring (CBT; Miklowitz, Goodwin, Bauer & Geddes, 2008).

The treatments listed in Table 10.1 have all been found in at least one study to delay relapses of BD when combined with pharmacotherapy. The control conditions vary and have included treatment as usual, individual supportive therapy, unstructured group support, and active clinical management. There are nonreplications as well: In a large-scale multicenter study, Scott et al. (2006) found that CBT was no more effective than treatment as usual in delaying recurrences. Post-hoc analyses, however, revealed that relative to treatment as usual, CBT was associated with longer time to recurrence among patients who had had fewer than 12 lifetime episodes, and less time to recurrence among patients with 12 or more prior episodes.

The large-scale Systematic Treatment Enhancement Program for BD (STEP-BD) attempted to examine the effects of psychosocial interventions in a practical clinical trial across 15 U.S. treatment centers (Miklowitz et al., 2007). In this trial, 293 bipolar I and II patients were randomly assigned to one of three intensive psychosocial interventions (30 sessions over 9 months of family-focused treatment, IPSRT, or CBT, or a control treatment called collaborative care [CC]). The CC involved three psychotherapy sessions over 6 weeks and focused on developing a relapse prevention plan. All patients were in an acute episode of bipolar depression at the time of randomization. All received "best practice" pharmacotherapy (i.e., mood stabilizers, atypical antipsychotic agents, or antidepressants, in various combinations) in combination with psychotherapy.

Over 1 year, being in any of the intensive psychotherapies was associated with a faster recovery from depression than being in CC. On average, patients in intensive treatment recovered within 169 days, as compared to 279 days in the CC condition. Patients in intensive treatment were also 1.6 times more likely than patients in CC to be clinically well in any given study month. Rates of recovery over 1 year were as follows: FFT, 77%; IPSRT, 65%; CBT, 60%; and CC, 52%. The differences among the three intensive modalities were not significant.

There are still many gaps in research on psychosocial treatment. For example, it is not clear which treatments are most effective for preventing symptoms of mania versus depression, or whether particular subgroups of patients respond more completely to individual, family, or group treatment. Few studies have identified the mechanisms of action of psychosocial interventions (for example, whether they enhance medication adherence, improve the patient's ability to recognize prodromal symptoms of recurrence, or increase insight or self-awareness). The applicability of psychosocial interventions to early-onset BD, or children at risk for developing the illness, has just begun to be systematically investigated (Fristad et al., 2009; Miklowitz et al., 2008; Miklowitz et al., 2011).

## DIAGNOSTIC CONSIDERATIONS

### THE BIPOLAR SPECTRUM

Controversy exists over how to draw the boundaries of BD. Although it has traditionally been conceptualized as a disease involving shifts between the dramatic poles of mania and depression, there is increasing recognition that many patients have bipolar spectrum disorders, which, depending on the definition, may include subsyndromal manic episodes, manic or hypomanic episodes triggered by antidepressants, subsyndromal mixed episodes, or agitated depression (Akiskal, Benazzi, Perugi, & Rihmer, 2005; Akiskal et al., 2000). For example, Smith, Harrison, Muir, and Blackwood (2005) observed that many young adults with recurrent depression have symptoms that would be best considered within the bipolar spectrum. In a sample of young adults treated for recurrent depression at a university health service, only 16% met the *DSM-IV* criteria for bipolar disorder and 83% for recurrent major depressive illness. When broader definitions of the bipolar spectrum were used, between 47% and 77% received bipolar diagnoses.

What is the evidence that spectrum patients are really bipolar in the classic sense? Although they do not necessarily follow the same course of illness patterns as patients with BD I or II, patients with subsyndromal forms of BD are more likely to have family histories of BD and higher rates of hypomania induced by antidepressants than people without subsyndromal BD symptoms. They also have high rates of suicide, marital disruption, and mental health service utilization (Judd & Akiskal, 2003; Smith et al., 2005).

Some researchers have examined the bipolar spectrum as a risk factor for the development of fully syndromal BD. Assessment instruments designed to identify persons at risk include the Temperament Evaluation of Memphis, Pisa, Paris, and San Diego—autoquestionnaire version (TEMPS-A; Akiskal et al., 2005). The TEMPS-A is a self- or parent-rated assessment of temperaments believed to precede the onset of full BD and to persist during the euthymic states. Although the TEMPS-A measures a range of mood-related symptoms and tendencies, a specific tendency toward high moods and mood variability, as captured on the cyclothymia subscale, predicted onset of BD in a 2-year follow-up of 80 children and adolescents with (Kochman et al., 2005).

The 79-item General Behavior Inventory (GBI; Depue, Kleinman, Davis, Hutchinson, & Krauss, 1985) evaluates lifetime experiences of depressive and manic symptoms, as well as mood variability, on 1–4 scales of frequency. High scores on the GBI during adolescence are associated with psychosocial impairment in adulthood (Klein & Depue, 1984), and a childhood version rated by parents discriminated pediatric BD from attention deficit hyperactivity disorder (ADHD; Danielson, Youngstrom, Findling, & Calabrese, 2003). Whereas the Klein et al. studies focused on the prognostic value of cyclothymic temperament, Reichart et al. (2005) found that higher scores on the GBI depression subscale were the best predictors of BD onset at 5-year follow-up among adolescents with depression.

Finally, the Hypomanic Personality Scale (Eckblad & Chapman, 1986) has been used to assess subsyndromal manic symptoms and related traits. Kwapil et al. (2000) found that high scores on this scale predicted the onset of bipolar spectrum disorders over a 13-year follow-up of a large sample of college students. Thus, self-report measures of spectrum symptoms and temperamental characteristics predict the onset of BDs in longitudinal studies.

These studies leave open the question of whether cyclothymic temperament or severe major depression are better predictors of onset of BD in adulthood. The NIMH Course and Outcome of Bipolar Youth (COBY) study provides strong empirical support for one approach to phenotyping high-risk youth. This long-term prospective study showed that youth characterized by (a) one *DSM-IV* symptom less than full criteria for a manic or hypomanic episode, (b) a clear change in functioning, and (c) a minimum symptom duration of 4 hours within a day and a minimum of four lifetime episodes, were at substantially elevated risk for "converting" to BD I or II by 4- to 5-year follow-up (Birmaher et al., 2009). When stratifying by family history for BD I or II, the risk of conversion in patients presenting with this BD-NOS phenotype was 52% over 4 years, compared to 32% in BD-NOS patients with negative BD family history. Thus, transient manic episodes, when present in a child with a bipolar first- or second-degree relative, are a high-risk phenotype for later bipolar onset.

Diagnosis in Children and Adolescents

Perhaps the most controversial diagnostic dilemma is where to draw the boundaries of the bipolar diagnosis in children. Before about 1980, belief was widespread that neither mania nor depression could occur before puberty, although individual case reports of the phenomenon existed (e.g., Anthony & Scott, 1960; Strecker,

1921). This belief has changed significantly in the past two decades (for review, see Luby & Navsaria, 2010). Unfortunately, no separate diagnostic criteria exist for juvenile BD patients, and as a result there is little agreement on the operational definition of a manic or mixed episode, whether well-demarcated episodes of mania and depression must occur or whether the symptoms can be chronic and unremitting, the minimum duration of episodes, and what constitutes a symptom (Biederman et al., 2003; Leibenluft, Charney, Towbin, Bhangoo, & Pine, 2003; McClellan, 2005). The reliability of the diagnosis appears to decrease with age (Meyer & Carlson, 2010).

One research group, led by Geller and colleagues (2002), has recommended that BD not be diagnosed in children unless elevated mood and grandiosity are present. Another group, led by Biederman, Wozniak, and colleagues (Biederman, Faraone, Chu, & Wozniak, 1999; Wozniak, Biederman, & Richards, 2001), emphasizes the roles of irritability, aggression, and mixed symptoms as core illness features. A third group (Leibenluft et al., 2003) has recommended that BD in children be divided into three phenotypes: (1) a narrow phenotype (meets *DSM-IV* criteria for mania or hypomania with elated mood and grandiosity); (2) an intermediate phenotype (meets *DSM-IV* criteria but with irritable mood only); and (3) a broad phenotype (e.g., mania that does not meet the duration criteria for bipolar I or II or is one symptom short).

Does childhood-onset BD develop into adult BD, or are they separate conditions? As indicated previously, the COBY study found clear evidence for a specific definition of BD-NOS—when combined with a family history of BD—as a high-risk phenotype. Another long-term study found developmental continuity for a narrow BD phenotype from late adolescence to early adulthood, but not for a broader BD phenotype marked by irritability and euphoria without the associated manic symptoms (Lewinsohn, Seeley, Buckley, & Klein, 2002). A 4-year follow-up of manic children (mean age 11) who met strict *DSM-IV* criteria revealed that the average duration of manic episodes was 79 weeks, and only 36% recovered fully within 1 year. At 4-year follow-up, 64% had a recurrence of mania. Follow-up into adulthood has not yet been accomplished (Geller, Tillman, Craney, & Bolhofner, 2004).

In a reanalysis of a large-scale longitudinal study of youths in semirural parts of New York (N = 776, mean age 13.8), two categories of risk were defined: (1) episodic irritability (based on the parents' and child's answer to questions such as "Are there times when [the child] feels irritable or jumpy?" and "Do these times last for a week or more?") and (2) chronic irritability (persistent arguing and temper tantrums across the home and school settings). Females exhibited higher levels of episodic and chronic irritability than males. Moreover, episodic irritability in adolescence predicted the onset of a mania by age 16 (Leibenluft, Cohen, Gorrindo, Brook, & Pine, 2006). In contrast, chronic irritability was associated with ADHD by midadolescence and major depressive illness in early adulthood. Episodic irritability was a unique predictor of mania by age 22, although this relationship was mediated by the cross-sectional correlation between episodic irritability and depression in early adolescence. Thus, the episodicity of symptoms is an important feature to assess when attempting to distinguish risk for BD from risk for other psychiatric syndromes among youths.

DUAL DIAGNOSIS

BD patients are highly likely to be diagnosed with one or more comorbid disorders. When 12-month prevalence rates in a community epidemiological sample are considered, the highest associations are found between mania/hypomania and ADHD, followed by oppositional defiant disorder, agoraphobia, panic disorder, generalized anxiety disorder, alcohol dependence, and drug abuse (Kessler et al., 2005). The prevalence of anxiety disorders in clinical and epidemiologic studies ranges from 10.6% to 62.5% for panic disorder, 7.8% to 47.2% for social anxiety disorder, 7% to 40% for posttraumatic stress disorder, 3.2% to 35% for obsessive-compulsive disorder, and 7% to 32% for generalized anxiety disorder (Simon et al., 2004). Taken together, at least some form of comorbid anxiety disorder is present for the majority of persons with bipolar disorder.

In the original Epidemiological Catchment Area Study, 6 of 10 patients with bipolar disorder had a lifetime history of alcohol or drug abuse (Regier et al., 1990). Other community and clinical population studies (Brady, Casto, Lydiard, Malcolm, & Arana, 1991; Goldberg, Garno, Leon, Kocsis, & Portera, 1999; Kessler et al., 1997) have documented rates of lifetime substance use disorder ranging from 21% to 45%. This represents a sixfold increase in substance use disorders among patients with BD relative to the general population. One study found that patients were more likely to use alcohol during depressive episodes and more likely to use cocaine and marijuana during manic episodes (Strakowski, DelBello, Fleck, & Arndt, 2000).

Comorbid diagnoses—and even subsyndromal symptoms of comorbid disorders—are associated with a poor prognosis of child and adult BD (Feske et al., 2000; Frank et al., 2002; Masi et al., 2004; Otto et al., 2006; Tohen, Waternaux, & Tsuang, 1990). For example, anxiety comorbidity has been linked with younger onset of BD, lower likelihood of recovery, poorer role functioning and quality of life, a greater likelihood of suicide attempts, and poorer response to medications (Henry et al., 2003; Simon et al., 2004). Studies have also documented lower recovery rates among patients with BD with a comorbid substance use disorder (Keller et al., 1986; Tohen et al., 1990) and a greater likelihood of rehospitalization (Brady et al., 1991; Reich, Davies, & Himmelhoch, 1974).

A separate issue is how to distinguish BD from comorbid disorders. A case in point is ADHD. In a sample of children, Geller et al. (1998) compared the frequency of symptoms that are considered classic or pathognomonic of mania versus those typically seen in either mania or ADHD. Elated mood, grandiosity, hypersexuality, decreased need for sleep, daredevil acts, and uninhibited people seeking were far more common in mania than ADHD. Distractibility, increased activity, and increased energy were observed in both disorders (see also Kim & Miklowitz, 2002). It is rare to see major depressive episodes in children with ADHD, and when the two do co-occur, the child is at high risk for developing BD (Chang, Steiner, & Ketter, 2000; Faraone, Biederman, Mennin, Wozniak, & Spencer, 1997a; Faraone et al., 1997b; Leibenluft et al., 2006).

## DIAGNOSTIC ASSESSMENT METHODS

Most patients with BD are diagnosed by a clinical interview; there are no biological tests that verify the diagnosis. The most prominent is the Structured Diagnostic

Interview for *DSM-IV* (SCID; First, Spitzer, Gibbon, & Williams, 1995). Despite impressive reliability and validity statistics for bipolar I disorder, the SCID and the Kiddie Schedule for Affective Disorders and Schizophrenia (KSADS) are not sensitive in identifying the milder forms of BD (Chambers et al., 1985; Kaufman et al., 1997). For example, the SCID may underestimate identification of hypomanic episodes when comparing with diagnoses based on interviews by experienced clinicians (Dunner & Tay, 1993). Current thinking about diagnostic assessments is that instruments like the SCID and KSADS should be supplemented by data from self-report questionnaires (especially those that examine subsyndromal forms of mania) as well as a thorough history of prior episodes involving an episode timeline, such as the National Institute of Mental Health (NIMH) Life Charting method (Leverich & Post, 1998). Life charting enables the clinician to investigate the frequency, severity, and timing of prior episodes; whether depressive, mixed, or manic episodes have dominated the clinical picture; and whether other disorders (e.g., substance dependence) preceded, coincided with, or developed after the onset of the mood disorder.

## ETIOLOGICAL CONSIDERATIONS

### HERITABILITY

Estimates of the heritability of BD range from 59% to 87% (McGuffin et al., 2003). Concordance rates for monozygotic twins averages 48%, whereas the concordance rate for dizygotic twins averages 6% (Barnett & Smoller, 2009; Willcutt & Mcqueen, 2010). One twin study found that the heritability for depression was correlated with the heritability of mania, but not so highly that these genetic vulnerabilities should be considered as overlapping (McGuffin et al., 2003).

The risk of BD among children of bipolar parents is 4 times greater than the risk among children of healthy parents. Children of bipolar parents, however, are also at approximately 2.7 times higher risk for developing nonaffective disorders (including ADHD and conduct disorder) than are the children of well parents. Thus, a proportion of the familial risk is not specific to bipolar illness (Hodgins et al., 2002; LaPalme, Hodgins, & LaRoche, 1997).

Several genomic regions relevant to BD have been identified, including 13q32, 22q11, 8p22, and 10p14 (Badner & Gershon, 2002; Berrettini, 2003), but effects have generally been small and findings have not been entirely consistent from study to study. One model (Murray et al., 2004) emphasizes the genetic overlap between BD and schizophrenia and common susceptibility genes that predispose individuals to dopamine dysregulation and psychosis. In addition to common susceptibilities, there are probably other genes whose expression affects neurodevelopment, illness-specific neurological changes, the likelihood of exposure to certain types of environments, and the eventual outcome of BD, schizoaffective disorder, or schizophrenia (Murray et al., 2004).

Genes that control circadian rhythms ("clock genes") may be involved in the risk for bipolar disorder and its recurrences (e.g., Benedetti et al., 2003). This hypothesis is consistent with observations about the dramatic role of sleep loss in mood recurrences. Laboratory mice with mutations in clock genes behave in ways that resemble people with mania (e.g., increases in activity, decreased sleep, reward-seeking behavior). These changes are reversed when mice are given lithium (Roybal et al., 2007).

## NEUROTRANSMITTER DYSREGULATION

Increasingly, BD is being described as an "impairment of synaptic and cellular plasticity" (Manji, 2009, p. 2). This means that people with BD have genetically influenced problems with information processing in synapses and circuits (the neuronal connections between one brain structure and others), rather than too much or too little of a certain chemical.

Traditional neurotransmitter models of mood disorders have focused on nor-epinephrine, dopamine, and serotonin (Charney, Menkes, & Heninger, 1981; Thase, Jindal, & Howland, 2002). It is now widely believed that dysregulations in these systems interact with deficits in other neurotransmitter systems, such as gamma-aminobutyric acid (GABA) and Substance P, to produce symptoms of mood disorders (Stockmeier, 2003). Given these complex interactions, current research focuses on the functioning of neurotransmitter systems rather than on simple models of neurotransmitter levels being either high or low. Current paradigms include measuring sensitivity of the postsynaptic receptors through pharmacological challenges, neuroimaging, or molecular genetic research. This type of research has progressed particularly rapidly in understanding dysregulation in serotonin and dopamine systems.

*Dopamine*   Among people without BD, several different dopamine agonists, including stimulants, have been found to trigger manic symptoms, including increases in mood, energy, and talkativeness (Willner, 1995). People with BD show pronounced behavioral effects to stimulants (Anand et al., 2000). Several paradigms have been used to challenge the dopamine system, including behavioral sensitization (the study of how repeated administration of dopamine agonists changes the sensitivity of dopaminergic reward pathways; Kalivas, Duffy, DuMars, & Skinner, 1988; Robinson & Becker, 1986) and sleep deprivation (which appears to interfere with normalizing the sensitivity of dopamine receptors; Ebert, Feistel, Barocks, Kaschka, & Pirner, 1994). Results obtained using these paradigms are consistent with the idea that BD is characterized by hypersensitivity of the dopamine system (Strakowski, Sax, Setters, & Keck, 1996; Strakowski, Sax, Setters, Stanton, & Keck, 1997).

Molecular genetic studies have not yet identified polymorphisms that could explain these effects. For example, BD has not been found to consistently relate to polymorphisms in the d1, d2, d3, and d4 receptor genes or the dopamine transporter genes (Chiaroni et al., 2000; Georgieva et al., 2002; Gorwood, Bellivier, Ades, & Leboyer, 2000; Lopez et al., 2005; Manki, Kanba, Muramatsu, & Higuchi, 1996; Muglia et al., 2002). In animal models, though, a set of candidate genes for BD have been identified that relate to modulating dopamine signaling within reward pathways (Ogden et al., 2004).

*Serotonin*   Neuroimaging studies indicate that mood disorders are generally associated with decreased sensitivity of the serotonin receptors (Stockmeier, 2003). The functioning of the serotonin system can also be tested by manipulating levels of tryptophan, the precursor to serotonin (Staley, Malison, & Innis, 1998). Findings of tryptophan-manipulation studies are consistent with the idea of serotonin receptor dysfunction among persons with a family history of BD (Sobcazk, Honig, Schmitt, & Riedel, 2003; Sobczak et al., 2002). Meta-analyses, however, find that BD is not consistently related to genes regulating serotonin receptors (Anguelova, Benkelfat, & Turecki, 2003) or to serotonin transporter genes (Lotrich & Pollock, 2004).

BRAIN REGIONS INVOLVED IN BIPOLAR DISORDER

Although findings are not entirely consistent, neuroimaging studies implicate a set of structures in the pathophysiology of BD. Many of these regions overlap substantially with those involved in emotional reactivity and regulation, and as such, many parallels are present with the brain correlates of unipolar depression (Davidson, Pizzagalli, & Nitschke, 2002; Mayberg, Keightley, Mahurin, & Brannan, 2004). Key structures include the amygdala, which is involved in the detection of the significance of emotionally salient stimuli, and a set of other regions involved in effective cognitive regulation of emotions and goal pursuit, such as regions of the prefrontal cortex, anterior cingulate, and hippocampus. One model suggests that mood disorders are characterized by increased activity in regions involved in emotional sensitivity, combined with diminished activity in regions involved in effective thinking and planning in response to emotional cues (Phillips, Drevets, Rauch, & Lane, 2003).

More specifically, several Positron Emission Tomography (PET) and functional Magnetic Resonance Imaging (fMRI) studies of neural activity during cognitive or emotional tasks have shown a pattern of amygdala hyperactivity among people with bipolar I disorder (Altshuler et al., 2005a; Chang et al., 2004; Kruger, Semi-nowicz, Goldapple, Kennedy, & Mayberg, 2003; Lawrence et al., 2004). Some adult studies correspondingly suggest above-average volume of the amygdala (Phillips et al., 2003).

Given that the neural regions involved in BD appear particularly tied to emotion reactivity and regulation, a central paradigm involves studying brain activity in response to positive and negative stimuli. Among such studies, increased neural activity has been consistently documented in reactions to mood-congruent stimuli, such as positive stimuli during manic periods, with some evidence for enhanced reactivity to negative stimuli during depressed periods (Johnson, Gruber, & Eisner, 2007).

People with BD also appear to demonstrate diminished activity of the hippo-campus and some regions of the prefrontal cortex (Kruger et al., 2003). In parallel with the findings of functional studies, structural studies have found that BD is associated with a smaller-than-average volume in the prefrontal cortex, basal ganglia, hippocampus, and anterior cingulate (Phillips et al., 2003). Findings regarding diminished volume of the hippocampus have been identified in juvenile BD (Frazier et al., 2005). Diminished function of the prefrontal cortex and related circuits might interfere with effective planning and goal pursuit in the context of emotion, leading to a low capacity to regulate emotion. Although prefrontal cortical deficits have been implicated in schizophrenia as well (Barch, 2005), recent research suggests that the prefrontal deficits in BD compared to schizophrenia may be more specific to the orbitofrontal cortex (Altshuler et al., 2005b; Cotter, Hudson, & Landau, 2005). Several recent studies have suggested diminished connectivity of regions of the prefrontal cortex with the amygdala while persons with bipolar disorder are viewing positive stimuli, although findings have not been congruent regarding which regions of the prefrontal cortex are implicated (Almeida et al., 2009; Versace et al., 2010; Wang et al., 2009).

Patterns of neural activation appear to shift with mood episodes. During depression, diminished activity in the anterior cingulate is observed (Mayberg et al., 2004). During mania, persons with BD may show diminished reactivity to negative stimuli compared with healthy or euthymic persons. For example, after viewing faces with different negative emotional expressions, patients with mania showed decreases in amygdala and subgenual anterior cingulate cortex activity compared to controls (Lennox, Jacob, Calder, Lupson, & Bullmore, 2004). Hence, brain regions involved in identifying the importance of negative stimuli appear to become less active during manic episodes.

Finally, given models of reward sensitivity in BD, the role of structures within the basal ganglia, including the nucleus accumbens (Knutson, Adams, Fong, & Hommer, 2001), has become an important focus of research. Both at rest and during motor tasks, the level of activity in the basal ganglia is positively correlated with the concurrent level of manic symptoms (Blumberg et al., 1999; Caligiuri et al., 2003).

Hence, one theory is that BD is related to dysregulation in brain regions relevant to emotional reactivity, such as the amygdala, as well as regions in the prefrontal cortex involved in the regulation of emotion and cognitive control. Much of this research demonstrates strong parallels with unipolar depression. Evidence suggests that neural activation is somewhat mood-state dependent. Regions involved in reward motivation are an important focus for research.

## CASE STUDY

### Case Identification and Presenting Complaints

Leonard, a 57-year-old White male, lived with his wife, Helen, and 15-year-old son in a rented house in the suburbs of a major metropolitan area. His wife requested treatment because of his angry outbursts, sleep disturbance, and bizarre preoccupations. He had become preoccupied with kickboxing and was spending hours on the Internet examining relevant websites and writing about it. She discovered that he had written a 500-page manuscript describing the mechanics of kickboxing, containing sections that were rambling, philosophical, and at times incoherent. She explained that he was frequently awake until 4 A.M. and went to bed smelling of alcohol. For nearly 5 years he had been unable to hold a job.

Leonard presented in his first interview as combative and oppositional. He admitted that he had been feeling "revved" over the past 2 weeks, that he felt full of energy and ideas, and that he needed little sleep, but he denied any negative effects of his symptoms. He described an incident that appeared to be related to his recent manic behavior. He had made contact with a kickboxing champion in another state and had started writing to this man about setting up a new television network devoted to kickboxing. He also claimed he was going to start his own studio. The plans seemed unrealistic given that he had little formal training in this sport and had no money to rent a studio. The kickboxing champion had stopped responding to Leonard's emails, which, Leonard claimed, might be because "he's raising money and wants to surprise me."

Leonard had one manic episode accompanied by hospitalization when he was in college. He had become entranced by a female professor and believed that she was related to him by blood. He began calling her continually and finally followed her out to a parking lot and tried to block her from getting into her car. A passerby called the police, and Leonard was taken to the hospital. He was admitted with the diagnosis of bipolar I, manic episode.

Since this time Leonard had functioned poorly. His work had been intermittent, and he had been fired several times because, as he explained, "My bosses are always idiots and I'm more than happy to tell them so." He had tried to set up a web-based business selling automobile window shields but had made little money. He met Helen during a hiking excursion for singles. They had married approximately 1 year after they met (a period of relative stability for Leonard) and had a child 1 year later.

Leonard had begun medication shortly after his son was born, explaining that he wanted to become a stable father. His psychiatrist recommended lithium carbonate 1,200 mg and divalproex sodium (Depakote) at 2,000 mg. Although Leonard did not have further manic episodes, he had several hypomanic periods and complained of an ongoing depression that never fully remitted. He had thought of suicide several times, and these fantasies usually had a grandiose quality. For example, he fantasized about setting himself on fire and then jumping from a tall building. He never made an attempt.

The clinician who evaluated Leonard administered the Structured Clinical Interview for *DSM-IV* (First et al., 1995), which involved an individual interview with him, followed by a separate interview with his wife. The interview confirmed the presence of elated and irritable mood for the past 2 weeks, along with inflated self-esteem, increased activity, decreased need for sleep, flight of ideas and racing thoughts, pressure of speech, and increased spending. His behavior did not require hospitalization but clearly interfered with his functioning. He was given a diagnosis of bipolar disorder I, manic episode and started on a regimen of lithium, divalproex, and an atypical antipsychotic agent, quetiapine (Seroquel).

## SUMMARY

Much progress has been made in clarifying the diagnostic boundaries, genetic pathways, and neurobiological mechanisms relevant to bipolar illness. New studies recognize the strong influence of psychosocial variables against this background of biological and genetic vulnerability. Psychotherapy is an effective adjunct to pharmacotherapy in the long-term maintenance treatment of the illness, notably interventions that focus on enhancing the patient's understanding of the disorder and effectiveness in coping with its cycling.

Major focal areas for future studies include clarifying the validity of the bipolar spectrum. It is unclear whether bipolar illness should include only *DSM IV*-defined bipolar I or bipolar II disorder or whether it should also include subsyndromal mixed presentations (e.g., depression with significant anxious-agitation), cyclothymia, or episodes of mania, hypomania, or depression that do not meet the full severity or duration criteria. Nowhere are these questions more critical than in defining childhood-onset BD, which is being diagnosed with increasing frequency. In the future, it may be that fMRI or other imaging techniques will identify brain changes uniquely associated with bipolar illness, but until that time we must rely on clinical interviews and supplemental questionnaires to diagnose these conditions. Research that improves the reliability, clinical utility, and consumer acceptance of existing diagnostic methods is therefore critical.

The interface between psychosocial and biological risk factors deserves considerable study, especially as these factors relate to different poles of the disorder. As we have summarized, life events involving goal attainment and factors that disrupt sleep are strongly correlated with the onset of manic episodes, although their role in predicting illness onset has not been established in longitudinal studies. High intrafamilial EE and negative life events stress are most consistently associated with depressive episodes. Laboratory-based translational research may help clarify the avenues from specific stressors to biological changes to manic versus depressive symptom exacerbations.

The optimal combinations of psychotherapy and pharmacotherapy must be identified in trials that sample populations of diverse ethnicity, socioeconomic status, psychiatric and medical comorbidity, and chronicity. Large-scale studies such as STEP-BD are a move in this direction, but even studies of this size can be underpowered for examining treatment effects within specific subgroups (e.g., patients with comorbid substance dependence, rapid-cycling patients, patients of African American or Latino heritage). Studies that adapt treatment methods to the cultural needs of specific populations are essential to moving the field forward.

Last, treatment studies should consider the synergy between biological and psychosocial interventions, and under what conditions combining one with the other will produce the most enduring effects. For example, drugs that stabilize mood symptoms may also energize patients to the extent that they become more amenable to the skill-oriented tasks of cognitive-behavioral treatment. Psychoeducational treatments may increase medication adherence, which in turn may allow patients to remain stable on fewer medications or on lower dosages. Interpersonal or family interventions that increase the patient's ability to benefit from social support and decrease the impact of family or life stressors may decrease the need for adjunctive antidepressants in long-term maintenance. Ideally, the next generation of clinical research in BD will address these questions.

## REFERENCES

Adler, A. (1964). *Problems of neurosis*. New York, NY: Harper & Row.

Akiskal, H. S., Benazzi, F., Perugi, G., & Rihmer, Z. (2005). Agitated "unipolar" depression reconceptualized as a depressive mixed state: Implications for the antidepressant-suicide controversy. *Journal of Affective Disorders, 85*, 245–258.

Akiskal, H. S., Bourgeois, M. L., Angst, J., Post, R., Moller, H., & Hirschfeld, R. (2000). Reevaluating the prevalence of and diagnostic composition within the broad clinical spectrum of bipolar disorders. *Journal of Affective Disorders, 59*(Suppl. 1), S5–S30.

Akiskal, H. S., Mendlowicz, M. V., Jean-Louis, G., Rapaport, M. H., Kelsoe, J. R., Gillin, J. C., & Smith, T. L. (2005). TEMPS-A: Validation of a short version of a self-rated instrument designed to measure variations in temperament. *Journal of Affective Disorders, 85*(1–2), 45–52.

Alloy, L. B., Reilly-Harrington, N., Fresco, D. M., Whitehouse, W. G., & Zechmeister, J. S. (1999). Cognitive styles and life events in subsyndromal unipolar and bipolar disorders: Stability and prospective prediction of depressive and hypomanic mood swings. *Journal of Cognitive Psychotherapy, 13*, 21–40.

Almeida, J. R., Versace, A., Mechelli, A., Hassel, S., Quevedo, K., Kupfer, D. J., & Phillips, M. L. (2009). Abnormal amygdala-prefrontal effective connectivity to happy faces differentiates bipolar from major depression. *Biological Psychiatry, 66*, 451–459.

Altshuler, L., Bookheimer, S., Proenza, M. A., Townsend, J., Sabb, F., Firestine, A., . . . Cohen, M. S. (2005a). Increased amygdala activation during mania: A functional magnetic resonance imaging study. *American Journal of Psychiatry, 162*, 1211–1213.

Altshuler, L. L., Bookheimer, S. Y., Townsend, J., Proenza, M. A., Eisenberger, N., Sabb, F., . . . Cohen, M. S. (2005b). Blunted activation in orbitofrontal cortex during mania: A functional magnetic resonance imaging study. *Biological Psychiatry, 58*(10), 763–769.

Altshuler, L., Suppes, T., Black, D., Nolen, W. A., Keck, P. E., Jr., Frye, M. A., . . . Post, R. (2003). Impact of antidepressant discontinuation after acute bipolar depression remission on rates of depressive relapse at 1-year follow-up. *American Journal of Psychiatry, 160*, 1252–1262.

American Psychiatric Association (APA). (2000). *Diagnostic and statistical manual of mental disorders* (4th ed., text revision; DSM-IV). Washington, DC: Author.

Anand, A., Verhoeff, P., Seneca, N., Zoghbi, S. S., Seibyl, J. P., Charney, D. S., . . . Cohen, M. S. (2000). Brain SPECT imaging of amphetamine-induced dopamine release in euthymic bipolar disorder patients. *American Journal of Psychiatry, 157*, 1109–1114.

Angst, J., Angst, F., Gerber-Werder, R., & Gamma, A. (2005). Suicide in 406 mood-disordered patients with and without long-term medication: A 40 to 44 years' follow-up. *Archives of Suicide Research, 9*(3), 279–300.

Anguelova, M., Benkelfat, C., & Turecki, G. (2003). A systematic review of association studies investigating genes coding for serotonin receptors and the serotonin transporter: I. Affective disorders. *Molecular Psychiatry, 8*, 574–591.

Anthony, E. J., & Scott, P. (1960). Manic-depressive psychosis in childhood. *Child Psychology and Psychiatry, 1*, 53–72.

Badner, J. A., & Gershon, E. S. (2002). Meta-analysis of whole-genome linkage scans of bipolar disorder and schizophrenia. *Molecular Psychiatry, 7*, 405–411.

Barbini, B., Colombo, C., Benedetti, F., Campori, C., Bellodi, L., & Smeraldi, E. (1998). The unipolar-bipolar dichotomy and the response to sleep deprivation. *Psychiatry Research, 79*, 43–50.

Barch, D. M. (2005). The cognitive neuroscience of schizophrenia. *Annual Review of Clinical Psychology, 1*, 321–353.

Barnett, J. H., & Smoller, J. W. (2009). The genetics of bipolar disorder. *Neuroscience, 164*(1), 331–343.

Benedetti, F., Serretti, A., Colombo, C., Barbini, B., Lorenzi, C., Campori, E., & Smeraldi, E. (2003). Influence of CLOCK gene polymorphism on circadian mood fluctuation and illness recurrence in bipolar depression. *American Journal of Medical Genetics, Part B Neuropsychiatric Genetics, 123B*(1), 23–26.

Berrettini, W. (2003). Evidence for shared susceptibility in bipolar disorder and schizophrenia. *American Journal of Medical Genetics, Part C, 123C*, 59–64.

Biederman, J., Faraone, S. V., Chu, M. P., & Wozniak, J. (1999). Further evidence of a bidirectional overlap between juvenile mania and conduct disorder in children. *Journal of the American Academy of Child and Adolescent Psychiatry, 38*, 468–476.

Biederman, J., Mick, E., Faraone, S. V., Spencer, T., Wilens, T. E., & Wozniak, J. (2003). Current concepts in the validity, diagnosis and treatment of paediatric bipolar disorder. *International Journal of Neuropsychopharmacology, 6*, 293–300.

Birmaher, B., Axelson, D., Goldstein, B., Strober, M., Gill, M. K., Hunt, J., . . . Keller, M. (2009). Four-year longitudinal course of children and adolescents with bipolar spectrum disorders: The Course and Outcome of Bipolar Youth (COBY) study. *American Journal of Psychiatry, 166*(7), 795–804.

Blumberg, H. P., Stern, E., Ricketts, S., Martinez, D., de Asis, J., White, T., . . . Silbersweig, D. A. (1999). Rostral and orbital prefrontal cortex dysfunction in the manic state of bipolar disorder. *American Journal of Psychiatry, 156*, 1986–1988.

Brady, K. T., Casto, S., Lydiard, R. B., Malcolm, R., & Arana, G. (1991). Substance abuse in an inpatient psychiatric sample. *American Journal of Drug and Alcohol Abuse, 17*, 389–397.

Brown, G. K., Beck, A. T., Steer, R. A., & Grisham, J. R. (2000). Risk factors for suicide in psychiatric outpatients: A 20-year prospective study. *Journal of Consulting and Clinical Psychology, 68*, 371–377.

Brown, G. W., & Andrews, B. (1986). Social support and depression. In R. Trumbull & M. H. Appley (Eds.), *Dynamics of stress: Physiological, psychological, and social perspectives* (pp. 257–282). New York, NY: Plenum Press.

Butzlaff, R. L., & Hooley, J. M. (1998). Expressed emotion and psychiatric relapse: A meta-analysis. *Archives of General Psychiatry, 55*, 547–552.

Calabrese, J. R., Fatemi, S. H., Kujawa, M., & Woyshville, M. J. (1996). Predictors of response to mood stabilizers. *Journal of Clinical Psychopharmacology, 16*(Suppl. 1), 24–31.

Caligiuri, M. P., Brown, G. G., Meloy, M. J., Eberson, S. C., Kindermann, S. S., Frank, L. R., . . . Lohr, J. B. (2003). An fMRI study of affective state and medication on cortical and subcortial regions during motor performance in bipolar disorder. *Psychiatry Research: Neuroimaging, 123*, 171–182.

Chambers, W. J., Puig-Antich, J., Hirsch, M., Paez, P., Ambrosini, P. J., Tabrizi, M. A., & Davies, M. (1985). The assessment of affective disorders in children and adolescents by semi-structured interview: Test-retest reliability. *Archives of General Psychiatry, 42*, 696–702.

Chang, K., Adleman, N. E., Dienes, K., Simeonova, D. I., Menon, V., & Reiss, A. (2004). Anomalous prefrontal-subcortical activation in familial pediatric bipolar disorder: A functional magnetic resonance imaging investigation. *Archives of General Psychiatry, 61*(8), 781–792.

Chang, K. D., Steiner, H., & Ketter, T. A. (2000). Psychiatric phenomenology of child and adolescent bipolar offspring. *Journal of the American Academy of Child and Adolescent Psychiatry, 39*, 453–460.

Charney, D. S., Menkes, D. B., & Heninger, G. R. (1981). Receptor sensitivity and the mechanism of action of antidepressants. *Archives of General Psychiatry, 38*, 1160–1180.

Chiaroni, P., Azorin, J. M., Dassa, D., Henry, J. M., Giudicelli, S., Malthiery, Y., & Planells, R. (2000). Possible involvement of the dopamine D3 receptor locus in subtypes of bipolar affective disorder. *Psychiatric Genetics, 10*, 43–49.

Colom, F., Vieta, E., Martinez-Aran, A., Reinares, M., Benabarre, A., & Gasto, C. (2000). Clinical factors associated with treatment noncompliance in euthymic bipolar patients. *Journal of Clinical Psychiatry, 61*, 549–555.

Colom, F., Vieta, E., Martinez-Aran, A., Reinares, M., Goikolea, J. M., Benabarre, A., . . . Corominas, J. (2003). A randomized trial on the efficacy of group psychoeducation in the prophylaxis of recurrences in bipolar patients whose disease is in remission. *Archives of General Psychiatry, 60*, 402–7.

Coryell, W., Endicott, J., Maser, J. D., Keller, M. B., Leon, A. C., & Akiskal, H. S. (1995). Long-term stability of polarity distinctions in the affective disorders. *American Journal of Psychiatry, 152*, 385–390.

Coryell, W., Scheftner, W., Keller, M., Endicott, J., Maser, J., & Klerman, G. L. (1993). The enduring psychosocial consequences of mania and depression. *American Journal of Psychiatry, 150*, 720–727.

Coryell, W. D. S., Turvey, C., Keller, M., Leon, A. C., Endicott, J., Schettler, P., . . . Mueller, T. (2003). The long-term course of rapid-cycling bipolar disorder. *Archives of General Psychiatry, 60*, 914–920.

Cotter, D., Hudson, L., & Landau, S. (2005). Evidence for orbitofrontal pathology in bipolar disorder and major depression, but not in schizophrenia. *Bipolar Disorders, 7*, 358–369.

Cuellar, A., Johnson, S. L., & Winters, R. (2005). Distinctions between bipolar and unipolar depression. *Clinical Psychology Review, 25*, 307–339.

Danielson, C. K., Youngstrom, E. A., Findling, R. L., & Calabrese, J. R. (2003). Discriminative validity of the general behavior inventory using youth report. *Journal of Abnormal Child Psychology, 31*, 29–39.

Davidson, R. J., Pizzagalli, D., & Nitschke, J. B. (2002). The representation and regulation of emotion in depression: Perspectives from affective neuroscience. In C. L. Hammen & I. H. Gotlib (Eds.), *Handbook of depression* (pp. 219–244). New York, NY: Guilford Press.

Depue, R. A., Kleinman, R. M., Davis, P., Hutchinson, M., & Krauss, S. P. (1985). The behavioral high-risk paradigm and bipolar affective disorder, Part VII: Serum free cortisol in nonpatient cyclothymic subjects selected by the General Behavior Inventory. *American Journal of Psychiatry, 142*, 175–181.

Depue, R. A., & Monroe, S. M. (1978). The unipolar-bipolar distinction in the depressive disorders. *Psychological Bulletin, 85*, 1001–1029.

Dion, G., Tohen, M., Anthony, W., & Waternaux, C. (1988). Symptoms and functioning of patients with bipolar disorder six months after hospitalization. *Hospital and Community Psychiatry, 39*, 652–656.

Dunner, D. L., & Tay, L. K. (1993). Diagnostic reliability of the history of hypomania in bipolar II patients and patients with major depression. *Comprehensive Psychiatry, 34*(5), 303–307.

Ebert, D., Feistel, H., Barocks, A., Kaschka, W. P., & Pirner, A. (1994). SPECT assessment of cerebral dopamine D2 receptor blockade in depression before and after sleep deprivation. *Biological Psychiatry, 35*, 880–885.

Eckblad, M., & Chapman, L. J. (1986). Development and validation of a scale for hypomanic personality. *Journal of Abnormal Psychology, 95*, 214–222.

Ehlers, C. L., Frank, E., & Kupfer, D. J. (1988). Social zeitgebers and biological rhythms. A unified approach to understanding the etiology of depression. *Archives of General Psychiatry, 45*, 948–952.

Ehlers, C. L., Kupfer, D. J., Frank, E., & Monk, T. H. (1993). Biological rhythms and depression: The role of zeitgebers and zeitstorers. *Depression, 1*, 285–293.

Eich, E., Macaulay, D., & Lam, R. W. (1997). Mania, depression, and mood dependent memory. *Cognition and Emotion, 11*, 607–618.

Eisner, L., Johnson, S. L., & Carver, C. S. (2008). Cognitive responses to failure and success relate uniquely to bipolar depression versus mania. *Journal of Abnormal Psychology, 117*, 154–163.

Ellicott, A., Hammen, C., Gitlin, M., Brown, G., & Jamison, K. (1990). Life events and the course of bipolar disorder. *American Journal of Psychiatry, 147*, 1194–1198.

Fagiolini, A., Kupfer, D. J., Masalehdan, A., Scott, J. A., Houck, P. R., & Frank, E. (2005). Functional impairment in the remission phase of bipolar disorder. *Bipolar Disorders, 7*, 281–285.

Faraone, S. V., Biederman, J., Mennin, D., Wozniak, J., & Spencer, T. (1997a). Attention-deficit hyperactivity disorder with bipolar disorder: A familial subtype? *Journal of the American Academy of Child and Adolescent Psychiatry, 36*, 1378–1387.

Faraone, S. V., Biederman, J., Wozniak, J., Mundy, E., Mennin, D., & O'Donnell, D. (1997b). Is comorbidity with ADHD a marker for juvenile-onset mania? *Journal of the American Academy of Child and Adolescent Psychiatry, 36*, 1046–1055.

Fawcett, J., Golden, B., & Rosenfeld, N. (2000). *New hope for people with bipolar disorder*. Roseville, CA: Prima Health.

Feske, U., Frank, E., Mallinger, A. G., Houck, P. R., Fagiolini, A., Shear, M. K., . . . Kupfer, D. J. (2000). Anxiety as a correlate of response to the acute treatment of bipolar I disorder. *American Journal of Psychiatry, 157*, 956–962.

First, M. B., Spitzer, R. L., Gibbon, M., & Williams, J. B. W. (1995). *Structured clinical interview for DSM-IV axis I disorders*. New York, NY: Biometrics Research Department, New York State Psychiatric Institute.

Frank, E., Cyranowski, J. M., Rucci, P., Shear, M. K., Fagiolini, A., Thase, M. E., . . . Kupfer, D. J. (2002). Clinical significance of lifetime panic spectrum symptoms in the treatment of patients with bipolar I disorder. *Archives of General Psychiatry, 59*, 905–911.

Frank, E., Kupfer, D. J., Thase, M. E., Mallinger, A. G., Swartz, H. A., Fagiolini, A. M., . . . Monk, T. (2005). Two-year outcomes for interpersonal and social rhythm therapy in individuals with bipolar I disorder. *Archives of General Psychiatry, 62*(9), 996–1004.

Frazier, J. A., Chiu, S., Breeze, J. L., Makris, N., Lange, N., Kennedy, D. N., . . . Biederman, J. (2005). Structural brain magnetic resonance imaging of limbic and thalamic volumes in pediatric bipolar disorder. *American Journal of Psychiatry, 162*, 1256–1265.

Fristad, M. A., Verducci, J. S., Walters, K., & Young, M. E. (2009). Impact of multifamily psychoeducational psychotherapy in treating children aged 8 to 12 years with mood disorders. *Archives of General Psychiatry, 66*(9), 1013–1021.

Garb, H. N. (1997). Racial bias, social class bias, and gender bias in clinical judgment. *Clinical Psychology: Science and Practice, 4*, 99–120.

Geller, B., Tillman, R., Craney, J. L., & Bolhofner, K. (2004). Four-year prospective outcome and natural history of mania in children with a prepubertal and early adolescent bipolar disorder phenotype. *Archives of General Psychiatry, 61*, 459–467.

Geller, B., Williams, M., Zimerman, B., Frazier, J., Beringer, I., & Warner, K. L. (1998). Prepubertal and early adolescent bipolarity differentiated from ADHD by manic symptoms, grandiose delusions, ultra-rapid or ultraradian cycling. *Journal of Affective Disorders, 51*, 81–91.

Geller, B., Zimerman, B., Williams, M., Bolhofner, K., Craney, J. L., Frazier, J., . . . Nickelsburg, M. J. (2002). *DSM-IV* mania symptoms in a prepubertal and early adolescent bipolar disorder phenotype compared to attention deficit hyperactive and normal controls. *Journal of the American Academy of Child and Adolescent Psychopharmacology, 12*, 11–25.

Georgieva, L., Dimitrova, A., Nikolov, I., Koleva, S., Tsvetkova, R., Owen, M. J., . . . Kirov, G. (2002). Dopamine transporter gene (DAT1) VNTR polymorphism in major psychiatric disorders: Family-based association study in the Bulgarian population. *Acta Psychiatrica Scandinavica, 105,* 396–399.

Ghaemi, S. N., Lenox, M. S., & Baldessarini, R. J. (2001). Effectiveness and safety of long-term antidepressant treatment in bipolar disorder. *Journal of Clinical Psychiatry, 62,* 565–569.

Gitlin, M. J., Swendsen, J., Heller, T. L., & Hammen, C. (1995). Relapse and impairment in bipolar disorder. *American Journal of Psychiatry, 152*(11), 1635–1640.

Goldberg, J., Garno, J., Leon, A., Kocsis, J., & Portera, L. (1999). A history of substance abuse complicates remission from acute mania in bipolar disorder. *Journal of Clinical Psychiatry, 60*(11), 733–740.

Goldberg, J. F. (2004). The changing landscape of psychopharmacology. In S. L. Johnson & R. L. Leahy (Eds.), *Psychological treatment of bipolar disorder* (pp. 109–138). New York, NY: Guilford Press.

Goldberg, J. F., Harrow, M., & Grossman, L. S. (1995). Course and outcome in bipolar affective disorder: A longitudinal follow-up study. *American Journal of Psychiatry, 152,* 379–385.

Goodwin, F. K., & Jamison, K. R. (1990). *Manic-depressive illness.* New York, NY: Oxford University Press.

Gorwood, P., Bellivier, F., Ades, J., & Leboyer, M. (2000). The DRD2 gene and the risk for alcohol dependence in bipolar patients. *European Psychiatry, 15,* 103–108.

Gunderson, J. G., Triebwasser, J., Phillips, K. A., & Sullivan, C. N. (1999). Personality and vulnerability to affective disorders. In R. C. Cloninger (Ed.), *Personality and psychopathology* (pp. 3–32). Washington, DC: American Psychiatric Press.

Harris, E. C., & Barraclough, B. (1997). Suicide as an outcome for mental disorders: A meta-analysis. *British Journal of Psychiatry, 170,* 205–208.

Harrow, M., Goldberg, J. F., Grossman, L. S., & Meltzer, H. Y. (1990). Outcome in manic disorders: A naturalistic follow-up study. *Archives of General Psychiatry, 47,* 665–671.

Heerlein, A., Richter, P., Gonzalez, M., & Santander, J. (1998). Personality patterns and outcome in depressive and bipolar disorders. *Psychopathology, 31,* 15–22.

Henry, C., Van den Bulke, D., Bellivier, F., Etain, B., Rouillon, F., & Leboyer, M. (2003). Anxiety disorders in 318 bipolar patients: Prevalence and impact on illness severity and response to mood stabilizer. *Journal of Clinical Psychiatry, 64,* 331–335.

Hillegers, M. H., Burger, H., Wals, M., Reichart, C. G., Verhulst, F. C., Nolen, W. A., & Ormel, J. (2004). Impact of stressful life events, familial loading and their interaction on the onset of mood disorders. *British Journal of Psychiatry, 185,* 97–101.

Hodgins, S., Faucher, B., Zarac, A., & Ellenbogen, M. (2002). Children of parents with bipolar disorder: A population at high risk for major affective disorders. *Child and Adolescent Psychiatric Clinics of North America, 11,* 533–553.

Jamison, K. R. (1993). *Touched with fire: Manic depressive illness and the artistic temperament.* New York, NY: Maxwell Macmillan International.

Jamison, K. R. (2000). Suicide and bipolar disorder. *Journal of Clinical Psychiatry, 61*(Suppl. 9), 47–56.

Jamison, K. R., & Baldessarini, R. J. (1999). Effects of medical interventions on suicial behavior. *Journal of Clinical Psychiatry, 60*(Suppl. 2), 4–6.

Johnson, R. E., & McFarland, B. H. (1996). Lithium use and discontinuation in a health maintenance organization. *American Journal of Psychiatry, 153,* 993–1000.

Johnson, S. L. (2005a). Life events in bipolar disorder: Towards more specific models. *Clinical Psychology Review, 25,* 1008–1027.

Johnson, S. L. (2005b). Mania and dysregulation in goal pursuit. *Clinical Psychology Review, 25,* 241–262.

Johnson, S. L., Cuellar, A., Ruggero, C., Perlman, C., Goodnick, P., White, R., & Miller, I. (2008). Life events as predictors of mania and depression in bipolar I disorder. *Journal of Abnormal Psychology, 117,* 268–277.

Johnson, S. L., Eisner, L., & Carver, C. S. (2009). Elevated expectancies among persons diagnosed with bipolar disorders. *British Journal of Clinical Psychology, 48,* 217–222.

Johnson, S. L., & Fingerhut, R. (2004). Negative cognitions predict the course of bipolar depression, not mania. *Journal of Cognitive Psychotherapy, 18,* 149–162.

Johnson, S. L., Gruber, J. L., & Eisner, L. R. (2007). Emotion and bipolar disorder. In J. Rottenberg & S. L. Johnson (Eds.), *Emotion and psychopathology* (pp. 123–150). Washington, DC: American Psychological Association.

Johnson, S. L., & Kizer, A. (2002). Bipolar and unipolar depression: A comparison of clinical phenomenology and psychosocial predictors. In I. H. Gotlib & C. Hammen (Eds.), *Handbook of depression* (pp. 141–165). New York, NY: Guilford Press.

Johnson, S. L., Meyer, B., Winett, C., & Small, J. (2000). Social support and self-esteem predict changes in bipolar depression but not mania. *Journal of Affective Disorders, 58,* 79–86.

Johnson, S. L., & Miller, I. (1997). Negative life events and time to recovery from episodes of bipolar disorder. *Journal of Abnormal Psychology, 106,* 449–457.

Johnson, S. L., Sandrow, D., Meyer, B., Winters, R., Miller, I., Solomon, D., & Keitner, G. (2000). Increases in manic symptoms following life events involving goal-attainment. *Journal of Abnormal Psychology, 109,* 721–727.

Johnson, S. L., Winett, C. A., Meyer, B., Greenhouse, W. J., & Miller, I. (1999). Social support and the course of bipolar disorder. *Journal of Abnormal Psychology, 108,* 558–566.

Jones, S. H., Hare, D. J., & Evershed, K. (2005). Actigraphic assessment of circadian activity and sleep patterns in bipolar disorder. *Bipolar Disorders, 7,* 176–186.

Judd, L. L., & Akiskal, H. S. (2003). The prevalence and disability of bipolar spectrum disorders in the U.S. population: Re-analysis of the ECA database taking into account subthreshold cases. *Journal of Affective Disorders, 73*(1-2), 123–131.

Judd, L. L., Akiskal, H. S., Schettler, P. J., Endicott, J., Maser, J., Solomon, D. A., . . . Keller, M. B. (2002). The long-term natural history of the weekly symptomatic status of bipolar I disorder. *Archives of General Psychiatry, 59,* 530–537.

Kalivas, P. W., Duffy, P., DuMars, L. A., & Skinner, C. (1988). Behavioral and neurochemical effects of acute and daily cocaine administration in rats. *Journal of Pharmacology and Experimental Therapeutics, 245*(2), 485–492.

Karkowski, L. M., & Kendler, K. S. (1997). An examination of the genetic relationship between bipolar and unipolar illness in an epidemiological sample. *Psychiatric Genetics, 7,* 159–163.

Kaufman, J., Birmaher, B., Brent, D., Rao, U., Flynn, C., Moreci, P., . . . Ryan, N. (1997). Schedule for Affective Disorders and Schizophrenia for School-Age Children—Present and Lifetime Version (K-SADS-PL): Initial reliability and validity data. *Journal of the American Academy of Child and Adolescent Psychiatry, 36,* 980–988.

Keck, P. E., Jr., McElroy, S. L., Strakowski, S. M., Bourne, M. L., & West, S. A. (1997). Compliance with maintenance treatment in bipolar disorder. *Psychopharmacology Bulletin, 33,* 87–91.

Keck, P. E., Jr., McElroy, S. L., Strakowski, S. M., West, S. A., Sax, K. W., Hawkins, J. M., . . . Haggard, P. (1998). Twelve-month outcome of patients with bipolar disorder following hospitalization for a manic or mixed episode. *American Journal of Psychiatry, 155,* 646–652.

Keller, M. B., Lavori, P. W., Coryell, W., Andreasen, N. C., Endicott, J., Clayton, P. J., . . . Hirschfeld, R. M. (1986). Differential outcome of pure manic, mixed/cycling, and pure depressive episodes in patients with bipolar illness. *Journal of the American Medical Association, 255*, 3138–3142.

Keller, M. B., Lavori, P. W., Coryell, W., Endicott, J., & Mueller, T. I. (1993). Bipolar I: A five-year prospective follow-up. *Journal of Nervous and Mental Disease, 181*, 238–245.

Kessler, R. C., Avenevoli, S., & Ries-Merikangas, K. (2001). Mood disorders in children and adolescents: An epidemiologic perspective. *Biological Psychiatry, 49*, 1002–1014.

Kessler, R. C., Chiu, W. T., Demler, O., & Walters, E. E. (2005). Prevalence, severity, and comorbidity of 12-month *DSM-IV* disorders in the National Comorbidity Survey Replication. *Archives of General Psychiatry, 62*, 617–627.

Kessler, R. C., Crum, R. C., Warner, L. A., Nelson, C. B., Schulenberg, J., & Anthony, J. C. (1997). Lifetime co-occurrence of *DSM-III-R* alcohol abuse and dependence with other psychiatric disorders in the National Comorbidity Survey. *Archives of General Psychiatry, 54*, 313–321.

Kilbourne, A. M., Bauer, M. S., Han, X., Haas, G. L., Elder, P., Good, C. B., . . . Pincus, H. (2005). Racial differences in the treatment of veterans with bipolar disorder. *Psychiatric Services, 56*, 1549–1555.

Kim, E. Y., & Miklowitz, D. J. (2002). Childhood mania, attention deficit hyperactivity disorder, and conduct disorder: A critical review of diagnostic dilemmas. *Bipolar Disorders, 4*, 215–225.

Kim, E. Y., & Miklowitz, D. J. (2004). Expressed emotion as a predictor of outcome among bipolar patients undergoing family therapy. *Journal of Affective Disorders, 82*, 343–352.

Klein, D. N., & Depue, R. A. (1984). Continued impairment in persons at risk for bipolar disorder: Results of a 19-month follow-up. *Journal of Abnormal Psychology, 93*, 345–347.

Knutson, B., Adams, C. M., Fong, G. W., & Hommer, D. (2001). Anticipation of increasing monetary reward selectively recruits nucleus accumbens. *Journal of Neuroscience, 21*(16), R C159.

Kochman, F. J., Hantouche, E. G., Ferrari, P., Lancrenon, S., Bayart, D., & Akiskal, H. S. (2005). Cyclothymic temperament as a prospective predictor of bipolarity and suicidality in children and adolescents with major depressive disorder. *Journal of Affective Disorders, 85* (1–2), 181–189.

Kowatch, R. A., Fristad, M., Birmaher, B., Wagner, K. D., Findling, R. L., Hellander, M., & The Child Psychiatric Workgroup on Bipolar Disorder. (2005). Treatment guidelines for children and adolescents with bipolar disorder. *Journal of the American Academy of Child and Adolescent Psychiatry, 44*(3), 213–235.

Kowatch, R. A., Sethuraman, G., Hume, J. H., Kromelis, M., & Weinberg, W. A. (2003). Combination pharmacotherapy in children and adolescents with bipolar disorder. *Biological Psychiatry, 53*, 978–984.

Kowatch, R. A., Youngstrom, E. A., Danielyan, A., & Findling, R. L. (2005). Review and meta-analysis of the phenomenology and clinical characteristics of mania in children and adolescents. *Bipolar Disorders, 7*(6), 483–496.

Kruger, S., Seminowicz, S., Goldapple, K., Kennedy, S. H., & Mayberg, H. S. (2003). State and trait influences on mood regulation in bipolar disorder: Blood flow differences with an acute mood challenge. *Biological Psychiatry, 54*, 1274–1283.

Kupfer, D. J., Frank, E., Grochocinski, V. J., Houck, P. R., & Brown, C. (2005). African-American participants in a bipolar disorder registry: clinical and treatment characteristics. *Bipolar Disorders, 7*(82–88).

Kwapil, T. R., Miller, M. B., Zinser, M. C., Chapman, L. J., Chapman, J., & Eckblad, M. (2000). A longitudinal study of high scorers on the hypomanic personality scale. *Journal of Abnormal Psychology, 109,* 222–226.

Lam, D. H., Watkins, E. R., Hayward, P., Bright, J., Wright, K., Kerr, N., . . . Sham, P. (2003). A randomized controlled study of cognitive therapy of relapse prevention for bipolar affective disorder: Outcome of the first year. *Archives of General Psychiatry, 60,* 145–152.

LaPalme, M., Hodgins, S., & LaRoche, C. (1997). Children of parents with bipolar disorder: A meta-analysis of risk for mental disorders. *Canadian Journal of Psychiatry, 42,* 623–631.

Lawrence, N. S., Williams, A. M., Surguladze, S., Giampietro, V., Brammer, M. J., Andrew, C., . . . Phillips, M. L. (2004). Subcortical and ventral prefrontal responses to facial expressions distinguish patients with BPD and major depression. *Biological Psychiatry, 55,* 578–587.

Leibenluft, E. (1997). Issues in the treatment of women with bipolar illness. *Journal of Clinical Psychiatry, 58* (Suppl. 15), 5–11.

Leibenluft, E., Albert, P. S., Rosenthal, N. E., & Wehr, T. A. (1996). Relationship between sleep and mood in patients with rapid-cycling bipolar disorder. *Psychiatry Research, 63,* 161–168.

Leibenluft, E., Charney, D. S., Towbin, K. E., Bhangoo, R. K., & Pine, D. S. (2003). Defining clinical phenotypes of juvenile mania. *American Journal of Psychiatry, 160,* 430–437.

Leibenluft, E., Cohen, P., Gorrindo, T., Brook, J. S., & Pine, D. S. (2006). Chronic vs. episodic irritability in youth: A community-based, longitudinal study of clinical and diagnostic associations. *Journal of Child and Adolescent Psychopharmacology, 16,* 456–466.

Lennox, R., Jacob, R., Calder, A. J., Lupson, V., & Bullmore, E. T. (2004). Behavioral and neurocognitive responses to sad facial affect are attenuated in patients with mania. *Psychological Medicine, 34,* 795–802.

Leverich, G. S., & Post, R. M. (1998). Life charting of affective disorders. *CNS Spectrums, 3,* 21–37.

Lewinsohn, P. M., Klein, D. N., & Seeley, J. R. (2000). Bipolar disorder during adolescence and young adulthood in a community sample. *Bipolar Disorders, 2,* 281–293.

Lewinsohn, P. M., Seeley, J. R., Buckley, M. E., & Klein, D. N. (2002). Bipolar disorder in adolescence and young adulthood. *Child and Adolescent Psychiatric Clinics of North America, 11,* 461–475.

Lopez, L. S., Croes, E. A., Sayed-Tabatabaei, F. A., Stephan, C., Van Broeckhoven, C., & Van Duijn, C. M. (2005). The dopamine D4 receptor gene 48-base-pair-repeat polymorphism and mood disorders: A meta-analysis. *Biological Psychiatry, 57,* 999–1003.

Lotrich, F. E., & Pollock, B. G. (2004). Meta-analysis of serotonin transporter polymorphisms and affective disorders. *Psychiatric Genetics, 14,* 121–129.

Lozano, B. L., & Johnson, S. L. (2001). Can personality traits predict increases in manic and depressive symptoms? *Journal of Affective Disorders, 63,* 103–111.

Luby, J. L., & Navsaria, N. (2010). Pediatric bipolar disorder: evidence for prodromal states and early markers. *Journal of Child Psychology and Psychiatry, 51,* 459–471.

Lyon, H. M., Startup, M., & Bentall, R. P. (1999). Social cognition and the manic defense: Attributions, selective attention, and self-schema in bipolar affective disorder. *Journal of Abnormal Psychology, 108,* 273–282.

Malhi, G. S., Adams, D., & Berk, M. (2009). Medicating mood with maintenance in mind: bipolar depression pharmacotherapy. *Bipolar Disorders, 11*(Suppl. 2), 55–76.

Malkoff-Schwartz, S., Frank, E., Anderson, B., Sherrill, J. T., Siegel, L., Patterson, D., & Kupfer, D. J. (1998). Stressful life events and social rhythm disruption in the onset of manic and depressive bipolar episodes: A preliminary investigation. *Archives of General Psychiatry, 55,* 702–707.

Malkoff-Schwartz, S., Frank, E., Anderson, B. P., Hlastala, S. A., Luther, J. F., Sherrill, J. T., . . . Kupfer, D. J. (2000). Social rhythm disruption and stressful life events in the onset of bipolar and unipolar episodes. *Psychological Medicine, 30,* 1005–1016.

Manji, H. (2009). The role of synpatic and cellular plasticity cascades in the pathophysiology and treatment of mood and psychotic disorders. *Bipolar Disorders,* 11(Suppl. 1), 2–3.

Manki, H., Kanba, S., Muramatsu, T., & Higuchi, S. (1996). Dopamine D2, D3 and D4 receptor and transporter gene polymorphisms and mood disorders. *Journal of Affective Disorders, 40,* 7–13.

Masi, G., Perugi, G., Toni, C., Millepiedi, S., Mucci, M., Bertini, N., & Akiskal, H. S. (2004). Obsessive-compulsive bipolar comorbidity: Focus on children and adolescents. *Journal of Affective Disorders, 78,* 175–183.

Mayberg, H. S., Keightley, M., Mahurin, R. K., & Brannan, S. K. (2004). Neuropsychiatric aspects of mood and affective disorders. In R. E. Hales & S. C. Yudofsky (Eds.), *Essentials of neuropsychiatry and clinical neurosciences* (pp. 489–517). Washington, DC: American Psychiatric Publishing.

McAllister-Williams, R. H. (2006). Relapse prevention in bipolar disorder: A critical review of current guidelines. *Journal of Psychopharmacology, 20* (2 Suppl.), 12–16.

McClellan, J. (2005). Commentary: Treatment guidelines for child and adolescent bipolar disorder. *Journal of the American Academy of Child and Adolescent Psychiatry, 44,* 236–239.

McGuffin, P., Rijsdijk, F., Andrew, M., Sham, P., Katz, R., & Cardno, A. (2003). The heritability of bipolar affective disorder and the genetic relationship to unipolar depression. *Archives of General Psychiatry, 60,* 497–502.

Merikangas, K. R., Akiskal, H. S., Angst, J., Greenberg, P. E., Hirschfeld, R. M. A., Petukhova, M., & Kessler, R. C. (2007). Lifetime and 12-month prevalence of bipolar spectrum disorder in the National Comorbidity Survey replication. *Archives of General Psychiatry, 64*(5), 543–552.

Meyer, S. E., & Carlson, G. A. (2010). Development, age of onset, and phenomenology in bipolar disorder. In D. J. Miklowitz & D. Cicchetti (Eds.), *Understanding bipolar disorder: a developmental psychopathology perspective* (pp. 35–66). New York, NY: Guilford Press.

Meyer, B., Johnson, S. L., & Carver, C. S. (1999). Exploring behavioral activation and inhibition sensitivities among college students at-risk for bipolar-spectrum symptomatology. *Journal of Psychopathology and Behavioral Assessment, 21,* 275–292.

Meyer, B., Johnson, S. L., & Winters, R. (2001). Responsiveness to threat and incentive in bipolar disorder: Relations of the BIS/BAS scales with symptoms. *Journal of Psychopathology and Behavioral Assessment, 23,* 133–143.

Miklowitz, D. J., Alatiq, Y., Geddes, J. R., Goodwin, G. M., & Williams, J. M. (2010). Thought suppression in patients with bipolar disorder. *Journal of Abnormal Psychology, 119*(2), 355–365.

Miklowitz, D. J., Axelson, D. A., Birmaher, B., George, E. L., Taylor, D. O., Schneck, C. D., . . . Brent, D. A. (2008). Family-focused treatment for adolescents with bipolar disorder: Results of a 2-year randomized trial. *Archives of General Psychiatry, 65*(9), 1053–1061.

Miklowitz, D. J., Chang, K. D., Taylor, D. O., George, E. L., Singh, M. K., Schneck, C. D., . . . Garber, J. (2011). Early psychosocial intervention for youth at risk for bipolar disorder: A 1-year treatment development trial. *Bipolar Disorders, 13*(1), 67–75.

Miklowitz, D. J., George, E. L., Richards, J. A., Simoneau, T. L., & Suddath, R. L. (2003). A randomized study of family-focused psychoeducation and pharmacotherapy in the outpatient management of bipolar disorder. *Archives of General Psychiatry, 60,* 904–912.

Miklowitz, D. J., Goldstein, M. J., Nuechterlein, K. H., Snyder, K. S., & Mintz, J. (1988). Family factors and the course of bipolar affective disorder. *Archives of General Psychiatry, 45,* 225–231.

Miklowitz, D. J., Goodwin, G. M., Bauer, M., & Geddes, J. R. (2008). Common and specific elements of psychosocial treatments for bipolar disorder: A survey of clinicians participating in randomized trials. *Journal of Psychiatric Practice, 14*(2), 77–85.

Miklowitz, D. J., Otto, M. W., Frank, E., Reilly-Harrington, N.A., Wisniewski, S. R., Kogan, J. N., & Sachs, G. S. (2007). Psychosocial treatments for bipolar depression: A 1-year randomized trial from the Systematic Treatment Enhancement Program. *Archives of General Psychiatry, 64*, 419–427.

Miklowitz, D. J. & Scott, J. (2009). Psychosocial treatments for bipolar disorder: Cost-effectiveness, mediating mechanisms, and future directions. *Bipolar Disorders, 11*, 110–122.

Monroe, S. M., Harkness, K., Simons, A., & Thase, M. (2001). Life stress and the symptoms of major depression. *Journal of Nervous and Mental Disease, 189*, 168–175.

Muglia, P., Petronis, A., Mundo, E., Lander, S., Cate, T., & Kennedy, J. L. (2002). Dopamine D4 receptor and tyrosine hydroxylase genes in bipolar disorder: Evidence for a role of DRD4. *Molecular Psychiatry, 7*, 860–866.

Murphy, F. C., Sahakian, B. J., Rubinsztein, J. S., Michael, A., Rogers, R. D., Robbins, T. W., & Paykel, E. S. (1999). Emotional bias and inhibitory control processes in mania and depression. *Psychological Medicine, 29*, 1307–1321.

Murray, R. M., Sham, P., Van Os, J., Zanelli, J., Cannon, M., & McDonald, C. (2004). A developmental model for similarities and dissimilarities between schizophrenia and bipolar disorder. *Schizophrenia Research, 71*, 405–416.

National Institute of Mental Health. (2001). Research Roundtable on Prepubertal Bipolar Disorder. *Journal of the American Academy of Child and Adolescent Psychiatry, 40*, 871–878.

Nowakowska, C., Strong, C. M., Santosa, C. M., Wang, P. W., & Ketter, T. A. (2005). Temperamental commonalities and differences in euthymic mood disorder patients, creative controls, and healthy controls. *Journal of Affective Disorders, 85*, 207–215.

Ogden, C. A., Rich, M. E., Schork, N. J., Paulus, M. P., Geyer, M. A., Lohr, J. B., . . . Niculescu, A. B. (2004). Candidate genes, pathways, and mechanisms for bipolar (manic-depressive) and related disorders: An expanded convergent functional genomics approach. *Molecular Psychiatry, 9*, 1007–1029.

Otto, M. W., Simon, N. M., Wisniewski, S. R., Miklowitz, D. J., Kogan, J. N., Reilly-Harrington, N. A., . . . STEP-BD Investigators. (2006). Prospective 12-month course of bipolar disorder in outpatients with and without anxiety comorbidity. *British Journal of Psychiatry, 189*, 20–25.

Pardoen, D., Bauewens, F., Dramaix, M., Tracy, A., Genevrois, C., Staner, L., & Mendlewicz, J. (1996). Life events and primary affective disorders: A one-year prospective study. *British Journal of Psychiatry, 169*, 160–166.

Patel, N. C., DelBello, M. P., Keck, P. E., Jr., & Strakowski, S. M. (2005). Ethnic differences in maintenance antipsychotic prescription among adolescents with bipolar disorder. *Journal of Child and Adolescent Psychopharmacology, 15*(6), 938–946.

Perlis, R. H., Miyahara, S., Marangell, L. B., Wisniewski, S. R., Ostacher, M., DelBello, M. P., . . . STEP-BD Investigators. (2004). Long-term implications of early onset in bipolar disorder: Data from the first 1,000 participants in the Systematic Treatment Enhancement Program for Bipolar Disorder (STEP-BD). *Biological Psychiatry, 55*, 875–881.

Perlis, R. H., Ostacher, M. J., Patel, J., Marangell, L. B., Zhang, H., Wisniewski, S. R., . . . Thase, M. E. (2006). Predictors of recurrence in bipolar disorder: Primary outcomes from the Systematic Treatment Enhancement Program for Bipolar Disorder (STEP-BD). *American Journal of Psychiatry, 163*(2), 217–224.

Perris, H. (1984). Life events and depression, Part 2: Results in diagnostic subgroups and in relation to the recurrence of depression. *Journal of Affective Disorders, 7*, 25–36.

Perry, A., Tarrier, N., Morriss, R., McCarthy, E., & Limb, K. (1999). Randomised controlled trial of efficacy of teaching patients with bipolar disorder to identify early symptoms of relapse and obtain treatment. *British Medical Journal, 16,* 149–153.

Phillips, M. L., Drevets, W. C., Rauch, S. L., & Lane, R. (2003). Neurobiology of emotion perception, Part II: Implications for major psychiatric disorders. *Biological Psychiatry, 54,* 515–528.

Post, R. M., Denicoff, K. D., Leverich, G. S., Altshuler, L. L., Frye, M. A., Suppes, T. M., . . . Nolen, W. A. (2003). Morbidity in 258 bipolar outpatients followed for 1 year with daily prospective ratings on the NIMH life chart method. *Journal of Clinical Psychiatry, 64,* 680–690.

Prien, R. F., & Potter, W. Z. (1990). NIMH Workshop report on treatment of bipolar disorder. *Psychopharmacology Bulletin, 26,* 409–427.

Rea, M. M., Tompson, M., Miklowitz, D. J., Goldstein, M. J., Hwang, S., & Mintz, J. (2003). Family focused treatment vs. individual treatment for bipolar disorder: Results of a randomized clinical trial. *Journal of Consulting and Clinical Psychology, 71,* 482–492.

Regeer, E. J., ten Have, M., Rosso, M. L., Hakkaart-van Roijen, L., Vollebergh, W., & Nolen, W. A. (2004). Prevalence of bipolar disorder in the general population: A reappraisal study of the Netherlands Mental Health Survey and Incidence Study. *Acta Psychiatrica Scandinavica, 110,* 374–382.

Regier, D. A., Farmer, M. E., Rae, D. S., Locke, B. Z., Keith, S. J., Judd, L. L., & Goodwin, F. K. (1990). Comorbidity of mental disorders with alcohol and other drug abuse: Results from the Epidemiologic Catchment Area (ECA) Study. *Journal of the American Medical Association, 264,* 2511–2518.

Reich, L. H., Davies, R. K., & Himmelhoch, J. M. (1974). Excessive alcohol use in manic-depressive illness. *American Journal of Psychiatry, 131*(1), 83–86.

Reichart, C. G., van der Ende, J., Wals, M., Hillegers, M. H., Nolen, W. A., Ormel, J., & Verhulst, F. C. (2005). The use of the GBI as predictor of bipolar disorder in a population of adolescent offspring of parents with a bipolar disorder. *Journal of Affective Disorders, 89*(1–3), 147–155.

Reilly-Harrington, N. A., Alloy, L. B., Fresco, D. M., & Whitehouse, W. G. (1999). Cognitive styles and life events interact to predict bipolar and unipolar symptomatology. *Journal of Abnormal Psychology, 108,* 567–578.

Rice, J., Reich, T., Andreasen, N. C., Endicott, J., Van Eerdewegh, M., Fishman, R., . . . Klerman, G. L. (1987). The familial transmission of bipolar illness. *Archives of General Psychiatry, 44,* 441–447.

Richards, R., Kinney, D. K., Lunde, I., Benet, M., & Merzel, A. P. (1988). Creativity in manic-depressives, cyclothymes, their normal relatives, and control subjects. *Journal of Abnormal Psychology, 97,* 281–288.

Robinson, T. E., & Becker, J. B. (1986). Enduring changes in brain and behavior produced by chronic amphetamine administration: A review and evaluation of animal models of amphetamine psychosis. *Brain Research Review, 11,* 157–198.

Roybal, K., Theobold, D., Graham, A., DiNieri, J. A., Russo, S. J., Krishnan, V., . . . McClung, C. A. (2007). Mania-like behavior induced by disruption of CLOCK. *Proceedings of the National Academy of Sciences USA, 104*(15), 6406–6411.

Ryan, N. D., Williamson, D. E., Iyengar, S., Orvaschel, H., Reich, T., Dahl, R. E., & Puig-Antich, J. (1992). A secular increase in child and adolescent onset affective disorder. *Journal of the American Academy of Child and Adolescent Psychiatry, 31,* 600–605.

Sachs, G. S., Nierenberg, A. A., Calabrese, J. R., Marangell, L. B., Wisniewski, S. R., Gyulai, L., . . . Thase, M. E. (2007). Effectiveness of adjunctive antidepressant treatment for bipolar depression. *New England Journal of Medicine, 356*(17), 1711–1722.

Sato, T., Bottlender, R., Kleindienst, N., & Moller, H. J. (2002). Syndromes and phenomenological subtypes underlying acute mania: A factor analytic study of 576 manic patients.
*American Journal of Psychiatry, 159*(6), 968–974.

Schneck, C. D., Miklowitz, D. J., Calabrese, J. R., Allen, M. H., Thomas, M. R., Wisniewski,
S. R., . . . Sachs, G. S. (2004). Phenomenology of rapid cycling bipolar disorder: Data from
the first 500 participants in the Systematic Treatment Enhancement Program for Bipolar
Disorder. *American Journal of Psychiatry, 161*, 1902–1908.

Scott, J., Paykel, E., Morriss, R., Bentall, R., Kinderman, P., Johnson, T., . . . Hayhurst, H. (2006).
Cognitive behaviour therapy for severe and recurrent bipolar disorders: A randomised
controlled trial. *British Journal of Psychiatry, 188*, 313–320.

Simeonova, D. I., Chang, K. D., Strong, C., & Ketter, T. A. (2005). Creativity in familial bipolar
disorder. *Journal of Psychiatric Research, 39*(6), 623–631.

Simon, G. E., Ludman, E. J., Unutzer, J., Bauer, M. S., Operskalski, B., & Rutter, C. (2005).
Randomized trial of a population-based care program for people with bipolar disorder.
*Psychological Medicine, 35*(1), 13–24.

Simon, N. M., Otto, M. W., Weiss, R., Bauer, M. S., Miyahara, S., Wisniewski, S. R., . . .
STEP-BD Investigators. (2004). Pharmacotherapy for bipolar disorder and comorbid
conditions: Baseline data from STEP-BD. *Journal of Clinical Psychopharmacology, 24*,
512–520.

Simoneau, T. L., Miklowitz, D. J., & Saleem, R. (1998). Expressed emotion and interactional patterns in the families of bipolar patients. *Journal of Abnormal Psychology, 107*,
497–507.

Smith, D. J., Harrison, N., Muir, W., & Blackwood, D. H. (2005). The high prevalence of bipolar
spectrum disorders in young adults with recurrent depression: Toward an innovative
diagnostic framework. *Journal of Affective Disorders, 84*, 167–178.

Sobczak, S., Honig, A., Schmitt, J. A., Jr., & Riedel, W. J. (2003). Pronounced cognitive deficits
following an intravenous L-tryptophan challenge in first-degree relatives of bipolar patients
compared to healthy controls. *Neuropsychopharmacology, 28*, 711–719.

Sobczak, S., Riedel, W. J., Booij, L., Aan het Rot, M., Deutz, N. E. P., & Honig, A. (2002).
Cognition following acute tryptophan depletion: Differences between first-degree relatives
of bipolar disorder patients and matched healthy control volunteers. *Psychological Medicine,
32*, 503–515.

Solomon, D. A., Leon, A. C., Endicott, J., Coryell, W. H., Mueller, T. I., Posternak, M. A., &
Keller, M. B. (2003). Unipolar mania over the course of a 20-year follow-up study. *American
Journal of Psychiatry, 160*, 2049–2051.

Staley, J. K., Malison, R. T., & Innis, R. B. (1998). Imaging of the serotonergic system:
Interactions of neuroanatomical and functional abnormalities of depression. *Biological
Psychiatry, 44*, 534–549.

Stern, G. S., & Berrenberg, J. L. (1979). Skill-set, success outcome, and mania as determinants of
the illusion of control. *Journal of Research in Personality, 13*, 206–220.

Stockmeier, C. A. (2003). Involvement of serotonin in depression: Evidence from postmortem
and imaging studies of serotonin receptors and the serotonin transporter. *Journal of
Psychiatric Research, 37*, 357–373.

Strakowski, S. M., DelBello, M. P., Fleck, D. E., & Arndt, S. (2000). The impact of substance
abuse on the course of bipolar disorder. *Biological Psychiatry, 48*, 477–485.

Strakowski, S. M., Keck, P. E., McElroy, S. L., West, S. A., Sax, K. W., Hawkins, J. M., . . .
Bourne, M. L. (1998). Twelve-month outcome after a first hospitalization for affective
psychosis. *Archives of General Psychiatry, 55*, 49–55.

Strakowski, S. M., Sax, K. W., Setters, M. J., & Keck, P. E., Jr., (1996). Enhanced response to repeated d-amphetamine challenge: Evidence for behavioral sensitization in humans. *Biological Psychiatry, 40*, 827–880.

Strakowski, S. M., Sax, K. W., Setters, M. J., Stanton, S. P., & Keck, P. E., Jr. (1997). Lack of enhanced behavioral response to repeated d-amphetamine challenge in first-episode psychosis: Implications for a sensitization model of psychosis in humans. *Biological Psychiatry, 42*, 749–755.

Strecker, E. A. (1921). The prognosis in manic-depressive psychosis. *New York Medical Journal, 114*, 209–211.

Strober, M., Morrell, W., Lampert, C., & Burroughs, J. (1990). Relapse following discontinuation of lithium maintenance therapy in adolescents with bipolar I illness: A naturalistic study. *American Journal of Psychiatry, 147*, 457–461.

Suppes, T., Baldessarini, R. J., Faedda, G. L., Tondo, L., & Tohen, M. (1993, September/October). Discontinuation of maintenance treatment in bipolar disorder: Risks and implications. *Harvard Review of Psychiatry, 1*, 131–144.

Suppes, T., Leverich, G. S., Keck, P. E., Nolen, W. A., Denicoff, K. D., Altshuler, L. L., . . . Post, R. M. (2001). The Stanley Foundation Bipolar Treatment Outcome Network, Part II: Demographics and illness characteristics of the first 261 patients. *Journal of Affective Disorders, 67*, 45–59.

Swann, A. C., Dougherty, D. M., Pazzaglia, P. J., Pham, M., & Moeller, F. G. (2004). Impulsivity: A link between bipolar disorder and substance abuse. *Bipolar Disorders, 6*, 204–212.

Thase, M. E., Jindal, R., & Howland, R. H. (2002). Biological aspects of depression. In I. H. Gotlib & C. L. Hammen (Eds.), *Handbook of depression* (pp. 192–218). New York, NY: Guilford Press.

Tohen, M., Waternaux, C. M., & Tsuang, M. T. (1990). Outcome in mania: A 4-year prospective follow-up of 75 patients utilizing survival analysis. *Archives of General Psychiatry, 47*, 1106–1111.

Tondo, L., & Baldessarini, R. J. (2000). Reducing suicide risk during lithium maintenance treatment. *Journal of Clinical Psychiatry, 61*(Suppl. 9), 97–104.

Versace, A., Thompson, W. K., Zhou, D., Almeida, J. R., Hassel, S., Klein, C. R., . . . Phillips, M. L. (2010). Abnormal left and right amygdala-orbitofrontal cortical functional connectivity to emotional faces: State versus trait vulnerability markers of depression in bipolar disorder. *Biological Psychiatry, 67*, 422–431.

Wang, F., Kalmar, J. H., He, Y., Jackowski, M., Chepenik, L. G., Edmiston, E. E., . . . Blumberg, H. P. (2009). Functional and structural connectivity between the perigenual anterior cingulate and amygdala in bipolar disorder. *Biological Psychiatry, 66*, 516–521.

Wehr, T. A., Sack, D. A., & Rosenthal, N. E. (1987). Sleep reduction as a final common pathway in the genesis of mania. *American Journal of Psychiatry, 144*, 210–214.

Weissman, M. M., & Myers, J. K. (1978). Affective disorders in a U.S. urban community: The use of research diagnostic criteria in an epidemiological survey. *Archives of General Psychiatry, 35*, 1304–1311.

Wickramaratne, P. J., Weissman, M. M., Leaf, J. P., & Holford, T. R. (1989). Age, period and cohort effects on the risk of major depression: Results from five United States communities. *Journal of Clinical Epidemiology, 42*, 333–343.

Willcutt, E., & Mcqueen, M. (2010). Genetic and environmental vulnerability to bipolar spectrum disorders. In D. J. Miklowitz & D. Cicchetti (Eds.), *Understanding bipolar disorder: A developmental psychopathology perspective*. New York, NY: Guilford Press.

Willner, P. (1995). Sensitization of dopamine D-sub-2- or D-sub-3-type receptors as a final common pathway in antidepressant drug action. *Clinical Neuropharmacology, 18*(Suppl. 1), S49–S56.

Wozniak, J., Biederman, J., & Richards, J. A. (2001). Diagnostic and therapeutic dilemmas in the management of pediatric-onset bipolar disorder. *Journal of Clinical Psychiatry, 62* (Suppl. 14), 10–15.

Yan, L. J., Hammen, C., Cohen, A. N., Daley, S. E., & Henry, R. M. (2004). Expressed emotion versus relationship quality variables in the prediction of recurrence in bipolar patients. *Journal of Affective Disorders, 83*, 199–206.

# CHAPTER 11

# Panic Disorder, Agoraphobia, Social Anxiety Disorder, and Specific Phobias

DAVID P. VALENTINER and THOMAS A. FERGUS

PANIC DISORDER, SOCIAL anxiety disorder, and specific phobias are prevalent and often quite debilitating. Anxiety disorders are a common type of diagnosable psychological problem in the United States, with almost one-third of the population meeting criteria for at least one anxiety disorder at some time in their life—a prevalence rate second only to substance use disorders (Aalto-Setaelae, Marttunen, Tuulio-Henriksson, & Loennqvist, 2001; Beckman et al., 1998; Kessler et al., 1994). In addition, these disorders lead to poor educational outcomes (Kessler, Foster, Saunders, & Stang, 1995). Goisman et al. (1994) found that about 50% of patients with panic disorder and/or agoraphobia were receiving unemployment, disability, welfare, social security payments, or some other form of financial assistance. Social anxiety disorder, the third most common psychiatric disorder in the United States (Keller, 2003), is associated with compromised functioning in school and at work (Liebowitz, Gorman, Fyer, & Klein, 1985; Turner, Beidel, Dancu, & Keys, 1986; Van Ameringen, Mancini, & Streiner, 1993; Wittchen & Beloch, 1996; Zhang, Ross, & Davidson, 2004). Anxiety disorders create an enormous burden on society, with annual costs estimated at $42.3 billion, or $1,542 per individual meeting the criteria for an anxiety disorder (Greenberg et al., 1999). Clearly, these disorders are common and substantially interfere with quality of life (Olatunji, Cisler, & Tolin, 2007).

## DESCRIPTION OF THE DISORDER

### PANIC ATTACKS

Panic attacks are defined as discrete periods of intense fear or discomfort that begin abruptly and reach their peak within 10 minutes. The *Diagnostic and Statistical Manual of Mental Disorders* (4th ed., text revision, *DSM-IV-TR*; American Psychiatric

Association, 2000) requires that at least four of the following 13 symptoms be present: palpitations, pounding heart, or accelerated heart rate; sweating; trembling or shaking; sensations of shortness of breath or smothering; feelings of choking; chest pain or discomfort; nausea or abdominal distress; feeling dizzy, unsteady, light-headed, or faint; derealization or depersonalization; fear of losing control or going crazy; fear of dying; paresthesias; and chills or hot flushes (i.e., heat sensations). Panic attacks occur in nonclinical populations, with about 6.3% of a community sample reporting having experienced a full-blown panic attack some time during their lives (Norton, Zvolensky, Bonn-Miller, Cox, & Norton, 2008) without debilitating conse-quences, development of a disorder, or treatment-seeking behavior.

Panic attacks also occur in the context of many mental disorders, especially anxiety disorders. For example, the acute fear responses that individuals with specific phobias experience in the presence of feared objects or situations (e.g., spider phobics' responses to spiders) sometimes meet the criteria for a panic attack. When a panic attack is triggered by exposure to or anticipation of a feared object or situation, it is considered to be a cued panic attack (also known as expected panic attacks). Cued panic attacks are most common among individuals with other anxiety disorders, including social anxiety disorder and specific phobias.

In addition to cued panic attacks, panic attacks can also be unexpected (or uncued). Unexpected panic attacks are not associated with any specific object or situation. Anyone, including individuals with no diagnoses, can experience cued or unexpected panic attacks. Cued panic attacks are not uncommon among individuals with social or specific phobias, but they also occur in a substantial number of patients with panic disorder (Craske et al., 2010). One issue that should be considered when diagnosing panic disorder is that the term "unexpected" may have different mean-ings across various cultural contexts (Lewis-Fernández et al., 2010).

## PANIC DISORDER WITH AND WITHOUT AGORAPHOBIA, AND AGORAPHOBIA WITHOUT A HISTORY OF PANIC

The diagnosis of panic disorder (with or without agoraphobia) requires recurrent and unexpected (uncued) panic attacks, followed by at least 1 month of concern about (a) additional attacks, (b) the implications of the attack, or (c) changes in behavior (APA, 2000). The *DSM-IV* does not recognize subtypes of panic disorder (e.g., respiratory, nocturnal, nonfearful, cognitive, and vestibular subtypes), although research on this possibility continues (see Kircanski, Craske, Epstein, & Wittchen, 2010).

Agoraphobia is a fear of being in public places or situations where escape might be difficult or where help may be unavailable if a panic attack occurred. Patients with agoraphobia avoid (or endure with marked distress) certain situations, includ-ing large stores; open or crowded public spaces; traveling in buses, trains, or cars; and being far or away from one's home (APA, 2000).

The *DSM-III* viewed agoraphobia as primary and panic attacks as a frequent but secondary feature. It included the diagnostic categories of "agoraphobia with panic attacks" and "agoraphobia without panic attacks." Subsequent revisions of the *DSM* have reversed this view and have included diagnostic categories of "panic disorder with agoraphobia," "panic disorder without agoraphobia," and an infrequently used category of "agoraphobia without panic disorder." This last category is used for patients who deny a history or have an unclear history of panic attacks, or who report histories of panic-like experiences (e.g., limited symptom panic attacks). Such cases may be difficult to differentiate from specific phobias, obsessive-compulsive disorder, and posttraumatic stress disorder. Although agoraphobia has most often been seen as a frequent but secondary feature of panic disorder since the publication of the *DSM-III-R*, some clinicians believe it is a distinctive disorder independent of panic disorder; an issue that can be considered through the continuation of a means for diagnosing agoraphobia separate from panic disorder (Wittchen, Gloster, Beesdo-Baum, Fava, & Craske, 2010).

## Social Anxiety Disorder

Social anxiety disorder, sometimes referred to as social phobia, is a marked and persistent fear of social or performance situations in which embarrassment may occur. Exposure or anticipation of the feared social situation almost invariably provokes anxiety or fear. Acute fear responses can take the form of situationally bound or predisposed panic attacks. Feared situations include performing certain activities in the presence of others (such as speaking, eating, drinking, or writing), or fearing that one may do something that will cause humiliation or embarrassment, such as saying something stupid or not knowing what to say, behaving inappropriately, or appearing overly anxious. The diagnosis requires that these feared situations are either avoided or endured with significant distress, and that the individual recognizes, at some time during the course of the disorder, the fear to be irrational (APA, 2000). Cultural factors are likely to affect the assessment of this requirement, as it implies a comparison to the patient's social reference group (Lewis-Fernández et al., 2010).

If an individual fears many or most social interactions, the generalized subtype should be specified. Generalized social anxiety disorder overlaps considerably with avoidant personality disorder, "so much so that they may be alternative conceptualizations of the same or similar conditions" (APA, 2000, p. 720). Individuals not assigned to the generalized subtype are commonly viewed as belonging to a nongeneralized subtype or to a specific subtype. The generalized subtype is associated with greater comorbidity, earlier age of onset, and greater heritability compared to the nongeneralized subtype, and is generally taken to be an indicator of greater severity, as is the overlapping diagnosis of avoidant personality disorder (Bögels et al., 2010).

Social anxiety disorder may subsume four other possible disorders. First, the separate diagnostic category of selective mutism may be an expression of social anxiety disorder during the developmental context of childhood (Bögels et al., 2010). This conceptualization of selective mutism treats the refusal to talk as a form of social avoidance. Continuation of a means for diagnosing selective mutism separate from social anxiety disorder will allow researchers to consider this possibility. Second, Feusner, Phillips, and Stein (2010) have suggested that the *DSM-5* should include a provisional diagnostic category for Olfactory Reference Disorder. This condition is characterized by a preoccupation with the erroneous belief that one emits an offensive body odor. Third, and closely related to Olfactory Reference Disorder, the *DSM-IV-TR* recognizes a culturally bound syndrome, Taijin Kyofusho, found mainly in Japan and South Korea. The Japanese characters for Taijin Kyofusho are read as Taein-kongpo in Korea, a term that is used interchangeably with social anxiety disorder (Kim, 2010). These conditions appear to be the same as anthropophobia, a condition recognized in the *ICD-10* (World Health Organization, 1992). These conditions involve a fear of offending and making others uncomfortable, such as through poor manners or bad odors, and have also been documented in Western cultures (Kim, Rapee, & Gaston, 2008; McNally, Cassiday, & Calamari, 1990). Lewis-Fernández et al. (2010) have suggested that the definition of social anxiety disorder could be broadened to subsume Taijin Kyofusho and equivalent conditions. Fourth, the *DSM-IV-TR* does not recognize test anxiety as a separate disorder but subsumes it within social anxiety disorder. LeBeau et al. (2010) suggested that one form of test anxiety may be a form of social anxiety disorder in that it involves social evaluative concerns and acute fear reactions, and a second form may be a form of generalized anxiety disorder in that involves anticipatory anxiety and worry.

By including the generalized subtype specifier, the *DSM-IV-TR* allows for the recognition that there may be two distinct conditions within the diagnostic category of social anxiety disorder. This might also, and perhaps more effectively, be accomplished by differentiating individuals who have acute fear reactions in a relatively circumscribed social performance situation, akin to specific phobias (see Hook & Valentiner, 2002), from those individuals who have relatively more chronic social anxiety (Bögels et al., 2010).

## SPECIFIC PHOBIAS

Specific phobias are marked and persistent fears of clearly discernible, circumscribed objects or situations. Exposure or anticipation of exposure to the feared object or situation almost invariably provokes anxiety or fear. Acute fear responses can take the form of situationally bound or predisposed panic attacks. Five subtypes of specific phobia are recognized by the *DSM-IV-TR* and are specified based on the type of object or situation that is feared: animals (e.g., dogs, snakes, spiders, etc.), natural environment (e.g., storms, water, heights, etc.), blood-injection-injury (BII; e.g., seeing blood, getting an injection with a syringe, etc.), situations (e.g., elevators, flying, etc.), and other (e.g., situations related to choking, vomiting, or illness; fear of falling without means of physical support, etc.). The diagnosis requires that these feared situations are either avoided or endured with significant distress (APA, 2000).

Although many individuals meet criteria for a specific phobia, very few seek treatment (Barlow, DiNardo, Vermilyea, Vermilyea, & Blanchard, 1986). Claustrophobia (fear of closed spaces) and acrophobia (fear of heights) are the most common subtypes seen in clinical settings (Emmelkamp, 1988). Those seeking treatment also show higher rates of comorbid diagnoses (Barlow, 1988). Although subtypes of specific phobia appear to have relatively distinctive ages of onset (Öst, 1987), they are generally accepted as constituting a single category. An exception is that the BII subtype may be or may subsume a disorder with distinct features and different etiological factors (LeBeau et al., 2010; Page, 1994).

## DIAGNOSTIC CONSIDERATIONS

Anxiety disorders identified in the *DSM-IV-TR* show considerable overlap and high rates of comorbidity. These observations suggest that a categorical approach to understanding these problems is not optimal. In addition, these problems do not appear to be discontinuous from normal (nonclinical) variation. Dimensional methods may more accurately model the nature of these problems (Krueger, 1999; Watson, 2005) and may eventually come into use. Given the usefulness of the diagnostic categories of panic disorder, social anxiety disorder, and specific phobias, it is not surprising that the definitions of these diagnoses have not changed substantially since the publication of the *DSM-III-R*.

One model for organizing internalizing problems involves distinguishing between distress and fear disorders (Krueger, 1999; Watson, 2005). Panic disorder and specific phobias involve acute fear reactions and avoidance behavior that appear to be controlled by specific stimuli. For panic disorder, the controlling stimulus is an internal sensation, such as a racing heart or dizziness. Each subtype of specific phobia is cued by a class of controlling stimuli (e.g., snakes, heights, etc.). Obsessive-compulsive disorder also involves a controlling stimulus (i.e., an intrusive thought or image). These fear disorders can be distinguished from distress disorders that include major depressive disorder, generalized anxiety disorder, and other internalizing disorders not characterized by an acute fear response.

Social anxiety disorders as a group appear to be distress disorders, showing closer relationships with depression and generalized anxiety than with panic disorder (Watson, 2005). However, for the nongeneralized subtype, acute fear reactions (including cued panic attacks) are often triggered by social situations, such as having to give a speech to an audience. Thus, generalized social anxiety disorder may be a distress disorder, and the nongeneralized subtype may be a fear disorder (Carter & Wu, 2010).

Although the *DSM-IV-TR* does not recognize higher-order classes of distress and fear disorders, there is good evidence for these superordinate classes because of patterns of comorbidity or co-occurrence of symptoms and patterns of shared heritable risk (Krueger, 1999). Presence (versus absence) of an acute fear response and avoidance behavior may be the key diagnostic distinction for fear disorders (versus distress disorders). Differential diagnosis within the fear disorder category (e.g., panic disorder versus animal phobia versus natural environment phobia) requires identification of the controlling stimuli. For example, if panic attacks only occur upon exposure to or anticipation of a specific stimulus, then panic disorder is not indicated and the specific stimulus provides a clue as to the subtype of specific phobia that best describes the condition.

Despite these open questions about the best way to conceptualize these types of problems, the *DSM-IV-TR* categories have proven to be quite useful, especially with regard to predicting prognosis and treatment response. These disorders are quite recognizable, with relatively good reliability of diagnosis using a semi-structured interview (Brown, Campbell, Lehman, Grisham, & Mancill, 2001). Social anxiety disorder appears to be frequently underdiagnosed, especially when a comorbid depressive disorder is present (Lecrubier & Weiller, 1997). Affecting the reliability of the diagnosis of specific phobias is the decision about whether clinically significant impairment (i.e., Criterion E) is present, which can be equivocal. Overall, however, there are many instances in which one of these diagnoses describes a patient's difficulties well. Treatment planning is greatly facilitated when working with a patient seeking treatment with problems that fit the diagnostic criteria for panic disorder, social anxiety disorder, or specific phobias. Pathological avoidance is a feature of these disorders. Such avoidance may reduce the willingness of patients to seek or accept help. In addition, such avoidance may influence the way in which a patient participates in treatment selection, perhaps increasing the appeal of approaches that do not involve confronting their fears (i.e., through exposure).

In addition, anxiety disorders present risk of suicide, especially when comorbid diagnoses (e.g., depression, personality disorders) are present (Cox, Direnfeld, Swinson, & Norton, 1994; Khan, Leventhal, Khan, & Brown, 2002; Warshaw, Dolan, & Keller, 2000). The subclinical symptoms that often accompany panic disorder and social anxiety disorder (Lecrubier & Weiller, 1997) may also elevate the risk for suicide.

## EPIDEMIOLOGY

### PANIC DISORDER

*Prevalence*   Lifetime prevalence rate of panic disorder with agoraphobia is estimated to be between approximately 1.5% and 5%, whereas the 12-month prevalence rate is estimated to be between approximately 1% and 2.7% (Barlow, 2002; Grant et al., 2006; Kessler, Berglund et al., 2005; Kessler, Chiu, Demler, & Walters, 2005).

*Gender*   The incidence of panic disorder is approximately two times higher in women than in men (Barlow, 2002; Bland, Orn, & Newman, 1988; Mathews, Gelder, & Johnston, 1981; Wittchen, Essau, Von Zerssen, Krieg, & Zaudig, 1992). Different hypotheses have been put forth to account for observed gender differences in relation to the incidence of panic disorder. These hypotheses include differences relating to the acceptability for women and men to report fear, as well as the higher prevalence of self-medication among men relative to women (Barlow, 2002). The gender distribution of panic disorder with agoraphobia is even more unbalanced, and the greater incidence in women than in men might also be due to gender role socialization (Bekker, 1996).

*Age of Onset*   Average age of onset for panic disorder ranges between approximately 19.7 and 32 years of age, with a mean age of onset of approximately 26.5 years of age (Burke, Burke, Regier, & Rae, 1990; Grant et al., 2006; McNally, 2001; Öst, 1987). Panic disorder typically appears during adulthood, although panic disorder in prepubescent children and older adults is possible (Barlow, 2002).

*Comorbidity*   Approximately half of individuals currently suffering from panic disorder also suffer from a comorbid psychological disorder, with comorbidity estimates ranging between approximately 51% and 60% (Brown, Antony, & Barlow, 1995; Brown et al., 2001). Among the most commonly co-occurring disorders, approximately 59% of individuals with panic disorder have a comorbid mood or anxiety disorder and 46% have a comorbid anxiety disorder alone. Among specific disorders, approximately 23% of individuals with panic disorder suffer from co-occurring major depressive disorder, 16% suffer from co-occurring generalized anxiety disorder, 15% suffer from co-occurring social anxiety disorder, and 15% suffer from co-occurring specific phobias (Brown et al., 2001). Panic disorders are also often accompanied by substance use disorders (Barlow, 2002), and this comorbidity appears to substantially reflect attempts at self-medication, and to a lesser degree common genetic vulnerability (Kushner, Abrams, & Borchardt, 2000).

*Clinical Course*   The clinical course for panic disorder is chronic and disabling without treatment. The 12-month remission rate for panic disorder is estimated to be approximately 17%, and the 5-year remission rate for panic disorder is estimated to be approximately 39% (Keller et al., 1994; Yonkers et al., 1998). Panic disorder is also associated with substantial social, occupational, and physical disability, including especially high rates of medical utilization (Barlow, 2002).

SOCIAL ANXIETY DISORDER

*Prevalence*   Lifetime prevalence rate of social anxiety disorder is estimated to be between approximately 5.0% and 13.3%, whereas the 12-month prevalence rate is estimated to be between approximately 2.8% and 6.8% (Grant et al., 2005; Kessler et al., 1994; Kessler, Berglund et al., 2005; Kessler, Chiu et al., 2005).

*Gender*   The incidence of social anxiety disorder is relatively equally represented between genders, with the sex ratio (1.4:1) only somewhat favoring women relative to men (Kessler, Berglund et al., 2005).

*Age of Onset*   Average age of onset for social anxiety disorder has been estimated to be approximately 15 years of age, with a median age of onset of approximately 12.5 years of age (Grant et al., 2005). Social anxiety disorder is typically especially prevalent among young (18–29 years of age) adults (Kessler, Berglund, et al., 2005).

*Comorbidity*   Approximately 46% of individuals currently suffering from social anxiety disorder also suffer from a comorbid Axis I disorder (Brown et al., 2001). Among the most commonly co-occurring disorders, approximately 45% of individuals with social anxiety disorder have a comorbid mood or anxiety disorder, and approximately 28% of individuals with social anxiety disorder have a comorbid anxiety disorder alone. Among specific disorders, approximately 14% of individuals with social anxiety disorder suffer from co-occurring major depressive disorder, and 13% of individuals with social anxiety disorder suffer from co-occurring generalized anxiety disorder (Brown et al., 2001). Other commonly comorbid disorders include substance use disorders (Grant et al., 2005).

*Clinical Course*   The clinical course for social anxiety disorder is chronic and disabling without treatment. The 12-month remission rate for social anxiety disorder is estimated to be approximately 7%, and the 5-year remission rate for social anxiety disorder is estimated to be approximately 27% (Yonkers, Bruce, Dyck, & Keller, 2003). Social anxiety disorder is also associated with substantial social, occupational, and physical disability, including especially high levels of scholastic difficulties (Stein & Kean, 2000).

## Specific Phobias

*Prevalence*   Lifetime prevalence rate for specific phobia is estimated to be between approximately 2% and 12.5%, whereas the 12-month prevalence rate is estimated to be between approximately 1.8% and 8.7% (Bland et al., 1988; Eaton, Dryman, & Weissman, 1991; Kessler, Berglund et al., 2005; Kessler, Chiu et al., 2005; Lindal & Stefansson, 1993; Stinson et al., 2007; Wittchen, Nelson, & Lachner, 1998). Among the specific phobias, animal phobia and height phobia are the most frequently diagnosed forms of specific phobia (Curtis, Magee, Eaton, Wittchen, & Kessler, 1998; Stinson et al., 2007).

*Gender*   The incidence of specific phobia is approximately four times higher in women than in men (Kessler, Berglund et al., 2005). However, research indicates that the incidence of phobias of heights, flying, injections, dentists, and injury do not significantly differ between women and men (Fredrikson, Annas, Fischer, & Wik, 1996). Different hypotheses have been put forth to account for observed gender differences in relation to the incidence of specific phobia. These hypotheses include differences relating to the reporting of fear between genders, as well as differences in the ways women and men are taught to deal with threatening stimuli (Barlow, 2002).

*Age of Onset*   Average age of onset for specific phobia typically occurs during adolescence. Specific estimates relating to the average age of onset for specific phobia are estimated to be between approximately 9.1 years of age and 16.1 years of age (Stinson et al., 2007; Thyer, Parrish, Curtis, Nesse, & Cameron, 1985), with a median age of onset of approximately 15 years of age (Magee, Eaton, Wittchen, McGonagle, & Kessler, 1996). Moreover, results suggest that particular specific phobias may have differential ages of onset. For example, animal phobia and BII phobia tend to begin in childhood, whereas situational phobia and phobia of heights tend to develop in adolescence or adulthood (e.g., Antony, Brown, & Barlow, 1997; Barlow, 2002; Himle, McPhee, Cameron, & Curtis, 1989; Marks & Gelder, 1966; Öst, 1987).

*Comorbidity*   Some data suggest that specific phobias are likely to co-occur with other specific phobias, with only 24.4% of individuals with specific phobias having a single specific phobia (Curtis et al., 1998). However, other findings suggest that the presence of multiple specific phobias is relatively rare (Fredrikson et al., 1996). Moreover, approximately 34% of individuals currently suffering from a specific phobia meet the criteria for an additional Axis I disorder, with mood and anxiety disorders being the most common co-occurring disorders (Brown et al., 2001). Among mood and anxiety disorders, some research has found especially high rates of co-occurring panic disorder in individuals suffering from specific phobias (Stinson et al., 2007). Other data suggest that specific phobias are rarely the principal diagnosis when they co-occur with other disorders, but they are often an additional diagnosis in relation to other disorders (Barlow, 2002; Sanderson, Di Nardo, Rapee, & Barlow, 1990).

*Clinical Course*   The clinical course for specific phobia is relatively chronic and disabling without treatment. The 15-month full remission rate is estimated to be approximately 19% (Trumpf, Becker, Vriends, Meyer, & Margraf, 2009). Specific phobia is also often associated with substantial social, occupational, and physical disability, including avoidance of medical procedures (Wolitzky-Taylor, Horowitz, Powers, & Telch, 2008).

## TREATMENT

### PHARMACOLOGICAL TREATMENTS

*Panic Disorder*   Many pharmacological agents have been used for the treatment of panic disorder with and without agoraphobia, including benzodiazepines, selective serotonin reuptake inhibitors (SSRIs), serotonin norepinephrine reuptake inhibitors (SNRIs), monoamine oxidase inhibitors (MAOIs), and tricyclic antidepressants (e.g., Ballenger et al., 1988; Barlow, Gorman, Shear, & Woods, 2000; Marks et al., 1993; Mavissakalian & Perel, 1999; Tesar et al., 1991; van Vliet, Westenberg, & Den Boer, 1993). Among these agents, a growing body of research suggests that SSRIs and SNRIs should be considered the front-line pharmacological agents for the treatment of panic disorder (Hoffman & Mathew, 2008; McHugh, Smits, & Otto, 2009; Pollack et al., 2007). Moreover, benzodiazepines are associated with abuse potential and may interfere with psychological interventions. That is, benzodiazepines interfere with the experience of anxiety during exposure to feared situations (Jorstad-Stein & Heimberg, 2009). For such reasons, benzodiazepines are often not considered first-line pharmacological agents for panic disorder.

*Social Anxiety Disorder*   Efficacious pharmacological agents for the treatment of social anxiety disorder include benzodiazepines, SSRIs, SNRIs, and MAOIs (e.g., Blackmore, Erwin, Heimberg, Magee, & Fresco, 2009; Blanco et al., 2003; Clark et al., 2003; Davidson et al., 2004; Gerlernter et al., 1991; Kobak, Greist, Jefferson, & Katzelnick, 2002; Ledley & Heimberg, 2005; Otto et al., 2000). Given the noted concerns surrounding benzodiazepines, SSRIs, SNRIs, and MAOIs are considered the first-line pharmacological agents for the treatment of social anxiety disorder (Jorstad Stein & Heimberg, 2009).

*Specific Phobias*   Extant data suggest that use of pharmacological agents, such as benzo-diazepines and sedatives, in the treatment of specific phobias is limited. Moreover, there exists a paucity of data relating to the efficacy of antidepressant medications as they relate to the treatment of specific phobias (Grös & Antony, 2006; Hamm, 2009).

### COGNITIVE-BEHAVIORAL TREATMENTS

*Panic Disorder*   Often considered to be a first-line treatment, panic disorder is often successfully treated with cognitive-behavioral treatment that incorporates psychoeducation, cognitive restructuring, and behavioral experiments. The behavioral experiments that incorporate interoceptive exposure attempt to modify appraisals and reactions to arousal-related sensations. During this interoceptive exposure, the feared arousal-related sensations are provoked to allow for disconfirmation of feared catastrophes associated with such sensations in the absence of maladaptive responses, such as avoidance (e.g., see McNally, 1990). Cognitive-behavioral treatments for panic disorder have been shown to be efficacious in both individual and group format, with 80% to 90% of patients showing marked improvement (e.g., Barlow et al., 2000; Clark et al., 2003; Hofmann & Smits, 2008; McHugh et al., 2009; Olatunji, Cisler, & Deacon, 2010; Öst, Thulin, & Ramnero, 2004; Penava, Otto, Maki, & Pollack, 1998; Telch et al., 1993). Moreover, treatment gains associated with cognitive-behavioral treatments for panic disorder have shown excellent maintenance, including at 2 years posttreatment (e.g., Craske, Brown, & Barlow, 1991).

*Social Anxiety Disorder*   Cognitive-behavioral treatments for social anxiety disorder include engagement in psychoeducation, cognitive restructuring, and behavioral experiments in an attempt to modify appraisals and reactions to social situations. Behavioral experiments often include in-session exposures, in which individuals engage in feared social situations to allow for disconfirmation of feared catastrophes associated with such situations in the absence of maladaptive responses, such as avoidance (e.g., see Clark & Wells, 1995). Cognitive-behavioral treatments for social anxiety disorder have been shown to be efficacious in both individual and group formats (Clark et al., 2006; Feske & Chambless, 1995; Heimberg & Becker, 2002; Jorstad-Stein & Heimberg, 2009; Olatunji et al., 2010; Ponniah & Hollon, 2008; Powers, Sigmarsson, & Emmelkamp, 2008). Moreover, treatment gains associated with cognitive-behavioral treatments for social anxiety disorder show excellent maintenance, including at 5 years posttreatment (e.g., Heimberg, Salzman, Holt, & Blendell, 1993). The newer formulations of cognitive-behavioral treatments (e.g., Clark, 2001; Clark & Wells, 1995; Hofmann & Otto, 2008), which appear to be more effective than earlier treatments, incorporate manipulation of self-focused attention, dropping of safety behaviors, reevaluation of social costs, and change in self-perceptions.

*Specific Phobias*   Cognitive-behavioral treatments for specific phobias typically involve exposure to feared stimuli. Such exposure allows for the disconfirmation of the expected catastrophes associated with coming into contact with feared stimuli in the absence of maladaptive responses, such as avoidance (e.g., see Antony & Swinson, 2000). Cognitive-behavioral treatments for specific phobia have been shown to be efficacious (e.g., Choy, Fyer, & Lipsitz, 2007; Hamm, 2009; Muhlberger, Herrmann, Wiedemann, Ellgring, & Pauli, 2001; Olatunji et al., 2010; Öst, 1989; Rothbaum, Hodges, Smith, Lee, & Price, 2000; Van Gerwen, Spinhoven, Diekstra, & Van Dyck, 2002; Wolitzky-Taylor et al., 2008). One version of this treatment, delivered during a single session lasting 2 to 4 hours, has been shown to be highly effective, with about 90% of patients showing marked improvement (Öst, 1989). Treatment gains associated with cognitive-behavioral treatments for specific phobia have shown excellent maintenance, including at 14 months posttreatment (e.g., Choy et al., 2007).

OTHER PSYCHOLOGICAL TREATMENTS

One additional emerging psychological treatment for anxiety disorders is acceptance and commitment therapy (ACT; Hayes, Luoma, Bond, Masuda, & Lillis, 2006). Broadly speaking, ACT seeks to reduce the extent to which individuals respond to thoughts and other inner experiences in ways that maintain and exacerbate emotional distress. Preliminary data indicate that ACT is an efficacious treatment for reducing anxiety symptoms (e.g., see Öst, 2008). Moreover, ACT-based treatments for panic disorder (Lopez & Salas, 2009) and social anxiety disorder (Dalrymple & Herbert, 2007) have been explicated. Other psychological treatments that have garnered some interest in the treatment of panic disorder, social anxiety disorder, and specific phobias include interpersonal therapy and psychoanalytic psychotherapy. High-quality randomized and controlled clinical trials have generally not yet been conducted, or have found no support for treating these disorders with these alternate psychological approaches, including Eye Movement Desensitization and Reprocessing (EMDR) therapy (e.g., Goldstein, de Beurs, Chambless, & Wilson, 2000). These treatments are not widely considered to be first-line treatments (Hamm, 2009; Jorstad-Stein & Heimberg, 2009; McHugh et al., 2009).

COMBINED PHARMACOLOGICAL AND PSYCHOLOGICAL TREATMENTS

*Traditional Pharmacological Agents*   Several studies have examined the combined effects of traditional pharmacological agents (e.g., antidepressants) and cognitive-behavioral treatments for panic disorder (e.g., Azhar, 2000; Barlow et al., 2000; Berger et al., 2004; Spinhoven, Onstein, Klinkhamer, Knoppert-van der Klein, 1996; Stein, Norton, Walker, Chartier, & Graham, 2000). In a review of such studies, Furukawa, Watanabe, and Churchill (2006) concluded that combined traditional pharmacological and psychological treatments in the treatment of panic disorder is modestly more efficacious relative to either pharmacological treatment or cognitive-behavioral treatments for panic disorder alone. However, such a combined approach is associated with greater dropouts and side effects relative to cognitive-behavioral treatments alone for panic disorder (e.g., Barlow et al., 2000).

Only a few known studies have examined whether a combined approach of traditional pharmacological agents and cognitive-behavioral treatments is efficacious for social anxiety disorder. Such findings have been mixed: One study found that a combined approach was superior to a psychological approach alone and pharmacological treatment alone (Blanco et al., 2010), one study found that a combined approach was *not* superior to a psychological approach alone or a pharmacological approach alone (Davidson et al., 2004), and one study found the psychological treatment alone to be especially beneficial at a 1-year follow-up (Blomhoff et al., 2001). No known studies have examined the efficacy of a combined approach in the treatment of specific phobias, although advantages of such an approach have been posited (e.g., Cottraux, 2004). Some researchers view the use of medications, particularly benzodiazepines, as antithetical to cognitive-behavioral treatment models if they are used to avoid feared somatic sensations (Bruce, Spiegel, & Hegel, 1999; Deacon & Abramowitz, 2005).

*D-cycloserine (DCS) and Related Issues* Among nontraditional pharmacological agents, DCS has emerged as a potentially important supplement to traditional cognitive-behavioral treatments for panic disorder, social anxiety disorder, and specific phobias. DCS is a drug approved by the U.S. Food and Drug Administration (FDA) for the treatment of tuberculosis. However, DCS also demonstrated enhancement in learning fear extinction in animal studies (Ledgerwood, Richardson, & Cranney, 2003). Thus, researchers began examining whether DCS might enhance the effects of exposure-based cognitive-behavioral interventions, including panic disorder, social anxiety disorder, and specific phobias (e.g., Guastella et al., 2008; Hofmann et al., 2006; Norberg, Krystal, & Tolin, 2008; Ressler et al., 2004). Supplementing traditional cognitive-behavioral treatments for such disorders with DCS has shown treatment enhancements at posttreatment and follow-up.

There is a clear parallel between the behavioral treatment of panic disorder, social anxiety disorder, and specific phobias using procedures that incorporate exposure, and the process of fear extinction, studied most extensively in rats. As agents and procedures that effect extinction processes using animal models are identified, translational work with humans may lead to innovative changes to the behavioral and cognitive-behavioral treatment protocols that are used for panic disorder, social anxiety disorder, and specific phobias. For example, extinction appears to involve the learning of safety associations that compete with fear associations, but alternate procedures can be used to *erase* fear associations, such as through specific chemical agents or behavioral procedures that interfere with reconsolidation (see Quirk et al., 2010). In addition, such research may help us to better understand how therapeutic effectiveness may be influenced by sleep routine, the time between therapy sessions, and other logistical factors.

## PREDICTORS OF TREATMENT OUTCOME

Symptom severity is generally associated with poorer treatment outcome. For example, higher levels of agoraphobia in panic disorder are associated with poorer treatment outcome (e.g., Cowley, Flick, & Roy-Byrne, 1996; Warshaw, Massion, Shea, Allsworth, & Keller, 1997). Moreover, higher depression symptoms and more avoidant personality traits are related to poorer treatment outcome for social anxiety disorder (Chambless, Tran, & Glass, 1997). Overall, the impact of comorbid conditions on treatment outcome has been met with mixed findings. For example, some research indicates that individuals with both panic disorder and co-occurring major depressive disorder have a poorer treatment outcome (Cowley et al., 1996), whereas other research has found that such a co-occurrence does not negatively impact treatment outcome (McLean, Woody, Taylor, & Koch, 1998; Tsao, Mystkowski, Zucker, & Craske, 2002). Moreover, results indicate that the presence of comorbid specific phobias and other anxiety disorders does not affect treatment outcome for specific phobias (Ollendick, Öst, Reuterskiöld, & Costa, 2010). Among several other examined treatment outcome variables (e.g., therapeutic alliance, treatment compliance), treatment expectance has garnered interest (Jorstad-Stein & Heimberg, 2009). For example, research indicates that lower levels of treatment expectancy are related to poorer outcome for social anxiety disorder treatment (Chambless et al., 1997).

## PSYCHOLOGICAL AND BIOLOGICAL ASSESSMENT

A multimodal approach is recommended to assess for panic disorder, social anxiety disorder, and specific phobias. This approach often includes the use of a clinical interview, self-report measures, and behavioral tests (e.g., see Antony, 1997; Barlow, 2002; Grös & Antony, 2006). Each of these three domains of assessment tools will be considered in turn. This section will conclude with a discussion about the emergence of biological assessments.

### CLINICAL INTERVIEWS

Clinical interviews provide detailed information relating to an individual's psychiatric history and current behavioral functioning. Clinical interviews can differ in regards to their format: Some clinical interviews are highly structured and directive, whereas other clinical interviews use an unstructured and conversational approach. When seeking a diagnosis, it is recommended to use more structured clinical interviews because of their increased standardization and reliability (Summerfeldt, Kloosterman, & Antony, 2010).

Two of the most commonly used semistructured clinical interviews for diagnosing anxiety disorders include the Anxiety Disorders Interview Schedule for *DSM-IV–Lifetime* (ADIS-IV-L; Di Nardo, Brown, & Barlow, 1994) and the Structured Clinical Interview for *DSM-IV* Axis I Disorders (SCID; First, Spitzer, Gibbon, & Williams, 1996). Although these interviews can be used to reach a diagnosis relating to a wide range of psychological disorders, both the ADIS-IV-L and the SCID can also be used to specifically assess whether an individual meets the diagnostic criteria for panic disorder, social anxiety disorder, or specific phobias. The ADIS-IV-L and the SCID both explicitly provide questions clinicians use when administering the interview. This structured format ensures that each individual is asked the same questions, in the same order, using the same terminology. However, subsequent questions, which may deviate from the standardized questions, can be used to further probe an individual's presenting problem(s). Both the ADIS-IV-L and the SCID have been shown to have good psychometric properties in prior studies (e.g., see Summerfeldt et al., 2010). Despite the ADIS-IV-L and the SCID providing a standardized, systematic, and valid assessment of panic disorder, social anxiety disorder, and specific phobias, both interviews require training and can be time-consuming to administer. Nonetheless, the use of such interviews is recommended when assessing for these three disorders.

### SELF-REPORT MEASURES

Self-report measures provide an efficient and cost-effective method to assess for panic disorder, social anxiety disorder, or specific phobias, as well as their associated symptomatology. There are several well-validated self-report measures (see Antony, Orsillo, & Roemer, 2001). Some of the most commonly used self-report measures to assess each disorder will be mentioned.

For panic disorder, well-validated and frequently used self-report measures include the Panic Disorder Severity Scale (PDSS; Shear et al., 1997) and the Panic and Agoraphobia Scale (PAS; Bandelow, 1999). The Agoraphobic Cognitions Questionnaire (ACQ; Chambless, Caputo, Bright, & Gallagher, 1984) and the Anxiety Sensitivity Index-3 (ASI-3; Taylor et al., 2007) are two frequently used measures to assess for panic-related cognitions and anxiety focused on physical sensations, respectively. For social anxiety disorder, well-validated and frequently used self-report measures include the Social Phobia and Anxiety Inventory (SPAI; Turner, Beidel, Dancu, & Stanley, 1989), the Social Interaction Anxiety Scale (SIAS; Mattick & Clarke, 1998), and the Social Phobia Scale (SPS; Mattick & Clarke, 1998). The Brief Fear of Negative Evaluation Scale (BFNES; Leary, 1983a) is a frequently used self-report measure to assess for the core cognition purported to underlie social anxiety disorder.

For specific phobias, the Fear Survey Schedule (FSS-II; Geer, 1965) is one well-validated and commonly used self-report measure to assess for specific phobias, although other promising self-report measures exist as well (e.g., Phobic Stimuli Response Scales, PSRS; Cutshall & Watson, 2004). Whereas the FSS-II assesses a broad range of specific phobias, self-report measures designed to assess certain types of specific phobias exist as well (e.g., Fear of Spiders Questionnaire, FSQ; Szymanski & O'Donohue, 1995; Blood-Injection Symptom Scale, BISS; Page, Bennett, Carter, Smith, & Woodmore, 1997). The Spence Child Anxiety Scale (SCAS; Spence, 1997, 1998; Spence, Barrett, & Turner, 2003) includes both self-report and parent informant versions for assessment of anxiety disorder symptoms in children and adolescents. In addition, the Social Phobia and Anxiety Inventory for Children (SPAI-C; Beidel, Turner, Hamlin, Morris, 2000) is a well-validated self-report measure for assessing social anxiety symptoms in children and adolescents.

## BEHAVIORAL TESTS

Although less frequently used in clinical practice, behavioral assessment strategies offer unique insights into the nature and expression of an individual's symptomatology. The chief goal of behavioral assessments is to evaluate an individual's distress during exposure to and avoidance of his or her feared stimulus. Such an assessment is commonly referred to as a behavioral approach test (BAT). BATs can differ in their orientations, with multiple-task BATs (i.e., BATs that require individuals to complete several fear-related tasks) generally being favored relative to single-task BATs. BATs are idiographic in nature, such that the exposed stimulus will be chosen based upon an individual's specific symptomatology. For example, an individual with spider phobia would likely be exposed to different stimuli relating to spiders, whereas an individual with social anxiety disorder would likely be exposed to different situations relating to social or performance situations. In the case of panic disorder, behavioral assessments include symptom induction tests that seek to identify sensations that trigger anxiety or fear for an individual. Subjective units of distress are often assessed during BATs, with higher units indicating higher levels of distress (e.g., Antony, 1997; Barlow, 2002; Grös & Antony, 2006).

Self-monitoring is another behavioral assessment strategy that is important in the assessment of anxiety disorders, particularly in panic disorder and social anxiety. Self-monitoring refers to recording thoughts or behavior in relation to specific situations. For panic disorder, self-monitoring typically occurs through recording information related to the occurrence of panic attacks. This information may include such things as the time of onset, intensity, situation, and location. If accompanied by agoraphobia, additional important information might include the frequency and duration of excursions from home, distance traveled, escape behaviors, safety behaviors, and level of anxiety (Barlow, 2002). For social anxiety disorder, self-monitoring ·could include the frequency and duration of social contacts, antecedents and consequences of these contacts, and level of anxiety experienced (e.g., Heimberg, Madsen, Montgomery, & McNabb, 1980). Despite the potentially useful information that accompanies behavioral assessment strategies, it is important to note that such strategies have been broadly criticized for poorer reliability and validity relative to structured clinical interviews and self-report measures. Moreover, behavioral assessment strategies can be prone to bias (e.g., observer bias, confirmation bias; Groth-Marnat, 2003). In addition to having potential assessment value, self-monitoring may also have therapeutic value by helping individuals become more aware of the automatic cognitions and behaviors that maintain their disorders.

BIOLOGICAL ASSESSMENT

Neuroanatomical differences are not sufficiently established to warrant routine assessment of neuroanatomy in individuals suffering from panic disorder, social anxiety disorder, and specific phobias (e.g., Britton & Rauch, 2009). Although their diagnostic value is limited, neuroanatomical assessment techniques are a promising area of research. Approaches used to assess the neuroanatomy of individuals suffering from panic disorder, social anxiety disorder, and specific phobias, as well as psychopathology more broadly, can be divided into two different methods: structural (anatomical) techniques and functional (physiological/neurochemical) techniques. These two sets of techniques will be briefly considered in turn.

Computerized tomography (CT) and magnetic resonance imaging (MRI) are two of the most common structural techniques used to examine how various parts of the brain relate to one another spatially. Of these two techniques, MRI produces better resolution than does CT and is thus the more often used technique. The most commonly used functional techniques include single photon emission computed tomography (SPECT), functional MRI (fMRI), and positron emission tomography (PET). Such functional techniques allow for the examination of changes in the brain's metabolism and blood flow. Both SPECT and PET use trace amounts of ligands that are labeled with radioactive isotopes, which in turn allow measurement of cerebral metabolism or cerebral blood flow. This radioactive dye is injected into the bloodstream, and SPECT or PET scanners detect the radiation emitted by the isotopes. PET allows for more precision and better resolution than does SPECT and is thus generally used more often. fMRI assesses cerebral blood flow in a similar fashion as the other two functional techniques, except fMRI has the advantage of not requiring any exposure to ionizing radiation. It is also important to note that structural methods and functional methods can be combined, such that a functional image can be placed on top of a structural image (i.e., image registration) to determine the exact structural location of the functional change (Andreasen, 2001).

## ETIOLOGICAL CONSIDERATIONS

BEHAVIORAL GENETICS

Behavioral genetic studies (e.g., studies of identical twins, adopted siblings, etc.) estimate that about 20% of the variance in panic disorder, social anxiety disorder, and specific phobias are attributable to heritable genetics (e.g., Hettema, Neale, Myers, Prescott, & Kendler, 2006). Familial factors (i.e., environmental factors shared by twins and siblings) account for less than 10% of the variance in the occurrence of the disorders, and the majority of the variance (perhaps as much as 70%) is attributed to unique environmental factors and measurement error. Although some behavioral genetics studies have resulted in higher estimates of the contribution of heritable genetics (perhaps as high as about 50% when correcting for measurement error; Kendler, Karkowski, & Prescott, 1999; Kendler, Myers, Prescott, & Neale, 2001), it is generally agreed that, compared to most other mental disorders, these anxiety disorders appear to be relatively less influenced by heritable genetics and relatively more influenced by environment or by gene-environment interactions. A notable exception to these findings is that the BII subtype of specific phobia appears to be relatively more heritable (Kendler et al., 1999, 2001). In addition, when social anxiety disorder subtypes are examined, the generalized subtype appears to involve somewhat greater heritable genetic risk than the nongeneralized subtype (Mannuzza et al., 1995; Stein et al., 1998).

Some of the hertiable genetic risk for panic disorder and specific phobias appears to be due to a general factor (perhaps neuroticism; Gray & McNaughton, 2000; Hettema et al., 2006) underlying most internalizing disorders (Krueger, 1999). A substantial part of the heritable genetic risk is specific to the group of disorders that involves acute fear reactions (Krueger, 1999). A modest amount of disorder-specific heritable genetic risk has been found for panic disorder (Hettema et al., 2006). It is also noteworthy that anxiety sensitivity (Stein, Lang, & Livesley, 1999), which is a risk factor for panic disorder (see Personality and Temperament: Anxiety Sensitivity), and behavioral inhibition (Hirschfield-Becker, Biederman, & Rosenbaum, 2004), which is a risk factor for social anxiety disorder (see Personality and Temperament: Behavioral Inhibition and Shy Temperament), are heritable. Although the largest portion of heritable genetic risk appears to involve a general factor underlying the entire class of disorders that involve acute fear reactions, unique environmental factors appear to play a considerable role, particularly with regard to which type of acute fear disorder develops.

BIOLOGICAL CONSIDERATIONS

The biological, cognitive, emotional, and behavioral responses to danger seen in humans, as in other species, increase survival and reproductive fitness. The neuro-anatomy, neurochemistry, and endocrinology underlying normal fear processes have been studied extensively (see Meaney, LeDoux, & Liebowitz, 2008). Normal fear and panic responses are often understood as part of a complex physical system involving neural, endocrinological, circulatory, muscular, and behavioral systems. This fight-or-flight system is designed to prevent or avoid physical danger and harm, and involves a fast and efficient response. Perceptions of immediate danger trigger a cascade of physical reactions that begin in the amygdala, which projects to the hypothalamus. The hypothalamus releases corticotropin-releasing factor (CRF), which triggers the pituitary to release adrenocorticotropic hormone (ACTH), which in turn triggers the adrenal cortex to release hormones, including cortisol. These hormones play a central role in regulating the body's preparation for stress. The hypothalamus also activates the sympathetic nervous system, resulting in a variety of bodily changes including the release of glucose from the liver; increases in heart rate, breathing, and blood pressure; a pattern of vasodilation and vasoconstriction that increases blood flow to the major muscles; and many other changes associated with preparation for the fight-or-flight response.

These physiological changes constitute the physical symptoms of panic attacks. Numbing and tingling in the fingers and toes and sensations in the stomach (nausea) and bladder are sometimes experienced as less blood reaches these nonvital areas; shaking and trembling are by-products of the readiness of the major muscles to expend energy; sweating is release of heat in preparation for physical exertion. Fear appears to be a preparation for a full panic response and involves a similar, though less dramatic, profile of physiological changes and symptoms. Thus, although we consider panic attacks and acute fear responses in the context of anxiety disorders to reflect pathology, the pathology does not appear to be due to the manner in which the hypothalamic-pituitary-adrenal (HPA) axis system is carrying out its function. The pathology usually appears to be due to the inappropriate triggering of the HPA axis, which typically works well to avoid physical danger and harm, even in individuals with panic disorder, social anxiety disorder, and specific phobias.

Consistent with this view, no abnormalities in the cardiovascular and vestibular systems have been consistently established for panic disorder (Jacob, Furman, Durrant, & Turner, 1996; Kathol et al., 1980; Shear, Devereaux, Kranier-Fox, Mann, & Frances, 1984). Anxiety disorders in general do, however, appear to be associated with greater reactivity in the amygdala (see Britton & Rauch, 2009; Meaney et al., 2008). For example, children with anxiety disorders, compared to controls, have increased amygdala activity when viewing fearful versus neutral faces (Pine et al., 2005). There is evidence that hyperventilation in patients with panic disorder may lead to decreased blood flow and changes in metabolism in and around the hippocampus, but it is not clear if these observations constitute differential processing compared to nondisordered individuals (Uhde & Singareddy, 2002). Overall, researchers have not identified neuroanatomical or neurochemical features that are specific to panic disorder, social anxiety disorder, or specific phobias (see Britton & Rauch, 2009).

Unlike other phobias, the BII subtype of specific phobia involves a parasympathetic response to feared stimuli. This response is distinct from fear responses in other phobias in that there is decreased blood pressure and vasodilation that results in pooling of the blood in the extremities. Page (1994) has suggested that this subtype can be further split into two distinct disorders, one that involves blood reactions, a parasympathetic response, and feelings of nausea and disgust; and the other that has a similar physiological reaction to that of other specific phobias and is characterized by fear of pain associated with needles and injury.

## Specific Genes

Research on specific genes that confer risk for panic disorder has led to conflicting findings (see Maron et al., 2008; Schmidt et al., 2000). Linkage and association studies have examined several candidate genes known to be involved in the development of the brain structures associated with fear and fear learning. One gene (COMT) involved with the degradation of dopamine in the prefrontal cortex appears to be associated with panic disorder (see Meaney et al., 2008). Also implicated are specific alleles of the serotonin transporter (5HTT) gene, which appear to play an important role in fear learning (Risbrough & Geyer, 2008). For example, in individuals who are carriers of particular alleles of 5HTT, the nonspecific experience of childhood maltreatment may lead to high levels of anxiety sensitivity (Stein, Schork, & Gelernter, 2008), a risk factor for panic disorder (see Personality and Temperament: Anxiety Sensitivity). Less research has examined specific genes that confer risk for social anxiety disorder and specific phobias. The development of new gene technologies is quite likely to facilitate the search for specific genes and clarify the ways in which genetic risk is conferred. Although this work is in an early stage, research on specific genes and gene-environment interactions are a promising approach for identifying the development of these (and other) disorders and for suggesting prevention strategies.

## Personality and Temperament

*Anxiety Sensitivity*   Anxiety sensitivity, or the fear of fear, can be viewed as both a cognitive variable and sometimes as a personality trait. This variable represents a relatively enduring tendency to negatively interpret the somatic sensations associated with anxiety and fear (Reiss & McNally, 1985). Anxiety sensitivity is often viewed as the key feature of panic disorder (McNally, 1990; Taylor, 1999). Scores on measures of this construct have differentiated individuals with panic disorder from those with most other anxiety disorders (all except posttraumatic stress disorder), individuals with anxiety disorders from those with other disorders, and individuals with other mental disorders from healthy individuals (Taylor, Koch, & McNally, 1992). Anxiety sensitivity predicts fear and panic reactions during lab challenges, such as $CO_2$ inhalation tasks, in individuals with panic disorder (Schmidt, 1999) and individuals who had never previously experienced a panic attack (Harrington, Schmidt, & Telch, 1996).

Evidence for anxiety sensitivity as a risk factor for the development of panic attacks comes from work by Schmidt, Lerew, and Jackson (1997, 1999). They followed Air Force recruits through the stressful experience of boot camp. Anxiety sensitivity before boot camp predicted panic attacks during boot camp, even after controlling for other variables, such as general neuroticism. These findings suggest that nonclinical elevations in anxiety sensitivity combine with stress to produce the first panic attacks. Panic attacks in the absence of objective external dangers may lead to an introspective process in search of an explanation for the aversive experience of panic, which may contribute to the development of the pathological levels of anxiety sensitivity sufficient to cause panic disorder. Although more research is needed to better understand how anxiety sensitivity develops—and how it contributes to the development of a full-blown panic disorder—anxiety sensitivity uniquely predicts panic attacks and related symptoms (Maller & Reiss, 1992; Schmidt et al., 1997, 1999) and the development of anxiety disorders (Calkins et al., 2009; Maller & Reiss, 1992).

*Behavioral Inhibition and Shy Temperament* Behavioral inhibition has been proposed as an enduring tendency to respond to unfamiliar events with anxiety (Kagan, Reznick, & Snidman, 1987). Behavioral inhibition is defined in infants as behavioral withdrawal and increased vigilance and arousal when confronted with novel (unfamiliar) situations. Behavioral inhibition has obvious similarities to both shyness and social anxiety. Behavioral inhibition during the first few years of life predicts inhibited behavior with peers later in childhood (Aksan & Kochanska, 2004) and social anxiety disorder in adolescence (Chronis-Tuscan et al., 2009; Hayward, Killen, Kraemer, & Taylor, 1998; Schwartz, Snidman, & Kagan, 1999) and adulthood (Kagan & Snidman, 1999). The relative stability of socially inhibited behavior from the first years of life until adulthood is consistent with the view of social anxiety disorder as rooted in relatively unchangeable, biologically based behavioral tendencies (i.e., temperament). It is notable, however, that a substantial number of children classified as having behavioral inhibition, perhaps a majority, do not go on to develop social anxiety disorder (Hayward et al., 1998; Kagan & Snidman, 1999; Schwartz et al., 1999; Wittchen, Stein, & Kessler, 1999). Studies of behavioral inhibition might also provide a means for understanding how parental variables contribute to the development of social anxiety disorder (Moehler et al., 2007) and how chronic inhibition in social behavior may develop through a dynamic interplay between child characteristics and parenting.

BEHAVIORAL CONSIDERATIONS

*Classical Conditioning* The definition of specific phobias as involving an acute fear response in the presence of a specific object or in a specific situation lends itself to analysis in terms of a learned association. Drawing upon the observation that fears can be acquired through a repeated process of paired learning, early behaviorists proposed that phobias are learned through classical conditioning. An early and famous demonstration of this approach involves the story of Little Albert, a 4-year-old boy who was conditioned to fear white rabbits after only a few conditioning trials (Watson & Rayner, 1920). Following this line of reasoning, a single conditioning trial with sufficiently severe unconditioned stimulus could result in learned fear (i.e., traumatic conditioning). Although classical conditioning of fear represents one way that a pathological association can be acquired, it does not account for the fact that most individuals with specific phobias have not experienced such events. Inconsistent with the classical conditioning model, many individuals with no prior experience with the fear object or situation meet the criteria for specific phobia, and many individuals with seemingly traumatic conditioning experiences do not develop phobias (Rachman, 1989). Nevertheless, the view of specific phobias as a learned association has persisted and proven to be quite useful.

*Operant Conditioning* Building on the idea of phobic fear as a learned association, Mowrer (1960) proposed that the avoidance behavior that accompanies phobic fear is maintained through a process of negative reinforcement. Escape and avoidance behaviors are negatively reinforced by the removal or prevention of negative affective states. This observation has become quite influential in treatment models for anxiety disorders, providing a compelling rationale for the prevention of compulsions in obsessive-compulsive disorder and for the reduction or elimination of avoidance and safety behaviors in panic disorder, social anxiety disorder, and specific phobias (e.g., Bennet-Levy et al., 2004). In addition to escape from and avoidance of feared situations, subtle in-situation avoidance behaviors have been identified as an important feature of these disorders (Helbig-Lang & Petermann, 2010). These behaviors are often referred to as safety behaviors. There is some evidence that avoidance and safety behaviors may play a role in the development of obsessive-compulsive disorder (Deacon & Maack, 2008), but the applicability of these ideas to panic disorder, social anxiety disorder, and specific phobias has not been examined. Operant behaviors are widely recognized as involved in the maintenance of anxiety disorders, but they are not usually seen as playing a substantial role in the early development of panic disorder, social anxiety disorder, or specific phobia.

*Vicarious Conditioning*   In addition to classical conditioning, vicarious conditioning (sometimes called observational learning or learning by modeling) is now widely recognized as a means for developing a learned association, functionally equivalent to learning by classical conditioning. Acquisition of fear by vicarious conditioning is well-illustrated in a study by Cook and Mineka (1990). In that study, lab-reared monkeys who had never seen a snake were shown a videotape of wild-reared monkeys displaying fear of live and toy snakes. This vicarious conditioning experience was sufficient for the lab-reared monkeys to acquire a fear of snakes. Such processes are widely accepted to be relevant to human learning processes (Mineka & Zinbarg, 2006).

Vicarious conditioning is believed to interact with temperament to predict the development of social anxiety disorder (Rapee & Spence, 2004). For example, de Rosnay, Cooper, Tsigaras, and Murray (2006) trained mothers to act in shy and nonshy manners with strangers. Their 12- to 14-month-old infants acted shyly in subsequent encounters with strangers following shy modeling (demonstrating vicarious learning), and this effect was particularly pronounced for those infants with an inhibited temperament.

*Informational Acquisition*   Rachman (1977) suggested that phobias might be acquired in three ways: (1) classical conditioning, (2) vicarious conditioning, and (3) informational acquisition. Information acquisition involves the development of a fear as a result of receiving information, such as from a parent or doctor. Both vicarious and informational learning has also been documented for social anxiety disorder (Mulkins & Bögels, 1999). For example, Barrett, Rapee, Dadds, and Ryan (1996) found that when presented with threatening scenarios, children with anxiety disorders and their parents independently chose avoidant responses and that children's selection of avoidant responses increased after they interacted with their parents; such a pattern was not apparent among aggressive children. This familial enhancement of avoidant responding in children with anxiety disorders is consistent with informational acquisition. The three-pathways model proposed by Rachman (1977) has also been applied to understand the retrospective accounts of the onset of many types of specific phobias (King, Eleonora, & Ollendick, 1998).

*Anxiety Versus Panic* Conditioning has also been applied to understanding the development of panic disorder. These efforts have sometimes been criticized as tautological because panic and anxiety are considered to be responses that become conditioned, but the conditioned stimuli are interoceptive symptoms associated with panic and anxiety (e.g., McNally, 1990). Bouton, Mineka, and Barlow (2001), however, point out that the tautology is resolved because panic and anxiety are distinct: Panic becomes conditioned to the symptoms of anxiety. Panic attacks in the context of panic disorder can be viewed as a highly generalized fear response, one in which one interoceptive stimulus (e.g., accelerated heart rate) may be sufficient to trigger an acute fear reaction even in the absence of any specific external stimulus.

PREPAREDNESS THEORY

One observation that challenges the behavioral view of phobias as learned associations is that common fears are not randomly distributed but are more frequently associated with stimuli that were objectively more dangerous during the evolution of the species. To account for this observation, Seligman (1971) proposed "preparedness theory," in which during the Paleolithic period of the evolution of the human species, survival and reproductive fitness was increased by a preparedness to fear and avoid objects and situations that were dangerous. Preparedness theory has led to a variety of hypotheses.

Work by Cook and Mineka (1990, 1991; mentioned in the description of vicarious conditioning) illustrates preparedness to acquire fear of stimuli relevant to survival. Although lab-reared monkeys who had never seen a snake quickly acquired fear when presented with a videotape model, illustrating vicarious learning, no such learning took place when they were presented with a videotape model of a monkey displaying fear of stimuli that are irrelevant to survival, such as flowers and toy rabbits. Also, this preferential conditioning did not occur with learning of other responses (e.g., appetitive). The greater fear conditioning to snake stimuli is explained by preparedness theory as being due to preparedness to acquire a fear of stimuli relevant to survival. The applicability of preferential conditioning in humans is somewhat less well-established (see Mineka & Zinbarg, 2006).

Another observation that is consistent with preparedness theory is the distribution of age of onset as a function of different types of specific phobia (Öst, 1987). Animal phobias tend to develop early (mean age of onset of 7 years of age), during an age when animals present the greatest objective threat. In contrast, claustrophobia tends to develop much later (mean age of onset of 20 years of age), during an age when taking refuge in an enclosed hiding place may be less advantageous.

Drawing upon preparedness theory, Mineka and Öhman (2001, 2002) proposed that humans are prepared to fear stimuli that are relevant to survival because we have evolved a module for fear learning that is encapsulated and relatively independent of cognitive processing. This view proposes that fears of survival-relevant stimuli are relatively automatic and involve central brain regions. There is evidence for several aspects of this model (see Mineka & Öhman, 2001; Mineka & Zinbarg, 2006), including evidence of slower extinction to survival-relevant stimuli and limited penetrability to conscious cognitive control for fear of stimuli that are relevant to survival (Öhman & Soares, 1998).

Related to preparedness theory, an ethological view of blood reactions has also been proposed (Thyer, Himle, & Curtis, 1985). Fainting appears to be an adaptive response to injury, because decreased blood pressure and raising the wound site relative to the heart reduces and slows blood loss. The high heritability of blood reactions might help explain the higher and relatively more specific heritability of the BII subtype of specific phobia (see Merckelbach & de Jong, 1997).

Disgust has been implicated as a distinct emotional state that is involved in many anxiety disorders (Woody & Teachman, 2000). For example, animal phobias can be differentiated into those that involve contamination threat and disgust reactions (e.g., fear of rats) and those that involve predators and do not include disgust reactions (e.g., fear of dogs; Matchett & Davey, 1991). Disgust also appears to be relevant to other specific phobias (e.g., BII phobias), to obsessive-compulsive washers, and perhaps to social anxiety disorder in the form of self-disgust (Amir, Najmi, Bomyea, & Burns, 2010). The role of disgust in these anxiety disorders appears to reflect an avoidance of disease that was also selected for during evolution (Matchett & Davey, 1991; Woody & Teachman, 2000).

## COGNITIVE CONSIDERATIONS

Cognitive biases have often been noted in individuals diagnosed with panic disorder, social anxiety disorder, and specific phobias. These phenomena are usually described using an information-processing framework for understanding pathological fear (Foa & Kozak, 1986; Lang, 1979; Rachman, 1980). Studies of these biases can be divided into those that focus on content (e.g., beliefs, expectancies, appraisals, etc.) and those that focus on process (e.g., attention, interpretation, memory, etc.). A key task in evaluating cognitive approaches to understanding the etiology of these disorders is to identify which biases play a causal role and which are simply features or by-products of the disorders.

*Situation-Specific Cognitions and Related Variables*   Approaches to understanding cognitive biases can be further divided into those that emphasize relatively enduring individual difference factors and situation-specific cognitions. Individual difference factors include anxiety sensitivity, which can be viewed as a tendency to engage in the situation-specific cognitions that cause panic attacks in the context of panic disorder (McNally, 1990). In addition, individual difference factors include beliefs, which can be viewed as the latent variables that interact with situational variables to produce the automatic cognitions that are the proximal determinants of fear, anxiety, and avoidance behavior (Beck & Emery, 2005). The individual difference variable of fear of negative evaluation (Leary, 1983b), which can be viewed as the tendency to overestimate the likelihood and importance of being negatively evaluated when in a social situation, has become the axiomatic dimension associated with social anxiety disorder.

Regarding situation-specific cognitions, panic disorder, social anxiety disorder, and specific phobias have been characterized by overestimations of fear and danger.

During the evolution of the danger and harm avoidance system, there were strong selection pressures against problems of underestimation of fear and danger, because such underestimation presented a great cost and relatively weaker pressure against overestimation because it rarely resulted in a loss of life. This naturally selected overprediction of fear (Rachman, 1995) is one of several situation-specific cognitions associated with panic disorder, social anxiety disorder, and specific phobias.

Examining situation-specific cognitions under a variety of names (including expectancies, concerns, automatic thoughts, catastrophic thoughts, and catastrophic misinterpretations), researchers have generally found that situation-specific cognitions are predictors of fear, anxiety, and avoidance behavior. For example, expectancies (Reiss & McNally, 1985) appear to be proximal cognitive determinants of fear and fear behavior (e.g., Valentiner, Telch, Petruzzi, & Bolte, 1996). The types of expectancies and concerns that are most important are believed to vary across different types of fear stimuli: Acrophobia is believed to involve expectances of falling (Menzies & Clarke, 1995), and claustrophobia is believed to involve expectancies of suffocation and entrapment (Radomsky, Rachman, Thordarson, McIsaac, Teachman, 2001; Valentiner et al., 1996). Panic attacks in the context of panic disorder are believed to involve automatic misinterpretation of bodily sensations, resulting in catastrophic thoughts related to heart dysfunction, suffocation, and mental control (Cox, 1996).

Another situation-specific cognitive variable that has been implicated for these disorders is self-efficacy, which is conceptualized as a higher-order cognitive process that incorporates lower-order cognitions, including estimates of one's coping capacities in addition to expectancies of anxiety and expectancies of danger (Bandura & Adams, 1977). Although there are methodological concerns about how the self-efficacy construct is typically operationalized, there is some evidence for self-efficacy as a unique predictor of fear and fear behavior for panic disorder (Cho, Smits, Powers, & Telch, 2007) and specific phobias (Valentiner et al., 1996).

Situation-specific cognitions and individual differences in the tendency to engage in situation-specific cognitions have proven to be useful to understanding panic disorder, social anxiety disorder, and specific phobias. These content variables predict changes in functioning over time and during treatment (e.g., Hoffman, 2004; Wilson & Rapee, 2005), and manipulations that target these cognitions appear to improve the ability of exposure-based treatment techniques in reducing symptoms of panic disorder (e.g., Murphy, Michelson, Marchione, Marchione, & Testa, 1998), social anxiety disorder (e.g., Kim, 2005), and specific phobias (e.g., Kamphuis & Telch, 2000). Little is known, however, about how such cognitions develop.

*Attentional Biases*   Regarding studies of cognitive biases that focus on process, a good deal of research has examined attentional processes. Anxiety has been found to be associated with biases in various attentional processes, namely orienting, engagement, and disengagement (see Ouimet, Gawronski, & Dozois, 2009). In addition, attentional biases have been found, using a variety of tasks, to occur in all anxiety disorders (see Cisler & Koster, 2010), including panic disorder (e.g., Buckley, Blanchard, & Hickling, 2002), social anxiety disorder (Amir, Elias, Klumpp, & Przeworski, 2003), and specific phobias (Watts, McKenna, Sharrock, & Trezise, 1986).

Some researchers (Bögels & Mansell, 2004), however, have viewed the evidence for attentional biases in social anxiety disorder as somewhat mixed. In addition, there may be differences in attentional biases as a function of social anxiety disorder subtype: McNeil et al. (1995) found evidence for cognitive interference (using the emotional Stoop task) on general social words and speech-specific words for the generalized subtypes of social anxiety disorder, but only for speech-specific words for the nongeneralized subtype.

The overall picture that emerges is one in which attentional biases are strongly implicated in anxiety disorders, including panic disorder, social anxiety disorder, and specific phobias. The attentional bias appears to be content-specific, with, for example, spider phobics showing attentional biases related to spider phobias (Watts et al., 1986). The pattern that emerges involves an attentional bias toward threatening stimuli evident early in the attentional process, followed by difficulty disengaging from threatening stimuli, and then later avoidance of threatening stimuli (Cisler & Koster, 2010). In addition, retraining of attentional bias appears to reduce fear and avoidance (Amir, Weber, Beard, Bomyea, & Taylor, 2008).

*Self-Focused Attention*   A cognitive process variable that appears to be particularly relevant to social anxiety is that of self-focused attention, or the tendency for socially anxious individuals to attend to internal stimuli rather than external, social stimuli. These internal stimuli are believed to include both interoceptive sensations (e.g., racing heart) and negative images of the self and behavior. Consistent with the social anxiety disorder model proposed by Clark and Wells (1995; see also Clark, 2001), self-focused attention when in social situations appears to be an important cognitive feature of the disorder, as well as an important factor in the maintenance of social anxiety (Bögels & Mansell, 2004), leading to an increased awareness of anxiety responses (Alden & Mellings, 2004) and a disruption of the realistic processing of the situation and other people's behaviors (Bögels & Lamers, 2002). Targeting self-focused attention appears to improve outcomes during exposure-based treatment for social anxiety disorder (Wells & Papageorgiou, 1998).

*Other Cognitive Processes*   A variety of other cognitive process variables has been proposed as involved in the development and maintenance of these disorders, particularly social anxiety disorder. For example, interpretation biases have been demonstrated for panic disorder (Westling & Öst, 1995) and social anxiety disorder (Amir, Foa, & Coles, 1998). Implicit memory bias has been found in panic disorder (Amir, McNally, Riemann, & Clements, 1996). Evidence for a memory bias in social anxiety disorder is weak, although some authors suggest that such a bias might only be evident in the context of an imminent social threat (Hirsch & Clark, 2004).

One cognitive process that has been shown to play a role in social anxiety disorder is post-event processing (cf. rumination), repetitive self-focused thought in which one's social performance is reconstructed and distorted to be consistent with the pathological beliefs underlying social anxiety (see Brozovich & Heimberg, 2008). Similar processes may be involved in the development of panic disorder and specific phobias, as Davey and Matchett (1994) have demonstrated that mental rehearsal of a conditioning trial can enhance conditioned fears.

CULTURE, SOCIALIZATION, AND THE SOCIAL ENVIRONMENT

Messages that parents give to their children about the meaning and importance of their interoceptive sensations, through parental reinforcement of illness behavior, may play a role in the development of panic attacks and panic disorder. A retrospective study by Stewart et al. (2001) provides evidence that childhood learning experiences with respect to arousing-reactive symptoms (e.g., racing heart, shortness of breath, etc.) but not arousing-nonreactive symptoms (e.g., colds, aches, rashes, etc.) contributed to the frequency and intensity of panic attacks. This effect appeared to be partially mediated by anxiety sensitivity.

Social factors appear to play an important role in the development and course of social anxiety disorder. For example, poorer social relationships have been observed for shy children (Gazelle & Ladd, 2003; Rubin, Wojslawowicz, Rose-Krasnor, Booth-LaForce, & Burgess, 2006) and for children (Alden & Taylor, 2004) and adults (Lampe, Slade, Issakidis, & Andrews, 2003; Whisman, Sheldon, & Goering, 2000) diagnosed with social anxiety disorder. The social deficits associated with social anxiety disorder and shyness include peer neglect (Gazelle & Ladd, 2003), fewer positive responses (Spence, Donovan, & Brechman-Toussaint, 2000), and peer victimization (Hawker & Boulton, 2000; La Greca & Harrison, 2005; McCabe, Antony, Summerfeldt, Liss, & Swinson, 2003; Siegel, La Greca, & Harrison, 2009; Storch & Masia-Warner, 2004). Social deficits, such as peer rejection, appear to be mediated by poor social skills (Greco & Morris, 2005), although individuals with social anxiety disorder do not always show poor social skills (e.g., Beidel, Turner, & Jacob, 1989). It should also be noted that peer victimization may be both a cause (Bond, Carlin, Thomas, Rubin, & Patton, 2001) and a consequence, as social anxiety predicts subsequent victimization (Siegel et al., 2009).

In a study by Daniels and Plomin (1985), mothers' sociability was significantly associated with the shyness of their adopted infants. As an adoption study, genetic effects could be ruled out. In addition, the effect was still evident after controlling for maternal shyness, largely ruling out interpretations in terms of modeling.

Overall, social anxiety appears to be influenced by the views that family and peers have about the individual, and social anxiety influences the social behavior that informs the impressions that family and peers have about the individual. Reciprocal effects between the individual and the social environment likely involve modeling; informational acquisition; selection, creation, and interpretation of social opportunities; and the internalization of messages that one receives about one's social value.

Culture may also play a role in the expression of panic disorder and other anxiety conditions. *Ataque de nervios* is an acute set of symptoms and behaviors that is somewhat reminiscent of a panic attack, although typically experienced in response to a stressful family event and incorporating a volitional behavior component (APA, 2000). It is not clear whether this and other culture-specific anxiety conditions represent an inapplicability of our nosological system to Latin American and Caribbean cultures, a culture-specific expression of known anxiety disorders such as panic disorder, or something else (Guarnaccia, Lewis-Fernandez, & Marano, 2003). In addition, the definitional requirement that panic attacks reach a peak within 10 minutes and the duration of panic attacks may vary as a function of culture (Lewis-Fernández et al., 2010).

Cultural factors likely play a role in the development of social anxiety. For example, culture-specific norms appear to impact the acceptability of socially inhibited behavior and affect the expression of social anxiety (Heinrichs et al., 2006). In addition, culture likely affects the expression of social anxiety. As discussed earlier, Taijin Kyofusho has been viewed as a culturally bound syndrome thought to appear only in Japan and Korea (APA, 2000; cf. anthropophobia, WHO, 1992). More information about the likely role of cultural attitudes, beliefs, norms, and practices on the development and expression of social anxiety is needed.

### LIFE EVENTS

Stress, including life events and chronic conditions such as maltreatment during childhood, appears to increase risk for a variety of mental disorders, including anxiety disorders (Allen Rapee, & Sandberg, 2008; Kessler, Davis, & Kendler, 1997; Phillips, Hammen, Brennan, Najman, & Bor, 2005). Stressful events also impact the maintenance and course of panic disorder (Craske, Rapee, & Barlow, 1988), agoraphobia (Rachman, 1984), social anxiety disorder (Mineka & Zinbarg, 1996), and specific phobias (Craske, 1991). Consistent with a conditioning model, individuals with social anxiety disorder retrospectively report greater incidence of traumatic social events than healthy controls, and this greater incidence appeared to be higher for those with the nongeneralized subtype compared to the generalized subtype (Stemberger, Turner, Beidel, & Calhoun, 1995). Some authors have argued that events that are characterized as unpredictable and uncontrollable are especially relevant to these disorders (Mineka & Zinbarg, 1996).

Early studies suggest that onset of panic disorder, social anxiety disorder, and specific phobias are sometimes triggered by the occurrence of a stressful life event. This phenomenon may reflect fear inflation (Mineka & Zinbarg, 1996; Rescorla, 1974), which takes place when a person or animal undergoes conditioning of mild fear, such as through classical conditioning, and then experiences an intense, unpaired exposure to the unconditioned stimulus, so the previously mild fear increases in strength. More recent evidence has found no greater rates of stressful life events prior to anxiety disorder onset than at other times (Calkins et al., 2009).

The phenomenon of latent inhibition, in which prior benign (nonfearful) exposure to a stimulus inhibits fear acquisition, is a well-established finding in the animal literature that informs how we think about fear learning in humans (see Mineka & Zinbarg, 2006). Prior exposure also reduces generalization of fear (Vervliet, Kindt, Vansteenwegen, & Hermans, 2010), an observation that may be especially relevant to the development of panic disorder, which is sometimes viewed as involving highly generalized fear responses (Gorman et al., 2001). Related to these ideas, positive control experiences early in life appear to provide protection against fear conditioning and the development of anxiety disorders (see Chorpita & Barlow, 1998).

### REFERENCES

Aalto-Setalae, T., Marttunen, M., Tuulio-Henriksson, A., & Loennqvist, J. (2001). One month prevalence of depression and other *DSM-IV* disorders among young adults. *Psychological Medicine, 31*, 791–801.

Aksan, N., & Kochanska, G. (2004). Links between systems of inhibition from infancy to preschool years. *Child Development, 75,* 1477–1490.

Alden, L. E., & Mellings, T. M. B. (2004). Generalized social phobia and social judgments: The salience of self- and partner-information. *Journal of Anxiety Disorders, 18,* 143–157.

Alden, L. E., & Taylor, C. T. (2004). Interpersonal processes in social phobia. *Clinical Psychology Review, 24,* 857–882.

Allen, J. L., Rapee, R. M., & Sandberg, S. (2008). Severe life events and chronic adversities as antecedents to anxiety in children: A matched control study. *Journal of Abnormal Child Psychology, 236,* 1047–1056.

American Psychiatric Association. (2000). *Diagnostic and Statistical Manual of Mental Disorders* (4th ed., text rev.). Washington DC: Author.

Amir, N., Elias, J., Klumpp, J., & Przeworski, A. (2003). Attentional bias to threat in social phobia: Facilitated processing of threat or difficulty disengaging attention from threat? *Behaviour Research and Therapy, 41,* 1325–1335.

Amir, N., Foa, E. B., & Coles, M. E. (1998). Negative interpretation bias in social phobia. *Behaviour Research and Therapy, 36,* 945–957.

Amir, N., McNally, R. J., Riemann, B. C., & Clements, C. (1996). Implicit memory bias for threat in panic disorder: Application of the 'white noise' paradigm. *Behaviour Research and Therapy, 34,* 157–162.

Amir, N., Najmi, S., Bomyea, J., & Burns, M. (2010). Disgust and anger in social anxiety. *International Journal of Cognitive Therapy, 3,* 3–10.

Amir, N., Weber, G., Beard, C., Bomyea, J., & Taylor, C. T. (2008). The effect of a single-session attention modification program on response to a public-speaking challenge in socially anxious individuals. *Journal of Abnormal Psychology, 117,* 860–868.

Andreasen, N. C. (2001). *Brave new brain.* New York, NY: Oxford University Press.

Antony, M. M. (1997). Assessment and treatment of social phobia. *Canadian Journal of Psychiatry, 42,* 826–834.

Antony, M. M., Brown, T. A., & Barlow, D. H. (1997). Heterogeneity among specific phobia types in *DSM-IV. Behaviour Research and Therapy, 35,* 1089–1100.

Antony, M. M., Orsillo, S. M., & Roemer, L. (Eds.). (2001). *Practitioner's guide to empirically based measures of anxiety.* New York, NY: Kluwer Academic/Plenum Publishers.

Antony, M. M., & Swinson, R. P. (2000). *Phobic disorders and panic in adults: A guide to assessment and treatment.* Washington, DC: American Psychological Association.

Azhar, M. Z. (2000). Comparison of fluvoxamine alone, fluvoxamine and cognitive psychotherapy and psychotherapy alone in the treatment of panic disorder in Kelantan—implications for management by family doctors. *Medical Journal of Malaysia, 55,* 402–408.

Ballenger, J. C., Burrows, G. D., DuPont, R. L., Jr., Lesser, I. M., Noyes, R., Jr., Pecknold, J. C., . . . Swinson, R. P. (1988). Alprazolam in panic disorder and agoraphobia: Results from a multicenter trial, I: Efficacy in short-term treatment. *Archives of General Psychiatry, 45,* 413–422.

Bandelow, B. (1999). *Panic and Agoraphobia Scale (PAS).* Seattle, WA: Hogrefe & Huber.

Bandura, A., & Adams, N. E. (1977). Analysis of self-efficacy theory of behavioral change. *Cognitive Therapy and Research, 1,* 287–310.

Barlow, D. H. (1988). *Anxiety and its disorders.* New York, NY: Guilford Press.

Barlow, D. H. (2002). *Anxiety and its disorders: The nature and treatment of anxiety and panic* (2nd ed.). New York, NY: Guilford Press.

Barlow, D. H., DiNardo, P. A., Vermilyea, B. B., Vermilyea, J. A., & Blanchard, E. B. (1986). Comorbidity and depression among the anxiety disorders: Issues in diagnosis and classification. *Journal of Nervous and Mental Disease, 174,* 63–72.

Barlow, D. H., Gorman, J. M., Shear, M. K., & Woods, S. W. (2000). Cognitive-behavioral therapy, imipramine, or their combination for panic disorder: A randomized controlled trial. *Journal of the American Medical Association, 283*, 2529–2536.

Barrett, P. M., Rapee, R. M., Dadds, M. M., & Ryan. S. (1996). Family enhancement of cognitive style in anxious and aggressive children. *Journal of Abnormal Child Psychology, 24*, 187–203.

Beck, A. T., & Emery, G. (2005). *Anxiety disorders and phobias: A cognitive perspective.* New York, NY: Basic Books.

Beekman, A. T., Bremmer, M. A., Deeg, D. J., van Balkom, A. J., Smith, J. H., de Beurs, E., . . . Tilburg, W. (1998). Anxiety disorders in later life: A report from the Longitudinal Aging Study Amsterdam. *International Journal of Geriatric Psychiatry, 13*, 717–726.

Beidel, D. C., Turner, S. M., Hamlin, K., & Morris, T. L. (2000). The Social Phobia and Anxiety Inventory for Children (SPAI-C): External and discriminant validity. *Behavior Therapy, 31*, 75–87.

Beidel, D. C., Turner, S. M., & Jacob, R. G. (1989). Assessment of social phobia: Reliability of an impromptu speech task. *Journal of Anxiety Disorders, 1; 3*, 149–158.

Bekker, M. H., Jr. (1996). Agoraphobia and gender: A review. *Clinical Psychology Review, 16*, 129–146.

Bennet-Levy, J., Butler, G., Fennell, M., Hackmann, A., Mueller, M., & Westbrook, D. (2004). *Oxford guide to behavioural experiments in cognitive therapy.* New York, NY: Oxford University Press.

Berger, P., Sachs, G., Amering, M., Holzinger, A., Bankier, B., & Katschnig, H. (2004). Personality disorder and social anxiety predict delayed response in drug and behavioral treatment of panic disorder. *Journal of Affective Disorders, 80*, 75–78.

Blackmore, M., Erwin, B. A., Heimberg, R. G., Magee, L., & Fresco, D. M. (2009). Social anxiety disorder and specific phobias. In M. G. Gelder, J. J. Lopez-Ibor, N. C. Andreason, & J. Geddes (Eds.), *New Oxford textbook of psychiatry* (2nd ed., pp. 739–750). Oxford, England: Oxford University Press.

Blanco, C., Heimberg, R. G., Schneier, F. R., Fresco, D. M., Chen, H., Turk, C. L., . . . Liebowitz, M. R. (2010). A placebo-controlled trial of phenelzine, cognitive behavioral group therapy and their combination for social anxiety disorder. *Archives of General Psychiatry, 67*, 286–295.

Blanco, C., Schneier, F. R., Schmidt A., Blanco-Jerez, C. R., Marshall, R. D., Sanchez-Lacay, A., & Liebowitz, M. R. (2003). Pharmacological treatment of social anxiety disorder: A meta-analysis. *Depression and Anxiety, 18*, 29–40.

Bland, R. C., Orn, H., & Newman, S. C. (1988). Lifetime prevalence rates of psychiatric disorders in Edmonton. *Acta Psychiatrica Scandinavica, 77*(Suppl. 338), 24–32.

Blomhoff, S., Haug, T. T., Hellström, K., Holme, I., Humble, M., Madsbu, H. P., & Wold, J. E. (2001). Randomised controlled general practice trial of sertraline, exposure therapy and combined treatment in generalized social phobia. *The British Journal of Psychiatry, 179*, 23–30.

Bögels, S. M., Alden, L., Beidel, D. C., Clark, L. A., Pine, D., Stein, M. B., & Voncken, M. (2010). Social anxiety disorder: Questions and answers for the *DSM-V. Depression and Anxiety, 27*, 168–189.

Bögels, S. M., & Lamers, C. T. J. (2002). The causal role of self-awareness in blushing-anxious, socially-anxious and social phobic individuals. *Behaviour Research and Therapy, 40*, 1367–1384.

Bögels, S. M., & Mansell, W. (2004). Attention processes in the maintenance and treatment of social phobia: Hypervigilance, avoidance, and self-focused attention. *Clinical Psychology Review, 24*, 827–856.

Bond, L., Carlin, J. B., Thomas, L., Rubin, K., & Patton, G. (2001). Does bullying cause emotional problems? A prospective study of young teenagers. *British Medical Journal, 323*, 480–484.

Bouton, M. E., Mineka, S., & Barlow, D. H. (2001). A modern learning-theory perspective on the etiology of panic disorder. *Psychological Review, 108*, 4–32.

Britton, J. C., & Rauch, S. L. (2009). Neuroanatomy and neuroimaging of anxiety disorders. In M. M. Antony & M. B. Stein (Eds.), *Oxford handbook of anxiety and related disorders* (pp. 97–110). New York, NY: Oxford University Press.

Brown, T. A., Antony, M. M., & Barlow, D. H. (1995). Long-term outcome in cognitive-behavioral treatment of panic disorder: Clinical predictors and alternative strategies for assessment. *Journal of Consulting and Clinical Psychology, 63*, 754–765.

Brown, T. A., Campbell, L. A., Lehman, C. C., Grisham, J. R., & Mancill, R. B. (2001). Current and lifetime comorbidity of the *DSM-IV* anxiety and mood disorders in a large clinical sample. *Journal of Abnormal Psychology, 110*, 49–58.

Brozovich, F., & Heimberg, R. G. (2008). An analysis of post-event processing in social anxiety disorder. *Clinical Psychology Review, 28*, 891–903.

Bruce, T. J., Spiegel, D. A., & Hegel, M. T. (1999). Cognitive-behavioral therapy helps prevent relapse and recurrence of panic disorder following alprazolam discontinuation: A long-term follow-up of the Peoria and Dartmouth studies. *Journal of Consulting and Clinical Psychology, 67*, 151–156.

Buckley, T. C., Blanchard, E. B., & Hickling, E. J. (2002). Automatic and strategic processing of threat stimuli: A comparison of PTSD, panic disorder, and non-anxiety controls. *Cognitive Therapy and Research, 26*, 97–115.

Burke, K. C., Burke, J. D., Jr., Regier, D. A., & Rae, D. S. (1990). Age of onset of selected mental disorders in five community populations. *Archives of General Psychiatry, 47*, 511–518.

Calkins, A. W., Otto, M. W., Cohen, L. S., Soares, C. N., Vitonis, A. F., Hearon, B. A., & Harlow, B. L. (2009). Psychosocial predictors of the onset of anxiety disorders in women: Results of a prospective 3-year longitudinal study. *Journal of Anxiety Disorders, 23*, 1165–1169.

Carter, S. A., & Wu, K. D. (2010). Relations among symptoms of social phobia subtypes, avoidant personality disorder, panic, and depression. *Behavior Therapy, 41*, 2–13.

Chambless, D. L., Caputo, G. C., Bright, P., & Gallagher, R. (1984). Assessment of "fear of fear" in agoraphobics: The Body Sensations Questionnaire and the Agoraphobic Cognitions Questionnaire. *Journal of Consulting and Clinical Psychology, 52*, 1090–1097.

Chambless, D. L., Tran, G. Q., & Glass, C. R. (1997). Predictors of response to cognitive-behavioral group therapy for social phobia. *Journal of Anxiety Disorders, 11*, 221–240.

Cho, Y., Smits, J. A., Jr., Powers, M. B., & Telch, M. J. (2007). Do changes in panic appraisal predict improvement in clinical status following cognitive-behavioral treatment of panic disorder? *Cognitive Therapy and Research, 31*, 695–707.

Chorpita, B. F., & Barlow, D. H. (1998). The development of anxiety: The role of control in the early environment. *Psychological Bulletin, 124*, 3–21.

Choy, Y., Fyer, A. J., & Lipsitz, J. D. (2007). Treatment of specific phobia in adults. *Clinical Psychology Review, 27*, 266–286.

Chronis-Tuscan, A., Degnan, K. A., Pine, D. S., Perea-Edgar, K., Henderson, H. A., Diaz, Y., . . . Fox, N. A. (2009). Stable early maternal report of behavioral inhibition predicts lifetime social anxiety disorder in adolescence. *Journal of the American Academy of Child and Adolescent Psychiatry, 48*, 928–935.

Cisler, J. M., & Koster, E.H.W. (2010). Mechanisms underlying attentional biases towards threat: An integrative review, *Clinical Psychology Review, 30*, 203–216.

Clark, D. M. (2001). A cognitive perspective on social phobia. In R. Crozier & L. E. Alden (Eds.), *International handbook of social anxiety: Concepts, research and interventions relating to the self and shyness* (pp. 405–430). Oxford, England: John Wiley & Sons.

Clark, D. M., Ehlers, A., Hackmann, A., McManus, F., Fennell, M., Grey, N., . . . Wild, J. (2006). Cognitive therapy versus exposure and applied relaxation in social phobia: a randomized controlled trial. *Journal of Consulting and Clinical Psychology, 74*, 568–578.

Clark, D. M., Ehlers, A., McManus, F., Hackmann, A., Fennell, M., Campbell, H., . . . Louis, B. (2003). Cognitive therapy vs. fluoxetine in generalized social phobia: a randomized placebo-controlled trial. *Journal of Consulting and Clinical Psychology, 71*, 1058–1067.

Clark, D. M., & Wells, A. (1995). A cognitive model of social phobia. In R. Heimberg, M. Liebowitz, D. A. Hope, & F. Schneier (Eds.), *Social phobia: Diagnosis, assessment and treatment* (pp. 69–93). New York, NY: Guilford Press.

Cook, M., & Mineka, S. (1990). Selective associations in the observational conditioning of fear in rhesus monkeys. *Journal of Experimental Psychology: Animal Behavior Processes, 16*, 372–389.

Cook, M., & Mineka, S. (1991). Selective associations in the origins of phobic fears and their implications for behavior therapy. In P. Martin (Ed.), *Handbook of behavior therapy and psychological science: An integrative approach* (pp. 413–434). Oxford, England: Pergamon Press.

Cottraux, J. (2004). Combining psychological and pharmacological treatment for specific phobias. *Psychiatry, 3*, 87–89.

Cowley, D. S., Flick, S. N., & Roy-Byrne, P. P. (1996). Long-term course and outcome in panic disorder: A naturalistic follow-up study. *Anxiety, 2*, 13–21.

Cox, B. J. (1996). The nature and assessment of catastrophic thoughts in panic disorder. *Behaviour Research and Therapy, 34*, 363–374.

Cox, B. J., Direnfeld, D. M., Swinson, R. P., & Norton, G. R. (1994). Suicidal ideation and suicide attempts in panic disorder and social phobia. *American Journal of Psychiatry, 151*, 882–887.

Craske, M. G. (1991). Phobic fear and panic attacks: The same emotional state triggered by different cues? *Clinical Psychology Review, 11*, 599–620.

Craske, M. G., Brown, T. A., & Barlow, D. H. (1991). Behavioral treatment of panic: A two-year follow-up. *Behavior Therapy, 22*, 289–304.

Craske, M. G., Kircanski, K., Epstein, A., Wittchen, H. U., Pine, D. S., Lewis-Fernández, R., & Hinton, D. (2010). Panic disorder: A review of *DSM-IV* panic disorder and proposals for DSM-V. *Depression and Anxiety, 27*, 93–112.

Craske, M. G., Rapee, R. M., & Barlow, D. H. (1988). The significance of panic expectancy for individual patterns of avoidance. *Behavior Therapy, 19*, 577–592.

Curtis, G. C., Magee, W. J., Eaton, W. W., Wittchen, H. U., & Kessler, R. C. (1998). Specific fears and phobias: Epidemiology and classification. *British Journal of Psychiatry, 173*, 212–217.

Cutshall, C., & Watson, D. (2004). The phobic stimuli response scales: A new self-report measure of fear. *Behaviour Research and Therapy, 42*, 1193–1201.

Dalrymple, K. L., & Herbert, J. D. (2007). Acceptance and Commitment Therapy for generalized social anxiety disorder: A pilot study. *Behavior Modification, 31*, 543–568.

Daniels, D., & Plomin, R. (1985). Origins of individual differences in infant shyness. *Developmental Psychology, 21*, 601–608.

Davey, G. C. L., & Matchett, G. (1994). Unconditioned stimulus rehearsal and the retention and enhancement of differential "fear" conditioning: Effects of trait and state anxiety. *Journal of Abnormal Psychology, 103*, 708–718.

Davidson, J. R., Foa, E. B., Huppert, J. D., Keefe, F. J., Franklin, M. E., Compton, J. S., . . . Gadde, K. M. (2004). Fluoxetine, comprehensive cognitive behavioral therapy, and placebo in generalized social phobia. *Archives of General Psychiatry, 61*, 1005–1013.

Deacon, B. J., & Abramowitz, J. S. (2005). Patients' perceptions of pharmacological and cognitive-behavioral treatment for anxiety disorders. *Behavior Therapy, 36*, 139–145.

Deacon, B. J., & Maack, D. J. (2008). The effects of safety behaviours on the fear of contamination: An experimental investigation. *Behaviour Research and Therapy, 46*, 537–547.

de Rosnay, M., Cooper, P., Tsigaras, N., & Murray, L. (2006). Transmission of social anxiety from mother to infant: An experimental study using a social referencing paradigm. *Behaviour Research and Therapy, 44*, 1165–1175.

Di Nardo, P. A., Brown, T. A., & Barlow, D. H. (1994). *Anxiety Disorders Interview Schedule for DSM-IV: Lifetime version (ADIS-IV-L).* San Antonio, TX: Psychological Corporation/Graywind Publications.

Eaton, W. W., Dryman, A., & Weissman, M. M. (1991). Panic and phobia. In L. N. Robins & D. A. Regier (Eds.), *Psychiatric disorders in America: The Epidemiological Catchment Area study.* New York, NY: Free Press.

Emmelkamp, P. M. G. (1988). Phobic disorders. In C. G. Last & M. Hersen (Eds.), *Handbook of Anxiety Disorders* (pp. 66–86). New York, NY: Pergamon.

Feske, U., & Chambless, D. L. (1995). Cognitive behavioral versus exposure only treatment for social phobia: A meta-analysis. *Behavior Therapy, 26*, 695–720.

Feusner, J. D., Phillips, K. A., & Stein, D. J. (2010). Olfactory reference syndrome: Issues for *DSM-V. Depression and Anxiety, 27*, 592–599.

First, M. B., Spitzer, R. L., Gibbon, M., & Williams, J. B. W. (1997). *Structured Clinical Interview for DSM-IV Axis I disorders (SCID-I): Clinician version.* Washington, DC: American Psychiatric Press.

Foa, E. B., & Kozak, M. J. (1986). Emotional processing of fear: Exposure to corrective information. *Psychological Bulletin, 99*, 20–35.

Fredrikson, M., Annas, P., Fischer, H., & Wik, G. (1996). Gender and age differences in the prevalence of specific fears and phobias. *Behaviour Research and Therapy, 26*, 241–244.

Furukawa, T. A., Watanabe, N., & Churchill, R. (2006). Psychotherapy plus antidepressant for panic disorder with and without agoraphobia: Systematic review. *The British Journal of Psychiatry, 188*, 305–312.

Gazelle, H., & Ladd, G. W. (2003). Anxious solitude and peer exclusion: A diathesis-stress model of internalizing trajectories in childhood. *Child Development, 74*, 257–278.

Geer, J. H. (1965). The development of a scale to measure fear. *Behaviour Research and Therapy, 3*, 45–53.

Gerlernter, C. S., Uhde, T. W., Cimbolic, P., Arnkoff, D. B., Vittone, B. J., Tancer, M. E., & Bartko, J. J. (1991). Cognitive-behavioral and pharmacological treatments of social phobia: a controlled study. *Archives of General Psychiatry, 48*, 938–945.

Goisman, R. M., Warshaw, M. G., Peterson, L. G., Rogers, M. P., Cuneo, P., Hunt, M. E., . . . Keller, M. B. (1994). Panic, agoraphobia, and panic disorder with agoraphobia: Data from a multicenter anxiety disorders study. *Journal of Nervous and Mental Disease, 182*, 72–79.

Goldstein, A. J., de Beurs, E., Chambless, D. L., & Wilson, K. A. (2000). EMDR for panic disorder with agoraphobia: Comparison with waiting list and credible attention placebo control conditions. *Journal of Consulting and Clinical Psychology, 68*, 947–956.

Gorman, J. M., Kent, J. M., Martinez, J. M., Browne, S. T., Coplan, J. D., & Papp, L. A. (2001). Physiological changes during carbon dioxide inhalation in patients with panic disorder, major depression, and premenstrual dysphoric disorder: Evidence for a central fear mechanism. *Archives of General Psychiatry, 58*, 125–131.

Grant, B. F., Hasin, D. S., Blanco, C., Stinson, F. S., Chou, P., Goldstein, R. B., . . . Huang, B. (2005). The epidemiology of social anxiety disorder in the United States: Results from the national epidemiologic survey on alcohol and related conditions. *Journal of Clinical Psychiatry, 66*, 1351–1361.

Grant, B. F., Hasin, D. S., Stinson, F. S., Dawson, D. A., Goldstein, R. B., Smith, S. M., . . . Huang, B. (2006). The epidemiology of *DSM-IV* panic disorder and agoraphobia in the

United States: Results from the national epidemiologic survey on alcohol and related conditions. *Journal of Clinical Psychiatry, 67,* 363–374.

Gray, J. A., & McNaughton, N. (2000). *The neurobiology of anxiety: An enquiry into the functions of the sept-hippocampal system* (2nd ed.). New York, NY: Oxford University Press.

Greco, L. A., & Morris, T. L. (2005). Factors influencing the link between social anxiety and peer acceptance: Contributions of social skills and close friendships during middle childhood. *Behavior Therapy, 36,* 197–205.

Greenberg, P. E., Sisitsky, T., Kessler, R. C., Finkelstein, S. N., Berndt, E. R., Davidson, J. R., . . . Fyer, A. J. (1999). The economic burden of anxiety disorders in the 1990s. *Journal of Clinical Psychiatry, 60,* 427–435.

Grös, D. F., & Antony, M. M. (2006). The assessment and treatment of specific phobias: A review. *Current Psychiatry Reports, 8,* 298–303.

Groth-Marnat, G. (2003). *Handbook of psychological assessment* (4th ed.). Hoboken, NJ: John Wiley & Sons.

Guarnaccia, P. J., Lewis-Fernandez, R., & Marano, M. R. (2003). Toward a Puerto Rican popular nosology: Nervios and Ataque de Nervios. *Culture, Medicine, and Psychiatry, 27,* 339–366.

Guastella, A. J., Richardson, R., Lovibond, P. F., Rapee, R. M., Gaston, J. E., Mitchell, P., & Dadds, M. R. (2008). A randomized controlled trial of D-cycloserine enhancement of exposure therapy for social anxiety disorder. *Biological Psychiatry, 63,* 544–549.

Hamm, A. O. (2009). Specific phobias. *Psychiatric Clinics of North America, 32,* 577–591.

Harrington, P. J., Schmidt, N. B., & Telch, M. J. (1996). Prospective evaluation of panic potentiation following 35% $CO_2$ challenge in nonclinical subjects. *American Journal of Psychiatry, 153,* 823–825.

Hawker, D. S., Jr., & Boulton, M. J. (2000). Twenty years' research on peer victimization and psychosocial maladjustment: A meta-analytic review of cross-sectional studies. *Journal of Child Psychology and Psychiatry, 41,* 441–455.

Hayes, S. C., Luoma, J. B., Bond, F. W., Masuda, A., & Lillis, J. (2006). Acceptance and commitment therapy: Model, processes, and outcomes. *Behaviour Research and Therapy, 44,* 1–26.

Hayward, C., Killen, J. D., Kraemer, H. C., & Taylor, C. B. (1998). Linking self-reported childhood behavioral inhibition to adolescent social phobia. *Journal of the American Academy of Child and Adolescent Psychiatry, 37,* 1308–1316.

Heimberg, R. G., & Becker, R. E. (2002). *Cognitive behavioral group therapy for social phobia: Basic mechanisms and clinical applications.* New York, NY: Guilford Press.

Heimberg, R. G., Madsen, C. H., Montgomery, D., & McNabb, C. E. (1980). Behavioral treatments for heterosocial problems: Effects on daily self-monitored and role played interactions. *Behavior Modification, 4,* 147–172.

Heimberg, R. G., Salzman, D. G., Holt, C. S., & Blendell, K. A. (1993). Cognitive-behavioral group treatment for social phobia: Effectiveness at five-year follow-up. *Cognitive Therapy and Research, 17,* 325–339.

Heinrichs, N., Rapee, R. M., Alden, L. A., Bögels, S. M., Hofmann, S. G., Oh, K. J., & Sakano, Y. (2006). Cultural differences in perceived norms and social anxiety. *Behaviour Research and Therapy, 41,* 209–221.

Helbig-Lang, S., & Petermann, F. (2010). Tolerate or eliminate?: A systematic review of the effects of safety behavior across anxiety disorders. *Clinical Psychology: Science and Practice, 17,* 218–233.

Hettema, J. M., Neale, M. C., Myers, J. M., Prescott, C. A., & Kendler, K. S. (2006). A population-based twin study of the relationship between neuroticism and internalizing disorders. *American Journal of Psychiatry, 163,* 857–864.

Himle, J. A., McPhee, K., Cameron, O. G., & Curtis, G. C. (1989). Simple phobia: Evidence for heterogeneity. *Psychiatry Research, 28,* 25–30.

Hirsch, C. R., & Clark, D. M. (2004). Information-processing bias in social phobia. *Clinical Psychology Review, 24,* 799–825.

Hirschfield-Becker, D. R., Biederman, J., & Rosenbaum, J. F. (2004). Behavioral inhibhition. In T. L. Morris & J. S. March (Eds.), *Anxiety disorders in children and adolescents* (pp. 27–58). New York, NY: Guilford Press.

Hoffman, E. J., & Mathew, S. J. (2008). Anxiety disorders: A comprehensive review of pharmacotherapies. *Mount Sinai Journal of Medicine, 75,* 248–262.

Hoffman, S. G. (2004). Cognitive mediation of treatment change in social phobia. *Journal of Consulting and Clinical Psychology, 72,* 392–399.

Hofmann, S. G., Meuret, A. E., Smits, J. A., Simon, N. M., Pollack, M. H., Eisenmenger, K., . . . Otto, M. W. (2006). Augmentation of exposure therapy with D-cycloserine for social anxiety disorder. *Archives of General Psychiatry, 63,* 298–304.

Hofmann, S. G., & Otto, M. W. (2008). *Cognitive-behavior therapy of social phobia: Evidence-based and disorder specific treatment techniques.* New York, NY: Routledge.

Hofmann, S. G., & Smits, J. A. (2008). Cognitive-behavioral therapy for adult anxiety disorders: A meta-analysis of randomized placebo-controlled trials. *Journal of Clinical Psychiatry, 69,* 621–632.

Hook, J. N., & Valentiner, D. P. (2002). Are specific and generalized social phobias qualitatively distinct? *Clinical Psychology: Science and Practice, 9,* 393–409.

Jacob, R. G., Furman, J. M., Durrant, J. D., & Turner, S. M. (1996). Panic, agoraphobia, and vestibular dysfunction. *American Journal of Psychiatry, 153,* 503–512.

Jorstad-Stein, E. C., & Heimberg, R. G. (2009). Social phobia: An updated on treatment. *Psychiatric Clinics of North America, 32,* 641–663.

Kagan, J., Reznick, J. S., & Snidman, N. (1987). The physiology and psychology of behavioral inhibition in children. *Child Development, 58,* 1459–1473.

Kagan, J., & Snidman, N. (1999). Early childhood predictors of adult anxiety disorders. *Biological Psychiatry, 46,* 1536–1541.

Kamphuis, J. H., & Telch, M. J. (2000). Effects of distraction and guided threat reappraisal on fear reduction during exposure-based treatments for specific fears. *Behaviour Research and Therapy, 38,* 1163–1181.

Kathol, R. G., Noyes, R., Slyman, D. J., Crowe, R. R., Clancy, J., & Kerber, R. E. (1980). Propranolol in chronic anxiety disorders. *Archives of General Psychiatry, 37,* 1361–1365.

Keller, M. B. (2003). The lifelong course of social anxiety disorder: A clinical perspective. *Acta Psychiatrica Scandinavica, 108,* 85–95.

Keller, M. B., Yonkers, K. A., Warshaw, M. G., Pratt, L. A., Golan, J., Mathews, A. O., . . . Lavori, P. (1994). Remission and relapse in subjects with panic disorder and agoraphobia: A prospective short interval naturalistic follow-up. *Journal of Nervous and Mental Disorders, 182,* 290–296.

Kendler, K., Karkowski, L., & Prescott, C. (1999). Fears and phobias: Reliability and heritability. *Psychological Medicine, 29,* 539–553.

Kendler, K., Myers, J., Prescott, C., & Neale, M. C. (2001). The genetic epidemiology of irrational fears and phobias in men. *Archives in General Psychiatry, 58,* 257–265.

Kessler, R. C., Berglund, P., Demler, O., Jin, R., Merikangas, K., & Walters, E. E. (2005). Lifetime prevalence and age-of-onset distributions of *DSM-IV* disorders in the national comorbidity survey replication. *Archives of General Psychiatry, 62,* 593–602.

Kessler, R. C., Chiu, W. T., Demler, O., & Walters, E. E. (2005). Prevalence, severity, and comorbidity of 12-month *DSM-IV* disorders in the national comorbidity survey replication. *Archives of General Psychiatry, 62,* 617–627.

Kessler, R. C., Davis, C. G., & Kendler, K. S., (1997). Childhood adversity and adult psychiatric disorder in the U.S. National Comorbidity Survey. *Psychological Medicine, 27,* 1101–1119.

Kessler, R. C., Foster, C. L., Saunders, W. B., & Stang, P. E. (1995). Social consequences of psychiatric disorders, I: Education attainment. *American Journal of Psychiatry, 152,* 1026–1032.

Kessler, R. C., McGonagle, K. A., Zhao, S., Nelson, C. B., Hughes, M., Eshleman, S., . . . Kendler, K. S. (1994). Lifetime and 12-month prevalence of *DSM-III-R* psychiatric disorders in the United States: Results from the National Comorbidity Survey. *Archives of General Psychiatry, 51,* 8–19.

Khan, A., Leventhal, R. M., Khan, S., & Brown, W. A. (2002). Suicide risk in patients with anxiety disorders: A meta-analysis of the FDA database. *Journal of Affective Disorders, 63,* 183–191.

Kim, E. J. (2005). The effect of the decreased safety behaviors on anxiety and negative thoughts in social phobics. *Journal of Anxiety Disorders, 19,* 69–86.

Kim, H. S. (2010). Personal communication.

Kim, J., Rapee, R. M., & Gaston, J. E. (2008). Symptoms of offensive type Taijin-Kyofusho among Australian social phobics. *Depression and Anxiety, 25,* 601–608.

King, N. J., Eleonora, G., & Ollendick, T. H. (1998). Etiology of childhood phobias: Current status of Rachman's three pathways theory. *Behaviour Research and Therapy, 36,* 297–309.

Kircanski, K., Craske, M. G., Epstein, A. M., & Wittchen, H. U. (2010). Subtypes of panic attacks: A critical review of the empirical literature. *Depression and Anxiety, 26,* 878–887.

Kobak, K. A., Greist, J. H., Jefferson, J. W., & Katzelnick, D. J. (2002). Fluoxetine in social phobia: A double-blind, placebo-controlled pilot study. *Journal of Clinical Psychopharmacology, 22,* 257–262.

Krueger, R. F. (1999). The structure of common mental disorders. *Archives of General Psychiatry, 56,* 921–926.

Kushner, M. G., Abrams, K., & Borchardt, C. (2000). The relationship between anxiety disorders and alcohol use disorders: A review of major perspectives and findings. *Clinical Psychology Review, 20,* 149–171.

La Greca, A. M., & Harrison, H. M (2005). Adolescent peer relations, friendships, and romantic relationships: Do they predict social anxiety and depression? *Journal of Clinical Child and Adolescent Psychology, 34,* 49–61.

Lampe, L., Slade, T., Issakidis, C., & Andrews, G. (2003). Social phobia in the Australian National Survey of Mental Health and Well-Being (NSMHWB). *Psychological Medicine, 33,* 637–646.

Lang, P. J. (1979). A bio-informational theory of emotional imagery. *Psychophysiology, 16,* 495–512.

Leary, M. R. (1983a). A brief version of the Fear of Negative Evaluation Scale. *Personality and Social Psychology Bulletin, 9,* 371–375.

Leary, M. R. (1983b). *Understanding social anxiety: Social, personality, and clinical perspectives.* Beverly Hills, CA: Sage.

LeBeau, R. T., Glenn, D., Liao, B., Wittchen, H. U., Beesdo-Baum, K., Ollendick, T., & Craske, M. G. (2010). Specific phobia: A review of *DSM-IV* specific phobia and preliminary recommendations for *DSM-V. Depression and Anxiety, 27,* 148–167.

Lecrubier, Y., & Weiller, E. (1997). Comorbidities in social phobia. *International Clinical Psychopharmacology, 12*(Suppl. 6), 17–21.

Ledgerwood, L., Richardson, R., & Cranney, J. (2003). Effects of D-Cycloserine on extinction of conditioned freezing. *Behavioral Neuroscience, 117,* 341–349.

Ledley, D. R., & Heimberg, R. G. (2005). Social anxiety disorder. In M. M. Antony, D. R. Ledley, & R. G. Heimberg (Eds.), *Improving outcomes and preventing relapse in cognitive-behavioral therapy* (pp. 38–76). New York, NY: Guilford Press.

Lewis-Fernández, R., Hinton, D. E., Laria, A. J., Patterson, E. H., Hofmann, S. G., Craske, M. G., . . . Liao, B. (2010). Culture and the anxiety disorders: Recommendations for *DSM-V*. *Depression and Anxiety, 27*, 212–229.

Liebowitz, M. R., Gorman, J. M., Fyer, A. J., & Klein, D. R. (1985). Social phobia. *Archives of General Psychiatry, 42*, 729–736.

Lindal, E., & Stefansson, J. G. (1993). The lifetime prevalence of anxiety disorders in Iceland as estimated by the U.S. National Institute of Mental Health Diagnostic Interview Schedule. *Acta Psychiatrica Scandinavica, 88*, 29–34.

Lopez, F. J. C., & Salas, S. V. (2009). Acceptance and Commitment Therapy (ACT) in the treatment of panic disorder: Some considerations from the research on basic processes. *International Journal of Psychology and Psychological Theory, 9*, 299–315.

Magee, W. J., Eaton, W. W., Wittchen, H.-U., McGonagle, K. A. & Kessler, R. C. (1996). Agoraphobia, simple phobia, and social phobia in the National Comorbidity Survey. *Archives of General Psychiatry, 53*, 159–168.

Maller, R. G., & Reiss, S. (1992). Anxiety sensitivity in 1984 and panic attacks in 1987. *Journal of Anxiety Disorders, 6*, 241–247.

Mannuzza, S., Schneier, F. R., Chapman, T. F., Liebowitz, M. R., Klein, D. F., & Fyer, A. J. (1995). Generalized social phobia: Reliability and validity. *Archives of General Psychiatry, 52*, 230–237.

Marks, I. M., & Gelder, M. G. (1966). Different ages of onset in varieties of phobia. *American Journal of Psychiatry, 123*, 218–221.

Marks, I. M., Swinson, R. P., Basoglu, M., Kuch, K., Noshirvani, H., O'Sullivan, G., . . . Wickwire, K. (1993). Alprazolam and exposure alone and combined in panic disorder with agoraphobia. A controlled study in London and Toronto. *The British Journal of Psychiatry, 162*, 776–787.

Maron, E., Tõru, I., Tasa, G., Must, A., Toover, E., Lang, A., . . . Shlik, J. (2008). Association testing of panic disorder candidate genes using CCK-4 challenge in healthy volunteers. *Neuroscience Letters, 446*, 88–92.

Matchett, G., & Davey, G. C. L. (1991). A test of a disease-avoidance model of animal phobias. *Behaviour Research and Therapy, 29*, 91–94.

Mathews, A. M., Gelder, M. G., & Johnston, D. W. (1981). *Agoraphobia: Nature and treatment.* New York, NY: Guilford Press.

Mattick, R. P., & Clarke, J. C. (1998). Development and validation of measures of social phobia scrutiny fear and social interaction anxiety. *Behaviour Research and Therapy, 36*, 455–470.

Mavissakalian, M. R., & Perel, J. M. (1999). Long-term maintenance and discontinuation of imipramine therapy in panic disorder with agoraphobia. *Archives of General Psychiatry, 56*, 821–827.

McCabe, R. E., Antony, M. M., Summerfeldt, L. J., Liss, A., & Swinson, R. P. (2003). Preliminary examination of the relationship between anxiety disorders in adults and self-reported history of teasing or bullying experiences. *Cognitive and Behaviour Therapy, 32*, 187–193.

McHugh, R. K., Smits, J. A., Jr., & Otto, M. W. (2009). Empirically supported treatments for panic disorder. *Psychiatric Clinics of North America, 32*, 593–610.

McLean, P. D., Woody, S., Taylor, S., & Koch, W. J. (1998). Comorbid panic disorder and major depression: Implications for cognitive-behavioral therapy. *Journal of Consulting and Clinical Psychology, 66*, 240–247.

McNally, R. J. (1990). Psychological approaches to panic disorder: A review. *Psychological Bulletin, 108*, 403–419.

McNally, R. J. (2001). Vulnerability to anxiety disorders in adulthood. In R. E. Ingram & J. M. Price (Eds.), *Vulnerability to psychopathology: Risk across the lifespan* (pp. 304–321). New York, NY: Guilford Press.

McNally, R. J., Cassiday, K. L., & Calamari, J. E. (1990). *Taijin-kyofu-sho* in a black American woman: Behavioral treatment of a "culture-bound" anxiety disorder. *Journal of Anxiety Disorders, 4*, 83–87.

McNeil, D. W., Ries, B. R., Taylor, L. J., Boone, M. L., Carter, L. E., Turk, C. L., & Lewin, M. R. (1995). Comparison of social phobia subtypes using stroop tests. *Journal of Anxiety Disorders, 9*, 47–57.

Meaney, M. J., LeDoux, J. E., & Liebowitz, M. L. (2008). Neurobiology of anxiety disorders. In A. Tasman, J. Kay, J. A. Lieberman, M. B. First, & M. May (Eds.), *Psychiatry* (3rd ed., pp. 317–328). Hoboken, NJ: John Wiley & Sons.

Menzies, R. G., & Clarke, J. C. (1995). Danger expectancies and insight in acrophobia. *Behaviour Research and Therapy, 33*, 215–221.

Merckelbach, H., & de Jong, P. J. (1997). Evolutionary models of phobias. In G. C. L. Davey (Ed.), *Phobias: A handbook of theory, research, and treatment (pp. 323–348–)*. Chichester, England: John Wiley & Sons.

Mineka, S., & Öhman, A. (2001). Fears, phobias, and preparedness: Toward an evolved module of fear learning. *Psychological Review, 108*, 483–522.

Mineka, S., & Öhman, A. (2002). Phobias and preparedness: The selective, automatic, and encapsulated nature of fear. *Biological Psychiatry, 15*, 927–937.

Mineka, S., & Zinbarg, R. (1996). Conditioning and ethological models of anxiety disorders. In D. A. Hope (Ed.), *Nebraska Symposium on Motivation, Volume 43: Perspectives on anxiety, panic, and fear: Current theory and research in motivation* (pp. 135–201). Lincoln: University of Nebraska Press.

Mineka, S., & Zinbarg, R. (2006). A contemporary learning theory perspective on the etiology of anxiety disorders. *American Psychologist, 61*, 10–26.

Moehler, E., Kagan, J., Parzer, P., Brunner, R., Reck, C., Wiebel, A., . . . Resch, F. (2007). Childhood behavioral inhibition and maternal symptoms of depression. *Psychopathology, 40*, 446–452.

Mowrer, O. H. (1960). *Learning theory and behavior*. New York, NY: John Wiley & Sons.

Muhlberger, A., Herrmann, M. J., Wiedemann, G. C., Ellgring, H., & Pauli, P. (2001). Repeated exposure of flight phobics to flights in virtual reality. *Behaviour Research and Therapy, 39*, 1033–1050.

Mulkins, S., & Bögels, S. M. (1999). Learning history in fear of blushing. *Behaviour Research and Therapy, 37*, 1159–1167.

Murphy, M. T., Michelson, L. K., Marchione, K., Marchione, N., & Testa, S. (1998). The role of self-directed in vivo exposure in combination with cognitive therapy, relaxation training, or therapist-assisted exposure in the treatment of panic disorder with agoraphobia. *Journal of Anxiety Disorders, 12*, 117–138.

Norberg, M. M., Krystal, J. H., & Tolin, D. F. (2008). A meta-analysis of d-cycloserine and the facilitation of fear extinction and exposure therapy. *Biological Psychiatry, 63*, 1118–1126.

Norton, P. J., Zvolensky, M. J., Bonn-Miller, M. O., Cox, B. J., & Norton, R. (2008). Use of the Panic Attack Questionnaire-IV to assess non-clinical panic attacks and limited symptom panic attacks in student and community samples. *Journal of Anxiety Disorders, 22*, 1159–1171.

Öhman, A., & Soares, J. J. F. (1998). Emotional conditioning to masked stimuli: Expectancies for aversive outcomes following nonrecognized fear-irrelevant stimuli. *Journal of Experimental Psychology: General, 127,* 69–82.

Olatunji, B. O., Cisler, J. M., & Deacon, B. J. (2010). Efficacy of cognitive behavioral therapy for anxiety disorders: A review of meta-analytic findings. *Psychiatric Clinics of North America, 33,* 557–577.

Olatunji, B. O., Cisler, J. M., & Tolin, D. T. (2007). Quality of life in the anxiety disorders: A meta-analytic review. *Clinical Psychology Review, 27,* 572–581.

Ollendick, T. H., Öst, L. G., Reuterskiöld, L., & Costa, N. (2010). Comorbidity in youth with specific phobias: Impact of comorbidity on treatment outcome and the impact of treatment on comorbid disorders. *Behaviour Research and Therapy, 48,* 827–831.

Öst, L. G. (1987). Age of onset in different phobias. *Journal of Abnormal Psychology, 96,* 223–229.

Öst, L. G. (1989). One-session treatment for specific phobias. *Behaviour Research and Therapy, 27,* 1–7.

Öst, L. G. (2008). Efficacy of the third wave of behavioral therapies: A systematic review and meta-analysis. *Behaviour Research and Therapy, 46,* 296–321.

Öst, L. G., Thulin, U., & Ramnero, J. (2004). Cognitive behavior therapy vs. exposure in vivo in the treatment of panic disorder with agoraphobia (corrected from agrophobia). *Behaviour Research and Therapy, 42,* 1105–1127.

Otto, M. W., Pollack, M. H., Gould, R. A., Worthington, J. J., McArdle, E. T., & Rosenbaum, J. F. (2000). A comparison of the efficacy of clonazepam and cognitive-behavioral group therapy for the treatment of social phobia. *Journal Anxiety Disorders, 14,* 345–358.

Ouimet, A. J., Gawronski, B., & Dozois, D. J. A. (2009). Cognitive vulnerability to anxiety: A review and an integrative model. *Clinical Psychology Review, 29,* 459–470.

Page, A. C. (1994). Blood-injury phobia. *Clinical Psychology Review, 14,* 443–461.

Page, A. C., Bennett, K. S., Carter, O., Smith, J., & Woodmore, K. (1997). The Blood-Injection Symptom Scale (BISS): Assessing a structure of phobic symptoms elicited by blood and injections. *Behaviour Research and Therapy, 35,* 457–464.

Penava, S. J., Otto, M. W., Maki, K. M., & Pollack, M. H. (1998). Rate of improvement during cognitive-behavioral group treatment for panic disorder. *Behaviour Research and Therapy, 36,* 665–673.

Phillips, N. K., Hammen, C. L., Brennan, P. A., Najman, J. M., & Bor, W. (2005). Early adversity and the prospective prediction of depressive and anxiety disorders in adolescents. *Journal of Abnormal Child Psychology, 33,* 13–24.

Pine, D. S., Klein, R. G, Mannuzza, S., Moulton, J. L., Lissek, S., Guardino, M., & Woldejar-wariat, G. (2005). Face-emotion processing in offspring at risk for panic disorder. *Journal of the American Academy of Child and Adolescent Psychiatry, 44,* 664–672.

Pollack, M., Mangano, R., Entsuah, R., Tzanis, E., Simon, N. M., & Zhang, Y. (2007). A randomized controlled trial of venlafaxine ER and paroxetine in the treatment of outpatients with panic disorder. *Psychopharmacology, 194,* 233–242.

Ponniah, K., & Hollon, S. D. (2008). Empirically supported psychological interventions for social phobia in adults: A qualitative review of randomized controlled trials. *Psychological Medicine, 38,* 3–14.

Powers, M. B., Sigmarsson, S. R., & Emmelkamp, P. M. G. (2008). A meta-analytic review of psychological treatments for social anxiety disorder. *International Journal of Cognitive Therapy, 1,* 94–113.

Quirk, G. J., Paré, D., Richardson, R., Herry, C., Monfils, M. H., Schiller, D., & Vicentic, A. (2010). Erasing fear memories with extinction training. *Journal of Neuroscience, 30,* 14993–14997.

Rachman, S. (1977). The condition theory of fear acquisition: A critical examination. *Behaviour Research and Therapy, 15,* 375–387.

Rachman, S. (1980). Emotional processing. *Behaviour Research and Therapy, 18,* 51–60.

Rachman, S. (1984). Agoraphobia: safety signal perspective. *Behavioral Research and Therapy, 22,* 59–70.

Rachman, S. (1989). *Fear and courage* (2nd ed., rev.). New York, NY: Freeman.

Rachman, S. (1995). The overprediction of fear: A review. *Behaviour Research and Therapy, 32,* 683–690.

Radomsky, A. S., Rachman, S., Thordarson, D. S., McIsaac, H. K., & Teachman, B. A. (2001). The claustrophobia questionnaire. *Journal of Anxiety Disorders, 15,* 287–297.

Rapee, R. M., & Spence, S. H. (2004). The etiology of social phobia: Empirical evidence and an initial model. *Clinical Psychology Review, 24,* 737–767.

Reiss, S., & McNally, R. (1985). Expectancy model of fear. In S. Reiss & R. R. Bootzin (Eds.), *Theoretical issues in behavior therapy* (pp. 107–122). New York, NY: Academic Press.

Rescorla, R. (1974). Effects of inflation on the unconditioned stimulus value following conditioning. *Journal of Comparative and Physiological Psychology, 86,* 101–106.

Ressler, K. J., Rothbaum, B. O., Tannenbaum, L., Anderson, P., Graap, K., Zimand, E., . . . David, M. (2004). Cognitive enhancers as adjuncts to psychotherapy: Use of D-cycloserine in phobic individuals to facilitate extinction of fear. *Archives of General Psychiatry, 61,* 1136–1144.

Risbrough, V. B., & Geyer, M. A. (2008). Preclinical approaches to understanding anxiety disorders. In M. Antony (Ed.), *Oxford handbook of anxiety and related disorders* (pp. 75–86). New York, NY: Oxford University Press.

Rothbaum, B. O., Hodges, L., Smith, S., Lee, J. H., & Price, L. (2000). A controlled study of virtual reality exposure therapy for the fear of flying. *Journal of Consulting and Clinical Psychology, 68,* 1020–1026.

Rubin, K., Wojslawowicz, J., Rose-Krasnor, L., Booth-LaForce, C., & Burgess, K. (2006). The friendships of shy/withdrawn children: Prevalence, stability, and relationship quality. *Journal of Abnormal Child Psychology, 34,* 139–153.

Sanderson, W. C., Di Nardo, P. A., Rapee, R. M., & Barlow, D. H. (1990). Syndrome comorbidity in patients diagnosed with a *DSM-III-R* anxiety disorder. *Journal of Abnormal Psychology, 99,* 308–312.

Schmidt, N. B. (1999). Examination of differential anxiety sensitivities in panic disorder: A test of anxiety sensitivity subdomains predicting fearful responding to a 35% $CO_2$ challenge. *Cognitive Therapy and Research, 23i,* 3–19.

Schmidt, N. B., Lerew, D. R., & Jackson, R. J. (1997). The role of anxiety sensitivity in the pathogenesis of panic: Prospective evaluation of spontaneous panic attacks during acute distress. *Journal of Abnormal Psychology, 106,* 355–364.

Schmidt, N. B., Lerew, D. R., & Jackson, R. J. (1999). Prospective evaluation of anxiety sensitivity in the pathogenesis of panic: Replication and extension. *Journal of Abnormal Psychology, 108,* 532–537.

Schmidt, N. B., Storey, J., Greenberg, B. D., Santiago, H. T., Li, Q., & Murphy, D. L. (2000). Evaluating gene X psychological risk factor effects in the pathogenesis of anxiety: A new model approach. *Journal of Abnormal Psychology, 109,* 308–320.

Schwartz, C. E., Snidman, N., & Kagan, J. (1999). Adolescent social anxiety as an outcome of inhibited temperament in childhood. *Journal of the American Academic of Child and Adolescent Psychiatry, 38,* 1008–1015.

Seligman, M. (1971). Phobias and preparedness. *Behavior Therapy, 2,* 307–320.

Shear, M. K., Brown, T. A., Sholomskas, D. E., Barlow, D. H., Gorman, J. M., Woods, S. W., & Cloitre, M. (1997). *Panic Disorder Severity Scale (PDSS)*. Pittsburgh, PA: Department of Psychiatry, University of Pittsburgh School of Medicine.

Shear, M. K., Devereux, R. B., Kranier-Fox, R., Mann, J. J., & Frances, A. (1984). Low prevalence of mitral valve prolapse in patients with panic disorder. *American Journal of Psychiatry, 141*, 302–303.

Siegel, R. S., La Greca, A. M., & Harrison, H. M. (2009). Peer victimization and social anxiety in adolescents: Prospective and reciprocal relationships. *Journal of Youth and Adolescence, 38*, 1096–1109.

Spence, S. H. (1997). Structure of anxiety symptoms among children: A confirmatory factor-analytic study. *Journal of Abnormal Psychology, 106*, 280–297.

Spence, S. H. (1998). A measure of anxiety symptoms among children. *Behaviour Research and Therapy, 36*, 545–566.

Spence, S. H., Barrett, P. M., & Turner, C. M. (2003). Psychometric properties of the Spence Children's Anxiety Scale with young adolescents. *Journal of Anxiety Disorders, 17*, 605–625.

Spence, S. H., Donovan, C., & Brechman-Toussaint, M. (2000). The treatment of childhood social phobia: The effectiveness of a social skills training-based, cognitive-behavioral intervention, with and without parental involvement. *Journal of Child Psychology and Psychiatry, 41*(6), 713–726.

Spinhoven, P., Onstein, E. J., Klinkhamer, R. A., & Knoppert-van der Klein, E. A. M. (1996). Panic management, trazodone and a combination of both in the treatment of panic disorder. *Clinical Psychology and Psychotherapy, 3*, 86–92.

Stein, M. B., Chartier, M. J., Hazen, A. L., Kozak, M. V., Tancer, M. E., Lander, S., . . . Walker, J. R. (1998). A direct-interview family study of generalized social phobia. *American Journal of Psychiatry, 155*, 90–97.

Stein, M. B., & Kean, Y. M. (2000). Disability and quality of life in social phobia: Epidemiologic findings. *American Journal of Psychiatry, 157*, 1606–1613.

Stein, M. B., Lang, K. L., & Livesley, W. J. (1999). Heritability of anxiety sensitivity: A twin study. *American Journal of Psychiatry, 156*, 246–251.

Stein, M. B., Norton, R. G., Walker, J. R., Chartier, M. J., & Graham, R. (2000). Do selective serotonin re-uptake inhibitors enhance the efficacy of very brief cognitive-behavioral therapy for panic disorder? A pilot study. *Psychiatry Research, 94*, 191–200.

Stein, M. B., Schork, N. J., & Gelernter, J. (2008). Gene-by-environment (serotonin transporter and childhood maltreatment) interaction for anxiety sensitivity, an intermediate phenotype for anxiety disorders. *Neuropsychopharmacology, 33*, 312–319.

Stemberger, R., Turner, S. M., Beidel, D. C., & Calhoun, K. S. (1995). Social phobia: An analysis of possible developmental factors. *Journal of Abnormal Psychology, 104*, 526–531.

Stewart, S. H., Taylor, S., Lang, K. L., Box, B. J., Watt, M. C., Fedroff, I. C., & Borger, S. C. (2001). Causal modeling of relations among learning history, anxiety sensitivity, and panic attacks. *Behaviour Research and Therapy, 39*, 443–456.

Stinson, F. S., Dawson, D. A., Chou, S. P., Smith, S., Goldenstein, R. B., Ruan, W. J., & Grant, B. F. (2007). The epidemiology of *DSM-IV* specific phobia in the USA: Results from the national epidemiologic survey on alcohol and related conditions. *Psychological Medicine, 37*, 1047–1059.

Storch, E. A., & Masia-Warner, C. (2004). The relationship of peer victimization to social anxiety and loneliness in adolescent females. *Journal of Adolescence, 27*, 351–362.

Summerfeldt, L. J., Kloosterman, P. H., & Antony, M. M. (2010). Structured and semi-structured diagnostic interviews. In M. M. Antony & D. H. Barlow (Eds.), *Handbook of assessment and treatment planning for psychological disorders* (pp. 95–137). New York, NY: Guilford Press.

Syzmanski, J., & O'Donohue, W. (1995). Fear of spiders questionnaire. *Journal of Behavior Therapy and Experimental Psychiatry, 26,* 31–34.

Taylor, S. (1999). *Anxiety sensitivity: Theory, research, and treatment of the fear of anxiety.* Mahwah, NJ: Erlbaum.

Taylor, S., Koch, W. J., & McNally, R. J. (1992). How does anxiety sensitivity vary across the anxiety disorders? *Journal of Anxiety Disorders, 6,* 249–259.

Taylor, S., Zvolensky, M. J., Cox, B. J., Deacon, B., Heimberg, R. G., Ledley, D. R., Cardenas, S. J. (2007). Robust dimensions of anxiety sensitivity: Development and initial validation of the Anxiety Sensitivity Index – 3. *Psychological Assessment, 19,* 176–188.

Telch, M. J., Lucas, J. A., Schmidt, N. B., Hanna, H. H., Jaimez, T. L., & Lucas, R. A. (1993). Group cognitive-behavioral treatment of panic disorder. *Behaviour Research and Therapy, 31,* 279–287.

Tesar, G. E., Rosenbaum, J. F., Pollack, M. H., Otto, M. W., Sachs, G. S., Herman, J. B., . . . Spier, S. A. (1991). Double-blind, placebo-controlled comparison of clonazepam and alprazolam for panic disorder. *Journal of Clinical Psychiatry, 52,* 69–76.

Thyer, B. A., Himle, J., & Curtis, G. C. (1985). Blood-injury-illness phobia: A review. *Journal of Clinical Psychology, 41,* 451–459.

Thyer, B. A., Parrish, R. T., Curtis, G. C., Nesse, R. M., & Cameron, O. G. (1985). Ages of onset of DSM-III anxiety disorders. *Comprehensive Psychiatry, 26,* 113–122.

Trumpf, J., Becker, E. S., Vriends, N., Meyer, A. H., & Margraf, J. (2009). Rates and predictors of remission in young women with specific phobia: A prospective community study. *Journal of Anxiety Disorders, 23,* 958–964.

Tsao, J. C. I., Mystkowski, J. L., Zucker, B. G., & Craske, M. G. (2002). Effects of cognitive-behavioral therapy for panic disorder on comorbid conditions: Replication and extension. *Behavior Therapy, 33,* 493–509.

Turner, S. M., Beidel, D. C., Dancu, C. V., & Keys, D. J. (1986). Psychopathology of social phobia and comparison to avoidant personality disorder. *Journal of Abnormal Psychology, 95,* 389–394.

Turner, S. M., Beidel, D. C., Dancu, C. V., & Stanley, M. A. (1989). An empirically derived inventory to measure social fears and anxiety: The Social Phobia and Anxiety Inventory. *Psychological Assessment, 1,* 35–40.

Uhde, T. W., & Singareddy, R. (2002). Biological research in anxiety disorders. In M. Maj (Ed.), *Psychiatry as a neuroscience* (pp. 237–285). Hoboken, NJ: John Wiley & Sons.

Valentiner, D. P., Telch, M. J., Petruzzi, D. C., & Bolte, M. C. (1996). Cognitive mechanisms in claustrophobia: An examination of Reiss and McNally's expectancy model and Bandura's self-efficacy theory. *Cognitive Therapy and Research, 20,* 593–612.

Van Ameringen, M., Mancini, C., & Streiner, D. (1993). Fluoxetine efficacy in social phobia. *Journal of Clinical Psychiatry, 54,* 27–32.

Van Gerwen, L. J., Spinhoven, P., Diekstra, R. F. W., & Van Dyck, R. (2002). Multicomponent standardized treatment program for fear of flying. Description and effectiveness. *Cognitive and Behavioral Practice, 9,* 138–149.

van Vliet, I. M., Westenberg, H. G., & Den Boer, J. A. (1993). MAO inhibitors in panic disorder: Clinical effects of treatment with brofaromine. A double-blind placebo-controlled study. *Psychopharmacology, 112,* 483–489.

Vervliet, B., Kindt, M., Vansteenwegen, D., & Hermans, D. (2010). Fear generalization in humans: Impact of prior non-fearful experiences. *Behaviour Research and Therapy, 48,* 1078–1084.

Warshaw, M. G., Dolan, R. T., & Keller, M. B. (2000). Suicidal behavior in patients with current or past panic disorder: Five years of prospective data from the Harvard/Brown Anxiety Research Program. *American Journal of Psychiatry, 157,* 1876–1879.

Warshaw, M. G., Massion, A. O., Shea, M. T., Allsworth, J., & Keller, M. B. (1997). Predictors of remission in patients with panic with and without agoraphobia: Prospective 5-year follow-up data. *Journal of Nervous and Mental Disease, 185*, 517–519.

Watson, D. (2005). Rethinking the mood and anxiety disorders: A quantitative hierarchical model for *DSM-V. Journal of Abnormal Psychology, 114*, 522–536.

Watson, J. B., & Rayner, R. (1920). Conditioning emotional reactions. *Journal of Experimental Psychology, 3*, 1–14.

Watts, F. N., McKenna, F. P., Sharrock, R., & Trezise, L. (1986). Color naming of phobia-related words. *British Journal of Psychology, 77*, 97–108.

Wells, A., & Papageorgiou, C. (1998). Social phobia: Effects of external attention on anxiety, negative beliefs, and perspective taking. *Behavior Therapy, 29*, 357–370.

Westling, B. E., & Öst, L. G. (1995). Cognitive bias in panic disorder patients and changes after cognitive-behavioral treatments. *Behaviour Research and Therapy, 33*, 585–588.

Whisman, M. A., Sheldon, C. T., & Goering, P. (2000). Psychiatric disorders and dissatisfaction with social relationships: Does type of relationship matter? *Journal of Abnormal Psychology, 109*, 803–808.

Wilson, J. K., & Rapee, R. M. (2005). The interpretation of negative social events in social phobia: Changes during treatment and relationship to outcome. *Behaviour Research and Therapy, 43*, 373–389.

Wittchen, H. U., & Beloch, E. (1996). The impact of social phobia on quality of life. *International Clinical Psychopharmacology, 11*(Suppl. 3), 15–23.

Wittchen, H. U., Essau, C. A., Von Zerseen, D., Krieg, J. C., & Zaudig, M. (1992). Lifetime and six-month prevalence of mental disorders in the Munich follow-up study. *European Archives of Psychiatry and Clinical Neuroscience, 241*, 247–258.

Wittchen, H. U., Gloster, A. T., Beesdo-Baum, K., Fava, G. A., & Craske, M. G. (2010). Agoraphobia: A review of the diagnostic classificatory position and criteria. *Depression and Anxiety, 27*, 113–133.

Wittchen, H. U., Nelson, C. B., & Lachner, G. (1998). Prevalence of mental disorders and psychosocial impairments in adolescents and young adults. *Psychological Medicine, 28*, 109–126.

Wittchen, H. U., Stein, M. B., & Kessler, R. C. (1999). Social fears and social phobia in a community sample of adolescents and young adults: Prevalence, risk factors, and comorbidity. *Psychological Medicine, 29*, 309–323.

Wolitzky-Taylor, K. B., Horowitz, J. D., Powers, M. B., & Telch, M. J. (2008). Psychological approaches in the treatment of specific phobias: A meta-analysis. *Clinical Psychology Review, 28*, 1021–1037.

Woody, S. R., & Teachman, B. A. (2000). Intersection of disgust and fear: Normative and pathological views. *Clinical Psychology: Science and Practice, 7*, 291–311.

World Health Organization. (1992). *The ICD 10 classification of mental and behavioral disorders: Clinical descriptions and diagnostic guidelines.* Geneva, Switzerland: Author.

Yonkers, K. A., Bruce, S. E., Dyck, I. R., & Keller, M. B. (2003). Chronicity, relapse, and illness – course of panic disorder, social phobia, and generalized anxiety disorder: Findings in men and women from 8 years of follow-up. *Depression and Anxiety, 17*, 173–179.

Yonkers, K. A., Zlotnick, C., Allsworth, J., Warshaw, M., Shea, T., & Keller, M. B. (1998). Is the course of panic disorder the same in men and women? *American Journal of Psychiatry, 155*, 596–602.

Zhang, W., Ross, J., & Davidson, J. R. T. (2004). Social anxiety disorder in callers to the Anxiety Disorders Association of America. *Depression and Anxiety, 20*, 101–107.

CHAPTER 12

# Generalized Anxiety Disorder, Posttraumatic Stress Disorder, and Obsessive-Compulsive Disorder

DANIEL CONYBEARE and EVELYN BEHAR


WORRY IS THE core criterion for generalized anxiety disorder (GAD; American Psychiatric Association [APA], 2000), and is typically defined as repetitive thinking about future potential threat, imagined catastrophes, uncertainties, and risks (Watkins, 2008). Individuals with GAD spend an excessive amount of time worrying and feeling anxious about a variety of topics and find it difficult to control the worry. The diagnosis also requires three or more of the following six symptoms: (1) restlessness or feeling keyed up or on edge; (2) being easily fatigued; (3) difficulty concentrating or mind going blank; (4) irritability; (5) muscle tension; and (6) sleep disturbance. Finally, the worry and anxiety are not confined to another disorder (e.g., worry about social evaluation only in the context of social anxiety disorder), and they lead to significant distress or impairment.

The diagnosis of GAD first appeared in the *DSM-III* (APA, 1980), but it was poorly defined, unreliable, and assigned only in the absence of other disorders (Mennin, Heimberg, & Turk, 2004). With publication of the *DSM-III-R* (APA, 1987), the diagnostic criteria for GAD were revised to include worry as the primary feature and to allow for primary diagnoses of GAD in the presence of other disorders. Despite these improvements, diagnostic reliability remained poor due to overly broad criteria for associated symptoms (Marten et al., 1993). The *DSM-IV* (APA, 1994) added the uncontrollability criterion and reduced the set of associated symptoms to reflect empirical findings and to improve specificity. As a result, diagnostic reliability of GAD improved but remains low relative to most of the other anxiety disorders (Brown, Di Nardo, Lehman, & Campbell, 2001).

Posttraumatic stress disorder (PTSD) is defined as a persistent and distressing reaction to one or more traumatic events. The symptoms include mentally reexperiencing the event, avoiding reminders of the event, and physiological hyperarousal (APA, 2000). First, the diagnosis requires (A) exposure to an actual or threatened traumatic event and an emotional response involving fear, helplessness, or horror.

Second, the individual reports symptoms from each of three clusters. Reexperiencing symptoms (B) include repetitive and intrusive memories of the event; nightmares about the event; acting or feeling as if the event were happening again; intense psychological distress to internal or external trauma cues; and physiological reactivity to internal and/or external trauma cues. Avoidance symptoms (C) include an inability to recall important aspects of the trauma; diminished interest or participation in important activities; feelings of detachment or estrangement from others; restricted range of affect; and a sense of a foreshortened future. Hyperarousal symptoms (D) include difficulty falling or staying asleep; irritability or anger; difficulty concentrating; hypervigilance; and exaggerated startle response. The symptoms endorsed in categories B, C, and D must have lasted at least 1 month. Finally, the symptoms must be accompanied by significant distress or impairment in social, occupational, or other areas of importance.

Obsessive-compulsive disorder (OCD) is characterized by intrusive thoughts (obsessions) and repetitive behaviors or mental acts (compulsions; APA, 2000). Obsessions are further defined as recurrent and persistent thoughts, impulses, or images that are deemed intrusive and inappropriate and lead to distress. Furthermore, the individual must attempt to ignore, suppress, or neutralize the obsessions with some other thought or action and recognize that the obsessions are not externally imposed (as in thought insertion). Compulsions are defined as repetitive behaviors (e.g., hand washing or checking) that are performed in response to obsessions and according to rigid rules. Moreover, compulsions are aimed at reducing distress caused by the obsessions or preventing some dreaded outcome (even though obsessions and compulsions may not be realistically connected). A diagnosis of OCD only requires obsessions or compulsions, despite the functional connection between the two and their frequent co-occurrence (see following section). Finally, the symptoms must be accompanied by marked distress or impairment, or consume more than 1 hour per day.

## CLINICAL FEATURES

The *DSM-IV-TR* (APA, 2000) defines *worry* as "anxious expectation." Elsewhere it has been described as "a chain of thoughts and images, negatively affect-laden and relatively uncontrollable; it is an attempt to engage in mental problem-solving on an issue whose outcome is uncertain but contains the possibility of one or more negative outcomes" (Borkovec, Robinson, Pruzinsky, & DePree, 1983; p. 10). Interpersonal concerns are the most commonly reported worry topic, regardless of GAD status (Roemer, Molina, & Borkovec, 1997). However, individuals with GAD are more likely than those without GAD to worry about minor or routine issues and health or illness (Craske, Rapee, Jackel, & Barlow, 1989; Roemer et al., 1997). They also report more worry topics overall and that their worry is less controllable and more realistic. Finally, although the diagnosis of GAD is categorical, taxometric analyses have found that worry exists on a continuum and may occur to a greater or lesser extent in a given individual (Olatunji, Broman-Fulks, Bergman, Green, & Zlomke, 2010; Ruscio, Borkovec, & Ruscio, 2001). Given that worry is the core diagnostic feature of GAD, these findings support a dimensional classification of the disorder.

Most of the physiological symptoms of GAD overlap with depression; in a nonclinical sample, only muscle tension was correlated with worry and not correlated with depression (Joormann & Stöber, 1999). Looking beyond *DSM-IV* criteria, GAD is also associated with gastrointestinal symptoms (e.g., diarrhea, heartburn) and aches and pains (e.g., neck ache, sore jaw), controlling for symptoms of depression (Aldao, Mennin, Linardatos, & Fresco, 2010).

The clinical picture of PTSD varies greatly, at least in terms of symptom severity; although the diagnosis is categorical, the disorder likely represents the extreme end of a dimensional response to trauma (Ruscio, Ruscio, & Keane, 2002). Indeed, a dimensional structure of PTSD is evident across veteran and civilian samples (Broman-Fulks et al., 2006; Forbes, Haslam, Williams, & Creamer, 2005; Ruscio et al., 2002). One of the implications of this dimensional structure is that milder symptoms of PTSD are qualitatively similar to more severe symptoms. These milder symptoms nonetheless may cause distress and impairment. Indeed, veterans with subthreshold PTSD underutilize mental health care, despite increased comorbidity and impairment compared to veterans without PTSD (Grubaugh et al., 2005). Among Iraq and Afghanistan War veterans specifically, subthreshold PTSD is associated with elevated levels of anger and hostility (Jakupcak et al., 2007), as well as poor physical health functioning (Jakupcak et al., 2008). Among civilians, subthreshold PTSD is associated with levels of impairment and suicidality that are equivalent to those observed in full PTSD (Zlotnick, Franklin, & Zimmerman, 2002).

Avoidance and numbing symptoms of PTSD likely represent separate factors, despite their current grouping under a single factor (Asmundson et al., 2000; Asmundson, Stapleton, & Taylor, 2004; King, Leskin, King, & Weathers, 1998; McWilliams, Cox, & Asmundson, 2005). In fact, avoidance may be more closely related to reexperiencing symptoms, whereas numbing may be more closely related to hyperarousal symptoms; two-factor models of PTSD find separate reexperiencing/avoidance and hyperarousal/numbing clusters (Buckley, Blanchard, & Hickling, 1996; Taylor, Kuch, Koch, Crockett, & Passey, 1998). The four-factor model (reexperiencing, avoidance, numbing, and hyperarousal) results in improved fit over the current three-factor model among epidemiological samples of unselected individuals (Elhai, Ford, Ruggiero, & Frueh, 2009) and individuals with PTSD (Cox, Mota, Clara, & Asmundson, 2008), and thus will likely be adopted for the *DSM-5* (Friedman, Resick, Bryant, & Brewin, 2010).

A review of research on PTSD, suicide, and comorbid conditions found that suicidality is elevated among individuals with PTSD, and that comorbid conditions further increase suicidality (Panagioti, Gooding, & Tarrier, 2009; Jakupcak et al., 2009). Among combat veterans, reexperiencing symptoms may be the best predictor of suicide, whereas arousal symptoms may best predict suicide in community samples (interestingly, avoidance/numbing is negatively correlated with suicide, at least in community samples; Panagioti et al., 2009). Suicidality is an important concern in PTSD, but perhaps not more so than in other disorders; one study found that the risk of suicidal ideation or attempts among individuals with PTSD was equivalent to the risk among those with substance dependence but lower than the risk among those with manic depressive disorder (MDD) and bipolar disorder (Fu et al., 2002).

The clinical picture of OCD is typically characterized by obsessions and compulsions; 96% of outpatients with OCD report experiencing both, whereas 2% report that obsessions are predominant and another 2% report that compulsions are predominant (Foa & Kozak, 1995). When identifying themselves based on categorical descriptions, 44.2% report that they are the "mixed" obsessive-compulsive type, 39.6% report that they are the "compulsive" type, and 22.2% report that they are the "obsessive" type. Furthermore, patients tend to perceive compulsions as being more severe than obsessions. Lastly, obsessions and compulsions are often functionally related. For example, contamination fears are often accompanied by repetitive cleaning, whereas self-doubt and dread are often accompanied by repetitive checking (Turner & Beidel, 1988).

Contamination was the most commonly endorsed primary obsession in the *DSM-IV* field trials, followed by fear of harming oneself or others (these topics were endorsed as primary by 37.8% and 23.6% of outpatients with OCD, respectively; Foa & Kozak, 1995). Other common topics of obsessions include symmetry, somatic sensations, religion, sexual urges, and hoarding. Checking is the most commonly endorsed primary compulsion (28.2%), followed by cleaning and washing (26.6%). Other common compulsions include repetition of various behaviors, mental rituals, ordering, hoarding, and counting.

The latent structure of OCD has been examined by several factor analytic studies. A review of 12 of those studies (including more than 2,000 patients with OCD) identified four common symptom dimensions: symmetry/ordering, hoarding, contamination, and obsessions/checking (Mataix-Cols, do Rosario-Campos, & Leckman, 2005). Moreover, those dimensions were temporally stable and may coexist within an individual. A recent meta-analysis confirmed this four-factor model (Bloch, Landeros-Weisenberger, Rosario, Pittenger, & Leckman, 2008). Taxometric analyses indicate that the severity of symptoms for all subtypes were dimensional in nature (subtypes in this study were based on high responsibility and threat estimation, high perfectionism and need for certainty, elevated concern for contamination, and frequent checking; Haslam, Williams, Kyrios, McKay, & Taylor, 2005).

## DIAGNOSTIC CONSIDERATIONS

Correctly classifying GAD may be particularly difficult due to high rates of comorbidity and symptom overlap with other disorders, especially MDD (Kessler, Chiu, Demler, & Walters, 2005). Twenty-six percent of those with a primary diagnosis of GAD also meet criteria for current MDD (Brown, Campbell, Lehman, Grisham, & Mancill, 2001). Moreover, when disregarding the *DSM-IV* hierarchy rule that prohibits the diagnosis of GAD when symptoms occur only during the course of a mood disorder, 67% of those with a primary diagnosis of MDD also meet diagnostic criteria for current GAD. In a longitudinal birth-cohort study, 12% of the sample had lifetime diagnoses of both GAD and MDD (Moffitt et al., 2007). Among those comorbid cases, 37% reported that GAD temporally preceded MDD, and 32% reported that MDD temporally preceded GAD.

Despite substantial comorbidity between GAD and MDD, a recent study found evidence that GAD was more similar to other anxiety disorders than it was to depression with respect to risk factors and temporal patterns (Beesdo, Pine, Lieb, &

Wittchen, 2010). Furthermore, a substantial proportion of GAD diagnoses occurs without comorbid depression, and levels of impairment between the two disorders are comparable (Kessler, DuPont, Berglund, & Wittchen, 1999). Thus, although GAD and MDD overlap considerably, evidence suggests that they occur independently and represent unique syndromes.

Although worry is the primary diagnostic and clinical feature of GAD, the majority of high worriers do not meet criteria for the disorder (Ruscio, 2002). However, compared to high worriers without GAD, high worriers with GAD report more distress and impairment associated with worry, indicating that worry is more harmful among certain individuals. High worriers with GAD are also more likely to perceive their worry as uncontrollable (Ruscio & Borkovec, 2004). Individuals who do not meet the "excessiveness of worry" criterion may present a milder form of GAD; they are less symptomatic overall and report fewer comorbid disorders compared to individuals with full GAD (Ruscio et al., 2005). Nonetheless, GAD without "excessive" worry is associated with considerable impairment, high rates of treatment seeking, and high rates of comorbidity.

Comorbidity is also a concern when diagnosing PTSD. The National Comorbidity Survey Replication (NCS-R; Kessler, Chiu et al., 2005) found that PTSD was significantly correlated with all of the internalizing disorders and the alcohol use disorders (but not drug abuse/dependence), whereas the original National Comorbidity Survey (Kessler, Sonnega, Bromet, Hughes, & Nelson, 1995) found that PTSD was correlated with all disorders studied, including drug abuse/dependence. When comorbid with mood disorders, PTSD is more likely to be primary, whereas it is more likely to be secondary when comorbid with anxiety disorders (Kessler et al., 1995). Lastly, trauma exposure is associated with increased rates of depression among individuals with PTSD but not among individuals who were exposed to trauma but did not develop PTSD (Breslau, Davis, Peterson, & Schultz, 2000).

In the Breslau et al. (2000) study, the relationship between PTSD and depression did not vary by trauma type, although a review of various samples and types of trauma found that certain patterns of comorbidity were more likely to result from certain types of trauma. Specifically, drug abuse was especially likely among American combat veterans, panic disorder was especially likely for traumas with high unpredictability and arousal, and somatization was especially likely for traumas involving physical suffering (Deering, Glover, Ready, Eddleman, & Alarcon, 1996). Increased rates of substance use disorders found among individuals with PTSD are not explained by presence of trauma alone; substance use disorders are not elevated among individuals with trauma exposure who do not meet the criteria for PTSD (Breslau, Davis, & Schultz, 2003). Importantly, PTSD and comorbid diagnoses may change over time within a given individual. A study of trauma survivors found that half of those who reported PTSD only at 3-month follow-up reported depression only at 12-month follow-up; likewise, half of those with depression only at 3-month follow-up reported PTSD only at 12-month follow-up (O'Donnell, Creamer, & Pattison, 2004).

An additional consideration when diagnosing PTSD is the nature of the traumatic event. PTSD-like reactions have been noted following a variety of nontraumatic events (e.g., divorce; Dreman, 1991), and in the absence of a traumatic event altogether (Gold, Marx, Soler-Baillo, & Sloan, 2005; Mol et al., 2005; Scott & Stradling, 1994).

Nonetheless, experiencing, witnessing, or being confronted with (i.e., learning about) a traumatic event is required for a diagnosis (Criterion A1). As previously mentioned, the diagnosis also requires that the individual report fear, helplessness, or horror in response to the trauma (Criterion A2). However, removing the A2 criterion does not substantially increase the rate of PTSD, suggesting that clinically significant symptoms occur in the absence of the specific emotional responses described in the *DSM-IV-TR* (Karam et al., 2010). Moreover, PTSD with criterion A2 does not differ from PTSD without criterion A2 in terms of persistence, suicidal ideation, or comorbidity. Similarly, A2 does not add to the ability of A1 to statistically predict the presence of PTSD (i.e., individuals who endorse both A1 and A2 are no more likely to report PTSD than are individuals who only endorse A1; Bedard-Gilligan & Zoellner, 2008). Lastly, from a theoretical perspective, requiring a particular emotional response as part of the traumatic event criterion confounds etiology (i.e., the traumatic event) with phenomenology (i.e., the symptoms experienced in response to the traumatic event; North, Suris, Davis, & Smith, 2009). For these reasons, the A2 criterion will likely be removed for the *DSM-5*.

Comorbidity may be less of a concern when diagnosing OCD, given its lower correlations with other disorders. For example, the NCS-R found that OCD was significantly correlated only to the occurrence of major depressive episodes, PTSD, and alcohol abuse, whereas GAD and PTSD were correlated with a variety of disorders (Kessler, Chiu et al., 2005). A large-scale study using the ADIS-IV-L found that OCD was associated with lower rates of comorbid disorders compared to GAD and PTSD; individuals with a principal diagnosis of OCD were only more likely to report a lifetime diagnosis of MDD, whereas individuals with a principal diagnosis of GAD or PTSD were more likely to report a variety of comorbid current and lifetime disorders (Brown, Campbell et al., 2001). Nonetheless, rates of comorbidity among individuals with OCD are substantial. Moreover, particular patterns of comorbidity may represent subtypes of OCD. A recent investigation utilizing latent class analysis reported that one subtype was most commonly associated with MDD, another subtype was associated with a variety of affective and anxiety disorders, and the final subtype was relatively strongly linked to tic disorder (Nestadt et al., 2009).

An additional concern when diagnosing OCD is to distinguish obsessions from other mental phenomena, such as worry or delusions. Obsessions typically reflect concerns about issues such as contamination, religion, and aggression, whereas worries tend to reflect concerns about everyday matters (although either may focus on health; Turner, Beidel, & Stanley, 1992). Moreover, obsessions may be experienced as thoughts, impulses, or images, and are typically strongly resisted, whereas worry is typically verbal-linguistic in nature and not as strongly resisted. Finally, obsessions tend to be ego-dystonic and perceived as "inappropriate," whereas worries are more likely to be ego-syntonic (Franklin & Foa, 2008; Turner et al., 1992).

Obsessions may also be confused with delusions. In a small sample of individuals with OCD, 28% reported some psychotic features, suggesting that OCD and psychotic symptoms may co-occur (Stanley, Turner, & Borden, 1990). Moreover, 25% of individuals with OCD strongly believe that their obsessions or compulsions are realistic (Kozak & Foa, 1994). Interestingly, degree of insight is not necessarily correlated with severity, indicating that an individual with perfect insight may have very severe symptoms; likewise, an individual with poor insight may have relatively mild symptoms (Eisen et al., 1998).

## EPIDEMIOLOGY

When *DSM-IV-TR* criteria are used, the 12-month prevalence of GAD is 3.1%, compared to 2.7% for panic disorder, 6.8% for social phobia, 8.7% for specific phobia, and 6.7% for MDD (Kessler, Chiu et al., 2005). Lifetime prevalence of *DSM-IV*-diagnosed GAD is 5.7%, compared to 4.7% for panic disorder, 12.1% for social phobia, 12.5% for specific phobia, and 16.6% for MDD (Kessler, Berglund et al., 2005). As noted previously, rates of comorbidity are substantial; the co-occurrence of GAD and at least one major depressive episode comprises one of the 12 most common pairs of disorders (Kessler, Chiu et al., 2005).

The 12-month prevalence of PTSD is 3.5% (Kessler, Chiu et al., 2005), and the lifetime prevalence is 6.8% (Kessler, Burglund et al., 2005). In an analysis of 10 different types of traumas (e.g., physical assault, fire, combat), tragic deaths were reported most frequently, sexual assault was most reliably associated with PTSD, and motor vehicle accidents were most adverse in terms of being both relatively frequent and symptom inducing (Norris, 1992). When PTSD occurs, however, the symptom presentation appears to be similar across different types of events; natural disasters (McFarlane, 1988), workplace accidents (Schottenfeld & Cullen, 1986), and wartime experiences (Keane & Fairbank, 1983) may all result in similar symptom patterns.

The 12-month prevalence of OCD is 1.0% (Kessler, Chiu et al., 2005), and the lifetime prevalence is 1.6% (Kessler, Berglund et al., 2005), indicating that OCD is less common than many other disorders. OCD may also differ from other disorders in terms of severity. In the NCS-R, approximately half of OCD cases were classified as serious, compared to 32.3% of GAD and 36.6% of PTSD cases (Kessler, Chiu et al., 2005).

## PSYCHOLOGICAL AND BIOLOGICAL ASSESSMENT

GAD is typically assessed by use of semistructured clinical interviews. The Anxiety Disorders Interview Schedule for *DSM-IV* (ADIS-IV; Brown, DiNardo, & Barlow, 1994) is a clinical interview commonly used to assess the presence of anxiety disorders. The ADIS-IV yields dimensional severity ratings at the symptom and disorder levels. The interviewer assigns a clinical severity rating (CSR) from 0 to 8 for each disorder with a typical dichotomous diagnostic cutoff of 4. For GAD, the interviewer further assigns dimensional scores on excessiveness and uncontrollability subscales for each of nine common worry domains. Inter-rater reliability for GAD is good for the CSR ($r = .72$), the composite scores for the excessiveness ($r = .73$) and uncontrollability ($r = .78$) of worry, and somatic tension and negative affect ($r = .83$; Brown, DiNardo et al., 2001). Inter-rater reliability is also good ($\kappa = .65$) for dichotomous diagnoses of current GAD. However, reliability for current diagnoses is notably higher among most of the other anxiety disorders, including specific phobia ($\kappa = .71$), social anxiety disorder ($\kappa = .77$), and panic disorder with agoraphobia ($\kappa = .81$).

GAD symptoms and trait worry can also be assessed with existing self-report measures, most notably the Generalized Anxiety Disorder Questionnaire—*DSM-IV* (GAD-Q-IV; Newman et al., 2002) and the Penn State Worry Questionnaire (PSWQ; Meyer, Miller, Metzger, & Borkovec, 1990). The GAD-Q-IV is a nine-item self-report measure of the symptoms of GAD, as outlined in the *DSM-IV-TR*, that have occurred during the past 6 months. The GAD-Q-IV assesses the excessiveness, frequency, and controllability of worry, the somatic symptoms of GAD, and interference and distress associated with both worry and physical symptoms. A dimensional scoring scheme with a cutoff score of 5.7 yields high sensitivity (83%) and specificity (89%) for identifying ADIS-IV-diagnosed GAD (Newman et al., 2002). The PSWQ is a 16-item self-report trait measure of the frequency and intensity of worry. The PSWQ has demonstrated high internal consistency and good retest reliability (Meyer et al., 1990) and identifies GAD cases with a sensitivity of .75 and specificity of .86 (Behar, Zuellig, & Borkovec, 2005). Furthermore, among a clinical sample receiving treatment for GAD, the PSWQ was uncorrelated with measures of anxiety and depression (Meyer et al., 1990). The latter finding suggests that trait worry can be differentiated from anxiety and depression, at least among individuals with GAD. Finally, individuals with GAD score higher on the PSWQ compared to individuals with other anxiety disorders (Brown, Antony, & Barlow, 1992).

PTSD is most commonly assessed using the Clinician-Administered PTSD Scale (CAPS; Blake et al., 1995). The CAPS includes a detailed assessment of each traumatic event, frequency and severity ratings for each symptom, and overall distress and impairment ratings. The CAPS has demonstrated excellent inter-item, inter-rater, and retest reliability, as well as convergent and discriminant validity and sensitivity to clinical change (Weathers, Keane, & Davidson, 2001). Several CAPS scoring algorithms have demonstrated good reliability and diagnostic utility (Weathers, Ruscio, & Keane, 1999). One method is to score a symptom as present if the frequency is greater than or equal to one and the intensity is greater than or equal to two, and to further require the endorsement of symptoms following *DSM-IV* criteria. This method favors sensitivity (.91) over specificity (.71), and thus may be better for screening purposes. Using a total dimensional cut-score of greater than or equal to 65, on the other hand, favors specificity (.91) over sensitivity (.82), and thus may be better for confirming a diagnosis (Weathers et al., 1999). The ADIS-IV can be used to assess PTSD, although inter-rater reliability for current diagnoses ($\kappa = .59$) is relatively low compared to the other anxiety disorders (Brown, Di Nardo et al., 2001).

Self-report questionnaires may also be used to assess PTSD. Commonly used measures include the PTSD Checklist (Weathers, Litz, Herman, Huska, & Keane, 1993), the Mississippi Scale for Combat-Related PTSD (Keane, Caddell, & Taylor, 1988), the PTSD Symptom Scale—Self-Report (PSS-SR; Foa, Riggs, Dancu, & Rothbaum, 1993), and the Posttraumatic Diagnostic Scale (PDS; Foa, Cashman, Jaycox, & Perry, 1997). An extensive list of measures used to assess PTSD is available from the National Center for PTSD (www.ptsd.va.gov).

Several physiological variables distinguish current PTSD from lifetime PTSD and no PTSD, including increased heart rate at rest and in response to non-trauma-related stressors, as well as increased heart rate, skin conductance, and diastolic blood pressure in response to trauma cues (Keane et al., 1988). However, the diagnostic utility of those physiological variables is limited; the optimal model correctly classified only approximately two-thirds of current PTSD cases, which was less accurate than interview-based and self-report assessments.

OCD is also typically assessed by use of semistructured clinical interviews. The ADIS-IV-L has demonstrated good retest reliability for lifetime diagnoses of OCD ($\kappa = .75$) and excellent inter-rater reliability for current diagnoses ($\kappa = .85$; Brown, Di Nardo et al., 2001). It also includes dimensional ratings of the persistence/distress and resistance associated with various types of obsessions, the severity of compulsions, and overall clinical severity. The Yale-Brown Obsessive-Compulsive Scale (Y-BOCS), another clinician-administered measure, is substantially shorter than the ADIS yet demonstrates good psychometric properties (Goodman, Price, Rasmussen, Mazure, Delgado et al., 1989; Goodman, Price, Rasmussen, Mazure, Fleischmann et al., 1989). The Y-BOCS has recently been revised to assess avoidance symptoms and the length of obsession-free intervals (instead of resistance to obsessions; Storch, Larson et al., 2010; Storch, Rasmussen et al., 2010).

Self-report measures of OCD with established reliability and validity include a self-report version of the Y-BOCS (Steketee, Frost, & Bogart, 1996) and the Obsessive-Compulsive Inventory—Revised, which assesses symptoms based on six categories of obsessions and compulsions (Foa et al., 2002). Given that family members may play a role in the maintenance of OCD symptoms (e.g., by participating in cleaning rituals or offering reassurance in response to contamination fears; Calvocoressi et al., 1995; Steketee, 1997), it may also be useful to assess the accommodation of symptoms by family members (Calvocoressi et al., 1999).

Although behavioral avoidance tests are typically used to assess fear and avoidance in phobias, they have also been used to assess OCD (Grabill et al., 2008). Behavioral avoidance tests are more difficult to implement, but at least one method is relatively straightforward and has good psychometric properties (Steketee, Chambless, Tran, Worden, & Gillis, 1996). The therapist and client jointly select three tasks that the client deems impossible to complete without significant anxiety or enactment of rituals. Each task is further broken down into seven steps, each of which is attempted sequentially. Scores are given in terms of subjective distress, avoidance of the task, and rituals performed during the task.

## ETIOLOGICAL CONSIDERATIONS

### BEHAVIORAL AND MOLECULAR GENETICS

A meta-analysis of family and twin studies found that genetic factors account for approximately 32% of the variance in liability to GAD (Hettema, Neale, & Kendler, 2001). Not surprisingly, there is considerable overlap in genetic liability for GAD and MDD, 25% of which is accounted for by neuroticism (Kendler, Gardner, Gatz, & Pedersen, 2007). Furthermore, a large twin study found that GAD and depression were linked to one genetic factor termed "anxious-misery," whereas the phobias were linked to another factor termed "fear" (panic disorder was linked to both factors, but less strongly; Kendler, Prescott, Myers, & Neale, 2003). A similar study examining only anxiety disorders found that GAD is linked to the same genetic factor as panic disorder and agoraphobia, whereas a different genetic factor was associated with situational and animal phobias (Hettema, Prescott, Myers, Neale, & Kendler, 2005). Despite genetic overlap, family studies suggest that GAD and panic disorder are somewhat distinct. For example, rates of GAD are higher among relatives of individuals with GAD compared to relatives of individuals with panic disorder (Noyes et al., 1992; Weissman, 1990).

Some studies have found associations between specific genes and GAD. Variation in the monoamine oxidase A (MAOA) serotonin transporter genes may confer increased risk for GAD. A polymorphism in the MAOA gene was associated with GAD but not panic disorder or MDD (Tadic et al., 2003), whereas a different MAOA polymorphism was associated with GAD, panic attacks, and possibly specific phobia and agoraphobia. Similarly, a variant in the serotonin transporter linked polymorphic region (5-HTTLPR) was overrepresented among individuals with GAD compared to normal controls (You, Hu, Chen, & Zhang, 2005). However, another study failed to replicate this finding (Samochowiec et al., 2004). Nonetheless, meta-analyses have concluded that the 5-HTTLPR polymorphism is associated with self-reported neuroticism and anxiety-related traits (Schinka, Busch, & Robichaux-Keene, 2004; Sen, Burmeister, & Ghosh, 2004), as well as amygdala activation during functional neuroimaging studies (Munafò, Brown, & Hariri, 2008). Moreover, presence of the 5-HTTLPR polymorphism moderates the relationship between childhood trauma and anxiety sensitivity, such that individuals with polymorphism and childhood trauma report the highest levels of anxiety sensitivity (Stein, Schork, & Gelernter, 2008). Thus, specific genetic polymorphisms may increase risk for GAD and anxiety-related traits (e.g., neuroticism and anxiety sensitivity).

Among veterans serving during the Vietnam War era, the liability to develop PTSD can be explained by (a) a genetic factor common to alcohol use and PTSD (accounting for 15.3% of the variance), (b) a genetic factor associated with PTSD but not with alcohol use (20.0% of the variance), and (c) unique environmental effects (54.0% of the variance; Xian et al., 2000). Another twin study of Vietnam War veterans found that the genetic factors that accounted for the relationship between combat exposure and PTSD also accounted for the relationship between combat exposure and alcohol use (McLeod et al., 2001). However, genetic factors contributed more to the relationship between combat exposure and PTSD as compared to environmental factors; genetic and environmental factors contributed equally to the relationship between combat exposure and alcohol use. Interestingly, the genetic factors that account for the presence of PTSD may also influence exposure to certain types of traumatic events. Concordance of both interpersonal violence and PTSD is higher among monozygotic twins compared to dizygotic twins (whereas other types of trauma, such as natural disasters and motor vehicle accidents, are not accounted for by genetic factors; Stein, Jang, Taylor, Vernon, & Livesley, 2002).

In terms of specific genetic markers, the 5-HTTLPR polymorphism is associated with increased risk to develop PTSD (and depression) among high-exposure hurricane survivors (but not among low-exposure survivors or survivors with high social support; Kilpatrick et al., 2003). A similar study in a community sample found that the 5-HTTLPR polymorphism is associated with increased risk of lifetime PTSD among individuals who reported both childhood and adult traumatic events

(Xie et al., 2009). A similar interaction has been reported for variants of polymorphisms in the FK506 binding protein 5 (FKBP5) gene, which is involved in regulating intracellular effects of cortisol. Individuals with these variants who had also experienced severe child abuse were at increased risk for PTSD after experiencing trauma as adults (Binder et al., 2008; Xie et al., 2010). This gene was underexpressed among survivors of the September 11, 2001 attacks on the World Trade Center who developed PTSD compared to those who did not (Yehuda et al., 2009). There is evidence for candidate genes in other systems (e.g., the dopamine system), but findings have been limited or inconsistent (Broekman, Olff, & Boer, 2007; Koenen, 2007; Koenen, Nugent, & Amstadter, 2008).

The previously mentioned meta-analysis of family studies on the anxiety disorders (Hettema, Neale, & Kendler, 2001) also found support for the familial aggregation of OCD. The rate of OCD among first-degree relatives of probands was 8.2%, compared to 2.0% among comparison relatives (the rates for panic disorder were 10.0% and 2.1%, respectively). A large-scale twin study found that 36% of the variance in factor-analytically-derived dimensions of rumination, contamination, and checking was accounted for by genetic factors (nonshared environment accounted for the rest of the variance; van Grootheest, Boomsma, Hettema, & Kendler, 2008).

Genetics may influence some types of OCD symptoms more than others. For example, taboo thoughts and hoarding were the most highly correlated symptom dimensions among OCD and non-OCD twin pairs (doubt/checking and contamination/cleaning dimensions were significantly but less strongly correlated, and symmetry/ordering was not correlated; Pinto et al., 2008). Certain symptom dimensions may also cluster with one another based on underlying genetic factors. A large-scale family study found that symptom factors representing doubt (including fears of harm and checking) and taboos (religious, sexual, and aggressive obsessions) share genetic influence, as do the factors representing hoarding/symmetry and contamination/cleaning (Katerberg et al., 2010). Finally, genetic influence is not uniform across individuals; a recent study identified two subtypes of OCD based on degree of familial association (Schooler, Revell, Timpano, Wheaton, & Murphy, 2008). The more familial type was associated with earlier age of onset and greater severity.

In terms of specific genetic markers, a recent association study found that OCD is associated with polymorphisms in the glutamate transporter gene (Wendland et al., 2009). OCD is also associated with the 5-HTT gene and other genes associated with serotonin (Hemmings & Stein, 2006). One study in particular found that the 5-HTTLPR polymorphism roughly doubles the risk of OCD (Hu et al., 2006).

## Neuroanatomy and Neurobiology

Patterns of connectivity between the amygdala, the medial prefrontal cortices, and other associated areas suggest the engagement of a compensatory, cognitive control system among individuals with GAD (Etkin, Prater, Schatzberg, Menon, & Greicius, 2009). Moreover, individuals with GAD fail to use the pregenual anterior cingulate to dampen amygdala activity and regulate emotions during laboratory emotional conflict tasks (Etkin, Prater, Hoeft, Menon, & Schatzberg, 2010). Interestingly, the medial prefrontal and anterior cingulate regions are associated with worry both in individuals with GAD and in normal controls, but only individuals with GAD show persistent activation in these areas following experimental worry periods (Paulesu et al., 2010). GAD is also associated with increased brain activity in response to both neutral and worry-related verbal statements, and reductions in that increased activity correspond to reductions in anxiety during treatment with citalopram (Hoehn-Saric, Schlund, & Wong, 2004). Lastly, individuals with GAD show increased gamma-band EEG activity in areas associated with negative emotion, as well as increased subjective negative emotion while worrying compared to individuals without GAD (Oathes et al., 2008). Moreover, both of these were attenuated following treatment for GAD.

The amygdala has been implicated in GAD, but the findings are not entirely clear. For example, individuals with GAD show increased activity in the amygdala in response to neutral and aversive pictures (relative to healthy controls; Nitschke et al., 2009). In response to fearful faces, however, individuals with GAD show decreased activity in the amygdala (relative to individuals with social anxiety disorder and healthy controls; Blair et al., 2008). Finally, the neurochemical under-pinnings of GAD likely involve abnormalities in several neurotransmitters, includ-ing gamma-aminobutyric acid (GABA), which is thought to mediate anxiety; norepinephrine (NE), a mediator of the sympathetic nervous system; and serotonin (5-HT), a target of efficacious pharmacologic treatment of GAD (Sinha, Mohlman, & Gorman, 2004).

Physiology of GAD is characterized by autonomic inflexibility; chronic tension and anxiety may lead to a restricted range of autonomic responses to environ-mental triggers (Thayer, Friedman, & Borkovec, 1996). GAD is associated with decreased vagal tone (an index of parasympathetic activity) and heart rate (Lyon-fields, Borkovec, & Thayer, 1995; Thayer et al., 1996). Importantly, physiological variables differ among individuals with GAD; only those high in baseline sympa-thetic arousal displayed reduced sympathetic response to a lab stressor (Fisher, Granger, & Newman, 2010).

Autonomic inflexibility has also been linked to panic disorder, and thus the physiological profile of GAD overlaps with other disorders (Hoehn-Saric et al., 2004). Nonetheless, research suggests that the physiological profile of GAD is related to a physiological-inhibitory effect of worry, the primary feature of the disorder. Worrying prior to exposure to a phobic image is associated with decreased heart rate response relative to neutral thinking or relaxation (Borkovec & Hu, 1990; Borkovec, Lyonfields, Wiser, & Deihl, 1993). Moreover, experimentally induced worry is also associated with decreased vagal tone, heart rate, and heart rate variability compared to neutral thinking among individuals with and without GAD (Thayer et al., 1996; Lyonfields et al., 1995). Worry is also associated with decreased heart rate response during subsequent anxiety-eliciting tasks (increased heart rate during exposure is a marker of emotional processing; Foa & Kozak, 1986) while simultaneously increasing subjective distress (e.g., Borkovec & Hu, 1990).

Several brain structures have been implicated in PTSD, including the amygdala, the medial prefrontal cortex, and the hippocampus. First, PTSD is associated with increased activation in the amygdala in response to trauma-related stimuli (Francati, Vermetten, & Bremner, 2007). This increased activity likely represents the neural substrates of exaggerated fear acquisition and expression and may explain the salience of trauma memories in PTSD (Rauch, Shin, & Phelps, 2006; Rauch, Shin, & Wright, 2003). Importantly, hyperactivity in the amygdala is not unique to PTSD; increased activity in response to disorder-related stimuli has also been noted in specific phobia and social anxiety disorder (Etkin & Wagner, 2007; Shin & Liberzon, 2010).

Second, PTSD is associated with deficient functioning in the medial prefrontal cortex (Francati et al., 2007; Shin & Liberzon, 2010). This deficiency is thought to underlie inadequate top-down modulation of the amygdala (Rauch et al., 2006). Moreover, the medial prefrontal cortex is thought to regulate processes that are important for habituation and extinction of fear responses, including emotional appraisal (Liberzon & Sripada, 2008).

Third, PTSD is associated with abnormalities in the hippocampus. These abnormalities may underlie difficulties contextualizing memories (e.g., recognizing that certain contexts are safe; Liberzon & Sripada, 2008; Rauch et al., 2006). A meta-analysis concluded that increased PTSD severity is associated with decreased volume of the hippocampus (as well as decreased volume in the amygdala and the anterior cingulate, a structure in the medial prefrontal cortex; Karl et al., 2006). Decreased hippocampal volume likely represents a risk factor for developing PTSD, as opposed to a neurobiological effect of trauma (McNally, 2003). Indeed, hippocampal volume does not change over time following trauma exposure (Bonne et al., 2001). Moreover, a study of veteran twin pairs discordant for combat exposure and PTSD found that PTSD severity among affected twins was negatively correlated with not only their own hippocampal volume but also that of their nonexposed co-twin (Gilbertson et al., 2002).

The neurochemical underpinnings of PTSD likely involve catecholamines (epinephrine, norepinephrine, and dopamine) and cortisol, a hormone involved in the neuroendocrine response to stress, as well as a variety of other neurotransmitters (Yehuda & Sarapas, 2010). Several studies have found that PTSD is associated with elevated levels of catecholamines at baseline and in response to challenge tasks (Yehuda, 2006). PTSD may also be characterized by disturbance of the hypothalamic-pituitary-adrenal axis, arising primarily from hypersensitivity of glucocorticoid (i.e., cortisol) receptors (Yehuda et al., 2009). This may represent a risk factor, although the research findings are not yet clearly integrated into a cohesive model. Lastly, PTSD is characterized by cardiovascular alterations. A meta-analysis concluded that heart rate and blood pressure were higher among individuals with PTSD compared to trauma-exposed individuals without PTSD and individuals with no trauma exposure (Buckley & Kaloupek, 2001).

Neurobiological models of OCD implicate the cortico-striato-thalamo-cortico (CSTC) circuit. This circuit connects regions that are involved in implicit behavioral responses and includes the orbitofrontal cortex, caudate nucleus, striatum, thalamus, and other associated subcortical regions (for a review, see Menzies et al., 2008). The orbitofronto-striatal model in particular posits that an imbalance between the excitatory and inhibitory control of that circuit mediates OCD, such that overactivity of the excitatory control leads to symptom expression. Structural and functional neuroimaging studies generally find abnormalities in the orbitofronto-striatal circuit (typically decreased volume and increased activation), supporting the role of this system in OCD. Moreover, functional abnormalities are reduced following successful drug or behavioral treatment of OCD, lending further support to the model (Baxter et al., 1992; Schwartz, Stoessel, Baxter, Martin, & Phelps, 1996). The orbitofronto-striatal model is also supported by neuropsychological research. Individuals with OCD typically show impairments in implicit behavioral learning paradigms and decreased behavioral inhibition as measured by neurocognitive tasks (Menzies et al., 2007; Menzies et al., 2008).

Some evidence suggests that the OCD symptom dimensions relate differentially to various areas of the brain. A functional imaging study found that the pattern of activation in response to evocative emotional stimuli varied based on stimuli content; washing, checking, hoarding, and non-OCD-related stimuli were each associated with differential patterns of activation of areas in the CSTC (Mataix-Cols et al., 2004). Furthermore, a structural imaging study found that symmetry/ordering, contamination/washing, and harm/checking symptoms were each associated with both distinct and overlapping patterns in white and grey matter volume (van den Heuvel et al., 2009).

### LEARNING, MODELING, AND LIFE EVENTS

Stressful life events are likely to influence development of GAD. For example, past traumatic events may contribute to feelings of anxious apprehension and the perception that the world is a dangerous place (Borkovec, Alcaine, & Behar, 2004). Traumatic events that occur after the onset of GAD may worsen anxiety and reinforce those perceptions of danger. In clinical and analogue samples, GAD is associated with a higher frequency of exposure to traumatic events (Roemer, Molina, Litz, & Borkovec, 1997). Individuals with GAD are also more likely to have experienced the death of a parent before the age of 16 compared to individuals with panic disorder and controls (Torgersen, 1986). Life events that contribute to GAD may differ from those that contribute to depression; events characterized by loss and danger may convey specific vulnerability to non-comorbid GAD, whereas loss and humiliation may be more specific to MDD (Kendler, Hettema, Butera, Gardner, & Prescott, 2003). Nonetheless, only approximately 50% of those with GAD report traumatic experiences (Roemer et al., 1997). Thus, if life events contribute to the development of GAD, they do not do so in all cases.

GAD is also associated with more anxiety problems among family members compared to nonanxious controls (McLaughlin, Behar, & Borkovec, 2008). A 32-year longitudinal study found several risk factors associated with GAD but not with MDD, including low socioeconomic status, maternal internalizing symptoms, mal-treatment, inhibited temperament, internalizing and conduct problems, and negative emotionality (Moffitt et al., 2007). Early childhood relationships may also contribute to the etiology of GAD. Compared to control participants, individuals with GAD report a history of rejection and neglect from their mothers, along with more frequent role-reversed/enmeshed relationships (in which the child must take care of the mother), as well as current feelings of vulnerability toward their mothers (Cassidy, Lichtenstein-Phelps, Sibrava, Thomas, & Borkovec, 2009).

Clearly, traumatic life events contribute to PTSD. Less clear is whether trauma exposure and PTSD share a dose-response relationship in which frequency and/or intensity of trauma correspond with symptom severity. Rates of PTSD vary based on the type of traumatic event, with assaultive violence and sexual assault being associated with the highest rates (Breslau et al., 1998; Norris, 1992). Furthermore, rates of PTSD among Vietnam War veterans roughly correspond to degree of combat exposure (Dohrenwend et al., 2006). However, PTSD severity does not directly correspond to severity of motor vehicle accidents among civilians (Schnyder, Moergeli, Klaghofer, & Buddeberg, 2001) or degree of torture among political prisoners (Başoğlu et al., 1994). Importantly, a dose-response relationship between trauma exposure and PTSD may be nonlinear; after a certain degree of trauma, continued exposure might not exacerbate symptoms any further (McNally, 2003).

PTSD may also be related to degree of trauma prior to the inciting event. Exposure to childhood physical or sexual abuse is associated with increased exposure to subsequent traumas and increased risk to develop PTSD following those subsequent traumas (Koenen, Moffitt, Poulton, Martin, & Caspi, 2007). A meta-analysis found that pretrauma risk factors for PTSD include psychiatric history and childhood abuse, whereas post-trauma risk factors include lack of social support and additional stressors (Brewin, Andrews, & Valentine, 2000).

Stress and trauma may also contribute to development of OCD. Among individuals with OCD, the occurrence of one or more traumatic events during the lifetime is associated with increased symptom severity, controlling for key variables such as age of onset and comorbidity (Cromer, Schmidt, & Murphy, 2007). Severity of childhood trauma appears to be greater for individuals with OCD compared to controls (individuals with trichotillomania, a putative obsessive-compulsive spectrum disorder, also reported greater childhood trauma; Lochner et al., 2002). Among children and adolescents, OCD is associated with more traumatic life events overall, as well as more events during the year before onset, an association that appears to be stronger for OCD than for other anxiety disorders (Gothelf, Aharonovsky, Horesh, Carty, & Apter, 2004). Although traumatic events may lead to onset of OCD or trigger relapse, classical conditioning is not a probable mechanism (de Silva & Marks, 1999). Indeed, individuals with OCD whose main concern is washing do not report past symptom-focused associative learning more frequently than do individuals without OCD (Jones & Menzies, 1998).

Cognitive Influences

Current cognitive-affective-behavioral conceptualizations of worry and GAD include the avoidance theory, the intolerance of uncertainty model, the meta-cognitive model, and emotion regulation models. The avoidance theory holds that the verbal-linguistic properties of worry preclude emotional processing. Indeed, worry is primarily verbal-linguistic as opposed to imagery based in nature (Behar, Zuellig, & Borkovec, 2005; Borkovec & Inz, 1990; Stöber, Tepperwien, & Staak, 2000), and it inhibits somatic arousal during a subsequent anxiety-inducing task (Borkovec & Hu, 1990; Borkovec et al., 1993; Peasley-Miklus & Vrana, 2000). Moreover, worry is associated with decreased anxious affect during subsequent periods of trauma recall (Behar et al., 2005) and depressive rumination (McLaughlin, Borkovec, & Sibrava, 2007). Lastly, individuals with GAD often report that worry serves as a distraction from more emotional topics (Borkovec & Roemer, 1995). Thus, it seems that worry precludes the somatic and emotional activation required for habituation to anxiety-provoking stimuli (Borkovec et al., 2004). Moreover, worry may be negatively reinforced via the removal of aversive and evocative images and emotional experiences.

Intolerance of uncertainty (IU) is defined as the tendency to respond negatively to uncertain situations in terms of cognition, affect, and behavior (Dugas, Buhr, & Ladouceur, 2004). IU is further defined as a schema through which an individual with GAD perceives the environment; for the individual with GAD, uncertain situations are unacceptable and distressing and may lead to worry (Dugas et al., 2004). Individuals with GAD consistently report greater levels of IU compared to nonclinical controls (Dugas, Gagnon, Ladouceur, & Freeston, 1998; Ladouceur, Blais, Freeston, & Dugas, 1998) and individuals with other anxiety disorders (Dugas, Marchand, & Ladouceur, 2005; Ladouceur et al., 1999). Finally, worry partially statistically mediates the relationship between IU and anxiety (Yook, Kim, Suh, & Lee, 2010).

The premise of the metacognitive model of GAD is that individuals with GAD experience two types of worry: Type 1 worry refers to worry about external threats and noncognitive internal triggers (e.g., physical symptoms), whereas Type 2 worry refers to meta-worry, or worry about worry (Wells, 1995, 2004). Positive beliefs about worry (e.g., that worrying will help avoid a catastrophe) give rise to Type 1 worry, whereas negative beliefs about worry (e.g., the belief that worry is uncontrollable) prompt Type 2 worry. Negative beliefs about worry may be more specific to GAD compared to positive beliefs about worry. Individuals with GAD perceive worry as more dangerous and uncontrollable than do individuals with other anxiety disorders and controls, even when controlling for Type 1 worry (Davis & Valentiner, 2000; Wells & Carter, 2001). Type 2 worry, on the other hand, may not be specific to GAD; individuals with GAD do not report greater positive beliefs about worry compared to anxious nonworriers (Davis & Valentiner, 2000), high worriers without GAD (Ruscio & Borkovec, 2004), and individuals with other anxiety disorders (Wells & Carter, 2001).

Emotion dysregulation models propose that individuals with GAD have difficulties understanding and modulating their emotions, and they may instead rely on suppression and control strategies (e.g., worry; Mennin, Heimberg, Turk, & Fresco, 2002). The model further describes specific components of emotion dysregulation in GAD, including heightened intensity of emotions (both positive and negative, but particularly negative; Turk, Heimberg, Luterek, Mennin, & Fresco, 2005), poor understanding of emotions, negative reactivity to emotions, and maladaptive management of emotions (Mennin, Heimberg, Turk, & Fresco, 2005; Mennin, Holaway, Fresco, Moore, & Heimberg, 2007). Both GAD analogue and clinical samples report higher emotion dysregulation compared to nonanxious participants, although individuals with depression report similar deficits. Moreover, self-report emotion dysregulation predicts severity of trait worry and analogue GAD status when controlling for negative affect (Salters-Pedneault, Roemer, Tull, Rucker, & Mennin, 2006), as well as dimensional GAD-Q-IV scores when controlling for symptoms of depression and anxious arousal (Roemer et al., 2009). The acceptance-based model also posits difficulties with emotional experiences in GAD, but instead focuses on fear and avoidance of internal experiences (Roemer, Salters,

Raffa, & Orsillo, 2005). Indeed, deficits in mindfulness account for unique variance in GAD symptom severity, even after controlling for emotion regulation and depressive and anxious symptoms (Roemer et al., 2009).

Cognitive influences of PTSD include maladaptive beliefs that one holds about the meaning of traumatic events (e.g., that one is at fault). Cognitive reprocessing therapy addresses these beliefs and improves PTSD symptoms, even in the absence of exposure exercises (Resick et al., 2008). Other possible cognitive mechanisms of PTSD include biases toward threat-related stimuli, which may specifically reflect a cognitive vulnerability to developing PTSD (Thrasher & Dalgleish, 1999). PTSD may also be influenced by perceived seriousness of threat, which in turn may be influenced by cognitive variables such as poor contextualization of autobiographical memory (Ehlers & Clark, 2000). Recent support for the importance of cognitive mechanisms include the finding that Iraq and Afghanistan War veterans with PTSD reported greater intrusion of combat-related thoughts during a thought suppression task compared to non-PTSD veterans, controlling for combat exposure (Aikins et al., 2009).

An important cognitive phenomenon in OCD is thought–action fusion, or the belief that thoughts are equal to actions (Shafran, Thordarson, & Rachman, 1996). Moral thought–action fusion refers to the belief that simply thinking an unacceptable thought is morally equivalent to performing an unacceptable action. Likelihood thought–action fusion refers to the belief that thinking about an event causes or increases the likelihood of that event actually occurring. Both types of thought–action fusion appear to be elevated among individuals with OCD (Shafran et al., 1996). A review concluded that thought–action fusion is indeed associated with OCD symptoms, but that it may also be elevated in other anxiety disorders, depressive symptoms, and eating disorders (Berle & Starcevic, 2005). Nonetheless, thought–action fusion seems to be fairly specific to OCD, at least as compared to panic disorder and GAD (Starcevic & Berle, 2006).

The cognitive appraisal model of OCD suggests that intrusive thoughts occur in individuals with and without OCD. Intrusive thoughts develop into obsessions, however, when they are appraised based on dysfunctional beliefs and misinterpretations, such as the overestimation of threat, excessive responsibility, or thought–action fusion (e.g., Freeston, Rhéaume, & Ladouceur, 1996; Rachman, 1998; Salkovskis, 1985, 1989). One study found that responsibility for harm and the need to control thoughts were elevated in OCD compared to other anxiety disorders (Steketee, Frost, & Cohen, 1998). However, a review concluded that when controlling for general distress, there is little evidence that individuals with OCD endorse relevant beliefs about intrusive thoughts more strongly compared to individuals with other anxiety disorders (Julien, O'Connor, Aardema, 2007). Although there is some evidence that beliefs about perfectionism/certainty are specifically related to ordering/counting and checking, the lack of overall elevated beliefs about intrusive thoughts, and the fact that many individuals with OCD do not report elevated dysfunctional beliefs, suggests that factors besides appraisals of intrusive thoughts contribute to obsessions.

OCD is also associated with a variety of neuropsychological impairments. One review concluded that deficits in organizational strategies and executive functioning were consistently found in OCD, and that memory impairments are most consistently found using tests that require implicit organization (Greisberg & McKay, 2003). A second review similarly concluded that OCD is related to impaired organizational ability, but especially at the level of encoding, as well as other, less consistently implicated executive functions (Kuelz, Hohagen, & Voderholzer, 2004). A third review concluded that OCD is associated with impairments in nonverbal memory, memory for one's own actions, decreased confidence in judgments about recognition memory, and reduced cognitive inhibition (Muller & Roberts, 2005). That review also found that OCD is associated with attentional biases toward threatening information. Finally, memory impairments may be more widespread among compulsive checkers compared to individuals with other types of OCD, although memory impairment is not necessarily an etiological factor (Woods, Vevea, Chambless, & Bayen, 2002).

## SEX AND RACIAL-ETHNIC CONSIDERATIONS

GAD is more prevalent among women compared to men. In a nationally representative sample, women were approximately twice as likely to report lifetime and 12-month diagnoses of GAD (Vesga-López et al., 2008). Women also reported greater disability from GAD. Given that the genetic contribution to GAD is equivalent among men and women, gender differences in prevalence are likely due to cognitive and environmental influences (Hettema, Prescott, & Kendler, 2001). Finally, although prevalence and severity differ between genders, rates of relapse and remission are similar (Yonkers, Bruce, Dyck, & Keller, 2003).

Rates of PTSD are approximately twice as high among women compared to men (Kessler et al., 1995), and the gender disproportion is even greater for subthreshold PTSD (Stein, Walker, Hazen, & Forde, 1997). Among men with PTSD, combat exposure and witnessing someone being badly injured are most commonly reported as the most upsetting trauma, whereas rape and sexual molestation are most commonly reported as the most upsetting trauma among women with PTSD (Kessler et al., 1995). Interestingly, the gender difference in prevalence is already apparent by adolescence (Kilpatrick et al., 2003).

The cultural context may influence some aspects of PTSD, but in general the disorder represents a coherent group of symptoms that occur across cultures (Hinton & Lewis-Fernández, 2010). Hispanic American Vietnam War veterans are almost twice as likely to report PTSD compared to Caucasian veterans (African American veterans reported PTSD at a rate between these two groups; Kulka et al., 1990). These differences can be explained by differences in trauma exposure, rather than a unique psychological vulnerability (Frueh, Brady, & Arellano, 1998).

Among adults, prevalence of OCD is elevated among females, although the gender difference appears to be smaller than for GAD and PTSD. In the Epidemiological Catchment Area study, the lifetime prevalence of OCD was 2.9% for females and 2.0% for males (12-month prevalence was 1.8% for females and 1.4% for males; Karno, Golding, Sorenson, & Burnam, 1988). The *DSM-IV* field trial found that 51% of those with OCD were female (Foa & Kozak, 1995). In contrast, among children and adolescents, the prevalence of OCD appears to be higher for males (Geller et al., 2001).

Cultural factors appear to influence the themes and content of OCD symptoms (Matsunaga & Seedat, 2007). In general, OCD content areas such as contamination and checking are prevalent in most cultures, whereas religious themes are most prevalent among cultures in which religion is prominent (Fontenelle, Mendlowicz, Marques, & Versiani, 2004; Karadağ, Oguzhanoglu, Özdel, Ateşci, & Amuk, 2006). Similar to Western cultures, the most common content areas among Turkish individuals with OCD are contamination and aggression (Karadağ et al., 2006). However, the most common topic of obsessions among Brazilians with OCD is aggression, and the most common topic among Middle Easterners with OCD is religion (Fontenelle et al., 2004). The most prominent obsessional themes among an Indonesian sample were related to social networks and status (e.g., needing to know the status of individual passersby), followed by religious and somatic obsessions (Lemelson, 2003). Among Orthodox Jewish individuals, OCD symptoms may reflect concerns about following religious practices that are already ritual-based in nature (Huppert, Siev, & Kushner, 2007). These types of cases require the utmost cultural sensitivity to (a) recognize the boundaries between religious customs and OCD rituals, and (b) treat the OCD symptoms while maintaining respect for religious practices.

In the United States, OCD among African Americans is persistent and associated with substantial distress and impairment, yet this group may receive evidence-based treatment at lower rates compared to other groups (Himle et al., 2008). In fact, minority groups are underrepresented in North American treatment trials for OCD, suggesting that efficacy of well-known treatments in non-Caucasian populations is not well established (Williams, Powers, Yun, & Foa, 2010). Moreover, self-report measures of OCD may be biased in that African Americans are more likely than Caucasians to endorse contamination items in the absence of clinically meaningful symptoms (Thomas, Turkheimer, & Oltmanns, 2000; Williams, Turkheimer, Schmidt, & Oltmanns, 2005).

## COURSE AND PROGNOSIS

GAD is associated with a later onset compared to the other anxiety disorders. Fifty percent of all lifetime cases of GAD begin by age 31; the corresponding ages for specific phobia, social phobia, OCD, and panic disorder are 7, 13, 19, and 24, respectively (Kessler, Berglund et al., 2005). Although this appears to suggest a later age of onset for GAD compared to other disorders, it may instead reflect the fact that the symptoms of GAD and associated impairment are recognized later during the course of the disorder. In terms of course, a naturalistic longitudinal study found that 42% of participants who reported GAD at baseline were still symptomatic at 12-year follow-up (Bruce et al., 2005). Although cognitive-behavioral therapy is effective for treating GAD (Borkovec & Ruscio, 2001) and reducing symptoms of comorbid Axis I disorders (Borkovec, Abel, & Newman, 1995), only 50% of patients achieve high end-state functioning as a result of treatment (Borkovec, Newman, Pincus, & Lytle, 2002).

The course of PTSD may begin immediately following or long after a traumatic event. Diagnostic criteria include a specifier for delayed onset, which is assigned when the full criteria are not met until 6 months following the trauma or later (although some symptoms may arise earlier; APA, 2000). Indeed, substantial rates of delayed-onset PTSD have been noted among U.S. peacekeepers who served in Somalia (Gray, Bolton, & Litz, 2007) and among civilian car accident victims (Buckley, Blanchard, & Hickling, 1996). These findings may partially be explained by exacerbation of symptoms over time; a review found that delayed-onset PTSD in the complete absence of prior symptoms was rare (Andrews, Brewin, Philpott, & Stewart, 2007). In terms of order of symptoms, a retrospective study of Vietnam War veterans with PTSD found that hyperarousal symptoms tend to arise prior to the emergence of other symptoms (Bremner, Southwick, Darnell, & Charney, 1996).

A prospective longitudinal study found that presence of avoidance symptoms specifically, as well as the occurrence of new traumatic events, contributed to the long-term maintenance of PTSD (Perkonigg et al., 2005). Indeed, efficacious treatments for PTSD include exposure exercises that counter maladaptive patterns of avoidance. These treatments include prolonged exposure (Foa, Hembree, et al., 2005; Foa, Rothbaum, Riggs, & Murdock, 1991) and cognitive reprocessing therapy (Monson et al., 2006; Resick, Nishith, Weaver, Astin, & Feuer, 2002). The focus in prolonged exposure is habituation to graded fear exposures, whereas the focus in cognitive reprocessing therapy is the modification of maladaptive trauma-related beliefs (e.g., denial or self-blame). However, cognitive reprocessing therapy includes written exposure exercises, and prolonged exposure includes cognitive restructuring. Adding cognitive restructuring to prolonged exposure does not increase efficacy (Foa, Hembree, et al., 2005), nor does adding writing exposure exercises to cognitive therapy (Resick et al., 2008), indicating that the therapies are efficacious in both their combined and component forms.

As previously mentioned, average age of onset for OCD is 19, although the age-of-onset distribution may be bimodal with modes in childhood and adulthood (as opposed to adolescence; Geller et al., 1998). The phenomenology is similar regardless of age of onset (Swedo, Rapoport, Leonard, Lenane, & Cheslow, 1989), although an early onset is associated with increased rates of tic disorders (do Rosario-Campos et al., 2001; Janowitz et al., 2009). Symptoms of OCD are highly stable over time, and change that does occur is typically within symptom dimensions as opposed to between symptom dimensions (e.g., the severity of a particular dimension might fluctuate, but rarely will an individual's symptoms completely shift from one dimension to another; Mataix-Cols et al., 2002).

Efficacious treatments for OCD include cognitive-behavioral therapies or antidepressants (Abramovitz, 1997; Kobak, Greist, Jefferson, Katzelnick, & Henk, 1998; van Balkom et al., 1994). The majority of patients completing exposure and ritual prevention (ERP; 86%) or ERP plus clomipramine (79%) responded to treatment, as defined by a score of moderately improved or better on the Clinical Global Impression scale (the response rate among completers was 48% for clomipramine and 10% for placebo; Foa, Liebowitz, et al., 2005).

Patients who endorse fears of disastrous consequences may benefit more from ERP compared to patients who do not endorse those fears, although extreme certainty that those feared consequences will occur is actually associated with worse outcome (Foa, Abramovitz, Franklin, & Kozak, 1999). A review of treatment moderators concluded that insight into the rationality of obsessions did not necessarily predict treatment outcome (Steketee & Shapiro, 1995). Among individuals receiving ERP or stress management training (an active control condition) to augment pharmacotherapy for OCD, treatment outcome was moderated by gender, such that ERP was more efficacious among males compared to females (Maher et al., 2010). Symptom severity was not related to outcome for ERP, although poor quality of life, greater comorbidity, and more unsuccessful trials of antidepressants predicted poorer outcome. Importantly, all of the moderators in this study combined accounted for a comparable amount of variance in outcome compared to the effects of treatment type. A review concluded that increased symptom severity is in fact associated with poorer outcome, although the findings are notably inconsistent (Keeley, Storch, Merlo, & Geffken, 2008). That review also concluded that the hoarding subtype of OCD or comorbid personality disorders also predicted worse outcome.

## LOOKING AHEAD TO *DSM-5*

Diagnostic criteria for GAD may undergo substantial changes in the *DSM-5* (Andrews et al., 2010). First, the name of the syndrome may be changed to General Anxiety and Worry Disorder to better represent worry, the core feature of the disorder. Second, the criterion that worry be "difficult to control" may be removed, because it adds little diagnostic validity and overlaps conceptually with the "excessiveness" criterion. Third, the duration requirement may be reduced from 6 months to 3 months to identify clinically significant cases and to improve reliability. Fourth, the list of associated symptoms (e.g., muscle tension) may be reduced to symptoms that are specific to GAD (as opposed to symptoms that overlap greatly with other disorders, such as sleep disturbance). Fifth, in accordance with theoretical models of GAD and consistent with the other anxiety disorders, behavioral criteria may be added. Behavioral criteria may include avoidance of and/or preparation for situations in which a negative outcome might occur, procrastination in behavior or decision making due to worry, and repeatedly seeking reassurance from others. Finally, the *DSM-5* may include dimensional severity and frequency ratings for certain symptoms.

Proposed modifications to the PTSD criteria include (a) removing the A2 criterion (reaction of fear, helplessness, or horror); (b) separating the avoidance and numbing symptoms into separate clusters; (c) broadening the numbing category to include negative cognitions and mood more generally, as well as replacing sense of foreshortened future with more broad negative expectations or beliefs about the self, others, or the world; (d) adding criteria for blame and guilt and for reckless or self-destructive behavior; and (e) restricting the definition of a traumatic event to something personally experienced or witnessed, or, if it occurred to a family member or close friend, that it be violent or accidental (Friedman et al., 2010).

The OCD work group has recommended that the disorder be grouped with other obsessive-compulsive spectrum disorders (such as body dysmorphic and Tourette's disorders), but that this group be subsumed under a category of anxiety and obsessive-compulsive spectrum disorders (Phillips et al., 2010; Stein et al., 2010). In terms of diagnostic criteria, proposed revisions include (a) minor adjustments to terminology (e.g., changing "inappropriate" to "unwanted" with respect to obsessions to avoid value-laden language); (b) adding specifiers for insight (delusional, poor, fair/good) and tic-related OCD; and (c) noting the symptom dimensions (e.g., contamination/cleaning) in the text (Leckman et al., 2010).

## CASE STUDIES

Emily is a 33-year-old woman who presented to her primary care physician complaining of stress and severe muscle tension. A psychological assessment revealed that Emily frequently and uncontrollably worries about the health and safety of herself and her family members, her performance at work, the quality of her relationships, and various miscellaneous matters. She also reported difficulty falling and staying asleep at night, as well as muscle tension and some feelings of irritability toward her family and coworkers. She further reported that her father died when she was 6 years old, and that her mother subsequently developed problems with anxiety and depression. Her mother became somewhat neglectful and actually required some emotional caretaking from Emily. Although she has "always been anxious," Emily's anxiety, worry, and associated symptoms have significantly worsened during the previous few years. Her symptoms are now causing significant distress and interfering with the quality of her work and her personal relationships.

Dylan is a 27-year-old Iraq War veteran who presented to the local VA primary care clinic requesting psychiatric services. Dylan served two tours of duty in Iraq and witnessed multiple roadside bombings in which members of his unit were injured or killed. His final tour ended 2 years ago, but his symptoms began shortly after the first roadside bombing. He is currently experiencing persistent nightmares that are thematically related to his trauma, intrusive memories, and intense distress when being confronted with reminders of his traumas. He also reported being unable to feel love and emotional connection, as well as feeling estranged from others. He avoids internal and external reminders of the event, which include thinking about the bombings and other graphic scenes from his service, as well as driving in general and overpasses in particular (one of the bombings occurred at an overpass). Lastly, he is experiencing marked irritability, anger, and hypervigilance, especially while driving. Because of his symptoms, Dylan's relationships have suffered and he is unable to work. Dylan's experiences in Iraq are consistent with the definition of a traumatic event, and his symptoms reflect chronic PTSD with acute onset.

Tom is a 51-year-old male who was brought to therapy by a family member. Tom reported obsessive thinking related to germs and contamination. He reported that thoughts of germs, contamination, and "dirty particles" often consume him. These thoughts elicit feelings of disgust, repulsion, and fear, and in response he engages in cleaning rituals. He cleans his house and office three times daily with alcohol, including his doorknob, telephone receiver, desk, and other areas to avoid contamination. He also reported concern about contamination by paper money. He finds it disgusting and smelly, and he will clean individual bills when symptoms are especially severe. He will not use his own toilet unless it was cleaned to his specific standards, and he refuses to use public restrooms. Nearly half of his days are spent thinking about contamination or engaging in cleaning rituals. Although he usually recognizes that his concerns are unrealistic, at times he is convinced that his fears of contamination and consequent cleaning rituals are justified. His wife accommodates his rituals by arranging her schedule accordingly and occasionally by helping to perform his rituals when their completion would otherwise make the couple late for important events. His symptoms began approximately 10 years ago and have worsened ever since. They currently cause him substantial distress and consume so much time that they significantly impair his work performance and interpersonal relationships.

## SUMMARY

GAD, PTSD, and OCD are each characterized by persistent anxiety, yet they are markedly distinct in their clinical presentations: GAD is characterized by uncontrollable and pervasive worry, as well as a variety of physical symptoms; PTSD is characterized by reexperiencing, avoidance, and hyperarousal symptoms that relate to one or more traumatic events; and OCD is characterized by intrusive and uncontrollable obsessions, as well as compulsions that are performed in response to those obsessions. Thus, anxiety and distress are related to a variety of topics among individuals with GAD, a particular traumatic event or series of events among individuals with PTSD, and specific irrational fears among individuals with OCD.

Biological models of these disorders highlight potentially unique neural correlates and physiological mechanisms, such as physiological inflexibility in GAD, reduced hippocampal volume in PTSD, and CSTC dysfunction in OCD. Nonetheless, some potential neurobiological mechanisms of anxiety (e.g., hyperactivity in the amygdala) seem to occur in a variety of disorders, and common versus specific genetic and environmental factors have not been clearly delineated. Moreover, consistently high rates of comorbidity suggest that these disorders rarely occur in isolation. These high rates of comorbidity, combined with the dimensional nature of these disorders, suggest that a given individual may experience any combination of symptoms at highly variable levels of severity.

In conclusion, we would like to highlight that GAD, PTSD, and OCD share certain characteristics, such as putative genetic (e.g., the 5-HTTLPR polymorphism) and environmental (i.e., stressful life events) etiological factors. Nonetheless, many characteristics of these disorders appear to be distinct, especially their clinical presentations. Although the nosology of *DSM-IV-TR* is imperfect, the diagnostic criteria characterize relatively distinct syndromes and are invaluable for clinical and research purposes. Indeed, appropriateness of a given psychotherapeutic treatment depends upon whether it has been shown to be efficacious for the particular disorder being treated. Thus, despite biological and etiological overlap, these disorders are in fact distinguishable, and accurate diagnosis is an essential first step in determining which treatment to provide to a given patient.

## REFERENCES

Abramowitz, J. S. (1997). Effectiveness of psychological and pharmacological treatments for obsessive-compulsive disorder: A quantitative review. *Journal of Consulting and Clinical Psychology, 65*(1), 44–52.

Aikins, D. E., Johnson, D. C., Borelli, J. L., Klemanski, D. H., Morrissey, P. M., Benham, T. L., . . . Tolin, D. F. (2009). Thought suppression failures in combat PTSD: A cognitive load hypothesis. *Behaviour Research and Therapy, 47,* 744–751.

Aldao, A., Mennin, D. S., Linardatos, E., & Fresco, D. M. (2010). Differential patterns of physical symptoms and subjective processes in generalized anxiety disorder and unipolar depression. *Journal of Anxiety Disorders, 24*, 250–259.

American Psychiatric Association. (1980). *Diagnostic and statistical manual of mental disorders* (3rd ed.). Washington, DC: Author.

American Psychiatric Association. (1987). *Diagnostic and statistical manual of mental disorders* (3rd ed., rev.). Washington, DC: Author.

American Psychiatric Association. (1994). *Diagnostic and statistical manual of mental disorders* (4th ed.). Washington, DC: Author.

American Psychiatric Association. (2000). *Diagnostic and statistical manual of mental disorders* (4th ed., text rev.). Washington, DC: Author.

Andrews, B., Brewin, C. R., Philpott, R., & Stewart, L. (2007). Delayed-onset posttraumatic stress disorder: A systematic review of the evidence. *American Journal of Psychiatry, 164*(9), 1319–1326.

Andrews, G., Hobbs, M. J., Borkovec, T. D., Beesdo, K., Craske, M. G., Heimberg, R. G., . . . Stanley, M. A. (2010). Generalized worry disorder: A review of *DSM-IV* generalized anxiety disorder and options for *DSM-V*. *Depression and Anxiety, 147*, 134–147.

Asmundson, G. J. G., Frombach, I., McQuaid, J., Pedrelli, P., Lenox, R., & Stein, M. B. (2000). Dimensionality of posttraumatic stress symptoms: A confirmatory factor analysis of *DSM-IV* symptom clusters and other symptom models. *Behaviour Research and Therapy, 38*, 203–214.

Asmundson, G. J. G., Stapleton, J. A., & Taylor, S. (2004). Are avoidance and numbing distinct PTSD symptom clusters? *Journal of Traumatic Stress, 17*(6), 467–475.

Başoğlu, M., Paker, M., Paker, O., Ozmen, E., Marks, I., Incesu, D., . . . Sarimurat, N. (1994). Psychological effects of torture: A comparison of tortured with nontortured political activists and Turkey. *American Journal of Psychiatry, 151*(1), 76–81.

Baxter, L. R., Schwartz, J. M., Bergman, K. S., Szuba, M. P., Guze, B. H., Mazziotta, J. C., . . . Phelps, M. E. (1992). Caudate glucose metabolic rate changes with both drug and behavior therapy for obsessive-compulsive disorder. *Archives of General Psychiatry, 49*(9), 681–689.

Bedard-Gilligan, M., & Zoellner, L. A. (2008). The utility of the A1 and A2 criteria in the diagnosis of PTSD. *Behaviour research and therapy, 46*, 1062–1069.

Beesdo, K., Pine, D. S., Lieb, R., & Wittchen, H. U. (2010). Incidence and risk patterns of anxiety and depressive disorders and categorization of generalized anxiety disorder. *Archives of General Psychiatry, 67*(1), 47–57.

Behar, E., Zuellig, A. R., & Borkovec, T. D. (2005). Thought and imaginal activity during worry and trauma recall. *Behavior Therapy, 36*, 157–168.

Berle, D., & Starcevic, V. (2005). Thought-action fusion: Review of the literature and future directions. *Clinical Psychology Review, 25*, 263–284.

Binder, E. B., Bradley, R. G., Liu, W., Epstein, M. P., Deveau, T. C., Mercer, K. B., . . . Ressler, K. J. (2008). Association of FKBP5 polymorphisms and childhood abuse with risk of post-traumatic stress disorder symptoms in adults. *Journal of the American Medical Association, 299*(11), 1291–1305.

Blair, K., Shaywitz, J., Smith, B. W., Rhodes, R., Geraci, M., Jones, M., . . . Pine, D. S. (2008). Response to emotional expressions in generalized social phobia and generalized anxiety disorder: Evidence for separate disorders. *American Journal of Psychiatry, 165*(9), 1193–1202.

Blake, D. D., Weathers, F. W., Nagy, L. M., Kaloupek, D. G., Gusman, F. D., Charney, D. S., & Keane, T. M. (1995). The development of a clinical-administered PTSD scale. *Journal of Traumatic Stress, 8*(1), 75–90.

Bloch, M. H., Landeros-Weisenberger, A., Rosario, M. C., Pittenger, C., & Leckman, J. F. (2008). Meta-analysis of the symptom structure of obsessive-compulsive disorder. *American Journal of Psychiatry*, *165*, 1532–1542.

Bonne, O., Brandes, D., Gilboa, A., Gomori, J. M., Shenton, M. E., Pitman, R. K., & Shalev, A. Y. (2001). Longitudinal MRI study of hippocampal volume in trauma survivors with PTSD. *The American Journal of Psychiatry*, *158*(8), 1248–1251.

Borkovec, T. D., Abel, J. L., & Newman, H. (1995). Effects of psychotherapy on comorbid conditions in generalized anxiety disorder. *Journal of Consulting and Clinical Psychology*, *63* (3), 479–483.

Borkovec, T. D., Alcaine, O. M., & Behar, E. (2004). Avoidance theory of worry and generalized anxiety disorder. In R. G. Heimberg, C. L. Turk, & D. S. Mennin (Eds.), *Generalized anxiety disorder: Advances in research and practice* (pp. 77–108). New York, NY: Guilford Press.

Borkovec, T. D., & Hu, S. (1990). The effect of worry on cardiovascular response to phobic imagery. *Behaviour Research and Therapy*, *28*(1), 69–73.

Borkovec, T. D., & Inz, J. (1990). The nature of worry in generalized anxiety disorder: A predominance of thought activity. *Behaviour Research and Therapy*, *28*(2), 153–158.

Borkovec, T. D., Lyonfields, J. D., Wiser, S. L., & Deihl, L. (1993). The role of worrisome thinking in the suppression of cardiovascular response to phobic imagery, *31*(3), 321–324.

Borkovec, T. D., Newman, M. G., Pincus, A. L., & Lytle, R. (2002). A component analysis of cognitive-behavioral therapy for generalized anxiety disorder and the role of interpersonal problems. *Journal of Consulting and Clinical Psychology*, *70*(2), 288–298.

Borkovec, T. D., Robinson, E., Pruzinsky, T., & DePree, J. A. (1983). Preliminary exploration of worry: Some characteristics and processes. *Behaviour Research and Therapy*, *21*, 9–16.

Borkovec, T. D., & Roemer, L. (1995). Perceived functions of worry among generalized anxiety disorder subjects: Distractions from more emotionally distressing topics? *Journal of Behavior Therapy and Experimental Psychiatry*, *26*(1), 25–30.

Borkovec, T. D., & Ruscio, A. M. (2001). Psychotherapy for generalized anxiety disorder. *Journal of Clinical Psychiatry*, *62*(11), 37–42.

Bremner, J. D., Southwick, S. M., Darnell, A., & Charney, D. S. (1996). Chronic PTSD in Vietnam combat veterans: Course of illness and substance abuse. *American Journal of Psychiatry*, *153*(3), 369–375.

Breslau, N., Davis, G. C., Peterson, E. L., & Schultz, L. R. (2000). A second look at comorbidity in victims of trauma: The posttraumatic stress disorder-major depression connection. *Biological Psychiatry*, *48*, 902–909.

Breslau, N., Davis, G. C., & Schultz, L. R. (2003). Posttraumatic stress disorder and the incidence of nicotine, alcohol, and other drug disorders in persons who have experienced trauma. *Archives of General Psychiatry*, *60*, 289–294.

Breslau, N., Kessler, R. C., Chilcoat, H. D., Schultz, L. R., Davis, G. C., & Andreski, P. (1998). Trauma and posttraumatic stress disorder in the community: The 1996 Detroit Area Survey of Trauma. *Archives of General Psychiatry*, *55*, 626–632.

Brewin, C. R., Andrews, B., & Valentine, J. D. (2000). Meta-analysis of risk factors for posttraumatic stress disorder in trauma-exposed adults. *Journal of Consulting and Clinical Psychology*, *68*(5), 748–766.

Broekman, B. F. P., Olff, M., & Boer, F. (2007). The genetic background to PTSD. *Neuroscience and Biobehavioral Reviews*, *31*, 348–362.

Broman-Fulks, J. J., Ruggiero, K. J., Green, B. A., Kilpatrick, D. G., Danielson, C. K., Resnick, H. S., & Saunders, B. E. (2006). Taxometric investigation of PTSD: Data from two nationally representative samples. *Behavior Therapy*, *37*(4), 364–380.

Brown, T. A., Antony, M. M., & Barlow, D. H. (1992). Psychometric properties of the Penn State Worry Questionnaire in a clinical anxiety disorders sample. *Behaviour Research and Therapy, 30*(1), 33–37.

Brown, T. A., Campbell, L. A., Lehman, C. L., Grisham, J. R., & Mancill, R. B. (2001). Current and lifetime comorbidity of the *DSM-IV* anxiety and mood disorders in a large clinical sample. *Journal of Abnormal Psychology, 110*(4), 585–599.

Brown, T. A., Di Nardo, P. A., & Barlow, D. H. (1994). *Anxiety Disorders Interview Schedule for DSM-IV*. Albany, NY: Graywind.

Brown, T. A., Di Nardo, P. A., Lehman, C. L., & Campbell, L. A. (2001). Reliability of *DSM-IV* anxiety and mood disorders: Implications for the classification of emotional disorders. *Journal of Abnormal Psychology, 110*(1), 49–58.

Bruce, S. E., Yonkers, K. A., Otto, M. W., Eisen, J. L., Weisberg, R. B., Pagano, M., . . . Keller, M. B. (2005). Influence of psychiatric comorbidity on recovery and recurrence in generalized anxiety disorder, social phobia, and panic disorder: A 12-year prospective study. *American Journal of Psychiatry, 162*(6), 1179–1187.

Buckley, T. C., Blanchard, E. B., & Hickling, E. J. (1996). A prospective examination of delayed onset PTSD secondary to motor vehicle accidents. *Journal of Abnormal Psychology, 105*(4), 617–625.

Buckley, T. C., & Kaloupek, D. G. (2001). A meta-analytic examination of basal cardiovascular activity in posttraumatic stress disorder. *Psychosomatic Medicine, 63*, 585–594.

Calvocoressi, L., Lewis, B., Harris, M., Trufan, S. J., Goodman, W. K., McDougle, C. J., & Price, L. H. (1995). Family accommodation in obsessive-compulsive disorder. *American Journal of Psychiatry, 152*, 441–443.

Calvocoressi, L., Mazure, C., Kasl, S., Skolnick, J., Fisk, D., Vegso, S., . . . Price, L. (1999). Family accommodation of obsessive-compulsive symptoms: Instrument development and assessment of family behavior. *Journal of Nervous and Mental Disease, 187*(10), 636–642.

Cassidy, J., Lichtenstein-Phelps, J., Sibrava, N. J., Thomas, C. L. J., & Borkovec, T. D. (2009). Generalized anxiety disorder: Connections with self-reported attachment. *Behavior Therapy, 40*, 23–38.

Cox, B. J., Mota, N., Clara, I., & Asmundson, G. J. G. (2008). The symptom structure of posttraumatic stress disorder in the National Comorbidity Replication Survey. *Journal of anxiety disorders, 22*, 1523–1528.

Craske, M. G., Rapee, R. M., Jackel, L., & Barlow, D. H. (1989). Qualitative dimensions of worry in *DSM-III-R* generalized anxiety disorder subjects and non anxious controls. *Behaviour Research and Therapy, 27*(4), 397–402.

Cromer, K. R., Schmidt, N. B., & Murphy, D. L. (2007). An investigation of traumatic life events and obsessive-compulsive disorder. *Behaviour Research and Therapy, 45*, 1683–1691.

Davis, R. N., & Valentiner, D. P. (2000). Does meta-cognitive theory enhance our understanding of pathological worry and anxiety? *Personality and Individual Differences, 29*(3), 513–526.

Deering, C. G., Glover, S. G., Ready, D., Eddleman, H. C., & Alarcon, R. D. (1996). Unique patterns of comorbidity in posttraumatic stress disorder from different sources of trauma. *Comprehensive Psychiatry, 37*(5), 336–346.

de Silva, P., & Marks, M. (1999). The role of traumatic experiences in the genesis of obsessive-compulsive disorder. *Behaviour Research and Therapy, 37*, 941–951.

Dohrenwend, B. P., Turner, J. B., Turse, N. A., Adams, B. G., Koenen, K. C., & Marshall, R. (2006). The psychological risks of Vietnam for U.S. veterans: A revisit with new data and methods. *Science, 313*, 979–982.

do Rosario-Campos, M. C., Leckman, J. F., Mercadante, M. T., Shavitt, R. G., Prado, H. D. S., Sada, P., . . . Miguel, E. C. (2001). Adults with early-onset obsessive-compulsive disorder. *American Journal of Psychiatry, 158*(11), 1899–1903.

Dreman, S. (1991). Coping with the trauma of divorce. *Journal of Traumatic Stress, 4*(1), 113–121.

Dugas, M. J., Buhr, K., & Ladouceur, R. (2004). The role of intolerance of uncertainty in etiology and maintenance. In R. G. Heimberg, C. L. Turk, & D. S. Mennin (Eds.), *Generalized anxiety disorder: Advances in research and practice* (pp. 143–163). New York, NY: Guilford Press.

Dugas, M. J., Gagnon, F., Ladouceur, R., & Freeston, M. H. (1998). Generalized anxiety disorder: A preliminary test of a conceptual model. *Behaviour Research and Therapy, 36* (2), 215–226.

Dugas, M. J., Marchand, A., & Ladouceur, R. (2005). Further validation of a cognitive-behavioral model of generalized anxiety disorder: Diagnostic and symptom specificity. *Journal of Anxiety Disorders, 19*(3), 329–343.

Ehlers, A., & Clark, D. M. (2000). A cognitive model of posttraumatic stress disorder. *Behaviour Research and Therapy, 38*(4), 319–345.

Eisen, J. L., Phillips, K. A., Baer, L., Beer, D. A., Atala, K. D., & Rasmussen, S. (1998). The Brown Assessment of Beliefs Scale: Reliability and validity. *American Journal of Psychiatry, 155*(1), 102–108.

Elhai, J. D., Ford, J. D., Ruggiero, K. J., & Frueh, B. C. (2009). Diagnostic alterations for posttraumatic stress disorder: Examining data from the National Comorbidity Survey Replication and National Survey of Adolescents. *Psychological Medicine, 39*, 1957–1966.

Etkin, A., Prater, K. E., Hoeft, F., Menon, V., & Schatzberg, A. F. (2010). Failure of anterior cingulate activation and connectivity with the amygdala during implicit regulation of emotional processing in generalized anxiety disorder. *American Journal of Psychiatry, 167*(5), 545–554.

Etkin, A., Prater, K. E., Schatzberg, A. F., Menon, V., & Greicius, M. D. (2009). Disrupted amygdalar subregion functional connectivity and evidence of a compensatory network in generalized anxiety disorder. *Archives of General Psychiatry, 66*(12), 1361–1372.

Etkin, A., & Wagner, T. D. (2007). Functional neuroimaging of anxiety: A meta-analysis of emotional processing in PTSD, social anxiety disorder, and specific phobia. *American Journal of Psychiatry, 164*(10), 1476–1488.

Fisher, A. J., Granger, D. A., & Newman, M. G. (2010). Sympathetic arousal moderates self-reported physiological arousal symptoms at baseline and physiological flexibility in response to a stressor in generalized anxiety disorder. *Biological Psychology, 83*, 191–200.

Foa, E. B., Abramowitz, J. S., Franklin, M. E., & Kozak, M. J. (1999). Feared consequences, fixity of belief, and treatment outcome in patients with obsessive-compulsive disorder. *Behavior Therapy, 30*, 717–724.

Foa, E. B., Cashman, L., Jaycox, L., & Perry, K. (1997). The validation of a self-report measure of posttraumatic stress disorder: The Posttraumatic Diagnostic Scale. *Psychological Assessment, 9*(4), 445–451.

Foa, E. B., Hembree, E. A., Cahill, S. P., Rauch, S. A. M., Riggs, D. S., Feeny, N. C., & Yadin, E. (2005). Randomized trial of prolonged exposure for posttraumatic stress disorder with and without cognitive restructuring: Outcome at academic and community clinics. *Journal of Consulting and Clinical Psychology, 73*(5), 953–964.

Foa, E. B., Huppert, J. D., Leiberg, S., Langner, R., Kichic, R., Hajcak, G., & Salkovskis, P. M. (2002). The Obsessive-Compulsive Inventory: Development and validation of a short version. *Psychological Assessment, 14*(4), 485–496.

Foa, E. B., & Kozak, M. J. (1986). Emotional processing of fear: Exposure to corrective information. *Psychological Bulletin, 99*(1), 20–35.

Foa, E. B., & Kozak, M. J. (1995). *DSM-IV* field trial: Obsessive-compulsive disorder. *American Journal of Psychiatry, 152,* 90–96.

Foa, E. B., Liebowitz, M. R., Kozak, M. J., Davies, S., Campeas, R., Franklin, M. E., . . . Tu, X. (2005). Randomized, placebo-controlled trial of exposure and ritual prevention, clompiramine, and their combination in the treatment of obsessive-compulsive disorder. *American Journal of Psychiatry, 162*(1), 151–161.

Foa, E. B., Riggs, D. S., Dancu, C. V., & Rothbaum, B. O. (1993). Reliability and validity of a brief instrument for assessing post-traumatic stress disorder. *Journal of Traumatic Stress, 6,* 459–473.

Foa, E. B., Rothbaum, B. O., Riggs, D. S., & Murdock, T. B. (1991). Treatment of posttraumatic stress disorder in rape victims: A comparison between cognitive-behavioral procedures and counseling. *Journal of Consulting and Clinical Psychology, 59*(5), 715–723.

Fontenelle, L. F., Mendlowicz, M. V., Marques, C., & Versiani, M. (2004). Trans-cultural aspects of obsessive-compulsive disorder: A description of a Brazilian sample and a systematic review of international clinical studies. *Journal of Psychiatric Research, 38,* 403–411.

Forbes, D., Haslam, N., Williams, B. J., & Creamer, M. (2005). Testing the latent structure of posttraumatic stress disorder: a taxometric study of combat veterans. *Journal of Traumatic Stress, 18*(6), 647–656.

Francati, V., Vermetten, E., & Bremner, J. D. (2007). Functional neuroimaging studies in posttraumatic stress disorder: Review of current methods and findings. *Depression and Anxiety, 24*(3), 202–218.

Franklin, M. E., & Foa, E. B. (2008). Obsessive-compulsive disorder. In D. H. Barlow (Ed.), *Clinical handbook of psychological disorders: A step-by-step treatment manual* (pp. 164–215). New York, NY: Guilford Press.

Freeston, M. H., Rhéaume, J., & Ladouceur, R. (1996). Correcting faulty appraisals of obsessional thoughts. *Behaviour Research and Therapy, 34*(5), 433–446.

Friedman, M. J., Resick, P. A., Bryant, R. A., & Brewin, C. R. (2010). Considering PTSD for *DSM-5. Depression and Anxiety.* Advance online publication. doi: 10.1002/da.20767

Frueh, B. C., Brady, K. L., & de Arellano, M. A. (1998). Racial differences in combat-related PTSD: Empirical findings and conceptual issues. *Clinical Psychology Review, 18*(3), 287–305.

Fu, Q., Heath, A. C., Bucholz, K. K., Nelson, E. C., Glowinski, A. L., Goldberg, J., . . . Eisen, S. A. (2002). A twin study of genetic and environmental influences on suicidality in men. *Psychological Medicine, 32,* 11–24.

Geller, D. A., Biederman, J., Faraone, S., Agranat, A., Cradock, K., Hagermoser, L., . . . Coffey, B. J. (2001). Developmental aspects of obsessive compulsive disorder: Findings in children, adolescents, and adults. *Journal of Nervous and Mental Disease, 189*(7), 471–477.

Geller, D. A., Biederman, J., Jones, J., Park, K., Schwartz, S., Shapiro, S., & Coffey, B. (1998). Is juvenile obsessive-compulsive disorder a developmental subtype of the disorder? A review of the pediatric literature. *Journal of the Academy of Child and Adolescent Psychiatry, 37*(4), 420–427.

Gilbertson, M. W., Shenton, M. E., Ciszewski, A., Kasai, K., Lasko, N. B., Orr, S. P., & Pitman, R. K. (2002). Smaller hippocampal volume predicts pathologic vulnerability to psychological trauma. *Nature Neuroscience, 5*(11), 1242–1247.

Gold, S. D., Marx, B. P., Soler-Baillo, J. M., & Sloan, D. M. (2005). Is life stress more traumatic than traumatic stress? *Journal of Anxiety Disorders, 19*(6), 687–698.

Goodman, W. K., Price, L. H., Rasmussen, S. A., Mazure, C., Delgado, P., Heninger, G. R., & Charney, D. S. (1989). The Yale-Brown Obsessive Compulsive Scale, II: Validity. *Archives of General Psychiatry, 46,* 1012–1016.

Goodman, W. K., Price, L. H., Rasmussen, S. A., Mazure, C., Fleischmann, R. L., Hill, C. L., & Charney, D. S. (1989). The Yale-Brown Obsessive Compulsive Scale, I: Development, use, and reliability, *46,* 1006–1011.

Gothelf, D., Aharonovsky, O., Horesh, N., Carty, T., & Apter, A. (2004). Life events and personality factors in children and adolescents with obsessive-compulsive disorder and other anxiety disorders. *Comprehensive Psychiatry, 45*(3), 192–198.

Grabill, K., Merlo, L., Duke, D., Harford, K. L., Keeley, M. L., Geffken, G. R., & Storch, E. A. (2008). Assessment of obsessive-compulsive disorder: A review. *Journal of Anxiety disorders, 22,* 1–17.

Gray, M. J., Bolton, E. E., & Litz, B. T. (2004). A longitudinal analysis of PTSD symptom course: Delayed-onset PTSD in Somalia peacekeepers. *Journal of Consulting and Clinical Psychology, 72*(5), 909–913.

Greisberg, S., & McKay, D. (2003). Neuropsychology of obsessive-compulsive disorder: A review and treatment implications. *Clinical Psychology Review, 23,* 95–117.

Grubaugh, A. L., Magruder, K. M., Waldrop, A. E., Elhai, J. D., Knapp, R. G., & Frueh, B. C. (2005). Subthreshold PTSD in primary care: Prevalence, psychiatric disorders, healthcare use, and functional status. *The Journal of Nervous and Mental Disease, 193,* 658–664.

Haslam, N., Williams, B. J., Kyrios, M., McKay, D., & Taylor, S. (2005). Subtyping obsessive-compulsive disorder: A taxometric analysis. *Behavior Therapy, 36,* 381–391.

Hemmings, S. M. J., & Stein, D. J. (2006). The current status of association studies in obsessive-compulsive disorder. *Psychiatric Clinics of North America, 29,* 411–444.

Hettema, J. M., Neale, M. C., & Kendler, K. S. (2001). A review and meta-analysis of the genetic epidemiology of anxiety disorders. *American Journal of Psychiatry, 158,* 1568–1578.

Hettema, J. M., Prescott, C. A., & Kendler, K. S. (2001). A population based twin study of generalized anxiety disorder in men and women. *Journal of Nervous and Mental Disease, 189,* 413–420.

Hettema, J. M., Prescott, C. A., Myers, J. M., Neale, M. C., & Kendler, K. S. (2005). The structure of genetic and environmental risk factors for anxiety disorders in men and women. *Archives of General Psychiatry, 62,* 182–189.

Himle, J. A., Muroff, J. R., Taylor, R. J., Baser, R. E., Abelson, J. M., Hanna, G. L., . . . Jackson, J. S. (2008). Obsessive-compulsive disorder among African Americans and blacks of Caribbean descent: Results from the National Survey of American Life. *Depression and Anxiety, 25,* 993–1005.

Hinton, D. E., & Lewis-Fernández, R. (2010). The cross-cultural validity of posttraumatic stress disorder: Implications for *DSM-5. Depression and Anxiety.* Advance online publication. doi: 10.1002/da.20753

Hoehn-Saric, R., Schlund, M. W., & Wong, S. H. Y. (2004). Effects of citalopram on worry and brain activation in patients with generalized anxiety disorder. *Psychiatry Research: Neuro-imaging, 131,* 11–21.

Hu, X. Z., Lipsky, R. H., Zhu, G., Akhtar, L. A., Taubman, J., Greenberg, B. D., . . . Goldman, D. (2006). Serotonin transporter promoter gain-of-function genotypes are linked to obsessive-compulsive disorder. *American Journal of Human Genetics, 78,* 815–826.

Huppert, J. D., Siev, J., & Kushner, E. S. (2007). When religion and obsessive-compulsive disorder collide: Treating scrupulosity in ultra-orthodox Jews. *Journal of Clinical Psychology, 63,* 925–941.

Jakupcak, M., Cook, J., Imel, Z., Fontana, A., Rosenheck, R., & McFall, M. (2009). Posttraumatic stress disorder as a risk factor for suicidal ideation in Iraq and Afghanistan War veterans. *Journal of Traumatic Stress, 22*(4), 303–306.

Jakupcak, M., Conybeare, D., Phelps, L., Hunt, S. C., Holmes, H. A., Felker, B., . . . McFall, M. E. (2007). Anger, hostility, and aggression among Iraq and Afghanistan War veterans reporting PTSD and subthreshold PTSD. *Journal of Traumatic Stress, 20*(6), 945–954.

Jakupcak, M., Luterek, J., Hunt, S. C., Conybeare, D., & McFall, M. (2008). Posttraumatic stress and its relationship to physical health functioning in a sample of Iraq and Afghanistan War veterans seeking postdeployment VA health care. *Journal of Nervous and Mental Disease, 196*, 425–428.

Janowitz, D., Grabe, H. J., Ruhrmann, S., Ettelt, S., Buhtz, F., Hochrein, A., . . . Wagner, M. (2009). Early onset of obsessive-compulsive disorder and associated comorbidity. *Depression and Anxiety, 26*, 1012–1017.

Jones, M., & Menzies, R. G. (1998). The relevance of associative learning pathways in the development of obsessive-compulsive washing. *Behaviour Research and Therapy, 36*, 273–283.

Joormann, J., & Stöber, J. (1999). Somatic symptoms of generalized anxiety disorder from the *DSM-IV*: Associations with pathological worry and depression symptoms in a nonclinical sample. *Journal of Anxiety Disorders, 13*(5), 491–503.

Julien, D., O'Connor, K. P., & Aardema, F. (2007). Intrusive thoughts, obsessions, and appraisals in obsessive-compulsive disorder: A critical review. *Clinical Psychology Review, 27*, 366–383.

Karadağ, F., Oguzhanoglu, N. K., Özdel, O., Ateşci, F. C., & Amuk, T. (2006). OCD symptoms in a sample of Turkish patients: A phenomenological picture. *Depression and Anxiety, 23*(3), 145–152.

Karam, E. G., Andrews, G., Bromet, E., Petukhova, M., Ruscio, A. M., Salamoun, M., . . . Kessler, R. C. (2010). The role of criterion A2 in the *DSM-IV* diagnosis of posttraumatic stress disorder. *Biological Psychiatry, 68*, 465–473.

Karl, A., Schaefer, M., Malta, L. S., Dörfel, D., Rohleder, N., & Werner, A. (2006). A meta-analysis of structural brain abnormalities in PTSD. *Neuroscience and Biobehavioral Reviews, 30*, 1004–1031.

Karno, M., Golding, J. M., Sorenson, S. B., & Burnam, M. A. (1988). The epidemiology of obsessive-compulsive disorder in five U.S. communities. *Archives of General Psychiatry, 45*(2), 1094–1099.

Katerberg, H., Delucchi, K. L., Stewart, S. E., Lochner, C., Denys, D. A., Stack, D. E., . . . Cath, D. C. (2010). Symptom dimensions in OCD: Item-level factor analysis and heritability estimates. *Behavior Genetics, 40*, 505–517.

Keane, T. M., Caddell, J. M., & Taylor, K. L. (1988). Mississippi Scale for combat-related posttraumatic stress disorder: Three studies in reliability and validity. *Journal of Consulting and Clinical Psychology, 56*, 85–90.

Keane, T. M., & Fairbank, J. A. (1983). Survey analysis of combat-related stress disorders in Viet Nam veterans. *American Journal of Psychiatry, 140*(3), 348–350.

Keeley, M. L., Storch, E. A., Merlo, L. J., & Geffken, G. R. (2008). Clinical predictors of response to cognitive-behavioral therapy for obsessive-compulsive disorder. *Clinical Psychology Review, 28*, 118–130.

Kendler, K. S., Gardner, C. O., Gatz, M., & Pedersen, N. L. (2007). The sources of co-morbidity between major depression and generalized anxiety disorder in a Swedish national twin sample. *Psychological Medicine, 37*, 453–462.

Kendler, K. S., Hettema, J. M., Butera, F., Gardner, C. O., & Prescott, C. A. (2003). Life event dimensions of loss, humiliation, entrapment, and danger in the prediction of onsets of major depression and generalized anxiety. *Archives of General Psychiatry, 60*, 789–796.

Kendler, K. S., Prescott, C. A., Myers, J., & Neale, M. C. (2003). The structure of genetic and environmental risk factors for common psychiatric and substance use disorders in men and women. *Archives of General Psychiatry, 60*, 929–937.

Kessler, R. C., Berglund, P., Demler, O., Jin, R., Merikangas, K. R., & Walters, E. E. (2005). Lifetime prevalence and age-of-onset distributions of *DSM-IV* disorders in the National Comorbidity Survey Replication. *Archives of General Psychiatry, 62*(6), 593–602.

Kessler, R. C., Chiu, W. T., Demler, O., & Walters, E. E. (2005). Prevalence, severity, and comorbidity of 12-month *DSM-IV* disorders in the National Comorbidity Survey Replication. *Archives of General Psychiatry, 62*, 617–627.

Kessler, R. C., DuPont, R. L., Berglund, P., & Wittchen, H.-U. (1999). Impairment in pure and comorbid generalized anxiety disorder and major depression at 12 months in two national surveys. *American Journal of Psychiatry, 156*, 1915–1923.

Kessler, R. C., Sonnega, A., Bromet, E., Hughes, M., & Nelson, C. B. (1995). Posttraumatic stress disorder in the National Comorbidity Survey. *Archives of General Psychiatry, 52*(12), 1048–1060.

Kilpatrick, D. G., Ruggiero, K. J., Acierno, R., Saunders, B. E., Resnick, H. S., & Best, C. L. (2003). Violence and risk of PTSD, major depression, substance abuse/dependence, and comorbidity: Results from the National Survey of Adolescents. *Journal of Consulting and Clinical Psychology, 71*(4), 692–700.

King, D. W., Leskin, G. A., King, L. A., & Weathers, F. W. (1998). Confirmatory factor analysis of the clinician-administered PTSD Scale: Evidence for the dimensionality of posttraumatic stress disorder. *Psychological Assessment, 10*(2), 90–96.

Kobak, K. A., Greist, J. H., Jefferson, J. W., Katzelnick, D. J., & Henk, H. J. (1998). Behavioral versus pharmacological treatments of obsessive-compulsive disorder: A meta-analysis. *Psychopharmacology, 136*, 205–216.

Koenen, K. C. (2007). Genetics of posttraumatic stress disorder: Review and recommendations for future studies. *Journal of Traumatic Stress, 20*(5), 737–750.

Koenen, K. C., Moffitt, T. E., Poulton, R., Martin, J., & Caspi, A. (2007). Early childhood factors associated with the development of post-traumatic stress disorder: Results from a longitudinal birth cohort. *Psychological Medicine, 37*, 181–192.

Koenen, K. C., Nugent, N. R., & Amstadter, A. B. (2008). Gene-environment interaction in posttraumatic stress disorder: Review, strategy and new directions for future research. *European Archives of Psychiatry and Clinical Neuroscience, 258*, 82–96.

Kozak, M. J., & Foa, E. B. (1994). Obsessions, overvalued ideas, and delusions in obsessive-compulsive disorder. *Behaviour Research and Therapy, 32*(3), 343–353.

Kuelz, A. K., Hohagen, F., & Voderholzer, U. (2004). Neuropsychological performance in obsessive-compulsive disorder: A critical review. *Biological Psychology, 65*, 185–236.

Kulka, R. A., Schlenger, W. E., Fairbank, J. A., Hough, R. L., Jordan, B. K., Marmar, C. R., & Weiss, D. S. (1990). *Trauma and the Vietnam War generation: Report of findings from the National Vietnam Veterans Readjustment Study*. Philadelphia, PA: Brunner/Mazel.

Ladouceur, R., Blais, F., Freeston, M. H., & Dugas, M. J. (1998). Problem solving and problem orientation in generalized anxiety disorder. *Journal of Anxiety Disorders, 12*(2), 139–152.

Ladouceur, R., Dugas, M. J., Freeston, M. H., Rhéaume, J., Blais, F., Boisvert, J. M., . . . Thibodeau, N. (1999). Specificity of generalized anxiety disorder symptoms and processes. *Behavior Therapy, 30*(2), 191–207.

Leckman, J. F., Denys, D., Simpson, H. B., Mataix-Cols, D., Hollander, E., Saxena, S., . . . Stein, D. J. (2010). Obsessive-compulsive disorder: A review of the diagnostic criteria and possible subtypes and dimensional specifiers for *DSM-V. Depression and Anxiety, 527*, 507–527.

Lemelson, R. (2003). Obsessive-compulsive disorder in Bali: The cultural shaping of a neuro-psychiatric disorder. *Transcultural Psychiatry, 40*, 377–408.

Liberzon, I., & Sripada, C. S. (2008). The functional neuroanatomy of PTSD: A critical review. *Progress in Brain Research, 167*, 151–169.

Lochner, C., du Toit, P. L., Zungu-Dirwayi, N., Marais, A., Kradenburg, J. van, Seedat, S., . . . Stein, D. J. (2002). Childhood trauma in obsessive-compulsive disorder, trichotillo-mania, and controls. *Depression and Anxiety, 68*, 66–68.

Lyonfields, J. D., Borkovec, T. D., & Thayer, J. F. (1995). Vagal tone in generalized anxiety disorder and the effects of aversive imagery and worrisome thinking. *Behavior Therapy, 26*, 457–466.

Maher, M. J., Huppert, J. D., Chen, H., Duan, N., Foa, E. B., Liebowitz, M. R., & Simpson, H. B. (2010). Moderators and predictors of response to cognitive-behavioral therapy augmenta-tion of pharmacotherapy in obsessive-compulsive disorder. *Psychological Medicine, 40*, 2013–2023.

Marten, P. A., Brown, T. A., Barlow, D. H., Borkovec, T. D., Shear, M. K., & Lydiard, R. B. (1993). Evaluating of the ratings comprising the associated symptom criteria of *DSM-III-R* gener-alized anxiety disorder. *Journal of Nervous and Mental Disease, 181*(11), 676–682.

Mataix-Cols, D., do Rosario-Campos, M. C., & Leckman, J. F. (2005). A multidimensional model of obsessive-compulsive disorder. *American Journal of Psychiatry, 162*, 228–238.

Mataix-Cols, D., Rauch, S. L., Baer, L., Eisen, J. L., Shera, D. M., Goodman, W. K., . . . Jenike, M. A. (2002). Symptom stability in adult obsessive-compulsive disorder: Data from a naturalistic two-year follow-up study. *American Journal of Psychiatry, 159*(2), 263–268.

Mataix-Cols, D., Wooderson, S., Lawrence, N., Brammer, M. J., Speckens, A., & Phillips, M. L. (2004). Distinct neural correlates of washing, checking, and hoarding symptom dimensions in obsessive-compulsive disorder. *Archives of General Psychiatry, 61*, 564–576.

Matsunaga, H., & Seedat, S. (2007). Obsessive-compulsive spectrum disorders: Cross-national and ethnic issues. *CNS Spectrums, 12*(5), 392–400.

McFarlane, A. C. (1988). The aetiology of post-traumatic stress disorders following a natural disaster. *British Journal of Psychiatry, 152*, 116–121.

McLaughlin, K. A., Behar, E., & Borkovec, T. D. (2008). Family history of psychological problems in generalized anxiety disorder. *Journal of Clinical Psychology, 64*, 905–919.

McLaughlin, K. A., Borkovec, T. D., & Sibrava, N. J. (2007). The effects of worry and rumination on affect states and cognitive activity. *Behavior Therapy, 38*, 23–38.

McLeod, D. S., Koenen, K. C., Meyer, J. M., Lyons, M. J., Eisen, S., True, W., & Goldberg, J. (2001). Genetic and environmental influences on the relationship among combat exposure, posttraumatic stress disorder symptoms, and alcohol use. *Journal of Traumatic Stress, 14*(2), 259–275.

McNally, R. J. (2003). Progress and controversy in the study of posttraumatic stress disorder. *Annual Review of Psychology, 54*, 229–252.

McWilliams, L. A., Cox, B. J., & Asmundson, G. J. G. (2005). Symptom structure of post-traumatic stress disorder in a nationally representative sample. *Journal of Anxiety Disorders, 19*, 626–41.

Mennin, D. S., Heimberg, R. G., & Turk, C. L. (2004). Clinical presentation and diagnostic features. In R. G. Heimberg, C. L. Turk, & D. S. Mennin (Eds.), *Generalized anxiety disorder: Advances in research and practice* (pp. 3–28). New York, NY: Guilford Press.

Mennin, D. S., Heimberg, R. G., Turk, C. L., & Fresco, D. M. (2002). Applying an emotion regulation framework to integrative approaches to generalized anxiety disorder. *Clinical Psychology Science and Practice, 9*, 85–90.

Mennin, D. S., Heimberg, R. G., Turk, C. L., & Fresco, D. M. (2005). Preliminary evidence for an emotion dysregulation model of generalized anxiety disorder. *Behaviour Research and Therapy, 43*, 1281–1310.

Mennin, D. S., Holaway, R. M., Fresco, D. M., Moore, M. T., & Heimberg, R. G. (2007). Delineating components of emotion and its dysregulation in anxiety and mood psychopathology. *Behavior Therapy, 38*, 284–302.

Menzies, L., Achard, S., Chamberlain, S. R., Fineberg, N., Chen, C. H., del Campo, N., . . . Bullmore, E. (2007). Neurocognitive endophenotypes of obsessive-compulsive disorder. *Brain, 130*, 3223–3236.

Menzies, L., Chamberlain, S. R., Laird, A. R., Thelen, S. M., Sahakian, B. J., & Bullmore, E. T. (2008). Integrating evidence from neuroimaging and neuropsychological studies of obsessive-compulsive disorder: The orbitofronto-striatal model revisited. *Neuroscience and Biobehavioral Reviews, 32*, 525–549.

Meyer, T. J., Miller, M. L., Metzger, R. L., & Borkovec, T. D. (1990). Development and validation of the Penn State Worry Questionnaire. *Behaviour Research and Therapy, 28*(6), 487–495.

Moffitt, T. E., Harrington, H., Caspi, A., Kim-Cohen, J., Goldberg, D., Gregory, A. M., & Poulton, R. (2007). Depression and generalized anxiety disorder: Cumulative and sequential comorbidity in a birth cohort followed prospectively to age 32 years. *Archives of General Psychiatry, 64*, 651–660.

Mol, S. S. L., Arntz, A., Metsemakers, J. F. M., Dinant, G., Vilters-Van Montfort, P. A. P., & Knottnerus, J. A. (2005). Symptoms of post-traumatic stress disorder after non-traumatic events: Evidence from an open population study. *British Journal of Psychiatry, 186*, 494–499.

Monson, C. M., Schnurr, P. P., Resick, P. A., Friedman, M. J., Young-Xu, Y., & Stevens, S. P. (2006). Cognitive processing therapy for veterans with military-related posttraumatic stress disorder. *Journal of Consulting and Clinical Psychology, 74*(5), 898–907.

Muller, J., & Roberts, J. E. (2005). Memory and attention in obsessive compulsive disorder: A review. *Journal of Anxiety Disorders, 19*, 1–28.

Munafò, M. R., Brown, S. M., & Hariri, A. R. (2008). Serotonin transporter (5-HTTLPR) genotype and amygdala activation: A meta-analysis. *Biological Psychiatry, 63*, 852–857.

Nestadt, G., Di, C. Z., Riddle, M. A., Grados, M. A., Greenberg, B. D., Fyer, A. J., . . . Roche, K. B. (2009). Obsessive-compulsive disorder: Subclassification based on co-morbidity. *Psychological Medicine, 39*, 1491–1501.

Newman, M. G., Zuellig, A. R., Kachin, K. E., Constantino, M. J., Przeworski, A., Erickson, T., & Cashman-McGrath, L. (2002). Preliminary reliability and validity of the generalized anxiety disorder questionnaire-IV: A revised self-report diagnostic measure of generalized anxiety disorder. *Behavior Therapy, 33*, 215–233.

Nitschke, J. B., Sarinopoulos, I., Oathes, D. J., Johnstone, T., Whalen, P. J., Davidson, R. J., & Kalin, N. H. (2009). Anticipatory activation in the amygdala and anterior cingulate in generalized anxiety disorder and prediction of treatment response. *American Journal of Psychiatry, 166*(3), 302–310.

Norris, F. H. (1992). Epidemiology of trauma: Frequency and impact of different potentially traumatic events on different demographics groups. *Journal of Consulting and Clinical Psychology, 60*(3), 409–418.

North, C. S., Suris, A. M., Davis, M., & Smith, R. P. (2009). Toward validation of the diagnosis of posttraumatic stress disorder. *American Journal of Psychiatry, 166*(1), 34–41.

Noyes, R., Woodman, C., Garvey, M. J., Cook, B. L., Suelzer, M., Clancy, J., & Anderson, D. J. (1992). Generalized anxiety disorder vs. panic disorder: Distinguishing characteristics and patterns of comorbidity. *Journal of Nervous and Mental Disease*, *180*(6), 369–379.

Oathes, D. J., Ray, W. J., Yamasaki, A. S., Borkovec, T. D., Castonguay, L. G., Newman, M. G., & Nitschke, J. (2008). Worry, generalized anxiety disorder, and emotion: Evidence from the EEG gamma band. *Biological Psychology*, *79*, 165–170.

O'Donnell, M. L., Creamer, M., & Pattison, P. (2004). Posttraumatic stress disorder and depression following trauma: Understanding comorbidity. *American Journal of Psychiatry*, *161*, 1390–1396.

Olatunji, B. O., Broman-Fulks, J. J., Bergman, S. M., Green, B. A., & Zlomke, K. R. (2010). A taxometric investigation of the latent structure of worry: Dimensionality and associations with depression, anxiety, and stress. *Behavior Therapy*, *41*, 212–228.

Panagioti, M., Gooding, P., & Tarrier, N. (2009). Post-traumatic stress disorder and suicidal behavior: A narrative review. *Clinical Psychology Review*, *29*, 471–482.

Paulesu, E., Sambugaro, E., Torti, T., Danelli, L., Ferri, F., Scialfa, G., . . . Sassaroli, S. (2010). Neural correlates of worry in generalized anxiety disorder and in normal controls: A functional MRI study. *Psychological Medicine*, *40*, 117–124.

Peasley-Miklus, C., & Vrana, S. R. (2000). Effect of worrisome and relaxing thinking on fearful emotional processing. *Behaviour Research and Therapy*, *38*, 129–144.

Perkonigg, A., Pfister, H., Stein, M. B., Höfler, M., Lieb, R., Maercker, A., & Wittchen, H. (2005). Longitudinal course of posttraumatic stress disorder and posttraumatic stress disorder symptoms in a community sample of adolescents and young adults. *American Journal of Psychiatry*, *162*(7), 1320–1327.

Phillips, K. A., Stein, D. J., Rauch, S. L., Hollander, E., Fallon, B. A., Barsky, A., . . . Leckman, J. (2010). Should an obsessive-compulsive spectrum grouping of disorders be included in *DSM-V*? *Depression and Anxiety*, *27*, 528–555.

Pinto, A., Greenberg, B. D., Grados, M. A., Bienvenu, O. J., Samuels, J. F., Murphy, D. L., . . . Nestadt, G. (2008). Further development of YBOCS dimensions in the OCD Collaborative Genetics Study: Symptoms vs. categories. *Psychiatry Research*, *160*, 83–93.

Rachman, S. (1998). A cognitive theory of obsessions: Elaborations. *Behaviour Research and Therapy*, *36*(4), 385–401.

Rauch, S. L., Shin, L. M., & Phelps, E. A. (2006). Neurocircuitry models of posttraumatic stress disorder and extinction: Human neuroimaging research—past, present, and future. *Biological Psychiatry 60*, 376–382.

Rauch, S. L., Shin, L. M., & Wright, C. I. (2003). Neuroimaging studies of amygdala function in anxiety disorders. *Annals of the New York Academy of Sciences*, *985*, 389–419.

Resick, P. A., Galovski, T. E., O'Brien Uhlmansiek, M., Scher, C. D., Clum, G. A., & Young-Xu, Y. (2008). A randomized clinical trial to dismantle components of cognitive processing therapy for posttraumatic stress disorder in female victims of interpersonal violence. *Journal of Consulting and Clinical Psychology*, *76*(2), 243–258.

Resick, P. A., Nishith, P., Weaver, T. L., Astin, M. C., & Feuer, C. A. (2002). A comparison of cognitive-processing therapy with prolonged exposure and a waiting condition for the treatment of chronic posttraumatic stress disorder in female rape victims. *Journal of Consulting and Clinical Psychology*, *70*(4), 867–879.

Roemer, L., Lee, J. K., Salters-Pedneault, K., Erisman, S. M., Orsillo, S. M., & Mennin, D. S. (2009). Mindfulness and emotion regulation difficulties in generalized anxiety disorder: Preliminary evidence for independent and overlapping contributions. *Behavior Therapy*, *40*, 142–154.

Roemer, L., Molina, S., & Borkovec, T. D. (1997). An investigation of worry content among generally anxious individuals. *Journal of Nervous and Mental Disease, 185*(5), 314–319.

Roemer, L., Molina, S., Litz, B. T., & Borkovec, T. D. (1997). Preliminary investigation of the role of previous exposure to potentially traumatic events in generalized anxiety disorder. *Depression and Anxiety, 4*, 134–138.

Roemer, L., Salters, K., Raffa, S. D., & Orsillo, S. M. (2005). Fear and avoidance of internal experiences in GAD: Preliminary tests of a conceptual model. *Cognitive Therapy and Research, 29*(1), 71–88.

Ruscio, A. M. (2002). Delimiting the boundaries of generalized anxiety disorder: Differentiating high worriers with and without GAD. *Journal of Anxiety Disorders, 16*, 377–400.

Ruscio, A. M., & Borkovec, T. D. (2004). Experience and appraisal of worry among high worriers with and without generalized anxiety disorder. *Behaviour Research and Therapy, 42*, 1469–1482.

Ruscio, A. M., Borkovec, T. D., & Ruscio, J. (2001). A taxometric investigation of the latent structure of worry. *Journal of Abnormal Psychology, 110*(3), 413–422.

Ruscio, A. M., Lane, M., Roy-Byrne, P., Stang, P. E., Stein, D. J., Wittchen, H., & Kessler, R. C. (2005). Should excessive worry be required for a diagnosis of generalized anxiety disorder? Results from the U.S. National Comorbidity Survey Replication. *Psychological Medicine, 35*, 1761–1772.

Ruscio, A. M., Ruscio, J., & Keane, T. M. (2002). The latent structure of posttraumatic stress disorder: A taxometric investigation of reactions to extreme stress. *Journal of Abnormal Psychology, 111*(2), 290–301.

Salkovskis, P. M. (1985). Obsessional-compulsive problems: A cognitive-behavioural analysis. *Behaviour Research and Therapy, 23*(5), 571–583.

Salkovskis, P. M. (1989). Cognitive-behavioural factors and the persistence of intrusive thoughts in obsessional problems. *Behaviour Research and Therapy, 27*(6), 677–682.

Salters-Pedneault, K., Roemer, L., Tull, M. T., Rucker, L., & Mennin, D. S. (2006). Evidence of broad deficits in emotion regulation associated with chronic worry and generalized anxiety disorder. *Cognitive Therapy and Research, 30*, 469–480.

Samochowiec, J., Hajduk, A., Samochowiec, A., Horodnicki, J., Stepień, G., Grzywacz, A., & Kucharska-Mazur, J. (2004). Association studies of MAO-A, COMT, and 5-HTT genes polymorphisms in patients with anxiety disorders of the phobic spectrum. *Psychiatry Research, 128*, 21–26.

Schinka, J. A., Busch, R. M., & Robichaux-Keene, N. (2004). A meta-analysis of the association between the serotonin transporter gene polymorphism (5-HTTLPR) and trait anxiety. *Molecular Psychiatry, 9*, 197–202.

Schnyder, U., Moergeli, H., Klaghofer, R., & Buddeberg, C. (2001). Incidence and prediction of posttraumatic stress disorder symptoms in severely injured accident victims. *American Journal of Psychiatry, 158*(4), 594–599.

Schooler, C., Revell, A. J., Timpano, K. R., Wheaton, M., & Murphy, D. L. (2008). Predicting genetic loading from symptom patterns in obsessive-compulsive disorder: A latent variable analysis. *Depression and Anxiety, 25*, 680–688.

Schottenfield, R. S., & Cullen, M. R. (1986). Recognition of occupation-induced posttraumatic stress disorders. *Journal of Occupational Medicine, 28*(5), 365–369.

Schwartz, J. M., Stoessel, P. W., Baxter, L. R., Martin, K. M., & Phelps, M. E. (1996). Systematic changes in cerebral glucose metabolic rate after successful behavior modification treatment of obsessive-compulsive disorder. *Archives of General Psychiatry, 53*(2), 109–113.

Scott, M. J., & Stradling, S. G. (1994). Post-traumatic stress disorder without the trauma. *British Journal of Clinical Psychology, 33*(1), 71–74.

Sen, S., Burmeister, M., & Ghosh, D. (2004). Meta-analysis of the association between a serotonin transporter promoter polymorphism (5-HTTLPR) and anxiety-related personality traits. *American Journal of Medical Genetics, 127B*, 85–99.

Shafran, R., Thordarson, D. S., & Rachman, S. (1996). Thought-action fusion in obsessive compulsive disorder. *Journal of Anxiety Disorders, 10*(5), 379–391.

Shin, L. M., & Liberzon, I. (2010). The neurocircuitry of fear, stress, and anxiety disorders. *Neuropsychopharmacology Reviews, 35*, 169–191.

Sinha, S. S., Mohlman, J., & Gorman, J. M. (2004). Neurobiology. In R. G. Heimberg, C. L. Turk, & D. S. Mennin (Eds.), *Generalized anxiety disorder: Advances in research and practice* (pp. 187–216). New York, NY: Guilford Press.

Stanley, M. A., Turner, S. M., & Borden, J. W. (1990). Schizotypal features in obsessive-compulsive disorder. *Comprehensive Psychiatry, 31*(6), 511–518.

Starcevic, V., & Berle, D. (2006). Cognitive specificity of anxiety disorders: A review of selected key constructs. *Depression and Anxiety, 23*(2), 51–61.

Stein, D. J., Fineberg, N. A., Bienvenu, O. J., Denys, D., Lochner, C., Nestadt, G., . . . Phillips, K. A. (2010). Should OCD be classified as an anxiety disorder in *DSM-V? Depression and Anxiety, 27*, 495–506.

Stein, M. B., Jang, K. L., Taylor, S., Vernon, P. A., & Livesley, W. J. (2002). Genetic and environmental influences on trauma exposure and posttraumatic stress disorder symptoms: A twin study. *American Journal of Psychiatry, 159*(10), 1675–1681.

Stein, M. B., Schork, N. J., & Gelernter, J. (2008). Gene-by-environment (serotonin transporter and childhood maltreatment) interaction for anxiety sensitivity, an intermediate phenotype for anxiety disorders. *Neuropsychopharmacology, 33*, 312–319.

Stein, M. B., Walker, J. R., Hazen, A. L., & Forde, D. R. (1997). Full and partial posttraumatic stress disorder: Findings from a community survey. *American Journal of Psychiatry, 154*(8), 1114–1119.

Steketee, G. (1997). Disability and family burden in obsessive-compulsive disorder. *Canadian Journal of Psychiatry, 42*, 919–928.

Steketee, G., Chambless, D. L., Tran, G. Q., Worden, H., & Gillis, M. (1996). Behavioral avoidance tests for obsessive compulsive disorder. *Behaviour Research and Therapy, 34*(1), 73–83.

Steketee, G., Frost, R., & Bogart, K. (1996). The Yale-Brown Obsessive Compulsive Scale: Interview versus self-report. *Behaviour Research and Therapy, 34*(8), 675–684.

Steketee, G., Frost, R. O., & Cohen, I. (1998). Beliefs in obsessive-compulsive disorder. *Journal of Anxiety Disorders, 12*(6), 525–537.

Steketee, G., & Shapiro, L. J. (1995). Predicting behavioral treatment outcome for agoraphobia and obsessive compulsive disorder. *Clinical Psychology Review, 15*(4), 317–346. DOI: 10.1016/0272-7358(95)00017-J

Stöber, J., Tepperwien, S., & Staak, M. (2000). Worrying leads to reduced concreteness of problem elaboration: Evidence for the avoidance theory of worry. *Anxiety, Stress, and Coping, 13*, 217–227.

Storch, E. A., Larson, M. J., Price, L. H., Rasmussen, S. A., Murphy, T. K., & Goodman, W. K. (2010). Psychometric analysis of the Yale-Brown Obsessive-Compulsive Scale Second Edition Symptom Checklist. *Journal of Anxiety Disorders, 24*, 650–656.

Storch, E. A., Rasmussen, S. A., Price, L. H., Larson, M. J., Murphy, T. K., & Goodman, W. K. (2010). Development and psychometric evaluation of the Yale-Brown Obsessive-Compulsive Scale—Second Edition. *Psychological Assessment, 22*(2), 223–232.

Swedo, S. E., Rapoport, J. L., Leonard, H., Lenane, M., & Cheslow, D. (1989). Obsessive-compulsive disorder in children and adolescents. *Archives of General Psychiatry, 46*, 335–341.

Tadic, A., Rujescu, D., Szegedi, A., Giegling, I., Singer, P., Möller, H. J., & Dahmen, N. (2003). Association of a MAOA gene variant with generalized anxiety disorder, but not with panic disorder or major depression. *American Journal of Medical Genetics and Neuropsychiatric Genetics, 117B*(1), 1–6.

Taylor, S., Kuch, K., Koch, W. J., Crockett, D. J., & Passey, G. (1998). The structure of posttraumatic stress symptoms. *Journal of Abnormal Psychology 107*(1), 154–160.

Thomas, J., Turkheimer, E., & Oltmanns, T. F. (2000). Psychometric analysis of racial differences on the Maudsley Obsessional Compulsive Inventory. *Assessment, 7*, 247–258.

Thayer, J. F., Friedman, B. H., & Borkovec, T. D. (1996). Autonomic characteristics of generalized anxiety disorder and worry. *Biological Psychiatry, 39*, 255–266.

Thrasher, S. M., & Dalgleish, T. (1999). Information processing research in PTSD. In W. Yule (Ed.), *Posttraumatic stress disorders* (pp. 176–192). Chichester, England: John Wiley & Sons.

Torgersen, S. (1986). Childhood and family characteristics in panic and generalized anxiety disorders. *American Journal of Psychiatry, 143*, 630–632.

Turk, C. L., Heimberg, R. G., Luterek, J. A., Mennin, D. S., & Fresco, D. M. (2005). Emotion dysregulation in generalized anxiety disorder: A comparison with social anxiety disorder. *Cognitive Therapy and Research, 29*(1), 89–106.

Turner, S. M., & Beidel, D. C. (1988). *Treating obsessive-compulsive disorder.* New York, NY: Pergamon Press.

Turner, S. M., Beidel, D. C., & Stanley, M. A. (1992). Are obsessional thoughts and worry different cognitive phenomena? *Clinical Psychology Review, 12*(2), 257–270.

van Balkom, A. J. L. M., van Oppen, P., Vermeulen, A. W. A., van Dyck, R., Nauta, M. C. E., & Vorst, H. C. M. (1994). A meta-analysis on the treatment of obsessive compulsive disorder: A comparison of antidepressants, behavior, and cognitive therapy. *Clinical Psychology Review, 14*(5), 359–381.

van den Heuvel, O. A., Remijnse, P. L., Mataix-Cols, D., Vrenken, H., Groenewegen, H. J., Uylings, H. B. M., . . . Veltman, D. J. (2009). The major symptom dimensions of obsessive-compulsive disorder are mediated by partially distinct neural systems. *Brain, 132*, 853–868.

van Grootheest, D. S., Boomsma, D. I., Hettema, J. M., & Kendler, K. S. (2008). Heritability of obsessive-compulsive symptom dimensions. *American Journal of Medical Genetics, 147B*, 473–478.

Vesga-López, O., Schneier, F. R., Wang, S., Heimberg, R. G., Liu, S. M., Hasin, D. S., & Blanco, C. (2008). Gender differences in generalized anxiety disorder from the National Epidemiological Survey on Alcohol and Related Conditions (NESARC). *Journal of Clinical Psychiatry, 69*(10), 1606–1616.

Watkins, E. R. (2008). Constructive and unconstructive repetitive thought. *Psychological Bulletin, 134*(2), 163–206.

Weathers, F. W., Keane, T. M., & Davidson, J. R. T. (2001). Clinician-administered PTSD scale: A review of the first ten years of research. *Depression and Anxiety, 13*(3), 132–156.

Weathers, F. W., Litz, B. T., Herman, D. S., Huska, J. A., & Keane, T. M. (1993, October). *The PTSD Checklist (PCL): Reliability, validity, and diagnostic utility.* Presentation at the International Society for Traumatic Stress Studies, San Antonio, TX.

Weathers, F. W., Ruscio, A. M., & Keane, T. M. (1999). Psychometric properties of nine scoring rules for the Clinician-Administered Posttraumatic Stress Disorder Scale. *Psychological Assessment, 11*(2), 124–133.

Weissman, M. M. (1990). Panic and generalized anxiety: Are they separate disorders? *Journal of Psychiatric Research, 24*(2), 157–162.

Wells, A. (1995). Meta-cognition and worry: A cognitive model of generalized anxiety disorders. *Behavioural and Cognitive Psychotherapy, 6,* 86–95.

Wells, A. (2004). A cognitive model of GAD: Metacognitions and pathological worry. In R. G. Heimberg, C. L. Turk, & D. S. Mennin (Eds.), *Generalized anxiety disorder: Advances in research and practice* (pp. 164–186). New York, NY: Guilford Press.

Wells, A., & Carter, K. (2001). Further tests of a cognitive model of generalized anxiety disorder: Metacognitions and worry in GAD, panic disorder, social phobia, depression, and nonpatients. *Behavior Therapy, 32*(1), 85–102.

Wendland, J. R., Moya, P. R., Timpano, K. R., Anavitarte, A. P., Kruse, M. R., Wheaton, M. G., . . . Murphy, D. L. (2009). A haplotype containing quantitative trait loci for SLC1A1 gene expression and its association with obsessive-compulsive disorder. *Archives of General Psychiatry, 66*(4), 408–416.

Williams, M., Powers, M., Yun, Y.-G., & Foa, E. B. (2010). Minority participation in randomized controlled trials for obsessive-compulsive disorder. *Journal of Anxiety Disorders, 24,* 171–177.

Williams, M. T., Turkheimer, E., Schmidt, K. M., & Oltmanns, T. F. (2005). Ethnic identification biases responses to the Padua Inventory for obsessive-compulsive disorder. *Assessment, 12,* 174–185.

Woods, C. M., Vevea, J. L., Chambless, D. L., & Bayen, U. J. (2002). Are compulsive checkers impaired in memory? A meta-analytic review. *Clinical Psychology: Science and Practice, 9,* 353–366.

Xian, H., Chantarujikapong, S., Scherrer, J. F., Eisen, S. A., Lyons, M. J., Goldberg, J., . . . True, W. R. (2000). Genetic and environmental influences on posttraumatic stress disorder, alcohol and drug dependence in twin pairs. *Drug and Alcohol Dependence, 61,* 95–102.

Xie, P., Kranzler, H. R., Poling, J., Stein, M. B., Anton, R. F., Brady, K., . . . Gelernter, J. (2009). Interactive effect of stressful life events and the serotonin transporter 5-HTTLPR genotype on posttraumatic stress disorder diagnosis in 2 independent populations. *Archives of General Psychiatry, 66*(11), 1201–1209.

Xie, P., Kranzler, H. R., Poling, J., Stein, M. B., Anton, R. F., Farrer, L. A., & Gelernter, J. (2010). Interaction of FKBP5 with childhood adversity on risk for post-traumatic stress disorder. *Neuropsychopharmacology, 35,* 1684–1692.

Yehuda, R. (2006). Advances in understanding neuroendocrine alterations in PTSD and their therapeutic implications. *Annals of the New York Academy of Sciences, 1071,* 137–166.

Yehuda, R., Cai, G., Golier, J. A., Sarapas, C., Galea, S., Ising, M., . . . Buxbaum, J. D. (2009). Gene expression patterns associated with posttraumatic stress disorder following exposure to the World Trade Center attacks. *Biological Psychiatry, 66,* 708–711.

Yehuda, R., & Sarapas, C. (2010). Pathogenesis of posttraumatic stress disorder and acute stress disorder. In D. J. Stein, E. Hollander, & B. O. Rothbaum (Eds.), *Textbook of anxiety disorders* (pp. 567–581). Arlington, VA: American Psychiatric Publishing.

Yonkers, K. A., Bruce, S. E., Dyck, I. R., & Keller, M. B. (2003). Chronicity, relapse, and illness—Course of panic disorder, social phobia, and generalized anxiety disorder: Findings in men and women from 8 years of follow-up. *Depression and Anxiety, 17*(3), 173–179.

Yook, K., Kim, K.-H., Suh, S. Y., & Lee, K. S. (2010). Intolerance of uncertainty, worry, and rumination in major depressive disorder and generalized anxiety disorder. *Journal of Anxiety Disorders, 24,* 623–628.

You, J. S., Hu, S. Y., Chen, B., & Zhang, H. G. (2005). Serotonin transporter and tryptophan hydroxylase gene polymorphisms in Chinese patients with generalized anxiety disorder. *Psychiatric Genetics, 15,* 7–11.

Zlotnick, C., Franklin, C. L., & Zimmerman, M. (2002). Does "subthreshold" posttraumatic stress disorder have any clinical relevance? *Comprehensive Psychiatry, 43*(6), 413–419.

# CHAPTER 13

# Somatoform Disorders

GORDON J. G. ASMUNDSON, MICHEL A. THIBODEAU, and DANIEL L. PELUSO

## DESCRIPTION OF THE DISORDER

The somatoform disorders, as described in the *Diagnostic and Statistical Manual of Mental Disorders, 4th edition, text revision* (*DSM-IV-TR*; American Psychiatric Association [APA], 2000), include somatization disorder, undifferentiated somatization disorder, conversion disorder, pain disorder, hypochondriasis, and body dysmorphic disorder. A not otherwise specified subcategory is also included for those presenting with relevant symptoms that do not meet criteria for one of the aforementioned somatoform disorders. The common feature of these disorders is bodily sensations (e.g., dyspnea, pain) or changes (e.g., subcutaneous lumps, rash)—interpreted by the person as being symptomatic of some disease process or physical anomaly—that occur in the absence of an identifiable general medical condition or direct influences of a substance or other mental health condition (e.g., panic disorder, depression) that satisfactorily explains the sensations or changes. Bodily sensations and changes are a common experience of day-to-day living for most people, and they typically remit without medical attention; however, available data suggest that about 25% of the population seeks medical attention when these sensations and changes persist (Kroenke, 2003). Up to 30% of those seeking medical attention will exhibit clinically significant distress about having an unidentified disease when there is no medical explanation for presenting "symptoms" (Fink, Sorensen, Engberg, Holm, & Munk-Jorgensen, 1999). This distress is associated with substantial impairment of personal, social, and professional functioning as well as considerable costs to health care (Hessel, Geyer, Hinz, & Brahier, 2005), even after controlling for medical and psychiatric comorbidity (Barsky, Orav, & Bates, 2005).

Some theorists suggest that the category of somatoform disorders needs to be extensively revised (Collimore, Asmundson, Taylor, & Abramowitz, 2009; Kroenke, Sharpe, Sykes, 2007; Noyes, Stuart, & Watson, 2008) or deleted altogether (e.g., Mayou, Kirmayer, Simon, Kroenke, & Sharpe, 2005), because the disorders do not seem to form a coherent category (Mayou et al., 2005). Bouman and Eifert (2009) point out that, while not explicit in the *DSM-IV-TR*, the somatoform disorders cluster into conditions characterized by (a) actual loss or alteration of body functions with little or no anxiety (i.e., somatization disorder, conversion disorder, and pain disorder) and (b) preoccupation with the body or its functioning accompanied by significant anxiety (i.e., hypochondriasis and body dysmorphic disorder). The extent to which these putative clusters accurately capture the complex nature of the disorders currently classified as somatoform disorders remains equivocal. For example, there is considerable evidence that anxiety is critical to the etiology and maintenance of physically unexplained chronic musculoskeletal pain (Asmundson, Norton, & Norton, 1999; Vlaeyen & Linton, 2000). Notwithstanding the lack of empirical support for the somatoform clusters suggested by Bouman and Eifert (2009), the idea that the somatoform disorders might comprise several distinct categories of disorders characterized by shared phenomenology has been considered by several theorists (Collimore et al., 2009); however, it does not appear that the proposed changes to the somatoform disorders in the *DSM-5* will involve reorganization purely along lines of shared phenomenology.

Despite prevalence and cost of the somatoform disorders, as well as a substantive increase in empirical attention during the past decade, they remain not well understood. In the sections that follow, we provide an overview of the general clinical profile, diagnostic considerations, and epidemiology of the somatoform disorders. We then turn attention to issues of assessment, etiological considerations, and course and prognosis. In each of these latter sections, we touch on issues germane to the collective category as well as its specific disorders. In the case study, we focus more specifically on an illustration of uncomplicated hypochondriasis. Given the potential importance of the *DSM-5* to future clinical practice and research endeavors, we end with consideration of reclassification suggestions and options for each of the somatoform disorders.

## CLINICAL PICTURE

While predicated on the shared perception that bodily sensations or changes are caused by a disease process or physical anomaly, the clinical profile for each of the somatoform disorders is unique. A brief overview of the clinical profile of each somatoform disorder is provided, along with reference to *DSM-IV-TR* diagnostic criteria.

### SOMATIZATION DISORDER

The main feature of somatization disorder is the presence of recurring and multiple physical complaints that began before the age of 30 years and are of clinical significance (Criterion A). These complaints are often vague in nature and do not have an identifiable organic basis or, when occurring in the context of a general medical condition, are in excess of what might be expected as a consequence of the condition (Criterion C). The *DSM-IV-TR* operationalizes physical complaints as clinically significant if they lead to medical intervention, including taking medication, or if they cause significant impairment in important areas of functioning. The multiple somatic complaints must not be produced or feigned (Criterion D) and must include each of (a) pain associated with at least four different locations (e.g., back, head, joints, stomach) or functions (e.g., urination, menstruation, intercourse), (b) two gastrointestinal complaints not related to pain (e.g., nausea, abdominal bloating, diarrhea, intolerance to certain foods), (c) one sexual or reproductive complaint not related to pain (e.g., irregular menses, erectile dysfunction, lack of sexual interest), and (d) at least one nonpain complaint suggestive of a neurological condition (Criterion B).

In cases where people do not meet full diagnostic criteria for somatization disorder, such as presenting with too few physical complaints to meet Criterion B, they may be diagnosed with undifferentiated somatization disorder. People with multiple somatic complaints tend to overestimate the probability of organic causes for their complaints and, despite assurances from physicians of no pathological findings, tend to misinterpret physician-provided information (Rief, Hiller, & Margraf, 1998) and selectively remember disease-based explanations for their complaints (Rief, Heitmuller, Reisberg, & Ruddel, 2006). As a means of coping, people with somatization disorder rely heavily on the relief provided by reassurance seeking and checking behaviors (e.g., palpating painful body regions, searching for information about disease in medical textbooks and on the Internet), tactics that ultimately prove ineffective in the long term and only perpetuate distress.

## CONVERSION DISORDER

Conversion disorder is manifestation of somatization wherein the person reports physical complaints that are limited to signs and symptoms suggestive of a neurological disorder or related general medical condition (Criterion A). These most often include paralysis, parasthesia, or blindness, as well as seizures or convulsions. The hallmark of conversion disorder is a lack of correspondence between specific presentations of signs and symptoms and medical understanding of the effects of corresponding neurologic damage. Instead, observed signs and symptoms appear to represent patient beliefs about how neurological deficits should present (Hurwitz, 2004). Onset typically follows a period of distress, such as that stemming from trauma (McFarlane, Atchison, Rafalowicz, & Papay, 1994; Roelofs, Keijsers, Hoogduin, Naring, & Moene, 2002; Van der Kolk et al., 1996) or physical injury (Stone et al., 2009); as such, psychological factors are considered as an essential feature of the diagnosis (Criterion B). Symptoms must not be intentionally produced or feigned (Criterion C) and must not be better accounted for by a general medical condition, direct effects of a substance, or culture-specific behaviors (Criterion D).

People with conversion disorder are often unaware of psychological factors associated with their condition, and many report an inability to control their symptoms. The symptoms must cause significant distress, impairment in important areas of functioning, or warrant medical attention (Criterion E), and they must not be limited to pain or sexual dysfunction or better explained by another mental disorder (Criterion F). Although not a diagnostic criteria for conversion disorder, lack of worry or concern about symptoms (i.e., *la belle indifference*) is mentioned in the *DSM-IV-TR* list of associated features. The available literature, however, fails to support the use of *la belle indifference* as a means of discriminating between conversion disorder and symptoms of organic pathology (Stone, Smyth, Carson, Warlow, & Sharpe, 2006).

## PAIN DISORDER

René Descartes (1596–1650) suggested that pain is a sensory experience resulting from stimulation of specific noxious receptors as a consequence of physical damage caused by injury or disease. Although elegant in its simplicity, this model is both reductionistic (i.e., all pain is directly linked to specific physical pathology) and exclusionary (i.e., social, psychological, behavioral mechanisms of illness are not of primary importance). Pain is currently understood as a complex perceptual phenomenon that involves many dimensions, including, but not limited to, intensity, quality, time course, and personal meaning (Merskey & Bogduk, 1994). It is adaptive in the short term, facilitating the ability to identify, respond to, and resolve physical pathology or injury; however, a significant number of people experience pain for periods that substantially exceed expected times for physical healing and are considered chronic (Waddell, 1987).

Chronic pain is operationalized in the *DSM-IV-TR* pain disorder diagnosis as that which has a duration of 6 months or more; however, other professional organizations (e.g., International Association for the Study of Pain, 1986) consider pain to be chronic if it persists for 3 months or longer. While not necessarily maladaptive (Turk & Rudy, 1987), chronic pain often leads to physical decline, limited functional ability, and emotional distress. These pain experiences are also associated with an increased probability of comorbid psychopathology (Asmundson & Katz, 2009), inappropriate use of medical services, reduced work performance or absenteeism, and high-cost insurance claims (Spengler, Bigos, & Martin, 1986; Stewart, Ricci, Chee, Morganstein, & Lipton, 2003).

The diagnosis of pain disorder is characterized by acute or chronic pain in one or more parts of the body that is severe enough to warrant clinical attention (Criterion A). There must be significant distress or impairment in social, occupational, and other important areas of functioning (Criterion B) and evidence suggesting that psychological factors are involved in the etiology, severity, exacerbation, and maintenance of pain (Criterion C). Psychological factors may include other Axis I or II conditions (also diagnosed but that do not fully account for the individual's pain experience) or subclinical symptoms (i.e., symptoms that do not reach the threshold for a disorder). The pain must not be intentionally produced or feigned (Criterion D), and it must not be better accounted for by another disorder (e.g., mood, anxiety, or psychotic disorder, or dyspareunia; Criterion E). Subtypes of pain disorder are defined according to associated factors (e.g., pain disorder associated with both psychological factors and a general medical condition).

## HYPOCHONDRIASIS

Hypochondriasis is characterized by the preoccupation with fears and beliefs about having a serious disease based on misinterpretation of benign (i.e., harmless) bodily sensations or changes (Criterion A). The focus of concern ranges from highly specific (e.g., "This pain in my gut is so bad. I must have stomach cancer") to vague and diffuse (e.g., "My whole body is aching. What could it be? Maybe it's ALS") and must persist despite appropriate medical evaluation and reassurance of good health (Criterion B). The concerns cannot be of delusional intensity or restricted to defects in appearance, as in the case of body dysmorphic disorder (Criterion C), and must cause significant distress or impairment in important areas of functioning (Criterion D) for at least 6 months (Criterion E). People with hypochondriasis typically resist the idea that they are suffering from a mental disorder and, like those with somatization disorder, come to rely on reassurance seeking and checking behaviors (e.g., palpating subcutaneous lumps, searching for information about disease in medical textbooks and on the Internet) to placate concerns about having a serious disease. While these behaviors can be effective in providing short-term relief, they perpetuate the condition in the long term (Taylor & Asmundson, 2004). Hypochondriasis *with poor insight* is diagnosed when, for most of the time during the course of the disorder, the person does not recognize that his or her concern about having a serious disease is excessive or unreasonable. Onset most often occurs when the person is under significant stress, seriously ill or recovering from a serious medical condition, or has lost a family member (Barsky & Klerman, 1983).

BODY DYSMORPHIC DISORDER

Body dysmorphic disorder is characterized by the preoccupation with either an imagined or exaggerated defect in physical appearance (Criterion A). Concerns might involve imagined or slight facial flaws (e.g., wrinkles, scars, facial asymmetry), the size or shape of a facial feature (e.g., nose, eyes, ears) or other body part (e.g., hair line, arms, sexual organs, breasts), general characteristics of the head (e.g., hair line), or overall body size or shape (Phillips, McElroy, Keck, Pope, & Hudson, 1993). The preoccupation must cause significant distress or functional impairment (Criterion B), and must not be better accounted for by another disorder (Criterion C). People with body dysmorphic disorder are reluctant to discuss appearance concerns with significant others or potential treatment providers and, as a consequence, do not receive targeted treatment (Wilhelm, Buhlmann, Hayward, Greenberg, & Dimaite, 2010). Their efforts to placate distress typically involve behavioral avoidance (e.g., turning down social opportunities, avoiding eye contact, staying away from mirrors or other reflective surfaces), ritualistic checking behaviors (e.g., staring in the mirror or other reflective surface, excessive grooming, reading about cosmetic surgery options), and attempts to conceal perceived defects (e.g., wearing a hat to cover hair line or shade face). People with body dysmorphic disorder tend to have poor insight regarding the unreasonable nature of their concerns and may be delusional (e.g., believe others are laughing or staring at their perceived defect; Phillips et al., 2006). Onset most often occurs in adolescence.

## DIAGNOSTIC CONSIDERATIONS (INCLUDING DUAL DIAGNOSIS)

To qualify for a somatoform disorder diagnosis, somatic signs and symptoms must be unexplained medically; that is, signs and symptoms must not be explained by organic pathology or physical deficit (APA, 2000). If an organic pathology or physical deficit is present, then concern must be in excess of that expected on the basis of the medical seriousness of the organic pathology or physical deficit. Ruling out an organic basis for somatic symptoms can pose a considerable challenge.

This determination depends, in large part, on sound clinical judgment and current medical knowledge. Because medical knowledge is perennially incomplete, some presentations of somatic signs and symptoms, both innocuous and serious, may arise from a specific physiological disturbance that is not identified. Sykes (2006) has argued that default attribution of medically unexplained somatic symptoms to psychopathology is untenable and has contributed to unjustified diagnoses of conditions characterized by somatic complaints as mental rather than physical disorders.

It is, however, important to understand that many benign physical factors can give rise to somatic signs and symptoms beyond organic pathology. Consider, for example, physical deconditioning. People with somatoform disorders and sub-syndromal presentations thereof often avoid physical exertion, including physical exercise, for fear that it will have harmful consequences. As a result, they become physically deconditioned. Physical deconditioning is associated with postural hypotension, muscle atrophy, and exertion-related breathlessness and fatigue, all of which can promote further inactivity and reinforce unfounded beliefs in people with somatoform disorders that they are ill (Taylor & Asmundson, 2004). In cases such as these, there appears to be ample foundation on which to conceptualize the presentation as having a psychological basis.

The diagnostic picture is further complicated in that there is no specific mention of the role of psychological factors in the *DSM-IV-TR* description of the somatoform disorders category, beyond the need for symptoms to cause significant distress. And, among the disorder subcategories, there is inconsistency in this regard; for example, descriptions of some of the somatoform disorders include mention of psychological factors (e.g., conversion and pain disorder are thought to be initiated, exacerbated, or maintained by psychological factors; hypochodriasis is defined by fears or preoccupations regarding the misattribution of benign somatic signs and symptoms as indicative of disease), while there is no reference to such factors for somatization disorder. Lack of coherence within the diagnostic subcategories contributes to existing concerns about the utility of the somatoform disorders as reflecting a coherent category of mental disorders (e.g., Mayou et al., 2005).

The seemingly insufficient rationale for conceptualizing somatoform disorders as a coherent class of mental disorders has led to the proposal of several diagnostic alternatives, including the dual diagnosis approach. For example, Mayou et al. (2005) propose that the somatoform disorders category be abolished and that its diagnostic subcategories be reassigned to other diagnostic categories or coded as part of a dual diagnosis. Irritable bowel syndrome provides an illustration for the dual diagnosis approach; it is classified both as a general medical condition and can receive an additional diagnosis (where appropriate) of a mental disorder or as a psychological factor affecting medical condition. The dual diagnosis approach provides a compelling potential diagnostic solution to problems associated with the somatoform disorders. Some argue that the dual diagnosis approach may also prevent diagnostic labels, like somatizer or hypochondriac, from being applied pejoratively or punitively (Sykes, 2006).

Although further research is required, there is evidence to support the notion that somatoform disorders require modification in order to facilitate accurate diagnoses (Noyes et al., 2008). The importance of diagnosis cannot be overstated, as any diagnosis carries significant implications for individuals receiving the diagnosis and their related experiences (e.g., stigmatization, interpretation of symptoms, nature of treatment, response to treatment). As Kirmayer and Looper (2007) note, diagnosis is a form of intervention and, as such, is a crucial element in shaping treatment and outcome. Changes for the forthcoming *DSM-5* have been proposed for the somatoform disorders and are discussed in subsequent sections.

## EPIDEMIOLOGY

Diagnosis of a somatoform disorder is dependent on the absence of identifiable organic pathology or physical deficit (APA, 2000); consequently, this class of disorders is a challenge to diagnose and to study from an epidemiological standpoint. Changes in classification and diagnosis, as well as the wide range and severity of somatic symptoms, have also proven a challenge to epidemiological investigation of the somatoform disorders. The somatoform disorders were not included in the large-scale national comorbidity surveys based on *DSM-III-R* (Kessler, 1994) and *DSM-IV-TR* (Kessler, Chiu, Demler, Merikangas, & Walters, 2005) criteria, nor were they examined in the recent World Health Organization World Mental Health Surveys initiative (Kessler & Üstün, 2008). Epidemiological researchers have often paired the class of somatoform disorders with other disorders (e.g., anxiety disorders; Bland, Orn, & Newman, 1988) or have excluded specific somatoform disorders from analyses due to low or high base rates or differences in classification methodologies (e.g., Leiknes, Finset, Moum, & Sandanger, 2008). As such, the prevalence of somatoform disorders as a class of disorders remains largely unstudied.

Presentation of somatic concerns that do not meet diagnostic criteria for a somatoform disorder or medical condition account for approximately half of all physician visits (Nimnuan, Hotopf, & Wessely, 2001), suggesting that subsyndromal somatoform symptoms are highly prevalent and costly (Barsky et al., 2005; Kirmayer & Robbins, 1991). As noted previously, few epidemiological studies have simultaneously assessed for all somatoform disorders; however, the few that have done so in community samples report 12-month prevalence ranging from 5.3% to 11% (Wittchen & Jacobi, 2005) and a lifetime prevalence of 32% (Grabe et al., 2003b). Somatoform disorders are more common in women (Wittchen & Jacobi, 2005), with perhaps the exception of hypochondriasis (Asmundson, Taylor, Sevgur, & Cox, 2001; Bleichhardt & Hiller, 2007). People with a somatoform disorder also frequently experience co-occurring mood disorders (Leiknes et al., 2008), anxiety disorders (Lowe et al., 2008), personality disorders (Bornstein & Gold, 2008; Sakai, Nestoriuc, Nolido, & Barsky, 2010), as well as other somatoform disorders (Leiknes et al., 2008).

Of the somatoform disorders, the least common are somatization disorder and conversion disorder. Somatization disorder occurs infrequently in the general population, with point prevalence (i.e., the proportion of cases at that time) and lifetime prevalence of less than 1% (Grabe et al., 2003b; Robins & Regier, 1991). Point prevalence in primary care settings vary but typically range from 1% to 5% (Dickinson et al., 2003; Gureje, Simon, Üstün, & Goldberg, 1997). The point and 12-month prevalence of conversion disorder in the general population are less than

0.1% (Akagi & House, 2001). Point prevalence in neurology and primary care settings have been reported as 1% (Smith, Clarke, Handrinos, Dunsis, & McKenzie, 2000) and 0.2% (De Waal, Arnold, Eekhof, & Van Hemert, 2004), respectively. Despite low prevalence of conversion disorder, medically unexplained neurological symptoms are present in approximately 11% to 35% of neurology patients (Carson et al., 2000; Snijders, de Leeuw, Klumpers, Kappelle, & van Gijn, 2004), suggesting that subsyndromal conversion may be more common than almost all neurological diseases.

Data from nationally representative German and U.S. samples indicate point prevalence for body dysmorphic disorder of approximately 1.8% (Buhlmann et al., 2010) and 2.4% (Koran, Abujaoude, Large, & Serpe, 2008), respectively. Another U.S. study has estimated the lifetime prevalence of body dysmorphic disorder as 1% (Bienvenu et al., 2000). Point prevalence of body dysmorphic disorder in psychiatric outpatient clinics is 3.2% (Zimmerman & Mattia, 1998), while in psychiatric inpatient settings it is 16% (Conroy et al., 2008). People with body dysmorphic disorder also frequently seek services in specialized medical settings (e.g., cosmetic surgery, dermatology; Aouizerate et al., 2003; Phillips, Dufresne, Wilkel, & Viottorio, 2000).

Hypochondriasis and pain disorder are the most common of the somatoform disorders and, based on the prevalence estimates detailed as follows, are as common as many of the major psychiatric disorders (e.g., panic disorder). Hypochondriasis, when assessed in the general population, has point and 12-month prevalence of approximately 0.4% (Bleichhardt & Hiller, 2007; Looper & Kirmayer, 2001) and 4.5% (Faravelli et al., 1997), respectively. Reported prevalence in primary care settings vary considerably based on methodology. Studies using diagnostic interviews have reported a point prevalence of 3% (Escobar et al., 1998) and a 12-month prevalence of 0.8% (Gureje, Üstün, & Simon, 1997), while a study using cutoff scores from self-report measures followed by interviews suggests a 12-month prevalence of 8.5% (Noyes et al., 1993). The lifetime prevalence of hypochondriasis is approximately 1% to 5% (APA, 2000).

While reported prevalence varies widely depending on sampling and assessment methods, most studies indicate that approximately 17% to 33% of the general population has current chronic pain (Blyth et al., 2001; Breivik, Collett, Ventafridda, Cohen, & Gallacher, 2006). Epidemiological studies of pain disorder face the additional challenge of having to account for psychological factors in the context of the pain experience. Studies of pain disorder in German nationally representative samples have reported a lifetime prevalence of 12.3% (Grabe et al., 2003a), a 12-month prevalence of 8.1% (Frohlich, Jacobi, & Wittchen, 2006), and a 6-month prevalence of 5.4% (Grabe et al., 2003a). Studies assessing prevalence in primary care samples have reported lifetime prevalence as 14.2% (Mergl et al., 2007) and point prevalence between 1.7% (De Waal et al., 2004) and 5.3% (Mergl et al., 2007).

## PSYCHOLOGICAL AND BIOLOGICAL ASSESSMENT

Individuals with somatoform disorders will typically present in medical settings rather than in mental health settings; indeed, they may often refuse a mental health referral because of a belief that their condition is purely organic. Cooperation between medical and mental health professionals aids the referral process and, due to the complexity of the factors involved (e.g., ruling out organic pathology), is typically necessary in making an accurate diagnosis. Throughout the course of assessing a person with a possible somatoform disorder, the mental health professional must seek to establish and maintain rapport and should clearly relay that, while probably not related to a disease process, the presenting issue is real and not feigned or "in the head" (Taylor & Asmundson, 2004). The general goals of assessment for the somatoform disorders are to rule out organic or substance-based explanations of presenting signs and symptoms, to determine the type and severity of signs and symptoms, and to facilitate appropriate treatment planning.

Because the diagnostic process relies heavily on the exclusion of general medical conditions, and 100% certainty is rarely if ever possible, false negatives will always remain a possibility (Taylor & Asmundson, 2004; Woolfolk, & Allen, 2007). In the case of somatization disorder and hypochondriasis, both of which involve numerous somatic complaints, the likelihood of falsely ruling out organic causes increases. Approximately 2% of persons presenting for cognitive behavioral assessment and treatment are misdiagnosed with hypochondriasis when they, in fact, have an underlying general medical condition (Warwick, Clark, Cobb, & Salkovskis, 1996). Gathering a detailed history of somatic complaints, past and current medical conditions, and medical professionals consulted is a crucial part of a comprehensive diagnostic process and may provide insight regarding the nature of the presenting condition. For example, individuals with hypochondriasis often seek medical attention as soon as they develop bodily sensations or changes, whereas those suffering from somatization disorder generally wait for several symptoms to develop before seeking medical assistance (Rief et al., 1998). A consult with the family physician may be necessary to determine the need for further medical assessments; however, caution is warranted, as further assessments may reinforce maladaptive coping (e.g., reassurance seeking) while also increasing the costs and potential risks associated with medical care.

Structured clinical interviews have proven to be the gold standard in the diagnosis of mental disorders, including somatoform disorders. Broad structured interviews that include sections on numerous mental disorders are the most commonly utilized. The Structured Clinical Interview for the *DSM-IV* (First, Spitzer, Gibbon, & Williams, 1996) and the Composite International Diagnostic Interview (CIDI; World Health Organization, 1990) based on the *International Statistical Classification of Diseases*, 10th edition, criteria (*ICD-10*; World Health Organization, 2007) are both used widely and have demonstrated efficacy and reliability in diagnosing somatoform disorders. Other useful structured interviews include the Somatoform Disorders Schedule (World Health Organization, 1994), the Schedules for Clinical Assessment in Neuropsychiatry (Wing et al., 1990), and the Diagnostic Interview Schedule (Robins, Helzer, Croughan, & Ratcliff, 1981). Interviews have also been designed to assess specific somatoform disorders, such as the Health Anxiety Interview (Taylor & Asmundson, 2004) for hypochondriasis and the Body Dysmorphic Disorder Examination (Rosen & Reiter, 1996) for severe symptoms of negative body image.

Structured clinical interviews can be supplemented with diarized monitoring of catastrophic thinking and maladaptive coping behaviors as well as information gleaned from standardized self-report measures. Self-report measures are efficient and effective screening tools that can provide invaluable information for case conceptualization and regular monitoring of treatment progress. The Screening for Somatoform Symptoms (Rief, Hiller, & Heuser, 1997), the Symptom Checklist–90, Revised (Derogatis, 1975), or the Patient Health Questionnaire–15 (Kroenke, Spitzer, & Williams, 2002) can be used to assess a broad range of somatoform symptoms. More specific information can be derived from a wide array of self-report measures that have been developed to assess the severity of specific somatoform symptoms. It is beyond the scope of this chapter to provide a comprehensive list of these measures; examples include the Health Attitude Survey (Noyes, Langbehn, Happel, Sieren, & Muller, 1999) for use in assessing attitudes and perceptions associated with somatization, the Whiteley Index (Pilowsky, 1967) for use in assessing cognitions associated with hypochondriasis, the Pain Catastrophizing Scale (Sullivan, Bishop, & Pivik, 1995) for assessing cognitions associated with pain disorder, and the Body Dysmorphic Disorder modification of the Yale-Brown Obsessive Compulsive Scale (Phillips et al., 1997). Medical service utilization and visual analogue scales pertaining to distressing thoughts and maladaptive coping behaviors can also be used to assess emotional and functional impact and to monitor treatment progress. Finally, measures of mood and anxiety can be useful in case conceptualization and monitoring and might include the Beck Depression Inventory–II (Beck, Steer, & Brown, 1996), the Beck Anxiety Inventory (Beck & Steer, 1993), and the original or recent 18-item expanded version of the Anxiety Sensitivity Index (Peterson & Reiss, 1987).

## ETIOLOGICAL CONSIDERATIONS

### BEHAVIORAL GENETICS AND MOLECULAR GENETICS

Heritability of somatoform disorders has been suggested by findings from behavioral (e.g., Kendler et al., 2011; Torgersen, 1986) and molecular (e.g., Hennings, Zill, & Rief, 2009) genetics studies. Somatoform symptom concordance rates between monozygotic twins are higher than between dizygotic twins, even when controlling for co-occurring psychiatric symptoms (Lembo, Zaman, Krueger, Tomenson, & Creed, 2009). A recent study concluded that while mood and somatoform disorders share common genetic factors (e.g., deregulation of serotonergic pathways), there are numerous genetic features unique to somatoform disorders (e.g., immunological deregulation, hypothalamic-pituitary-adrenal [HPA] axis responses; Rief, Hennings, Riemer, & Euteneuer, 2010). The role of specific genetic markers in the development of somatoform symptoms remains unclear; however, research in this area is ongoing, and genetic factors are now being considered within the context of psychological models of various somatoform disorders (e.g., Taylor, Jang, Stein, & Asmundson, 2008; Veale, 2004).

### NEUROANATOMY AND NEUROBIOLOGY

Researchers have reported neurological correlates for each of body dysmorphic disorder (e.g., Feusner, Yaryura-Tobias, & Saxena, 2008), conversion disorder (e.g.,

Vuilleumier, 2005), somatization disorder (e.g., Hakala, Vahlberg, Niemi, & Karlsson, 2006), pain disorder and fibromyalgia (e.g., Wood, Glabus, Simpson, & Patterson, 2009), and hypochondriasis (e.g., Atmaca, Sec, Yildirim, Kayali, & Korkmaz, 2010). The HPA axis has been a focus of research in this area. A recent longitudinal study reported preliminary evidence that cortisol deregulation in the HPA axis may predate the development of somatic symptoms in some people (Tak & Rosmalen, 2010). The HPA axis controls glandular and hormonal responses to stress and, when stressors (e.g., chronic pain, anxiety) have a chronic course, may lead to hypocortisolism (i.e., adrenal insufficiency), which induces greater stress and enhances experiences of pain and fatigue (Fries, Hesse, Hellhammer, & Hellhammer, 2005). Increases in these experiences typically exacerbate somatic symptoms or lead to behaviors that exacerbate or maintain somatoform disorders (Taylor & Asmundson, 2004). The second somatosensory area (SII) of the cerebral cortex, which is involved in the analysis and evaluation of complex patterns of somesthetic input (e.g., perception of pain, sensations from visceral structures, gastric sensations), has also been implicated as a source of the somatic perturbation associated with the somatoform disorders (Miller, 1984); however, despite its appeal as a neural structure underlying this class of disorders, people with somatoform disorders do not typically show abnormalities in sensory acuity.

## Learning, Modeling, and Life Events

Early childhood experiences of illness and perceptions of significant illness in others are associated with the experience of medically unexplained symptoms in adulthood (Hotopf, Wilson-Jones, Mayou, Wadsworth, & Wessely, 2000). Likewise, parents who fear disease, who are preoccupied with their bodies, and who overreact to minor ailments experienced by their children are more likely to have children with the same tendencies, both during childhood and adulthood (Craig, Boardman, Mills, Daly-Jones, & Drake, 1993; Hotopf, Mayou, Wadsworth, & Wessely, 1999; Marshall, Jones, Ramchandani, Stein, & Bass, 2007). In addition, childhood physical and sexual abuse and neglect have been associated with increased physician visits during adulthood (Fiddler, Jackson, Kapur, Wells, & Creed, 2004) and with hypochondriasis (Barsky, Wool, Barnett, & Cleary, 1994), as have other stressful life events unrelated to disease; however, it is noteworthy that increased prevalence of abuse and other stressful life events are characteristic of people with a variety of psychiatric conditions (e.g., panic disorder; Taylor, 2009), not just the somatoform disorders.

## Cognitive Influences

Greater focus on somatic sensations and pain is associated with greater experiences of those sensations (Brown, 2004; Ursin, 2005). When attention is directed to the body, the intensity of perceived sensations increases (Mechanic, 1983; Pennebaker, 1980). People with somatoform disorders spend a considerable amount of time focusing on their bodies, thereby increasing their chances of noticing somatic sensations and changes. They also tend to believe that somatic sensations and changes are indicative of disease or are otherwise harmful in some way (Barsky,

1992; Taylor & Asmundson, 2004; Vervoort, Goubert, Eccleston, Bijttebier, & Crombez, 2006). These beliefs increase the attention directed to somatic sensations and changes and, in turn, increase associated distress.

SEX AND RACIAL-ETHNIC CONSIDERATIONS

As noted in the Epidemiology section, the somatoform disorders are more prevalent in women than in men, perhaps with the exception of hypochondriasis. There are several possible explanations for this difference. Because women are more likely to seek medical services (Corney, 1990; Kessler et al., 2008), they may be more prone to diagnostic biases wherein physicians consider somatic symptoms presented by a woman as more likely to be psychological than organic in nature (e.g., Martin, Gordon, & Lounsbury, 1998). Women also tend to experience higher rates of psychopathology (Kessler et al., 2008). Shared etiological or maintenance factors between mental disorders may make it more likely that women are at a higher risk of developing a somatoform disorder. There is evidence that women tend to focus more on their bodies (Beebe, 1995) and are more fearful of some of their bodily sensations (Stewart, Taylor, & Baker, 1997), further increasing their risk for developing somatoform disorders. Other putative sex differences have been proposed (e.g., differential experiences of abuse; HPA axis dysregulation) but warrant further empirical scrutiny in the context of their role in somatoform disorder etiology.

Somatic sensations and changes are common in all cultural groups; however, presentation varies widely depending on sociocultural norms (Kirmayer & Young, 1998). Cultural factors, such as socially transmitted values, beliefs, and expectations, can influence how a person interprets somatic sensations and changes, and whether treatment seeking is initiated. Some cultures appear to be more distressed by gastrointestinal sensations (e.g., excessive concerns about constipation in the United Kingdom), whereas others are more distressed by cardiopulmonary (e.g., excessive concerns about low blood pressure in Germany) and immunologically based (e.g., excessive concerns about viruses and their effects in the United States and Canada) symptoms (Escobar, Allen, Hoyos Nervi, & Gara, 2001). Whether one seeks care for somatic concerns also appears to vary as a function of culture, with those of Chinese, African American, Puerto Rican, and other Latin American descent presenting with more medically unexplained somatic symptoms than those from other groups (Escobar et al., 2001). Whether concern over somatic sensations and changes is excessive needs to be judged in the context of the individual's cultural background.

## COURSE AND PROGNOSIS

Somatoform disorders vary considerably in course and prognosis, in part because the disorders are heterogeneous in presentation and involve substantial comorbidity with mood and anxiety disorders, personality disorders, and, in some cases, general medical conditions. Certain prognostic indicators are common across somatoform disorders; for example, comorbidity with other psychiatric disorders contributes to a more chronic and persistent course (e.g., Rief, Hiller, Geissner, & Fichter, 1995).

The presence of fewer somatic symptoms, few or no comorbid conditions, identifiable stressors at the time of onset, high intellectual functioning, as well as sound social support networks are typically associated with good prognosis. Also indicative of good prognosis is the development of a strong therapeutic alliance between the patient and care provider, wherein the patient believes that the care provider views the patient's presenting signs and symptoms as legitimate, albeit probably not due to an organic pathology or physical defect (Taylor & Asmundson, 2004).

Despite heterogeneous presentation of this class of disorder, psychosocial interventions have demonstrated efficacy across the various somatoform disorders. Specifically, cognitive-behavioral therapy (CBT) has demonstrated to be superior to standard medical care in improving somatic complaints/somatization (Allen, Woolfolk, Escobar, Gara, & Hamer, 2006; Speckens, Van Hemert, Bolk, Rooijmans, & Hengeveld, 1996) and reducing health-related anxiety (Barsky & Ahern, 2004). Likewise, CBT and, to a lesser extent, physical rehabilitation have been recommended for treating conversion disorder (Halligan, Bass, & Marshall, 2001), and CBT has proven effective in the treatment of chronic pain (Morley, Eccleston, & Williams, 1999). Psychiatric consultation letters to primary care physicians describing somatization and providing recommendations for primary care have also been shown to significantly improve physical functioning and reduce the cost of medical care (Rost, Kashner, & Smith, 1994).

## LOOKING AHEAD TO *DSM-5*

Nosological classification continues to be a challenge for the somatoform disorders. The key assumption underlying somatoform disorders is the notion that medically unexplained somatic distress is attributable to psychopathology. This issue, combined with the limited ability to identify and measure organic causes for all somatic perturbations, has made classification challenging. As a consequence, there have been several recommendations for revisions to the somatoform disorders category for the forthcoming *DSM-5*, including renaming certain disorders, renaming the category, and reassigning some disorders to other diagnostic categories (APA, 2011).

Hypochondriasis provides a good illustration of the suggested changes. Hypochondriasis is proposed to be renamed as illness anxiety disorder given its empirically supported conceptualization as a form of health anxiety (Collimore et al., 2009; Noyes et al., 2008; Taylor & Asmundson, 2004). The working group has, at present, chosen to characterize the condition by use of the term *illness anxiety* despite use of the term *health anxiety* in the extant literature as well as in the diagnostic nomenclature of one of the other proposed additions to this category of disorders (i.e., complex somatic symptom disorder). Converging evidence also strongly suggests that hypochondriasis (or illness anxiety disorder) be reclassified as an anxiety disorder given that anxiety is a core feature of hypochondriasis, and empirically supported etiological conceptualizations of hypochondriasis (i.e., CBT model) are very similar to other anxiety disorders (e.g., catastrophic misinterpretations of bodily symptoms; Collimore et al., 2009; Taylor & Asmundson, 2004); however, at this point, it appears that the proposed illness anxiety disorder will remain in the somatoform disorders.

Among other changes to the category, the name *somatoform disorders* has been proposed to be changed to *somatic symptom disorders* because presentations of medical illness and somatic symptoms are also central among other disorders (i.e., factitious disorders, psychological factors affecting medical condition). More substantive changes include proposed exclusion of medically unexplained symptoms as a core feature of several disorders (APA, 2011). In addition, (a) various disorders will be collapsed and subsumed under a single diagnosis due to overlapping symptoms (e.g., somatic symptoms and cognitive distortions); specifically, somatization disorder, undifferentiated somatization disorder, and pain disorder (associated with psychological factors or with both psychological factors and a general medical condition) are all to be subsumed as part of the new complex somatic symptom disorder; (b) conversion disorder will be renamed as functional neurological symptoms; (c) somatoform disorder not otherwise specified will be renamed as somatic symptom disorder not elsewhere classified; and, (d) although still under review, body dysmorphic disorder may be reassigned to the anxiety disorders, obsessive-compulsive spectrum disorders, or subsumed under complex somatic symptom disorder.

Under the new diagnostic rubric, disorders are to be characterized by somatic symptoms and associated distress and dysfunction. Somatic symptoms, in turn, may be precipitated, exacerbated, or perpetuated by biological, psychological, and social factors. The following is the provisional taxonomy for the newly proposed somatic symptom disorder category and a brief explanation of core features of the disorders therein.

### PSYCHOLOGICAL FACTORS AFFECTING MEDICAL CONDITION

This new disorder is characterized by the presence of one or more clinically significant psychological or behavioral factors that adversely affect a somatic symptom or medical condition (i.e., by increasing the risk for suffering, death, or disability). Psychological factors include psychological distress, interpersonal interaction, and maladaptive health behaviors, and these factors may influence the course of treatment or constitute an additional health risk factor. The somatic symptoms or medical condition, in turn, can be exacerbated by the presence of psychological features.

### COMPLEX SOMATIC SYMPTOM DISORDER

This disorder is characterized by one or several distressing symptoms and maladaptive or excessive responses to such symptoms or associated health concerns. Somatic symptoms can vary from specific (e.g., localized pain) to generalized (e.g., extreme fatigue) and must be disproportionate and persistent in the context of the medical seriousness of the presenting symptoms; that is, the somatic signs and symptoms must be typically appraised as harmful and threatening despite contradictory evidence. High levels of health-related anxiety are proposed as a component of complex somatic symptom disorder; however, if health-related anxiety is present with only minimal somatic symptoms, then illness anxiety disorder may be a more appropriate diagnosis. This latter distinction is still under discussion.

### Simple (or Abridged) Somatic Symptom Disorder

To meet diagnostic criteria for this new disorder, a person must have at least one distressing or disabling somatic symptom (e.g., pain) as well as at least one of (a) disproportionate and persistent concerns about the medical seriousness of the presenting symptom, (b) high level of health-related anxiety, or (c) excessive time and energy devoted to these symptoms or health concerns (i.e., core features of complex somatic symptom disorder) experienced for at least 1 month.

### Illness Anxiety Disorder

This proposed disorder is characterized by elevated levels of illness (or health) anxiety; that is, anxiety associated with innocuous somatic symptoms that is distressing and/or disruptive. Individuals receiving this diagnosis must be pre-occupied with having or developing a serious illness and will present with the maladaptive behavioral patterns (e.g., excessive checking and reassurance seeking) and maladaptive avoidance characteristic of the *DSM-IV-TR* hypochondriasis over a chronic course.

### Functional Neurological Symptoms

This proposed disorder will, in essence, replace *DSM-IV-TR* conversion disorder. Unlike current diagnostic criteria for conversion disorder, psychological factors are not the essential feature of functional neurological symptoms, although they may be related to the onset of the symptoms.

### Factitious Disorder

Factitious disorder is characterized by longstanding and persistent problems of illness perception and identity, typically associated with unexplained or unexpected somatic symptoms. In factitious disorder, individuals simulate (e.g., exaggerate, fabricate, simulate, induce) psychological or medical impairment in themselves or others, including pets, in the absence of obvious gain.

### Pseudocyesis

This proposed disorder is characterized by false beliefs of being pregnant that are accompanied by objective signs of pregnancy (e.g., nausea, reduced menstrual flow, subjective sensation of fetal movement). The symptoms are not better accounted for by a general medical condition that precipitates endocrine changes, though such changes may be present.

## CASE STUDY

### Case Identification

The basic features of this case are undisguised; however, in line with Clifft's (1986) guidelines, identifying information has been altered or omitted to protect confidentiality and privacy.

Jacob is a 37-year-old Caucasian male who has been married for 10 years and has a 5-year-old daughter and a 6-month-old son. He currently resides with his wife and children in an upper-middle-class suburban neighborhood. His family is financially secure, and he is not involved in any legal proceedings. Jacob is employed full time as an electrical engineer for a large company, a job he has held for the past 6 years. He enjoys a variety of sports, walking the family dog, and spending time with his family. Until recently, he was active as a competitive triathlete. His job requires that he travel periodically, with absences from home and his family for up to 1 month at a time. He reports that job demands increase in the months prior to extended travel and that his next lengthy trip is fast approaching in 10 weeks.

## PRESENTING COMPLAINTS

Jacob was referred by his family physician for assessment and, if appropriate, treatment of increasing anxiety over his physical well-being that was negatively impacting on his work (e.g., spending excessive amounts of time searching medical information on the Internet instead of working) as well as leisure and family (e.g., withdrawing from physical activity and shared leisure activities) functioning. These concerns started 9 months ago, when his father died of heart complications associated with amyloidosis, a disease wherein amyloid proteins build up in specific organs and, over time, disrupt organ function and eventually lead to failure of the affected organs. There is a rare form—hereditary amyloidosis—that is most frequently passed from father to son and for which there are no preventive measures other than not having children. There is no cure for amyloidosis, and the effects do not become apparent until later in life (i.e., over the age of 50 years). Beginning shortly after his father's death, Jacob became increasingly aware of and concerned by somatic sensations in his body—heart palpitation and racing, upper body aches and pain, dizziness, and blurred vision—all of which were similar to those initially experienced by his father. He feared that he may also have amyloidosis and might die from it. His fears were exacerbated upon the birth of his son, with specific concerns that he had passed on the condition and that his son would eventually succumb as well.

## HISTORY

Jacob had no prior history of mental health problems or treatment and, aside from chicken pox and tonsillitis as a child, had been physically healthy throughout his life. The report from his physician confirmed that, despite numerous visits regarding various somatic complaints over the past months, there was no evidence of an organic basis for Jacob's concerns. The physician report also indicated that Jacob was physically healthy and that he and his son had a pending appointment for genetic testing to rule out the genetic profile for hereditary amyloidosis. Jacob reported having a loving and supportive relationship with his wife, although she was becoming increasingly concerned by his condition and, at times, annoyed at his growing reluctance to actively play with their children. Until recently, he was exercising five or six times per week and had competed in numerous triathlons; however, because of growing concerns about his health, he had significantly cut down his frequency of training and was not competing in order to "avoid physical exertion" for fear that his heart would "explode." In place of training, he was spending hours checking the Internet for medical information.

Jacob was assessed using the Health Anxiety Interview (Taylor & Asmundson, 2004), a semistructured interview that permits detailed assessment of the *DSM-IV-TR* hypochondrias and related conditions (i.e., disease phobia, delusional disorder—somatic type), as well as the Structured Clinical Interview for *DSM-IV* (First et al., 1996) and a battery of self-report questionnaires. The latter included (a) the Beck Depression Inventory–II, a measure of depression over the past 2 weeks (Beck et al., 1996), (b) the Beck Anxiety Inventory, a measure of general anxiety over the past week (Beck & Steer, 1993), (c) the Anxiety Sensitivity Index (Peterson & Reiss, 1987), a measure of the fear of arousal-related bodily sensations, and (d) the Whiteley Index (Pilowsky, 1967), a measure of the core features of hypochondriasis, including disease fear, disease conviction, and bodily preoccupation. The structured interview and self-report data provided detailed data regarding general features of Jacob's distress, as well as specific features of his health-related concerns.

Jacob met the *DSM-IV-TR* diagnostic criteria for hypochondriasis. He presented with several specific concerns, including (a) daily concerns that bodily changes and sensations (e.g., heart palpitations and racing, upper body aches and pain, dizziness, blurred vision) were signs of physical disease (hypochondriasis Criterion A) despite medical evidence to the contrary (hypochondriasis Criterion B), (b) daily concerns about the future-oriented health and well-being of his 6-month-old son, (c) considerable distress at work due to his inability to focus on work-related tasks (hypochondriasis Criterion D), and (d) considerable distress due to his increasing hesitation to do any physical activity, including leisure activities with his wife and playing with his daughter and son (hypochondriasis Criterion D). His concerns had, as noted previously, begun around the time of his father's death 9 months prior (hypochondriasis Criterion E) and were deemed to not be delusional in nature or restricted to concerns about appearance (hypochondriasis Criterion C).

It is noteworthy that hypochondriasis is diagnosed only when general medical conditions are ruled out as sufficient causes of the presenting concerns. Given that the effects of amyloidosis are typically not evident until later in life, and that Jacob was in his mid-thirties, it was deemed unlikely that amyloid deposits were responsible for the bodily sensations he was experiencing. It is also noteworthy that Jacob and his son completed genetic testing just prior to 6-month follow-up and were found to not have the genetic profile for hereditary amyloidosis. At the time of assessment, Jacob's score on the Whiteley Index was moderate overall (score = 8; possible range 0–14), characterized by significant disease fear (score = 3; possible range 0–4) and bodily preoccupation (score = 3; possible range 0–3) but little disease conviction (score = 0; possible range 0–3). The latter is indicative of good prognosis with treatment (Taylor & Asmundson, 2004).

He did not meet diagnostic criteria for other Axis I diagnoses. Scores on the Beck Depression Inventory (score = 13; possible range 0–63) and Beck Anxiety Inventory (score = 26; possible range 0–63) suggest a mildly depressed mood and moderate general anxiety, respectively. The absence of comorbid Axis I diagnoses, along with depression and general anxiety in the mild to moderate range, are also indicative of good prognosis with treatment (Taylor & Asmundson, 2004). His score on the Anxiety Sensitivity Index (score = 26; possible range 0–64) indicates strong beliefs that arousal-related bodily sensations have harmful consequences, which, when considered in the context of his significant disease fear and bodily preoccupation, suggest that attention-focusing exercises (e.g., Furer, Walker, & Stein, 2007; Wells, 1997) and interoceptive exposure (Taylor & Asmundson, 2004) may prove to be particularly beneficial additions to treatment.

## SUMMARY

Conditions characterized by significant concern over somatic signs and symptoms, often presenting as medically unexplainable, are associated with significant emotional distress, cognitions characterized by catastrophic thinking, maladaptive coping behaviors typically manifest as excessive checking and reassurance seeking, limitations in social and occupational functioning, and excessive use of health care resources. These conditions are represented by the disorders subsumed under the current *DSM-IV-TR* somatoform disorders as well as their subsyndromal presentations. Changes proposed for the *DSM-5* may improve the utility of this category of disorders by promoting more accurate diagnosis and, should this be accomplished, may help direct appropriate treatment resources to optimize outcomes. The burden on the health care system and the personal distress associated with somatic symptoms highlight the need for appropriate reconceptualization of disorders characterized by somatic symptom presentation; however, some investigators have suggested that there is insufficient empirical evidence to warrant change at this time and that the proposed changes may be premature (Taylor, 2009). Indeed, it remains unclear at this time whether proposed changes for the *DSM-5* reflect the extant empirical evidence and clinical wisdom that has accumulated since the release of the *DSM-IV* in 1994. It also remains unclear if, or how, the proposed changes to classification will facilitate efforts to identify underlying mechanisms or provide more effective treatment.

## REFERENCES

Akagi, H., & House, A. (2001). The epidemiology of hysterical conversion. In P. Halligan, C. Bass, & J. Marshall (Eds.), *Contemporary approaches to the study of hysteria*. Oxford, England: Oxford University Press.

Allen, L. A., Woolfolk, R. L., Escobar, J. I., Gara, M. A., & Hamer, R. M. (2006). Cognitive-behaviour therapy for somatization disorder. *Psychosomatic Medicine, 63*, 93–94.

American Psychiatric Association. (2000). *Diagnostic and statistical manual of mental disorders* (4th ed., text rev; DSM-IV-TR). Washington, DC: Author.

American Psychiatric Association. (2011). Proposed draft revisions to *DSM* disorders and criteria. Retrieved from www.dsm5.org/ProposedRevisions/Pages/Default.aspx

Aouizerate, B., Pujol, H., Grabot, D., Faytout, M., Suire, K., Braud, C., . . . Tignol, J. (2003). Body dysmorphic disorder in a sample of cosmetic surgery applicants. *European Psychiatry, 18*, 365–368.

Asmundson, G. J. G., & Katz, J. (2009). Understanding the co-occurrence of anxiety disorders and chronic musculoskeletal pain: The state-of-the-art. *Depression and Anxiety, 26*, 888–901.

Asmundson, G. J. G., Norton, P. J., & Norton, G. R. (1999). Beyond pain: The role of fear and avoidance in chronicity. *Clinical Psychology Review, 19*, 97–119.

Asmundson, G. J. G., Taylor, S., Sevgur, S., & Cox, B. J. (2001). Health anxiety: Classification and clinical features. In G. J. G. Asmundson, S. Taylor, & B. J. Cox (Eds.), *Health anxiety: Clinical and research perspectives on hypochondriasis and related disorders* (pp. 3–21). New York, NY: John Wiley & Sons.

Atmaca, M., Sec, S., Yildirim, H., Kayali, A., & Korkmaz, S. (2010). A volumetric MRI analysis of hypochondriac patients. *Bulletin of Clinical Psychopharmacology, 20*, 293–299.

Barsky, A. J. (1992). Amplification, somatization, and the somatoform disorders. *Psychosomatics, 33*, 28–34.

Barsky, A. J., & Ahern, D. K. (2004). Cognitive behaviour therapy for hypochondriasis: A randomized controlled trial. *Journal of the American Medical Association, 291*, 1464–1470.

Barsky, A. J., & Klerman, G. L. (1983). Overview: Hypochondriasis, bodily complaints, and somatic style. *American Journal of Psychiatry, 140*, 273–283.

Barsky, A. J., Orav, E. J., & Bates, D. W. (2005). Somatization increases medical utilization and costs independent of psychiatric and medical comorbidity. *Archives of General Psychiatry, 62*, 903–910.

Barsky, A., Wool, C., Barnett, M., & Cleary, P. (1994). Histories of childhood trauma in adult hypochondriacal patients. *American Journal of Psychiatry, 151*, 397–401.

Beck, A. T., & Steer, R. A. (1993). *Manual for the Beck Anxiety Inventory.* San Antonio, TX: Psychological Corporation.

Beck A. T., Steer, R. A., & Brown, G. K. (1996). *Manual for the Beck Depression Inventory—II.* San Antonio, TX: Psychological Corporation.

Beebe, D. W. (1995). The Attention of Body Shape Scale: A new measure of body focus. *Journal of Personality Assessment, 65*, 486–501.

Bienvenu, O. J., Samuels, J. F., Riddle, M. A., Hochn Saric, R., Liang, K.-Y., Cullen, B. A. M., . . . Nestadt, G. (2000). The relationship of obsessive-compulsive disorder to possible spectrum disorders: Results from a family study. *Biological Psychiatry, 48*, 287–293.

Bland, R. C., Orn, H., & Newman, S. C. (1988). Lifetime prevalence of psychiatric disorders in Edmonton. *Acta Psychiatrica Scandinavica, 77*, 24–32.

Bleichhardt, G., & Hiller, W. (2007). Hypochondriasis and health anxiety in the German population. *British Journal of Health Psychology, 12*, 511–523.

Brown, R. J. (2004). Psychological mechanisms of medically unexplained symptoms: An integrative conceptual model. *Psychological Bulletin, 130*, 793–812.

Blyth, F. M., March, L. M., Brnabic, A. J., Jorm, L. R., Williamson, M., & Cousins, M. J. (2001). Chronic pain in Australia: A prevalence study. *Pain, 89*, 127–134.

Bornstein, R. F., & Gold, S. H. (2008). Comorbidity of personality disorders and somatization disorder: A meta-analytic review. *Journal of Psychopathology and Behavioral Assessment, 30*, 154–161.

Bouman, T. K., & Eifert, G. H. (2009). Somatoform disorders. In P. H. Blaney & T. Millon (Eds.), *Oxford textbook of psychopathology* (2nd ed., pp. 482–505). New York, NY: Oxford University Press.

Breivik, H., Collett, B., Ventafridda, V., Cohen, R., & Gallacher, D. (2006). Survey of chronic pain in Europe: Prevalence, impact on daily life, and treatment. *European Journal of Pain, 10*, 287–333.

Buhlmann, U., Glaesmer, H., Mewes, R., Fama, J. M., Wilhelm, S., Brähler, E., & Rief, W. (2010). Updates on the prevalence of body dysmorphic disorder: A population-based survey. *Psychiatry Research, 178,* 171–175.

Carson, A. J., Ringbauer, B., Stone, J., McKenzie, L., Warlow, C., & Sharpe, M. (2000). Do medically unexplained symptoms matter? A prospective cohort study of 300 new referrals to neurology outpatient clinics. *Journal of Neurology Neurosurgery and Psychiatry, 68,* 207–210.

Clifft, M. A. (1986). Writing about psychiatric patients. Guidelines for disguising case material. *Bulletin of the Menninger Clinic, 50,* 511–524.

Collimore, K. C., Asmundson, G. J. G., Taylor, S., & Abramowitz, J. S. (2009). Classification of hypochondriasis and other somatoform disorders. In D. McKay, J. S. Abramowitz, S. Taylor, & G. J. G. Asmundson (Eds.), *Current perspectives on the anxiety disorders: Implications for DSM-V and beyond* (pp. 431–452). New York, NY: Springer.

Conroy, M., Menard, W., Fleming-Ives, K., Modha, P., Cerullo, H., & Phillips, K. A. (2008). Prevalence and clinical characteristics of body dysmorphic disorder in an adult inpatient setting. *General Hospital Psychiatry, 30,* 67–72.

Corney, R. H. (1990). Sex differences in general practice attendance and help seeking for minor illness. *Journal of Psychosomatic Research, 34,* 525–534.

Craig, T. K., Boardman, A. P., Mills, K., Daly-Jones, O., & Drake, H. (1993). The South London Somatisation Study, I: Longitudinal course and the influence of early life experiences. *The British Journal of Psychiatry, 163,* 579–588.

De Waal, M. W. M., Arnold, I. A., Eekhof, J. A. H., & Van Hemert, A. M. (2004). Somatoform disorders in general practice: Prevalence, functional impairment and comorbidity with anxiety and depressive disorders. *British Journal of Psychiatry, 184,* 470–476.

Derogatis, L. R. (1975). *SCL-90-R: Administration, scoring and procedures manual-II for the revised version and other instruments of the psychopathology rating scale series.* Towson, MD: Clinical Psychometric Research.

Dickinson, W. P., Dickinson, L. M., deGruy, F. V., Candib, L. M., Main, D. S., Libby, A.M., & Rost, K. (2003). The somatization in primary care study: A tale of three diagnoses. *General Hospital Psychiatry, 25,* 1–7.

Escobar, J. I., Allen, L. A., Hoyos Nervi, C., & Gara, M. A. (2001). General and cross-cultural considerations in a medical setting for patients presenting with medically unexplained symptoms. In G. J. G. Asmundson, S. Taylor, & B. J. Cox (Eds.), *Health anxiety: Clinical and research perspectives on hypochondriasis and related conditions* (pp. 220–245). New York, NY: John Wiley & Sons.

Escobar, J. I., Gara, M., Waitzkin, H., Silver, R. C., Holman, A., & Compton, W. (1998). *DSM-IV* hypochondriasis in primary care. *General Hospital Psychiatry, 20,* 155–159.

Faravelli, C., Salvatori, S., Galassi, F., Aiazzi, L., Drei, C., & Cabras, P. (1997). Epidemiology of somatoform disorders: A community survey in Florence. *Social Psychiatry and Psychiatric Epidemiology, 32,* 24–29.

Feusner, J. D., Yaryura-Tobias, J., & Saxena, S. (2008). The pathophysiology of body dysmorphic disorder. *Body image, 5,* 3–12.

Fiddler, M., Jackson, J., Kapur, N., Wells, A., & Creed, F. (2004). Childhood adversity and frequent medical consultations. *General hospital psychiatry, 26,* 367–377.

Fink, P., Sorensen, L., Engberg, M., Holm, M., & Munk-Jorgensen, P. (1999). Somatization in primary care: Prevalence, health care utilization, and general practitioner recognition. *Psychosomatics, 40,* 330–338.

First, M. B., Spitzer, R. L., Gibbon, M., & Williams, J. B. W. (1996). *Structured Clinical Interview for DSM-IV Axis I Disorders—Patient edition.* New York: New York State Psychiatric Institute, Biometrics Research Department.

Fries, E., Hesse, J., Hellhammer, J., & Hellhammer, D. H. (2005). A new view on hypocortisolism. *Psychoneuroendocrinology, 30,* 1010–1016.

Frohlich, C., Jacobi, F., & Wittchen, H. U. (2006). *DSM-IV* pain disorder in the general population: An exploration of the structure and threshold of medically unexplained pain symptoms. *European Archives of Psychiatry and Clinical Neuroscience, 256,* 187–196.

Furer, P., Walker, J. R., & Stein, M. B. (2007). *Treating health anxiety and fear of death.* New York, NY: Springer.

Grabe, H. J., Meyer, C., Hapke, U., Rumpf, H. J., Freyberger, H. J., Dilling, H., & John, U. (2003a). Somatoform pain disorder in the general population. *Psychotherapy and Psychosomatics, 72,* 88–94.

Grabe, H. J., Meyer, C., Hapke, U., Rumpf, H. J., Freyberger, H. J., Dilling, H., & John, U. (2003b). Specific somatoform disorder in the general population. *Psychosomatics, 44,* 304–311.

Gureje, O., Simon, G. E., Üstün, T. B., & Goldberg, D. P. (1997). Somatization in cross-cultural perspective: A world health organization study in primary care. *American Journal of Psychiatry, 154,* 989–995.

Gureje, O., Üstün, T. B., & Simon, G. E. (1997). The syndrome of hypochondriasis: A cross-national study in primary care. *Psychological Medicine, 27,* 1001–1010.

Hakala, M., Vahlberg, T., Niemi, P. M., & Karlsson, H. (2006). Brain glucose metabolism and temperament in relation to severe somatization. *Psychiatry and Clinical Neurosciences, 60,* 669–675.

Halligan, P. W., Bass, C., & Marshall, J. C. (Eds.). (2001). *Contemporary approach to the study of hysteria: Clinical and theoretical perspectives.* Oxford, England: Oxford University Press.

Hennings, A., Zill, P., & Rief, W. (2009). Serotonin transporter gene promoter polymorphism and somatoform symptoms. *The Journal of Clinical Psychiatry, 70,* 1536–1539.

Hessel, A., Geyer, M., Hinz, A., & Brahier, E. (2005). Utilization of the health care system due to somatoform complaints: Results of a representative survey. *Zeitschrift fur Psychosomatische Medizin und Psychotherapie, 51,* 38–56.

Hotopf, M., Mayou, R., Wadsworth, M., & Wessely, S. (1999). Childhood risk factors for adults with medically unexplained symptoms: Results from a national birth cohort study. *American Journal of Psychiatry, 156,* 1796–1800.

Hotopf, M., Wilson-Jones, C., Mayou, R., Wadsworth, M., & Wessely, S. (2000). Childhood predictors of adult medically unexplained hospitalisations: Results from a national birth cohort study. *British Journal of Psychiatry, 176,* 273–280.

Hurwitz, T. A. (2004). Somatization and conversion disorder. *Canadian Journal of Psychiatry, 49,* 172–178.

International Association for the Study of Pain. (1986). Classification of chronic pain: Descriptions of chronic pain syndromes and definitions of pain terms. *Pain Supplement, 3,* 1–222.

Kendler, K., Aggen, S. H., Knudsen, G. P., Røysamb, E., Neale, M. C., & Reichborn-Kjennerud, T. (2011). The structure of genetic and environmental risk factors for syndromal and subsyndromal common *DSM-IV* axis I and all axis II disorders. *The American Journal of Psychiatry, 168,* 29–39.

Kessler, R. C. (1994). The National Comorbidity Survey of the United States. *International Review of Psychiatry, 6,* 365–376.

Kessler, R. C., Berglund, P. A., Chiu, W.-T., Demler, O., Glantz, M., Lane, M. C., . . . Wells, K. B. (2008). The national comorbidity survey replication (NCS-R): Cornerstone in improving mental health and mental health care in the United States. In R. C. Kessler & T. B. Üstün (Eds.), *The WHO World Mental Health Surveys: Global Perspectives on the Epidemiology of Mental Disorders* (pp. 165–209). New York, NY: Cambridge University Press.

Kessler, R. C., Chiu, W. T., Demler, O., Merikangas, K. R., & Walters, E. E. (2005). Prevalence, severity, and comorbidity of 12-month *DSM-IV* disorders in the national comorbidity survey replication. *Archives of General Psychiatry, 62*, 617–627.

Kessler, R. C., & Üstün, T. B. (2008). *The WHO World Mental Health Surveys: Global perspectives on the epidemiology of mental disorders.* New York, NY: Cambridge University Press.

Kirmayer, L. J., & Looper, K. J. (2007). Somatoform disorders. In M. Hersen, S. Turner, & D. Beidel (Eds.), *Adult psychopathology* (5th ed., pp. 410–472). Hoboken, NJ: John Wiley & Sons.

Kirmayer, L. J., & Robbins, J. M. (1991). Three forms of somatization in primary care: Prevalence, co-occurrence, and sociodemographic characteristics. *The Journal of Nervous and Mental Disease, 179*, 647–655.

Kirmayer, L. J., & Young, A. (1998). Culture and somatization: clinical, epidemiological, and ethnographic perspectives. *Psychosomatic Medicine, 60*, 420–430.

Koran, L. M., Abujaoude, E., Large, M. D., Serpe, R. T. (2008). The prevalence of body dysmorphic disorder in the United States adult population. *CNS Spectrums, 13*, 1–7.

Kroenke, K. (2003). Patients presenting with somatic complaints: Epidemiology, psychiatric co-morbidity and management. *International Journal of Methods in Psychiatric Research, 12*, 34–43.

Kroenke, K., Sharpe, M., & Sykes, R. (2007). Revising the classification of somatoform disorders: Key questions and preliminary recommendations. *Psychosomatics, 48*, 277–285.

Kroenke, K., Spitzer, R. L., & Williams, J. B. W. (2002). The PHQ-15: Validity of a new measure for evaluating the severity of somatic symptoms. *Psychosomatic Medicine, 64*, 258–266.

Leiknes, K. A., Finset, A., Moum, T., & Sandanger, I. (2008). Overlap, comorbidity, and the use of and stability of somatoform disorders current versus lifetime criteria. *Psychosomatics, 49*, 152–162.

Lembo, A. J., Zaman, M., Krueger, R. F., Tomenson, B. M., & Creed, F. H. (2009). Psychiatric disorder, irritable bowel syndrome, and extra-intestinal symptoms in a population-based sample of twins. *The American Journal of Gastroenterology, 104*, 686–694.

Looper, K. J., & Kirmayer, L. J. (2001). Hypochondriacal concerns in a community population. *Psychological Medicine, 31*, 577–584.

Lowe, B., Spitzer, R. L., Williams, J. B. W., Mussell, M., Schellberg, D., & Kroenke, K. (2008). Depression, anxiety and somatization in primary care: Syndrome overlap and functional impairment. *General Hospital Psychiatry, 30*, 191–199.

Marshall, T., Jones, D. P. H., Ramchandani, P. G., Stein, A., & Bass, C. (2007). Intergenerational transmission of health beliefs in somatoform disorders: exploratory study. *The British Journal of Psychiatry, 191*, 449–50.

Martin, R., Gordon, E. E., & Lounsbury, P. (1998). Gender disparities in the attribution of cardiac-related symptoms: Contribution of common sense models of illness. *Health Psychology, 17*, 346–357.

Mayou, R., Kirmayer, L. J., Simon, G., Kroenke, K., & Sharpe, M. (2005). Somatoform disorders: Time for a new approach in *DSM-V*. *American Journal of Psychiatry, 162*, 847–855.

McFarlane, A. C., Atchison, M., Rafalowicz, E., & Papay, P. (1994). Physical symptoms in posttraumatic stress disorder. *Journal of Psychosomatic Research, 38*, 715–726.

Mechanic, D. (1983). Adolescent health and illness behavior: review of the literature and a new hypothesis for the study of stress. *Journal of Human Stress, 9*, 4–13.

Mergl, R., Seidscheck, I., Allgaier, A. K., Moller, H. J., Hegerl, U., & Henkel, V. (2007). Depressive, anxiety, and somatoform disorders in primary care: Prevalence and re-cognition. *Depression and Anxiety, 24*, 185–195.

Merskey, H., & Bogduk, N. (1994). *Classification of chronic pain, description of chronic pain syndromes and definitions of pain terms.* Seattle, WA: IASP Press.

Miller, L. (1984). Neuropsychological concepts of somatoform disorders. *International Journal of Psychiatry in Medicine, 14*, 31–46.

Morley, S., Eccleston, C., & Williams, A. (1999). Systematic review and meta analysis of randomised controlled trials of cognitive behavioral therapy and behavior therapy for chronic pain in adults, excluding headache. *Pain, 80*, 1–13.

Nimnuan, C., Hotopf, M., & Wessely, S. (2001). Medically unexplained symptoms: An epidemiological study in seven specialities. *Journal of Psychosomatic Research, 51*, 361–367.

Noyes, R., Kathol, R. G., Fisher, M. M., Phillips, B. M., Suelzer, M. T., & Holt, C. S. (1993). The validity of DSM-III-R hypochondriasis. *Archives of General Psychiatry, 50*, 961–970.

Noyes, R., Langbehn, D. R., Happel, R. L., Sieren, L. R., & Muller, B. A. (1999). Health Attitude Survey: A scale for assessing somatizing patients. *Psychosomatics, 40*, 470–478.

Noyes, R., Stuart, S. P., & Watson, D. B. (2008). A reconceptualization of the somatoform disorders. *Psychosomatics, 49*, 14–22.

Pennebaker, J. W. (1980). Perceptual and environmental determinants of coughing. *Basic and Applied Social Psychology, 1*, 83–91.

Peterson, R. A., & Reiss, S. (1987). *Test manual for the Anxiety Sensitivity Index.* Orland Park, IL: International Diagnostic Systems.

Phillips, K. A., Didie, E. R., Menard, W., Pagano, M. E., Fay, C., & Weisberg, R. B. (2006). Clinical features of body dysmorphic disorder in adolescents and adults. *Psychiatry Research, 141*, 305–314.

Phillips, K. A., Dufresne, R. G., Wilkel, C. S., & Viottorio, C. C. (2000). Rate of body dysmorphic disorder in dermatology patients. *Journal of the American Academy of Dermatology, 42*, 436–441.

Phillips, K. A., Hollander, E., Rasmussen, S. A., Aronowitz, B. R., DeCaria, C., & Goodman, W. K. (1997). A severity rating scale for body dysmorphic disorder: Development, reliability, and validity of a modified version of the Yale-Brown Obsessive Compulsive Scale. *Psychopharmocological Bulletin, 33*, 17–22.

Phillips, K. A., McElroy, S. L., Keck, P. E., Pope, H. G., & Hudson, J. I. (1993). Body dysmorphic disorder: 30 cases of imagined ugliness. *The American Journal of Psychiatry, 150*, 302–308.

Pilowsky, I. (1967). Dimensions of hypochondriasis. *The British Journal of Psychiatry, 113*, 89–93.

Rief, W., Heitmuller, A. M., Reisberg, K., & Ruddel, H. (2006). Why reassurance fails in patients with unexplained symptoms—An experimental investigation of remembered probabilities. *PLoS Medicine, 3*, 1266–1272.

Rief, W., Hennings, A., Riemer, S., & Euteneuer, F. (2010). Psychobiological differences between depression and somatization. *Journal of Psychosomatic Research, 68*, 495–502.

Rief, W., Hiller, W., Geissner, E., & Fichter, M. M. (1995). A two-year follow-up study of patients with somatoform disorders. *Psychosomatics, 36*, 376–386.

Rief, W., Hiller, W., Heuser, J. (1997). SOMS—Screening für somatoforme Störungen. Manual Zum Fragebogen (SOMS—the Screening for Somatoform Symptoms—Manual). Berne, Switzerland: Huber.

Rief, W., Hiller, W., & Margraf, J. (1998). Cognitive aspects of hypochondriasis and somatization syndrome. *Journal of Abnormal Psychology, 107*, 587–595.

Robins, L. N., Helzer, J. E., Croughan, J., & Ratcliff, K. S. (1981). National Institute of Mental Health diagnostic interview schedule: Its history, characteristics, and validity. *Archives of General Psychiatry, 38*, 381–389.

Robins, L. N., & Regier, D. (1991). *Psychiatric disorders in America: The Epidemiologic Catchment Area Study.* New York, NY: Free Press.

Roelofs, K., Keijers, G. P. J., Hoogduin, C. A. L., Naring, G. W. B., & Moene, F. C. (2002). Childhood abuse in patients with conversion disorder. *American Journal of Psychiatry, 159,* 1908–1913.

Rosen, J. C., & Reiter, J. (1996). Development of the Body Dysmorphic Disorder Examination. *Behaviour Research and Therapy, 34,* 755–766.

Rost, K., Kashner, T. M., & Smith, G. R., Jr. (1994). Effectiveness of psychiatric intervention with somatization disorder patients: Improved outcomes at reduced cost. *General Hospital Psychiatry, 16,* 381–387.

Sakai, R., Nestoriuc, Y., Nolido, N. V., & Barsky, A. J. (2010). The prevalence of personality disorders in hypochondriasis. *Journal of Clinical Psychiatry, 71,* 41–47.

Smith, C. G., Clarke, D. M., Handrinos, D., Dunsis, A., & McKenzie, D. P. (2000). Consultation-liaison psychiatrists' management of somatoform disorders. *Psychosomatics, 41,* 481–489.

Snijders, T. J., de Leeuw, F. E., Klumpers, U. M. H., Kappelle, L. J., & van Gijn, J. (2004). Prevalence and predictors of unexplained neurological symptoms in an academic neurology outpatient clinic: An observational study. *Journal of Neurology, 251,* 66–71.

Speckens, A. E., Van Hemert, A. M., Bolk, J. H., Rooijmans, H. G. M., & Hengeveld, M. W. (1996). Unexplained physical symptoms: Outcome, utilization of medical care and associated factors. *Psychological Medicine, 26,* 745–752.

Spengler, D. M., Bigos, S. J., & Martin, N. A. (1986). Back injuries in industry: A retrospective study, Part 1: Overview and cost analysis. *Spine, 11,* 241–245.

Stewart, S. H., Taylor, S., & Baker, J. M. (1997). Gender differences in dimensions of anxiety sensitivity. *Journal of Anxiety Disorders, 11,* 179–200.

Stewart, W. F., Ricci, J. A., Chee, E., Morganstein, D., & Lipton, R. (2003). Lost productive time and cost due to common pain conditions in the U.S. workforce. *JAMA: The Journal of the American Medical Association, 290,* 2443–2454.

Stone J., Carson, A., Aditya, H., Presscott, R., Zaubi, M., Warlow, C., & Sharpe, M. (2009). The role of physical injury in motor and sensory conversion symptoms: A systematic and narrative review. *Journal of Psychosomatic Research, 66,* 383–390.

Stone, J., Smyth, R., Carson, A., Warlow, C., & Sharpe, M. (2006). La belle indifference in conversion symptoms and hysteria. *British Journal of Psychiatry, 188,* 204–209.

Sullivan, M. J. L., Bishop, S. R., & Pivik, J. (1995). The Pain Catastrophizing Scale: Development and validation. *Psychological Assessment, 7,* 524–532.

Sykes, R. (2006). Somatoform disorders in *DSM-IV*: Mental of physical disorders? *Journal of Psychosomatic Research, 60,* 341–344.

Tak, L. M., & Rosmalen, J. G. M. (2010). Dysfunction of stress responsive systems as a risk factor for functional somatic syndromes. *Journal of Psychosomatic Research, 68,* 461–468.

Taylor, S. (2009). Is it time to revise the classification of somatoform disorders? [Review of *Somatic presentations of mental disorders: Refining the research agenda for DSM-V,* by Dimsdale et al. (Eds.).] *PsycCRITIQUES—Contemporary Psychology: APA Review of Books, 54*(36), Article 7 (http://psycnet.apa.org/critiques/54/36/7.html).

Taylor, S., & Asmundson, G. J. G. (2004). *Treating health anxiety: A cognitive-behavioral approach.* New York, NY: Guilford Press.

Taylor, S., Jang, K. L., Stein, M. B., & Asmundson, G. J. G. (2008). A behavioral-genetic analysis of health anxiety: Implications for the cognitive-behavioral model of hypochondriasis. *Journal of Cognitive Psychotherapy, 22,* 143–153.

Torgersen, S. (1986). Genetics of somatoform disorders. *Archives of General Psychiatry, 43,* 502–505.

Turk, D. C., & Rudy, T. E. (1987). Towards a comprehensive assessment of chronic pain patients. *Behaviour Research and Therapy, 25,* 237–249.

Ursin, H. (2005). Press stop to start: The role of inhibition for choice and health. *Psychoneuroendocrinology, 30,* 1059–1065.

Van der Kolk, B. A., Pelcovitz, D., Roth, S., Mandel, F. S., McFarlane, A., & Herman, J. L. (1996). Dissociation, somatization, and affect dysregulation: The complexity of adaptation to trauma. *American Journal of Psychiatry, 153,* 83–93.

Veale, D. (2004). Advances in a cognitive behavioural model of body dysmorphic disorder. *Body Image, 1,* 113–125.

Vervoort, T., Goubert, L., Eccleston, C., Bijttebier, P., & Crombez, G. (2006). Catastrophic thinking about pain is independently associated with pain severity, disability, and somatic complaints in school children and children with chronic pain. *Journal of Pediatric Psychology, 31,* 674–683.

Vlaeyen, J. W. S., & Linton, S. J. (2000). Fear-avoidance and its consequences in chronic musculoskeletal pain. *Pain, 85,* 317–332.

Vuilleumier, P. (2005). Hysterical conversion and brain function. *Progress in Brain Research, 150,* 309–329.

Waddell, G. (1987). A new clinical model for the treatment of low back pain. *Spine, 12,* 623–644.

Warwick, H. M., Clark, D. M., Cobb, A. M., & Salkovskis, P. M. (1996). A controlled trial of cognitive-behavioural treatment of hypochondriasis. *British Journal of Psychiatry, 169,* 189–195.

Wells, A. (1997). *Cognitive therapy for anxiety disorders.* New York, NY: John Wiley & Sons.

Wilhelm, S., Buhlmann, U., Hayward, L. C., Greenberg, J. L., & Dimaite, R. (2010). A cognitive-behavioral treatment approach for body dysmorphic disorder. *Cognitive and Behavioral Practice, 17,* 241–247.

Wing, J. K., Babor, T., Brugha, T., Burke, J., Cooper, J. E., Giel, R., & Sartorius, N. (1990). SCAN: Schedules for Clinical Assessment in Neuropsychiatry. *Archives of General Psychiatry, 47,* 589–593.

Wittchen, H. U., & Jacobi, F. (2005). Size and burden of mental disorders in Europe: A critical review and appraisal of 27 studies. *European Neuropsychopharmacology, 15,* 357–376.

Wood, P. B., Glabus, M. F., Simpson, R., & Patterson, J. C. (2009). Changes in gray matter density in fibromyalgia: correlation with dopamine metabolism. *The Journal of Pain, 10,* 609–618.

Woolfolk, R. L., & Allen, L. A. (2007). *Treating Somatization: A cognitive-behavioral approach.* New York, NY: Guilford Press.

World Health Organization. (1990). *The Composite International Diagnostic Interview (CIDI).* Geneva, Switzerland: Author.

World Health Organization. (1994). *Somatoform disorders schedule (SDS).* Geneva, Switzerland: Author.

World Health Organization. (2007). *International Statistical Classification of Diseases and Related Health Problems, 10th Revision (ICD-10).* Geneva, Switzerland: Author.

Zimmerman, M., & Mattia, J. I. (1998). Body dysmorphic disorder in psychiatric outpatients: Recognition, prevalence, comorbidity, demographic, and clinical correlates. *Comprehensive Psychiatry, 39,* 265–270.

# CHAPTER 14

# Dissociative Disorders

STEVEN JAY LYNN, JOANNA BERG, SCOTT LILIENFELD, HARALD MERCKELBACH,
TIMO GIESBRECHT, MICHELLE ACCARDI, and COLLEEN CLEERE

## INTRODUCTION

The most recent edition of the *Diagnostic and Statistical Manual of Mental Disorders*
(*DSM-IV-TR*; American Psychiatric Association [APA], 2000) defines *dissociative
disorders* as conditions marked by disruptions in "consciousness, memory, identity,
or perception" (p. 519). *DSM-IV-TR* identifies four major dissociative disorders:
dissociative amnesia, dissociative fugue, depersonalization disorder, and dissociative identity disorder (formerly called multiple personality disorder), plus a fifth
residual category of Dissociative Disorder Not Otherwise Specified (NOS). Additionally, dissociative trance disorder is listed in the appendix of *DSM-IV-TR* and is
believed by its proponents to be characterized by an involuntary state of trance
outside of accepted cultural or religious practices that causes significant clinical
distress (see Cardeña, Duijl, Weiner, & Terhune, 2009, for a discussion of trance/
possession phenomena).

Some epidemiological studies among psychiatric inpatients and outpatients have
reported the prevalence of dissociative disorders as exceeding 10% (Ross, Anderson,
Fleischer, & Norton, 1991; Sar, Tutkun, Alyanak, Bakim, & Barai, 2000; Tutkun et al.,
1998), and a recent study among women in the general population in Turkey even
reported a prevalence of 18.3% for lifetime diagnoses of a dissociative disorder (Sar,
Akyüz, & Dogan, 2007). In contrast, many authors would take issue with these high
prevalence in both clinical and nonclinical samples. Indeed, as our discussion will
reveal, estimates of the prevalence of dissociative disorders vary widely and are
associated with considerable controversy.

Many authors regard symptoms of derealization (i.e., an alteration in the perception of one's surroundings so that a sense of reality of the external world is lost, APA,
2000), depersonalization (i.e., a sensation of being an outside observer of one's body
and "feeling like an automaton or as if one is living in a dream or a movie" [APA,
2000, p. 530]), and dissociative amnesia (i.e., extensive forgetting typically associated
with highly aversive events) as core features of dissociation. However, the concept
of dissociation is semantically open and lacks a precise and generally accepted

definition (Giesbrecht, Lynn, Lilienfeld, & Merckelbach, 2008). This definitional ambiguity is related, in no small measure, to the substantial diversity of experiences that fall under the rubric of "dissociation." Dissociative symptoms range in their manifestation from common cognitive failures (e.g., lapses in attention), to non-pathological absorption and daydreaming, to more pathological manifestations of dissociation, as represented by the dissociative disorders (Holmes et al., 2005).

This variability raises the possibility that some of these symptoms are milder manifestations of the same etiology or have different etiologies and biological substrates, raising questions about whether dissociation is a unitary conceptual domain (Hacking, 1995; Holmes, et al., 2005; Jureidini, 2003). Indeed, van der Hart and his colleagues (van der Hart, Nijenhuis, Steele, & Brown, 2004, 2006) have distinguished ostensibly trauma-related or pathological dissociation, which they term *structural dissociation of the personality*, from nonpathological dissociative experiences (e.g., altered sense of time, absorption). Structural dissociation, in turn, can be subdivided into levels that encompass primary, in which there exists one apparently normal part of the personality (ANP) and one emotional part of the personality (EP), secondary structural dissociation, purportedly associated with a single ANP and further division of the EP, and tertiary dissociation, ostensibly limited to dissociative identity disorder (DID) and characterized with several ANPs and EPs. However, as our review will demonstrate, researchers' attempts to discriminate pathological from nonpathological dissociative experiences psychometrically have been subject to criticism and have been less than uniformly successful (Giesbrecht et al., 2008; Modestin & Erni, 2004; Waller, Putnam, & Carlson, 1996; Waller & Ross, 1997).

Other researchers (Allen, 2001; Cardeña, 1994; Holmes et al., 2005) have proposed two distinct forms of dissociation: detachment and compartmentalization. Detachment consists of depersonalization and derealization, which we describe in some detail later, and related phenomena, like out-of-body experiences. Psychopathological conditions that reflect symptoms of detachment include depersonalization disorder (DPD) and feelings of detachment that occur during flashbacks in post-traumatic stress disorder (PTSD). Compartmentalization, in contrast, ostensibly encompasses dissociative amnesia, marked by extensive forgetting of autobiographical material, and somatoform dissociation, such as sensory loss and "unexplained" neurological symptoms (Nijenhuis, Spinhoven, van Dyck, van der Hart, & Vanderlinden, 1998). The core feature of compartmentalization is a deficit in deliberate control of processes or actions that would normally be amenable to control, as is evident in dissociative identity disorder or somatization disorder. Although clinicians may find it helpful to subdivide dissociative symptoms into different symptom clusters (Bernstein-Carlson & Putnam, 1993), attempts to differentiate such clusters on a psychometric basis have not been consistently successful.

Dissociation is often presumed to reflect a splitting of consciousness, although it must be distinguished from the superficially similar but much debated concept of Freudian repression. Specifically, dissociation can be described as a horizontal split (i.e., the consciousness is split into two or more pieces, but they operate in parallel). In contrast, repression is more akin to a vertical split, in which consciousness is arranged in levels, and traumatic or otherwise undesirable memories are ostensibly pushed downward and rendered more or less inaccessible.

Although the existence of dissociation as a clinical symptom is not in dispute, dissociative disorders are among the most controversial psychological disorders. Disagreement generally centers on the etiology of these disorders, with advocates often arguing for largely trauma-based origins (e.g., Gleaves, 1996). In this light, dissociative symptoms are regarded as manifestations of a coping mechanism that mitigates the impact of highly aversive or traumatic events (Gershuny & Thayer, 1999; Nijenhuis, van der Hart, & Steel, 2010). In contrast, skeptics often emphasize the role of social influences, including cultural expectancies and inadvertent therapist cueing of symptoms (e.g., Lilienfeld et al., 1999; McHugh, 2008). As discussed later in the chapter, the controversies stemming from etiology and classification of dissociative disorders extend to their assessment and treatment. We will focus our discussion on chronic dissociative symptoms, rather than dissociation at the time of a highly aversive event (i.e., peritraumatic dissociation). However, we will present several state measures of dissociation, because researchers not infrequently consider changes in dissociation in the context of research on more chronic presentations of dissociation.

## DISSOCIATIVE AMNESIA

According to the *DSM-IV-TR*, dissociative amnesia is the "inability to recall important personal information, usually of a traumatic or stressful nature, that is too extensive to be explained by ordinary forgetfulness" (APA, 2000, p. 519). The diagnosis of dissociative amnesia requires that these symptoms not be attributable to substance use or to a neurological or medical condition such as age-related cognitive loss, and that they must cause significant distress, impairment of functioning in major aspects of daily life, or both.

This disorder, formerly referred to as psychogenic amnesia, often presents as retrospective amnesia for some period or series of periods in a person's life, frequently involving a traumatic experience. *DSM-IV-TR* lists several subtypes of dissociative amnesia. In localized amnesia, the individual cannot recall any information from a specific period of time, such as the first few hours after a car accident. Selective amnesia involves the loss of memories from some, but not all, events from a specific period of time. In generalized amnesia, individuals cannot recall anything about their entire lives; in continuous amnesia, individuals cannot recall anything that occurred after a particular event, up to and including the present. Finally, systematized amnesia consists of the "loss of memory for certain categories of information" (APA, 2000, p. 520): For example, an individual might display amnesia for all information regarding only one person. These last three types of dissociative amnesia—generalized, continuous, and systematized—are much less common than the others, and may be manifestations of more complex dissociative disorders, such as dissociative identity disorder rather than dissociative amnesia alone.

*Diagnostic Considerations* Some workers in the field have argued that the scientific evidence for the existence of dissociative amnesia is unconvincing, and that barring brain injury or substance abuse or dependence, individuals who have experienced trauma do not forget those events (e.g., McNally, 2003; Pope, Hudson, Bodkin, & Oliva, 1998). Certain cases of purported traumatic amnesia are in fact attributable to organic or other nondissociative causes. For example, in a critique of a case put forth by Brown, Scheflin, and Hammond (1997) as a convincing demonstration of dissociative amnesia, McNally (2004) discussed a study (Dollinger, 1985) of two children who witnessed a playmate get struck and killed by lightning, and who were later diagnosed with dissociative amnesia. Yet as McNally noted, this diagnosis was clearly mistaken, as the children had also been struck by lightning and knocked unconscious.

Amusingly, and perhaps tellingly, Pope, Poliakoff, Parker, Boynes, and Hudson (2007) offered a reward of $1,000 to "the first individual who could find a case of dissociative amnesia for a traumatic event in any fictional or nonfictional work before 1800" (p. 225) on the basis that whereas the vast majority of psychological symptoms can be found in literature or records dating back centuries, dissociative amnesia appears only in more modern literature beginning in the late 1800s. More than 100 individuals came forward with examples, but none met the diagnostic criteria for the disorder (although the prize later went to someone who discovered a case of dissociative amnesia in a 1786 opera, *Nina*, by the French composer Nicholas Dalayrac). Although Pope and colleagues' challenge does not prove anything regarding the validity of the disorder, its relative scarcity and apparently recent (perhaps post-late-18th-century) development raise troubling questions about its existence as a genuine entity in nature.

A special form of dissociative amnesia is crime-related amnesia. Many perpetrators of violent crimes claim to experience great difficulty remembering the essential details of the crimes they committed (Moskowitz, 2004). Memory loss for crime has been reported in 25% to 40% of homicide cases and severe sex offenses. Nevertheless, skeptics believe that genuine dissociative amnesia in these cases is rare. They have pointed out that trauma victims (e.g., concentration camp survivors) almost never report dissociative amnesia (Merckelbach, Dekkers, Wessel, & Roefs, 2003). For example, Rivard and colleagues (2002) examined a large sample of police officers involved in critical shooting incidents and found no reports of amnesia. Also, recent laboratory research shows that when participants encode information while in a survival mode, this manipulation yields superior memory effects (Nairne & Pandeirada, 2008). This finding is difficult to reconcile with the idea of experiencing dissociative amnesia while committing a crime. Thus, it is likely that feigning underlies most claims of crime-related amnesia (Van Oorsouw & Merckelbach, 2010).

*Epidemiology*   Because dissociative amnesia is so controversial and rates of reporting vary so widely, it is difficult to obtain reliable epidemiological information, although general population estimates range from .2% to more than 7% (Dell, 2009). The *DSM-IV-TR* states that dissociative amnesia can present in any age group, although it is more difficult to diagnose in younger children due to possible confusion with other disorders and conditions, including inattention, anxiety, oppositional behavior, and learning disorders. Other sources (e.g., Coons, 1998) suggest that most cases occur in individuals in their 30s or 40s. The prevalence of dissociative amnesia is approximately equal between genders.

The number of episodes of dissociative amnesia is variable. There may be just one episode of amnesia, or there may be multiple episodes, with each episode lasting anywhere from minutes to years. Individuals who have experienced one episode may be more likely to develop amnesia for future traumatic events, and the episodes of amnesia may resolve spontaneously or they may become chronic (APA, 2000, p. 521). Seventy-five percent of cases last between 24 hours and 5 days.

DISSOCIATIVE FUGUE

Dissociative fugue (previously called psychogenic fugue), arguably the most controversial dissociative disorder after DID, is defined in the *DSM-IV-TR* as a period of "sudden, unexpected travel away from home or one's customary place of work" (APA, 2000, p. 519). This "fugue" (which has the same etymology as the word "fugitive") or escape is accompanied by amnesia regarding one's past, as well as confusion about one's personal identity, sometimes to the extent of adopting an entirely new identity. If and when this identity develops, it is often characterized by higher levels of extraversion than the individual displayed pre-fugue, and he or she usually presents as well-integrated and nondisordered.

Periods of fugue vary considerably across individuals, both in duration and in distance traveled. In some cases, the travel can be a brief and relatively short trip, whereas in more extreme cases it can involve traveling thousands of miles and even crossing national borders. While in the dissociative fugue state, individuals often appear to be devoid of psychopathology; if they attract attention at all, it is usually because of amnesia or confusion about personal identity.

*Diagnostic Considerations*   Reportedly, the disorder often develops as a result of traumatic or stressful events, which has led to controversy and ambiguity regarding the relationship between dissociative fugue and PTSD. Other precipitants that have been associated with the development of dissociative fugue include war or natural disasters, as well as the avoidance of various stressors, such as marital discord or financial or legal problems (Coons, 1998). Such avoidance suggests that clinicians must be certain to rule out malingering and factitious disorders before diagnosing dissociative fugue. For an historical overview and a critical analysis of dissociative fugue, we refer the reader to Hacking (1995).

Dissociative fugue may manifest with symptoms other than those in *DSM-IV-TR*, including depression, anxiety, dysphoria, grief, shame, guilt, stress, and aggressive or suicidal impulses (APA, 2000). Episodes of fugue must not occur solely within the course of dissociative identity disorder and must not be attributable to substance abuse or dependence, or to a medical condition. The symptoms must cause significant distress, impairment of functioning in major aspects of daily life, or both.

Certain culture-bound syndromes exhibit similar symptoms to, and may meet diagnostic criteria for, dissociative fugue. These include *amok*, present in Western Pacific cultures (which has given rise to the colloquialism "running amok"); *pibloktok*, present in native cultures of the Arctic; and Navajo "frenzy" witchcraft, all of which are marked by "a sudden onset of a high level of activity, a trancelike state, potentially dangerous behavior in the form of running or fleeing, and ensuing exhaustion, sleep, and amnesia" for the duration of the episode (APA, 2000, p. 524; Simons & Hughes, 1985).

*Epidemiology*    DSM-IV-TR places the population prevalence estimate of dissociative fugue at .02%, with the majority of cases occurring in adults (APA, 2000, p. 524). Ross (2009b) observed that in the approximately 3,000 individuals he treated in his trauma program over a 12-year period, he encountered fewer than 10 individuals with pure dissociative amnesia or pure dissociative fugue, although he noted that symptoms of amnesia and fugue were common in the patients he admitted.

### DEPERSONALIZATION DISORDER

Depersonalization disorder (DPD) is one of the most common dissociative disorders and perhaps the least controversial. The disorder is marked by a "persistent or recurring feeling of being detached from one's mental processes or body" (APA, 2000, p. 530), but it must be accompanied by intact reality testing, thereby indicating that individuals are aware that the sensations are not real and that they are not experiencing a break from reality akin to psychosis. Nearly 50% of adults have experienced at least one episode of depersonalization in their lifetimes, usually in adolescence, though a single episode is not sufficient to meet criteria for the disorder (Aderibigbe, Bloch, & Walker, 2001).

Greatly contributing to our knowledge about depersonalization symptoms has been the development of well-validated screening instruments, notably the Cambridge Depersonalization Scale (CDS; Sierra & Berrios, 2000; Sierra, Baker, Medford & David, 2005). Depersonalization episodes are not uncommonly triggered by intense stress and are often associated with high levels of interpersonal impairment (APA, 2000, p. 531; Simeon et al., 1997). Episodes of depersonalization or derealization (the sensation that the external world is dreamlike or unreal) are also frequently associated with panic attacks, unfamiliar environments, perceived threatening social interactions, the ingestion of hallucinogens, depression, and PTSD (Simeon, Knutelska, Nelson, & Guralnik, 2003). Individuals with DPD are also more likely than healthy individuals to report a history of emotional abuse. In contrast, general dissociation scores are better predicted by a history of combined emotional and sexual abuse (Simeon, Guralnik, Schmeidler, Sirof, & Knutelska, 2001).

*Diagnostic Considerations*    Because depersonalization and derealization are common, DPD should be diagnosed only if these symptoms are severe enough to cause distress, impairment in functioning, or both. The distress associated with DPD may be extreme, with sufferers reporting they feel robotic, unreal, and "unalive." They may fear becoming psychotic, losing control, and suffering permanent brain damage (Simeon, 2009a). Individuals with DPD may perceive an alteration in the size or shape of objects around them. Other people may appear mechanical or unfamiliar, and affected individuals may experience a disturbance in their sense of time (Simeon & Abugel, 2006).

A diagnosis of DPD requires that the symptoms do not occur exclusively in the course of another mental disorder, nor can they be attributable to substance abuse or dependence or to a general medical condition. Furthermore, DPD should not be diagnosed solely in the context of meditative or trance practices. Symptoms of other disorders, such as anxiety disorders, major depression, and hypochondriasis, and certain personality disorders, especially avoidant, borderline, and obsessive-compulsive, may also be present (Simeon et al., 1997). Depersonalization and derealization symptoms are often also part of the symptom picture of acute stress disorder (ASD; APA, 2000), which is often a precursor to PTSD.

*Epidemiology*   The lifetime population prevalence of DPD is unknown, although it may be as high as 2% (Ross, 1991), suggesting that DPD might be as or more common than schizophrenia and bipolar disorder. DPD is diagnosed almost equally often in women as in men (Simeon et al., 2003). It frequently presents for treatment in adolescence or adulthood, even as late as the 40s, though its onset may be earlier. Estimates of the age of onset of DPD range from 16.1 (Simeon et al., 1997) to 22 years (Baker et al., 2003).

The onset and course of DPD vary widely across individuals. Some people experience a sudden onset and others a more gradual onset; some experience a chronic form of the disorder, whereas others experience it episodically. In about two-thirds of people with DPD, the course is chronic, and symptoms of depersonalization are present most of the time, if not continually. Episodes of depersonalization may last from hours to weeks or months, and in more extreme cases, years or decades (Simeon, 2009a).

### DISSOCIATIVE IDENTITY DISORDER

Dissociative identity disorder (DID) is the most controversial dissociative disorder and easily among the most controversial disorders in *DSM-IV-TR*. DID is defined as the existence of at least two "distinct identities or personality states that recurrently take control of the individual's behavior (p. 519)" in conjunction with "an inability to recall important personal information that is too extensive to be explained by ordinary forgetfulness" (APA, 2000, p. 526). This disorder, formerly known as multiple personality disorder, reflects a "failure to integrate various aspects of identity, memory, and consciousness" (APA, 2000, p. 526), and is therefore better described as "identity fragmentation" than as the "proliferation of separate personalities."

The primary identity or personality in an individual with DID often carries the individual's given name and tends to be "passive, dependent, guilty, and depressed." Other personalities, called "alters," may be assertive or even aggressive and hostile, and these more-dominant identities usually possess more complete memories regarding the individual's actions and history. Within one individual, there can often be anywhere between 2 and 100 or more personalities, with approximately 50% of individuals reporting 10 or fewer distinct identities—although extreme cases of many as 4,500 alters have been reported (Acocella, 1999). Reported identities are usually just "regular" people, but more extreme and bizarre cases exist. There have been reports of identities claiming to be Mr. Spock from *Star Trek*, the rock star Madonna, the bride of Satan, and even a lobster.

*Diagnostic Considerations*   To meet criteria for DID, an individual's symptoms cannot be attributable to substance use or to a medical condition; when the disorder is assessed in children, the symptoms must not be confused with imaginary play.

Researchers have documented substantial comorbidity of DID with other disorders. For example, Ellason, Ross, and Fuchs (1996) reported that DID patients met criteria for an average of 8 Axis I disorders and 4.5 Axis II disorders. One-half to two-thirds of patients with DID meet diagnostic criteria for borderline personality disorder (BPD; Coons, Bowman, & Milstein, 1988; Horevitz & Braun, 1984). Conversely, Sar, Akyuz, Kugu, Ozturk, & Ertem-Vehid (2006) found that 72.5% of patients screened for BPD had a dissociative disorder. In one study, researchers (Kemp, Gilbertson, & Torem, 1988) reported no significant differences between BPD and DID patients on measures of personality traits, cognitive and adaptive functioning, and clinician ratings, suggesting noteworthy commonalities between the two conditions. Histories of sexual and physical abuse are also commonly reported in both patient groups, and BPD patients score well above general population norms on measures of dissociation (Lauer, Black, & Keen, 1993). Indeed, Lauer and his colleagues (Lauer et al., 1993) suggested that DID is an epiphenomenon of the combination of BPD with high suggestibility.

Individuals with DID often experience additional symptoms, including self-mutilation, suicidal or aggressive behavior, as well as major depression, substance abuse, and sexual, eating, and sleep disorders (Fullerton et al., 2000; North, Ryall, Ricci, & Wetzel, 1993; Ross, 1997). Accordingly, some clinicians have argued that the DID diagnosis really is a severity marker identifying extreme variants of a host of other disorders (for an extensive discussion, see North, Ryall, Ricci & Wetzel, 1993).

Many DID patients meet the criteria for schizoaffective disorder (Lauer et al., 1993), and as many as half have received a previous diagnosis of schizophrenia (Ross & Norton, 1988). Indeed, auditory and visual hallucinations are common in both DID and schizophrenia. However, patients with DID commonly report that hallucinated voices originate inside of their heads, whereas patients with schizophrenia tend to perceive the origin of voices outside of their heads and possess less insight into the nature of their symptoms (Coons, 1998; Kluft, 1993).

DID patients have been reported to endorse more positive symptoms (e.g., delusions, hallucinations, and suspiciousness) and Schneiderian first-rank symptoms, which include themes of passivity, than do schizophrenic patients (Ellason & Ross, 1995; Steinberg, Rounsaville, & Cichetti, 1990). Ellason and Ross (1995) argued that the presence of positive symptoms can be used to formulate an accurate differential diagnosis between the two disorders, although further research regarding this possibility is necessary (for further diagnostic considerations, see Steinberg & Siegel, 2008).

PTSD is one of the most commonly comorbid conditions with DID (Loewenstein, 1991). Moreover, PTSD patients are more likely to present with symptoms of dissociation (e.g., numbing, amnesia, flashback phenomena) than patients with major depression, schizophrenia, and schizoaffective disorder (Bremner, Steinberg, Southwick, Johnson, & Charney, 1993).

*Epidemiology*   DID may be episodic or continuous, and in some cases may remit after the late 40s (APA, 2000). There are documented cases of DID extending decades and arguably even centuries, and the concept of fragmented or multiple personalities is an ancient one. That said, the number of cases has increased exponentially in the last few decades. Prior to 1970, there were approximately 80 reported cases, but by 1986 that number had ballooned to approximately 6,000. As of 1998, there were approximately 40,000 cases (Lilienfeld & Lynn, 2003).

Population prevalence estimates vary widely, from extremely rare (e.g., Piper, 1997; Rifkin, Ghisalbert, Dimatou, Jin, & Sethi, 1998) to rates approximating that of schizophrenia (1% to 2%; Coons, 1998; Ross, 1997). Estimates of DID in inpatient settings range from 1% to 9.6% (Rifkin et al., 1998; Ross, Duffy, & Ellason, 2002). In addition to the dramatic increase in DID's prevalence over the past few decades, there has been an increase in the number of alters reported, from only two or three separate identities to an average of approximately 16 (interestingly, the exact number reported by Sybil; see following discussion) by 1990.

DID is between 3 and 9 times more common in women than men, and women also tend to have more identities (an average of 15, as compared with the male average of eight; APA, 2000). However, this imbalanced sex ratio may be an artifact of selection and referral biases (Lynn, Fassler, Knox, & Lilienfeld, 2009). In particular, a large proportion of males with DID may end up in prisons (or other forensic settings) rather than in clinical settings (Putnam & Loewenstein, 2000).

Skeptics of the disorder argue that its proliferation is in part a function of media exposure. In 1976, the movie *Sybil* was released, documenting the real-life story of a woman who had supposedly experienced severe child abuse and later developed 16 personalities (but see "Etiological Considerations" for evidence calling into question significant details of the Sybil case). In addition to the number of cases increasing after the release of this movie, the number of individuals reporting child abuse as a cause of DID also rose drastically (Lilienfeld & Lynn, 2003; Spanos, 1996). In contrast, proponents of the disorder respond that clinicians are simply better equipped to identify the disorder now that more attention is paid to it (Gleaves, May, & Cardeña, 2001). We elaborate on this etiological debate later in the chapter.

## PSYCHOLOGICAL ASSESSMENT

A variety of assessment instruments are available to evaluate dissociation and dissociative disorders. In this section, we review commonly used structured interview and self-report measures.

*Structured Interview Measures*  The Structured Clinical Interview for *DSM-IV* (SCID-D; Steinberg, 1985) and its revision (SCID-D-R; Steinberg, 1994) are semistructured interviews that systematically assess five core symptoms of dissociation: amnesia, depersonalization, derealization, identity confusion, and identity alteration. The SCID-D incorporates the *DSM-IV* criteria for dissociative disorders. The full 250-item administration may take 2 to 3 hours for psychiatric patients with dissociative symptoms; however, nondissociative psychiatric patients may complete the interview in 30 to 90 minutes, and nonpsychiatric participants may finish in 30 minutes. The severity of each of the five core symptoms is scored in terms of distress, dysfunctionality, frequency, duration, and course.

The revised scale was administered in NIMH field trials that encompassed 350 interviews of dissociative and nondissociative adults. Reports from the field trials

($N = 141$ mixed psychiatric patients) revealed that the inter-examiner and temporal reliability of the SCID-D-R ranges from very good to excellent (weighted kappa .77–.86) for both the presence and extent of dissociative symptoms over three time periods. For type of dissociative disorder, inter-examiner agreement ranged from .72–.86, and test-retest reliability for the overall presence of a dissociative disorder was good (.88 over a 7-day period). The SCID-D-R possesses good convergent validity and is capable of distinguishing DID patients from patients with anxiety disorders, substance abuse, personality disorders, eating disorders, and psychotic disorders (Cardeña, 2008). The SCID-D may also be useful in detecting malingering, as it can discriminate DID from feigning. It also appears to distinguish DID from schizophrenia (Welburn et al., 2003). Nevertheless, Kihlstrom (2005, p. 3) countered that "even with relatively strict criteria in place, it can be difficult to discriminate between dissociative disorders and bipolar disorder, borderline personality disorder, and even schizophrenia."

The Dissociative Disorders Interview Schedule (DDIS; Ross et al., 1989) is a structured interview used to assist in the diagnosis of dissociative disorders, as well as conditions that often co-occur with it, including somatization disorder, major depressive disorder, and borderline personality disorder. The interview has been used for clinical and research purposes and consists of 16 sections with a total of 131 questions. The interview is highly structured to minimize interviewer confirmation bias and sequenced so that indirect questions about secondary features of DID precede increasingly specific questions.

In the original validation study, 80 psychiatric patients from specialized research clinics were interviewed. Patients diagnosed with DID ($n = 20$) were compared with patients with panic disorder ($n = 20$), eating disorder ($n = 20$), and schizophrenia ($n = 20$). For DID, the DDIS yielded a sensitivity of 90% and a specificity of 100% [see also Ross et al., (1992) who demonstrated high agreement (94.1%) of DDIS classification using the DDIS with independent clinical evaluation]. The authors reported that inter-rater reliability was adequate ($r = .68$; Ross, Norton, & Wozney, 1989). The DDIS has demonstrated good convergent validity, as indexed by high correlations of DID diagnosis scores with the DES ($r = .67–.78$; Cardeña, 2008). Nevertheless, the authors (Ross et al., 1989) cautioned that depersonalization disorder cannot be reliably diagnosed using the DDIS (inter-rater reliability $= .56$).

The Clinician Administered Dissociation State Scale (CADSS; Bremner et al., 1998) was developed to assess dissociative states. The clinician verbally administers 19 subject-rated items on a Likert-type scale ranging from 0 (not at all) to 4 (extremely). Three subscales subsume the subject-rated items: amnesia, depersonalization, and derealization. The clinician also observes the participant's behavior during the interview and rates eight behaviors presumed to indicate the presence of a dissociative state on the same Likert-type scale as the subject-rated items.

In the original study, the CADSS was administered to patients with combat-related PTSD and a comorbid dissociative disorder (PTSD/dissociative) ($n = 68$). These patients were compared with patients with schizophrenia ($n = 22$), mood disorders ($n = 15$), healthy controls ($n = 8$), and combat veterans without PTSD ($n = 11$). The CADSS discriminated between patients with PTSD and comorbid dissociative disorders (86% of cases) and patients with the comparison conditions. Furthermore, the CADSS detected changes in dissociative symptoms before and after patients with PTSD participated in a traumatic memories group. These patients showed a significant increase in symptoms compared with baseline, suggesting that the CADSS may be sensitive enough to capture changes in repeated measures designs. Inter-rater reliability was excellent for the total scale (ICC = .92) and for the subject-rated portion (ICC = .99), but was markedly lower for the observer ratings (ICC = .34). The internal consistency of the CADSS was good to excellent for the total scale ($\alpha$ = .94), subjective portion ($\alpha$ = .94), observer ratings ($\alpha$ = .90), and for the individual subscales ($\alpha$ = .74–.90).

*Self-Report Measures*    The Dissociative Experiences Scale (DES; Bernstein-Carlson & Putnam, 1986) and its revision (DES-II; Bernstein-Carlson & Putnam, 1993) are brief self-report measures of dissociation that can be used in both research and clinical settings to assess individuals within normal and psychiatric populations. Participants rate 28 items pertaining to dissociative experiences in terms of the frequency they are experienced, from 0% to 100%. In the original sample, the test-retest reliability among 192 participants was .84 over a period of 4 to 8 weeks, and split half reliability coefficients ranged from .71 to .96, indicating good internal consistency. In addition, DES scores differentiated participants with a dissociative disorder (e.g., DID) from those without a dissociative disorder (e.g., normal adults, late adolescent college students, alcoholics, phobics). A cutoff of 30 correctly identified 74% of patients with DID and 80% of subjects without DID in a multicenter study (Carlson, Putnam, Ross, Torem, et al., 1991).

The DES is the most frequently used self-report measure of dissociation (Brand, Armstrong, & Loewenstein, 2006). However, researchers have questioned whether the scale is unidimensional, as would be expected of a factorially pure measure of dissociation. Carlson, Putnam, Ross, Anderson, et al. (1991) reported a three-factor solution—amnesia, absorption (related to openness to experience), and depersonalization (also see Ross, Ellason, & Anderson, 1995; Sanders & Green, 1994)—and others (Ray & Faith, 1994) have identified four factors. In contrast, Waller (1995) reanalyzed Carlson, Putnam, Ross, Anderson, and colleagues' (1991) data and concluded that their three-factor solution could reflect the skewed distribution of the items, and thus might be a statistical artifact reflecting the presence of difficulty factors (that is, factors induced by similar levels of skewness across the items; see also Holmes et al., 2005; Wright & Loftus, 1999).

Waller, Putnam, and Carlson (1996) responded to criticisms that the DES contains a substantial number of nonpathological items that tap absorption (e.g., "Some people find that when they are watching television or a movie they become so absorbed in the story that they are unaware of other events happening around them.") by developing the DES-Taxon (DES-T) scale. This eight-item scale contains items from the original DES that measure pathological dissociation, including derealization, depersonalization, psychogenic amnesia, and identity alteration. Waller and Ross (1997) estimated that the general population base rate of pathological dissociation is 3.3%. Of course, being classified as a taxon member (i.e., distinct type or latent class) cannot be equated with DID (Modestin & Erni, 2004), as the prevalence of DID in the general population is almost certainly much lower than 3%. Although the resulting scale was stricter in the criteria for establishing evidence of pathologic dissociation, the data supporting its validity are mixed.

Simeon and colleagues (Simeon et al., 1998) found that the DES-T sum score is superior to the standard DES at distinguishing patients with depersonalization disorders from control subjects. However, later studies revealed that the DES-T: (a) classified only 64% of patients with DPD as having a dissociative disorder (Simeon et al., 2003); (b) produced high false-positive rates (Giesbrecht, Merckelbach, & Geraerts, 2007); and (c) lacked temporal stability for taxon membership probability (Watson, 2003). Nevertheless, many studies have documented significant differences between people who score high versus low on both the DES and the DES-T with respect to a variety of measures of memory and cognition (Giesbrecht et al., 2008).

The Adolescent Dissociative Experiences Scale (A-DES; Armstrong, Putnam, Carlson, Libero, & Smith, 1997) is a 30-item self-report measure designed exclusively for use with adolescent populations. The scale is intended to serve as a screening tool for dissociative disorders among adolescents and to trace the developmental trajectories of normal and pathological dissociation over time. The A-DES items are rated on an 11-point Likert-type scale and comprise the following subscales: dissociative amnesia, absorption and imaginative involvement, passive influence, and depersonalization and derealization. The A-DES was normed using a group of healthy adolescents in junior high and high school populations (Smith & Carlson, 1996) and a group of adolescent clinical patients (Armstrong et al., 1997). The authors reported excellent internal consistency for the total score ($\alpha = .93$) and subscales ($\alpha = .72-.85$). Nevertheless, there are questions concerning the A-DES's convergent validity. In a sample of 331 nonreferred youths, Muris, Merckelbach, and Peeters (2003) reported that A-DES scores are not only significantly related to PTSD symptoms and fantasy proneness but also to other anxiety symptoms.

The Multidimensional Inventory of Dissociation (MID 5.0; Dell, 2006) is a recently developed self-report measure used to assess the symptom-domain of DID and the phenomenological domain of dissociation. The MID 5.0 contains 168 dissociation items and 50 validity items rated on a 0–10 Likert-type scale. The MID shows promising convergent validity with other psychiatric diagnoses (e.g., it distinguishes among individuals with DID, dissociative disorder NOS, mixed psychiatric, and nonclinical adults; Dell, 2002) and self-report measures (e.g., correlations with the DES = .90; Dell, 2006), as well as structural validity (e.g., factor analyses isolated a single overarching factor of pathological dissociation; see Dell, 2006). Nevertheless, these findings have yet to be replicated by independent research groups. The author reported good-to-excellent internal consistency of the 23 dissociation scales ($\alpha = .84-.96$) and temporal stability (4- to 8-week test-retest interval; $rs = .82-.97$) in a large clinical sample. These latter results were replicated in Israel and Germany (see Dell, 2006).

The Somatoform Dissociation Questionnaire (SDQ-20; Nijenhuis, Spinhoven, van Dyck, van der Hart, & Vanderlinden, 1996) is a self-report measure designed to evaluate the presence of somatoform responses associated with dissociative states that cannot be medically explained. Participants rate items on a 5-point Likert-type scale. Twenty of the 75 original items discriminated outpatients with dissociative disorders from nondissociative psychiatric outpatients and comprised the final scale. The authors reported excellent internal consistency ($\alpha = .95$) and higher scores among patients with DID compared with patients with dissociative disorder NOS. The authors also reduced the SDQ-20 to a five-item screen for dissociative disorders (SDQ-5, Nijenhuis et al., 1997). For dissociative disorders among psychiatric patients, the SDQ-5 exhibited a sensitivity of 94% and a specificity of 98% (Nijenhuis et al., 1998).

The Dissociation Questionnaire (DIS-Q; Vanderlinden, van Dyck, Vandereycken, & Vertommen, 1991) was developed to account for sociocultural differences in European populations as well as to assess a broad spectrum of dissociative experiences. The authors generated items from existing dissociation questionnaires and clinical experience. Participants rate items on a 1–5 Likert-type scale; the final 63-item scale was normed on 374 participants from the general population in Belgium and the Netherlands. Four factors comprise the DIS-Q (i.e., identity confusion, loss of control, amnesia, and absorption). Internal consistency of the subscales ($\alpha = .67$–$.94$) and the overall scale ($\alpha = .96$) were good to excellent, as was test-retest reliability over a period of 3 to 4 weeks. The authors report successful discrimination of patients with dissociative disorders and nondissociative disorders with the exception of PTSD. Within the dissociative disorders, the DIS-Q successfully discriminated DID from dissociative disorder NOS.

The State Scale of Dissociation (SSD; Kruger & Mace, 2002) is a self-report inventory designed to detect changes in dissociative states, rather than traits. The SSD was developed using existing scales, the *DSM-IV*, and the *ICD-10*, along with the aid of clinical experts. The 56-item scale is scored on a Likert-type scale from 0–9 and broken down into seven subscales: derealization, depersonalization, identity confusion, identity alteration, conversion, amnesia, and hypermnesia (remembering things too well). In the original study, the SSD was administered to 130 patients with major depression (n = 19), schizophrenia (n = 18), alcohol withdrawal (n = 20), dissociative disorders (n = 10), and healthy controls (n = 63). A score of more than 3.9 nearly doubled the certainty of a diagnosis of a dissociative disorder, although an important limitation is the small sample of dissociative patients. The internal consistency of the SSD was good to excellent for the total scale ($\alpha = .97$), and correlations between the SSD and the DES among people with a dissociative disorder were $r = .81$, and $r = .57$ in healthy controls. Following a brief grounding activity (53 minutes, during which participants completed several other scales), the SSD scores among all participants decreased significantly on retest, suggesting that the SSD is sensitive to short-term changes in dissociative states across diagnostic groups.

The Cambridge Depersonalization Scale (CDS; Sierra & Berrios, 2000) consists of 29 items that ask respondents to rate recent depersonalization symptoms on a 5-point frequency scale (anchors: 0 = never; 5 = all the time) and a 6-point duration scale (anchors: 1 = few seconds; 6 = more than a week). The scale differentiates patients with DPD from other patient groups (e.g., patients with epilepsy, anxiety disorders) and from healthy controls (Sierra & Berrios, 2000). Sierra and Berrios (2000, 2001) reported good internal consistency for the CDS (e.g., $\alpha = .89$). An exploratory factor analysis identified four factors that accounted for 73.3% of the variance: anomalous body experience, emotional numbing, anomalous subjective recall, and alienation from surroundings (Sierra et al., 2005).

Assessment is often an ongoing process in psychotherapy, and much information can be gleaned in the absence of standardized tests of dissociative experiences and symptoms. In this regard, some caveats are in order. Less formal assessment procedures that even subtly suggest a history of abuse or validate the manifestation of alters with separate histories (e.g., personality "system mapping" to establish contact with nonforthcoming alters, providing names to alters, prompting or suggesting the emergence appearance of alters) should be avoided. A concern is that therapists who repeatedly ask leading questions such as "Is it possible that there is another part of you with whom I haven't yet spoken?" may elicit via suggestion previously "latent alters" that ostensibly account for their clients' otherwise enigmatic behaviors (e.g., self-mutilation, rapid and intense mood shifts). Repeated questioning about historical events is not helpful, as it can lead patients to mistakenly believe that they have significant gaps (e.g., amnesia) in their autobiographical memories of childhood (Belli, Winkielman, Read, Schwartz, & Lynn, 1998). Assessors should also eschew the use of hypnosis to recover allegedly dissociated or repressed memories given that hypnosis does not enhance the overall accuracy of memories and is associated with a heightened risk for confabulation (Lynn, Knox, Fassler, Lilienfeld, & Loftus, 2004).

## CASE STUDY

### Case Identification and Presenting Complaints

The patient, a 47-year-old Caucasian female, first presented with dissociative symptoms to a health professional during a routine pelvic examination (see Colletti, Lynn, & Laurence, 2010, for a more complete description). During the exam, she exhibited dramatic changes in her demeanor. In quick succession, her emotions vacillated unpredictably, ranging from calm and composed, to scared and vulnerable, to angry and aggressive. The physician referred her for psychotherapy, insofar as her histrionic presentation was at sharp variance with what he observed during prior office visits.

### History

When the patient initiated treatment with a psychotherapist, she insisted that her problems were the product of stress at work related to serious medical concerns (e.g., lupus, peripheral neuralgia, among others) that interfered with her job performance. Nevertheless, the therapist, a graduate student at a psychological clinic, noted that her mood and behavior fluctuated dramatically both within and between sessions, with episodes of anger and anxiety flaring up frequently and unpredictably within sessions. Over the next 2 years, the patient recounted a history of sexual assault 7 years prior to treatment, the death of a sibling, intense and sometimes unstable interpersonal relationships, and sexual abuse in childhood. Emotional outbursts during sessions escalated; seemingly innocuous statements by the therapist could trigger memories of highly aversive events. The patient began to experience more frequent crises in and out of sessions as well as emotional lability, often alternating between speaking in a childlike voice and as an angry adult, only to later apologize and express deep regret. Her memory for what transpired when she appeared to be enacting different "identities" was spotty and at times devoid of meaningful content.

After 2 years of treatment, the graduate student transferred the case to his supervisor, who witnessed increased irritability, vitriolic anger, and flashback-like experiences in session that were followed by amnesia, depersonalization, derealization, and problems in focusing attention. The patient reported feeling "spaced out" in session, and reported that she often was aware of "missing time" at home, and experienced difficulties recalling anything beyond the gist of the previous session. At the start of treatment with her second therapist, she met the criteria for borderline personality disorder and posttraumatic stress disorder, and DID was considered a rule-out diagnosis. She reported hearing "voices in my head" and experienced herself as "splitting off" into an angry "adult protector" or defender of others and childlike aspects of herself that required protection. One major diathesis for her dissociative symptoms appeared to be a history of fantasy versus reality-based coping originating in childhood. She became aware of this style of coping when her sister died when the patient was 5 years old, and she experienced guilt for not somehow preventing her death. She stated that she began, from that time forward, to think of herself as split into angry and protective "parts." As therapy progressed, she reported more frequent episodes of depersonalization and disturbing episodes of amnesia, as well as disorientation at times of high stress. She also reported more incidents of abuse during childhood, and her therapist felt her presentation now met the criteria for DID.

At this time, SJL, one of the authors of this chapter, was invited to serve as a consultant and co-therapist. The therapists conveyed the consistent message that although at times the patient felt as if she housed distinct personalities, she truly embodied only one personality. The therapists implemented a multifaceted treatment that included (a) elements of affect management and problem-solving to contend with anger; (b) CBT techniques including activity scheduling for depressed mood, progressive muscle and hypnosis-based relaxation, and rational disputation of maladaptive thoughts; (c) mindfulness-based techniques for detaching from negative and self-deprecating cognitions and moods; and (d) affect containment methods derived from dialectical behavior therapy. After 3 years of treatment, the patient exhibited no signs of "personality split" and only occasional episodes of depersonalization, with improved functioning and mood stabilization.

### ASSESSMENT

The patient met all of the diagnostic criteria for DID, including her enacting distinct "identities" during sessions and reports of such alterations outside of sessions. She also reported amnesia associated with dissociative episodes, and she was troubled by her failure to recall key interpersonal interactions that others remembered well. The patient was not assessed at the outset of treatment, although later in treatment after SJL came onboard, she was evaluated with the DES and scored in the clinical range (i.e., 39) and met diagnostic criteria for DID based on the SCID-D (Steinberg, 1994).

# ETIOLOGICAL CONSIDERATIONS

## Behavioral Genetics

Limited research is available on the behavioral genetics of dissociative disorders. The evidence indicates that DID co-aggregates within biological families (APA, 1994), although data on intact family members are indeterminate with regard to genetic versus shared environmental causation. Using twin registry data, Jang, Paris, Zweig-Frank, and Livesley (1998) reported that 48% of the variability in DES-T scores is attributable to genes and that the other 52% of the variance can be attributed to nonshared environment. When the researchers considered nonpathological dissociation scores, excluding taxon items, genetic influences accounted for 55% of the variance, whereas nonshared environmental influences accounted for 45% of the variance. Similarly, a study of children and adolescents found a substantial genetic (59% genes, 41% nonshared environment) contribution to dissociation scores (Becker-Blease et al., 2004). In contrast, a study (Waller & Ross, 1997) based on 280 identical twins and 148 fraternal twins found no evidence for genetic influences. Approximately 45% of the variance on a measure of pathological dissociation (DES-T) was attributable to shared environmental influences, with the remaining variance due to nonshared environmental influences. Adoption studies would help clarify the extent to which the familial clustering of dissociative disorders is due to genes, shared environment, or both.

## Neuroanatomy, Neurobiology, Physiology, and Pharmacology

Drugs, notably low doses of the anesthetic ketamine, often produce dreamlike states and dissociative symptoms. Krystal et al. (1994) found that ketamine produces alterations in the perception of time (i.e., slowing) and alterations in the vividness, form, and context of sensory experiences, all possibly attributable to diminished NMDA-related neurotransmission (Simeon, 2004). Interestingly, cannabinoids, including marijuana, which induce dissociative experiences, may similarly affect NMDA receptors (Simeon et al., 2003). The fact that hallucinogens (e.g., LSD), which frequently elicit depersonalization reactions in healthy participants, are agonists of serotonin $5\text{-HT}_{2A}$ and $5\text{-HT}_{2C}$ receptors implies that serotonin also may mediate dissociation (Simeon, 2004). Research that establishes links between drugs that produce dissociative symptoms in conjunction with changes in specific neurotransmitter systems holds the potential to shed light on the neurobiological basis of these dissociative symptoms (Giesbrecht et al., 2008).

Simeon et al. (2000) used positron emission tomography (PET) and magnetic resonance imaging (MRI) to compare 8 participants with DPD with 24 healthy participants. The researchers found that depersonalization is associated with functional abnormalities in sequential hierarchical areas—secondary and cross-modal—of the sensory cortex (visual, auditory, and somatosensory), as well as areas responsible for integrated body schemas. Specifically, DPD patients showed lower metabolic activity in right Brodman's areas 21 and 22 of the superior and middle temporal gyri, and higher metabolism in parietal Brodmann's areas 7B and 39 and left occipital Brodmann's area 19. The researchers contended that these findings are compatible with the phenomenological conceptualization of depersonalization as a dissociation of perceptions, as well as with the subjective symptoms of DPD.

In a fascinating study, Sang, Jáuregui-Renaud, Green, Bronstein, and Gresty (2006) showed that disorienting vestibular stimulation produced by caloric irrigation of the ear labyrinths engendered depersonalization in healthy participants and symptoms (e.g., feeling spaced out, body feels strange/not in control of self) similar to those experienced by patients with vestibular disease. The researchers suggested that depersonalization/derealization experiences may "occur because distorted vestibular signals mismatch with sensory input to create an incoherent frame of spatial reference which makes the patient feel that he or she is detached or separated from the world" (p. 760).

In a later study, the researchers (Jáuregui-Renaud, Sang, Gresty, Green, & Bronstein, 2008b) found that patients with peripheral vestibular disease reported a higher prevalence of depersonalization/derealization symptoms and greater errors on a body rotation test of updating spatial orientation compared with healthy control participants. The investigators claimed that their findings support their theory that DPD symptoms sometimes reflect a mismatch between disordered vestibular input and other sensory signals of orientation. This claim was supported in a study in which patients with vestibular disease and patients with retinal disease reported more symptoms of depersonalization than patients with hearing loss and healthy participants (Jáuregui-Renaud, Ramos-Toledo, Aguilar-Bolaños, Montaño-Velazquez, & Pliego-Maldonado, 2008a). Depersonalization and derealization experiences may well be the product of mismatches or lack of integration between multisensory inputs (e.g., vestibular, visual, proprioceptive) that produces dysfunctional neural representations that in turn generate an altered sense of self and reality (Aspell & Blanke, 2009).

Out-of-body experiences (OBEs), which are intimately related to depersonalization, are increasingly being studied in the laboratory (e.g., Ehrsson, 2007; Lenggenhager, Tadi, Metzinger, & Blanke, 2007) and are coming to be understood in terms of the scrambling of the senses (e.g., touch and vision) when people's usual experience of their physical body becomes disrupted. In addition, scientists are identifying the brain location of OBEs by stimulating the vestibular cortex, the superior temporal gyrus, and the place where the brain's right temporal and parietal lobes join (Blanke, Ortigue, Landis, & Seeck, 2002; Blanke & Thut, 2007; Cheyne & Girard, 2009; De Ridder, Van Laere, Dupont, Menovsky, & Van de Heyning, 2007; Persinger, 2001).

Ehrrson (2007) provided participants with goggles that permitted them to view a video display of themselves relayed by a camera placed behind them. This setup created the illusion that their bodies, viewed from the rear, were standing in front of them. Ehrrson touched participants with a rod in the chest while he used cameras to make it appear that the visual image was being touched at the same time. Participants reported the eerie sensation that their video double was also being touched. In short, they reported that they could experience the touch in a location outside their physical bodies (see also Aspell, Lenggenhager, & Blanke, 2009; Lenggenhager et al., 2007). When visual sensory impressions combine with physical sensations, they can deceive people into believing that their physical selves are separate from their bodies (Cheyne & Girard, 2009; Terhune, 2009), suggesting a physiological genesis of at least some depersonalization experiences. Relatedly, disruptions in somatosensory signals may explain why some people experience OBEs during sleep paralysis (Nelson, Mattingly, Lee, & Schmitt, 2006) and during general anesthesia when they retain partial awareness (Bunning & Blanke, 2005). Nevertheless, researchers have little understanding of how stressors and other precipitants of depersonalization and derealization create and maintain the symptoms of dissociative disorders.

Researchers have devoted considerable attention to describing physiological differences among alters in DID and have reported inter-identity differences in terms of heart rates, voice pitch, eyeglass prescriptions, handedness, handwriting, allergies, or pain tolerance (see Lilienfeld & Lynn, 2003). Nevertheless, it is unclear whether such differences validate the existence of alters, as many of these differences may merely reflect differences in mood, differences stemming from the unconscious role-playing of different identities, or both. Also, some authors have pointed out that one may obtain similar intra-individual differences when healthy actors are instructed to role-play alters (Merckelbach, Devilly & Rassin, 2002). Moreover, Allen and Movius (2000) suggested that some of these apparent differences may reflect Type I errors given the large number of psychophysiological variables analyzed in many of these studies.

Tsai, Condie, Wu, and Chang (1999) used MRI with a 47-year-old female with DID in an attempt to corroborate a history of childhood abuse. The authors drew upon previous investigations that had reported a reduction in hippocampal volume following combat trauma (e.g., Bremner, Randall, Scott, & Bronen, 1995) and early abuse (Bremner, Randall, Vermetten, & Staub, 1997; Stein, Koverola, Hanna, & Torchia, 1997) to hypothesize that DID patients— given their presumed history of early abuse—would similarly exhibit decreased hippocampal volume. As predicted, they found significant bilateral reductions in hippocampal volume in their patient with DID. Nevertheless, this finding must be interpreted cautiously for two major reasons (Lilienfeld & Lynn, 2003): (1) Because it is based on only one patient, its generalizability to other individuals with DID is unclear; and (2) decreased hippocampal volume is not specific to PTSD or to other conditions secondary to trauma, and has also been reported in schizophrenia (Nelson, Saykin, Flashman, & Riordan, 1998) and depression (Bremner et al., 2000). Consequently, decreased hippocampal volume may be a nonspecific marker of long-term stress (Sapolsky, 2000) that is present in many psychiatric conditions.

## LEARNING, MODELING, AND LIFE EVENTS

Some cases of (mis)diagnosed dissociative disorders are probably a product of malingering. Estimates suggest that malingering or other forms of feigning (e.g., the faking seen in factitious disorders) account for 2% to 10% of diagnoses of inpatient dissociative disorders (Friedl & Draijer, 2000; Pope, Jonas, & Jones, 1982). There is widespread agreement that DID can be successfully malingered. For example, Kenneth Bianchi, one of the two Hillside Stranger murderers, is widely believed to have faked DID to escape criminal responsibility (Orne, Dinges, & Orne, 1984). In one survey, experienced neuropsychologists estimated the prevalence of feigned dissociative symptoms in cases involved in litigation to be about 10% (Mittenberg,

Patton, Canyock & Condit, 2002). Nevertheless, cases of malingered DID are believed to be quite rare outside of forensic settings, and the substantial majority of individuals with this condition do not appear to be intentionally fabricating their symptoms.

## THE POSTTRAUMATIC VERSUS THE SOCIOCOGNITIVE MODELS OF DISSOCIATION

There is little dispute that some individuals meet the diagnostic criteria for DID, display unpredictable and sometimes bizarre shifts in mood and behavior, and are convinced that they house compartmentalized "personalities" engendered by severe early physical abuse, sexual abuse, or both. Nevertheless, over the past 25 years, controversy has swirled around the question of whether the symptoms of DID are naturally occurring responses to early trauma (Gleaves, 1996), as the posttraumatic model (PTM) of dissociation holds, or are largely socially constructed and culturally influenced, as the sociocognitive model (SCM) of dissociation holds (Spanos, 1994).

Proponents of the PTM (Gleaves, 1996; Gleaves, May, & Cardeña, 2001; Ross, 1997) argue that DID is a posttraumatic condition that arises primarily from a history of severe physical and/or sexual abuse in childhood. Advocates of the PTM contend that such abuse is a crucial contributor to DID: The child compartmentalizes the abuse so that he or she feels as though it is happening to someone else (Ross, 1997). Moreover, alters or ego states supposedly arise as a means of coping with the intense emotional pain of the trauma (see Lilienfeld & Lynn, 2003, for an explanation and critique). PTM theories variously emphasize the effects of childhood abuse and early traumatic experiences on producing (a) patterns of disorganized interpersonal attachment (Liotti, 1999, 2009) that engender dissociation; (b) structural dissociation (i.e., the development of different "parts" of the personality to handle different functions in "defense" and everyday life; Steele, van der Hart, Nijenhuis, 2009); (c) disturbances in the self-system that integrates "identity-mind-body-world-time" into a coherent whole; in this view, alters are conceptualized as "younger self-systems (ego-states) that are 'trapped' in a past trauma" (p. 283, Beere, 2009); (d) developmental deficits that degrade self-regulation and promote fragmentation of the self (Carlson, Yates, Sroufe, 2009); and (e) a dissociative information processing style related to feelings of being betrayed by a trusted caregiver (Barlow & Freyd, 2009; Freyd, 1996).

These diverse theories are ostensibly supported by very high rates—sometimes exceeding 90%—of reported histories of severe child abuse among patients diagnosed with DID and other severe dissociative disorders (Gleaves, 1996). Nevertheless, critics of the PTM (see Giesbrecht et al., 2008; Giesbrecht, Lynn, Lilienfeld, & Merckelbach, 2010; Lilienfeld et al., 1999; Merckelbach & Muris, 2001; Spanos, 1994, 1996) have questioned the validity of the child-abuse or maltreatment–DID link for the following five reasons:

1. Many studies that purport to confirm this association lack objective corroboration of child abuse (e.g. Coons, Bowman, & Milstein, 1988). For example, Sanders and Giolas (1991) found a correlation of $r = .44$ between the DES and scores on a child abuse questionnaire. Yet when a psychiatrist (unaware of the

dissociative status of participants) provided more objective ratings of trauma based on hospital records, the authors found a nonsignificant *negative* correlation between ratings of traumatic experiences and dissociation ($r = -.21$).

2. The overwhelming majority of studies investigating the link between self-reported trauma and dissociation are based on cross-sectional designs that do not permit researchers to draw causal inferences (Merckelbach & Muris, 2001) and that are subject to retrospective biases. Prospective studies that circumvent the pitfalls of retrospective reporting often fail to substantiate a consistent link between childhood abuse and dissociation in adulthood (Dutra, Bureau, Holmes, Lyubchik, & Lyons-Ruth, 2009; Noll, Trickett, & Putnam, 2003; Ogawa, Sroufe, Weinfield, Carlson, & Egeland, 1997; but see Bremner, 2010).

3. Researchers rarely control for potentially comorbid psychopathological syndromes and symptoms known to be related to dissociative disorders (e.g., anxiety, eating, personality disorders, impulsivity, schizotypal traits; see Giesbrecht et al., 2008).

4. The reported high levels of child abuse among DID patients may be attributable to selection and referral biases common in psychiatric samples. For example, patients who are abused are more likely than other patients to enter treatment (Pope & Hudson, 1995).

5. Correlations between abuse and psychopathology tend to decrease substantially or disappear when participants' perception of family pathology is controlled statistically (Nash, Hulsey, Sexton, Haralson, & Lambert, 1993).

Based on these five points of contention, Lilienfeld and Lynn (2003) noted that the available evidence provides little or no warrant for concluding that early abuse plays a causal role in DID.

In contrast to the PTM, proponents of the SCM (Spanos, 1994, 1996; see also Aldridge-Morris, 1989; Lilienfeld et al., 1999; Lynn & Pintar, 1997; McHugh, 1993; Merskey, 1992; Sarbin, 1995) contend that DID results from inadvertent therapist cueing (e.g., suggestive questioning regarding the existence of possible alters, hypnosis, sodium amytal), media influences (e.g., television and film portrayals of DID, such as *Sybil*), and broader sociocultural expectations regarding the presumed clinical features of DID.

Advocates of the SCM cite the following findings (Lilienfeld & Lynn, 2003; Lilienfeld et al., 1999) as consistent with the SCM or as challenges to the PTM:

1. The number of patients with DID, along with the number of alters per DID individual, have increased dramatically over the past few decades (Elzinga, van Dyck, & Spinhoven, 1998; North et al., 1993), although the number of alters at the time of initial diagnosis appears to have remained constant (Ross, Norton, & Wozney, 1989).

2. The massive increase in reported cases of DID followed closely upon the release of the best-selling book *Sybil* (Schreiber, 1973) in the 1970s, which told the story of a young woman with 16 personalities who reported a history of severe child abuse at the hands of her mother. As noted earlier, this book was turned into a widely viewed television film starring Sally Fields in 1976.

Interestingly, however, a well-known psychiatrist who was involved closely with the Sybil case later contended that Sybil's presentation of DID was largely or entirely the product of therapeutic suggestion. Herbert Spiegel, who served as a backup therapist for Sybil, maintained that Sybil's primary therapist, Cornelia Wilbur, frequently encouraged her to develop and display different personalities in therapy. According to Rieber (2006), who possessed tapes of conversations between Sybil and Cornelia Wilbur, Spiegel referred to Sybil as a "brilliant hysteric," with multiple identities fabricated to please the all-too-credulous Wilbur. Spiegel further maintained that Wilbur and Flora Schreiber, who authored the best-selling book about Sybil, insisted that Sybil be described in the book as a "multiple" to make the book more appealing (Acocella, 1999). Rieber concluded that "the three women—Wilbur, Schreiber, and Sybil—are responsible for shaping the modern myth of multiple personality disorder" (Rieber, 1999, p. 109). In short, increases in the diagnosis of DID and the number of alters per DID patient coincide with dramatically increased therapist and public awareness of the major features of DID (Fahy, 1988).

3. Mainstream treatment techniques for DID often reinforce patients' displays of multiplicity (e.g., asking questions like, "Is there another part of you with whom I have not spoken?"), reify alters as distinct personalities (e.g., therapists calling different alters by different names, mapping their "personality systems"), and encourage patients to establish contact and dialogue with presumed latent alters (Spanos, 1994, 1996). A case in point is the $N = 1$ within-subject study by Kohlenberg (1973), who showed that the behavioral displays of alter personalities can depend on reinforcement contingencies: The patient's alters soon "disappeared" after hospital staff stopped attending to them.

4. Many or most DID patients show few or no clear-cut signs of this condition (e.g., alters) prior to psychotherapy (Kluft, 1984).

5. The number of alters per DID individual tends to increase substantially over the course of DID-oriented psychotherapy (Piper, 1997).

6. Psychotherapists who use hypnosis tend to have more DID patients in their caseloads than do psychotherapists who do not use hypnosis (Powell & Gee, 1999).

7. The majority of diagnoses of DID derive from a relatively small number of psychotherapists, many of whom are specialists in DID (Mai, 1995).

8. Laboratory studies suggest that nonclinical participants who are provided with appropriate cues and prompts can reproduce many of the overt features of DID (Spanos, Weekes, & Bertrand, 1985; Stafford & Lynn, 2002).

9. Until fairly recently, diagnoses of DID were limited largely to North America, where the condition has received widespread media publicity (Spanos, 1996), although DID is now being diagnosed with considerable frequency in some countries (e.g., Holland) in which it has recently become more widely publicized. Manifestations of DID symptoms also vary across cultures. For example, in India, the transition period as the individual shifts between alter personalities is typically preceded by sleep, a presentation that reflects common media portrayals of DID in India (North et al., 1993). There are indications that both research interest in DID and media coverage of the

condition are waning, so it will be interesting to see whether this change heralds drops in prevalence (Pope, Barry, Bodkin & Hudson, 2006).

10. Laboratory research challenges the assertion that consciousness can be separated into multiple streams by amnesic barriers to form independently functioning alter personalities (Kong, Allen, & Glisky, 2008; Lynn et al., 2004).

These 10 sources of evidence do not imply that DID can typically be created *in vacuo* by iatrogenic (therapist-induced) or sociocultural influences. SCM theorists acknowledge that iatrogenic and sociocultural influences typically operate on a backdrop of preexisting psychopathology and exert their impact primarily on individuals who are seeking a causal explanation for their instability, identity problems, and impulsive and seemingly inexplicable behaviors. Indeed, the SCM is entirely consistent with findings, reviewed earlier, that many or most patients with DID meet criteria for BPD, a condition marked by extremely labile behaviors.

## Cognitive Mechanisms of Dissociation

Despite subjective reports of profound cognitive disturbances like amnesia, feelings of unreality, and identity alterations, researchers have found evidence for only relatively subtle and specific cognitive deficits in highly dissociative individuals. Such individuals usually fall within the normative range on tests of intellectual ability and standard neuropsychological tests (Giesbrecht et al., 2008). Indeed, whereas most studies, with few exceptions (but see Prohl, Resch, Parzer, & Brunner, 2001), fail to report any link between dissociation and working memory capacity, some report that dissociative individuals exhibit *superior* verbal working memory capacity or performance (Giesbrecht et al., 2008).

When cognitive deficits in dissociative patients are identified, they tend to be quite specific. For example, Guralnik, Schmeidler, and Simeon (2000) found that DPD patients exhibited deficits in visual perception and visual-spatial reasoning for both two- and three-dimensional stimuli. Patients' visual and verbal short-term memory capacity was also compromised, for both abstract and meaningful information, especially under information overload conditions. DPD participants experienced difficulty with early stimulus-encoding tasks under conditions of heightened distraction, to which they responded with more omission errors. Accordingly, DPD appears to be characterized by vulnerability in early information processing at the level of perception and attention (for a replication, see Guralnik, Giesbrecht, Knutelska, Sirroff, & Simeon, 2007).

Simeon and colleagues (Simeon, Hwu, & Knutelska, 2007) found evidence for a relationship between the dissociative symptoms of DPD patients, temporal disintegration (i.e., problems in memory regarding the chronology and dating of events), and total DES scores, as well as a positive correlation between temporal disintegration and DES absorption scores. They concluded that the dissociative dimension of absorption is a significant predictor of temporal disintegration.

The relative absence of a measurable general neuropsychological deficit in patients with dissociative disorders is noteworthy, as it differentiates them from those with most other severe psychiatric disorders, such as schizophrenia and bipolar disorder. These other conditions overlap with the dissociative disorders, but unlike them, are marked by a wide range of neuropsychological deficits (Heinrichs & Zakzanis, 1998). In addition, different dissociative disorders appear related to different cognitive deficiencies. DID is characterized mainly by performance fluctuations [e.g., increased scatter on the Wechsler Adult Intelligence Scale (Wechsler, 1981); Rossini, Schwartz, & Braun, 1996; reduced P300 amplitudes, but only during acute dissociative episodes in DID patients], whereas DPD is associated with disruptions in early stages of information processing (Guralnik et al., 2000). However, few investigations have controlled for general distress and psychopathology, or for scores on openness to experience, which is moderately associated with both dissociative tendencies (Kihlstrom, Glisky, & Angiulo, 1994) and with crystallized intelligence (DeYoung, Peterson, & Higgins, 2005). Interestingly, as we have noted earlier, dissociative individuals sometimes exhibit a performance advantage relative to nondissociative individuals (e.g., Chiu, Yeh, Huang, Wu, & Chiu, 2009).

Much of the literature on cognitive mechanisms of dissociation is more consistent with the SCM rather than the PTM. As already noted, proponents of the PTM typically argue that individuals who undergo horrific trauma in early life often dissociate or compartmentalize their personalities into discrete alters, segregated by amnesic barriers, as a means of coping with the intense emotional pain of the trauma. However, studies of amnesia among patients with DID have generally not reported findings commensurate with the existence of true amnesia among so-called alter personalities (Giesbrecht et al., 2010). For example, researchers have found little or no evidence for inter-identity amnesia using objective measures (e.g., behavioral tasks or event related potentials) of memory (e.g., Allen & Movius, 2000; Huntjens et al., 2006; Huntjens et al., 2007; Kong et al., 2008).

If dissociative symptoms attenuate the impact of traumatic events, individuals with heightened levels of dissociation should exhibit slower or impaired processing of threat-related information. Nevertheless, patients with DID and other "high dissociators" display *better* memory for to-be-forgotten sexual words in directed forgetting tasks (Elzinga, de Beurs, Sergeant, Van Dyck, & Phaf, 2000; see also Cloitre, Cancienne, Brodsky, Dulit, & Perry, 1996), a finding strikingly discrepant with the presumed defensive function of dissociation. Research on nonclinical samples (e.g., Candel, Merckelbach, & Kuijpers, 2003) showing that dissociation is not associated with inferior memory performance has been replicated in patients with DPD (Montagne et al., 2007). Studies of cognitive inhibition in high dissociative clinical (Dorahy, Irwin, & Middleton, 2002; Dorahy, McCusker, Loewenstein, Colbert, & Mulholland, 2006; Dorahy, Middleton, & Irwin, 2005) and nonclinical (Giesbrecht, Merckelbach, & Smeets, 2006) samples typically find a breakdown in such inhibition, which stands in sharp contrast with the widespread idea that amnesia (i.e., extreme inhibition) is a core feature of dissociation (Anderson et al., 2004). Research also finds mixed support at best for the contention that highly dissociative individuals are superior to low dissociators in dividing their attention. In two samples, Devilly et al. (2007) failed to replicate DePrince and Freyd's (2001) findings of superior forgetting of trauma-related words in high versus low dissociator college students in a divided attention task (see also Giesbrecht & Merckelbach, 2009). Giesbrecht et al. (2010) contended that the findings we have reviewed challenge the widespread assumption that dissociation is related to avoidant information processing and suggested that apparent gaps in memory in inter-identity amnesia, or dissociative amnesia more generally, could reflect intentional failures to report (McNally, 2003; Pope et al., 2006).

Giesbrecht and colleagues (Giesbrecht et al., 2008, 2010) further argued that dissociation is marked by a propensity toward pseudomemories, possibly mediated by heightened levels of interrogative suggestibility, fantasy proneness, and cognitive failures. They noted that at least 10 studies from diverse laboratories have confirmed a link between dissociation and fantasy proneness (Giesbrecht, Merckelbach, Kater, & Sluis, 2007), and that heightened levels of fantasy proneness are associated with both the tendency to overreport autobiographical memories (Merckelbach, Muris, Horselenberg, & Stougie, 2000) and the false recall of aversive memory material (Giesbrecht, Geraerts, & Merckelbach, 2007).

These authors contended that the relationship between dissociation and fantasy proneness may explain why individuals with high levels of dissociation are more prone than other individuals to develop false memories of emotional childhood events (e.g., a severe animal attack; Porter, Birt, Yuille, & Lehman, 2000), and further pointed to data revealing links between hypnotizability, dissociative symptoms (Frischholz, Lipman, Braun, & Sachs, 1992), and high scores on the Gudjonsson Suggestibility Scale (GSS; Gudjonnson, 1984; Merckelbach, Muris, Rassin, & Horselenberg, 2000; Wolfradt & Meyer, 1998). Similarly, researchers have shown that dissociation increases the risk of commission (e.g., confabulations/false positives, problems discriminating perception from vivid imagery, errors in response to misleading questions) rather than omission memory errors; the latter type of error is presumably associated with dissociative amnesia (Giesbrecht et al., 2008; Holmes et al., 2005).

These findings, taken together with research demonstrating a consistent link between dissociation and cognitive failures (Merckelbach, Horselenberg, & Schmidt, 2002; Merckelbach, Muris, & Rassin, 1999; Wright & Osborne, 2005), point to an association between heightened risk of confabulation and possibly pseudomemories that raise serious questions regarding the accuracy of retrospective reports of traumatic experiences. In addition, these findings severely limit the inferences that we can draw from studies that rely exclusively on self-reports to establish a connection between trauma and dissociation (Merckelbach & Jelicic, 2004; Merckelbach, Muris, Horselenberg, & Stougie, 2000).

Still, these findings do not exclude some role for trauma in the genesis of dissociation and dissociative disorders. Suggestibility, cognitive failures, and fantasy proneness might contribute to an overestimation of a genuine, although perhaps weak or modest, link between dissociation and trauma. Alternatively, early trauma might predispose individuals to develop high levels of fantasy proneness (Lynn, Rhue, & Green, 1988), absorption (Tellegen & Atkinson, 1974), or related traits. In turn, such traits may render individuals susceptible to the iatrogenic and cultural influences posited by the SCM, thereby increasing the likelihood that they will develop DID following exposure to these influences. This and even more sophisticated etiological models of DID have yet to be subjected to direct empirical tests. In the next section, we examine a novel theory that provides a possible basis of rapprochement between the PTM and the SCM.

Sleep, Memory, and Dissociation{.sc}

A recent theory linking sleep, memory problems, and dissociation may provide a conceptual bridge between the PTM and the SCM. In a review of 19 studies, van der Kloet, Merckelbach, Giesbrecht, and Lynn (2011) concluded that the extant research provides strong support for a link between dissociative experiences and a labile sleep-wake cycle that is evident across a range of phenomena, including waking dreams, nightmares, and hypnogogic (occurring while falling asleep) and hypnopompic (occurring after falling sleep) hallucinations. Studies that offered evidence for a link between dissociative experiences and sleep disturbances relied on clinical and nonclinical samples, and, with only one exception, yielded correlations in the range of .30 to .55, suggesting that unusual sleep experiences and dissociation are discriminable yet related constructs. Moreover, researchers (Giesbrecht, Smeets, Leppink, Jelicic, & Merckelbach, 2007) have shown that sleep loss induced in the laboratory intensifies dissociative symptoms, whereas a sleep hygiene intervention in a clinical setting decreases dissociative symptoms (van der Kloet, Giesbrecht, Lynn, Merckelbach, & de Zutter, in press), suggesting a possible causal link between sleep experiences and dissociation.

These findings suggest an intriguing interpretation of the link between dissociative symptoms and deviant sleep phenomena (see also Watson, 2001). Individuals with a labile sleep-wake cycle—perhaps associated with a genetic propensity or perhaps a by-product of intrusions of trauma-related memories—experience intrusions of sleep phenomena (e.g., dreamlike experiences) into waking consciousness, which in turn foster fantasy proneness, depersonalization, and derealization. These disruptions of the sleep-wake cycle, in turn, degrade memory (Hairston & Knight, 2004) and attentional control (Williamson, Feyer, Mattick, Friswell, & Finlay-Brown, 2001), thereby accounting for, or contributing to, the attention deficits and cognitive failures evidenced by highly dissociative individuals (Giesbrecht, Merckelbach, Geraerts, & Smeets, 2004) and dissociative patients (Dorahy, McCusker, Loewenstein, Colbert, & Mulholland, 2006; Guralnik et al., 2007).

Accordingly, the sleep-dissociation perspective may explain both (1) how highly aversive events disrupt the sleep-wake cycle and increase vulnerability to dissociative symptoms, and (2) why dissociation, trauma, fantasy proneness, and cognitive failures overlap. Thus, the sleep-dissociation perspective is commensurate with the possibility that trauma mediated by sleep disturbances plays a pivotal role in the genesis of dissociation and suggests that previously competing theoretical perspectives may be amenable to integration. The SCM holds that patients become convinced they possess separate indwelling identities as a byproduct of suggestive media, sociocultural, and psychotherapeutic influences. These patients' sensitivity to suggestive influences may arise from their propensity to fantasize, memory errors, increased salience of negative memories, and difficulties in distinguishing fantasy and reality brought about by disruptions in the sleep cycle.

Treatment

*Depersonalization and Derealization*   The available research evidence provides few guidelines for the treatment of dissociative disorders. Pharmacological treatments have proven to be of little help in improving symptoms of DPD or other dissociative disorders. For example, only a small proportion of people with DPD exhibit a clinically meaningful or even partial response to selective serotonin reuptake inhibitors or benzodiazepines. Although stimulant medications may improve concentration in individuals with DPD, they have little effect on the core symptoms of depersonalization (Simeon, et al., 1997, 2003). Moreover, the symptoms of depersonalization are no more responsive to fluoxetine (Simeon, Guralnik, Schmeidler, & Knutelska, 2004) or lamotrigine (Sierra, Phillips, Krystal, & David, 2003) than they are to a placebo. According to Simeon (2009b), the well-documented lack of response to anxioloytics or mood stabilizers among DPD patients suggests that this condition cannot be reduced to a mood or anxiety spectrum disorder, "despite being often triggered by, or co-occurring with, the latter" (p. 439). However, the fact that treatment response differs across disorders does not necessarily preclude commonalities in etiology.

The literature on psychotherapy with patients with DPD is similarly scant. An open study conducted by Hunter, Baker, Phillips, Sierra, and David (2005) examined the effects of cognitive-behavioral therapy (CBT) in DPD. The investigators taught patients to interpret their symptoms in a nonthreatening way. Although there were dramatic improvements in the patient sample and follow-up results were on the whole promising, the results must be interpreted with caution given the absence of a randomized control group. More rigorous trials are needed to confirm the merits of CBT and other psychotherapeutic approaches in patients with DPD.

*Dissociative Identity Disorder*   Individuals with DID are typically in treatment for an average of 6 to 7 years before being diagnosed with this condition (Gleaves, 1996). Advocates of the PTM see this finding as evidence that individuals with DID are underdiagnosed, whereas advocates of the SCM see it as evidence that patients who are later diagnosed with DID typically enter treatment with few or no symptoms of the disorder. The treatment outcome literature for DID is sparse. According to Brand, Classen, McNary, and Zaveri (2009), only eight studies have examined treatment outcomes for DID and other dissociative disorders. More recently, Brand's research team reported a naturalistic study of DID and DD-NOS treatment by community clinicians. Nevertheless, there are no randomized controlled trials on DID. Furthermore, studies do not permit an evaluation of the extent to which symptom reduction in dissociative patients is due to regression to the mean, the passage of time, placebo effects, or other artifacts. Other methodological problems include variability in treatments offered to patients (e.g., Choe & Kluft, 1995), lack of controls for nonspecific effects (e.g., Ellason & Ross, 1997), dropout rates as high as 68% (Gantt & Tinnin, 2007), and the failure to document clinically meaningful changes following treatment. As a consequence, one cannot draw confident conclusions regarding treatment efficacy from the extant literature.

Importantly, some literature suggests that patients treated with commonly used DID interventions that involve identifying alters, addressing "parts," and recovering memories deteriorate significantly over the course of treatment. In one study, the majority of patients developed "florid posttraumatic stress disorder during treatment" (Dell & Eisenhower, 1990, p. 361). Moreover, after treatment commences, patients report increased suicide attempts, hallucinations, severe dysphoria, and chronic crises (Piper & Merskey, 2004). Studies that compare negative sequelae across DID and conventional therapies are therefore a priority.

Assuming that future studies establish that certain sleep deviations serve as causal antecedents of dissociative symptoms, it will be imperative to study the effects of treatment interventions focused on sleep normalization in dissociative patients (Hamner, Brodrick, & Labbate, 2001; Merckelbach & Giesbrecht, 2006). Previous studies that have examined the effectiveness of sleep medication in PTSD (Van Liempt, Vermetten, Geuze, & Westenberg, 2006) and DID (Loewenstein, Hornstein, & Farber, 1988) have yielded promising results

## LOOKING AHEAD TO *DSM-5*

Workers in the field have offered suggestions for changes in the upcoming revision of the *DSM*, due out in 2013. For example, Schore (2009) observed that the definition of dissociation in the *DSM-5*

> must include a developmental model of dissociative phenomena, arguing that mal-treatment in childhood is associated with an impairment of higher corticolimbic modulation of the vagal circuit of emotional regulation on the right side of the brain that generates the psychobiological state of dissociation. (p. 130)

Although the neurobehavioral underpinnings of dissociative phenomena may one day be identified and incorporated into future iterations of the *DSM*, Schore's basic premise that maltreatment is the root cause of all or most dissociative phenomena is not unambiguously supported by the research literature.

A significant problem for the *DSM* is the vague nature of the diagnostic criteria for dissociative disorders. For example, the central diagnostic criterion for disso-ciative amnesia is vague and subjective in stipulating that one or more episodes of inability to recall important information must be "... too extensive to be explained by ordinary forgetfulness" (p. 522). The reliability of judgments of what constitutes "ordinary forgetfulness" is questionable, and what is "ordinary" will probably depend heavily on a variety of factors, including the situational context and presence of comorbid conditions. Indeed, questions concerning the validity of dissociative amnesia as a diagnostic entity are supported by markedly different prevalence in the general population across cultures: 0.2% in China, 0.9% and 7.3% in Turkey, and 3.0% in Canada (Dell, 2009). These varying prevalence estimates could reflect genuine cultural differences, but they could just as plausibly reflect different interviewer criteria for evaluating amnesia.

The *DSM* is similarly imprecise about what counts as a "distinct" personality or personality state in DID, which requires the presence of "two or more distinct identities or personality states" (p. 529). Worse still, there are no objective, observable criteria to evaluate not only "identities" or "personality states," but also the question of whether "at least two of these identities or personality states recurrently take control of the person's behavior" (p. 529). In fact, the claim of distinct personality states, as proposed by *DSM-5* working criteria, can rest entirely on self-report and does not require observation by others. Definitional ambiguity regarding "personalities" or "personality states" and dissociative amnesia also poses difficulties for Ross's (2009a) proposal that the *DSM-5* include a new subtype of schizophrenia; namely, schizophrenia, dissociative type. This subtype would include dissociative amnesia and the presence of two or more distinct identities or personality states.

Definitional imprecision also spills over into the diagnosis of DD-NOS, which is the most prevalent dissociative disorder in psychiatric settings (Dell, 2009). A person could qualify for a diagnosis of DD-NOS if there are prominent features of DID but if two or more distinct personality states or amnesia for important personal information are not present. Again, the lack of clarity regarding amnesia and identities are problematic in this context, as is the vagueness surrounding "states of dissociation" in arriving at a DD-NOS diagnosis in individuals who have been subjected to prolonged and intense coercive persuasion (e.g., brainwashing).

Dissociative trance disorder, currently in the *DSM-IV* Appendix, is classified in the current manual as a DD-NOS. Cardeña and his associates suggested that possession and trance phenomena ". . . may be the most common dissociative presentation in non-Western cultures (p. 178), although there is scant evidence for this assertion. As Cardeña et al. (2009) noted with respect to the criteria for this disorder, it is unfortunate that ". . . not a single published project . . . has systematically applied them." The authors further observed that ". . . diagnostic criteria for dissociative trance disorder would seem to be a nosological must for *DSM-V*" (p. 178), and called for researchers to evaluate the reliability and validity of the proposed criteria.

Questions also persist about the taxonic nature of dissociation and the role of more nonpathological or normative traits or experiences, including cognitive failures, fantasy proneness, and suggestibility in the genesis of dissociative experiences. Ross (2009b) suggested that because the individuals with "pure dissociative amnesia" he has interviewed score low on the DES and do not seem to be members of the dissociative taxon, they may suffer from a distinct type of dissociative disorder. Although Ross's anecdotal observations have not been replicated, he noted that the "*DSM-V* Dissociative Disorders Committee should consider whether the issue of taxon membership deserves comment in the *DSM-V* texts about dissociative amnesia and dissociative fugue" (p. 430).

The difficulties in diagnosing DID have led some workers in the field to question whether the disorder can even be reliably diagnosed. Piper and Merskey (2004), for example, went so far as to write that

> . . . with manifestations that are visible to only some clinicians and on only some occasions; with symptoms that cannot be distinguished from other psychiatric disorders or from malingering; with unacceptably vague diagnostic criteria; and with patients who initially deny their symptoms, show no signs of the condition's essential feature, and know nothing of either their traumatic histories or the presence of alters—simply cannot be reliably diagnosed." (p. 681; but see Gleaves & Cardeña, 2001, for a competing view)

## SUMMARY

Dissociative disorders, especially DID and dissociative fugue, are among the most controversial diagnoses in all of descriptive psychopathology, and for good reason.

Although dissociation is unquestionably a genuine subjective experience, serious questions remain concerning the assessment, etiology, and treatment of most dissociative disorders.

The etiological issues are a particular sticking point, and they appear no closer to resolution with the impending publication of *DSM-5*. Although some authors (e.g., Gleaves, 1996) maintain that DID and perhaps other dissociative disorders stem primarily from early child abuse and maltreatment, others (e.g., Spanos, 1994) maintain that these conditions are largely socially and culturally influenced products that are aided and abetted by therapist prompting and cueing of symptoms—a view that is supported by multiple sources of admittedly circumstantial evidence (Lilienfeld et al., 1999). It remains to be seen whether new and promising models, such as those linking sleep deprivation to dissociative symptoms (van der Kloet et al., 2011) may provide common ground between these competing theories of the genesis of dissociative disorders. In the meantime, clinicians who work with dissociative patients should bear in mind the powerful historical lesson imparted by the literature on DID: In their well-meaning efforts to unearth psychopathology, assessors and therapists may inadvertently end up creating it (Lilienfeld et al., 1999).

## REFERENCES

Acocella, J. (1999). *Creating hysteria: Women and multiple personality disorder*. San Francisco, CA: Jossey-Bass.

Aderibigbe, Y. A., Bloch, R. M., & Walker, W. R. (2001). Prevalence of depersonalization and derealization experiences in a rural population. *Social Psychiatry and Psychiatric Epidemiology, 36*, 63–69.

Aldridge-Morris, R. (1989). *Multiple personality: An exercise in deception*. Hillsdale, NJ: Erlbaum.

Allen, J. G. (2001). *Traumatic relationships and serious mental disorders*. New York, NY: John Wiley & Sons.

Allen, J. J. B., & Movius, H. L., II. (2000). The objective assessment of amnesia in dissociative identity disorder using event-related potentials. *International Journal of Psychophysiology, 38*, 21–41.

American Psychiatric Association. (1994). *Diagnostic and statistical manual of mental disorders* (4th ed.). Washington, DC: Author.

American Psychiatric Association. (2000). *Diagnostic and statistical manual of mental disorders* (4th ed., text rev.). Washington, DC: Author.

Anderson, M. C., Ochsner, K. N., Kuhl, B., Cooper, J., Robertson, E., Gabrieli, S. W., . . . Gabrieli, J. D. (2004). Neural systems underlying the suppression of unwanted memories. *Science, 303*, 232–235.

Armstrong, J., Putnam, F., Carlson, E., Libero, D., & Smith, S. (1997). Development and validation of a measure of adolescent dissociation: The Adolescent Dissociative Experiences Scale. *Journal of Nervous and Mental Disorders, 185*, 491–497.

Aspell, J. E., & Blanke, O. (2009). Understanding the out-of-body experience from a neuroscientific perspective. In C. Murray (Ed.), *Psychological and scientific perspectives on out-of-body and near death experiences*. New York, NY: Nova Science.

Aspell, J. E., Lenggenhager, B., & Blanke, O. (2009). Keeping in touch with one's self: Multisensory mechanisms of self-consciousness. *PLoS ONE, 4*(8), e6488. doi: 10.1371/journal.pone.0006488

Baker, D., Hunter, E., Lawrence, E., Medford, M., Patel, N., Senior, C., . . . David, A. S. (2003). Depersonalisation disorder: Clinical features of 204 cases. *British Journal of Psychiatry, 182,* 428–433.

Barlow, M. R., & Freyd, J. J. (2009). Adaptive dissociation: Information processing and response to betrayal. In P. F. Dell & J. A. O'Neil (Eds.), *Dissociation and the dissociative disorders* (pp. 93–105). New York, NY: Routledge/Taylor Francis.

Becker-Blease, K. A., Deater-Deckard, K., Eley, T., Freyd, J. J., Stevenson, J., & Plomin, R. (2004). A genetic analysis of individual differences in dissociative behaviors in childhood and adolescence. *Journal of Child Psychology and Psychiatry and Allied Disciplines, 45,* 522–532.

Beere, D. B. (2009). The self-system as a mechanism for the dissociative disorders: An extension of the perceptual theory of dissociation. In P. F. Dell & J. A. O'Neil (Eds.), *Dissociation and the dissociative disorders* (pp. 277–286). New York, NY: Routledge/Taylor Francis.

Belli, R. F., Winkielman, P., Read, J. D., Schwarz, N., & Lynn, S. J. (1998). Recalling more childhood events leads to judgments of poorer memory: Implications for the recovered/false memory debate. *Psychonomic Bulletin & Review, 5,* 318–323.

Bernstein-Carlson, E. B., & Putnam, F. W. (1986). Development, reliability, and validity of a dissociation scale. *Journal of Nervous and Mental Disease, 174,* 727–735.

Bernstein-Carlson, E., & Putnam, F. W. (1993). An update on the Dissociative Experiences Scale. *Dissociation, 6,* 19–27.

Blanke, O., Ortigue, S., Landis, T., & Seeck, M. (2002). Neuropsychology: Stimulating illusory own-body perceptions. *Nature, 419*(6904), 269–270.

Blanke, O., & Thut, G. (2007). Inducing out of body experiences. In G. Della Sala (Ed.), *Tall tales.* Oxford, England: Oxford University Press.

Brand, B. L., Armstrong, J. G., & Loewenstein, R. J. (2006). Psychological assessment of patients with dissociative identity disorder. *Psychiatric Clinics of North America, 29,* 145–168.

Brand, B., Classen, C. C., McNary, S. W., & Zaveri, P. (2009). A review of dissociative disorders treatment studies. *Journal of Nervous and Mental Disease, 197,* 646–694.

Bremner, J. D. (2010). Cognitive processes in dissociation: Comment on Giesbrecht et al. (2008). *Psychological Bulletin, 136*(1), 1–6.

Bremner, J. D., Krystal, J. H., Putnam, F. W., Southwick, S. M., Marmar, C., Charney, D. S., & Mazure, C. M. (1998). Measurement of dissociative states with the Clinician Administered Dissociative States Scale (CADSS). *Journal of Traumatic Stress, 11,* 125–136.

Bremner, J. D., Narayan, M., Anderson, E. R., Staib, L. H., Miller, H. L., & Charney, D. S. (2000). Hippocampal volume reduction in major depression. *American Journal of Psychiatry, 157,* 115–117.

Bremner, J. D., Randall, P., Scott, T. M., & Bronen, R. (1995). MRI-based measurement of hippocampal volume in patients with combat-related posttraumatic stress disorder. *American Journal of Psychiatry, 152,* 973–981.

Bremner, J. D., Randall, P., Vermetten, E., & Staib, L. (1997). Magnetic resonance imaging-based measurement of hippocampal volume in posttraumatic stress disorder related to childhood physical and sexual abuse: A preliminary report. *Biological Psychiatry, 41,* 23–32.

Bremner, J. D., Steinberg, M., Southwick, S. M., Johnson, D. R., & Charney, D. S. (1993). Use of the Structured Clinical Interview for DSM-IV-Dissociative Disorders for systematic assessment of dissociative symptoms in posttraumatic stress disorder. *American Journal of Psychiatry, 150,* 1011–1014.

Brown, D. P., Scheflin, A. W., & Hammond, D. C. (1997). *Memory, trauma, treatment, and the law.* New York, NY: W. W. Norton.

Bunning, S., & Blanke, O. (2005). The out-of-body experience: Precipitating factors and neural correlates. In S. Laureys (Ed.), *Progress in brain research, Vol. 150: The boundaries of consciousness: Neurobiology and neuropatholoy* (pp. 331–350). Maryland Heights, MO: Elsevier.

Candel, I., Merckelbach, H., & Kuijpers, M. (2003). Dissociative experiences are related to commissions in emotional memory. *Behaviour Research and Therapy, 41*, 719–725.

Cardeña, E. (1994). The domain of dissociation. In S. J. Lynn, & J. W. Rhue (Eds.), *Dissociation: Clinical and theoretical perspectives* (pp. 15–31). New York, NY: Guilford Press.

Cardeña, E. (2008). Dissociative disorders measures. In A. J. Rush, M. First, & D. Blacker (Eds.), *Handbook of psychiatric measures* (2nd ed., pp. 677–690). Arlington, VA: American Psychiatric Publishing.

Cardeña, E., van Duijl, M., Weiner, L. A., & Terhune, D. (2009). Possession/trance phenomena. In P. Dell & J. A. O'Neil (Eds.), *Dissociation and the dissociative disorders: DSM-V and Beyond* (pp. 171–181). New York, NY: Routledge/Taylor & Francis.

Carlson, E. B., Putnam, F. W., Ross, C. A., Anderson, G., Clark, P., Torem, M., . . . Braun, B. G. (1991). Factor analysis of the Dissociative Experiences Scale: A multicenter study. In B. G. Braun & E. B. Carlson (Eds.), *Proceedings of the Eighth International Conference on Multiple Personality and Dissociative States*. Chicago, IL: Rush.

Carlson, E. B., Putnam, F. W., Ross, C. A., Torem, M., Coons, P., Bowman, E. S., . . . Braun, B. G. (1991). Validity of the Dissociative Experiences Scale in screening for multiple personality disorder: A multicenter study. *American Journal of Psychiatry, 150*(7), 1030–1036.

Carlson, E. A., Yates, T. M., & Sroufe, L. A. (2009). Dissociation and development of the self. In P. F. Dell & J. A. O'Neil (Eds.), *Dissociation and the dissociative disorders* (pp. 39–52). New York, NY: Routledge/Taylor Francis.

Cheyne, J. A., & Girard, T. A. (2009). The body unbound: Vestibular-motor hallucinations and out-of-body experiences. *Cortex, 45*(2), 201–215.

Chiu, C.-D.Yeh, Y.-Y., Huang, Y.-M., Wu, Y.-C., & Chiu, Y.-C. (2009). The switching function of nonclinical dissociators under negative emotion. *Journal of Abnormal Psychology, 118*(1), 214–222.

Choe, B. M., & Kluft, R. P. (1995). The use of the DES in studying treatment outcome with dissociative identity disorder: A pilot study. *Dissociation, 8*, 160–164.

Cloitre, M., Cancienne, J., Brodsky, B., Dulit, R., & Perry, S. W. (1996). Memory performance among women with parental abuse histories: Enhanced directed forgetting or directed remembering? *Journal of Abnormal Psychology, 105*, 204–211.

Colletti, G., Lynn, S. J., & Laurence, J.-R. (2010). Hypnosis and the treatment of dissociative identity disorder. In S. J. Lynn, I. Kirsch, & J. W. Rhue (Eds.), *Handbook of clinical hypnosis* (2nd ed., pp. 433–452). Washington, DC: American Psychological Association.

Coons, P. M. (1988). Schneiderian first rank symptoms in schizophrenia and multiple personality disorder. *Acta Psychiatrica Scandinavica, 77*, 235.

Coons, P. M. (1998). The dissociative disorders: Rarely considered and underdiagnosed. *The Psychiatric Clinics of North America, 21*, 637–648.

Coons, P. M., Bowman, E. S., & Milstein, V. (1988). Multiple personality disorder: A clinical investigation of 50 cases. *Journal of Nervous and Mental Disease, 176*, 519–527.

Dell, P. F. (2002). Dissociative phenomenology of dissociative identity disorder. *Journal of Nervous and Mental Disease, 190*(1), 10–15.

Dell, P. F. (2006). The Multidimensional Inventory of Dissociation (MID): A comprehensive measure of pathological dissociation. *Journal of Trauma and Dissociation, 7*(2), 77–106.

Dell, P. F. (2009). The long struggle to diagnose multiple personality disorder (MPD): Partial MPD. In P. F. Dell & J. A. O'Neil (Eds.), *Dissociation and the dissociative disorders: DSM-5 and beyond* (pp. 403–428). New York, NY: Routlege/Taylor & Francis.

Dell, P. F., & Eisenhower, J. W. (1990). Adolescent multiple personality disorder: A preliminary study of eleven cases. *Journal of the Academy of Child and Adolescent Psychiatry, 29*, 359–366.

DePrince, A. P., & Freyd, J. J. (2001). Memory and dissociative tendencies: The roles of attentional context and word meaning in a directed forgetting task. *Journal of Trauma and Dissociation, 2*, 67–82.

De Ridder, D., Van Laere, K., Dupont, P., Menovsky, T., & Van de Heyning, P. (2007). Visualizing out-of-body experience in the brain. *The New England Journal of Medicine, 357* (18), 1829–1833.

Devilly, G. J., Ciorciari, J., Piesse, A., Sherwell, S., Zammit, S., Cook, F., & Turton, C. (2007). Dissociative tendencies and memory performance on directed forgetting tasks. *Psychological Science, 18*, 212–217.

DeYoung, C. G., Peterson, J. B., & Higgins, D. M. (2005). Sources of openness/intellect: Cognitive and neuropsychological correlates of the fifth factor of personality. *Journal of Personality, 73*, 825–858.

Dollinger, S. J. (1985). Lightning strike disaster among children. *British Journal of Medical Psychology, 58*, 375–383.

Dorahy, M. J., Irwin, H. J., & Middleton, W. (2002). Cognitive inhibition in dissociative identity disorder (DID): Developing an understanding of working memory function in DID. *Journal of Trauma and Dissociation, 3*, 111–132.

Dorahy, M. J., McCusker, C. G., Loewenstein, R. J., Colbert, K., & Mulholland, C. (2006). Cognitive inhibition and interference in dissociative identity disorder: The effects of anxiety on specific executive functions. *Behaviour Research and Therapy, 44*, 749–764.

Dorahy, M. J., Middleton, W., & Irwin, H. J. (2005). The effect of emotional context on cognitive inhibition and attentional processing in dissociative identity disorder. *Behaviour Research and Therapy, 43*, 555–568.

Dutra, L., Bureau, J. F., Holmes, B., Lyubchik, A., & Lyons-Ruth, K. (2009). Quality of early care and childhood trauma: A prospective study of developmental pathways to dissociation. *Journal of Nervous and Mental Disease, 197*(6), 383–390.

Ehrsson, H. (2007). The experimental induction of out-of-body experiences. *Science, 317*(5841), 1048.

Ellason, J. W., & Ross, C. A. (1995). Positive and negative symptoms in dissociative identity disorder and schizophrenia: A comparative analysis. *Journal of Nervous and Mental Disease, 183*(4), 236–241.

Ellason, J. W., & Ross, C. A. (1997). Two-year follow-up of inpatients with dissociative identity disorder. *American Journal of Psychiatry, 154*, 832–839.

Ellason, J. W., Ross, C. A., & Fuchs, D. L. (1996). Lifetime Axis I and II comorbidity and childhood trauma history in dissociative identity disorder. *Psychiatry, 59*, 255–261.

Elzinga, B. M., de Beurs, E., Sergeant, J. A., Van Dyck, R., & Phaf, R. H. (2000). Dissociative style and directed forgetting. *Cognitive Therapy and Research, 24*, 279–295.

Elzinga, B. M., van Dyck, R., & Spinhoven, P. (1998). Three controversies about dissociative identity disorder. *Clinical Psychology and Psychotherapy, 5*, 13–23.

Fahy, T. A. (1988). The diagnosis of multiple personality disorder: A critical review. *British Journal of Psychiatry, 153*, 597–606.

Freyd, J. J. (1996). *Betrayal trauma theory: The logic of forgetting childhood abuse.* Cambridge, MA: Harvard University Press.

Friedl, M. C., & Draijer, N. (2000). Dissociative disorders in Dutch psychiatric inpatients. *American Journal of Psychiatry, 157*, 1012–1013.

Frischholz, E. J., Lipman, L. S., Braun, B. G., & Sachs, R. G. (1992). Psychopathology, hypnotizability and dissociation. *American Journal of Psychiatry, 149,* 1521–1525.

Fullerton, C., Ursano, R., Epstein, R., Crowley, B., Vance, K., Kao, T.-C., & Baum, A. (2000). Posttraumatic dissociation following motor vehicle accidents: Relationship to prior trauma and prior major depression. *Journal of Nervous and Mental Disease, 188*(5), 267–272.

Gantt, L., & Tinnin, L.W. (2007). Intensive trauma therapy of PTSD and dissociation: An outcome study. *The Arts in Psychotherapy, 34,* 69–80.

Gershuny, B. S., & Thayer, J. F. (1999). Relations among psychological trauma, dissociative phenomena, and trauma-related distress: A review and integration. *Clinical Psychology Review, 19,* 631–637.

Giesbrecht, T., Geraerts, E., & Merckelbach, H. (2007). Dissociation, memory commission errors, and heightened autonomic reactivity. *Psychiatry Research, 150,* 277.

Giesbrecht, T., Lynn, S. J., Lilienfeld, S., & Merckelbach, H. (2008). Cognitive processes in dissociation: An analysis of core theoretical assumptions. *Psychological Bulletin, 134,* 617–647.

Giesbrecht, T., Lynn, S. J., Lilienfeld, S., & Merckelbach, H. (2010). Cognitive processes, trauma, and dissociation: Misconceptions and misrepresentations (Reply to Bremner, 2009). *Psychological Bulletin, 136,* 7–11.

Giesbrecht, T., & Merckelbach, H. (2009). Betrayal trauma theory of dissociative experiences: Stroop and directed forgetting findings. *American Journal of Psychology, 122,* 337–348.

Giesbrecht, T., Merckelbach, H., & Geraerts, E. (2007). The dissociative experiences taxon is related to fantasy proneness. *Journal of Nervous and Mental Disease, 195,* 769–772.

Giesbrecht, T., Merckelbach, H., Geraerts, E., & Smeets, E. (2004). Disruptions in executive functioning and dissociation in undergraduate students. *Journal of Nervous and Mental Disease, 192,* 567–569.

Giesbrecht, T., Merckelbach, H., Kater, M., & Sluis, A. F. (2007). Why dissociation and schizotypy overlap: The joint influence of fantasy proneness, cognitive failures, and childhood trauma. *Journal of Nervous and Mental Disease, 195,* 812–818.

Giesbrecht, T., Merckelbach, H., & Smeets, E. (2006). Thought suppression, dissociation, and context effects. *Netherlands Journal of Psychology, 62,* 73–80.

Giesbrecht, T., Smeets, T., Leppink, J., Jelicic, M., & Merckelbach, H. (2007). Acute dissociation after 1 night of sleep loss. *Journal of Abnormal Psychology, 116,* 599–606.

Gleaves, D. H. (1996). The sociocognitive model of dissociative identity disorder: A re-examination of the evidence. *Psychological Bulletin, 120,* 142–159.

Gleaves, D. H., May, M. C., & Cardeña, E. (2001). An examination of the diagnostic validity of dissociative identity disorder. *Clinical Psychology Review, 21,* 577–608.

Gudjonsson, G. H. (1984). A new scale of interrogative suggestibility. *Personality and Individual Differences, 5,* 303–314.

Guralnik, O., Giesbrecht, T., Knutelska, M., Sirroff, B., & Simeon, D. (2007). Cognitive functioning in depersonalization disorder. *Journal of Nervous and Mental Disease, 195,* 983–988.

Guralnik, O., Schmeidler, J., & Simeon, D. (2000). Feeling unreal: Cognitive processes in depersonalization. *American Journal of Psychiatry, 157,* 103–109.

Hacking, I. (1995). *Rewriting the soul: Multiple personality and the sciences.* Princeton, NJ: Princeton University Press.

Hairston, I. S., & Knight, R. T. (2004). Neurobiology—Sleep on it. *Nature, 430,* 27–28.

Hamner, M. B., Broderick, P. S., & Labbate, L. S. (2001). Gabapentin in PTSD: A retrospective clinical series of adjunctive therapy. *Annals of Clinical Psychiatry, 13,* 141–146.

Heinrichs, R. W., & Zakzanis, K. K. (1998). Neurocognitive deficit in schizophrenia: A quantitative review of the evidence. *Neuropsychology, 12,* 426–445.

Holmes, E. A., Brown, R. J., Mansell, W., Fearon, R., Hunter, E. C. M., Frasquilho, F., & Oakley, D. A. (2005). Are there two qualitatively distinct forms of dissociation? A review and some clinical implications. *Clinical Psychology Review, 25,* 1–23.

Horevitz, R. P., & Braun, B. G. (1984). Are multiple personalities borderline? *Psychiatric Clinics of North America, 7,* 69–87.

Hunter, E. C. M., Baker, D., Phillips, M. L., Sierra, M., & David, A. S. (2005). Cognitive behaviour therapy for depersonalization disorder: An open study. *Behaviour Research and Therapy, 43,* 1121–1130.

Huntjens, R. J. C., Peters, M. L., Woertman, L., Bovenschen, L. M., Martin, R. C., & Postma, A. (2006). Inter-identity amnesia in dissociative identity disorder: A simulated memory impairment? *Psychological Medicine, 36,* 857–863.

Huntjens, R. J. C., Peters, M. L., Woertman, L., van der Hart, O., & Postma, A. (2007). Memory transfer for emotionally valenced words between identities in dissociative identity disorder. *Behaviour Research and Therapy, 45,* 775–789.

Jang, K. L., Paris, J., Zweig-Frank, H., & Livesley, W. J. (1998). Twin study of dissociative experiences. *Journal of Abnormal Psychology, 186,* 345–351.

Jáuregui-Renaud, K., Ramos-Toledo, V., Aguilar-Bolanos, M., Montaño-Velazquez, B., & Pliego-Maldonado, A. (2008a). Symptoms of detachment from the self or from the environment in patients with an acquired deficiency of the special senses. *Journal of Vestibular Research, 18,* 129–137.

Jáuregui-Renaud, K., Sang, F. Y., Gresty, M. A., Green, D. A., & Bronstein, A. M. (2008b). Depersonalization/derealization symptoms and updating orientation in patients with vestibular disease. *Journal of Neurology, Neurosurgery, and Psychiatry, 79*(3), 276–283.

Jureidini, J. (2003). Does dissociation offer a useful explanation for psychopathology? *Psychopathology, 37,* 259–265.

Kemp, K., Gilbertson, A. D., & Torem, M. (1988). The differential diagnosis of multiple personality disorder from borderline personality disorder. *Dissociation, 1,* 41–46.

Kihlstrom, J. F. (2005). Dissociative disorders. *Annual Review of Clinical Psychology, 1,* 1–27.

Kihlstrom, J. F., Glisky, M. L., & Angiulo, M. J. (1994). Dissociative tendencies and dissociative disorders. *Journal of Abnormal Psychology, 103,* 117–124.

Kluft, R. P. (1984). Treatment of multiple personality disorders: A study of 33 cases. *Psychiatric Clinics of North America, 7,* 9–29.

Kluft, R. P. (1993). Multiple personality disorders. In D. Spiegel (Ed.), *Dissociative disorders: A clinical review* (pp. 14–44). Lutherville, MD: Sidran Press.

Kohlenberg, R. J. (1973). Behavioristic approach to multiple personality: A case study. *Behavior Therapy, 4,* 137–140.

Kong, L. L., Allen, J. J. B., & Glisky, E. L. (2008). Interidentity memory transfer in dissociative identity disorder. *Journal of Abnormal Psychology, 117,* 686–692.

Kruger, C., & Mace, C. J. (2002). Psychometric validation of the State Scale of Dissociation (SSD). *Psychology and Psychotherapy: Theory, Research, and Practice, 75,* 33–51.

Krystal, J. H., Karper, L. P., Seibyl, J. P., Freeman, G. K., Delaney, R., Bremner, J. D., . . . Charney, D. S. (1994). Subanesthetic effects of the noncompetitive NMDA antagonist, ketamine, in humans: Psychotomimetic, perceptual, cognitive, and neuroendocrine responses. *Archives of General Psychiatry, 51,* 199–214.

Lauer, J., Black, D. W., & Keen, P. (1993). Multiple personality disorder and borderline personality disorder: Distinct entities or variations on a common theme. *Annals of Clinical Psychiatry, 5*, 129–134.

Lenggenhager, B., Tadi, T., Metzinger, T., & Blanke, O. (2007). Video ergo sum: Manipulating bodily self-consciousness. *Science, 317*(5841), 1096–1099.

Lilienfeld, S. O., & Lynn, S. J. (2003). Dissociative identity disorder: Multiple personalities, multiple controversies. In S. O. Lilienfeld, S. J. Lynn, & J. M. Lohr (Eds.), *Science and pseudoscience in clinical psychology* (pp. 109–142). New York, NY: Guilford Press.

Lilienfeld, S. O., Lynn, S. J., Kirsch, I., Chaves, J., Sarbin, T., Ganaway, G., & Powell, R. (1999). Dissociative identity disorder and the sociocognitive model: Recalling the lessons of the past. *Psychological Bulletin, 125*, 507–523.

Liotti, G. (1999). Understanding the dissociative processes: The contribution of attachment theory. *Psychoanalytic Inquiry, 19*, 757–783.

Liotti, G. (2009). Attachment and dissociation. In P. F. Dell & J. A. O'Neil (Eds.), *Dissociation and the dissociative disorders* (pp. 53–66). New York, NY: Routledge/Taylor Francis.

Loewenstein, R. J. (1991). An office mental status examination for complex chronic dissociative symptoms and multiple personality disorder. In R. J. Loewenstein (Ed.), *Psychiatric clinics of North America* (Vol. 14, pp. 567–604). Philadelphia, PA: W. B. Saunders.

Loewenstein, R. J., Hornstein, N., & Farber, B. (1988). Open trial of clonazepam in the treatment of posttraumatic stress symptoms in MPD. *Dissociation, 1*, 3–12.

Lynn, S. J., Fassler, O., Knox, J., & Lilienfeld, S. O. (2009). Dissociation and dissociative identity disorder: Treatment guidelines and cautions. In J. Fisher & W. O'Donohue (Eds.), *Practitioner's guide to evidence-based psychotherapy.*

Lynn, S. J., Knox, J., Fassler, O., Lilienfeld, S. O., & Loftus, E. (2004). Trauma, dissociation, and memory. In J. Rosen (Ed.), *Posttraumatic stress disorder: Issues and controversies.* Hoboken, NJ: John Wiley & Sons.

Lynn, S. J., & Pintar, J. (1997). A social narrative model of dissociative identity disorder. *Australian Journal of Clinical and Experimental Hypnosis, 25*, 1–7.

Lynn, S. J., Rhue, J., & Green, J. (1988). Multiple personality and fantasy-proneness: Is there an association or dissociation? *British Journal of Experimental and Clinical Hypnosis, 5*, 138–142.

Mai, F. M. (1995). Psychiatrists attitudes to multiple personality disorder: A questionnaire study. *Canadian Journal of Psychiatry, 40*, 154–157.

McHugh, P. R. (1993). Multiple personality disorder. *Harvard Mental Health Newsletter, 10*(3), 4–6.

McHugh, P. R. (2008). *Try to remember: Psychiatry's clash over meaning.* New York, NY: Dana Press.

McNally, R. J. (2003). Recovering memories of trauma: A view from the laboratory. *Current Directions in Psychological Science, 12*, 32–35.

McNally, R. J. (2004). The science and folklore of traumatic amnesia. *Clinical Psychology: Science and Practice, 11*, 29–33.

Merckelbach, H., Dekkers, T., Wessel, I., & Roefs, A. (2003). Dissociative symptoms and amnesia in Dutch concentration camp survivors. *Comprehensive Psychiatry, 44*, 65–69.

Merckelbach, H., Devilly, G. J., & Rassin, E. (2002). Alters in dissociative identity disorder: Metaphors or genuine entities? *Clinical Psychology Review, 22*, 481–497.

Merckelbach, H., & Giesbrecht, T. (2006). Subclinical dissociation, schizotypy, and traumatic distress. *Personality and Individual Differences, 40*, 365–374.

Merckelbach, H., Horselenberg, R., & Schmidt, H. (2002). Modeling the connection between self-reported trauma and dissociation in a student sample. *Personality and Individual Differences, 32*, 695–705.

Merckelbach, H., & Jelicic, M. (2004). Dissociative symptoms are related to endorsement of vague trauma items. *Comprehensive Psychiatry, 45*, 70–75.

Merckelbach, H., & Muris, P. (2001). The causal link between self-reported trauma and dissociation: A critical review. *Behaviour Research and Therapy, 39*, 245–254.

Merckelbach, H., Muris, P., Horselenberg, R., & Stougie, S. (2000). Dissociative experiences, response bias, and fantasy proneness in college students. *Personality and Individual Differences, 28*, 49–58.

Merckelbach, H., Muris, P., & Rassin, E. (1999). Fantasy proneness and cognitive failures as correlates of dissociative experiences. *Personality and Individual Differences, 26*, 961–967.

Merckelbach, H., Muris, P., Rassin, E., & Horselenberg, R. (2000). Dissociative experiences and interrogative suggestibility in college students. *Personality and Individual Differences, 29*, 1133–1140.

Merskey, H. (1992). The manufacture of personalities: The production of multiple personality disorder. *British Journal of Psychiatry, 160*, 327–340.

Mittenberg, W., Patton, C., Canyock, E. M., & Condit, D. C. (2002). Base rates of malingering and symptom exaggeration. *Journal of Clinical and Experimental Neuropsychology, 24*, 1094–1102.

Modestin, J., & Erni, T. (2004). Testing the dissociative taxon. *Psychiatry Research, 126*, 77–82.

Montagne, B., Sierra, M., Medford, N., Hunter, E. C. M., Baker, D., Kessels, R. P. C., . . . David, A. S. (2007). Emotional memory and perception of emotional faces in patients suffering from depersonalization disorder. *British Journal of Psychology, 98*, 517–527.

Moskowitz, A. (2004). Dissociation and violence: A review of the literature. *Trauma, Violence, and Abuse, 5*, 21–46.

Muris, P., Merckelbach, H., & Peeters, E. (2003). The links between the adolescent Dissociative Experiences Scale (A-DES), fantasy proneness, and anxiety symptoms. *Journal of Nervous and Mental Disease, 191*, 18–24.

Nairne, J. S., Pandeirada, J. N. S. (2008). Adaptive memory: Remembering with a stone-age brain. *Current Directions in Psychological Science, 17*, 239–243.

Nash, M. R., Hulsey, T. L., Sexton, M. C., Harralson, T. L., & Lambert, W. (1993). Long-term sequelae of childhood sexual abuse: Perceived family environment, psychopathology, and dissociation. *Journal of Consulting and Clinical Psychology, 61*, 276–283.

Nelson, K. R., Mattingly, M., Lee, S. A., & Schmitt, F. A. (2006). Does the arousal system contribute to near death experience? *Neurology, 66*(7), 1003–1009.

Nelson, M. D., Saykin, A. J., Flashman, L. A., & Riordan, H. J. (1998). Hippocampal volume reduction as assessed by magnetic resonance imaging: A meta-analytic study. *Archives of General Psychiatry, 55*, 433–440.

Nijenhuis, E. R., Spinhoven, P., Van Dyck, R., Van der Hart, O., & Vanderlinden, J. (1996). The development and psychometric characteristics of the Somatoform Dissociation Questionnaire (SDQ-20). *Journal of Nervous and Mental Disease, 184*, 688–694.

Nijenhuis, E. R. S., Spinhoven, P., Van Dyck, R., Van der Hart, O., & Vanderlinden, J. (1997). The development of the Somatoform Dissociation Questionnaire (SDQ 5) as a screening instrument for dissociative disorders. *Acta Psychiatrica Scandinavica, 96*, 311–318.

Nijenhuis, E. R. S., Spinhoven, P., Van Dyck, R., Van der Hart, O., & Vanderlinden, J. (1998). Psychometric characteristics of the Somatoform Dissociation Questionnaire: A replication study. *Psychotherapy and Psychosomatics, 67*, 17–23.

Nijenhuis, E., van der Hart, O., & Steel, C. (2010). Trauma-related structural dissociation of the personality. *Activitas Nervosa Superior, 52*, 1–23.

Noll, J., Trickett, P., & Putnam, F. W. (2003). A prospective investigation of the impact of childhood sexual abuse on the development of sexuality. *Journal of Consulting and Clinical Psychology, 71*(3), 575–586.

North, C. S., Ryall, J. M., Ricci, D. A., & Wetzel, R. D. (1993). *Multiple personalities, multiple disorders: Psychiatric classification and media influence.* Oxford, England: Oxford University Press.

Ogawa, J. R., Sroufe, L. A., Weinfield, N. S., Carlson, E. A., & Egeland, B. (1997). Development and the fragmented self: Longitudinal study of dissociative symptomatology in a non-clinical sample. *Development and Psychopathology, 9,* 855–879.

Orne, M. T., Dinges, D. F., & Orne, E. C. (1984). On the differential diagnosis of multiple personality in the forensic context. *International Journal of Clinical and Experimental Hypnosis, 32,* 118–169.

Persinger, M. M. (2001). The neuropsychiatry of paranormal experiences. *Neuropsychiatric Practice and Opinion, 13,* 521–522.

Piper, A. (1997). *Hoax and reality: The bizarre world of multiple personality disorder.* Northvale, NJ: Jason Aronson.

Piper, A., & Merskey, H. (2004). The persistence of folly: Critical examination of dissociative identity disorder, Part II: The defence and decline of multiple personality or dissociative identity disorder. *Canadian Journal of Psychiatry, 49,* 678–683.

Pope, H. G., Barry, S., Bodkin, A., & Hudson, J. I. (2006). Tracking scientific interest in the dissociative disorders: A study of scientific publication output, 1984–2003. *Psychotherapy & Psychosomatics, 75,* 19–24.

Pope, H. G., & Hudson, J. I. (1995). Does childhood sexual abuse cause adult psychiatric disorders? Essentials of methodology. *Journal of Psychiatry & Law, 12,* 363–381.

Pope, H. G., Hudson, J. I., Bodkin, J. A., & Oliva, P. (1998). Questionable validity of 'dissociative amnesia' in trauma victims: Evidence from prospective studies. *The British Journal of Psychiatry, 172,* 210–215.

Pope, H. G., Jonas, J. M., & Jones, B. (1982). Factitious psychosis: Phenomenology, family history, and long-term outcome of nine patients. *American Journal of Psychiatry, 139,* 1480–1483.

Pope, H. G., Poliakoff, M. B., Parker, M. P., Boynes, M., & Hudson, J. I. (2007). Is dissociative amnesia a culture-bound syndrome? Findings from a survey of historical literature. *Psychological Medicine, 37,* 225–233.

Porter, S., Birt, A. R., Yuille, J. C., & Lehman, D. R. (2000). Negotiating false memories: Interviewer and rememberer characteristics relate to memory distortion. *Psychological Science, 11,* 507–510.

Powell, R. A., & Gee, T. L. (1999). The effects of hypnosis on dissociative identity disorder: A reexamination of the evidence. *Canadian Journal of Psychiatry, 44,* 914–916.

Prohl, J., Resch, F., Parzer, P., & Brunner, R. (2001). Relationship between dissociative symptomatology and declarative and procedural memory in adolescent psychiatric patients. *Journal of Nervous and Mental Disease, 198,* 602–607.

Putnam, F. W., & Lowenstein, R. J. (2000). Dissociative identity disorder. In B. J. Sadock & V. A. Sadock (Eds.), *Kaplan and Sadock's comprehensive textbook of psychiatry* (7th ed., Vol. 1, pp. 1552–1564). Philadelphia, PA: Lippincott, Williams, & Wilkins.

Ray, W., & Faith, M. (1994). Dissociative experiences in a college age population. *Personality and Individual Differences, 18,* 223–230.

Rieber, R. W. (1999). Hypnosis, false memory and multiple personality: A trinity of affinity. *History of Psychiatry, 10,* 3–11.

Rieber, R. W. (2006). *The bifurcation of the self: The history and theory of dissociation and its disorders*. New York, NY: Springer.

Rifkin, A., Ghisalbert, D., Dimatou, S., Jin, C., & Sethi, M. (1998). Dissociative identity disorder in psychiatric inpatients. *American Journal of Psychiatry, 155*, 844–845.

Rivard, J. M., Dietz, P., Matell, D., & Widawski, M. (2002). Acute dissociative responses in law enforcement officers involved in critical shooting incidents. *Journal of Forensic Sciences, 47*, 1093–1100.

Ross, C. A. (1991). High and low dissociators in a college student population. *Dissociation: Progress in the Dissociative Disorders, 4*(3), 147–151.

Ross, C. A. (1997). *Dissociative identity disorder: Diagnosis, clinical features, and treatment of multiple personality*. New York, NY: John Wiley & Sons.

Ross, C. A. (2009a). The theory of a dissociative subtype of schizophrenia. In P. Dell & J. A. O'Neil (Eds.), *Dissociation and the dissociative disorders: DSM-V and beyond* (pp. 557–568). New York, NY: Routledge/Taylor Francis.

Ross, C. A. (2009b). Dissociative amnesia and dissociative fugue. In P. Dell & J. A. O'Neil (Eds.), *Dissociation and the dissociative disorders: DSM-V and beyond* (pp. 429–434). New York, NY: Routledge/Taylor Francis.

Ross, C. A., Anderson, G., Fleisher, W. P., & Norton, G. R. (1991). The frequency of multiple personality disorder among psychiatric inpatients. *American Journal of Psychiatry, 148*, 1717–1720.

Ross, C. A., Anderson, G., Fraser, G. A., Reagor, P., Bjornson, L., & Miller, S. D. (1992). Differentiating multiple personality disorder and dissociative disorder not otherwise specified. *Dissociation, 5*, 88–91.

Ross, C. A., Duffy, C. M. M., & Ellason J. W. (2002). Prevalence, reliability and validity of dissociative disorders in an inpatient setting. *Journal of Trauma & Dissociation, 3*, 7–17.

Ross, C. A., Ellason, J. W., & Anderson, G. (1995). A factor analysis of the dissociative experiences scale (DES) in dissociative identity disorder. *Dissociation, 8*, 229–235.

Ross, C. A., Heber, S., Norton, G. R., Anderson, D., Anderson, G., & Barchet, P. (1989). The Dissociative Disorders Interview Schedule: A structured interview. *Dissociation, 2*, 169–189.

Ross, C. A., & Norton, G. R. (1988). Multiple personality patients with a past diagnosis of schizophrenia. *Dissociation, 1*(2), 39–42.

Ross, C. A., Norton, G. R., & Wozney, K. (1989). Multiple personality disorder: An analysis of 236 cases. *Canadian Journal of Psychiatry, 34*, 413–418.

Rossini, E. D., Schwartz, D. R., & Braun, B. G. (1996). Intellectual functioning of inpatients with dissociative identity disorder and dissociative disorder not otherwise specified. Cognitive and neuropsychological aspects. *Journal of Nervous and Mental Disease, 184*, 289–294.

Sanders, B., & Giolas, M. H. (1991). Dissociation and childhood trauma in psychological disturbed adolescents. *American Journal of Psychiatry, 148*, 50–54.

Sanders, B., & Green, A. (1994). The factor structure of dissociative experiences in college students. *Dissociation, 7*, 23–27.

Sang, F. Y. P., Jáuregui-Renaud, K., Green, D. A., Bronstein, A. M., & Gresty, M. A. (2006). Depersonalisation/derealisation symptoms in vestibular disease. *Journal of Neurology, Neurosurgery, and Psychiatry, 77*, 760–766.

Sapolsky, R. M. (2000). Glucocorticoids and hippocampal atrophy in neuropsychiatric disorders. *Archives of General Psychiatry, 57*, 925–935.

Sar, V., Akyüz, G., & Dogan, O. (2007). Prevalence of dissociative disorders among women in the general population. *Psychiatry Research, 149*(1–3), 169–176.

Sar, V., Akyuz, G., Kugu, N., Ozturk, E., & Ertem-Vehid, H. (2006). Axis I dissociative disorder comorbidity in borderline personality disorder and reports of childhood trauma. *Journal of Clinical Psychiatry, 67*(10), 1583–1590.

Sar, V., Tutkun, H., Alyanak, B., Bakim, B., & Barai, I. (2000). Frequency of dissociative disorders among psychiatric outpatients in Turkey. *Comprehensive Psychiatry, 41,* 216–222.

Sarbin, T. R. (1995). On the belief that one body may be host to two or more personalities. *International Journal of Clinical and Experimental Hypnosis, 43,* 163–183.

Schore, A. N. (2009). Attachment trauma and the developing right brain: Origins of pathological dissociation. In P. F. Dell & J. A. O'Neil (Eds.), *Dissociation and dissociative disorders: DSM-5 and beyond* (pp. 107–143). New York, NY: Routledge/Taylor & Francis.

Schreiber, F. R. (1973). *Sybil.* New York, NY: Warner.

Sierra, M., Baker, D., Medford, N. & David, A. S. (2005). Unpacking the depersonalization syndrome: An exploratory factor analysis on the Cambridge Depersonalization Scale (CDS). *Psychological Medicine, 35,* 1523–1532.

Sierra, M., & Berrios, G. E. (2000). The Cambridge Depersonalisation Scale: A new instrument for the measurement of depersonalization. *Psychiatry Research, 93,* 163–164.

Sierra, M., & Berrios, G. E. (2001). The phenomenological stability of depersonalization: Comparing the old with the new. *Journal of Nervous and Mental Disease, 189,* 629–636.

Sierra, M., Phillips, M. L., Krystal, J., & David, A. S. (2003). A placebo-controlled, crossover trial of lamotrigine in depersonalization disorder. *Journal of Psychopharmacology, 17,* 103–105.

Simeon, D. (2004). Depersonalization disorder: A contemporary overview. *CNS Drugs, 18,* 343–354.

Simeon, D. (2009a). Depersonalization disorder. In P. F. Dell & J. A. O'Neil (Eds.), *Dissociation and dissociative disorders: DSM-5 and beyond* (pp. 435–446). New York, NY: Routledge/Taylor & Francis.

Simeon, D. (2009b). Neurobiology of depersonalization disorder. In P. F. Dell & J. A. O'Neil (Eds.), *Dissociation and dissociative disorders: DSM-5 and beyond* (pp. 367–372). New York, NY: Routledge/Taylor & Francis.

Simeon, D., & Abugel, J. (2006). *Feeling unreal: Depersonalization disorder and the loss of the self.* New York, NY: Oxford University Press.

Simeon, D., Gross, S., Guralnik, O., Stein, D. J., Schmeidler, J., & Hollander, E. (1997). Feeling unreal: 30 cases of DSM-III-R depersonalization disorder. *American Journal of Psychiatry, 154,* 1107–1113.

Simeon, D., Guralnik, O., Gross, S., Stein, D. J., Schmeidler, J., & Hollander, E. (1998). The detection and measurement of depersonalization disorder. *Journal of Nervous and Mental Disease, 186,* 536–542.

Simeon, D., Guralnik, O., Hazlett, E. A., Spiegel-Cohen, J., Hollander, E., & Buchsbaum, M. S. (2000). Feeling unreal: A PET study of depersonalization disorder. *American Journal of Psychiatry, 157,* 1782–1788.

Simeon, D., Guralnik, O., Schmeidler, J., & Knutelska, M. (2004). Fluoxetine therapy in depersonalization disorder: randomized clinical trial. *British Journal of Psychiatry, 185,* 31–36.

Simeon, D., Guralnik, O., Schmeidler, J., Sirof, B., & Knutelska, M. (2001). The role of childhood interpersonal trauma in depersonalization disorder. *American Journal of Psychiatry, 158,* 1027–1033.

Simeon, D., Hwu, R., & Knutelska, M. (2007). Temporal disintegration in depersonalization disorder. *Journal of Trauma and Dissociation, 8,* 11–24.

Simeon, D., Knutselska, M., Nelson, D., & Guralnik, O. (2003). Feeling unreal: A depersonalization disorder update of 117 cases. *The Journal of Clinical Psychiatry, 64*, 990–997.

Simons, R. C., & Hughes, C. C. (Eds.). (1985). *The culture-bound syndromes: Folk illnesses of psychiatric and anthropological interest.* Dordrecht, The Netherlands: D. Reidel Publishing.

Smith, S. R., & Carlson, E. B. (1996). Reliability and validity of the Adolescent Dissociative Experiences Scale. *Dissociation, 9*, 125–129.

Spanos, N. P. (1994). Multiple identity enactments and multiple personality disorder: A sociocognitive perspective. *Psychological Bulletin, 116*, 143–165.

Spanos, N. P. (1996). *Multiple identities and false memories: A sociocognitive perspective.* Washington, DC: American Psychiatric Association.

Spanos, N. P., Weekes, J. R., & Bertrand, L. D. (1985). Multiple personality: A social psychological perspective. *Journal of Abnormal Psychology, 94*, 362–376.

Stafford, J., & Lynn, S. J. (2002). Cultural scripts, childhood abuse, and multiple identities: A study of role-played enactments. *International Journal of Clinical & Experimental Hypnosis, 50*, 67–85.

Steele, K., van der Hart, O., & Nijenhuis, E. (2009). The traum-related structural dissociation of the personality. In P. F. Dell & J. A. O'Neil (Eds.), *Dissociation and the dissociative disorders* (pp. 239–258). New York, NY: Routledge/Taylor Francis.

Stein, M. B., Koverola, C., Hanna, C., & Torchia, M. G. (1997). Hippocampal volume in women victimized by childhood sexual abuse. *Psychological Medicine, 27*, 951–959.

Steinberg, M. (1985). *Structured clinical interview for DSM-III-R dissociative disorders (SCID-D).* New Haven, CT: Yale University School of Medicine.

Steinberg, M. (1994). *Structured clinical interview for DSM-IV dissociative disorders revised (SCID-D-R).* Washington, DC: American Psychiatric Press.

Steinberg, M., Rounsaville, B., & Cichetti, D., (1990). The Structured Clinical Interview for DSM-III-R dissociative disorders: Preliminary report on a new diagnostic instrument. *American Journal of Psychiatry, 147*, 76–82.

Steinberg, M., & Siegel, H. D. (2008). Advances in assessment: The differential diagnosis of dissociative identity disorder and schizophrenia. In A. Moskowitz, I. Schäfer, & M. J. Dorahy (Eds.), *Psychosis, trauma, and dissociation: Emerging perspectives on severe psychopathology* (pp. 177–189). Chichester, England: John Wiley & Sons.

Tellegen, A., & Atkinson, G. (1974). Openness to absorbing and self-altering experiences ("absorption"), a trait related to hypnotic susceptibility. *Journal of Abnormal Psychology, 83*, 268–277.

Terhune, D. B. (2009). The incidence and determinants of visual phenomenology during out-of-body experiences. *Cortex, 45*(2), 236–242.

Tsai, G. E., Condie, D., Wu, M.-T., & Chang, I.-W. (1999). Functional magnetic resonance imaging of personality switches in a woman with dissociative identity disorder. *Harvard Review of Psychiatry, 72*, 119–122.

Tutkun, H., Sar, V., Yargic, L. L., Özpulat, T., Yank, M., & Kiziltan, E. (1998). Frequency of dissociative disorders among psychiatric inpatients in a Turkish University Clinic. *American Journal of Psychiatry, 155*, 800–805.

van der Hart, O., Nijenhuis, E., Steele, K., & Brown, D. (2004). Trauma-related dissociation: Conceptual clarity lost and found. *Australian and New Zealand Journal of Psychiatry, 38*, 906–914.

van der Hart, O., Nijenhuis, E., Steele, K., & Brown, D. (2006). *The haunted self: Structural dissociation and the treatment of chronic traumatization.* New York, NY: W. W. Norton.

van der Kloet, D., Giesbrecht, T., Lynn, S. J., Merckelbach, H., & de Zutter, A. (in press). Sleep normalization and decrease in dissociative experiences: Evaluation in an inpatient sample. *Journal of Abnormal Psychology.*

van der Kloet, D., Merckelbach, H., Giesbrecht, T., & Lynn, S. J. (2011). *Dissociation, sleep, and memory: A heuristic integrative model.* Manuscript submitted for publication.

Vanderlinden, J., Van Dyck, R., Vandereycken, W., & Vertommen, H. (1991). Dissociative experiences in the general population in the Netherlands and Belgium: A study with the Dissociative Questionnaire (DIS-Q). *Dissociation: Progress in the Dissociative Disorders, 4,* 180–184.

Van Liempt, S., Vermetten, E., Geuze, E., & Westenberg, H. (2006). Pharmacotherapeutic treatment of disordered sleep in posttraumatic stress disorder: A systematic review. *International Journal of Clinical Psychopharmacology, 21*(4), 193–202.

Van Oorsouw, K., & Merckelbach, H. (2010). Detecting malingered memory problems in the civil and criminal arena. *Legal and Criminological Psychology, 15,* 97–114.

Waller, N. G. (1995). *The Dissociative Experiences Scale: The 12th Mental Measurements Yearbook* (pp. 317–318). Lincoln, NE: The Buros Institute of Mental Measurements.

Waller, N. G., Putnam, F. W., & Carlson, E. B. (1996). Types of dissociation and dissociation and dissociative types: A taxometric analysis of dissociative experiences. *Psychological Methods, 1,* 300–321.

Waller, N. G., & Ross, C. A. (1997). The prevalence and biometric structure of pathological dissociation in the general population: Taxometric and behavior genetic findings. *Journal of Abnormal Psychology, 106,* 499–510.

Watson, D. (2001). Dissociations of the night: Individual differences in sleep-related experiences and their relation to dissociation and schizotypy. *Journal of Abnormal Psychology, 110,* 526–535.

Watson, D. (2003). Investigating the construct validity of the dissociative taxon: Stability analysis of normal and pathological dissociation. *Journal of Abnormal Psychology, 112,* 298–305.

Wechsler, D. (1981). *Wechsler Adult Intelligence Scale-Revised.* San Antonio, TX: The Psychological Corporation.

Welburn, K. R., Fraser, G. A., Jordan, S. A., Cameron, C., Webb, L. M., & Raine, D. (2003). Discriminating dissociative identity disorder from schizophrenia and feigned dissociation on psychological tests and structured interview. *Journal of Trauma & Dissociation, 4*(2), 109–130.

Williamson, A. M., Feyer, A. M., Mattick, R. P., Friswell, R., & Finlay-Brown, S. (2001). Developing measures of fatigue using an alcohol comparison to validate the effects of fatigue on performance. *Accident Analysis and Prevention, 33,* 313–326.

Wolfradt, U., & Meyer, T. (1998). Interrogative suggestibility, anxiety and dissociation among anxious patients and normal controls. *Personality and Individual Differences, 25,* 425–432.

Wright, D. B., & Loftus, E. F. (1999). Measuring dissociation: Comparison of alternative forms of the dissociative experiences scale. *American Journal of Psychology, 112,* 497–519.

Wright, D. B., & Osborne, J. E. (2005). Dissociation, cognitive failures, and working memory. *American Journal of Psychology, 118,* 103–113.

# CHAPTER 15

# Sexual Dysfunctions and Paraphilias

LORI A. BROTTO and CAROLIN KLEIN

T HE SEXUAL AND gender identity disorders are classified according to the *Diagnostic and Statistical Manual of Mental Disorders*, 4th Edition, Text Revised (DSM-IV-TR; American Psychiatric Association [APA], 2000) and are divided into three groups: (1) sexual dysfunctions, which characterize sexual problems related to the sexual response cycle or pain; (2) paraphilias, which are recurrent, sexually arousing fantasies, urges, or behaviors involving nonconventional or nonconsenting persons and/or objects; and (3) gender identity disorder, which involves strong discomfort with one's own sex and the desire to be the other sex (APA, 2000). In this chapter we will focus on the sexual dysfunctions and paraphilias, whereas gender identity disorder will be covered in a separate chapter. In part, this division is attributed to the fact that the former relate to sex, whereas the latter relates to gender. Furthermore, it has been suggested that the categorization of gender identity variants be moved to a nonpsychiatric disorders section of the *DSM*, declared as a nonpsychiatric medical condition, or removed from the *DSM* altogether (Meyer-Bahlburg, 2010), whereas sexual dysfunctions and paraphilias are likely to remain "as neighbors" in the *DSM*. We will organize our remarks about each of these categories according to the more broad headings of epidemiology, assessment and diagnosis, and treatment, and we will also consider proposals for revised criteria in the *DSM-5*.

## PART I: SEXUAL DYSFUNCTIONS

### DESCRIPTION OF SEXUAL DISORDERS

Nearly 15 years have passed since the approval and subsequent widespread availability of the oral treatments for male sexual dysfunction (e.g., sildenafil, vardenafil, and tadalafil); as a result, research exploring the pathophysiology, epidemiology, assessment, and treatment of sexual dysfunctions has had an unprecedented surge. Methodological sophistication has soared, particularly in the area of neural imaging for low desire and genetic studies of orgasmic dysfunction and dyspareunia. As experts are critically examining diagnostic criteria in preparation for the 5th edition of the

*Diagnostic and Statistical Manual of Mental Disorders* (2013) and the 11th edition of the *International Classification of Diseases* (2014), there has also been an intensified examination of the reliability and validity of these categories of sexual disorders.

The disorders of sexual dysfunction are divided in the *DSM-IV-TR* according to whether they relate to problems in desire, arousal, orgasm, or pain. This classification system is based on Masters and Johnson's four-stage human sexual response cycle (Masters & Johnson, 1966), which was based on observations of 700 men and women studied in their St. Louis clinic in the 1960s and 1970s. On the basis of arousal patterns, they formulated their model in which sexual stimulation is thought to proceed through a linear sequence of excitement, plateau, orgasm, and resolution. Subsequently, both American psychiatrists Harold Lief (1977) and Helen Singer Kaplan (1979) strongly advocated that desire be added to the human sexual response cycle and that it be acknowledged as the beginning of healthy sexual responding. Lief further coined the term "inhibited sexual desire," which was added to the *DSM-III*. The disorders of sexual pain were not a component of Masters and Johnson's cycle; however, their prevalence in the general population necessitated their inclusion into the taxonomy.

This four-category system of diagnosing sexual dysfunctions has been commonplace since *DSM-III* in 1980. However, given numerous criticisms about this linear response cycle, particularly when conceptualizing women's sexual problems, more recently there have been attempts to refine these categories. In particular, concerns about the lack of generalizability of the sexual response cycle for women are that (1) it is based on the sexual response patterns of men; (2) it assumes a linear progression of sexual experience from desire to arousal to orgasm; however, healthy sexual experiences can progress in any order and do not need to proceed in this sequence for satisfaction to occur; (3) many of the experiences that are considered normal parts of female sexual response (e.g., fantasizing) are not reported in all women; and (4) characteristics of the sample on which the human sexual response cycle were based are considered biased (Hill & Preston, 1996; Klusmann, 2002; Regan & Berscheid, 1996). Thus, alternative conceptualizations have been offered. One of these was proposed by the "Definitions Committee" sponsored by the American Foundation for Urologic Diseases in which an international panel of experts in women's sexual dysfunction was convened to revise existing criteria for the female sexual dysfunctions (Basson et al., 2003). The committee retained the four categories; however, some criteria were improved and/or deleted based upon the evidence-based literature.

An alternative system for classifying sexual dysfunctions as "problems" was proposed by the New View Task Force, led by sexologist Leonore Tiefer. The resultant "New View Document" (Kaschak & Tiefer, 2002; Tiefer, 2001) was a radical departure from the *DSM* classification system and suggested that sexual problems in women have been overdiagnosed and medicalized, and the designating of "dysfunctions" is unhelpful. This alternate system proposes that sexual problems can be a result of sociocultural, political, or economic factors; partner and relationship status; psychological factors; or medical factors, and removes the emphasis on biological components of sexual complaints. Empirical support for the New View system is sparse; however, some data suggest that 98% of the sexual issues in one sample of British women could be classified by the New View scheme (Nicholls, 2008).

We now turn to the specific sexual dysfunctions in men and women. The *DSM-IV-TR* (APA, 2000) divides these into (1) Sexual Desire Disorders, (2) Sexual Arousal

Disorders, (3) Orgasmic Disorders, (4) Sexual Pain Disorders, (5) Sexual Dysfunction due to a General Medical Condition, and (6) Sexual Dysfunction Not Otherwise Specified (NOS). In addition, each sexual dysfunction diagnosis has several specifiers, including Lifelong (i.e., the person has always had the problem) versus Acquired (i.e., the problem is new in onset); Generalized (i.e., the problem exists in all sexual situations and with all partners) versus Situational (i.e., the problem occurs in only select situations or with certain partners); and if the dysfunction is due to psychological factors or to combined psychological and biological factors.

## CLINICAL PICTURE

### HYPOACTIVE SEXUAL DESIRE DISORDER

Hypoactive Sexual Desire Disorder (HSDD) is defined as "persistently or recurrently deficient (or absent) sexual fantasies and desire for sexual activity" (APA, 2000). Although no distinction is made in the *DSM-IV-TR* between HSDD in men and women, we discuss these phenomena separately by gender given that they are experienced and expressed differently (Baumeister, Catanese, & Vohs, 2001).

In men, Maurice (2005) operationalized low sexual desire as (1) reduced sexual thoughts, fantasies, and dreams, (2) reduced sexual behavior with a partner, and (3) reduced sexual behavior with oneself through masturbation. HSDD in women has been the focus of much recent media attention given the promising findings of testosterone for women's complaints of absent desire, and also because of recent controversies over how to best define low desire. In particular, there is a high degree of overlap between sexual desire and arousal in women (e.g., Brotto, Heiman, & Tolman, 2009), leading to the suggestion that sexual desire and sexual arousal may be indistinguishable for women and may, therefore, be merged in future diagnostic systems (Brotto, 2010a; Graham, 2010).

### SEXUAL AVERSION DISORDER

Although classified as a sexual desire disorder, much less is known about Sexual Aversion Disorder (SAD) than HSDD. Originally described by Kaplan (1987), SAD is defined as "persistent or recurrent extreme aversion to, and avoidance of, all (or almost all) genital sexual contact with a sexual partner," (APA, 2000). The aversion and subsequent avoidance are highly distressing and are thought to be due to a marked anxiety response that may focus either directly on genital sexual contact or on other nongenital aspects of sexual expression such as kissing or hugging (Katz, Gipson, Kearl, & Kriskovich, 1989). Individuals with SAD may experience panic attacks that lead to impairment in their interpersonal relations as well as avoidance of all potential sexual encounters. There has been virtually no empirical data on SAD in the past 20 years, and very little is known about its prevalence, etiology, and course.

### SEXUAL AROUSAL DISORDERS

Arousal disorders are diagnosed according to impairments in physical genital response. Interestingly, whereas earlier editions of the *DSM* also included attention to subjective sexual arousal, the *DSM-IV-TR* focuses only on genital lubrication (in women) and erectile function (in men). In men, Erectile Disorder (ED), also often referred to in the medical field as Erectile Dysfunction, is defined as "persistent or recurrent inability to attain, or to maintain until completion of sexual activity, an adequate erection," which causes distress (APA, 2000). In women, Female Sexual Arousal Disorder (FSAD) is defined as "persistent or recurrent inability to attain, or to maintain until completion of the sexual activity an adequate lubrication, swelling response of sexual excitement" (APA, 2000). In the gyneco-logic setting, it has been estimated that as many as 75% of women seeking routine care complain of inadequate genital lubrication (Nusbaum, Gamble, Skinner, & Heiman, 2000). In the clinical setting, however, arousal complaints that are inde-pendent of desire and/or orgasm complaints are rarely seen, suggesting that FSAD may not exist independent of other sexual difficulties (Segraves & Segraves, 1991). Others have argued that there may be subtypes of FSAD, which reflect various combinations of purely subjective (i.e., mental or psychological) versus physiolog-ical arousal difficulties (Basson, 2002). Most recently, FSAD has been criticized for focusing exclusively on genital lubrication and not on impairments in subjective sexual arousal (Graham, 2010)—the latter of which are more often the presenting complaint in the clinical setting.

A relatively new clinical syndrome, Persistent Genital Arousal Disorder (PGAD), has been described as "spontaneous intrusive and unwanted genital arousal in the absence of sexual interest and desire" (Basson et al., 2003; Leiblum & Nathan, 2001). Women with PGAD experience persistent and unwanted genital arousal that is often only temporarily relieved by orgasm. Research on PGAD is relatively new, and epidemiological and pathophysiology data are extremely limited.

### ORGASMIC DISORDERS

Orgasm disorders in men are divided into Premature Ejaculation (PE) and Male Orgasmic Disorder (MOD)—the former defined as ejaculation too early and the latter as ejaculation later than desired—with both causing significant distress. Given that the prevalence, etiology, and treatments for these ejaculatory disorders in men are very different, we discuss them separately.

*Premature Ejaculation*   The *DSM-IV-TR* defines PE, also often referred to as rapid ejaculation and early ejaculation, as "persistent or recurrent ejaculation with minimal sexual stimulation before, on, or shortly after penetration and before the person wishes it" (APA, 2000). Men with PE report lack of control over ejaculation and fewer than desired number of thrusts during intercourse (Rowland et al., 2004). PE has an impact on the man's partner, given that the defining criterion is that ejaculation takes place before, on, or shortly after penetration *with a partner*. In fact, men with PE report fulfilling a partner's needs as being very important to their own rating of sexual satisfaction (Rowland et al., 2004), and Symonds et al. (Symonds, Roblin, Hart, & Althof, 2003) found that 50% of men reported distress-ing effects of their PE on either finding new relationships or on not satisfying a current partner.

*Male Orgasmic Disorder*   Also known as delayed or retarded ejaculation, MOD is defined as "persistent or recurrent delay in, or absence of, orgasm following a normal sexual excitement phase during sexual activity that the clinician, taking into account the person's age, judges to be adequate in focus, intensity, and duration" (APA, 2000). Because the delay leads to extended sexual activity, some have suggested that it provides a prolonged period of penetration, thus enhancing a female partner's potential for pleasure. Although this may be true, MOD is associated with significant distress in both the man and his partner.

*Female Orgasmic Disorder*   The study of women's orgasms originated with Freud, who described clitoral orgasms as immature and vaginal orgasms as sexually mature—a theory that has now been discarded. The *DSM-IV-TR* defines Female Orgasmic Disorder (FOD) as "persistent or recurrent delay in, or absence of, orgasm following a normal sexual excitement phase. If there is insufficient arousal leading to anorgasmia, the diagnosis is simply one of FSAD and not FOD (Brotto, Bitzer, Laan, Leiblum, & Luria, 2010). Women exhibit wide variability in the type or intensity of stimulation that triggers orgasm. The diagnosis of FOD should be based on the clinician's judgment that the woman's orgasmic capacity is less than would be reasonable for her age, sexual experience, and the adequacy of sexual stimulation she receives (APA, 2000). Women who are able to reach orgasm via clitoral stimulation only and not through vaginal penetration do not have an orgasm dysfunction.

SEXUAL PAIN DISORDERS

Because Masters and Johnson's human sexual response cycle formed the basis for the classification of sexual dysfunctions within the *DSM*, the inclusion of the sexual pain disorders may appear perplexing. This has been an area of intense controversy with sexual pain experts, who argue that sexual pain disorders should be placed with other disorders of pain in the somatoform disorders section of the *DSM* (Binik, 2005, 2010a). Compared to sexual pain disorders in women, comparably less has been published on sexual pain in men.

*Dyspareunia in Women*   Vulvodynia describes chronic vulvar pain or discomfort, but it is not a specific diagnosis. Provoked Vestibulodynia (PVD; formerly Vulvar Vestibulitis Syndrome) is the most common cause of dyspareunia and is diagnosed when there is sharp, shooting pain upon direct stimulation of the vulvar vestibule.

*Vaginismus*   Vaginismus is characterized by significant tension of the pelvic floor, not due to a structural/physical abnormality, which prevents penetration of the vagina. It is often associated with a phobic-like avoidance of sexual and genital contact, as well as fear and anticipation of pain. Vaginismus is highly comorbid with dyspareunia, such that women with vaginismus who are phobic of pain often experience vulvo-vaginal pain, and women with dyspareunia experience vaginismus. Because they are often difficult to differentiate (de Kruiff, Ter Kuile, Weijenborg, & Van Lankveld, 2000), there is a proposal that they be merged into one condition for *DSM-5* (Binik, 2010a, 2010b).

## DIAGNOSTIC CONSIDERATIONS

Primary care providers are often the first point of contact for individuals with sexual concerns. Adequate assessment requires a thorough biopsychosocial approach, including attention to early family history, relationship and sexual history, and psychiatric status and history, and may require the assistance of a sexual health expert. In some cases, preexisting and confounding contributors may be directly responsible for the sexual issues. For example, relationship factors can mask as sexual dysfunction, as these constructs are highly correlated (e.g., Dennerstein, Lehert, Guthrie, & Burger, 2007). Problems in the relationship can directly impact sexual functioning, and difficulties expressing one's sexual needs can negatively impact sexual desire. In general, men have more difficulty than women with discussing emotional and sexual issues (Banmen & Vogel, 1985). It is important to note that some decline in sexual function is normative with age and relationship duration (Klusmann, 2002) and should not be considered a sexual dysfunction. The clinician is advised to take into account factors that affect sexual function, such as age, novelty of the sexual partner or situation, and recent frequency of sexual activity, before making a sexual diagnosis.

Sometimes a sexual difficulty may be an adaptive reaction to a stressful or aversive situation. For example, in homosexuals who are ashamed or insecure about their sexual orientation and who are, thus, in heterosexual relationships, sexual desire may be low in response to individuals of the opposite sex but may be satisfactory toward individuals of the desired sex (Sandfort & de Keizer, 2001). In this case, a diagnosis of sexual desire disorder would not be warranted. Balon (2010) has suggested that a clinician consider "Adjustment Disorder with Disturbed Sexual Functioning" to account for situations where sexual difficulties emerge in response to an identifiable stressor and cease once the stressor has ended. This would orient treatment to the stressor and may reduce the likelihood of prematurely resorting to pharmacological aids.

## EPIDEMIOLOGY

In the past decade, there have been several international surveys aimed at determining the prevalence of sexual difficulties. The National Health and Social Life Survey (NHSLS), a population-based study of 3,159 American men and women between the ages of 18 and 59 (Laumann, Gagnon, Michael, & Michaels, 1994), had an excellent response rate (79%) and used a combination of face-to-face interviews and questionnaires. The authors inquired about (1) lack of sexual desire, (2) arousal difficulties, (3) problems achieving climax or ejaculation, (4) anxiety about sexual performance, (5) climaxing or ejaculating too quickly, (6) pain during intercourse, and (7) not finding sex pleasurable. The NHSLS found a total prevalence for sexual difficulties of 43% in women and 31% in men (Laumann, Paik, & Rosen, 1999), although these figures may be inflated because the study did not inquire about distress arising from sexual complaints.

The specific prevalence rates for each sexual difficulty in men and women are presented in Tables 15.1 and 15.2, respectively. Being married and having a higher educational level were each associated with significantly lower rates of sexual

**Table 15.1**

Prevalence (%) of Sexual Difficulties According to Age in Men Aged 18–59 (n = 1249) in the National Health and Social Life Survey (Laumann et al., 1999)

| Sexual Difficulty | Age | | | |
|---|---|---|---|---|
| | 18–29 | 30–39 | 40–49 | 50–59 |
| Lack of interest in sex | 14 | 13 | 15 | 17 |
| Unable to achieve orgasm | 7 | 7 | 9 | 9 |
| Climax too early | 30 | 32 | 28 | 31 |
| Sex not pleasurable | 10 | 8 | 9 | 6 |
| Anxious about performance | 19 | 17 | 19 | 14 |
| Trouble maintaining or achieving an erection | 7 | 9 | 11 | 18 |

difficulties in men and women. Differences according to ethnic status were more prominent for women than for men, with African American women reporting lower levels of sexual desire and pleasure than Caucasian women, but Caucasian women reporting more sexual pain than African American women. In contrast, both groups had higher rates of sexual difficulty than Hispanic women. Emotional or stress-related problems were strongly associated with sexual difficulties, whereas physical health-related problems were more predictive of sexual dysfunction in men only. A decline in social status was related to an increased risk for all types of sexual difficulty for women but only with erectile disorder in men. Quality of life significantly predicted sexual difficulties, particularly for women (Laumann et al., 1999).

Another epidemiological survey assessed 1,335 women and 1,475 men aged 18 to 74 who lived in Sweden (Fugl-Meyer & Sjogren Fugl-Meyer, 1999), and a third study assessed 13,882 women and 13,618 men from 29 countries (Global Study of Sexual Attitudes and Behaviors [GSSAB; Laumann et al., 2005]), with the latter collecting information on the prevalence of sexual concerns in men and women aged 40 to 80, as well as additional important information on correlates of sexual difficulties. Data from each of these studies are discussed as follows.

**Table 15.2**

Prevalence (%) of sexual difficulties according to age in women aged 18–59 (n = 1486) in the National Health and Social Life Survey (Laumann et al., 1999).

| Sexual Difficulty | Age | | | |
|---|---|---|---|---|
| | 18–29 | 30–39 | 40–49 | 50–59 |
| Lack of interest in sex | 32 | 32 | 30 | 27 |
| Unable to achieve orgasm | 26 | 28 | 22 | 23 |
| Exerienced pain during sex | 21 | 15 | 13 | 8 |
| Sex not pleasurable | 27 | 24 | 17 | 17 |
| Anxious about performance | 16 | 11 | 11 | 6 |
| Trouble lubricating | 19 | 18 | 21 | 27 |

## HYPOACTIVE SEXUAL DESIRE DISORDER

Based on the findings from the NHSLS, low desire occurs in approximately 15% of American men and 30% of American women aged 19 to 59 (Laumann et al., 1999). These numbers are in line with those of the Swedish study, which found the prevalence of low sexual desire to be approximately 16% in men and between 27% to 34% in women (Fugl-Meyer & Sjogren Fugl-Meyer, 1999). Men aged 66 to 74 reported the highest prevalence of low desire at 41% (Fugl-Meyer & Sjogren Fugl-Meyer, 1999). The GSSAB found a very high prevalence of HSDD in women aged 40 to 80 from the Middle East and Southeast Asia (43%; Laumann et al., 2005), while the prevalence in men was found to be approximately 22% to 28%. Among women seeking routine gynecologic care, the rate of low sexual interest has been found to be even higher, at 87% (Nusbaum et al., 2000); however, when including distress in the diagnosis, the prevalence of low desire in women may drop to less than 10% (Bancroft, Loftus, & Long, 2003).

## SEXUAL AROUSAL DISORDERS

According to the NHSLS, the prevalence of ED is 7% in men aged 18 to 29 and 18% in men aged 50 to 59 (Laumann et al., 1999). Difficulties in attaining an erection are age-associated, with a prevalence of 24% being found in men aged 66 to 74 (Fugl-Meyer & Sjogren Fugl-Meyer, 1999), and a prevalence of 58% being found in men aged 75 to 79 (Monga, Bettencourt, & Barrett-Connor, 2002). Outpatient settings reveal much higher rates of ED. For example, of 1,352 Polish men seeking routine care in an outpatient setting, 43% met criteria for ED (Haczynski et al., 2006). There are also cross-cultural differences in ED prevalence, as shown in the GSSAB study, where there was double the rate in East (27.1%) and Southeast (28.1%) Asia compared to Western countries (Laumann et al., 2005).

Using the *DSM-IV-TR* definition of FSAD, which focuses on an insufficient lubrication-swelling response, prevalence rates range from 10.9% to 31.2% (Laumann et al., 1999; Mercer et al., 2003; Oberg, Fugl-Meyer, & Fugl-Meyer, 2004; Witting et al., 2008), with higher rates once again being found in Southeast (34.2%) and East (37.9%) Asia (Laumann et al., 2005). Bancroft and colleagues (2003) defined low arousal somewhat differently (i.e., decreased sexual arousal during sexual activity, decreased genital tingling, and decreased enjoyment of genital touch) and found this affected 12.2% of women. The only other study to assess the prevalence of subjective sexual arousal difficulties found a prevalence of 17% (Dunn, Croft, and Hackett, 1998). It is notable that the latter subjective arousal impairments are more commonly the presenting complaint in sex therapy clinics, whereas difficulties with lubrication are more likely to present at gynecologic offices or that of the primary care provider.

## PREMATURE EJACULATION

PE affects approximately 30% of men aged 18 to 59 (Laumann et al., 1999) and is, therefore, considered the most prevalent male sexual dysfunction. This prevalence is relatively uniform around the world, except in the Middle East, where rates are much lower at approximately 12.4% (Laumann et al., 2005); however, controversy in what defines "too early" has led to differing prevalence rates, as the national probability study in Sweden found a prevalence of only 9% (Fugl-Meyer & Sjogren Fugl-Meyer, 1999).

## MALE ORGASMIC DISORDER

Delayed is much less prevalent than rapid or premature ejaculation, with its prevalence ranging from 2% to 8% (Fugl-Meyer & Sjogren Fugl-Meyer, 1999; Laumann et al., 1999). Among older men, the prevalence ranges between 9.1% (Northern Europe) to 21.1% (Southeast Asia; Laumann et al., 2005).

## FEMALE ORGASMIC DISORDER

The prevalence in Swedish and American probability samples ranges between 22% to 25% (Fugl-Meyer & Sjogren Fugl-Meyer, 1999; Laumann et al., 1999), with the highest prevalence in the youngest age cohort, perhaps due to a lack of sexual skill and high partner turnover. Rates of anorgasmia are also culturally determined, with the highest prevalence of FOD (41.2%) being in women from Southeast Asia (Laumann et al., 2005).

## DYSPAREUNIA

Pain elicited from sexual activity affects approximately 14% of American women (Laumann et al., 1999), 30% of East Asian and Southeast Asian women (Laumann et al., 2005), and is one of the most common sexual complaints expressed during routine gynecologic examinations (72%; Nusbaum et al., 2000). Among sexually active adolescent women, the prevalence of pain with intercourse is 20% (Landry & Bergeron, 2009). The prevalence of vaginismus ranges from 1% to 6% of women based on a large review (Weijmar Schultz & Van de Wiel, 2005). Estimates of the prevalence of male dyspareunia are sparse, ranging from 3% to 5% in Western countries to 10% to 12% in the Middle East and Southeast Asia (Laumann et al., 2005). Approximately 14% of gay men experience anodyspareunia (Damon & Rosser, 2005).

Across epidemiological studies, there are methodological concerns that raise doubt about the accuracy of these figures and concerns about the potential for the medicalization of sexuality (Tiefer, 2002). In part, this debate is centered on the notion that a sexual difficulty is not necessarily a dysfunction if such a large proportion of the population experiences it. Thus, Bancroft and colleagues (2003) assessed the extent to which sexual difficulties were associated with distress about the sexual relationship and distress about one's own sexuality. They suggested that 24% of the sample experienced a sexual problem that evoked distress (almost half that reported by the NHSLS), and that the findings from the NHSLS are likely inflated. Furthermore, other researchers note that the positive relationship between low desire and age disappears when distress is taken into account (Hayes, Dennerstein, Bennett, Fairley, 2008). Finally, several studies have found a high prevalence of sexual satisfaction despite the presence of sexual symptoms (i.e., low desire, problematic arousal; Cain et al., 2003).

## PSYCHOLOGICAL AND BIOLOGICAL ASSESSMENT

A thorough biopsychosocial interview is considered foundational in the assessment of sexual difficulties. An important aspect in assessing sexual dysfunction is determining whether the problem is related to a psychological versus a biological/organic etiology or both. It is also important for the clinician to distinguish lifelong (primary) versus acquired (secondary) and generalized versus situational difficulties as these may point to important etiological factors. For example, clinicians should inquire about morning erections to gain a sense of the degree to which ED is situational or generalized. Complete loss of morning erections suggests a vascular or neurological component to the ED, and a referral to a qualified urologist is indicated.

Assessment involves face-to-face interviews of the presenting person, together with and separately from the partner, covering known and supposed predisposing, precipitating, and perpetuating issues relevant to the sexual difficulty. These include assessments of mood and general psychiatric status, medications and medical comorbidities, psychosexual history, and personal history. Although many self-report questionnaires are available, none can replace a thorough clinical interview (Brotto et al., 2010).

Accurate assessment of medical factors often requires physical and laboratory examinations. In men, testosterone that is free, bound to albumin, and bound to SHBG should be measured first thing in the morning. A thorough assessment of arousal dysfunction in women involves separately assessing for difficulties in mental sexual arousal versus genital excitement and includes a physical examination of the level of voluntary control of the pelvic floor muscles, pelvic floor muscle tonus, presence of vaginal wall prolapse, signs of vaginal atrophy, size of introitus, presence of discharge, evidence of infection (acute or chronic), epithelial disorders, and/or pain.

The diagnosis of PVD is made with the cotton swab test in which the vestibule is palpated with a cotton swab and the woman reports areas of particular tenderness or pain. In addition to pain and tenderness upon touch, there is erythema (redness) in the area of the vestibule (Friedrich, 1987). During such an assessment, it is important for the clinician to elicit as much information as possible regarding the qualities of pain (location, intensity, characteristics). Because the elicitation of pain may evoke distressing emotions for the woman, it is important for the clinician to be sensitive to the woman's emotional state and only conduct the genital exam if sufficient explanation and preparation has been given.

With respect to vaginismus, the vaginal muscle spasm that is featured in the *DSM-IV-TR* definition (APA, 2000) is considered to be an unreliable characteristic of the disorder (Reissing, Binik, Khalifé, Cohen & Amsel, 2004); therefore, confirmation of its presence is not a prerequisite for making a diagnosis. Instead, the diagnosis is largely based on the patient's self-report of difficulties with intercourse, including anticipation of pain, anxiety, and phobic avoidance.

Assessment of PE in clinical trials has adopted the stop-watch technique in which the duration of time between penetration and ejaculation is monitored, usually by the man's partner. This additional layer of performance anxiety may artificially inflate the man's dysfunction, leaving this technique suboptimal, particularly when making a diagnosis of PE. Accurate assessment can also be confounded by embarrassment

(Symonds et al., 2003). Grenier and Byers (2001) found marked differences in the prevalence of PE depending on the operational definition of "rapid." They concluded that a multifaceted approach should include assessment of behavior, affect, self-efficacy, and the degree of severity of different dimensions of PE.

## ETIOLOGICAL CONSIDERATIONS

As implied in the previous section on assessment, all of the sexual dysfunctions are considered to be biopsychosocial in their etiology. Although previous editions of the *DSM-IV-TR* offered the specifiers "due to psychological factors" or "due to combined factors" (APA, 2000), it is now recognized that this delineation is rarely possible. Perhaps unlike any other area of function, sexual functioning involves an integration of all organ systems of the body, the vascular system, muscles, and the brain, making multidisciplinary collaboration the norm rather than the exception.

### HYPOACTIVE SEXUAL DESIRE DISORDER

Low desire in both men and women is considered to result from a combination of organic and psychological factors. In women, relationship duration, age, feelings for one's partner, and depression have all been associated with HSDD (Brotto et al., 2010). In fact, 27% to 62% of women with low desire also meet criteria for a depressive disorder (Hartmann, Heiser, Ruffer-Hesse, & Kloth, 2002; Phillips & Slaughter, 2000). Interestingly, a few studies report that depressed mood is associated with increased frequency of masturbation (Cyranowski et al., 2004; Frolich & Meston, 2002)—one potential index of sexual desire. Low testosterone and testosterone metabolites have not been found to significantly differentiate women with and without HSDD, although the latter are found to have lower levels of the androgen precursor, dihydroepiandrosterone (DHEA; Basson, Brotto, Petkau, & Labrie, 2010). Women with HSDD show different patterns of neural activation particularly in neural circuits involved with encoding arousing stimuli, retrieval of past erotic situations, or both (Arnow et al., 2009).

Recent studies on cultural influences in low desire have shown women from East Asian heritage to have lower levels of desire compared to women from European descent. Moreover, among the East Asian women, those with higher levels of mainstream (i.e., Westernized) acculturation had higher sexual desire than those who retained their culture or heritage (Woo, Brotto, & Gorzalka, 2011). The variable "sex guilt," or "a generalized expectancy for self-mediated punishment for violating or for anticipating violating standards of proper sexual conduct," has been shown to mediate the relationship between culture and sexual desire in women. Therefore, sex guilt may be a future treatment target among ethnic minority women presenting with sexual desire complaints (Woo et al., 2011).

Androgen deprivation and hyperprolactinemia seem to play a more pertinent role in HSDD in men (Brotto, 2010b). Hyperprolactinemia may result from antipsychotic medications or prolactin-secreting tumors. With respect to androgen deprivation, as men age, sex hormone binding globulin (SHBG) levels increase, thereby decreasing the level of free testosterone. Similarly, bioavailable testosterone begins to decline when men are in their 30s and 40s, and continues to decline throughout the life span

(Seidman, 2003). A syndrome known as Androgen Deficiency in the Aging Male (ADAM) or Partial ADAM (PADAM) can include fatigue, depression, reduced sex drive, erectile disorder, and changes in mood and cognition (Morales, Heaton, & Carson, 2000). There is significant comorbidity between ED and HSDD in men such that men experiencing erectile difficulties eventually have reduced levels of desire.

## AROUSAL DISORDERS

In men, hypothyroidism, hypogonadism, and hyperprolactinemia are also associated with ED (Morales et al., 2004). Radical genital or pelvic surgeries can result in a sudden loss of erectile function, such as the case with prostate cancer surgery (Bolt, Evans, & Marshall, 1987; Stanford et al., 2000), especially if the procedure did not involve nerve-sparing techniques. Among men treated for diabetes, the prevalence of ED is 28% (Feldman, Goldstein, Hatzichristou, Krane, & McKinlay, 1994). Overall, any medical condition that causes blood vessel damage will likely negatively impact erectile function. Although often presumed to have an exclusive organic etiology, it is suspected that there are many cases of ED where psychological factors are responsible but go unrecognized. For example, major depressive disorder has been strongly associated with ED (Araujo, Durante, Feldman, Goldstein, & McKinley, 1998). Distinguishing ED that is secondary to the depression itself versus as a result of antidepressant use (Ferguson, 2001) is an important consideration.

Performance anxiety is also strongly associated with erectile dysfunction. Anxiety or stress may activate the sympathetic nervous system, which can both increase smooth muscle tone and interfere with signals from the sacral spinal cord. The man with no prior history of ED who fails to reach an erection one time due to stress or other factors may become concerned about his future erectile ability such that his ED is maintained by performance anxiety. Implicit in this example is the phenomenon that factors that maintain a sexual dysfunction may not be the same factors that initially triggered the complaint.

Using the current definition of FSAD in women, which focuses on insufficient lubrication, it is assumed that many, if not most, of these cases may be attributable to insufficient estrogen as during menopause (Brotto et al., 2010). However, using vaginal photoplethysmography as an indirect measure of genital vagocongestion, several studies of women with FSAD have found normal levels of genital arousal despite self-reported impaired genital responsivity (Laan, van Driel, & van Lunsen, 2008). For this reason, it is assumed that impairments in genital blood flow do not underlie the genital arousal complaints of women with FSAD. The reasons for women's lack of awareness of their genital responding, otherwise known as desynchrony, compared to men (Chivers, Seto, Lalumiere, Laan, & Grimbos, 2010) has become the focus of study because it may shed light on different models of sexual responding between the sexes.

## PREMATURE EJACULATION

The precise etiology of PE is unknown, but a combination of psychological, biological, and behavioral components likely contribute. Much of the research exploring etiology in PE is based on rodent studies in which serotonergic disruption is the primary etiological factor. Stimulation of $5\text{-HT}_{1A}$ receptors in rats leads to rapid ejaculation, whereas hyposensitivity at the $5\text{-HT}_{2C}$ receptor shortens ejaculation time (Waldinger, 2002). Studies in rodents have led Waldinger, a leading authority on PE, to formulate the Ejaculation Threshold Hypothesis, which posits that men with PE have a lower ejaculatory setpoint (threshold) due to low serotonin neurotransmission, leading them to tolerate only a very low amount of sexual arousal prior to ejaculation (Waldinger, 2005). There is also evidence of a genetic predisposition to PE given the finding that 71% of first-degree relatives of men with PE also have the condition (Waldinger, Rietschel, Nothen, Hengeveld, & Olivier, 1998).

Acquired and/or situational PE may suggest a more psychological etiology related to early sexual experiences, low frequency of sexual activity, or poor ejaculatory control techniques. Among men with PE, 50% of the female partners meet criteria for anorgasmia and 54% meet criteria for hypoactive sexual desire (Fugl-Meyer & Sjogren Fugl-Meyer, 1999), suggesting a reciprocal relationship between PE and women's sexual complaints. The possibility that performance anxiety leads to loss of ejaculatory control was forwarded by Masters and Johnson (1970), but more recent research does not support the role for anxiety in PE in the clinical or the laboratory setting (Strassberg, Kelly, Carroll, & Kircher, 1987). Instead, high anxiety, if present, may be the consequence, rather than the cause, of PE.

## MALE ORGASMIC DISORDER

Waldinger (2005) has speculated that organic factors related to genetics have a likely role in the etiology of MOD. In particular, aberrations in the serotonergic system, such as hyperactivity at the $5\text{-HT}_{2C}$ receptor and hypoactivity at the $5\text{-HT}_{1A}$ receptor, have been found in rodent studies to be related to delayed ejaculation. Androgen deficiency with aging and/or hypogonadism is also linked to MOD, as are age and prostate disease (Laumann et al., 2005). Injury to the lumbar sympathetic ganglia (i.e., such as from multiple sclerosis) may also lead to MOD. One chart review has suggested that idiosyncratic masturbatory style (e.g., using rapid stimulation or pressure in a manner that is not easily duplicated by partnered sexual activity), as well as using a variant sexual fantasy (e.g., fantasy about S&M), act as predisposing factors for MOD (Perelman, 2006).

## FEMALE ORGASMIC DISORDER

The same organic factors implicated in retarded ejaculation in men have been associated with FOD in women (e.g., neurologic injury, SSRI use, alcohol). There may also be a genetic aspect to orgasmic difficulties in women given the finding of higher correlations between orgasmic frequency during masturbation and orgasmic frequency during sexual intercourse in monozygotic twins compared to dizygotic twins (Dunne et al., 1997). In addition, the heritability for orgasm problems with intercourse is 31% to 34%, and the rate for orgasm problems in masturbation is 37% to 45% (Dunn, Cherkas, & Spector, 2005).

Psychological factors found to be associated with anorgasmia in women include lower educational levels, high religiosity, sex guilt (Laumann et al., 1999), and a dim outlook for the future (Laumann et al., 2005). Although sexual abuse has been associated with anorgasmia in some studies, other studies have failed to find such a relationship. There does not appear to be a correlation between relationship satisfaction and orgasmic ability, given that many women are sexually satisfied with their partners despite not consistently or, perhaps, ever attaining orgasm with intercourse (Basson, 2004).

## Dyspareunia

Pelvic or vulvar surgeries, chemotherapy, or radiation have all been associated with dyspareunia (Amsterdam, Carter, & Krychman, 2006), as have menopausal changes due to loss of estrogen and subsequent loss of elasticity in the vaginal tissues. In PVD specifically, biological etiological factors have included yeast infections, use of oral contraceptives, early menarche, a genetic predisposition, human papillomavirus, and urethral conditions or infections (Pukall, Payne, Kao, Khalifé, & Binik, 2005). Assessment with functional magnetic resonance imaging (fMRI) indicates that women with PVD have a more general hypersensitivity to touch and pain compared to unaffected women (Pukall, Strigo, et al., 2005).

Although psychological factors are not considered primary in dyspareunia, personality and psychiatric symptoms can exacerbate pain as well as pain-induced affect. Among the many psychological factors correlated with PVD are anxiety, depression, low self-esteem, harm avoidance, somatization, shyness, and pain catastrophization (as summarized in Pukall, Payne, et al., 2005).

## Vaginismus

Weijmar Schultz and van de Wiel (2005) summarize eight major theories of the etiology of vaginismus. One theory is a behavioral view in which a conditioned anxiety reaction results in vaginal muscle spasm. This conditioning may have taken place during one episode of learning (e.g., as in the case of sexual assault with forced penetration) or over repeated trials (e.g., as in the case of voluntary intercourse in a woman with dyspareunia). The fear of pain from intercourse and the subsequent avoidance of any genital contact maintains the phobic anxiety in vaginismus.

According to the overactive pelvic floor muscle view (Weijmar Schultz & van de Wiel, 2005), vaginismus should be regarded as a pelvic floor dysfunction and not as a sexual dysfunction. Because conditioning is the likely mechanism behind the overactive pelvic floor muscles, physiotherapy with biofeedback is the most logical treatment approach (Rosenbaum, 2003).

The interactional view (Weijmar Schultz & van de Wiel, 2005) suggests that vaginismus maintains balance between partners. Although research on this view is sparse, it is not uncommon in the clinical setting for male partners to be passive, dependent, anxious, and lacking in self-confidence. There is also evidence that these partners suffer from sexual dysfunction themselves (Lamont, 1978); therefore, vaginismus maintains balance in the sexless relationship.

## COURSE, PROGNOSIS, AND TREATMENT

As implied in the section on etiology, there has been a pendulum shift in the past decade, with much research attention focused on finding effective pharmacological treatments for the most prevalent sexual complaints (low desire in women, erectile and ejaculation difficulties in men). As a result, there has been a recent dearth of randomized controlled trials of psychological treatments, and much of the information on efficacy of psychological treatments is based on studies conducted in the 1970s and 1980s. However, psychological treatments are effective and needed (Heiman, 2002).

### HYPOACTIVE SEXUAL DESIRE DISORDER IN MEN

Treatment for HSDD largely depends on the presumed etiology and can involve any combination of psychotherapy (either alone or with the partner), medications, or hormonal therapy. Psychological therapy may involve exploration of couple issues, including anger, trust, exploration of an affair, and feelings of attractiveness. Treatment may also encourage the use of fantasies, erotic stimuli, and other forms of sexual activity besides intercourse. Unfortunately, there are no controlled publications on the efficacy of psychological treatment without concomitant medication treatment for HSDD in men.

Among the pharmacological treatments for low desire, bupropion (marketed as the antidepressant Wellbutrin) is a norepinephrine and dopamine agonist that has been found to have an efficacy rate of approximately 86% in nondepressed men with HSDD (Crenshaw, Goldberg, & Stern, 1987). Testosterone replacement has been the primary hormonal treatment studied for men with HSDD and is administered as an injection, a patch, or a gel. In a recent meta-analysis of the effects of testosterone on sexual dysfunction in men with heterogeneous sexual complaints, testosterone treatment improved sexual desire among men with clinically low levels of testosterone but not in men with normal levels (Isidori et al., 2005).

### HYPOACTIVE SEXUAL DESIRE DISORDER IN WOMEN

Much recent attention has been focused on finding an effective dose and method of administration of testosterone for improving women's sexual desire, and several randomized, placebo-controlled trials investigating a transdermal testosterone patch for improving desire in postmenopausal women receiving estrogen replacement have shown a benefit (e.g., Davis et al., 2006; Kroll et al., 2004). However, given a concern over the lack of long-term safety data, particularly with the possible link of testosterone and breast cancer (Tworoger et al., 2005), the testosterone patch did not receive regulatory approval by the Food and Drug Administration (FDA) and, therefore, continues to be prescribed "off-label" until sufficient long-term safety data are accrued.

The failed antidepressant and serotonin-1A receptor agonist/2A antagonist and dopamine-4 receptor partial agonist, flibanserin, had been shown to significantly improve sexual desire among women with HSDD (Clayton, Dennerstein, Pyke, & Sand, 2010). However, it was rejected by the FDA in 2010 due to the relatively minimal benefit beyond placebo and the concern over side effects. Flibanserin continues to be tested in clinical trials at the current time.

The synthetic hormone tibolone, which has estrogenic, androgenic, and progestogenic effects, has been found to significantly increase sexual desire, frequency of sexual fantasies, and sexual arousability in a randomized, double-blind study of postmenopausal women free of sexual complaints (Laan, van Lunsen, & Everaerd, 2001); however, although it is licensed for the treatment of menopausal symptoms in Europe, it does not have FDA approval in the United States.

Cognitive and behavioral therapies (CBT) for low desire have moderate empirical support. For example, Trudel and colleagues (Trudel et al., 2001) compared the effects of CBT to a wait-list control in 74 couples in which women met criteria for HSDD. Treatment included psychoeducation, skills and emotional training, and couple assignments in a group format. After 12 weeks, 74% of women no longer met diagnostic criteria for HSDD, and this stabilized to 64% after 1-year follow-up. In addition to significantly improved sexual desire, women also reported improved quality of marital life and perception of sexual arousal.

Interestingly, CBT addressing a different aspect of the sexual response cycle—namely, orgasm—is also effective in increasing sexual desire in women (Hurlbert, 1993) and provides additional evidence that components of sexual response are highly correlated. Several studies including both members of the couple, which tested the efficacy of marital therapy for women's low desire, have also found promising effects on sexual desire (Fish, Busby, & Killian, 1994; MacPhee, Johnson, & Van der Veer, 1995).

Most recently, two uncontrolled trials have found significant beneficial effects of a mindfulness-based CBT for women with mixed desire and arousal difficulties (Brotto et al., 2008; Brotto, Basson, & Luria, 2008). These findings emphasize the importance of mindfully participating in the body and its sensations during sexual activity. Whether such mindfulness-based interventions show benefit above and beyond treatment as usual or a placebo group is currently being investigated.

### SEXUAL AVERSION DISORDER

Systematic desensitization was effective in two case studies of women with SAD (Finch, 2001; Kingsberg & Janata, 2003), although, in general, SAD is less responsive to behavioral treatment than is HSDD (Schover & LoPiccolo, 1982). We were unable to locate any published efficacy studies on treatment of SAD in men.

### ERECTILE DISORDER

With the approval of sildenafil citrate (Viagra, Pfizer Inc.) in the United States in 1998, treatment for ED is vastly different then it was a decade ago. Sildenafil is a phosphodiesterase type-5 (PDE5) inhibitor that has become a first-line treatment for ED. All PDE5 inhibitors work by inhibiting the action of PDE5, a molecule in the corpus cavernosum of the penis that is involved in detumescence (loss of erection). There are almost 2,000 published studies in various subgroups of men with ED ranging in age from 19 to 87 years. The drug, in 20, 50, or 100 mg doses, is taken 1 hour before planned sexual activity with a low-fat meal and must be combined with subjective or mechanical sexual stimulation. Its effectiveness ranges from 43% for men with radical prostatectomy, to 59% of those with diabetes, and to 84% for men with ED due to psychological causes (Osterloh & Riley, 2002).

Tadalafil (Cialis, Lilly ICOS LLC.) is a newer PDE5 inhibitor with a 17.5-hour half-life, which promotes greater sexual spontaneity—an important factor for some couples. A large analysis of 2,100 men taking tadalafil found that the drug was significantly more effective than placebo among all subgroups of men studied, including those with diabetes, hypertension, cardiovascular disease, hyperlipidemia, depression, and benign prostatic hyperplasia, and across ethnocultural groups (Lewis et al., 2005).

Vardenafil (Levitra, Bayer) is another PDE5 inhibitor that has been found to be particularly effective for two difficult-to-treat groups: namely, men with diabetes and men who have undergone a radical prostatectomy. More than 70% of men in both groups responded to vardenafil with improved erections (Brock et al., 2001; Goldstein, Fischer, Taylor, & Thibonnier, 2001).

Before the approval of the PDE5 inhibitors, injectable and intraurethral treatments were considered the mainstay of ED treatment. Traditionally reserved for men with an organic basis to their ED, these techniques involve intracavernosal injection of alprostadil (prostaglandin E1) directly into the penis, and, unlike the oral medications, sexual stimulation is not necessary for an erection. Although these treatments were found to be highly effective in 87% of men (Linet & Ogrinc, 1996), the side effects of penile pain or prolonged erections make compliance a concern. Alprostadil can also be delivered directly into the urethra as MUSE (medicated urethral system for erection). This mode of delivery is favorable for men who cannot tolerate oral medications or injections. Approximately 70% of men respond positively to MUSE (Padma-Nathan et al., 1997), which requires some training from a sexual health clinician for proper insertion. Testosterone therapy, both alone (Isidori et al., 2005) and in combination with a PDE5 inhibitor (Shabsigh, 2005), has also been found effective in the treatment of erectile disorder.

Vacuum constriction devices (VCD) and constriction rings are also available for ED and do not require administration/ingestion of a medication. A VCD is a cylindrical tube that is placed over the flaccid penis, and a vacuum draws blood into the penis either manually or with a battery-operated motor. A constriction ring is then typically placed over the base of the penis to sustain the erection for intercourse. Although very effective for men who cannot tolerate medical forms of ED treatment, it does require a certain degree of manual dexterity and is not suitable for men with sickle cell disease, leukemia, or who are using anticoagulation treatments (Wylie & MacInnes, 2005).

Psychological techniques can be essential for couples in which relationship discord and difficulties in communication are related to the ED. However, considerably less research has examined the efficacy of psychological therapies for men with ED, although multiple case reports indicate benefit from combined oral medications plus cognitive behavioral therapies (McCarthy, 1998; Perelman, 2002; Segraves, 1999).

FEMALE SEXUAL AROUSAL DISORDER

Given the high degree of comorbidity between arousal, desire, and orgasm complaints, there have been no published trials testing the efficacy of a psychological intervention for FSAD alone. Instead, there have been numerous recent investigations of pharmacologic treatments, particularly for women with genital sexual arousal disorder; however, all remain unregulated for use for this condition. The dopaminergic agonist apomorphine SL was found to significantly improve sexual arousal, desire, orgasm, satisfaction, and enjoyment when taken daily at 2–3 mg doses but not when taken on an as-needed basis (Caruso et al., 2004). Phentolamine mesylate, commonly used to treat ED, significantly improved self-reported lubrication and tingling sensations, but had no effect on physiological sexual arousal, subjective pleasure, or arousal in postmenopausal women when administered orally (Rosen, Phillips, Gendrano, & Ferguson, 1999). In a much larger, double-blind replication of the study, vaginally applied phentolamine significantly increased physiological arousal in postmenopausal women receiving hormone replacement (Rubio-Aurioles et al., 2002).

The remarkable success of the PDE5 inhibitors for men has initiated a race to find efficacious treatments for women's sexual arousal complaints. However, studies using sildenafil have yielded conflicting findings (Basson & Brotto, 2003; Basson, McInnes, Smith, Hodgson, & Koppiker, 2002; Berman, Berman, Toler, Gill, & Haughie, 2003; Caruso, Intelisano, Lupo, & Agnello, 2001), and there are no published investigations of either vardenafil or tadalafil in women with FSAD.

Currently, one product has been approved by the FDA for the treatment of FSAD. The EROS Clitoral Therapy Device (CTD; Urometrics, St. Paul, MN) is a small, hand-held, battery-operated device that is placed over the clitoris and increases blood flow through gentle suction. The EROS-CTD was found to significantly improve all measures of sexual response and satisfaction in women with FSAD (Billups et al., 2001) and in women with arousal complaints secondary to radiation therapy for cervical cancer (Schroder et al., 2005), but lack of a control condition and the fact that women were required to use the device several times per week for the duration of the study makes it difficult to ascertain whether positive effects were due to the suction, per se (in which case a vibrator might suffice), or to nonspecific attentional factors.

PREMATURE EJACULATION

Seman's Squeeze technique is a highly effective behavioral treatment for PE. The method requires the man to provide direct feedback to his partner when he feels an ejaculatory urge. The couple discontinues sexual stimulation, and the partner applies pressure to the glans of the penis until the urge is reduced (Masters & Johnson, 1970; Semans, 1956). The technique can be used during masturbation before attempting it with a partner. The efficacy of the Squeeze technique is approximately 60% (Metz, Pryor, Nesvacil, Abuzzahab, & Koznar, 1997). The Stop-Pause approach is very similar but, because it involves a reduction in penile stimulation as the man nears ejaculatory inevitability, it better simulates natural behaviors during intercourse (Kaplan, 1989). Sexual stimulation is resumed once the man feels control over his ejaculation. Although early studies by Masters and Johnson and Kaplan found efficacy rates nearing 100%, more recent controlled trials find efficacy in the range of 64% (Hawton, Catalan, Martin, & Fagg, 1986). Other behavioral interventions such as self-administered psychological treatment (Trudel & Proulx, 1987) or pelvic floor rehabilitation (Giuseppe & Nicastro, 1996) have been reported successful in uncontrolled trials.

Based on the hypothesis that a low ejaculatory setpoint due to low serotonin neurotransmission may underlie some forms of PE, selective serotonin reuptake inhibitors (SSRIs) have become a mainstay of pharmacological treatment. This SSRI effect takes advantage of one of the negative side effects of SSRI use—namely delayed orgasm in men and women. Several dozen trials examining the efficacy of SSRIs in PE have been conducted, and a recent meta-analysis of daily SSRI use showed paroxetine to have the greatest efficacy in delaying ejaculation (Kara et al., 1996).

Pharmacological treatment for PE may also include topical local anaesthetics applied to the penis. For example, lidocaine and/or prilocaine appear to be effective in about 85% of men (Xin, Choi, Lee, & Choi, 1997). Finally, a comparison of behavior therapy with and without sildenafil shows the combination to significantly delay time to ejaculation (Tang, Ma, Zhao, Liu, & Chen, 2004).

## MALE ORGASMIC DISORDER

In cases of an organic etiology, amelioration of the underlying biological factors is an important first line of treatment. This may include switching the patient to a different antidepressant, androgen administration, or attempts to control diabetic neuropathy. Kaplan (1974) described a shaping procedure in which a male partner with situational MOD masturbates in front of his female partner on the other side of the room and subsequently masturbates while moving progressively closer and closer to her, with the goal of eventual ejaculation inside the vagina. No controlled trials exist, but clinical observation supports its efficacy for a large proportion of men. In addition, individual or couple therapy may be warranted if there are perpetuating interpersonal factors.

## FEMALE ORGASMIC DISORDER

Both psychological and pharmacological treatments have been found to be effective for FOD. Directed Masturbation exercises (Masters & Johnson, 1970) are designed to teach women to focus on sexually erotic cues, not focus on distracting nonsexual cues, and apply graded stimulation to the clitoris in an effort to become orgasmic with masturbation. The self-help book *Becoming Orgasmic: A Sexual Growth Program for Women* recommends these exercises (Heiman & LoPiccolo, 1987) and has an approximate 90% efficacy rate.

Because anxiety may act as a cognitive distraction, thereby distracting the woman away from sexual cues, anxiety reduction is often a target in treatment. Systematic desensitization involves training the woman to relax the muscles of her body while simultaneously presenting her with sexual anxiety-evoking stimuli. Sensate focus involves having a partner touch the woman, with her verbal guidance, while she focuses on relaxation (Masters & Johnson, 1970). These interventions were efficacious when treatment was administered by a therapist, or in a group or self-help format (Libman et al., 1984).

In the Coital Alignment Technique (CAT), the man is in the superior position and shifts forward such that the base of his penis makes direct contact with the woman's clitoris. This ensures constant clitoral stimulation and results in improved coital orgasmic ability in approximately 56% of women (Hurlbert & Apt, 1995). The EROS-CTD, described earlier for FSAD, has also been found to significantly improve orgasmic ability in women with FOD (Billups et al., 2001).

Several placebo-controlled studies have examined the efficacy of pharmacologic treatments for FOD. For example, pre- and postmenopausal women with low arousal and anorgasmia showed significant improvements with sildenafil (Basson & Brotto, 2003; Caruso et al., 2001). In a double-blind trial of 100 mg sildenfil versus placebo for women with SSRI-induced FOD, there were significantly fewer sexual side effects in the sildenafil group (Nurnberg et al., 2008). However, given the study's highly selective inclusion criteria and the difficulties in recruiting participants to the trial, the generalizability of these findings remains tentative.

## DYSPAREUNIA

There are four general categories of treatment for PVD, the most common cause of dyspareunia: (1) medical, (2) psychological, (3) physical, and (4) surgical. Among the medical treatments for PVD, suggestions include hygiene modification and sitz baths, topical anesthetics or corticosteroids, oral treatments in the form of low-dose antidepressants, anticonvulsants, oral corticosteroids, or antifungals, and injectable treatments. Unfortunately, there is a lack of randomized double-blind and prospective studies assessing these treatments, so precise efficacy rates are not available.

Behavioral treatments such as CBT adopt pain control strategies as their primary target and include Kegel exercises, vaginal dilatation, relaxation, and cognitive challenging (Bergeron & Binik, 1998). Physiotherapy with pelvic floor biofeedback has also been found to be very effective (Bergeron et al., 2002). Surgery, usually in the form of vestibulectomy, involves excision of the hymen and sensitive areas of the vestibule. Recent studies demonstrate a high degree of efficacy (73% to 90%; Gaunt, Good, & Stanhope, 2003; Lavy, Lev-Sagie, Hamani, Zacut, & Ben-Chetrit, 2005); however, results are lower for women with acquired PVD, who also have a higher rate of recurrence (Rettenmaier, Brown, & Micha, 2003).

In the only published, randomized, head-to-head comparison of 12-week group CBT, pelvic floor physiotherapy, and vestibulectomy, 78 women were followed for a 2-year period (Bergeron et al., 2001). All groups experienced a significant reduction in pain at post-treatment and at 6-months follow-up, with the vestibulectomy group showing the greatest degree of improvement (Bergeron et al., 2001). All groups also significantly improved on measures of psychological and sexual function. A 2.5-year follow-up of the study found continued improvement in all three groups, with no significant treatment differences in pain from intercourse, sexual functioning, or intercourse frequency (Bergeron, Khalifé, Glazer, & Binik, 2008).

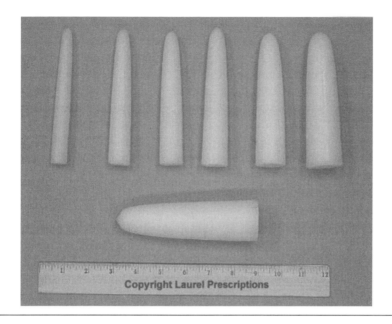

**Figure 15.1**   Vaginal dilators (Laurel Prescriptions, Vancouver, Canada) for the treatment of vaginismus. *Source:* © Laurel Prescriptions.

VAGINISMUS

According to the behavioral view, treatment of vaginismus involves a reconditioning of the body's response to feared objects such as the penis, a speculum, or a tampon, much like the treatment approach for other specific phobias. Using a systematic desensitization approach, the woman is asked to create a hierarchy of feared objects, which she will then progressively work through to insert vaginally over the course of treatment. Simultaneously, the woman is taught to engage in activity incompatible with tension or anxiety, such as relaxation and diaphragmatic breathing. Highly useful as an object of insertion is the vaginal dilator (or insert or accommodator), shown in Figure 15.1 (Laurel Prescriptions, Vancouver, Canada), which can be made of wax, plastic, silicone, or other nonirritating substances. Research examining the efficacy of this behavioral approach combined with cognitive elements found it to be highly effective for nearly all women in reducing vaginismus, anxiety, and improving the couple relationship (Kabakci & Batur, 2003). A prospective study of CBT in women with vaginismus was found to be effective, and benefits were mediated by changes in fear of intercourse and changes in avoidance behavior (ter Kuile et al., 2007).

LOOKING AHEAD TO *DSM-5*

The highly subjective nature of sexual difficulties raises challenges in establishing objective criteria for determining dysfunction. *DSM-5* will retain criterion B, which is focused on the distressing nature of the sexual difficulty. Specifically, "The disturbance causes clinically significant distress or impairment" is proposed for inclusion for all of the sexual dysfunctions.

Because of considerable criticism of the *DSM-IV-TR* criteria for HSDD in women, in that the focus on reduced sexual fantasies and lack of spontaneous thinking about sexual activity may be quite normative for women, the proposal for *DSM-5* has been to merge HSDD with FSAD and expand upon the definition of desire (Brotto, 2010a; Graham, 2010). Specifically, the Sexual Dysfunctions sub-workgroup for *DSM-5* has suggested that a new disorder, Sexual Interest/Arousal Disorder, replace HSDD and FSAD and that a polythetic list of criteria be adopted whereby three of six symptoms for a duration of 6 months or more are required, in addition to associated distress, in order to meet criteria. The revised diagnosis has received significant support but also criticism—the latter focused on concerns about diagnostic ambiguity (Derogatis et al., 2010).

A similar criterion set has been proposed to replace HSDD for men; however, there is significantly less empirical data to support a change in criteria for men compared to women (Brotto, 2010b). Nevertheless, the finding that men, across ages, often confound definitions of desire and subjective sexual arousal supports an expanded definition of low desire in men. The proposed changes to the sexual dsyfunctions for *DSM-5* are summarized in Table 15.3.

## CASE STUDY

### Hypoactive Sexual Desire Disorder in a Man

Robert is a 64-year-old married, Caucasian, heterosexual man. He and his wife, Cecile, age 58, have been married for 36 years and have three adult children ages 35, 31, and 28. Robert presented to his primary care doctor with complaints of "lost libido," which he thought might be due to a "hormonal imbalance." Robert's physician conducted a brief but focused assessment of his loss of desire, focusing on how Robert defined desire, the impact on his self-esteem and relationship, and an exploration of other contributing factors in Robert (and Cecile's) lives. The physician ordered a complete hormone profile, focusing on Robert's levels of bioavailable testosterone. Robert reported that in the past 5 years he became less interested in sex, thought about sex less than once per week (previously he would think about it daily), and only very reluctantly initiated sexual activity. He became quite anxious about sex in the evenings, which was typically when sexual activity would occur. Although Cecile was not present during this appointment, Robert noted that Cecile had also experienced a reduction in sexual interest, and that she had increased vaginal dryness over the past few years coinciding with menopause.

When asked what steps Robert and Cecile have taken on their own to improve Robert's desire for sex, he stated that they were unsure, and this is what prompted their speaking to the physician. Robert noted that there had also been recent problems with his erectile capacity. He was unable to reach an erection in approximately 50% of his sexual attempts. Robert concluded the appointment by stating that these changes were quite distressing to him, and he worried about becoming less attractive to Cecile. Therefore, he was quite motivated for treatment. The physician referred Robert and Cecile to a sex therapist to provide some educational information on normative sexual function changes with age and relationship duration, and to discuss with Robert and Cecile sexual skills (e.g., sensate focus) that might improve

**Table 15.3**

Proposed Criteria for the Sexual Dysfunctions for *DSM-5*

| *DSM-IV-TR* Disorder | Proposed Disorder Name for *DSM-5* | Proposed Criteria for *DSM-5* |
|---|---|---|
| Hypoactive Sexual Desire Disorder<br><br>Female Sexual Arousal Disorder | Sexual Interest/Arousal Disorder in Women | A. Lack of sexual interest/arousal of at least 6 months' duration as manifested by at least three of the following indicators:<br>  1. Absent or reduced frequency or intensity of interest in sexual activity<br>  2. Absent or reduced frequency or intensity of sexual/erotic thoughts or fantasies<br>  3. Absence or reduced frequency of initiation of sexual activity and is typically unreceptive to a partner's attempts to initiate<br>  4. Absent/reduced frequency or intensity of sexual excitement/pleasure during sexual activity on most sexual encounters<br>  5. Sexual interest/arousal is absent or infrequently elicited by any internal or external sexual/erotic cues (e.g., written, verbal, visual, etc.)<br>  6. Absent/reduced frequency or intensity of genital and/or nongenital sensations during sexual activity on most sexual encounters<br>B. The problem causes clinically significant distress or impairment.<br>C. The sexual dysfunction is not better accounted for by another Axis I disorder (except another Sexual Dysfunction) and is not due to the effects of a substance (e.g., a drug of abuse, a medication) or a general medical condition |
| Hypoactive Sexual Desire Disorder | Hypoactive Sexual Desire Disorder in Men | A. Persistently or recurrently deficient (or absent) sexual fantasies and desire for sexual activity. The judgment of deficiency or absence is made by the clinician, taking into account factors that affect sexual functioning, such as age and the context of the person's life<br>B. The disturbance causes marked distress or interpersonal difficulty<br>C. The sexual dysfunction is not better accounted for by another Axis I disorder (except another Sexual Dysfunction) and is not due exclusively to the direct physiological effects of a substance (e.g., a drug of abuse, a medication) or a general medical condition |
| Sexual Aversion Disorder | Other Specified Sexual Dysfunction | This condition will be removed from the *DSM-5*. The symptom of fear and avoidance of all or almost all sexual contact that causes clinically significant distress or impairment might be considered as an "other specified sexual dysfunction." |

*(continued)*

**Table 15.3**
(*Continued*)

| *DSM-IV-TR* Disorder | Proposed Disorder Name for *DSM-5* | Proposed Criteria for *DSM-5* |
|---|---|---|
| Male Erectile Disorder | Erectile Disorder | A. At least one of the three following symptom(s) must have been present for 6 months or more and be experienced on most occasions of sexual activity:<br>   1. Inability to obtain an erection during sexual activity<br>   2. Inability to maintain an erection until the completion of sexual activity<br>   3. Marked decrease in erectile rigidity that intereferes with function (e.g., penetration or pleasure)<br>B. The problem causes clinically significant distress or impairment<br>C. The sexual dysfunction is not better accounted for by another Axis I disorder (except another Sexual Dysfunction) and is not due to the effects of a substance (e.g., a drug of abuse, a medication) or a general medical condition |
| Female Orgasmic Disorder | Female Orgasmic Disorder | A. At least one of the two following symptoms where the symptom(s) must have been present for at least 6 months and be experienced on most occasions of sexual activity:<br>   1. Marked delay in, marked infrequency, or absence of orgasm<br>   2. Markedly reduced intensity of orgasmic sensation<br>B. The problem causes clinically significant distress or impairment<br>C. The sexual dysfunction is not better accounted for by another Axis I disorder (except another Sexual Dysfunction) and is not due to the effects of a substance (e.g., a drug of abuse, a medication) or a general medical condition |
| Male Orgasmic Disorder | Delayed Ejaculation | A. At least one of the two following symptoms must have been present for 6 months or more and be experienced on most occasions of sexual activity:<br>   1. Marked delay in ejaculation<br>   2. Marked infrequency or absence of ejaculation<br>B. The problem causes clinically significant distress or impairment.<br>C. The sexual dysfunction is not better accounted for by another Axis I disorder (except another Sexual Dysfunction) and is not due to the effects of a substance (e.g., a drug of abuse, a medication) or a general medical condition |

| | | |
|---|---|---|
| Premature Ejaculation | Early Ejaculation | A. The following symptom must have been present for at least 6 months and be experienced on most occasions of sexual activity: Persistent or recurrent pattern of ejaculation occurring during partnered sexual activity within approximately one minute of beginning of sexual activity and before the person wishes it. |
| | | B. The problem causes clinically significant distress or impairment. |
| | | C. The sexual dysfunction is not better accounted for by another Axis I disorder (except another Sexual Dysfunction) and is not due to the effects of a substance (e.g., a drug of abuse, a medication) or a general medical condition |
| Dyspareunia Vaginismus | Genito-Pelvic Pain/ Penetration Disorder | A. Persistent or recurrent difficulties for at least 6 months with one or more of the following: |
| | | 1. Inability to have vaginal intercourse/penetration |
| | | 2. Marked vulvovaginal or pelvic pain during vaginal intercourse/penetration attempts |
| | | 3. Marked fear or anxiety either about vulvovaginal or pelvic pain or vaginal penetration |
| | | 4. Marked tensing or tightening of the pelvic floor muscles during attempted vaginal penetration |
| | | B. The problem causes clinically significant distress or impairment |
| | | The sexual dysfunction is not better accounted for by another Axis I disorder (except another Sexual Dysfunction) and is not due to the effects of a substance (e.g., a drug of abuse, a medication) or a general medical condition |

563

the quality of their sexual interactions. The sex therapist could also address Robert's anxiety as well as perform a more thorough assessment of mood and lifestyle factors. Although the physician suggested examining Robert's hormonal profile, he knew that Robert was otherwise "hormonally healthy" and showed no clinical signs of hypogonadism.

## SUMMARY OF SEXUAL DYSFUNCTIONS

The past 10 years have seen an unprecedented increase in research aimed at understanding the etiology, pathophysiology, prevalence, diagnostic features of, and treatments for sexual dysfunction. The increased presence of the pharmaceutical industry's interests in this field has led to increased research funding, but this boom has also been associated with caution and criticism for fear of medicalizing conditions that many argue are largely influenced (and created) by sociopolitical and psychological pressures. Interested readers are encouraged to regularly read the *DSM-5* development website of the American Psychiatric Association (www.dsm5 .org) as new criteria are deliberated.

## PART II: PARAPHILIAS

### DESCRIPTION OF PARAPHILIAS

The paraphilias, as defined in the *DSM-IV-TR* (APA, 2000), refer to sexual disorders of "recurrent, intense sexual urges, fantasies, or behaviors that involve unusual objects, activities, or situations and cause clinically significant distress or impairment in social, occupational, or other important areas of functioning" (p. 535). The paraphilias fall into one of three types, involving sexual arousal toward nonhuman objects, sexual arousal toward children or other nonconsenting individuals, or sexual arousal related to the suffering or humiliation of oneself or others.

The term *paraphilia* was coined by Stekel in 1923 and translates into love (*philia*) beyond the usual (*para*; Money, 1984). Although paraphilias are often associated with sexual offending, the two terms are not synonymous. As Krueger and Kaplan (2001) point out, paraphilias refer to a type of mental disorder. In contrast, "sexual offender" is a legal term that denotes individuals who have been convicted of a sexual offense. Nevertheless, many sexual offenders do meet diagnostic criteria for one or more paraphilias, and some individuals diagnosed with a paraphilia have committed sexual offenses; thus, the two phenomena are by no means mutually exclusive (McElroy et al., 1999).

As a result of the association between paraphilias and sexual offending, much of the research on paraphilias has been based on samples of convicted sexual offenders. Unfortunately, this leads to three major confounds. First, many sexual offenders were never formally diagnosed with a paraphilia. Second, the generalizability of the samples to all individuals with paraphilias is suspect, because individuals convicted of a sexual offense often represent the more severe end of the spectrum. Third, the veracity of self-reports by sexual offenders needs to be considered, because these individuals often have high motivations to appear less "deviant" in their sexual interests. As a result, they may under- and over-report certain fantasies and experiences. As a consequence of these issues, there is an increasing call for more research based on non-criminological samples (e.g., Kramer, 2011; Okami & Goldberg, 1992).

## CLINICAL PICTURE

### Exhibitionism

Exhibitionism, involving recurrent and intense sexually arousing fantasies, sexual urges, or behaviors of exposing one's genitals to an unsuspecting stranger over a period of at least 6 months, is one of the most commonly reported paraphilias (Firestone, Kingston, Wexler, & Bradford, 2006; Långström & Seto, 2006; Murphy, 1997). Exhibiting may consist of showing the genitals to, and/or actively masturbating in front of, a stranger. Often, the victim's shock is sexually arousing to the perpetrator, and in most cases there is no other contact. To meet *DSM-IV-TR* criteria, the individual must either have acted on the sexual urges or fantasies or have experienced marked distress or interpersonal difficulty as a result of the sexual interest (APA, 2000).

Although primarily a disorder of men, female exhibitionism has been reported (e.g., Bader, Schoeneman-Morris, Scalora, & Casady, 2008; Federoff, Fishell, & Federoff, 1999). The majority of victims of exhibitionism are females, including both children and adolescents (Bader et al., 2008), although exhibitionists who prefer to expose themselves to children may have a different disorder from those who prefer to expose themselves to adults (Murphy & Page, 2008).

Exhibitionists are a heterogeneous group whose education, intelligence, and socioeconomic status do not differ from the general population (Blair & Lanyon, 1981). Initial investigations found high rates of shy and nonassertive personalities (Ellis & Brancale, 1956), but later studies utilizing more standardized assessment instruments did not find abnormal or specific personality patterns (Langevin, Paitich, Freeman, Mann, & Handy, 1978; Langevin et al., 1979; Smukler & Schiebel, 1975), nor did they find that psychopathology symptoms differed from other sexual or non-sexual offenders (Murphy, Haynes, & Worley, 1991; Murphy & Peters, 1992). Moreover, the majority of exhibitionists are married or in common-law relationships and enjoy nonpathological sexual relationships with their partners (Langevin & Lang, 1987; Maletzky, 1991).

Cox and Maletzky (1980) found that, in comparison to those with other paraphilias, exhibitionists are least likely to see their behavior as harmful to their victims—a factor likely to influence both motivations for, and success of, treatment. Relatedly, they are more likely to underreport or minimize their exhibitionistic and other paraphilic fantasies and behaviors (McConaghy, 1993; McConaghy, Blaszcyzynski, & Kidson, 1988), and among all individuals with paraphilias, exhibitionists were most likely to have committed other sexual offenses (Freund & Blanchard, 1986; Langevin & Lang, 1987).

### Fetishism

Fetishism involves recurrent sexual arousal (fantasies, urges, or behaviors) toward nonliving objects, present for at least 6 months and accompanied by clinically significant distress or impairment (APA, 2000). The objects are not limited to female clothing used in cross-dressing or to devices specifically designed for tactile genital stimulation, such as vibrators.

Fetish objects can take many forms, including clothing (particularly underwear and stockings), footwear, diapers, gloves, and certain fabrics or materials such as rubber and leather. Sexual arousal may take the form of looking at, fondling, smelling, licking, sucking, cutting, burning, stealing, or seeing someone else dressed in the fetish objects (Chalkley & Powell, 1983). As with exhibitionism and, in fact, all of the paraphilias, fetishism is largely a disorder found in men, although there are a few reports of women engaged in this behavior (Zavitzianos, 1971).

## FROTTEURISM

Frotteurism is sexual arousal, in the form of sexual urges, fantasies, and/or behaviors, involving touching and rubbing against nonconsenting individuals. The sexual urges, fantasies, or behaviors must be recurrent over at least a 6-month period; however, unlike fetishism but similar to exhibitionism, clinically significant distress or impairment is not required if the individual has acted on the urges (APA, 2000). Although numerous researchers (e.g., Freund, 1990; Freund, Seto, & Kuban, 1996) include both touching and rubbing under the definition of frotteurism, others have differentiated frotteurism from toucherism (e.g., Adams & McAnulty, 1993). The latter refers to sexual arousal from touching exclusively with the hands, rather than touching with, for example, the groin.

Frotteurism generally takes place in crowded places, such as on public transportation or on busy sidewalks, where escape for the frotteur is feasible (APA, 2000). While engaging in frotteuristic activities, the frotteur "usually fantasizes an exclusive, caring relationship with the victim" (APA, 2000, p. 570). Frotteurism, as with most paraphilias, appears to occur mainly in men, although a few cases of frotteurism in women have been reported (Fedoroff et al., 1999; Kar & Koola, 2007). Krueger and Kaplan (1997) note that, "men who engage in frotteurism have large numbers of victims, are not often arrested, and, when apprehended, do not serve long sentences" (p. 145).

Very little published data exist on frotteurism. For example, Krueger and Kaplan (1997) found only 17 studies published on the topic between 1966 and 1997 on Psychlit and Medline. Our own search from 1997 to 2010 yielded only an additional 12 publications.

## PEDOPHILIA

Pedophilia refers to a disorder involving sexual arousal toward a prepubescent child. To meet criteria, the sexual urges, fantasies, or behaviors must be recurrent over at least 6 months, and the individual must either have experienced consequent distress or interpersonal difficulty, or have acted on the urges. Moreover, the individual must be at least 16 years of age and at least 5 years older than the prepubescent target of arousal (APA, 2000).

*Pedophilia* is a term that is often incorrectly used interchangeably with *child molestation*. Although they can overlap, similar to the terms *paraphilia* and *sexual offender*, *pedophilia* describes the diagnostic term for a mental disorder, whereas *child molester* refers to any individual who has engaged in sexual activity with a pre-pubescent or pubescent child. As Barbaree and Seto (1997) point out, some pedophiles who have recurrent sexual fantasies or urges involving prepubescent children but without action would not be considered child molesters; conversely, individuals who have engaged in sexual activity with a minor once or even on occasion, but who do not experience recurrent fantasies, urges, or behaviors over a 6-month period, would not be diagnosed with pedophilia.

Individuals with pedophilia may be sexually aroused by girls, boys, both girls and boys, and even to both adults and children (APA, 2000). Furthermore, sexual arousal may be specific to children of particular ages. While pedophilia involving girl victims is more frequent, the average number of victims is higher in pedophiles attracted to boys (Abel & Osborn, 1992). In addition, the rate of recidivism of male-preferential pedophilia is higher than that of female-preferential pedophilia (Abel & Osborn, 1992; Maletzky, 1993). Although originally believed to be a disorder specific to males, child sexual molestation by women has been reported in the literature (e.g., Cavanaugh-Johnson, 1988; Lane, 1991; Wijkman, Bijleveld, & Hendriks, 2010).

Compared to other paraphilias, an extensive literature exists for pedophilia (although much is based on child molesters who were never formally diagnosed with the disorder). A relatively high proportion of convicted child molesters experienced sexual abuse as children (50%, versus 20% in non–sex offenders; Dhawan & Marshall, 1996), as well as nonsexual abuse and neglect (Davidson, 1983; Finkelhor, 1979, 1984; Marshall, Hudson, & Hodkinson, 1993); however, child molesters did not suffer from higher rates of psychopathology or personality disturbances than nonmolesters (Abel, Rouleau, & Cunningham-Rathner, 1986; Mohr, Turner, & Jerry, 1964).

Finkelhor (1984) proposed that child molesters may suffer from a lack of empathy toward their victims that disinhibits restrictions the individual would otherwise have against offending. This finding has some support (Fernandez, Marshall, Lightbody, & O'Sullivan, 1999), although empathy toward adults and children more generally (i.e., not victims) does not differ from that of nonoffenders (Fernandez et al., 1999; Marshall, Hudson, Jones, & Fernandez, 1995). Thus, child molesters may push away empathic feelings toward their victims, but they do not suffer from any pervasive empathy deficits.

## SEXUAL MASOCHISM

Sexual arousal in response to being humiliated, bound, or beaten characterizes sexual masochism. Sexual arousal occurs in the form of fantasies, urges, or behaviors over a minimum of 6 months, and the person must suffer consequent distress or impairment in at least one important area of functioning. Furthermore, the sexual arousal must be in response to actual, not simulated, humiliation, bondage, or beatings (APA, 2000).

Although pain through being slapped, spanked, or whipped is considered sexually arousing by most sexual masochists (Baumeister, 1989; Moser & Levitt, 1987), many sexual masochists use little or no pain (Baumeister & Butler, 1997), instead becoming aroused through loss of control by being bound or becoming aroused by carrying out humiliating acts such as wearing diapers, licking their partner's shoes, or having to display themselves while naked. Other masochistic activities include the use of electrical shocks, piercing (infibulation), being urinated or defecated on, being subjected to verbal abuse, self-mutilation, and oxygen deprivation (hypoxyphilia). Although many sexual masochists appear to practice these activities with safety in mind—by, for example, prearranging a signal with their partners to indicate when to stop (Scott, 1983; Weinberg & Kamel, 1983)—masochistic behaviors can lead to serious injuries and death (Agnew, 1986; Hucker, 1985). This is particularly true for activities involving oxygen deprivation, such as hanging or the use of ligatures, plastic bags, scarves, and chemicals.

The ratio of men to women who meet the criteria for this disorder is much smaller than that of the other paraphilias, with approximately 20 men having the disorder for every woman (APA, 2000). Gender differences in preferences for various masochistic activities reveal that pain and humiliation are the preferred forms of masochism for women; however, women prefer less-severe forms of pain than men (Baumeister, 1989). Being forced to be a slave and anal penetration have been found to be somewhat equally enjoyed by both sexes (Baumeister, 1989).

Interestingly, sexual masochism seems to be fairly modern when compared to the other paraphilias and also appears to be limited to Western cultures (Baumeister, 1989). Furthermore, it has been associated with increased socioeconomic functioning, with community samples of individuals who practice sexual masochism evidencing a higher level of education, higher income, and higher occupational status as compared to norms for the general population (for a review, see Weinberg, 2006). These findings have been corroborated by the demographics of those involved in S&M (sadism and masochism) organizations (Moser & Levitt, 1987; Scott, 1983; Spengler, 1977).

In line with the correlation between sexual masochism and socioeconomic status, research has found that sexual masochists are well-adjusted individuals who are often quite successful and above norms on measures of mental health (Cowan, 1982; Moser & Levitt, 1987; Scott, 1983; Spengler, 1977; Weinberg, 2006). In fact, a recent study that measured hormone levels before and after participation in consensual, sadomasochistic activities revealed reductions in cortisol following the sadomasochistic activities, indicating reduced physiological stress with this behavior (Sagarin, Cutler, Cuther, Lawler-Sagarin, & Matuszewich, 2009). Furthermore, this study also found that indices of relationship closeness increased following engagement in positively experienced sadomasochistic activities.

Some investigators have examined whether masochistic individuals enjoy pain, humiliation, and/or loss of control outside of sexual activity; however, there appears to be no relationship between sexual masochism and nonsexual forms of masochism (i.e., self-defeating behaviors or enjoyment of nonsexual painful behaviors such as going to the dentist; Baumeister, 1989, 1991; Baumeister & Scher, 1988; Berglas & Baumeister, 1993; Friedman, 1991; Scott, 1983; Weinberg, Williams, & Moser, 1984).

## Sexual Sadism

Sexual sadism, in some ways the complementary opposite of sexual masochism, involves recurrent sexual arousal over a 6-month period in response to fantasies, urges, or behaviors involving the psychological or physical suffering of another. The urges and/or fantasies must have been carried out, must be distressing, or must cause interpersonal difficulty (APA, 2000).

As with sexual masochism, many individuals with sexual sadism engage in this behavior consensually and take precautions to ensure that their behavior does not exceed a certain threshold of pain or injury. However, sexual sadism can lead to serious injury or death, particularly when individuals with sexual sadism have a comorbid diagnosis of antisocial personality disorder (APA, 2000). Although the lay public often associates torture and cruelty to sexual sadism, it should be noted that these violent behaviors are not always accompanied by sexual arousal (Dietz, Hazelwood, & Warren, 1990; Hazelwood, Dietz, & Warren, 1992). Furthermore, it has been suggested that a sexual interest in power, and not the infliction of pain, is at the core of sexual sadism (Cross & Matheson, 2006). As with all of the paraphilias, sexual sadism appears to be more common in men than in women (e.g., Breslow, Evans, & Langley, 1985, 1995).

## TRANSVESTIC FETISHISM

Specific to heterosexual men, transvestic fetishism is characterized by at least 6 months of recurrent sexual arousal associated with wearing women's clothing (cross-dressing) that is accompanied by significant distress or impairment (APA, 2000). Of all of the disorders in the *DSM-IV-TR*, this is the only disorder for which the diagnostic criteria specify both the gender and sexual orientation of the individual; however, it should be noted that homosexual men have also been found to report sexual arousal to cross-dressing, albeit to a significantly lesser extent than heterosexual men (Blanchard & Collins, 1993; Docter & Prince, 1997).

Transvestic fetishism can be associated with gender dysphoria and a desire to transition to the female role, particularly when transvestic fetishism is associated with autogynephilia (sexual arousal in response to the idea or image of oneself as a women; Blanchard, 2005). In fact, the *DSM-IV-TR* states that, in many individuals with transvestic fetishism:

> Sexual arousal is produced by the accompanying thought or image of the person as a female. . . . These images can range from being a woman with female genitalia to that of a view of the self fully dressed as a woman with no real attention to genitalia. (APA, 2000, p. 574)

In contrast, other individuals with transvestic fetishism are content with their gender and only cross-dress in sexual situations.

The childhood and adolescent behaviors of men with transvestic fetishism are consistent with those of other heterosexual men and unlike the childhood and adolescent behaviors often seen in homosexual men (Buhrich & McConaghy, 1985; Doorn, Poortinga, & Verschoor, 1994; Zucker & Bradley, 1995). Similarly, as adults, men with transvestic fetishism generally have masculine occupations and hobbies (Chung & Harmon, 1994).

Transvestic fetishism must be distinguished from transvestic behavior. While the former involves sexual arousal in response to cross-dressing, this is not necessarily the case in the latter. Nonsexual transvestic behaviors can be found, for example, in men who cross-dress for entertainment purposes (colloquially referred to as "drag queens").

### Voyeurism

Voyeurism refers to recurrent, intense sexual arousal, as demonstrated by fantasies, urges, or behaviors, of seeing an unsuspecting person who is naked, in the process of undressing, or engaging in sexual activity. As with the other paraphilias, the *DSM-IV-TR* diagnostic criteria require the behavior to cause significant distress or inter-personal difficulty, or to be present in the form of actual voyeuristic activities (APA, 2000). Abel et al. (1986) and Marshall and Eccles (1991) examined interpersonal skills and sexual functioning in voyeurs and found that these individuals have deficits in social and assertiveness skills as well as sexual knowledge, and that they also have higher rates of sexual dysfunctions and difficulties with intimacy than do non-voyeurs. Nevertheless, approximately half have been found to be involved in marital relationships (Gebhard, Gagnon, Pomeroy, & Christenson, 1965).

### Paraphilia Not Otherwise Specified

The diagnosis of paraphilia not otherwise specified is given to those paraphilias that do not meet the criteria for any of the eight specific paraphilias previously reviewed. These include paraphilias such as necrophilia (sexual activity with corpses), zoo-philia (sexual arousal involving activity with animals), coprophilia (sexual arousal involving activity with feces), klismaphelia (sexual arousal involving enemas), and urophilia (sexual arousal involving urination). Very little is known about these paraphilias because they appear to occur relatively infrequently.

## DIAGNOSTIC CONSIDERATIONS

Several diagnostic considerations are relevant to the paraphilias. First, paraphilias must be differentiated from nonpsychopathological sexual urges, fantasies, and behaviors. Paraphilias are based on the presence of clinically significant distress, impairment, or harm to others, examples that include sexual urges, fantasies, or behaviors that require the participation of nonconsenting individuals, that result in contact with the law, and/or that interfere with relationship or sexual function-ing (APA, 2000). This definition of clinically significant distress, impairment, or harm is particularly important, because it is not uncommon for individuals with paraphilias to "assert that the behavior causes them no distress and that their only problem is social dysfunction as a result of the reaction of others to their behavior" (APA, 2000, p. 567).

Second, paraphilias must be distinguished not only from nonpathological sexual interests, but also from each other. For example, transvestic fetishism must be distinguished from fetishism and sexual masochism. Both transvestic fetishism and fetishism can involve articles of feminine clothing, making it necessary to distinguish between a sexual interest in cross-dressing (necessary for a diagnosis of transvestic fetishism) and a sexual interest in the articles of clothing themselves (necessary for a diagnosis of fetishism). Similarly, sexual masochism can involve humiliation via dressing in women's clothing, and thus must be distinguished from transvestic fetishism and fetishism by the fact that the interest in cross-dressing seen in sexual masochism is specific to the humiliation felt while engaging in this behavior.

Distinguishing among the paraphilias can be complicated by the fact that the presence of one paraphilia is associated with a significantly elevated risk of having additional paraphilias (e.g., Kafka & Hennen, 1999; Price, Gutheil, Commons, Kafka, & Dodd-Kimmey, 2001). For example, transvestic fetishism has been associated with autoerotic asphyxia—a form of sexual masochism—(Blanchard & Hucker, 1991), as well as with exhibitionism, voyeurism, and pedophilia (e.g., Långström & Zucker, 2005). Similarly, significant comorbidity has been found among exhibitionism, voyeurism, and frotteurism (Freund, 1990; Långström & Seto, 2006). In fact, in one study, only 10.4% of 561 nonincarcerated paraphiliacs had only one paraphilia (Abel, Becker, Cunningham-Rathner, Mittelman, & Rouleau, 1988).

Finally, the paraphilias need to be distinguished from other nonparaphilic disorders. For example, significant overlap can exist between transvestic fetishism and gender identity disorder, whereby individuals may meet the criteria exclusively for either gender identity disorder or transvestic fetishism, but where it is also possible for individuals with transvestic fetishism to experience gender dysphoria but not meet the full criteria for gender identity disorder. In this case, a *DSM-IV-TR* diagnosis of transvestic fetishism with the specifier "with gender dysphoria" would be given (APA, 2000).

As the *DSM-IV-TR* notes, other disorders that must be differentiated from the paraphilias include mental retardation, dementia, personality disorders, personality change due to a general medical condition, substance intoxication, mania, and schizophrenia. In these conditions:

> [T]here may be a decrease in judgment, social skills, or impulse control that, in rare instances, leads to unusual sexual behavior. This can be distinguished from a Paraphilia by the fact that the unusual sexual behavior is not the individual's preferred or obligatory pattern, the sexual symptoms occur exclusively during the course of these mental disorders, and the unusual sexual acts tend to be isolated rather than recurrent and usually have a later age of onset. (APA, 2000, p. 568)

## EPIDEMIOLOGY

The incidence and prevalence of the paraphilias is unknown due to their secretive and often illegal nature. Therefore, frequency estimates are generally based on small, nonrepresentative samples, most often involving convicted sexual offenders. This research is, nonetheless, useful in deriving a preliminary indication of the occurrence of this group of disorders.

### EXHIBITIONISM

As previously noted, exhibitionism is one of the most common paraphilias and may be the most common sexual offense (e.g., Bartosh, Garby, Lewis, & Gray, 2003;

Firestone et al., 2006). With respect to prevalence, studies have found that exhibitionism accounts for between one-third and two-thirds of all sexual offenses reported to police in Canada, the United States, and Europe (e.g., Gebhard et al., 1965; Smukler & Shiebel, 1975). Although estimates have varied, up to 20% of women may be victims of exhibitionism (Kaplan & Krueger, 1997; Meyer, 1995). Corroborating this high number of victims, Abel and Rouleau (1990) found that 25% of offenders in their outpatient clinics had a history of exhibitionism and that these 142 offenders reported a total of 72,074 victims. In one nonoffender study, 2% admitted to a history of exhibitionism (Templeman & Stinnett, 1991); however, in a more recent study involving a nationally representative sample of 2,450 adults in Sweden, more than 4% of males and 2% of females reported a history of at least one instance of exhibitionistic behavior for the purposes of sexual arousal (Långström & Seto, 2006).

## Fetishism

Fetishism is a rare condition (APA, 2000). Chalkley and Powell (1983) reported that 0.8% of patients seen in three psychiatric hospitals over a period of 20 years met the criteria, and Curren (1954) found that only 5 out of 4,000 clients seen in private practice had a primary diagnosis of fetishism; however, as Mason (1997) notes, clinicians likely see only a small minority of the total number of individuals with fetishistic interests considering the wide proliferation of organizations and materials catering to these individuals. Nevertheless, it is unlikely that the majority of these individuals meet *DSM-IV-TR* criteria for fetishism, given that many do not experience distress or impairment.

## Frotteurism

Abel et al. (1988) interviewed 561 nonincarcerated paraphiliacs and found that 62 (11%) had a primary diagnosis of frotteurism, leading them to conclude that frottage is not the uncommon paraphilic act it has sometimes been touted to be. These rates are in line with other studies (Bradford, Boulet, & Pawlak, 1992; Kafka & Hennen, 2002), although even higher rates were found by Templeman and Stinnett (1991), who asked 60 college-aged men about frotteuristic activities and found that 35% indicated that they had engaged in frottage. Interestingly, a study of 33 adult men and 28 adult women in India revealed higher rates of reported sexual interests in frotteurism in women (14.3%) than in men (9.1%; Kar & Koola, 2007); this finding is very surprising given that paraphilias are generally considered to be very uncommon in women, with the exception of sexual masochism.

## Pedophilia

Although a substantial amount of research has been conducted on pedophilia, its prevalence is unknown. Seto (2009) has extrapolated that the upper limit for the prevalence of pedophilia is likely around 5%. This is based on the fact that several small convenience-sample surveys with men have revealed rates of between 3% to 9% for self-reported sexual fantasies or sexual contact involving prepubescent children (e.g., Fromuth, Burkhart, & Jones, 1991; Templeman & Stinnett, 1991), but also on the fact that these rates are likely to overestimate the prevalence of pedophilia because these surveys did not assess the intensity, persistence, or presence of distress/impairment related to the sexual fantasies/behaviors.

## SEXUAL MASOCHISM

Baumeister (1989) estimated that between 5% and 10% of the population has engaged in some form of masochistic activities based on a literature review of findings from other studies. He further hypothesized that double this number have had fantasies about sexual masochism but that less than 1% of the population likely engages in masochistic sexual activities on a regular basis.

Since Baumeister's (1989) review, more recent studies have been conducted with both clinical and nonclinical populations. In studies with sexual offenders, the rates of sexual masochism have ranged from 2% (Becker, Stinson, Tromp, & Messer, 2003) to just over 5% (Hill, Habermann, Berner, & Briken, 2006). Higher percentages—but still in line with the review by Baumeister (1989)—have been found in studies of outpatient males seeking treatment for paraphilic or paraphilia-related disorders, with between 9% and 11% of the samples meeting criteria for sexual masochism (Kafka & Prentky, 1994; Kafka & Hennen, 2002, 2003). With respect to nonclinical populations, an Australian study that assessed participation in bondage, discipline, sadomasochism, dominance, or submission via telephone survey revealed that 2.0% of men and 1.4% of women acknowledged having engaged in these activities at some point in their lives (Richters, Grulich, De Visser, Smith, & Rissel, 2003).

Paraphilic interests, in general, are rarely known to occur in women, with the exception of sexual masochism. In line with the notion that sexual masochism is not specific to males, a recent literature review of studies that have assessed women's rape fantasies revealed that between 31% and 57% of women have had sexual fantasies involving forced sexual activities, and that, of these women, 9% to 17% reported that these fantasies were either their most frequent or their most preferred fantasies (Critelli & Bivona, 2008).

## SEXUAL SADISM

Several studies have been conducted on the extent of sexual sadism in clinical and nonclinical samples. Of studies with convicted sexual offenders, rates of sexual sadism have ranged substantially, from 4% to 9% in some studies (e.g., Becker, Stinson, Tromp, & Messer, 2003; Elwood, Doren, & Thornton, 2010; Levenson, 2004) to upwards of 35% in other studies (e.g., Berger, Berner, Bolterauer, Gutierrez, & Berger, 1999; Hill et al., 2006).

In a study of 561 adult males seeking outpatient treatment for possible paraphilias, 28 (5%) of participants met the criteria for sexual sadism (Abel et al., 1987; Abel et al., 1988), consistent with a more recent study with 120 outpatient males with paraphilias or paraphilia-related disorders, 60 of whom were sex offenders (Kafka & Hennen, 2002, 2003). Another study of 63 outpatient males found 12% of the sample meeting criteria for sexual sadism (Kafka & Prentky, 1994).

With respect to nonclinical samples, Hunt (1974) surveyed both men and women on their sexual experiences and found that 5% of men and 2% of women endorsed becoming sexually aroused to inflicting pain on others. Crepault and Couture (1980) assessed rates of sexually sadistic fantasies in a community sample of men and found that 11% had fantasies of beating up a woman and 15% had fantasies of humiliating a woman. Arndt, Foehl, and Good (1985) found that half of their sample of men and one-third of their sample of women indicated having had prior fantasies of tying up their partners.

## VOYEURISM

Along with exhibitionism, voyeurism is one of the most common paraphilias and one of the most common sexual offences (e.g., Bradford et al., 1992; Långström & Seto, 2006). In the study by Långström & Seto (2006), involving 2,450 adult men and women from a nationally representative sample in Sweden, 12% of men and 4% of women acknowledged at least one instance of sexual arousal in response to viewing unsuspecting individuals engaging in sexual activities. Much higher rates were found in a study of 33 adult men and 28 adult women in India (Kar & Koola, 2007), where 55% of the men and 25% of the women in the sample had engaged in voyeuristic activities. Furthermore, 3% of these men reported that voyeurism was a necessary component for sexual gratification. These high rates are in line with at least one study of 60 male college students in the United States, in which 42% engaged in voyeuristic activities and 53% reported an interest in voyeurism (Templeman & Stinnett, 1991). Meyer (1995) has posited that up to 20% of women have been targeted by voyeurs.

## TRANSVESTIC FETISHISM

Since the publication of the fifth edition of this volume, the first population-based study on transvestic fetishism has been conducted (Långström & Zucker, 2005). This study found that 2.8% of 1,279 Swedish men, and 0.4% of 1,171 Swedish women reported sexual arousal in response to cross-dressing. The percentage for men is consistent with another, subsequent study, which also found that 3% of a small sample of men (n = 33) acknowledged engaging in cross-dressing for sexual purposes (Kar & Koola, 2007). Interestingly, this latter study found a higher rate of transvestism (7.1%) in the 28 women in the sample.

## PSYCHOLOGICAL AND BIOLOGICAL ASSESSMENT

Assessment strategies include questionnaires and self-report measures, as well as objective, physiological measures, such as the plethysmograph, the polygraph, and measures of visual reaction time. Two challenges inherent in measuring paraphilic interests are (1) the fact that sexuality is typically a private matter and many individuals are uncomfortable discussing their interests and/or behaviors that carry a social stigma, and (2) the ethical aspects of assessment whereby some techniques are invasive and/or involve the presentation of potentially disturbing sexual stimuli. All of these techniques suffer from problems with reliability, validity, and vulnerability to dissimulation to varying degrees. Therefore, no one technique should be used in isolation.

One of the most widely used self-report measures is the Clarke Sexual History Questionnaire for Males (Paitich, Langevin, Freeman, Mann, & Handy, 1977), a 190-item questionnaire that assesses a wide range of sexual experiences, including paraphilic experiences, their frequency, and their age of onset. Another self-report measure, the Multiphasic Sex Inventory (Nichols & Molinder, 1984, 1992), assesses paraphilic sexual preferences, sexual knowledge, and sexual dysfunction. The Wilson Sex Fantasy Questionnaire (Wilson, 1978) is a further standardized, commonly used instrument. Unfortunately, all of these measures have the potential for biased or dishonest responses.

Card sort techniques contain rating scales composed of pictorial or written sexual stimuli that individuals are asked to view and then rate according to the degree of sexual arousal elicited. Examples include the Sexual Interest Card Sort Questionnaire (Holland, Zolondek, Abel, Jordan, & Becker, 2000) and Laws' (1986) Sexual Deviance Card Sort. Clinicians can also develop their own card sorts specific to what they know about a client, or they can ask their clients to record their daily sexual fantasies and urges and then rate the corresponding degree of sexual arousal (Maletzky, 1997).

A review by Schiavi, Derogatis, Kuriansky, O'Connor, and Sharpe (1979) of 50 self-report instruments used with sexual offenders found little evidence for their validity; however, their usefulness may lie in their ability to be used in conjunction with historical information that allows examination of inconsistencies (Kaplan & Krueger, 1997) or bias (Abel & Rouleau, 1990).

Because of the difficulties with self-report, many clinicians and researchers depend on objective measures. Of these, phallometric assessment is considered to be the most reliable and valid and the least prone to dissimulation (Quinsey, 1988; Quinsey & Earls, 1990; Seto, 2001). This technique involves the psychophysiological recording of sexual arousal through a device that measures either volumetric or circumferential changes in penile tumescence in response to sexual stimuli. The stimuli can take various forms, such as videos, audiotapes, photographs, and written text. Consistent increases in penile tumescence to specific sexual stimuli relative to other sexual and nonsexual stimuli are considered to indicate sexual preferences for those stimuli (Freund, 1963). The use of stimuli depicting individuals of all ages and both sexes, engaged in various sexual and nonsexual activities, reliably discriminates sexual from nonsexual offenders, including child molesters and non–child molesters (Barbaree & Marshall, 1989; Freund & Blanchard, 1989); rapists and nonrapists (Harris, Rice, Chaplin, & Quinsey, 1999; Lalumiere & Quinsey, 1994); men who admit to sadistic fantasies, cross-dress, or expose their genitals in public from men who do not (Freund, Seto, & Kuban, 1996; Seto & Kuban, 1996); and incest offenders and nonoffenders (Barsetti, Earls, & Lalumiere, 1998; Chaplin, Rice, & Harris, 1995). Phallometry also has high predictive power for sexual and violent recidivism (Malcolm, Andrews, & Quinsey, 1993; Rice, Harris, & Quinsey, 1990; Seto, 2001), similar to that of psychopathy diagnoses and criminal history (Hanson & Bussiere, 1998). Sexual interests, as measured through phallometric testing, are considered to be the most consistently identifiable distinguishing characteristics of sexual offenders compared to general psychopathology, empathy, and social skills (Quinsey & Lalumiere, 1996; Seto & Lalumiere, 2001).

Phallometric testing is not without its criticisms. For example, group discrimination is not perfect, with the distributions of phallometric scores overlapping between sex offenders and nonoffenders (Seto, 2001). Furthermore, while the specificity of phallometry is very high (i.e., the test is able to accurately identify men who have not committed a sexual offense as nondeviant 90% to 97.5% of the time), the sensitivity of the test (i.e., the ability of the test to identify men who have committed a sexual offense as deviant), appears to only be between 44% and 50% (Freund & Watson, 1991; Lalumiere & Quinsey, 1993). In addition, in 21% of participants assessed with phallometric testing, no clear diagnosis with respect to paraphillic sexual preferences was possible (Freund & Blanchard, 1989).

Furthermore, a lack of standardization in stimuli, testing procedures, and data analysis results in considerable variability in procedures, data interpretation, and outcome across phallometric laboratories (Howes, 1995), making it difficult to evaluate the technical adequacy of different phallometric studies, replicate experiments, and account for discrepancies between studies (Schouten & Simon, 1992). There are also ethical concerns because sexual stimuli that depict violent sexual behavior or sexual images of children are usually presented. Finally, although phallometric testing is much less susceptible than self-report to response bias or dissimulation, some participants can alter their physiological responses in a socially desirable direction (see Freund, Watson, & Rienzo, 1988, for a review; Lalumiere & Earls, 1992), an issue that has an impact on the procedure's sensitivity. Furthermore, the ability of participants to control, or alter, their physiological responses increases with subsequent testing (Quinsey, Rice, & Harris, 1995), suggesting that multiple assessments give participants the opportunity to learn how to alter their responses so they appear less sexually deviant (Lalumiere & Harris, 1998).

The polygraph (also known as the "lie detector") is another psychophysiological assessment technique used with individuals who have been accused or convicted of a sexual offense. However, unlike the plethysmograph, which is used to assess current sexual interests, the polygraph assesses past sexual behaviors and deceitfulness by measuring galvanic skin response, heart rate, blood pressure, and respiration. Changes in arousal are associated with involuntary responses to fear, based on the assumption that when people lie, they fear that their lie will be discovered, leading to measurable physiological increases. As Branaman and Gallagher (2005) indicate, the validity of the polygraph largely depends on the types of questions asked during the assessment. This has led to significant caution because the implications of incorrectly identifying someone as having committed sexual offenses are numerous and severe. Furthermore, skeptics note that some individuals may feel coerced into admitting to offenses they never committed (Cross & Saxe, 1992, 2001). Because of these concerns, the polygraph is not generally admissible in court.

Another objective assessment is visual reaction time (also referred to as viewing time). Similar to phallometric testing, this strategy involves showing pictures of various sexual and nonsexual stimuli. Participants are informed that the technique assesses sexual interests through their self-reported ratings of sexual attractiveness to each picture. However, participants do not know that the procedure involves the unobtrusive recording of the length of time they view each stimuli. The technique is based on findings that individuals view images they find sexually stimulating longer than those they do not (Lang, Searles, Lauerman, & Adesso, 1980; Quinsey, Rice, Harris, & Reid, 1993). Visual reaction time has similar reliability and validity as phallometric testing (Abel, Huffman, Warberg, & Holland, 1998; Letourneau, 2002), with the added advantages of greater efficiency, less intrusiveness, and less technological complexity than phallometry (Abel et al., 1998; Harris, Rice, Quinsey, & Chaplin, 1996). Because the technique is less intrusive and thus less ethically controversial, it has also been used with adolescent sexual offenders with promising results (Abel et al., 2004).

## ETIOLOGICAL CONSIDERATIONS

Numerous theories have been proposed to explain how the paraphilias develop; however, empirical evidence is either lacking or contradictory, and, as a result, no individual theory satisfactorily explains the development of paraphilic sexual interests. Nevertheless, knowledge of these theories provides some insight into current thinking about how paraphilic sexual disorders develop and the rationale behind various treatment approaches.

### NEUROANATOMY AND NEUROBIOLOGY

Cases in which individuals developed paraphilic sexual interests following brain injuries and degenerative brain diseases (see Langevin, 1990, for a review) have led to hypotheses that the paraphilias may be caused by certain neurological abnormalities, particularly temporal lobe and limbic area abnormalities. Unfortunately, these findings are not uniform, and they fail to account for a large number of individuals with paraphilias (Hucker et al., 1988; O'Carroll, 1989; Tarter, Hegadus, Alterman, & Katz-Garris, 1983). Further, numerous studies have found that temporal lobe disorders are generally associated with hyposexuality, not hypersexuality (Miller, Darby, Swartz, Yener, & Mena, 1995; Rosenblum, 1974).

New research suggests possible neurobiological underpinnings of paraphilic interests. In particular, research by Cantor and colleagues (Cantor et al., 2008), which compared the MRI scans of a sample of 65 pedophiles to a sample of 62 nonsexual offenders, found that pedophilic men had significantly less white matter in the superior fronto-occipital fasciculus and the right arcuate fasciculus regions of the brain. These regions of the brain, located in the temporal and parietal lobes, are comprised of axons that connect to other brain regions, thereby suggesting differences in the connectivity of the various regions of the brain in pedophiles versus nonpedophiles. Specifically, Cantor et al. (2008) surmised that because the superior fronto-occipital fasciculus and arcuate fasciculus connect those regions of the brain that respond to sexual cues, pedophilia may be the result of a partial disconnection within the network that recognizes sexually relevant stimuli.

As Cantor et al. (2008) point out, it must be acknowledged that it is unknown whether these differences are the cause or the result of pedophilia, or due to an unknown third variable. However, given that these two regions of the brain are not generally associated with changes following environmental stimulation, the possibility that these changes are the result of pedophilia is unlikely. Furthermore, the relatively lower volumes of white matter found in pedophiles are congruent with neuropsychological findings that pedophilic men have lower IQs (Cantor, Blanchard, Christensen, Dickey, & Klassen, 2004; Cantor, Blanchard, Robichaud, & Christensen, 2005), poorer visuospatial and verbal memory abilities (Cantor et al., 2004), higher rates of being non-right-handed (Cantor et al., 2004, 2005), higher rates of head injuries that resulted in unconsciousness in childhood (Blanchard et al., 2002; Blanchard et al., 2003), and higher rates of having failed grades in school or having been placed in special education programs (Cantor et al., 2006), than nonpedophilic men. These characteristics may also be the result of reduced white matter volume and, in the case of handedness, become apparent very early in life (i.e., in utero). As such, the possibility that pedophilia leads to a lower volume of white matter over time is unlikely, and it is more likely that pedophilia is the result of an anomaly in early neurodevelopment (Blanchard et al., 2002).

### LEARNING, MODELING, AND LIFE EVENTS

Behavioral theories of paraphilias have garnered much attention from clinicians and researchers, and have shaped many of the psychotherapeutic approaches used to treat paraphilic interests. Behavioral theories posit that paraphilias develop through operant or classical conditioning in which the object of paraphilic attention becomes paired with sexual arousal, resulting in abnormal arousal patterns. In essence, sexual arousal becomes the conditioned response to the paraphilic target and is reinforced through masturbation and orgasm.

Research by Rachman and colleagues (Rachman, 1966; Rachman & Hodgson, 1968) demonstrated that sexual arousal can, in fact, be conditioned; they conditioned a sexual response to a picture of a pair of boots by pairing the picture of the boots with photographs of nude adult women. However, the responses were easily extinguished, leading others to argue that the behavioral theory is not sufficient on its own to explain the maintenance of such behaviors throughout an individual's life (Bancroft, 2009).

Modeling and the effects of early life events have also been hypothesized to play a causal role. The belief that negative and disruptive early childhood and family functioning may lead to paraphilias comes from research indicating high rates of childhood abuse (both sexual and nonsexual), neglect, and disturbed family relations in paraphilic individuals (e.g., Marshall et al., 1993; Saunders, Awad, & White, 1986). Marshall and colleagues (1993) suggest that these negative experiences serve as templates for future relationships, leading to distrust or ambivalence with appropriate partners and teaching individuals to be abusive toward others. McGuire, Carlisle, and Young (1965) more specifically hypothesized that individuals who experience sexual abuse as children go on to use thoughts of the abuse during masturbation in adolescence, thus pairing abusive thoughts with the pleasure of masturbation, and leading to specific, paraphilic sexual preferences.

These hypotheses, however, fail to account for the many individuals who have experienced abuse and dysfunctional family relationships who do not go on to develop paraphilias and, conversely, the many individuals with paraphilias who have no history of familial instability or victimization (Murphy, Haynes, & Page, 1992; Murphy & Smith, 1996).

COGNITIVE INFLUENCES

Cognitive-behavioral theories have emphasized the role of cognitions in the etiology of sexual offending (e.g., Ward, Hudson, & Marshall, 1995). Cognitive distortions include beliefs and ways of thinking that minimize or deny harm and attribute blame to victims or to other external factors, resulting in a lack of empathy toward victims. These distorted beliefs facilitate and justify further sexual offending (Abel, Becker, & Cunningham-Rathner, 1984) and have, thus, become the target of most treatment efforts with sexual offenders. However, evidence is lacking that these cognitions cause paraphilic sexual interests to develop. In fact, even the extent to which they cause initial instances of sexual offending, versus emerging after the fact, remains unclear. Of note is that researchers have found that child molesters are not lacking in general empathy (i.e., they have not been found to be less empathic compared to non–child molesters), but that they are lacking in specific empathy toward their victims (Marshall, Jones, Hudson, & McDonald, 1994).

## COURSE, PROGNOSIS, AND TREATMENT

Paraphilias most commonly first appear in adolescence (e.g., Abel, Osborn, & Twigg, 1993; McConaghy, 1993; Zucker & Bradley, 1995), with charges and convictions most frequently occurring in early adulthood (e.g., Berah & Meyers, 1983). The course has generally been found to be chronic (e.g., Gosselin & Wilson, 1980), and, at least in the case of sexual sadism, the severity may increase over time (APA, 2000).

Due to ethical and methodological limitations in conducting empirical investigations of treatment efficacy with paraphilic individuals (such as randomly assigning convicted offenders to a no-treatment control group), and because most paraphilias have extremely low base rates, leading to difficulties with acquiring adequate sample sizes, efficacy rates for the treatment of the paraphilias has not been conclusive. In fact, some professionals have argued that there currently is no empirical basis indicating that treatment for sexual offenders is superior to placebo (e.g., Furby, Weinrott, & Blackshaw, 1989). Treatment of paraphilias with nonoffending individuals is often focused on helping them understand that paraphilias are lifelong and that people do not choose what will interest them sexually. In addition, treatment may focus on how the interests can be managed in ways that do not involve illegal activities or risks to physical health and safety, and in ways that do not affect social and/or occupational functioning.

## LOOKING AHEAD TO *DSM-5*

Several significant changes to the paraphilia diagnoses are being proposed for the fifth edition of the *Diagnostic and Statistical Manual of Mental Disorders* (*DSM-5*). These include two broad changes to the way disorders in this section of the *DSM* are conceptualized and diagnosed, the addition of two new diagnoses, and changes to the diagnostic criteria of the currently recognized paraphilias.

### DISTINCTION BETWEEN PARAPHILIAS AND PARAPHILIC DISORDERS

The first of the broad changes that the American Psychiatric Association's *DSM-5* Workgroup on Sexual and Gender Identity Disorders (hereafter referred to as the "Workgroup") has proposed is that a distinction be made between *paraphilias* and *paraphilic disorders*. Under the proposed revisions, the former would denote sexual desires, urges, and/or behaviors that are non-normative but not necessarily psychopathological. In contrast, the latter term is being suggested to refer to paraphilias that cause stress or impairment to the individual, or harm to others. For example, the term *exhibitionism* under the proposed revisions would denote the presence of a paraphilia involving a non-normative sexual interest in exposing oneself to unsuspecting individuals. In contrast, the term *exhibitionistic disorder* would denote the presence of exhibitionism together with significant distress, impairment, or harm to others. The former would be "ascertained," after which the latter could be "diagnosed" *if* distress, impairment, and/or harm to others is present. In other words, as noted by the Workgroup, "having a paraphilia would be a necessary but not a sufficient condition for having a paraphilic disorder" (APA, 2010, Rationale section).

By distinguishing non-normative but nonharmful sexual interests from those that are harmful and/or distressing, the Workgroup highlighted that paraphilias are not, in and of themselves, psychiatric disorders. Furthermore, the Workgroup points out that this proposed revision eliminates the prior discrepancy in which someone with a pervasive, non-normative sexual interest (e.g., a sexual interest in experiencing pain or humiliation) could only be described as having that interest (i.e., being a sexual masochist) when the sexual interest was accompanied by distress, impairment, or harm to others.

### CRITERION B SEXUAL BEHAVIORS CLAUSE

The second broad change is that those paraphilic disorders that often involve nonconsenting individuals (i.e., exhibitionistic disorder, frotteuristic disorder, voyeuristic disorder, pedohebephilic disorder, and sexual sadism disorder) require a minimum number of victims in order for the "significant distress, impairment, or harm to others" criterion (Criterion B) to be met in cases where the individual denies the paraphilic preference. The Workgroup proposed this change because a significant number of individuals who have been arrested or convicted of a sexual offense deny paraphilic urges or fantasies, likely to avoid legal and social repercussions. This denial precludes clinicians from being able to rely on patient self-reports when assessing the paraphilias. Thus, the change promoted allows for a diagnosis of a paraphilia in cases where a specific number of separate victims have been identified, despite denial of paraphilic sexual interests by the patient. Furthermore, this change addresses past criticisms regarding what defines "recurrent" in Criterion A when referring to the presence of paraphilic sexual urges, fantasies, and behaviors. The proposed specific minimum number of victims varies across the paraphilias (see APA, 2010, Rationale section for details).

## Hypersexual Disorder

One of the new diagnoses proposed for consideration is Hypersexual Disorder. This disorder relates to what is often termed "sexual addiction" in the media, and is being proposed to refer to recurrent and intense sexual fantasies, urges, and behaviors over at least a 6-month time period that are associated with at least four of the following: (1) an excessive amount of time is consumed by sexual urges and fantasies, as well as by planning for, and engaging in, sexual behaviors; (2) the individual repeatedly engages in sexual fantasies, urges, and behaviors in response to anxiety, depression, boredom, irritability, or other dysphoric mood states, or (3) in response to stressful life events; (4) the individual has made repeated but unsuccessful attempts to control or significantly reduce the sexual fantasies, urges, and behaviors; and (5) the individual engages in sexual behaviors without regard for the risk of either physical or emotional harm to self or others.

In addition, sexual fantasies, urges, and behaviors must result in clinically significant distress and/or impairment, cannot be due to the direct physiological effects of a substance, or be directly attributable to the consequences of a manic episode. Finally, the proposed diagnostic criteria require that the individual be at least 18 years of age.

Hypersexual Disorder is being conceptualized "as primarily a nonparaphilic sexual desire disorder with an impulsivity component" (Kafka, 2010, p. 377). Currently, these difficulties are diagnosed as a Sexual Disorder Not Otherwise Specified (Sexual Disorder NOS).

## Paraphilic Coercive Disorder

The other new proposed disorder is what has been termed Paraphilic Coercive Disorder. This proposed diagnosis refers to recurrent and intense sexual fantasies, urges, or behaviors, over a period of at least 6 months, pertaining to sexual coercion (Criterion A), that result in clinically significant distress or impairment or forced sex with at least three nonconsenting individuals on separate occasions (Criterion B). According to the proposed diagnostic criteria, the diagnosis is not made if the criteria for Sexual Sadism Disorder are met (Criterion C).

## Other Proposed Changes

In addition to the significant, conceptual changes described previously, the *DSM-5* Workgroup is proposing only minor changes to the diagnostic criteria for exhibitionistic disorder, fetishistic disorder, frotteuristic disorder, voyeuristic disorder, sexual sadism disorder, sexual masochistic disorder, and transvestic disorder.

## Pedohebephilic Disorder

Of all of the revisions to the current paraphilias that are being proposed for *DSM-5*, the Workgroup is suggesting that the diagnosis of pedophilia undergo the most significant changes. First is that the name of the disorder be changed to differentiate between a paraphilia and a paraphilic disorder. Second, the Workgroup is advocating that a distinction be made between a sexual interest in prepubescent children (pedophilia) and pubescent children (hebephilia). Pubescent children are generally those between the ages of approximately 11 to 15 (see Blanchard, 2010). Thus, the *DSM-5* Workgroup is proposing that the name of the disorder be changed to Pedohebephilic Disorder and that the specifiers delineate between "Pedophilic type—Sexually Attracted to Prepubescent Children (Generally Younger than 11)," "Hebephilic Type—Sexually Attracted to Pubescent Children (Generally Age 11 through 14)," and "Pedohebephilic Type—Sexually Attracted to Both" (APA, 2010, Pedohebephilic Disorder section).

Proposed changes to the specific diagnostic criteria for Pedohebephilic Disorder include a change to Criterion A that would allow for the ascertainment of pedohebephilia based on either (or both) recurrent and intense sexual fantasies, urges, or behaviors over at least a 6-month period involving prepubescent or pubescent children, or equal or greater sexual arousal to prepubescent or pubescent children than to physically mature individuals. With respect to changes to Criterion B, the *DSM-5* Workgroup is proposing that this criterion be met when at least one of the following signs or symptoms is present: (1) there is significant distress or impairment as a result of the sexual attraction to children; (2) the person has acted on the pedohebephilic interest with at least two prepubescent children, or with at least three pubescent children, on separate occasions; and (3) the person has a history of at least 6 months' duration of repeated pornography use that depicts prepubescent or pubescent children, and the person experiences greater arousal from this type of pornography than from pornography depicting physically mature individuals. The proposed change to Criterion C involves raising the minimum age for the diagnosis from 16 to 18, although the requirement that the individual be at least 5 years older than the children in Criteria A and B remains unchanged.

## CASE STUDY

John is a 21-year-old, single, heterosexual, Caucasian male who resides with his parents and two younger siblings. He has a college diploma and is currently employed in the sales industry. John's probation officer referred John to a behavioral sexology clinic following John's conviction for committing an indecent act (also known as "indecent exposure" or "public indecency"). John was charged and convicted of committing an indecent act after he drove his car alongside two females, ages 14 and 20, exposed his penis, and then masturbated to the point of ejaculation before driving away. John has no criminal record for any prior sexual or nonsexual offenses; however, John acknowledged a sexual interest in exhibitionism and a prior history of exposing himself to strangers. He reported that he spontaneously began to have fantasies about exposing himself to unsuspecting women when he was approximately 18 or 19 years of age. His fantasies of exhibitionism involve the unsuspecting woman becoming intrigued and aroused by his exhibitionism and this leading to consensual partnered sexual activities. At the same time, John acknowledged that, while this is his fantasy, he has never actually believed that this would happen in reality.

John reported that he exposed himself for the first time when he was 19 years old. He was driving in his car, with no prior intention of exposing himself, when he drove past an attractive, adult female walking on the street. John reported that he developed a strong urge to expose himself to her. He maneuvered his car in such a way that she walked by him and could see in his window, and he then masturbated to the point of ejaculation. According to John, the female noticed what he was doing but gave no reaction. John felt very guilty after the incident. Nonetheless, he noticed that his fantasies and urges to expose himself increased.

John's second instance of exposing himself occurred when he was in college. He was in the college library when he saw an attractive female studying in a study carrel across from him. John once again exposed his penis and masturbated to the point of ejaculation, after which he ran out of the library and again felt very guilty.

With respect to the incident that resulted in John's conviction and subsequent referral to the behavioral sexology clinic, John reported that he had purposely gotten in his car and driven around searching for an attractive female to expose himself to after experiencing strong urges to do so. He reported that he then saw the two victims, the older of whom he found attractive. He pulled up to them, exposed himself, and masturbated to the point of ejaculation. He then drove away but was contacted by police an hour later.

John expressed a lot of guilt about his exhibitionistic urges and behaviors. He acknowledged that he continues to have urges to expose himself since the index offense but reported that he has been able to refrain from acting out on the urges by reminding himself of his arrest and conviction. At the same time, he expressed concern that thinking of the index offence may not be enough to resist his urges in the future.

With respect to other sexual interests, John reported that he is sexually attracted exclusively to females who are approximately his age. He reported no sexual attraction to prepubescent or pubescent females. He similarly reported that he has no sexual interest in cross-dressing, leather, latex, rough or violent sexual behavior, or being humiliated. He reported no interest in voyeurism beyond viewing "amateur" pornographic videos that advertise that the performers are unaware of being filmed. He reported no concerns pertaining to sexual functioning or gender identity.

Assessment involved a comprehensive psychosexual history, including information about his exhibitionistic fantasies, urges, and behaviors, information about other paraphilic and nonparaphilic interests and behaviors, general mental and physical health, and social and interpersonal functioning. Through this psychosexual history, John met *DSM-IV-TR* criteria for exhibitionism.

John did not report any other paraphilic sexual interests; however, given the nature of the referral and the additional fact that one of the two victims of the index offense was 14 years of age, corroborative objective assessment via phallometric testing was deemed appropriate. Phallometric testing was not indicative of a sexual interest in either prepubescent or pubescent children. Thus, John's final diagnosis was exhibitionism, and it was concluded that he could potentially benefit from participation in cognitive-behavioral/relapse prevention treatment for his sexual offending behaviors.

## SUMMARY

Often associated with sexual deviance and sexual offending, the paraphilias are one of the most controversial groups of disorders. This controversy stems from disagreements over such issues as whether the paraphilias should be categorized as mental disorders or instead be seen simply as variants of human sexuality; arguments over why certain sexual behaviors are included under the paraphilias (such as fetishism) while others are not (such as rape); and arguments over the specific diagnostic criteria for each of the paraphilias. This controversy is furthered by the limited amount of sound empirical research—particularly epidemiological research—with individuals with these conditions. However, assessment and treatment of the paraphilias have advanced significantly toward more effective, efficient, and ethical techniques. With the upcoming publication of the fifth edition of the *Diagnostic and Statistical Manual of Mental Disorders*, it will be interesting to see how revisions to the current diagnostic criteria for the paraphilias will impact on the diagnosis, classification, and understanding of these phenomena.

## REFERENCES

Abel, G. G., Becker, J. V., & Cunningham-Rathner, J. (1984). Complications, consent and cognitions in sex between children and adults. *International Journal of Law and Psychiatry, 7,* 89–103.

Abel, G. G., Becker, J. V., Cunningham-Rathner, J., Mittelman, M., & Rouleau, J. (1988). Multiple paraphilic diagnoses among sex offenders. *Bulletin of the American Academy of Psychiatry and the Law, 16,* 153–168.

Abel, G. G., Becker, J. V., Mittelman, M., Cunningham-Rathner, J., Rouleau, J. L., & Murphy, W. D. (1987). Self-reported sex crimes of nonincarcerated paraphiliacs. *Journal of Interpersonal Violence, 2,* 3–25.

Abel, G. G., Huffman, J., Warberg, B., & Holland, C. L. (1998). Visual reaction time and plethysmography as measures of sexual interest in child molesters. *Sexual Abuse: A Journal of Research and Treatment, 10,* 81–95.

Abel, G. G., Jordan, A., Rouleau, J. L., Emerick, R., Barboza-Whitehead, S., & Osborn, C. (2004). Use of visual reaction time to assess male adolescents who molest children. *Sexual Abuse: A Journal of Research and Treatment, 16,* 255–265.

Abel, G. G., & Osborn, C. (1992). The paraphilias: The extent and nature of sexually deviant and criminal behavior. *Clinical Forensic Psychiatry, 15,* 675–687.

Abel, G., Osborn, C., & Twigg, D. (1993). Sexual assault through the life span: Adult offenders with juvenile histories. In H. E. Barbaree, W. Marshall, & S. M. Hudson (Eds.), *The juvenile sex offender* (pp. 104–117). New York, NY: Guilford Press.

Abel, G. G., & Rouleau, J. L. (1990). The nature and extent of sexual assault. In W. L. Marshall, D. R. Laws, & H. E. Barbaree (Eds.), *Handbook of sexual assault: Issues, theories, and treatment of the offender* (pp. 9–21). New York, NY: Plenum Press.

Abel, G. G., Rouleau, J. L., & Cunningham-Rathner, J. (1986). Sexually aggressive behavior. In W. J. Curran, A. L. McGarry, & S. Shah (Eds.), *Forensic psychiatry and psychology: Perspectives and standards for interdisciplinary practice* (pp. 289–313). Philadelphia, PA: F. A. Davis.

Adams, H. E., & McAnulty, R. D. (1993). Sexual disorders: The paraphilias. In P. B. Sutker & H. E. Adams (Eds.), *Comprehensive handbook of psychopathology* (2nd ed., pp. 563–579). New York, NY: Plenum.

Agnew, J. (1986). Hazards associated with anal erotic activity. *Archives of Sexual Behavior, 15,* 307–314.

American Psychiatric Association. (2000). *Diagnostic and statistical manual of mental disorders* (4th edition, text revision; DSM-IV-TR). Washington, DC: American Psychiatric Association.

American Psychiatric Association. (2010). DSM-5 development, sexual and gender identity disorders. Retrieved December 1, 2011 from www.dsm5.org/ProposedRevisions/Pages/SexualandGenderIdentityDisorders.aspx.

Amsterdam, A., Carter, L., & Krychman, M. (2006). Prevalence of psychiatric illness in women in an oncology sexual health population: A retrospective pilot study. *Journal of Sexual Medicine, 3,* 292–295.

Araujo, A. B., Durante, R., Feldman, H. A., Goldstein, I., & McKinley, J. B. (1998). The relationship between depressive symptoms and male erectile dysfunction: Cross-sectional results from the Massachusetts Male Aging Study. *Psychosomatic Medicine, 60,* 458–465.

Arndt, W., Foehl, J., & Good, F. (1985). Specific sexual fantasy themes: A multidimensional study. *Journal of Personality and Social Psychology, 48,* 472–480.

Arnow, B. A., Millheiser, L., Garrett, A., Lake Polan, M., Glover, G. H., Lightbody, A., . . . Desmond, J. E. (2009). Women with hypoactive sexual desire disorder compared to normal females: a functional magnetic resonance imaging study. *Neuroscience, 158,* 484–502.

Bader, S. M., Schoeneman-Morris, K. A., Scalora, M. J., & Casady, T. K. (2008). Exhibitionism: Findings from a Midwestern police contact sample. *International Journal of Offender Therapy and Comparative Criminology, 52,* 270–279.

Balon, R. (2010). Proposal to introduce adjustment disorder with disturbed sexual functioning into the revised classifications of *DSM* and *ICD*. *Journal of Sex and Marital Therapy, 36,* 1–5.

Bancroft, J. (2009). *Human sexuality and its problems* (3rd ed.). Edinburgh, Scotland: Churchill Livingstone.

Bancroft, J., Loftus, J., & Long, S. J. (2003). Distress about sex: A national survey of women in heterosexual relationships. *Archives of Sexual Behavior, 32,* 193–208.

Banmen, J., & Vogel, N. A. (1985). The relationship between marital quality and interpersonal sexual communication. *Family Therapy, 12,* 45–58.

Barbaree, H. E., & Marshall, W. L. (1989). Erectile responses among heterosexual child molesters, father-daughter incest offenders, and matched non-offenders: Five distinct age preference profiles. *Canadian Journal of Behavioral Science, 21,* 70–82.

Barbaree, H. E., & Seto, M. C. (1997). Pedophilia: Assessment and treatment. In D. R. Laws & W. O'Donohue (Eds.), *Sexual deviance: Theory, assessment, and treatment* (pp. 175–193). New York, NY: Guilford Press.

Barsetti, I., Earls, C. M., & Lalumiere, M. L. (1998). The differentiation of intrafamilial and extrafamilial heterosexual child molesters. *Journal of Interpersonal Violence, 13,* 275–286.

Bartosh, D. L., Garby, T., Lewis, D., & Gray, S. (2003). Differences in predictive validity of actuarial risk assessments in relation to sex offender type. *International Journal of Offender Therapy and Comparative Criminology, 47,* 422–438.

Basson, R. (2002). A model of women's sexual arousal. *Journal of Sex and Marital Therapy, 28,* 1–10.

Basson, R. (2004). Pharmacotherapy for sexual dysfunction in women. *Expert Opinion in Pharmacotherapy, 5,* 1045–1059.

Basson, R., & Brotto, L. A. (2003). Sexual psychophysiology and effects of sildenafil citrate in oestrogenised women with acquired genital arousal disorder and impaired orgasm: A randomised controlled trial. *British Journal of Obstetrics and Gynaecology, 110,* 1014–1024.

Basson, R., Brotto, L. A., Petkau, J. A., & Labrie, F. (2010). Role of androgens in women's sexual dysfunction. *Menopause, 17*, 962–971.

Basson, R., Leiblum, S. L., Brotto, L. A., Derogatis, L., Fourcroy, J., Fugl-Meyer, K., . . . Schultz, W. W. (2003). Definitions of women's sexual dysfunctions reconsidered: Advocating expansion and revision. *Journal of Psychosomatic Obstetrics and Gynaecology, 24*, 221–229.

Basson, R., McInnes, R., Smith, M. D., Hodgson, G., & Koppiker, N. (2002). Efficacy and safety of sildenafil citrate in women with sexual dysfunction associated with female sexual arousal disorder. *Journal of Women's Health and Gender-Based Medicine, 11*, 367–377.

Baumeister, R. F. (1989). *Masochism and the self.* Hillsdale, NJ: Erlbaum.

Baumeister, R. F. (1991). *Escaping the self: Alcoholism, spirituality, masochism, and other flights from the burden of selfhood.* New York, NY: Basic Books.

Baumeister, R. F., & Butler, J. L. (1997). Sexual masochism: Deviance without pathology. In D. R. Laws & W. O'Donohue (Eds.), *Sexual deviance: Theory, assessment, and treatment* (pp. 225–239). New York, NY: Guilford Press.

Baumeister, R. F., Catanese, K. R., & Vohs, K. D. (2001). Is there a gender difference in strength of sex drive? Theoretical views, conceptual distinctions, and a review of relevant evidence. *Personality and the Social Psychology Review, 5*, 242–273.

Baumeister, R. F., & Scher, S. J. (1988). Self-defeating behavior patterns among normal individuals: Review and analysis of common self-destructive tendencies. *Psychological Bulletin, 104*, 3–22.

Becker, J. V., Stinson, J., Tromp, S., & Messer, G. (2003). Characteristics of individuals petitioned for civil commitment. *International Journal of Offender Therapy and Comparative Criminology, 47*, 185–195.

Berah, E. F., & Meyers, R. G. (1983). The offense records of a sample of convicted exhibitionists. *Bulletin of the American Academy of Psychiatry and the Law, 11*, 365–369.

Berger, P., Berner, W., Bolterauer, J., Gutierrez, K., & Berger, K. (1999). Sadistic personality disorder in sex offenders: Relationship to antisocial personality disorder and sexual sadism. *Journal of Personality Disorders, 13*, 175–186.

Bergeron, S., & Binik, Y. M. (1998). *Treatment manual for cognitive-behavioural group therapy with women suffering from vulvar vestibulitis syndrome.* Unpublished treatment manual. Montreal, Canada: McGill University.

Bergeron, S., Binik, Y. M., Khalife, S., Pagidas, K., Glazer, H. I., Meana, M., & Amsel, R. (2001). A randomized comparison of group cognitive behavioural therapy, surface eletromyographic biofeedback, and vestibulectomy in the treatment of dyspareunia resulting from vulvar vestibulitis. *Pain, 91*, 297–306.

Bergeron, S., Brown, C., Lord, M. J, Oala, M., Binik, Y. M., & Khalife, S. (2002). Physical therapy for vulvar vestibulitis syndrome: a retrospective study. *Journal of Sex and Marital Therapy, 28*, 183–192.

Bergeron, S., Khalifé, S., Glazer, H. I., & Binik, Y. M. (2008). Surgical and behavioral treatments for vestibulodynia: two-and-one-half year follow-up and predictors of outcome. *Obstetrics and Gynecology, 111*, 159–166.

Berglas, S. C., & Baumeister, R. F. (1993). *Your own worst enemy: Understanding the paradox of self-defeating behavior.* New York, NY: Basic Books.

Berman, J. R., Berman, L. A., Toler, S. M., Gill, J., Haughie, S., & Sildenafil Study Group. (2003). Safety and efficacy of sildenafil citrate for the treatment of female sexual arousal disorder: A double-blind, placebo controlled study. *Journal of Urology, 170*, 2333–2338.

Billups, K. L., Berman, L., Berman, J., Metz, M. E., Glennon, M. E., & Goldstein, I. (2001). A new non-pharmacological vacuum therapy for female sexual dysfunction. *Journal of Sex and Marital Therapy, 27*, 435–441.

Binik, Y. M. (2005). Should dyspareunia be retained as a sexual dysfunction in *DSM-V*? A painful classification decision. *Archives of Sexual Behavior, 34,* 11–21.

Binik, Y. M. (2010a). The *DSM* diagnostic criteria for dyspareunia. *Archives of Sexual Behavior, 39,* 292–303.

Binik, Y. M. (2010b). The *DSM* diagnostic criteria for vaginismus. *Archives of Sexual Behavior, 9,* 861–873.

Blair, C. D., & Lanyon, R. I. (1981). Exhibitionism: Etiology and treatment. *Psychological Bulletin, 89,* 439–463.

Blanchard, R. (2005). Early history of the concept of autogynephilia. *Archives of Sexual Behavior, 34,* 439–446.

Blanchard, R. (2010). The *DSM* diagnostic criteria for pedophilia. *Archives of Sexual Behavior, 39,* 304–316.

Blanchard, R., Christensen, B. K., Strong, S. M., Cantor, J. M., Kuban, M. E., Klassen, P., . . . Blak, T. (2002). Retrospective self-reports of childhood accidents causing unconsciousness in phallometrically diagnosed pedophiles. *Archives of Sexual Behavior, 31,* 511–526.

Blanchard, R., & Collins, P. (1993). Men with sexual interest in transvestites, transsexuals and she-males. *Journal of Nervous and Mental Disease, 181,* 570–575.

Blanchard, R., & Hucker, S. J. (1991). Age, transvestism, bondage, and concurrent paraphilic activities in 117 fatal cases of autoerotic asphyxia. *British Journal of Psychiatry, 159,* 371–377.

Blanchard, R., Kuban, M. E., Klassen, P., Dickey, R., Christensen, B. K., Cantor, J. M., & Blak, T. (2003). Self-reported head injuries before and after age 13 in pedophilic and non-pedophilic men referred for clinical assessment. *Archives of Sexual Behavior, 32,* 573–581.

Bolt, J. W., Evans, C., & Marshall, V. R. (1987). Sexual dysfunction after prostatectomy. *British Journal of Urology, 59,* 319–322.

Bradford, J., Boulet, J., & Pawlak, A. (1992). The paraphilias: A multiplicity of deviant behaviors. *Canadian Journal of Psychiatry, 37,* 104–108.

Branaman, T. F., & Gallagher, S. N. (2005). Polygraph testing in sex offender treatment: A review of limitations. *American Journal of Forensic Psychology, 23,* 45–64.

Breslow, N., Evans, N., & Langley, J. (1985). On the prevalence and roles of females in sadomasochistic sub-culture: Report of an empirical study. *Archives of Sexual Medicine, 14,* 303–317.

Breslow, N., Evans, L., & Langley, J. (1995). On the prevalence and roles of females in the sadomasochistic subculture: Report of an empirical study. In T. S. Weinberg (Ed.), *S & M studies in dominance and submission* (pp. 249–267). Amherst, NY: Prometheus Books.

Brock, G., Iglesias, J., Toulouse, K., Ferguson, K. M., Pullman, W. E., & Anglin, G. (2001). *Efficacy and safety of tadalafil (IC351) treatment for ED.* Paper presented at the 16th Congress of the European Association of Urology, Geneva, Switzerland.

Brotto, L. A. (2010a). The *DSM* diagnostic criteria for hypoactive sexual desire disorder in women. *Archives of Sexual Behavior, 39,* 221–239.

Brotto, L. A. (2010b). The *DSM* diagnostic criteria for hypoactive sexual desire disorder in men. *Journal of Sexual Medicine, 7,* 2015–2030.

Brotto, L. A., Basson, R., & Luria, M. (2008). A mindfulness-based group psychoeducational intervention targeting sexual arousal disorder in women. *Journal of Sexual Medicine, 5,* 1646–1659.

Brotto, L. A., Bitzer, J., Laan, E., Leiblum, S., & Luria, M. (2010). Women's sexual desire and arousal disorders. *Journal of Sexual Medicine, 7,* 586–614.

Brotto, L. A., Heiman, J. R., Goff, B., Greer, B., Lentz, G. M., Swisher, E., . . . van Blaricom, A. (2008). A psychoeducational intervention for sexual dysfunction in women with gynecologic cancer. *Archives of Sexual Behavior, 37,* 317–329.

Brotto, L. A., Heiman, J. R., & Tolman, D. L. (2009). Narratives of desire in mid-age women with and without arousal difficulties. *Journal of Sex Research, 46*, 387–398.

Buhrich, N., & McConaghy, N. (1985). Preadult feminine behaviors of male transvestites. *Archives of Sexual Behavior, 14*, 413–419.

Cain, V. S., Johannes, C. B., Avis, N. E., Mohr, B., Schocken, M., Skurnick J., & Ory, M. (2003). Sexual functioning and practices in a multi-ethnic study of midlife women: Baseline results from SWAN. *Journal of Sex Research, 40*, 266–276.

Cantor, J. M., Blanchard, R., Christensen, B. K., Dickey, R., & Klassen, P. E. (2004). Intelligence, memory, and handedness in pedophilia. *Neuropsychology, 18*, 3–14.

Cantor, J. M., Blanchard, R., Robichaud, L. K., & Christensen, B. K. (2005). Quantitative reanalysis of aggregate data on IQ in sexual offenders. *Psychological Bulletin, 131*, 555–568.

Cantor, J. M., Kabani, N., Christensen, B. K., Zipursky, R. B., Barbaree, H. E., Dickey, R., . . . Blanchard, R. (2008). Cerebral white matter deficiencies in pedophilic men. *Journal of Psychiatric Research, 42*, 167–183.

Cantor, J. M., Kuban, M. E., Blak, T., Klassen, P. E., Dickey, R., & Blanchard, R. (2006). Grade failure and special education placement in sexual offenders' educational histories. *Archives of Sexual Behavior, 35*, 743–751.

Caruso, S., Agnello, C., Intelisano, G., Farina, M., Di Mari, L., & Cianci, A. (2004). Placebo-controlled study on efficacy and safety of daily apomorphine SL intake in premenopausal women affected by hypoactive sexual desire disorder and sexual arousal disorder. *Urology, 63*, 955–959.

Caruso, S., Intelisano, G., Lupo, L., & Agnello, C. (2001). Premenopausal women affected by sexual arousal disorder treated with sildenafil: A double-blind, cross-over, placebo-controlled study. *British Journal of Obstetrics and Gynaecology, 108*, 623–628.

Cavanaugh-Johnson, T. (1988). Child perpetrators: Children who molest children. *Child Abuse and Neglect, 12*, 219–229.

Chalkley, A. J., & Powell, G. E. (1983). The clinical description of forty-eight cases of sexual fetishism. *British Journal of Psychiatry, 142*, 292–295.

Chaplin, T. C., Rice, M. E., & Harris, G. T. (1995). Salient victim suffering and the sexual responses of child molesters. *Journal of Consulting and Clinical Psychology, 63*, 249–255.

Chivers, M. L., Seto, M. C., Lalumiere, M. L., Laan, E., & Grimbos, T. (2010). Agreement of self-reported and genital measures of sexual arousal in men and women: A meta-analysis. *Archives of Sexual Behavior, 39*, 5–56.

Chung, Y. B., & Harmon, L. W. (1994). The career interests and aspirations of gay men: How sex-role orientation is related. *Journal of Vocational Behavior, 45*, 223–239.

Clayton, A. H., Dennerstein, L., Pyke, R., & Sand, M. (2010). Flibanserin: A potential treatment for hypoactive sexual desire disorder in premenopausal women. *Women's Health, 6*, 639–653.

Cowan, L. (1982). *Masochism: A Jungian view.* Dallas, TX: Spring.

Cox, D. J., & Maletzky, B. M. (1980). Victims of exhibitionism. In D. J. Cox & R. J. Daitzman (Eds.), *Exhibitionism: Description, assessment and treatment* (pp. 289–293). New York, NY: Garland.

Crenshaw, T. L., Goldberg, J. P., & Stern, W. C. (1987). Pharmacologic modification of psychosexual dysfunction. *Journal of Sex and Marital Therapy, 13*, 239–252.

Crepault, E., & Couture, M. (1980). Men's erotic fantasies. *Archives of Sexual Behavior, 9*, 565–581.

Critelli, J. W., & Bivona, J. M. (2008). Women's erotic rape fantasies: An evaluation of theory and research. *Journal of Sex Research, 45*, 57–70.

Cross, P. A., & Matheson, K. (2006). Understanding sadomasochism: An empirical examination of four perspectives. *Journal of Homosexuality, 50*, 133–166.

Cross, T. P., & Saxe, L. (1992). A critique of the validity of polygraph testing in child sexual abuse cases. *Journal of Child Sexual Abuse, 1*, 19–33.

Cross, T. P., & Saxe, L. (2001). Polygraph testing and sexual abuse: The lure of the magic lasso. *Child Maltreatment, 6*, 195–206.

Curren, D. (1954). Sexual perversion. *Practitioner, 172*, 440–445.

Cyranowski, J. M., Bromberger, J., Youk, A., Matthews, K., Kravitz, H., & Powell, L. H. (2004). Lifetime depression and sexual function in women at midlife. *Archives of Sexual Behavior, 33*, 539–548.

Damon, W., & Rosser, B. R. (2005). Anodyspareunia in men who have sex with men: Prevalence, predictors, consequences and the development of *DSM* diagnostic criteria. *Journal of Sex and Marital Therapy, 31*, 129–141.

Davidson, A. T. (1983). Sexual exploitation of children: A call to action. *Journal of the National Medical Association, 75*, 925–927.

Davis, S. R., van der Mooren, M. J., van Lunsen, R. H. W., Lopes, P., Ribot, C., Rees, M., . . . Purdie, D. W. (2006). Efficacy and safety of a testosterone patch for the treatment of hypoactive sexual desire disorder in surgically menopausal women: A randomized, placebo-controlled trial. *Menopause, 13*, 387–396.

de Kruiff, M. E., Ter Kuile, M. M., Weijenborg, P. T., & Van Lankveld, J. J. (2000). Vaginismus and dyspareunia: Is there a difference in clinical presentation? *Journal of Psychosomatic Obstetrics and Gynaecology, 21*, 149–155.

Dennerstein, L., Lehert, P., Guthrie, J. R., & Burger, H. G. (2007). Modeling women's health during the menopausal transition: A longitudinal analysis. *Menopause, 14*, 53–62.

Derogatis, L. R., Laan, E., Brauer, M., van Lunsen, R. H., Jannini, E. A., Davis, S. R., . . . Goldstein, L. (2010). Responses to the proposed *DSM-V* changes. *Journal of Sexual Medicine, 7*, 1998–2014.

Dhawan, S., & Marshall, W. L. (1996). Sexual abuse histories of sexual offenders. *Sexual Abuse: A Journal of Research and Treatment, 8*, 7–15.

Dietz, P. E., Hazelwood, R. R., & Warren, J. (1990). The sexually sadistic criminal and his offenses. *Bulletin of the American Academy of Psychiatry and the Law, 18*, 163–178.

Docter, R. F., & Prince, V. (1997). Transvestism: A survey of 1032 cross-dressers. *Archives of Sexual Behavior, 26*, 589–605.

Doorn, C. D., Poortinga, J., & Verschoor, A. M. (1994). Cross-gender identity in transvestites and male transsexuals. *Archives of Sexual Behavior, 23*, 185–201.

Dunn, K. M., Cherkas, L. F., & Spector, T. D. (2005). Genetic influences on variation in female orgasmic function: A twin study. *Biology Letters, 1*, 260–263.

Dunn, K. M., Croft, P. R., & Hackett, G. I. (1998). Sexual problems: A study of the prevalence and need for health care in the general population. *Family Practice, 15*, 519–524.

Dunne, M. P., Martin, N. G., Statham, D. J., Slutskie, W. S., Dinwiddie, S. H., Bucholz, K. K., . . . Heath, A. C. (1997). Genetic and environmental contributions to variance in age at first sexual intercourse. *Psychological Bulletin, 8*, 211–216.

Ellis, A., & Brancale, R. (1956). *The psychology of sex offenders.* Springfield, IL: Charles C. Thomas.

Elwood, R. W., Doren, D. M., & Thornton, D. (2010). Diagnostic and risk profiles of men detained under Wisconsin's sexually violent person law. *International Journal of Offender Therapy and Comparative Criminology, 54*, 187–196.

Federoff, J. P., Fishell, A., & Federoff, B. (1999). A case series of women evaluated for paraphilic sexual disorders. *The Canadian Journal of Human Sexuality, 8*, 127–140.

Feldman, H. A., Goldstein, I., Hatzichristou, D. G., Krane, R. J., & McKinlay, J. B. (1994). Impotence and its medical and psychosocial correlates: Results of the Massachusetts Male Aging Study. *Journal of Urology, 151*, 54–61.

Ferguson, J. M. (2001). The effects of antidepressants on sexual functioning in depressed patients: A review. *Journal of Clinical Psychiatry, 62* (Suppl 3), 22–34.

Fernandez, Y. M., Marshall, W. L., Lightbody, S., & O'Sullivan, C. (1999). The child molester empathy measure: Description and examination of its reliability and validity. *Sexual Abuse: A Journal of Research and Treatment, 11,* 17–32.

Finch, S. (2001). Sexual aversion disorder treated with behavioural desensitization. *Canadian Journal of Psychiatry, 46,* 563–564.

Finkelhor, D. (1979). *Sexually victimized children.* New York, NY: Free Press.

Finkelhor, D. (1984). *Child sexual abuse: New theory and research.* New York, NY: Free Press.

Firestone, P., Kingston, D., Wexler, A., & Bradford, J. M. (2006). Long-term followup of exhibitionists: Psychological, phallometric, and offense characteristics. *Journal of the American Academy of Psychiatry and the Law, 34,* 349–359.

Fish, L. S., Busby, D., & Killian, K. (1994). Structural couple therapy in the treatment of inhibited sexual desire. *American Journal of Family Therapy, 22,* 113–125.

Freund, K. (1963). A laboratory method for diagnosing predominance of homo- or hetero-erotic interest in the male. *Behavior Research and Therapy, 1,* 85–93.

Freund, K. (1990). Courtship disorders. In W. L. Marshall, D. R. Laws, & H. E. Barbaree (Eds.), *Handbook of sexual assault: Issues, theories, and treatment of the offender* (pp. 195–207). New York, NY: Plenum.

Freund, K., & Blanchard, R. (1986). The concept of courtship disorder. *Journal of Sex and Marital Therapy, 12,* 79–92.

Freund, K., & Blanchard, R. (1989). Phallometric diagnosis of pedophilia. *Journal of Consulting and Clinical Psychology, 57,* 100–105.

Freund, K., Seto, M. C., & Kuban, M. (1996). Two types of fetishism. *Behavior Research and Therapy, 34,* 687–694.

Freund, K., & Watson, R. J. (1991). Assessment of the sensitivity and specificity of a phallometric test: An update of phallometric diagnosis of pedophilia. *Psychological Assessment, 3,* 254–260.

Freund, K., Watson, R., & Rienzo, D. (1988). Signs of feigning in the phallometric test. *Behavior Research and Therapy, 26,* 105–112.

Friedman, R. C. (1991). The depressed masochistic patient: Diagnostic and management considerations—a contemporary psychoanalytic perspective. *Journal of the American Academy of Psychoanalysis, 19,* 9–31.

Friedrich, E. G. (1987). Vulvar vistibulitis syndrome. *Journal of Reproductive Medicine, 32,* 110–114.

Frolich, P., & Meston, C. (2002). Sexual functioning and self-reported depressive symptoms among college women. *Journal of Sex Research, 39,* 321–325.

Fromuth, M. E., Burkhart, B. R., & Jones, C. W. (1991). Hidden child molestation: An investigation of adolescent perpetrators in a nonclinical sample. *Journal of Interpersonal Violence, 6,* 376–384.

Fugl-Meyer, A. R., & Sjogren Fugl-Meyer, K. (1999). Sexual disabilities, problems and satisfaction in 18-74 year old Swedes. *Scandinavian Journal of Sexology, 2,* 79–105.

Furby, L., Weinrott, M. R., & Blackshaw, L. (1989). Sex offender recidivism: A review. *Psychological Bulletin, 105,* 3–30.

Gaunt, G., Good, A., & Stanhope, C. R. (2003). Vestibulectomy for vulvar vestibulitis. *Journal of Reproductive Medicine, 48,* 591–595.

Gebhard, P. H., Gagnon, J. H., Pomeroy, W. B., & Christenson, C. V. (1965). *Sex offenders: An analysis of types.* New York, NY: Harper & Row.

Giuseppe, L., & Nicastro, A. (1996). A new treatment for premature ejaculation: The rehabilitation of the pelvic floor. *Journal of Sex & Marital Therapy, 22*, 22–26.

Goldstein, I., Fischer, J., Taylor, T., & Thibonnier, M. (2002). Influence of HbA1c on the efficacy and safety of vardenafil for the treatment of erectile dysfunction in men with diabetes. *Diabetes, 51* (Suppl 2), A98.

Gosselin, C., & Wilson, G. (1980). *Sexual variations*. London, England: Faber & Faber.

Graham, C. A. (2010). The *DSM* diagnostic criteria for female sexual arousal disorder. *Archives of Sexual Behavior, 39*, 240–255.

Grenier, G., & Byers, E. S. (2001). Operationalizing early or premature ejaculation. *Journal of Sex Research, 38*, 369–378.

Haczynski, J., Lew-Starowicz, Z., Darewicz, B., Krajka, K., Piotrowicz, R., & Ciesielska, B. (2006). The prevalence of erectile dysfunction in men visiting outpatient clinics. *International Journal of Impotence Research, 18*, 359–363.

Hanson, P. K., & Bussiere, M. T. (1998). Predicting relapse: A meta-analysis of sexual offender recidivism studies. *Journal of Consulting and Clinical Psychology, 66*, 348–362.

Harris, G. T., Rice, M. E., Chaplin, T. C., & Quinsey, V. L. (1999). Dissimulation in phallometric testing of rapists' sexual preferences. *Archives of Sexual Behavior, 28*, 223–232.

Harris, G. T., Rice, M. E., Quinsey, V. L., & Chaplin, T. C. (1996). Viewing time as a measure of sexual interest among child molesters and normal heterosexual men. *Behavior Research Therapy, 34*, 389–394.

Hartmann, U., Heiser, K., Ruffer-Hesse, C., & Kloth, G. (2002). Female sexual desire disorders: Subtypes, classification, personality factors and new directions for treatment. *World Journal of Urology, 20*, 79–88.

Hawton, K., Catalan, J., Martin, P., & Fagg, J. (1986). Long-term outcome of sex therapy. *Behavioral Research and Therapy, 24*, 665–675.

Hazelwood, R. R., Dietz, P. E., & Warren, J. (1992). The criminal sexual sadist. *FBI Law Enforcement Bulletin, 61*, 12–20.

Hayes, R. D., Dennerstein, L., Bennett, C. M., & Fairley, C. K. (2008). What is the "true" prevalence of female sexual dysfunctions and does the way we assess these conditions have an impact? *Journal of Sexual Medicine, 5*, 777–787.

Heiman, J. R. (2002). Psychologic treatments for female sexual dysfunction: Are they effective and do we need them? *Archives of Sexual Behavior, 31*, 445–450.

Heiman, J. R., & LoPiccolo, J. (1987). *Becoming orgasmic: A sexual and personal growth program for women* (rev. and expanded ed.). New York, NY: Simon & Schuster.

Hill, A., Habermann, N., Berner, W., & Briken, P. (2006). Sexual sadism and sadistic personality disorders in sexual homicide. *Journal of Personality Disorders, 20*, 671–684.

Hill, C. A., & Preston, L. K. (1996). Individual differences in the experience of sexual motivation: Theory and measurement of dispositional sexual motives. *Journal of Sex Research, 33*, 27–45.

Holland, L. A., Zolondek, S. C., Abel, G. G., Jordan, A. D., & Becker, J. V. (2000). Psychometric analysis of the Sexual Interest Cardsort Questionnaire. *Sexual Abuse: A Journal of Research and Treatment, 12*, 107–122.

Howes, R. J. (1995). A survey of plethysmographic assessment in North America. *Sexual Abuse: A Journal of Research and Treatment, 7*, 9–24.

Hucker, S. J. (1985). Self-harmful sexual behavior. *Psychiatric Clinics of North America, 8*, 323–337.

Hucker, S., Langevin, R., Dickey, R., Handy, L., Chambers, J., Wright, S., Bain, J., & Wortzman, G. (1988). Cerebral damage and dysfunction in sexually aggressive men. *Annals of Sex Research, 1*, 33–47.

Hunt, M. (1974). *Sexual behavior in the 1970's*. New York, NY: Playboy Press.

Hurlbert, D. F. (1993). A comparative study using orgasm consistency training in the treatment of women reporting hypoactive sexual desire. *Journal of Sex and Marital Therapy, 19*, 41–55.

Hurlbert, D. F., & Apt, C. (1995). The coital alignment technique and direct masturbation: A comparison study on female orgasm. *Journal of Sex and Marital Therapy, 21*, 21–29.

Isidori, A. M., Giannetta, E., Gianfrilli, D., Greco, E. A., Bonifacio, V., Aversa, A., . . . Lenzi, A. (2005). Effects of testosterone on sexual function in men: Results of a meta-analysis. *Clinical Endocrinology, 63*, 381–394.

Kabakci, E., & Batur, S. (2003). Who benefits from cognitive behavioural therapy for vaginismus? *Journal of Sex and Marital Therapy, 29*, 277–288.

Kafka, M. P. (2010). Hypersexual disorder: A proposed diagnosis for *DSM-5*. *Archives of Sexual Behavior, 39*, 377–400.

Kafka, M. P., & Hennen, J. (1999). The paraphilia-related disorders: An empirical investigation of nonparaphilic hypersexuality disorders in outpatient males. *Journal of Sex and Marital Therapy, 25*, 305–319.

Kafka, M. P., & Hennen, J. (2002). A *DSM-IV* Axis I comorbidity study of males (n = 120) with paraphilia-related disorders. *Sexual Abuse: A Journal of Research and Treatment, 14*, 349–366.

Kafka, M. P., & Hennen, J. (2003). Hypersexual desire in males: Are males with paraphilias different from males with paraphilia-related disorders? *Sexual Abuse: A Journal of Research and Treatment, 15*, 307–321.

Kafka, M. P., & Prentky, R. A. (1994). Preliminary observations of *DSM-III-R* Axis I comorbidity in men with paraphilias and paraphilia-related disorders. *Journal of Clinical Psychiatry, 55*, 481–487.

Kaplan, H. S. (1974). Retarded ejaculation. In H. S. Kaplan (Ed.), *The new sex therapy* (pp. 316–338). New York, NY: Brunner Mazel.

Kaplan, H. S. (1979). *Disorders of sexual desire*. New York, NY: Brunner Mazel.

Kaplan, H. S. (1987). *Sexual aversion, sexual phobias, and panic disorder*. New York, NY: Brunner Mazel.

Kaplan, H. S. (1989). *Premature ejaculation: Overcoming early ejaculation*. New York, NY: Brunner Mazel.

Kaplan, M. S., & Krueger, R. B. (1997). Voyeurism: Psychopathology and theory. In D. R. Laws & W. O'Donohue (Eds.), *Sexual deviance: Theory, assessment, and treatment* (pp. 297–310). New York, NY: Guilford Press.

Kar, N., & Koola, M. M. (2007). A pilot survey of sexual functioning and preferences in a sample of English-speaking adults from a small South Indian town. *Journal of Sexual Medicine, 4*, 1254–1261.

Kara, H., Aydin, S., Yucel, M., Agargun, M. Y., Odabas, O., & Yilmaz, Y. (1996). The efficacy of fluoextine in the treatment of premature ejaculation: A double-blind placebo controlled study. *Journal of Urology, 156*, 1631–1632.

Kaschak, E., & Tiefer, L. (2002). *A new view of women's sexual problems*. Binghamton, NY: Haworth Press.

Katz, R. C., Gipson, M. T., Kearl, A., & Kriskovich, M. (1989). Assessing sexual aversion in college students. *Journal of Sex and Marital Therapy, 15*, 135–140.

Kingsberg, S. A., & Janata, J. W. (2003). The sexual aversions. In S. B. Levine, C. B. Risen, & S. E. Althof (Eds.), *Handbook of clinical sexuality for mental health professionals* (pp. 153–165). New York, NY: Brunner-Routledge.

Klusmann, D. (2002). Sexual motivation and the duration of partnership. *Archives of Sexual Behavior, 31,* 275–287.

Kramer, R. (2011). APA guidelines ignored in development of diagnostic criteria for pedohebephilia. *Archives of Sexual Behavior, 40*(2), 233–235.

Kroll, R., Davis, S., Moreau, M., Waldbaum, A., Shifren, J., & Wekselman, K. (2004). Testosterone transdermal patch (TTP) significantly improved sexual function in naturally menopausal women in a large phase III study. *Fertility and Sterility, 82* (Suppl. 2), S77–S78.

Krueger, R. B., & Kaplan, M. S. (1997). Frotteurism: Assessment and treatment. In D. R. Laws & W. O'Donohue (Eds.), *Sexual deviance: Theory, assessment, and treatment* (pp. 131–151). New York, NY: Guilford Press.

Krueger, R. B., & Kaplan, M. S. (2001). The paraphilic and hypersexual disorders: An overview. *Journal of Psychiatric Practice, 7,* 391–403.

Laan, E., van Driel, E. M., & van Lunsen, R. H. (2008). Genital responsiveness in healthy women with and without sexual arousal disorder. *Journal of Sexual Medicine, 5,* 1424–1435.

Laan, E., van Lunsen, R. H., & Everaerd, W. (2001). The effects of tibolone on vaginal blood flow, sexual desire and arousability in postmenopausal women. *Climacteric, 4,* 28–41.

Lalumiere, M. L., & Earls, C. M. (1992). Voluntary control of penile responses as a function of stimulus duration and instructions. *Behavioral Assessment, 14,* 121–132.

Lalumiere, M. L., & Harris, G. T. (1998). Common questions regarding the use of phallometric testing with sexual offenders. *Sexual Abuse: A Journal of Research and Treatment, 10,* 227–237.

Lalumiere, M. L., & Quinsey, V. L. (1993). The sensitivity of phallometric measures with rapists. *Annals of Sex Research, 6,* 123–138.

Lalumiere, M. L., & Quinsey, V. L. (1994). The discriminability of rapists from non-sex offenders using phallometric measures: A meta-analysis. *Criminal Justice and Behavior, 21,* 150–175.

Lamont, J. A. (1978). Vaginismus. *American Journal of Obstetrics and Gynecology, 131,* 632–636.

Landry, T., & Bergeron, S. (2009). How young does vulvo-vaginal pain begin? Prevalence and characteristics of dyspareunia in adolescents. *Journal of Sexual Medicine, 6,* 927–935.

Lane, S. (1991). The sexual abuse cycle. In G. D. Ryan & S. L. Lane (Eds.), *Juvenile sexual offending: Causes, consequences, and correction* (pp. 103–141). Lexington, MA: Lexington Books.

Lang, A. R., Searles, J., Lauerman, R., & Adesso, V. (1980). Expectancy, alcohol, and sex guilt as determinants of interest in and reaction to sexual stimuli. *Journal of Abnormal Psychology, 95,* 150–158.

Langevin, R. (1990). Sexual anomalies and the brain. In W. L. Marshall, D. R. Laws, & H. E. Barbaree (Eds.), *Handbook of sexual assault: Issues, theories, and treatment of the offender* (pp. 103–113). New York, NY: Plenum Press.

Langevin, R., & Lang, R. A., (1987). The courtship disorders. In G. O. Wilson (Ed.), *Variant sexuality: Research and theory* (pp. 202–228). London, England: Croom Helm.

Langevin, R., Paitich, D., Freeman, R., Mann, K., & Handy, L. (1978). Personality characteristics and sexual anomalies in males. *Canadian Journal of Behavioral Science, 10,* 222–238.

Langevin, R., Paitich, D., Ramsey, G., Anderson, C., Kamrad, J., Pope, S., . . . & Newman, S. (1979). Experimental studies of the etiology of genital exhibitionism. *Archives of Sexual Behavior, 8,* 307–331.

Långström, N., & Seto, M. C. (2006). Exhibitionistic and voyeuristic behavior in a Swedish national population survey. *Archives of Sexual Behavior, 35,* 427–435.

Långström, N., & Zucker, K. J. (2005). Transvestic fetishism in the general population. *Journal of Sex & Marital Therapy, 31,* 87–95.

Laumann, E. O., Gagnon J. H., Michael R. T., & Michaels, S. (1994). *The social organization of sexuality: Sexual practices in the United States.* Chicago, IL: University of Chicago Press.

Laumann, E. O., Nicolosi, A., Glasser, D. B., Paik, A., Gingell, C., Moreira, E., . . . the GSSAB Investigators' Group. (2005). Sexual problems among women and men aged 40-80 years: Prevalence and correlates identified in the Global Study of Sexual Attitudes and Behaviors. *International Journal of Impotence Research, 17,* 39–57.

Laumann E. O., Paik, A., & Rosen, R. C. (1999). Sexual dysfunction in the United States. *Journal of the American Medical Association, 281,* 537–544.

Lavy, Y., Lev-Sagie, A., Hamani, Y., Zacut, D., & Ben-Chetrit, A. (2005). Modified vulvar verstibulectomy: Simple and effective surgery for the treatment of vulvar verstibulitis. *European Journal of Obstetric & Gynecology and Reproductive Biology, 120,* 91–95.

Laws, D. R. (1986). *Sexual deviance card sort.* Tampa, FL: Florida Mental Health Institute. Unpublished manuscript.

Leiblum, S. R., & Nathan, S. G. (2001). Persistent sexual arousal syndrome: A newly discovered pattern of female sexuality. *Journal of Sex and Marital Therapy, 24,* 365–380.

Letourneau, E. J. (2002). A comparison of objective measures of sexual arousal and interest: Visual reaction time and penile plethysmography. *Sexual Abuse: A Journal of Research and Treatment, 14,* 207–223.

Levenson, J. S. (2004). Sexual predator civil commitment: A comparison of selected and released offenders. *International Journal of Offender Therapy and Comparative Criminology, 48,* 638–648.

Lewis, R. W., Sadovsky, R., Eardley, I., O'Leary, M., Seftel, A., Wang, W. C., . . . Ahuja, S. (2005). The efficacy of tadalafil in clinical populations. *Journal of Sexual Medicine, 2,* 517–531.

Libman, E., Fichten, C. S., Brender, W., Burstein, R., Cohen, J., & Binik, Y. M. (1984). A comparison of three therapeutic formats in the treatment of secondary orgasmic dysfunction. *Journal of Sex and Marital Therapy, 10,* 147–159.

Lief, H. I. (1977). Inhibited sexual desire. *Medical Aspects of Human Sexuality, 7,* 94–95.

Linet, O. I., & Ogrinc, F. G. (1996). Efficacy and safety of intracavernosal alprostadil in men with erectile dysfunction. *New England Journal of Medicine, 334,* 873–877.

MacPhee, D. C., Johnson, S. M., & Van der Veer, M. M. (1995). Low sexual desire in women: The effects of marital therapy. *Journal of Sex and Marital Therapy, 21,* 159–182.

Malcolm, P. B., Andrews, D. A., & Quinsey, V. L. (1993). Discriminant and predictive validity of phallometrically measured sexual age and gender preference. *Journal of Interpersonal Violence, 8,* 486–501.

Maletzky, B. M. (1991). *Treating the sexual offender.* Newbury Park, CA: Sage.

Maletzky, B. M. (1993). Factors associated with success and failure in the behavioral and cognitive treatment of sexual offenders. *Annals of Sex Research, 6,* 241–258.

Maletzky, B. M. (1997). Exhibitionism: Assessment and treatment. In D. R. Laws & W. O'Donohue (Eds.), *Sexual deviance: Theory, assessment, and treatment* (pp. 40–74). New York, NY: Guilford Press.

Marshall, W. L., & Eccles, A. (1991). Issues in clinical practice with sex offenders. *Journal of Interpersonal Violence, 6,* 68–93.

Marshall, W. L., Hudson, S. M., & Hodkinson, S. (1993). The importance of attachment bonds in the development of juvenile sex offending. In H. E. Barbaree, W. L. Marshall, & S. M. Hudson (Eds.), *The juvenile sex offender* (pp. 164–181). New York, NY: Guilford Press.

Marshall, W. L., Hudson, S. M., Jones, R., & Fernandez, Y. M. (1995). Empathy in sex offenders. *Clinical Psychology Review, 15,* 99–113.

Marshall, W. L., Jones, R., Hudson, S. M., & McDonald, E. (1994). Generalised empathy in child molesters. *Journal of Child Sexual Abuse, 2*, 61–68.

Mason, F. L. (1997). Fetishism: Psychopathology and theory. In D. R. Laws & W. O'Donohue (Eds.), *Sexual deviance: Theory, assessment, and treatment* (pp. 75–91). New York, NY: Guilford Press.

Masters, W. H., & Johnson, V. E. (1966). *Human sexual response*. Boston, MA: Little, Brown.

Masters, W. H., & Johnson, V. E. (1970). *Human sexual inadequacy*. Boston, MA: Little, Brown.

Maurice, W. L. (2005). Male hypoactive sexual desire disorder. In R. Balon & R. T. Seagraves (Eds.), *Handbook of sexual dysfunction* (pp. 67–109). Boca Raton, FL: Taylor & Francis Group.

McCarthy, B. W. (1998). Integrating sildenafil into cognitive-behavioral couple's sex therapy. *Journal of Sex Education and Therapy, 23*, 302–308.

McConaghy, N. (1993). *Sexual behavior: Problems and management*. New York, NY: Plenum Press.

McConaghy, N., Blaszcyzynski, A., & Kidson, W. (1988). Treatment of sex offenders with imaginal desensitization and/or medroxyprogesterone. *Acta Psychiatrica Scandinavica, 77*, 199–206.

McElroy, S. L., Soutullo, C. A., Taylor, P., Nelson, E. B., Beckman, D. A., Brusman, L. A., . . . Keck, P. E., Jr. (1999). Psychiatric features of 36 men convicted of sexual offenses. *Journal of Clinical Psychiatry, 60*, 414–420.

McGuire, R. J., Carlisle, J. M., & Young, B. G. (1965). Sexual deviations as conditioned behavior: A hypothesis. *Behavior Research and Therapy, 2*, 185–190.

Mercer, C. H., Fenton, K. A., Johnson, A. M., Wellings, K., Macdowall, W., McManus, S., . . . Erens, B. (2003). Sexual function problems and help seeking behaviour in Britain: National probability sample survey. *British Medical Journal, 327*, 426–427.

Metz, M. E., Pryor, J. L., Nesvacil, L. J., Abuzzahab, F., Sr., & Koznar, J. (1997). Premature ejaculation: A psychophysiological review. *Journal of Sex and Marital Therapy, 23*, 3–23.

Meyer, J. K. (1995). Paraphilias. In H. I. Kaplan & B. J. Sadock (Eds.), *Comprehensive textbook of psychiatry VI* (Vol. 1, 6th ed. pp. 1334–1347). Baltimore, MD: Williams & Wilkins.

Meyer-Bahlburg, H. F. L. (2010). From mental disorder to iatrogenic hypogonadism: Dilemmas in conceptualizing gender identity variants as psychiatric conditions. *Archives of Sexual Behavior, 39*, 461–476.

Miller, B. L., Darby, A. L., Sartz, J. R., Yener, G. G., & Mena, I. (1995). Dietary changes, compulsions and sexual behavior in frontotemporal degeneration. *Dementia, 6*, 195–199.

Mohr, J. W., Turner, R. E., & Jerry, M. B. (1964). *Pedophilia and exhibitionism*. Toronto, Canada: University of Toronto Press.

Money, J. (1984). Paraphilias: Phenomenology and classification. *American Journal of Psychotherapy, 38*, 164–179.

Monga, M., Bettencourt, R., & Barrett-Connor, E. (2002). Community-based study of erectile dysfunction and sildenafil use: The Rancho Bernardo study. *Urology, 59*, 753–757.

Morales, A., Buvat, J., Gooren, L. J., Guay, A. T., Kaufman, J.-M., Tan, H. M., & Torres, L. O. (2004). Endocrine aspects of sexual dysfunction in men. *Journal of Sexual Medicine, 1*, 69–81.

Morales, A., Heaton, J. P. W., & Carson, C. C., III. (2000). Andropause: A misnomer for a true clinical entity. *Journal of Urology, 163*, 705–712.

Moser, C., & Levitt, E. E. (1987). An exploratory-descriptive study of a sadomasochistically oriented sample. *Journal of Sex Research, 23*, 322–337.

Murphy, W. D. (1997). Exhibitionism: Psychopathology and theory. In D. R. Laws & W. O'Donohue (Eds.), *Sexual deviance: Theory, assessment, and treatment* (pp. 22–39). New York, NY: Guilford Press.

Murphy, W. D., Haynes, M. R., & Page, I. J. (1992). Adolescent sex offenders. In W. O'Donohue & J. H. Geer (Eds.), *The sexual abuse of children: Clinical issues* (Vol. 2, pp. 395–429). Hillsdale, NJ: Erlbaum.

Murphy, W. D., Haynes, M. R., & Worley, P. J. (1991). Assessment of adult sexual interest. In C. R. Hollin & K. Howells (Eds.), *Clinical approaches to sex offenders and their victims* (pp. 77–92). West Sussex, England: John Wiley & Sons.

Murphy, W., & Page, I. (2008). Exhibitionism: Psychopathology and theory. In D. R. Laws & W. T. O'Donohue (Eds.), *Sexual deviance: theory, assessment, and treatment* (2nd ed., pp. 61–75). New York, NY: Guilford Press.

Murphy, W. D., & Peters, J. M. (1992). Profiling child sexual abusers: Psychological considerations. *Criminal Justice and Behavior, 19*, 24–37.

Murphy, W. D., & Smith, T. A. (1996). Sex offenders against children: Empirical and clinical issues. In J. Briere, L. Berliner, J. A. Bulkley, C. Jenny, & T. Reid (Eds.), *The APSAC handbook on child maltreatment* (pp. 175–191). Thousand Oaks, CA: Sage.

Nicholls, L. (2008). Putting the New View classification scheme to an empirical test. *Feminism and Psychology, 18*, 515–526.

Nichols, H. R., & Molinder, I. (1984). *The Multiphasic Sex Inventory manual.* Tacoma, WA: Author.

Nichols, H. R., & Molinder, I. (1992). *The Multiphasic Sex Inventory manual.* Tacoma, WA: Author.

Nurnberg, H. G., Hensley, P. L., Heiman, J. R., Croft, H. A., Debattista, C. & Paine, S. (2008). Sildenafil treatment of women with antidepressant-associated sexual dysfunction: a randomized controlled trial. *Journal of the American Medical Association, 300*, 395–404.

Nusbaum, M. R., Gamble, G., Skinner, B., & Heiman, J. (2000). The high prevalence of sexual concerns among women seeking routine gynecological care. *Journal of Family Practice, 49*, 229–232.

Oberg, K., Fugl-Meyer, A. R., Fugl-Meyer, K. S. (2004). On categorization and quantification of women's sexual dysfunctions: an epidemiological approach. *International Journal of Impotence Research, 16*, 261–269.

O'Carroll, R. (1989). A neuropsychological study of sexual deviation. *Sexual and Marital Therapy, 4*, 59–63.

Okami, P., & Goldberg, A. (1992). Personality correlates of pedophilia: Are they reliable indicators? *Journal of Sex Research, 29*, 297–328.

Osterloh, I. H. & Riley, A. (2002). Clinical update on sildenafil citrate. *British Journal of Clinical Pharmacology, 53*, 219–223.

Padma-Nathan, H., Hellstrom, W. J., Kaiser, F. E., Labasky, R. F., Lue, T. F., Nolten, W. E., . . . Gesundheit, N. (1997). Treatment of men with erectile dysfunction with transurethral alprostadil: Medicated Urethral System for Erection (MUSE) Study Group. *New England Journal of Medicine, 336*, 1–7.

Paitich, D., Langevin, R., Freeman, R., Mann, K., & Handy, L. (1977). The Clarke Sexual History Questionnaire: A clinical sex history questionnaire for males. *Archives of Sexual Behavior, 6*, 421–435.

Perelman, M. A. (2002). FSD partner issues: Expanding sex therapy with sildenafil. *Journal of Sex and Marital Therapy, 28* (Suppl 1), 195–204.

Perelman, M. A. (2006). *Masturbation is a key variable in the treatment of retarded ejaculation by health care professionals.* Poster presented at the annual meeting of the International Society for the Study of Women's Sexual Health, Lisbon, Portugal.

Phillips, L., Jr., & Slaughter, J. R. (2000). Depression and sexual desire. *American Family Physician, 62*, 782–786.

Price, M., Gutheil, T. G., Commons, M. L., Kafka, M. P., & Dodd-Kimmey, S. (2001). Telephone scatologia: Comorbidity and theories of etiology. *Psychiatric Annals, 31,* 226–232.

Pukall, C. F., Payne, K. A., Kao, A., Khalifé, S., & Binik, Y. M. (2005). In R. Balon & R. T. Segraves (Eds.), *Handbook of sexual dysfunction* (pp. 249–272). Boca Raton, FL: Taylor & Francis Group.

Pukall, C. F., Strigo, I. A., Binik, Y. M., Amsel, R., Khalifé, S., & Bushnell, M. C. (2005). Neural correlates of painful genital touch in women with vulvar vestibulitis syndrome. *Pain, 115,* 117–118.

Quinsey, V. L. (1988). Assessments of the treatability of forensic patients. *Behavioral Sciences and the Law, 6,* 443–452.

Quinsey, V. L., & Earls, C. M. (1990). The modification of sexual preferences. In W. L. Marshall, D. R. Laws, & H. E. Barbaree (Eds.), *Handbook of sexual assault: Issues, theories, and treatment of the offender* (pp. 343–361). New York, NY: Plenum Press.

Quinsey, V. L., & Lalumiere, M. L. (1996). *Assessment of sexual offenders against children.* Newbury Park, CA: Sage.

Quinsey, V. L., Rice, M. E., & Harris, G. T. (1995). The actuarial prediction of sexual recidivism. *Journal of Interpersonal Violence, 10,* 85–105.

Quinsey, V. L., Rice, M. E., Harris, G. T., & Reid, K. S. (1993). The phylogenetic and ontogenetic development of sexual age preferences in males: Conceptual and measurement issues. In H. E. Barbaree, W. L. Marshall, & S. M. Hudson (Eds.), *The juvenile sex offender* (pp. 143–163). New York, NY: Guilford Press.

Rachman, S. (1966). Sexual fetishism: An experimental analogue. *Psychological Record, 16,* 293–296.

Rachman, S., & Hodgson, R. J. (1968). Experimentally-induced "sexual fetishism": Replication and development. *Psychological Record, 18,* 25–27.

Regan, P., & Berscheid, C. E. (1996). Belief about the state, goals, and objects of sexual desire. *Journal of Sex and Marital Therapy, 22,* 110–120.

Reissing, E. D., Binik, Y. M., Khalifé, S., Cohen, D., & Amsel, R. (2004). Vaginal spasm, pain, and behavior: An empirical investigation of the diagnosis of vaginismus. *Archives of Sexual Behavior, 33,* 5–17.

Rettenmaier, M. A., Brown, J. V., & Micha, J. P. (2003). Modified vestibulectomy is inadequate treatment for secondary vulvar vestibulitis. *Journal of Gynecologic Surgery, 19,* 13–17.

Rice, M. E., Harris, G. T., & Quinsey, V. L. (1990). A follow-up of rapists assessed in a maximum security psychiatric facility. *Journal of Interpersonal Violence, 5,* 435–448.

Richters, J., Grulich, A. E., De Visser, R. O., Smith, A. M. A., & Rissel, C. E. (2003). Sex in Australia: Autoerotic, esoteric and other sexual practices engaged in by a representative sample of adults. *Australian and New Zealand Journal of Public Health, 27,* 180–190.

Rosen, R. C., Phillips, N. A., Gendrano, N. C., 3rd, & Ferguson, D. M. (1999). Oral phentolamine and female sexual arousal disorder: A pilot study. *Journal of Sex and Marital Therapy, 25,* 137–144.

Rosenbaum, T. Y. (2003). Physiotherapy treatment of sexual pain disorders. *Journal of Sex and Marital Therapy, 31,* 329–340.

Rosenblum, J. A. (1974). Human sexuality and the cerebral cortex. *Diseases of the Nervous System, 35,* 268–271.

Rowland, D., Perelman, M., Althof, S., Barada, J., McCullough, A., Bull, S., . . . Ho, K. F. (2004). Self-reported premature ejaculation and aspects of sexual functioning and satisfaction. *Journal of Sexual Medicine, 1,* 225–232.

Rubio-Aurioles, E., Lopez, M., Lipezker, M., Lara, C., Ramirez, A., Rampazzo, C., . . . Lammers, P. (2002). Phentolamine mesylate in postmenopausal women with female sexual arousal disorder: A psychophysiological study. *Journal of Sex and Marital Therapy, 28* (Suppl 1), 205–215.

Sagarin, B. J., Cutler, B., Cuther, N., Lawler-Sagarin, K. A., & Matuszewich, L. (2009). Hormonal changes and couple bonding in consensual sadomasochistic activity. *Archives of Sexual Behavior, 38*, 186–200.

Sandfort, T. G., & de Keizer, M. (2001). Sexual problems in gay men: An overview of empirical research. *Annual Review of Sex Research, 12*, 93–120.

Saunders, E., Awad, G. A., & White, G. (1986). Male adolescent sexual offenders: The offender and the offense. *Canadian Journal of Psychiatry, 31*, 542–549.

Schiavi, R. C., Derogatis, L. R., Kuriansky, J., O'Connor, D., & Sharpe, L. (1979). The assessment of sexual function and marital interaction. *Journal of Sex and Marital Therapy, 5*, 169–224.

Schouten, P. G. W., & Simon, W. T. (1992). Validity of phallometric measures with sex offenders: Comments on the Quinsey, Laws, and Hall debate. *Journal of Consulting and Clinical Psychology, 60*, 812–814.

Schover, L. R., & LoPiccolo, J. (1982). Treatment effectiveness for dysfunctions of sexual desire. *Journal of Sex and Marital Therapy, 8*, 179–197.

Schroder, M., Mell, L. K., Hurteau, J. A., Collins, Y. C., Rotmensch, J., Waggoner, S. E., . . . Mundt, A. J. (2005). Clitoral therapy device for treatment of sexual dysfunction in irradiated cervical cancer patients. *International Journal of Radiation Oncology Biology, and Physics, 61*, 1078–1086.

Scott, G. G. (1983). *Dominant women, submissive men.* New York, NY: Praeger.

Segraves, K. B., & Segraves, R. T. (1991). Hypoactive sexual desire disorder: Prevalence and comorbidity in 906 subjects. *Journal of Sex and Marital Therapy, 17*, 55–58.

Segraves, R. T. (1999). Case Report, two additional uses for sildenafil in psychiatric patients. *Journal of Sex and Marital Therapy, 25*, 265–266.

Seidman, S. N. (2003). Testosterone deficiency and mood in aging men: Pathogenic and therapeutic interactions. *Journal of Clinical Psychiatry, 4*, 14–20.

Semans, J. H. (1956). Premature ejaculation. *Southern Medical Journal, 49*, 353–358.

Seto, M. C. (2001). The value of phallometry in the assessment of male sex offenders. *Journal of Forensic Psychology Practice, 1*, 65–75.

Seto, M. C. (2009). Pedophilia. *Annual Review of Clinical Psychology, 5*, 391–407.

Seto, M. C., & Kuban, M. (1996). Criterion-related validity of a phallometric test for paraphilic rape and sadism. *Behavior Research and Therapy, 34*, 175–183.

Seto, M. C., & Lalumiere, M. L. (2001). A brief screening scale to identify pedophilic interests among child molesters. *Sexual Abuse: A Journal of Research and Treatment, 13*, 15–25.

Shabsigh, R. (2005). Testosterone therapy in erectile dysfunction and hypogonadism. *Journal of Sexual Medicine, 2*, 785–792.

Smukler, A. J., & Schiebel, D. (1975). Personality characteristics of exhibitionists. *Diseases of the Nervous System, 36*, 600–603.

Spengler, A. (1977). Manifest sadomasochism of males: Results of an empirical study. *Archives of Sexual Behavior, 6*, 441–456.

Stanford, J. L., Feng, Z., Hamilton, A. S., Gilliland, F. D., Stephenson, R. A., Eley, J. W., . . . Potosky, A. L. (2000). Urinary and sexual function after radical prostatectomy for clinically localized prostate cancer: The prostate cancer outcomes study. *Journal of the American Medical Association, 283*, 354–360.

Stekel, W. (1923). *Der fetischismus dargestellt für Ärzte und Kriminalogen. Störungen des Trieb- und Affektlebens (die parapathischen Erkrankungen).* Berlin/Wien: Urban & Schwarzenberg.

Strassberg, D. S., Kelly, M. P., Carroll, C., & Kircher, J. C. (1987). The psychophysiological nature of premature ejaculation. *Archives of Sexual Behavior, 16*, 327–336.

Symonds, T., Roblin, D., Hart, K., & Althof, S. (2003). How does premature ejaculation impact a man's life? *Journal of Sex and Marital Therapy, 29,* 361–370.

Tang, W., Ma, L., Zhao, L., Liu, Y., & Chen, Z. (2004). Clinical efficacy of Viagra with behavior therapy against premature ejaculation. *Zhonghua Nan Ke Xue, 10,* 366–370.

Tarter, R. E., Hegadus, A. M., Alterman, A. I., & Katz-Garris, L. (1983). Cognitive capacities of juvenile, violent, nonviolent, and sexual offenders. *Journal of Nervous and Mental Disease, 171,* 564–567.

Templeman, T. L., & Stinnett, R. D. (1991). Patterns of sexual arousal and history in a "normal" sample of young men. *Archives of Sexual Behavior, 20,* 137–150.

ter Kuile, M. M., van Lankveld, J. J., de Groot, E., Melles, R., Neffs, J. & Zandbergen, M. (2007). Cognitive-behavioral therapy for women with lifelong vaginismus: Process and prognostic factors. *Behaviour Research and Therapy, 45,* 359–373.

Tiefer, L. (2001). A new view of women's sexual problems: Why new? Why now? *Journal of Sex Research, 38,* 89–96.

Tiefer, L. (2002). Sexual behaviour and its medicalisation. Many (especially economic) forces promote medicalisation. *British Medical Journal, 325,* 45.

Trudel, G., Marchand, A., Ravart, M., Aubin, S., Turgeon, L., & Fortier, P. (2001). The effect of a cognitive behavioral group treatment program on hypoactive sexual desire in women. *Sexual and Relationship Therapy, 16,* 145–164.

Trudel, G. & Proulx, S. (1987). Treatment of premature ejaculation by bibliotherapy: An experimental study. *Sex & Marital Therapy, 2,* 163–167.

Tworoger, S. S., Missmer, S. A., Barbieri, R. L., Willett, W. C., Colditz, G. A., & Hankinson, R. G. (2005). Plasma sex hormone concentrations and subsequent risk of breast cancer among women using postmenopausal hormones. *Journal of the National Cancer Institute, 97,* 595–602.

Waldinger, M. D. (2002). The neurobiological approach to early ejaculation. *Journal of Urology, 168,* 2359–2367.

Waldinger, M. D. (2005). Male ejaculation and orgasmic disorders. In R. Balon & R. T. Segraves (Eds.), *Handbook of sexual dysfunction* (pp. 215–248). Boca Raton, FL: Taylor & Francis Group.

Waldinger, M. D., Rietschel, M., Nothen, M. M., Hengeveld, M. W., & Olivier, B. (1998). Familial occurrence of primary premature ejaculation. *Psychiatric Genetics, 8,* 37–40.

Ward, T., Hudson, S. M., & Marshall, W. L. (1995). Cognitive distortions and affective deficits in sex offenders: A cognitive deconstructionist interpretation. *Sex Abuse, 7,* 67–83.

Weijmar Schultz, W. C. M., & Van de Weil, H. B. M. (2005). Vaginismus. In R. Balon & R. T. Segraves (Eds.), *Handbook of sexual dysfunction* (pp. 43–65). Boca Raton, FL: Taylor & Francis Group.

Weinberg, T. A. (2006). Sadomasochism and the social sciences: A review of the sociological and social psychological literature. *Journal of Homosexuality, 50,* 17–40.

Weinberg, T., & Kamel, W. L. (Eds.). (1983). *S and M: Studies in sadomasochism.* Buffalo, NY: Prometheus.

Weinberg, T. S., Williams, C. J., & Moser, C. (1984). The social constituents of sadomasochism. *Social Problems, 31,* 379–389.

Wijkman, M., Bijleveld, C., & Hendriks, J. (2010). Women don't do such things! Characteristics of female sex offenders and offender types. *Sexual Abuse: A Journal of Research and Treatment, 22,* 135–156.

Wilson, G. (1978). *The secrets of sexual fantasy.* London: Dent.

Witting, K., Santtila, P., Varjonen, M., Jern, P., Johansson, A., von der Pahlen, B., & Sandnabba, K. (2008). Female sexual dysfunction, sexual distress, and compatibility with partner. *Journal of Sexual Medicine, 5,* 2587–2599.

Woo, J. S. T., Brotto, L. A., & Gorzalka, B. B. (2011). The role of sex guilt in the relationship between culture and women's sexual desire. *Archives of Sexual Behavior, 40*, 385–394.

Wylie, K. & MacInnes, I. (2005). Erectile Dysfunction. In R. Balon & R. T. Segraves (Eds.), *Handbook of sexual dysfunction* (pp. 155–191). Boca Raton, FL: Taylor & Francis Group.

Xin, Z. C., Choi, Y. D., Lee, S. H., & Choi, H. K. (1997). Efficacy of a topical agent SS-cream in the treatment of premature ejaculation: Preliminary clinical studies. *Yonsei Medical Journal, 38*, 91–95.

Zavitzianos, G., (1971). Fetishism and exhibitionism in the female and their relationship to psychopathology and kleptomania. *International Journal of Psycho-Analysis, 52*, 297–305.

Zucker, K. J., & Bradley, S. J. (1995). *Gender identity disorder and psychosexual problems in children and adolescents.* New York, NY: Guilford Press.

# CHAPTER 16

# Gender Identity Disorders

ANNE A. LAWRENCE and KENNETH J. ZUCKER

## DESCRIPTION OF THE DISORDERS

The gender identity disorders (GIDs) are a diverse group of psychosexual disorders in which affected persons express a strong identification with the other sex and marked discomfort with their assigned sex or gender role (American Psychiatric Association [APA], 2000). The most widely recognized and severe of the GIDs is transsexualism, in which affected persons express an intense and persistent desire to live and be recognized as members of the other sex and make their bodies resemble those of the other sex. Less severe and less widely known types of GIDs also exist, however, and may be more prevalent than transsexualism.

HISTORY AND TERMINOLOGY

Individuals who wish to live as members of the other sex have been recognized since antiquity in many different societies worldwide (Green, 1969). The German physicians Krafft-Ebing (1903/1965) and Hirschfeld (1910/1991) described patients who would now be diagnosed as having GIDs. Christine Jorgensen's widely reported sex reassignment in 1952 brought the phenomenon of transsexualism to public attention in Western countries (Meyerowitz, 2002). By the 1960s, academic medical centers in the United States and Western Europe were offering surgical sex reassignment to carefully selected patients. In 1980, the GIDs were first recognized as psychiatric diagnoses in the third edition of the *Diagnostic and Statistical Manual of Mental Disorders* (*DSM-III*) (APA, 1980).

Terminology related to the GIDs has evolved over time. The term *transsexualism* was first used in the 1950s to describe persons who wanted to live as members of the other sex and undergo surgical sex reassignment or had actually done so. Transsexualism was thought to represent an incongruence between biologic sex and *gender identity*, "a person's inner conviction of being male or female" (APA, 2000, p. 823). In addition to a cross-gender (i.e., disordered) gender identity, transsexuals experienced *gender*

Acknowledgment: Dr. Zucker is the Chair of the DSM-5 Workgroup on Sexual and Gender Identity Disorders.

*dysphoria*, "aversion to some or all of those physical characteristics or social roles that connote one's own biological sex" (APA, 2000, p. 823).

Starting with the *DSM-III* (APA, 1980), the categories of GIDs applicable to adults have usually included one principal diagnosis with specific criteria and a residual diagnosis without specific criteria. In the *DSM-III*, the principal diagnosis was Transsexualism. In the *DSM-IV* (APA, 1994) and *DSM-IV-TR* (APA, 2000), Gender Identity Disorder (GID) became the principal diagnosis; the residual diagnosis was called Gender Identity Disorder Not Otherwise Specified (GIDNOS). Many clinicians have continued to use the term *transsexualism*, however, in part because it remains an official diagnosis in the *International Classification of Diseases* (World Health Organization, 1992). Some authorities consider transsexualism and GID to be synonymous terms (Selvaggi et al., 2005; Simon, Zsolt, Fogd, & Czobor, 2011), whereas others reserve the term transsexualism for GID that is irreversible (Sohn & Bosinski, 2007) or severe and accompanied by the desire for sex reassignment (APA, 2000). The distinction may be of limited practical importance, because much of the research relevant to understanding GID in adults has been conducted with persons who would meet criteria for transsexualism by most definitions. Adults with GID, especially those who request or have completed sex reassignment, are commonly referred to as male-to-female (MtF) and female-to-male (FtM) transsexuals.

GIDNOS is a nonspecific diagnosis that can be given to persons with many different types of disturbances in gender identity. For example, the diagnosis is applicable to men who wish to undergo or have undergone castration and who identify as neither male nor female but as eunuchs (Johnson, Brett, Roberts, & Wassersug, 2007).

Men who engage in erotic cross-dressing can be diagnosed with Transvestic Fetishism (TF), a paraphilia discussed in greater detail in Chapter 15, Sexual Dysfunctions and Paraphilias. TF is mentioned here because some experts (e.g., Levine, 1993) argue that cross-dressing always implies a degree of cross-gender identity. This suggests that some men who meet diagnostic criteria for TF would also meet diagnostic criteria for GID or GIDNOS. The text discussion of GIDNOS in the *DSM-IV-TR* (APA, 2000) implies that cross-dressing per se can provide a sufficient basis for assigning a diagnosis of GIDNOS (Lawrence, 2009b), and the text discussion of GID states explicitly that patients can be diagnosed with both TF and GID.

The terms *transgender* and *transgenderism* are used informally to describe persons who report or exhibit significant cross-gender identity or behavior, whether or not they meet full diagnostic criteria for transsexualism, GID, GIDNOS, or TF. It should also be noted that some people will use these terms as a marker of their self-identity (e.g., "I'm a trans person").

## CLINICAL PICTURE

### Clinical Presentation

Gender dysphoria, gender identity–related concerns, and requests for approval for sex reassignment are frequent presenting complaints of patients with GIDs. Patients with GIDs sometimes present with other clinical concerns, however, including paraphilias, sexual dysfunctions, depression, or other general psychiatric conditions (Levine, 1993).

Persons with GIDs may want the anatomy, the gender role, or the sexuality of the other sex, or any combination of these (Carroll, 1999), but persons with severe GID or transsexualism typically want both the anatomy and the gender role of the other sex (Deogracias et al., 2007). An intense feeling of "wrong embodiment," manifesting as gender dysphoria related to sexed body characteristics and a strong desire to acquire the anatomy of the other sex, is sometimes considered the essential feature of severe GID or transsexualism (Bower, 2001; Prosser, 1998); however, not all patients with GIDs experience intense anatomic dysphoria. In some patients, especially those with GIDNOS, gender dysphoria may primarily involve a desire for the gender role or sexuality of the other sex.

CLINICAL FEATURES OF TRANSSEXUAL SUBTYPES

The *DSM-III* recognized that Transsexualism was a "heterogeneous disorder" (APA, 1980, p. 261), and subsequent research has confirmed the diversity of clinical presentations in adults with GIDs. Biologic sex and sexual orientation are two features that account for much of this diversity (Lawrence, 2010b). Adult males with GID are different, and more variable, in clinical presentation than adult females with GID. In particular, adult males with GID/transsexualism who are exclusively sexually attracted to men—called *homosexual* MtF transsexuals, because they are homosexual relative to biologic sex—are dramatically different in clinical presentation from adult males with GID/transsexualism who are sexually attracted to women, women and men, or neither sex—called *nonhomosexual* MtF transsexuals (Blanchard, 1985, 1989b; see also Lawrence, 2010b). Homosexual and nonhomosexual MtF transsexuals appear to represent distinctly different clinical spectra (Whitam, 1987) and possibly reflect entirely different etiologies (Freund, 1985; Smith, van Goozen, Kuiper, & Cohen-Kettenis, 2005a). Among adult females with GID/transsexualism, homosexual FtM transsexuals (exclusively attracted to women) also differ from their nonhomosexual FtM counterparts, but the differences are less pronounced and less well documented. Key features of these four typological categories are summarized in Table 16.1.

*Homosexual MtF Transsexuals*   Most MtF transsexuals who are exclusively sexually attracted to men were conspicuously feminine as children; many or most probably would have met diagnostic criteria for GID during childhood and adolescence.

**Table 16.1**
Adult GID/Transsexual Subtypes

| Homosexual Male-to-Female | Nonhomosexual Male-to-Female |
|---|---|
| attracted only to men | attracted to women, women and men, or neither |
| conspicuously feminine during childhood | not conspicuously feminine during childhood |
| rarely sexually aroused by cross-dressing | usually sexually aroused by cross-dressing |
| usually transition in 20s or early 30s | usually transition in late 30s, 40s, 50s, or later |
| Homosexual Female-to-Male | Nonhomosexual Female-to-Male |
| attracted only to women | attracted to men or women and men |
| conspicuously masculine during childhood | less conspicuously masculine during childhood |
| sexual attitudes are strongly male-typical | sexual attitudes are less male-typical |
| usually transition in 20s or early 30s | usually transition in 20s or early 30s |

Homosexual MtF transsexuals are also extremely feminine as adults (Blanchard, 1988; Whitam, 1987, 1997) and are more feminine in appearance than their non-homosexual counterparts (Smith et al., 2005b). They rarely report any history of sexual arousal with cross-dressing (Blanchard, 1985, 1989b). Whitam (1987) observed that, "in most societies these persons regard themselves as homosexuals and are regarded by more masculine homosexuals as a natural part of the homosexual world" (p. 177); clinicians may find it useful to adopt this perspective as well. Homosexual MtF transsexuals usually seek sex reassignment in their 20s or early 30s (Blanchard, Clemmensen, & Steiner, 1987; Smith et al., 2005b). In past decades, most MtF transsexuals who underwent sex reassignment in the United States, Canada, and western European countries were homosexual in orientation; currently, most MtF transsexuals who undergo sex reassignment in these countries are non-homosexual (Lawrence, 2010c).

*Nonhomosexual MtF Transsexuals*    Most MtF transsexuals currently seen by clinicians in the United States and many Western countries are nonhomosexual in orientation. They may describe themselves as sexually attracted to women, women and men, or neither, but their primary sexual attraction is toward females. They are also sexually attracted, however, to the thought or image of themselves as females, a paraphilic sexual interest called *autogynephilia* ("love of oneself as a woman"; Blanchard, 1989a, 1989b). The most common manifestation of autogynephilia is erotic cross-dressing. Most nonhomosexual MtF transsexuals give a history of erotic cross-dressing or cross-gender fantasy (Blanchard, 1985; Lawrence, 2005), and sexual arousal with cross-dressing is extremely common, perhaps almost universal, in nonhomosexual MtF transsexuals (Blanchard, Racansky, & Steiner, 1986). Anatomic autogynephilia, or sexual arousal to the idea of having female anatomic features, such as breasts or a vulva, is especially characteristic of men who seek surgical sex reassignment (Blanchard, 1993). It is conceptually useful to think of nonhomosexual MtF transsexuals as heterosexual men with an unusual paraphilic sexual interest that makes them want to *become what they love* (Lawrence, 2007) by turning their bodies into facsimiles of the persons they find sexually desirable, women (Freund & Blanchard, 1993). Nonhomosexual MtF transsexuals often have other paraphilic sexual interests, especially sexual masochism (e.g., Bolin, 1988; Walworth, 1997). Some nonhomosexual MtF transsexuals develop a secondary sexual interest in men, because they are aroused by the idea of taking a woman's sexual role with a man, thereby having their "physical attractiveness as women validated by others" (Blanchard, 1989b, p. 622).

Nonhomosexual MtF transsexuals usually were not conspicuously feminine during childhood nor are they as adults (Blanchard, 1990; Whitam, 1997). Some report mild gender nonconformity during childhood (Buhrich & McConaghy, 1977) but less so than homosexual MtF transsexuals (see Zucker et al., in press). They are also less feminine in appearance than their homosexual counterparts (Smith et al., 2005b). They usually seek sex reassignment in their mid-30s or later (Blanchard et al., 1987; Smith et al., 2005b) and not uncommonly in their 50s or 60s (Lawrence, 2003). However, it should also be noted that in the current generation of transsexuals, individuals may be coming out at earlier ages, and this appears to be true for both the homosexual and nonhomosexual subtypes (see Zucker et al., in press).

*Homosexual and Nonhomosexual FtM Transsexuals*   There are also two subtypes of FtM transsexuals based on sexual orientation, but these are less dissimilar than the two MtF subtypes. Homosexual and nonhomosexual FtM transsexuals, for example, apply for sex reassignment at roughly similar ages (Smith et al., 2005b), but the FtM subtypes also display some significant differences. Homosexual FtM transsexuals, who are exclusively sexually attracted to women, were invariably conspicuously masculine during childhood (Smith et al., 2005b); most probably would have met diagnostic criteria for GID during childhood and adolescence. Nonhomosexual FtM transsexuals, who are sexually attracted to men or both women and men, "may have been girls with neutral interests or with some tomboy characteristics" (Smith et al., 2005b, p. 159) but were usually less conspicuously and pervasively masculine during childhood. The sexual attitudes of homosexual FtM transsexuals are male-typical in many respects: They display greater sexual than emotional jealousy and report more sexual partners, more interest in visual sexual stimuli, and greater desire for phalloplasty than nonhomosexual FtM transsexuals (Chivers & Bailey, 2000). Nonhomosexual FtM transsexuals report sexual attitudes that are less male-typical (Chivers & Bailey, 2000). They are also more likely to have comorbid psychopathology (Smith et al., 2005b), for reasons that are not well understood. Sexual arousal to cross-dressing or cross-gender fantasy does not appear to be a significant factor in the development of nonhomosexual FtM trans-sexualism (Smith et al., 2005b). Nonhomosexual FtM transsexuals were once believed to be rare, but they now comprise roughly 10% to 20% of FtM transsexuals in northern European countries (Kreukels et al., in press).

## DIAGNOSTIC CONSIDERATIONS

### DSM-IV-TR DIAGNOSES

In the *DSM-IV-TR*, a diagnosis of GID requires both a "strong and persistent cross-gender identification" and "persistent discomfort with [one's] sex or sense of inappropriateness in the gender role of that sex" (APA, 2000, p. 581); however, these two symptoms seem to represent the same underlying construct (Paap et al., 2011). There is also a requirement of "clinically significant distress or impairment in social, occupational, or other important areas of functioning" (APA, 2000, p. 581). The presence of a physical intersex condition—a *disorder of sex development* (DSD) is now the preferred term—is an exclusion criterion for GID, because these disorders appear to manifest differently in persons with DSDs (Meyer-Bahlburg, 1994). A person with a DSD who would otherwise meet diagnostic criteria for GID would instead receive a diagnosis of GIDNOS in the *DSM-IV-TR* (APA, 2000, p. 582).

### DIFFERENTIAL DIAGNOSIS

Differential diagnostic considerations for the diagnoses of GID and GIDNOS include TF; Schizophrenia, Bipolar Disorder, and other psychotic conditions; Dissociative

Identity Disorder; some Cluster B personality disorders; Body Dysmorphic Disorder; and gender nonconformity.

As previously noted, TF can co-occur with both GID and GIDNOS (see Blanchard, 2010). It is useful to think of TF and the nonhomosexual type of male GID as points on a spectrum of symptomatology, rather than as discrete entities (Lawrence, 2009b). In persons with TF, the absence of a strong and persistent cross-gender identification or gender dysphoria would presumably exclude the diagnosis of GID, and perhaps the diagnosis of GIDNOS as well. Many cross-dressing men who meet diagnostic criteria for TF, however, report cross-gender identities of some strength and also symptoms of gender dysphoria, based on their stated wish to take feminizing hormones (Docter & Prince, 1997).

Patients with schizophrenia, bipolar disorder, and other psychotic disorders sometimes experience delusional beliefs of being or becoming the other sex (Habermeyer, Kamps, & Kawohl, 2003; Manderson & Kumar, 2001); treatment of the psychotic condition usually leads to resolution of the cross-gender identification, but GID and psychotic diagnoses do, on rare occasions, co-occur (Baltieri & De Andrade, 2009; Haberman, Hollingsworth, Falek, & Michael, 1975). Cross-gender ideation sometimes occurs in Dissociative Identity Disorder (Modestin & Ebner, 1995; Saks, 1998); transsexuals display fewer dissociative symptoms than patients with dissociative disorders (Kersting et al., 2003) but more than nonclinical controls. Persons with Antisocial Personality Disorder have been known to seek sex reassignment in the absence of gender dysphoria (Laub & Fisk, 1974). Some theorists (e.g., Lothstein, 1984; Person & Ovesey, 1974) have proposed that the identity diffusion associated with borderline personality disturbances might manifest as gender dysphoria, implying that Borderline Personality Disorder (BPD) could be a possible differential diagnosis. Wilkinson-Ryan and Westen (2000) found that patients with BPD were more conflicted or unsure about their gender identity than nonclinical controls, but Singh, McMain, and Zucker (2011) found no individuals meeting criteria for GID among 100 women diagnosed with BPD. Pfäfflin (2007) suggested that Body Dysmorphic Disorder focused on the genitals could be mistaken for GID; absence of a desire for the anatomy and gender role of the other sex would exclude the latter diagnosis (see also Phillips et al., 2010). Persons with nonpathological gender nonconformity sometimes report significant cross-gender identification or a preference for the gender role of the other sex but may not experience enough distress or functional impairment to meet diagnostic criteria for any GID.

## Comorbid Psychiatric Conditions and Dual Diagnoses

Estimates vary on the prevalence of comorbid Axis I conditions in persons with GIDs. Cole, O'Boyle, Emory, and Meyer (1997) found that only 6% of MtF transsexuals and 4% of FtM transsexuals gave a history of treatment for another Axis I disorder, excluding substance abuse. Prevalence estimates based on clinicians' interviews and evaluations are generally higher, suggesting important method variance across studies: Haraldsen and Dahl (2000) observed that 33% of a mixed group of MtF and FtM patients had another current Axis I disorder; the figure reported by Bodlund and Armelius (1994) was 44%. Hepp, Kraemer, Schnyder, Miller, and Delsignore (2005) found another current Axis I disorder in 40% of MtF and 36% of FtM transsexuals. De Cuypere, Jannes, and Rubens (1995), on the other hand, diagnosed a current comorbid Axis I disorder in only 23% of MtF and 0% of FtM patients. Most recently, Hoshiai et al. (2010) reported a current prevalence of comorbid psychiatric disorder in 19% of MtF and 12.0% of FtM patients from Japan. Reported lifetime prevalence figures for Axis I disorders in MtF transsexuals include 21% (Verschoor & Poortinga, 1988), 45% (De Cuypere et al., 1995), and 80% (Hepp et al., 2005). In FtM transsexuals, reported lifetime prevalence figures for Axis I disorders include 33% (Verschoor & Poortinga, 1998), 39% (De Cuypere et al., 1995), and 55% (Hepp et al., 2005). Most of these figures are consistent with those found in other clinical populations but exceed those of nonclinical populations. Affective and adjustment disorders are among the most common comorbid Axis I conditions. A lifetime history of suicidal ideation and self-mutilation was quite high in both MtF (76% and 31%, respectively) and FtM (71% and 32%, respectively), as reported on by Hoshiai et al. (2010).

Comorbid substance abuse ("dual diagnosis") is often considered separately from other Axis I disorders. Prevalence estimates for comorbid substance abuse among transsexuals cover a wide range. Verschoor and Poortinga (1988) reported a lifetime history of substance abuse in only 11% of MtF and 4% of FtM patients. Cole et al. (1997), Hepp et al. (2005), and De Cuypere et al. (1995) found higher lifetime prevalence figures: 29%, 50%, and 50%, respectively, in MtF transsexuals and 26%, 36%, and 62%, respectively, in FtM transsexuals.

Reported prevalence figures for comorbid Axis II personality disorders are more consistent: Observed prevalence figures in mixed groups of MtF and FtM transsexuals include 20% (Haraldsen & Dahl, 2000), 33% (Bodlund & Armelius, 1994), and 42% (Hepp et al., 2005). Miach, Berah, Butcher, and Rouse (2000) found personality disorders in 29% of MtF transsexuals, whereas De Cuypere et al. (1995) reported personality disorders in 23% of FtM patients but in 70% of MtF patients—the last figure a notable outlier. These figures are similar to those seen in other clinical populations but higher than in nonclinical populations. Cluster B personality disorders, especially BPD, are the most commonly reported comorbid Axis II disorders.

When there is psychiatric comorbidity in patients with GID, how might this be best understood? There are at least four ways in which to formulate it: (1) It might be explained by the social stigma that results from the patient's non-normative gender identity (e.g., Clements-Nolle, Guzman, & Harris, 2008; Herbst et al., 2008; Koken, Bimbi, & Parsons, 2009; Melendez & Pinto, 2007); (2) it can be conceptualized as a causal factor in understanding the genesis of the GID (e.g., de Vries et al., 2010); (3) the presence of such difficulties might be related to generic risk factors that operate in the individual and/or the family of origin (e.g., genetics, parental psychopathology, social and economic adversity, etc.); and (4) it could be argued that the inherent distress associated with a GID leads to other psychiatric problems. Levine and Solomon (2009) have provided a useful essay for clinicians that can help them sort out which of these factors might be operative in an individual case.

# EPIDEMIOLOGY

## PREVALENCE AND SEX RATIO

Population-based data from European countries provide the best estimates of the prevalence of transsexualism and GID in Western societies (Zucker & Lawrence, 2009). In Belgium, the prevalence of transsexualism, defined as having undergone sex reassignment, is 1:12,900 for adult males and 1:33,800 for adult females (De Cuypere et al., 2007). Data from the Netherlands are similar: 1:11,900 adult males and 1:30,400 adult females (Bakker, van Kesteren, Gooren, & Bezemer, 1993). Primary care physicians in Scotland reported a prevalence of gender dysphoria, treated with cross-sex hormone therapy or sex reassignment surgery (SRS), of 1:12,800 in adult males patients and 1:52,100 in adult females patients (Wilson, Sharp, & Carr, 1999); the overall prevalence of gender dysphoria, treated or untreated, was 1:7,400 in males and 1:31,200 in females. Based on New Zealand passport data, Veale (2008) reported somewhat higher rates: 1:3,630 in males and 1:22,714 in females. In most Western countries, MtF transsexualism is two or three times as prevalent as FtM transsexualism (Garrels et al., 2000; Landén, Wålinder, & Lundström, 1996).

Transsexualism is apparently becoming more prevalent. Studies conducted in Sweden in the 1960s reported a prevalence of 1:37,000 in adult males and 1:103,000 in adult females (Landén et al., 1996), roughly one-third of current estimates. The observed increase in prevalence probably reflects a lower threshold at which individuals consider themselves to be appropriate candidates for sex reassignment.

Two recent surveys revealed that 2.7% and 2.8% of adult males reported having experienced sexual arousal in association with cross-dressing (Ahlers et al., 2011; Långström & Zucker, 2005), suggesting that autogynephilic cross-dressers are probably the most numerous transgender subgroup. Some of these cross-dressers, however, probably do not experience sufficient cross-gender identity or gender dysphoria to meet diagnostic criteria for GID or GIDNOS, nor sufficient distress or functional impairment to meet diagnostic criteria for GID, GIDNOS, or TF.

## AGE OF ONSET

Some persons with GID report that they were aware of their transgender feelings from their earliest memories. The cross-gender behaviors and interests of most homosexual MtF and FtM transsexuals, and some nonhomosexual FtM transsexuals, were usually evident in early childhood. Nonhomosexual MtF transsexuals typically report that they experienced their first desire to be the other sex or to change sex in middle childhood but sometimes as late as adolescence or adulthood (Lawrence, 2005; Nieder et al., in press; Zucker et al., in press).

# PSYCHOLOGICAL AND BIOLOGICAL ASSESSMENT

## PSYCHOLOGICAL ASSESSMENT

Psychological assessment in known or suspected cases of GID involves determining the presence or absence of a GID, evaluating the nature and severity of the GID, and assessment of comorbid psychopathology. In adults, GIDs are diagnosed primarily on the basis of self-report: "There are no so-called objective tests, either medical or psychological, that serve as proof of the diagnosis" (Pfäfflin, 2007, p. 176). The clinician should obtain information about the client's psychosexual development, gender identification, sexual orientation, and feelings concerning sexed body characteristics and assigned gender role. Clients sometimes deliberately or inadvertently provide misleading information to caregivers, especially if they are eager to be approved for treatment (Walworth, 1997). Clinicians should not uncritically accept self-reported sexual orientation in male GID patients with a history of sexual attraction to women: Many such patients develop secondary sexual attraction to men in connection with their cross-gender identification and inaccurately describe themselves as exclusively attracted to men, whereas experienced clinicians often judge otherwise (Nieder et al., in press).

Questionnaires and scales for the objective assessment of GID exist but are not yet widely used in clinical practice. The gender-related scales of the Minnesota Multiphasic Personality Inventory-2 (*Mf*, *GM*, and *GF*; Butcher et al., 2001; Martin & Finn, 2010) provide objective measures of clients' gender-typical or atypical attitudes and interests (see, e.g., Gómez-Gil, Vidal-Hagemeijer, & Salmero, 2008). The Feminine Gender Identity Scale for Males (Freund, Langevin, Satterberg, & Steiner, 1977) and Masculine Gender Identity Scale for Females (Blanchard & Freund, 1983) have rarely been used outside of research settings. The Utrecht Gender Dysphoria Scale (Cohen-Kettenis & van Goozen, 1997; see also Cohen-Kettenis & Pfäfflin, 2010) unfortunately has not been published in English. The Gender Identity/Gender Dysphoria Questionnaire for Adolescents and Adults (Deogracias et al., 2007) is a recently developed, published instrument with good sensitivity and specificity; it has been cross-validated (Singh et al., 2010) and seems destined to achieve widespread acceptance.

The specific focus of gender dysphoria can vary considerably among clients with GIDs. Gender dysphoria may involve dissatisfaction with the sexed body characteristics, gender role, or sexuality of natal sex, or any combination; the specific pattern may affect treatment planning. Intensity of gender dysphoria not only varies among clients but can also vary over time in the same client. Gender dysphoria often intensifies following significant crises or losses (Levine, 1993; Lothstein, 1979; Roback, Fellemann, & Abramowitz, 1984) but may moderate or remit when these have been resolved.

As noted previously, comorbid mental health problems are prevalent in persons with GIDs. Treatment of comorbid psychotic, affective, and anxiety disorders may be required before a GID can be confidently diagnosed. Satisfactory control of comorbid mental health problems is a precondition for approval for genital SRS (Meyer et al., 2001).

BIOLOGICAL ASSESSMENT

Physical examination and laboratory testing are of limited value in the assessment of GIDs. In principle, physical examination could help ascertain the presence or absence of an intersex condition, which might lead to a diagnosis of GIDNOS rather than GID. Some gender identity clinics routinely perform karyotyping in GID evaluations, but the procedure is expensive and the results will be normal in roughly 97% of patients with known or suspected GID (Bearman, 2007; Inoubli et al., 2011). Nonautosomal positive findings in males will usually represent Kleinfelter syndrome (47, XXY) or an XYY karyotype (Buhrich, Barr, & Lam-Po-Tang, 1978; Snaith, Penhale, & Horsfield, 1991; Taneja, Ammini, Mohapatra, Saxena, & Kucheria, 1992; see also Mouaffak, Gallarda, Baup, Olié, & Klebs, 2007). Bearman suggested that, if karyotyping is performed at all, it should be offered only to male patients with hypogonadism, tall stature, gynecomastia, or learning disorders. There are two case reports in the literature showing sex chromosome abnormalities in FtM patients (Khandelwal, Agarwal, & Jiloha, 2010; Turan et al., 2000).

Over the years, evidence for an elevated rate of polycystic ovary syndrome (PCOS) in FtM transsexuals has been inconsistent. For example, Baba et al. (2007) reported an astonishing prevalence of 58% in a Japanese sample. In contrast, a well-controlled study using more rigorous definition of PCOS found a prevalence rate of only 11.5% in Dutch FtM transsexuals, which was not significant from the 9.6% found in health controls (Mueller et al., 2008). Because PCOS may be related to both prenatal and postnatal levels of androgen, it would probably be useful for it to be ruled out as part of routine endocrinological evaluations.

## CLINICAL COURSE, PROGNOSIS, AND TREATMENT

### Clinical Course

The clinical course of GID is variable, not easily predictable, and not well understood, even in persons who have been carefully evaluated and diagnosed with GID (Meyer et al., 2001). There are at least four recognized outcomes of severe gender dysphoria or GID/transsexualism (Carroll, 1999): (1) unresolved or unknown, (2) acceptance of natal gender, (3) part-time cross-gender expression, and (4) full-time cross-living and sex reassignment.

*Unresolved or Unknown Outcomes*   As many as half of clients who undergo evaluation or psychotherapy for GID may withdraw from treatment (Carroll, 1999). They may find the process prohibitively expensive, become impatient with a prolonged evaluation process, or feel ambivalent or hopeless about achieving a satisfactory solution to their gender concerns. Some clients who drop out subsequently resume treatment, but otherwise little is known about the natural history of GIDs in these individuals.

*Acceptance of Natal Gender*   Acceptance of natal gender was once considered the optimal outcome for patients with GIDs. There have been no convincing demonstrations, however, that any form of psychiatric treatment can eliminate gender dysphoria or facilitate acceptance of natal gender in adults with GIDs; however, some adults with GIDs do appear to accept their natal gender (Marks, Green, & Mataix-Cols, 2000; Shore, 1984). Acceptance of natal gender sometimes occurs in persons who undergo treatment of comorbid psychological problems, are unwilling to risk losing their employment or their families, hold religious beliefs that condemn sex reassignment, or have physical characteristics that make it impossible for them to pass convincingly as members of the other sex (Carroll, 1999; Shore, 1984). Nonhomosexual gender dysphoric men sometimes successfully postpone treatment until they have completed parental or spousal obligations (Blanchard, 1994). The Standards of Care (SOC; Meyer et al., 2001) suggest various "options for gender adaptation" for individuals who decide not to live part- or full-time in a cross-gender role.

*Part-Time Cross-Gender Behavior*    Persons with GIDs may decide to live part-time in their preferred gender role and part-time as members of their natal sex. They sometimes use masculinizing or feminizing hormone therapy or undergo surgical procedures to facilitate this process. Docter and Prince (1997) surveyed more than 1,000 heterosexual cross-dressers, none of whom lived full-time as women, and found that 17% would seek sex reassignment if possible, 28% considered their feminine self their preferred gender identity, and nearly 50% were either using feminizing hormones or wanted to do so. Many of these persons presumably had a persistent cross-gender identity of some strength and experienced some degree of gender dysphoria, yet decided to live only part-time as women. Adult females with GIDs sometimes live part-time in the cross-gender role as well, but this rarely becomes a focus of clinical attention and has not been as thoroughly documented.

*Full-Time Cross-Living and Sex Reassignment*    Many clients with a presenting complaint of GID/transsexualism will want to undergo sex reassignment and live full-time as members of the other sex. In reality, full-time and part-time cross-gender behavior do not represent distinctly demarcated outcomes but rather points on a spectrum of options available to persons with GID, involving many possible choices of presentation, cross-gender role assumption, and anatomic modification. Some persons who live full-time in the cross-gender role do not undergo SRS and may not use cross-sex hormone therapy; some persons who use cross-sex hormones and undergo SRS do not present themselves unambiguously as members of the other sex, but as gender-ambiguous, androgynous, or visibly transgendered individuals.

The decision to undertake full-time cross-living and sex reassignment and the process of actualizing this decision typically occurs in stages, similar to the stages of coming out for lesbians and gay men. Several multistage models of transsexual coming out have been proposed (e.g., Devor, 2004; Gagne, Tewksbury, & McGaughey, 1997; Lewins, 1995). These typically involve acknowledging gender dysphoria, questioning and information gathering, developing a transsexual identity, disclosing one's situation to significant others, cross-living, undergoing surgical sex reassignment if desired, and experiencing further evolution of gender identity after transition (Devor, 2004).

TREATMENT

*Standards of Care for Gender Identity Disorders*    The World Professional Association for Transgender Health, formerly the Harry Benjamin International Gender Dysphoria Association, promulgates SOC for the treatment of GIDs. The SOC are updated regularly; the most recent edition was published 10 years ago (Meyer et al., 2001), and a new edition is expected in 2011 or 2012 (Coleman, 2009). The SOC reflect the consensus opinions of experienced professionals but rarely a higher quality of empirical evidence (Cohen-Kettenis & Gooren, 1999). They are nevertheless an important resource for treatment of clients with GIDs, although some clients contest them (see Green, 2008).

The SOC describe four main treatment modalities for GID: psychotherapy, cross-sex hormone therapy, real-life experience in the desired gender role, and sex reassignment surgery (SRS)—a term that usually denotes feminizing genitoplasty in MtF transsexuals but can denote either mastectomy with chest reconstruction or masculinizing genitoplasty in FtM transsexuals. Not all patients with GID desire all of these therapeutic modalities. Some patients, for example, are satisfied with cross-sex hormone therapy and full-time or part-time cross-living. The SOC state that hormone therapy, the real-life experience, and nongenital surgery can be provided separately or in any combination, but that feminizing or masculinizing genitoplasty should ordinarily be provided only to patients who have previously used cross-sex hormone therapy for at least one year and have successfully completed a minimum one-year, full-time real-life experience in the desired gender role (Meyer et al., 2001).

*Psychotherapy*   Individual psychotherapy is not required by the SOC but is strongly encouraged (Meyer et al., 2001; see also Bockting, 2008). Psychotherapy is not intended to cure gender dysphoria but to allow the client to explore his or her evolving identity, discuss relationship and employment issues, and consider treatment options. Seikowski (2007) argued that psychotherapy was most appropriate for patients with some type of personality disorder, but not for the majority. Persons with GID can also benefit from group psychotherapy (Stermac, Blanchard, Clemmensen, & Dickey, 1991), which can reduce feelings of isolation and provide opportunities to receive and give support, including advice about grooming and social presentation.

*Cross-Sex Hormone Therapy*   Cross-sex hormone therapy suppresses or minimizes the secondary sex characteristics of a person's natal sex and promotes the development of the secondary sex characteristics of the other sex. Recent review articles and expert guidelines describe the management of cross-sex hormone therapy (e.g., Gooren & Delemarre-van de Waal, 2007; Hembree et al., 2009). The SOC (Meyer et al., 2001) discuss eligibility criteria for cross-sex hormone therapy. Hormone therapy is usually prescribed for persons diagnosed with GID/transsexualism, but it also can be prescribed for transgender persons who do not wish to live full-time in a cross-gender role or who do not desire SRS.

Hormone therapy for MtF transsexuals usually involves a combination of estrogens and antiandrogens. Feminizing hormone therapy typically results in breast growth, decreased muscle mass, reduction in the growth of facial and body hair, slowing of scalp hair loss, and decreased sexual interest. Leavitt, Berger, Hoeppner, and Northrop (1980) found that hormone-treated MtF transsexuals displayed better psychological adjustment than an untreated comparison group.

Hormone therapy for FtM transsexuals usually involves only testosterone. Masculinizing hormone therapy causes increased facial and body hair, increased muscle mass, male pattern scalp hair loss, deepening of the voice, clitoral enlargement, and suppression of menses. Masculinizing hormone therapy also has emotional and psychological effects, including increased aggressiveness, anger-proneness, and sexual interest (van Goozen, Cohen-Kettenis, Gooren, Frijda, & Van de Poll, 1995).

*Real-Life Experience in the Desired Gender Role*   Real-life experience in the desired gender role helps clients decide whether cross-living offers a better quality of life. Clients can undertake a real-life experience without professional help, and some clients will already be living full-time in a cross-gender role when they are first seen by clinicians. It is not always easy to decide, however, whether clients are living full-time in their desired gender roles, especially given that the SOC do not require clients to live as typical members of the other sex, but merely to live in whatever gender role is congruent with their gender identity.

Being regarded as a member of one's preferred sex during the real-life experience is usually easier for FtM than MtF transsexuals. Attribution of male status results from observing signs of masculinization, whereas attribution of female status occurs by a process of exclusion, when few or no signs of masculinization are observed (Kessler & McKenna, 1978). Although it is almost impossible for either MtF or FtM transsexuals to remove all physical signs of their natal sex, residual signs of maleness in MtF transsexuals will often prevent their being regarded as unequivocally female, whereas residual signs of femaleness in FtM transsexuals will rarely prevent their being regarded as unequivocally male.

The SOC describe the real-life experience as a reversible step that, if successfully completed, allows clients and caregivers to consider the irreversible step of genital SRS with greater confidence (Meyer et al., 2001). In practice, however, the real-life experience may have irreversible social and economic consequences of its own, which clients may consider more serious than the potential consequences of genital surgery. The SOC also do not specify what a successful real-life experience should look like. Improvement in social and psychological functioning in the desired gender role is one possible measure of success, but such improvement can be difficult to demonstrate if negative social and economic consequences of prejudice and discrimination overshadow the psychological benefits of living in the desired gender role (Levy, Crown, & Reid, 2003).

## Sex Reassignment Surgery

*Feminizing Genitoplasty in MtF transsexuals.* Genital SRS for MtF transsexuals yields excellent cosmetic and functional results and a high degree of patient satisfaction (Gijs & Brewaeys, 2007; Giraldo, Mora, Solano, Gonzáles, & Smith-Fernández, 2002). All elements of MtF sex reassignment provide relief of gender dysphoria (Kuiper & Cohen-Kettenis, 1988), but genital SRS offers particular social and psychological benefits. In a prospective controlled study of MtF SRS outcomes, patients who received expedited SRS reported better psychosocial outcomes than did waitlist controls (Mate-Kole, Freschi, & Robin, 1990). Good surgical results and absence of complications are associated with greater subjective satisfaction and better psychosocial outcomes (Lawrence, 2003; Ross & Need, 1989; Schroder & Carroll, 1999).

*Reduction Mammaplasty and Chest Reconstruction in FtM transsexuals.* This is the surgical procedure that FtM transsexuals most frequently undergo and is arguably the most important one (Monstrey, Ceulemans, & Hoebeke, 2007). It is often performed early in the sex reassignment process, which the SOC explicitly allow.

*Masculinizing Genitoplasty in FtM transsexuals.* There are no truly satisfactory genital SRS techniques available to FtM transsexuals, and many FtM transsexuals forego this procedure entirely. Two genital SRS techniques have been most widely utilized in FtM transsexuals. In *metoidioplasty,* the hypertrophied clitoris is used to create a microphallus; in *phalloplasty* techniques, skin flaps or free skin grafts are used to create a neophallus that usually allows standing urination (Monstrey et al., 2007). Often the labia majora are fused to create a neoscrotum and testicular prostheses are inserted. Complications related to graft/flap necrosis and urinary leakage or obstruction are common following phalloplasty.

*Results of Sex Reassignment*    Most studies of the outcomes of the sex reassignment process have involved transsexuals who have undergone genital SRS, or chest reconstruction in the case of FtM transsexuals. Nearly all such studies conclude that sex reassignment generally, and SRS specifically, results in substantial relief of gender dysphoria, high levels of patient satisfaction, favorable (or at least not worsened) psychosocial outcomes, and a low prevalence of regret (Gijs & Brewaeys, 2007; Green & Fleming, 1990; Murad et al., 2010). Factors associated with favorable outcomes of SRS include careful diagnostic screening of candidates, availability of social support, psychological stability, and freedom from surgical complications. Some studies have found that nonhomosexual MtF transsexuals are more likely to experience regret after SRS than their homosexual counterparts (Blanchard, Steiner, Clemmensen, & Dickey, 1989; Smith, van Goozen, Kuiper, & Cohen-Kettenis, 2005a), but one large study did not confirm this impression (Lawrence, 2003).

## ETIOLOGICAL CONSIDERATIONS

It is important to recognize the limitations of theories and research findings relevant to understanding the etiology of adult GID/transexualism. Much of the relevant research has addressed the etiology of GID as it manifests in children (for a review, see Zucker & Bradley, 1995), but most cases of childhood GID remit before adulthood (Drummond, Bradley, Badali-Peterson, & Zucker, 2008; Green, 1987; Singh, Bradley, & Zucker, 2010; Wallien and Cohen-Kettenis, 2008); there is even a recent study that showed that some children who had transitioned socially to live as a member of the other gender "reverted" to living in the gender role that matched their natal sex (Steensma, Biemond, de Boer, & Cohen-Kettenis, in press). Moreover, most research has been conducted in males with GID; females with GID have received less attention. In addition, theorists and researchers often have not distinguished between homosexual and nonhomosexual transsexual subtypes, even though these may have different etiologies.

### BEHAVIORAL GENETICS AND MOLECULAR GENETICS

*Behavioral Genetics*    Studies of the co-occurrence of behavioral traits within families and especially within monozygotic (MZ) twin pairs are the usual methods of estimating the influence of genetic factors on behavioral traits (e.g., GID, gender dysphoria, or gender nonconformity). Gómez-Gil et al. (2010) summarized the published MZ twin data: In males, six pairs concordant and five pairs nonconcordant for transsexualism have been reported; in females, one pair concordant and four pairs nonconcordant have been described. There have also been two large studies of co-occurring GID or transsexualism in first-degree relatives of persons with GID or transsexualism: Green (2000) reported 10 instances of co-occurring transsexualism or transvestism in the siblings, parents, or children of roughly 1,500 transsexual probands, and Gómez-Gil et al. (2010) reported 12 cases of co-occurring trans-sexualism in the siblings of 995 transsexual probands. In the latter study, the prevalence of transsexualism in siblings of transsexuals was 1 in 211, much higher than in the general population.

The best-known investigation of the heritability of GID in children was con-ducted by Coolidge, Thede, and Young (2002), who studied 96 MZ and 61 dizygotic twin pairs, ages 4 to 17 years. They assessed GID using a six-item scale based on *DSM-IV* criteria, but none of the twins had been diagnosed clinically with GID. Coolidge et al. reported that heritability accounted for 62% of the variance in GID scores and nonshared environment accounted for 38%. The prevalence of GID in the children was 2.3%, however, suggesting that the authors' threshold for ascer-taining the condition was too low: Their conclusions about heritability arguably addressed childhood gender nonconformity, rather than genuine GID. Two other studies that explicitly addressed the heritability of childhood gender non-conformity reached different conclusions, perhaps because of their different methodology: Bailey, Dunne, and Martin (2000) found that heritability accounted for 50% of variance in recalled childhood gender nonconformity among men and 37% among women, with nonshared environment accounting for the rest. Knafo, Iervolino, and Plomin (2005) found that heritability accounted for about 27% of variance in parent-reported gender atypicality in boys ages 3 to 4, with shared environment accounting for about 57% and nonshared environment accounting for 16%; the comparable figures for girls were heritability 42%, shared environment 43%, and nonshared environment 15%. It is important to note that childhood gender atypicality usually does not lead to GID in adulthood, but it is one of the antecedents of homosexual MtF and FtM transsexualism and appears to be at least partly heritable.

*Molecular Genetics*   Sexual differentiation of the mammalian brain is influenced by prenatal sex hormone activity (Garcia-Falgueras & Swaab, 2010; Gooren, 2006; Sánchez, Bocklandt, & Vilain, 2009; Savic, Garcia-Falgueras, & Swaab, 2010; Swaab, 2004). Consequently, researchers have hypothesized that abnormalities in genes that code for sex hormone receptors or for enzymes that catalyze the synthesis or metabolism of sex hormones might show associations with GID/transsexualism. Candidate genes include those coding for the androgen receptor (AR), estrogen receptor alpha (ERα), estrogen receptor beta (ERβ), and progesterone receptor (PR), and for the enzymes aromatase (CYP19), 17-alpha-hydroxylase (CYP17), and 5-alpha-reductase, type II (SRD5A2). Most studies have investigated differences between transsexual patients and same-sex controls in mean repeat numbers of specific polymorphisms in candidate genes or in the frequencies of specific mutant alleles or genotypes. None have attempted to differentiate between transsexual subtypes.

Henningsson et al. (2005) found no significant differences between MtF trans-sexuals and male controls for the AR or CYP19 genes, but they did find a significant difference for the ERβ gene. Hare et al. (2009) examined the same three candidate genes in MtF transsexuals and male controls, but they obtained different results: No significant differences for the CYP19 or ERβ genes, but a significant difference for the AR gene, albeit using a one-tailed test; a two-tailed test would have been non-significant (moreover, the false-positive rate among the controls was substantial). Bentz et al. (2007) reported no differences between MtF transsexuals and male controls or FtM transsexuals and female controls for the SRD5A2 gene. Bentz et al. (2008) found no differences between MtF transsexuals and male controls for CPY17 alleles and genotypes, but they did find a significant difference in the case of FtM transsexuals and female controls. Ujike et al. (2009) detected no significant differences between MtF transsexuals and male controls or FtM transsexuals and female controls for the AR, ERα, ERβ, PR, or CYP19 genes.

In summary, there is little or no evidence at present that abnormalities related to molecular genetics account for GID/transsexualism: Most investigations have yielded negative results, and most positive results have not been replicated by other investigators.

### NEUROANATOMY AND NEUROBIOLOGY

*Neuroanatomy*   The central subdivision of the bed nucleus of the stria terminalis (BSTc), a hypothalamic or limbic nucleus, is sexually dimorphic: it is significantly larger and contains a larger number of neurons in men than in women. Zhou, Hofman, Gooren, and Swaab (1995) conducted a postmortem study of six MtF transsexuals and found that mean BSTc size was small and female-typical, a sex-reversed pattern. The MtF transsexuals supposedly included both homosexual and nonhomosexual types. Kruijver et al. (2000) studied the same six MtF transsexuals and found that mean neuron number in the BSTc was also sex-reversed. Similar postmortem findings in a gender dysphoric man who had never received hormone therapy suggested that cross-sex hormone therapy could not account for the sex-reversed pattern. Kruijver et al. proposed that "transsexualism may reflect a form of brain hermaphroditism" (p. 2041).

The validity of this putative marker was challenged by the discovery that the BSTc does not become sexually dimorphic until adulthood, long after the symptoms of MtF transsexualism typically appear (Chung, De Vries, & Swaab, 2002). Magnetic resonance imaging (MRI) studies also demonstrated that hormone therapy in MtF transsexuals was associated with significant reductions in the volume of the brain globally and the hypothalamus particularly (Hulshoff Pol et al., 2006). Hulshoff Pol et al. conjectured that, in the Zhou/Kruijver studies, "the altered size of the bed nucleus of the stria terminalis could have been due to the exposure of cross-sex hormones in adult life" (p. S108). Also using MRI, Schiltz et al. (2007) found that male pedophiles, too, had a lower than expected BST volume; noting the similar findings in MtF transsexuals, they proposed that "these alterations may not be specific to pedophilia but may rather be a feature of sexual abnormalities in general" (p. 744). Additional information about the sexual orientation of the six Zhou/Kruijver MtF transsexuals, reported by

Garcia-Falgueras and Swaab (2008), was consistent with the hypothesis that all were nonhomosexual.

In summary, a sex-reversed BSTc size and neuron number may be a marker for paraphilic male sexuality or for only nonhomosexual MtF transsexualism, rather than for all types of MtF transsexualism. Alternatively, the BSTc findings may be attributable to the effects of transgender hormone therapy. In a related postmortem study of 12 MtF transsexuals, including the six Zhou/Kruijver subjects, Garcia-Falgueras and Swaab (2008) found that the volume and neuron number of yet another sexually dimorphic hypothalamic nucleus, INAH-3, was sex-reversed; probably 11 of the 12 MtF transsexuals were nonhomosexual. Further research will be needed to confirm or disconfirm these findings and clarify their implications for understanding the etiology of GID.

A few neuroanatomic studies of untreated GID patients have been conducted using neuroimaging techniques. Luders et al. (2009) used MRI to compare regional gray matter volumes in 24 MtF transsexuals (6 homosexual, 18 nonhomosexual) and male and female control subjects; the pattern observed in the MtF transsexuals more closely matched the male controls. In one of the rare studies of FtM transsexuals, Rametti et al. (2011) compared 18 homosexual FtM transsexuals to male and female control subjects, using an MRI technique called diffusion tensor imaging to examine a measure of the directional organization of specific white matter regions; the pattern in the FtM transsexuals more closely approximated that found in the male control subjects. These findings have yet to be confirmed, and their implications for understanding the etiology of GID remain to be determined.

*Neurophysiology* Several neurophysiological studies of transsexuals have been conducted using neuroimaging; most have involved nonhomosexual MtF transsexuals primarily or exclusively, and none of the findings have yet been confirmed by other investigators. Berglund, Lindström, Dhejne-Helmy, and Savic (2008) studied the effect of inhaling odorous steroid compounds on regional cerebral blood flow in the hypothalamus in 12 nonhomosexual MtF transsexuals and in male and female control subjects, using positron emission tomography; they found that the MtF transsexuals showed a pattern of activation intermediate between the male and female control subjects, but closer to the latter. Gizewski et al. (2008) used functional MRI (fMRI) to study patterns of cerebral activation in response to visual erotic stimuli in 12 MtF transsexuals, 10 of whom were nonhomosexual, and in male and female control subjects; they reported that the activation pattern in the transsexuals more closely matched that of the female controls.

Schöning et al. (2010) examined cerebral activation patterns during a mental rotation task in 11 untreated MtF transsexuals, 11 hormone-treated MtF transsexuals, and male control subjects, using fMRI; the transsexuals were described as more variable in sexual orientation than the control subjects, but no further detail was provided. All three groups activated the classical cerebral mental rotation network, but with some regional differences between the controls and the two transsexual groups, which did not differ from each other. Carrillo et al. (2010) also used fMRI to study cerebral activation during a mental rotation task in 18 MtF transsexuals, 19 FtM transsexuals, and male and female control subjects; all of the transsexuals were nominally homosexual and all were hormone-treated.

The general activation pattern was similar in all groups; the MtF transsexuals showed a specific activation pattern that differed from both male and female controls, whereas the specific activation patterns of the FtM transsexuals and the two control groups did not differ. The proximate causes of these neuro-physiological findings are unknown, and the implications of these findings for understanding the etiology of GID remain to be determined.

### LEARNING, MODELING, AND LIFE EVENTS

Early psychoanalytic theorists viewed parenting behavior as etiologically important in childhood GID. Stoller (1968, 1975) emphasized maternal parenting style: He believed that the mother's excessive closeness to her son ("blissful symbiosis"; Stoller, 1975, p. 37) was largely responsible for the development of transsexualism in boys, whereas the mother's inability to achieve emotional closeness with an "unfeminine" daughter contributed significantly to the development of transsexu-alism in girls. Moberly (1986), in contrast, believed that transsexualism reflected a "same-sex developmental deficit" (p. 205), in which the child's inability to identify with the same-sex parent led to a defensive opposite-sex identification.

Although these psychoanalytic formulations may now seem overly simplistic, parenting behavior may nevertheless be etiologically important. Zucker and Bradley (1995) observed that the mothers of boys with GID often have a history of significant psychopathology (see also Zucker et al., 2003), which is positively correlated with their reinforcement of feminine behaviors in their sons; the authors proposed that the mothers of boys who develop GID may be unwilling or unable to limit or discourage their sons' cross-gender behavior. Something similar may occur with girls with GID: Maternal psychopathology may again be associated with an inability to limit cross-gender expression (Zucker & Bradley, 1995). Consistent with these observations, Simon et al. (2011) reported that, compared with nonclinical control subjects, adult MtF and FtM transsexuals described their mothers as less caring and affective but more controlling. MtF transsexuals also described their mothers as more unreliable and abusive yet less demanding; they described their fathers as less caring, reliable, and available.

### COGNITIVE INFLUENCES

Cognitive factors appear to play a limited role in the etiology of GIDs in adults. Most relevant theory and research has focused on a few specific areas: childhood devel-opment of cognitive schemas concerning gender, cognitive comparisons of self and others during transgender coming out, and cognitive contributions to cross-gender identity formation in transvestism and nonhomosexual MtF transsexualism.

Children develop cognitive schemas concerning gender identity and gender stereotypes during early and middle childhood (Martin, Ruble, & Szkrybalo, 2002). Some children with GID develop gender schemas that include a cross-gender identity, but the reasons for this are unclear: Perhaps these children observe that their behaviors and interests conform to opposite-sex gender stereotypes and mislabel themselves accordingly (Zucker & Bradley, 1995). While such a cognitive process could explain the mechanism of cross-gender identity formation in children with GID, it does not explain the origins of the sex-atypical behaviors and interests that are the putative objects of cognitive appraisal. Moreover, most children with GID do not go on to become adults with GID.

Cognitive comparisons of self and others concerning gender-related interests and behaviors is a recognized mechanism of identity formation and consolidation in the process of coming out for transsexuals and other transgender persons. Devor (2004) observed that transgender persons typically employ "a number of techniques of identity comparison to try to determine if there is an identity in which they can comfortably live their lives in their originally assigned gender and sex" (pp. 50–51). They subsequently undertake a similar cognitive process as they try to find an authentic identity within the other gender.

Docter's (1988) theory of gender identity formation in transvestism (including TF) and nonhomosexual MtF transsexualism stressed the importance of fully enacting the cross-gender role through complete cross-dressing and public presentation. Implicitly, this is a cognitive process, grounded in self-observation ("I dress and behave like a female; therefore I *am*, in some sense, female"). Docter described the process of reconciling core gender identity and the emergent cross-gender identity as an attempt to resolve cognitive dissonance. He observed that this process could lead to integration of the cross-gender identity into the existing male self-system (i.e., a revised cognitive schema) or reorganization of the self-system to give primacy to the cross-gender identity (i.e., an alternative cognitive schema).

*Sex and Ethnicity Considerations* As previously noted, biological sex is a key feature that explains much of the diversity in the GIDs. Adult GID is two to three times more common in males than in females, perhaps because autogynephilia accounts for many cases of male GID, whereas the analogous paraphilia in females is probably rare (Lawrence, 2009a) and accounts for few, if any, cases of female GID. TF appears to be an exclusively male phenomenon (APA, 2000).

The clinical manifestations of GIDs differ substantially in males and females. Males with GID are diverse with respect to sexual orientation, age at clinical presentation, and congruence between physical appearance and desired gender role; females with GID are more homogeneous with respect to these variables. Cross-sex hormone therapy is highly effective in masculinizing the appearance of FtM transsexuals but much less effective in feminizing the appearance of MtF transsexuals. Genital SRS techniques for MtF transsexuals are highly refined and generally yield excellent results, whereas most FtM transsexuals forego genital SRS altogether, for want of a genuinely satisfactory technique.

The role of ethnicity in accounting for the etiology and clinical manifestations of GID is incompletely understood, but there is a significant association between ethnicity and MtF transsexual typology across national cultures, and probably within national cultures. In Asian, Polynesian, and Latin American countries, most MtF transsexuals (or, at least, the cultural equivalents of MtF transsexuals) are homosexual in orientation (e.g., Collumbien et al., 2009; Ellingson & Odo, 2008; Infante, Sosa-Rubi, & Cuadra, 2009; Johnson, 1997; Khan et al., 2009; Khan, Rehan, Qayyum, & Khan, 2008; Koon, 2002; Kulick, 1998; Nanda, 1994), whereas in the United States, Canada, and most western European countries, the majority of MtF transsexuals are currently nonhomosexual in orientation (for review, see Lawrence, 2010c). Societal individualism appears to mediate the relationship between ethnicity and MtF transsexual typology: Nonhomosexual MtF transsexuals are relatively more prevalent in more individualistic societies and less prevalent in less individualistic societies (Lawrence, 2010c). There is also evidence of a significant association between ethnicity and MtF transsexual typology within the United States. Hwahng and Nuttbrock (2007) reported that Black and Hispanic transgender and transsexual males in New York City were more likely than their White counterparts to be homosexual in orientation. In a subsequent, larger study of transgender and transsexual males in New York City, most of whom were Black or Hispanic, the correlation between nonhomosexual orientation and White ethnicity was .60 (Nuttbrock et al., 2011; see also Lawrence, 2010a). Similarly, Kellogg, Clements-Nolle, Dilley, Katz, and McFarland (2001) observed that, in a predominantly (71%) non-White sample of transgender and transsexual men in San Francisco, about 64% were probably homosexual in orientation, a much higher percentage than has typically been observed among predominantly White MtF transsexual samples in the United States (Lawrence, 2010c).

## LOOKING AHEAD TO *DSM-5*

The Sexual and Gender Identity Disorders Workgroup is one of 13 diagnostic groups assembled by the *DSM-5* Task Force to propose revisions for the forthcoming fifth edition of the *DSM* (scheduled for publication in May 2013). The Gender Identity Disorders subworkgroup has published four review articles, including one on adolescents and adults (Cohen-Kettenis & Pfäfflin, 2010; see also Drescher, 2010; Meyer-Bahlburg, 2010, Zucker, 2010). Here, we will summarize five components of the literature reviews on GID and recommended changes.

### NAME CHANGE

The GID subworkgroup initially recommended a change in name of the GID diagnosis to that of Gender Incongruence. This was guided by two main considerations: (1) It was argued that the term "gender incongruence" captured in a succinct manner the core presenting complaint of most patients, namely, the felt discordance between one's felt gender identity and somatic sex (see www .dsm5.org; (2) the deletion of the word "disorder" from the name of the diagnosis was motivated, in part, by the suggestion of some critics that this would help reduce the stigma among a marginalized population. Regarding the latter, some critics have suggested that the proposed name change is more appearance than substance (e.g., Lawrence, 2010d), and others have recommended an alternative diagnostic label of Gender Dysphoria (e.g., De Cuypere, Knudson, & Bockting, 2010). Although public commentary on the dsm5.org website was strongly supportive of the proposed name change to Gender Incongruence (see also Vance et al., 2010), the GID subworkgroup subsequently recommended the diagnostic label of Gender Dysphoria (see www.dsm5.org), which was the preferred term recommended by members of the World Professional Association for Transgender Health

(De Cuypere et al., 2010). The term "gender dysphoria" has a long history of usage in clinical sexology and thus will likely be quite familiar to most clinicians in the field. Although the diagnostic label has not been finalized, it should be noted that in *DSM-IV-TR* there are other diagnoses in which the term "disorder" is not present (e.g., anorexia nervosa, encopresis, enuresis).

## Modification of Diagnostic Criteria

Table 16.2 shows the diagnostic criteria for GID for adolescents and adults. One criticism of the current criteria is that they are a bit vague (see Cohen-Kettenis & Pfäfflin, 2010; Zucker, 2006). For example, the symptom pertaining to a "stated desire to be the other sex" makes no formal reference to intensity or duration. The proposed revised criteria are shown in Table 16.3. It can be seen that these proposed criteria are more detailed and are guided by the conceptual formulation of gender incongruence. In addition, the proposed criteria have collapsed the Point A and B criterion on the grounds that the symptom cluster very likely represents one underlying construct (see Deogracias et al., 2007; Papp et al., 2011; Singh et al., 2010). The recommendation of a minimum of two symptoms for the diagnosis was based, in part, on a secondary data analysis that yielded excellent specificity and sensitivity rates (see www.dsm5.org). Lastly, the proposed lower bound of a 6-month duration criterion has been recommended to rule-out transient symptoms of gender incongruence.

### Table 16.2
*DSM-IV-TR* Criteria for Gender Identity Disorder (Adolescent and Adults)

A  A strong and persistent cross-gender identification (not merely a desire for any perceived cultural advantages of being the other sex).

In adolescents and adults, the disturbance is manifested by symptoms such as a stated desire to be the other sex, frequent passing as the other sex, desire to live or be treated as the other sex, or the conviction that he or she has the typical feelings and reactions of the other sex.

B. Persistent discomfort with his or her sex or sense of inappropriateness in the gender role of that sex.

In adolescents and adults, the disturbance is manifested by symptoms of such as preoccupation with getting rid of primary and secondary sex characteristics (e.g., request for hormones, surgery, or other procedures to physically alter sexual characteristics to simulate the other sex) or belief that he or she was born the wrong sex.

C. The disturbance is not concurrent with a physical intersex condition.

D. The disturbance causes clinically significant distress or impairment in social, occupational, or other important areas of functioning.

**Specify if (for sexually mature individuals):**

- Sexually Attracted to Males
- Sexually Attracted to Females
- Sexually Attracted to Both
- Sexually Attracted to Neither

*Note:* Only criteria for adolescents and adults are listed.

**Table 16.3**

Proposed *DSM-5* Criteria for Gender Dysphoria (Adolescents and Adults)

A.   A marked incongruence between one's experienced/expressed gender and assigned gender, of at least 6 months' duration, as manifested by two or more of the following indicators:

  1.   a marked incongruence between one's experienced/expressed gender and primary and/or secondary sex characteristics (or, in young adolescents, the anticipated secondary sex characteristics)

  2.   a strong desire to be rid of one's primary and/or secondary sex characteristics because of a marked incongruence with one's experienced/expressed gender (or, in young adolescents, a desire to prevent the development of the anticipated secondary sex characteristics)

  3.   a strong desire for the primary and/or secondary sex characteristics of the other gender

  4.   a strong desire to be of the other gender (or some alternative gender different from one's assigned gender)

  5.   a strong desire to be treated as the other gender (or some alternative gender different from one's assigned gender)

  6.   a strong conviction that one has the typical feelings and reactions of the other gender (or some alternative gender different from one's assigned gender)

B. The condition is associated with clinically significant distress or impairment in social, occupational, or other important areas of functioning, or with a significantly increased risk of suffering, such as distress or disability.

**Subtypes**

With a disorder of sex development

Without a disorder of sex development

**Specifier**

Post-transition, that is, the individual has transitioned to full-time living in the desire gender (with or without legalization of gender change) and has undergone (or is undergoing) at least one cross-sex medical procedure or treatment regiment, namely, regular cross-sex hormone treatment or gender reassignment surgery confirming the desire gender (e.g., penectomy, vaginoplasty in a natal male, mastectomy, phalloplasty in a natal female).

*Source:* www.dsm5.org (as of May 4, 2011).

DISTRESS AND IMPAIRMENT

In the *DSM-IV-TR*, distress and impairment were added as a criterion for most diagnoses, in an effort to formally define the cutpoint for a mental disorder definition. In the work of the DSM-5 Task Force, there have been discussions about whether or not to retain this criterion for all diagnoses. On the one hand, it has been argued that some diagnoses clearly require this criterion; on the other hand, it has been argued that distress and/or impairment should be evaluated independently of the clinical symptomatology. In medicine, "a wart is a wart" regardless of whether it causes distress and/or impairment. The Gender Identity Disorders subworkgroup provisionally recommended that distress and/or impairment be evaluated on a separate axis (for criticisms, see De Cuypere et al., 2010; Lawrence, 2010d). Subsequently, however, the subworkgroup recommended that a distress/impairment criterion be included, as it is quite likely that this criterion will be required across all diagnoses in the *DSM-5* (see www.dsm5.org).

SUBTYPES

In the *DSM-IV-TR*, there is one specifier for GID, namely the patient's sexual orientation. The GID subworkgroup has recommended the deletion of this criterion, in part because it is, nowadays, less germane to treatment decisions (Cohen-Kettenis & Pfäfflin, 2010). The subworkgroup has, however, recognized the importance of sexual orientation subtypes for research purposes, and this will be emphasized in the text. Age of onset was considered by the subworkgroup as the basis for an alternative subtype system, but this parameter is not always easy to operationalize (for review, see Lawrence, 2010b), and sexual orientation may be an easier construct to measure (Lawrence, 2010b).

For *DSM-5*, the GID subworkgroup has provisionally recommended that subtypes be based on the presence or absence of a DSD. Although there are differences in the natural history of gender incongruence between individuals with and without a co-occurring DSD and at least some differences in underlying causal mechanisms, there are also similarities. Accordingly, some have argued that the inclusion of DSD subtyping will facilitate access to appropriate psychosocial and medical care (Richter-Appelt & Sandberg, 2010).

SHOULD THE DIAGNOSIS OF GID BE DELETED FROM THE *DSM-5*?

Perhaps the most radical proposal for the *DSM-5* is the argument that GID should be deleted on the grounds that it does not meet the criteria for the definition of a mental disorder (for review, see Meyer-Bahlburg, 2010; for a critique, see Lawrence, 2011). Many transgender activists argue in favor of deletion, but others do not, in part because it is believed that this would threaten access to medical care (see Drescher, 2010; Vance et al., 2010). Others suggest that GID should be reclassified as a neurological condition, but the evidence for this suggestion is quite weak; indeed, many other *DSM* diagnoses probably have a much stronger neurobiological substrate evidence base than GID, but this has not precluded their retention as a psychiatric condition based on clinical phenomenology. If GID is not considered a psychiatric disorder, and if the evidence is quite weak for reclassifying it as a physical condition, then the only remaining options would be to consider the request for hormonal and sex-reassignment surgery to be elective in nature (akin to other forms of cosmetic surgery). Many care providers would find this option problematic. In some respects, GID is a good example of a behavioral condition that straddles the interface between the mind and the body.

## CASE STUDY

CASE IDENTIFICATION AND PRESENTING COMPLAINTS[*]

Jordan is a 22-year-old natal (biological) female who was referred by her college counselor for an assessment regarding her strong feelings of gender dysphoria (gender incongruence). When not living on campus, Jordan resided with her parents and a younger sibling. Her parents were both professionals and worked full-time. Jordan reported that her parents had a "weird" relationship, that her mother had

---

[*]We have used Clifft's (1986) guidelines for confidentiality in reporting clinical material.

just had an affair, and that her parents might separate. On the WAIS-IV, Jordan obtained a Full-Scale IQ of 103 (average range).

## HISTORY AND ASSESSMENT

Jordan recalled a childhood in which she never felt like other girls. She related more comfortably with her male classmates and enjoyed a variety of stereotypical masculine activities. In particular, she recalled a longstanding fascination with science fiction and, as an adolescent and young adult, would attend Star Trek conventions. She identified most closely with the character Spock (originally portrayed by Leonard Nimoy). Jordan recalled never liking to wear girl-typical clothes in childhood, but noted that her mother was a "feminist," so this was not a source of strain between them. Although Jordan identified more with the boys, she wore her hair very long and so was never mistaken as a boy in her social environment. In childhood, Jordan recalled that she never voiced a desire to be a boy, but felt, in retrospect, that she did not "fit in" with the other girls in her neighborhood and at school. Jordan did not recall being teased as a youngster for her gender-related behavior, but she felt estranged and "alienated" from her peers.

As Jordan started to go through puberty, she began to develop a strong aversion to her female body characteristics. She did not like her monthly menstrual periods and was "horrified" as her breasts began to grow. At the time of assessment, Jordan's main request was to have a bilateral mastectomy. She was less interested in cross-sex hormone therapy and had not yet contemplated whether she wanted surgery to create a neophallus. In terms of Jordan's social appearance, she presented as an androgynous youth, with short hair and a casual clothing style (she cut her hair short after high school graduation, to which she wore a suit and tie). She concealed her large breasts with layers of T-shirts and a sweatshirt. The clinical impression was that Jordan would likely be perceived by naïve others to be male, based on her physical presentation and gender-ambiguous name.

During adolescence, Jordan reported long periods of depression. She engaged in frequent self-cutting of her wrists and the upper portion of her legs and had frequent suicidal ideation. In adolescence, Jordan became aware of sexual attraction directed toward other girls, and there was a period in which she secretly self-identified as a lesbian; however, until she attended college, Jordan had had no interpersonal sexual relationships. Jordan felt quite alienated from both boys and girls her age and considered herself to be a "loner." Her only solace was attending Star Trek conventions and conversing via the Internet with other Star Trek aficionados. By the time Jordan graduated from high school, she became increasingly aware that she did not "feel" like a female, and she began to read on the Internet about transsexualism and transgenderism. She commented during the assessment that "I think I meet the criteria for gender identity disorder." She was extremely subdued as she said this and cried. In college, Jordan's depression deepened, and she sought out counseling at the health center and eventually revealed her gender dysphoric feelings. In college, Jordan has had one long-term sexual relationship with a girl who self-identifies as heterosexual and whom Jordan stated "accepts me as a guy." They would kiss and Jordan would engage in manual-genital exploration with her partner, but she would not let her partner touch her ("I have 'no-touch zones,' which she accepts").

When asked about her own ideas about her gender identity development, Jordan commented that she never felt particularly close to either of her parents, but, if anything, she identified more with her father because they shared an interest in science. Jordan talked at length about how her mother always would "rant on and on" about the "objectification" of women and that her mother would leave the family room at home if Jordan's father was watching television in which "good-looking women with their breasts partially exposed" were present. Jordan said that her mother found these portrayals of women to be "disgusting." Jordan recalled that "My mom always talked about women being the sex objects of men." Jordan recalled feeling ashamed of her own breast development, but that she could not talk about this with her mother as "My mom is sex phobic."

Based on the assessment, Jordan clearly met the *DSM-IV-TR* criteria for GID (Points A, B, and D), with sexual attraction to females as a specifier. She also met criteria for Dysthymic Disorder. After the assessment, Jordan entered weekly psychotherapy for a year with a clinical psychology trainee who worked in a specialized gender identity service. Therapy focused on helping Jordan consolidate a male gender identity and role, gradually transitioning to living as a male. Jordan did not identify himself to others as transgendered, but as a "guy." Jordan's depression began to lift, and there was a marked diminution of suicidal ideation and self-cutting. Two years after the assessment, Jordan received a bilateral mastectomy and thereafter began a regimen of cross-sex hormone therapy. The major crisis during treatment was that Jordan's girlfriend ended their relationship, which resulted in a transient period of intense depression. In general, Jordan reports greater comfort with himself as a guy, although he struggles with the fact that "I have nothing between my legs." Nonetheless, Jordan feels that he will be able to establish new romantic partnerships with understanding heterosexual women.

## SUMMARY

The GIDs comprise a heterogeneous group of conditions involving dissatisfaction with the body, the sexuality, or the gender role associated with a person's natal sex. Biologic sex (male vs. female) and sexual orientation (homosexual vs. nonhomosexual) define four GID subtypes that differ in clinical presentation. Outcomes in the GIDs can include acceptance of natal gender, part-time cross-gender behavior, or sex reassignment and full-time cross-living. Individual and group psychotherapy can benefit some persons with GIDs. Treatment with cross-sex hormone therapy and SRS usually provides significant relief of gender dysphoria, high levels of patient satisfaction, and favorable psychosocial outcomes.

## REFERENCES

Ahlers, C. J., Schaefer, G. A., Mundt, I. A., Roll, S., Englert, H., Willich, S. N., & Beier, K. M. (2011). How unusual are the contents of paraphilias? Paraphilia-associated sexual arousal patterns in a community-based sample of men. *Journal of Sexual Medicine, 8*, 1362–1370.

American Psychiatric Association. (1980). *Diagnostic and statistical manual of mental disorders* (3rd ed.). Washington, DC: Author.

American Psychiatric Association. (1994). *Diagnostic and statistical manual of mental disorders* (4th ed.). Washington, DC: Author.

American Psychiatric Association. (2000). *Diagnostic and statistical manual of mental disorders* (4th ed., text revision). Washington, DC: Author.

Baba, T., Endo, T., Honnma, H., Kitajima, Y., Hayashi, T., Ikeda, H., . . . Saito, T. (2007). Association between polycystic ovary syndrome and female-to-male transsexuality. *Human Reproduction, 22,* 1011–1016.

Bailey, J. M., Dunne, M. P., & Martin, N. G. (2000). Genetic and environmental influences on sexual orientation and its correlates in an Australian twin sample. *Journal of Personality and Social Psychology, 78,* 524–536.

Bakker, A., van Kesteren, P. J., Gooren, L. J. G., & Bezemer, P. D. (1993). The prevalence of transsexualism in The Netherlands. *Acta Psychiatrica Scandinavica, 87,* 237–238.

Baltieri, A., & De Andrade, A. G. (2009). Schizophrenia modifying the expression of gender identity disorder. *Journal of Sexual Medicine, 6,* 1185–1118.

Bearman, G. (2007). Karyotyping and genetics in the transgendered population. In R. Ettner, S. Monstrey, & A. E. Eyler (Eds.), *Principles of transgender medicine and surgery* (pp. 223–233). Binghamton, NY: Haworth Press.

Bentz, E. K., Hefler, L. A., Kaufmann, U., Huber, J. C., Kolbus, A., & Tempfer, C. B. (2008). A polymorphism of the CYP17 gene related to sex steroid metabolism is associated with female-to-male but not male-to-female transsexualism. *Fertility and Sterility, 90,* 56–59.

Bentz, E. K., Schneeberger, C., Hefler, L. A., van Trotsenburg, M., Kaufmann, U., Huber, J. C., & Tempfer, C. B. (2007). A common polymorphism of the SRD5A2 gene and transsexualism. *Reproductive Science, 14,* 705–709.

Berglund, H., Lindström, P., Dhejne-Helmy, C., & Savic, I. (2008). Male-to-female transsexuals show sex-atypical hypothalamus activation when smelling odorous steroids. *Cerebral Cortex, 18,* 1900–1908.

Blanchard, R. (1985). Typology of male-to-female transsexualism. *Archives of Sexual Behavior, 14,* 247–261.

Blanchard, R. (1988). Nonhomosexual gender dysphoria. *Journal of Sex Research, 24,* 188–193.

Blanchard, R. (1989a). The classification and labeling of nonhomosexual gender dysphorias. *Archives of Sexual Behavior, 18,* 315–334.

Blanchard, R. (1989b). The concept of autogynephilia and the typology of male gender dysphoria. *Journal of Nervous and Mental Disease, 177,* 616–623.

Blanchard, R. (1990). Gender identity disorders in adult men. In R. Blanchard & B. Steiner (Eds.), *Clinical management of gender identity disorders in children and adults* (pp. 49–76). Washington, DC: American Psychiatric Press.

Blanchard, R. (1993). Varieties of autogynephilia and their relationship to gender dysphoria. *Archives of Sexual Behavior, 22,* 241–251.

Blanchard, R. (1994). A structural equation model for age at clinical presentation in non-homosexual male gender dysphorics. *Archives of Sexual Behavior, 23,* 311–320.

Blanchard, R. (2010). The DSM diagnostic criteria for transvestic fetishism. *Archives of Sexual Behavior, 39,* 363–372.

Blanchard, R., Clemmensen, L. H., & Steiner, B. W. (1987). Heterosexual and homosexual gender dysphoria. *Archives of Sexual Behavior, 16,* 139–152.

Blanchard, R., & Freund, K. (1983). Measuring masculine gender identity in females. *Journal of Consulting and Clinical Psychology, 51,* 205–214.

Blanchard, R., Racansky, I. G., & Steiner, B. W. (1986). Phallometric detection of fetishistic arousal in heterosexual male cross-dressers. *Journal of Sex Research, 22,* 452–462.

Blanchard, R., Steiner, B. W., Clemmensen, L., & Dickey, R. (1989). Prediction of regrets in postoperative transsexuals. *Canadian Journal of Psychiatry, 34,* 43–45.

Bockting, W. O. (2008). Psychotherapy and the real-life experience: From gender dichotomy to gender diversity. *Sexologies, 17*, 211–224.

Bodlund, O., & Armelius, K. (1994). Self-image and personality traits in gender identity disorders: An empirical study. *Journal of Sex & Marital Therapy, 20*, 303–317.

Bolin, A. (1988). *In search of Eve: Transsexual rites of passage.* New York, NY: Bergin & Garvey.

Bower, H. (2001). The gender identity disorders in the DSM-IV classification: A critical evaluation. *Australian and New Zealand Journal of Psychiatry, 35*, 1–8.

Buhrich, N., Barr, R., & Lam-Po-Tang, P. R. (1978). Two transsexuals with 47-XYY karyotype. *British Journal of Psychiatry, 133*, 77–81.

Buhrich, N., & McConaghy, N. (1977). Can fetishism occur in transsexuals? *Archives of Sexual Behavior, 6*, 223–235.

Butcher, J. N., Graham, J. R., Ben-Porath, Y. S., Telligen, A., Dahlstrom, W. G., & Kaemmer, B. (2001). *MMPI-2 (Minnesota Multiphasic Personality Inventory-2) manual for administration, scoring, and interpretation* (revised ed.). Minneapolis: University of Minnesota Press.

Carrillo, B., Gómez-Gil, E., Rametti, G., Junque, C., Gomez, A., Karadi, K., . . . Guillamon, A. (2010). Cortical activation during mental rotation in male-to-female and female-to-male transsexuals under hormonal treatment. *Psychoneuroendocrinology, 35*, 1213–1222.

Carroll, R. A. (1999). Outcomes of treatment for gender dysphoria. *Journal of Sex Education and Therapy, 24*, 128–136.

Chivers, M. L., & Bailey, J. M. (2000). Sexual orientation of female-to-male transsexuals: A comparison of homosexual and nonhomosexual types. *Archives of Sexual Behavior, 29*, 259–278.

Chung, W. C., De Vries, G. J., & Swaab, D. F. (2002). Sexual differentiation of the bed nucleus of the stria terminalis in humans may extend into adulthood. *Journal of Neuroscience, 22*, 1027–1033.

Clements-Nolle, K., Guzman, R., & Harris, S. G. (2008). Sex trade in a male-to-female transgender population: Psychosocial correlates of inconsistent condom use. *Sexual Health, 5*, 49–54.

Clifft, M. A. (1986). Writing about psychiatric patients: Guidelines for disguising case material. *Bulletin of the Menninger Clinic, 50*, 511 524.

Cohen-Kettenis, P. T., & Gooren, L. J. G. (1999). Transsexualism: A review of etiology, diagnosis and treatment. *Journal of Psychosomatic Research, 46*, 315–333.

Cohen-Kettenis, P. T., & Pfäfflin, F. (2010). The DSM diagnostic criteria for gender identity disorder in adolescents and adults. *Archives of Sexual Behavior, 39*, 499–513.

Cohen-Kettenis, P. T., & van Goozen, S. H. M. (1997). Sex reassignment of adolescent transsexuals: A follow-up study. *Journal of the American Academy of Child and Adolescent Psychiatry, 36*, 263–271.

Cole, C. M., O'Boyle, M., Emory, L. E., & Meyer, W. J. (1997). Comorbidity of gender dysphoria and other major psychiatric diagnoses. *Archives of Sexual Behavior, 26*, 13–26.

Coleman, E. (2009). Toward Version 7 of the World Professional Association for Transgender Health's *Standards of Care*: Medical and therapeutic approaches to treatment. *International Journal of Transgenderism, 11*, 215–219.

Collumbien, M., Querishi, A. A., Mayhew, S. H., Rizvi, N., Rabbani, A., Rolfe, B., . . . Rahat, N. (2009). Understanding the context of male and transgender sex work using peer ethnography. *Sexually Transmitted Infections, 85* (Suppl. II), ii3–ii7.

Coolidge, F. L., Thede, L. L., & Young, S. E. (2002). The heritability of gender identity disorder in a child and adolescent twin sample. *Behavior Genetics, 32*, 251–257.

De Cuypere, G., Jannes, C., & Rubens, R. (1995). Psychosocial functioning of transsexuals in Belgium. *Acta Psychiatrica Scandinavica, 91*, 180–184.

De Cuypere, G., Knudson, G., & Bockting, W. (2010). Response of the World Professional Association for Transgender Health to the proposed DSM-5 criteria for Gender Incongruence. *International Journal of Transgenderism, 12,* 119–123.

De Cuypere, G., Van Hemelrijck, M., Michel, A., Carael, B., Heylens, G., Rubens, R., . . . Monstrey, S., (2007). Prevalence and demography of transsexualism in Belgium. *European Psychiatry, 22,* 137–141.

Deogracias, J. J., Johnson, L. L., Meyer-Bahlburg, H. F. L., Kessler, S. J., Schober, J. M., & Zucker, K. J. (2007). The Gender Identity/Gender Dysphoria Questionnaire for Adolescents and Adults. *Journal of Sex Research, 44,* 370–379.

Devor, A. H. (2004). Witnessing and mirroring: A fourteen stage model of transsexual identity formation. *Journal of Gay & Lesbian Psychotherapy, 8*(1/2), 41–67.

de Vries, A. L. C., Noens, I. L., Cohen-Kettenis, P. T., van Berckelaer-Onnes, I. A., & Doreleijers, T. A. H. (2010). Autism spectrum disorders in gender dysphoric children and adolescents. *Journal of Autism and Developmental Disorders, 40,* 930–936.

Docter, R. F. (1988). Transvestites and transsexuals: Toward a theory of cross-gender behavior. New York, NY: Plenum.

Docter, R. F., & Prince, V. (1997). Transvestism: A survey of 1032 cross-dressers. *Archives of Sexual Behavior, 26,* 589–605.

Drescher, J. (2010). Queer diagnoses: Parallels and contrasts in the history of homosexuality, gender variance, and the *Diagnostic and Statistical Manual. Archives of Sexual Behavior, 39,* 427–460.

Drummond, K. D., Bradley, S. J., Badali-Peterson, M., & Zucker, K. J. (2008). A follow-up study of girls with gender identity disorder. *Developmental Psychology, 44,* 34–45.

Ellingson, L., & Odo, C. (2008). HIV risk behaviors among *Mahuwahine* (Native Hawaiian) transgender women. *AIDS Education and Prevention, 20,* 558–569.

Freund, K. (1985). Cross gender identity in a broader context. In B. W. Steiner (Ed.), *Gender dysphoria: Development, research, management* (pp. 259–324). New York, NY: Plenum.

Freund, K., & Blanchard, R. (1993). Erotic target location errors in male gender dysphorics, paedophiles, and fetishists. *British Journal of Psychiatry, 162,* 558–563.

Freund, K., Langevin, R., Satterberg, J., & Steiner, B. (1977). Extension of the Gender Identity Scale for Males. *Archives of Sexual Behavior, 6,* 507–519.

Gagne, P., Tewksbury, R., & McGaughey, D. (1997). Coming out and crossing over: Identity formation and proclamation in a transgender community. *Gender & Society, 11,* 478–508.

Garcia-Falgueras, A., & Swaab, D. F. (2008). A sex difference in the hypothalamic uncinate nucleus: Relationship to gender identity. *Brain, 131,* 3132–3146.

Garcia-Falgueras, A., & Swaab, D. F. (2010). Sexual hormones and the brain: An essential alliance for sexual identity and sexual orientation. In S. Loche, M. Cappa, L. Ghizzoni, M. Maghnie, & M. O. Savage (Eds.), *Pediatric neuroendocrinology* (pp. 22–35). Basel, Switzerland: Karger.

Garrels, L., Kockott, G., Michael, N., Preuss, W., Renter, K., Schmidt, G., . . . Windgassen, K. (2000). Sex ratio of transsexuals in Germany: The development over three decades. *Acta Psychiatrica Scandinavica, 102,* 445–448.

Gijs, L., & Brewaeys, A. (2007). Surgical treatment of gender dysphoria in adults and adolescents: Recent developments, effectiveness, and challenges. *Annual Review of Sex Research, 18,* 178–224.

Giraldo, F., Mora, M. J., Solano, A., Gonzáles, C., & Smith-Fernández, V. (2002). Male perineogenital anatomy and clinical applications in genital reconstructions and male-to-female sex reassignment surgery. *Plastic and Reconstructive Surgery, 109,* 1301–1310.

Gizewski, E. R., Krause, E., Schlamann, M., Happich, F., Ladd, M. E., Forsting, M., & Senf, W. (2008). Specific cerebral activation due to visual erotic stimuli in male-to-female transsexuals compared with male and female controls: An fMRI study. *Journal of Sexual Medicine, 6,* 440–448.

Gómez-Gil, E., Esteva, I., Almaraz, M. C., Pasaro, E., Segovia, S., & Guillamon, A. (2010). Familiality of gender identity disorder in non-twin siblings. *Archives of Sexual Behavior, 39,* 546–552.

Gómez-Gil, E., Vidal-Hagemeijer, A., & Salamero, M. (2008). MMPI-2 characteristics of transsexuals requesting sex reassignment: Comparison of patients in prehormonal and presurgical phases. *Journal of Personality Assessment, 90,* 368–374.

Gooren, L. (2006). The biology of human psychosexual differentiation. *Hormones and Behavior, 50,* 589–601.

Gooren, L. J., & Delemarre-van de Waal, H. A. (2007). Hormone treatment of adult and juvenile transsexual patients. In R. Ettner, S. Monstrey, & A. E. Eyler (Eds.), *Principles of transgender medicine and surgery* (pp. 73–88). Binghamton, NY: Haworth Press.

Green, R. (1969). Mythological, historical, and cross-cultural aspects of transsexualism. In R. Green & J. Money (Eds.), *Transsexualism and sex reassignment* (pp. 13–22). Baltimore. MD: Johns Hopkins Press.

Green, R. (1987). *The "sissy boy syndrome" and the development of homosexuality.* New Haven, CT: Yale University Press.

Green, R. (2000). Family cooccurrence of "gender dysphoria": Ten sibling or parent-child pairs. *Archives of Sexual Behavior, 29,* 499–507.

Green, R. (2008). Potholes in the interview road with gender dysphoric patients: Contentious areas in clinical practice. *Sexologies, 17,* 245–257.

Green, R., & Fleming, D. T. (1990). Transsexual surgery follow-up: Status in the 1990s. *Annual Review of Sex Research, 1,* 163–174.

Haberman, M., Hollingsworth, F., Falek, A., & Michael, R. P. (1975). Gender identity confusion, schizophrenia and a 47 XYY karyotype: A case report. *Psychoneuroendocrinology, 1,* 207–209.

Habermeyer, E., Kamps, I., & Kawohl, W. (2003). A case of bipolar psychosis and transsexualism. *Psychopathology, 36,* 168–170.

Haraldsen, I. R., & Dahl, A. A. (2000). Symptom profiles of gender dysphoric patients of transsexual type compared to patients with personality disorders and healthy adults. *Acta Psychiatrica Scandinavica, 102,* 276–281.

Hare, L., Bernard, P., Sánchez, F. J., Baird, P. N., Vilain, E., Kennedy, T., & Harley, V. R. (2009). Androgen receptor repeat length polymorphism associated with male-to-female transsexualism. *Biological Psychiatry, 65,* 93–96.

Hembree, W. C., Cohen-Kettenis, P., Delemarre-van de Waal, H. A., Gooren, L. J., Meyer, W. J., Spack, N. P., . . . Montori, V. M. (2009). Endocrine treatment of transsexual persons: An Endocrine Society clinical practice guideline. *Journal of Clinical Endocrinology and Metabolism, 94,* 3132–3154.

Henningsson, S., Westberg, L., Nilsson, S., Lundström, B., Ekselius, L., Bodlund, O., . . . Landén, M. (2005). Sex steroid-related genes and male-to-female transsexualism. *Psychoneuroendocrinology, 30,* 657–664.

Hepp, U., Kraemer, B., Schnyder, U., Miller, N., & Delsignore, A. (2005). Psychiatric comorbidity in gender identity disorder. *Journal of Psychosomatic Research, 58,* 259–261.

Herbst, J. H., Jacobs, E. D., Finlayson, T. J., McKleroy, V. S., Neumann, M. S., & Crepaz, N. (2008). Estimating HIV prevalence and risk behaviors of transgender persons in the United States: A systematic review. *AIDS & Behavior, 12,* 1–17.

Hirschfeld, M. (1991). *Transvestites: The erotic drive to cross-dress* ( M. A. Lombardi-Nash, Trans.). Buffalo, NY: Prometheus Books. (Original work published 1910.)

Hoshiai, M., Matsumoto, Y., Sato, T., Ohnishi, M., Okabe, N., Kishimoto, Y., . . . Kuroda, S. (2010). Psychiatric comorbidity among patients with gender identity disorder. *Psychiatry and Clinical Neurosciences, 64*, 514–519.

Hulshoff Pol, H. E., Cohen-Kettenis, P. T., Van Haren, N. E., Peper, J. S., Brans, R. G., Cahn, W., . . . Kahn, R. S. (2006). Changing your sex changes your brain: Influences of testosterone and estrogen on adult human brain structure. *European Journal of Endocrinology, 155* (Suppl. 1), S107–S114.

Hwahng, J. S., & Nuttbrock, L. (2007). Sex workers, fem queens, and cross-dressers: Differential marginalizations and HIV vulnerabilities among three ethnocultural male-to-female transgender communities in New York City. *Sexuality Research & Social Policy, 4*(4), 36–59.

Infante, C., Sosa-Rubi, S. G., & Cuadra, S. M. (2009). Sex work in Mexico: Vulnerability of male, *travesti*, transgender and transsexual sex workers. *Culture, Health & Sexuality, 11*, 125–137.

Inoubli, A., De Cuypere, G., Rubens, R., Heylens, G., Elaut, E., Van Caenegem, E., . . . T'Sjoen, G. (2011). Karyotyping, is it worthwhile in transsexualism? *Journal of Sexual Medicine, 8*, 475–478.

Johnson, M. (1997). *Beauty and power: Transgendering and cultural transformation in the southern Philippines*. Oxford, England: Berg.

Johnson, T. W., Brett, M. A., Roberts, L. F., & Wassersug, R. J. (2007). Eunuchs in contemporary society: Characterizing men who are voluntarily castrated (part I). *Journal of Sexual Medicine, 4*, 930–945.

Kellogg, T. A., Clements-Nolle, K., Dilley, J., Katz, M. H., & McFarland, W. (2001). Incidence of human immunodeficiency virus among male-to-female transgendered persons in San Francisco. *Journal of Acquired Immune Deficiency Syndromes, 28*, 380–384.

Kersting, A., Reutemann, M., Gast, U., Ohrmann, P., Suslow, T., Michael, N., & Arolt, V. (2003). Dissociative disorders and traumatic childhood experiences in transsexuals. *Journal of Nervous and Ment Disease, 191*, 182–189.

Kessler, S. J., & McKenna, W. (1978). *Gender: An ethnomethodological approach*. Chicago, IL: University of Chicago Press.

Khan, S. I., Hussain, M. I., Parveen, S., Bhuiyan, M. I., Gourab, G., Sarker, G. F., . . . Sikder, J. (2009). Living on the extreme margin: Social exclusion of the transgender population (*Hijra*) in Bangladesh. *Journal of Health, Population, and Nutrition, 27*, 441–451.

Khan, A. A., Rehan, N., Qayyum, K., & Khan, A. (2008). Correlates and prevalence of HIV and sexually transmitted infections among Hijras (male transgenders) in Pakistan. *International Journal of STD & AIDS, 19*, 817–820.

Khandelwal, A., Agarwal, A., & Jiloha, R. C. (2010). A 47,XXY female with gender identity disorder [Letter to the Editor]. *Archives of Sexual Behavior, 39*, 1021–1023.

Knafo, A., Iervolino, A. C., & Plomin. R. (2005). Masculine girls and feminine boys: Genetic and environmental contributions to atypical gender development in early childhood. *Journal of Personality and Social Psychology, 88*, 400–412.

Koken, J. A., Bimbi, D. S., & Parsons, J. T. (2009). Experiences of familial acceptance-rejection among transwomen of color. *Journal of Family Psychology, 23*, 853–860.

Koon, T. Y. (2002). *The Mak Nyahs: Malaysian male to female transsexuals*. Singapore: Eastern Universities Press.

Krafft-Ebing, R. (1965). *Psychopathia sexualis* (F. S. Klaf, Trans.). New York, NY: Stein and Day. (Original work published 1903.)

Kreukels, B. P., Haraldsen, I. R., De Cuypere, G., Richter-Appelt, H., Gijs, L., & Cohen-Kettenis, P. T. (in press). A European network for the investigation of gender incongruence: The ENIGI initiative. *European Psychiatry*.

Kruijver, F. P., Zhou, J. N., Pool, C. W., Hofman, M. A., Gooren, L. J., & Swaab, D. F. (2000). Male-to-female transsexuals have female neuron numbers in a limbic nucleus. *Journal of Clinical Endocrinology and Metabolism, 85,* 2034–2041.

Kuiper, B., & Cohen-Kettenis, P. T. (1988). Sex reassignment surgery: A study of 141 Dutch transsexuals. *Archives of Sexual Behavior, 17,* 439–457.

Kulick, D. (1998). *Travesti: Sex, gender, and culture among Brazilian transgendered prostitutes.* Chicago, IL: University of Chicago Press.

Landén, M., Wålinder, J., & Lundström, B. (1996). Prevalence, incidence, and sex ratio of transsexualism. *Acta Psychiatrica Scandinavica, 93,* 221–223.

Långström, N., & Zucker, K. J. (2005). Transvestic fetishism in the general population: Prevalence and correlates. *Journal of Sex & Marital Therapy, 31,* 87–95.

Laub, D. R., & Fisk, N. M. (1974). A rehabilitation program for gender dysphoria syndrome by surgical sex change. *Plastic and Reconstructive Surgery, 53,* 388–403.

Lawrence, A. A. (2003). Factors associated with satisfaction or regret following male-to-female sex reassignment surgery. *Archives of Sexual Behavior, 32,* 299–315.

Lawrence, A. A. (2005). Sexuality before and after male-to-female sex reassignment surgery. *Archives of Sexual Behavior, 34,* 147–166.

Lawrence, A. A. (2007). Becoming what we love: Autogynephilic transsexualism conceptualized as an expression of romantic love. *Perspectives in Biology and Medicine, 50,* 506–520.

Lawrence, A. A. (2009a). Erotic target location errors: An underappreciated paraphilic dimension. *Journal of Sex Research, 46,* 194–215.

Lawrence, A. A. (2009b). Transgenderism in nonhomosexual males as a paraphilic phenomenon: Implications for case conceptualization and treatment. *Sexual and Relationship Therapy, 24,* 188–206.

Lawrence, A. A. (2010a). A validation of Blanchard's typology: Comment on Nuttbrock et al. (2010) [Letter to the Editor]. *Archives of Sexual Behavior, 39,* 1011–1015.

Lawrence, A. A. (2010b). Sexual orientation versus age of onset as bases for typologies (subtypes) of gender identity disorder in adolescents and adults. *Archives of Sexual Behavior, 39,* 514–545.

Lawrence, A. A. (2010c). Societal individualism predicts prevalence of nonhomosexual orientation in male-to-female transsexualism. *Archives of Sexual Behavior, 39,* 573–583.

Lawrence, A. A. (2010d). Proposed revisions to gender identity disorder diagnoses in the DSM-5 [Letter to the Editor]. *Archives of Sexual Behavior, 39,* 1253–1260.

Lawrence, A. A. (2011). Do some men who desire sex reassignment have a mental disorder? Comment on Meyer-Bahlburg (2010)[Letter to the Editor]. *Archives of Sexual Behavior, 40,* 651–654.

Leavitt, F., Berger, J. C., Hoeppner, J.-A., & Northrop, G. (1980). Presurgical adjustment in male transsexuals with and without hormonal treatment. *Journal of Nervous and Mental Disease, 168,* 693–697.

Levine, S. B. (1993). Gender-disturbed males. *Journal of Sex & Marital Therapy, 19,* 131–141.

Levine, S. B., & Solomon, A. (2009). Meanings and political implications of "psychopathology" in a gender identity clinic: A report of 10 cases. *Journal of Sex & Marital Therapy, 35,* 40–57.

Levy, A., Crown, A., & Reid, R. (2003). Endocrine intervention with transsexuals. *Clinical Endocrinology, 59,* 409–418.

Lewins, F. (1995). *Transsexualism in society: A sociology of male-to-female transsexuals.* South Melbourne: MacMillan Education Australia.

Lothstein, L. M. (1979). The aging gender dysphoria (transsexual) patient. *Archives of Sexual Behavior, 8,* 431–444.

Lothstein, L. M. (1984). Psychological testing with transsexuals: A 30-year review. *Journal of Personality Assessment, 48*, 500–507.

Luders, E., Sánchez, F. J., Gaser, C., Toga, A. W., Narr, K. L., Hamilton L. S., & Vilain, E. (2009). Regional gray matter variation in male-to-female transsexualism. *NeuroImage, 46*, 904–907.

Manderson, L., & Kumar, S. (2001). Gender identity disorder as a rare manifestation of schizophrenia. *Australian and New Zealand Journal of Psychiatry, 35*, 546–547.

Marks, I., Green, R., & Mataix-Cols, D. (2000). Adult gender identity disorder can remit. *Comprehensive Psychiatry, 41*, 273–275.

Martin, C. L., Ruble, D. N., & Szkrybalo, J. (2002). Cognitive theories of early gender development. *Psychological Bulletin, 128*, 903–933.

Martin, H., & Finn, S. E. (2010). *Masculinity and femininity in the MMPI-2 and MMPI-A.* Minneapolis: University of Minnesota Press.

Mate-Kole, C., Freschi, M., & Robin, A. (1990). A controlled study of psychological and social change after surgical gender reassignment in selected male transsexuals. *British Journal of Psychiatry, 157*, 261–264.

Melendez, R. M., & Pinto, R. (2007). "It's really a hard life": Love, gender and HIV risk among male-to-female transgender persons. *Culture, Health & Sexuality, 9*, 233–245.

Meyer, W., Bockting, W. O., Cohen-Kettenis, P., Coleman, E., DiCeglie, D., Devor H., . . . Wheeler, C. C. (2001). *The standards of care for gender identity disorders, sixth version.* Düsseldorf, Germany: Symposion.

Meyer-Bahlburg, H. F. L. (1994). Intersexuality and the diagnosis of gender identity disorder. *Archives of Sexual Behavior, 23*, 21–40.

Meyer-Bahlburg, H. F. L. (2010). From mental disorder to iatrogenic hypogonadism: Dilemmas in conceptualizing gender identity variants as psychiatric conditions. *Archives of Sexual Behavior, 39*, 461–476.

Meyerowitz, J. (2002). *How sex changed: A history of transsexuality in the United States.* Cambridge, MA: Harvard University Press.

Miach, P. P., Berah, E. F., Butcher, J. N., & Rouse, S. (2000). Utility of the MMPI-2 in assessing gender dysphoric patients. *Journal of Personality Assessment, 75*, 268–279.

Moberly, E. R. (1986). Attachment and separation: The implications for gender identity and for the structuralization of the self: A theoretical model for transsexualism, and homosexuality. *Psychiatric Journal of the University of Ottawa, 11*, 205–209.

Modestin, J., & Ebner, G. (1995). Multiple personality disorder manifesting itself under the mask of transsexualism. *Psychopathology, 28*, 317–321.

Monstrey, S., Ceulemans, P., & Hoebeke, P. (2007). Surgery: Female-to-male patient. In R. Ettner, S. Monstrey, & A. E. Eyler (Eds.), *Principles of transgender medicine and surgery* (pp. 135–168). Binghamton, NY: Haworth Press.

Mouaffak, F., Gallarda, T., Baup, N., Olié, J.-P., & Krebs, M.-O. (2007). Gender identity disorders and bipolar disorder associated with the ring Y chromosome [Letter to the Editor]. *American Journal of Psychiatry, 164*, 1122–1123.

Mueller, A., Gooren, L. J., Naton-Schöotz, S., Cupisti, S., Beckmann, M., & Dittrich, R. (2008). Prevalence of polycystic ovary syndrome and hyperandrogenemia in female-to-male transsexuals. *Journal of Clinical Endocrinology and Metabolism, 93*, 1408–1411.

Murad, M. H., Elamin, M. B., Garcia, M. A., Mullan, R. J., Murad, A., Erwin, P. J., & Montori, V. M. (2010). Hormonal therapy and sex reassignment: A systematic review and meta-analysis of quality of life and psychosocial outcomes. *Clinical Endocrinology, 72*, 214–231.

Nanda, S. (1994). Hijras: An alternative sex and gender role in India. In G. Herdt (Ed.), *Third sex, third gender: Beyond sexual dimorphism in culture and history* (pp. 373–417). New York, NY: Zone Books.

Nieder, T. O., Herff, M., Cerwenka, S., Preuss, W. F., Cohen-Kettenis, P. T., De Cuypere, G., . . . Richter-Appelt, H. (in press) Age of onset and sexual orientation in transsexual males and females. *Journal of Sexual Medicine.*

Nuttbrock, L., Bockting, W. O., Mason, M., Hwahng, S., Rosenblum, A., Macri, M., & Becker, J. (2011). A further assessment of Blanchard's typology of homosexual versus non-homosexual or autogynephilic gender dysphoria. *Archives of Sexual Behavior, 40,* 247–257.

Paap, M. C., Kreukels, B. P., Cohen-Kettenis, P. T., Richter-Appelt, H., De Cuypere, G., & Haraldsen, I. R. (2011). Assessing the utility of diagnostic criteria: A multisite study on gender identity disorder. *Journal of Sexual Medicine, 8,* 180–190.

Person, E., & Ovesey, L. (1974). The transsexual syndrome in males. I. Primary transsexualism. *American Journal of Psychotherapy, 28,* 4–20.

Pfäfflin, F. (2007). Mental health issues. In R. Ettner, S. Monstrey, & A. E. Eyler (Eds.), *Principles of transgender medicine and surgery* (pp. 169–184). Binghamton, NY: Haworth Press.

Phillips, K. A., Wilhelm, S., Koran, L. M., Didie, E. R., Fallon, B. A., Feusner, J., Stein, D. J. (2010). Body dysmorphic disorder: Some key issues for DSM-V. *Depression and Anxiety, 27,* 573–591.

Prosser, J. (1998). *Second skins: The body narratives of transsexuality.* New York, NY: Columbia University Press.

Rametti, G., Carrillo, B., Gómez-Gil, E., Junque, C., Segovia, S., Gomez, A., & Guillamon, A. (2011). White matter microstructure in female to male transsexuals before cross-sex hormonal treatment. A diffusion tensor imaging study. *Journal of Psychiatric Research, 45,* 199–204.

Richter-Appelt, H., & Sandberg, D. E. (2010). Should disorders of sex development be an exclusion criterion for gender identity disorder in DSM 5? *International Journal of Transgenderism, 12,* 94–99.

Roback, H. B., Fellemann, E. S., & Abramowitz, S. I. (1984). The mid-life male sex-change applicant: A multiclinic survey. *Archives of Sexual Behavior, 13,* 141–153.

Ross, M. W., & Need, J. A. (1989). Effects of adequacy of gender reassignment surgery on psychological adjustment: A follow-up of fourteen male-to-female patients. *Archives of Sexual Behavior, 18,* 145–153.

Saks, B. M. (1998). Transgenderism and dissociative identity disorder: A case study. *International Journal of Transgenderism, 2*(2). Retrieved from www.iiav.nl/ezines/web/IJT/97-03/numbers/symposion/ijtc0404.htm

Sánchez, F. J., Bocklandt, S., & Vilain, E. (2009). The biology of sexual orientation and gender identity. In D. W. Pfaff, A. P. Arnold, A. M. Etgen, S. E. Fahrbach, & R. T. Rubin (Eds.), *Hormones, brain and behavior* (Vol. 4, 2nd ed; pp. 271–289). San Diego, CA: Academic Press.

Savic, I., Garcia-Falgueras, & Swaab, D. F. (2010). Sexual differentiation of the human brain in relation to gender identity and sexual orientation. *Progress in Brain Research, 186,* 41–62.

Schiltz, K., Witzel, J., Northoff, G., Zierhut, K., Gubka, U., Fellmann, H., . . . Bogerts, B. (2007). Brain pathology in pedophilic offenders: Evidence of volume reduction in the right amygdala and related diencephalic structures. *Archives of General Psychiatry, 64,* 737–746.

Schöning, S., Engelien, A., Bauer, C., Kugel, H., Kersting, A., Roestel, C., . . . Konrad, C. (2010). Neuroimaging differences in spatial cognition between men and male-to-female transsexuals before and during hormone therapy. *Journal of Sexual Medicine, 7,* 1858–1867.

Schroder, M., & Carroll, R. (1999). New women: Sexological outcomes of male-to-female gender reassignment surgery. *Journal of Sex Education and Therapy, 24,* 137–146.

Seikowski, K. (2007). Psychotherapy and transsexualism. *Andrologia, 39,* 248–252.

Selvaggi, G., Ceulemans, P., De Cuypere, G., VanLanduyt, K., Blondeel, P., Hamdi, M., . . . Monstrey, S. (2005). Gender identity disorder: General overview and surgical treatment for vaginoplasty in male-to-female transsexuals. *Plastic and Reconstructive Surgery, 116,* 135e–145e.

Shore, E. S. (1984). The former transsexual: A case study. *Archives of Sexual Behavior, 13,* 277–285.

Simon, L., Zsolt, U., Fogd, D., & Czobor, P. (2011). Dysfunctional core beliefs, perceived parenting behavior and psychopathology in gender identity disorder: A comparison of male-to-female, female-to-male transsexual and nontranssexual control subjects. *Journal of Behavior Therapy and Experimental Psychiatry, 42,* 38–45.

Singh, D., Bradley, S. J., & Zucker, K. J. (2010, June). *A follow-up study of boys with gender identity disorder.* Poster presented at the University of Lethbridge Workshop, The Puzzle of Sexual Orientation: What Is It and How Does It Work?, Lethbridge, Alberta, Canada.

Singh, D., Deogracias J. J., Johnson, L. L., Bradley, S. J., Kibblewhite, S. J., Owen-Anderson, A., . . . Zucker, K. J. (2010). The Gender Identity/Gender Dysphoria Questionnaire for Adolescents and Adults: Further validity evidence. *Journal of Sex Research, 47,* 49–58.

Singh, D., McMain, S., & Zucker, K. J. (2011). Gender identity and sexual orientation in women with borderline personality disorder. *Journal of Sexual Medicine, 8,* 447–454.

Smith, Y. L. S., van Goozen, S. H. M., Kuiper, A. J., & Cohen-Kettenis, P. T. (2005a). Sex reassignment: Outcomes and predictors of treatment for adolescent and adult transsexuals. *Psychological Medicine, 35,* 89–99.

Smith, Y. L. S., van Goozen, S. H. M., Kuiper, A. J., & Cohen-Kettenis, P. T. (2005b). Transsexual subtypes: Clinical and theoretical significance. *Psychiatry Research, 137,* 151–160.

Snaith, R. P., Penhale, S., & Horsfield, P. (1991). Male-to-female transsexual with XYY karyotype. *Lancet, 337,* 557–558.

Sohn, M., & Bosinski, H. A. (2007). Gender identity disorders: Diagnostic and surgical aspects. *Journal of Sexual Medicine, 4,* 1193–1207.

Steensma, T. D., Biemond, R., de Boer, F., & Cohen-Kettenis, P. T. (in press) Desisting and persisting gender dysphoria after childhood: A qualitative follow-up study. *Clinical Child Psychology and Psychiatry.*

Stermac, L., Blanchard, R., Clemmensen, L. H., & Dickey, R. (1991). Group therapy for gender-dysphoric heterosexual men. *Journal of Sex & Marital Therapy, 17,* 252–258.

Stoller, R. J. (1968). *Sex and gender, Vol. 1: On the development of masculinity and femininity.* New York, NY: Science House.

Stoller, R. J. (1975). *Sex and gender, Vol. 2: The transsexual experiment.* New York, NY: Jason Aronson.

Swaab, D. F. (2004). Sexual differentiation of the human brain: Relevance for gender identity, transsexualism, and sexual orientation. *Gynecological Endocrinology, 19,* 301–312.

Taneja, N., Ammini, A. C., Mohapatra, I., Saxena, S., & Kucheria, K. (1992). A transsexual male with 47,XYY karyotype. *British Journal of Psychiatry, 161,* 698–699.

Turan, M. T., Esel, E., Dündar, M., Candemir, Z., Bastürk, M., Sofuoglu, S., & Ozkul, Y. (2000). Female-to-male transsexual with 47,XXX karyotype. *Biological Psychiatry, 48,* 1116–1117.

Ujike, H., Otani, K., Nakatsuka, M., Ishii, K., Sasaki, A., Oishi, T., . . . Kuroda, S. (2009). Association study of gender identity disorder and sex hormone-related genes. *Progress in Neuro-Psychopharmacology & Biological Psychiatry, 33,* 1241–1244.

van Goozen, S. H., Cohen-Kettenis, P. T., Gooren, L. J. G., Frijda, N. H., & Van de Poll, N. E. (1995). Gender differences in behaviour: Activating effects of cross-sex hormones. *Psychoneuroendocrinology, 20,* 343–363.

Vance, S. R., Cohen-Kettenis, P. T., Drescher, J., Meyer-Bahlburg, H. F. L., Pfäfflin, F., & Zucker, K. J. (2010). Opinions about the *DSM* gender identity disorder diagnosis: Results from an international survey administered to organizations concerned with the welfare of transgender people. *International Journal of Transgenderism, 12,* 1–14.

Veale, J. F. (2008). Prevalence of transsexualism among New Zealand passport holders. *Australian and New Zealand Journal of Psychiatry, 42,* 887–889.

Verschoor, A. M., & Poortinga, J. (1988). Psychosocial differences between Dutch male and female transsexuals. *Archives of Sexual Behavior, 17,* 173–178.

Wallien, M. S., & Cohen-Kettenis, P. T. (2008). Psychosexual outcome of gender-dysphoric children. *Journal of the American Academy of Child and Adolescent Psychiatry, 47,* 1413–1423.

Walworth, J. R. (1997). Sex-reassignment surgery in male-to-female transsexuals: Client satisfaction in relation to selection criteria. In B. Bullough, V. L. Bullough, & J. Elias (Eds.), *Gender blending* (pp. 352–369). Amherst, NY: Prometheus Books.

Whitam, F. L. (1987). A cross-cultural perspective on homosexuality, transvestism, and transsexualism. In G. D. Wilson (Ed.), *Variant sexuality: Research and theory* (pp. 176–201). Baltimore, MD: Johns Hopkins University Press.

Whitam, F. L. (1997). Culturally universal aspects of male homosexual transvestites and transsexuals. In B. Bullough, V. L. Bullough, & J. Elias (Eds.), *Gender blending* (pp. 189–203). *Amherst, NY:* Prometheus Books.

Wilkinson-Ryan, T., & Westen, D. (2000). Identity disturbance in borderline personality disorder: An empirical investigation. *American Journal of Psychiatry, 157,* 528–541.

Wilson, P., Sharp, C., & Carr, S. (1999). The prevalence of gender dysphoria in Scotland: A primary care study. *British Journal of General Practice, 49,* 991–992.

World Health Organization. (1992). *International statistical classification of diseases and related health problems* (10th revision, Vol. 1) Geneva, Switzerland: Author.

Zhou, J. N., Hofman, M. A., Gooren, L. J., & Swaab, D. F. (1995). A sex difference in the human brain and its relation to transsexuality. *Nature, 378,* 68–70.

Zucker, K. J. (2006). Gender identity disorder. In D. A. Wolfe & E. J. Mash (Eds.), *Behavioral and emotional disorders in adolescents: Nature, assessment, and treatment* (pp. 535–562). New York: Guilford Press.

Zucker, K. J. (2010). The DSM diagnostic criteria for gender identity disorder in children. *Archives of Sexual Behavior, 39,* 477–498.

Zucker, K. J., & Bradley, S. J. (1995). *Gender identity disorder and psychosexual problems in children and adolescents.* New York, NY: Guilford Press.

Zucker, K. J., Bradley, S. J., Ben-Dat, D. N., Ho, C., Johnson, L., & Owen, A. (2003). Psychopathology in the parents of boys with gender identity disorder [Letter to the Editor]. *Journal of the American Academy of Child and Adolescent Psychiatry, 42,* 2–4.

Zucker, K. J., Bradley, S. J., Owen-Anderson, A., Kibblewhite, S. J., Wood, H., Singh, D., & Choi, K. (in press) Demographics, behavior problems, and psychosexual characteristics of adolescents with gender identity disorder or transvestic fetishism. *Journal of Sex & Marital Therapy.*

Zucker, K. J., & Lawrence, A. A. (2009). Epidemiology of gender identity disorder. *International Journal of Transgenderism, 11,* 8–18.

# CHAPTER 17

# Eating Disorders

CYNTHIA M. BULIK, SARA E. TRACE, and SUZANNE E. MAZZEO

## DESCRIPTION OF THE DISORDERS

Eating disorders represent a category of partially overlapping syndromes, all of which have some clinical features marked by eating dysregulation. We will focus our discussion on anorexia nervosa (AN), bulimia nervosa (BN), and eating disorders not otherwise specified (EDNOS), with special emphasis on binge eating disorder (BED) which will be liberated from its current position in the Appendix of *DSM-IV* to be an officially recognized eating disorder in *DSM-5*. Eating disorders are serious mental illnesses that are influenced by both genetic and environmental factors. The syndromes are partially overlapping, as considerable diagnostic flux occurs over time, with individuals migrating from one clinical presentation to another, and because several diagnostic features are shared across disorders. Nonetheless, pure forms of each of the presentations also exist.

## CLINICAL PICTURE

Table 17.1 presents current *DSM-IV* diagnostic criteria for AN, BN, and BED. AN, the most visible eating disorder, is a serious psychiatric illness characterized by an inability to maintain a normal healthy body weight (< 85% of ideal body weight) or, in individuals who are still growing, failure to make expected increases in weight (and often height) and bone density. Despite increasing weight loss and frank emaciation, individuals with AN strive for additional weight loss, see themselves as fat even when they are severely underweight, and often engage in unhealthy weight-loss behaviors (e.g., purging, dieting, excessive exercise, fasting).

AN is further characterized by shape and weight playing a central role in self-evaluation. Although amenorrhea of at least 3 months is a diagnostic criterion, there are no meaningful differences between individuals with AN who do and do not menstruate (Gendall et al., 2006; Watson & Andersen, 2003), and this criterion is likely to be eliminated in the future. AN presents either as the restricting subtype in which low weight is achieved and maintained through energy restriction and increased physical activity only, as well as the binge-purge subtype in which the

637

**Table 17.1**

Diagnostic Criteria: Anorexia Nervosa, Bulimia Nervosa, and Binge-Eating Disorder

### *DSM-IV* Criteria for Anorexia Nervosa (307.10)

A.  Refusal to maintain body weight at or above a minimally normal weight for age and height (e.g., weight loss leading to maintenance of body weight less than 85% of that expected or failure to make expected weight gain during period of growth, leading to body weight less than 85% of that expected).
B.  Intense fear of gaining weight or becoming fat, even though underweight.
C.  Disturbance in the way in which one's body weight or shape is experienced, undue influence of body weight or shape on self-evaluation, or denial of the seriousness of the current low body weight.
D.  In postmenarchal females, amenorrhea i.e., the absence of at least three consecutive cycles. (A woman is considered to have amenorrhea if her periods occur only following hormone, e.g., estrogen administration.)

*Specify type:*

Restricting Type: During the current episode of anorexia nervosa, the person has not regularly engaged in binge-eating or purging behavior (i.e., self-induced vomiting or the misuse of laxatives, diuretics, or enemas).

Binge-Eating/Purging Type: During the current episode of anorexia nervosa, the person has regularly engaged in binge-eating or purging behavior (i.e., self-induced vomiting or the misuse of laxatives, diuretics, or enemas).

### *DSM-IV* Criteria for Bulimia Nervosa (307.51)

A.  Recurrent episodes of binge eating. An episode of binge eating is characterized by both of the following:
    1.  Eating, in a discrete period of time (e.g., within any 2-hour period), an amount of food that is definitely larger than most people would eat during a similar period of time and under similar circumstances
    2.  A sense of lack of control over eating during the episode (e.g., a feeling that one cannot stop eating or control what or how much one is eating)
B.  Recurrent inappropriate compensatory behavior in order to prevent weight gain, such as self-induced vomiting; misuse of laxatives, diuretics, enemas, or other medications; fasting or excessive exercise
C.  The binge eating and inappropriate compensatory behaviors both occur, on average, at least twice a week for 3 months
D.  Self-evaluation is unduly influenced by body shape and weight
E.  The disturbance does not occur exclusively during episodes of anorexia nervosa

*Specify type:*

Purging type: During the current episode of bulimia nervosa, the person has regularly engaged in self-induced vomiting or the misuse of laxatives, diuretics, or enemas

Nonpurging type: During the current episode of bulimia nervosa, the person has used inappropriate compensatory behaviors, such as fasting or excessive exercise, but has not regularly engaged in self-induced vomiting or the misuse of laxatives, diuretics, or enemas

### *DSM-IV* Criteria for Binge-Eating Disorder (307.50)

A.  Recurrent episodes of binge eating. An episode of binge eating is characterized by both of the following:
    1.  Eating, in a discrete period of time (e.g., within any 2-hour period), an amount of food that is definitely larger than most people would eat in a similar period of time under similar circumstances
    2.  The sense of lack of control over eating during the episode (e.g., a feeling that one cannot stop eating or control what or how much one is eating)

B. Binge-eating episodes are associated with three (or more) of the following:

1. eating much more rapidly than normal
2. eating until feeling uncomfortably full
3. eating large amounts of food when not feeling physically hungry
4. eating alone because of being embarrassed by how much one is eating
5. feeling disgusted with oneself, depressed, or very guilty after overeating

C. Marked distress regarding binge eating is present
D. The binge eating occurs, on average, at least 2 days a week for 6 months
   Note: The method of determining frequency differs from that used for bulimia nervosa; future research should address whether the preferred method of setting a frequency threshold is counting the number of days on which binges occur or counting the number of episodes of binge eating
E. The binge eating is not associated with the regular use of inappropriate compensatory behavior (e.g., purging, fasting, excessive exercise, etc.) and does not occur exclusively during the course of anorexia nervosa or bulimia nervosa

---

individual regularly engages in binge-eating or purging behavior (i.e., self-induced vomiting or the misuse of laxatives, diuretics, or enemas).

BN is characterized by recurrent binge eating episodes, which are followed by inappropriate compensatory behaviors (such as self-induced vomiting, laxative or diuretics misuse, fasting, and excessive exercise). Binge eating is defined as the consumption of an abnormally large amount of food accompanied by a subjective feeling of loss of control over eating. BN is only diagnosed if AN criteria are not met. Thus, to be diagnosed with BN, individuals should have a body mass index (BMI) greater than $17.5 \, kg/m^2$ or the equivalent in children and adolescents. The *DSM* distinguishes two BN subtypes based on the nature of the individual's compensatory behavior: purging (including vomiting and misuse of laxatives, diuretics, diet pills, or enemas) and nonpurging (restricted eating and excessive exercise). While the *ICD-10* (WHO, 1992) acknowledges alternate periods of starvation in BN, due to societal pathologizing of vomiting and laxative misuse compared with exercise or restrictive eating, only the former purging behaviors are described.

BN onset most frequently occurs in adolescence or early adulthood, and women with this disorder are typically of normal body weight (American Psychiatric Association [APA], 1994). As is the case in AN, approximately 90% of BN cases occur in women. However, it has been argued that BN diagnostic criteria are gender-biased. Men who seek treatment for BN tend to manifest a greater reliance on nonpurging forms of compensatory behavior such as excessive exercise (Anderson & Bulik, 2003; Lewinsohn, Seeley, Moerk, & Striegel-Moore, 2002). It is important to consider such gender differences in the clinical presentation of BN to revise estimates of the prevalence of this diagnosis (Anderson & Bulik, 2003).

Eating disorders not otherwise specified (EDNOS) is a diagnostic category for individuals whose eating behaviors, while clinically significant, do not meet AN or BN criteria. The *DSM-IV* includes six different examples of EDNOS presentations:

1. All features of AN except amenorrhea
2. All features of AN except remaining in a normal weight range
3. All criteria for BN except frequency of binge eating or purging or duration of 3 months

4. Regular inappropriate compensatory behavior after eating small amounts of food
5. Chewing and spitting out food
6. Binge eating disorder (BED)

EDNOS is an example of the Not Otherwise Specified (NOS) category in the *DSM-IV* (APA, 2000). The NOS categories of the *DSM* were created to include atypical presentations of disorders encountered in clinical practice (Fairburn & Bohn, 2005). According to the *DSM*, the NOS diagnoses are intended to "indicate a category within a class of disorders that is residual to the specific categories in that class . . ." (APA, 1980, 1987). Yet, the prevalence of EDNOS is greater than the combined prevalence of AN and BN in clinical samples (Dalle Grave, Calugi, Brambilla, & Marchesini, 2008; Ricca et al., 2001; Rockert, Kaplan, & Olmsted, 2007; Turner & Bryant-Waugh, 2003; Williamson, Gleaves, & Savin, 1992). More than half (50% to 70%) of patients presenting with eating disorder psychopathology meet criteria for EDNOS (Ricca et al., 2001; Turner & Bryant-Waugh, 2003). Four studies of outpatient adult eating disorder samples found that EDNOS was the most common diagnosis, with an average weighted prevalence of 60% (Martin, Williamson, & Thaw, 2000; Ricca et al., 2001; Turner & Bryant-Waugh, 2003). In addition, Turner and Bryant-Waugh reported that only 33% of individuals seeking treatment in their study met AN or BN criteria. Thus, clinically significant eating disorders incorporate a broader range of symptomatology than that accounted for by the standard AN and BN diagnoses (Wade, Bergin, Tiggemann, Bulik, & Fairburn, 2006; Wade, 2007).

Furthermore, the severity of pathology and psychosocial impairment is comparable among individuals with EDNOS, AN, and BN (Fairburn & Bohn, 2005; Keel, Gravener, Joiner, & Haedt, 2010). Clinical descriptions of EDNOS are consistent in stating that most cases have features similar to AN and BN (Crow, Agras, Halmi, Mitchell, & Kraemer, 2002; Waller, 1993; Walsh & Garner, 1997). Three studies (Fairburn & Cooper, 2007; Ricca et al., 2001; Turner & Bryant-Waugh, 2003) using the Eating Disorder Examination (EDE; Cooper & Fairburn, 1987) found that individuals with EDNOS presented with significant cognitive symptomatology related to eating, shape, and weight, suggesting that these partial syndromes are clinically significant.

In addition, in the study by Turner and Bryant-Waugh, individuals with EDNOS scored similarly to individuals with AN and BN on several EDE items, again suggesting comparable clinical impairment among EDNOS, AN, and BN. Fairburn and Bohn's work offered further support for this finding and noted that the similarity extends to the severity of associated psychological features, course of illness, and degree of psychosocial impairment. That so many patients presenting for treatment receive an EDNOS diagnosis, however, suggests that the nomenclature for eating disorders is imperfect. Moreover, there is a paucity of investigations on the nature of the highly heterogeneous category of EDNOS and on the treatment and outcome of specific EDNOS presentations.

In the *DSM-IV*, BED is included as a disorder requiring further study, and patients meeting criteria for this diagnosis technically fall within the EDNOS category. Binge eating was first noted in a subset of obese individuals by Stunkard in 1959

(Stunkard, 1959). BED has had a slow and controversial evolution in the psychiatric nosology for eating disorders (Fairburn, Welch, & Hay, 1993; Spitzer et al., 1993a, 1993b; Walsh, 1992). Individuals with BED engage in regular binge eating, which is defined in the same manner as in BN; it requires consumption of an unusually large amount of food accompanied by a sense of loss of control over eating. The frequency required (twice per week) is the same as in BN, although this criterion does not have strong empirical support (Garfinkel et al., 1995; Sullivan, Bulik, & Kendler, 1998). Unlike BN, individuals with BED do not regularly engage in compensatory behaviors. Several other criteria in the provisional BED diagnosis, including duration and binge frequency, also require further empirical support (Latner & Clyne, 2008; Striegel-Moore & Franko, 2003).

## DIAGNOSTIC CONSIDERATIONS

As suggested in the previous discussion of EDNOS, the current classification system for eating disorders is suboptimal (e.g., Bulik, Brownley, & Shapiro, 2007; Chavez & Insel, 2007; Clinton & Norring, 2005; Thomas, Vartanian, & Brownell, 2009; Wade, 2007; Walsh & Sysko, 2009). With the publication of *DSM-5* slated for 2013, investigation of the validity of the current classification system is a research focus (Hebebrand & Bulik, in press; Walsh & Sysko, 2009).

Clinton and Norring (2005) argue that the *DSM-IV* diagnostic criteria (APA, 1994) are based largely on clinical opinion and consensus rather than empirical data. One criticism of the *DSM-IV* is that the eating disorder diagnoses might not be mutually exclusive. For example, individuals often report diagnostic crossover from one eating disorder diagnosis to another (Milos, Spindler, Schnyder, & Fairburn, 2005; Tozzi et al., 2005). Indeed, when BN was first described by Gerald Russell (Russell, 1979), he characterized it as an "ominous variant" of AN, because many of his patients with BN had AN histories. Empirical data support this clinical observation, although estimates vary widely; overall between 8% and 62% of individuals initially diagnosed with AN develop bulimic symptoms during the course of their illness (Bulik, Sullivan, Fear, & Pickering, 1997; Eckert, Halmi, Marchi, Grove, & Crosby, 1995; Eddy et al., 2002; Strober, Freeman, & Morrell, 1997; Tozzi et al., 2005). Although AN and BN are conceptualized as distinct diagnoses, most clinicians and researchers agree that these two categories represent only a small component of the eating disorder continuum (e.g., Keel, Haedt, & Edler, 2005).

Given this lack of diagnostic clarity, several researchers have recently highlighted the importance of considering putative endophenotypes or component phenotypes of eating disorders to inform eating disorder classification (Bulik, Hebebrand, et al., 2007). Endophenotypes occur between a distal genotype and the disease (phenotype) and include biological and psychological characteristics (Gottesman & Gould, 2003). An endophenotypic approach acknowledges several common personality characteristics and comorbid psychiatric diagnoses among individuals with eating disorders and their biological relatives who are not affected with eating disorders.

For example, individuals with AN often manifest a specific cluster of personality traits, including perfectionism, obsessionality, anxiety, harm avoidance, and low self-esteem (Cassin & von Ranson, 2005; Fassino, Amianto, Gramaglia, Facchini, &

Abbate Daga, 2004; Klump et al., 2000). Furthermore, both these personality characteristics and anxiety disorders often precede AN onset (Bulik, Sullivan, Fear, & Joyce, 1997; Kaye et al., 2004). Major depression and anxiety disorders frequently co-occur with AN (Bulik, Sullivan, Fear, & Joyce, 1997; Fernandez-Aranda et al., 2007; Godart, Flament, Perdereau, & Jeammet, 2002; Godart, Flament, Lecrubier, & Jeammet, 2000; Kaye et al., 2004), and longitudinal research suggests that depression often persists following recovery from AN (Sullivan, Bulik, Fear, & Pickering, 1998).

Some personality features common among individuals with AN are also manifested by many women with BN, such as high harm avoidance, perfectionism, and low self-esteem. However, other personality features appear more specific to BN, including higher novelty seeking, higher impulsivity, lower self-directedness, and lower cooperativeness (Bulik, Sullivan, Carter, & Joyce, 1995; Fassino et al., 2004; Steiger et al., 2004).

Comorbid psychiatric disorders are very common among individuals with BN, occurring among nearly 80% of patients (Fichter & Quadflieg, 1997). These comorbidities include anxiety disorders, major depression, dysthymia, substance use, and personality disorders (Braun, Sunday, & Halmi, 1994; Brewerton et al., 1995; Bulik et al., 2004; Perez, Joiner, & Lewinsohn, 2004).

Finally, BED also commonly co-occurs with numerous other psychiatric diagnoses, including mood, anxiety, and substance abuse disorders (Grucza & Beirut, 2007; Johnson, Spitzer, & Williams, 2001; Marcus, Wing, & Fairburn, 1995; Striegel-Moore et al., 2001; Wilfley, Freidman, et al., 2000). Recent data from the National Comorbidity Study Replication (Hudson, Hiripi, Pope, & Kessler, 2007) indicate that BED is a chronic condition associated with significant impairment in daily functioning. Binge eating is also associated with numerous psychosocial problems, particularly depression and anxiety. Furthermore, the association between binge eating and psychological distress has been found in both treatment-seeking (Decaluwe & Braet, 2003; Glasofer et al., 2007) and non-treatment-seeking samples (Ledoux, Choquet, & Manfredi, 1993) and in diverse ethnic groups (Glasofer et al., 2007; Isnard et al., 2003; Marcus, Bromberger, Wei, Brown, & Kravitz, 2007; Striegel-Moore, Wilfley, Pike, Dohm, & Fairburn, 2000). Finally, most adults with BED are obese, and thus, are at risk for medical complications associated with overweight (Hudson et al., 2007). Yet, the negative psychological impact of BED does not appear to be attributable to obesity; obese individuals with BED report substantially poorer psychological functioning than do obese individuals without BED (Grucza, Przybeck, & Cloninger, 2007).

## EPIDEMIOLOGY

Lifetime prevalence estimates of *DSM-IV* AN, BN, and BED from a nationally representative population sample of women over age 18 are .9%, 1.5%, and 3.5% and in men .3%, .5%, and 2.0%, respectively (Hudson et al., 2007). The prevalence of subthreshold AN, defined as at least one criterion short of threshold, is greater and ranges from 0.37% to 1.3% (Hoek, 1991). The gender ratio for AN is approximately 9:1, women to men (APA, 1994). Awareness of these disorders has increased; however, the data on changing incidence are conflicting. Some studies report increasing incidence (e.g., Eagles, Johnston, Hunter, Lobban, & Millar, 1995; Jones,

Fox, Babigan, & Hutton, 1980; Møller-Madsen & Nystrup, 1992), whereas others describe stable prevalence (e.g., Hall & Hay, 1991; Hoek et al., 1995). The peak age of onset for AN is between 15 and 19 years (Lucas, Beard, O'Fallon, & Kurland, 1988). However, anecdotal reports suggest new-onset cases in mid- and late-life (Beck, Casper, & Andersen, 1996; Inagaki et al., 2002) and increasing presentations in children (Rosen, 2010).

The prevalence of BN in the United States is estimated to be 1.5% for women and 0.5% for men (Hudson et al., 2007). The prevalence of subthreshold behaviors is considerably higher, with 4.9% of women and 4% of men endorsing any binge eating. Similar to AN, reports suggest that more children and older adults are presenting with BN (Marcus et al., 2007; Rosen, 2010).

The prevalence of BED in the United States has been estimated at 3.5% for women and 2% for men (Hudson et al., 2007). In a population-based study of female twins, 37% of obese women (BMI $\geq$ 30) reported binge eating (Bulik, Sullivan, & Kendler, 2002), representing 2.7% of the female population studied. Community studies of obese individuals have found a prevalence of BED between 5% and 8% (Bruce & Agras, 1992; Bruce & Wilfley, 1996). The sex distribution in BED is more equal than in AN or BN (Hudson et al., 2007) with few differences in prevalence across races or ethnic groups (Alegria et al., 2007; Marcus et al., 2007).

## PSYCHOLOGICAL AND BIOLOGICAL ASSESSMENT

Careful and accurate assessment of eating disorders, which are frequently complex and have multiple presentations, is critical for effective treatment and research. The general goal of psychological assessment is to elicit information that accurately describes symptomatology, accurately characterizes diagnostic profile, and indicates appropriate treatment recommendations (Peterson & Mitchell, 2005). Assessing individuals with eating disorders is often challenging secondary to denial of the illness and hidden signs and symptoms (Palmer, 2003; Schacter, 1999; Tury, Gulec, & Kohls, 2010; Vitousek, Daly, & Heiser, 1991). The use of active listening skills is important for developing rapport (Keel, 2001), and motivational interviewing techniques (Miller & Rollnick, 2002), which encourage rolling with resistance, avoiding arguments, and expressing empathy, are often helpful for conducting a successful assessment.

Clinical interviews in eating disorders are used to elicit the patient's perspective of the development of his or her difficulties and frequently include the reason for the assessment/primary complaint, history of present illness, medical complications, treatment history, and coexisting conditions (Peterson, 2005). A combination of structured interviews, self-report measures, and medical assessments may also be employed to obtain a more complete clinical picture. In the case of minors, corroborating information, such as reports from parents or school officials, is additionally informative (Lock, Le Grange, Agras, & Dare, 2001).

### STRUCTURED INTERVIEWS

Structured interviews are essential for clarifying differential diagnostic issues and assessing psychiatric comorbidity. Structured interviews are advantageous in that they allow for active involvement of the interviewer, who can help clarify concepts or answer questions that may arise during the assessment. Obvious drawbacks to structured interviews include greater financial cost and clinician burden (Grilo, 2005).

For untrained interviewers, the two dominant instruments for assessing Axis I pathology are the Diagnostic Interview Schedule (DIS; Robins, Helzer, Croughan, & Ratcliff, 1981) and the Composite International Diagnostic Interview (CIDI; World Health Organization, 1990). The various versions of the Structured Clinical Interview for *DSM-IV* (SCID; First, Spitzer, Gibbon, & Williams, 2002), which has excellent validity and reliability (Grilo, 2005; Zanarini et al., 2000), are recommended for assessing Axis I pathology in adults by trained interviewers.

Several clinician-based structured or semistructured interviews have been developed specifically for assessing eating disorder symptomatology. The Eating Disorder Examination (EDE; Cooper & Fairburn, 1987) is well-established (Wilfley, Schwartz, Spurrell, & Fairburn, 2000) and widely used. It includes 33 items that measure behavioral and psychological traits in AN and BN and, with the exception of the diagnostic items, focuses on the 28 days preceding the assessment. Items are rated on a 7-point Likert-type scale, with higher scores indicating greater pathology, and comprise the following scales: dietary restraint, eating concern, weight concern, and shape concern. The EDE has high inter-rater reliability (Cooper & Fairburn, 1987; Grilo, Masheb, Lozano-Blanco, & Barry, 2004; Rizvi, Peterson, Crow, & Agras, 2000), adequate internal consistency (Beumont, Kopec-Schrader, Talbot, & Touyz, 1993; Cooper, Cooper, & Fairburn, 1989), and good discriminative validity for distinguishing those with eating disorders from healthy individuals (Cooper et al., 1989; Wilson & Smith, 1989). Other popular structured interviews for assessing disordered eating include the Interview for Diagnosis of Eating Disorders (IDED; Williamson, 1990) and the Structured Interview for Anorexic and Bulimic Disorders (SIAB-EX; Fichter et al., 1998). For a full review of these and other structured interviews in eating disorders see Grilo, 2005.

The IDED-IV (Kutlesic, Williamson, Gleaves, Barbin, & Murphy-Eberenz, 1998) is another semistructured interview primarily used for differential diagnosis of *DSM-IV* AN, BN, and EDNOS. The IDED-IV differs from the EDE in that it does not focus on frequency and severity data, but rather on differential diagnosis. Four studies support the psychometric properties of this instrument (Kutlesic et al., 1998).

The current version of the SIAB-EX (Fichter et al., 1998) assesses specific criteria for AN and BN (including subtypes), consistent with both the *DSM-IV* and the *ICD-10*. There is also an algorithm that allows the data to be used to generate the BED research diagnosis and other eating disorder syndromes currently falling under the EDNOS category. The SIAB-EX has demonstrated good internal consistency, factor structure, interrater reliability, and convergent and discriminant construct validity (Fichter & Quadflieg, 2000, 2001). Overall, the EDE and the SIAB-EX have been shown to produce generally similar findings. However, areas of divergence do exist, many of which could be attributable to the differences in criteria and time frames for assessment (Fichter & Quadflieg, 2001).

SELF-REPORTS

Many self-report measures are available for assessing disordered eating both in research and clinical settings. Self-report assessments can be used for a variety of purposes, including identifying clinical features, quantifying symptoms, and verifying diagnoses. They are particularly useful for assessing change over time and are time and cost effective because they can be completed independently by the patient (Peterson & Mitchell, 2005). Two of the most widely used self-report questionnaires for assessing disordered eating include the Eating Disorder Inventory (EDI) and the Eating Disorder Examination-Questionnaire (EDE-Q).

The EDI (Garner, Olmsted, & Polivy, 1983, 1984), which assess eating disorder symptoms and associated psychological traits, is useful for differentiating levels of eating disorder severity and for assessing treatment outcome (Williamson, Anderson, Jackman, & Jackson, 1995). This assessment is described by the authors as "investigator-based," emphasizing that it is the investigator's job to make final judgments about what symptoms and behaviors are present (e.g., to determine what constitutes a binge). The EDI has 64 questions answered on a 6-point Likert-type scale and is comprised of the following eight subscales: drive for thinness, bulimia, body dissatisfaction, ineffectiveness, perfectionism, interpersonal distress, interoceptive awareness, and maturity fears. A revised version of the EDI, the EDI-2, was published in 1991 and includes 27 additional questions. The eight scales from the EDI were retained, and three additional scales—asceticism, impulse regulation, and social insecurity—were incorporated (Garner, 1991).

The third version of the scale, EDI-3 (Garner, 2004), retained the same items as the EDI-2 but has a slightly different factor structure (Garner, Olmsted, & Polivy, 2008). It contains 91 items rated on a 0-to-4-point scoring system. The three subscales assessing eating pathology added in the EDI-2 (drive for thinness, bulimia, and body dissatisfaction) remain largely unchanged, and the general psychology subscales include low self-esteem, personal alienation, interpersonal insecurity, interpersonal alienation, interoceptive deficits, emotional dysregulation, perfectionism, asceticism, and maturity fears. Scoring for the EDI-3 includes the following six composite scores: eating disorder risk, ineffectiveness, interpersonal problems, affective problems, over control, and general psychological maladjustment, as well as infrequency and negative impression scores. The EDI-3 has yielded reliable and valid scores (Garner, 2004).

The EDE-Q (Fairburn & Beglin, 1994), another widely used self-report measure of eating disorder symptoms, assesses severity of eating pathology and associated disturbances over the past 28 days. It is most often used in research, but it can be applied in clinical settings as well (Peterson & Mitchell, 2005). The EDE-Q was adapted from the structured interview EDE (Cooper & Fairburn, 1987), and like the EDE, it consists of 33 items and four subscales (restraint, eating concern, shape concern, and weight concern). The subscales and total scores are based on averages from 0 to 6, with higher scores indicating greater pathology. The EDE-Q has been described as an accurate method for assessing binge eating (Wilson, Nonas, & Rosenbaum, 1993) and shows acceptable reliability and validity (Fairburn & Cooper, 1993).

There are numerous other self-report assessments for eating disorders, including the Multiaxial Assessment of Eating Disorder Symptoms (MAEDS; Anderson, Williamson, Duchmann, Gleaves, & Barbin, 1999), the Stirling Eating Disorder Scales (SEDS; Williams et al., 1994), the Anorexia Nervosa Inventory for Self-Rating (ANIS; Fichter & Keeser, 1980), the Three Factor Eating Questionnaire (TFEQ; Stunkard &

Messick, 1985), the Binge Eating Scale (BES; Gormally, Black, Daston, & Rardin, 1982), and the Questionnaire for Eating and Weight Patterns–Revised (QEWP-R; Yanovski, 1993). A full review of these and other self-report measures for assessing disordered eating can be found in Peterson and Mitchell (2005), or Tury, Gulec, and Kohls (2010).

MEDICAL ASSESSMENT

Careful medical assessment, both initially and as indicated throughout the duration of eating disorder treatment, is critical for effective treatment (Crow, 2005). Documentation of medical complications is imperative, not only for treatment planning but also for service authorization by insurance companies. Although all eating disorder presentations require medical monitoring, low-weight patients, individuals with purging behaviors, and obese individuals with binge-eating behavior (or a combination of these behaviors) are typically at the greatest risk for medical complications (e.g., Crow, Salisbury, Crosby, & Mitchell, 1997; Harris & Barraclough, 1998; Kohn, Golden, & Shenker, 1998).

Low-weight individuals are particularly vulnerable to medical morbidity and mortality (Harris & Barraclough, 1998). A BMI below 13 is associated with less favorable outcome (Hebebrand et al., 1997), and low weight is associated with increased likelihood of sudden cardiac death. AN, BN, and EDNOS are all associated with increased mortality (Crow et al., 2009). Evidence of medical complications might also encourage otherwise resistant patients to enter treatment. A standard initial assessment for low-weight individuals should include a complete blood count, an electrolyte battery (including phosphorus, calcium, and magnesium), an electrocardiogram, liver function tests, and a dual-energy X-ray absorptiometry (DEXA) scan (Crow, 2005). Blood pressure and pulse should also be documented, as dehydration can lead to orthostatic hypotension. The patient should be monitored carefully though the refeeding process, as provision of adequate calories may lead to a drop in serum phosphorus, which is associated with mortality (Kohn et al., 1998) both in hospital (Ornstein, Golden, Jacobson, & Shenker, 2003) and outpatient settings (Winston & Wells, 2002).

Electrolyte disturbance is the most commonly recognized complication of purging behaviors (Crow et al., 1997). Although not sensitive to vomiting frequency, hypokalemia is a marker of vomiting behavior (Crow et al., 1997). Another common complication of self-induced vomiting is parotid hypertrophy, or painless swelling of the parotid glands, which may persist for months following cessation of purging (Ogren, Huerter, Pearson, Antonson, & Moore, 1987). Dental complications, including dental enamel erosion on the lingual surfaces of teeth (Little, 2002), may occur in individuals who vomit frequently and, thus, continued dental monitoring is important. A smaller number of individuals with purging behaviors report gastrointestinal symptoms, including intestinal bleeding, hematemesis (vomiting blood), the passing of melanotic stools, or blood in the stools. Although rare, esophageal tears, gastric erosions, hemorrhoids, and gastric rupture may also occur (Cuellar, Kaye, Hsu, & Van Thiel, 1988; Cuellar & Van Thiel, 1986). Abuse of laxatives and emetics are also associated with significant medical morbidity. The use of syrup of Ipecac should signal a medical and cardiac evaluation, as it is associated with severe cardiac effects.

BED, which is among the most common of eating disorder presentations, is often associated with co-occurring conditions (Crow, 2005), including Type II diabetes mellitus and obesity. There is some evidence to suggest that obese individuals with Type II diabetes mellitus who also binge eat experience worse outcomes than their non-binge eating peers (Goodwin, Hoven, & Spitzer, 2003; Mannucci et al., 2002). Binge eating appears to be associated with medical problems independent of obesity (Bulik et al., 2002). Moreover, BED may confer a risk of components of the metabolic syndrome (cluster of related risk factors for atherosclerotic cardio-vascular disease, including abdominal obesity, dyslipidemia, hypertension, and abnormal glucose metabolism) beyond the risk attributable to obesity alone (Hudson et al., 2010).

The growing interest in eating disorders over the last 20 years has resulted in the development of numerous assessment tools for research and clinical purposes. Accurate assessment of individuals with disordered eating requires a multidisci-plinary approach to address both the psychological and biological factors under-lying etiology.

## ETIOLOGICAL CONSIDERATIONS

Although numerous psychological, social, and biological factors have been impli-cated as potential causes of eating disorders, few specific risk factors have been consistently identified across studies, and the etiology of these disorders is not fully understood (Jacobi, Hayward, de Zwaan, Kraemer, & Agras, 2004; Striegel-Moore & Bulik, 2007). Common risk factors across eating disorders include female sex, race or ethnicity, childhood eating and gastrointestinal problems, elevated concerns about shape and weight, negative self evaluation, prior history of sexual abuse and other adverse events, and presence of additional psychiatric diagnoses (Jacobi et al., 2004). Developmentally, prematurity, smallness for gestational age, and cephalohematoma have been identified as possible risk factors for AN (Cnattingius, Hultman, Dahl, & Sparen, 1999).

Current studies suggest that eating disorders are caused by a variety of factors, including both genetic (e.g., Bulik, Slof-Op't Landt, van Furth, & Sullivan, 2007; Slof-Op 't Landt et al., 2005) and environmental influences (e.g., Becker & Hamburg, 1996; Garner & Garfinkel, 1980; Striegel-Moore & Bulik, 2007). Contemporary understand-ing of eating disorders incorporates both genetic and environmental factors into causal models. Previously, an overemphasis on sociocultural factors ignored the fact that although social pressures toward thinness are ubiquitous, only a fraction of individuals exposed to these factors develop eating disorders. Therefore, a clearer understanding of vulnerability has led to the model that individuals who are more genetically predisposed to eating disorders are those who are also more vulnerable to environmental triggers of illness—typically ones that result in dieting, drive for thinness, and persistent negative energy balance.

Environmental influences that might serve as eating disorder triggers include the media's idealization of the thin body ideal and pressure to achieve an unrealistically thin body type (Irving, 1990; Levine & Harrison, 2004). Sociocultural models of disordered eating (Polivy & Herman, 1985; Striegel-Moore, Silberstein, & Rodin, 1986) suggest that the perception of a discrepancy between the self and the thin ideal leads to psychological discomfort. In turn, a desire to ameliorate this discomfort might result in eating disordered behavior. Striegel-Moore and Bulik report that cultural models of eating disorders are supported by the following: (a) the high percentage of female cases of disordered eating; (b) the increase in incidence of eating disorders in women coinciding with the decreasing body-weight ideal for women; (c) the reported higher incidence of eating disorders in cultures that emphasize thinness; and (d) the significant association between thin ideal internalization and disordered eating.

In a community-based case-control study, Fairburn et al. (1998) found significant differences in exposure to risk factors between women with BED and healthy controls, but surprisingly few differences between women with BED and BN. Specifically, compared with controls, women with BED reported more adverse childhood experiences, parental depression, personal vulnerability to depression, and exposure to negative comments about weight, shape, and eating.

Other studies have indicated that environmental factors, including parental and peer behaviors, contribute to both risk and protection from eating pathology (Enten & Golan, 2009; Twamley & Davis, 1999). For example, Twamley and Davis reported that low family pressures to control weight moderated the relation between exposure to thin norms and internalization of these messages. In addition, other environmental variables including social pressure could amplify or mitigate the risk of eating disorders (Striegel-Moore et al., 1986). For example, individuals exposed to peer teasing might be more likely to develop disordered eating (Thompson, Coovert, Richards, Johnson, & Cattarin, 1995; Thompson & Heinberg, 1993). Similarly, individuals from higher social classes might be more prone to develop disordered eating as they presumably have more time, attention, and resources available to focus on the achievement of cultural beauty ideals (Striegel-Moore & Bulik, 2007). Although these factors might influence eating disorder etiology, they are likely not solely responsible for their development (Striegel-Moore & Bulik, 2007). Personality traits such as perfectionism as well as social anxiety, elevated weight, and high impulsivity might also play important etiological roles. These sociocultural and environmental factors likely combine with genetic influences (Strober, Freeman, Lampert, Diamond, & Kaye, 2000) to contribute to the development of disordered eating, as is described in the next section.

## Behavioral Genetics and Molecular Genetics

AN was originally believed to be a culturally determined disorder; however, with advances in technology, the past decade of biological and genetic research has revealed that AN is familial and that genetic factors account for the majority of variance in liability to the disorder (Bulik et al., 2006; Klump, Miller, Keel, McGue, & Iacono, 2001). In this section, we review results of family, twin, and molecular genetic studies. Family studies investigate the degree to which a particular trait runs in families. Although they are a valuable tool, family studies cannot tell us why a trait runs in families—whether due to genetic factors, environmental factors, or some combination of both.

Twin studies allow us to decompose the variance of a trait into genetic and environmental sources by comparing the similarities and differences between monozygotic (MZ) and dizygotic (DZ) twin pairs. Although twin studies could reveal the proportion of individual differences in disordered eating that is due to genetic factors, they are unable to identify which specific genes are involved.

Molecular genetic studies provide greater clarity regarding which genes influence risk for a trait or disorder. Association studies examine a genetic variant's association with a trait; if the variant and trait are correlated, there is said to be an association between the two. Association studies that involve a single gene or set of genes that have a hypothesized association with the trait under study are referred to as candidate gene studies. Molecular genetic designs that do not focus on one particular gene or set of genes include linkage and genome-wide association studies (GWAS). Linkage identifies chromosomal regions that house predisposing or protective genes and allow us to narrow the search from the entire human genome to specific regions. GWAS examines 300,000 to 1,000,000 genetic markers scattered across the genome, comparing cases with the trait to controls. If a genetic variant is more frequent in cases, the variant is said to be associated with the trait. GWAS represents an agnostic search of the human genome and as such is a genetic discovery tool.

Candidate gene association studies for AN have examined primarily genes involved in the serotonergic, catecholaminergic, and dopaminergic systems and those affecting appetite and weight regulation. Although the serotonergic system has received significant research attention, results regarding its importance to eating disorders are inconclusive. One meta-analysis of studies investigating *5-HTTLPR* and AN suggests that carriers of the short allele are at increased risk for this eating disorder (Calati, De Ronchi, Bellini, & Serretti, 2011). A recent comprehensive review of all candidate gene association studies conducted for AN (175 association studies of 128 polymorphisms related to 43 genes) points to promising although not conclusive evidence for genes related to mood regulation [brain-derived neurotrophic factor *(BDNF)* and *SK3* channel], the hedonic reward system [catecholamine O methyl-transferase *(COMT)* and opioid receptor-1 *(OPRD1)*], and appetite [agouti-related protein *(AGRP)*] (Rask-Andersen, Olszewski, Levine, & Schioth, 2010).

A small number of linkage and GWAS studies have been performed investigating AN. Linkage studies identified chromosomes 1, 4, 11, 13, and 15 as possible regions of interest (Bacanu et al., 2005; Devlin et al., 2002; Grice et al., 2002). A subsequent study of candidate genes on chromosome 1 revealed associations with the serotonergic *(5-HTR1D)* and opioidergic *(OPRD1)* neurotransmitter system (Bergen et al., 2003). A genome-wide case-control association study using 23,465 highly polymorphic microsatellite markers to identify genomic loci related to AN reported 10 loci to be significantly associated with this disorder (Nakabayashi et al., 2009). To narrow the region relevant to this association, a single nucleotide polymorphism analysis was performed; regions on chromosome 1 and 11 remained significant. A second GWAS of AN confirmed prior observations of *5-HTR1D* and *OPRD1* as potential susceptibility genes. Yet, no polymorphisms reached genome-wide significance (Wang et al., in press).

Like AN, BN runs in families. First-degree relatives of individuals with BN are 4 to 10 times more likely to have the disorder themselves (Lilenfeld et al., 1998). In studies of female twins, the estimated heritability of BN ranges between 54% and 83% in females (see Slof-Op't Landt et al., 2005, for a review).

As is the case in AN, molecular genetic studies of BN have generally focused on the serotonergic, dopaminergic, catecholamineric, and appetite systems. Significant associations have emerged between BN and *5-HT2A* and *5-HTTLPR*. However, meta-analytic results did not identify an association between *5-HTTLPR* and BN across studies (Lee & Lin, 2010). Studies investigating associations between serotonin receptor genes and BN have also yielded mixed results (see Scherag, Hebebrand, & Hinney, 2010, for a review). Nonetheless, associations have been identified between several traits related to BN and the serotonin system, including minimum lifetime BMI (*5-HT1B*), impulsiveness (*5-HT2A* and *5-HTTLPR*), and affective dysregulation in females (*5-HTTLPR*) (see Scherag et al., 2010, for a review). Furthermore, a gene–environment interaction was identified in one study; within a sample of individuals with BN, carriers of the *5-HTTLPR* short allele who reported physical or sexual abuse also manifested greater sensation seeking, insecure attachment, and dissocial behavior (Steiger et al., 2007, 2008). The existence of this type of gene–environment interaction might explain some of the inconsistent results regarding serotonin to date.

Studies investigating genes within the dopamine and catecholamine systems and those genes involved in appetite have also yielded inconsistent findings. Sporadic associations were found between BN and the dopamine transporter gene (*DAT1*) (Shinohara et al., 2004) and *COMT* (Mikolajczyk, Grzywacz, & Samochowiec, 2010), respectively. In addition, a few studies have identified an association between BN and preproghrelin (Miyasaka et al., 2006) and *BDNF*, yet these results require replication.

Linkage has identified one region of interest on chromosome 10 for BN (Bulik et al., 2003). No GWAS of BN have been conducted to date. In sum, results of molecular genetic studies of BN remain inconclusive and are limited by the use of small samples, which provide relatively low power. Like the other eating disorders, BED also aggregates within families (Hudson et al., 2006). Twin studies have yielded heritability estimates ranging from 41% to 57% (Javaras et al., 2008; Reichborn-Kjennerud, Bulik, Sullivan, Tambs, & Harris, 2004).

Genes associated with obesity have also been investigated for their potential role in BED, given the positive correlation between these conditions. *MC4R* (which is associated with obesity) was examined as an early candidate for BED (Branson et al., 2003), although this finding is not consistently replicated across studies (Hebebrand et al., 2004). Positive associations with *5-HTTLPR* and *DAT1, BDNF,* and ghrelin have also been identified in BED (Davis et al., 2007; Monteleone, Tortorella, Castaldo, Di Filippo, & Maj, 2007; Monteleone, Tortorella, Castaldo, & Maj, 2006; Monteleone, Zanardini, et al., 2006; Shinohara et al., 2004); however, these results require confirmation and replication, and the field awaits more comprehensive genome-wide approaches.

## NEUROANATOMY AND NEUROBIOLOGY

Neurobiological vulnerabilities contribute to eating disorder pathogenesis (Kaye, 2008; Treasure & Campbell, 1994), and brain structural and functional abnormalities are consistently found in individuals with eating disorders (Frank, Bailer, Henry, Wagner, & Kaye, 2004). Improvements in technology over the last decade, particularly in neuroimaging and genetics, have greatly enhanced our ability to characterize the complex neuronal systems involved in disordered eating (Kaye, 2008). However, these techniques are relatively new, and our understanding of the relation between biological vulnerabilities and subsequent changes in brain pathways contributing to disordered eating are limited. Neurobiological investigations of disordered eating are further complicated by state-related effects from changes in diet and weight, which might impact neuronal processes. Nonetheless, central nervous system (CNS) dysregulation of neuropeptides (Bailer & Kaye, 2003) and monoamines (Bailer et al., 2007; Kaye, 2008), as well as brain structural abnormalities (Artmann, Grau, Adelmann, & Schleiffer, 1985; Heinz, Martinez, & Haenggeli, 1977; Joos et al., 2010; Krieg, Lauer, & Pirke, 1989), have been specifically implicated in the neurobiology of disordered eating.

*Neuropeptides*   Neuropeptides involve a complicated interplay between the peripheral system and the CNS (Morton, Cummings, Baskin, Barsh, & Schwartz, 2006), and opioid peptides, corticotropin-releasing hormone (CRH), vasopressin, oxytocin, neuropeptide-Y, Peptide YY (PYY), cholecystokinin (CCK), leptin, ghrelin, and gastrin-releasing peptides are reported to play an important role in the regulation of feeding behavior (Bailer & Kaye, 2003; Kelley et al., 2002). Specifically, individuals with AN have state-dependent altered levels of CRH (Licinio, Wong, & Gold, 1996), neuropeptide-Y (NPY), beta-endorphin, and leptin that normalize with weight restoration (Bailer & Kaye, 2003; Kaye, 2008), whereas individuals with BN demonstrate state-related reductions in cholecystokinin (CCK) response (Brewerton, Lydiard, Laraia, Shook, & Ballenger, 1992; Kaye et al., 1987; Lesem, Berrettini, Kaye, & Jimerson, 1991) and beta-endorphin levels.

A number of the CNS neuropeptides implicated in AN and BN are also involved in regulating cognitive functioning, mood, the autonomic nervous system, and hormone secretion (Jimerson & Wolfe, 2006). While abnormalities in neuropeptide systems typically remit following recovery from AN and BN, malnutrition in combination with neuropeptide alterations can exaggerate symptoms of increased satiety and dysphoric mood, which might perpetuate eating disordered behavior (Bailer & Kaye, 2003); see Bailer and Kaye for a full review of how neuropeptides influence AN and BN.

Neuropeptides are also implicated in BED, and both human and animal studies suggest that binge eating alters the endogenous opioid system (Bencherif et al., 2005; Boggiano & Chandler, 2006; Colantuoni et al., 2001; Munsch, Biedert, Meyer, Herpertz, & Beglinger, 2009). Individuals with BED have higher meal-induced levels of CCK and PYY than controls (Munsch et al., 2009). Furthermore, both obese and nonobese women with binge eating demonstrate decreased levels of ghrelin in the morning, compared with nonobese healthy women and obese non-binge eating women (Monteleone et al., 2005). However, these findings have not been consistently replicated across studies (Geliebter, Hashim, & Gluck, 2008; Munsch et al., 2009).

*Monoamines*   The monoamine system, including serotonin (5-HT), dopamine (DA), and norepinephrine (NE), has also been implicated in the development and maintenance of disordered eating (Hildebrandt, Alfano, Tricamo, & Pfaff, 2010; Kaye, Fudge, & Paulus, 2009; Steiger, 2004). The 5-HT system is critical in regulating appetite, anxiety, and impulse control (Fairbanks, Melega, Jorgensen, Kaplan, & McGuire, 2001), and the effects of 5-HT manipulation on eating behaviors have been demonstrated in both animal and human models (e.g., Blundell, 1986; Mancilla-Diaz, Escartin-Perez, Lopez-Alonso, & Cruz-Morales, 2002). Studies of individuals with eating disorders document alterations in 5-HT metabolism, receptor sensitivity, and transporter activity (Frank & Kaye, 2005). As a general trend, decreased 5-HT is associated with increased feeding (Brewerton, 1995), leading to the expectancy that AN would coincide with increased 5-HT.

At first glance, individuals with AN appear to contradict expectation with regards to levels of 5-HT. Individuals with AN have significant reductions in cerebral spinal fluid 5-hydroxyindoleacetic acid (CSF 5-HIAA) compared with controls (Kaye et al., 2009), suggesting reduced 5-HT activity. However, CSF 5-HIAA levels are elevated following long-term recovery from AN (Kaye, 2008), indicating that AN may correspond to a primary state of increased 5-HT and that diminished 5-HT activity may be a result of malnutrition, rather than a trait-related feature. Overall, the field is embracing more complex systems- and pathway-driven models of disease to understand the complex way in which both serotonin and other neurotransmitters are implicated in disease etiology (Kaye, 2008; Kaye et al., 2009).

Findings in acute BN are generally compatible with a low 5-HT hypothesis (decreased 5-HT promotes increased feeding). Individuals with BN demonstrate decreased CSF 5-HIAA levels (Kaye, 2008) that are inversely related to binging and purging frequency (Jimerson, Lesem, Kaye, & Brewerton, 1992), reduced platelet binding of 5-HT uptake inhibitors, reduced availability of central transporters, and decreased neuroendocrine responses to 5-HT precursors and 5-HT agonists/partial agonists. However, similar to individuals with AN, following recovery, they have elevated levels of CSF 5-HIAA compared to controls (Kaye, 2008). These findings further support the hypothesis that both AN and BN might involve elevated 5-HT activity (Steiger, 2004). Increased 5-HT activity has also been associated with behavioral characteristics, including obsessionality and rigidity, which are frequently found in individuals recovered from AN and BN (Kaye, Gwirtsman, George, & Ebert, 1991; Kaye, 1997). Abnormalities in 5-HT have also been implicated in binge eating (Akkermann, Nordquist, Oreland, & Harro, 2010) and in the frequency of binge eating for individuals with BN (Jimerson et al., 1992; Monteleone, Brambilla, Bortolotti, Ferraro, & Maj, 1998). Decreased 5-HT responses are hypothesized to contribute to blunted satiety, which may increase propensity for binge eating (Chiodo & Latimer, 1986).

Further support of the role of 5-HT in eating disorders is provided by studies indicating that selective serotonin reuptake inhibitors (SSRIs) are fairly efficacious in treating BN and BED (see Brownley, Berkman, Sedway, Lohr, & Bulik, 2007; Shapiro et al., 2007 for reviews). Fluoxetine is the only FDA-approved medication for the treatment of any eating disorder. Fewer investigations have examined the effectiveness of SSRIs in treating AN, and in the small number of available studies (Attia, Haiman, Walsh, & Flater, 1998; Ferguson, La Via, Crossan, & Kaye, 1999; Kaye et al., 2001; Rosenblum & Forman, 2003; Vaswani, Linda, & Ramesh, 2003; Walsh et al., 2006), results were mixed.

In summary, significant evidence suggests an overall dysregulation of 5-HT in eating disorders (Steiger, 2004), which persists following recovery. Together, these results suggest that patterns of 5-HT dysregulation might vary by eating disorder subtype, suggesting that underlying pathophysiology might differ across varying eating disorders presentations (Kaye, 2008).

Dopamine is another monoamine hypothesized to contribute to disordered eating (Bello & Hajnal, 2010; Frank & Kaye, 2005; Jimerson et al., 1992; Kaye, Frank, & McConaha, 1999), and it is known to be involved in the reward and motivational aspects of feeding behavior (Erlanson-Albertsson, 2005; Szczypka, Rainey, & Palmiter, 2000). Individuals in recovery from restricting-type AN (AN-R) show lower CSF levels of the DA metabolite homovanillic acid (HVA; (Kaye et al., 1999), which is typically considered an indicator of reduced dopamine function and reduced dopamine turnover (dopamine to HVA ratio). Individuals recovered from AN-R and binge-purge type AN (AN-BP) also demonstrate increased binding of D2/D3 receptors in the anteroventral striatum (AVS; Frank et al., 2005), including the nucleus accumbens, a brain region implicated in the response to reward stimuli (Delgado, Nystrom, Fissell, Noll, & Fiez, 2000; Montague, Hyman, & Cohen, 2004).

Individuals with BN, particularly those with high binge frequency, also have significantly lower HVA levels (Jimerson et al., 1992; Kaplan, Garfinkel, Warsh, & Brown, 1989; Kaye et al., 1990). However, Jimerson et al. (1992) found that after weight restoration and normalization of food intake, individuals recovered from BN did not differ significantly from controls on HVA concentrations, suggesting that abnormalities in the dopamine system in BN might be state dependent. Lastly, DA has also been hypothesized to play a role in binge eating disorder by modulating reward pathways (Bello & Hajnal, 2010; Mathes, Brownley, Mo, & Bulik, 2009).

Norepinephrine (NE) transmission in the medial prefrontal cortex is also implicated in food-related motivational behavior in animal models (Ventura, Latagliata, Morrone, La Mela, & Puglisi-Allegra, 2008; Ventura, Morrone, & Puglisi-Allegra, 2007). Although few investigations have specifically examined the role of NE in disordered eating, it plays a central role in CNS modulation of energy balance, which has downstream effects on satiety, hunger, and feeding behavior (Hainer, Kabrnova, Aldhoon, Kunesova, & Wagenknecht, 2006).

*Structural Abnormalities*   Brain structural abnormalities in eating disorders have been investigated using computerized tomography (CT) and magnetic resonance imaging (MRI). Functional imaging studies, including positron emission tomography (PET), single photon emission computer tomography (SPECT), and functional magnetic resonance imaging (fMRI), have also been employed to provide information about the cerebral activity of a system or receptor being studied.

Neuroimaging studies with CT show neuroanatomical changes in individuals with AN, including cerebral atrophy and enlarged ventricles (Artmann et al., 1985; Heinz et al., 1977; Krieg et al., 1989; Lankenau, Swigar, Bhimani, Luchins, & Quinlan, 1985; Nussbaum, Shenker, Marc, & Klein, 1980). MRI studies in AN also demonstrate increased volumes of CSF in association with deficits in both total gray matter and total white matter volumes (Castro-Fornieles et al., 2010; Joos et al., 2010; Katzman et al., 1996) and enlarged ventricles (Golden et al., 1996). There is much debate over whether these changes persist after successful treatment and weight restoration. Several investigations have reported that neuroanatomical changes persist following normalization of weight (Artmann et al., 1985; Krieg et al., 1989), while other studies have found that structural brain abnormalities are reversible after long-term recovery (Golden et al., 1996; Wagner et al., 2005). Although definitive conclusions cannot be drawn, if lasting brain abnormalities in AN do occur, they might represent residual damage to the brain or persistent abnormal metabolism (Husain et al., 1992). They could also represent underdeveloped areas that originally contributed to the eating pathology (Artmann et al., 1985).

Fewer neuroimaging studies have been conducted in patients with BN, and findings regarding structural abnormalities are mixed. Several studies support structural changes in BN, including cerebral atrophy and decreased ventrical size (Hoffman et al., 1989; Krieg et al., 1989). However, other studies find no evidence for neuroanatomical abnormalities in BN (Husain et al., 1992; Joos et al., 2010). Taken together, results from these studies indicate that neuroanatomical abnormalities often occur in individuals with eating disorder, particularly AN. Additional prospective studies are needed to understand whether these abnormalities are a cause or an effect of the disordered eating behavior.

## Learning, Modeling, and Life Events

As noted previously, biology only accounts for part of the liability to developing an eating disorder. It is hypothesized that environment, via channels such as learning, modeling, and life events, can contribute to eating disorders risk either directly or indirectly through their influence on genetic expression.

*Life Events*   Stressful life events have long been hypothesized to play an important role in eating disorder etiology (Klump, Wonderlich, Lehoux, Lilenfeld, & Bulik, 2002; Pike et al., 2006; Schmidt, Troop, & Treasure, 1999; Welch, Doll, & Fairburn, 1997). However, research in this area is fraught with methodological challenges. Many studies have relied exclusively on case reports, and few included control groups of individuals without eating disorders (Schmidt et al., 1999). Nonetheless, one investigation suggested that women with BN were more likely than controls to experience certain stressful life events (e.g., a major move, illness, pregnancy, physical abuse, and sexual abuse) during the year prior to the beginning of their illness. However, there was no association between BN status and the occurrence of other life events (e.g., bereavement, illness of a close relative, friend or partner, and beginning or ending a romantic relationship) in the last year. In addition, 29% of women with BN experienced none of the life events assessed in the 12 months prior to the onset of their diagnosis.

Adverse life events (in the year prior to BED onset) are also associated with BED risk (Pike et al., 2006). In a study comparing women with BED with psychiatric and nonclinical controls, those with BED were most likely to report significant changes in life circumstances and relationships during the previous year. Furthermore, compared with the nonclinical controls, women with BED more commonly reported specific adverse events, including physical abuse, perceived risk of physical abuse, safety concerns, stress, and experiences of weight- and shape-related criticism. These findings suggest that some stressful life events might increase BN and BED susceptibility, but this risk is not uniform and is likely mediated by cognitive processes, such as appraisal and distress tolerance, which are discussed in the following section.

*Distress Tolerance*    Perhaps one reason for the somewhat inconsistent findings regarding the impact of stressful life events is that the impact of these experiences is influenced by the way in which they are appraised and how well individuals cope in response to them. Numerous studies have documented the link between cognitive appraisal and psychological outcomes (Folkman, Lazarus, Dunkel-Schetter, DeLongis, & Gruen, 1986; Folkman, Lazarus, Gruen, & DeLongis, 1986). More recently, the construct of distress tolerance has received attention in the area of eating disorders. This construct seems especially relevant to individuals with eating disorders, as emotion regulation difficulties have long been identified in affected individuals and across eating disorder subtypes (deZwaan, Biener, Bach, Wiesnagrotzki, & Stacher, 1996; Heatherton & Baumeister, 1991), and more recent research has linked poor distress tolerance and eating disorder symptomatology. Future research should investigate whether treatments that focus on strengthening distress tolerance skills [e.g., Dialectical Behavioral Therapy (Linehan, 1993)] effectively reduce eating disorder symptomatology.

### Cognitive Functioning

The possibility that there is CNS dysfunction in affected individuals has been explored though a variety of mechanisms, including neuropsychological performance (Duchesne et al., 2004). Cognitive functions implicated in AN include decreased attentional capability (Ferraro, Wonderlich, & Jocic, 1997; Green, Elliman, Wakeling, & Rogers, 1996; Jones, Duncan, Brouwers, & Mirsky, 1991), memory (Kingston, Szmukler, Andrewes, Tress, & Desmond, 1996; Mathias & Kent, 1998), visuo-spatial construction (Thompson & Spana, 1991), learning capacity (Witt, Ryan, & Hsu, 1985), and executive functioning (Kingston et al., 1996; Szmukler et al., 1992). Cognitive functioning in BN has been less extensively studied and has largely focused on decreased attention and executive functioning (McKay, Humphries, Allen, & Clawson, 1986; Steiger, Lehoux, & Gauvin, 1999).

Various deficits in executive functioning have been noted in the eating disorder literature (Cooper, Anastasiades, & Fairburn, 1992; Fassino et al., 2002; Kemps, Tiggemann, & Marshall, 2005; Koba, Horie, & Nabeta, 2002; Tchanturia et al., 2004; Zastrow et al., 2009). For example, individuals with AN score lower than controls on executive functioning tasks (Lena, Fiocco, & Leyenaar, 2004). Fassino et al. (2002), and Koba et al. (2002) found that individuals with AN made significantly more errors on the Wisconsin Card Sorting Task (WCST; Berg, 1948), a test of frontal lobe functioning implicated in executive functioning. In addition, Tchanturia et al. (2004) found that individuals with AN performed significantly worse than controls on multiple tests of mental flexibility, another indicator of executive functioning.

Set-shifting, or the ability to move back and forth between tasks or mental sets, is an important component of executive functioning (Miyake et al., 2000). Set-shifting ability is essential for cognitive-behavioral flexibility, allowing an individual to adapt his or her behavior to meet the changing demands of the environment. Problems in set shifting might manifest in a variety of forms of cognitive inflexibility (e.g., rigid approaches to problem solving) or response inflexibility (e.g., perseverative or stereotyped behavior; Roberts, Tchanturia, Stahl, Southgate, & Treasure, 2007). Recent research has suggested that set-shifting difficulties might be related to the development of disordered eating (Roberts et al., 2007; Steinglass, Walsh, & Stern, 2006; Tchanturia et al., 2004; Zastrow et al., 2009).

For example, individuals with AN perform poorly on set-shifting tasks compared to controls. A 2007 systematic review and meta-analysis (Roberts et al., 2007) examined set-shifting in eating disorders. Fifteen papers that administered at least one of six neuropsychological set-shifting tasks—including the Trail Making Test (TMT; Reitan, 1958), the WCST (Berg, 1948), the Brixton Task (Burgess & Shallice, 1997), the Haptic Illusion (Tchanturia, Serpell, Troop, & Treasure, 2001; Uznadze, 1966), the CatBat Task (Eliava, 1964), and the set-shifting subset of the Cambridge Neuropsychological Tests Automated Battery (CANTAB; Downes et al., 1989) to individuals with eating disorders—were reviewed. A consistent deficit was observed that traversed diagnoses, state of illness, and the majority of the set-shifting assessment measures used. The size of the pooled effect between tasks ranged from small (TMT), to moderate (WCST and CatBat task), to large (Haptic Illusion). Although this study employed a limited amount of data from recovered/weight-restored subgroups of individuals with AN, preliminary results suggest that deficits in set shifting, particularly as measured by the TMT, the Haptic Illusion, and the CatBat, remain following weight restoration (Roberts et al., 2007).

A 2004 study by Tchanturia et al. (2004) examined whether suboptimal set shifting was state or trait related by examining set shifting in individuals with current or past AN. The association of these deficits with obsessive-compulsive behaviors and traits was also explored. The authors compared set-shifting abilities in female individuals with current AN (AN-R, $n = 20$; AN-BP, $n = 14$) prior to receiving treatment, individuals with past AN in long-term recovery ($n = 18$, stable body mass for minimum of a year, regular menses for a year, and no psychotropic medication for a year), and healthy controls ($n = 36$). Participants were given a battery of neuropsychological tests assessing various facets of set shifting and executive functioning. A computerized version of the TMT (Kravariti, Morris, Rabe-Hesketh, Murray, & Frangou, 2003; Reitan, 1958) assessed rapid simple alternation between mental sets; the Brixton Test (Burgess & Shallice, 1997), the Set Flexibility Picture Test (Surguladze, 1995), and the Cat Bat Test were used to assess problem solving and set shifting. The Uznadze Illusion Task (Uznadze, 1966) was used to assess perceptual set shifting. Lastly, a verbal fluency test (as described in Lezak, 1995) assessed cognitive retrieval and flexibility in cognitive search options. In addition, a semistructured interview evaluated obsessive-compulsive traits in childhood and adulthood.

Scores of individuals with current AN-R or AN-BP on several set-shifting tasks (e.g., including the TMT and the Brixton Illusion) were significantly lower than those of the recovered and control groups. Individuals recovered from AN had significantly more illusions on the Uznadze Illusion Task and made more errors on the Set Flexibility Picture Test, relative to the control group. Overall, the individuals recovered from AN obtained scores that were between those of individuals with current AN and healthy controls, suggesting that nutritional status might play some role but is not entirely responsible for the mental inflexibility associated with AN.

Across studies, findings suggest that executive functioning deficits might be related to an underlying biological vulnerability to AN. Neurobiological deficits found among individuals with AN might mirror the behavioral and personality character- istics, such as rigidity and inflexibility, observed within this diagnostic group (see reviews by Braun & Chouinard, 1992; Lauer, 2002).

## SEX AND RACIAL-ETHNIC CONSIDERATIONS

African American women's risk for AN and BN is lower than that of White women (Hoek, 2006; Striegel-Moore et al., 2003); thus, for many years, eating disorders were often considered illnesses that affected White women nearly exclusively (Becker, Franko, Speck, & Herzog, 2003). This cultural stereotype appears to have influenced clinicians as well, as studies show that women of color are less likely to be identified as having an eating disorder (even when their symptoms are consistent with diagnosis) or referred for eating disorder treatment.

As noted previously, lifetime prevalence estimates of *DSM-IV* AN, BN, and BED from a nationally representative population sample of women over age 18 are .9%, 1.5%, and 3.5% (Hudson et al., 2007). Prevalence estimates vary across racial and ethnic groups, however. The lifetime prevalence of eating disorders among African American adult females from a U.S. population-based survey is 0.14% for AN, 1.90% for BN, 2.36% for BED, and 5.82% for any binge-eating behavior (Taylor, Caldwell, Baser, Faison, & Jackson, 2007). Other studies have reported slightly lower prevalence estimates in African American women (Striegel-Moore et al., 2003). One set of lifetime prevalence estimates among Latinas are 0.12% for AN, 1.91% for BN, 2.31% for BED, and 5.80% for any binge eating (Alegria et al., 2007). The prevalence of eating disorders among Asian women has been estimated to be 0.12% for AN, 1.42% for BN, 2.67% for BED, and 4.71% for any binge eating (Nicdao, Hong, & Takeuchi, 2007). These numbers are subject to interpretation, as another study found no difference in binge-eating frequency by race (Reagan & Hersch, 2005).

African American women's risk for binge eating and BED may indeed be equal to, or possibly even greater, than that of White women (Striegel-Moore, Wilfley et al., 2000). For example, Striegel-Moore et al. reported that African American women endorsed binge-eating symptoms (with a frequency and duration consist- ent with *DSM* criteria) more often than White women. Another study (Taylor et al., 2007) found that BED was not only more common than either AN or BN among African American women, but also was the most chronic eating disorder diagnosis, with a mean duration of over 7 years. These findings are consistent with those of other studies with respect to the clinical significance and prevalence of binge-eating behaviors among African American adults (Marcus et al., 2007; Striegel-Moore, Wilfley et al., 2000). Another significant concern regarding eating disorders among African Americans is that rates of treatment seeking for eating disorders are significantly lower among this group than among White women (Becker et al., 2003; Cachelin, Veisel, Barzengarnazari, & Striegel-Moore, 2000). These findings suggest that many African American women with clinically significant binge-eating behaviors remain untreated.

The few extant studies on eating disorders in Latinos suggest prevalence estimates on par with Whites in the United States (Alegria et al., 2007; Reyes-Rodriguez et al., 2010). Studies of eating disordered attitudes and behaviors indicate considerable concern amongst Latinas. Pumariega (1986) found that 20% of young Hispanic urban high school students scored 30 or higher, the screening threshold, on the Eating Attitudes Test (EAT). Binge eating has also been reported to be more severe in Latinas than in Whites or African Americans (Fitzgibbon et al., 1998). Latina girls report greater body dissatisfaction than White girls (Robinson et al., 1996) and more disturbed eating attitudes and behaviors than African American girls (Vander Wal & Thomas, 2004). Weight-related concerns and behaviors are prevalent among adolescents, regardless of their ethnic or racial origin (Neumark-Sztainer et al., 2002).

Although research is emerging regarding the prevalence of eating disorders across racial and ethnic groups, much less is known about the treatment of eating disorders in diverse populations. The majority of studies comprising the evidence base have been conducted primarily on White samples. Research testing the appropriateness of standard eating disorders treatments and the optimal approaches to cultural adaptation of treatments for diverse populations remains in its infancy.

## COURSE AND PROGNOSIS

AN has serious medical and psychological consequences, many of which persist even after recovery. In addition to the eating-related symptomatology, many other comorbidities of this disorder, including depression, anxiety, social withdrawal, heightened self-consciousness, fatigue, and multiple medical complications, cause considerable impairment (Berkman, Lohr, & Bulik, 2007). For example, the social toll of AN interferes with normal adolescent development (Bulik, 2002). Across psychiatric disorders, the highest risks of premature death, from both natural and unnatural causes, are from substance abuse and eating disorders (Harris & Barraclough, 1998).

AN history is further associated with reproductive problems (Bulik et al., 1999; Micali, Simonoff, & Treasure, 2007; Micali & Treasure, 2009), osteoporosis (Mehler & MacKenzie, 2009), continued low BMI (Sullivan, Bulik, Fear, et al., 1998), and major depression (Fernandez-Aranda et al., 2007). Given the high morbidity and mortality associated with AN, it is critical to develop effective treatments. Initial treatment typically includes a comprehensive medical evaluation and nutritional counseling. Less medically compromised cases of AN are most often treated on an outpatient basis by mental health providers, with primary care physicians managing medical issues. Treatment guidelines or position papers outlining recommended AN treatment have been developed by numerous professional organizations, including the American Psychiatric Association (APA, 2006), the National Institute for Clinical Excellence (NICE, 2004), the Society for Adolescent Medicine (Golden et al., 2003), the American Academy of Pediatrics (AAP, 2003), and the Royal Australian and New Zealand College of Psychiatrists (Beumont et al., 2004).

AN treatment also typically involves psychotherapeutic intervention. Individual, family, and group psychotherapy for AN are conducted from a multitude of theoretical perspectives (e.g., cognitive-behavioral, interpersonal, behavioral, and psychodynamic). The APA Working Group on Eating Disorders has recommended hospitalization for individuals below 75% of ideal body weight (APA, 2006). However, in addition to weight, parameters such as medical complications, suicidality, previous treatment success, psychiatric comorbidities, social support, role impairment, and availability of other treatment options should all be considered in level-of-care decisions (APA, 2006). Currently, no medications are effective in the treatment of AN (Bulik, Berkman, Brownley, Sedway, & Lohr, 2007). Although commonly prescribed, SSRIs tend to be ineffective in the underweight state, especially in the absence of dietary tryptophan to subsidize the synthesis of serotonin. All treatment commonly involves highly specialized multidisciplinary teams, including psychologists, psychiatrists, internists or pediatricians, nutritionists, social workers, and nurse specialists.

Among individuals hospitalized for AN, lengths of stay are much shorter in the United States, compared with those in Europe and New Zealand. For example, Striegel-Moore et al. found the average length of stay within the United States was 26 days (according to an insurance database of approximately 4 million individuals) (Striegel-Moore, Leslie, Petrill, Garvin, & Rosenheck, 2000). This is substantially shorter than stays found in other countries, including New Zealand (72 days; McKenzie & Joyce, 1992) and Europe, which ranges from 40.6 days (Finland) to 135.8 days (Switzerland) (Matthias, 2005). Moreover, AN treatment costs in the United States were higher than those for obsessive-compulsive disorder and comparable to those for schizophrenia, both of which occur at similar rates to AN (Striegel-Moore, Leslie, et al., 2000).

Although BN is not frequently associated with the severe medical complications more commonly found among those with AN, patients with BN report physical symptoms such as fatigue, lethargy, bloating, and gastrointestinal problems. Frequent vomiting is associated with electrolyte abnormalities, metabolic alkalosis, erosion of dental enamel, swelling of the parotid glands, and scars and calluses on the backs of their hands (Mitchell & Crow, 2006). Laxative misuse often causes edema, fluid loss and subsequent dehydration, electrolyte abnormalities, metabolic acidosis, and potentially permanent loss of normal bowel function (Mitchell & Crow, 2006).

In the United States, most BN treatment is conducted on an outpatient basis. A comprehensive medical evaluation is typically recommended, given the frequency of medical and nutritional complications within this patient population. If significant medical complications related to BN present, or if the affected individual is pregnant or unable to bring her binge-purge behaviors under control in outpatient treatment, partial hospitalization or inpatient treatment may be warranted.

Once medical issues are assessed and under control, psychotherapy (individual and/or group) is typically the primary treatment for BN. As is the case with AN, the theoretical perspectives used in these psychotherapeutic interventions can vary; however, cognitive-behavioral and interpersonal psychotherapy are commonly used. In 1996, the Food and Drug Administration (FDA) approved fluoxetine for the treatment of BN. Currently, this is the only FDA-approved medication for the treatment of any eating disorder.

Given that BED has only recently entered the psychiatric nomenclature, minimal population-based data are available regarding the morbidity and mortality related to this diagnosis. However, most adults with BED are obese and, thus, are at risk for medical complications associated with overweight (Hudson et al., 2007; Hudson et al., 2010; Striegel-Moore et al., 2001). Yet, the negative psychological impact of BED does not appear to be attributable to obesity; obese individuals with BED report substantially poorer psychological functioning than do obese individuals without BED (Grucza et al., 2007). Many adults with BED report that their symptoms began in childhood (Abbott et al., 1998). Thus, it seems important that future research investigate further the correlates of binge eating in childhood. Within the United States, BED treatment is typically conducted on an outpatient basis. Psychological and nutritional interventions aim to reduce binge eating and control weight (Brownley et al., 2007). Common psychotherapeutic approaches include cognitive-behavioral and interpersonal psychotherapy; nutritional approaches include behavioral self-management strategies and facilitating hunger and satiety awareness (Brownley et al., 2007). Pharmacotherapy targeting both the core symptoms of binge eating and weight loss are also available as off-label interventions (Brownley et al., 2007).

## LOOKING AHEAD TO *DSM-5*

Several changes have been proposed for *DSM-5*, although controversy still exists regarding the appropriateness of the changes (Hebebrand & Bulik, 2010), as well as the extent to which the new criteria will be able to capture the presentation of eating disorders, especially in children (Knoll, Bulik, & Hebebrand, 2011). For AN, proposed changes include replacement of the terms "refusal" with "restriction" and the term "denial" with "persistent lack of recognition." In addition, the criterion A will be substantially rephrased to focus on the importance of energy homeostasis for maintenance of a "markedly low body weight." The criterion B now additionally refers to "persistent behavior to avoid weight gain, even though at a markedly low body weight." Finally, the *DSM-IV* criterion D (amenorrhea) will be omitted. For BN, it is proposed that the frequency criterion for binge eating and purging be reduced from twice per week to once per week and that the nonpurging subtype be eliminated. BED will be included as an officially recognized eating disorder. Considerable thought has gone into the reconceptualization of the EDNOS category, which is to be replaced by a section entitled Feeding and Eating Conditions Not Elsewhere Classified. This section will include a listing of conditions that should be considered only if the individual has a feeding or eating problem that is judged to be of clinical significance that does not meet the criteria for any of the primary feeding or eating disorders. Presentations include atypical AN (all AN criteria except sufficient weight loss), subthreshold BN (low frequency or limited duration), subthreshold BED (low frequency or limited duration), purging disorder (recurrent purging behavior to influence weight or shape, such as self-induced vomiting, misuse of laxatives, diuretics, or other medications, in the absence of binge eating) and night eating syndrome (recurrent episodes of night eating, as manifested by eating after awakening from sleep or excessive food consumption after the evening meal). The extent to which these proposed new criteria will more accurately "carve nature at its joints" remains unknown.

## CASE STUDY

Referral

Wendy was a 35-year-old married white female who was referred for treatment for an eating disorder after passing out at the finish line of a half marathon.

### Presenting Complaints

The emergency room discharge note indicated that Wendy was 5 feet 6 inches tall and 95 pounds (BMI 16.3 kg/m$^2$). She was severely dehydrated, her potassium was 2.5 (normal range 3.5–5 mEq/L), and her EKG indicated a prolonged QT interval. Pulse and blood pressure were low. The physician noted scrapes on her knuckles (Russell's sign) indicative of purging and referred her to the eating disorders team for follow-up.

### History

Wendy was a competitive runner with hopes of qualifying for the Olympics. Two years ago, while on a training run on trails, she was attacked by a man who tried to rape her. She screamed and fought and managed to get away by running out of the forest as fast as she could, but she continued to have flashbacks to this attack every day when she was training on the streets or trails. Prior to the attack, all of her attention was on training. She was a healthy eater, focused on performance rather than appearance, and adhered strictly to the recommendations of her trainer and sports dietitian. After the attack, she became increasingly anxious and had difficulty keeping up her training schedule. Her race times were increasing, as was her weight. She lost two races to one of her main competitors, and when she saw a picture of herself coming in second in the paper, she became fixated on her weight. She was up to 125 pounds, which was higher than she had ever been before. She started cutting back on calories, which she found easy to do. Wendy stated, "I was training hard and pushing through pain to get through marathons, so that dealing with hunger is a piece of cake in comparison."

One evening she went out for pizza and beer with her partner and some friends. She went to the restroom and was overcome by anxiety about what she had eaten. She decided to vomit and, much to her surprise, she felt less anxious afterward. At that point, she rationalized that this would be a way to keep people off her case about not eating enough; she could eat, but then get rid of it whenever she wanted. Soon the urge to vomit became overwhelming, and it seemed to be the only way she could control her anxiety. She started a few times a week, but she was soon up to 5 to 10 times a day. Her weight continued to drop and her times kept getting worse. Her coach and trainer were worried about her health, but she denied any problems. She started having difficulty concentrating at work, was sleeping poorly, and withdrew almost completely from her family and friends. She also withdrew from her husband. Even though they had been talking about starting a family, she became less and less interested in having sex and started even disliking being touched. She spent hours in the bathroom scrutinizing her body—checking to see if her shape had changed, pinching the skin on her waist to make sure her shape wasn't changing, and weighing herself sometimes 10 times per day. She became convinced that the only way to start winning again was to get down to 90 pounds. She was restricting her intake to about 800 calories per day, restricting fluids, and was vomiting several times per day. She made it through the half marathon on sheer will, but passing out at the finish line was the final event that brought her into treatment.

ASSESSMENT

On clinical interview, Wendy demonstrated significant weight loss below 85% of expected weight for her age and sex. She presented with clear drive for thinness, fear of weight gain, and denial of illness. Her body image was distorted, as she continued to see herself as fat even though she was 95 pounds and 5 feet 6 inches tall. There were no other medical explanations for her weight loss. She denied objective binge eating (eating unusually large amounts of food and feeling out of control) but endorsed subjective binge eating (feeling out of control when eating regular or small amounts of food). She also admitted to regular purging via self-induced vomiting. She had not menstruated for the previous 6 months. Wendy met the diagnostic criteria for anorexia nervosa, purging subtype.

Clinical interview also indicated that she experienced posttraumatic stress symptoms secondary to the attack while running. She completed three self-report forms—the Eating Disorders Inventory (EDI) and the Beck Depression and Anxiety Inventories. Results indicated high scores on drive for thinness, body dissatisfaction, and perfectionism on the EDI. Her BDI scores indicated mild depression and no suicidal ideation, and a BAI score of 38 indicated high anxiety consistent with her clinical interview.

## SUMMARY

Our understanding of eating disorders had advanced remarkably over the past decade. Once thought to be largely disorders of choice of primarily sociocultural origin, it is now common knowledge that genes and biology play an important role in risk. The classification scheme for eating disorders will soon undergo a shuffle that will hopefully capture natural variation of eating pathology more sensibly, with a greater proportion of affected individuals representing the "rules" rather than the "exceptions." Further advancements to understanding the eating disorders are likely to come from neurobiological and genetic research, and these discoveries will facilitate our ability to understand why some individuals are more vulnerable to environmental insults than others. Ironically, the thorough study of biology may provide the biggest boost for our understanding of the role of environment as causal in eating disorders. This work may also assist in identifying risk factors, which will fuel prevention efforts.

As work in the eating disorders field is additionally challenged by the new world context of escalating obesity, eating disorders researchers must partner with obesity researchers both to share findings and to ensure that prevention and treatment efforts in one area do not increase the risk for development of pathology in the other area. For example, obesity prevention efforts cannot inadvertently lead to more disordered eating behavior in attempts to control weight, and eating disorders treatment should not inadvertently increase the risk for the development of obesity. Animal models of component features of eating disorders (e.g., driven physical activity, binge eating) might also shed valuable light on underlying neurobiological mechanisms that initiate and maintain dysregulated behavior. The integration of research findings from cell to population are required to complete the complex picture of these perplexing disorders that stand at the intersection of psyche and soma.

## REFERENCES

Abbott, D. W., de Zwaan, M., Mussell, M. P., Raymond, N. C., Seim, H. C., Crow, S. J., . . . Mitchell, J. E. (1998). Onset of binge eating and dieting in overweight women: Implications for etiology, associated features and treatment. *Journal of Psychosomatic Research, 44*, 367–374.

Akkermann, K., Nordquist, N., Oreland, L., & Harro, J. (2010). Serotonin transporter gene promoter polymorphism affects the severity of binge eating in general population. *Progress in Neuropsychopharmacology & Biological Psychiatry, 34*, 111–114.

Alegria, M., Woo, M., Cao, Z., Torres, M., Meng, X. L., & Striegel-Moore, R. (2007). Prevalence and correlates of eating disorders in Latinos in the United States. *International Journal of Eating Disorders, 40* (Suppl.), S15–S21.

American Academy of Pediatrics. (2003). Identifying and treating eating disorders. *Pediatrics, 111*, 204–211.

American Psychiatric Association. (1980). *Diagnostic and statistical manual of mental disorders* (3rd ed.). Washington, DC: Author.

American Psychiatric Association. (1987). *Diagnostic and statistical manual of mental disorders* (3rd ed., revised). Washington, DC: Author.

American Psychiatric Association. (1994). *Diagnostic and statistical manual of mental disorders* (4th ed.). Washington, DC: Author.

American Psychiatric Association. (2000). *Diagnostic and statistical manual of mental disorders* (4th ed., revised). Washington, DC: Author.

American Psychiatric Association. (2006). Practice guideline for the treatment of patients with eating disorders (3rd ed.). Accessed at www.psychiatryonline.com/pracGuide/loadGuidelinePdf.aspx?file=EatingDisorders3ePG_04-28-06

Anderson, C., & Bulik, C. (2003). Gender differences in compensatory behaviors, weight and shape salience, and drive for thinness. *Eating Behaviors, 5*, 1–11.

Anderson, D. A., Williamson, D. A., Duchmann, E. G., Gleaves, D. H., & Barbin, J. M. (1999). Development and validation of a multifactorial treatment outcome measure for eating disorders. *Assessment, 6*, 7–20.

Artmann, H., Grau, H., Adelmann, M., & Schleiffer, R. (1985). Reversible and non-reversible enlargement of cerebrospinal fluid spaces in anorexia nervosa. *Neuroradiology, 27*, 304–312.

Attia, E., Haiman, C., Walsh, B. T., & Flater, S. R. (1998). Does fluoxetine augment the inpatient treatment of anorexia nervosa? *American Journal of Psychiatry, 155*, 548–551.

Bacanu, S., Bulik, C., Klump, K., Fichter, M., Halmi, K., Keel, P., . . . Devlin, B. (2005). Linkage analysis of anorexia and bulimia nervosa cohorts using selected behavioral phenotypes as quantitative traits or covariates. *American Journal of Medical Genetics Part B Neuropsychiatric Genetics, 139*, 61–68.

Bailer, U. F., Frank, G. K., Henry, S. E., Price, J. C., Meltzer, C. C., Mathis, C. A., . . . Kaye, W. H. (2007). Exaggerated 5-HT1A but normal 5-HT2A receptor activity in individuals ill with anorexia nervosa. *Biological Psychiatry, 61*, 1090–1099.

Bailer, U. F., & Kaye, W. H. (2003). A review of neuropeptide and neuroendocrine dysregulation in anorexia and bulimia nervosa. *Current Drug Targets CNS Neurological Disorders*, 2, 53–59.

Beck, D., Casper, R., & Andersen, A. (1996). Truly late onset of eating disorders: A study of 11 cases averaging 60 years of age at presentation. *International Journal of Eating Disorders*, 20, 389–395.

Becker, A. E., Franko, D. L., Speck, A., & Herzog, D. B. (2003). Ethnicity and differential access to care for eating disorder symptoms. *International Journal of Eating Disorders*, 33, 205–212.

Becker, A. E., & Hamburg, P. (1996). Culture, the media, and eating disorders. *Harvard Review of Psychiatry*, 4, 163–167.

Bello, N. T., & Hajnal, A. (2010). Dopamine and binge eating behaviors. *Pharmacology Biochemistry and Behavior*, 97, 25–33.

Bencherif, B., Guarda, A. S., Colantuoni, C., Ravert, H. T., Dannals, R. F., & Frost, J. J. (2005). Regional mu-opioid receptor binding in insular cortex is decreased in bulimia nervosa and correlates inversely with fasting behavior. *Journal of Nuclear Medicine*, 46, 1349–1351.

Berg, E. A. (1948). A simple objective technique for measuring flexibility in thinking. *Journal of General Psychology*, 39, 15–22.

Bergen, A. W., van den Bree, M. B. M., Yeager, M., Welch, R., Ganjei, J. K., Haque, K., . . . Kaye, W. H. (2003). Candidate genes for anorexia nervosa in the 1p 33-36 linkage region: Serotonin 1D and delta opioid receptor loci exhibit significant association to anorexia nervosa. *Molecular Psychiatry*, 8, 397–406.

Berkman, N. D., Lohr, K. N., & Bulik, C. M. (2007). Outcomes of eating disorders: A systematic review of the literature. *International Journal of Eating Disorders*, 40, 293–309.

Beumont, P., Hay, P., Beumont, D., Birmingham, L., Derham, H., Jordan, A., . . . Royal Australian and New Zealand College of Psychiatrists Clinical Practice Guidelines Team for Anorexia Nervosa. (2004). Australian and New Zealand clinical practice guidelines for the treatment of anorexia nervosa. *Australia and New Zealand Journal of Psychiatry*, 38, 659–670.

Beumont, P. J., Kopec-Schrader, E. M., Talbot, P., & Touyz, S. W. (1993). Measuring the specific psychopathology of eating disorder patients. *Australia and New Zealand Journal of Psychiatry*, 27, 506–511.

Blundell, J. E. (1986). Serotonin manipulations and the structure of feeding behaviour. *Appetite*, 7 (Suppl.), 39–56.

Boggiano, M. M., & Chandler, P. C. (2006). Binge eating in rats produced by combining dieting with stress. *Current Protocols in Neuroscience, Chapter 9* Unit 9.23A.

Branson, R., Potoczna, N., Kral, J., Lentes, K., Hoehe, M., & Horber, F. (2003). Binge eating as a major phenotype of melanocortin 4 receptor gene mutations. *New England Journal of Medicine*, 348, 1096–1103.

Braun, C. M. J., & Chouinard, M. J. (1992). Is anorexia nervosa a neuropsychological disease? *Neuropsychology Bulletin*, 3, 171–212.

Braun, D. L., Sunday, S. R., & Halmi, K. A. (1994). Psychiatric comorbidity in patients with eating disorders. *Psychological Medicine*, 24, 859–867.

Brewerton, T. (1995). Toward a unified theory of serotonin dysregulation in eating and related disorders. *Psychoneuroendocrinology*, 20, 561–590.

Brewerton, T., Lydiard, B., Laraia, M., Shook, J., & Ballenger, J. (1992). CSF b-endorphin and dynorphin in bulimia nervosa. *American Journal of Psychiatry*, 149, 1086–1090.

Brewerton, T., Lydiard, R., Herzog, D., Brotman, A., O'Neil, P., & Ballenger, J. (1995). Comorbidity of Axis I psychiatric disorders in bulimia nervosa. *Journal of Clinical Psychiatry*, 56, 77–80.

Brownley, K. A., Berkman, N. D., Sedway, J. A., Lohr, K. N., & Bulik, C. M. (2007). Binge eating disorder treatment: A systematic review of randomized controlled trials. *International Journal of Eating Disorders, 40,* 337–348.

Bruce, B., & Agras, W. S. (1992). Binge eating in females: A population-based investigation. *International Journal of Eating Disorders, 12,* 365–373.

Bruce, B., & Wilfley, D. (1996). Binge eating among the overweight population: A serious and prevalent problem. *Journal of the American Dietetic Association, 96,* 58–61.

Bulik, C., Klump, K., Thornton, L., Kaplan, A., Devlin, B., Fichter, M., . . . Kaye, W. H. (2004). Alcohol use disorder comorbidity in eating disorders: A multicenter study. *Journal of Clinical Psychiatry, 65,* 1000–1006.

Bulik, C., Sullivan, P., Carter, F., & Joyce, P. (1995). Temperament, character, and personality disorder in bulimia nervosa. *Journal of Nervous and Mental Disease, 183,* 593–598.

Bulik, C., Sullivan, P., Fear, J., & Joyce, P. (1997). Eating disorders and antecedent anxiety disorders: A controlled study. *Acta Psychiatrica Scandinavica, 96,* 101–107.

Bulik, C., Sullivan, P. F., Fear, J., & Pickering, A. (1997). Predictors of the development of bulimia nervosa in women with anorexia nervosa. *Journal of Nervous and Mental Disease, 185,* 704–707.

Bulik, C., Sullivan, P., Fear, J., Pickering, A., Dawn, A., & McCullin, M. (1999). Fertility and reproduction in women with a history of anorexia nervosa: A controlled study. *Journal of Clinical Psychiatry, 60,* 130–135.

Bulik, C., Sullivan, P., Tozzi, F., Furberg, H., Lichtenstein, P., & Pedersen, N. (2006). Prevalence, heritability and prospective risk factors for anorexia nervosa. *Archives of General Psychiatry, 63,* 305–312.

Bulik, C. M. (2002). Eating disorders in adolescents and young adults. *Child and Adolescent Psychiatry Clinics of North America, 11,* 201–218.

Bulik, C. M., Berkman, N. D., Brownley, K. A., Sedway, J. A., & Lohr, K. N. (2007). Anorexia nervosa treatment: A systematic review of randomized controlled trials. *International Journal of Eating Disorders, 40,* 310–320.

Bulik, C. M., Brownley, K. A., & Shapiro, J. R. (2007). Diagnosis and management of binge eating disorder. *World Psychiatry, 6,* 142–148.

Bulik, C. M., Devlin, B., Bacanu, S. A., Thornton, L., Klump, K. L., Fichter, M. M., & Kaye, W. H. (2003). Significant linkage on chromosome 10p in families with bulimia nervosa. *American Journal of Human Genetics, 72,* 200–207.

Bulik, C. M., Hebebrand, J., Keski-Rahkonen, A., Klump, K. L., Reichborn-Kjennerud, T., Mazzeo, S. E., & Wade, T. D. (2007). Genetic epidemiology, endophenotypes, and eating disorder classification. *International Journal of Eating Disorders, 40* (Suppl.), S52–S60.

Bulik, C. M., Slof-Op't Landt, M. C., van Furth, E. F., & Sullivan, P. F. (2007). The genetics of anorexia nervosa. *Annual Review of Nutrition, 27,* 263–275.

Bulik, C. M., Sullivan, P. F., & Kendler, K. S. (2002). Medical and psychiatric morbidity in obese women with and without binge-eating. *International Journal of Eating Disorders, 32,* 72–78.

Burgess, P. W., & Shallice, T. (1997). *The Hayling and Brixton Tests.* Bury St. Edmunds, England: Thames Valley Test Company.

Cachelin, F. M., Veisel, C., Barzengarnazari, E., & Striegel-Moore, R. H. (2000). Disordered eating, acculturation, and treatment-seeking in a community sample of Hispanic, Asian, Black and White women. *Psychology of Women Quarterly, 24,* 244–253.

Calati, R., De Ronchi, D., Bellini, M., & Serretti, A. (2011). The 5-HTTLPR polymorphism and eating disorders: A meta-analysis. *International Journal of Eating Disorders, 44*(3), 191–199.

Cassin, S. E., & von Ranson, K. M. (2005). Personality and eating disorders: A decade in review. *Clinical Psychology Review, 25,* 895–916.

Castro-Fornieles, J., Caldú, X., Andrés-Perpiñá, S., Lázaro, L., Bargalló, N., Falcón, C., . . . Junqué, C. (2010). A cross-sectional and follow-up functional MRI study with a working memory task in adolescent anorexia nervosa. *Neuropsychologia, 48*(14), 4111–4116.

Chavez, M., & Insel, T. R. (2007). Eating disorders: National Institute of Mental Health's perspective. *American Psychologist, 62,* 159–166.

Chiodo, J., & Latimer, P. R. (1986). Hunger perceptions and satiety responses among normal-weight bulimics and normals to a high-calorie, carbohydrate-rich food. *Psychological Medicine, 16,* 343–349.

Clinton, D., & Norring, C. (2005). The comparative utility of statistically derived eating disorder clusters and *DSM-IV* diagnoses: Relationship to symptomatology and psychiatric comorbidity at intake and follow-up. *Eating Behaviors, 6,* 403–418.

Cnattingius, S., Hultman, C., Dahl, M., & Sparen, P. (1999). Very preterm birth, birth trauma, and the risk of anorexia nervosa among girls. *Archives of General Psychiatry, 56,* 634–638.

Colantuoni, C., Schwenker, J., McCarthy, J., Rada, P., Ladenheim, B., Cadet, J. L., . . . Hoebel, B. G. (2001). Excessive sugar intake alters binding to dopamine and mu-opioid receptors in the brain. *Neuroreport, 12,* 3549–3552.

Cooper, M. J., Anastasiades, P., & Fairburn, C. G. (1992). Selective processing of eating-, shape-, and weight-related words in persons with bulimia nervosa. *Journal of Abnormal Psychology, 101,* 352–355.

Cooper, Z., Cooper, P., & Fairburn, C. (1989). The validity of the eating disorder examination and its subscales. *British Journal of Psychiatry, 154,* 807–812.

Cooper, Z., & Fairburn, C. (1987). The eating disorders examination: A semi-structured interview for the assessment of the specific psychopathology of eating disorders. *International Journal of Eating Disorders, 6*(1), 1–8.

Crow, S. (2005). Medical complications of eating disorders. In S. Wonderlich, J. Mitchell, M. de Zwann, & H. Steiger (Eds.), *Eating disorders review, Part I* (pp. 127–136). Milton Keynes, England: Radcliffe.

Crow, S., Agras, W., Halmi, K., Mitchell, J., & Kraemer, H. (2002). Full syndromal vs. subthreshold anorexia nervosa, bulimia nervosa, and binge eating disorder: A multicenter study. *International Journal of Eating Disorders, 32,* 309–318.

Crow, S. J., Peterson, C. B., Swanson, S. A., Raymond, N. C., Specker, S., Eckert, E. D., & Mitchell, J. E. (2009). Increased mortality in bulimia nervosa and other eating disorders. *American Journal of Psychiatry, 166,* 1342–1346.

Crow, S. J., Salisbury, J. J., Crosby, R. D., & Mitchell, J. E. (1997). Serum electrolytes as markers of vomiting in bulimia nervosa. *International Journal of Eating Disorders, 21,* 95–98.

Cuellar, R. E., Kaye, W. H., Hsu, L. K., & Van Thiel, D. H. (1988). Upper gastrointestinal tract dysfunction in bulimia. *Digestive Diseases and Sciences, 33,* 1549–1553.

Cuellar, R. E., & Van Thiel, D. H. (1986). Gastrointestinal consequences of the eating disorders: Anorexia nervosa and bulimia. *American Journal of Gastroenterology, 81,* 1113–1124.

Dalle Grave, R., Calugi, S., Brambilla, F., & Marchesini, G. (2008). Personality dimensions and treatment drop-outs among eating disorder patients treated with cognitive behavior therapy. *Psychiatry Research, 158,* 381–388.

Davis, C., Levitan, R. D., Kaplan, A. S., Carter, J., Reid, C., Curtis, C., . . . Kennedy, J. L. (2007). Dopamine transporter gene (DAT1) associated with appetite suppression to methylphenidate in a case-control study of binge eating disorder. *Neuropsychopharmacology, 32,* 2199–2206.

Decaluwe, V., & Braet, C. (2003). Prevalence of binge-eating disorder in obese children and adolescents seeking weight-loss treatment. *International Journal of Obesity and Related Metabolic Disorders, 27,* 404–409.

Delgado, M. R., Nystrom, L. E., Fissell, C., Noll, D. C., & Fiez, J. A. (2000). Tracking the hemodynamic responses to reward and punishment in the striatum. *Journal of Neurophysiology, 84*, 3072–3077.

Devlin, B., Bacanu, S., Klump, K., Bulik, C., Fichter, M., Halmi, K., . . . Kaye, W. H. (2002). Linkage analysis of anorexia nervosa incorporating behavioral covariates. *Human Molecular Genetics, 11*, 689–696.

de Zwaan, M., Biener, D., Bach, M., Wiesnagrotzki, S., & Stacher, G. (1996). Pain sensitivity, alexithymia, and depression in patients with eating disorders: Are they related? *Journal of Psychosomatic Research, 41*, 65–70.

Downes, J. J., Roberts, A. C., Sahakian, B. J., Evenden, J. L., Morris, R. G., & Robbins, T. W. (1989). Impaired extra-dimensional shift performance in medicated and unmedicated Parkinson's disease: Evidence for a specific attentional dysfunction. *Neuropsychologia, 27*, 1329–1343.

Duchesne, M., Mattos, P., Fontenelle, L. F., Veiga, H., Rizo, L., & Appolinario, J. C. (2004). Neuropsychology of eating disorders: a systematic review of the literature. *Revista Brasileira de Psiquiatria, 26*, 107–117.

Eagles, J., Johnston, M., Hunter, D., Lobban, M., & Millar, H. (1995). Increasing incidence of anorexia nervosa in the female population of northeast Scotland. *American Journal of Psychiatry, 152*, 1266–1271.

Eckert, E. D., Halmi, K. A., Marchi, P., Grove, W., & Crosby, R. (1995). Ten-year follow-up of anorexia nervosa: Clinical course and outcome. *Psychological Medicine, 25*, 143–156.

Eddy, K., Keel, P., Dorer, D., Delinsky, S., Franko, D., & Herzog, D. (2002). Longitudinal comparison of anorexia nervosa subtypes. *International Journal of Eating Disorders, 31*, 191–201.

Eliava, N. (1964). *A problem of set in cognitive psychology*. Tbilisi, Georgia: Academic Press.

Enten, R. S., & Golan, M. (2009). Parenting styles and eating disorder pathology. *Appetite, 52*, 784–787.

Erlanson-Albertsson, C. (2005). How palatable food disrupts appetite regulation. *Basic Clinical Pharmacology and Toxicology, 97*, 61–73.

Fairbanks, L. A., Melega, W. P., Jorgensen, M. J., Kaplan, J. R., & McGuire, M. T. (2001). Social impulsivity inversely associated with CSF 5-HIAA and fluoxetine exposure in vervet monkeys. *Neuropsychopharmacology, 24*, 370–378.

Fairburn, C., & Cooper, Z. (1993). The eating disorders examination (12th ed.). In C. Fairburn & G. Wilson (Eds.), *Binge-eating: Nature, assessment and treatment* (pp. 317–360). New York, NY: Guilford Press.

Fairburn, C. G., & Beglin, S. J. (1994). Assessment of eating disorders: Interview or self-report questionnaire? *International Journal of Eating Disorders, 16*(4), 363–370.

Fairburn, C. G., & Bohn, K. (2005). Eating disorder NOS (EDNOS): An example of the troublesome "not otherwise specified" (NOS) category in *DSM-IV*. *Behaviour Research and Therapy, 43*, 691–701.

Fairburn, C. G., & Cooper, Z. (2007). Thinking afresh about the classification of eating disorders. *International Journal of Eating Disorders, 40* (Suppl.), S107–S110.

Fairburn, C. G., Doll, H. A., Welch, S. L., Hay, P. J., Davies, B. A., & O'Connor, M. E. (1998). Risk factors for binge eating disorder: A community-based, case-control study. *Archives of General Psychiatry, 55*, 425–432.

Fairburn, C. G., Welch, S. L., & Hay, P. J. (1993). The classification of recurrent overeating: The "binge eating disorder" proposal. *International Journal of Eating Disorders, 13*, 155–159.

Fassino, S., Amianto, F., Gramaglia, C., Facchini, F., & Abbate Daga, G. (2004). Temperament and character in eating disorders: Ten years of studies. *Eating and Weight Disorders, 9*, 81–90.

Fassino, S., Piero, A., Daga, G. A., Leombruni, P., Mortara, P., & Rovera, G. G. (2002). Attentional biases and frontal functioning in anorexia nervosa. *International Journal of Eating Disorders, 31,* 274–283.

Ferguson, C. P., La Via, M. C., Crossan, P. J., & Kaye, W. H. (1999). Are serotonin selective reuptake inhibitors effective in underweight anorexia nervosa? *International Journal of Eating Disorders, 25,* 11–17.

Fernandez-Aranda, F., Pinheiro, A., Tozzi, F., Thornton, L., Fichter, M., Halmi, K., . . . Bulik, C. M. (2007). Symptom profile and temporal relation of major depressive disorder in females with eating disorders. *Australian and New Zealand Journal of Psychiatry, 41,* 24–31.

Ferraro, F., Wonderlich, S., & Jocic, Z. (1997). Performance variability as a new theoretical mechanism regarding eating disorders and cognitive processing. *Journal of Clinical Psychology, 53,* 117–121.

Fichter, M., Herpertz, S., Quadflieg, N., & Herpertz-Dahlmann, B. (1998). Structured interview for anorexic and bulimic disorders for *DSM-IV* and *ICD-10*: Updated (third) revision. *International Journal of Eating Disorders, 24,* 227–249.

Fichter, M., & Quadflieg, N. (1997). Six-year course of bulimia nervosa. *International Journal of Eating Disorders, 22,* 361–384.

Fichter, M., & Quadflieg, N. (2001). The structured interview for anorexic and bulimic disorders for *DSM-IV* and *ICD-10* (SIAB-EX): Reliability and validity. *European Psychiatry, 16,* 38–48.

Fichter, M. M., & Keeser, W. (1980). [The anorexia nervosa inventory for self-rating (ANIS) (author's translation)]. *Archiv für Psychiatrie Nervenkrankheiten, 228,* 67–89.

Fichter, M. M., & Quadflieg, N. (2000). Comparing self-and expert rating: A self-report screening version (SIAB-S) of the structured interview for anorexic and bulimic syndromes for DSM-IV and ICD-10 (SIAB-EX). *European Archives of Psychiatry and Clinical Neurosciences, 250,* 175–185.

First, M. B., Spitzer, R., Gibbon, M., & Williams, J. B. (2002). *Structured Clinical Interview for DSM-IV-TR Axis I disorders, research version, patient edition. (SCID-I/P).* New York: Biometrics Research, New York State Psychiatric Institute.

Fitzgibbon, M. L., Spring, B., Avellone, M. E., Blackman, L. R., Pingitore, R., & Stolley, M. R. (1998). Correlates of binge eating in Hispanic, black, and white women. *International Journal of Eating Disorders, 24,* 43–52.

Folkman, S., Lazarus, R., Dunkel-Schetter, C., DeLongis, A., & Gruen, R. (1986). Dynamics of a stressful encounter: Cognitive appraisal, coping, and encounter outcomes. *Journal of Personality and Social Psychology, 50,* 992–1003.

Folkman, S., Lazarus, R., Gruen, R., & DeLongis, A. (1986). Appraisal, coping, health status, and psychological symptoms. *Journal of Personality and Social Psychology, 50,* 571–579.

Frank, G. K., Bailer, U. F., Henry, S., Wagner, A., & Kaye, W. H. (2004). Neuroimaging studies in eating disorders. *CNS Spectrums, 9,* 539–548.

Frank, G. K., Bailer, U. F., Henry, S. E., Drevets, W., Meltzer, C. C., Price, J. C., . . . Kaye, W. H. (2005). Increased dopamine D2/D3 receptor binding after recovery from anorexia nervosa measured by positron emission tomography and [11c]raclopride. *Biological Psychiatry, 58,* 908–912.

Frank, G. K., & Kaye, W. H. (2005). Positron emission tomography studies in eating disorders: Multireceptor brain imaging, correlates with behavior and implications for pharmacotherapy. *Nuclear Medicine Biology, 32,* 755–761.

Garfinkel, P., Lin, E., Goering, P., Spegg, C., Goldbloom, D., Kennedy, S., . . . Woodside, D. B. (1995). Bulimia nervosa in a Canadian community sample: prevalence and comparison of subgroups. *American Journal of Psychiatry, 152,* 1052–1058.

Garner, D. (1991). *Eating disorders inventory-2: Professional manual.* Odessa, FL: Psychological Assessment Resources.

Garner, D., & Garfinkel, P. (1980). Socio-cultural factors in the development of anorexia nervosa. *Psychological Medicine, 10,* 647–656.

Garner, D., Olmsted, M., & Polivy, J. (1983). Development and validation of a multi-dimenional eating disorder inventory for anorexia nervosa and bulimia. *International Journal of Eating Disorders, 2,* 15–34.

Garner, D., Olmsted, M., & Polivy, J. (1984). *Eating disorders inventory manual.* New York, NY: Psychological Assessment Resources.

Garner, D. M. (2004). *Eating disorders inventory-3.* Lutz, FL: Psychological Assessment Resources.

Garner, D. M., Olmsted, M. P., & Polivy, J. (2008). Eating disorders inventory-3 (EDI-3). In A. J. Rush, M. B. First, & D. Blacker (Eds.), *Handbook of psychiatric measures* (2nd ed. ed., pp. 626–628). Washington, DC: American Psychiatric Publishing.

Geliebter, A., Hashim, S. A., & Gluck, M. E. (2008). Appetite-related gut peptides, ghrelin, PYY, and GLP-1 in obese women with and without binge eating disorder (BED). *Physiology and Behavior, 94,* 696–699.

Gendall, K., Joyce, P., Carter, F., McIntosh, V., Jordan, J., & Bulik, C. (2006). The psychobiology and diagnostic significance of amenorrhea in patients with anorexia nervosa. *Fertility and Sterility, 85,* 1531–1535.

Glasofer, D. R., Tanofsky-Kraff, M., Eddy, K. T., Yanovski, S. Z., Theim, K. R., Mirch, M. C., . . . Yanovski, J. A. (2007). Binge eating in overweight treatment-seeking adolescents. *Journal of Pediatric Psychology, 32,* 95–105.

Godart, N., Flament, M., Perdereau, F., & Jeammet, P. (2002). Comorbidity between eating disorders and anxiety disorders: A review. *International Journal of Eating Disorders, 32,* 253–270.

Godart, N. T., Flament, M. F., Lecrubier, Y., & Jeammet, P. (2000). Anxiety disorders in anorexia nervosa and bulimia nervosa: co-morbidity and chronology of appearance. *European Psychiatry, 15,* 38–45.

Golden, N., Katzman, D., Kreipe, R., Stevens, S., Sawyer, S., Rees, J., . . . Rome, E. S. (2003). Eating disorders in adolescents: Position paper of the Society for Adolescent Medicine. *Journal of Adolescent Health, 33,* 496–503.

Golden, N. H., Ashtari, M., Kohn, M. R., Patel, M., Jacobson, M. S., Fletcher, A., & Shenker, I. R. (1996). Reversibility of cerebral ventricular enlargement in anorexia nervosa, demonstrated by quantitative magnetic resonance imaging. *Journal of Pediatrics, 128,* 296–301.

Goodwin, R. D., Hoven, C. W., & Spitzer, R. L. (2003). Diabetes and eating disorders in primary care. *International Journal of Eating Disorders, 33,* 85–91.

Gormally, J., Black, S., Daston, S., & Rardin, D. (1982). The assessment of binge-eating severity among obese persons. *Addictive Behaviors, 7,* 47–55.

Gottesman, I., & Gould, T. (2003). The endophenotype concept in psychiatry: Etymology and strategic intentions. *American Journal of Psychiatry, 160,* 636–645.

Green, M. W., Elliman, N. A., Wakeling, A., & Rogers, P. J. (1996). Cognitive functioning, weight change and therapy in anorexia nervosa. *Journal of Psychiatric Research, 30,* 401–410.

Grice, D. E., Halmi, K. A., Fichter, M. M., Strober, M., Woodside, D. B., Treasure, J. T., . . . Berrettini, W. H. (2002). Evidence for a susceptibility gene for anorexia nervosa on chromosome 1. *American Journal of Human Genetics, 70,* 787–792.

Grilo, C. M. (2005). *Structured instruments.* In J. E. Mitchell & C. B. Peterson (Eds.), *Assessment of eating disorders* (pp. 79–97). New York, NY: Guilford Press.

Grilo, C. M., Masheb, R. M., Lozano-Blanco, C., & Barry, D. T. (2004). Reliability of the Eating Disorder Examination in patients with binge eating disorder. *International Journal of Eating Disorders, 35*, 80–85.

Grucza, R., & Beirut, L. (2007). Co-occurring risk factors for alcohol dependence and habitual smoking: Update on findings from the Collaborative Study on the Genetics of Alcoholism. *Alcohol Research & Health, 29*, 172–177.

Grucza, R. A., Przybeck, T. R., & Cloninger, C. R. (2007). Prevalence and correlates of binge eating disorder in a community sample. *Comprehensive Psychiatry, 48*, 124–131.

Hainer, V., Kabrnova, K., Aldhoon, B., Kunesova, M., & Wagenknecht, M. (2006). Serotonin and norepinephrine reuptake inhibition and eating behavior. *Annals of the New York Academy of Sciences, 1083*, 252–269.

Hall, A., & Hay, P. J. (1991). Eating disorder patient referrals from a population region 1977–1986. *Psychological Medicine, 21*, 697–701.

Harris, E. C., & Barraclough, B. (1998). Excess mortality of mental disorder. *British Journal of Psychiatry, 173*, 11–53.

Heatherton, T. F., & Baumeister, R. F. (1991). Binge eating as escape from self-awareness. *Psychological Bulletin, 110*, 86–108.

Hebebrand, J., & Bulik, C. M. (2010). Critical appraisal of the provisional *DSM-5* criteria for anorexia nervosa and an alternative proposal. *International Journal of Eating Disorders.*

Hebebrand, J., Geller, F., Dempfle, A., Heinzel-Gutenbrunner, M., Raab, M., Gerber, G., . . . Hinney, A. (2004). Binge-eating episodes are not characteristic of carriers of melanocortin-4 receptor gene mutations. *Molecular Psychiatry, 9*, 796–800.

Hebebrand, J., Himmelmann, G., Herzog, W., Herpertz-Dahlmann, B., Steinhausen, H., Amstein, M., . . . Schäfer, H. (1997). Prediction of low body weight at long-term follow-up in acute anorexia nervosa by low body weight at referral. *American Journal of Psychiatry, 154*, 566–569.

Heinz, E. R., Martinez, J., & Haenggeli, A. (1977). Reversibility of cerebral atrophy in anorexia nervosa and Cushing's syndrome. *Journal of Computer Assisted Tomography, 1*, 415–418.

Hildebrandt, T., Alfano, L., Tricamo, M., & Pfaff, D. W. (2010). Conceptualizing the role of estrogens and serotonin in the development and maintenance of bulimia nervosa. *Clinical Psychology Reviews, 30*, 655–668.

Hoek, H., Bartelds, A., Bosveld, J., van der Graaf, Y., Limpens, V., Maiwald, M., & Spaaij, C. J. (1995). Impact of urbanization on detection rates of eating disorders. *American Journal of Psychiatry, 152*, 1272–1278.

Hoek, H. W. (1991). The incidence and prevalence of anorexia nervosa and bulimia nervosa in primary care. *Psychological Medicine, 21*, 455–460.

Hoek, H. W. (2006). Incidence, prevalence and mortality of anorexia nervosa and other eating disorders. *Current Opinion in Psychiatry, 19*, 389–394.

Hoffman, G. W., Ellinwood, E. H., Jr., Rockwell, W. J., Herfkens, R. J., Nishita, J. K., & Guthrie, L. F. (1989). Cerebral atrophy in bulimia. *Biological Psychiatry, 25*, 894–902.

Hudson, J., Lalonde, J., Pindyck, L., Bulik, C., Crow, S., McElroy, S . . . & Pope, H.G., Jr. (2006). Binge-eating disorder as a distinct familial phenotype in obese inviduals. *Archives of General Psychiatry, 63*, 313–319.

Hudson, J. I., Hiripi, E., Pope, H. G., Jr., & Kessler, R. C. (2007). The prevalence and correlates of eating disorders in the National Comorbidity Survey Replication. *Biological Psychiatry, 61*, 348–358.

Hudson, J. I., Lalonde, J. K., Coit, C. E., Tsuang, M. T., McElroy, S. L., Crow, S. J., . . . Pope, H. G., Jr. (2010). Longitudinal study of the diagnosis of components of the metabolic syndrome in individuals with binge-eating disorder. *American Journal of Clinical Nutrition*, *91*, 1568–1573.

Husain, M. M., Black, K. J., Doraiswamy, P. M., Shah, S. A., Rockwell, W. J., Ellinwood, E. H., Jr., & Krishnan, K. R. (1992). Subcortical brain anatomy in anorexia and bulimia. *Biological Psychiatry*, *31*, 735–738.

Inagaki, T., Horiguchi, J., Tsubouchi, K., Miyaoka, T., Uegaki, J., & Seno, H. (2002). Late onset anorexia nervosa: Two case reports. *International Journal of Psychiatry Medicine*, *32*, 91–95.

Irving, L. M. (1990). Mirror images: Effects of the standard of beauty on the self- and body-esteem of women exhibiting varying levels of bulimic symptoms. *Journal of Social and Clinical Psychology*, 230–242.

Isnard, P., Michel, G., Frelut, M. L., Vila, G., Falissard, B., Naja, W., . . . Mouren Simeoni, M. C. (2003). Binge eating and psychopathology in severely obese adolescents. *International Journal of Eating Disorders*, *34*, 235–243.

Jacobi, C., Hayward, C., de Zwaan, M., Kraemer, H., & Agras, W. (2004). Coming to terms with risk factors for eating disorders: Application of risk terminology and suggestions for a general taxonomy. *Psychological Bulletin*, *130*, 19–65.

Javaras, K. N., Laird, N. M., Reichborn-Kjennerud, T., Bulik, C. M., Pope, H. G., Jr., & Hudson, J. I. (2008). Familiality and heritability of binge eating disorder: Results of a case-control family study and a twin study. *International Journal of Eating Disorders*, *41*, 174–179.

Jimerson, D., Lesem, M., Kaye, W., & Brewerton, T. (1992). Low serotonin and dopamine metabolite concentrations in cerebrospinal fluid from bulimic patients with frequent binge episodes. *Archives of General Psychiatry*, *49*, 132–138.

Jimerson, D., & Wolfe, B. (2006). Psychobiology of eating disorders. In S. A. Wonderlich, J. Mitchell, M. De Zwann, & H. Steiger (Eds.), *Annual review of eating disorders, Part 2*. (Vol. 1-15). Abington England: Radcliffe.

Johnson, J. G., Spitzer, R. L., & Williams, J. B. (2001). Health problems, impairment and illnesses associated with bulimia nervosa and binge eating disorder among primary care and obstetric gynaecology patients. *Psychological Medicine*, *31*, 1455–1466.

Jones, B., Duncan, C., Brouwers, P., & Mirsky, A. (1991). Cognition in eating disorders. *Journal of Clinical and Experimental Neuropsychology*, *13*, 711–728.

Jones, D., Fox, M., Babigan, H., & Hutton, H. (1980). Epidemiology of anorexia nervosa in Monroe County, New York: 1960-76. *Psychosomatic Medicine*, *42*, 551–558.

Joos, A., Kloppel, S., Hartmann, A., Glauche, V., Tuscher, O., Perlov, E., . . . Tebarst van Elst, L. (2010). Voxel-based morphometry in eating disorders: correlation of psychopathology with grey matter volume. *Psychiatry Research*, *182*, 146–151.

Kaplan, A. S., Garfinkel, P. E., Warsh, J. J., & Brown, G. M. (1989). Clonidine challenge test in bulimia nervosa. *International Journal of Eating Disorders*, *8*, 425–435.

Katzman, D. K., Lambe, E. K., Mikulis, D. J., Ridgley, J. N., Goldbloom, D. S., & Zipursky, R. B. (1996). Cerebral gray matter and white matter volume deficits in adolescent girls with anorexia nervosa. *Journal of Pediatrics*, *129*, 794–803.

Kaye, W., Ballenger, J., Lydiard, R., Stuart, G., Laraia, M., O'Neil, P., . . . Hsu, G. (1990). CSF monoamine levels in normal weight bulimia: Evidence for altered noradrenergic activity. *American Journal of Psychiatry*, 1990b, 225–229.

Kaye, W., Berrettini, W., Gwirtsman, H., Chretien, M., Gold, P., George, D., . . . Ebert, M. H. (1987). Reduced cerebrospinal fluid levels of immunoreactive propiomelanocortin related peptides (including beta-endorphin) in anorexia nervosa. *Life Sciences*, *52*, 2147–2155.

Kaye, W., Bulik, C., Thornton, L., Barbarich, B. S., Masters, K., & Group, P. F. C. (2004). Comorbidity of anxiety disorders with anorexia and bulimia nervosa. *American Journal of Psychiatry*, *161*, 2215–2221.

Kaye, W., Gwirtsman, H., George, D., & Ebert, M. (1991). Altered serotonin activity in anorexia nervosa after long-term weight restoration: Does elevated CSF-5HIAA correlate with rigid and obsessive behavior? *Archives of General Psychiatry, 48*, 556–562.

Kaye, W., Nagata, T., Weltzin, T., Hsu, L., Sokol, M., McConaha, C., . . . Deep, D. (2001). Double-blind placebo-controlled administration of fluoxetine in restricting- and restricting-purging-type anorexia nervosa. *Biological Psychiatry, 49*, 644–652.

Kaye, W. H. (1997). Persistent alterations in behavior and serotonin activity after recovery from anorexia and bulimia nervosa. *Annals of the New York Academy of Sciences, 817*, 162–178.

Kaye, W. H. (2008). Neurobiology of anorexia and bulimia nervosa. *Physiology and Behavior, 94*, 121–135.

Kaye, W. H., Frank, G. K., & McConaha, C. (1999). Altered dopamine activity after recovery from restricting-type anorexia nervosa. *Neuropsychopharmacology, 21*, 503–506.

Kaye, W. H., Fudge, J. L., & Paulus, M. (2009). New insights into symptoms and neurocircuit function of anorexia nervosa. *Nature Reviews Neuroscience, 10*, 573–584.

Keel, P., Haedt, A., & Edler, C. (2005). Purging disorder: An ominous variant of bulimia nervosa? *International Journal of Eating Disorders, 38*, 191–199.

Keel, P. K. (2001). Basic counseling techniques. In J. E. Mitchell (Ed.), *The outpatient treatment of eating disorders: A guide for therapists, dietitions, and physicians* (pp. 119–143). Minneapolis: University of Minnesota Press.

Keel, P. K., Gravener, J. A., Joiner, T. E., Jr., & Haedt, A. A. (2010). Twenty-year follow-up of bulimia nervosa and related eating disorders not otherwise specified. *International Journal of Eating Disorders, 43*, 492–497.

Kelley, A. E., Bakshi, V. P., Haber, S. N., Steininger, T. L., Will, M. J., & Zhang, M. (2002). Opioid modulation of taste hedonics within the ventral striatum. *Physiology and Behavior, 76*, 365–377.

Kemps, E., Tiggemann, M., & Marshall, K. (2005). Relationship between dieting to lose weight and the functioning of the central executive. *Appetite, 45*, 287–294.

Kingston, K., Szmukler, G., Andrewes, D., Tress, B., & Desmond, P. (1996). Neuropsychological and structural brain changes in anorexia nervosa before and after refeeding. *Psychological Medicine, 26*, 15–28.

Klump, K. L., Bulik, C. M., Pollice, C., Halmi, K. A., Fichter, M. M., Berrettini, W. H., . . . Kaye, W. H. (2000). Temperament and character in women with anorexia nervosa. *Journal of Nervous and Mental Disease, 188*, 559–567.

Klump, K. L., Miller, K. B., Keel, P. K., McGue, M., & Iacono, W. G. (2001). Genetic and environmental influences on anorexia nervosa syndromes in a population-based twin sample. *Psychological Medicine, 31*, 737–740.

Klump, K. L., Wonderlich, S., Lehoux, P., Lilenfeld, L. R., & Bulik, C. M. (2002). Does environment matter? A review of nonshared environment and eating disorders. *International Journal of Eating Disorders, 31*, 118–135.

Knoll, S., Bulik, C., & Hebebrand, J. (2011). Do the currently proposed *DSM-5* criteria for anorexia nervosa adequately consider developmental aspects in children and adolescents? *European Child and Adolescent Psychiatry, 20*(2), 96–101.

Koba, T., Horie, S., & Nabeta, Y. (2002). Impaired performance on Wisconsin card sorting test in patients with eating disorders: a preliminary study. *Seishin Igaku, 44*, 681–683.

Kohn, M. R., Golden, N. H., & Shenker, I. R. (1998). Cardiac arrest and delirium: Presentations of the refeeding syndrome in severely malnourished adolescents with anorexia nervosa. *Journal of Adolescent Health, 22*, 239–243.

Kravariti, E., Morris, R. G., Rabe-Hesketh, S., Murray, R. M., & Frangou, S. (2003). The Maudsley early onset schizophrenia study: Cognitive function in adolescents with recent onset schizophrenia. *Schizophrenia Research, 61,* 137–148.

Krieg, J. C., Lauer, C., & Pirke, K. M. (1989). Structural brain abnormalities in patients with bulimia nervosa. *Psychiatry Research, 27,* 39–48.

Kutlesic, V., Williamson, D. A., Gleaves, D. H., Barbin, J. M., & Murphy-Eberenz, K. P. (1998). The Interview for the Diagnosis of Eating Disorders-IV: Application to *DSM-IV* diagnostic criteria. *Psychological Assessment, 10,* 41–48.

Lankenau, H., Swigar, M. E., Bhimani, S., Luchins, D., & Quinlan, D. M. (1985). Cranial CT scans in eating disorder patients and controls. *Comprehensive Psychiatry, 26,* 136–147.

Latner, J. D., & Clyne, C. (2008). The diagnostic validity of the criteria for binge eating disorder. *International Journal of Eating Disorders, 41,* 1–14.

Lauer, C. J. (2002). Neruopsychological findings in eating disorders. In H. D'haenen, J. A. den Boer, H. Westenberg, & P. Willner (Eds.), *Biological psychiatry* (pp. 1167–1173). Swansey, England: John Wiley & Sons.

Ledoux, S., Choquet, M., & Manfredi, R. (1993). Associated factors for self-reported binge eating among male and female adolescents. *Journal of Adolescence, 16,* 75–91.

Lee, Y., & Lin, P. Y. (2010). Association between serotonin transporter gene polymorphism and eating disorders: a meta-analytic study. *International Journal of Eating Disorders, 43*(6), 498–504.

Lena, S. M., Fiocco, A. J., & Leyenaar, J. K. (2004). The role of cognitive deficits in the development of eating disorders. *Neuropsychology Reviews, 14,* 99–113.

Lesem, M., Berrettini, W., Kaye, W., & Jimerson, D. (1991). Measurement of CSFdynorphin A 1-8 immunoreactivity in anorexia nervosa and normal-weight bulimia. *Biological Psychiatry, 29,* 244–252.

Levine, M. P., & Harrison, K. (2004). The role of mass media in the perpetuation and prevention of negative body image and disordered eating. In J. K. Thompson (Ed.), *Handbook of eating disorders and obesity* (pp. 695–717). Hoboken, NJ: John Wiley & Sons.

Lewinsohn, P., Seeley, J., Moerk, K , & Striegel-Moore, R. (2002). Gender differences in eating disorder symptoms in young adults. *International Journal of Eating Disorders, 32,* 426–440.

Lezak, M. D. (1995). *Neuropsychological assessment.* Oxford, England: Oxford University Press.

Licinio, J., Wong, M., & Gold, P. (1996). The hypothalamic-pituitary-adrenal axis in anorexia nervosa. *Psychiatry Research, 62,* 75–83.

Lilenfeld, L., Kaye, W., Greeno, C., Merikangas, K., Plotnikov, K., Pollice, C., . . . Nagy, L. (1998). A controlled family study of restricting anorexia and bulimia nervosa: Comorbidity in probands and disorders in first-degree relatives. *Archives of General Psychiatry, 55,* 603–610.

Linehan, M. (1993). *Cognitive-behavioral treatment of borderline personality disorder.* New York, NY: Guilford Press.

Little, J. W. (2002). Eating disorders: dental implications. *Oral Surgery, Oral Medicine, Oral Pathology, Oral Radiology & Endodontics, 93,* 138–143.

Lock, J., Le Grange, D., Agras, W., & Dare, C. (2001). *Treatment manual for anorexia nervosa: A family-based approach.* New York, NY: Guilford Press.

Lucas, A. R., Beard, C. M., O'Fallon, W. M., & Kurland, L. T. (1988). Anorexia nervosa in Rochester, Minnesota: A 45-year study. *Mayo Clinic Proceedings, 63,* 433–442.

Mancilla-Diaz, J. M., Escartin-Perez, R. E., Lopez-Alonso, V. E., & Cruz-Morales, S. E. (2002). Effect of 5-HT in mianserin-pretreated rats on the structure of feeding behavior. *European Neuropsychopharmacology, 12,* 445–451.

Mannucci, E., Tesi, F., Ricca, V., Pierazzuoli, E., Barciulli, E., Moretti, S., . . . Rotella, C. M. (2002). Eating behavior in obese patients with and without type 2 diabetes mellitus. *International Journal of Obesity and Related Metabolic Disorders, 26,* 848–853.

Marcus, M., Wing, R., & Fairburn, C. (1995). Cognitive treatment of binge-eating versus behavioral weight control in the treatment of binge-eating disorder. *Annals of Behavioral Medicine, 17,* 5090.

Marcus, M. D., Bromberger, J. T., Wei, H. L., Brown, C., & Kravitz, H. M. (2007). Prevalence and selected correlates of eating disorder symptoms among a multiethnic community sample of midlife women. *Annals of Behavioral Medicine, 33,* 269–277.

Martin, C. K., Williamson, D. A., & Thaw, J. M. (2000). Criterion validity of the multiaxial assessment of eating disorders symptoms. *International Journal of Eating Disorders, 28,* 303–310.

Mathes, W. F., Brownley, K. A., Mo, X., & Bulik, C. M. (2009). The biology of binge eating. *Appetite, 52,* 545–553.

Mathias, J. L., & Kent, P. S. (1998). Neuropsychological consequences of extreme weight loss and dietary restriction in patients with anorexia nervosa. *Journal of Clinical and Experimental Neuropsychology, 20,* 548–564.

Matthias, R. (2005). Care provision for patients with eating disorders in Europe: What patients get treatment where? *European Eating Disorders Review, 13,* 159–168.

McKay, S. E., Humphries, L. L., Allen, M. E., & Clawson, D. R. (1986). Neuropsychological test performance of bulimia patients. *International Journal of Neuroscience, 30,* 73–80.

McKenzie, J. M., & Joyce, P. R. (1992). Hospitalization for anorexia nervosa. *International Journal of Eating Disorders, 11,* 235–241.

Mehler, P. S., & MacKenzie, T. D. (2009). Treatment of osteopenia and osteoporosis in anorexia nervosa: A systematic review of the literature. *International Journal of Eating Disorders, 42,* 195–201.

Micali, N., Simonoff, E., & Treasure, J. (2007). Risk of major adverse perinatal outcomes in women with eating disorders. *British Journal of Psychiatry, 190,* 255–259.

Micali, N., & Treasure, J. (2009). Biological effects of a maternal ED on pregnancy and foetal development: A review. *European Eating Disorders Review, 17,* 448–454.

Mikolajczyk, E., Grzywacz, A., & Samochowiec, J. (2010). The association of catechol-O-methyltransferase genotype with the phenotype of women with eating disorders. *Brain Research, 1307,* 142–148.

Miller, W. R., & Rollnick, S. (2002). *Motivational Interviewing: Preparing people for change* (2nd ed.). New York, NY: Guilford Press.

Milos, G., Spindler, A., Schnyder, U., & Fairburn, C. G. (2005). Instability of eating disorder diagnoses: Prospective study. *British Journal of Psychiatry, 187,* 573–578.

Mitchell, J. E., & Crow, S. (2006). Medical complications of anorexia nervosa and bulimia nervosa. *Current Opinions in Psychiatry, 19,* 438–443.

Miyake, A., Friedman, N. P., Emerson, M. J., Witzki, A. H., Howerter, A., & Wager, T. D. (2000). The unity and diversity of executive functions and their contributions to complex "Frontal Lobe" tasks: A latent variable analysis. *Cognitive Psychology, 41,* 49–100.

Miyasaka, K., Hosoya, H., Sekime, A., Ohta, M., Amono, H., Matsushita, S., . . . Funakoshi, A. (2006). Association of ghrelin receptor gene polymorphism with bulimia nervosa in a Japanese population. *Journal of Neural Transmission, 113,* 1279–1285.

Møller-Madsen, S., & Nystrup, J. (1992). Incidence of anorexia nervosa in Denmark. *Acta Psychiatrica Scandinavica, 86,* 187–200.

Montague, P. R., Hyman, S. E., & Cohen, J. D. (2004). Computational roles for dopamine in behavioural control. *Nature, 431,* 760–767.

Monteleone, P., Brambilla, F., Bortolotti, F., Ferraro, C., & Maj, M. (1998). Plasma prolactin response to D-fenfluramine is blunted in bulimic patients with frequent binge episodes. *Psychological Medicine, 28*, 975–983.

Monteleone, P., Fabrazzo, M., Tortorella, A., Martiadis, V., Serritella, C., & Maj, M. (2005). Circulating ghrelin is decreased in non-obese and obese women with binge eating disorder as well as in obese non-binge eating women, but not in patients with bulimia nervosa. *Psychoneuroendocrinology, 30*, 243–250.

Monteleone, P., Tortorella, A., Castaldo, E., Di Filippo, C., & Maj, M. (2007). The Leu72Met polymorphism of the ghrelin gene is significantly associated with binge eating disorder. *Psychiatric Genetics, 17*, 13–16.

Monteleone, P., Tortorella, A., Castaldo, E., & Maj, M. (2006). Association of a functional serotonin transporter gene polymorphism with binge eating disorder. *American Journal of Medical Genetics Part B Neuropsychiatric Genetics, 141B*, 7–9.

Monteleone, P., Zanardini, R., Tortorella, A., Gennarelli, M., Castaldo, E., Canestrelli, B., Maj, M. (2006). The 196G/A (val66met) polymorphism of the BDNF gene is significantly associated with binge eating behavior in women with bulimia nervosa or binge eating disorder. *Neuroscience Letters, 406*, 133–137.

Morton, G. J., Cummings, D. E., Baskin, D. G., Barsh, G. S., & Schwartz, M. W. (2006). Central nervous system control of food intake and body weight. *Nature, 443*, 289–295.

Munsch, S., Biedert, E., Meyer, A. H., Herpertz, S., & Beglinger, C. (2009). CCK, ghrelin, and PYY responses in individuals with binge eating disorder before and after a cognitive behavioral treatment (CBT). *Physiology and Behavior, 97*, 14–20.

Nakabayashi, K., Komaki, G., Tajima, A., Ando, T., Ishikawa, M., Nomoto, J., . . . Shirasawa, S. (2009). Identification of novel candidate loci for anorexia nervosa at 1q41 and 11q22 in Japanese by a genome-wide association analysis with microsatellite markers. *Journal of Human Genetics, 54*, 531–537.

National Institute for Health and Clinical Excellence (NICE). (2004). Eating disorders: Core interventions in the treatment and management of anorexia nervosa, bulimia nervosa, and related eating disorders. Accessed at: www.nice.org.uk/page.aspx?o=101239

Neumark-Sztainer, D., Croll, J., Story, M., Hannan, P. J., French, S. A., & Perry, C. (2002). Ethnic/racial differences in weight-related concerns and behaviors among adolescent girls and boys: Findings from Project EAT. *Journal of Psychosomatic Research, 53*, 963–974.

Nicdao, E. G., Hong, S., & Takeuchi, D. T. (2007). Prevalence and correlates of eating disorders among Asian Americans: Results from the National Latino and Asian American Study. *International Journal of Eating Disorders, 40* (Suppl.), S22–S26.

Nussbaum, M., Shenker, I. R., Marc, J., & Klein, M. (1980). Cerebral atrophy in anorexia nervosa. *Journal of Pediatrics, 96*, 867–869.

Ogren, F. P., Huerter, J. V., Pearson, P. H., Antonson, C. W., & Moore, G. F. (1987). Transient salivary gland hypertrophy in bulimics. *Laryngoscope, 97*, 951–953.

Ornstein, R. M., Golden, N. H., Jacobson, M. S., & Shenker, I. R. (2003). Hypophosphatemia during nutritional rehabilitation in anorexia nervosa: Implications for refeeding and monitoring. *Journal of Adolescent Health, 32*, 83–88.

Palmer, R. L. (2003). Death in anorexia nervosa. *Lancet, 361*, 1490.

Perez, M., Joiner, T. J., & Lewinsohn, P. (2004). Is major depressive disorder or dysthymia more strongly associated with bulimia nervosa? *International Journal of Eating Disorders, 36*, 55–61.

Peterson, C. B. (2005) Conducting the diagnostic interview. In J. E. Mitchell & C. B. Peterson (Eds.), *Assessment of eating disorders* (pp. 98–119). New York, NY: Guilford Press.

Peterson, C. B., & Mitchell, J. E. (2005). Self-report measures. In J. E. Mitchell & C. B. Peterson (Eds.), *Assessment of eating disorders* (pp. 98–119). New York, NY: Guilford Press.

Pike, K. M., Wilfley, D., Hilbert, A., Fairburn, C. G., Dohm, F. A., & Striegel-Moore, R. H. (2006). Antecedent life events of binge-eating disorder. *Psychiatry Research, 142*, 19–29.

Polivy, J., & Herman, C. P. (1985). Dieting and binging: a causal analysis. *American Psychologist, 40*, 193–201.

Pumariega, A. J. (1986). Acculturation and eating attitudes in adolescent girls: A comparative and correlational study. *Journal of the American Academy of Child Psychiatry, 25*, 276–279.

Rask-Andersen, M., Olszewski, P. K., Levine, A. S., & Schioth, H. B. (2010). Molecular mechanisms underlying anorexia nervosa: focus on human gene association studies and systems controlling food intake. *Brain Research Reviews, 62*, 147–164.

Reagan, P., & Hersch, J. (2005). Influence of race, gender, and socioeconomic status on binge eating frequency in a population-based sample. *International Journal of Eating Disorders, 38*, 252–256.

Reichborn-Kjennerud, T., Bulik, C., Sullivan, P., Tambs, K., & Harris, J. (2004). Psychiatric and medical symptoms in binge eating in the absence of compensatory behaviors. *Obesity Research, 12*, 1445–1454.

Reitan, R. (1958). Validity of the Trial Making Test as an indication of organic brain damage. *Perceptual and Motor Skills, 8*, 127–130.

Reyes-Rodriguez, M. L., Franko, D. L., Matos-Lamourt, A., Bulik, C. M., Von Holle, A., Camara-Fuentes, L. R., . . . Suárez-Torres, A. (2010). Eating disorder symptomatology: Prevalence among Latino college freshmen students. *Journal of Clinical Psychology, 66*, 666–679.

Ricca, V., Mannucci, E., Mezzani, B., Di Bernardo, M., Zucchi, T., Paionni, A., . . . Faravelli, C. (2001). Psychopathological and clinical features of outpatients with an eating disorder not otherwise specified. *Eating and Weight Disorders, 6*, 157–165.

Rizvi, S. L., Peterson, C. B., Crow, S. J., & Agras, W. S. (2000). Test-retest reliability of the eating disorder examination. *International Journal of Eating Disorders, 28*, 311–316.

Roberts, M. E., Tchanturia, K., Stahl, D., Southgate, L., & Treasure, J. (2007). A systematic review and meta-analysis of set-shifting ability in eating disorders. *Psychological Medicine, 37*, 1075–1084.

Robins, L., Helzer, J., Croughan, J., & Ratcliff, K. (1981). National Institute of Mental Health diagnostic interview schedule: Its history, characteristics, and validity. *Archives of General Psychiatry, 38*, 381–389.

Robinson, T. N., Killen, J. D., Litt, I. F., Hammer, L. D., Wilson, D. M., Haydel, K. F., . . . Taylor, C. B. (1996). Ethnicity and body dissatisfaction: Are Hispanic and Asian girls at increased risk for eating disorders? *Journal of Adolescent Health, 19*, 384–393.

Rockert, W., Kaplan, A. S., & Olmsted, M. P. (2007). Eating disorder not otherwise specified: the view from a tertiary care treatment center. *International Journal of Eating Disorders, 40* (Suppl.), S99–S103.

Rosen, D. S. (2010). Identification and management of eating disorders in children and adolescents. *Pediatrics, 126*, 1240–1253.

Rosenblum, J., & Forman, S. F. (2003). Management of anorexia nervosa with exercise and selective serotonergic reuptake inhibitors. *Current Opinions in Pediatrics, 15*, 346–347.

Russell, G. F. M. (1979). Bulimia nervosa: An ominous variant of anorexia nervosa. *Psychological Medicine, 9*, 429–448.

Schacter, D. L. (1999). The seven sins of memory. Insights from psychology and cognitive neuroscience. *American Psychologist, 54*, 182–203.

Scherag, S., Hebebrand, J., & Hinney, A. (2010). Eating disorders: The current status of molecular genetic research. *European Child and Adolescent Psychiatry, 19*, 211–226.

Schmidt, U., Troop, N., & Treasure, J. (1999). Events and the onset of eating disorders: Correcting an "age old" myth. *International Journal of Eating Disorders, 25*, 83–88.

Shapiro, J. R., Berkman, N. D., Brownley, K. A., Sedway, J. A., Lohr, K. N., & Bulik, C. M. (2007). Bulimia nervosa treatment: A systematic review of randomized controlled trials. *International Journal of Eating Disorders, 40,* 321–336.

Shinohara, M., Mizushima, H., Hirano, M., Shioe, K., Nakazawa, M., Hiejima, Y., . . . Kanba, S. (2004). Eating disorders with binge-eating behaviour are associated with the s allele of the 3'-UTR VNTR polymorphism of the dopamine transporter gene. *Journal of Psychiatry and Neuroscience, 29,* 134–137.

Slof-Op't Landt, M., van Furth, E., Meulenbelt, I., Slagboom, P., Bartels, M., Boomsma, D., & Bulik, C. M. (2005). Eating disorders: From twin studies to candidate genes and beyond. *Twin Research and Human Genetics, 16,* 467–482.

Spitzer, R. L., Stunkard, A., Yanovski, S., Marcus, M. D., Wadden, T., Wing, R., . . . Hasin, D. (1993). Binge eating disorder should be included in *DSM-IV*: A reply to Fairburn et al.'s "The classification of recurrent overeating: The binge eating disorder proposal." *International Journal of Eating Disorders, 13,* 161–169.

Steiger, H. (2004). Eating disorders and the serotonin connection: State, trait and developmental effects. *Journal of Psychiatry and Neuroscience, 29,* 20–29.

Steiger, H., Gauvin, L., Israel, M., Kin, N., Young, S., & Roussin, J. (2004). Serotonin function, personality-trait variations, and childhood abuse in women with bulimia-spectrum eating disorders. *Journal of Clinical Psychiatry, 65,* 830–837.

Steiger, H., Lehoux, P. M., & Gauvin, L. (1999). Impulsivity, dietary control and the urge to binge in bulimic syndromes. *International Journal of Eating Disorders, 26,* 261–274.

Steiger, H., Richardson, J., Joober, R., Gauvin, L., Israel, M., Bruce, K. R., . . . Young, S. N. (2007). The 5HTTLPR polymorphism, prior maltreatment and dramatic-erratic personality manifestations in women with bulimic syndromes. *Journal of Psychiatry and Neuroscience, 32,* 354–362.

Steiger, H., Richardson, J., Joober, R., Israel, M., Bruce, K. R., Ng Ying Kin, N. M., . . . Gauvin, L. (2008). Dissocial behavior, the 5HTTLPR polymorphism, and maltreatment in women with bulimic syndromes. *American Journal of Medical Genetics Part B Neuropsychiatric Genetics, 147B,* 128–130.

Steinglass, J., Walsh, B., & Stern, Y. (2006). Set shifting deficit in anorexia nervosa. *Journal of the International Neuropsychological Society, 12,* 431–435.

Striegel-Moore, R., Dohm, F., Kraemer, H., Taylor, C., Daniels, S., Crawford, P., & Schreiber, G. B. (2003). Eating disorders in white and black women. *American Journal of Psychiatry, 160,* 1326–1331.

Striegel-Moore, R., Leslie, D., Petrill, S., Garvin, V., & Rosenheck, R. (2000). One-year use and cost of inpatient and outpatient services among female and male patients with an eating disorder: Evidence from national database of health insurance claims. *International Journal of Eating Disorders, 27,* 381–389.

Striegel-Moore, R., Silberstein, L., & Rodin, J. (1986). Toward an understanding of risk factors for bulimia. *American Psychologist, 41,* 246–263.

Striegel-Moore, R. H., & Bulik, C. M. (2007). Risk factors for eating disorders. *American Psychologist, 62,* 181–198.

Striegel-Moore, R. H., Cachelin, F. M., Dohm, F. A., Pike, K. M., Wilfley, D. E., & Fairburn, C. G. (2001). Comparison of binge eating disorder and bulimia nervosa in a community sample. *International Journal of Eating Disorders, 29,* 157–165.

Striegel-Moore, R. H., & Franko, D. L. (2003). Epidemiology of binge eating disorder. *International Journal of Eating Disorders, 34* (Suppl.), S19–S29.

Striegel-Moore, R. H., Wilfley, D. E., Pike, K. M., Dohm, F. A., & Fairburn, C. G. (2000). Recurrent binge eating in black American women. *Archives of Family Medicine, 9,* 83–87.

Strober, M., Freeman, R., Lampert, C., Diamond, J., & Kaye, W. (2000). Controlled family study of anorexia nervosa and bulimia nervosa: Evidence of shared liability and transmission of partial syndromes. *American Journal of Psychiatry, 157*, 393–401.

Strober, M., Freeman, R., & Morrell, W. (1997). The long-term course of severe anorexia nervosa in adolescents: Survival analysis of recovery, relapse, and outcome predictors over 10–15 years in a prospective study. *International Journal of Eating Disorders, 22*, 339–360.

Stunkard, A., & Messick, S. (1985). Three-factor eating questionnaire to measure dietary restraint, disinhibition, and hunger. *Journal of Psychosomatic Research, 29*, 71–83.

Stunkard, A. J. (1959). Eating patterns and obesity. *Psychiatric Quarterly, 33*, 284–295.

Sullivan, P. F., Bulik, C. M., Fear, J. L., & Pickering, A. (1998). Outcome of anorexia nervosa. *American Journal of Psychiatry, 155*, 939–946.

Sullivan, P. F., Bulik, C. M., & Kendler, K. S. (1998). The epidemiology and classification of bulimia nervosa. *Psychological Medicine, 28*, 599–610.

Surguladze, S. (1995). Insight and characteristics of fixed set in patients with schizophrenia. *Journal of Georgian Medicine, 2*, 59–60.

Szczypka, M. S., Rainey, M. A., & Palmiter, R. D. (2000). Dopamine is required for hyperphagia in Lep(ob/ob) mice. *Nature Genetics, 25*, 102–104.

Szmukler, G., Andrewes, D., Kingston, K., Chen, L., Stargatt, R., & Stanley, R. (1992). Neuropsychological impairment in anorexia nervosa before and after refeeding. *Journal of Clinical and Experimental Neuropsychology, 14*, 347–352.

Taylor, J. Y., Caldwell, C. H., Baser, R. E., Faison, N., & Jackson, J. S. (2007). Prevalence of eating disorders among Blacks in the National Survey of American Life. *International Journal of Eating Disorders, 40*, 10–14.

Tchanturia, K., Morris, R. G., Anderluh, M. B., Collier, D. A., Nikolaou, V., & Treasure, J. (2004). Set shifting in anorexia nervosa: an examination before and after weight gain, in full recovery and relationship to childhood and adult OCPD traits. *Journal of Psychiatry Research, 38*, 545–552.

Tchanturia, K., Serpell, L., Troop, N., & Treasure, J. (2001). Perceptual illusions in eating disorders: Rigid and fluctuating styles. *Journal of Behavior Therapy and Experimental Psychiatry, 32*, 107–115.

Thomas, J. J., Vartanian, L. R., & Brownell, K. D. (2009). The relationship between eating disorder not otherwise specified (EDNOS) and officially recognized eating disorders: Meta-analysis and implications for DSM. *Psychological Bulletin, 135*, 407–433.

Thompson, J. K., Coovert, M. D., Richards, K. J., Johnson, S., & Cattarin, J. (1995). Development of body image, eating disturbance, and general psychological functioning in female adolescents: Covariance structure modeling and longitudinal investigations. *International Journal of Eating Disorders, 18*, 221–236.

Thompson, J. K., & Heinberg, L. J. (1993). Preliminary test of two hypotheses of body image disturbance. *International Journal of Eating Disorders, 14*, 59–63.

Thompson, J. K., & Spana, R. E. (1991). Visuospatial ability, accuracy of size estimation, and bulimic disturbance in a noneating-disordered college sample: A neuropsychological analysis. *Perceptual and Motor Skills, 73*, 335–338.

Tozzi, F., Thornton, L., Klump, K., Bulik, C., Fichter, M., Halmi, K., . . . Kaye, W. H. (2005). Symptom fluctuation in eating disorders: Correlates of diagnostic crossover. *American Journal of Psychiatry, 162*, 732–740.

Treasure, J., & Campbell, I. (1994). The case for biology in the aetiology of anorexia nervosa. *Psychological Medicine, 24*, 3–8.

Turner, H., & Bryant-Waugh, R. (2003). Eating disorders not otherwise specified (EDNOS): Profiles of clients presenting at a community eating disorders service. *European Eating Disorders Review, 12*, 18–26.

Tury, F., Gulec, H., & Kohls, E. (2010). Assessment methods for eating disorders and body image disorders. *Journal of Psychosomatic Research, 69*, 601–611.

Twamley, E. W., & Davis, M. C. (1999). The sociocultural model of eating disturbances in young women: The effects of personal attributes and family environment. *Journal of Social and Clinical Psychology, 18*, 467–489.

Uznadze, D. N. (1966). *The psychology of set.* New York, NY: Consultants' Bureau.

Vander Wal, J., & Thomas, N. (2004). Predictors of body image dissatisfaction and disturbed eating attitudes and behaviors in African American and Hispanic. *Eating Behaviors, 5,* 291–301.

Vaswani, M., Linda, F. K., & Ramesh, S. (2003). Role of selective serotonin reuptake inhibitors in psychiatric disorders: A comprehensive review. *Progress in Neuropsychopharmacology and Biological Psychiatry, 27*, 85–102.

Ventura, R., Latagliata, E. C., Morrone, C., La Mela, I., & Puglisi-Allegra, S. (2008). Prefrontal norepinephrine determines attribution of "high" motivational salience. *PLoS One, 3*, e3044.

Ventura, R., Morrone, C., & Puglisi-Allegra, S. (2007). Prefrontal/accumbal catecholamine system determines motivational salience attribution to both reward-and aversion-related stimuli. *Proceedings of the National Academy of Science USA, 104*, 5181–5186.

Vitousek, K., Daly, M., & Heiser, C. (1991). Reconstructing the internal world of the eating-disordered individual: Overcoming denial and distortionin self-report. *International Journal of Eating Disorders, 10*, 647–666.

Wade, T., Bergin, J., Tiggemann, M., Bulik, C., & Fairburn, C. (2006). Prevalence and long-term course of eating disorders in an adult Australian cohort. *Australian and New Zealand Journal of Psychiatry, 40*, 121–128.

Wade, T. D. (2007). Epidemiology of eating disorders: Creating opportunities to move the current classification paradigm forward. *International Journal of Eating Disorders, 40* (Suppl.), S27–S30.

Wagner, A., Greer, P., Bailer, U. F., Frank, G. K., Henry, S. E., Putnam, K., . . . Kaye, W. H. (2005). Normal brain tissue volumes after long-term recovery in anorexia and bulimia nervosa. *Biological Psychiatry, 59*, 291–293.

Waller, G. (1993). Association of sexual abuse and borderline personality disorder in eating disordered women. *International Journal of Eating Disorders, 13*, 259–263.

Walsh, B. (1992). Diagnostic criteria for eating disorders in *DSM-IV*: Work in progress. *International Journal of Eating Disorders, 11*, 301–304.

Walsh, B. T., & Garner, D. M. (1997). Diagnostic issues. In D. M. Garner & P. E. Garfinkel (Eds.), *Handbook of treatment for eating disorders* (2nd ed., pp. 25–33). New York, NY: Guilford Press.

Walsh, B. T., Kaplan, A. S., Attia, E., Olmsted, M., Parides, M., Carter, J. C., . . . Rockert, W. (2006). Fluoxetine after weight restoration in anorexia nervosa: A randomized controlled trial. *Journal of the American Medical Association, 295*, 2605–2612.

Walsh, B. T., & Sysko, R. (2009). Broad categories for the diagnosis of eating disorders (BCD-ED): An alternative system for classification. *International Journal of Eating Disorders, 42*, 754–764.

Wang, K., Zhang, H., Bloss, C. S., Duvvuri, V., Kaye, W., Schork, N. J., . . . Hakonarson, H. (in press). A genome-wide association study on common SNPs and rare CNVs in anorexia nervosa. *Molecular Psychiatry.*

Watson, T., & Andersen, A. (2003). A critical examination of the amenorrhea and weight criteria for diagnosing anorexia nervosa. *Acta Psychiatrica Scandinavica, 108*, 175–182.

Welch, S., Doll, H., & Fairburn, C. (1997). Life events and the onset of bulimia nervosa: A controlled study. *Psychological Medicine, 27*, 515–522.

Wilfley, D., Freidman, M., Dounchis, J., Stein, R., Welch, R., & Ball, S. (2000). Comorbid psychopathology in binge eating disorder: relation to eating disorder severity at baseline and following treatment. *Journal of Consulting and Clinical Psychology, 68*, 641–649.

Wilfley, D. E., Schwartz, M. B., Spurrell, E. B., & Fairburn, C. G. (2000). Using the eating disorder examination to identify the specific psychopathology of binge eating disorder. *International Journal of Eating Disorders, 27,* 259–269.

Williams, G. J., Power, K. G., Miller, H. R., Freeman, C. P., Yellowlees, A., Dowds, T., . . . Parry-Jones, W. L. (1994). Development and validation of the Stirling Eating Disorder Scales. *International Journal of Eating Disorders, 16,* 35–43.

Williamson, D. A. (1990). *Assessment of eating disorders: Obesity, anorexia, and bulimia nervosa.* New York, NY: Pergamon Press.

Williamson, D. A., Anderson, D. A., Jackman, L. P., & Jackson, S. R. (1995). Assessment of eating disordered thoughts, feelings, and behaviours. In D. B. Allison (Ed.), *Handbook of assessment methods for eating behaviours and weight related problems. Measures, theory and research* (pp. 347–386). London, England: Sage.

Williamson, D. A., Gleaves, D. H., & Savin, S. S. (1992). Empirical classification of eating disorders not otherwise specified: Support for *DSM-IV* changes. *Psychopathology and Behavioral Assessment, 14,* 201–216.

Wilson, G., Nonas, C., & Rosenbaum, G. (1993). Assessment of binge-eating on obese patients. *International Journal of Eating Disorders, 13,* 25–33.

Wilson, G. T., & Smith, D. (1989). Assessment of bulimia nervosa: An evaluation of the Eating Disorder Examination. *International Journal of Eating Disorders, 8,* 173–179.

Winston, A. P., & Wells, F. E. (2002). Hypophosphatemia following self-treatment for anorexia nervosa. *International Journal of Eating Disorders, 32,* 245–248.

Witt, E., Ryan, C., & Hsu, L. (1985). Learning deficits in adolescents with anorexia nervosa. *Journal of Nervous and Mental Disease, 173,* 182–184.

World Health Organization (WHO). (1990). *Composite International Diagnostic Interview (CIDI).* Geneva, Switzerland: Author.

World Health Organization (WHO). (1992). *International statistical classification of diseases and related health problems* (10th ed., ICD-10). Geneva, Switzerland: Author.

Yanovski, S. Z. (1993). Binge eating disorder: current knowledge and future directions. *Obesity Research, 1,* 306–324.

Zanarini, M. C., Skodol, A. E., Bender, D., Dolan, R., Sanislow, C., Schaefer, E., . . . Gunderson, J. G. (2000). The Collaborative Longitudinal Personality Disorders Study: Reliability of axis I and II diagnoses. *Journal of Personality Disorders, 14,* 291–299.

Zastrow, A., Kaiser, S., Stippich, C., Walther, S., Herzog, W., Tchanturia, K., . . . Friederich, H. C. (2009). Neural correlates of impaired cognitive-behavioral flexibility in anorexia nervosa. *American Journal of Psychiatry, 166,* 608–616.

# CHAPTER 18

# Personality Disorders

CHRISTOPHER J. HOPWOOD and KATHERINE M. THOMAS

ERSONALITY DISORDERS (PDs) represent a major public health concern, as more than 1 in 10 adults in the community meet the diagnostic criteria for at least one PD (Torgersen, 2005; Torgersen, Kringlen, & Cramer, 2001) and PD diagnoses are associated with increased risk for hospitalization (Bender et al., 2001), criminal behavior (Johnson et al., 2000), suicidal behavior (Soloff, Lis, Kelly, & Cornelius, 1994), and dysfunction at work and in relationships (Grant et al., 2004; Skodol et al., 2002; Torgersen, 2005). Relatively few evidence-based treatments are available for PDs (Matusiewicz, Hopwood, Banducci, & Lejuez, 2010), which are notoriously difficult to treat and interfere with treatment of other kinds of disorders (Cyranowski et al., 2004; Feske et al., 2004; Reich, 2003). The wide-ranging clinical importance of normative personality traits thought to predispose personality and other forms of psychopathology is also well-documented (e.g., Lahey, 2009; Ozer & Benet-Martinez, 2006; Roberts, Kuncel, Shiner, Caspi, & Goldberg, 2007). For instance, in one recent study, Cuijpers et al. (2010) estimated that the direct and indirect medical costs for individuals in the top 5% of neuroticism scores are $12,362 per person per year, compared with $7,851 for individuals with mood disorders and $3,641 for the average person.

Despite the clinical significance of personality and personality pathology, representing PDs in a manner that is scientifically valid and clinically useful continues to pose a major challenge. As publication of the *DSM-5* nears, the view that the *DSM-III* and *DSM-IV* model of PDs that has guided recent research and practice is substantially flawed has been commonly advanced, and many alternatives have been suggested (Borsnstein, 1997; Clark, 2007; Hopwood et al., 2011; Krueger et al., 2011; Westen, Shedler, & Bradley, 2006; Widiger & Mullins-Sweat, 2009). Changes to the PDs in the *DSM-5* are likely to be dramatic (Bender et al., 2011; Krueger et al., 2011a, b; Skodol et al., 2011). The new framework has the potential to increase clinical utility and efficiency, more closely link the PDs with evidence-based models of personality and personality pathology, and ultimately lead to an increased focus on personality and PD among clinicians and scholars, with a corresponding improvement in practice and research. However, the proposed *DSM-5* model is not without critics, who have expressed concerns both about its clinical utility (Bornstein, 2011b; Clarkin & Huprich, 2011; Shedler et al., 2010) and its evidentiary basis (Samuel, 2011; Widiger, 2011; Zimmerman, 2011).

We begin this chapter by discussing several concepts relevant to the definition of personality pathology and PD. We next describe the *DSM-IV* PDs in an historical context, review research on the prevalence, etiology, and course of personality pathology, and describe several approaches to its assessment. We close with an evaluation of the *DSM-5* proposal, highlighting differences between the *DSM-IV* and *DSM-5* approaches to PD diagnosis in the context of a clinical case.

## DEFINING PERSONALITY: TRAITS, DYNAMICS, PATHOLOGY, AND DISORDERS

Personality is a broad concept with considerable room for theoretical variation in terms of emphasis on different, even nonoverlapping, components. One way to organize divergent theoretical perspectives is to differentiate those aspects of personality on which they focus. For instance, a protracted rivalry exists in academic personality psychology between those who focus on its more stable or dynamic aspects that extend to the problem of how to classify personality pathology (Wright, 2011). There are also vigorous debates between those who would prefer a more conservative approach to *DSM-5* involving the retention of categorical PD constructs (e.g., Bornstein, 2011a; Gunderson, 2010; Shedler et al., 2010) and those who would overhaul the model more dramatically by utilizing a completely dimensional approach (e.g., Widiger & Mullins-Sweat, 2009; Krueger et al., 2011a).

The *DSM-III* and *DSM-IV* circumvented conceptual debates somewhat by focusing on atheoretical descriptions of personality pathology. The *DSM-IV* defines PD as "an enduring pattern of inner experience and behavior that deviates markedly from the expectations of the individual's culture, is pervasive and inflexible, has an onset in adolescence or early adulthood, is stable over time, and leads to distress or impairment" (APA, 2000, p. 685). The *DSM-IV* describes 10 instantiations of PD, organized into three clusters: Cluster A: schizotypal, schizoid, and paranoid; Cluster B: antisocial, borderline, histrionic, and narcissistic; and Cluster C: avoidant, dependent, and obsessive-compulsive.

These specific PDs, their clustering, and their criteria were selected as much based on clinical legacy in the medical and psychoanalytic perspectives on personality, and the collective wisdom of a specific group of committee members with diverse theoretical perspectives, as they were for their empirical support or conceptual coherence (Widiger, 1993). While the atheoretical approach of the *DSM-III* and *DSM-IV* had many advantages, notably including its apparently having affected a dramatic increase in PD research, it has become clear that important conceptual issues must be addressed more directly for PD classification to move forward. To clarify some of these conceptual issues, we will begin by distinguishing four broad domains of personality that are relevant to debates on the nature of personality and related pathology: traits, dynamics, pathology, and disorders. These definitions will provide a framework for discussing various perspectives on PD classification in the remainder of this chapter.

PERSONALITY TRAITS

Personality traits are enduring features of personality that are (a) cultural universal (McCrae & Terracciano, 2005), (b) heritable (Jang, Livesley, & Vernon, 1996), (c) linked to specific neurobiological structures (DeYoung, 2010) and pathways (Depue & Lenzenweger, 2005), (d) well-characterized in terms of content and course (Soldz & Valliant, 2002), (e) valid for predicting a host of important life outcomes (Roberts et al., 2007), and (f) amenable to reliable assessment, particularly via self-report questionnaires (Samuel & Widiger, 2006). The Five-Factor Model (FFM) currently represents the most viable model of normative personality traits, having the advantage of decades of empirical justification (Digman, 1990) and extensive theoretical articulation (Costa & McCrae, 2006). In the FFM, five normally distributed traits represent the broadest level of variation in personality: neuroticism, extraversion, openness to experience, agreeableness, and conscientiousness. These traits provide a context for all human behavior, and certain constellations of these traits make personality pathology in general and certain forms of PD more or less likely (Morey et al., 2002; Samuel & Widiger, 2008; Saulsman & Page, 2004).

From the perspective of the *DSM-IV*, personality traits such as those of the FFM are enduring features with broad implications for behavior across many situations. These features become clinically relevant when they are "inflexible and maladaptive and cause significant functional impairment or subjective distress" (APA, 2000, p. 686). This distinction implies a discontinuity between traits and their maladaptive consequences under conditions of inflexibility and extremity. However, an explicit linkage between traits and associated dysfunction invites a dimensional view of personality pathology, in which differences between trait and PD are quantitative rather than qualitative. Indeed, evidence suggests that the cluster model of the *DSM-IV* is not valid (Lenzenweger & Clarkin, 2005) and that the disorders are overlapping blends of polythetic and potentially common traits (Widiger et al., 1991), suggesting scientific advantages to viewing personality pathology dimensionally. These potential advantages have led some theorists to suggest defining PDs as reflecting extreme or maladaptive variants of normative traits (Widiger, 1993).

However, several research findings prescribe pause in equating personality pathology with extreme scores on normative traits (Hopwood, 2011). First, relations between normative traits and PDs are not unique or special; normative traits relate systematically to most forms of psychopathology (Cuijpers et al., 2010), just as they relate to a wide variety of individual differences in human behavior (Ozer & Benet-Martinez, 2006). Second, there are potential structural differences between normal and pathological personality traits (Krueger et al., 2011a, b). Third, personality traits and disorders can be distinguished empirically in terms of stability and incremental validity (Hopwood & Zanarini, 2010; Morey et al., 2007; Morey & Zanarini, 2000; Warner et al., 2004). Stable trait concepts are also limited for conceptualizing dynamic and contingent aspects of social behavior and emotional experiences related to personality and related pathology, which we describe next.

PERSONALITY DYNAMICS

Mischel's 1968 text *Personality and Assessment* initiated a major conflict in personality psychology between those who view personality as comprising stable traits and those who see personality primarily as a function of situational contingencies (see *Journal of Research in Personality*, issue 43[2]). Although it has been difficult and contentious, this debate has had several positive consequences. With regard to personality stability, trait psychologists were prompted to develop methods that could more convincingly show that traits can be reliably assessed, are stable, and are valid predictors of important behaviors. Equally relevant to contemporary models of PD, this debate led to the development of new models for understanding how traits and situations interact in "*if . . . then*" behavioral signatures (Mischel & Shoda, 1995). For instance, *if* a conscientious person is on the clock, *then* she will typically attend to her work. This logic extends to PD (Wright, 2011): *If* a person with borderline PD is exposed to rejection, *then* he will tend to react in a self-damaging manner. Notably, this formulation, while inconsistent with a simple trait-behavior formulation of personality (Clarkin & Huprich, 2011), is consonant with several previous models, including Lewin's (1936) classic equation that personality is a function of the person and the environment, or object-relations models that assert that behavior is influenced by the elicitation of self-other dyad units by the parameters of current, actual social situations (Kernberg & Caligor, 2005). As such, the concept of the behavioral signature both reemphasizes and builds upon a long tradition in personality and clinical psychology that emphasizes the moderation of trait-relevant behavior by situational contingencies.

Understanding dynamic elements of personality may be particularly important given recent research suggesting that PD symptoms vary in their stabilities (McGlashan et al., 2005). However, research aimed at conceptualizing the behavioral signatures associated with PDs is just beginning. Most of the work in this area has involved borderline PD, likely because intraindividual variability in emotion and behavior is thematic of the disorder (Schmideberg, 1959). Research using ecological momentary assessment—in which assessments occur several times per day over several days—has generally showed increased variability in mood, interpersonal behavior, and self-esteem among borderline individuals (Sadikaj, Russell, Moskowitz, & Paris, 2010; Trull et al., 2008; Zeigler-Hill & Abraham, 2006). Ongoing and future work exploring the intraindividual dynamics associated with particular kinds of personality problems will be important for assimilating dynamic behavioral signatures into conceptualizations of personality pathology and PD.

## SEVERITY OF PERSONALITY PATHOLOGY

Several PD theorists have distinguished defining features of personality pathology from the stylistic manifestations of personality disorders (Bornstein, 2011a; Kernberg, 1984; Livesley, 1998; Pincus, 2005; Pincus & Hopwood, in press). From this perspective, personality pathology indicates whether a person has a clinically significant PD diagnosis as well as the overall level or severity of personality-related dysfunction, whereas PDs (described later) reflect symptom constellations that vary across individuals, independent of the severity of their overall personality pathology. For example, the *DSM-IV* distinguishes the defining characteristics of PD in general from symptom criteria for 10 specific PD types. However, in the *DSM-IV* model, personality pathology is not quantified, and the PD symptoms conflate aspects of pathological severity and its stylistic manifestations. This conflation likely contributes to unnecessarily high comorbidity among the PDs (Parker et al., 1998).

Empirical research supports the distinction between personality pathology and stylistic aspects of PDs. Parker et al. (2004) derived two higher-order factors from an assessment of the basic elements of personality pathology, which they labeled cooperativeness (ability to love) and coping (ability to work). These factors correlated nonspecifically with PDs and differentiated clinical and nonclinical samples. Hopwood et al. (2011) factor-analyzed PD symptoms after variance in each symptom associated with a general pathology factor was removed. The severity composite explained most of the variance in functional outcomes, but the five stylistic dimensions, which were labeled peculiarity, deliberateness, instability, withdrawal, and fearfulness, incremented this composite for predicting several specific outcomes. Importantly, these stylistic dimensions were completely independent of the overall level of personality pathology severity and were mostly independent of normative traits. Morey et al. (2011) assessed personality pathology with items from questionnaires designed to assess global personality dysfunction. By refining these item sets using a host of psychometric procedures, they showed, in two large and diverse samples, that greater severity was associated with greater likelihood of PD diagnosis and higher rates of comorbidity.

## PERSONALITY DISORDER STYLE

Delineating stylistic aspects of PD would represent a significant challenge even if global personality pathology were effectively separated from PD features. The *DSM-IV* proposes 10 PDs, but given the conflation of severity and style in the *DSM-IV* (Parker et al., 1998), it is possible that fewer than 10 stylistic dimensions would be sufficient for depicting the stylistic variability in PD expression. The Hopwood et al. (2011) study discussed previously identified five reliable PD dimensions, although that study was constrained by the *DSM-IV* content that was factor-analyzed. To the degree that the *DSM-IV* symptom criteria are not comprehensive (e.g., they do not include symptoms from appendicized diagnoses and may not fully capture the content of some disorders [e.g., Pincus et al., 2011]), it is possible that other important dimensions exist. Thus, an important question for ongoing research is: How many PD dimensions are there?

We will discuss this issue in more detail as follows, but for now we suggest that decisions about what PDs to keep or remove and whether PDs should be conceptualized as polythetic syndromes or trait constellations should be based on empirical evidence. Given that evidence is currently insufficient for such decisions, whatever is decided for *DSM-5* will be necessarily questionable and temporary. For this reason, it is wise that the *DSM-5* is being conceived of as a living document subject to ongoing empirical and conceptual refinement (Krueger et al., 2011a, b). From our perspective, the process for making decisions about which PD constructs are sufficiently valid for routine clinical consideration should be regarded as a psychometric matter (Loevinger, 1957).

The PDs listed in the *DSM-IV* and its appendix offer a reasonable starting point as a list of hypothetical constructs in the PD domain (MacCorquodale & Meehl, 1948).

The first step in establishing their construct validity would involve describing their theoretical contents thoroughly. Next, these contents would be measured using multiple assessment methods in diverse samples. The constructs would then be refined based on the psychometric considerations, including (a) replicability of factor structure, (b) discriminant validity relative to one another, personality pathology, and normative traits, (c) freedom from bias, (d) reliability, and (e) criterion validity. Clinically efficient methods for their assessment would then be developed and field tested, permitting subjugation to further refinement through psychometric procedures. Ideally, the resulting constructs would provide a means for developing a coherent theory of PD style that could facilitate clinical formulations, future research, and testable inferences about dynamic processes.

Several investigators have undertaken projects along these lines, leading to the development of Clark's (1993) *Schedule for Nonadaptive and Adaptive Personality*, Livesley and Jackson's (2006) *Dimensional Assessment of Personality Problems*, and the *DSM-5* trait proposal (Krueger et al., 2011a, b). This line of work provides an important foundation for the process of depicting PD and delineates areas needing further study. For example, because all of these research programs have relied nearly exclusively on self-report questionnaires, which may be limited in some respects for assessing PD (Huprich & Bornstein, 2007), future investigations should employ multiple assessment methods. Second, variance in the structure of each of these models needs to be resolved to build consensual models of PD. Third, each of these models has been guided by an underlying trait perspective on PD classification, and the integration of these approaches with other theoretical approaches, including those that emphasize dynamic or potentially discontinuous aspects of PD or that separate personality pathology from PD, remain unclear.

## The Separation of Personality Pathology and Disorder

Separating severity and style has the potential to improve diagnostic efficiency and predictive validity. This two-part model of personality pathology and PD is analogous to common conceptions of intelligence involving a general component (i.e., *g* or IQ) and specific components (e.g., verbal versus nonverbal abilities). Clinical diagnosis is determined by the standing on the general component; just as mental retardation is defined by a particularly low IQ score, the diagnosis of personality pathology could be defined by a particularly low score on a measure of general personality functioning. More specific predictions about impairment can be made when severity and stylistic elements are distinguished. For example, clinicians would predict that any individual with mental retardation would do poorly in schoolwork relative to most other students, but they would further predict that individuals with personal strengths in verbal versus nonverbal abilities would perform relatively better in reading than mathematics classes. Analogously, severity of personality pathology may permit predictions about the overall level of treatment needed (e.g., inpatient versus outpatient), whereas PD style permits predictions about how pathology will manifest (e.g., as impulsive social behavior or social withdrawal) and what treatment techniques might be most effective (e.g., group versus individual therapy, pharmacotherapy).

One general issue that requires reconciliation in distinguishing personality pathology severity from style involves their differential association with some PD constructs. Specifically, the terms *borderline* and *narcissism* are treated as distinct disorders in the *DSM-IV*, but they have historically been employed as a general term for personality pathology in several major theories (e.g., Kernberg, 1984; Kohut, 1971). Indeed, empirical models of personality organization appear to relate, conceptually and empirically, to these two PDs (Morey, 2005; Morey et al., 2011). So are narcissistic and borderline PDs discrete, stylistic elements of PD, or are they proxies for personality pathology? These are the kinds of theoretical questions that require resolution through empirical procedures if the field is to make progress toward a more scientifically valid and clinically useful model of personality pathology and disorder. We will return to contemporary issues in PD classification at the end of the chapter. First, we review the historical context of current operationalizations and empirical evidence relating to the prevalence, etiology, and course of PDs as defined by the *DSM-IV*.

## DIAGNOSTIC CONSIDERATIONS: AN HISTORICAL BACKDROP TO THE *DSM-IV*

Clinicians have been interested in pathological manifestations of personality for as long as they have been deriving psychopathology taxonomies. Among the first material approaches on record occurred in the fourth century B.C., when Hippocrates translated the philosophies of ancient Mesopotamia (Sudhoff, 1926) into a taxonomy consisting of four temperaments that he believed corresponded to imbalance in bodily humors: choleric (irritable), melancholic (sad), sanguine (optimistic), and phlegmatic (apathetic). It is notable how similar these temperaments are to contemporary models of human personality (i.e., irritable ~ disagreeable, sad ~ neurotic, sanguine ~ extraverted, and phlegmatic ~ [un]conscientious). Hippocrates developed a taxonomy for psychiatric conditions based on these temperamental factors and other conditions, which included six classes of disease: phrenitis, mania, melancholia, epilepsy, hysteria, and Scythian disease (Menninger, 1963). Clinical theorists such as Galen added complexity to early Greek models throughout the Middle Ages and Renaissance, but the quasi-medical approach to classification and basic categories remained fairly similar and continued to be influenced somewhat by supernatural assumptions.

In the 17th century, scientific approaches began to supplant concepts that were rooted in clinical descriptions colored by metaphysical theories. The enhanced focus on falsifiable methods from the 17th century onward paved the way for contemporary models in descriptive psychiatry. Emil Kraepelin, who produced nine volumes of clinical psychiatry textbooks from 1883 to 1927 that represented a standard text on psychiatric classification during his lifetime and for many years to follow, is widely regarded as the pioneer of this movement. The aspect of his approach that set him apart from previous theorists was his focus on the course of disorders, in addition to their signs and symptoms. The concept of course is particularly important for PDs, which have been distinguished from other disorders based on the presumption that they are relatively more enduring. Given his focus on course and the historical importance of personality pathology, it is not surprising that many of the concepts in Kraepelin's textbook are easily identified in the *DSM* PDs. This link is also due to Kraepelin's influence on early-20th-century efforts to categorize mental disorders in the United States (Menninger, 1963). In the middle of that century, Kraepelinian concepts were blended with psychoanalytic ideas by major figures such as Adolf Meyer and William Alanson White, who contributed significantly to the conceptual models of psychopathology underlying the first *DSM*.[1]

### *DSM-I* AND *DSM-II*

PDs have appeared in every edition of the *Diagnostic and Statistical Manual of Mental Disorders* (DSM; American Psychiatric Association [APA], 1952; 1968; 1980; 1987; 1994; 2000). In the *DSM-I*, they were

> characterized by developmental defects or pathological trends in personality structure, with minimal subjective anxiety, and little or no sense of distress. In most instances, the disorder is manifested by a lifelong pattern of action or behavior, rather than by mental or emotional symptoms. (APA, 1952, p. 34)

These three pillars of PD definition have persisted in subsequent editions: PDs are thought to be developmental, stable, and ego-syntonic.

The *DSM-I* employed a narrative rating system for diagnosing PDs, meaning that clinicians were expected to determine a diagnosis based on the perceived match between a patient's behavior and a description of pathological prototypes in the manual. PDs in *DSM-I* were separated into distinct groups. Personality pattern disturbances were regarded as "deep-seated," "with little room for regression." These included the inadequate, schizoid, cyclothymic, and paranoid types. Personality trait disturbances referred to conditions brought about by stress, which were thought to indicate latent weaknesses in the underlying personality structure. These included emotional instability, passive aggression, compulsivity, and an "other" category. Sociopathic personality disturbances were similar to personality trait disturbances, but their manifestation was thought to be driven primarily by a mismatch between an individual's behavior and cultural norms. Such disturbances included antisocial and dyssocial reactions, sexual deviance, and substance abuse.

Although the second edition of the *DSM* (APA, 1968) brought with it some theoretical and classificatory changes to the PDs, it remained very similar in underlying approach and in content to the first edition. The primary change was the removal of the three diagnostic subcategories in favor of the more straightforward depiction of 10 distinct types, largely carrying over from *DSM-I*. Specifically, dependent and aggressive subtypes of passive aggressive personality were collapsed, compulsive personality was reconceptualized and renamed obsessive-compulsive personality, dyssocial personality was renamed explosive personality,

---

1. Kraepelin's conceptualizations also profoundly influenced theories of psychiatric classification in other countries, and the World Health Organization's *International Classification of Diseases* (ICD) PD model significantly parallels that of the *DSM-IV*.

and asthenic personality, conceptualized as involving dependency and compromised character strength, was added. Finally, although PDs continued to be differentiated from other disorders in terms of their supposed ego-syntonicity, the assertion that patients with PDs routinely did not experience distress as a result of their personality pathology was tempered (Oldham, 2005).

## DSM-III AND DSM-IV

In order to improve diagnostic reliability, *DSM-III* categories were rated based on atheoretical, behavioral symptom criteria rather than prototype descriptions that were rooted in the formulations of specific theories and required relatively more clinical inference. The *DSM-III* also introduced the multiaxial system, in which a distinction was made between Axis I conditions (thought to be acute, ego-dystonic, and relatively amenable to treatment) and Axis II conditions (thought to be enduring, ego-syntonic, and relatively resistant to treatment), with PDs belonging to Axis II. Four *DSM-II* PDs were either eliminated (inadequate and asthenic) or moved to Axis I (cyclothymic and explosive). Schizoid PD was separated into schizoid (defined by interpersonal aloofness), schizotypy (defined by odd behavior), and avoidant (defined by fear of interpersonal criticism/embarrassment) PDs. Two new PD diagnoses, borderline and narcissistic, were introduced in *DSM-III*. Finally, the PDs were grouped into three clusters based on their degree of shared phenomenology: Cluster A consisted of schizoid, schizotypal, and paranoid; Cluster B of borderline, histrionic, narcissistic, and antisocial; and Cluster C of obsessive-compulsive, avoidant, dependent, and passive-aggressive.

The *DSM-IV* largely retained this system, with three major exceptions: (1) the antisocial criteria were simplified somewhat; (2) a paranoid/dissociation criterion was added to borderline; and (3) passive-aggressive PD was appendicized. The rationale for removing passive-aggressive PD was that it referred to a narrow behavioral tendency, rather than a broad personality syndrome (Millon & Radovanov, 1995), although this view has been challenged on rational (Wetzler & Morey, 1999) and empirical (Hopwood et al., 2009) grounds. Finally, personality pathology was formally operationalized, separately from the criteria of each specific PD. It was defined as (a) an enduring pattern of inner experience and behavior that deviates markedly from the expectations of the individual's culture and is manifested in at least two of the following areas: cognition, affectivity, interpersonal functioning, or impulsive control; (b) pervasive across a broad range of personal and social situations; (c) leading to clinically significant impairment in social, occupational, or other important areas of functioning; (d) stable with an onset that can be traced back at least to adolescence or early adulthood; (e) not better accounted for by another mental disorder; and (f) not due to the direct physiological effects of a substance or medical condition. Criteria sets were polythetic for all PDs, whereas in the *DSM-III* criteria for some PDs had been more typological and impressionistic due to limited theoretical and empirical understanding. For example, a patient would have to meet all three of the *DSM-III-R* dependent PD criteria for the diagnosis, including passively allowing others to assume responsibility, subordinating needs to others, and lacking self-confidence. In the *DSM-IV*, a patient would need to meet five of eight symptoms, including difficulties initiating projects on one's own and urgently seeking new relationships for support when old relationships end. While this change enhanced the reliability of the PDs (Pfohl, Coryell, Zimmerman, & Stangl, 1986), the increased use of polythetic criteria may have also worsened the problems of construct heterogeneity and diagnostic overlap (Gunderson, 2010).

## CLINICAL PICTURE: THE *DSM-IV* PERSONALITY DISORDERS

Having described the clinical importance of personality pathology, defined the central concepts of personality and related pathology, and reviewed the history of PD taxonomy, we will now focus on clinical manifestations of the PDs listed in the *DSM-IV-TR* (APA, 2000). Cluster A consists of paranoid, schizoid, and schizotypal PDs, which are thought to share odd and eccentric features. These disorders are associated with psychotic disorders phenomenologically and etiologically (Maier, Lichtermann, Minges, & Heun, 1994) but are distinguished by their lack of persistent psychotic symptoms (i.e., hallucinations and delusions). *Paranoid* PD is defined by a pervasive pattern of distrust and beliefs that others' motives are malevolent. Symptoms involve suspiciousness and consequent social dysfunction, loose and hyper-vigilant thinking, and resentment. *Schizoid* PD is characterized by a pervasive pattern of social detachment and restricted emotional expression. Symptoms include disinterest in relationships and preference for solitude, limited pleasure in sex or other activities commonly regarded as pleasurable, and emotional flatness. The defining feature of *schizotypal* PD is a pervasive pattern of interpersonal deficits, cognitive or perceptual distortions, and eccentric behavior. It is diagnosed by symptoms related to loose or eccentric perceptions and cognitions, flat affect, mistrustfulness, and profound social dysfunction.

Antisocial, borderline, histrionic, and narcissistic PDs comprise Cluster B, which is regarded as the "dramatic, erratic, and emotional" group (APA, 2000). Individuals with these disorders tend to experience emotional dysregulation and behave impulsively. *Antisocial* PD is marked by a pervasive pattern of disregard for the rights and wishes of others (APA, 2000). The *DSM-IV* requires evidence of childhood conduct disorder for a diagnosis of antisocial PD, and additionally includes symptoms of socially non-normative behavior, dishonesty, impulsivity, aggression, lack of empathy, and irresponsibility. *Borderline* PD is characterized by "stable instability" (Schmideberg, 1959) in emotions, interpersonal behavior, and identity. Emotional dysregulation, including anger and emptiness, is thought to be triggered by concerns about abandonment, which is followed by maladaptive coping, including impulsive and suicidal behavior (Zanarini & Frankenburg, 2007). *Histrionic* PD is characterized by excessive emotionality and attempts to obtain attention from others. This desire to be the center of attention often comes at the cost of deep and meaningful interpersonal relationships, as histrionic individuals tend to have relatively superficial interpersonal interactions and shallow emotions. The core of *narcissistic* PD involves grandiose thoughts and behaviors, a need for excessive admiration from others, and a lack of empathy. It is commonly believed that arrogant and haughty behavior is undergirded by feelings of vulnerability and inadequacy.

Cluster C includes avoidant, dependent, and obsessive-compulsive PDs, which are grouped together based on their common thread of anxiety and fearfulness.

*Avoidant* PD is characterized by social inhibition rooted in feelings of inadequacy and fears of negative evaluations from others (APA, 2000). Symptoms include avoidance of social and occupational opportunities, fears of shame and ridicule, and negative self-concept. *Dependent* PD is defined by an excessive need to be cared for by others that leads to submissive, clingy behavior. Symptoms include difficulties making autonomous decisions or expressing disagreement with others, nonassertiveness, preoccupation with abandonment, and maladaptive or self-defeating efforts to seek and maintain relationships. *Obsessive-compulsive* PD is defined by a preoccupation with order, perfection, and control in which flexibility, efficiency, and even task completion are often sacrificed. Symptoms include preoccupation with rules and order, perfectionism, workaholism, interpersonal inflexibility, frugality, and stubbornness.

## RESEARCH ON THE *DSM-IV* PERSONALITY DISORDERS

### Epidemiology

One of the principal advantages of the *DSM-III* and *DSM-IV* model of PDs has been its contribution to the increase in PD research since its publication. However, to the extent that a majority of this research has been based on the *DSM* conception of PDs, its utility is constrained by the validity of the model. Epidemiology instantiates this paradox. Although the development of reliable PD criteria has made it more possible to evaluate the prevalence of PDs, calculating the prevalence of PDs assumes that they are categorical taxa, even though the weight of evidence suggests they are not (Trull & Durrett, 2005), and diagnostic cutoffs in the *DSM-IV* are thus commonly regarded as essentially arbitrary (Cooper, Balsis, & Zimmerman, 2010). As such, it is not clear what to make of PD prevalence rates. With this caveat in mind, we review the results of several epidemiological studies on PD based on *DSM* diagnostic cutoffs.

Overall prevalence estimates indicate that more than 10% of individuals suffer from a PD during their lifetime (Grant et al., 2004; Lenzenweger, Loranger, Korfine, & Neff, 1997; Samuels et al., 2002; Torgersen, 2005; Torgerson et al., 2001). Although prevalence for individual PDs are more variable across studies, research suggests that prevalence ranges between .5% and 5%, with paranoid, avoidant, and obsessive-compulsive PDs being relatively common and dependent and narcissistic PDs being relatively uncommon. PD prevalence is considerably higher in psychiatric settings: research indicates that nearly half of clinical outpatients and more than half of clinical inpatients meet the diagnostic criteria for a PD (Molinari, Ames, & Essa, 1994; Zimmerman, Rothschild, & Chelminski, 2005), making PDs among the most commonly encountered disorders in psychiatric settings. The two most commonly occurring PDs among psychiatric patients are borderline, 10% to 20% (APA, 2000; Zimmerman et al., 2005) and dependent PD. Rates of dependent PD are particularly high among inpatients, 15% to 25% (Jackson et al., 1991; Oldham, 2005), relative to outpatients, 0% to 7% (Mezzich, Fabrega, & Coffman, 1987; Poldrugo & Forti, 1988; Zimmerman et al., 2005).

In contrast, somewhat lower occurrence has been observed for paranoid (2% to 4%; Zimmerman et al., 2005), schizoid, and schizotypal (1% to 2%; Stuart et al., 1998; Zimmerman et al., 2005) patients in clinical settings. The relatively low prevalence may relate to the impact of the paranoia and social avoidance that characterizes these disorders on treatment seeking. Indeed, prevalence estimates for schizoid PD among a homeless population are as high as 14% (Rouff, 2000). Likewise, antisocial PD is seen in 1% to 4% of individuals in a clinical population (Zimmerman et al., 2005), but estimates are considerably higher in prison and substance abuse populations, indicating that individuals with this type of pathology are unlikely to initiate psychological treatment. Somewhat lower prevalence has been observed for narcissistic (2%; Torgersen et al., 2001) and obsessive-compulsive (3% to 9%; Zimmerman et al., 2005) PDs in clinical settings, perhaps owing to the limited functional impact of these PDs relative to others. Rates of histrionic and avoidant PD in clinical patients have been estimated at 10% to 15% (APA, 2000; Zimmerman et al., 2005).

ETIOLOGY

Despite extensive theorizing, empirical evidence regarding the etiology of PDs is quite limited (Paris, 2011; Skodol et al., 2011). Factors contributing to this gap between theory and evidence include a history of underfunding for PD research relative to research on Axis I conditions and various conceptual problems discussed throughout this chapter. Nevertheless, we briefly review etiological contributions related to genes, neurobiology, learning, and cognition presently.

*Genetics* While the broad heritability of personality traits is well-established (McGue, Bacon, & Lykken, 1993; Plomin, DeFries, Craig, & McGuggin, 2003), the heritability of personality pathology and disorders remains more ambiguous (Lenzenweger & Clarkin, 2005). A twin study by Torgersen and colleagues (2000) indicated that the overall 58% of the variance in PDs were due to genes, with specific heritability estimates for each PD as follows: paranoid (.30), schizoid (.31), schizotypal (.62), borderline (.69), histrionic (.67), narcissistic (.77), avoidant (.31), dependent (.55), and obsessive-compulsive (.78). Notably, shared family environment influences were also particularly important in predicting borderline PD. These results led the authors to conclude that PDs may have even stronger genetic influences than most Axis I disorders, similar to broad dimensions of normative personality. Rates of antisocial PD were too low to be included in the Torgersen et al. (2000) study; however, work by other researchers has broadly evidenced that the heritability of aggression is between 44% to 72% (Siever, 2008). A meta-analysis suggests the importance of both genetic and environmental influences on antisocial behavior in men and women, though this influence was measured on antisocial behaviors as opposed to antisocial PD (Rhee & Waldman, 2002). Evidence also suggests higher rates of schizotypal (Kendler et al., 2006) and borderline (Links, Steiner, & Huxley, 1988) PDs among family members of individuals with those disorders, and increased rates of Cluster C PDs among individuals who have relatives with Axis I anxiety disorders (Reich, 1991).

Evidence also suggests interactive effects between genes and the environment, such as the finding that associations between a polymorphism on the MAOA gene is associated with antisocial traits only in individuals who have been exposed to trauma (Caspi et al., 2002). Evidence suggesting an interaction between genes and the early attachment environment may also be crucial in subsequent development of PDs (Siever & Weinstein, 2009). The interplay of genes and environment in the genesis of psychopathology is quite complicated (e.g., Burt, 2009), and much more research is needed with respect to the etiology of PDs. Beyond a basic decomposition of the etiological components of personality pathology and specific PDs, research should begin focusing more on molecular models and the interplay between behavior genetic and environmental risk factors.

*Neurobiology* As with etiology and despite a recent rise in interest in understanding neurological risk factors for the development of PDs (for a review, see Siever & Weinstein, 2009), potential neurobiological endophenotypes for PDs are largely unknown (Paris, 2011; Skodol et al., 2011). It is widely presumed that endophenotypes are more likely to reflect neurobiological dimensions that underlie personality pathology rather than point to pathways to specific PDs. Potential dimensions include those related to cognitive dysregulation, impulsivity, and emotional dysregulation (Depue & Lenzenweger, 2005; Siever & Weinstein, 2009). We will briefly review these three classes of potential endophenotypes and their implications for PDs.

Cluster A PDs, and particularly schizotypal, share features of *cognitive dysregulation* with schizophrenia, including distorted perception and disrupted attention. Cognitive dysregulation is thought to relate to reduced dopamine reactivity in the frontal cortex (Abi-Dargham et al., 1998; Siever & Weinstein, 2009), as well as structural anomalies found in psychotic disorders such as increased ventricular volume (Hazlett et al., 2008). The influence of common endophenotypes represents a promising explanation for descriptive and phenomenological similarities between Cluster A PDs and psychotic disorders (Depue & Lenzenweger, 2005).

*Impulsivity* is a reaction to emotional provocation, implicating a failure in higher-order mental processes that may predispose several PDs, and particularly those in Cluster B (Siever & Weinstein, 2009). Indeed, there is evidence of reduced cortical activation during impulsive behavior (New et al., 2004) and evidence that serotonin plays an important mediating role in the top-down regulation of impulsive, and particularly aggressive, impulses (Brown et al., 1982; Coccaro, Gabriel, & Siever, 1990; Winstanley, Theobald, Dalley, Glennon, & Robbins, 2004) generated from limbic structures (Herpetz et al., 2001).

*Emotional dysregulation* is also related to Cluster B PDs, and it often takes the form of aggressive behavior, making it difficult to distinguish descriptively from impulsivity. Emotional dysregulation is associated with amygdala hyperreactivity (Donegan et al., 2003; Herpertz et al. 2001), suggesting that it may be dynamically related to impulsive behavior: Hypersensitivity to threat leads to emotion dysregulation, and failure to modulate the urge to act based on dysregulated emotion by cortical structures leads to impulsive, often aggressive, behavior. Anxiety is thought to underlie Cluster C PDs, which are responsive to chemical manipulations of serotonin and dopamine (Schneier, Blanco, Anita, & Liebowitz, 2002), suggesting common endophenotypes with mood and anxiety disorders (DeYoung, 2010).

*Learning and Cognition* A large body of theory and empirical evidence supports links among attachment patterns, developmental trauma, and PDs. In particular, attachment patterns are related to the stylistic expression of PD (Meyer & Pilkonis,

2005), and childhood maltreatment is associated with the development of personality pathology in general (Johnson, Cohen, Brown, Smailes, & Bernstein, 1999) and some PDs specifically (e.g., borderline; Zanarini, Gunderson, Marino, & Schwartz, 1989). Several theories have been organized specifically around the interpersonal antecedents of personality pathology. For instance, Benjamin (1996) has formulated each of the *DSM-IV* PDs in terms of specific and testable developmental patterns. She has also outlined a broad framework for conceptualizing developmental "copy processes" that could usefully inform research in this area (Critchfield & Benjamin, 2010). Unfortunately, research is currently too limited to speak with confidence regarding the interpersonal mechanisms that generate or maintain PD; more research is certainly needed on this important but neglected issue.

Cognitive theorists implicate three fundamental aspects of cognition in the development of PDs: automatic thoughts, cognitive distortions, and interpersonal strategies (Pretzer & Beck, 2005). From this perspective, individuals apply automatic (i.e., implicit or unconscious) thoughts to events they encounter that are rooted in deep-seated ways of interpreting the world, learned in early childhood. For some individuals, these automatic thoughts may lead to cognitive distortions, which, in turn, result in maladaptive interpersonal strategies that reinforce and maintain an individual's personality pathology. Several automatic thoughts and cognitive distortions have been hypothesized for specific PDs (Beck & Freeman, 1990). For example, individuals with avoidant PD may be prone to automatic thoughts such as "I am incompetent," whereas individuals with obsessive-compulsive PD are more likely to employ dichotomous thinking (Beck & Freeman, 1990). As with interpersonal models, further research is needed on cognitive models of the genesis and maintenance of personality pathology.

## COURSE AND PROGNOSIS

According to the *DSM-IV*, individuals cannot be diagnosed with personality pathology before age 18, even though pathological personality features should be present during adolescence and early adulthood for a diagnosis during adulthood. This definition is sensitive to the ill-formed nature of personality during the transition to adulthood (Arnett, 2000) and the possibility that personality problems in childhood may reflect developmental challenges that would remit with maturity (although see Shiner, 2009). There is no upper restriction on PD diagnosis in the *DSM-IV*, but most PDs tend to decline in middle age (although see Tackett, Balsis, Oltmanns, & Krueger, 2009). As such, PDs as conceptualized in the *DSM-IV* can generally be regarded as disorders of young to middle adulthood. Within this period, PDs have long been presumed to be stable and pervasive. This assumption has caused significant skepticism regarding prognosis. However, recent research suggests some optimism for therapeutic improvement in that the stability of PDs seems to be lower than was once thought, and treatments have shown benefit for at least some PD symptoms. This research and its implications for conceptualizing personality pathology are discussed presently.

*Course*   Several longitudinal studies of PD in adult clinical samples in the past few decades have shed significant light on the course of PDs (see the special issue of *Journal of Personality Disorders*, volume 20, 2006, for a review of these studies). The Collaborative Longitudinal Personality Disorders (CLPS) study followed individuals with PDs or major depression for 10 years. Early research from this study found that PDs declined rapidly over the first 2 years of follow-up (Grilo et al., 2004). Later research showed that PD features were less stable than personality traits (Morey et al., 2007), and that some PD features declined more rapidly than others (McGlashan et al., 2005), leading to the proposal that personality pathology reflects a hybrid combination of stable, enduring personality traits and dynamic, environmentally contingent symptoms. Zanarini's McLean Study of Adult Development (MSAD) is an ongoing study that has followed individuals with borderline PD and a comparison clinical sample without borderline PD for more than 16 years. As in CLPS, remission from borderline PD was more rapid than anticipated in the MSAD (Zanarini, Frankenburg, Hennen, Reich, & Silk, 2007), and again temperamental and acute symptoms were identified (Zanarini et al., 2007; Hopwood, Donnellan, & Zanarini, 2010). Lenzenweger's Longitudinal Study of Personality Disorder similarly showed, in a college student sample followed for 4 years, that there exists "compelling evidence of change in PD features over time and does not support the assumption that PD features are trait-like, enduring, and stable over time" (Lenzenweger, 2006, p. 662).

Overall, these findings suggest that some aspects of personality pathology are stable, as has been historically assumed, whereas other aspects appear to operate more like the symptoms of Axis I disorders: They are malleable and perhaps reactive to the influence of environmental dynamics. Thus it may be possible, diagnostically, to distinguish aspects of PD that are due to temperamental diatheses from those that are due to dynamic environmental processes, or the interaction between traits and contexts. These promising findings also suggest that some aspects of PD may be subject to change through psychological treatment, a topic to which we now turn.

*Treatment Effects*   There is limited evidence that psychopharmacology is effective for treating PD, with results mostly suggesting that targeted use of medication may benefit certain symptom constellations (e.g., the emotional lability of borderline PD or the cognitive slippage of schizotypal PD; Siever & Weinstein, 2009) but not treat the totality of PD symptoms. Nevertheless, polypharmacy for PDs is common (Zanarini, Frankenburg, Hennen, & Silk, 2004). Perhaps in part because of the longstanding belief that PDs are intractable, relatively few psychosocial treatments have been developed for personality pathology, and most of them have been developed for a single disorder, borderline PD (Matusiewicz et al., 2010). Several issues complicate the effectiveness of psychosocial treatments, including relatively high rates of early dropout (particularly in BPD, c.f. Skodol, Buckley, & Charles, 1983), substantial diagnostic complexity (McGlashan et al., 2000), and the tendency for PD treatment to be unpleasant for clinicians, who may consequently exhibit iatrogenic behavior.

That said, some headway is being made with regard to borderline PD, with several treatments showing benefit in controlled research, including dialectical behavior therapy (Linehan, 1993), transference-focused therapy (Clarkin, Levy, Lenzenweger, & Kernberg, 2007), schema-focused therapy (Giesen-Bloo et al., 2006), psychiatric management (Gunderson, 2008), and mentalization-based therapy (Bateman & Fonagy, 2004). It is notable that these therapeutic models come from very different theoretical backgrounds, yet they share several features, including a highly structured therapeutic frame, a focus on the relationship between therapist and client, and a focus on managing self-damaging behavior through contracting and explicit crisis plans. The treatments also tend to show similar effects in controlled research (Clarkin et al., 2007). One potential conclusion to draw from the similarity of these treatments is that, in dealing with complex phenomena such as PDs, it is more helpful to integrate the wisdom of multiple perspectives than to cling to theoretical dogma. This lesson may fruitfully translate to the issue of PD classification, to which we now turn.

## ASSESSMENT

The manner in which personality pathology and PD are assessed varies across theoretical and measurement approaches, with preferences for particular methods often being related to underlying theoretical assumptions. Common assessment methods are thus organized as follows according to their underlying theoretical foundation. Specifically, we distinguish *DSM*-based, trait, and psychoanalytic approaches to the assessment of personality pathology and PD.

### DSM-IV

The most common and widely accepted method for assessing personality pathology and PD involves translating the *DSM-IV* PD symptoms into questions that individuals can endorse or not, and then determining whether they meet criteria based on the number of symptoms endorsed. Assessing PDs based on *DSM* symptoms can occur either via interview or questionnaire; clinicians tend to prefer unstructured interviews, whereas researchers tend to prefer semistructured interviews or self-report inventories (Widiger & Samuel, 2005). Structured and semistructured interviews are more reliable than unstructured interviews (Rogers, 2001), but unstructured interviews may have the advantages of allowing dynamics between patients and clinicians to occur more naturally and of not requiring patients to have insight into their own personality pathology (Westen, 1997). Conventionally, clinician or research interviews have been regarded as the criterion method for determining whether an individual has a PD. This is partially based on the belief that clinicians are better able to infer meanings and motivations behind client behaviors than individuals with PDs, who are commonly thought to lack insight regarding their pathology.

Numerous measures exist for assessing PDs using the *DSM* model (Widiger & Samuel, 2005). Among the more commonly employed instruments are the clinician-administered *Structured Clinical Interview for DSM-IV TR Axis II Personality Disorders* (SCID-II; First et al., 1997) and the self-report *Personality Disorder Questionnaire* (Hyler, 1994). Given that rates of PD are lower by interview than self-report (Clark & Harrison, 2001; Hopwood et al., 2008), a method advocated by First et al. (1997) and others is to screen for PDs using a self-report questionnaire and then use a clinician-administered semistructured interview as a follow-up procedure to determine whether an individual meets diagnostic criteria for disorders endorsed by self-report.

A primary advantage of the *DSM* symptom–based method is that it provides a consensual way to evaluate PDs and thus increases confidence among clinicians and researchers that they are assessing the same constructs. However, agreement among

DSM-based measures is surprisingly poor (Skodol, Rosnick, Kellman, Oldham, & Hyler, 1991), and assessing PDs from the *DSM* perspective is limited to the degree that the *DSM-III* and *DSM-IV* model is of questionable validity, as many have suggested. Several authors have argued that a more theoretically coherent model is needed to improve methods for assessing personality pathology and disorders. Trait and psychoanalytic models, which are described as follows, may offer desirable theoretical coherence.

## TRAIT MODELS

Building upon consistent evidence that personality traits such as those of the FFM systematically relate to *DSM* PDs (Samuel & Widiger, 2008; Saulsman & Page, 2004), trait researchers have developed methods for deriving PD prototype scores that can be utilized to determine the degree to which a given individual's FFM profile is consistent with a prototypical FFM profile for a given PD (Miller, Bagby, Pilkonis, Reynolds, & Lynam, 2005). A potential advantage to FFM assessment methods is that normal and pathological personality can be evaluated within the same model. This would permit, for example, an assessment of personality strengths that may not be afforded by an exclusive focus on PD constructs. However, one potential limitation to this approach is the possibility that normative measures such as those based on the FFM do not effectively assess some important aspects of personality pathology and disorder (Hopwood, 2011; Krueger et al., 2011a, b; although see also Haigler & Widiger, 2001). It is also possible that the self-report method, on which most trait research relies heavily, may be limited for some aspects of personality pathology assessment (Huprich & Bornstein, 2007).

A related approach to PD assessment involves focusing on maladaptive traits rather than general personality, as in the FFM. The two predominant measures that are used in this regard are the *Dimensional Assessment of Personality Pathology* (Livesley & Jackson, 2006), which was initially developed to test the structure of the *DSM* model but later reformulated as a trait model, and the *Schedule for Nonadaptive and Adaptive Personality* (Clark, 1993), which was developed to provide a means for dimensionally assessing clinically relevant personality and personality pathology traits. Both measures consist of higher-order factors that resemble subsets of FFM traits (Widiger, Livesley, & Clark, 2009) and lower-order factors that assess pathological personality traits. Recently, Krueger and colleagues have developed a questionnaire that is similar to these measures to serve as the basis for pathological trait assessment in the *DSM-5* (Krueger et al., 2011a, 2011b, in review).

## PSYCHOANALYTIC ASSESSMENT

Unlike trait psychologists, psychoanalytically oriented clinicians and researchers tend to prefer clinician ratings or performance-based assessment over self-report methods. There has also been increased interest among psychoanalytic researchers and clinicians in using prototypes to assess PDs. The *Shedler and Westen Assessment Procedure* (SWAP; Westen & Shedler, 1999) is a prototype-based clinician rating method informed by psychoanalytic theory. On the SWAP, clinicians describe their patients' personalities by sorting 200 cards that are applicable to varying degrees to the patient being rated. These sorts can then be compared with prototypes to determine the most likely diagnosis. Evidence suggesting that clinicians tend to think of patients in prototypical terms rather than trait profiles (Rottman, Woo-kyoung, Sanislow, & Kim, 2009; Westen et al., 2006) makes the SWAP and similar procedures appealing. However, prototypes are not without limitations, mainly owing to their potential unreliability (Zimmerman, 2011) and the loss of information that occurs when ratings are made globally. For instance, if a patient is a good match to a given prototype, that could either mean the patient moderately matches nearly all features of the description or matches some features of the description extremely well and others not so well.

Another approach involves using measures that assess features of psychoanalytic theories that deviate from the *DSM* model. For instance, psychoanalysts have developed the *Psychodynamic Diagnostic Manual* (PDM Task Force, 2006; see also *Journal of Personality Assessment* special issue 2, 2011) for this purpose. Other examples include the *Structured Interview of Personality Organization* (Stern et al., 2010) and the *Inventory of Personality Organization* (Kernberg & Clarkin, 1995), which are based on Kernberg's (1984) model of personality pathology. An appealing feature of this model is that it explicitly separates personality pathology (i.e., personality organization) from PDs. However, thus far these measures have been subjected to limited psychometric research.

A third historically psychoanalytic approach to assessing personality pathology involves performance-based assessment methods in which individuals provide open-ended responses to novel stimuli. For example, the *Rorschach Inkblot Method* (Huprich, 2005), in which individuals describe what images they see in a series of inkblots, the Thematic Apperception Test, in which individuals produce stories to go along with pictures, and sentence completion tests (e.g., Hy & Loevinger, 1996) are commonly employed performance-based assessments. Scoring methods have also been developed to score patient narratives as a way of evaluating concepts that are important in psychoanalytic theory, such as defense mechanisms (Cramer, 1991) and the quality of object relations (Westen, 1995).

The primary strengths of psychoanalytic approaches to PD assessment include that they are embedded in a coherent theory of personality pathology and that they may be better suited than interviews and self-reports for identifying pathological personality processes that are outside of individuals' awareness (Huprich & Bornstein, 2007). However, there is limited empirical support for psychoanalytic approaches to PD assessment relative to *DSM*-based and trait assessment instruments, and using methods that are informed heavily by nonconsensual theories risks returning to a time when clinicians used the same terms to mean different things. Furthermore, clinician ratings and performance-based methods are time-consuming relative to questionnaires. Thus, the utility of psychoanalytic approaches could be better judged if they were made as efficient as possible and linked better empirically to other approaches to PD assessment.

SUMMARY

Overall, any assessment method designed to evaluate complicated constructs such as personality pathology and PDs is likely to have strengths and weaknesses.

The optimal strategy is therefore to use multiple assessment methods from varying theoretical perspectives. One example of a more comprehensive approach is the LEAD standard (Pilkonis, Heape, Ruddy, & Serrao, 1991), in which all available current and historical data from any methods are evaluated by a team of expert clinicians to derive the most reliable possible diagnosis.

## THE *DSM-5*

Personality pathology is likely to be significantly reconceptualized in the *DSM-5* (Skodol et al., 2011). In this section, we describe widely recognized problems with the *DSM-IV* model that led to this reconceptualization, the current *DSM-5* proposal, and the impact of the *DSM-5* on scientific validity and clinical utility. We conclude by highlighting differences between the *DSM-IV* and *DSM-5* approach to PD diagnosis with a case study.

### CRITICISMS OF THE *DSM-IV*

Although the *DSM-III* and *DSM-IV* model has catalyzed PD research, the research it has stimulated has contributed to the identification of several limitations of the *DSM-III* and *DSM-IV* system (Clark, 2007). Many limitations relate to the categorical model of PD, which appears to fit nature poorly (Trull & Durrett, 2005), worsens reliability (Heumman & Morey, 1990), and necessitates arbitrary diagnostic cutoffs (Skodol et al., 2011). Others, such as profound diagnostic overlap (Clark, 2007; Oldham, Skodol, Kellman, Hyler, & Rosnick, 1992) and the common use of a not-otherwise-specified category (Verheul & Widiger, 2004), appear to relate to the questionable empirical structure of the PDs (Hopwood et al., 2011). The polythetic format of PD criteria (Krueger et al., 2011a, b), conflation of personality severity and style in PD symptoms (Parker et al., 1998), and the arbitrary diagnostic cutoffs contribute to problematic diagnostic heterogeneity. *DSM-IV* constructs also conflate relatively stable traits with more dynamic symptoms (McGlashan et al., 2005; Zanarini et al., 2007). Finally, as discussed previously, although the *DSM-III* and *DSM-IV* have promoted PD research in general, some PDs are woefully neglected in the research literature, and the *DSM-IV* has not led to the development of effective treatments for most PDs (Widiger & Mullins-Sweatt, 2009).

### THE *DSM-5* PROPOSAL

The *DSM-5* model was designed to address some of these problems toward improving the scientific validity and clinical utility of PD diagnosis. We will first describe the basic elements of the proposal. We will then describe the degree to which it has improved the scientific validity and clinical utility of PD assessment.

The *DSM-5* model as currently proposed[2] (Krueger et al., 2011a, b; Morey et al., 2011; Skodol et al., 2011) includes a general definition of personality pathology which is quantified, six PDs defined by a mix of symptom deficits and pathological traits,

---

2. Note that further changes to the proposal based on feedback and field studies are possible prior to the publication of *DSM-5*.

and a hierarchical system of pathological traits. The general definition of personality pathology is quantified in terms of levels of functioning on two dimensions rated on a five-point scale: self (i.e., self-definition and autonomy) and interpersonal (i.e., intimacy and empathy). Any patient in the diagnostic range would be assessed for the presence of six potential PDs: antisocial, avoidant, borderline, narcissistic, obsessive-compulsive, and schizotypal; the other four *DSM-IV* PDs (schizoid, para-noid, histrionic, and dependent) have been eliminated. There are five criteria for each PD. Criterion A involves the core deficits in self and interpersonal functioning that are specific to that disorder. Criterion B lists the traits that are also thought to undergird each disorder. Criteria C through E specify that these features must be stable, deviant, and not better accounted for by other conditions, respectively. Importantly, patients would need to meet every sub-criterion to meet a diagnosis, although this issue continues to be under active discussion among the *DSM-5* workgroup. Any patient with personality pathology who does meet the criteria for a specific disorder would be classified as PD-trait specified. This specification would be based on a hierarchical model with five higher-order traits (negative affectivity, detachment, antagonism, disinhibition, and psychoticism) and 25 lower order traits (Krueger et al., 2011a, 2011b, in review). These traits could also be used to supplement PD diagnoses, for instance when a patient meets criteria for a certain PD and has several other significant traits, or to describe a patient without any PD diagnosis but with some pathological traits.

## THE SCIENTIFIC VALIDITY OF THE *DSM-5* PROPOSAL

The *DSM-5* proposal appears to improve the scientific validity of PD diagnosis in several respects relative to its predecessor. Research discussed earlier supports the quantification of a general personality pathology factor in terms of levels of functioning, and the contents of this rating scale are based on empirical evidence (Morey et al., 2011) rooted in a large body of theoretical considerations and clinical observations (Bender, Morey, & Skodol, 2011). The PDs that are included retain several concepts such as borderline personality, psychopathy, and schizotypy, with considerable construct validity, and the transition to a more personality-based model of psychopathy (Hare, 1991) improves the definition of that construct considerably. The traits incorporate a dimensional perspective and appear to capture the major traits of other dimensional models (Krueger et al., in review; Wright et al., in review), addressing the most common evidence-based critique of the *DSM-IV* PDs.

However, several aspects of the *DSM-5* have been questioned on empirical grounds. Because the model is so new and uses a somewhat novel approach to PD assessment, critics have argued that not enough is known about its validity (Shedler et al., 2010; Zimmerman, 2011). For instance, the content of the retained PD constructs are changing considerably and although initial evidence suggests that the *DSM-5* covers the content described in the *DSM-IV* relatively well (Hopwood et al., in review), the change from polythetic to absolute criteria may have unintended effects such as significantly lowering the prevalence of the PDs. Some have also questioned whether the proposed trait structure will hold up in future research, particularly since it deviates from other models significantly in its employment of unipolar, as opposed to bipolar, traits (Samuel, 2011). This approach also likely contributes to some odd facet-domain relationships, such as the loading of submissiveness onto negative affectivity (Widiger, 2011, although see also Krueger et al., 2011a).

There is also significant controversy regarding decisions about which PD constructs to retain. The response from the clinical and research community to an initial proposal to delete narcissistic PD (e.g., Pincus, et al., 2011) contributed to the *DSM-5* workgroup's decision to include that disorder in its second proposal. However, paranoid, schizoid, histrionic, and dependent PDs did not return. Individuals with pathology described by these terms in the *DSM-IV* would therefore be trait specified in the *DSM-5*. Decisions regarding which PDs to retain were based primarily on evidence concerning the prevalence of these conditions and the overall body of research for each PD (Skodol et al., 2011). However it is predictable that clinicians and researchers would hesitate to delete PDs that they have grown accustomed to. Furthermore, losing both dependent and histrionic PDs means that the *DSM-5* may be limited in its assessment of pathology related to interpersonal warmth and excessive needs for affiliation, a feature these disorders share (Widiger, 2010) and which are not well-represented in the pathological trait model (Pincus et al., 2011).

## The Clinical Utility of the *DSM-5* Proposal

According to First and colleagues (2004), clinical utility involves the clinician's ability to communicate; select effective interventions; predict course, prognosis, and future management needs; and differentiate disorder from nondisorder to determine who might benefit from treatment. The degree to which the *DSM-5* model improves upon the *DSM-IV* can be evaluated in each of these areas.

In terms of communication, the levels of functioning index and any reduction in diagnostic overlap and construct heterogeneity that results from the move from polythetic to type diagnosis would tend to facilitate communication. However, communication may be hampered by the loss of several PDs with which clinicians are familiar (Clarkin & Huprich, 2011). Trait approaches may be unfamiliar to clinicians, who may also find the trait system of the *DSM-5* overly complex (Clarkin & Huprich, 2011). However, trait ratings solve the problem posed by the regular diagnosis of PD NOS (Krueger et al., 2011a, b), and over time clinicians will likely become more familiar with the *DSM-5* traits. It is also useful to note that the 25 facets of the *DSM-5* represent a dramatic reduction from the 79 to 99 symptom criteria of *DSM-III* and *DSM-IV* (Krueger et al., 2011a, b). Finally, although it is clinically important to depict personality-related strengths (e.g., Bornstein, 2011a; Hopwood, 2011), the *DSM-5* provides no mechanism for doing so, as all of the elements of PD diagnosis are pathological.

Overall, the *DSM-IV* has not been particularly useful to clinicians wishing to select effective interventions, as there are no evidence-based interventions for most PDs, and treatments that do exist are only modestly helpful (Matusiewicz et al., 2010). There are reasons to think that the *DSM-5* model could lead to more effective interventions. For instance, the development of treatment methods to differentially target personality pathology or particular types/traits of PD style could enhance the specificity of therapeutic techniques. However, the issue of treatment selection has rarely been discussed in debates about how to classify PDs, suggesting that improvements in this regard attributable to the *DSM-5* are likely to be modest (Clarkin & Huprich, 2011).

Several aspects of the *DSM-5* PD proposal may improve clinical predictions about course and prognosis. Dimensional models of PD are more stable and more valid for predicting prospective outcomes (Morey et al., 2007), suggesting that their incorporation in the *DSM-5* should improve clinical predictions. The separation of levels of functioning from PD styles may improve prognostic predictions if, for instance, it is shown that personality pathology is more stable than PD instantiations. However, given that the *DSM-5* proposal is quite new and the publication deadline is relatively soon, there will not be enough time to research the use of the proposed model to make predictions about course. As discussed earlier, for this reason it is wise that the *DSM-5* is being regarded as a living document that can be modified in order to incorporate new information, such as the stability and long-term predictive validity of different elements of PD diagnosis (Krueger et al., 2011a). However, this otherwise appealing feature may contribute to clinician confusion and diagnostic unreliability any time the model is modified.

The *DSM-5* has perhaps made the most significant progress in terms of helping clinicians differentiate disorder from nondisorder. The quantification of levels provides clinicians with a clear basis for determining a patient's diagnostic standing. Replacement of polythetic criteria and arbitrary thresholds with clinical types with absolute criteria (i.e., the patient must meet every criterion for the diagnosis) will reduce heterogeneity within PD types and the option to diagnose a patient with a trait specification will eliminate PD not otherwise specified as a diagnosis and permit a more precise depiction of PD style.

## CASE STUDY

We will demonstrate differences between the *DSM-IV* and *DSM-5* proposal using the case of Elaine, a 28-year-old single, unemployed woman. Elaine presented for an evaluation at a low-fee outpatient clinic unkempt and in clear distress, although her behavior was appropriate and she established rapport readily. The clinician experienced her as thoughtful, warm, and insightful and reported that she had provoked in him a strong desire to be helpful to her. Elaine sought psychotherapy shortly after her life circumstances had worsened considerably. She had been evicted from her apartment 1 month prior and had been living in a homeless shelter. During that time, she had stolen money to buy alcohol and food. She had begun cutting herself on her arms and legs with thumb tacks and broken glass in moments of acute despair, something she had done on a few occasions during dramatic romantic break-ups in adolescence, but which she had discontinued since that time. She denied suicidal intent but acknowledged multiple potentially self-harming behaviors, such as promiscuous sex and careless substance use, in the past and present.

Elaine described being the lone child in an intact, middle-class family as "mostly okay," although she also reported being estranged from her physically abusive father for the 10 years since she had moved out of her parents' house. She maintained a close relationship with her mother, but their contact was somewhat limited due to the ongoing rupture between Elaine and her father. She also had several close friends whom she felt she could trust, although she reported feeling too ashamed to turn to them for help when she really needed it. During adolescence and early adulthood, Elaine had been convicted several times for petty theft. She reported that she had generally stolen or shoplifted with or for her boyfriends in the distant past, but that in the previous few years she had primarily shoplifted alcohol or food for her own consumption. Elaine did well academically and reported many positive social experiences and stable friendships during adolescence, although this time was also colored by several emotionally charged and disruptive romantic breakups. She described several instances in which she behaved in a manner she later regarded as embarrassing in order to attract the attention of a potential suitor. For instance, when Elaine was 16, she shared seductive pictures of herself with a boy that she liked, who then showed the pictures to his friends. When she learned he had done this, she drank heavily, had a sexual liaison with the boy's friend, and threw a rock through his bedroom window. She was charged, convicted, and put on probation, which she later violated; her social reputation also predictably suffered.

Elaine's personality problems were exacerbated 3 years prior to her visit when she witnessed the death of her daughter in an automobile accident. Elaine had been driving, but the accident was not her fault. After being left by her daughter's father shortly after conception, she had cared for her daughter alone and reported that doing so was her main motivation to limit her drinking and work reliably. Following the accident, Elaine had persistent posttraumatic symptoms, including reexperiencing, avoidance of social events, exaggerated startle, nightmares, and generalized anxiety. She had a history of alcohol abuse that reached dependence in the last 2 years and had become sufficiently severe to cost her a job 6 months prior to her presentation. She also reported that following the accident, she became disinterested in a committed relationship with a man, although she continued to have multiple sexual relationships.

In terms of personality diagnosis, Elaine has several borderline characteristics with some historical precedent but which had become more severe following her daughter's death. She claimed that every man with whom she had ever had a close romantic relationship had been verbally or physically abusive. She described a host of brief and volatile relationships characterized by a pattern of events involving intense anger over seemingly minor issues, followed by impulsive behavior such as substance abuse or infidelity, and a deep sense of emptiness and regret. She reported feeling so ashamed of herself and angry at her partner following these episodes that she would end relationships rather than acknowledging her behavior or attempting to repair the relationship. Notably, Elaine also reported impulsive, and often attention-seeking, behavior associated with a particularly positive mood. She said that when she felt good, she "just doesn't want it to end," so she "lets it all hang out," which typically involves behaviors such as substance abuse and promiscuous sex that ultimately lead to her feeling lonely and empty.

*DSM-IV* Diagnosis

From the perspective of the *DSM-IV* Axis II, Elaine would meet seven of nine criteria for borderline PD: unstable relationships, identity disturbance, impulsivity, suicidal gestures, affective instability, emptiness, and anger. She would not meet the criteria for dissociative symptoms/paranoid ideation. Although her thinking became somewhat loose during moments of extreme distress, this symptom was not severe enough to be rated as fully present. She also denied abandonment concerns. Elaine would also meet criteria for antisocial PD, having met for adolescent conduct disorder and six of seven antisocial criteria (failure to conform, deceitfulness, impulsivity, irritability, recklessness, irresponsibility) and for histrionic PD, having five of eight symptoms (inappropriate sexuality, rapidly shifting emotions, use of appearance for attention, impressionistic speech, and theatricality). She would, therefore, be well categorized, from a *DSM-IV* perspective, as having prominent Cluster B personality pathology and in particular borderline, antisocial, and histrionic features.

### DSM-5 DIAGNOSIS

*DSM-5*[3] PD diagnosis occurs in several steps. The first involves rating overall personality pathology. A rating of 3, indicating serious impairment, seemed most appropriate for Elaine in terms of both self- and interpersonal functioning. Her self-system was poorly regulated and unstable, with some boundary definition problems and a fragile self-concept. Her sense of agency was weak, and she commonly felt empty. She often experienced life as meaningless or dangerous. There was sufficient self-functioning that a rating of 4, indicating extreme impairment, did not seem warranted. She was able to regulate her self-states more often than not, and she was able to articulate a unique identity. There was some evidence of agency and transient fulfillment. Interpersonally, she was able to have stable attachments to individuals outside of romantic relationships, and in these contexts was generally able to understand others' behaviors and motivations empathically. However, she was not able to use these relationships when she needed social support the most, and the negative impacts of her interpersonal dysfunction in romantic relationships were profound.

Elaine did not meet the criteria for any of the PD types, including borderline or antisocial. For borderline, she was missing some criterion A features such as perceptual dysregulation and a desire to avoid abandonment, and she did not have the required criterion B traits risk taking or hostility (scores on these traits range from 0 – not present to 3 – present). Most of the criterion A and B features for antisocial were absent. Thus, she would be classified as PD trait specified, with prominent negative affectivity (emotional lability and anxiousness) and disinhibition (recklessness, impulsivity, and irresponsibility).

Is this an improvement? The *DSM-5* framework appears to offer a richer description than the *DSM-IV*, in that it quantifies personality pathology, separates personality pathology from PD features, and lists PD features in more detail. Furthermore, the *DSM-IV* antisocial diagnosis was accurate given her symptoms but did not seem

---

3. Specific criteria for *DSM-5* PD diagnosis are available at the American Psychiatric Association website: www.dsm5.org/PROPOSEDREVISIONS/Pages/PersonalityandPersonalityDisorders.aspx

to capture her very well. That said, from a clinical perspective the term borderline does seem to describe Elaine overall, and perhaps more efficiently than the trait specified diagnosis. The question of optimal models of PD diagnosis cannot be answered using a single study or single case example, and it is likely that there will be strengths and weaknesses of any model of PD. Thus this question will need to be answered by the future researchers and clinicians who use the *DSM-5*.

**Table 18.1**
Elaine's *DSM-5* Personality Disorder Trait Profile

| | |
|---|---|
| Negative Affectivity | 3 |
| Emotional Lability | 3 |
| Anxiousness | 3 |
| Submissiveness | 1 |
| Separation Insecurity | 2 |
| Perseveration | 0 |
| Hostility | 1 |
| Restricted Affectivity | 0 |
| Detachment | 1 |
| Social Withdrawal | 1 |
| Suspisciousness | 2 |
| Depressivity | 2 |
| Anhedonia | 1 |
| Intimacy Avoidance | 0 |
| Antagonism | 1 |
| Callousness | 0 |
| Manipulativeness | 1 |
| Grandiosity | 0 |
| Attention Seeking | 2 |
| Deceitfulness | 1 |
| Disinhibition | 3 |
| Impulsivity | 3 |
| Distractibility | 2 |
| Recklessness | 3 |
| Irresponsibility | 3 |
| Rigid Perfectionism | 0 |
| Risk Taking | 0 |
| Psychoticism | 1 |
| Unusual Perceptions/Experiences | 0 |
| Eccentricity | 0 |
| Perceptual Dysregulation | 2 |

## SUMMARY

In this chapter, we have described personality pathology and PDs, reviewed their history, clinical presentation, and construct validity, and compared the *DSM-IV* and *DSM-5* models of PD with a clinical case. In general, it can be concluded that personality pathology is common and associated with profound functional impairments and personal and societal costs. Although recent research advances provide new, promising methods for assessing and treating PDs, much remains unknown about how to assess and treat personality problems. The upcoming *DSM-5* could contribute to further understanding and clinical utility. However, there is a long history of research and clinical neglect on PDs, so understanding of many aspects of personality pathology is severely limited. Future directions for research include better understanding associations between normative traits and personality-related impairments, developing stronger links between research and practice, and incorporating dynamic elements of personality into existing models. Advances in these areas should contribute to an improved understanding of etiology and ultimately to more effective assessment and treatment methods.

## REFERENCES

Abi-Dargham, A., Gil, R., Krystal, J., Baldwin, R. M., Seibyl, J. P., Bowers, M., . . . Laruelle, M. (1998). Increased stiatal dopamine transmission in schizophrenia: Confirmed in a second cohort. *American Journal of Psychiatry, 155*, 761–767.

American Psychiatric Association. (1952). *Diagnostic and statistical manual of mental disorders.* Washington, DC: Author.

American Psychiatric Association. (1968). *Diagnostic and statistical manual of mental disorders* (2nd ed.). Washington, DC: Author.

American Psychiatric Association. (1980). *Diagnostic and statistical manual of mental disorders* (3rd ed.). Washington, DC: Author.

American Psychiatric Association. (1987). *Diagnostic and statistical manual of mental disorders* (3rd ed., text rev.). Washington, DC: Author.

American Psychiatric Association. (1994). *Diagnostic and statistical manual of mental disorders* (4th ed.). Washington, DC: Author.

American Psychiatric Association. (2000). *Diagnostic and statistical manual of mental disorders* (4th ed., text rev.). Washington, DC: Author.

Arnett, J. J. (2000). Emerging adulthood: A theory of development from the late teens through the twenties. *American Psychologist, 55*, 469–480.

Bateman, A. W., & Fonagy, P. (2004). Mentalization-based treatment of BPD. *Journal of Personality Disorders, 18*, 36–51.

Beck, A. T., & Freeman, A. F. (1990). *Cognitive therapy of personality disorders.* New York, NY: Guilford Press.

Bender, D. S., Dolan, R. T., Skodol, A. E., Sanislow, C. A., Dyck, I. R., McGlasgan, T. H., . . . Gunderson, J. G. (2001). Treatment utilization by patients with personality disorders. *The American Journal of Psychiatry, 158*, 295–302.

Bender, D. S., Morey, L. C., & Skodol, A. E. (2011). Toward a model for assessing level of personality functioning in *DSM-5*: An empirical review. *Journal of Personality Assessment, 93*, 332–346.

Benjamin, L. S. (1996). *Interpersonal diagnosis and treatment of personality disorders* (2nd ed.). New York, NY: Guilford Press.

Bornstein, R. F. (1997). Dependent personality disorder in the *DSM-IV* and beyond. *Clinical Psychology: Science and Practice, 4*, 175–187.

Bornstein, R. F. (2011a). Toward a multidimensional model of personality disorder diagnosis: Implications for *DSM-5. Journal of Personality Assessment, 93*, 362–369.

Bornstein, R. F. (2011b). Reconceptualizing personality pathology in *DSM-5*: Limitations in evidence for eliminating dependent personality disorder and other *DSM-IV* syndromes. *Journal or Personality Disorders, 25*, 235–247.

Brown, G. L., Eberth, M. H., Goyer, P. F., Jimerson, D. C., Klein, W. J., Bunney, W. E., & Goodwin, F. K. (1982). Aggression, suicide, and serotonin: Relationships to CSF amine metabolites. *American Journal of Psychiatry, 139*, 741–746.

Burt, S. A. (2009). Rethinking environmental contributions to child and adolescent psychopathology: A meta-analysis of shared environmental influences. *Psychological Bulletin, 135*, 608–637.

Caspi, A., McClay, J., Moffitt, T. E., Mill, J., Martin, J., Craig, I. W., . . . Poulton, R. (2002). Role of genotype in the cycle of maltreated children. *Science, 297*, 851–854.

Clark, L. A. (1993). *Manual for the schedule for nonadaptive and adaptive personality*. Minneapolis: University of Minnesota Press.

Clark, L. A. (2007). Assessment and diagnosis of personality disorder: Perennial issues and emerging conceptualization. *Annual Review of Psychology, 58*, 227–258.

Clark, L. A., & Harrison, J. A. (2001). Assessment instruments. In W. J. Livesley (Ed.), *Handbook of personality disorders: Theory, research, and treatment* (pp. 277–306). New York, NY: Guilford Press.

Clarkin, J. F., & Huprich, S. K. (2011). Do DSM-V personality disorder proposals meet criteria for clinical utility? *Journal of Personality Disorders, 25*(2), 192–205.

Clarkin, J. F., Levy, K. N., Lenzenweger, M. F., & Kernberg, O. (2007). Evaluating three treatments for borderline personality disorder: A multiwave study. *The American Journal of Psychiatry, 164*, 6922–6928.

Coccaro, E. F., Gabriel, S., & Siever, L. J. (1990). Buspirone challenge: Preliminary evidence for a role for 5-HT-1A receptors in impulsive aggressive behavior in humans. *Psychopharmacology Bulletin, 26*, 393–405.

Cooper, L. D., Balsis, S., & Zimmerman, M. (2010). Challenges associated with a polythetic diagnostic system: Criteria combinations in the personality disorders. *Journal of Abnormal Psychology, 119*(4), 886–895.

Costa, P. T., Jr., & McCrae, R. R. (2006). Trait and factor theories. In M. Hersen & J. C. Thomas (Eds.), *Comprehensive handbook of personality and psychopathology, Vol. 1: Personality and everyday functioning* (pp. 96–114). Hoboken, NJ: John Wiley & Sons.

Cramer, P. (1991). Anger and the use of defense mechanisms in college students. *Journal of Personality, 59*, 39–55.

Critchfield, K. L., & Benjamin, L. S. (2010). Assessment of repeated relational patterns for individual cases using the SASB-Based Intrex Questionnaire. *Journal of Personality Assessment, 92*, 480–489.

Cuijpers, P., Smit, F., Penninx, B. W. J. H., De Graaf, R., ten Have, M., & Beekman, A. T. F. (2010). Economic costs of neuroticism: A population-based study. *Archives of General Psychiatry, 67*, 1086–1093.

Cyranowski, J. M., Frank, E., Winter, E., Rucci, P., Novick, D., Pilkonis, P., . . . Kupfer, D. J. (2004). Personality pathology and outcome in recurrently depressed women over 2 years of maintenance interpersonal psychotherapy. *Psychological Medicine: A Journal of Research in Psychiatry and the Allied Sciences, 34,* 659–669.

Depue, R. A., & Lenzenweger, M. F. (2005). A neurobehavioral dimensional model of personality disturbance. In M. F. Lenzenweger & J. F. Clarkin (Eds.), *Major theories of personality disorder* (2nd ed., pp. 391–453). New York, NY: Guilford Press.

DeYoung, C. G. (2010). Mapping personality traits onto brain systems: BIS, BAS, FFFS, and beyond. *European Journal of Personality, 24,* 404–422.

Digman, J. M. (1990). Personality structure: Emergence of the five-factor model. *Annual Review of Psychology, 41,* 417–440.

Donegan, N. H., Sanislow, C. A., Blumberg, H. P., Fulbright, R. K., Lacadie, C., Skudlarski, P., . . . Wexler, B. E. (2003). Amygdala hyperreactivity in borderline personality disorder: implications for emotional dysregulation. *Biological Psychiatry, 54,* 1284–1293.

Feske, U., Mulsant, B. H., Pilkonis, P. A., Soloff, P., Dolata, D., Sackeim, H. A., & Haskett, R. F. (2004). Clinical outcome of ECT in patients with major depression and comorbid borderline personality disorder. *The American Journal of Psychiatry, 161,* 2073–2080.

First, M. B., Gibbon, R. L., Spitzer, R. L., Williams, J. B. W., & Benjamin, L. S. (1997). *Structured Clinical Interview for DSM-IV Axis II personality disorders* (SCID-II). Washington, DC: American Psychiatric Press.

First, M. B., Pincus, H. A., Levine, J. B., Williams, J. B. W., Ustun, B., & Peele, R. (2004). Clinical utility as a criterion for revising psychiatric diagnoses. *American Journal of Psychiatry, 161,* 946–954.

Garno, J., Goldberg, J., Ramirez, P., & Ritzler, B. (2005). Bipolar disorder with comorbid cluster B personality disorder features: Impact on suicidality. *Journal of Clinical Psychiatry, 66,* 339–345.

Giesen-Bloo, J., van Dyck, R., Spinhoven, P., van Tilburg, W., Dirksen, C., van Asselt, T., . . . Arntz, A. (2006). Outpatient psychotherapy for borderline personality disorder: Randomized trial of schema-focused therapy vs transference-focused psychotherapy. *Archives of General Psychiatry, 63,* 649–658.

Grant, B. F., Hasin, D. S., Stinson, F. S., Dawson, D. A., Chou, S. P., Ruan, W. J., & Pickering, R. P. (2004). Prevalence, correlates, and disability of personality disorders in the United States: Results from the National Epidemiologic Survey on alcohol and related conditions. *Journal of Clinical Psychiatry, 65,* 948–958.

Grilo, C. M., Shea, M. T., Sanislow, C. A., Skodol, A. E., Gunderson, J. G., Stout, R. L., . . . McGlashan, T. H. (2004). Two-year stability and change of schizotypal, borderline, avoidant, and obsessive-compulsive personality disorders. *Journal of Consulting and Clinical Psychology, 72,* 767–775.

Grilo, C. M., Stout, R. L., Markowitz, J. C., Sanislow, C. A., Ansell, E. B., Skodol, A. E., . . . McGlashan, T. H. (2010). Personality disorders predict relapse after remission from an episode of major depressive disorder: A 6-year prospective study. *Journal of Clinical Psychiatry, 71,* 1629–1635.

Gunderson, J. G. (2008). *Borderline personality disorder: A clinical guide* (2nd ed.). Arlington, VA: American Psychiatric Publishing.

Gunderson, J. G. (2010). Commentary on "Personality traits and the classification of mental disorders: Toward a more complete integration in *DSM-5* and an empirical model of psychopathology." *Personality Disorders: Theory, Research, and Treatment 1,* 119–122.

Haigler, E. D., & Widiger, T.A. (2001). Experimental manipulations of NEO PI-R items. *Journal of Personality Assessment, 77,* 339–358.

Hare, R. D. (1991). *The Hare psychopathy checklist—Revised manual.* Toronto, Canada: Multi-Health Systems.

Hazlett, E. A., Buchsbaum, M. S., Mehmet, H. M., Newmark, R., Goldstein, K. E., Zelmanova, Y., . . . Siever, L. J. (2008). Cortical gray and white matter volume in unmedicated schizotypal and schizophrenia patients. *Schizophrenia Research, 1*, 111–123.

Herpertz, S. C., Dietrich, T. M., Wenning, B., Krings, T., Erberich, S. G., Willmes, K., . . . Sass, H. (2001). Evidence of abnormal amygdala functioning in borderline personality disorder: A functional MRI study. *Biological Psychiatry, 50*, 292–298.

Heumman, K. A., & Morey, L. C. (1990). Reliability of categorical and dimensional judgments of personality disorder. *American Journal of Psychiatry, 147*, 498–500.

Hopwood, C. J. (2011). Personality traits in the DSM-5. *Journal of Personality Assessment, 93*, 398–405.

Hopwood, C. J., Donnellan, M. B., & Zanarini, M. C. (2010). Temperamental and acute symptoms of borderline personality disorder: associations with normal personality traits and dynamic relations over time. *Psychological Medicine, 40*, 1871–1878.

Hopwood, C. J., Malone, J. C., Ansell, E. B., Sanislow, C. A., Grilo, C. M., McGlashan, T. H., . . . Morey, L. C. (2011). Personality assessment in DSM-V: Empirical support for rating severity, style, and traits. *Journal of Personality Disorders, 25*, 305–320.

Hopwood, C. J., Morey, L. C., Edelen, M. O., Shea, M. T., Grilo, C. M., Sanislow, C. A., . . . Skodol, A. E. (2008). A comparison of interview and self-report methods for the assessment of borderline personality disorder criteria. *Psychological Assessment, 20*, 81–85.

Hopwood, C. J., Morey, L. C., Markowitz, J. C., Pinto, A., Skodol, A. E., Gunderson, J. G., . . . Sanislow, C. A. (2009). The construct validity of passive-aggressive personality disorder. *Psychiatry: Interpersonal and Biological Processes, 72*, 256–267.

Hopwood, C. J., & Thomas, K. M. (in press). Paranoid and schizoid personality disorders. In T. A. Widiger (Ed.), *Oxford handbook of personality disorders*. Oxford, England: Oxford University Press.

Hopwood, C. J., Thomas, K. M., Markon, K. E., Wright, A. G. C., & Krueger, R. F. (in review). DSM-5 personality traits and DSM-IV disorders.

Hopwood, C. J., & Zanarini, M. C. (2010). Five-factor trait instability in borderline relative to other personality disorders. *Personality Disorders: Theory, Research, and Treatment, 1*, 158–166.

Huprich, S. K. (2005). *Rorschach assessment of personality disorders*. Mahwah, NJ: Erlbaum.

Huprich, S. K. & Bornstein, R. F. (2007). An overview of issues related to categorical and dimensional models of personality disorders assessment. *Journal of Personality Assessment, Special Issue: Dimensional Verses Categorical Personality Disorder Diagnosis: Implications from and for Psychological Assessment, 89*, 3–15.

Hy, L. X., & Loevinger, J. (1996). *Measuring ego development* (2nd ed.). Mahwah, NJ: Erlbaum.

Hyler, S. E. (1994). *Personality Diagnostic Questionnaire-4 (PDQ-4)*. New York: New York State Psychiatric Institute.

Jackson, H. J., Whiteside, H. L., Bates, G. W., Bell, R., Rudd, R. P., & Edwards, J. (1991). Diagnosing personality disorders in psychiatric inpatients. *Acta Psychiatrica Scandinavica, 83*, 206–213.

Jang, K. L., Livesley, W. J., & Vernon, P. A. (1996). Heritability of the big five personality dimensions and their facets: A twin study. *Journal of Personality, 64*, 577–591.

Johnson, J. G., Cohen, P., Brown, J., Smailes, E., & Bernstein, D. P. (1999). Childhood maltreatment increases risk for personality disorders during early adulthood. *Archives of General Psychiatry, 56*, 600–606.

Johnson, J. G., Cohen, P., Kasen, S., Skodol, A. E., Hamagami, F., & Brook, J. S. (2000). Age-related change in personality disorder trait levels between early adolescence and adulthood: A community-based longitudinal investigation. *Acta Psychiatrica Scandinavica, 102*, 265–275.

Kendler, K. S., Czajkowski, N., Tambs, K., Torgersen, S., Aggen, S. H., Neale, M. C., & Reichborn-Kjennerud, T. (2006). Dimensional representations of *DSM-IV* Cluster A personality disorders in a population-based sample of Norwegian twins: A multivariate study. *Psychological Medicine: A Journal of Research in Psychiatry and the Allied Sciences, 36,* 1583–1591.

Kernberg, O. F. (1984). *Severe personality disorders.* New Haven, CT: Yale University Press.

Kernberg, O. F., & Caligor, E. (2005). A psychoanalytic theory of personality disorders. In M. F. Lenzenweger & J. F. Clarkin (Eds.), *Major theories of personality disorder* (2nd ed., pp. 391–453). New York, NY: Guilford Press.

Kernberg, O. F., & Clarkin, J. F. (1995). *The inventory of personality organization.* White Plains, NY: Hospital-Cornell Medical Center.

Kohut, H. (1971). *The analysis of the self.* New York, NY: International Universities Press

Krueger, R. F., Eaton, N. R., Clark, L. A., Watson, D. W., Derringer, J., Skodol, A., & Livesley, W. J. (2011a). Deriving an empirical structure of personality pathology for *DSM-5*. *Journal of Personality Disorders, 25*(2), 170–191.

Krueger, R. F., Eaton, N. R., Derringer, J., Markon, K. E., Clark, L. A., Watson, D., & Livesley, W. J. (2011b). Personality in *DSM-5*: Helping delineate personality disorder content and framing the meta-structure. *Journal of Personality Assessment, 93,* 325–331.

Krueger, R.F., Derringer, J., Markon, K.E., Watson, D., & Skodol, A.E. (in review). Constructing a personality inventory for DSM-5.

Lahey, B. B. (2009). The public health significance of neuroticism. *American Psychologist, 4,* 241–256.

Lenzenweger, M. F. (2006). The longitudinal study of personality disorders: History, design considerations, and initial findings. *Journal of Personality Disorders, 20,* 645–670.

Lenzenweger, M. F., & Clarkin, J. F. (2005). The personality disorders: History, classification, and research issues. In M. F. Lenzenweger & J. F. Clarkin (Eds.), *Major theories of personality disorder* (2nd ed., pp. 391–453). New York, NY: Guilford Press.

Lenzenweger, M. F., Loranger, A. W., Korfine, L., & Neff, C. (1997). Detecting personality disorders in a nonclinical population: Application of a 2-stage for case identification. *Archives of General Psychiatry, 54,* 4345–4351.

Lewin, K. (1936). *Principles of topological psychology.* New York, NY: McGraw-Hill.

Linehan, M. (1993). *Cognitive-behavioral treatment of borderline personality disorder.* New York, NY: Guilford Press.

Links, P. S., Steiner, M., & Huxley, G. (1988). The occurrence of borderline personality disorder in the families of borderline patients. *Journal of Personality Disorders, 2,* 14–20.

Livesley, W. J. (1998). Suggestions for a framework for an empirically based classification of personality disorder. *The Canadian Journal of Psychiatry, 43,* 137–147.

Livesley, W. J., & Jackson, D. N. (2006). *Dimensional assessment of personality problems.* Port Huron, MI: Sigma Assessment Systems.

Loevinger, J. (1957). Objective tests as instruments of psychological theory. *Psychological Reports, 3,* 635–694.

MacCorquodale, K., & Meehl, P. E. (1948). On a distinction between hypothetical constructs and intervening variables. *Psychological Review, 55,* 95–107.

Maier, W., Lichtermann, D., Minges, J., & Heun, R. (1994). Personality disorders among the relatives of schizophrenia patients. *Schizophrenia Bulletin, 20,* 481–493.

Matusiewicz, A. K., Hopwood, C. J., Banducci, A. N., & Lejuez, C. W. (2010). The effectiveness of cognitive behavioral therapy for personality disorders. *Psychiatric Clinics of North America, 33,* 657–685.

McCrae, R. R., & Terracciano, A. (2005). Universal features of personality traits from the observer's perspective: Data from 50 cultures. *Journal of Personality and Social Psychology, 88*, 547–561.

McGlashan, T. H., Grilo, C. M., Sanislow, C. A., Ralevski, E., Morey, L. C., Gunderson, J. G., . . . Pagano, M. (2005). Two-year prevalence and stability of individual *DSM-IV* criteria for schizotypal, borderline, avoidant, and obsessive-compulsive personality disorders: Toward a hybrid model of axis II disorders. *American Journal of Psychiatry, 162*, 883–889.

McGlashan, T. H., Grilo, C. M., Skodol, A. E., Gunderson, J. G., Shea, M. T., Morey, L. C., . . . Stout, R. L. (2000). The Collaborative Longitudinal Personality Disorders Study: Baseline Axis I/II and II/II diagnostic co-occurrence. *Acta Psychiatrica Scandinavica 102*, 256–264.

McGue, M., Bacon, S., & Lykken, D. T. (1993). Personality stability and change in early adulthood: A behavioral genetic analysis. *Developmental Psychology, 29*, 196–109.

Menninger, K. A. (1963). *The vital balance: The life process in mental health and illness.* New York, NY: Viking Press.

Meyer, B., & Pilkonis, P. A. (2005). An attachment model of personality. In M. F. Lenzenweger & J. F. Clarkin (Eds.), *Major theories of personality disorder* (2nd ed., pp. 231–281). New York, NY: Guilford Press.

Mezzich, J. E., Fabrega, H., Jr., & Coffman, G. A. (1987). Multiaxial characterization of depressive patients. *Journal of Nervous and Mental Disease, 175*, 339–346.

Miller, J. D., Bagby, R. M., Pilkonis, P. A., Reynolds, S. K., & Lynam, D. R. (2005). A simplified technique for scoring *DSM-IV* personality disorders with the five-factor model. *Assessment, 12*, 404–415.

Millon, T., & Radovanov, J. (1995). Passive-aggressive (negativistic) personality disorder. In W. Livesley (Ed.), *The DSM-IV personality disorders: Diagnosis and of self-defeating personality disorder* (pp. 312–325). New York, NY: Guilford Press.

Mischel, W. (1968). *Personality and assessment.* New York, NY: John Wiley & Sons.

Mischel, W., & Shoda, Y. (1995). A cognitive-affective system theory of personality: Reconceptualizing situations, dispositions, dynamics, and invariance in personality structure. *Psychological Review, 102*, 246–268.

Molinari, V., Ames, A., & Essa, M. (1994). Prevalence of personality disorders in two geropsychiatric inpatient units. *Journal of Geriatric Psychiatry and Neurology, 7*, 209–215.

Morey, L. C. (2005). Personality pathology as pathological narcissism. In M. Maj, H. S. Akiskal, J. E. Mezzich, & A. Okasha (Eds.), *Evidence and experience in psychiatry, Vol. 8: Personality disorders* (pp. 328–331). Hoboken, NJ: John Wiley & Sons.

Morey, L. C., Berghuis, H., Bender, D. S., Verheul, R., Krueger, R. F., & Skodol, A. E. (2011). Empirical articulation of a core dimension of personality pathology. *Journal of Personality Assessment, 93*, 347–353.

Morey, L. C., Gunderson, J. G., Quigley, B. D., Shea, M. T., Skodol, A. E., McGlashan, T. H., . . . Zanarini, M. C. (2002). The representation of borderline, avoidant, obsessive-compulsive, and schizotypal personality disorders by the five-factor model. *Journal of Personality Disorders, 16*, 215–234.

Morey, L. C., Hopwood, C. J., Gunderson, J. G., Skodol, A. E., Shea, M. T., Yen, S., McGlashan, T. H. (2007). Comparison of alternate models for personality disorders. *Psychological Medicine, 37*, 7983–7994.

Morey, L. C., Hopwood, C. J., Markowitz, J. C., Gunderson, J. G., Grilo, C. M., McGlashan, T. H., . . . Skodol, A. E. (in review). Comparison of alternative models for personality disorders, II: 6-, 8-, and 10-year follow-up.

Morey, L. C., & Zanarini, M. C. (2000). Borderline personality: Traits and disorder. *Journal of Abnormal Psychology, 109,* 733–737.

New, A. S., Buchsbaum, M. S., Hazlett, F. A., Goodman, M., Koenigsberg, I I., Lo, J., . . . Siever, L. J. (2004). Fluoxetine increases relative metabolic rate in prefrontal cortex in impulsive aggression. *Psychopharmacology, 176,* 451–458.

Oldham, J. M. (2005). Guideline watch: Practice guideline for the treatment of patients with borderline personality disorder. *Focus, 3,* 396–400.

Oldham, J. M., Skodol, A. E., Kellman, H. D., Hyler, S. E., & Rosnick, L. (1992). Diagnosis of DSM-III-R personality disorders by two structured interviews: Patterns of comorbidity. *American Journal of Psychiatry, 149,* 213–220.

Ozer, D. J., & Benet-Martinez, V. (2006). Personality and the prediction of consequential outcomes. *Annual Review of Psychology, 57,* 401–421.

Paris, J. (2011). Endophenotypes and the diagnosis of personality disorders. *Journal of Personality Disorders, 25*(2), 260–268.

Parker, G., Hadzi-Pavlovic, D., Both, L., Kumar, S., Wilhelm, K., & Olley, A. (2004). Measuring disordered personality functioning: To love and to work reprised. *Acta Psychiatrica Scandinavica, 110,* 230–239.

Parker, G., Roussos, J., Wilhelm, K., Mitchell, P., Austin, M. P., & Hadzi-Pavlovic, D. (1998). On modelling personality disorders: Are personality style and disordered functioning independent or interdependent constructs? *Journal of Nervous and Mental Disease, 186,* 709–715.

PDM Task Force. (2006). *Psychodynamic diagnostic manual.* Silver Springs, MD: Alliance of Psychoanalytic Organizations.

Pfohl, B., Coryell, W., Zimmerman, M., & Stangl, D. (1986). *DSM-III* personality disorders: Diagnostic overlap and internal consistency of individual *DSM-III* criteria. *Comprehensive Psychiatry, 27,* 21–34.

Pilkonis, P. A., Heape, C. L., Ruddy, J., & Serrao, P. (1991). Validity in the diagnosis of personality disorders: The use of the LEAD standard. *Psychological Assessment: A Journal of Consulting and Clinical Psychology, 3,* 46–54.

Pincus, A. L. (2005). A contemporary integrative interpersonal theory of personality disorders. In M. F. Lenzenweger & J. F. Clarkin (Eds.), *Major theories of personality disorder* (2nd ed., pp. 391–453). New York, NY: Guilford Press.

Pincus, A. L. (in press). Some comments on nosology, diagnostic process, and narcissistic personality disorder in the *DSM-5* proposal for personality and personality disorder disorders. *Personality Disorders: Theory, Research, and Treatment.*

Pincus, A. L. & Hopwood, C. J. (in press). A contemporary interpersonal model of personality pathology and personality disorder. In T. A. Widiger (Ed.), *Oxford handbook of personality disorders.* Oxford, England: Oxford University Press.

Pincus, A. L., Wright, A. G. C., Hopwood, C. J., & Krueger, R. F. (2011). An interpersonal analysis of pathological personality traits in DSM-5. *Society for Interpersonal Theory and Research, Zurich, Switzerland.*

Plomin, R., DeFries, J. C., Craig, I. W., & McGuggin, P. (2003). Behavioral genetics. In R. Plomin, J. C. DeFries, I. W. Craig, & P. McGuggin (Eds.), *Behavioral genetics in the postgenomic era* (pp. 531–540). Washington, DC: American Psychological Association.

Poldrugo, F., & Forti, B. (1988). Personality disorders and alcoholism treatment outcome. *Drug and Alcohol Dependence, 21,* 171–176.

Pretzer, J. L., & Beck, A. T. (2005). A cognitive theory of personality disorders. In M. F. Lenzenweger & J. F. Clarkin (Eds.), *Major theories of personality disorder* (2nd ed., pp. 391–453). New York, NY: Guilford Press.

Reich, J. (1991). Using the family history method to distinguish relatives of patients with dependent personality disorder from relatives of controls. *Psychiatry Research, 39*, 227–237.

Reich, J. (2003). The effects of Axis II disorders on the outcome of treatment of anxiety and unipolar depressive disorders: A review. *Journal of Personality Disorders, 17*, 387–405.

Rhee, S. H., & Waldman, I. D. (2002). Genetic and environmental influences on antisocial behavior: A meta-analysis of twin and adoption studies. *Psychological Bulletin, 128*, 490–529.

Roberts, B. W., Kuncel, N. R., Shiner, R., Caspi, A., & Goldberg, L. R. (2007). The power of personality: The comparative validity of personality traits, socioeconomic status, and cognitive ability for predicting important life outcomes. *Perspectives on Psychological Science, 2*, 313–345.

Rogers, R. (2001). *Diagnostic and structured interviewing: A handbook for psychologists.* New York, NY: Guilford Press.

Rottman, B. M., Woo-kyoung, A., Sanislow, C. A., & Kim, N. S. (2009). Can clinicians recognize *DSM-IV* personality disorders from five-factor model descriptions of patient cases. *American Journal of Psychiatry, 166*, 427–433.

Rouff, L. (2000). Schizoid personality traits among the homeless mentally ill: A quantitative and qualitative report. *Journal of Social Distress & the Homeless, 9*, 127–141.

Sadikaj, G., Russell, J. J., Moskowitz, D. S., & Paris, J. (2010). Affect dysregulation in individuals with borderline personality disorder: Persistence and interpersonal triggers. *Journal of Personality Assessment, 92*, 490–500.

Samuel, D. B. (2011). Assessing personality in the *DSM-5*: The utility of bipolar constructs. *Journal of Personality Assessment, 93*, 390–397.

Samuel, D. B., & Widiger, T. A. (2006). Clinician's judgments of clinical utility: A comparison of the *DSM-IV* and five-factor models of personality. *Journal of Abnormal Psychology, 115*, 298–308.

Samuel, D. B., & Widiger, T. A. (2008). A meta-analytic review of the relationships between the five-factor model and DSM-IV-TR personality disorders: A facet level analysis. *Clinical Psychology Review, 28*, 1326–1342.

Samuels, J., Eaton, W. W., Bienvenu, O. J., III, Brown, C. H., Costa, P. T., Jr., & Nestadt, G. (2002). Prevalence and correlates of personality disorders in a community sample. *British Journal of Psychiatry, 180*, 536–542.

Saulsman, L. M., & Page, A. C. (2004). The five-factor model and personality disorder empirical literature: A meta-analytic review. *Clinical Psychology Review, 23*, 1055–1085.

Schmideberg, M. (1959). The borderline patient. In S. Arieti (Ed.), *American handbook of psychiatry* (Vol. I, pp. 398–416). New York, NY: Basic Books.

Schneier, F. R., Blanco, C., Anita. S. X., & Liebowitz, M. R. (2002). The social anxiety spectrum. *Psychiatric Clinics of North America, 25*, 757–774.

Shedler, J., Beck, A., Fonagy, P., Gabbard, G. O., Gunderson, J., Kernberg, O. F., . . . Westen, D. (2010). Personality disorders in *DSM-5*. *The American Journal of Psychiatry, 167*, 1026–1028.

Shiner, R. L. (2009). The development of personality disorders: Perspectives from normal personality development in childhood and adolescence. *Development and Psychopathology, 21*, 715–734.

Siever, L. J. (2008). Neurobiology of aggression and violence. *The American Journal of Psychiatry, 165*, 429–442.

Siever, L. J., & Weinstein, L. N. (2009). The neurobiology of personality disorders: Implications for psychoanalysis. *Journal of the American Psychoanalytic Association, 57*, 361–398.

Skodol, A. E., Bender, D. S., Morey, L. C., Clark, L. A., Oldham, J. M., Alarcon, R. D., . . . Siever, L. J. (2011). Personality disorder types proposed for *DSM-5. Journal of Personality Disorders, 25*(2), 136–169.

Skodol, A. E., Buckley, P., & Charles, E. (1983). Is there a characteristic pattern to the treatment of history of clinic outpatients with borderline personality? *Journal of Nervous and Mental Disease, 171*, 405–410.

Skodol, A. E., Oldham, J. M., & Gallaher, P. E. (1999). Axis II comorbidity of substance use disorders among patients referred for treatment of personality disorders. *The American Journal of Psychiatry, 156*, 733–738.

Skodol, A. E., Rosnick, L., Kellman, D., Oldham, J. M., & Hyler, S. (1991). Development of a procedure for validating structured assessments of Axis II. In A. E. Skodol, L. Rosnick, D. Kellman, J. M. Oldham, & S. Hyler (Eds.), *Personality disorders: New perspectives on diagnostic validity*. Washington, DC: American Psychiatric Association.

Skodol, A. E., Siever, L. J., Livesley, W. J., Gunderson, J. G., Pfohl, B., & Widiger, T. A. (2002). The borderline diagnosis II: Biology, genetics, and clinical course. *Biological Psychiatry, 51*, 951–963.

Soldz, S., & Valliant, G. E. (2002). The big five personality traits and the life course: A 45-year longitudinal study. *Journal of Research in Personality, 33*, 208–232.

Soloff, P. H., Lis, J. A., Kelly, T., & Cornelius, J. R. (1994). Risk factors for suicidal behavior borderline personality disorder. *The American Journal of Psychiatry, 151*, 1316–1323.

Stern, B. L., Caligor, E., Clarkin, J. F., Critchfield, K. L., Horz, S., MacCornack, V., . . . Kernberg, O. F. (2010). Structured Interview of Personality Organization (STIPO): Preliminary psychometrics in a clinical sample. *Journal of Personality Assessment, 92*, 35–44.

Stuart, S., Pfohl, B., Battaglia, M., Bellodi, L., Grove, W., & Cadoret, R. (1998). The cooccurrence of DSM-III-R personality disorders. *Journal of Personality Disorders, 12*, 302–315.

Sudhoff, K. (1926). *Essays in the history of medicine* (pp. 67–87). New York, NY: Medical Life Press.

Tackett, J. L., Balsis, S., Oltmanns, T. F., & Krueger, R. F. (2009). A unifying perspective on personality pathology across the life span: Developmental considerations for the fifth edition of the Diagnostic and Statistical Manual for Mental Disorders. *Developmental Psychopathology, 21*, 687–713.

Torgersen, S. (2005). Epidemiology. In J. M. Oldham, A. E. Skodol, & D. Bender (Eds.), *Textbook of personality disorders* (pp. 129–141). Washington, DC: American Psychiatric Press.

Torgersen, S., Kringlen, E., & Cramer, V. (2001). The prevalence of personality disorders in a community sample. *Archives of General Psychiatry, 58*, 590–596.

Torgersen, S., Lygren, S., Oien, P. A., Skre, I., Onstad, S., Edvardsen, J., . . . Kringlen, E. (2000). A twin study of personality disorders. *Comprehensive Psychiatry, 41*, 416–425.

Trull, T. J., & Durrett, C. A. (2005). Categorical and dimensional models of personality disorder. *Annual Review of Clinical Psychology, 1*, 355–380.

Trull, T. J., Solhan, M. B., Tragesser, S. L., Jahng, S., Wood, P. K, Piasecki, T. M., & Watson, D. (2008). Affective instability: Measuring a core feature of borderline personality disorder with ecological momentary assessment. *Journal of Abnormal Psychology, 117*, 647–661.

Verheul, R., & Widiger, T. A. (2004). A meta-analysis of the prevalence and usage of the Personality Disorder Not Otherwise Specified (PDNOS) diagnosis. *Journal of Personality Disorders, 18*, 309–319.

Warner, M. B., Morey, L. C., Finch, J. F., Gunderson, J. G., Skodol, A. E., Sanislow, C. A., . . . Grilo, C. M. (2004). The longitudinal relationship of personality traits and disorders. *Journal of Abnormal Psychology, 113*, 217–227.

Westen, D. (1995). A clinical-empirical model of personality: Life after the Mischelian ice and the NEO-lithic era. *Journal of Personality, 63*, 495–591.

Westen, D. (1997). Divergences between clinical and research methods for assessing personality disorders: Implications for research and the evolution of Axis II. *American Journal of Psychiatry, 154*, 895–903.

Westen, D., DeFife, J. A., Bradley, B., & Hilsenroth, M. J. (2010). Prototype personality diagnosis in clinical practice: A viable alternative for *DSM-5* and *ICD-11*. *Professional Psychology: Research and Practice, 41*, 482–487.

Westen, D., & Shedler, J. (1999). Revising and assessing Axis II, part II: Toward an empirically-based and clinically useful classification of personality disorders. *American Journal of Psychiatry, 156*, 273–285.

Westen, D., Shedler, J., Bradley, R. (2006). A prototype approach to personality disorder diagnosis. *The American Journal of Psychiatry, 163*, 846–856.

Wetzler, S., & Morey, L. C. (1999). Passive-aggressive personality disorder: The demise of a syndrome. *Psychiatry: Interpersonal and Biological Processes, 62*, 49–59.

Widiger, T. A. (1993). The DSM-III-R categorical personality disorder diagnoses: A critique and an alternative. *Psychological Inquiry, 4*, 75–90.

Widiger, T. A. (2003). Personality disorder and Axis I psychopathology: the problematic boundary of Axis I and Axis II. *Journal of Personality Disorders, 17*, 90–108.

Widiger, T. A. (2010). Personality, interpersonal circumplex, and *DSM-5*: A commentary on five studies. *Journal of Personality Assessment, 92*, 528–532.

Widiger, T. A. (2011). The *DSM-5* dimensional model of personality disorder: Rationale and empirical support. *Journal of Personality Disorders, 25*(2), 222–234.

Widiger, T. A., Frances, A. J., Harris, M., Jacobsberg, L., Fyer, M., & Manning, D. (1991). Comorbidity among Axis II disorders. In J. Oldham (Ed.), *Personality disorders: New perspectives on diagnostic validity* (pp. 163–194). Washington, DC: American Psychiatric Press.

Widiger, T. A., Livesley, W. J., & Clark, L. E. A. (2009). An integrative dimensional classification of personality disorder. *Psychological Assessment, 21*, 243–255.

Widiger, T. A., & Mullins-Sweatt, S. N. (2009). Five-factor model of personality disorders: A proposal for DSM-V. *Annual Review of Clinical Psychology*, 197–220.

Widiger, T. A., & Samuel, D. B. (2005). Evidence-based assessment of personality disorders. *Psychological Assessment, 17*, 278–287.

Winstanley, C. A., Theobald, D. E., Dalley, J. W., Glennon, J. C., & Robbins, T. W. (2004). 5-HT$_{2A}$ and 5-HT$_{2C}$ receptor antagonists have opposing effects on a measure of impulsivity: Interactions with global 5-HT depletion. *Psychopharmacology, 176*, 379–385.

Wright, A. G. C. (2011). Qualitative and quantitative distinctions in personality disorder. *Journal of Personality Assessment, 93*, 370–379.

Wright, A. G. C., Thomas, K. M., Hopwood, C. J., Markon, K. E., Pincus, A. L., & Krueger, R. F. (in review). Empirical examination of the DSM-5 personality trait structure.

Zanarini, M. C., & Frankenburg, F. R. (2007). The essential nature of borderline psychopathology. *Journal of Personality Disorders, 21*, 518–535.

Zanarini, M. C., & Frankenburg, F. R., Hennen, J., Reich, D. B., & Silk, K. R. (2007). Prediction of the 10-year course of borderline personality disorder. *The American Journal of Psychiatry, 163*, 827–832.

Zanarini, M. C., Frankenburg, F. R., Hennen, J., & Silk, K. R. (2004). Mental health service utilization by borderline personality disorder patients and Axis II comparison subjects followed prospectively for 6 years. *Journal of Clinical Psychiatry, 65*, 28–36.

Zanarini, M. C., Gunderson, J. G., Marino, M. F., & Schwartz, E. O. (1989). Childhood experiences of borderline patients. *Comprehensive Psychiatry, 30,* 18–25.

Zeigler-Hill, V., & Abraham, J. (2006). Borderline personality features: Instability of self-esteem and affect. *Journal of Social and Clinical Psychology, 25,* 668–687.

Zimmerman, M. (2011). A critique of the proposed prototype rating system for personality disorders in *DSM-5. Journal of Personality Disorders, 25*(2), 206–221.

Zimmerman, M., Rothschild, L., & Chelminski, I. (2005). The prevalence of *DSM-IV* personality disorders in psychiatric outpatients. *American Journal of Psychiatry, 162,* 1911–1918.

# CHAPTER 19

# Sleep Disorders

THOMAS W. UHDE, BERNADETTE M. CORTESE, and ANDREI VEDENIAPIN

## INTRODUCTION

Sleep complaints are common in the general population and even more prevalent among individuals seeking consultation or treatment from mental health professionals. The *Diagnostic and Statistical Manual of Mental Disorders* (DSM-IV; American Psychiatric Association [APA], 2000) categorizes sleep disorders into four categories: (1) primary sleep disorders; (2) sleep disorders related to another mental disorder; (3) sleep disorders related to a general medical condition; and (4) substance-induced sleep disorders. In this chapter, we focus on the primary sleep disorders, which are subdivided into *dyssomnia* and *parasomnia*. Dyssomnias are conditions where there is a disturbance in the amount and/or quality of sleep or there is a mismatch between the expected demands of the individual in terms of normal work or social functions and the timing of sleep (e.g., circadian rhythm sleep disorder). Parasomnias are sleep disorders characterized by abnormal behaviors (e.g., sleepwalking) or physiological events (e.g., profuse sweating and tachycardia), which take place either during sleep or within a specific sleep stage (e.g., REM-stage sleep) or during transitions into or out of sleep.

The intent of this chapter is to review the dyssomnias and parasomnias that are most relevant to the mental health professional (i.e., sleep syndromes that are most likely to present in clinical practice). Information that will assist clinicians in correctly differentiating the dyssomnias and parasomnias from sleep disorders that are related to another mental disorder or general medical condition or a substance-induced sleep disorder will be discussed in the sections titled "Diagnostic Considerations."

Because primary sleep disorders [i.e., conditions that cannot be exclusively explained on the basis of another coexisting mental disorder or medical condition or the use, misuse, or discontinuation of a licit (e.g., prescribed medication, caffeine) or illicit (e.g., cocaine) substance] are thought to be caused by a fundamental disturbance in brain mechanisms that mediate sleep functions, we briefly review the neuroscience of sleep. We also provide an overview of three laboratory indices [e.g., multiple sleep latency test (MSLT), Apnea-Hypopnea Index (AHI), and Periodic

Limb Movement Index in Sleep (PLMS-I)] that are used as aids in the diagnosis of sleep disorders.

## NEUROSCIENCE OF SLEEP

At a fundamental level, sleep is exemplified by decreased consciousness, decreased responses to external stimuli, and decreased overall motor activity compared to wakefulness. Several brain neuroanatomical structures, genes, and neurotransmitter pathways play a role in sleep; however, no specific neurobiological mechanism(s) have been identified that specifically control the onset, maintenance, or termination of sleep. Electroencephalography (EEG), combined with electro-oculography (EOG) and electromyography (EMG), are the basis upon which the two major types of sleep (i.e., rapid eye movement [REM] versus non-REM sleep), the stages of sleep (Stages 1–4), and sleep architecture are defined.

### POLYSOMNOGRAPHY (PSG)

When electrodes are placed on the head to record surface brain activity, the resultant information is referred to as electroencephalography (EEG). In order to obtain a comprehensive profile of objective sleep, EEG information must be combined with EOG and EMG recordings; these data together are referred to as polysomnography (PSG). EEG brainwaves are defined by the amplitude, frequency, and their form/shape. All of these constructs are relevant to interpreting types and stages of sleep. *Amplitude* refers to the magnitude of the brainwave [from its valley-to-peak (measured in microvolts)], and *frequency* is the number of peak-to-peak brainwaves over time [measured in cycles per second, referred to as Hertz (Hz)]. Brainwave frequencies are described using the Greek alphabet: Beta (12–30 Hz), Alpha (8–12 Hz), Theta (4–7 Hz), and Delta (up to 4 Hz). Electro-oculography (EOG) measures the movement of the eye. During the phase of sleep most commonly associated with vivid images and dreaming, the eyes move, which is referred to as rapid eye movement (REM) sleep. Electromyography (EMG) measures muscle tone and activity. With the exception of the heart, eye, and respiratory muscles, there is a loss of muscle tone in all other major muscle groups during REM sleep.

### TYPES OF SLEEP

Sleep is divided into two major types: REM and non-REM sleep. Vivid images and dreaming occur during REM sleep. The brainwaves of REM sleep are similar or essentially identical to the brainwaves of wakefulness (i.e., low voltage, high frequency). For this reason, REM sleep is often referred to as "paradoxical" or "active" sleep. REM sleep is distinguished from wake states on the PSG by the appearance of unique low-amplitude, high-frequency brainwaves (taking on a "sawtooth" shape/form) in the presence of muscle atonia and rapid eye movements. Non-REM sleep is basically any sleep state that is not REM sleep. Rechtschaffen and Kales (1968) originally defined four stages (I–IV) of non-REM sleep, which reflect lighter-to-deeper stages of sleep. In 2007, the American Academy of Sleep

Medicine established a new nomenclature. Essentially, the original Rechtschaffen and Kales (1968) criteria for Stages 3 and 4 sleep have been combined into a single category, which is still commonly referred to as "slow wave," "deep," or "delta" sleep.

## SLEEP STAGES

*Stage 1/N1* is the transition from wakefulness to sleep. *Stage 2/N2* is the stage of sleep associated with a predominance of theta waves, with the appearance of highly characteristic sleep spindle and K-complex wave forms. (K-complexes are increased in restless legs syndrome.) *Stage 3–4/N3* is known as "deep sleep," "slow-wave sleep," or "delta sleep." Some patients report dream content during stage 3–4/N3 sleep, but such reports are infrequent, and the images are much less vivid compared to dreams emerging from REM sleep.

## SLEEP ARCHITECTURE

Sleep architecture refers to the cyclical pattern in the types (REM and non-REM) and stages of sleep. In healthy adults, there is a predictable pattern in the progression of REM and non-REM sleep. In healthy normal adults, it takes approximately 15–20 minutes to achieve stage 2/N2 sleep and 30–50 minutes to move from stage 2/N2 to deep sleep. After a period of deep sleep, there is a transition back toward lighter (stage 2/N2) sleep followed by REM sleep. Following the first REM sleep period, this cycle repeats itself, with progressively longer REM periods throughout the night. Each sleep cycle lasts approximately 90–120 minutes, with four to five cycles per 8-hour night. The proportion of time for an adult in each of these types and phases of sleep are 25% REM and 75% non-REM sleep [stage 1/N1 (5%), stage 2/N2 (45%–55%), stage 3–4/N3 or slow-wave sleep (15%–25%)]. Abnormalities in the timing, distribution, and/or proportion of different types and phases of sleep are prevalent in the dyssomnias.

## SLEEP INDICES

Three commonly used sleep indices are relevant to mental health professionals. Each of these measures provides an index of severity regarding a specific aspect of sleep and, in some cases (i.e., AHI, PLMSI), the test results are used in part to diagnose selective sleep disorders [AHI (sleep-related breathing disorder); PLMS-I (periodic limb movement of sleep disorder)].

*Multiple Sleep Latency Test (MSLT)* The Multiple Sleep Latency Test (MSLT) is a measure of daytime sleepiness, developed by Carskadon and Dement (1997). The test consists of four to five distinct 20-minute sessions, separated by 2-hour intervals, where the individual is placed in a comfortable, dark sleep environment (i.e., sleep laboratory) and asked to take a nap. The first nap period begins within 3 hours after awakening from the previous night's sleep. The main purpose of this test is to determine sleep latency and, if present, the onset of REM-stage sleep. Sleep latencies greater than 10 minutes (including an inability to fall asleep) are considered normal in well-rested individuals, whereas people who fall asleep within 5 minutes are judged to be sleep deprived (i.e., suffering from pathological sleepiness). The MSLT is an objective measure of daytime sleep propensity, and the appearance of REM sleep within 20 minutes is suggestive, but not diagnostic, of narcolepsy.

*Apnea-Hypopnea Index (AHI)*   The AHI provides useful information regarding the severity of abnormal breathing, which may include (a) not breathing at all (i.e., apnea) or (b) having insufficient rate or depth of breathing (i.e., hypopneas). In both cases, the major medical concern is that repeated decreases in blood oxygen levels (referred to as *desaturations*) will lead to brain damage or excessive daytime sleepiness. Multiple arousals, associated with sleep apneas or hypopneas, are considered risk factors for high blood pressure and cardiovascular diseases. To be considered a genuine apnea or hypopnea event, it must last for 10 seconds or longer. The AHI is calculated by taking the total number of apnea plus hypopnea events per night, divided by the total number of sleep hours. AHI values above 5 are considered clinically relevant but mild. AHI values above 30 are generally considered consistent with a severe sleep-related breathing disorder.

*Periodic Limb Movement Index (PLMI)*   This measure quantifies the severity of muscle contractions and is referred to as the periodic limb movement in sleep index (PLMS-I). The PLMS-I uses EMG data from muscles on the front part of the leg (i.e., anterior tibialis), which records muscle contractions lasting several seconds (usually up to 5 to 10 seconds) with 20 seconds or more contraction-free periods before another burst of muscle contractions. Similar to the AHI, the PLMS-I is calculated by taking the total number of muscle movements/contraction episodes divided by the total sleep hours. PLMS-Is over 5 are judged to be clinically relevant.

## DYSSOMNIAS

### Description of Disorders

Dyssomnias are primary sleep disorders where there is abnormality in the amount of sleep, quality of sleep, or timing of sleep, which cannot be explained exclusively by another mental disorder, sleep disorder, or the direct physiological effects of a substance. There may be problems falling asleep, staying asleep, or achieving restful sleep. Dyssomnias include primary insomnia, primary hypersomnia, narcolepsy, breathing-related sleep disorder, circadian rhythm sleep disorder, and dyssomnia not otherwise specified.

### Clinical Picture

Insomnia is one of the most prevalent complaints among patients seeking treatment from primary care physicians and mental health professionals.

*Primary Insomnia* is largely a subjective complaint of one or more of the following: delayed sleep onset, difficulty maintaining sleep, multiple awakenings from sleep, early morning awakenings, or the failure to feel refreshed after sleeping (i.e., non-restorative sleep). Current *DSM-IV* criteria (see Table 19.1) require at least 1 month of

**Table 19.1**

Diagnostic Criteria for 307.42 Primary Insomnia

A. The predominant complaint is difficulty initiating or maintaining sleep or nonrestorative sleep, for at least a month.
B. The sleep disturbance (or associated daytime fatigue) causes clinically significant distress or impairment in social, occupational, or other important areas of functioning.
C. The sleep disturbance does not occur exclusively during the course of narcolepsy, breathing-related sleep disorder, circadian rhythm sleep disorder, or a parasomnia.
D. The disturbance does not occur exclusively during the course of another mental disorder (e.g., major depressive disorder, generalized anxiety disorder, a delirium).
E. The disturbance is not due to the direct physiological effects of a substance (e.g., a drug of abuse, a medication) or a general medical condition.

insomnia, as well as secondary impairment in daytime functions (e.g., difficulty concentrating, poor work performance).

*Primary Hypersomnia* (see Table 19.2) is excessive sleepiness for a minimum of 1 month (or less if recurrent). Hypersomnia is clinically demonstrated either by unusually long sleep episodes or by abnormal amounts of sleeping when the person is expected to be alert. There may be daily episodes of daytime sleep. The person with primary hypersomnia sleeps at least 8 hours in a single night and often will sleep 10–14 hours during his or her normal sleeping period.

*Narcolepsy* is characterized by excessive daytime drowsiness, emotion-triggered muscle atonia/weakness (i.e., cataplexy), sleep paralysis, and hypnagogic/hypno-pompic hallucinations. According to the *DSM-IV*, narcolepsy is defined as irresistible attacks of refreshing sleep with either one or both of the following: cataplexy or recurrent intrusions of REM-related phenomena such as hypnopompic or hynagogic hallucinations or sleep paralysis. The severity of sleepiness ranges

**Table 19.2**

Diagnostic Criteria for 307.44 Primary Hypersomnia

A. The predominant complaint is excessive sleepiness for at least 1 month (or less if recurrent) as evidenced by either prolonged sleep episodes or daytime sleep episodes that occur almost daily.
B. The excessive sleepiness causes clinically significant distress or impairment in social, occupational, or other important areas of functioning.
C. The excessive sleepiness is not better accounted for by insomnia and does not occur exclusively during the course of another sleep disorder (e.g., narcolepsy, breathing-related sleep disorder, circadian rhythm sleep disorder, or a parasomnia) and cannot be accounted for by an inadequate amount of sleep.
D. The disturbance does not occur exclusively during the course of another mental disorder.
E. The disturbance is not due to the direct physiological effects of a substance (e.g., a drug of abuse, a medication) or a general medical condition.

*Specify if:*

**Recurrent:** If there are periods of excessive sleepiness that last at least 3 days occurring several times a year for at least 2 years.

from feelings of drowsiness while engaged in boring tasks (often requiring naps) to pervasive sleepiness and full-blown sleep attacks. It is widely known that narcoleptics have trouble staying awake. Less appreciated is that narcolepsy is also associated with insomnia. Thus, patients with narcolepsy have problems with maintaining *both* sleep and alertness under the appropriate circumstances.

*Breathing-Related Sleep Disorder* is characterized by sleep disruptions that lead to excessive sleepiness or insomnia, which can be attributed to a sleep-related breathing condition (obstructive or central sleep apnea or central alveolar hypoventilation). Among the sleep-disordered breathing syndromes, there are two major types of sleep apnea, central and obstructive. Mental health professionals overwhelmingly tend to work with individuals suffering from obstructive sleep apnea and, therefore, this disorder is highlighted in this chapter. Patients with obstructive sleep apnea have a mechanical blockage of their upper airway (e.g., enlarged tonsils, increased collapsibility of the upper airway related to reductions in genioglossus muscle activity), which results in decreased airflow and/or significant decreases in arterial blood oxygenation or sleep arousals (see Apnea-Hypopnea Index for details).

*Circadian Rhythm Sleep Disorder* is a recurrent or repeating pattern of problems with remaining alert or sleeping at appropriate times. The *DSM-IV* recognizes four subtypes: delayed sleep phase type, jet lag type, shift work type, and unspecified type. The jet lag and shift work types are almost always caused by a significant external change in the person's sleep-wake schedule. As a result, there is a misalignment of the required sleep schedule with the person's natural biological rhythms.

Several dyssomnias, which are subsumed under the *DSM-IV* diagnosis of 307.47 Dyssomnia Not Otherwise Specified, also come to the attention of mental health professionals. Examples are restless legs syndrome (RLS), periodic leg movement disorder (PLMDS), and sleep deprivation that causes abnormal levels of sleepiness. Restless legs syndrome is characterized by a "creepy crawly"-like feeling, usually in the lower legs, that is partially or totally relieved by getting up and moving around; frequently, the uncomfortable feeling returns as soon as the person rests or tries to return to sleep. The abnormal sensations are typically in the legs, but they may also occur in the arms. Periodic leg movements or nocturnal myoclonus are muscle contractions lasting several seconds alternating with contraction-free periods before another burst of muscle contractions. The contraction-free periods last about 20–30 seconds. Frequent muscular contractions and limb jerks can produce sleep interruptions and multiple awakenings throughout the night. The limb movements in patients with PLMD are stereotyped and involve extension of the big toe along with flexion of the ankle, knee, and sometimes the hip. Patients with RLS often display evidence on PSG-EMG of periodic leg movements, whereas most people with PLMD, as classified by the International Classification of Sleep Disorders (ICSD) [revised by the American Academy of Sleep Medicine (2005)], do not suffer from RLS. Patients with RLS or PLMD are often unaware of their sleep-related limb movements. The problem is often identified by the bed partner and/or self-discovered by virtue of bed covers being in total disarray after awakening. Periodic limb movements are suppressed during REM-stage sleep. The *severity* of sleep-related periodic limb movements is documented by PMLS-I scores (see "Sleep Indices"). Of interest, a majority of older women have PLMS-I over 5, and up to 50% will have PLMS-I greater than the clinically accepted diagnostic cutoff of 15 per hour. Periodic leg movements that cause frequent arousals and full awakenings from sleep are associated with decreased sleep efficiency, decreased total sleep time, and greater and lesser time, respectively, in light versus deep sleep. Arousals and awakenings from sleep may result in excessive daytime drowsiness.

## DIAGNOSTIC CONSIDERATIONS

The first task of mental health professionals is to establish that sleep complaints are not solely caused by an underlying medical disorder, another sleep disorder, or a substance-related disorder. From a clinical perspective, this is often difficult to determine with certainty. Moreover, dyssomnias are not automatically eliminated as an added sleep disorder diagnosis in the presence of a co-existing psychiatric disorder. This is important to remember, because there is a growing consensus that the independent treatment of a dyssomnia plus the psychiatric disorder may be necessary to achieve an optimal outcome.

Any medical disease, mental disorder, or sleep disorder that can cause insomnia is technically part of the differential diagnosis of primary insomnia. On a practical level, primary insomnia is increasingly likely to be the diagnosis with the exclusion of each medical and mental disorder known to cause insomnia. Within this context, two anxiety disorders (i.e., generalized anxiety disorder and posttraumatic stress disorder) are commonly associated with problems initiating, maintaining, or achieving restful sleep. Insomnia is reported in up to 70% of patients with generalized anxiety disorder (GAD; Monti and Monti, 2000; Ohayon, Caulet, & Lemoine, 1998), and the *quality* of insomnia in GAD is nearly identical to that of patients with primary insomnia. In both primary insomnia and insomnia associated with GAD, patients often worry about obtaining sufficient sleep at night and report difficulty falling asleep and maintaining sleep. Both primary insomnia and GAD patients report being keyed up (alternating with fatigue) and having difficulty concentrating. Thus, it is not feasible to use qualitative differences in making the diagnosis of primary insomnia versus insomnia as a core component of GAD.

Posttraumatic stress disorder (PTSD) is also associated with insomnia, often severe insomnia. Unlike primary insomnia, nightmares are also a feature of PTSD. The content of PTSD-related nightmares often contains features of the original trauma, including the experience of reliving the traumatic event (Mellman & Hipolito, 2006). The presence of trauma-related nightmares linked to real-life traumatic events are the key feature that distinguishes primary insomnia from the sleep problems reported by patients suffering from PTSD.

According to the *DSM-IV*, a person would meet criteria for narcolepsy by having attacks of refreshing sleep that occur daily over at least 3 months *plus* recurrent episodes of sleep paralysis. This would be known among sleep medicine experts as narcolepsy without cataplexy, and its validity as a true form of narcolepsy is questioned by some clinicians. Normal healthy individuals without narcolepsy can report sleep paralysis, which is self-limiting and not an absolute indicator of underlying neuropathology. Sleep paralysis, therefore, is not diagnostic of narcolepsy.

In contrast, cataplexy that is triggered by strong emotions (e.g., laughter, anger, or fear) where the atonia/weakness affects the knees, face, neck/head, or muscles of the lower or upper extremities is almost always a sign of narcolepsy. Thus, emotion-linked cataplexy is pathognomonic of narcolepsy. Unlike seizures, there is no clouding or loss of consciousness associated with cataplexy. A minority of narcoleptic patients (approximately 30%) suffer from excessive daytime sleepiness and sleep-onset REM but putatively have no history of cataplexy. Cataplexy, therefore, may be a marker of severity and/or increased loss of hypocretin neurons. Because narcoleptic patients may nod off or withdraw from social engagements at work, they are sometimes perceived as lazy, shy, or suffering from an Axis II personality disorder. Without a careful history, narcolepsy also may be confused with major depression, primary insomnia, or social anxiety disorder.

Breathing-related sleep disorder (i.e., obstructive sleep apnea) is a serious condition that left untreated leads to impaired memory and work performance, poor motor coordination, and poor executive functions. Risk factors are obesity, large neck circumference ($>$ 17 inches), increasing age (over 40% in the elderly), male gender, positive family history, or any medical condition that obstructs or impairs the patency of the upper airway. Patients presenting with depression or fatigue or an inability to achieve refreshed sleep should be automatically assessed for possible sleep-related breathing disorders. Normal or even underweight individuals can rarely be diagnosed with obstructive sleep apnea.

Traveling to another location, especially across time-zones, results in a misalignment of circadian rhythms; that is, the sleep-wake cycle is temporarily out-of-phase with the person's biological (e.g., thermoregulation, hypothalamic-pituitary-adrenal axis) circadian rhythms. With these types of externally induced circadian rhythm disturbances (e.g., jet lag, shift work), there is a strong sleep propensity during times that the individual needs to be awake and, conversely, a natural alertness during periods when the person is attempting to sleep. In most healthy people who have crossed several time zones, their circadian-based, biological rhythms will synchronize with their new sleep-wake cycle after several days. It may be possible to accelerate this process by administering melatonin and light exposure at the appropriate times in relation to their new sleep-wake requirements. In patients with mental disorders, travel across time zones can markedly exacerbate or trigger a reemergence of psychiatric symptoms, particularly in patients with major depression. The circadian rhythm disturbances associated with travel east across several time zones has been proposed as a biological model for major depression.

Individuals with restless legs syndrome, which will be a separate diagnosis in *DSM-5*, have classic complaints (e.g., creepy-crawly feelings in the legs). There are clear-cut urges to physically get up and move around, which temporarily reduces "tension" in the legs. A high proportion (up to 75%) of patients with restless legs syndrome develop repeated limb movements in sleep, which are characterized by muscle twitches and jerks every 20–40 seconds throughout the night. While restless legs syndrome is commonly associated with sleep-related periodic limb movements, most individuals with PLMD, as defined by the International Classification of Sleep Disorders (ICSD), do not suffer from dysesthesias and/or restless legs syndrome. In PLMD, the muscle disturbances are not simply hypnic reflexes (i.e., the jerks associated with the early phase of sleep onset) but flexing of toes, knees, and ankles, which is outside the person's awareness. There are hundreds of these movements throughout the night, although there is a large variance in the night-to-night frequency in limb movements. Talking with the patient's bed partner is valuable, because this person will inevitably report extreme restlessness *throughout* the night, which is easily confirmed by polysomnography. Fibromyalgia, anemia, kidney disorders, and other sleep disorders such as sleep apnea may present with or exacerbate the severity of periodic limb movements or restless legs syndrome.

## EPIDEMIOLOGY

Complaints of difficulty initiating or maintaining sleep or difficulty obtaining restful sleep (i.e., nonrestorative sleep) are common (approximately 20%) in the general population. Insomnia is more prevalent in women and older patients. When more restrictive and hierarchical diagnostic criteria are used to diagnose primary insomnia, the prevalence rate drops to approximately 6 percent (Ohayon & Sagales, 2010). Approximately 10% of patients who seek treatment for excessive daytime sleepiness suffer from primary hypersomnia, but the lifetime prevalence in the general population is unknown. The prevalence of classic narcolepsy with emotion-triggered cataplexy is approximately 0.02% to 0.05% of the U.S. population, with an equal incidence in men and women.

For unknown reasons, the prevalence of narcolepsy is quite different in different regions of the world, with Japan having about 1 person in 600 affected, or a 0.17% rate. The prevalence in Israel is about 1 in 500,000. Like most medical syndromes, growth in scientific knowledge about a disease entity leads to the discovery of various subtypes and milder forms of the illness. Thirty percent of narcoleptics are estimated to suffer from narcolepsy without cataplexy (perhaps a less severe form of narcolepsy), and less than 25% experience all four components of the narcoleptic tetrad (i.e., excessive daytime sleepiness, cataplexy, sleep paralysis, and hallucinations) at any point during their course of illness.

The Kleine-Levin form of narcolepsy is more common in men than women. The prevalence of breathing-related sleep disorder is 2% to 3% in women and up to 7% in adult males. Although the prevalence in Caucasian and African American populations is similar, there is some evidence for an earlier age of onset and greater severity in African Americans. The lifetime prevalence for circadian rhythm sleep disorder is unknown. The elderly tend to have a higher prevalence of phase-advanced sleep patterns (early to sleep, early to rise) compared to younger and middle-aged adults. In contrast, 5% to 10% of adolescents report phase-delayed patterns (late to sleep, late to rise). Up to 60% of shift workers experience delayed sleep phase type of circadian disturbances. A number of syndromes are subsumed under the dyssomnia not otherwise specified category, several of which in the literature are diagnosed using quite different criteria. There are estimated lifetime prevalence rates as high as 10% for restless legs syndrome, although the prevalence drops to approximately 2% to 3% or less if one considers only those individuals with more severe forms. There is a two-fold greater prevalence in women, with increasing severity in older individuals. Restless legs syndrome does exist in childhood, but its true prevalence is unknown; it is possible that the childhood variants may be attributed to stress and/or anxiety disorders.

PSYCHOLOGICAL AND BIOLOGICAL ASSESSMENT

There is no single brain region that regulates sleep or wakefulness, nor has there been a neurotransmitter that exclusively turns on or turns off sleep. However, there is a complex network of brain regions and neuronal pathways that regulate selective components of sleep (e.g., homeostasis). Polysomnography (PSG) is not generally employed as a tool in the diagnosis of primary insomnia. No objective findings on PSG (e.g., sleep architecture, proportion of time in sleep stages) are specific to primary insomnia. Research will determine whether presleep and sleep EEG power spectra will emerge as diagnostic aids in the future. The MSLT is an adjunctive tool to obtain an objective measure of sleepiness. MSLT-derived sleep latencies, however, reflect an integration of sleep propensity and physiological arousal. To the extent that insomnia is a condition of hyperarousal, MSLT sleep latencies are often normal (or even prolonged). This may even be the case in patients whose subjective experience is an inability to obtain sufficient quantities of sleep.

In primary hypersomnia, the PSG will typically show decreased sleep latency, increased total sleep time, and normal (or increased) sleep efficiency. The amount of time in deep sleep may be increased. The average MSLT sleep latency is short (< 5 minutes). Kleine-Levin hypersomnia is associated with increased sleep propensity on MSLT. A distinctive PSG feature of narcolepsy is sleep-onset REM. The first REM period in healthy individuals takes place about 90 minutes after sleep onset. In patients with narcolepsy, the first REM period often takes place in less than 20 minutes or, in some cases, "the moment the head hits the pillow"; thus, the term *sleep-onset REM*. Sleep-onset REM also may take place during daytime naps, particularly in those narcoleptic patients with sleep deprivation. Although the presence of sleep-onset REM (SOREM) on the MSLT is highly suggestive of narcolepsy, MSLT SOREM is not a definitive confirmation of narcolepsy (Mignot et al., 2002).

If there are no identified mechanical blockages (e.g., enlarged tonsils or craniofacial abnormalities) or endocrine disorders, continuous positive airway pressure (CPAP) is the treatment of choice for sleep-related breathing disorder (i.e., obstructive sleep apnea). CPAP is highly effective but associated with poor compliance, which can be attributed to the cumbersome nature of the equipment as well as the lack of awareness on the part of patients that they are truly suffering from abnormal breathing. The development of specific cognitive-behavioral treatments for sleep apnea that target compliance problems will be a focus of research in the future. The majority of people with sleep-related breathing disorder are overweight [Body Mass Index (BMI) 25–29.9 kg/m$^2$] or obese (BMI > 30 kg/m$^2$).

There is no diagnostic test for circadian rhythm sleep disorder (see Table 19.3). A history of external changes in the timing of sleep makes it fairly easy to identify jet lag and shift work types of circadian rhythm sleep disorder. Delayed sleep phase type of disturbance is also easily identified by sleep history and a few classic features (e.g., these individuals almost always report having extreme difficulty waking up).

**Table 19.3**

Diagnostic Criteria for 307.45 Circadian Rhythm Sleep Disorder

A. A persistent or recurrent pattern of sleep disruption leading to excessive sleepiness or insomnia that is due to a mismatch between the sleep-awake schedule required by a person's environment and his or her circadian sleep-wake pattern.

B. The sleep disturbance causes clinically significant distress or impairment in social, occupational, or other important areas of functioning.

C. The disturbance does not occur exclusively during the course of another sleep disorder or other mental disorder.

D. The disturbance is not due to the direct physiological effects of a substance (e.g., a drug of abuse, a medication) or a general medical condition.

Specify type:

**Phase-Delayed Sleep Type:** A persistent pattern of late sleep onset and late awakening times, with an inability to fall asleep and awaken at a desired earlier time

**Jet Lag Type:** Sleepiness and alertness that occur at an inappropriate time of day relative to local time, occurring after repeated travel across more than one time zone

**Shift Work Type:** Insomnia during the major sleep period or excessive sleepiness during the major awake period associated with night shift work or frequently changing shift work

**Unspecified Type**

The person with a delayed sleep phase type of circadian rhythm disorder may have multiple alarm clocks set and/or push the snooze button(s) 30 to 40 times before achieving full awakening. With the exception of phase-advanced sleep-wake patterns, many of the circadian rhythm sleep disorders of the unspecified type are probably rare (or, at least, not commonly recognized) in mental health clinics.

Several of the unspecified types mimic mood and anxiety disorders. Examples include individuals with so-called "free-running" and "irregular" sleep-wake patterns. The "free-runner" has a gradual delay each night in the time of sleep onset and awakens a little later each morning. This person's sleep-wake cycle is gradually delayed by short periods (15–30 minutes) each night throughout the 24-hour clock period. The person with a "free-running" sleep-wake cycle is locked into a natural sleep-wake biological rhythm, which is just slightly greater than 24 hours. Some people have unidentifiable or irregular sleep-wake cycles (i.e., there is no discernible pattern). Although a stable advanced sleep-wake cycle is a common variant in older people, it is given the unspecified type designation in *DSM-IV*. It should be emphasized that none of these advanced, delayed, free-running, or irregular sleep-wake patterns are considered pathological in the absence of clinically significant distress or impairment.

The diagnosis of restless legs syndrome (i.e., dyssomnia not otherwise specified) is made on the basis of history and ruling out other possible medical or neurological diseases. Patients with restless legs syndrome often meet ICSD criteria for periodic limb movement disorder (PLMD). On PSG-EMG there will often be limb movements at sleep onset.

ETIOLOGICAL CONSIDERATIONS

Several neurotransmitter systems (e.g., noradrenergic, GABAergic, serotonergic, and hypocretinergic) are involved in the regulation of arousal systems in both sleep and wakefulness. These same transmitter-receptor systems are implicated in the anxiety disorders, especially GAD, panic disorder, and PTSD. Perhaps this explains in part the high prevalence of insomnia in anxiety disorders and the difficult challenge of separating primary insomnia from the *DSM-IV* disorders of insomnia related to panic disorder or GAD.

Primary hypersomnia is heritable in some but not all family pedigrees. There are two major patterns: gradual and recurrent. Some people gradually develop hypersomnia, which evolves into a chronic pattern of excessive daytime sleepiness and an inability to obtain restorative sleep. These individuals appear to be sluggish or even drunk and experience automatic behaviors (e.g., driving a car past the turn-off without awareness that they have missed the exit). Disturbances in hypothalamic functions have been proposed for this type of primary hypersomnia, although there is no definitive proof of this theory. There is also a recurrent form of primary hypersomnia, which is characterized by repeated bouts of excessive daytime sleepiness lasting from 2 to 30 or more days. These individuals demonstrate largely normal cognitive, emotional, and behavioral functions between episodes of hypersomnia. This form of primary hypersomnia is specified in *DSM-IV* as *recurrent* if there are periods of excessive sleepiness that last for at least 3 days on several occasions within at least two consecutive 12-month periods.

Among sleep medicine experts, this subtype of primary hypersomnia is referred to as the Kleine-Levin syndrome. Patients with Kleine-Levin hypersomnia often demonstrate compulsive eating and inappropriate sexuality (e.g., public masturbation) or other bizarre behaviors during bouts of hypersomnia. Overt sexual impulsivity is almost twice as prevalent in men as women with the Kleine-Levin subtype. Patients with recurrent primary hypersomnia are much more likely to demonstrate neurological problems such as impaired memory, gait disturbances, and autonomic nervous system dysfunctions (e.g., sweating, flushing, low blood pressure, and bradycardia) (Billiard, Jaussent, Dauvilliers, & Besset, in press). Lesions in the frontal and occipital lobes, hippocampus, amygdala, and pontine locus coeruleus have been associated with hypersomnia, inappropriate sexual behaviors, and compulsive eating.

First-degree relatives of probands with narcolepsy have an increased risk compared to relatives of unaffected probands. However, only 25% of monozygotic twins are concordant for narcolepsy, which suggests a strong environmental influence. The discovery of narcoleptic dogs and a mutation of the hypocretin gene catapulted narcolepsy into the forefront of sleep research. Interestingly, while a mutated hypocretin-2 receptor gene produces narcolepsy in dogs, no such mutation has been discovered in narcoleptic humans. What have been identified are human leukocyte antigen susceptibility factors for narcolepsy (HLA-DR2 and HLA-DQB1*0602) and low cerebrospinal fluid levels of hypocretin-1 in narcoleptics with cataplexy (Lin & Mignot, 2007; Mignot et al., 2002). There also appears to be a loss of hypothalamic hypocretinergic neurons in postmortem patients with narcolepsy (Blouin et al., 2005). The hypocretin neurotransmitter system is largely excitatory and stimulates neuronal activity in multiple projection areas in the brain, including interfacing with acetylcholine and noradrenergic (i.e., locus ceruleus) nuclei, which are, respectively, involved in REM and muscle atonia.

More than 86% of obese patients with type 2 diabetes have a sleep-related breathing disorder (Foster et al., 2009), and overweight and obese people report getting less sleep than do patients of normal weight. People who self-report less than 7 hours of sleep per night are at greater risk for developing obesity (Gangwisch et al., 2005). Also, Nordin and Kaplan (2010) found that complaints of sleep initiation or maintaining sleep are a predictor of significant weight gain when tracked over an approximately 29-year period of time. Thus, there appears to be a bidirectional relationship between insomnia and obesity. Insomnia and sleep-related breathing disturbances are so prevalent in overweight and obese individuals that it may be impossible to determine whether sleep complaints are due to a dyssomnia or secondary to obesity or an admixture of both situations. It is possible that the early diagnosis and treatment of insomnia will prevent the later sequential development of obesity, sleep apnea, and sleep deprivation–related neurological impairments.

Circadian rhythm sleep disorder must be distinguished from normal adaptations to external changes in the sleep-wake cycle and phase-delayed or phase-advanced sleep-wake cycles that cause no distress or impairment. A phase-advanced sleep-wake cycle (not unusual for older people) is not itself evidence of a sleep disorder.

The familial pattern of dyssomnia not otherwise specified (i.e., restless legs syndrome) has been appreciated since its first description by Ekbom (1944). There is an approximately 83% concordance in monozygotic twins. Desautels and coworkers (2001) identified the first locus linked to restless legs syndrome on chromosome 12. In total, four genes and six loci have been linked to restless legs syndrome. Data suggest that brain iron levels may be decreased in restless legs syndrome.

Course and Prognosis

The thorny issue for clinicians is what to do with patients who suffer from insomnia (or hypersomnia) that could be caused by an underlying medical, psychiatric, or sleep disorder. In theory, if the underlying disease is effectively treated, then the insomnia (or hypersomnia) should resolve. When this is the case, it is justified to focus exclusively on the underlying medical, psychiatric, or other sleep condition (e.g., sleep apnea). Often, however, this is not what takes place. Even dramatic improvements in the underlying medical (e.g., fibromyalgia), sleep (e.g., sleep apnea), or psychiatric (e.g., major depression) disorder(s) may not be associated with parallel improvements in the insomnia (or hypersomnia). In such situations, the patient requires separate treatment for the sleep problem and, depending on the course of illness, would receive a diagnosis of primary insomnia (or primary hypersomnia) or insomnia (or hypersomnia) related to another mental disorder or 780.XX sleep disorder due to a general medical disorder. The critical issue is that the person should receive targeted and comprehensive treatment for *both* the dyssomnia and any other coexisting disorder(s). Identifying and developing targeted treatments for the dyssomnias and any coexisting disorder will improve the long-term course, prognosis, and well-being of the patient.

# PARASOMNIAS

## DESCRIPTION OF DISORDERS

According to the *DSM-IV*, parasomnias are characterized by either abnormal behaviors or physiological events that occur in association with sleep or emerge during a specific sleep stage (e.g., REM behavior disorder) or during sleep-wake transitions (e.g., recurrent isolated sleep paralysis). Isolated parasomnias are probably much more prevalent in the general population than is generally appreciated. Patients with parasomnias often come to the attention of mental health providers due to their associated bizarre, wild, and sometimes dangerous behaviors. Serious self-inflicted injuries and aggression, including homicidal behaviors, have been linked to parasomnias.

## CLINICAL PICTURE

All people experience bad dreams or nightmares. Thus, the experience of a single nightmare or even many nightmares is not itself indicative of a sleep disorder and/or the need for treatment. To a large extent, a person is defined as having a nightmare disorder when he or she experiences great distress and/or is impaired by the episodes. As reviewed in the "Types of Sleep" section, nightmares take place during REM-stage sleep and are characterized by vivid images and, at times, elaborate content. Nightmares are typically associated with content-relevant emotions (e.g., fear when the dream involves threats to one's well-being).

There are four *DSM-IV* criteria for *Nightmare Disorder*. The word-for-word criteria are:

A. Repeated awakenings from the major sleep period or naps with detailed recall of extended and frightening dreams, usually involving threats to survival, security, or self-esteem. The awakenings generally occur during the second half of the sleep period.

B. On awakening from the frightening dreams, the person rapidly becomes oriented and alert (in contrast to the confusion and disorientation seen in sleep terror disorder and some forms of epilepsy).

C. The dream experience, or the sleep disturbance resulting from the awakening causes clinically significant distress or impairment in social, occupational, or other important areas of functioning; and

D. The nightmares do not occur exclusively during the course of another mental disorder (e.g., a delirium, posttraumatic stress disorder) and are not due to the direct physiological effects of a substance (e.g., a drug of abuse, a medication) or a general medical condition.

*Sleep Terror Disorder* is a condition characterized by repeated arousals from sleep, which are heralded by yelling, screaming, or crying. The person appears frightened. These abrupt, fear-like awakenings typically take place during the first third of the sleep period. It is very difficult for an observer to awaken the person and terminate the episode (see Table 19.4). There is no dream recall and, in fact, there is amnesia for the event upon awakening to full consciousness the next day. There

**Table 19.4**

Diagnostic Criteria for 307.46 Sleep Terror Disorder

A.  Recurrent episodes of abrupt awakening from sleep, usually occurring during the first third of the major sleep episode and beginning with a panicky scream.

B.  Intense fear and signs of autonomic arousal, such as tachycardia, rapid breathing, and sweating, during each episode.

C.  Relative unresponsiveness to the efforts of others to comfort the person during the episode.

D.  No detailed dream is recalled and there is amnesia for the episode.

E.  The episodes cause clinically significant distress or impairment in social, occupational, or other important areas of functioning.

F.  The disturbance is not due to the direct physiological effects of a substance (e.g., a drug of abuse, a medication) or a general medical condition.

must be evidence of significant clinical distress or impairment as a consequence of these events, which cannot be exclusively attributed to another medical, substance, or mental disorder.

*Sleepwalking Disorder* is characterized by its namesake (i.e., repeated complex motor behaviors that involve getting out of bed and walking around; see Table 19.5). Like sleep terror disorder, there is amnesia the next morning about the event. During the events themselves, which may last from a few minutes to as long as 30–45 minutes, the individual often has a blank stare and does not appear to be aware of his or her surroundings. Similar to sleep terror events, the patient is very difficult to awaken or terminate the episode.

*Parasomnia Not Otherwise Specified* incorporates several sleep-related disturbances that are characterized by either abnormal behaviors and/or physiological events that take place during sleep or in relation to specific sleep stages or during transitions into or out of sleep. Examples include REM behavior disorder, sleep paralysis, sleep panic attacks, sexual behavior in sleep (i.e., sexsomnia), and sleep-related eating. With the exception of sleep panic attacks and sleep paralysis, where the patients are fully alert after awakening, there is often confusion during or immediately after awakening in

**Table 19.5**

Diagnostic Criteria for 307.46 Sleepwalking Disorder

A.  Repeated episodes of rising from bed during sleep and walking about, usually occurring during the first third of the major sleep episode.

B.  While sleepwalking, the person has a blank, staring face, is relatively unresponsive to the efforts of others to communicate with him or her, and can be awakened only with great difficulty.

C.  On awakening (either from the sleepwalking episode or the next morning), the person has amnesia for the episode.

D.  Within several minutes after awakening from the sleepwalking episode, there is no impairment of mental activity or behavior (although there may initially be a short period of confusion or disorientation).

E.  The sleepwalking causes clinically significant distress or impairment in social, occupational, or other important areas of functioning.

F.  The disturbance is not due to the direct physiological effects of a substance (e.g., a drug of abuse, a medication) or a general medical condition.

patients with REM behavior disorder, sexsomnia, and sleep-related eating. In addition, patients with REM behavior disorder, sexsomnia, and sleep-related eating (as well as sleep terror and sleepwalking disorders) are unable to remember most or any of their behaviors or events that took place during the sleep-related episode. Many of these conditions come to the attention of mental health professionals via the patients themselves or family members and, in cases involving sexsomnia, increasingly by the legal-justice system.

REM behavior disorder, as indicated by its name, is a disorder of REM sleep. It will be removed from the Parasomnia Not Otherwise Specified category in *DSM-5* and stand alone as a diagnostic entity. The fundamental feature of this parasomnia is an absence of the muscle paralysis that is normally associated with REM-stage sleep (i.e., there is REM without muscle atonia). Behaviors may range from a hand movement or facial expression to very complex motor behaviors. There appear to be strong emotions (e.g., anger) associated with many of the behaviors (e.g., punching or shouting). Although REM behaviors may appear bizarre, on close examination they often make sense when understood within the context of the dream content.

Sleep paralysis, like REM sleep behavior disorder, is linked to disturbances in REM-stage sleep. The phenomenon of paralysis takes place while the person is "going into" (i.e., hypnogogic) or "coming out" (i.e., hypnopompic) of sleep. Sleep paralysis refers to the experience of being unable to move, which is a normal physiological state in REM-stage sleep (i.e., muscle atonia). Thus, being unable to move is not abnormal; what is abnormal is that the person is fully aware of his or her physiological state of paralysis. This conscious awareness is a frightening experience (i.e., the inability to move despite major efforts to do so). REM-related muscle atonia may be an evolutionary adaptation to promote safety by preventing individuals from acting out their dream content. Most sleep medicine textbooks describe sleep paralysis as a "border" or "transition" state between being asleep versus being awake. In addition to muscle paralysis (except for respiratory and eye muscles), patients with sleep paralysis may experience a range of sensory sensations from simple "feelings" ("I feel an evil presence") to elaborate and detailed events involving any combination of sensory modalities. Visual experiences are lifelike in quality (e.g., "a woman was standing by my bed"), but they may also include auditory, telepathic, olfactory, somatosensory, or gustatory sensations that are integrated into the experience ("She was very old, with deep crevices in her face. . . . She also had a hard-to-describe but strong musty odor. . . . The smell was horrible and I wanted to throw up. . . .").

Sleep panic attacks are fearful arousals to full consciousness, lasting 2 to 8 minutes. Unlike confusional arousals from delta sleep, sleep panic attacks are associated with complete awakenings to full alertness. The next morning, patients have full and accurate recall of the previous night's panic attacks. There are no dreams, vivid images, or cognitions *during* sleep panic attacks. Sleep panic arousals are characterized by profound fear and frequently (but not always) physiological hyperarousal (e.g., tachycardia, increased respiratory rate, increased blood pressure), but changes in heart and respiratory rate are inconsistent, and any associated increases are less impressive than those observed in sleep terror disorder. After *awakening*, patients may develop fear-related cognitions, with content focused on worries about death and dying. As few as one sleep panic attack can lead to secondary (i.e., conditioned or context-specific) avoidance behaviors. Thus, patients with sleep panic attacks often develop a fear of sleep and the sleeping environment.

Patients with sexsomnia may engage in the full range of human sexual behaviors (e.g., masturbation, intercourse). These behaviors are often abrupt in onset and appear senseless and without motivation or purpose. The sexual behaviors are often outside the norm for the individual compared to his or her sexual activities during waking, fully conscious states. The sexual acts can be aggressive in nature, reflecting rape, sadomasochistic, or humiliating motifs. Actions tend to develop abruptly during partial awakenings after 1 or more hours of sleep. There is amnesia for the events with a sense of guilt, shame, or disgust upon realization of the sexual acts.

Sleep-related eating disorder is defined as recurrent episodes of involuntary eating after having fallen asleep (in contrast to eating at night while awake and before sleep onset). While this condition would be diagnosed as a parasomnia not otherwise specified in *DSM-IV*, the ICDS classification recognizes this as a distinct disorder requiring one or more of the following: (a) consumption of peculiar forms or combinations of food (i.e., foods that would not normally be consumed by the individual); (b) insomnia and complaints of nonrestorative sleep, fatigue, or day-time sleepiness related to multiple episodes of awakening to eat; (c) sleep-related injury; (d) dangerous behaviors performed in pursuit of food or while cooking food; (e) morning anorexia; and (f) negative health consequences. People with sleep-related eating disorder often discover the next morning that they have been in the kitchen cooking and find evidence of food consumption. It is presumed that these individuals are confused as a consequence of their sleep-related eating disorder and that this disorientation accounts for the consumption of peculiar foods and/or drinks or, infrequently, dangerous substances. Little is known about the long-term course of sleep-related eating disorder. Over the short term, patients are at increased risk for harm due to burns while cooking, falls or tripping over objects or barriers in search for food, or consuming toxic substances.

DIAGNOSTIC CONSIDERATIONS

In other classification systems, sleep terror, sleepwalking, sexsomnia, and sleep-related eating would all be considered confusional arousal disorders. Consistent with this concept, the *DSM-5* will subsume sleep terror and sleepwalking disorders within a group of non-REM parasomnias identified as confusional arousal disorders. These sleep-related disorders share in common partial arousals in delta or deep sleep. The behaviors associated with confusional arousals are very often out-of-character for the person. There is blurred or no recall of the events after later awakening and achieving a state of full consciousness (i.e., there is amnesia for the event). One can conceptualize these syndromes, therefore, as conditions wherein the individual is able to perform motor functions ranging from simple acts (e.g., sitting up in bed) to complex behaviors (e.g., driving a car) during periods of impaired consciousness (i.e., partial awareness or, more typically, being totally unaware of physical surroundings and associated circumstances). Another theoretical model is to conceptualize these syndromes as a transient, sleep-related uncoupling of higher cognitive functions from intact motor behaviors. It is not unusual for an individual with one type of confusional arousal to suffer from a second or even third type of disorder of arousal. Some investigators view sleep terror and sleepwalking as simply clinical variants of a common diathesis. This view is supported by (a) high comorbidity of sleepwalking in patients with sleep terror disorder; (b) children with sleep terrors often become adult sleepwalkers; and (c) sleep terrors and sleepwalking often co-occur in the same sleep event.

Unlike the non-REM confusional arousals of sleep terror, sleepwalking, sexsomnia, and sleep-related eating, individuals with *nightmares* are fully alert and aware of their surroundings after awakening. And, unlike sleep paralysis, nightmares are easily identified as unreal events (i.e., *after awakening*, patients are fully aware that the dream event did not actually take place in physical reality). The conditions most likely to be confused with nightmare disorder are different for children and adults. Nightmares in children are often confused with sleep terrors by parents. The child with sleep terrors has no recollection of the episode; the only memory associated with sleep terrors may be the image of a parent vigorously attempting to awaken the child from sleep. Sleep terrors are common in children but less prevalent in adults and can be easily distinguished from dreams in a number of ways (e.g., sleep terrors arise from delta sleep and there is amnesia for the episode, whereas nightmares are REM events that are often recalled in great detail by the person). Nightmares in children are linked to high levels of waking anxiety, anxiety proneness, and/or stressful events, whereas this is not necessarily the case in adults. In both children and adults with nightmares, a critical component of the workup is to evaluate for a history of trauma and to rule out posttraumatic stress disorder.

The symptoms of recurrent sleep paralysis disorder are poignant and, in most cases, are easily distinguished from other sleep disorders. The main challenge is to determine whether there is additional evidence of cataplexy and excessive daytime drowsiness to justify a diagnosis of narcolepsy. Although both sleep paralysis and sleep panic attacks are frightening, sleep panic attacks are not associated with muscle paralysis *during sleep*. We recently reported (Cortese & Uhde, 2006) that some patients with sleep panic attacks report freezing/immobilizations *during wake panic attacks* but not, to our knowledge, during sleep. The investigation of possibly overlapping motor pathways in the pathophysiology of sleep paralysis and sleep panic attacks deserves attention (Flosnik, Cortese, & Uhde, 2009). Clearly, however, patients with sleep panic attacks do not report visitation experiences and/or report hynagogic or hypnopompic hallucinations. Time misperception is commonly associated with sleep paralysis. Experiential time during sleep paralytic events is often much greater than actual clock time. Sometimes this experiential time versus clock time is appreciated by the patient ("It seemed like hours, but I know it was only a few minutes") both during and immediately after the paralytic episodes, whereas other patients report being in some type of time warp. Whether the latter could be characterized as a dissociative phenomenon is undetermined. In any case, we have never seen time misperception of this nature in patients with sleep panic attacks. Neither sleep paralysis nor sleep panic attacks are accompanied by amnesia or confusional arousals or clouding of consciousness.

In patients with sexual behavior disorders in sleep, Kleine-Levin syndrome along with seizure disorders should be kept in mind. Sexual gestures, body thrusts, sexual moaning, and other sexual-like automatisms have been associated with seizures. Serotonin selective reuptake inhibitors (SSRIs) are reported to induce unwanted sexual behaviors in both wake and sleep states. Finally, malingering should be part of the differential diagnosis, especially when the patient has been charged with a crime or has a history of sociopathy and the diagnosis of a medical problem (e.g., sleep disorder) might be leveraged to his or her advantage.

In summary, the differential diagnosis of patients with parasomnias can be a challenge. Frontal and temporal lobe pathology, mainly seizure disorders, may have some similarities to parasomnias, especially those associated with confusion; however, episodes taking place during *both waking and sleeping states* and that have focal or stereotypical motor behaviors are associated with seizures and not parasomnias (Nickell & Uhde, 1991). The sun-downing phenomenon needs to be considered in the elderly with apparent disorientation and/or walking around aimlessly. As many of the non-REM parasomnias often coexist, the biggest challenge for the clinician will be differentiating among the various types.

EPIDEMIOLOGY

Nightmares appear to be more prevalent in both younger and older women than in men and decrease in both men and women with older age. Up to 5% of children experience one or more nightmares per week. Thirty percent of children will experience at least one lifetime sleep terror event, historically called *pavor nocturnus*, with a peak onset around 12 years of age. About 2.2% of the population overall suffers from sleep terrors, without any gender predominance. Nightmares are much more common than sleep terrors, but the two syndromes are often confused, especially in children. Children with the onset of sleep terrors before the age of 10 are more likely to suffer from sleep terrors in adulthood, and up to 75% of patients with sleep terrors will report sleepwalking. Sleepwalking is common in childhood and, like sleep terror disorder, also peaks around 12 years of age. Patients with sleepwalking may later develop sleep terrors or vice versa, and both sleep terrors and sleepwalking can coexist within the same episode.

REM sleep behavior disorder usually appears for the first time in adulthood, although it has been reported in childhood. Most information comes from clinical samples with a high male predominance. When the diagnosis is made in younger individuals, particularly those without coexisting neurological problems, there is close to a 1:1 gender ratio. The best available information suggests an approximate prevalence of 0.5% in the general population. Most cases come to the attention of clinicians when the patient is older than 50 years of age. The lifetime prevalence of sleep paralysis is close to 50% but drops off to 6% to 10% in people reporting recurrent isolated episodes of sleep paralysis (i.e., excluding individuals where sleep paralysis is part of narcolepsy). Patients with recurrent isolated sleep paralysis typically report their initial episode during early childhood, although the onset may occur at any time. In our clinical sample and others (Cheyne, 2005), there is a much higher prevalence in women compared with men.

Sleep panic attacks are two to three times more prevalent in women than men. The lifetime prevalence of panic disorder has been estimated to be as high as 5%. Approximately 65% of patients with *DSM-III/IV* panic disorder report at least one lifetime episode of sleep panic, and 30% to 45% report frequent sleep panic attacks (Singareddy & Uhde, 2009; Uhde, 2000). The lifetime and point prevalence of patients with exclusive sleep panic attacks (i.e., no history of wake panic attacks) is unknown. Information on sexsomnia is largely based on clinical samples, where there is a predominance of men in middle-age adulthood. Survey data, however, indicate that in nonclinical populations there is a wide range in age and a higher prevalence in women than previously appreciated (Trajanovic, Mangan, & Sapiro, 2007). Information regarding the epidemiology and prevalence of sleep-related eating is also limited. Four percent of college students report symptoms consistent with this syndrome, which markedly increases among patients with eating disorders. There appears to be an approximately 2:1 to 3:1 female/male ratio.

## PSYCHOLOGICAL AND BIOLOGICAL ASSESSMENT

Similar to patients with sleep panic attacks, patients with recurrent nightmares tend to experience decreased frequency and severity of nightmares when they are studied in the sleep laboratory environment. This improvement is attributed to the positive impact of safety cues (i.e., being monitored by staff and physicians). Nightmare sufferers do not demonstrate impressive differences from healthy normal controls on measures of sleep-onset latency or sleep efficiency. Increased gross motor activity, which is sufficient to meet criteria for periodic limb movement disorder, is sometimes observed in individuals with frequent nightmares. There may be modest increases in heart and respiratory rate, but these increases are less dramatic than what is observed in night terrors. Sleep terror episodes may be triggered by auditory-induced arousals during post-recovery delta sleep after 24 hours of total sleep deprivation. These events may also take place during transitions from delta sleep to REM sleep (Broughton, 2000). Hypersynchronous slow-wave sleep may develop just before an episode of sleep terror with the rapid appearance of a waking EEG pattern (Broughton, 1968). Increased fragmented sleep with multiple arousals during delta sleep is associated with sleep terrors and sleepwalking. Sleepwalkers have decreased EEG power in the delta band (0.75–4.5 Hz), with the most significant difference between sleepwalkers and normal controls being in the first non-REM cycle. Other lines of evidence in sleepwalkers suggest that after partial arousals there may be high-voltage theta/delta mixed in with alpha and beta wave activity.

REM sleep behavior disorder symptoms tend to take place during the second half of the sleep cycle. The behavioral events are noted during REM-stage sleep, and muscle activity is present during more than 50% of the REM period. Because this is a condition characterized by REM sleep without muscle paralysis, the diagnosis can be easily established by combining the PSG with careful video monitoring. Extra EMG leads should be placed on different muscle groups of the body, because selective areas may be associated with increased muscle tone, activity, or frank movement (e.g., arms but not legs).

The belief that isolated sleep paralysis is a REM-related event is mainly based upon extrapolations from patients' self-reports. Our cohort of subjects with isolated sleep paralysis report two peak time periods: (1) within the first 2 hours of sleep and (2) early in the morning. Our experience is consistent with the observations of other investigators (Cheyne, 2002; Girard & Cheyne, 2006). However, sleep paralysis episodes can take place at any point throughout the sleep night. The phenomenon of sleep paralysis clearly suggests a REM-related event, and some evidence suggests that paralysis can be induced in sleep paralysis–prone individuals by interrupting the first REM period.

The physiology of sleep paralysis is similar to cataplexy insofar as both phenomena are characterized by muscle atonia: One condition (sleep paralysis) emerges during transitions into and/or out of sleep and the other (cataplexy) that takes place during alert wakefulness. Both sleep paralysis and cataplexy, together with hallucinations and excessive daytime drowsiness, are components of the so-called narcoleptic tetrad (see "Narcolepsy").

Sleep panic attacks occur during the first half of the sleep period, almost always within 3 hours of sleep onset (Craske & Barlow, 1989; Mellman & Uhde, 1988). Sleep panic attacks are non-REM events, which typically take place during one of the first two non-REM cycles. Sleep panic attacks are abrupt awakenings and almost always emerge during the transition from late stage 2 to early delta sleep (Mellman & Uhde, 1988; Uhde, 2000). There is no seizure activity on EEG, although sleep-related seizures can be associated with anxiety or even panic-like episodes (Nickell & Uhde, 1991). Thus, sleep-related seizures are part of the differential diagnosis of sleep panic attacks. As a consequence of developing a conditioned fear of sleep, many patients with sleep panic attacks will have prolonged sleep latencies, decreased sleep efficiencies, and decreased total sleep times. However, these findings are not consistent across all studies, and there is a subgroup with sleep state misperception. Sex-related behaviors in sexsomnia, which may include sex talking (i.e., "dirty talk") are associated with abrupt arousals from delta sleep.

### Etiological Considerations

Given the longheld view that patients with distressing nightmares tend to have increased neuroticism and anxiety-like psychopathology during wakefulness, one might expect to find a genetic association between nightmares and anxiety disorders. The best available information, however, suggests that while nightmare disorder and GAD appear to be heritable conditions, there has yet to be identified common gene(s) that confer this comorbidity. There is a strong heritability associated with sleep terror and sleepwalking disorders. These disorders arise out of delta sleep (stage 4/N3), and confusional arousals can be triggered out of deep sleep by stimuli administered during (or mini-arousals developing during) phases of sleep where there is strong homeostatic pressure for wakefulness. Pedigree studies suggest a very high rate of heritability for sleep terrors (Kales et al., 1980), with many pedigrees also demonstrating a high prevalence of sleep terror and sleepwalking comorbidity. Probands with a positive sleepwalking history have a fivefold greater concordance for sleepwalking in monozygotic compared to dizygotic twins. There also appear to be high rates of comorbid sleepwalking, restless legs syndrome, periodic limb movement disorder, and sleep-disordered breathing, as well as bulimia and anorexia, in patients with sleep-related eating disorders. There is no information about the genetics of sleep-related eating disorder, although clock gene knockouts are known to shift major food consumption to the inactive, light phase in mice (Turek, et al., 2005). There is no information about the genetics of sexsomnia behaviors, although it is common to find a positive family history.

Early reports suggested that the narcolepsy HLA-type also occurred in REM sleep behavior disorder. However, this now appears unlikely; and, there is no evidence for HLA-DR 2 haplotype being associated in Parkinson's patients "with" versus "without" concomitant REM sleep behavior disorder. At the present time, there is no genetic test for REM sleep behavior disorder, either as a primary condition or complication of other medical conditions associated with REM without atonia. Selective lesions of subnuclei in the reticular formation and the locus ceruleus, as well as pure pontine infarctions in humans, are known to produce REM behaviors without atonia. These observations support brainstem abnormalities in the pathophysiology for many REM behaviors without atonia. Given that REM behavior disorder also may present years in advance of multiple system atrophy and Parkinson's disease, disorders characterized in part by abnormal accumulations of alpha-synucelein that destroy dopamine-producing cells, one wonders whether some types of REM sleep behavior disorder may prove to be a synucleinopathy. Little is known about the genetics of recurrent isolated sleep paralysis. There is a higher prevalence in African Americans compared to non-African Americans in the same geographical region, and within affected individuals the paralytic frequency is greater in African American than Caucasians.

## Course and Prognosis

The peak ages for experiencing "distressing" nightmares are 10–29 for women and 30–49 for men (Nielsen, 2010). Frequent nightmares, particularly if they are coupled with full awakenings and delayed return to sleep, may produce clinically significant insomnia. Unlike patients with sleep panic attacks, most patients with nightmares do not develop a fear of sleeping. Both the degree of distress and frequency of nightmares are employed as guideposts in making treatment decisions, but neither of these constructs are well-established predictors of treatment response. In psychoanalytic practice, a great deal of attention in the past was paid to the interpretation of dreams. In today's nonpsychoanalytically based practices, most clinicians engage clients in a review of their dreams only to the extent that anxiety dreams or nightmares are impairing and/or significantly distressing to the patients. Some data suggest that the preexisting level of waking psychological disturbance or neuroticism, rather than the frequency of nightmares per se, is most likely to predict distress and/or impairment from nightmares (Belicki, 1992). In terms of nightmares associated with life-threatening events or situations that threaten bodily integrity, the natural course is an initial peak in trauma-related nightmares followed by a progressive decrease and then disappearance over several months. Within the context of PTSD-related nightmares, those individuals whose nightmares fail to extinguish over several months ultimately require treatment.

At the present time, it is impossible to predict who will or will not follow a positive extinction versus nonextinction pattern and, therefore, our current ability to provide early interventions after a traumatic exposure is limited. Individuals with persistent PTSD-related nightmares will likely show dysfunctions in other areas of work, social, and interpersonal performance. In both children and adults, with or without known antecedent traumatic exposures, evidence of ongoing fear of sleep/sleeping or intense distresses about dream content are reasonable indications for treatment. Children with sleep terrors are often sleepwalkers too; and childhood sleep terror disorder can become a sleepwalking disorder in adulthood. Injuries including bone fractures, lacerations, walking into a wall, and aggressive behaviors toward others, including loved ones, often precipitate evaluation by sleep medicine or mental health professionals. Sleepwalkers appear confused and disoriented when engaged in their activities, which range from simple tasks such as hand gestures or turning on a bedside lamp to quite complex behaviors such as walking down the street to an all-night deli and ordering food. Episodes may last from a few seconds to up to 30–40 minutes. The behaviors undertaken by sleepwalkers are frequently out of character, and there is confusion immediately after awakening with a lack of memory for the sleepwalking events.

Unlike patients with sleep terrors or other confusional states that arise from delta sleep, patients with REM sleep behavior disorder tend to remain in the bed (or in the area where they were sleeping) when they act out dreams. An exact diagnosis of idiopathic REM behavior disorder is often challenging, because REM-related behaviors without atonia often coexists with confusional arousal disorders, narcolepsy, and neurodegenerative diseases. In some cases, symptoms of REM sleep without atonia may herald the onset of narcolepsy. Sleep-related seizures should be considered in the differential diagnosis, both of which can be associated with abrupt and violent behaviors.

Tricyclic, serotonin selective reuptake inhibitor (SSRI) and serotonin-norepinephrine reuptake inhibitor (SNRI) antidepressants may induce and worsen preexisting symptoms of REM sleep behavior disorder. In patients with violent behaviors, there may be self-injury or injuries inflicted on the bed partner. As one might imagine, the bed partner may become extremely frightened of the person with REM sleep behavior disorder. In patients with violent behaviors, there is a risk of serious, even life-threatening injuries. Some investigators have suggested that REM without atonia may be an early symptom of neurodegenerative diseases such as Parkinson's disease and multiple system atrophy, which may emerge 10 or more years later (Mahowald, Bramer Bornemann, & Schenck, 2010). Patients with recent-onset REM behavior without atonia deserves a careful documentation of their course of illness, with a comprehensive workup including polysomnography with EEG synchronized video recording. Patients should be evaluated for the presence of coexisting neurological disorders (i.e., seizures and neurodegenerative disorders) as well as the use of psychotropic medications. Because the motor manifestation of REM sleep behavior disorder can be frightening and/or dangerous, it is useful to tell the patient and his or her family that the person is taking actions that would be appropriate if the dreams were real events.

Initial episodes of sleep paralysis are unequivocally frightening (e.g., "the most horrifying thing that has happened to me in my life"). There is almost always a fight-or-flight response, although with sleep paralysis the person can neither put up a defense nor flee the situation. This realization only magnifies the fear and causes a sense of total vulnerability. Some individuals recognize the paralysis as a true physiological state of muscle weakness, whereas others report being "controlled by an evil force" or "frozen with fear." Isolated sleep paralysis ranges in frequency from a single lifetime episode to multiple episodes in a single night. Similar to patients with panic attacks, the *frequency* of paralytic events does not strongly predict the degree of psychological distress. Unlike patients with sleep panic attacks, it is unusual for patients with recurrent isolated sleep paralysis to develop a conditioned fear of sleep. Rarely, sleep paralysis may be associated with spiritual experiences. These individuals describe a sense of well-being connected to their sensory-related experiences.

Most people with recurrent episodes of sleep paralysis who seek treatment, even well-educated professionals and scientists, struggle with trying to comprehend the "true nature" of these lifelike events. Episodes may emerge at any time during the sleep night or during daytime naps. Many patients with recurrent sleep paralysis cannot distinguish between wakefulness, sleep states, or transitions into or out of sleep. Stressful life events may trigger a return or series of sleep paralytic events after having been quiescent for many years. The cultural background and heritage of the patient is particularly relevant in treating sleep paralysis. The depiction of the "evil presence" is remarkably similar across cultures, even among people who had no prior knowledge of the phenomenon (for a superb review, see Hufford, 1982). The hypnagogic/hypnopompic "visitor" is often an old woman who has been given various names (e.g., old hag, succubus) to describe the associated experience ("being held down by ghosts," "witch riding my back," "sucking the breath out of me"). Patients from Western and/or European backgrounds are exceedingly cautious about telling anybody, especially mental health professionals, about their hallucination-related visitation experiences. Patients are relieved to talk with a mental health professional who is knowledgeable about the syndrome. Education is a core element of treatment.

Little is known about patients who *exclusively* experience sleep panic attacks. The majority of patients with *DSM-III/IV* diagnosed panic disorder, however, also report sleep panic attacks. It is important to take a thorough history regarding sleep panic attacks, particularly among men, because they often downplay their importance or hide their existence. Some victims are simply too embarrassed to talk about their sleep panic attacks, especially if they are associated with a fear of sleep/sleeping. Several lines of evidence suggest important differences between patients with sleep panic attacks—that is, patients who experience *both* sleep and wake panic attacks versus patients who experience panic attacks only during wakefulness: (1) sleep panic attacks may be more often associated with trauma (Freed, Craske, & Greher, 1999); (2) comorbid depression is unusually high in patients with sleep panic attacks (Agaragun & Kara, 1998; Uhde, 2000); and (3) very restricted sleep (i.e., less than 5 hours of sleep per night) is greater in patients with sleep panic attacks (20.6%) compared to those with only wake panic attacks (2%) (Singareddy & Uhde, 2009).

Some couples enjoy previously unexplored and out-of-character behaviors that take place as part of sleep-related sex. This should be kept in mind insofar as not all sleep-related sexual behaviors require treatment. Patients with sexsomnia, who wish to prevent dangerous or aggressive sleep-related behaviors, often have an appreciation for predisposing conditions such as alcohol, medications, or other substances. The patient, bed partner, and therapist should design a treatment plan that eliminates or reduces predisposing risk factors. With both sexsomnia and sleep-related eating, education is a major component of treatment. It is helpful to educate patients and families about sleep-wake mechanisms involved in the parasomnias. It is common for family members to believe that sleepwalking, sleep-related sex, REM sleep aggression, and other disturbing parasomnia-related behaviors are under the direct conscious control of the patient. The medical facts, as well as available treatments, should be highlighted. Good sleep hygiene (particularly avoiding sleep deprivation), limiting alcohol and sedative use, and maintaining a safe sleep environment (i.e., eliminating situations such as open windows that increase the risk of physical harm) should be incorporated into the management of parasomnias. There is a tendency to try to awaken the person out of a confusional state. This is often a mistake insofar as attempts to interrupt sleep may only worsen the situation, which may lead to bodily harm to a person trying to be helpful. Criminal behavior conducted in a person with a confusional parasomnia presents several legal questions, which will often require consultation.

## LOOKING AHEAD TO *DSM-5*

In the years since the publication of *DSM-IV*, scientific advances in sleep physiology and genetics, as well as the development of evidence-based treatments for sleep disorders, have, in part, driven the need for an update of the current diagnostic criteria for sleep-wake disorders. The primary goal of the Sleep-Wake Disorders Workgroup (Reynolds & Redline, 2010), the panel of sleep experts responsible for the *DSM-5* revision on sleep-wake disorders, was to simplify the classification of the sleep-wake disorders so that general mental health and medical clinicians have improved recognition of these conditions, can make the proper referrals to sleep specialists, and facilitate the appropriate treatment for sleep disorders that are comorbid with other health conditions.

The main changes regarding the nosology of sleep-wake disorders in *DSM-5* are proposed as follows:

1. The diagnoses of insomnia or hypersomnia related to another mental condition or related to a general medical condition will be replaced by "Insomnia Disorder" or "Hypersomnia Disorder" with concurrent specification of clinically comorbid medical and/or psychiatric conditions.
2. The current Breathing-Related Sleep Disorder will be divided into separate sleep-wake diagnoses for Obstructive and Central Sleep Apnea.
3. Rapid Eye Movement Behavior Disorder and Restless Legs Syndrome will be classified independently, removing them from the "Not Otherwise Specified" classification.
4. Sleepwalking and Sleep Terror Disorders will be subsumed under the diagnosis of "Confusional Arousal Disorders," a collection of NREM parasomnias.

5. A number of different types of circadian rhythm disorders, (e.g., advanced sleep phase, free-running, and irregular sleep-wake types) are proposed additions to the *DSM-5*.

## CASE STUDY

Panic Disorder With Agoraphobia and Sleep Disorder Related to Another Mental Disorder

Ms. Case is a 30-year-old married, normal weight African American woman with an 8-year history of panic disorder with agoraphobia. Her first daytime panic attack occurred while shopping. There were no major life stressors at the time. She described her first lifetime panic attack as "out of the blue" and "not like anything I'd ever experienced before." She had 15 panic attacks over the next 2 months, always while she was fully awake. These attacks were characterized by tachycardia, chest tightness, sweating (over her lip and hands), and a strange feeling of floating and "time standing still." During this first wake episode she thought she was dying from a heart attack. A medical and neurological workup was negative. The ER physician prescribed a medication for her "anxiety" but she was noncompliant ("I didn't want to put drugs in my body"). She later worked with a therapist. This was helpful in dealing with what she perceived as minor family issues (e.g., her husband was complaining that she never wanted to do anything fun anymore). Over the next several years, her wake panic attacks decreased in frequency and she learned "how to handle them." Now and then, usually after the flu or a limited-symptom panic attack, she would become a "little concerned" about having an undiagnosed medical problem. This "little concern" became outright terror, associated with nonstop cognitions about dying, after experiencing her first of many subsequent *sleep panic attacks*. She perceived her sleep panic attacks as more unpredictable and serious than her wake panic attacks. Her sleep panic symptoms were very similar to her wake panic attacks and included a pounding heart ("beating out of my chest"), numbness in her hands, choking (without regurgitation), and feeling unreal. She also reported being hot and sweating. What made her most afraid, however, was her inability to "catch my breath . . . I cannot get enough air." Ms. Case developed a fear of sleep, which resulted in maladaptive sleep habits (e.g., sleeping in a chair rather than the bed and making her husband promise to watch her sleep in order to wake her up if she stopped breathing). The husband reported that he had never witnessed his wife stop breathing and that she snored only when she had a "bad cold." The patient's fear of sleep led to a pattern of insomnia, with fragmented sleep and periods of sleep deprivation lasting 24 or more hours. Most recently, she reports the reemergence of "bad" daytime wake and sleep panic attacks.

The patient also had a history of nightmares. Her sleep panic attacks, however, were qualitatively different from her nightmares (i.e., there was no dream content or visual images associated with her panic attacks) and her nightmares caused no impairment (e.g., "My nightmares won't kill me"). She also reported a history since childhood of isolated episodes of sleep paralysis. While she remembers these childhood events as frightening [especially when she could not "run away" from the old woman (i.e. hypnagogic hallucinations)], they are no longer distressing.

In fact, these episodes of isolated sleep paralysis with hynagogic hallucinations often have an ineffable, positive, spiritual-like quality.

Because of Ms. Case's concerns about breathing, she obtained a sleep study. Except for difficulty falling asleep (it took her almost 2 hours to achieve sustained stage two sleep), she did not experience any type of frightening arousal and her AHI was well within normal limits.

This case illustrates the value of (a) obtaining a longitudinal perspective; (b) determining the degree of distress and impact of the patient's sleep complaints on work, social, and other important areas of function; and (c) appraising the merits of treating the sleep problem(s) as a distinct disorder(s). This individual clearly suffers from longstanding panic disorder with agoraphobia. While the wake panic attacks may have decreased in frequency and the associated avoidance behaviors are downplayed by the patient, it would be a mistake to ignore the negative impact of wake panic attacks and agoraphobia on this person's overall health and well-being. Thus, she meets criteria for 300.21 Panic Disorder with Agoraphobia. The emergence of sleep panic attacks after years of having wake panic attacks presents several interesting diagnostic dilemmas. One could view the presence of sleep panic attacks in this case as just a symptom variant of panic disorder with agoraphobia. This viewpoint argues for a single diagnosis (i.e., panic disorder with agoraphobia). A single diagnosis might unwittingly lead some clinicians to presume that the use of well-established, empirically proven treatments for wake panic attacks will be equally effective in the treatment of sleep panic attacks. While research is necessary to answer this question, common sense warrants the targeted treatment of sleep panic attacks, conditioned fear of sleep, and the resultant chronic-intermittent sleep deprivation (i.e., insomnia). A separate sleep disorder diagnosis, therefore, is justified.

What is the appropriate sleep disorder diagnosis? *DSM-IV* guidelines highlight the *consequences* of sleep panic attacks (i.e., insomnia), insofar as sleep panic attacks disrupt the continuity of sleep and decrease the total amount of sleep. From this *DSM-IV* reference point, the added diagnosis would be 307.42 Insomnia Related to Panic Disorder with Agoraphobia. Sleep panic attacks, however, represent a specific subtype of parasomnias (Singareddy & Uhde, 2010). The *DSM-IV* does not provide guidelines for the diagnosis of individuals who experience sleep panic attacks in the absence of wake panic attacks. In such a situation, or even in a patient who has been free of wake panic attacks for an extended (e.g., years) period of time, it would be justified to designate the diagnosis as 307.47 Parasomnia Not Otherwise Specified. This patient also had a history of nightmares. Insufficient information was provided to ascertain whether Ms. Case would have met criteria for 307.47 Nightmare Disorder in the past, but she clearly was not distressed or disturbed by dreams, nor was there any evidence for interpersonal, social, or occupational impairment related to her dream experiences. Also, no information was provided regarding a history of sexual, physical, or life-threatening trauma, which would have been critical information in the event that her nightmares did cause significant distress or impairment.

In such a scenario, the clinician must determine whether the nightmares are limited to a sleep disorder (i.e., nightmare disorder) or associated with post-traumatic stress disorder, or both. It should be noted that this patient could easily distinguish among her various sleep events: nightmares (dreams), sleep panic attacks, and episodes of sleep paralysis. Sleep paralysis is prevalent as a normal self-limiting phenomenon in the general population. Isolated episodes of sleep paralysis, even on a recurrent basis in the absence of cataplexy, are not indicative of neurological disease. But, like nightmares, they can be terrifying and lead to impairment. Making this determination is important. In Ms. Case, the visitation experiences (not described in detail) were mainly enjoyable and had a positive impact on her philosophical outlook on life. If these sleep events had been significantly distressing, she would qualify for an additional diagnosis of 307.47 Parasomnia Not Otherwise Specified.

Even though Ms. Case had a normal Body Mass Index (BMI), snored only during "bad colds," and even then "not loudly," it was appropriate to obtain an objective sleep PSG to rule out 780.59 Breathing-Related Sleep Disorder. Normal-weight, nonsnoring people can have sleep apnea, and the absence of these clinical features should not be used to rule out a breathing-related sleep disorder. If there had been objective PSG/AHI evidence of sleep apnea, which also produced significant insomnia, then a breathing-related sleep disorder should be added as another Axis I disorder and listed as a medical condition on Axis III.

Patients with comorbid panic attacks and sleep apnea report more frequent panic attacks when their apnea is poorly controlled but show remarkable improvement after CPAP treatment. Would objective evidence of obstructive sleep apnea on PSG/AHI justify the removal of the diagnosis of insomnia related to panic disorder with agoraphobia (or parasomnia not otherwise specified) on the basis that the sleep panic attacks and associated insomnia were simply a manifestation of hypoxia related to a breathing-related disorder? In our experience, CPAP treatment will often be associated with improvements in anxiety in panic disorder patients with comorbid obstructive sleep apnea. But, this improvement is only partial, even when there is a return to totally normal pulmonary indices and oxygen saturation levels. Sleep deprivation is well-known to trigger the recrudescence and severity of panic attacks (Uhde, 2000). We propose that the *worsening* of anxiety symptoms in panic disorder patients with sleep apnea is due to sleep deprivation (caused by the multiple apnea-related awakenings) rather than being caused by abnormally low arterial oxygen (Singareddy & Uhde, 2010). If there had been evidence of obstructive sleep apnea, Ms. Case's history and present illness would justify the following diagnoses: (a) panic disorder with agoraphobia; (b) insomnia related to panic disorder with agoraphobia (or parasomnia not otherwise specified); and (c) breathing-related sleep disorder.

Overall, this case underscores the importance of carefully examining the degree of impairment and whether the sleep problems are sufficiently severe to warrant independent attention. As with this case, it is very common for the same person to report multiple parasomnias.

## SUMMARY

*DSM-IV* identifies two types of *primary* sleep disorders: dyssomnias and parasomnias. The chief characteristics of dyssomnias are disturbances in the amount of sleep (e.g., too little, oversleeping), quality of sleep (e.g., nonrefreshed), or timing of sleep (e.g., mismatches between the sleep-wake schedule with the person's external demands), whereas parasomnias are characterized by abnormal behavioral (e.g., walking, eating) or physiological (e.g., tachycardia, hyperventilation) events that are associated with sleep, specific sleep stages (e.g., REM-stage sleep), or sleep-wake transitions. The primary sleep disorders are distinguished from secondary sleep problems (i.e., sleep disturbances that are caused by a substance or another mental or a medical disorder).

The identification of the main clinical features of the primary sleep disorders (dyssomnias and parasomnias) is straightforward: The biggest challenge is to rule out other possible causes of the symptoms. This is not always easy, as there are many common symptoms within and across the primary sleep disorders. Moreover, there is a high rate of comorbidity among the sleep disorders and between sleep disorders and mental disorders. For example, the sleep complaints in primary insomnia are essentially identical to those reported by patients with generalized anxiety disorder. If the symptoms of insomnia are tightly linked to the onset, course, and treatment of anxiety, then the patient is given a single diagnosis of generalized anxiety disorder. On the other hand, if the insomnia and anxiety have distinctly different illness patterns, then separate diagnoses of primary insomnia and generalized anxiety disorder are appropriate. In practical reality, there are many underappreciated situations where the insomnia is temporally associated with an underlying mental disorder (e.g., generalized anxiety disorder), but the person's chief complaint is insomnia, not anxiety. Typically, such patients will openly identify insomnia as the preferred target of treatment. In this situation, the patient would be given two diagnoses: Generalized Anxiety Disorder and 307.42 Insomnia Related to Generalized Anxiety Disorder.

As with all patients complaining of sleep problems, it is critical to rule out sleep problems that are *directly related* to an underlying medical condition or a substance or medication. In the latter case, the sleep complaints must have developed either during or within 1 month of a period of intoxication or withdrawal from the substance in order to meet criteria for a substance-induced sleep disorder. The classic example of a drug-induced sleep problem is caffeine, which interestingly can be associated with insomnia during the intoxication phase and either insomnia or hypersomnia during acute withdrawal (Uhde, 1995). In the case of insomnia exclusively associated with caffeine intoxication, the patient would be given a diagnosis of 292.89 Caffeine-Induced Sleep Disorder, Insomnia Type, With Onset During Intoxication.

One of the most valuable tools to ascertain whether a sleep disorder is primary (dyssomnias or parasomnias) versus the manifestation of another mental or sleep disorder, general medical condition, or a substance-related problem is to use life-charting methods (Roy-Byrne et al., 1985; Uhde et al., 1985) to plot the *temporal relationship* among major life events, medical illnesses, and ratings of sleep, anxiety, and mood. It is also critical to assess the history of medications, alcohol, and other substances over the entire lifetime of the individual. The life-charting strategy, even if applied in a speedy manner, often uncovers important relationships that were previously unrecognized by both the patient and the clinician (Roy-Byrne et al., 1985). While this approach has not been validated in patients with primary sleep disorders per se, there is strong evidence for its utility in the assessment of complex psychiatric disorders (Denicoff et al., ). This method has great potential as a diagnostic aid in evaluating the time course and relationship of primary and secondary sleep problems in patients who present with complex sleep, mental, and medical disorders.

## REFERENCES

Agaragun, M. Y., & Kara, H. (1998). Recurrent sleep panic, insomnia, and suicidal behavior in patients with panic disorder. *Comprehensive Psychiatry, 39*, 149–151.

American Academy of Sleep Medicine. (2005). *International classification of sleep disorders* (2nd ed.). Westchester, IL: American Academy of Sleep Medicine.

American Psychiatric Association. (2000). *Diagnostic and statistical manual of mental disorders* (4th ed., rev.). Washington, DC: Author.

Belicki, K. (1992). Nightmare frequency versus nightmare distress: Relation to psycho-pathology and cognitive style. *Journal of Abnormal Psychology, 101*, 592–597.

Billiard, M., Jaussent, I., Dauvilliers, Y., & Besset, A. (in press). Recurrent hypersomnia: A review of 339 cases. *Sleep Medicine Reviews*, doi: 10.1016/j.smrv.2010.08.001

Blouin, A. M., Thannickal, T. C., Worley, P. F., Baraban, J. M., Reti, I. M., & Siegel, J. M. (2005). Narp immunostaining of human hypocretin (orexin) neurons: Loss in narcolepsy. *Neurology, 65*(8): 1189–1192.

Broughton, R. J. (1968). Sleep disorders: Disorders of arousal? *Science, 159*, 1070–1078.

Broughton, R. J. (2000). NREM arousal parasomnias. In M. Kryger, T. Roth, & W. Dement (Eds.), *Principles and practice of sleep medicine* (3rd ed., pp. 693–706). Philadelphia, PA: W. B. Saunders.

Carskadon, M. A., & Dement, W. C. (1997). Sleep tendency: An objective measure of sleep loss. *Sleep Research, 6*, 200.

Cheyne, J. A. (2002). Situational factors affecting sleep paralysis and associated hallucinations: position and timing effects. *Journal of Sleep Research, 11*, 169–177.

Cheyne, J. A. (2005). Sleep paralysis episode frequency and number, types and structure of associated hallucination. *Journal of Sleep Research, 14*, 319–324.

Cortese, B. M., & Uhde, T. W. (2006). Immobilization panic. *American Journal of Psychiatry, 163*, 1453–1454.

Craske, M. G., & Barlow, D. H. (1989). Nocturnal panic. *Journal of Nervous and Mental Disease, 177*, 160–168.

Denicoff, K. D., Ali, S. O., Sollinger, A. B., Smith-Jackson, E. E., Leverich, G. S., Post, R. M. (2002). Utility of the daily prospective National Institute of Mental Health Life-Chart Method (NIMH-LCM-p) ratings in clinical trials of bipolar disorder. *Depression and Anxiety, 15*(1),1–9.

Desautels, A., Turecki, G., Montplaisir, J., Sequeira, A., Verner, A., & Rouleau, G. A. (2001). Identification of a major susceptibility locus for restless legs syndrome on chromosome 12q. *American Journal of Human Genetics, 69*, 1266–1270.

Ekbom, K. A. (1994). Asthenia crurum paraesthetica (Irritable Legs). *Acta Medica Scandinavia, 118*, 197.

Flosnik, D. L., Cortese, B. M., & Uhde, T. W. (2009). Cataplexy in anxious patients: Is subclinical narcolepsy underrecognized in anxiety disorders. *Journal of Clinical Psychiatry, 70*(6), 810–816.

Foster, G. D., Sander, M. H., Millman, R., Zammit, G., Borradaile, K. E., Newman, A. B., . . . Kuna, S. T. (2009). Obstructive sleep apnea among obese patients with type 2 diabetes. *Diabetes Care, 32*, 1017–1019.

Freed, S., Craske, M. G., & Greher, M. R. (1999). Nocturnal panic and trauma. *Depression and Anxiety, 9*, 141–145.

Gangwisch, J. E., Malaspina, D., Boden-Albala, B., & Heymsfield, S. B. (2005). Inadequate sleep as a risk factor for obesity: Analyses of the NHANES I. *Sleep, 28*, 1289–1296.

Girard, T. A., & Cheyne, J. A. (2006). Timing of spontaneous sleep paralysis episodes. *Journal of Sleep Research, 5*, 222–229.

Hufford, D. J. (1982). *The terror that comes in the night: An experience-centered study of supernatural assault traditions.* Philadelphia: University of Pennsylvania Press.

Kales, J. D., Kales, A., Soldatos, C. R., Caldwell, A. B., Charney, D. S., & Martin, E. D. (1980). Night terrors: Clinical characteristics and personality patterns. *Arch Gen Psychiatry, 37*(12): 1413–1417.

Lin, L., & Mignot, E. (2007). HLA and narcolepsy: Present status and relationship with familial history and hypocretin deficiency. In C. Bassetti, M. Billiard, and E. Mignot (Eds.), *Narcolepsy and hypersomnia* (pp. 411–426). New York, NY: Decker/Taylor & Francis.

Mahowald, M. W., Bramer Bornemann, M. A., & Schenck, C. H. (2010). The early and accurate objective diagnosis of RBD—Why should we care? *Movement Disorders, 13*, 2003–2005.

Mellman, T. A., & Hipolito, M. M. (2006). Sleep disturbances in the aftermath of trauma and posttraumatic stress disorder. *CNS Spectrum, 11*, 611–615.

Mellman, T. A., & Uhde, T. W. (1988). Electroencephalographic sleep in panic disorder: A focus on sleep-related panic attacks. *Archives of General Psychiatry, 46*, 178–184.

Mignot, E., Lammers, G. J., Ripley, B., Okun, M., Nevsimalova, S., Overeem, S., . . . Nishino, S. (2002). The role of cerebrospinal fluid hypocretin measurement in the diagnosis of narcolepsy and other parasomnias. *Archives of Neurology*, 1553–1562.

Monti, J. M., & Monti, D. (2000). Sleep disturbance in generalized anxiety disorder and its treatment. *Sleep Medicine Review, 4*, 263–276.

Nickell, P. V., & Uhde, T. W. (1991). Anxiety disorders and epilepsy. In O. Devinsky & W. H. Theodore (Eds.), *Epilepsy and behavior* (pp. 67–84). New York, NY: Wiley-Liss.

Nielsen, T. (2010). Nightmares associated with the eveningness chronotype. *Journal of Biological Rhythms, 25*, 53–62.

Nordin, M., & Kaplan, R. M. (2010). Sleep discontinuity and impaired sleep continuity affect transition to and from obesity over time: Results from the Alameda county study. *Scandinavian Journal of Public Health*, 200–207.

Ohayon, M. M., Caulet, M., & Lemoine, P. (1998). Comorbidity of mental and insomnia disorders in the general population. *Comprehensive Psychiatry, 39*, 185–197.

Ohayon, M. M., & Sagales, T. (2010). Prevalence of insomnia and sleep characteristics in the general population of Spain. *Sleep Medicine, 11*, 1010–1018.

Rechtschaffen, A., & Kales, A. (Eds.). (1968). *A manual of standardized terminology, techniques, and scoring system for sleep stages of human subjects.* Washington, DC: Public Health Service, U.S. Government Printing Service.

Reynolds, C. F., 3rd, & Redline, S. (2010). DSM-V Sleep-Wake Disorders Workgroup and Advisors. The DSM-V sleep-wake disorders nosology: An update and an invitation to the sleep community. *Sleep, 33*, 10–11.

Roy-Byrne, P. P., Post, R. M., Uhde, T. W., Porcu, T., & Davis, D. (1985). The longitudinal course of recurrent affective illness: Life chart data from research patients at NIMH. *Acta Psychiatrica Scandinavia, 71*, 1–34.

Singareddy, R., & Uhde, T. W. (2009). Nocturnal sleep panic and depression: Relationship to subjective sleep in panic disorder. *Journal of Affective Disorders, 112*, 262–266.

Singareddy, R., & Uhde, T. W. (2010). Sleep panic arousals. In M. Thorpy & G. Plazzi (Eds.), *The parasomnias and other sleep-related movement disorders* (pp. 278–288). Cambridge, England: Cambridge University Press.

Trajanovic, N. N., Mangan, M., & Sapiro, C. M. (2007). Sexual behavior in sleep: An internet survey. *Social Psychiatry and Psychiatric Epidemiology, 42*, 1024–1031.

Turek, F. W., Joshu, C., Kohsaka, A., Lin, E., Ivanova, G., McDearmon, E., . . . Bass, J. (2005). Obesity and metabolic syndrome in circadian clock mutant mice. *Science, 13*, 1043–1045.

Uhde, T. W. (1995). Caffeine-induced anxiety: An ideal chemical model of panic disorder. In G. M. Asnis & H. M. van Praag (Eds.), *Einstein monograph series in psychiatry* (pp. 181–205). New York, NY: Wiley-Liss.

Uhde, T. W. (2000). The anxiety disorders. In M. H. Kryger, T. Roth, & W. Dement (Eds.), *Principles and practice in sleep medicine* (3rd ed., pp. 1123–1139). Philadelphia, PA: W. B. Saunders.

Uhde, T. W., Boulenger, J. P., Roy-Byrne, P. P., Geraci, M. F., Vittone, B. J., & Post, R. M. (1985). Longitudinal course of panic disorder: Clinical and biological considerations. *Progress in Neuro-Psychopharmacology and Biological Psychiatry, 9*, 39–51.

Uhde, T. W., Cortese, B. M., & Vedniapin, A. (2009). Anxiety and sleep problems: Emerging concepts and theoretical implications. *Current Psychiatry Reports, 11*, 269–276.

# Author Index

# Subject Index